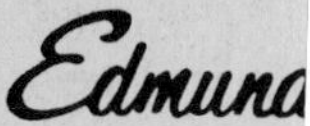

$10,000 WHEEL N' DEAL GIVEAWAY

Edmund's is giving away $1,000 a month to lucky readers selected at random – see our announcement on the back cover of this book. To enter the drawing, complete the form below or provide the same information on a piece of paper and mail to:

Edmund Publications Corporation
300 N. Sepulveda Blvd., Suite 2050
El Segundo, CA 90245

NAME ____________________

ADDRESS ____________________

CITY, STATE, ZIP ____________________

TELEPHONE ____________________

NAME AND YEAR OF DESIRED AUTOMOBILE ____________________

NAME, ADDRESS, AND CONTACT OF A DEALER IN YOUR AREA LISTED IN EDMUND'S AUTOMOBILE DEALER DIRECTORY (page 217) OR OBTAINED BY CALLING **1-800-996-AUTO** ____________________

WHEEL'n'DEAL GIVEAWAY OFFICIAL RULES. 1. Using the Automobile Dealer Directory in the back of this book, select the dealer nearest you for your desired vehicle. Simply enter and send us the name, address, and contact person for this dealer. NO PURCHASE IS NECESSARY TO PARTICIPATE OR WIN. 2. $1,000 cash prize will be awarded each month to a single entrant. Prizes will be awarded through hand-drawn drawings from all eligible entry forms timely received. The drawings will be under supervision of an independent organization (Edmund Publications' promotions department) whose decisions are final, binding and conclusive on all matters. Prizes will be awarded only if prize winner complies with these official rules. Only one winner per name or household. All prizes will be awarded. 3. Drawings will be held on the 25th day of each month starting January 1995, with the last drawing on October 25, 1995. Entry forms must be received by Edmund Publications by the end of business on the (20th) day of the month to be eligible to participate in the drawing for that month and all subsequent drawings. All eligible entry forms timely received will be automatically entered into each subsequent monthly drawing. Edmund Publications is not and will not be responsible for illegible, damaged, late, lost, or misdirected entry forms. 4. Winners will be notified by First Class Mail on or before the 15th day of the month following each drawing. Prize winners will be required to sign (a) a declaration of eligibility and release form whereby winners consent to the commercial use of their name for advertising without additional compensation and (b) any forms required by tax authorities within 21 days of notification or forfeit the prize. 5. Payment of all applicable federal, state and local taxes is the sole responsibility of and must be paid by the winner. 6. Contest is open to residents of the United States who are 18 years or older. Employees and their immediate families of Edmund Publications or any dealer listed in the Automobile Dealer Directory, or any company or individual engaged in the development, production or execution of this promotion are not eligible to participate. Residents of Florida are eligible to participate and to win prizes. Void where prohibited or restricted by law. 7. For a list of prize winners, official entry forms, or a copy of these official rules, send a stamped self-addressed envelope to: Wheel'n'Deal Giveaway, c/o Edmund Publications Corp., 300 N. Sepulveda Blvd., Suite 2050, El Segundo, CA 90245. 8. Odds of winning are determined by the total number of entry forms received.

Most people have three things in common when they buy a car.

1995

Edmund's

USED CARS PRICES & RATINGS

"THE ORIGINAL CONSUMER PRICE AUTHORITY"

Publisher: Peter Steinlauf

USED CARS PRICES & RATINGS

TABLE OF CONTENTS

SPRING 1995 VOL U2901-9504

Published by:
Edmund Publications Corp.
300 N Sepulveda Suite 2050
El Segundo, CA 90245

ISBN: 0-87759-456-2
ISSN: 1079-1515

Editor-in-Chief:
Michael G. Samet, Ph. D.

Automotive Editor:
Christian Wardlaw

Copy Editor:
William Badnow

Creative Design:
Debra Katzir

Cover Design:
Jozsef Nagy

Information Technology:
Victor Friedman
David Samet

Advertising Manager:
Brenda Davis

Printed in the United States

Cover: 1993 Dodge Intrepid

Edmund's books are available at special quantity discounts when purchased in bulk by credit unions, corporations, organizations, and other special interest groups. Custom covers and/or customized copy on available pages may also be prepared to fit particular needs.

REGIONAL PRICE DIFFERENCES: The pricing information contained in Edmund's *Used Cars Prices and Ratings* represents an average value for a vehicle regardless of geographical location. Bear in mind that there are minor regional differences in values for some vehicles-especially trucks-due to climate, local culture, and current trends. Price data suggest that for areas approximately west of the Mississippi River, 5% should be added to the values in this guide.

Look for the Automobile Dealer Directory on page 379.
Enter Edmund's Wheel N'Deal Giveaway (see page 1).

NOTE: All information and prices published herein are gathered from sources which, in the editor's opinion, are considered reliable, but under no circumstances is the reader to assume that this information is official or final. All prices are represented as average approximations only. Unless otherwise noted, all prices are subject to change without notice. The publisher does not assume responsibility for errors of omission, commission, or interpretation. ◆ All consumer information and pricing services advertised herein are not operated by nor are they the responsibility of the publisher. The publisher assumes no responsibility for claims made by advertisers regarding their products or services.

INTRODUCTION

PRICING AND RATING A VEHICLE

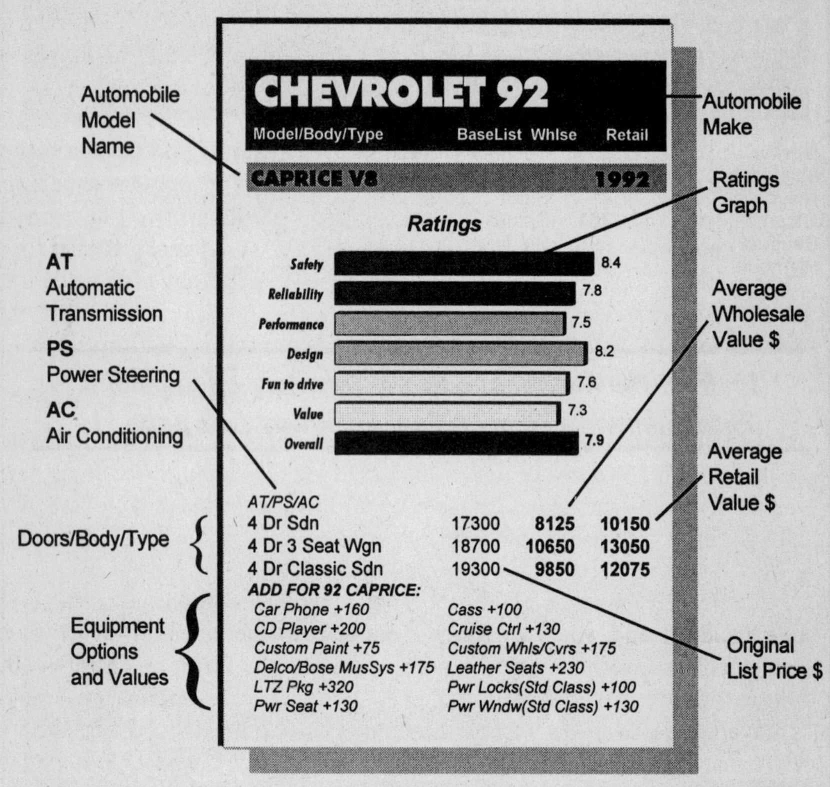

Sample Listing

The data in this book have been compiled and organized to enable you to determine the fair market value for American and imported used cars, pickup trucks, vans, and sport utilities, with model years between 1986 and 1994. The illustration on the preceding page and the paragraphs below provide descriptions of the used car listings and instructions on how to price an automobile.

INTRODUCTION

Price Listings. The vehicles in *Edmund's Used Car Prices and Ratings* are listed in alphabetical order by automobile make, irrespective of their country of origin (either American or imported). See the <u>Table of Contents</u> for a listing of automobile makes and their corresponding page numbers. Within each make (e.g., Acura, Chevrolet, Ford), all automobile models are arranged alphabetically, irrespective of their type (car or truck). To distinguish the trucks from the cars, all listings of pickups, vans, and sport utilities appear on a shaded gray background.

As shown in the sample listing on the previous page, for each vehicle (Model/Body/Type) with its basic included equipment, Edmund's gives: the **Wholesale** price [the current, approximate average price a seller can expect to receive from an automobile <u>dealer</u> for a clean vehicle], and the **Retail** price [the current, approximate average price a buyer can expect to pay an automobile <u>dealer</u> for a clean vehicle]. In addition, for each manufacturer-installed option or accessory, an approximate value is provided which is to be *added* or *deducted* from both the Wholesale and Retail price of the automobile. All price data are based on seasonally adjusted national averages.

Ratings. For many used cars (1989 to 1994), ratings on six separate dimensions and overall (derived from *Edmund's Used Car Ratings* book) are presented in graphic and numerical form, on a 1 to 10 scale where 10 is best. The rating dimensions are defined and derived as follows.

Safety encompasses multiple factors including the avoidance of automobile accidents and, when an accident does occur, the potential for physical damage to the automobile and resulting injury to the driver and passengers. Our safety rating, therefore, factors in automobile weight and maneuverability, availability of special safety features (anti-lock brakes, driver and passenger airbags), government crash test results for driver and passenger, reported occupant injury histories, and the level of required manufacturer's recalls to fix or adjust safety equipment.

Reliability refers to mechanical and operational dependability, or the extent to which the automobile is likely to be maintained trouble free. Edmund's rating is based on the number, if any, of the manufacturer's recalls for mechanical defects for the particular automobile model, as well as on frequency reports by automobile owners of problems and difficulties experienced. In the computation of our reliability rating, the observed recalls and trouble spots are each individually weighted by their respective severity.

INTRODUCTION

Performance is a measure of how well an automobile responds to the operational demands put to it by the driver. Edmund's performance rating is derived and combined from several evaluative factors including ride, steering, handling, power, acceleration, braking distance, cornering, and parking ease.

Design, or ergonomics, reflects the degree to which the manufacturer has thought out, configured, and put together the automobile to make it a user friendly machine, and to meet the comfort and convenience needs of the driver and passengers. Edmund's human factored procedure for rating automotive design includes measures of driver and passenger comfort, visibility, arrangement and operation of both the displays and controls, driving position (how the driver sits vis a vis the equipment), interior and exterior workmanship, and functional versatility of the vehicle; it does not include an index of aesthetic design, per se, as found in the eye of the beholder.

Fun to Drive refers to the enjoyment you can experience while driving an automobile. Edmund's special formula is based upon the combination of ten selected performance and design factors that contribute, in our opinion, to the "fun-to-drive" feeling.

Value reflects cost and utility factors involved in automobile ownership other than the purchase price. Our value rating for a used car goes up based on higher owner satisfaction reports, fuel efficiency, and price retention levels; and it goes down based on higher maintenance, repair, and insurance costs. A high theft rating, or tendency for the vehicle to be stolen, also decreases the value rating.

Edmund's ***Overall*** rating for a used automobile is obtained through an exclusive combination formula that weights the relative contributions (to the overall rating) of the six rating dimensions such that the level of importance (weight) is highest for Safety and Reliability, mid-level for Performance and Design, and lowest for Fun to Drive and Value. Of course, when comparing two or more vehicles, readers with specific preferences or utilities for the various rating dimensions can develop and apply (to the individual ratings) their own personalized weighting schemes.

INTRODUCTION

Automobile Condition. When pricing a specific vehicle, its condition must be taken into account. The clean vehicle priced in this book is defined as an automobile in fine physical and mechanical condition. A vehicle in better condition (e.g. a Cream Puff or Extra Clean car) commands a higher than average price, and one in worse condition (e.g. a car showing obvious wear and tear, or a Rough car needing mechanical repair) has a lower than average value. In fact, for vehicles needing reconditioning or repairs, the cost of this work should be deducted from the value of a clean car of the same make and model year.

Loan Value. Edmund's does <u>not</u> list the loan value for an automobile, which is the amount of money a bank or credit organization will lend on its purchase. Typically, the loan value on a clean used automobile can be calculated as about 85-90% of its Wholesale value. Of course, this percentage can vary depending on the particular vehicle and the applicant's credit history.

Trade-In Value. Edmund's also does <u>not</u> list the average amount you can expect to get from an automobile dealer on a used car when you trade it in for a new car. Typically, a dealer will low-ball your trade-in; that is, they will offer you much less for it than it's actually worth. Try to get Edmund's listed wholesale value or better, and not less than $300 below Edmund's listed wholesale value.

Pricing a Vehicle. Below most model names, which are highlighted in a gray background bar, you'll find an abbreviated list of key features (e.g. *FWD* for Front Wheel Drive, *AT* for Automatic Transmission, etc.) which are already factored into the prices given for those models. Next to each vehicle identified, the average current dealer **Wholesale** and **Retail** prices are given. If you are buying or selling a car yourself without going through an automobile dealer, the final negotiated price will usually fall somewhere between the **Wholeale** and **Retail** listed values (after adjustments are made for equipment and mileage) depending, of course, on the vehicle's condition.

Price Adjustment For Equipment. After the price listings for most newer models, you'll find an *ADD FOR* and, sometimes, a *DEDUCT FOR* list of equipment options with corresponding price-adjustment values. These equipment price lists appear directly below each set of automobile models and/or at the end of the listings for all the car and truck models within a given automobile make and year; option tables specific to American truck-type vehicles (shaded listings) appear in the later format.

INTRODUCTION

To adjust the average price of the vehicle, *add* or *subtract* the listed value of each relevant optional equipment item [except for equipment listed as standard (Std) for that model]; the same adjustment amount should be made for both the Wholesale and Retail price. For older model years, no adjustments are necessary for optional equipment since their presence or absence no longer impacts upon the average price of the vehicle. A key to the abbreviations used in the automobile and options listings is provided as part of these instructions on pages 16 and 17.

Mileage Adjustment. There is one more step to take before a final price estimate is reached. Check the appropriate mileage table (pages 18-21) to determine what amount, if any, should be *added to* or *subtracted from* the price based on whether the vehicle's current mileage is either below or above average mileage levels, respectfully. Select the mileage table to be used according to the **Wholesale** value of the vehicle after adjusting for optional equipment.

Four mileage tables are provided as follows:

Table	Wholesale Value of Automobile
1	Under $4,000
2	$4,000 to $10,000
3	$10,000 to $15,000
4	Above $15,000

To adjust value for mileage, go to the table corresponding to the wholesale value of the vehicle, and locate the cell in the table determined by the vehicle's mileage and the model year; and then take the dollar figure in that cell and either *add it* (if it has a + sign) or *subtract it* (if it has a - sign) from the estimated vehicle price – whether **Wholesale** or **Retail**.

Pricing Examples:

1) 1987 Toyota Celica (4 Cylinder) 2-Door GT Coupe (Front Wheel Drive/ Automatic Transmission/Power Steering/Air Conditioning) with 85,000 miles. Note that any optional equipment on this car would no longer be factored into the car's value [see listing on page 361, and Mileage Table 1 on page 14]:

Wholesale = $3,400 + 0 = **$3,400**
Retail = $4,825 + 0 = **$4,825**

2) **1991 Chevrolet Cavalier** (4 Cylinder) 4-Door RS Sedan (Front Wheel Drive/ Automatic Transmission/Power Steering/Air Conditioning) with cassette, cruise control, sunroof, no air conditioning, and 43,000 miles [see listing on page 70 and Mileage Table 2 on page 19]:

Wholesale = $4,700 + 35 + 75 + 115 - 390 + 670 = **$5,205**
Retail = $6,175 + 35 + 75 + 115 - 390 + 670 = **$6,680**

3) **1992 Honda Accord** (4 Cylinder) 5-Door EX Wagon (Front Wheel Drive/ Automatic Transmission/Power Steering/Air Conditioning) with custom wheels and 47,000 miles [see listings on page 185, and Mileage Table 3 on page 16]:

Wholesale = $13,000 + 160 + 0 = **$13,160**
Retail = $15,500 + 160 + 0 = **$15,660**

4) **1993 Ford Explorer** (V6 ½ Ton) 4-Door Wagon 2WD (Automatic Transmission/Power Steering/Air Conditioning) with the XLT Package, Leather Seats, and 15,000 miles [see listings on pages 99 and 101, and Mileage Table 4 on page 17]:

Wholesale = $15,825 + 700 + 250 + 1130 = **$19,205**
Retail = $18,700 + 700 + 250 + 1130 = **$20,780**

Validating Model Year. To validate the model year for a used automobile, check the letter in the **tenth** position of the VIN (Vehicle Identification Number). The VIN is usually located on the dashboard near the lower left corner of the windshield. The illustration below shows the letter and the corresponding year for a vehicle. For example, below is the VIN for a 1987 Chevrolet Cavalier. Note that the letter in the tenth position of the VIN is an **H** – indicating a 1987 automobile.

1G1JE1119**H**J162212

LETTER	YEAR	LETTER	YEAR
B	1981	J	1988
C	1982	K	1989
D	1983	L	1990
E	1984	M	1991
F	1985	N	1992
G	1986	P	1993
H	1987	Q	1994

Mileage Adjustment Table 1

(based on driving average of 14,000 miles per year)

*Add (+) or deduct (-) dollar amount according to mileage and model year**

USED CARS WITH WHOLESALE VALUE UNDER $4,000

Mileage	1994	1993	1992	1991	1990	1989	1988	1987	1986/85
0–7,000	+210	+270	+280	+290	+330	+390	+390	+400	+400
7–14,000	+120	+210	+260	+270	+330	+360	+360	+390	+390
14–21,000	0	+140	+260	+260	+310	+340	+340	+380	+380
21–28,000	-50	+60	+250	+260	+290	+330	+330	+370	+370
28–35,000	-190	0	+160	+250	+270	+320	+320	+360	+360
35–42,000	-330	-170	+80	+240	+250	+290	+300	+340	+340
42–49,000	-420	-310	0	+210	+230	+270	+290	+320	+320
49–56,000	-520	-450	-150	+130	+190	+240	+260	+300	+300
56–63,000	-570	-550	-290	0	+100	+170	+210	+270	+270
63–70,000	-610	-590	-400	-40	0	+90	+160	+210	+210
70–77,000	-640	-620	-510	-190	-160	0	+60	+160	+160
77–84,000	-650	-640	-590	-330	-300	-110	0	+50	+130
84–91,000	-660	-650	-630	-480	-390	-280	-170	0	+50
91–98,000	-670	-660	-650	-560	-540	-460	-360	-170	0
98,000 +	-670	-670	-670	-620	-620	-570	-570	-330	-310

*Do not add or deduct more than 40% of the automobile's wholesale value.

Mileage Adjustment Table 2

(based on driving average of 14,000 miles per year)
*Add (+) or deduct (-) dollar amount according to mileage and model year**

USED CARS WITH WHOLESALE VALUE $4,000 TO $10,000

Mileage	1994	1993	1992	1991	1990	1989	1988	1987	1986/85
0–7,000	+670	+870	+910	+920	+1060	+1160	+1240	+1260	+1270
7–14,000	+390	+670	+850	+860	+1040	+1130	+1180	+1230	+1250
14–21,000	0	+440	+830	+840	+980	+1090	+1120	+1200	+1220
21–28,000	-170	+180	+800	+820	+920	+1050	+1060	+1160	+1170
28–35,000	-590	0	+510	+800	+870	+1000	+1010	+1120	+1130
35–42,000	-1060	-530	+240	+760	+800	+920	+970	+1060	+1070
42–49,000	-1320	-970	0	+670	+740	+870	+920	+1010	+1020
49–56,000	-1640	-1430	-480	+410	+600	+760	+840	+930	+940
56–63,000	-1820	-1740	-920	0	+320	+540	+680	+840	+850
63–70,000	-1950	-1860	-1260	-140	0	+290	+500	+670	+670
70–77,000	-2020	-1970	-1610	-610	-520	0	+180	+500	+520
77–84,000	-2070	-2030	-1880	-1050	-960	-340	0	+160	+420
84–91,000	-2100	-2080	-1990	-1540	-1230	-880	-540	0	+170
91–98,000	-2130	-2110	-2070	-1790	-1720	-1470	-1140	-550	0
98,000 +	-2140	-2140	-2130	-1960	-1960	-1820	-1820	-1050	-980

*Do not add or deduct more than 40% of the automobile's wholesale value.

Mileage Adjustment Table 3

(based on driving average of 14,000 miles per year)
*Add (+) or deduct (-) dollar amount according to mileage and model year**

USED CARS WITH WHOLESALE VALUE $10,000 TO $15,000

Mileage	1994	1993	1992	1991	1990	1989	1988	1987	1988/85
0–7,000	+1190	+1550	+1630	+1640	+1890	+2060	+2080	+2250	+2280
7–14,000	+690	+1190	+1500	+1540	+1850	+1990	+2010	+2200	+2230
14–21,000	0	+780	+1400	+1500	+1750	+1940	+1950	+2150	+2180
21–28,000	-310	+330	+1400	+1460	+1650	+1860	+1880	+2060	+2090
28–35,000	-1060	0	+910	+1430	+1550	+1790	+1800	+2010	+2030
35–42,000	-1890	-950	+430	+1360	+1430	+1640	+1730	+1910	+1930
42–49,000	-2360	-1740	0	+1190	+1310	+1550	+1650	+1800	+1830
49–56,000	-2930	-2550	-860	+730	+1060	+1360	+1500	+1680	+1690
56–63,000	-3250	-3100	-1650	0	+560	+960	+1210	+1530	+1540
63–70,000	-3490	-3330	-2250	-250	0	+530	+890	+1190	+1200
70–77,000	-3610	-3530	-2880	-1090	-930	0	+310	+900	+930
77–84,000	-3690	-3630	-3360	-1880	-1710	-610	0	+290	+750
84–91,000	-3750	-3710	-3550	-2750	-2190	-1560	-960	0	+300
91–98,000	-3800	-3770	-3690	-3190	-3080	-2630	-2040	-980	0
98,000 +	-3820	-3820	-3800	-3500	-3250	-3250	-3250	-1880	-1750

*Do not add or deduct more than 40% of the automobile's wholesale value.

Edmund's

Mileage Adjustment Table 4

(based on driving average of 14,000 miles per year)

*Add (+) or deduct (-) dollar amount according to mileage and model year**

USED CARS WITH WHOLESALE VALUE OVER $15,000

Mileage	1994	1993	1992	1991	1990	1989	1988	1987	1986/85
0–7,000	+1710	+2230	+2300	+2360	+2720	+2990	+3190	+3240	+3280
7–14,000	+990	+1710	+2200	+2210	+2660	+2900	+3040	+3170	+3200
14–21,000	0	+1130	+2100	+2160	+2520	+2810	+2820	+3100	+3130
21–28,000	-440	+470	+2060	+2100	+2380	+2700	+2720	+2970	+3010
28–35,000	-1520	0	+1310	+2050	+2230	+2570	+2590	+2900	+2920
35–42,000	-2720	-1370	+620	+1960	+2050	+2360	+2480	+2750	+2770
42–49,000	-3400	-2500	0	+1710	+1890	+2230	+2380	+2600	+2630
49–56,000	-4210	-3670	-1240	+1040	+1530	+1960	+2160	+2410	+2430
56–63,000	-4680	-4460	-2380	0	+810	+1390	+1750	+2200	+2210
63–70,000	-5020	-4790	-3240	-360	0	+760	+1280	+1710	+1730
70–77,000	-5200	-5080	-4140	-1570	-1330	0	+450	+1300	+1330
77–84,000	-5320	-5220	-4840	-2700	-2470	-880	0	+410	+1080
84–91,000	-5400	-5340	-5110	-3960	-3150	-2250	-1390	0	+430
91–98,000	-5470	-5430	-5310	-4590	-4430	-3780	-2930	-1400	0
98,000 +	-5500	-5500	-5480	-5470	-5040	-5040	-4680	-2700	-2520

*Do not add or deduct more than 40% of the automobile's wholesale value.

ABBREVIATIONS

16V	16 Valve Engine
2WD	Two Wheel Drive
4SP	4 Speed Transmission
4SPD	4 Speed Transmission
4WD	Four Wheel Drive
4WS	Four Wheel Steering
5SP	5 Speed Transmission
5SPD	5 Speed Transmission
5SPD/AT	5 Speed or Automatic Transmission
6SP	6 Speed Transmission
6SPD	6 Speed Transmission
ABS	Anti-Lock Braking System
AC	Air Conditioning
ALUM	Aluminum
ANT	Antenna
AT	Automatic Transmission
AUTO	Automatic
AWD	All Wheel Drive
CD	Compact Disc
CNTRY	Country
CONV	Convertible
CPE	Coupe
CRS	Cruise
CTRL	Control
CUST	Custom
CVRS	Covers
CYL	Cylinder
DFRS	Dual Facing Rear Seats
DLX	Deluxe
DOHC	Dual Overhead Camshaft
DRW	Dual Rear Wheels
DR	Door
ENG	Engine
EQUIP	Equipment
EXT	Extended
FBK	Fastback
FWD	Front Wheel Drive
GRP	Group
HBK	Hatchback
HD	Heavy Duty
HT	Hardtop
L	Liter
LB	Longbed
LBK	Liftback
LD	Light Duty
LKS	Locks
LTD	Limited
LTHR	Leather
LUGRK	Luggage Rack
LUX	Luxury
LWB	Long Wheelbase
MPG	Miles Per Gallon
N/A	Not Available
NBK	Notchback
OD	Overdrive
P/U	Pickup Truck
PASS	Passenger
PDL	Power Door Locks
PERF	Performance
PKG	Package
PKUP	Pickup Truck
PNT	Paint
PREM	Premium
PS	Power Steering
PW	Power Windows
PWR	Power
RWD	Rear Wheel Drive
RDSTR	Roadster
RR	Rear
SB	Shortbed
SDN	Sedan
SEFI	Sequential Fuel Injection
SFTTP	Soft Top
SNRF	Sunroof
SOHC	Single Overhead Camshaft
SP	Speed
SPD	Speed
SPKRS	Speakers
SPT	Sport
SRS	Supplemental Restraint System (Airbag)
ST	Seat(s)
STD	Standard
STS	Seats
SWB	Short Wheelbase
SYS	System
TP	Tape
TPI	Tuned Port Injection
TRANS	Transmission
TRBO	Turbo
TURB	Turbo
W/T	Work Truck
WGN	Station Wagon
WHLS	Wheels
W/	With

ACURA

ACURA Japan

1992 Acura Integra 4-Dr RS Sedan

For an Acura dealer in your area, see our Dealer Directory (pg 217)

1994 ACURA

INTEGRA 4 Cyl 1994

Model/Body/Type	BaseList	Whlse	Retail
FWD/AT/PS/AC			
3 Dr RS Hbk	14670	**12975**	**15475**
4 Dr RS Sdn	15580	**13275**	**15775**
3 Dr LS Hbk	17210	**14550**	**17125**
4 Dr LS Sdn	17450	**14825**	**17425**
3 Dr GS-R Hbk (5 spd)	19440	**16325**	**19000**
4 Dr GS-R Sdn (5 spd)	19980	**16625**	**19425**

LEGEND V6 1994

Ratings

Rating	Score
Safety	8.4
Reliability	8.4
Performance	8.2
Design	8.3
Fun to drive	8
Value	7.5
Overall	8.3

Model/Body/Type	BaseList	Whlse	Retail
FWD/AT/PS/AC			
4 Dr L Sdn	33800	**26300**	**30225**
2 Dr L Cpe	37700	**28575**	**32625**
4 Dr LS Sdn	38600	-	-
2 Dr LS Cpe	41500	-	-
4 Dr GS Sdn	40700	-	-

NSX V6 1994

Model/Body/Type	BaseList	Whlse	Retail
5SP-AT/PS/AC			
2 Dr Cpe	72500	-	-

VIGOR 5 Cyl 1994

Model/Body/Type	BaseList	Whlse	Retail
FWD/AT/PS/AC			
4 Dr LS Sdn	26350	**19875**	**23100**
4 Dr GS Sdn	28350	-	-

ADD FOR ALL 94 ACURA:

Anti-Theft/Recovery Sys +365
Car Phone(Vigor,Legend,NSX) +230
Custom Whls +205
Leather Seats(Leg 4Dr L) +365

DEDUCT FOR ALL 94 ACURA:

No AC -680
No Auto Trans -590

1993 ACURA

INTEGRA 4 Cyl 1993

Ratings

Rating	Score
Safety	7.1
Reliability	9.5
Performance	8.6
Design	8.2
Fun to drive	8.5
Value	8.1
Overall	8.5

Model/Body/Type	BaseList	Whlse	Retail
FWD/AT/PS/AC			
3 Dr RS Hbk	12930	**10575**	**12775**
4 Dr RS Sdn	13855	**10750**	**13100**
3 Dr LS Hbk	14835	**11550**	**13925**
4 Dr LS Sdn	15585	**11750**	**14200**
3 Dr GS Hbk	17005	**13025**	**15525**
4 Dr GS Sdn	17545	**13225**	**15725**
3 Dr GS-R Hbk (5 spd)	18260	**13450**	**15975**

Model/Body/Type	BaseList	Whlse	Retail

LEGEND V6 1993

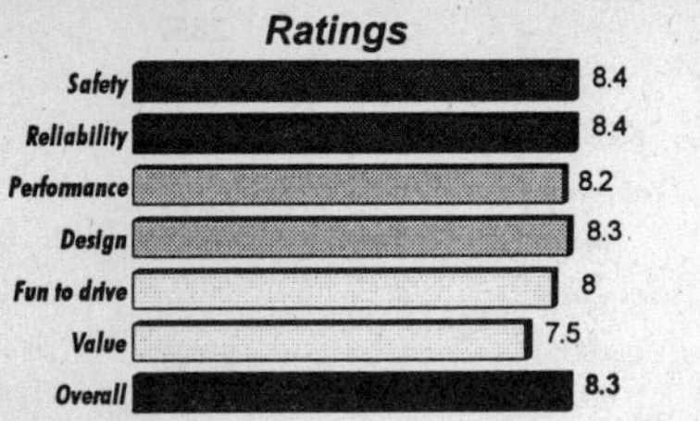

Ratings

Rating	Score
Safety	8.4
Reliability	8.4
Performance	8.2
Design	8.3
Fun to drive	8
Value	7.5
Overall	8.3

FWD/AT/PS/AC

Model/Body/Type	BaseList	Whlse	Retail
4 Dr Sdn	29200	**22300**	**25950**
4 Dr L Sdn	31200	**23700**	**27450**
2 Dr L Cpe	34450	**25100**	**29000**
4 Dr LS Sdn	35700	**26000**	**29900**
2 Dr LS Cpe	37850	**27450**	**31500**

NSX V6 1993

5SP-AT/PS/AC

Model/Body/Type	BaseList	Whlse	Retail
2 Dr Cpe	68000	**46750**	**51100**

VIGOR 5 Cyl 1993

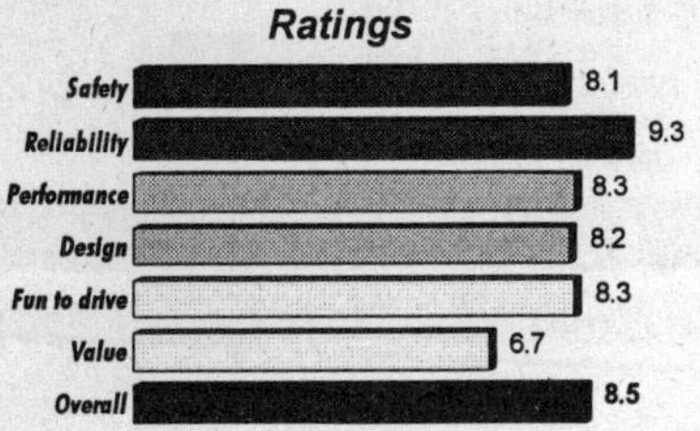

Ratings

Rating	Score
Safety	8.1
Reliability	9.3
Performance	8.3
Design	8.2
Fun to drive	8.3
Value	6.7
Overall	8.5

FWD/AT/PS/AC

Model/Body/Type	BaseList	Whlse	Retail
4 Dr LS Sdn	24265	**16725**	**19675**
4 Dr GS Sdn	26750	**18375**	**21475**

ADD FOR ALL 93 ACURA:

Car Phone(Vigor,Legend,NSX) +175
Cass(RS) +100
Custom Whls(RS) +175
Leather Seats(Std VigGS,LegLS,NSX) +315

DEDUCT FOR ALL 93 ACURA:

No AC -545
No Auto Trans -505

1992 ACURA

INTEGRA 4 Cyl 1992

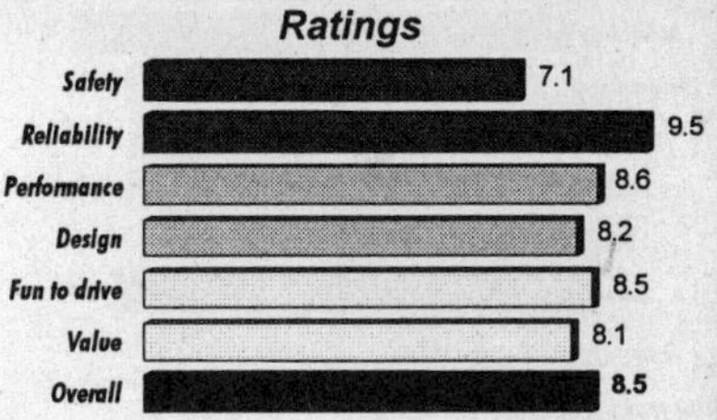

Ratings

Rating	Score
Safety	7.1
Reliability	9.5
Performance	8.6
Design	8.2
Fun to drive	8.5
Value	8.1
Overall	8.5

FWD/AT/PS/AC

Model/Body/Type	BaseList	Whlse	Retail
3 Dr RS Hbk	12335	**9875**	**12025**
4 Dr RS Sdn	13260	**10050**	**12225**
3 Dr LS Hbk	14240	**10700**	**13050**
4 Dr LS Sdn	14990	**10900**	**13250**
3 Dr GS Hbk	16410	**12100**	**14575**
4 Dr GS Sdn	16950	**12300**	**14775**
3 Dr GS-R Hbk (5 spd)	17910	**12525**	**15000**

LEGEND V6 1992

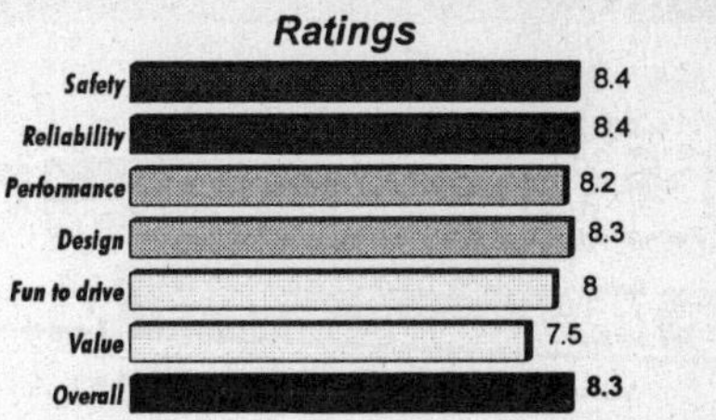

Ratings

Rating	Score
Safety	8.4
Reliability	8.4
Performance	8.2
Design	8.3
Fun to drive	8
Value	7.5
Overall	8.3

FWD/AT/PS/AC

Model/Body/Type	BaseList	Whlse	Retail
4 Dr Sdn	27450	**19050**	**22425**
4 Dr L Sdn	29850	**20350**	**23825**
2 Dr L Cpe	31300	**21650**	**25250**
4 Dr LS Sdn	34350	**22500**	**26175**
2 Dr LS Cpe	35700	**23800**	**27550**

NSX V6 1992

5SP-AT/PS/AC

Model/Body/Type	BaseList	Whlse	Retail
2 Dr Cpe	63000	**43050**	**47825**

ACURA 92-90

VIGOR 5 Cyl — 1992

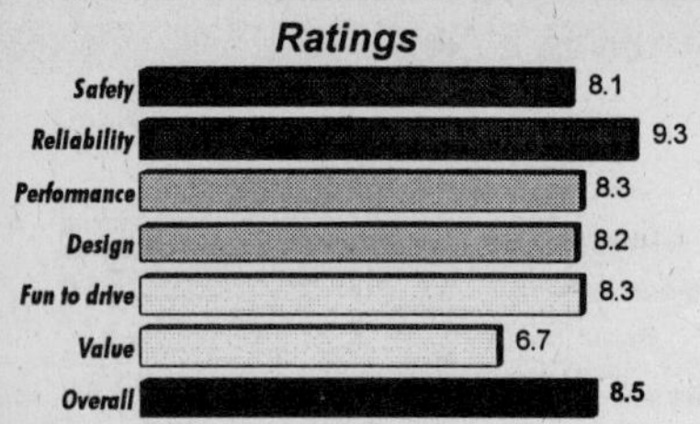

Model/Body/Type	BaseList	Whlse	Retail
FWD/AT/PS/AC			
4 Dr LS Sdn	23265	**14250**	**16950**
4 Dr GS Sdn	25250	**15425**	**18200**

ADD FOR ALL 92 ACURA:

Car Phone(Vigor,Legend,NSX) +160
Cass(RS) +75
Custom Whls(RS) +160
Leather Seats(Std VigorGS,LegendLS,NSX) +275

DEDUCT FOR ALL 92 ACURA:

No AC -505
No Auto Trans -470

1991 ACURA

INTEGRA 4 Cyl — 1991

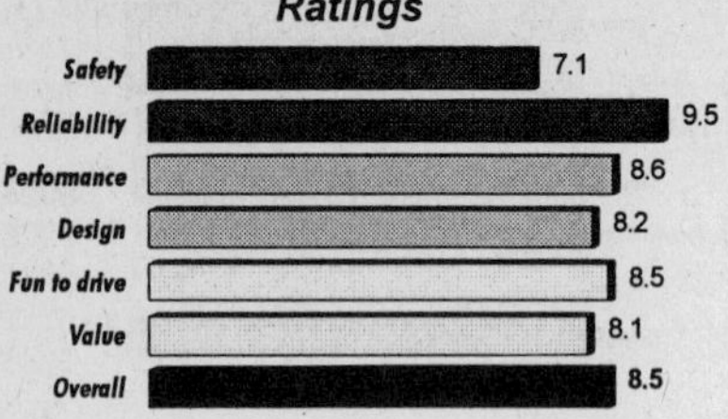

Model/Body/Type	BaseList	Whlse	Retail
FWD/AT/PS/AC			
3 Dr RS Hbk	11950	**8850**	**10850**
4 Dr RS Sdn	12850	**9050**	**11050**
3 Dr LS Hbk	13825	**9625**	**11675**
4 Dr LS Sdn	14545	**9800**	**11950**
3 Dr GS Hbk	15925	**10575**	**12800**
4 Dr GS Sdn	16450	**10775**	**13125**

LEGEND V6 — 1991

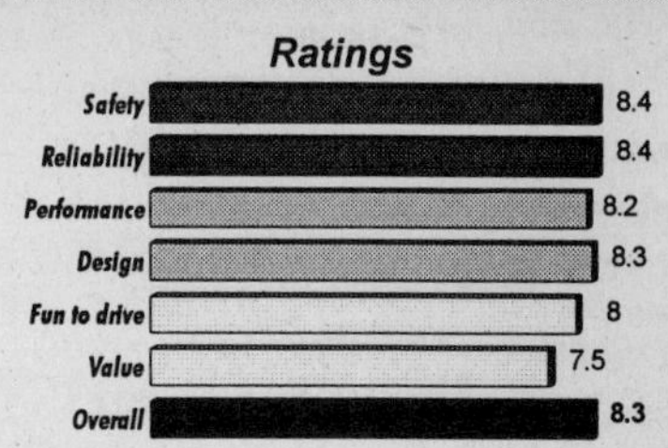

Model/Body/Type	BaseList	Whlse	Retail
FWD/AT/PS/AC			
4 Dr Sdn	26800	**16550**	**19725**
4 Dr L Sdn	28800	**17600**	**20900**
2 Dr L Cpe	30900	**18900**	**22250**
4 Dr LS Sdn	33400	**19475**	**22900**
2 Dr LS Cpe	35500	**20775**	**24275**

NSX V6 — 1991

Model/Body/Type	BaseList	Whlse	Retail
5SP-AT/PS/AC			
2 Dr Cpe	60000	**39325**	**44050**

ADD FOR ALL 91 ACURA:

Car Phone(Legend,NSX) +135
Cass(RS) +60
Custom Whls(RS) +135
Leather Seats(Std LegendLS,NSX) +215

DEDUCT FOR ALL 91 ACURA:

No AC -470
No Auto Trans -430

1990 ACURA

INTEGRA 4 Cyl — 1990

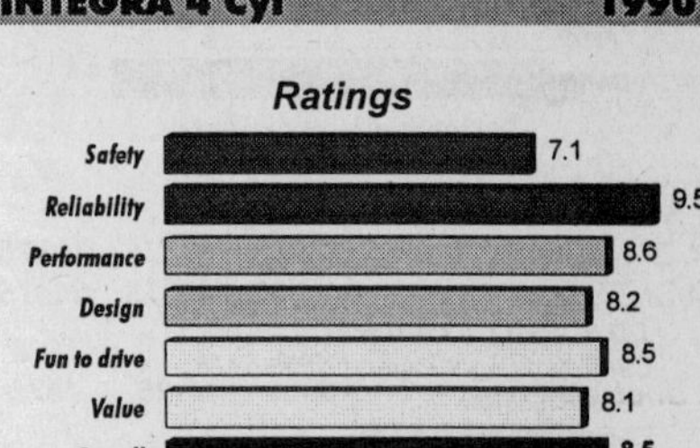

Model/Body/Type	BaseList	Whlse	Retail
FWD/AT/PS/AC			
3 Dr RS Hbk	11950	**7150**	**9025**
4 Dr RS Sdn	12850	**7350**	**9225**
3 Dr LS Hbk	13725	**7875**	**9800**
4 Dr LS Sdn	14545	**8075**	**9975**
3 Dr GS Hbk	15825	**8650**	**10575**
4 Dr GS Sdn	15950	**8850**	**10850**

LEGEND V6 1990

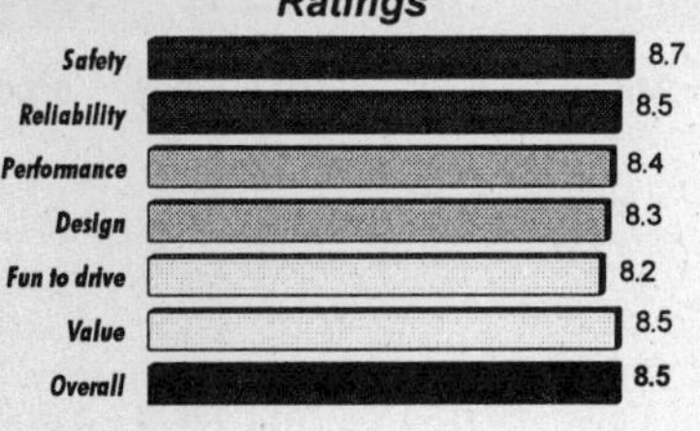

Model/Body/Type	BaseList	Whlse	Retail
FWD/AT/PS/AC			
4 Dr Sdn	22600	**10825**	**13575**
2 Dr Cpe	24760	**12050**	**14875**
4 Dr L Sdn	25900	**11800**	**14625**
2 Dr L Cpe	27325	**13050**	**15925**
4 Dr LS Sdn	29610	**12775**	**15650**
2 Dr LS Cpe	30690	**14025**	**16975**

ADD FOR ALL 90 ACURA:

Cass(RS) +60
Custom Whls(RS) +115
Leather Seats(Std Legend LS) +160
Pwr Sunroof(Base Legend Sdn) +390

DEDUCT FOR ALL 90 ACURA:

No AC -430
No Auto Trans -390

1989 ACURA

INTEGRA 4 Cyl 1989

Model/Body/Type	BaseList	Whlse	Retail
FWD/AT/PS/AC			
3 Dr RS Hbk	11260	**5200**	**6900**
5 Dr RS Hbk	12060	**5400**	**7125**
3 Dr LS Hbk	13070	**5875**	**7625**
5 Dr LS Hbk	13900	**6125**	**7825**

LEGEND V6 1989

Ratings

Rating	Score
Safety	8.7
Reliability	8.5
Performance	8.4
Design	8.3
Fun to drive	8.2
Value	8.5
Overall	8.5

Model/Body/Type	BaseList	Whlse	Retail
FWD/AT/PS/AC			
4 Dr Sdn	22600	**8125**	**10325**
2 Dr Cpe	24760	**9325**	**11675**
4 Dr L Sdn	25900	**9075**	**11425**
2 Dr L Cpe	27325	**10200**	**12850**
4 Dr LS Sdn	29160	**9775**	**12300**
2 Dr LS Cpe	30040	**10900**	**13650**

ADD FOR ALL 89 ACURA:

Cass(RS) +35
Custom Whls +75
Leather Seats(Std Legend LS) +135
Pwr Sunroof(Base Legend Sdn) +330

DEDUCT FOR ALL 89 ACURA:

No AC -390
No Auto Trans -350

1988 ACURA

INTEGRA 4 Cyl 1988

Model/Body/Type	BaseList	Whlse	Retail
FWD/AT/PS/AC			
3 Dr RS Hbk	10545	**3600**	**5025**
5 Dr RS Hbk	11300	**3800**	**5275**
3 Dr LS Hbk	12240	**4125**	**5675**
5 Dr LS Hbk	13030	**4325**	**5875**
3 Dr SE Hbk	13670	**4350**	**5875**

LEGEND V6 1988

Model/Body/Type	BaseList	Whlse	Retail
FWD/AT/PS/AC			
4 Dr Sdn	21010	**6350**	**8375**
2 Dr Cpe	23096	**7475**	**9700**
4 Dr L Sdn	24998	**7125**	**9300**
2 Dr L Cpe	26578	**8250**	**10475**
4 Dr LS Sdn	27541	**7850**	**10050**
2 Dr LS Cpe	28377	**9000**	**11325**

DEDUCT FOR ALL 88 ACURA:

No AC -330
No Auto Trans -290

ACURA 87-86

1987 ACURA

Model/Body/Type	BaseList	Whlse	Retail
INTEGRA 4 Cyl			**1987**
FWD/AT/PS/AC			
3 Dr RS Hbk	9859	**3050**	**4400**
5 Dr RS Hbk	10559	**3225**	**4625**
3 Dr LS Hbk	11359	**3450**	**4850**
5 Dr LS Hbk	12159	**3650**	**5075**
LEGEND V6			**1987**
FWD/AT/PS/AC			
4 Dr Sdn	19898	**5175**	**7150**
2 Dr Cpe	22458	**6250**	**8275**
4 Dr L Sdn	23198	**5800**	**7775**
2 Dr L Cpe	26108	**6850**	**9000**
2 Dr LS Cpe	27958	**7400**	**9625**

1986 ACURA

Model/Body/Type	BaseList	Whlse	Retail
INTEGRA			**1986**
FWD			
3 Dr RS Hbk	9298	**2025**	**3450**
5 Dr RS Hbk	9948	**2175**	**3650**
3 Dr LS Hbk	10593	**2400**	**3925**
5 Dr LS Hbk	11343	**2575**	**4125**
LEGEND			**1986**
FWD			
4 Dr Sdn	19298	**4300**	**6100**

Model/Body/Type	BaseList	Whlse	Retail

ALFA ROMEO Italy

1991 Alfa Romeo 164

For an Alfa Romeo dealer in your area, see our Dealer Directory (pg 217)

1994 ALFA ROMEO

164 V6 1994

AT/PS/AC

Model/Body/Type	BaseList	Whlse	Retail
4 Dr LS Sdn	34890	-	-
4 Dr S Quadrifoglio (5 spd)	37690	-	-

SPIDER 4 Cyl 1994

5SP/PS/AC

Model/Body/Type	BaseList	Whlse	Retail
2 Dr Conv	22590	-	-
2 Dr Veloce Conv	27590	-	-

1993 ALFA ROMEO

164 V6 1993

AT/PS/AC

Model/Body/Type	BaseList	Whlse	Retail
4 Dr L Sdn	30240	16075	18875
4 Dr S Sdn (5 spd)	34990	18725	21850

SPIDER 4 Cyl 1993

5SP/PS/AC

Model/Body/Type	BaseList	Whlse	Retail
2 Dr Conv	21764	13100	15600
2 Dr Veloce Conv	24870	14850	17450

ADD FOR ALL 93 ALFA ROMEO:
Auto Trans(Spider) +430
Car Phone(164) +175
CD Player +195
DEDUCT FOR ALL 93 ALFA ROMEO:
No AC -545
No Auto Trans -505

1992 ALFA ROMEO

164 V6 1992

AT/PS/AC

Model/Body/Type	BaseList	Whlse	Retail
4 Dr L Sdn	29490	13800	16475
4 Dr S Sdn (5 spd)	34990	16250	19075

SPIDER 4 Cyl 1992

5SP/PS/AC

Model/Body/Type	BaseList	Whlse	Retail
2 Dr Conv	21264	12175	14650
2 Dr Veloce Conv	24309	13775	16300

ADD FOR ALL 92 ALFA ROMEO:
Auto Trans(Spider) +390
Car Phone(164) +160
CD Player +175
DEDUCT FOR ALL 92 ALFA ROMEO:
No AC -505
No Auto Trans -470

1991 ALFA ROMEO

164 V6 1991

AT/PS/AC

Model/Body/Type	BaseList	Whlse	Retail
4 Dr Sdn	24500	8675	10750
4 Dr L Sdn	27500	10400	12725
4 Dr S Sdn (5 spd)	29500	11300	13750

SPIDER 4 Cyl 1991

5SP/PS/AC

Model/Body/Type	BaseList	Whlse	Retail
2 Dr Conv	20950	9725	11850
2 Dr Veloce Conv	22950	10950	13300

ADD FOR ALL 91 ALFA ROMEO:
Auto Trans(Spider) +350
Car Phone(164) +135
Detachable Hardtop +430
Pwr Sunroof +350
DEDUCT FOR ALL 91 ALFA ROMEO:
No AC -470
No Auto Trans -430

1990 ALFA ROMEO

SPIDER 4 Cyl 1990

AC

Model/Body/Type	BaseList	Whlse	Retail
2 Dr Veloce Conv	20950	9425	11450
2 Dr Quadrifoglio Conv	23950	10100	12275
2 Dr Graduate Conv	16950	8025	9950

ADD FOR ALL 90 ALFA ROMEO:
Cass(Graduate) +60
DEDUCT FOR ALL 90 ALFA ROMEO:
No AC -430

Model/Body/Type	BaseList	Whlse	Retail

1989 ALFA ROMEO

MILANO V6			1989
AT/AC			
4 Dr Gold Sdn	18475	4900	6575
4 Dr Platinum Sdn	22500	5300	7000
4 Dr 3.0L Sdn (5 spd)	22700	5925	7650

SPIDER 4 Cyl			1989
AC			
2 Dr Veloce Conv	20200	7550	9450
2 Dr Quadrifoglio Conv	23400	8225	10150
2 Dr Graduate Conv	16700	6375	8125

ADD FOR ALL 89 ALFA ROMEO:
Cass(Graduate) +35
Pwr Sunroof +250

DEDUCT FOR ALL 89 ALFA ROMEO:
No AC -390
No Auto Trans(164) -350

1988 ALFA ROMEO

MILANO V6			1988
AT/AC			
4 Dr Gold Sdn	17550	2950	4300
4 Dr Platinum Sdn	21450	3175	4575
4 Dr 3.0L Verde Sdn (5 spd)	21650	3675	5100

SPIDER 4 Cyl			1988
AC			
2 Dr Veloce Conv	19380	5875	7600
2 Dr Quadrifoglio Conv	22440	6500	8250
2 Dr Graduate Conv	15950	4775	6425

DEDUCT FOR ALL 88 ALFA ROMEO:
No AC -330
No Auto Trans(164) -290

1987 ALFA ROMEO

MILANO V6			1987
AC			
4 Dr Silver Sdn	12850	2275	3500

SPIDER 4 Cyl			1987
AC			
2 Dr Veloce Conv	16995	4600	6175
2 Dr Quadrifoglio Conv	20500	5125	6825
2 Dr Graduate Conv	13995	3600	5025

ADD FOR ALL 87 ALFA ROMEO:
Platinum Pkg +430

1986 ALFA ROMEO

GTV-6			1986
2 Dr Cpe	16500	2900	4225

SPIDER			1986
2 Dr Veloce Conv	16995	3700	5100
2 Dr Quadrifoglio Conv	19600	4100	5575
2 Dr Graduate Conv	13995	2825	4150

1985 ALFA ROMEO

GTV-6			1985
2 Dr Cpe	16500	2425	3700

SPIDER			1985
2 Dr Veloce Conv	16500	3150	4525
2 Dr Graduate Conv	13495	2325	3575

AMC
USA

1986 AMC Alliance Convertible

For a dealer in your area, see our Dealer Directory (pg 217)

1987 AMERICAN MOTORS

Model/Body/Type	BaseList	Whlse	Retail
ALLIANCE 4 Cyl			**1987**
FWD/AT/PS/AC			
4 Dr Sdn	6399	550	1350
2 Dr Sdn	6199	450	1275
3 Dr Hbk	6199	500	1300
4 Dr L Sdn	7000	700	1525
2 Dr L Sdn	6725	600	1400
3 Dr L Hbk	6775	650	1450
5 Dr L Hbk	7050	750	1575
2 Dr L Conv	10899	1850	2925
4 Dr DL Sdn	7700	850	1700
2 Dr DL Sdn	7425	750	1575
3 Dr DL Hbk	7475	800	1625
5 Dr DL Hbk	7750	875	1725
2 Dr DL Conv	11899	2000	3100
3 Dr GS Hbk	8299	925	1800
2 Dr GTA Sdn (5 spd)	8999	950	1825
2 Dr GTA Conv (5 spd)	12899	2150	3225
EAGLE 4WD V6			**1987**
AT/PS/AC			
4 Dr Sdn	11150	1075	2075
4 Dr Wgn	11943	1275	2275
4 Dr Limited Wgn	12653	1625	2700

1986 AMERICAN MOTORS

Model/Body/Type	BaseList	Whlse	Retail
ALLIANCE 4 Cyl			**1986**
FWD			
4 Dr Sdn	5995	225	1150
2 Dr Sdn	5895	200	1050
4 Dr L Sdn	6645	350	1275
2 Dr L Sdn	6395	275	1200
2 Dr L Conv	10345	1300	2350
4 Dr DL Sdn	7245	450	1375
2 Dr DL Sdn	6995	375	1300
2 Dr DL Conv	11345	1375	2475
EAGLE V6			**1986**
4WD			
4 Dr Sdn	10615	850	1800
4 Dr Wgn	11385	1025	2050
4 Dr Limited Wgn	12075	1325	2375
ENCORE 4 Cyl			**1986**
FWD			
3 Dr S Lbk	6545	250	1175
5 Dr S Lbk	6795	325	1275
3 Dr Electronic Lbk	7275	375	1325
3 Dr LS Lbk	7145	375	1325
5 Dr LS Lbk	7395	475	1400
3 Dr GS Lbk	7695	600	1550

1985 AMERICAN MOTORS

Model/Body/Type	BaseList	Whlse	Retail
ALLIANCE			**1985**
FWD			
2 Dr Sdn	6161	200	950
4 Dr L Sdn	6761	250	1175
2 Dr L Sdn	6511	200	1075
2 Dr L Conv	10295	1075	2100
4 Dr DL Sdn	7361	325	1275
2 Dr DL Sdn	7111	250	1175
2 Dr DL Conv	11295	1150	2175
4 Dr Limited Sdn	7861	475	1400
EAGLE			**1985**
4WD			
4 Dr Sdn	10457	625	1600
4 Dr Wgn	11217	825	1775
4 Dr Limited Wgn	11893	1075	2125
ENCORE			**1985**
FWD			
3 Dr Lbk	5959	200	950
3 Dr S Lbk	6409	200	1075
5 Dr S Lbk	6659	250	1175
3 Dr LS Lbk	7109	275	1200
5 Dr LS Lbk	7359	350	1275
3 Dr GS Lbk	7609	450	1375

AUDI

Germany

1991 Audi 100 Quattro

For an Audi dealer in your area, see our Dealer Directory (pg 217)

1994 AUDI

90 V6 — 1994

Model/Body/Type	BaseList	Whlse	Retail
FWD/AT/PS/AC			
4 Dr S Sdn	27820	**20650**	**24150**
4 Dr CS Sdn	30770	**22825**	**26525**
4 Dr CS Quattro Sport (5 spd)	34420	-	-

100 V6 — 1994

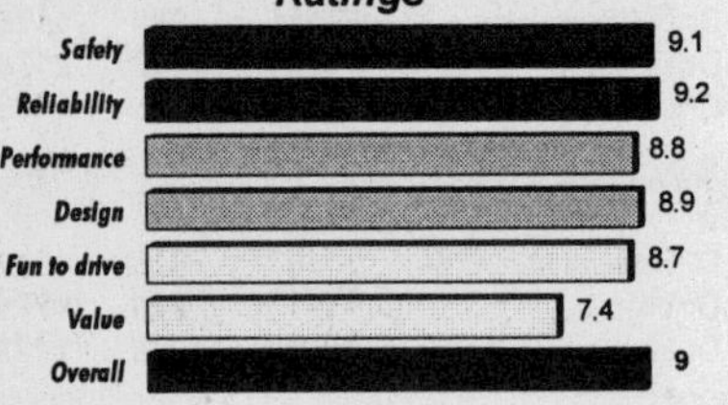

Model/Body/Type	BaseList	Whlse	Retail
FWD/AT/PS/AC			
4 Dr S Sdn	35120	**24650**	**28475**
4 Dr S Wgn	38070	**26925**	**30950**
4 Dr CS Sdn	40570	**28600**	**32650**
4 Dr CS Quattro Sdn	43020	-	-
4 Dr CS Quattro Wgn	47020	-	-
4 Dr S4 Sdn (5 spd)	49070	-	-
4 Dr V8 Quattro Sdn	58700	-	-

ADD FOR ALL 94 AUDI:

Anti-Theft/Recovery Sys +365
Car Phone(Std S4,V8) +230
CD Player(Std V8) +340
Leather Seats(90S +100S) +365
Pwr Sunroof(90S) +635

DEDUCT FOR ALL 94 AUDI:

No Auto Trans -680

1993 AUDI

90 V6 — 1993

Model/Body/Type	BaseList	Whlse	Retail
FWD/AT/PS/AC			
4 Dr S Sdn	25850	**16750**	**19925**
4 Dr CS Sdn	28700	**18700**	**22050**
4 Dr CS Quattro Sport Sdn (5 spd)	32250	**20975**	**24475**

100 V6 — 1993

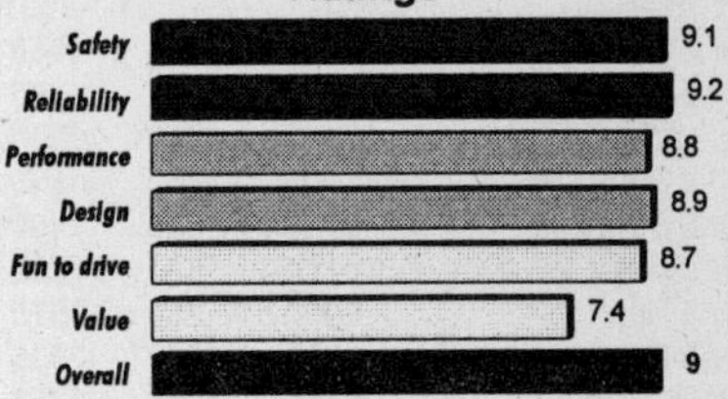

Model/Body/Type	BaseList	Whlse	Retail
FWD/AT/PS/AC			
4 Dr Sdn	30400	**18350**	**21700**
4 Dr S Sdn	33250	**20125**	**23575**
4 Dr CS Sdn	37750	**21900**	**25525**
4 Dr CS Quattro Sdn	40950	**24800**	**28650**
4 Dr CS Quattro Wgn	44250	**26650**	**30650**
4 Dr S4 Sdn (5 spd)	46850	**32500**	**36500**
4 Dr V8 Quattro Sdn	56400	**37600**	**42125**

ADD FOR ALL 93 AUDI:

Car Phone(Std S4,V8) +175
CD Player(Std V8) +290
Leather Seats(100S) +315
Pwr Sunroof(90S) +505

DEDUCT FOR ALL 93 AUDI:

No Auto Trans -585

Model/Body/Type	BaseList	Whlse	Retail

1992 AUDI

80 5 Cyl — 1992

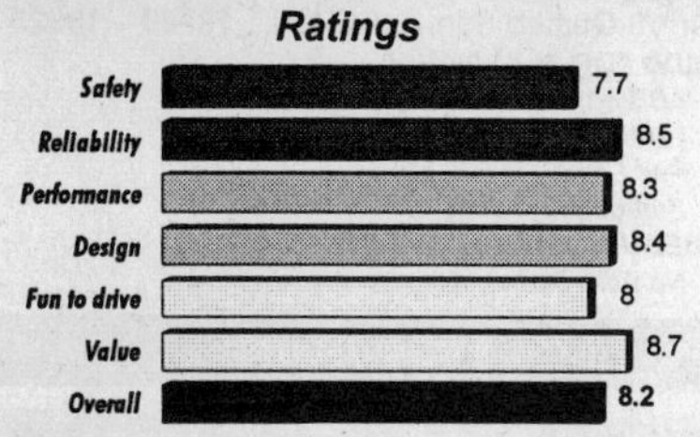

FWD/AT/PS/AC

Model/Body/Type	BaseList	Whlse	Retail
4 Dr Sdn	22650	**10825**	**13575**
4 Dr Quattro Sdn(5 spd)	26250	**12900**	**15775**

100 V6 — 1992

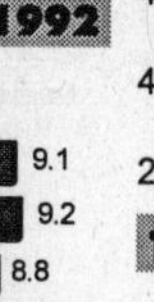

FWD/AT/PS/AC

Model/Body/Type	BaseList	Whlse	Retail
4 Dr Sdn	27700	**16150**	**19250**
4 Dr S Sdn	29900	**17475**	**20775**
4 Dr CS Sdn	32900	**18725**	**22075**
4 Dr CS Quattro Sdn	36400	**21400**	**24900**
4 Dr CS Quattro Wgn	40800	**23000**	**26700**
4 Dr S4 Sdn (5 spd)	43750	**29175**	**33275**
4 Dr V8 Quattro Sdn	53100	**31450**	**35550**

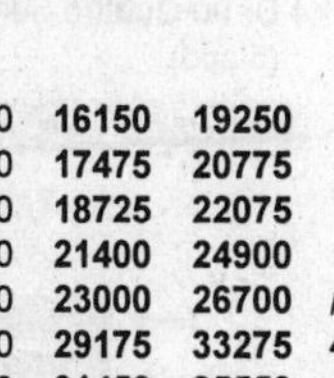

ADD FOR ALL 92 AUDI:

Car Phone(Std S4,V8) +160
CD Player(Std V8) +250
Leather Seats(100S,100CS Sdns) +275
Pwr Sunroof(80) +470

DEDUCT FOR ALL 92 AUDI:

No Auto Trans -545

1991 AUDI

80/90 5 Cyl — 1991

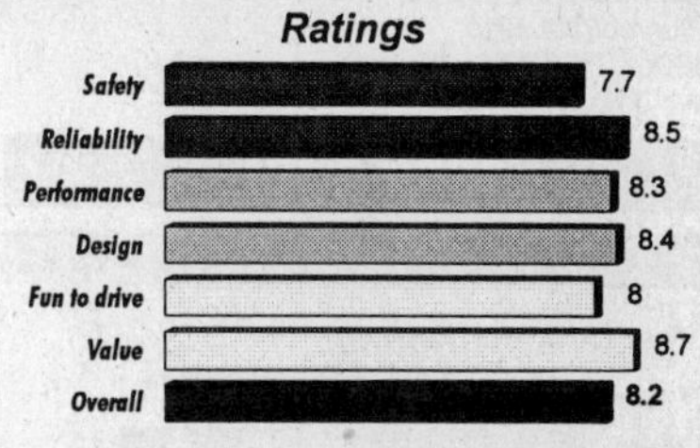

FWD/AT/PS/AC

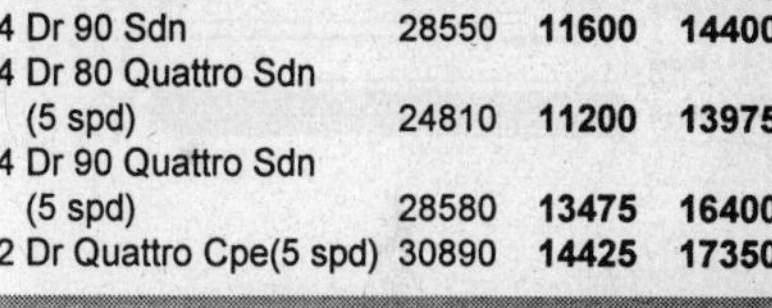

Model/Body/Type	BaseList	Whlse	Retail
4 Dr 80 Sdn	21045	**9375**	**11750**
4 Dr 90 Sdn	28550	**11600**	**14400**
4 Dr 80 Quattro Sdn (5 spd)	24810	**11200**	**13975**
4 Dr 90 Quattro Sdn (5 spd)	28580	**13475**	**16400**
2 Dr Quattro Cpe(5 spd)	30890	**14425**	**17350**

100/200 5 Cyl — 1991

Ratings

Safety 8.1
Reliability 6.7
Performance 8.9
Design 8.3
Fun to drive 8.3
Value 7.5
Overall 7.8

FWD/AT/PS/AC

Model/Body/Type	BaseList	Whlse	Retail
4 Dr 100 Sdn	28150	**11375**	**14150**
4 Dr 100 Quattro Sdn (5 spd)	30510	**13150**	**16050**
4 Dr 200 Turbo Sdn	34580	**14400**	**17325**
4 Dr 200 Turbo Quattro Sdn (5 spd)	42400	**16150**	**19250**
4 Dr 200 Turbo Quattro Wgn (5 spd)	42400	**16500**	**19600**
4 Dr V8 Quattro Sdn	50200	**22900**	**26600**

AUDI

AUDI 92-89

ADD FOR ALL 91 AUDI:
ABS(Base 80) +315
Car Phone(Std 200 Quattro Sdn,V8) +135
Leather Seats(Std Quattro Cpe,200,V8) +215
Pwr Seats(Std 200,V8) +135
Sunroof(80) +215
DEDUCT FOR ALL 91 AUDI:
No Auto Trans -505

1990 AUDI

80 4 Cyl/90 5 Cyl — 1990

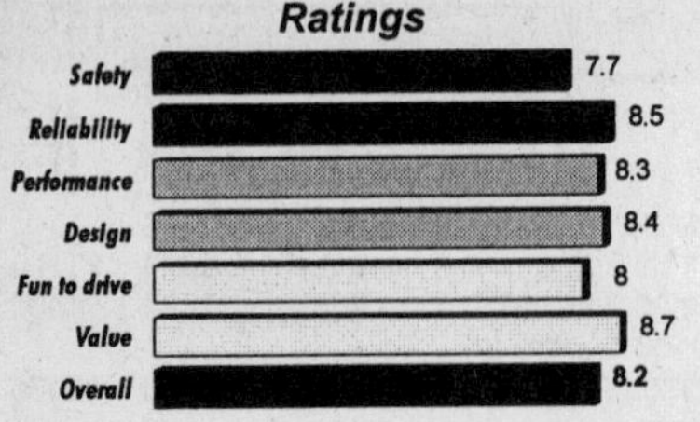

Model/Body/Type	BaseList	Whlse	Retail
FWD/AT/PS/AC			
4 Dr 80 Sdn	19485	**7425**	**9650**
4 Dr 90 Sdn	24575	**9675**	**12200**
4 Dr 80 Quattro Sdn (5 spd)	22800	**9100**	**11450**
4 Dr 90 Quattro Sdn (5 spd)	27500	**11275**	**14050**
2 Dr Quattro Cpe(5 spd)	29750	**12300**	**15125**

100/200 5 Cyl — 1990

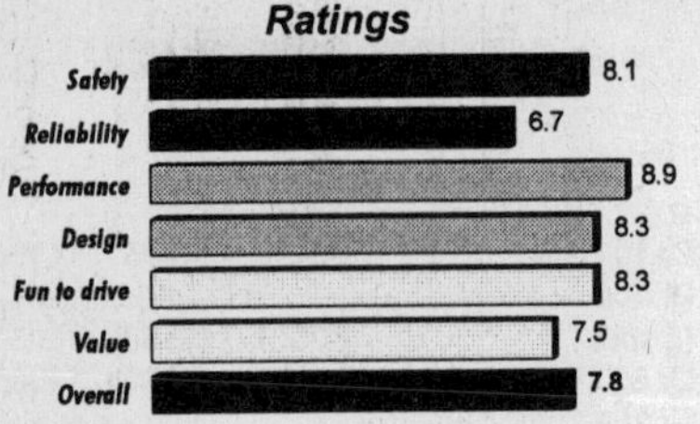

Model/Body/Type	BaseList	Whlse	Retail
FWD/AT/PS/AC			
4 Dr 100 Sdn	26900	**8975**	**11300**
4 Dr 100 Quattro Sdn (5 spd)	29470	**10475**	**13150**
4 Dr 200 Turbo Sdn	33405	**11250**	**14025**
4 Dr 200 Turbo Quattro Sdn (5 spd)	35805	**12800**	**15675**
4 Dr 200 Turbo Quattro Wgn (5 spd)	36930	**13125**	**16025**
4 Dr V8 Quattro Sdn	47450	**16750**	**19925**

ADD FOR ALL 90 AUDI:
ABS(80) +275
Leather Seats(Std Cpe,200,V8) +160
Pwr Seats(Std 200,V8) +115
Sunroof(80) +160
DEDUCT FOR ALL 90 AUDI:
No Auto Trans -470

1989 AUDI

80 4 Cyl/90 5 Cyl — 1989

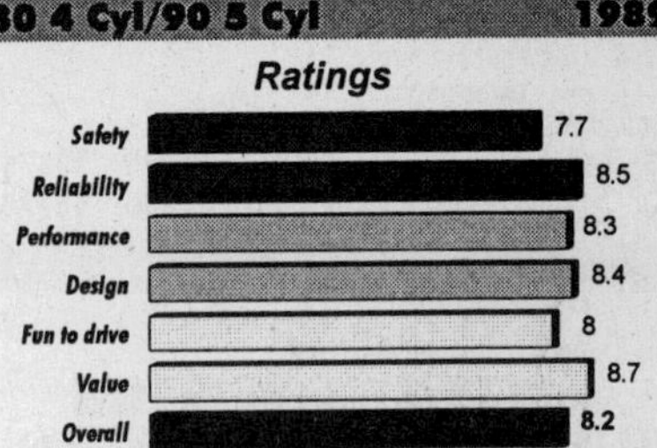

Model/Body/Type	BaseList	Whlse	Retail
FWD/AT/PS/AC			
4 Dr 80 Sdn	19350	**5650**	**7600**
4 Dr 90 Sdn	25310	**7600**	**9825**
4 Dr 80 Quattro Sdn (5 spd)	23610	**7150**	**9350**
4 Dr 90 Quattro Sdn (5 spd)	28840	**9150**	**11500**

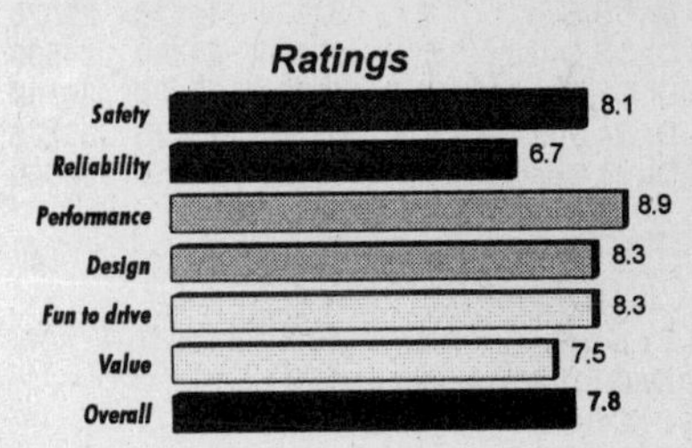

Model/Body/Type	BaseList	Whlse	Retail
FWD/AT/PS/AC			
4 Dr 100 E Sdn	24980	6175	8175
4 Dr 100 Sdn	27480	7100	9275
4 Dr 100 Wgn	28960	7375	9600
4 Dr 100 Quattro Sdn (5 spd)	30805	8525	10750
4 Dr 200 Turbo Sdn	32455	9150	11500
4 Dr 200 Turbo Quattro Sdn (5 spd)	36355	10525	13200
4 Dr 200 Turbo Quattro Wgn (5 spd)	37855	10825	13575

ADD FOR ALL 89 AUDI:
Cass(80) +75
Leather Seats(Std 90,200,Quattro) +135
Pwr Seats(Std 200) +100
Pwr Sunroof(80) +330
DEDUCT FOR ALL 89 AUDI:
No Auto Trans -430

1988 AUDI

80 4 Cyl/90 4-5 Cyl — 1988

Model/Body/Type	BaseList	Whlse	Retail
FWD/AT/PS/AC			
4 Dr 80 Sdn	18600	4225	5975
4 Dr 90 Sdn	24330	5725	7675
4 Dr 80 Quattro Sdn (5 spd)	22700	5600	7550
4 Dr 90 Quattro Sdn (5 spd)	27720	7100	9275

5000 5 Cyl — 1988

Model/Body/Type	BaseList	Whlse	Retail
FWD/AT/PS/AC			
4 Dr S Sdn	22180	4600	6400
4 Dr S Wgn	23620	4850	6725
4 Dr CS Turbo Sdn	30010	5975	7975
4 Dr S Quattro Sdn (5 spd)	26490	5875	7850
4 Dr CS Turbo Quattro Sdn (5 spd)	33800	7250	9450
4 Dr CS Turbo Quattro Wgn (5 spd)	35250	7525	9775

DEDUCT FOR ALL 88 AUDI:
No Auto Trans -390

1987 AUDI

4000 4-5 Cyl — 1987

Model/Body/Type	BaseList	Whlse	Retail
FWD/AT/PS/AC			
4 Dr S Sdn	15875	2550	4000
2 Dr GT Cpe	17580	3175	4750
4 Dr CS Quattro Sdn (5 spd)	19850	3225	4825

5000 5 Cyl — 1987

Model/Body/Type	BaseList	Whlse	Retail
FWD/AT/PS/AC			
4 Dr S Sdn	20060	2825	4350
4 Dr S Wgn	21390	3075	4650
4 Dr CS Turbo Sdn	26640	3725	5400
4 Dr CS Turbo Quattro Sdn (5 spd)	31250	4850	6725
4 Dr CS Turbo Quattro Wgn (5 spd)	32555	5075	7025

1986 AUDI

4000 — 1986

Model/Body/Type	BaseList	Whlse	Retail
FWD			
4 Dr S Sdn	14230	1950	3125
2 Dr GT Cpe	15555	2425	3675
4 Dr CS Quattro Sdn (5 spd)	17800	2675	3975

5000 — 1986

Model/Body/Type	BaseList	Whlse	Retail
FWD			
4 Dr S Sdn	18065	2225	3425
4 Dr S Wgn	19750	2425	3675
4 Dr CS Turbo Sdn	24570	2775	4075
4 Dr CS Turbo Quattro Sdn (5 spd)	27975	3950	5375
4 Dr CS Turbo Quattro Wgn (5 spd)	29185	4175	5675

1985 AUDI

4000 — 1985

Model/Body/Type	BaseList	Whlse	Retail
4 Dr S Sdn	13950	1400	2500
2 Dr GT Cpe	15250	1825	3025
4 Dr S Quattro Sdn	17450	2125	3300

5000 — 1985

Model/Body/Type	BaseList	Whlse	Retail
4 Dr S Sdn	17710	1775	2950
4 Dr S Wgn	19370	1950	3125
4 Dr Turbo Sdn	23875	2025	3200

BMW — Germany

1988 BMW 325

For a BMW dealer in your area, see our Dealer Directory (pg 217)

1994 BMW

3-Series — 1994

AT/PS/AC

Model/Body/Type	BaseList	Whlse	Retail
4 Cyl Models			
318is 2 Dr Cpe	25800	**21500**	**25075**
318i 4 Dr Sdn	24675	**20600**	**24100**
318i 2 Dr Conv	29900	-	-
6 Cyl Models			
325is 2 Dr Cpe	32200	**26325**	**30250**
325i 4 Dr Sdn	30850	**25325**	**29200**
325i 2 Dr Conv	38800	-	-

5-Series 6 Cyl — 1994

AT/PS/AC

Model/Body/Type	BaseList	Whlse	Retail
525i 4 Dr Sdn	38425	**31000**	**35025**
525i 5 Dr Touring Wgn	40600	-	-
530i 4 Dr Sdn	40000	-	-
530i 5 Dr Touring Wgn	44000	-	-
540i 4 Dr Sdn	47000	-	-

7-Series V8 — 1994

AT/PS/AC

Model/Body/Type	BaseList	Whlse	Retail
740i 4 Dr Sdn	55950	-	-
740iL 4 Dr Sdn	59950	-	-
750iL 4 Dr Sdn(V12)	83950	-	-

8-Series V12 — 1994

AT/PS/AC

Model/Body/Type	BaseList	Whlse	Retail
840Ci 2 Dr Cpe	68100	-	-
850Ci 2 Dr Cpe	85500	-	-
850CSi 2 Dr Cpe	98500	-	-

ADD FOR ALL 94 BMW:

Anti-Theft/Recovery Sys +365
CD Player(Std 750iL,850Ci +CSi) +340
Car Phone(Std 750iL,850Ci +CSi) +230
Leather Seats(325i 4Dr) +590
Sports Pkg +365
Traction Ctrl(Std 530i Wgn +750 +840 +850) +955

DEDUCT FOR ALL 94 BMW:

No Auto Trans -680

1993 BMW

3-Series — 1993

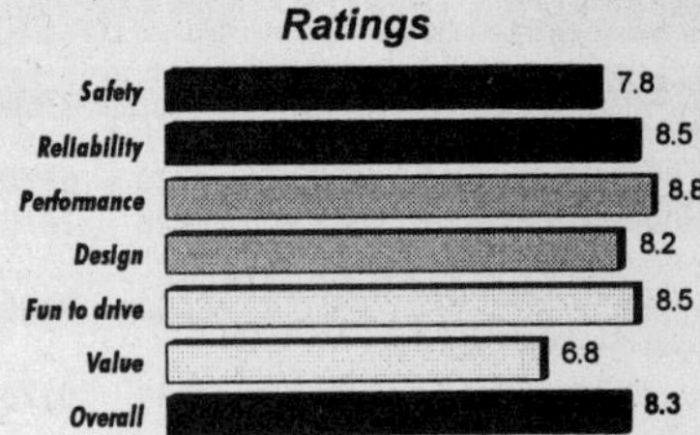

AT/PS/AC

Model/Body/Type	BaseList	Whlse	Retail
4 Cyl Models			
318is 2 Dr Cpe	24810	**19350**	**22725**
318i 4 Dr Sdn	23710	**18550**	**21900**
6 Cyl Models			
325is 2 Dr Cpe	30950	**24000**	**27750**
325i 4 Dr Sdn	29650	**23100**	**26800**
325i 2 Dr Conv (5 spd)	36320	**28625**	**32675**

5-Series 6 Cyl — 1993

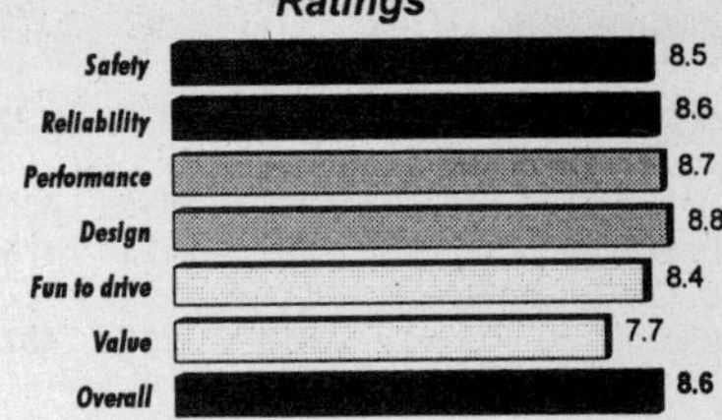

Model/Body/Type	BaseList	Whlse	Retail
AT/PS/AC			
525i 4 Dr Sdn	37100	**26950**	**30975**
525i 5 Dr Touring Wgn	39800	**28125**	**32150**
535i 4 Dr Sdn	44350	**32325**	**36325**
M5 4 Dr Sdn (5 spd)	60700	**44900**	**49150**

7-Series V8 — 1993

Model/Body/Type	BaseList	Whlse	Retail
AT/PS/AC			
740i 4 Dr Sdn	54000	**36800**	**41025**
740iL 4 Dr Sdn	58000	**38975**	**43550**
750iL 4 Dr Sdn(V12)	80900	**48850**	**54325**

8-Series V12 — 1993

Model/Body/Type	BaseList	Whlse	Retail
AT/PS/AC			
850Ci 2 Dr Cpe	83400	**52950**	**57650**

ADD FOR ALL 93 BMW:
CD Player(Std 750iL,850Ci) +290
Car Phone(Std 750iL,850Ci) +175
Leather Seats(325i 4D,525i Touring) +470
Sports Pkg +315
DEDUCT FOR ALL 93 BMW:
No Auto Trans -585

1992 BMW

3-Series — 1992

Ratings

Rating	Score
Safety	7.8
Reliability	8.5
Performance	8.8
Design	8.2
Fun to drive	8.5
Value	6.8
Overall	8.3

Model/Body/Type	BaseList	Whlse	Retail
5SP/PS/AC			
4 Cyl Models			
318is 2 Dr Cpe	23600	**15500**	**18550**
318i 4 Dr Sdn	22900	**14800**	**17800**
318i 2 Dr Conv	28870	**19050**	**22425**
6 Cyl Models			
325is 2 Dr Cpe	29100	**19900**	**23375**
325i 4 Dr Sdn	27990	**19150**	**22525**
325i 2 Dr Conv	36320	**24575**	**28375**

5-Series 6 Cyl — 1992

Ratings

Rating	Score
Safety	8.5
Reliability	8.6
Performance	8.7
Design	8.8
Fun to drive	8.4
Value	7.7
Overall	8.6

Model/Body/Type	BaseList	Whlse	Retail
AT/PS/AC			
525i 4 Dr Sdn	35600	**22750**	**26450**
525i 5 Dr Touring Wgn	38600	**23750**	**27500**
535i 4 Dr Sdn	44350	**27675**	**31775**
M5 4 Dr Sdn (5 spd)	58600	**36600**	**40800**

7-Series 6 Cyl — 1992

Model/Body/Type	BaseList	Whlse	Retail
AT/PS/AC			
735i 4 Dr Sdn	52990	**30375**	**34475**
735iL 4 Dr Sdn	56950	**32575**	**36575**
750iL 4 Dr Sdn(V12)	76500	**44050**	**48725**

8-Series V12 — 1992

Model/Body/Type	BaseList	Whlse	Retail
AT/PS/AC			
850i 2 Dr Cpe	78500	**47950**	**52875**

ADD FOR ALL 92 BMW:
Car Phone(Std 750iL,850i) +160
CD Player(Std 750iL,850i) +250
Leather Seats(325i 4D,525i) +410
DEDUCT FOR ALL 92 BMW:
No Auto Trans -545

1991 BMW

3-Series 1991

Ratings

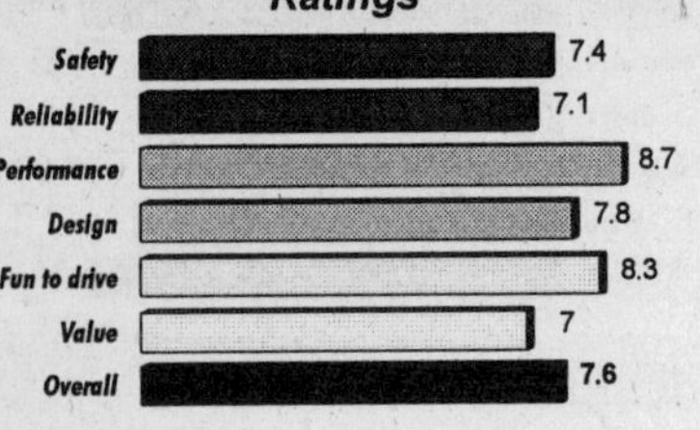

5SP/PS/AC

Model/Body/Type	BaseList	Whlse	Retail
4 Cyl Models			
318is 2 Dr Cpe	21500	**10350**	**13000**
318i 4 Dr Sdn	19900	**10075**	**12675**
318i 2 Dr Conv	28500	**15125**	**18150**
M3 2 Dr Cpe	35900	**19425**	**22825**
6 Cyl Models			
325i 2 Dr Cpe	24600	**14525**	**17475**
325i 4 Dr Sdn	26400	**14425**	**17350**
325i 2 Dr Conv	34550	**20725**	**24225**
325iX 4WD 2 Dr Cpe	31100	**17050**	**20275**
325iX 4WD 4 Dr Sdn	31900	**16975**	**20175**

5-Series 6 Cyl 1991

Ratings

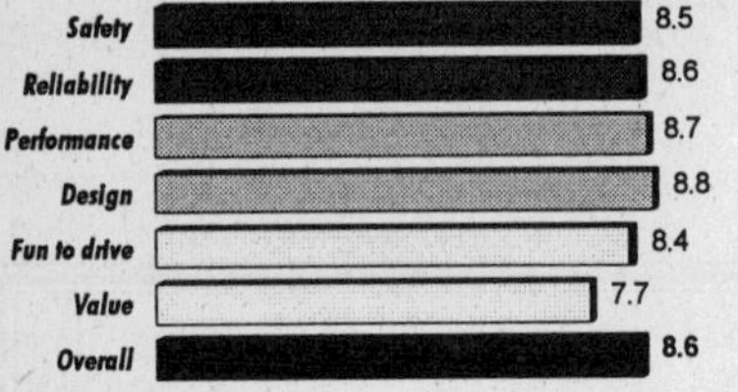

AT/PS/AC

Model/Body/Type	BaseList	Whlse	Retail
525i 4 Dr Sdn	34500	**18675**	**22025**
535i 4 Dr Sdn	42600	**22725**	**26425**
M5 4 Dr Sdn (5 spd)	56600	**31125**	**35150**

7-Series 6 Cyl 1991

AT/PS/AC

Model/Body/Type	BaseList	Whlse	Retail
735i 4 Dr Sdn	50900	**24575**	**28375**
735iL 4 Dr Sdn	55000	**26650**	**30650**
750iL 4 Dr Sdn(V12)	74000	**32800**	**36825**

8-Series V12 1991

AT/PS/AC

Model/Body/Type	BaseList	Whlse	Retail
850i 2 Dr Cpe	73600	**38675**	**43250**

ADD FOR ALL 91 BMW:
Car Phone(Std 750iL,850i) +135
CD Player(Std 750iL,850i) +195
Leather Seats(325 Sdn,525i) +350
Sport Pkg +625
Sunroof(318) +215
DEDUCT FOR ALL 91 BMW:
No Auto Trans -505

1990 BMW

3-Series 6 Cyl 1990

Ratings

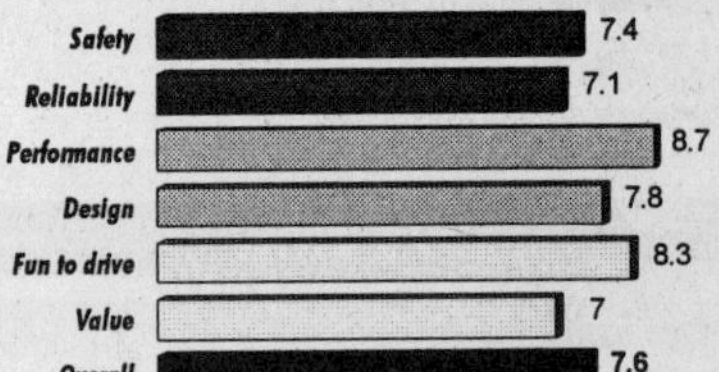

AT/PS/AC

Model/Body/Type	BaseList	Whlse	Retail
M3 2 Dr Cpe (4 Cyl,5 Spd)	34950	**16075**	**19175**
325i 2 Dr Cpe	24650	**11800**	**14600**
325i 4 Dr Sdn	25450	**11700**	**14525**
325is 2 Dr Cpe	28950	**13475**	**16400**
325i 2 Dr Conv	33850	**17575**	**20875**
325iX 4WD 2 Dr Cpe	29950	**14075**	**17000**
325iX 4WD 4 Dr Sdn	30750	**13975**	**16925**

5-Series 6 Cyl 1990

Ratings

Safety 8.5
Reliability 8.6
Performance 8.7
Design 8.8
Fun to drive 8.4
Value 7.7
Overall 8.6

AT/PS/AC

Model/Body/Type	BaseList	Whlse	Retail
525i 4 Dr Sdn	33200	**15450**	**18500**
535i 4 Dr Sdn	41500	**18750**	**22100**

BMW

7-Series 6 Cyl — 1990

AT/PS/AC

Model/Body/Type	BaseList	Whlse	Retail
735i 4 Dr Sdn	49000	**19450**	**22850**
735iL 4 Dr Sdn	53000	**20975**	**24475**
750iL 4 Dr Sdn(V12)	70000	**25250**	**29125**

ADD FOR ALL 90 BMW:
CD Player(Std 750iL) +135
Leather Seats(325 Sdn,525i) +290
DEDUCT FOR ALL 90 BMW:
No Auto Trans -470

1989 BMW

3-Series 6 Cyl — 1989

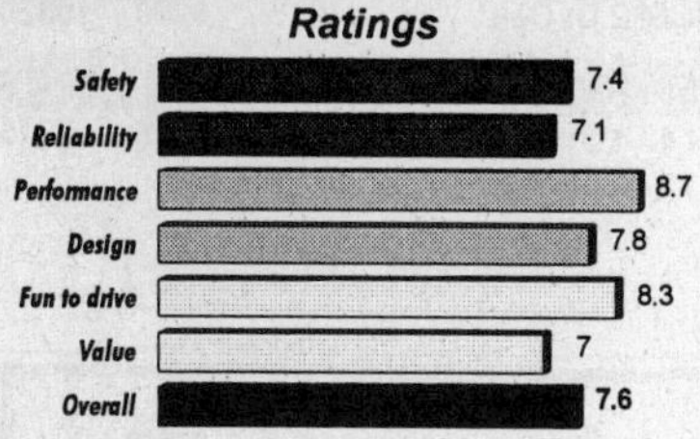

AT/PS/AC

Model/Body/Type	BaseList	Whlse	Retail
M3 2 Dr Cpe (4 Cyl,5 Spd)	34950	**12675**	**15525**
325i 2 Dr Cpe	24650	**8975**	**11300**
325i 4 Dr Sdn	25450	**8875**	**11200**
325is 2 Dr Cpe	28950	**10575**	**13225**
325i 2 Dr Conv	33850	**14525**	**17475**
325iX 4WD 2 Dr Cpe	29950	**10900**	**13650**
325iX 4WD 4 Dr Sdn	30750	**10800**	**13525**

5-Series 6 Cyl — 1989

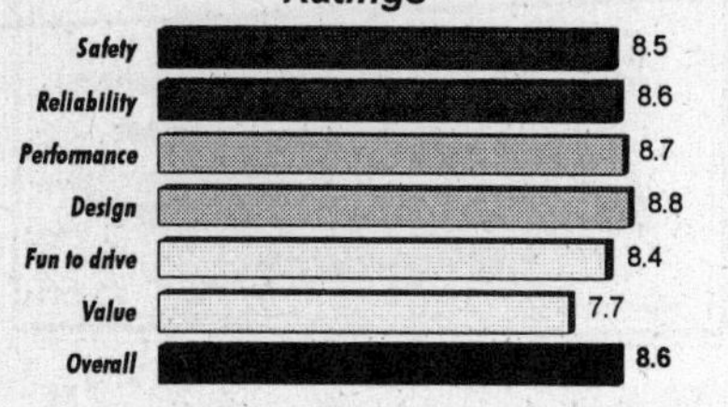

AT/PS/AC

Model/Body/Type	BaseList	Whlse	Retail
525i 4 Dr Sdn	37000	**13075**	**15975**
535i 4 Dr Sdn	43600	**15825**	**18900**

6-Series 6 Cyl — 1989

AT/PS/AC

Model/Body/Type	BaseList	Whlse	Retail
635CSi 2 Dr Cpe	47000	**14175**	**17125**

7-Series 6 Cyl — 1989

AT/PS/AC

Model/Body/Type	BaseList	Whlse	Retail
735i 4 Dr Sdn	54000	**15450**	**18500**
735iL 4 Dr Sdn	58000	**16975**	**20175**
750iL 4 Dr Sdn(V12)	70000	**20000**	**23475**

ADD FOR ALL 89 BMW:
CD Player(Std 750iL) +100
DEDUCT FOR ALL 89 BMW:
No Auto Trans -430

1988 BMW

3-Series 6 Cyl — 1988

AT/PS/AC

Model/Body/Type	BaseList	Whlse	Retail
M3 2 Dr Cpe (4 Cyl,5 Spd)	34000	**11025**	**13775**
325 2 Dr Cpe	23750	**7200**	**9400**
325 4 Dr Sdn	24400	**7125**	**9300**
325is 2 Dr Cpe	28400	**8750**	**11050**
325i 4 Dr Sdn	28400	**8650**	**10900**
325i 2 Dr Conv	32500	**12500**	**15350**
325iX 4WD 2 Dr Cpe (5 spd)	32800	**9200**	**11550**

5-Series 6 Cyl — 1988

AT/PS/AC

Model/Body/Type	BaseList	Whlse	Retail
528e 4 Dr Sdn	31500	**6775**	**8950**
535i 4 Dr Sdn	36000	**9425**	**11800**
535is 4 Dr Sdn	36900	**9975**	**12575**
M5 4 Dr Sdn (5 spd)	46500	**14125**	**17050**

6-Series 6 Cyl — 1988

AT/PS/AC

Model/Body/Type	BaseList	Whlse	Retail
635CSi 2 Dr Cpe	46000	**12350**	**15175**
M6 2 Dr Cpe (5 spd)	55900	**17800**	**21100**

7-Series 6 Cyl — 1988

AT/PS/AC

Model/Body/Type	BaseList	Whlse	Retail
735i 4 Dr Sdn	53000	**11675**	**14500**
735iL 4 Dr Sdn	58000	**12950**	**15825**
750iL 4 Dr Sdn(V12)	67000	**15425**	**18475**

DEDUCT FOR ALL 88 BMW:
No Auto Trans -390

BMW 87-85

1987 BMW

Model/Body/Type	BaseList	Whlse	Retail
3-Series 6 Cyl			**1987**
AT/PS/AC			
325 2 Dr Cpe	21475	**5925**	**7900**
325 4 Dr Sdn	22015	**5825**	**7800**
325es 2 Dr Cpe	24370	**6500**	**8550**
325e 4 Dr Sdn	25150	**6400**	**8425**
325is 2 Dr Cpe	26990	**7200**	**9400**
325i 4 Dr Sdn	26990	**7125**	**9300**
325i 2 Dr Conv	28875	**11125**	**13875**
5-Series 6 Cyl			**1987**
AT/PS/AC			
528e 4 Dr Sdn	28330	**5525**	**7475**
535i 4 Dr Sdn	33600	**7700**	**9925**
535is 4 Dr Sdn	35200	**8525**	**10750**
6-Series 6 Cyl			**1987**
AT/PS/AC			
635CSi 2 Dr Cpe	46965	**11175**	**13950**
L6 2 Dr Cpe	49500	**11525**	**14325**
M6 2 Dr Cpe (5 spd)	55950	**15600**	**18675**
7-Series 6 Cyl			**1987**
AT/PS/AC			
735i 4 Dr Sdn	42475	**9075**	**11425**
L7 4 Dr Sdn	46675	**9800**	**12350**

1986 BMW

Model/Body/Type	BaseList	Whlse	Retail
3-Series			**1986**
325 2 Dr Cpe	19560	**4975**	**6875**
325 4 Dr Sdn	20055	**4875**	**6750**
325es 2 Dr Cpe	21950	**5375**	**7300**
325e 4 Dr Sdn	22650	**5275**	**7200**
5-Series			**1986**
524td 4 Dr Sdn	25560	**3700**	**5400**
528e 4 Dr Sdn	26280	**4800**	**6650**
535i 4 Dr Sdn	31175	**6400**	**8400**
6-Series			**1986**
635CSi 2 Dr Cpe	41965	**9875**	**12075**
7-Series			**1986**
735i 4 Dr Sdn	38280	**7075**	**9125**
L7 4 Dr Sdn	42920	**7725**	**9800**

1985 BMW

Model/Body/Type	BaseList	Whlse	Retail
3-Series			**1985**
318i 4 Dr Sdn	16925	**3075**	**4700**
318i 2 Dr Cpe	16430	**3150**	**4775**
325e 4 Dr Sdn	21105	**4125**	**5875**
325e 2 Dr Cpe	20970	**4200**	**5975**
5-Series			**1985**
524td 4 Dr Sdn	24560	**3150**	**4775**
528e 4 Dr Sdn	24565	**3950**	**5725**
535i 4 Dr Sdn	30760	**5175**	**7100**
6-Series			**1985**
635CSi 2 Dr Cpe	41315	**8250**	**10325**
7-Series			**1985**
735i 4 Dr Sdn	36880	**5725**	**7625**

BUICK USA

1992 Buick Roadmaster Sedan

For a Buick dealer in your area, see our Dealer Directory (pg 217)

1994 BUICK

CENTURY 1994

FWD/AT/PS/AC

Model/Body/Type	BaseList	Whlse	Retail
4 Cyl Models			
4 Dr Special Sdn	15495	**12500**	**14975**
4 Dr Special Wgn	16345	**13050**	**15550**
4 Dr Custom Sdn	16695	**12950**	**15450**
V6 Models			
4 Dr Special Sdn	16105	**13100**	**15600**
4 Dr Special Wgn	16955	**13650**	**16175**
4 Dr Custom Sdn	17305	**13550**	**16075**

ADD FOR 94 CENTURY:

Anti-Theft/Recovery Sys +365 — Cass +115
CD Player +230 — Cruise Ctrl +160
Custom Whls/Cvrs +205 — Driver Side Airbag +320
Leather Seats +275 — Luggage Rack +115
Pwr Seat +160 — Pwr Wndw +160
Third Seat +205

LE SABRE V6 1994

FWD/AT/PS/AC

Model/Body/Type	BaseList	Whlse	Retail
4 Dr Custom Sdn	20860	**16250**	**19075**
4 Dr Limited Sdn	24420	**18450**	**21575**

ADD FOR 94 LE SABRE:

Anti-Theft/Recovery Sys +365 — Car Phone +230
Cass +135 — CD Player +275
Cruise Ctrl +180 — Custom Whls/Cvrs +230
Leather Seats +320

PARK AVENUE V6 1994

FWD/AT/PS/AC

Model/Body/Type	BaseList	Whlse	Retail
4 Dr Sdn	26999	**21025**	**24500**
4 Dr Ultra Sdn	31699	**23850**	**27600**

ADD FOR 94 PARK AVENUE:

Anti-Theft/Recovery Sys +365 — Car Phone +230
CD Player +340 — Delco/Bose Mus Sys +295
Lthr Seats(Std Ultra) +365 — Pwr Sunroof +635

REGAL V6 1994

FWD/AT/PS/AC

Model/Body/Type	BaseList	Whlse	Retail
4 Dr Custom Sdn	18299	**13550**	**16075**
2 Dr Custom Cpe	17999	**13550**	**16075**
4 Dr Limited Sdn	19799	**14900**	**17500**
4 Dr Gran Sport Sdn	20299	**15500**	**18075**
2 Dr Gran Sport Cpe	19999	**15500**	**18075**

ADD FOR 94 REGAL:

Anti-Theft/Recovery Sys +365 — Cass +115
CD Player +230 — Cruise Ctrl +160
Custom Whls/Cvrs +205 — Leather Seats +275
Pwr Seat +160 — Pwr Sunroof +545

ROADMASTER V8 1994

AT/PS/AC

Model/Body/Type	BaseList	Whlse	Retail
4 Dr Sdn	23999	**18550**	**21675**
4 Dr Limited Sdn	26399	**20300**	**23525**
4 Dr 3 Seat Estate Wgn	25599	**20725**	**23975**

ADD FOR 94 ROADMASTER:

Anti-Theft/Recovery Sys +365 — Car Phone +230
CD Player +275 — Custom Whls/Cvrs +230
Leather Seats +320 — Vinyl Roof +135

SKYLARK 1994

FWD/AT/PS/AC

Model/Body/Type	BaseList	Whlse	Retail
Quad 4 Models			
2 Dr Custom Cpe	13599	**10775**	**13125**
4 Dr Custom Sdn	13599	**10775**	**13125**
4 Dr Limited Sdn	16199	**12025**	**14525**
V6 Models			
2 Dr Custom Cpe	14009	**11000**	**13325**
4 Dr Custom Sdn	14009	**11000**	**13325**
4 Dr Limited Sdn	16609	**12225**	**14700**
2 Dr Gran Sport Cpe	18299	**13175**	**15675**
4 Dr Gran Sport Sdn	18299	**13175**	**15675**

ADD FOR 94 SKYLARK:

Anti-Theft/Recovery Sys +365 — Cass +115
CD Player +230 — Cruise Ctrl(Custom) +160
Custom Whls/Cvrs +205 — Pwr Seat +160
Pwr Wndw(Custom) +160

DEDUCT FOR 94 SKYLARK:

No AC -680

1993 BUICK

CENTURY 1993

Ratings

Rating	Score
Safety	6.7
Reliability	6.5
Performance	7
Design	7.8
Fun to drive	6.9
Value	7.5
Overall	6.8

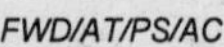

FWD/AT/PS/AC

Model/Body/Type	BaseList	Whlse	Retail
4 Cyl Models			
4 Dr Special Sdn	14205	**8700**	**10700**
4 Dr Special Wgn	14960	**9200**	**11225**
4 Dr Custom Sdn	15905	**9100**	**11125**
2 Dr Custom Cpe	15620	**9000**	**11000**
4 Dr Custom Wgn	17250	**9600**	**11650**
4 Dr Limited Sdn	16865	**9925**	**12075**
V6 Models			
4 Dr Special Sdn	14865	**9250**	**11275**
4 Dr Special Wgn	15620	**9750**	**11875**
4 Dr Custom Sdn	16565	**9650**	**11700**
2 Dr Custom Cpe	16280	**9550**	**11600**
4 Dr Custom Wgn	17910	**10100**	**12275**
4 Dr Limited Sdn	17525	**10425**	**12650**

ADD FOR 93 CENTURY:

Cass +100 · *CD Player +200*
Cruise Ctrl +130 · *Custom Whls/Cvrs +175*
Driver Side Airbag +320 · *Leather Seats +230*
Luggage Rack +75 · *Pwr Seat +130*
Pwr Wndw +130 · *Third Seat +160*
Tilt Whl +100

LE SABRE V6 1993

Ratings

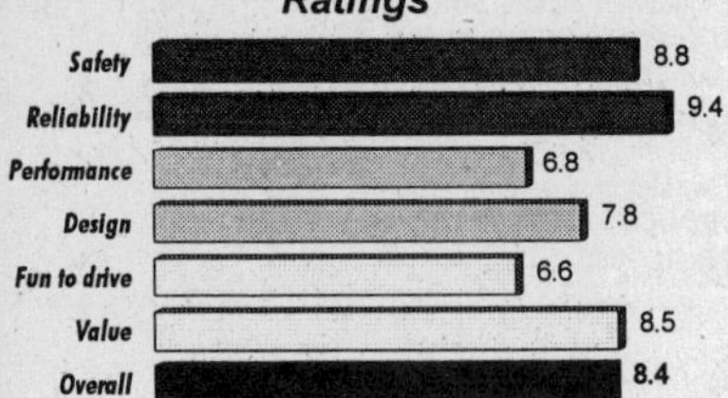

FWD/AT/PS/AC

Model/Body/Type	BaseList	Whlse	Retail
4 Dr Custom Sdn	19935	**13125**	**15750**
4 Dr Limited Sdn	21735	**14525**	**17225**

ADD FOR 93 LE SABRE:

Car Phone +175 · *Cass +115*
CD Player +230 · *Cruise Ctrl +160*
Custom Whls/Cvrs +200 · *Leather Seats +275*
Pwr Seat +160

PARK AVENUE V6 1993

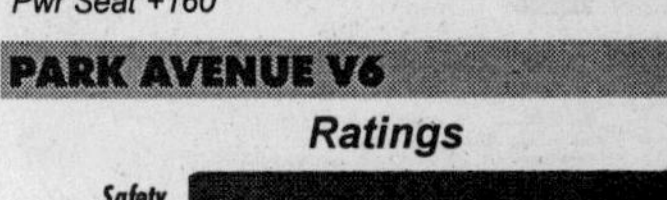

Ratings

Rating	Score
Safety	9
Reliability	8.2
Performance	7.6
Design	7.8
Fun to drive	7.5
Value	7.9
Overall	8.2

FWD/AT/PS/AC

Model/Body/Type	BaseList	Whlse	Retail
4 Dr Sdn	26040	**16900**	**20075**
4 Dr Ultra Sdn	29395	**19450**	**22850**

ADD FOR 93 PARK AVENUE:

Car Phone +175 · *CD Player +290*
Custom Paint +115 · *Delco/Bose Mus Sys +250*
Lthr Seats(Std Ultra) +320 · *Pwr Sunroof +505*
Vinyl Roof +200

REGAL V6 1993

Ratings

FWD/AT/PS/AC

Model/Body/Type	BaseList	Whlse	Retail
4 Dr Custom Sdn	16865	**10450**	**12675**
2 Dr Custom Cpe	16610	**10450**	**12675**
4 Dr Limited Sdn	18460	**11675**	**14125**
2 Dr Limited Cpe	18260	**11675**	**14125**
4 Dr Gran Sport Sdn	19310	**12175**	**14550**
2 Dr Gran Sport Cpe	19095	**12175**	**14550**

Model/Body/Type	BaseList	Whlse	Retail

ADD FOR 93 REGAL:

ABS(Std Ltd,GS) +390 | *Cass +100*
CD Player +200 | *Cruise Ctrl +130*
Cust Pnt(Std GS 4Dr) +75 | *Custom Whls/Cvrs +175*
Leather Seats +230 | *Pwr Seat +130*
Pwr Sunroof +430 | *Pwr Wndw +130*

RIVIERA V6 1993

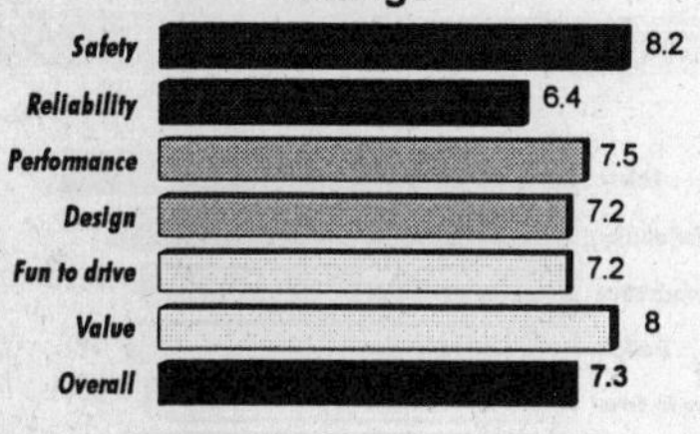

FWD/AT/PS/AC

Model/Body/Type	BaseList	Whlse	Retail
2 Dr Cpe	26320	**17675**	**20975**

ADD FOR 93 RIVIERA:

Car Phone +175 | *CD Player +290*
Custom Paint +115 | *Delco/Bose Mus Sys +250*
Leather Seats +320 | *Pwr Sunroof +505*
Vinyl Roof +200

ROADMASTER V8 1993

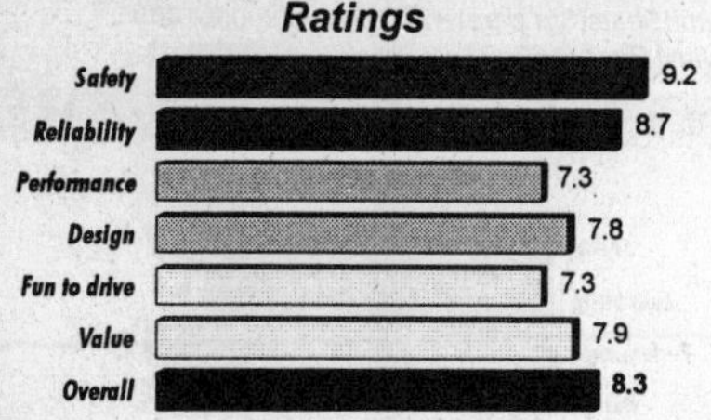

AT/PS/AC

Model/Body/Type	BaseList	Whlse	Retail
4 Dr Sdn	22555	**15175**	**17925**
4 Dr Limited Sdn	24920	**16775**	**19725**
4 Dr 3 Seat Estate Wgn	23850	**17175**	**20175**

ADD FOR 93 ROADMASTER:

Car Phone +175 | *CD Player +230*
Custom Whls/Cvrs +200 | *Leather Seats +275*
Vinyl Roof +115

SKYLARK 1993

Ratings

Safety 6.9
Reliability 8.8
Performance 7.6
Design 7.1
Fun to drive 7.2
Value 7.5
Overall 7.8

FWD/AT/PS/AC

Model/Body/Type	BaseList	Whlse	Retail
Quad 4 Models			
2 Dr Custom Cpe	12955	**8750**	**10750**
4 Dr Custom Sdn	12955	**8750**	**10750**
2 Dr Limited Cpe	13875	**9050**	**11050**
4 Dr Limited Sdn	13875	**9050**	**11050**
V6 Models			
2 Dr Custom Cpe	13415	**8950**	**10950**
4 Dr Custom Sdn	13415	**8950**	**10950**
2 Dr Limited Cpe	14335	**9250**	**11275**
4 Dr Limited Sdn	14335	**9250**	**11275**
2 Dr Gran Sport Cpe	15760	**10575**	**12775**
4 Dr Gran Sport Sdn	15760	**10575**	**12775**

ADD FOR 93 SKYLARK:

Cass +100 | *CD Player +200*
Cruise Ctrl +130 | *Custom Paint +75*
Custom Whls/Cvrs +175 | *Pwr Seat +130*
Pwr Wndw +130 | *Tilt Whl +100*

DEDUCT FOR 93 SKYLARK:

No AC -545

1992 BUICK

CENTURY 1992

Ratings

Rating	Score
Safety	6.7
Reliability	6.5
Performance	7
Design	7.8
Fun to drive	6.9
Value	7.5
Overall	6.8

FWD/AT/PS/AC

Model/Body/Type	BaseList	Whlse	Retail
4 Cyl Models			
4 Dr Special Sdn	13795	**6500**	**8250**
4 Dr Custom Sdn	14755	**6850**	**8675**
2 Dr Custom Cpe	14550	**6725**	**8550**
4 Dr Custom Wgn	15660	**7275**	**9150**
4 Dr Limited Sdn	15695	**7550**	**9450**
4 Dr Limited Wgn	16395	**8000**	**9925**
V6 Models			
4 Dr Special Sdn	14505	**7000**	**8825**
4 Dr Custom Sdn	15465	**7325**	**9200**
2 Dr Custom Cpe	15260	**7225**	**9100**
4 Dr Custom Wgn	16370	**7775**	**9700**
4 Dr Limited Sdn	16405	**8050**	**9975**
4 Dr Limited Wgn	17105	**8500**	**10400**

ADD FOR 92 CENTURY:

Cass +75
Cruise Ctrl +115
Leather Seats +200
Pwr Seat +115
Third Seat +130
Woodgrain +130
CD Player +175
Custom Whls/Cvrs +160
Luggage Rack +60
Pwr Wndw +115
Tilt Whl +75

LE SABRE V6 1992

Ratings

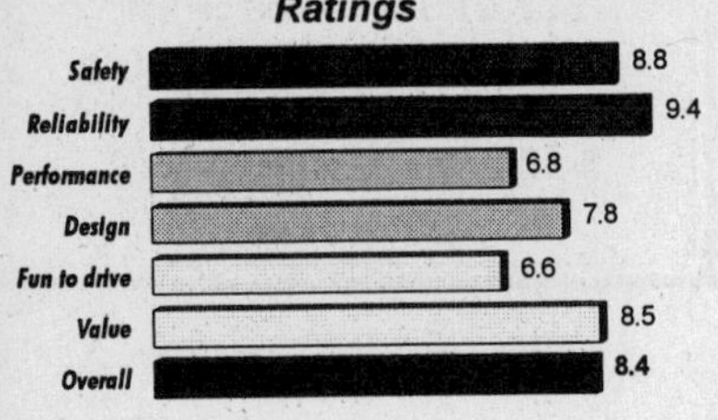

FWD/AT/PS/AC

Model/Body/Type	BaseList	Whlse	Retail
4 Dr Custom Sdn	18695	**10300**	**12625**
4 Dr Limited Sdn	20775	**11525**	**14000**

ADD FOR 92 LE SABRE:

ABS(Std Ltd) +345
Cass +100
Cruise Ctrl +130
Leather Seats +230
Pwr Seat +130
Car Phone +160
CD Player +200
Custom Whls/Cvrs +175
Pwr Locks +100
Vinyl Roof +100

PARK AVENUE V6 1992

Ratings

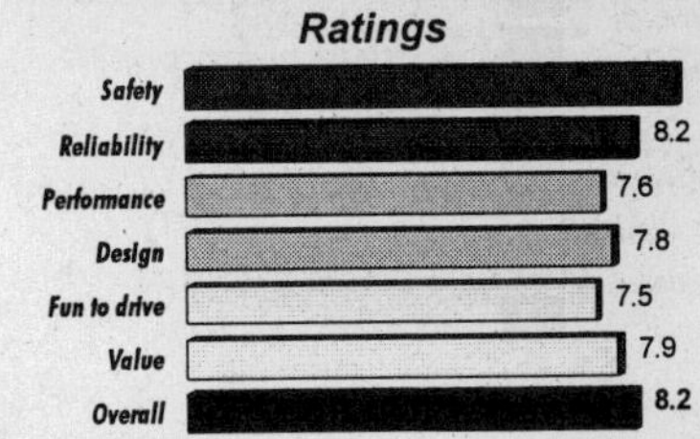

FWD/AT/PS/AC

Model/Body/Type	BaseList	Whlse	Retail
4 Dr Base Sdn	25285	**13425**	**16325**
4 Dr Ultra Sdn	28780	**15850**	**18925**

ADD FOR 92 PARK AVENUE:

Car Phone +160
Custom Paint +100
Lthr Seats(Std Ultra) +275
Vinyl Roof +160
CD Player +250
Delco/Bose Mus Sys +230
Pwr Sunroof +465

REGAL V6 1992

Ratings

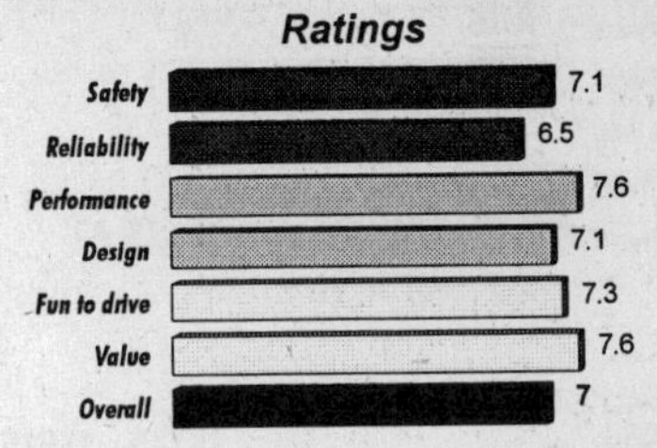
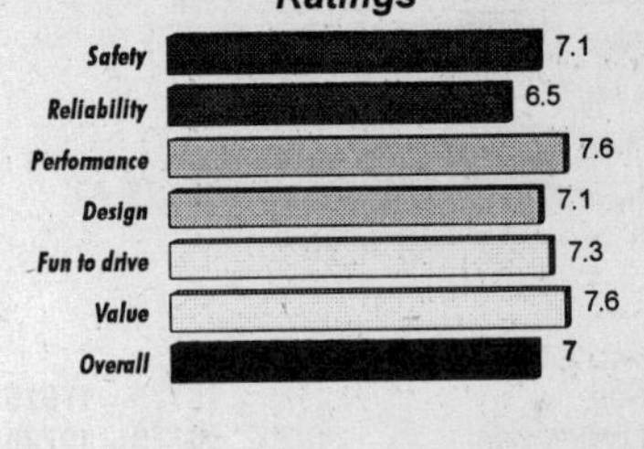

FWD/AT/PS/AC

Model/Body/Type	BaseList	Whlse	Retail
4 Dr Custom Sdn	16865	**8000**	**9925**
2 Dr Custom Cpe	16610	**8000**	**9925**
4 Dr Limited Sdn	18110	**8875**	**10875**
2 Dr Limited Cpe	17790	**8875**	**10875**
4 Dr Gran Sport Sdn	19300	**9525**	**11475**
2 Dr Gran Sport Cpe	18600	**9525**	**11475**

Model/Body/Type	BaseList	Whlse	Retail

ADD FOR 92 REGAL:
ABS(Std Ltd,GS) +345 *Cass +75*
CD Player +175 *Cruise Ctrl +115*
Cust Pnt(Std GS 4Dr) +60 *Custom Whls/Cvrs +160*
Leather Seats +200 *Pwr Seat +115*
Pwr Sunroof +390 *Pwr Wndw +115*

RIVIERA V6 1992

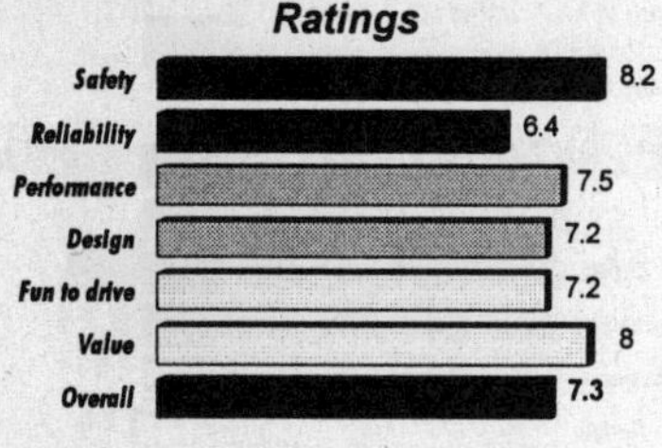

FWD/AT/PS/AC

Model/Body/Type	BaseList	Whlse	Retail
2 Dr Cpe	25415	**14625**	**17600**

ADD FOR 92 RIVIERA:
Car Phone +160 *CD Player +250*
Custom Paint +100 *Delco/Bose Mus Sys +230*
Leather Seats +275 *Pwr Sunroof +465*
Vinyl Roof +160

ROADMASTER V8 1992

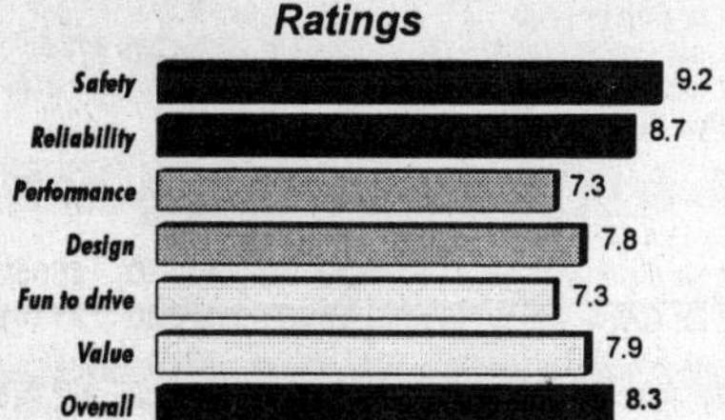

AT/PS/AC

Model/Body/Type	BaseList	Whlse	Retail
4 Dr Base Sdn	21865	**11650**	**14225**
4 Dr Limited Sdn	24195	**13075**	**15700**
4 Dr 3 Seat Estate Wgn	23040	**13900**	**16575**

ADD FOR 92 ROADMASTER:
Car Phone +160 *CD Player +200*
Custom Whls/Cvrs +175 *Leather Seats +230*
Vinyl Roof +100

SKYLARK 1992

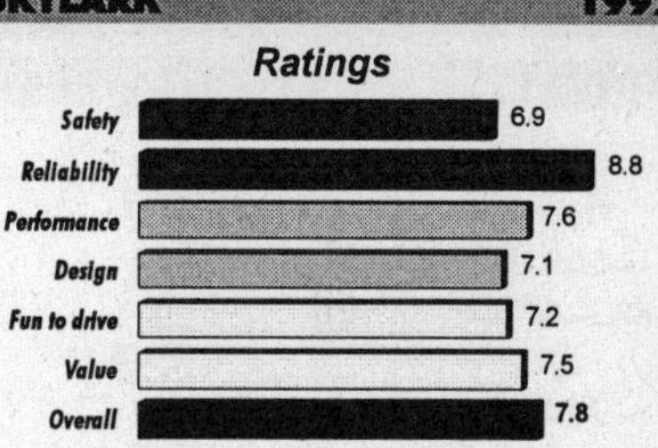

FWD/AT/PS/AC

Model/Body/Type	BaseList	Whlse	Retail
Quad 4 Models			
2 Dr Cpe	13560	**7075**	**8900**
4 Dr Sdn	13560	**7075**	**8900**
V6 Models			
2 Dr Cpe	14020	**7250**	**9125**
4 Dr Sdn	14020	**7250**	**9125**
2 Dr Gran Sport Cpe	15555	**8675**	**10675**
4 Dr Gran Sport Sdn	15555	**8675**	**10675**

ADD FOR 92 SKYLARK:
Cass(Std GS) +75 *CD Player +175*
Cruise Ctrl +115 *Custom Paint +60*
Pwr Seat +115 *Pwr Wndw +115*
Tilt Whl +75

DEDUCT FOR 92 SKYLARK:
No AC -505

Model/Body/Type	BaseList	Whlse	Retail

1991 BUICK

CENTURY 1991

Ratings

Safety 6.7
Reliability 6.5
Performance 7
Design 7.8
Fun to drive 6.9
Value 7.5
Overall 6.8

FWD/AT/PS/AC

Model/Body/Type	BaseList	Whlse	Retail
4 Cyl Models			
4 Dr Special Sdn	13240	**5000**	**6650**
4 Dr Custom Sdn	13685	**5300**	**7000**
2 Dr Custom Cpe	13785	**5200**	**6900**
4 Dr Custom Wgn	15310	**5725**	**7425**
4 Dr Limited Sdn	14795	**5875**	**7625**
4 Dr Limited Wgn	16230	**6275**	**8050**
V6 Models			
4 Dr Special Sdn	13950	**5475**	**7150**
4 Dr Custom Sdn	14395	**5775**	**7475**
2 Dr Custom Cpe	14495	**5700**	**7375**
4 Dr Custom Wgn	16020	**6175**	**7900**
4 Dr Limited Sdn	15505	**6350**	**8100**
4 Dr Limited Wgn	16940	**6725**	**8550**

ADD FOR 91 CENTURY:

Cass +60 | *CD Player +160*
Cruise Ctrl +100 | *Custom Whls/Cvrs +130*
Leather Seats +160 | *Luggage Rack +35*
Pwr Locks +60 | *Pwr Seat +100*
Pwr Wndw +100 | *Third Seat +115*
Tilt Whl +60 | *Woodgrain +115*

LE SABRE V6 1991

Ratings

Safety 7.8
Reliability 8.2
Performance 7
Design 8.2
Fun to drive 6.8
Value 8.6
Overall 7.8

FWD/AT/PS/AC

Model/Body/Type	BaseList	Whlse	Retail
2 Dr Cpe	17180	**7350**	**9375**
4 Dr Custom Sdn	17080	**7500**	**9525**
4 Dr Limited Sdn	18430	**8425**	**10475**
2 Dr Limited Cpe	18330	**8275**	**10300**

ADD FOR 91 LE SABRE:

ABS +320 | *Car Phone +130*
Cass +75 | *Cruise Ctrl +115*
Custom Whls/Cvrs +160 | *Leather Seats +200*
Pwr Locks +75 | *Pwr Seat +115*
Pwr Wndw +115 | *Vinyl Roof +75*

PARK AVENUE V6 1991

Ratings

Safety 9
Reliability 8.2
Performance 7.6
Design 7.8
Fun to drive 7.5
Value 7.9
Overall 8.2

FWD/AT/PS/AC

Model/Body/Type	BaseList	Whlse	Retail
4 Dr Sdn	24385	**10575**	**13225**
4 Dr Ultra Sdn	27420	**12800**	**15675**

ADD FOR 91 PARK AVENUE:

Car Phone +130 | *CD Player +200*
Cust Pnt(Std Ultra) +75 | *Custom Whls/Cvrs +175*
Delco/Bose Mus Sys +200 | *Lthr Seats(Std Ultra) +215*
Pwr Sunroof +430 | *Vinyl Roof +130*

REATTA V6 1991

FWD/AT/PS/AC

Model/Body/Type	BaseList	Whlse	Retail
2 Dr Cpe	29300	**13150**	**16050**
2 Dr Conv	35965	**17800**	**21100**

REGAL V6 1991

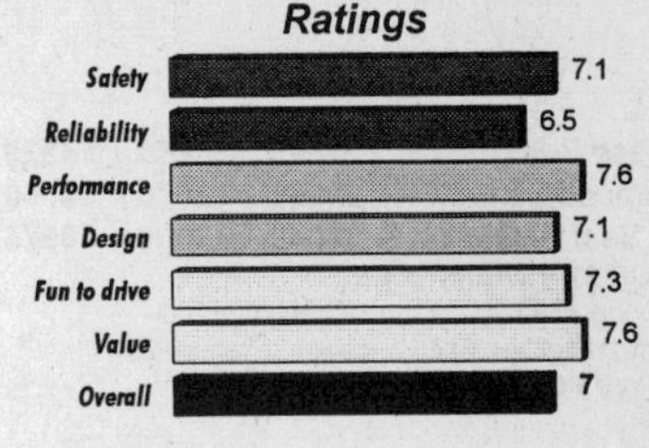

BUICK

Model/Body/Type	BaseList	Whlse	Retail
FWD/AT/PS/AC			
4 Dr Custom Sdn	15910	**6875**	**8700**
2 Dr Custom Cpe	15690	**6875**	**8700**
4 Dr Limited Sdn	16735	**7425**	**9300**
2 Dr Limited Cpe	16455	**7425**	**9300**

ADD FOR 91 REGAL:

ABS +320 | *Cass +60*
CD Player +160 | *Cruise Ctrl +100*
Custom Paint +35 | *Custom Whls/Cvrs +130*
Gran Sport Pkg +320 | *Leather Seats +160*
Pwr Locks +60 | *Pwr Seat +100*
Pwr Sunroof +345 | *Pwr Wndw +100*

RIVIERA V6 1991

Ratings

Rating	Score
Safety	8.2
Reliability	6.4
Performance	7.5
Design	7.2
Fun to drive	7.2
Value	8
Overall	7.3

Model/Body/Type	BaseList	Whlse	Retail
FWD/AT/PS/AC			
2 Dr Cpe	24560	**11425**	**14200**

ADD FOR 91 RIVIERA:

Car Phone +130 | *CD Player +200*
Custom Paint +75 | *Custom Whls/Cvrs +175*
Delco/Bose Mus Sys +200 | *Leather Seats +215*
Pwr Sunroof +430 | *Vinyl Roof +130*

ROADMASTER V8 1991

Ratings

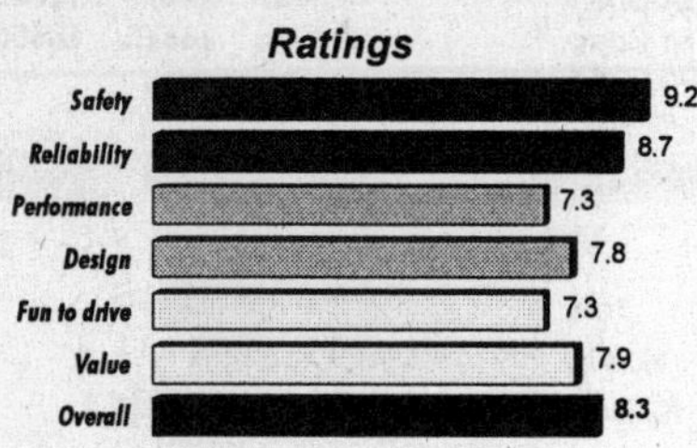

Model/Body/Type	BaseList	Whlse	Retail
AT/PS/AC			
4 Dr 3 Seat Estate Wgn	21445	**11725**	**14300**

ADD FOR 91 ROADMASTER:

Car Phone +130 | *CD Player +160*
Leather Seats +200

SKYLARK 1991

Ratings

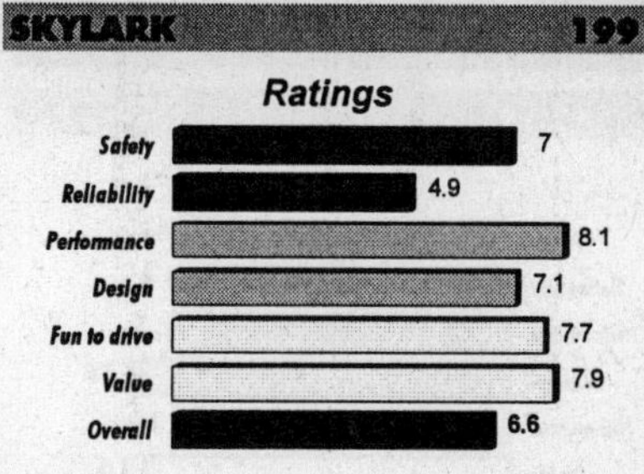

Model/Body/Type	BaseList	Whlse	Retail
FWD/AT/PS/AC			
4 Cyl Models			
2 Dr Cpe	10825	**5225**	**6925**
4 Dr Sdn	10725	**5225**	**6925**
2 Dr Custom Cpe	12020	**5725**	**7425**
4 Dr Custom Sdn	12020	**5725**	**7425**
2 Dr Gran Sport Cpe	13665	**6250**	**8000**
4 Dr Luxury Edit Sdn	13865	**6450**	**8200**
V6 Models			
2 Dr Cpe	11535	**5675**	**7350**
4 Dr Sdn	11435	**5675**	**7350**
2 Dr Custom Cpe	12730	**6125**	**7850**
4 Dr Custom Sdn	12730	**6125**	**7850**
2 Dr Gran Sport Cpe	14375	**6650**	**8425**
4 Dr Luxury Edit Sdn	14575	**6850**	**8675**

ADD FOR 91 SKYLARK:

ABS +320 | *Cass(Std GS) +60*
Cruise Ctrl +100 | *Cust Pnt(Std LE) +35*
Custom Whls/Cvrs +130 | *Pwr Locks +60*
Pwr Seat +100 | *Pwr Wndw +100*
Quad 4 Engine +275 | *Tilt Whl +60*

DEDUCT FOR 91 SKYLARK:

No AC -465

CENTURY 1990

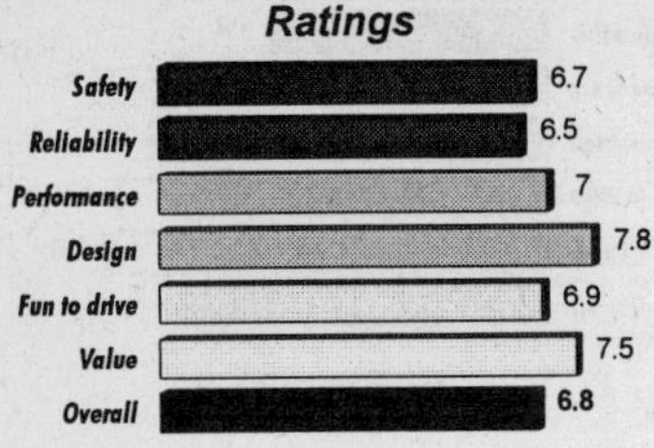

FWD/AT/PS/AC

Model/Body/Type	BaseList	Whlse	Retail
4 Cyl Models			
4 Dr Custom Sdn	13150	**3850**	**5325**
2 Dr Custom Cpe	13250	**3750**	**5225**
4 Dr Custom Wgn	14570	**4200**	**5725**
4 Dr Limited Sdn	14075	**4375**	**5925**
4 Dr Limited Wgn	15455	**4700**	**6325**
V6 Models			
4 Dr Custom Sdn	13860	**4250**	**5800**
2 Dr Custom Cpe	13960	**4150**	**5700**
4 Dr Custom Wgn	15280	**4600**	**6175**
4 Dr Limited Sdn	14785	**4750**	**6375**
4 Dr Limited Wgn	16165	**5075**	**6750**

ADD FOR 90 CENTURY:

Cass +60 | *Cruise Ctrl +75*
Custom Whls/Cvrs +115 | *Leather Seats +115*
Luggage Rack +35 | *Pwr Locks +60*
Pwr Seat +75 | *Pwr Wndw +75*
Third Seat +100 | *Tilt Whl +60*
Woodgrain +100

ELECTRA V6 1990

FWD/AT/PS/AC

Model/Body/Type	BaseList	Whlse	Retail
4 Dr Limited Sdn	20225	**6950**	**9100**
4 Dr Park Ave Sdn	21750	**7800**	**10000**
4 Dr Park Ave Ultra Sdn	27825	**9900**	**12475**
4 Dr T Type Sdn	23025	**7350**	**9575**

ADD FOR 90 ELECTRA:

ABS(Std T,Ultra) +275 | *Cabriolet Roof +230*
CD Player +130 | *Cust Pnt(Std Ultra) +60*
Custom Whls/Cvrs +130 | *Delco/Bose Mus Sys +130*
Lthr Seats(Std Ultra) +160 | *Pwr Sunroof +390*
Vinyl Roof +100

ESTATE WAGON V8 1990

AT/PS/AC

Model/Body/Type	BaseList	Whlse	Retail
4 Dr 3 Seat Wgn	17940	**6100**	**7950**

ADD FOR 90 ESTATE WAGON:

Leather Seats +130 | *Luggage Rack +35*
Woodgrain +130

LE SABRE V6 1990

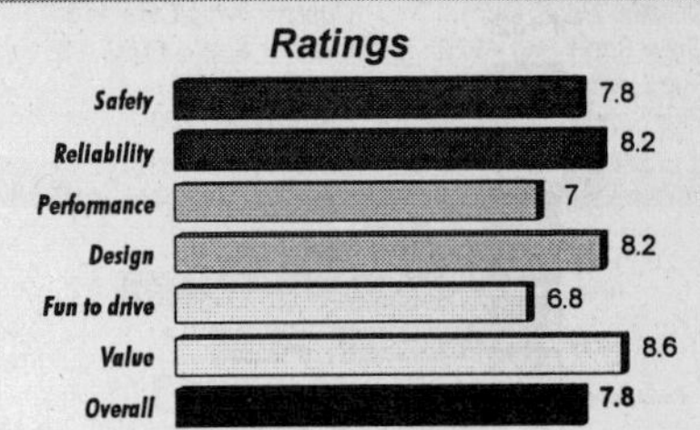

FWD/AT/PS/AC

Model/Body/Type	BaseList	Whlse	Retail
2 Dr Cpe	16145	**6050**	**7925**
4 Dr Custom Sdn	16050	**6200**	**8075**
4 Dr Limited Sdn	17400	**7050**	**9025**
2 Dr Limited Cpe	17300	**6900**	**8850**

ADD FOR 90 LE SABRE:

ABS +275 | *Cass +75*
Cruise Ctrl +100 | *Custom Whls/Cvrs +115*
Leather Seats +130 | *Pwr Locks +60*
Pwr Seat +100 | *Pwr Wndw +100*
Vinyl Roof +60

REATTA V6 1990

FWD/AT/PS/AC

Model/Body/Type	BaseList	Whlse	Retail
2 Dr Cpe	28335	**9475**	**11850**
2 Dr Conv	34995	**13575**	**16500**

ADD FOR 90 REATTA:

CD Player +130 | *Pwr Sunroof +390*

REGAL V6 1990

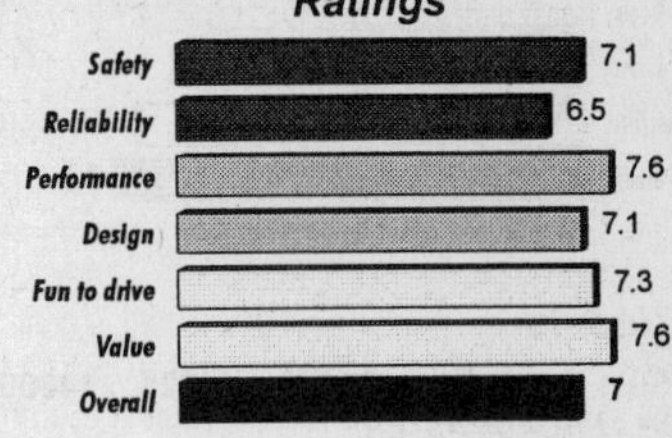

Model/Body/Type	BaseList	Whlse	Retail
FWD/AT/PS/AC			
2 Dr Custom Cpe	15200	**6275**	**8025**
2 Dr Limited Cpe	15860	**6750**	**8600**

ADD FOR 90 REGAL:

ABS +275	*Cass +60*
CD Player +115	*Cruise Ctrl +75*
Custom Paint +20	*Custom Whls/Cvrs +115*
Gran Sport Pkg +275	*Leather Seats +115*
Pwr Locks +60	*Pwr Seat +75*
Pwr Sunroof +320	*Pwr Wndw +75*

RIVIERA V6 1990

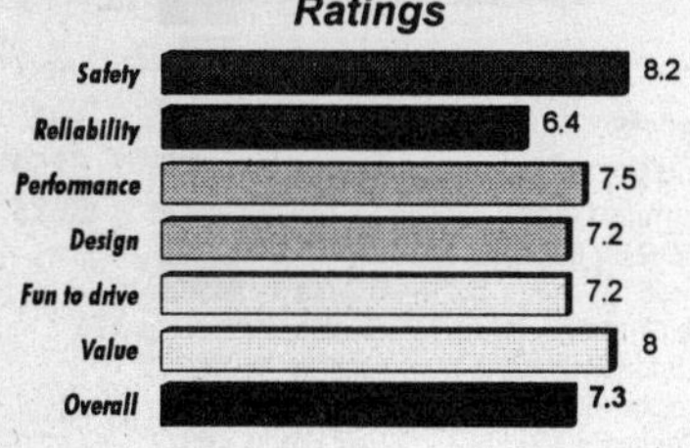

Model/Body/Type	BaseList	Whlse	Retail
FWD/AT/PS/AC			
2 Dr Cpe	23040	**8550**	**10800**

ADD FOR 90 RIVIERA:

ABS +275	*Cabriolet Roof +230*
CD Player +130	*Custom Paint +60*
Custom Whls/Cvrs +130	*Delco/Bose Mus Sys +130*
Leather Seats +160	*Pwr Sunroof +390*
Vinyl Roof +100	

SKYLARK 1990

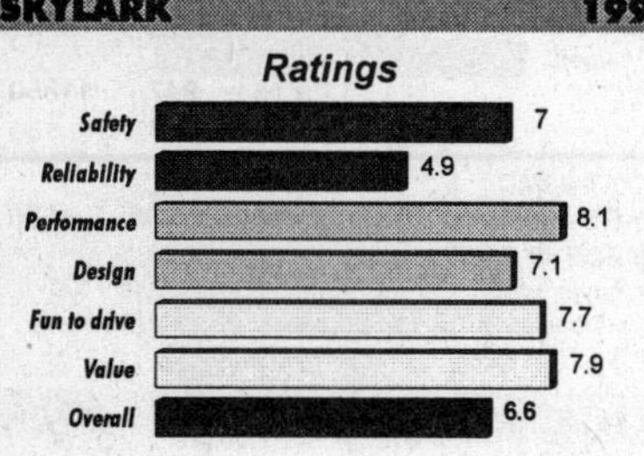

Model/Body/Type	BaseList	Whlse	Retail
FWD/AT/PS/AC			
4 Cyl Models			
2 Dr Cpe	10565	**4250**	**5800**
4 Dr Sdn	10465	**4250**	**5800**
2 Dr Custom Cpe	11460	**4675**	**6250**
4 Dr Custom Sdn	11460	**4675**	**6250**
2 Dr Gran Sport Cpe	12935	**5075**	**6750**
4 Dr Luxury Edit Sdn	13145	**5275**	**7000**
V6 Models			
2 Dr Custom Cpe	12170	**4975**	**6650**
4 Dr Custom Sdn	12170	**4975**	**6650**
2 Dr Gran Sport Cpe	13645	**5425**	**7150**
4 Dr Luxury Edit Sdn	13855	**5675**	**7350**

ADD FOR 90 SKYLARK:

Cass(Std GS) +60	*Cruise Ctrl +75*
Cust Pnt(Std LE) +20	*Custom Whls/Cvrs +115*
Pwr Locks +60	*Pwr Seat +75*
Pwr Wndw +75	*Quad 4 Engine +230*
Tilt Whl +60	

DEDUCT FOR 90 SKYLARK:

No AC -430

1989 BUICK

CENTURY 1989

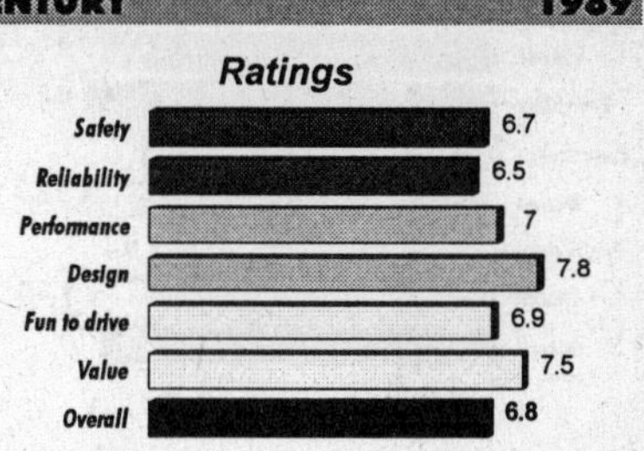

Model/Body/Type	BaseList	Whlse	Retail
FWD/AT/PS/AC			
4 Cyl Models			
4 Dr Custom Sdn	12429	**3125**	**4500**
2 Dr Custom Cpe	12199	**3025**	**4375**
4 Dr Custom Wgn	13156	**3375**	**4800**
4 Dr Limited Sdn	13356	**3550**	**4975**
4 Dr Limited Estate Wgn	13956	**3850**	**5325**
V6 Models			
4 Dr Custom Sdn	13139	**3450**	**4850**
2 Dr Custom Cpe	12909	**3350**	**4775**
4 Dr Custom Wgn	13866	**3750**	**5225**
4 Dr Limited Sdn	14066	**3925**	**5400**
4 Dr Limited Wgn	14666	**4225**	**5775**

ADD FOR 89 CENTURY:

Cass +35	*Cruise Ctrl +60*
Custom Whls/Cvrs +75	*Luggage Rack +20*
Pwr Locks +35	*Pwr Seat +60*
Pwr Wndw +60	*Third Seat +75*
Tilt Whl +35	*Woodgrain +75*

DEDUCT FOR 89 CENTURY:

No AC -390

BUICK 89

Model/Body/Type	BaseList	Whlse	Retail

ELECTRA V6 — 1989

FWD/AT/PS/AC

Model/Body/Type	BaseList	Whlse	Retail
4 Dr Limited Sdn	18525	**5250**	**7200**
4 Dr Park Ave Sdn	20460	**6000**	**8000**
4 Dr Park Ave Ultra Sdn	26218	**7825**	**10025**
4 Dr T-Type Sdn	21325	**5600**	**7550**

ADD FOR 89 ELECTRA:
CD Player +100 · *Custom Whls/Cvrs +100*
Delco/Bose Mus Sys +115 · *Lthr Seats(Std Ultra) +130*
Pwr Sunroof +330 · *Vinyl Roof +75*

ELECTRA ESTATE WAGON V8 — 1989

AT/PS/AC

Model/Body/Type	BaseList	Whlse	Retail
4 Dr 3 Seat Wgn	19905	**5925**	**7900**

ADD FOR 89 ELECTRA ESTATE WAGON:
Leather Seats +115

LE SABRE V6 — 1989

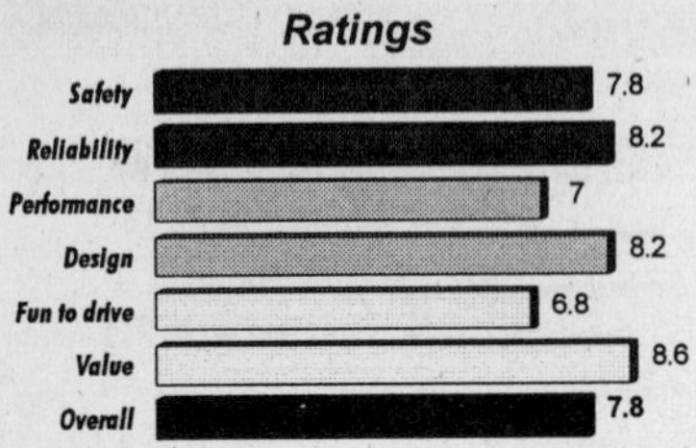

Ratings

Category	Rating
Safety	7.8
Reliability	8.2
Performance	7
Design	8.2
Fun to drive	6.8
Value	8.6
Overall	7.8

FWD/AT/PS/AC

Model/Body/Type	BaseList	Whlse	Retail
2 Dr Cpe	15425	**4450**	**6150**
4 Dr Custom Sdn	15330	**4600**	**6325**
4 Dr Limited Sdn	16730	**5325**	**7150**
2 Dr Limited Cpe	16630	**5175**	**7025**
2 Dr T-Type Cpe	17327	**5300**	**7150**

ADD FOR 89 LE SABRE:
Cass(Std T) +60 · *Cruise Ctrl(Std T) +75*
Custom Whls/Cvrs +75 · *Leather Seats +115*
Pwr Locks +35 · *Pwr Seat +75*
Pwr Wndw +75 · *Vinyl Rf(Std Ltd Cpe) +35*

LE SABRE ESTATE WAGON V8 — 1989

AT/PS/AC

Model/Body/Type	BaseList	Whlse	Retail
4 Dr 3 Seat Wgn	16770	**4450**	**6150**

REATTA V6 — 1989

FWD/AT/PS/AC

Model/Body/Type	BaseList	Whlse	Retail
2 Dr Cpe	26700	**8075**	**10275**

ADD FOR 89 REATTA:
Pwr Sunroof +330

REGAL V6 — 1989

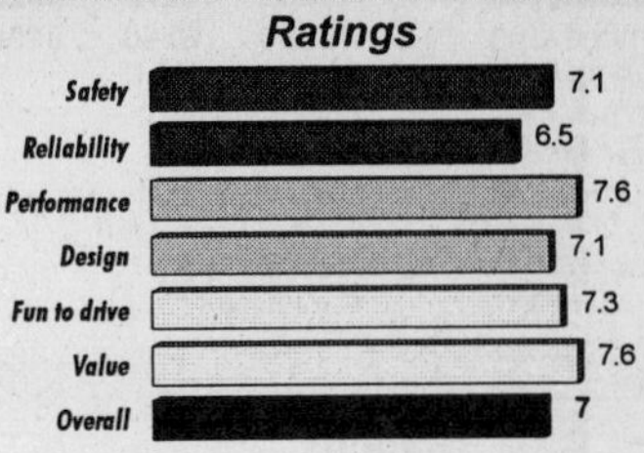

Ratings

Category	Rating
Safety	7.1
Reliability	6.5
Performance	7.6
Design	7.1
Fun to drive	7.3
Value	7.6
Overall	7

FWD/AT/PS/AC

Model/Body/Type	BaseList	Whlse	Retail
2 Dr Custom Cpe	14214	**4575**	**6150**
2 Dr Limited Cpe	14739	**4950**	**6625**

ADD FOR 89 REGAL:
Cass +35 · *CD Player +75*
Cruise Ctrl +60 · *Custom Whls/Cvrs +75*
Gran Sport Pkg +230 · *Leather Seats +75*
Pwr Locks +35 · *Pwr Seat +60*
Pwr Sunroof +250 · *Pwr Wndw +60*

RIVIERA V6 — 1989

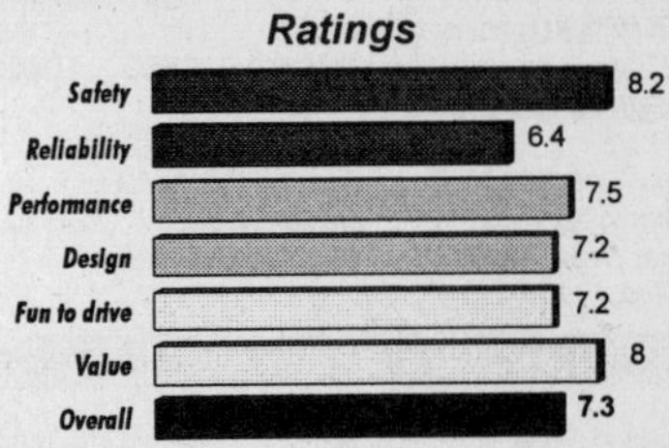

Ratings

Category	Rating
Safety	8.2
Reliability	6.4
Performance	7.5
Design	7.2
Fun to drive	7.2
Value	8
Overall	7.3

FWD/AT/PS/AC

Model/Body/Type	BaseList	Whlse	Retail
2 Dr Cpe	22540	**6500**	**8550**

ADD FOR 89 RIVIERA:
CD Player +100 · *Custom Whls/Cvrs +100*
Delco/Bose Mus Sys +115 · *Leather Seats +130*
Pwr Sunroof +330 · *Vinyl Roof +75*

SKYHAWK 4 Cyl — 1989

FWD/AT/PS/AC

Model/Body/Type	BaseList	Whlse	Retail
4 Dr Sdn	9285	**3250**	**4575**
2 Dr Cpe	9285	**3175**	**4475**
2 Dr Cpe S/E	10380	**3575**	**4900**
4 Dr Wgn	10230	**3450**	**4775**

ADD FOR 89 SKYHAWK:
Cass +20 · *Cruise Ctrl +35*
Pwr Locks +20 · *Tilt Whl +20*

DEDUCT FOR 89 SKYHAWK:
No AC -320 · *No Auto Trans -275*

SKYLARK 1989

Ratings

Rating	Score
Safety	7
Reliability	4.9
Performance	8.1
Design	7.1
Fun to drive	7.7
Value	7.9
Overall	6.6

FWD/AT/PS/AC

Model/Body/Type	BaseList	Whlse	Retail
4 Cyl Models			
2 Dr Custom Cpe	11115	**3325**	**4750**
4 Dr Custom Sdn	11115	**3325**	**4750**
2 Dr Limited Cpe	12345	**3700**	**5125**
4 Dr Limited Sdn	12345	**3700**	**5125**
V6 Models			
2 Dr Custom Cpe	11825	**3650**	**5075**
4 Dr Custom Sdn	11825	**3650**	**5075**
2 Dr Limited Cpe	13055	**4025**	**5550**
4 Dr Limited Sdn	13055	**4025**	**5550**

ADD FOR 89 SKYLARK:

Cass +35 *Cruise Ctrl +60*
Custom Whls/Cvrs +75 *Pwr Locks +35*
Pwr Seat +60 *Pwr Wndw +60*
Quad 4 Engine +215 *S/E Pkg +250*
Tilt Whl +35

DEDUCT FOR 89 SKYLARK:

No AC -390

1988 BUICK

CENTURY 1988

FWD/AT/PS/AC

Model/Body/Type	BaseList	Whlse	Retail
4 Cyl Models			
4 Dr Custom Sdn	11793	**2175**	**3350**
2 Dr Custom Cpe	11643	**2100**	**3250**
4 Dr Custom Wgn	12345	**2400**	**3625**
4 Dr Limited Sdn	12613	**2575**	**3825**
2 Dr Limited Cpe	12410	**2475**	**3725**
4 Dr Limited Estate Wgn	13077	**2825**	**4150**
V6 Models			
4 Dr Custom Sdn	12403	**2500**	**3750**
2 Dr Custom Cpe	12253	**2400**	**3625**
4 Dr Custom Wgn	12955	**2750**	**4025**
4 Dr Limited Sdn	13223	**2925**	**4275**
2 Dr Limited Cpe	13020	**2825**	**4150**
4 Dr Limited Wgn	13687	**3150**	**4550**

DEDUCT FOR 88 CENTURY:

No AC -330

ELECTRA V6 1988

FWD/AT/PS/AC

Model/Body/Type	BaseList	Whlse	Retail
4 Dr Limited Sdn	17479	**3375**	**5000**
4 Dr Park Ave Sdn	19464	**4000**	**5725**
4 Dr T-Type Sdn	20229	**3700**	**5350**

ELECTRA ESTATE WAGON V8 1988

AT/PS/AC

Model/Body/Type	BaseList	Whlse	Retail
4 Dr 3 Seat Wgn	18954	**4050**	**5800**

LE SABRE V6 1988

FWD/AT/PS/AC

Model/Body/Type	BaseList	Whlse	Retail
2 Dr Cpe	14560	**3150**	**4700**
4 Dr Custom Sdn	14405	**3275**	**4850**
4 Dr Limited Sdn	15745	**3950**	**5600**
2 Dr Limited Cpe	16350	**3800**	**5400**
2 Dr T-Type Cpe	16518	**3925**	**5575**

LE SABRE ESTATE WAGON V8 1988

AT/PS/AC

Model/Body/Type	BaseList	Whlse	Retail
4 Dr 3 Seat Wgn	16040	**2850**	**4325**

REATTA V6 1988

FWD/AT/PS/AC

Model/Body/Type	BaseList	Whlse	Retail
2 Dr Cpe	25000	**6025**	**8025**

REGAL V6 1988

FWD/AT/PS/AC

Model/Body/Type	BaseList	Whlse	Retail
2 Dr Custom Cpe	12449	**3300**	**4725**
2 Dr Limited Cpe	12782	**3600**	**5025**

DEDUCT FOR 88 REGAL:

No AC -330

RIVIERA V6 1988

FWD/AT/PS/AC

Model/Body/Type	BaseList	Whlse	Retail
2 Dr Cpe	21615	**4325**	**6125**
2 Dr T-Type Cpe	23380	**4800**	**6675**

SKYHAWK 4 Cyl 1988

FWD/AT/PS/AC

Model/Body/Type	BaseList	Whlse	Retail
4 Dr Sdn	8884	**2275**	**3375**
2 Dr Cpe	8884	**2175**	**3250**
2 Dr Cpe S/E	9979	**2500**	**3650**
4 Dr Wgn	9797	**2425**	**3575**

DEDUCT FOR 88 SKYHAWK:

No AC -250 *No Auto Trans -230*

SKYLARK 1988

FWD/AT/PS/AC

Model/Body/Type	BaseList	Whlse	Retail
4 Cyl Models			
2 Dr Custom Cpe	10684	**2275**	**3500**
4 Dr Custom Sdn	10399	**2275**	**3500**
2 Dr Limited Cpe	11791	**2625**	**3875**
4 Dr Limited Sdn	11721	**2625**	**3875**

BUICK 88-86

Model/Body/Type	BaseList	Whlse	Retail
V6 Models			
2 Dr Custom Cpe	11344	**2575**	**3825**
4 Dr Custom Sdn	11059	**2575**	**3825**
2 Dr Limited Cpe	12451	**2925**	**4275**
4 Dr Limited Sdn	12381	**2925**	**4275**

ADD FOR 88 SKYLARK:
Quad 4 Engine +200
DEDUCT FOR 88 SKYLARK:
No AC -330

1987 BUICK

CENTURY V6 — 1987

FWD/AT/PS/AC

Model/Body/Type	BaseList	Whlse	Retail
4 Dr Custom Sdn	11599	**1775**	**2925**
2 Dr Custom Cpe	11454	**1700**	**2800**
4 Dr Custom Wgn	12088	**2000**	**3150**
4 Dr Limited Sdn	12203	**2150**	**3300**
2 Dr Limited Cpe	12007	**2050**	**3200**
4 Dr Limited Estate Wgn	12608	**2325**	**3550**

DEDUCT FOR 87 CENTURY:
4 Cyl Engine -250

ELECTRA V6 — 1987

FWD/AT/PS/AC

Model/Body/Type	BaseList	Whlse	Retail
4 Dr Limited Sdn	16902	**2525**	**3975**
4 Dr T-Type Sdn	18224	**2800**	**4325**
4 Dr Park Ave Sdn	18769	**3050**	**4625**
2 Dr Park Ave Cpe	18577	**2900**	**4450**

ELECTRA ESTATE WAGON V8 — 1987

AT/PS/AC

Model/Body/Type	BaseList	Whlse	Retail
4 Dr Wgn	17697	**2900**	**4450**

LE SABRE V6 — 1987

FWD/AT/PS/AC

Model/Body/Type	BaseList	Whlse	Retail
4 Dr Sdn	13438	**2300**	**3625**
4 Dr Custom Sdn	13616	**2600**	**3950**
2 Dr Custom Cpe	13616	**2450**	**3775**
4 Dr Limited Sdn	14918	**3150**	**4700**
2 Dr Limited Cpe	14918	**3025**	**4525**
2 Dr T-Type Cpe	15521	**3125**	**4650**

LE SABRE ESTATE WAGON V8 — 1987

AT/PS/AC

Model/Body/Type	BaseList	Whlse	Retail
4 Dr Wgn	14724	**2050**	**3275**

REGAL V6 — 1987

AT/PS/AC

Model/Body/Type	BaseList	Whlse	Retail
2 Dr Cpe	11562	**2450**	**3700**
2 Dr Limited Cpe	12303	**2750**	**4025**
2 Dr T-Type Turbo Cpe	14857	**4400**	**5950**
2 Dr T-Type Turbo Grand National Cpe	15136	**8250**	**10150**

ADD FOR 87 REGAL:
V8 Engine +290

RIVIERA V6 — 1987

FWD/AT/PS/AC

Model/Body/Type	BaseList	Whlse	Retail
2 Dr Cpe	20337	**3225**	**4825**
2 Dr T-Type Cpe	22181	**3600**	**5250**

SKYHAWK 4 Cyl — 1987

FWD/AT/PS/AC

Model/Body/Type	BaseList	Whlse	Retail
4 Dr Custom Sdn	8559	**1725**	**2750**
2 Dr Custom Cpe	8522	**1650**	**2625**
4 Dr Custom Wgn	9249	**1825**	**2900**
4 Dr Limited Sdn	9503	**1950**	**3025**
2 Dr Limited Cpe	9445	**1850**	**2925**
4 Dr Limited Wgn	9841	**2075**	**3150**
3 Dr Sport Hbk	8965	**1725**	**2750**

ADD FOR 87 SKYHAWK:
4 Cyl Turbo Eng +100

SKYLARK 4 Cyl — 1987

FWD/AT/PS/AC

Model/Body/Type	BaseList	Whlse	Retail
4 Dr Custom Sdn	9915	**1800**	**2950**
4 Dr Limited Sdn	11003	**2100**	**3250**

ADD FOR 87 SKYLARK:
V6 Engine +205

SOMERSET 4 Cyl — 1987

FWD/AT/PS/AC

Model/Body/Type	BaseList	Whlse	Retail
2 Dr Custom Cpe	9957	**1800**	**2950**
2 Dr Limited Cpe	11003	**2100**	**3250**

ADD FOR 87 SOMERSET:
V6 Engine +205

1986 BUICK

CENTURY — 1986

FWD

Model/Body/Type	BaseList	Whlse	Retail
4 Dr Custom Sdn	10663	**1375**	**2450**
2 Dr Custom Cpe	10487	**1300**	**2350**
4 Dr Custom Wgn	11083	**1525**	**2625**
4 Dr Limited Sdn	11164	**1675**	**2800**
2 Dr Limited Cpe	10979	**1575**	**2700**
4 Dr Limited Estate Wgn	11544	**1775**	**2975**
4 Dr T-Type Sdn	12223	**1700**	**2825**

ELECTRA — 1986

FWD

Model/Body/Type	BaseList	Whlse	Retail
4 Dr Sdn	15588	**2075**	**3500**
2 Dr Cpe	15396	**1950**	**3350**
4 Dr Park Ave Sdn	17338	**2375**	**3900**
2 Dr Park Ave Cpe	17158	**2250**	**3750**
4 Dr T-Type Sdn	16826	**2225**	**3700**

ELECTRA ESTATE WAGON — 1986

Model/Body/Type	BaseList	Whlse	Retail
4 Dr Wgn	16402	**2100**	**3525**

Model/Body/Type	BaseList	Whlse	Retail
LE SABRE			**1986**
FWD			
4 Dr Custom Sdn	12511	1800	3225
2 Dr Custom Cpe	12511	1700	3100
4 Dr Limited Sdn	13633	2200	3675
2 Dr Limited Cpe	13633	2100	3525
LE SABRE ESTATE WAGON V8			**1986**
4 Dr Wgn	13597	1450	2800
REGAL V6			**1986**
2 Dr Cpe	10654	1850	3050
2 Dr Limited Cpe	11347	2125	3300
2 Dr T-Type Turbo Cpe	13714	3325	4725
2 Dr T-Type Turbo Grand National Cpe	14349	6400	8050
RIVIERA			**1986**
FWD			
2 Dr T-Type Cpe	21577	3100	4700
2 Dr Cpe	19831	2825	4400
SKYHAWK			**1986**
FWD			
4 Dr Custom Sdn	8073	1200	2225
2 Dr Custom Cpe	7844	1100	2150
4 Dr Custom Wgn	8426	1250	2275
4 Dr Limited Sdn	8598	1375	2450
2 Dr Limited Cpe	8388	1300	2350
4 Dr Limited Wgn	8910	1425	2525
3 Dr Sport Hbk	8405	1200	2225
3 Dr T-Type Hbk	9668	1525	2625
2 Dr T-Type Cpe	8971	1425	2525
SKYLARK			**1986**
FWD			
4 Dr Custom Sdn	9620	1350	2425
4 Dr Limited Sdn	10290	1575	2700
SOMERSET			**1986**
FWD			
2 Dr Custom Cpe	9425	1350	2425
2 Dr Limited Cpe	10095	1575	2700
2 Dr T-Type Cpe	11390	1825	3025

1985 BUICK

Model/Body/Type	BaseList	Whlse	Retail
CENTURY			**1985**
FWD			
4 Dr Custom Sdn	9805	1150	2175
2 Dr Custom Cpe	9637	1075	2100
4 Dr Custom Wgn	10201	1275	2300
4 Dr Limited Sdn	10272	1350	2425
2 Dr Limited Cpe	10101	1275	2325
4 Dr Limited Estate Wgn	10639	1475	2575
4 Dr T-Type Sdn	11418	1400	2500
2 Dr T-Type Cpe	11249	1400	2500
ELECTRA			**1985**
FWD			
4 Dr Sdn	13850	1625	3000
2 Dr Cpe	13673	1500	2850
4 Dr Park Ave Sdn	15752	1900	3300
2 Dr Park Ave Cpe	15596	1775	3175
4 Dr T-Type Sdn	15053	1775	3175
2 Dr T-Type Cpe	14876	1675	3050
4 Dr Estate Wgn	15323	1975	3400
LE SABRE			**1985**
FWD			
4 Dr Custom Sdn	10993	1375	2700
2 Dr Custom Cpe	10843	1275	2550
4 Dr Limited Sdn	12306	1675	3050
2 Dr Limited Cpe	12141	1550	2900
4 Dr Estate Wgn	12704	1400	2725
REGAL			**1985**
2 Dr Cpe	9928	1400	2500
2 Dr Limited Cpe	10585	1650	2775
2 Dr T-Type Turbo Cpe	12640	2650	3950
2 Dr T-Type Turbo Grand National Cpe	13315	4250	5725
RIVIERA			**1985**
FWD			
2 Dr T-Type Turbo Cpe	17654	1425	2750
2 Dr Cpe	16710	1900	3300
2 Dr Conv	26797	5100	7025
SKYHAWK			**1985**
FWD			
4 Dr Custom Sdn	7581	900	1875
2 Dr Custom Cpe	7365	825	1775
4 Dr Custom Wgn	7919	925	1925
4 Dr Limited Sdn	8083	1075	2100
2 Dr Limited Cpe	7883	975	2000
4 Dr Limited Wgn	8379	1100	2150
2 Dr T-Type Cpe	8437	1125	2175
SKYLARK			**1985**
FWD			
4 Dr Custom Sdn	7707	875	1825
4 Dr Limited Sdn	8283	1000	2025
SOMERSET REGAL			**1985**
FWD			
2 Dr Custom Cpe	8857	1225	2275
2 Dr Limited Cpe	9466	1425	2525

Model/Body/Type	BaseList	Whlse	Retail

CADILLAC USA

1992 Cadillac Allante

For a Cadillac dealer in your area, see our Dealer Directory (pg 217)

1994 CADILLAC

DE VILLE V8 1994

FWD/AT/PS/AC

Model/Body/Type	BaseList	Whlse	Retail
4 Dr Sdn	32990	**26000**	**29900**
4 Dr Concours Sdn	36590	**29400**	**33525**

ELDORADO V8 1994

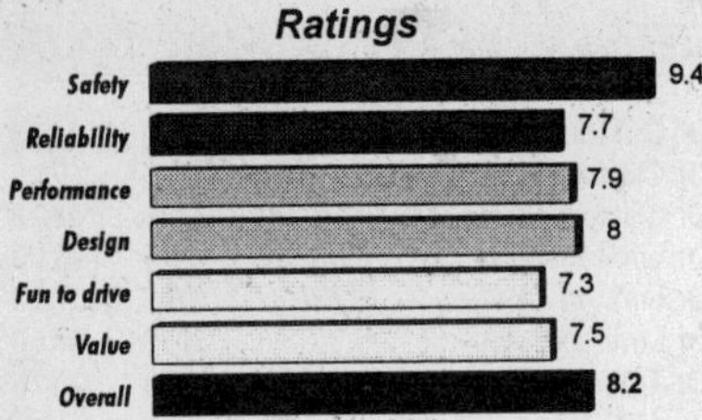

FWD/AT/PS/AC

Model/Body/Type	BaseList	Whlse	Retail
2 Dr Cpe	37290	**28175**	**32200**
2 Dr Touring Cpe	40590	**31175**	**35200**

FLEETWOOD V8 1994

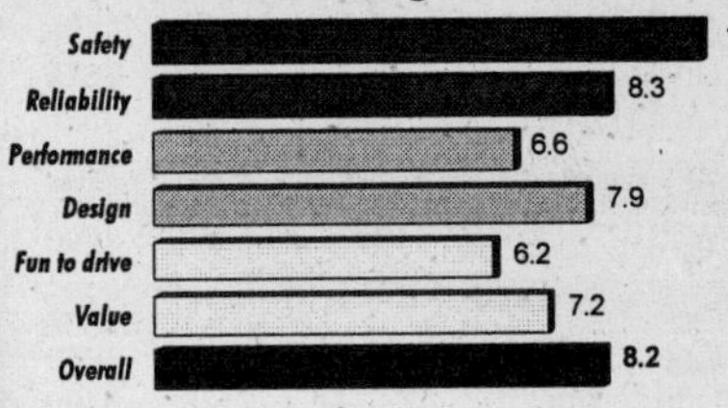

AT/PS/AC

Model/Body/Type	BaseList	Whlse	Retail
4 Dr Sdn	33990	**24250**	**28000**

SEVILLE V8 1994

Ratings

Rating	Score
Safety	8.9
Reliability	7.8
Performance	8.4
Design	7.9
Fun to drive	8
Value	7.9
Overall	8.2

FWD/AT/PS/AC

Model/Body/Type	BaseList	Whlse	Retail
4 Dr Luxury Sdn	40990	**31250**	**35300**
4 Dr Touring Sdn	44890	**34550**	**38400**

ADD FOR ALL 94 CADILLAC:

Anti-Theft/Recovery Sys +365
Brougham(Fleetwood) +1090
Car Phone +230
CD Player +340
Custom Paint +135
Custom Wheels +275
Delco/Bose Mus Sys +295
Leather Seats(Std Touring,Concours) +365
Pwr Sunroof +635
Vinyl Roof +230

1993 CADILLAC

ALLANTE V8 1993

FWD/AT/PS/AC

Model/Body/Type	BaseList	Whlse	Retail
2 Dr Conv	59975	**35100**	**39075**

Model/Body/Type	BaseList	Whlse	Retail

DE VILLE V8 1993

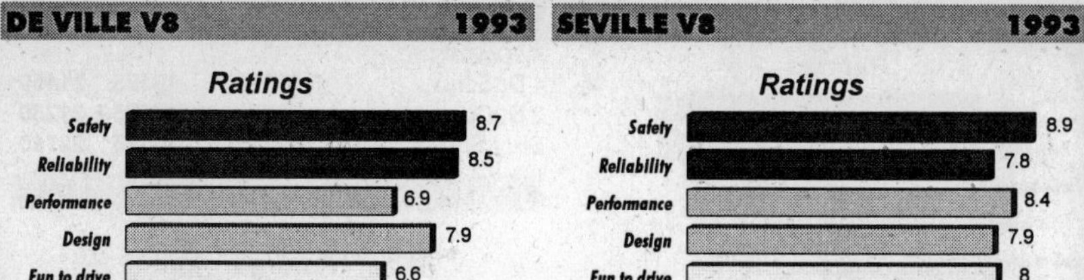

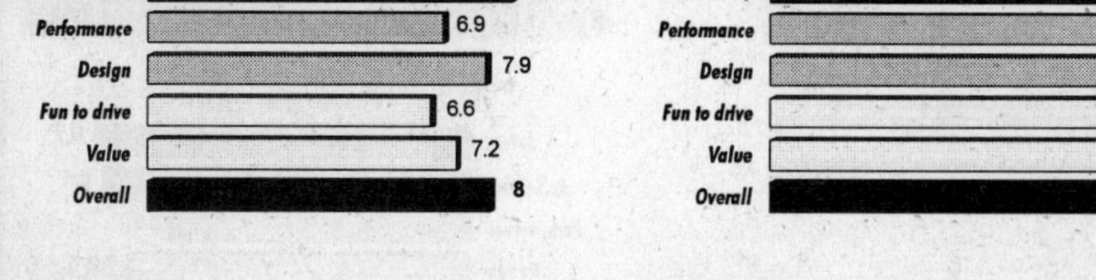

FWD/AT/PS/AC

Model/Body/Type	BaseList	Whlse	Retail
4 Dr Sdn	32990	**19000**	**22350**
2 Dr Cpe	33915	**18800**	**22150**
4 Dr Touring Sdn	36310	**21450**	**25025**

ELDORADO V8 1993

Ratings

Safety	9.4
Reliability	7.7
Performance	7.9
Design	8
Fun to drive	7.3
Value	7.5
Overall	8.2

FWD/AT/PS/AC

Model/Body/Type	BaseList	Whlse	Retail
2 Dr Cpe	33990	**24150**	**27900**

FLEETWOOD V8 1993

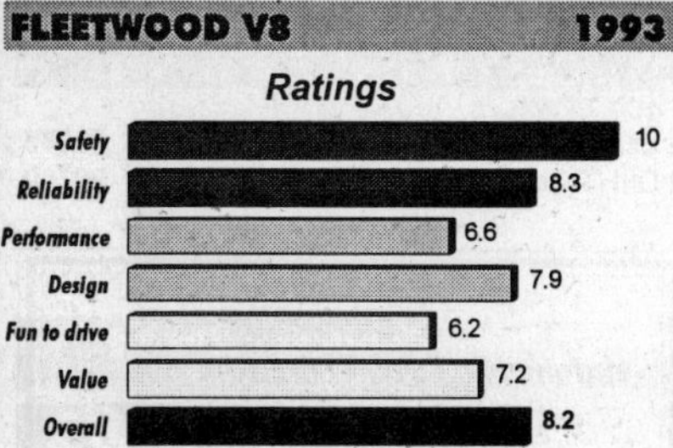

AT/PS/AC

Model/Body/Type	BaseList	Whlse	Retail
4 Dr Sdn	33990	**22325**	**25975**

SEVILLE V8 1993

Ratings

Safety	8.9
Reliability	7.8
Performance	8.4
Design	7.9
Fun to drive	8
Value	7.9
Overall	8.2

FWD/AT/PS/AC

Model/Body/Type	BaseList	Whlse	Retail
4 Dr Sdn	36990	**25275**	**29150**
4 Dr Touring Sdn	41990	**28475**	**32525**

SIXTY SPECIAL V8 1993

FWD/AT/PS/AC

Model/Body/Type	BaseList	Whlse	Retail
4 Dr Sdn	37230	**22425**	**26100**

ADD FOR ALL 93 CADILLAC:

Brougham(Fleetwood) +855
Car Phone +175
CD Player(Std Allante) +290
Custom Paint +115
Delco/Bose Mus Sys(Std Touring,Allante) +250
Eldorado Sport Cpe +1290
Eldorado Touring Cpe +2500
Leather Seats(Std Touring,Allante) +320
Pwr Sunroof +505
Removable Hardtop(Allante) +795
Vinyl Roof(Std Sixty Special) +175
Wire Whl Covers,Locking(DeVille) +230

1992 CADILLAC

ALLANTE V8 1992

FWD/AT/PS/AC

Model/Body/Type	BaseList	Whlse	Retail
2 Dr Conv	57170	**26450**	**30450**
2 Dr HT Conv	62790	**29175**	**33275**

See the Automobile Dealer Directory on page 379 for a Dealer near you!

CADILLAC

CADILLAC 92-91

Model/Body/Type	BaseList	Whlse	Retail

BROUGHAM V8 — 1992

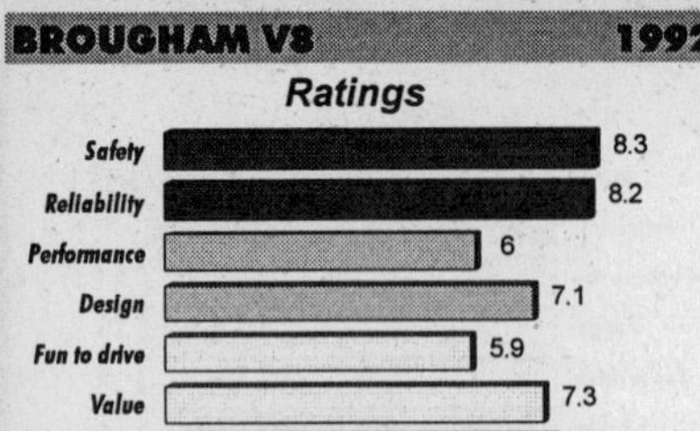

Model/Body/Type	BaseList	Whlse	Retail
AT/PS/AC			
4 Dr Sdn	31740	**16525**	**19700**

DE VILLE V8 — 1992

Model/Body/Type	BaseList	Whlse	Retail
FWD/AT/PS/AC			
4 Dr Sdn	31740	**15750**	**18825**
2 Dr Cpe	31740	**15550**	**18625**
4 Dr Touring Sdn	35190	**17825**	**21125**

ELDORADO V8 — 1992

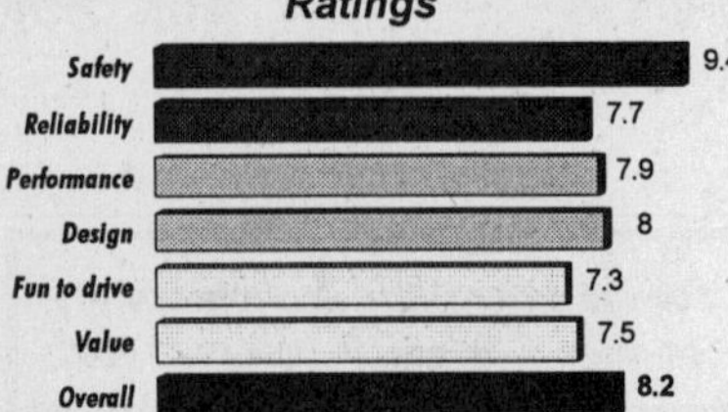

Model/Body/Type	BaseList	Whlse	Retail
FWD/AT/PS/AC			
2 Dr Cpe	32470	**18975**	**22325**

FLEETWOOD V8 — 1992

Model/Body/Type	BaseList	Whlse	Retail
FWD/AT/PS/AC			
4 Dr Sdn	36360	**18125**	**21450**
2 Dr Cpe	36360	**17925**	**21250**
Sixty Special Sdn	39860	**19375**	**22750**

SEVILLE V8 — 1992

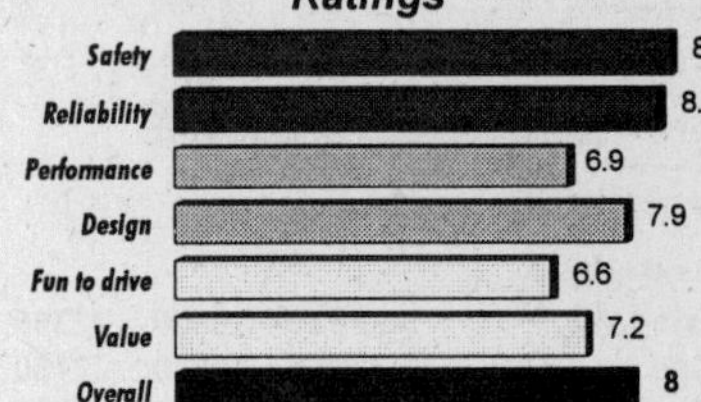

Model/Body/Type	BaseList	Whlse	Retail
FWD/AT/PS/AC			
4 Dr Sdn	34975	**20625**	**24125**
4 Dr Touring Sdn	37975	**23200**	**26925**

ADD FOR ALL 92 CADILLACS:

Brougham d'Elegance +835
Cabriolet Roof(Std Fleetwood Cpe) +375
Car Phone +160
CD Player(Std Allante) +250
Cust Whls(Brougham) +215
Custom Paint +100
Delco/Bose Mus Sys(Std Allante) +230
Eldorado Touring Cpe +760
Leather Seats(Std Tour,60Sp,Allante) +275
Pwr Sunroof +465
Vinyl Roof(DeVille) +160
Wire Whl Covers,Locking(Std Fltwd,60 Sp) +215

1991 CADILLAC

ALLANTE V8 — 1991

Model/Body/Type	BaseList	Whlse	Retail
FWD/AT/PS/AC			
2 Dr Conv	55250	**22400**	**26075**
2 Dr HT Conv	60800	**24850**	**28700**

Model/Body/Type	BaseList	Whlse	Retail

BROUGHAM V8 1991

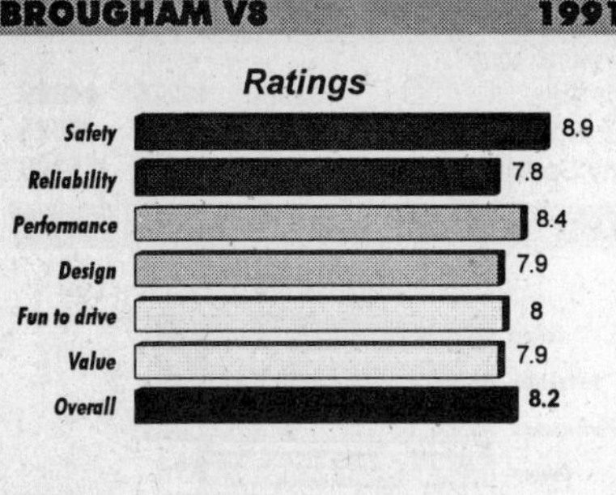

AT/PS/AC

Model/Body/Type	BaseList	Whlse	Retail
4 Dr Sdn	30225	**13450**	**16375**

DE VILLE V8 1991

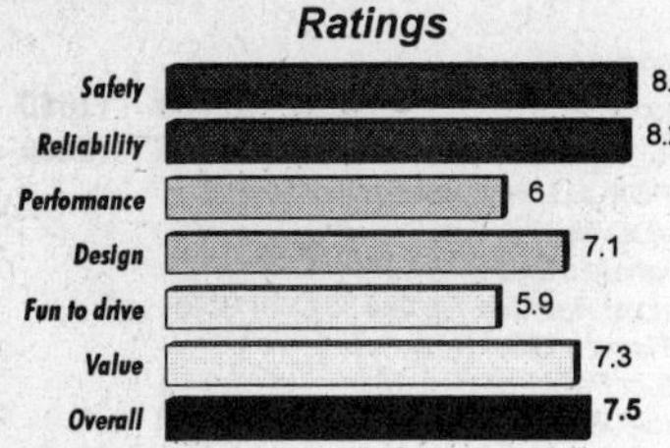

FWD/AT/PS/AC

Model/Body/Type	BaseList	Whlse	Retail
4 Dr Sdn	30455	**13000**	**15875**
2 Dr Cpe	30205	**12800**	**15675**
4 Dr Touring Sdn	33455	**14850**	**17875**

ELDORADO V8 1991

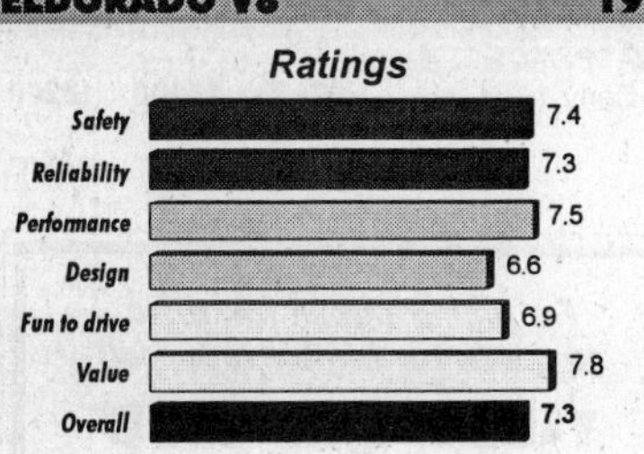

FWD/AT/PS/AC

Model/Body/Type	BaseList	Whlse	Retail
2 Dr Cpe	31245	**14450**	**17375**

FLEETWOOD V8 1991

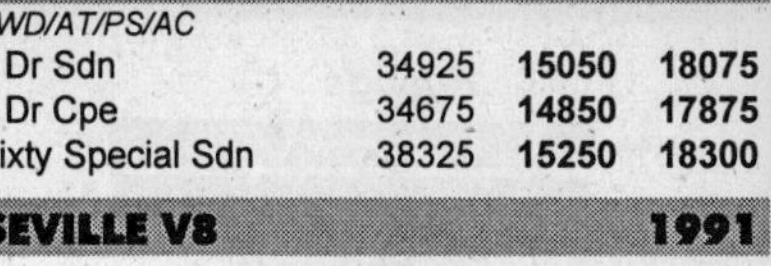

FWD/AT/PS/AC

Model/Body/Type	BaseList	Whlse	Retail
4 Dr Sdn	34925	**15050**	**18075**
2 Dr Cpe	34675	**14850**	**17875**
Sixty Special Sdn	38325	**15250**	**18300**

SEVILLE V8 1991

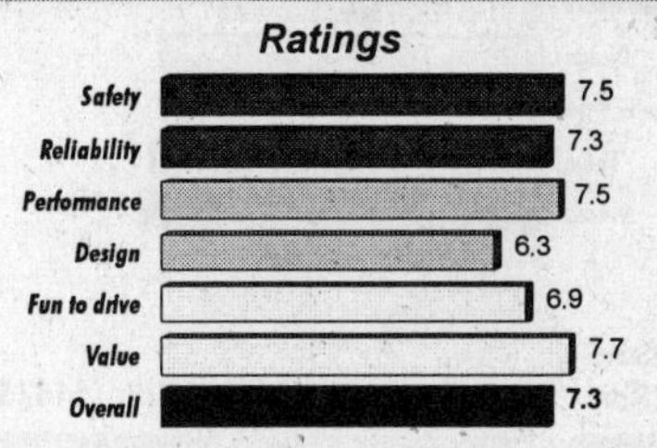

FWD/AT/PS/AC

Model/Body/Type	BaseList	Whlse	Retail
4 Dr Sdn	33935	**13950**	**16900**
4 Dr Touring Sdn	37135	**16175**	**19275**

ADD FOR ALL 91 CADILLAC:

Brougham d'Elegance +795
Cabriolet Roof(Std Fleetwood Cpe) +330
Car Phone +130
CD Player(Std Allante) +200
Cust Whls(Brougham) +175
Custom Paint +75
Delco/Bose Mus Sys(Std Allante) +200
Eldorado Biarritz +955
Eldorado Touring Cpe +580
Leather Seats(Std Tour,60Special,Allante) +215
Pwr Sunroof +430
Wire Whl Covers,Locking(Std Fltwd,60Spc) +175

1990 CADILLAC

ALLANTE V8 1990

FWD/AT/PS/AC

Model/Body/Type	BaseList	Whlse	Retail
2 Dr Conv	51550	**18200**	**21525**
2 Dr HT Conv	57183	**20250**	**23725**

CADILLAC

CADILLAC 90-89

Model/Body/Type	BaseList	Whlse	Retail

BROUGHAM V8 1990

Ratings

Rating	Score
Safety	8.3
Reliability	8.2
Performance	6
Design	7.1
Fun to drive	5.9
Value	7.3
Overall	7.5

AT/PS/AC

Model/Body/Type	BaseList	Whlse	Retail
4 Dr Sdn	27400	**9325**	**11675**

DE VILLE V8 1990

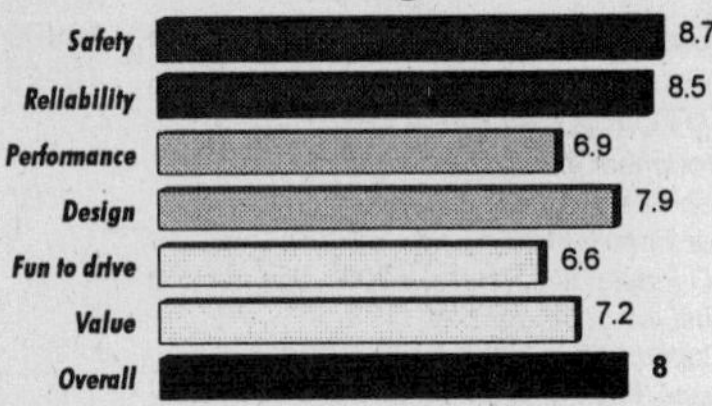

FWD/AT/PS/AC

Model/Body/Type	BaseList	Whlse	Retail
4 Dr Sdn	27540	**9975**	**12550**
2 Dr Cpe	26960	**9800**	**12325**

ELDORADO V8 1990

FWD/AT/PS/AC

Model/Body/Type	BaseList	Whlse	Retail
2 Dr Cpe	28855	**11225**	**14000**

FLEETWOOD V8 1990

FWD/AT/PS/AC

Model/Body/Type	BaseList	Whlse	Retail
4 Dr Sdn	32980	**11275**	**14050**
2 Dr Cpe	32400	**11075**	**13825**
Sixty Special Sdn	36980	**12450**	**15300**

SEVILLE V8 1990

Ratings

Rating	Score
Safety	7.5
Reliability	7.3
Performance	7.5
Design	6.3
Fun to drive	6.9
Value	7.7
Overall	7.3

FWD/AT/PS/AC

Model/Body/Type	BaseList	Whlse	Retail
4 Dr Sdn	31830	**10850**	**13600**
4 Dr Touring Sdn	36320	**12775**	**15650**

ADD FOR ALL 90 CADILLAC:

ABS(DeVille,Eldorado,BaseSeville) +275
Brougham d'Elegance +705
Cabriolet Roof(Std Fleetwood Cpe) +275
CD Player +130
Custom Paint +60
Custom Whls(Brougham, DeVille) +130
Delco/Bose Mus Sys(Std Allante) +130
Eldorado Biarritz +835
Leather Seats(Std Tour,60Sp,Allante) +160
Pwr Sunroof +390
Wire Whl Covers,Locking(Std Fltwd,60Spc) +130

1989 CADILLAC

ALLANTE V8 1989

FWD/AT/PS/AC

Model/Body/Type	BaseList	Whlse	Retail
2 Dr Conv	57183	**16100**	**19200**

Model/Body/Type	BaseList	Whlse	Retail

BROUGHAM V8 1989

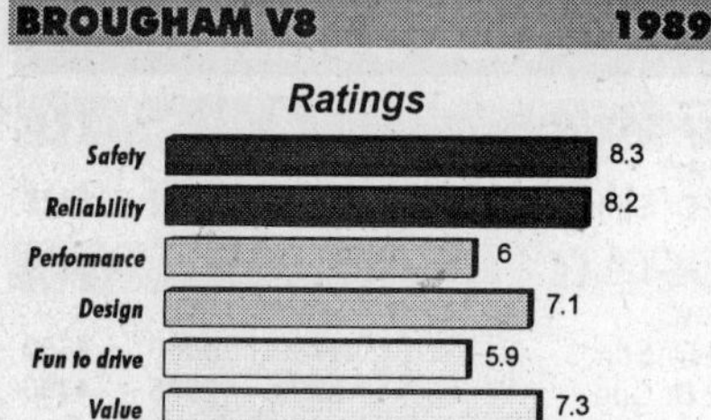

Model/Body/Type	BaseList	Whlse	Retail
AT/PS/AC			
4 Dr Sdn	25699	**6850**	**9000**

DE VILLE V8 1989

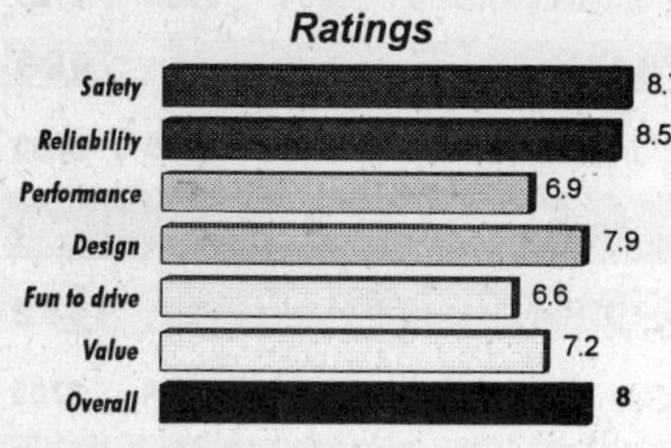

Model/Body/Type	BaseList	Whlse	Retail
FWD/AT/PS/AC			
4 Dr Sdn	25435	**7700**	**9925**
2 Dr Cpe	24960	**7500**	**9725**

ELDORADO V8 1989

Ratings

Safety 7.4
Reliability 7.3
Performance 7.5
Design 6.6
Fun to drive 6.9
Value 7.8
Overall 7.3

Model/Body/Type	BaseList	Whlse	Retail
FWD/AT/PS/AC			
2 Dr Cpe	26738	**8400**	**10625**

FLEETWOOD V8 1989

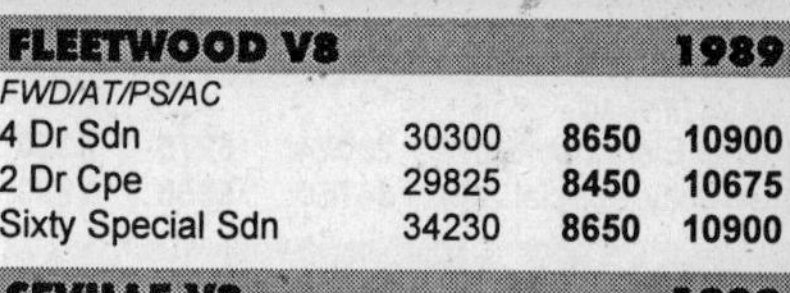

Model/Body/Type	BaseList	Whlse	Retail
FWD/AT/PS/AC			
4 Dr Sdn	30300	**8650**	**10900**
2 Dr Cpe	29825	**8450**	**10675**
Sixty Special Sdn	34230	**8650**	**10900**

SEVILLE V8 1989

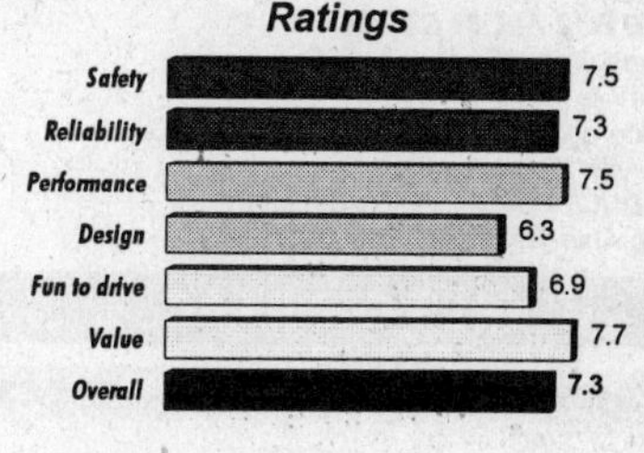

Model/Body/Type	BaseList	Whlse	Retail
FWD/AT/PS/AC			
4 Dr Sdn	29750	**8250**	**10475**

ADD FOR ALL 89 CADILLAC:

Brougham d'Elegance +605
Cabriolet Roof(Std Fleetwood Cpe) +215
CD Player +100
Custom Whls(Brougham,DeVille) +100
Delco/Bose Mus Sys(Std Allante) +115
Eldorado Biarritz +760
Leather Seats(Std 60Spc,Allante) +130
Pwr Sunroof +330
STS Pkg +1340
Wire Whl Covers,Locking(Std Fltwd,60Spc) +100

1988 CADILLAC

ALLANTE V8 1988

Model/Body/Type	BaseList	Whlse	Retail
FWD/AT/PS/AC			
2 Dr Conv	56533	**13700**	**16625**

BROUGHAM V8 1988

Model/Body/Type	BaseList	Whlse	Retail
AT/PS/AC			
4 Dr Sdn	23846	**4800**	**6675**

CIMARRON V6 1988

Model/Body/Type	BaseList	Whlse	Retail
FWD/AT/PS/AC			
4 Dr Sdn	16071	**2900**	**4450**

DE VILLE V8 1988

Model/Body/Type	BaseList	Whlse	Retail
FWD/AT/PS/AC			
4 Dr Sdn	23404	**5475**	**7425**
2 Dr Cpe	23049	**5250**	**7200**

ELDORADO V8 1988

Model/Body/Type	BaseList	Whlse	Retail
FWD/AT/PS/AC			
2 Dr Cpe	24891	**5650**	**7600**

FLEETWOOD V8 — 1988

FWD/AT/PS/AC

Model/Body/Type	BaseList	Whlse	Retail
4 Dr D'Elegance Sdn	28024	**6275**	**8300**
4 Dr Sixty Special Sdn	34750	**5950**	**7950**

SEVILLE V8 — 1988

FWD/AT/PS/AC

Model/Body/Type	BaseList	Whlse	Retail
4 Dr Sdn	27627	**6225**	**8250**

ADD FOR ALL 88 CADILLAC:

Brougham d'Elegance +545
DeVille Touring +375
Eldorado Biarritz +605
Seville Elegante +895

DEDUCT FOR ALL 88 CADILLAC:

No Auto Trans -390

1987 CADILLAC

ALLANTE V8 — 1987

FWD/AT/PS/AC

Model/Body/Type	BaseList	Whlse	Retail
2 Dr Conv	54700	**11575**	**14375**

BROUGHAM V8 — 1987

AT/PS/AC

Model/Body/Type	BaseList	Whlse	Retail
4 Dr Sdn	22637	**3575**	**5225**

CIMARRON V6 — 1987

FWD/AT/PS/AC

Model/Body/Type	BaseList	Whlse	Retail
4 Dr Sdn	15032	**2175**	**3525**

DEDUCT FOR 87 CIMARRON:

4 Cyl Engine -250

DE VILLE V8 — 1987

FWD/AT/PS/AC

Model/Body/Type	BaseList	Whlse	Retail
4 Dr Sdn	21659	**3975**	**5725**
2 Dr Cpe	21316	**3775**	**5475**

ELDORADO V8 — 1987

FWD/AT/PS/AC

Model/Body/Type	BaseList	Whlse	Retail
2 Dr Cpe	23740	**4450**	**6250**

FLEETWOOD V8 — 1987

FWD/AT/PS/AC

Model/Body/Type	BaseList	Whlse	Retail
4 Dr D'Elegance Sdn	26104	**4475**	**6275**
4 Dr Sixty Special Sdn	34850	**4500**	**6275**
4 Dr Limousine	36510	**4375**	**6150**
4 Dr Formal Limousine	38580	**5725**	**7675**

SEVILLE V8 — 1987

FWD/AT/PS/AC

Model/Body/Type	BaseList	Whlse	Retail
4 Dr Sdn	26326	**4425**	**6200**

ADD FOR ALL 87 CADILLAC:

Brougham d'Elegance +390
DeVille Touring +250
Eldorado Biarritz +505
Seville Elegante +705

1986 CADILLAC

CIMARRON — 1986

FWD

Model/Body/Type	BaseList	Whlse	Retail
4 Dr Sdn	13738	**1750**	**3125**

DE VILLE — 1986

FWD

Model/Body/Type	BaseList	Whlse	Retail
4 Dr Sdn	19669	**3050**	**4650**
2 Dr Cpe	19990	**2875**	**4450**

ELDORADO — 1986

FWD

Model/Body/Type	BaseList	Whlse	Retail
2 Dr Cpe	24251	**3825**	**5550**

FLEETWOOD — 1986

FWD

Model/Body/Type	BaseList	Whlse	Retail
4 Dr Brougham Sdn	21265	**3150**	**4775**
4 Dr Limousine	33895	**4025**	**5775**
4 Dr Formal Limousine	36934	**5200**	**7125**

SEVILLE — 1986

FWD

Model/Body/Type	BaseList	Whlse	Retail
4 Dr Sdn	26756	**3925**	**5700**

1985 CADILLAC

CIMARRON — 1985

FWD

Model/Body/Type	BaseList	Whlse	Retail
4 Dr Sdn	13447	**1375**	**2700**

DE VILLE — 1985

FWD

Model/Body/Type	BaseList	Whlse	Retail
4 Dr Sdn	18571	**2625**	**4175**
2 Dr Cpe	17990	**2475**	**4025**

ELDORADO — 1985

FWD

Model/Body/Type	BaseList	Whlse	Retail
2 Dr Cpe	20931	**2825**	**4400**
2 Dr Biarritz Conv	32105	**6450**	**8450**

FLEETWOOD — 1985

FWD

Model/Body/Type	BaseList	Whlse	Retail
4 Dr Sdn	21040	**2925**	**4525**
2 Dr Cpe	21069	**2800**	**4375**
4 Dr Brougham Sdn	21402	**2450**	**4000**
2 Dr Brougham Cpe	20798	**2325**	**3850**
4 Dr Limousine	32640	**2975**	**4575**

SEVILLE — 1985

FWD

Model/Body/Type	BaseList	Whlse	Retail
4 Dr Sdn	23259	**2825**	**4400**

Model/Body/Type	BaseList	Whlse	Retail

CHEVROLET USA

1992 Chevrolet Corvette Convertible

For a Chevrolet dealer in your area, see our Dealer Directory (pg 217)

1994 CHEVROLET

ASTRO VAN V6 1/2 Ton 1994

AT/PS/AC

Model/Body/Type	BaseList	Whlse	Retail
Cargo Van	15344	-	-
Extended Cargo Van	15817	-	-
CS Van	16278	**14500**	**17250**
Extended CS Van	16580	**15525**	**18400**

REFER TO 94 CHEV. TRUCK OPTIONS TABLE Pg 60

BERETTA 1994

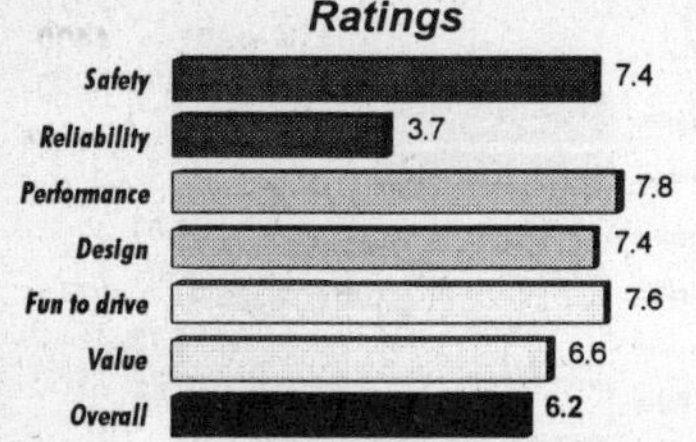

FWD/AT/PS/AC

4 Cyl Models

Model/Body/Type	BaseList	Whlse	Retail
2 Dr Cpe	12415	**9775**	**11800**
2 Dr Z26 Cpe	15310	**11500**	**13825**

V6 Models

Model/Body/Type	BaseList	Whlse	Retail
2 Dr Cpe	13690	**10250**	**12350**
2 Dr Z26 Cpe	15835	**12375**	**14775**

ADD FOR 94 BERETTA:

Anti-Theft/Recovery Sys +365
Cass(Std Z26) +90 *CD Player +205*
Cruise Ctrl +135 *Pwr Wndw +135*
Sunroof +275 *Tilt Whl +90*

DEDUCT FOR 94 BERETTA:

No Auto Trans -500

BLAZER V8 1/2 Ton 1994

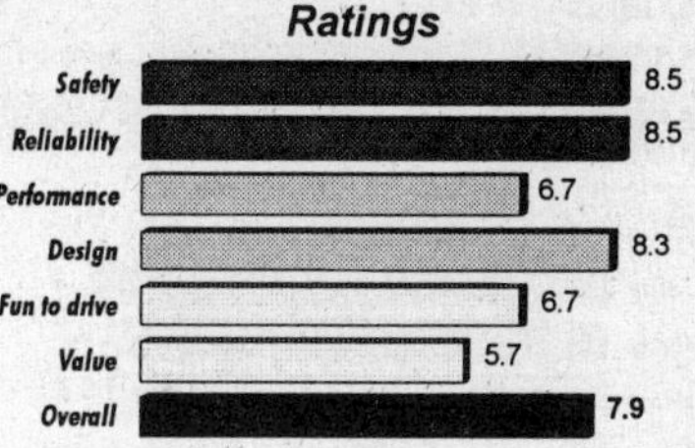

4WD/AT/PS/AC

Model/Body/Type	BaseList	Whlse	Retail
2 Dr Utility	21225	20600	23925

REFER TO 94 CHEV. TRUCK OPTIONS TABLE Pg 60

C1500/C2500/C3500 PKUP V8 1994

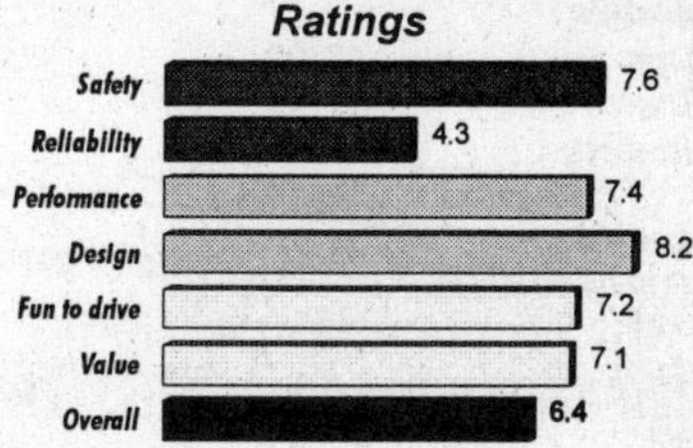

AT/PS/AC

C1500 Pickup 1/2 Ton

Model/Body/Type	BaseList	Whlse	Retail
Fleetside WT 6 1/2' (V6)	12354	-	-
Fleetside WT 8' (V6)	12554	-	-
Sportside 6 1/2'	14690	**14050**	**16825**
Fleetside 6 1/2'	14027	**13650**	**16400**
Fleetside 8'	14307	**13750**	**16500**
Fleetside Ext Cab 6 1/2'	15854	**15500**	**18375**
Fleetside Ext Cab 8'	16697	**15600**	**18475**
Sportside Ext Cab 6 1/2'	16266	**15900**	**18800**

Model/Body/Type	BaseList	Whlse	Retail
C2500 Pickup 3/4 Ton			
Fleetside 8'	15114	**14575**	**17350**
Fleetside Ext Cab 6 1/2'	17642	**16350**	**19275**
Fleetside Ext Cab 8'	18529	**16450**	**19375**
C3500 Pickup 1 Ton			
Fleetside 8'	16847	**15200**	**18625**
Fleetside Ext Cab 8'	20092	**17075**	**20700**
Fleetside Crew Cab 8'	19356	**17225**	**20875**

ADD FOR 94 C1500/C2500/C3500 PKUP:
Silverado Pkg +775 *Sport Pkg +820*
V8 6.5L Diesel Engine +730
V8 6.5L Turbo Diesel Engine +1045
DEDUCT FOR 94 C1500/C2500/C3500 PKUP:
V6 Eng -590
REFER TO 94 CHEV. TRUCK OPTIONS TABLE Pg 60

CAMARO 1994

AT/PS/AC

Model/Body/Type	BaseList	Whlse	Retail
V6 Models			
2 Dr Cpe	13399	-	-
2 Dr Conv	18745	-	-
V8 Models			
2 Dr Z28 Cpe	16779	-	-
2 Dr Z28 Conv	22075	-	-

ADD FOR 94 CAMARO:
T-Top +815

CAPRICE CLASSIC V8 1994

AT/PS/AC

Model/Body/Type	BaseList	Whlse	Retail
4 Dr Sdn	18995	**13975**	**16650**
4 Dr LS Sdn	21435	**16100**	**18925**
4 Dr 3 Seat Wgn	21180	**16475**	**19300**
4 Dr Impala SS	21920	-	-

ADD FOR 94 CAPRICE CLASSIC:
Anti-Theft/Recovery Sys +365
Car Phone +230 *Cass(Base) +135*
CD Player +275
Cruise Ctrl(Std LS,Impala) +180
Custom Whls/Cvrs +230 *Lthr Sts(Std Impala) +320*
Pwr Locks(Std LS,Impala) +135
Pwr Seat(Std Impala) +180
Pwr Wndw(Std LS,Impala) +180
Woodgrain(S/W) +230

CAVALIER 1994

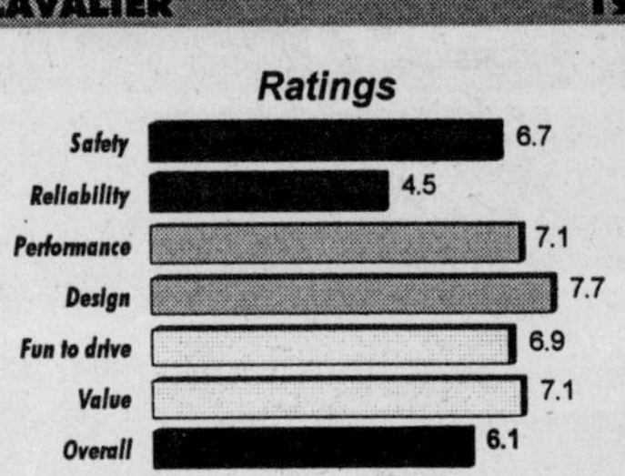

FWD/AT/PS/AC

Model/Body/Type	BaseList	Whlse	Retail
4 Cyl Models			
4 Dr VL Sdn	8995	**8150**	**9975**
2 Dr VL Cpe	8845	**8050**	**9900**
4 Dr RS Sdn	11315	**8900**	**10800**
2 Dr RS Cpe	10715	**8800**	**10675**
2 Dr RS Conv	16995	**12725**	**15125**
4 Dr Wgn	10785	**9350**	**11275**
V6 Models			
2 Dr Z24 Cpe	13995	**11975**	**14350**
2 Dr Z24 Conv	19995	**15925**	**18525**

ADD FOR 94 CAVALIER:
Anti-Theft/Recovery Sys +365
Cass(Std Z24) +90
CD Player +205 *Cruise Ctrl +135*
Luggage Rack(S/W) +115 *Pwr Wndw(Std Conv) +135*
Sunroof +275 *Tilt Whl(Std Z24) +70*
V6 Eng(Std Z24) +455
DEDUCT FOR 94 CAVALIER:
No AC -590 *No Auto Trans -500*

CORSICA 1994

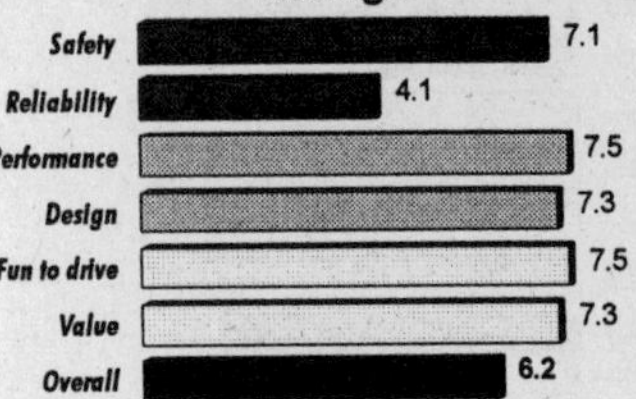

FWD/AT/PS/AC

Model/Body/Type	BaseList	Whlse	Retail
4 Cyl Models			
4 Dr Sdn	13145	**9275**	**11200**

Model/Body/Type	BaseList	Whlse	Retail
V6 Models			
4 Dr Sdn	13865	**9800**	**11850**

ADD FOR 94 CORSICA:
Anti-Theft/Recovery Sys +365
Cass +90
CD Player +205 *Cruise Ctrl +135*
Pwr Wndw +135 *Sunroof +275*
Tilt Whl +90

DEDUCT FOR 94 CORSICA:
No Auto Trans -500

CORVETTE V8 1994

AT-6SP

Model/Body/Type	BaseList	Whlse	Retail
2 Dr Cpe	36185	**26800**	**30825**
2 Dr Conv	42960	**31625**	**35725**
2 Dr ZR1 Cpe	67443	-	-

ADD FOR 94 CORVETTE:
Anti-Theft/Recovery Sys +365
Car Phone +230 *CD Player(Std ZR1) +340*
Delco/Bose Music Sys(Std ZR1) +295
Removable Glass Rf +680 *Removable Hardtop +910*

G10/G20/G30 VANS V8 1994

AT/PS/AC

Model/Body/Type	BaseList	Whlse	Retail
G10 Van 1/2 Ton			
Chevy Van	15709	**13425**	**16150**
G20 Van 3/4 Ton			
Chevy Van	15678	**13725**	**16475**
Sportvan	18648	**15275**	**18125**
G30 Van 1 Ton			
Chevy Van	16010	-	-
Sportvan	20000	-	-
Ext Chevy Van	18130	-	-
Ext Sportvan	21156	-	-
Cutaway	16738	-	-

DEDUCT FOR 94 G10/G20/G30 VAN:
V6 Eng -590

REFER TO 94 CHEV. TRUCK OPTIONS TABLE Pg 60

LUMINA V6 1994

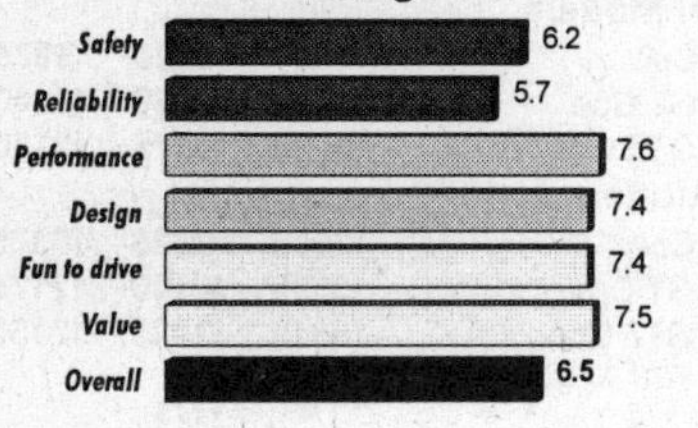

FWD/AT/PS/AC

Model/Body/Type	BaseList	Whlse	Retail
4 Dr Sdn	15305	**11075**	**13425**
4 Dr Euro Sdn	16515	**12600**	**15075**
2 Dr Euro Cpe	16875	**12600**	**15075**
2 Dr Z34 Cpe	19310	**15125**	**17750**

ADD FOR 94 LUMINA:
ABS(Std Euro +Z34) +430
Anti-Theft/Recovery Sys +365
Cass(Std Euro +Z34) +115 *CD Player +230*
Cruise Ctrl(Std Z34) +160 *Delco/Bose Mus Sys +205*
Euro 3.4 Pkg +635 *Pwr Seat +160*
Pwr Wndw(Std Euro 2Dr +Z34) +160

LUMINA APV V6 1994

FWD/AT/PS/AC

Model/Body/Type	BaseList	Whlse	Retail
Cargo Van	15485	-	-
Wagon	16815	**15025**	**17850**

REFER TO 94 CHEV. TRUCK OPTIONS TABLE Pg 60

S10 BLAZER V6 1/2 Ton 1994

Ratings

Rating	Score
Safety	6.7
Reliability	6.6
Performance	7.3
Design	8.2
Fun to drive	7.1
Value	7.1
Overall	7

AT/PS/AC

Model/Body/Type	BaseList	Whlse	Retail
2 Dr Utility	15938	**14900**	**17725**
4 Dr Utility	16728	**16650**	**19675**
2 Dr 4WD Utility	17239	**16600**	**19625**
4 Dr 4WD Utility	18962	**18300**	**21475**

ADD FOR 94 S10 BLAZER:
Tahoe LT Pkg +1545 *Tahoe Pkg(Std 4Dr) +775*

REFER TO 94 CHEV. TRUCK OPTIONS TABLE Pg 60

S10 PICKUPS V6 1/2 Ton 1994

AT/PS/AC

Model/Body/Type	BaseList	Whlse	Retail
Fleetside 6'	9655	**9400**	**11625**
Fleetside 7 1/3'	9955	**9500**	**11725**
Fleetside Ext Cab 6'	11790	**11000**	**13500**

ADD FOR 94 S10 PICKUP:
LS Pkg(Std S19) +635 *SS Pkg +775*

DEDUCT FOR 94 S10 PICKUP:
4 Cyl Eng -545

REFER TO 94 CHEV. TRUCK OPTIONS TABLE Pg 60

Model/Body/Type	BaseList	Whlse	Retail

SUBURBAN V8 1994

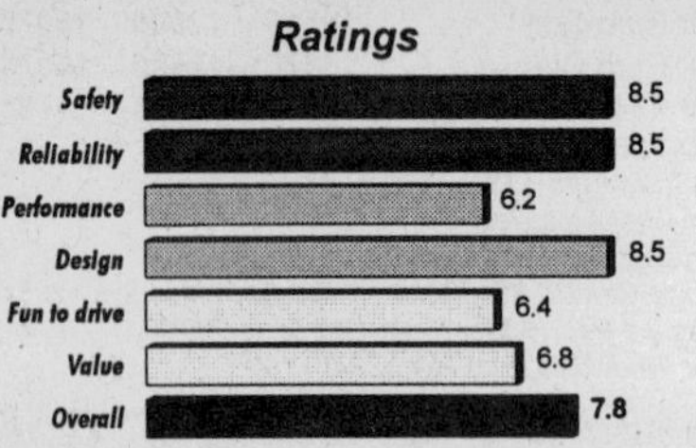

AT/PS/AC

Model/Body/Type	BaseList	Whlse	Retail
C1500 Suburbn 1/2 Ton	20166	**22100**	**25575**
C2500 Suburbn 3/4 Ton	21398	**22850**	**26375**

REFER TO 94 CHEV. TRUCK OPTIONS TABLE Pg 60

94 CHEVROLET TRUCK OPTIONS TABLE

ADD FOR ALL 94 CHEVROLET TRUCKS:

15 Pass Seating +375
4-Whl Drive(Std Blazer V8) +1265
AC-Rear +375
Bed Liner +125
Cass(Std S-10 BlazerTah/TahLT,S-10 LS,SS) +105
CD Player +205
Cruise Ctrl(Std S-10 Blazer Tahoe LT) +125
Cstm Whls(Std C1500/C2500 Sport, S-10 Blazer,Tahoe LT) +145
Dual Rear Whls +415
Fiberglass Cap +250
Leather Seats(Std S-10 Blazer Tahoe LT) +250
Luggage Rack(Std S-10 Blazer Tahoe LT) +80
Privacy Glass(Std S-10 Blazer Tahoe LT) +145
Pwr Locks(Std S-10 Blazer Tahoe LT) +105
Pwr Seats(Std S-10 Blazer Tahoe LT) +125
Pwr Wndw(Std S-10 Blazer Tahoe LT) +145
Running Boards +145
Slider Wndw +80
Sunroof-Manual +145
Tilt Whl(Std S-10 Blazer Tahoe LT) +105
Towing Pkg +185
V8 6.2L Diesel Engine +470

DEDUCT FOR ALL 94 CHEVROLET TRUCKS:

No AC -435
No AM/FM Radio -105
No Auto Trans -415
No Pwr Steering -185

1993 CHEVROLET

ASTRO VAN V6 1/2 Ton 1993

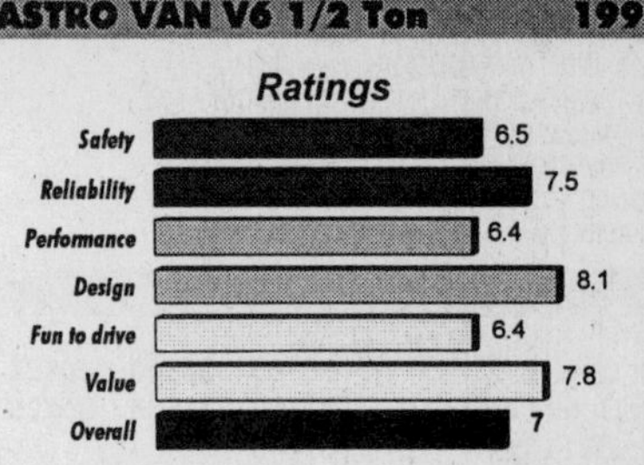

AT/PS/AC

Model/Body/Type	BaseList	Whlse	Retail
Cargo Van	14695	**10475**	**12875**
Extended Cargo Van	15365	**11500**	**14050**
CS Van	15605	**12100**	**14775**
Extended CS Van	16295	**13125**	**15825**

REFER TO 93 CHEV. TRUCK OPTIONS TABLE Pg 64

BERETTA 1993

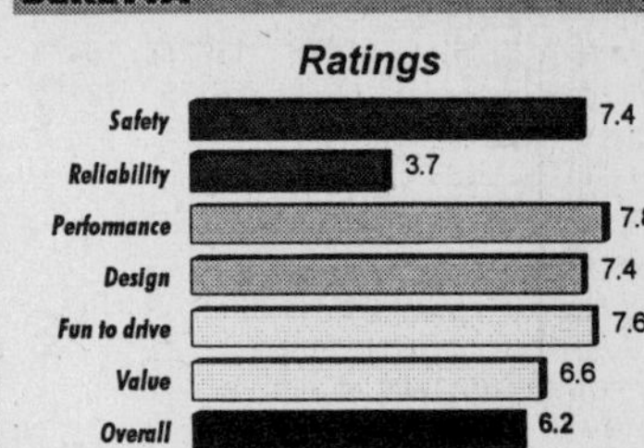

FWD/AT/PS/AC

Model/Body/Type	BaseList	Whlse	Retail
4 Cyl Models			
2 Dr Cpe	11395	**8025**	**9875**
2 Dr GT Cpe	12995	**9650**	**11600**
2 Dr GTZ Cpe	15995	**10575**	**12700**
V6 Models			
2 Dr Cpe	11995	**8525**	**10375**
2 Dr GT Cpe	13595	**10100**	**12175**
2 Dr GTZ Cpe	15845	**11425**	**13750**

ADD FOR 93 BERETTA:

Cass +75 · *CD Player +175*
Cruise Ctrl +115 · *Custom Whls/Cvrs +160*
Pwr Locks +75 · *Pwr Wndw +115*
Sunroof +200 · *Tilt Whl +75*

DEDUCT FOR 93 BERETTA:

No AC -465 · *No Auto Trans -430*

CHEVROLET

Model/Body/Type	BaseList	Whlse	Retail

BLAZER V8 1/2 Ton 1993

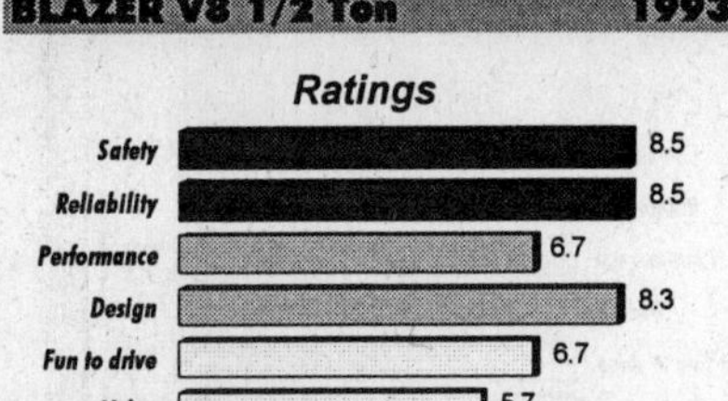

4WD/AT/PS/AC

Model/Body/Type	BaseList	Whlse	Retail
2 Dr Utility	20005	**17000**	**20050**

REFER TO 93 CHEV. TRUCK OPTIONS TABLE Pg 64

C1500/C2500/C3500 PKUP V8 1993

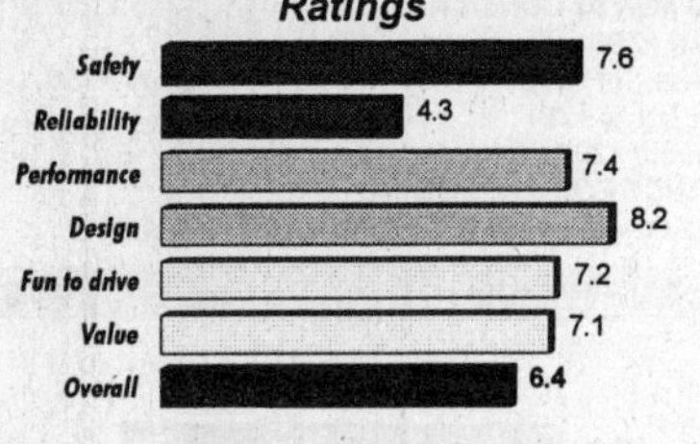

AT/PS/AC

Model/Body/Type	BaseList	Whlse	Retail
C1500 Pickup 1/2 Ton			
Fleetside WT 8' (V6)	11225	**10000**	**12325**
Sportside 6 1/2'	13985	**11775**	**14425**
Fleetside 6 1/2'	13585	**11475**	**14025**
Fleetside 8'	13885	**11575**	**14150**
Fleetside Ext Cab 6 1/2'	15130	**13100**	**15800**
Fleetside Ext Cab 8'	15390	**13200**	**15925**
Sportside Ext Cab 6 1/2'	15530	**13400**	**16125**
Fleetside 454SS	21240	**14900**	**17725**
C2500 Pickup 3/4 Ton			
Fleetside 8'	14425	**12300**	**14950**
Fleetside Ext Cab 6 1/2'	16240	**13850**	**16600**
Fleetside Ext Cab 8'	16520	**13950**	**16700**
C3500 Pickup 1 Ton			
Fleetside 8'	16164	**12850**	**16100**
Fleetside Ext Cab 8'	17824	**14400**	**17700**
Fleetside Crew Cab 8'	18144	**14550**	**17875**

ADD FOR 93 C1500/C2500/C3500 PKUP:

Silverado Pkg +545 — *Sport Pkg +585*
V8 6.5L Turbo Dsl Eng +700

DEDUCT FOR 93 C1500/C2500/C3500 PKUP:

V6 Eng -470

REFER TO 93 CHEV. TRUCK OPTIONS TABLE Pg 64

CAMARO 1993

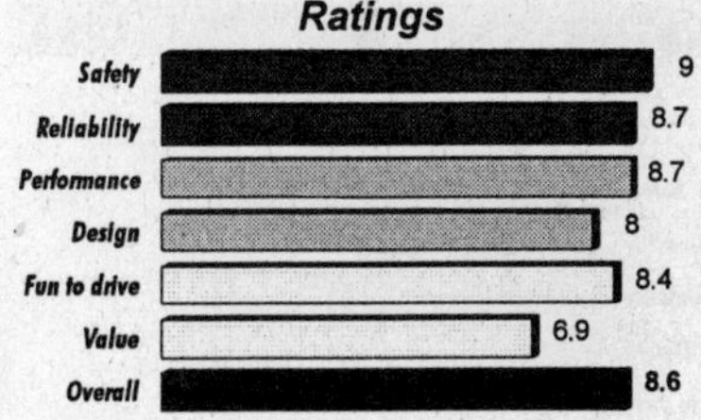

AT/PS/AC

Model/Body/Type	BaseList	Whlse	Retail
V6 Models			
2 Dr Cpe	13399	**12875**	**15375**
V8 Models			
2 Dr Z28 Cpe	16779	**16200**	**18875**

ADD FOR 93 CAMARO:

CD Player +200 — *Cruise Ctrl +130*
Custom Whls/Cvrs +175 — *Delco/Bose Mus Sys +175*
Pwr Locks +100 — *Pwr Seat +130*
Pwr Wndw +130 — *Cass(Std Z28) +100*
T-Top +625

DEDUCT FOR 93 CAMARO:

No AC -545 — *No Auto Trans(V6) -505*

CAPRICE CLASSIC V8 1993

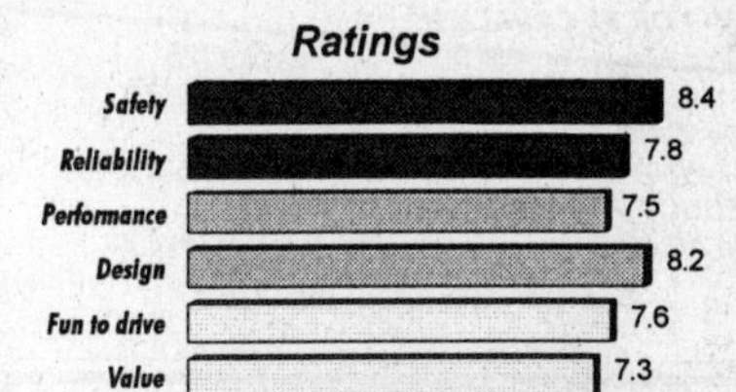

AT/PS/AC

Model/Body/Type	BaseList	Whlse	Retail
4 Dr Sdn	17995	**11000**	**13400**
4 Dr LS Sdn	19995	**12800**	**15400**
4 Dr 3 Seat Wgn	19575	**13200**	**15825**

Model/Body/Type	BaseList	Whlse	Retail

ADD FOR 93 CAPRICE CLASSIC:

Car Phone +175	*Cass +115*
CD Player +230	*Cruise Ctrl +160*
Custom Paint +100	*Custom Whls/Cvrs +200*
Delco/Bose Mus Sys +200	
Leather Seats +275	*LTZ Pkg +390*
Pwr Locks(Std LS) +115	
Pwr Seat +160	*Pwr Wndw(Std LS) +160*
Woodgrain +200	

CAVALIER 1993

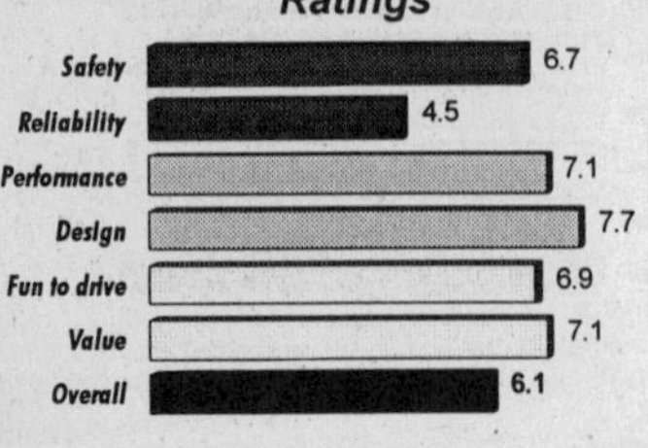

FWD/AT/PS/AC

Model/Body/Type	BaseList	Whlse	Retail
4 Cyl Models			
4 Dr VL Sdn	8620	**6925**	**8675**
2 Dr VL Cpe	8520	**6825**	**8550**
4 Dr VL Wgn	9735	**6425**	**9100**
4 Dr RS Sdn	9620	**7550**	**9375**
2 Dr RS Cpe	9520	**7450**	**9250**
2 Dr RS Conv	15395	**11100**	**13400**
4 Dr RS Wgn	10785	**7950**	**9800**
V6 Models			
2 Dr Z24 Cpe	12500	**10475**	**12600**
2 Dr Z24 Conv	18305	**14175**	**16650**

ADD FOR 93 CAVALIER:

Cass +75	*CD Player +175*
Cruise Ctrl +115	*Luggage Rack +75*
Pwr Wndw(Std Cnv) +115	*Sunroof +200*
Tilt Whl +75	*V6 Eng(Std Z24) +345*

DEDUCT FOR 93 CAVALIER:

No AC -465	*No Auto Trans -430*

CORSICA 1993

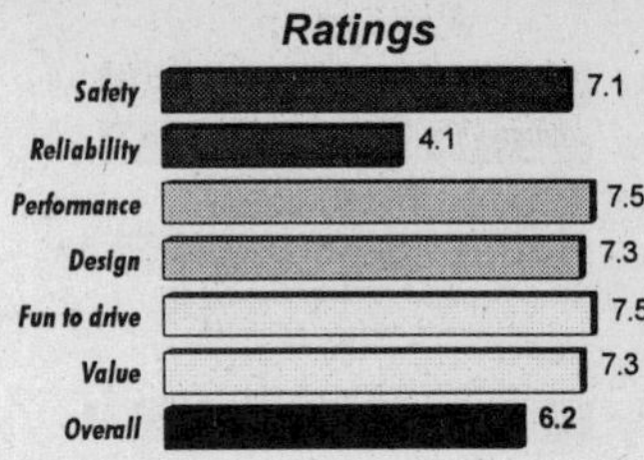

FWD/AT/PS/AC

Model/Body/Type	BaseList	Whlse	Retail
4 Cyl Models			
4 Dr LT Sdn	11395	**7525**	**9325**
V6 Models			
4 Dr LT Sdn	11995	**8025**	**9875**

ADD FOR 93 CORSICA:

Cass +75	*CD Player +175*
Cruise Ctrl +115	*Custom Whls/Cvrs +160*
Pwr Locks +75	*Pwr Wndw +115*
Sunroof +200	*Tilt Whl +75*

DEDUCT FOR 93 CORSICA:

No AC -465	*No Auto Trans -430*

CORVETTE V8 1993

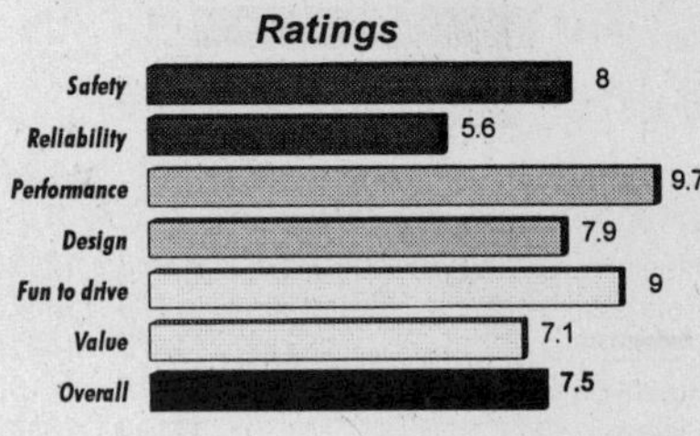

AT-6SP

Model/Body/Type	BaseList	Whlse	Retail
2 Dr Cpe	34595	**23950**	**27700**
2 Dr Conv	41195	**28375**	**32425**
2 Dr ZR1 Cpe	66278	**36275**	**40200**

ADD FOR 93 CORVETTE:

Car Phone +175	*CD Player(Std ZR1) +290*
Delco/Bose Music Sys(Std ZR1) +250	
Lthr Seats(Std ZR1) +320	*Removable Glass Rf +545*
Removable Hardtop +820	

G10/G20/G30 VANS V8 — 1993

Ratings

Safety 6.7
Reliability 5.9
Performance 5.7
Design 7.2
Fun to drive 5.3
Value 7.4
Overall 6.2

AT/PS/AC

Model/Body/Type	BaseList	Whlse	Retail
G10 Van 1/2 Ton			
Chevy Van	14600	**11750**	**14400**
Sportvan	16360	**13075**	**15775**
G20 Van 3/4 Ton			
Chevy Van	14720	**12000**	**14625**
Sportvan	17250	**13500**	**16225**
G30 Van 1 Ton			
Chevy Van	15040	**12500**	**15725**
Sportvan	19000	**13850**	**17150**
Ext Chevy Van	17530	**13150**	**16425**
Ext Sportvan	20485	**14500**	**17825**

DEDUCT FOR 93 G10/G20/G30 VAN:
V6 Eng -470
REFER TO 93 CHEV. TRUCK OPTIONS TABLE Pg 64

LUMINA — 1993

Ratings

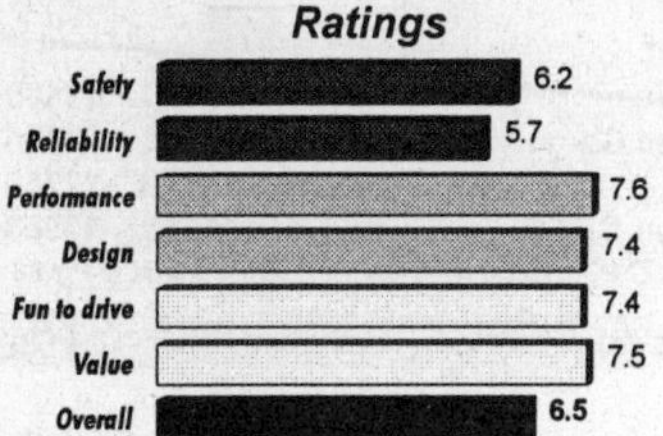

FWD/AT/PS/AC

Model/Body/Type	BaseList	Whlse	Retail
4 Cyl Models			
4 Dr Sdn	13400	**8600**	**10525**
V6 Models			
4 Dr Sdn	14010	**9150**	**11175**
2 Dr Cpe	14690	**9150**	**11175**
4 Dr Euro Sdn	15800	**10575**	**12775**
2 Dr Euro Cpe	15600	**10575**	**12775**
2 Dr Z34 Cpe	18400	**13025**	**15525**

ADD FOR 93 LUMINA:
ABS(Std Euro,Z34) +390
CruiseCtrl(Std Z34) +130
Euro 3.4 Pkg +465
Pwr Wndw +130
Tilt Whl(Std Z34) +100
CD Player +200
Delco/Bose Mus Sys +175
Pwr Seat +130
Cass(Std Z34) +100
DEDUCT FOR 93 LUMINA:
No AC -545

LUMINA APV V6 — 1993

Ratings

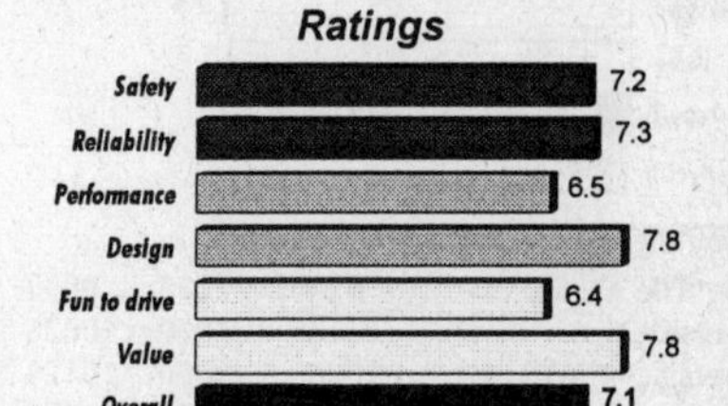

FWD/AT/PS/AC

Model/Body/Type	BaseList	Whlse	Retail
Cargo Van	14695	**9875**	**12175**
Wagon	15895	**12025**	**14650**
LS Wagon	17995	**12800**	**15475**

REFER TO 93 CHEV. TRUCK OPTIONS TABLE Pg 64

S10 BLAZER V6 1/2 Ton — 1993

Ratings

Safety 6.7
Reliability 6.6
Performance 7.3
Design 8.2
Fun to drive 7.1
Value 7.1
Overall 7

AT/PS/AC

Model/Body/Type	BaseList	Whlse	Retail
2 Dr Utility	14823	**12350**	**15000**
4 Dr Utility	15783	**13900**	**16650**
2 Dr 4WD Utility	16583	**14000**	**16775**
4 Dr 4WD Utility	17953	**15500**	**18375**

ADD FOR 93 S10 BLAZER:
Tahoe LT Pkg +1175
Tahoe Pkg +545
REFER TO 93 CHEV. TRUCK OPTIONS TABLE Pg 64

CHEVROLET 93-92

Model/Body/Type	BaseList	Whlse	Retail

S10 PICKUPS V6 1/2 Ton 1993

Ratings

Rating	Score
Safety	6.6
Reliability	5.2
Performance	7.6
Design	8.2
Fun to drive	7.4
Value	7.3
Overall	6.5

AT/PS/AC

Model/Body/Type	BaseList	Whlse	Retail
Fleetside EL 6'	8745	**7725**	**9800**
Fleetside 6'	10130	**7950**	**10025**
Fleetside 7 1/3'	10430	**8050**	**10125**
Fleetside Ext Cab 6'	11630	**9350**	**11575**

ADD FOR 93 S10 PICKUP:
Tahoe Pkg +545
DEDUCT FOR 93 S10 PICKUP:
4 Cyl Eng -430
REFER TO 93 CHEV. TRUCK OPTIONS TABLE Pg 64

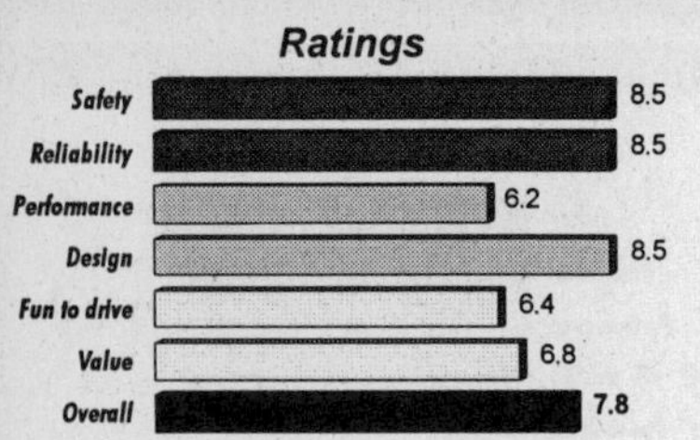

AT/PS/AC

Model/Body/Type	BaseList	Whlse	Retail
C1500 Suburbn 1/2 Ton	19080	**18525**	**21725**
C2500 Suburbn 3/4 Ton	20285	**19175**	**22400**

REFER TO 93 CHEV. TRUCK OPTIONS TABLE Pg 64

93 CHEVROLET TRUCK OPTIONS TABLE

ADD FOR ALL 93 CHEVROLET TRUCKS:
15 Pass Seating +375
4-Whl Drive(Std Blazer V8) +1265
AC-Rear +375
Bed Liner +125
Cass(Std S-10 BlazerTah/TahLT,S-10 Tah) +105
CD Player +205
Cruise Ctrl(Std S-10 Blazer Tahoe LT) +125
Cstm Whls(Std C1500/C2500 Sport, S-10 Blazer Tahoe LT,S-10 4x4 Tahoe) +145
Dual Rear Whls +415
Fiberglass Cap +250
Leather Seats(Std S-10 Blazer Tahoe LT) +250
Luggage Rack(Std S-10 Blazer Tahoe LT) +80
Privacy Glass(Std S-10 Blazer Tahoe LT) +145
Pwr Locks(Std S-10 Blazer Tahoe LT) +105
Pwr Seats(Std S-10 Blazer Tahoe LT) +125
Pwr Wndw(Std S-10 Blazer Tahoe LT) +145
Running Boards +145
Slider Wndw(Std S-10 Reg Cab Tahoe) +80
Sunroof-Manual +145
Tilt Whl(Std S-10 Blazer Tahoe LT) +105
Towing Pkg +185
V8 6.2L Diesel Engine +470
DEDUCT FOR ALL 93 CHEVROLET TRUCKS:
No AC -435
No AM/FM Radio -105
No Auto Trans -415
No Pwr Steering -185

1992 CHEVROLET

ASTRO VAN V6 1/2 Ton 1992

AT/PS/AC

Model/Body/Type	BaseList	Whlse	Retail
Cargo Van	13995	**8900**	**11100**
Extended Cargo Van	14665	**9850**	**12150**
CS Van	15185	**10375**	**12750**
Extended CS Van	15875	**11350**	**13900**

REFER TO 92 CHEV. TRUCK OPTIONS TABLE Pg 68

BERETTA 1992

Model/Body/Type	BaseList	Whlse	Retail
FWD/AT/PS/AC			
4 Cyl Models			
2 Dr Cpe	10999	**6350**	**7950**
2 Dr GT Cpe	12575	**7750**	**9600**
2 Dr GTZ Cpe	15590	**8650**	**10500**
V6 Models			
2 Dr Cpe	11609	**6775**	**8525**
2 Dr GT Cpe	13185	**8200**	**10050**
2 Dr GTZ Cpe	15440	**9400**	**11325**

ADD FOR 92 BERETTA:

Cass +60 *CD Player +160*
Cruise Ctrl +100 *Custom Whls/Cvrs +130*
Pwr Locks +60 *Pwr Wndw +100*
Sunroof +160 *Tilt Whl +60*

DEDUCT FOR 92 BERETTA:

No AC -430 *No Auto Trans -390*

BLAZER V8 1/2 Ton 1992

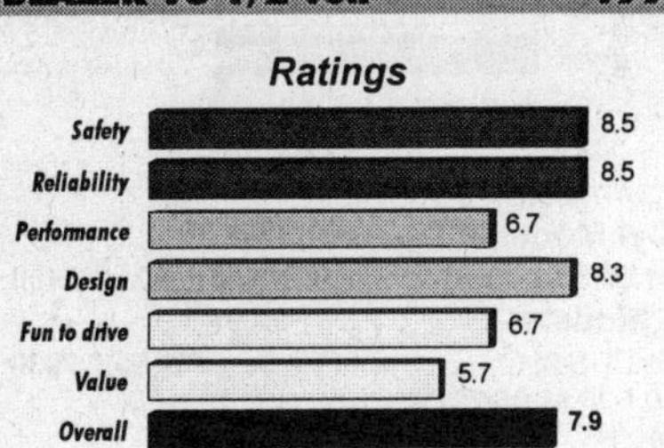

Model/Body/Type	BaseList	Whlse	Retail
4WD/AT/PS/AC			
2 Dr Utility	19280	**14500**	**17250**

REFER TO 92 CHEV. TRUCK OPTIONS TABLE Pg 68

C1500/C2500/C3500 PKUP V8 1992

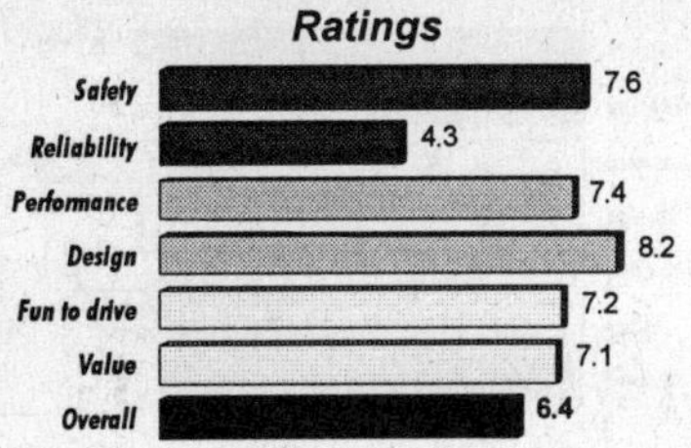

Model/Body/Type	BaseList	Whlse	Retail
AT/PS/AC			
C1500 Pickup 1/2 Ton			
Fleetside WT 8' (V6)	10600	**9200**	**11425**
Sportside 6 1/2'	13495	**10775**	**13275**
Fleetside 6 1/2'	13095	**10525**	**12925**
Fleetside 8'	13395	**10625**	**13125**
Fleetside Ext Cab 6 1/2'	14045	**11975**	**14600**
Fleetside Ext Cab 8'	14335	**12050**	**14725**
Sportside Ext Cab 6 1/2'	14445	**12200**	**14850**
Fleetside 454SS	20585	**13600**	**16350**
C2500 Pickup 3/4 Ton			
Fleetside 8'	14035	**11225**	**13775**
Fleetside Ext Cab 6 1/2'	15155	**12550**	**15225**
Fleetside Ext Cab 8'	15435	**12650**	**15325**
C3500 Pickup 1 Ton			
Fleetside 8'	15588	**11800**	**14975**
Fleetside Ext Cab 8'	16658	**13150**	**16425**
Fleetside Crew Cab 8'	17407	**13350**	**16625**

ADD FOR 92 C1500/C2500/C3500 PKUP:

Scottsdale Pkg +315 *Silverado Pkg +505*
Sport Pkg +545

DEDUCT FOR 92 C1500/C2500/C3500 PKUP:

V6 Eng -430

REFER TO 92 CHEV. TRUCK OPTIONS TABLE Pg 68

CAMARO 1992

Ratings

Rating	Score
Safety	7.1
Reliability	4.5
Performance	8
Design	6.6
Fun to drive	7.9
Value	6.8
Overall	6.4

Model/Body/Type	BaseList	Whlse	Retail
AT/PS/AC			
V6 Models			
2 Dr RS Cpe	12075	**9225**	**11250**
2 Dr RS Conv	18055	**13425**	**15950**
V8 Models			
2 Dr RS Cpe	12444	**9725**	**11850**
2 Dr RS Conv	18424	**13925**	**16475**
2 Dr Z28 Cpe	16055	**12500**	**14975**
2 Dr Z28 Conv	21500	**16750**	**19525**

ADD FOR 92 CAMARO:

5.7L V8 Eng +605 *Cass +75*
CD Player +175 *Cruise Ctrl +115*
Delco/Bose Mus Sys +160 *Leather Seats +200*
Pwr Locks +75 *Pwr Seat +115*
Pwr Wndw +115 *T-Top +565*

DEDUCT FOR 92 CAMARO:

No AC -505 *No Auto Trans -465*

CHEVROLET

CHEVROLET 92

CAPRICE V8 — 1992

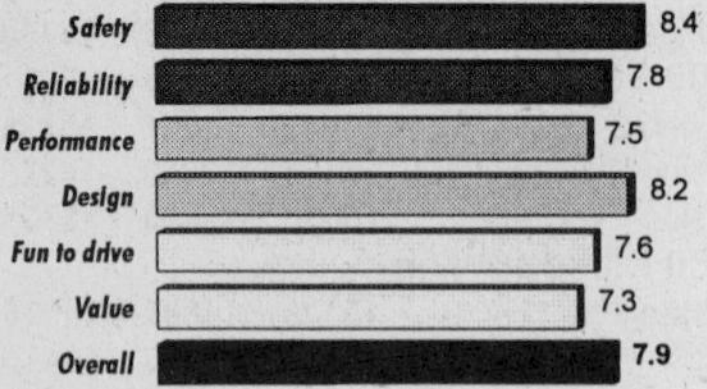

AT/PS/AC

Model/Body/Type	BaseList	Whlse	Retail
4 Dr Sdn	17300	**8125**	**10150**
4 Dr 3 Seat Wgn	18700	**10650**	**13050**
4 Dr Classic Sdn	19300	**9850**	**12075**

ADD FOR 92 CAPRICE:

Car Phone +160 — *Cass +100*
CD Player +200 — *Cruise Ctrl +130*
Custom Paint +75 — *Custom Whls/Cvrs +175*
Delco/Bose MusSys +175 — *Leather Seats +230*
LTZ Pkg +320 — *Pwr Locks(Std Class) +100*
Pwr Seat +130 — *Pwr Wndw(Std Class) +130*

CAVALIER — 1992

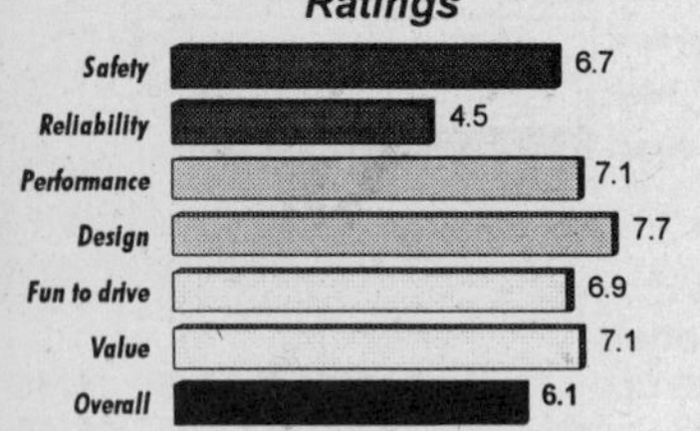

FWD/AT/PS/AC

Model/Body/Type	BaseList	Whlse	Retail
4 Cyl Models			
4 Dr VL Sdn	8999	**5425**	**7000**
2 Dr VL Cpe	8899	**5325**	**6875**
4 Dr VL Wgn	10099	**5800**	**7350**
4 Dr RS Sdn	10199	**6050**	**7625**
2 Dr RS Cpe	9999	**5950**	**7525**
2 Dr RS Conv	15395	**9475**	**11425**
4 Dr RS Wgn	11199	**6400**	**8000**
V6 Models			
2 Dr Z24 Cpe	12995	**8900**	**10800**
2 Dr Z24 Conv	18305	**12350**	**14750**

ADD FOR 92 CAVALIER:

Cass +60 — *CD Player +160*
Cruise Ctrl +100 — *Luggage Rack +60*
Pwr Wndw(Std Conv) +100 — *Sunroof +160*
Tilt Whl +60 — *V6 Eng(Std Z24) +320*

DEDUCT FOR 92 CAVALIER:

No AC -430 — *No Auto Trans -390*

CORSICA — 1992

Ratings

Rating	Score
Safety	7.1
Reliability	4.1
Performance	7.5
Design	7.3
Fun to drive	7.5
Value	7.3
Overall	6.2

FWD/AT/PS/AC

Model/Body/Type	BaseList	Whlse	Retail
4 Cyl Models			
4 Dr LT Sdn	10999	**5850**	**7400**
V6 Models			
4 Dr LT Sdn	11609	**6275**	**7900**

ADD FOR 92 CORSICA:

Cass +60 — *CD Player +160*
Cruise Ctrl +100 — *Custom Whls/Cvrs +130*
Pwr Locks +60 — *Pwr Wndw +100*
Sunroof +160 — *Tilt Whl +60*

DEDUCT FOR 92 CORSICA:

No AC -430 — *No Auto Trans -390*

CORVETTE V8 — 1992

AT-6SP

Model/Body/Type	BaseList	Whlse	Retail
2 Dr Cpe	33635	**21325**	**24825**
2 Dr Conv	40145	**25550**	**29425**
2 Dr ZR1 Cpe	65318	**29025**	**33100**

Model/Body/Type	BaseList	Whlse	Retail

ADD FOR 92 CORVETTE:
Car Phone +160 *CD Player(Std ZR1) +250*
Delco/Bose Music Sys(Std ZR1) +230
Lthr Seats(Std ZR1) +275 *Removable Glass Rf +485*
Removable Hardtop +740

G10/G20/G30 VANS V8 — 1992

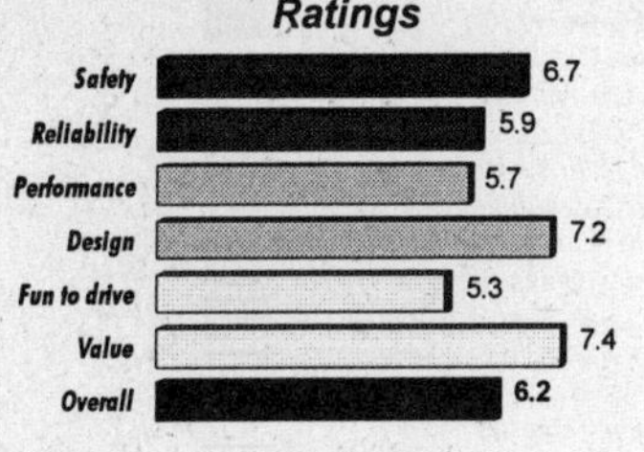

AT/PS/AC

Model/Body/Type	BaseList	Whlse	Retail
G10 Van 1/2 Ton			
Chevy Van	14315	**10150**	**12525**
Sportvan	16045	**11475**	**14025**
G20 Van 3/4 Ton			
Chevy Van	14535	**10350**	**12725**
Sportvan	17185	**11800**	**14475**
G30 Van 1 Ton			
Chevy Van	14555	**10800**	**13850**
Sportvan	18935	**12100**	**15275**
Ext Chevy Van	17345	**11375**	**14475**
Ext Sportvan	20465	**12675**	**15900**

DEDUCT FOR 92 G10/G20/G30 VAN:
V6 Eng -430
REFER TO 92 CHEV. TRUCK OPTIONS TABLE Pg 68

LUMINA — 1992

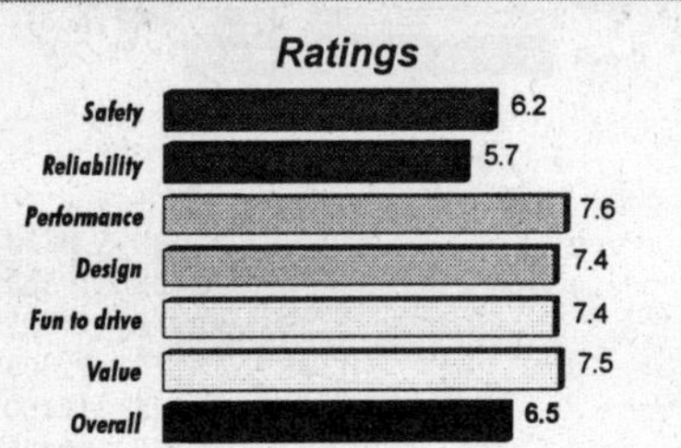

FWD/AT/PS/AC

Model/Body/Type	BaseList	Whlse	Retail
4 Cyl Models			
4 Dr Sdn	13400	**6250**	**8000**
2 Dr Cpe	13200	**6250**	**8000**
V6 Models			
4 Dr Sdn	14060	**6725**	**8550**
2 Dr Cpe	13860	**6725**	**8550**
4 Dr Euro Sdn	15800	**8150**	**10050**
2 Dr Euro Cpe	15600	**8150**	**10050**
2 Dr Z34 Cpe	18400	**10525**	**12750**

ADD FOR 92 LUMINA:
ABS(Std Euro,Z34) +345 *CD Player +175*
CruiseCtrl(Std Z34) +115 *Delco/Bose Mus Sys +160*
Euro 3.4 Pkg +405 *Pwr Locks +75*
Pwr Seat +115 *Pwr Wndw +115*
Cass(Std Z34) +75 *Tilt Whl(Std Z34) +75*

DEDUCT FOR 92 LUMINA:
No AC -505

LUMINA APV V6 — 1992

Ratings

Rating	Score
Safety	7.2
Reliability	7.3
Performance	6.5
Design	7.8
Fun to drive	6.4
Value	7.8
Overall	7.1

FWD/AT/PS/AC

Model/Body/Type	BaseList	Whlse	Retail
Cargo Van	14375	**7650**	**9750**
Wagon	15570	**9700**	**11975**
CL Wagon	17355	**10325**	**12700**

REFER TO 92 CHEV. TRUCK OPTIONS TABLE Pg 68

S10 BLAZER V6 1/2 Ton — 1992

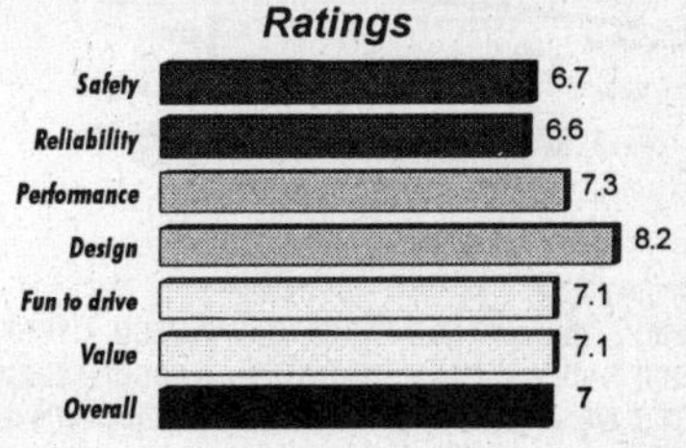

AT/PS/AC

Model/Body/Type	BaseList	Whlse	Retail
2 Dr Utility	14823	**11100**	**13625**
4 Dr Utility	15783	**12450**	**15125**
2 Dr 4WD Utility	16583	**12675**	**15350**
4 Dr 4WD Utility	17953	**14050**	**16825**

Model/Body/Type	BaseList	Whlse	Retail

ADD FOR 92 S10 BLAZER:
Sport Pkg +545 *Tahoe LT Pkg +935*
REFER TO 92 CHEV. TRUCK OPTIONS TABLE Pg 68

S10 PICKUPS V6 1/2 Ton 1992

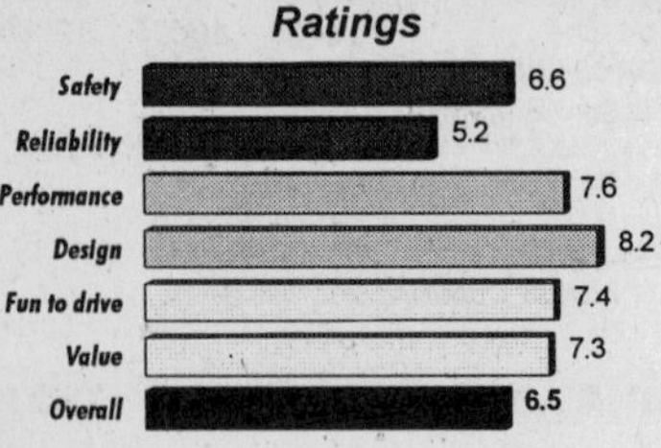

AT/PS/AC			
Fleetside EL 6'	8722	**6650**	**8650**
Fleetside 6'	9858	**6875**	**8875**
Fleetside 7 1/3'	10158	**7000**	**8975**
Fleetside Maxi-Cab 6'	11358	**8100**	**10175**

ADD FOR 92 S10 PICKUP:
Tahoe Pkg +470
DEDUCT FOR 92 S10 PICKUP:
4 Cyl Eng -430
REFER TO 92 CHEV. TRUCK OPTIONS TABLE Pg 68

SUBURBAN V8 1992

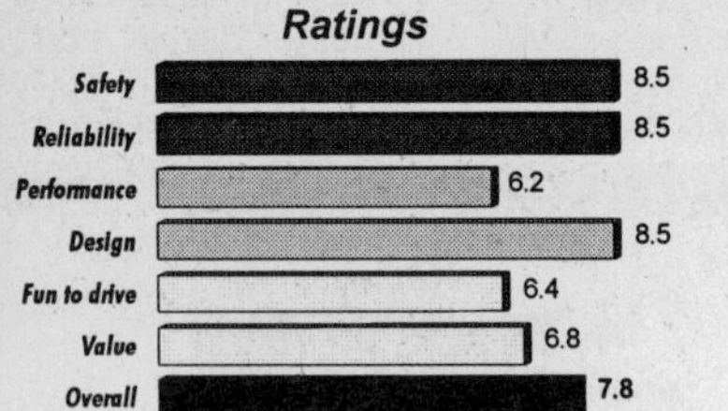

AT/PS/AC			
C1500 Suburbn 1/2 Ton	18155	**15700**	**18575**
C2500 Suburbn 3/4 Ton	19359	**16300**	**19225**

REFER TO 92 CHEV. TRUCK OPTIONS TABLE Pg 68

92 CHEVROLET TRUCK OPTIONS TABLE

ADD FOR ALL 92 CHEVROLET TRUCKS:
15 Pass Seating +330
4-Whl Drive(Std Blazer V8) +1200
AC-Rear +315
Bed Liner +105
Cass(Std C1500/C2500Silverado, S-10 BlazerTahoe LT,S-10 Tahoe) +80
CD Player +170
Cruise Ctrl(Std S-10 Blazer Tahoe LT) +80
Custom Whls(Std C1500/2500 Sport, S-10 Blazer Tahoe LT) +125
Dual Rear Whls +375
Fiberglass Cap +205
Leather Seats(Std S-10 Blazer Tahoe LT) +205
Privacy Glass(Std S-10 Blazer Tahoe LT) +125
Pwr Locks(Std S-10 Blazer Tahoe LT) +80
Pwr Seats(Std S-10 Blazer Tahoe LT) +105
Pwr Wndw(Std S-10 Blazer Tahoe LT) +105
Running Boards +125
Sunroof-Manual +105
Towing Pkg +145
V8 6.2L Diesel Engine +430
DEDUCT FOR ALL 92 CHEVROLET TRUCKS:
No AC -375
No Auto Trans -330
No Pwr Steering -145

1991 CHEVROLET

ASTRO VAN V6 1/2 Ton 1991

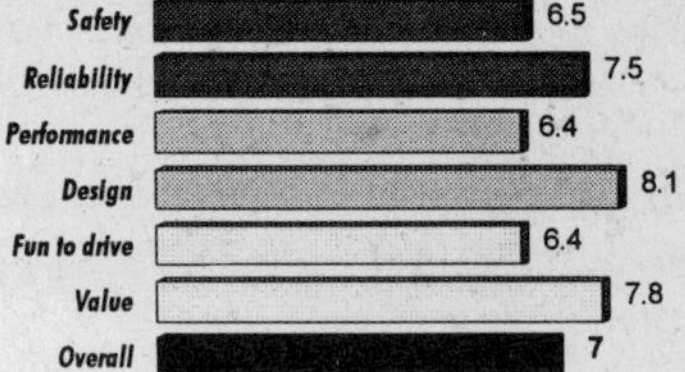

AT/PS/AC			
Cargo Van	13460	**7525**	**9600**
Extended Cargo Van	14130	**8425**	**10525**
CS Van	14580	**8975**	**11175**
CL Van	15660	**9575**	**11800**
LT Van	17210	**10125**	**12450**
Extended CS Van	15270	**9850**	**12150**
Extended CL Van	16350	**10400**	**12775**
Extended LT Van	17900	**11000**	**13525**

REFER TO 91 CHEV. TRUCK OPTIONS TABLE Pg 73

Model/Body/Type	BaseList	Whlse	Retail

BERETTA 1991

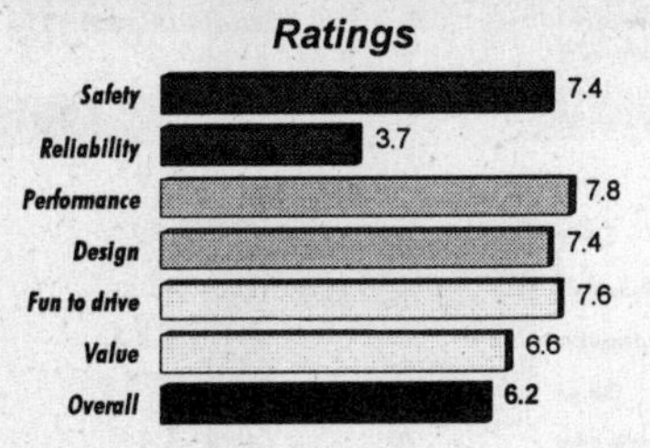

FWD/AT/PS/AC

Model/Body/Type	BaseList	Whlse	Retail
4 Cyl Models			
2 Dr Cpe	10365	**5200**	**6725**
2 Dr GTZ Cpe	14550	**7125**	**8875**
V6 Models			
2 Dr Cpe	11050	**5650**	**7150**
2 Dr GT Cpe	13150	**6875**	**8600**

ADD FOR 91 BERETTA:

Cass +35 *CD Player +115*
Cruise Ctrl +75 *Custom Whls/Cvrs +115*
Pwr Locks +35 *Pwr Wndw +75*
Sunroof +115 *Tilt Whl +35*

DEDUCT FOR 91 BERETTA:

No AC -390 *No Auto Trans -345*

BLAZER V8 1/2 Ton 1991

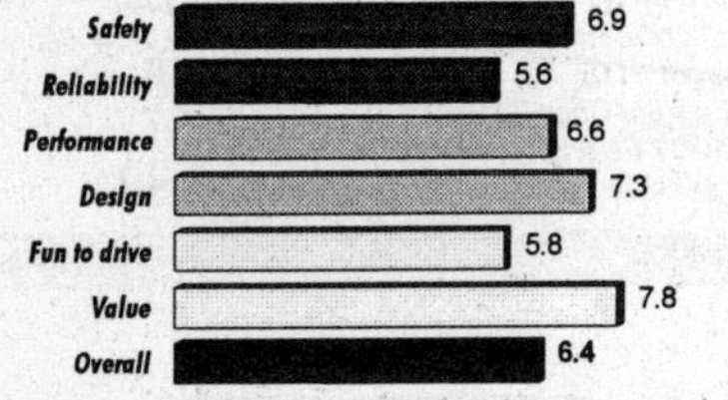

4WD/AT/PS/AC

Model/Body/Type	BaseList	Whlse	Retail
2 Dr Utility	17590	**11050**	**13575**

REFER TO 91 CHEV. TRUCK OPTIONS TABLE Pg 73

C1500/C2500/C3500 PKUP V8 1991

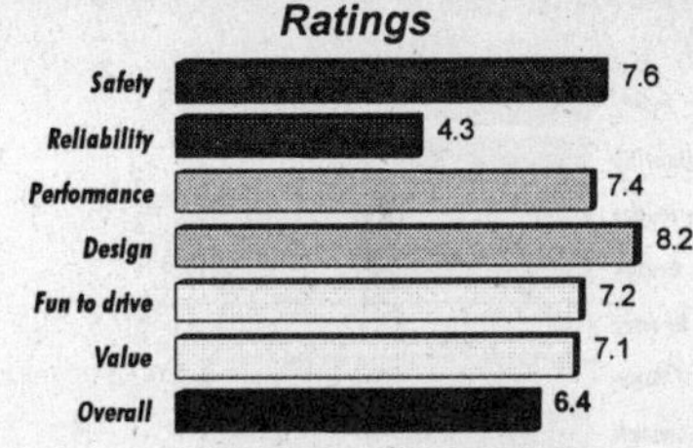

AT/PS/AC

Model/Body/Type	BaseList	Whlse	Retail
C1500 Pickup 1/2 Ton			
Fleetside WT 8' (V6)	10625	**7900**	**9975**
Sportside 6 1/2'	12455	**9400**	**11625**
Fleetside 6 1/2'	12115	**9200**	**11425**
Fleetside 8'	12415	**9300**	**11525**
Fleetside Ext Cab 6 1/2'	13065	**10275**	**12650**
Fleetside Ext Cab 8'	13365	**10375**	**12750**
Fleetside 454SS	19610	**11925**	**14550**
C2500 Pickup 3/4 Ton			
Fleetside 8'	13055	**9825**	**12100**
Fleetside Ext Cab 6 1/2'	14175	**10825**	**13350**
Fleetside Ext Cab 8'	14455	**10925**	**13450**
C3500 Pickup 1 Ton			
Fleetside 8'	15785	**10325**	**13275**
Fleetside Ext Cab 8'	16855	**11475**	**14550**
Fleetside Bonus Cab 8'	16258	**11525**	**14600**
Fleetside Crew Cab 8'	16798	**11725**	**14850**

ADD FOR 91 C1500/C2500/C3500 PKUP:

Scottsdale Pkg +275 *Z71 Pkg +115*

DEDUCT FOR 91 C1500/C2500/C3500 PKUP:

V6 Eng -390

REFER TO 91 CHEV. TRUCK OPTIONS TABLE Pg 73

Model/Body/Type	BaseList	Whlse	Retail

CAMARO 1991

Ratings

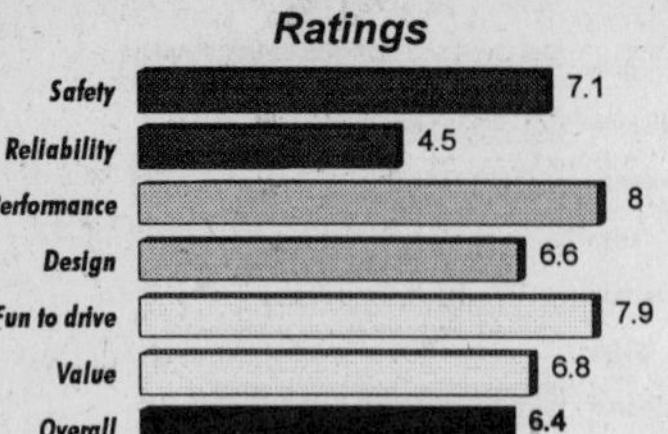

AT/PS/AC

Model/Body/Type	BaseList	Whlse	Retail
V6 Models			
2 Dr RS Cpe	12180	**6950**	**8775**
2 Dr RS Conv	17960	**10950**	**13300**
V8 Models			
2 Dr RS Cpe	12530	**7375**	**9250**
2 Dr RS Conv	18310	**11425**	**13775**
2 Dr Z28 Cpe	15445	**9925**	**12075**
2 Dr Z28 Conv	20815	**13950**	**16500**

ADD FOR 91 CAMARO:
5.7L V8 Eng +545 *Cass +60*
CD Player +160 *Cruise Ctrl +100*
Leather Seats +160 *Pwr Locks +60*
Pwr Seat +100 *Pwr Wndw +100*
T-Top +525

DEDUCT FOR 91 CAMARO:
No AC -465 *No Auto Trans -430*

CAPRICE V8 1991

Ratings

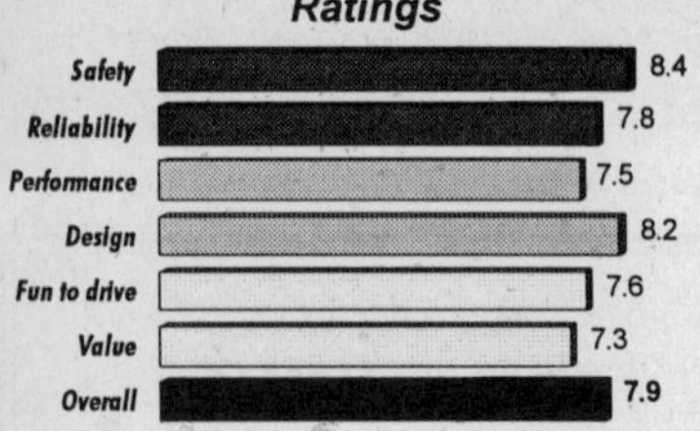

AT/PS/AC

Model/Body/Type	BaseList	Whlse	Retail
4 Dr Sdn	16515	**6500**	**8400**
4 Dr 3 Seat Wgn	17875	**8925**	**11000**
4 Dr Classic Sdn	18470	**8025**	**10050**

ADD FOR 91 CAPRICE:
Car Phone +130 *Cass +75*
CD Player +160 *Cruise Ctrl +115*
Custom Paint +60 *Custom Whls/Cvrs +160*
Delco/Bose Mus Sys +130 *Leather Seats +200*
LTZ Pkg +275 *Pwr Locks(Std Class) +75*
Pwr Seat +115 *Pwr Wndw(Std Class) +115*
Tilt Whl +75

CAVALIER 1991

Ratings

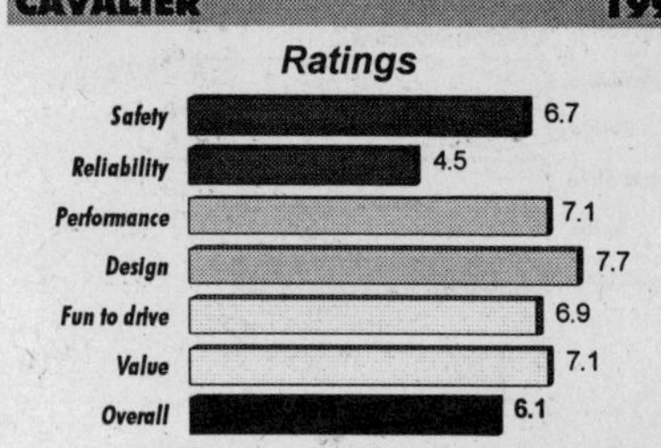

FWD/AT/PS/AC

Model/Body/Type	BaseList	Whlse	Retail
4 Cyl Models			
4 Dr VL Sdn	8270	**4175**	**5575**
2 Dr VL Cpe	7995	**4075**	**5475**
4 Dr VL Wgn	9225	**4475**	**5875**
4 Dr RS Sdn	9265	**4700**	**6175**
2 Dr RS Cpe	9065	**4625**	**6100**
4 Dr RS Wgn	10270	**4975**	**6500**
V6 Models			
2 Dr RS Conv	15214	**7875**	**9750**
2 Dr Z24 Cpe	12050	**7275**	**9075**

ADD FOR 91 CAVALIER:
Cass +35 *CD Player +115*
Cruise Ctrl +75 *Luggage Rack +35*
Pwr Locks(Std Conv) +35 *Pwr Wndw(Std Conv) +75*
Sunroof +115 *Tilt Whl +35*
V6Eng(Std Conv,Z24) +250

DEDUCT FOR 91 CAVALIER:
No AC -390 *No Auto Trans -345*

CORSICA 1991

Ratings

Model/Body/Type	BaseList	Whlse	Retail
FWD/AT/PS/AC			
4 Cyl Models			
4 Dr LT Nbk	10070	**4725**	**6200**
4 Dr LT Hbk	10745	**4900**	**6425**
V6 Models			
4 Dr LT Nbk	10755	**5100**	**6625**
4 Dr LT Hbk	11430	**5300**	**6850**

ADD FOR 91 CORSICA:

Cass +35 | *CD Player +115*
Cruise Ctrl +75 | *Custom Whls/Cvrs +115*
Pwr Locks +35 | *Pwr Wndw +75*
Sunroof +115 | *Tilt Whl +35*

DEDUCT FOR 91 CORSICA:

No AC -390 | *No Auto Trans -345*

CORVETTE V8 1991

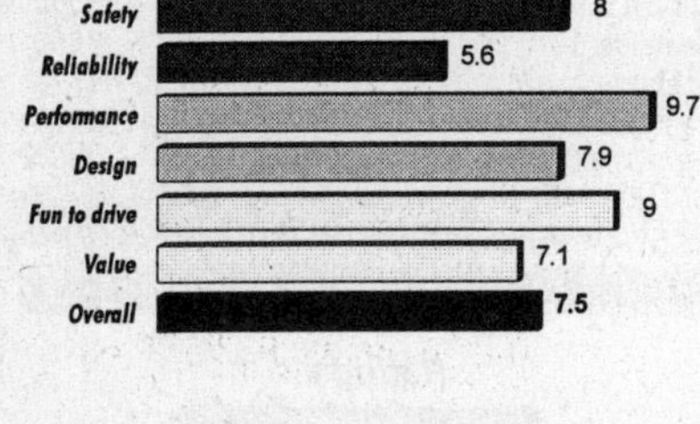

Model/Body/Type	BaseList	Whlse	Retail
AT-6SP			
2 Dr Hbk Cpe	32455	**18550**	**21900**
2 Dr Conv	38770	**22650**	**26325**
2 Dr ZR1 Cpe	64138	**28325**	**32375**

ADD FOR 91 CORVETTE:

Car Phone +130 | *CD Player(Std ZR1) +200*
Delco/Bose Music Sys(Std ZR1) +200
Lthr Seats(Std ZR1) +215 | *Removable Glass Rf +450*
Removable Hardtop +680

G10/G20/G30 VANS V8 1991

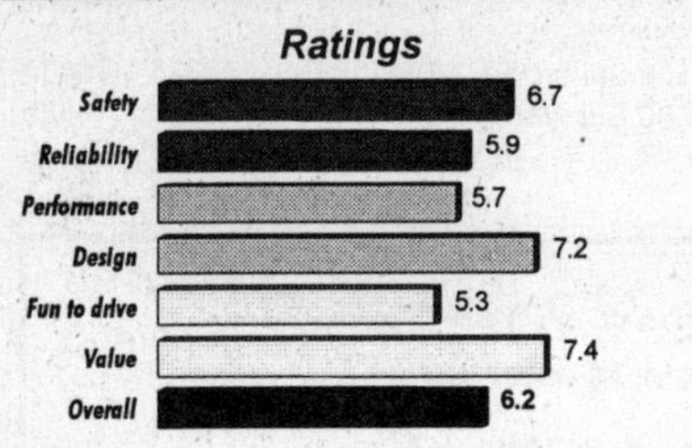

Model/Body/Type	BaseList	Whlse	Retail
AT/PS/AC			
G10 Van 1/2 Ton			
Chevy Van	13610	**7900**	**9975**
Sportvan	15340	**9200**	**11425**
Beauville	17180	**10250**	**12625**
G20 Van 3/4 Ton			
Chevy Van	13790	**8050**	**10125**
Sportvan	16440	**9475**	**11700**
Beauville	17320	**10400**	**12775**
G30 Van 1 Ton			
Chevy Van	13850	**8475**	**11075**
Sportvan	18230	**9775**	**12600**
Beauville	19110	**10700**	**13725**
Ext Chevy Van	16640	**9000**	**11750**
Ext Sportvan	19760	**10225**	**13175**
Ext Beauville	20570	**11225**	**14300**

DEDUCT FOR 91 G10/G20/G30 VAN:

V6 Eng -390

REFER TO 91 CHEV. TRUCK OPTIONS TABLE Pg 73

LUMINA 1991

Ratings

Safety 6.2
Reliability 5.7
Performance 7.6
Design 7.4
Fun to drive 7.4
Value 7.5
Overall 6.5

Model/Body/Type	BaseList	Whlse	Retail
FWD/AT/PS/AC			
4 Cyl Models			
4 Dr Sdn	12870	**4800**	**6450**
2 Dr Cpe	12670	**4800**	**6450**
V6 Models			
4 Dr Sdn	13530	**5225**	**6925**
2 Dr Cpe	13330	**5225**	**6925**
4 Dr Euro Sdn	14995	**6575**	**8350**
2 Dr Euro Cpe	14795	**6575**	**8350**
2 Dr Z34 Cpe	17275	**8925**	**10925**

ADD FOR 91 LUMINA:

Cass(Std Z34) +60 | *CruiseCtrl(Std Z34) +100*
Delco/Bose Mus Sys +130 | *Pwr Locks +60*
Pwr Seat +100 | *Pwr Wndw +100*
Tilt Whl(Std Z34) +60

DEDUCT FOR 91 LUMINA:

No AC -465

CHEVROLET 91

LUMINA APV V6 — 1991

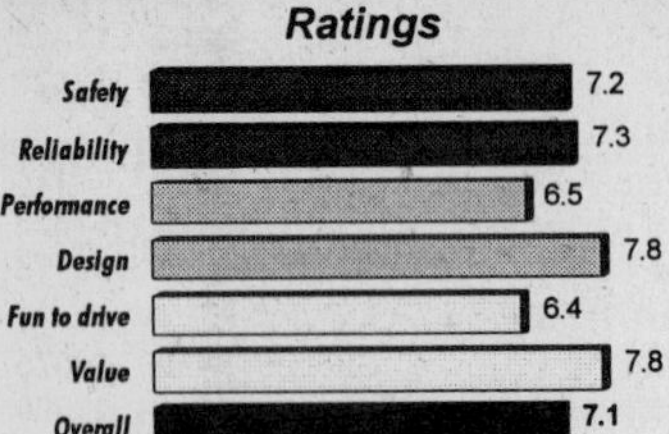

Model/Body/Type	BaseList	Whlse	Retail
FWD/AT/PS/AC			
Cargo Van	13592	**6125**	**8050**
Wagon	14730	**8000**	**10075**
CL Wagon	16450	**8600**	**10700**

REFER TO 91 CHEV. TRUCK OPTIONS TABLE Pg 73

S10 BLAZER V6 1/2 Ton — 1991

Model/Body/Type	BaseList	Whlse	Retail
AT/PS/AC			
2 Dr Utility	13845	**9125**	**11325**
4 Dr Utility	15085	**10200**	**12575**
2 Dr 4WD Utility	15575	**10600**	**13100**
4 Dr 4WD Utility	17215	**11750**	**14400**

REFER TO 91 CHEV. TRUCK OPTIONS TABLE Pg 73

S10 PICKUPS V6 1/2 Ton — 1991

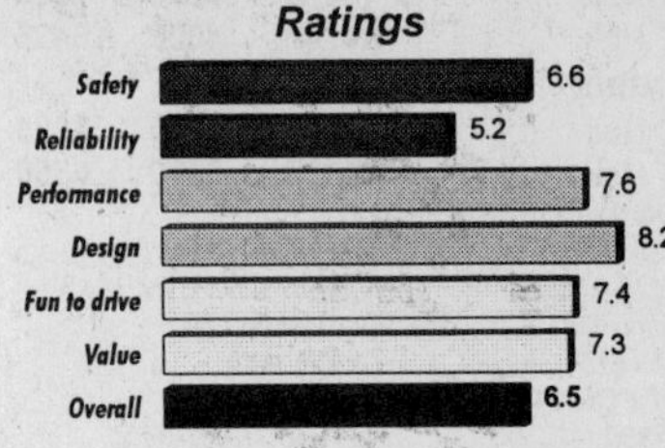

Model/Body/Type	BaseList	Whlse	Retail
AT/PS/AC			
Fleetside EL 6' (4 cyl,5 spd)	8382	**4750**	**6550**
Fleetside 6'	9700	**5775**	**7650**
Fleetside 7 1/3'	9870	**5875**	**7775**
Fleetside Ext Cab 6'	10970	**6825**	**8825**

DEDUCT FOR 91 S10 PICKUP:

4 Cyl Eng -350

REFER TO 91 CHEV. TRUCK OPTIONS TABLE Pg 73

SUBURBAN V8 — 1991

Ratings

Safety 7
Reliability 6
Performance 5.9
Design 7.5
Fun to drive 5.5
Value 7.5
Overall 6.4

Model/Body/Type	BaseList	Whlse	Retail
AT/PS/AC			
R1500 Suburbn 1/2 Ton	16720	**13325**	**16050**
R2500 Suburbn 3/4 Ton	18265	**13875**	**16625**

REFER TO 91 CHEV. TRUCK OPTIONS TABLE Pg 44

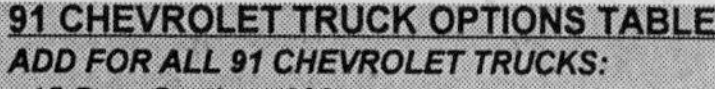

91 CHEVROLET TRUCK OPTIONS TABLE

ADD FOR ALL 91 CHEVROLET TRUCKS:

15 Pass Seating +290
4-Whl Drive(Std Blazer V8) +1140
AC-Rear +250
Bed Liner +80
CD Player +125
Custom Whls +105
Dual Rear Whls +330
Fiberglass Cap +170
Leather Seats +170
Privacy Glass +105
Pwr Seats +80
Pwr Wndw +80
Running Boards +105
Sunroof-Manual +80
Towing Pkg +105
V8 6.2L Diesel Engine +390

DEDUCT FOR ALL 91 CHEVROLET TRUCKS:

No AC -315
No Auto Trans -250
No Pwr Steering -105

1990 CHEVROLET

ASTRO VAN V6 1/2 Ton — 1990

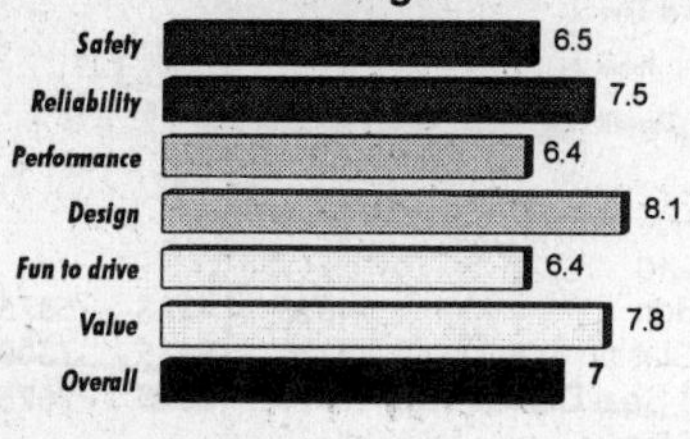

AT/PS/AC

Model/Body/Type	BaseList	Whlse	Retail
Cargo Van	12095	**5925**	**7825**
Extended Cargo Van	13397	**6725**	**8725**
CS Van	13790	**7250**	**9300**
CL Van	14830	**7750**	**9825**
LT Van	16325	**8350**	**10425**
Extended CS Van	14492	**8075**	**10150**
Extended CL Van	15532	**8575**	**10675**
Extended LT Van	17027	**9175**	**11375**

DEDUCT FOR 90 ASTRO VAN:

4 Cyl Eng -275

REFER TO 90 CHEV. TRUCK OPTIONS TABLE Pg 77

BERETTA — 1990

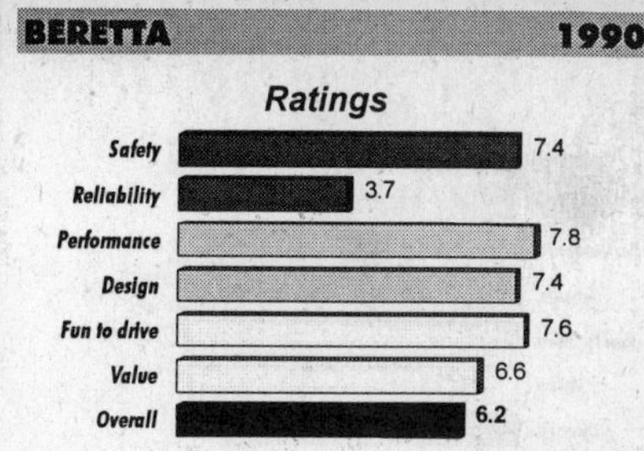

FWD/AT/PS/AC

Model/Body/Type	BaseList	Whlse	Retail
4 Cyl Models			
2 Dr Cpe	10320	**4475**	**5875**
2 Dr GTZ Cpe	13750	**5875**	**7475**
V6 Models			
2 Dr Cpe	11050	**4800**	**6275**
2 Dr GT Cpe	12500	**5875**	**7450**

ADD FOR 90 BERETTA:

Cass +35
Custom Whls/Cvrs +75
Pwr Wndw +60
Tilt Whl +35
Cruise Ctrl +60
Pwr Locks +35
Sunroof +100

DEDUCT FOR 90 BERETTA:

No AC -345
No Auto Trans -320

BLAZER V8 1/2 Ton — 1990

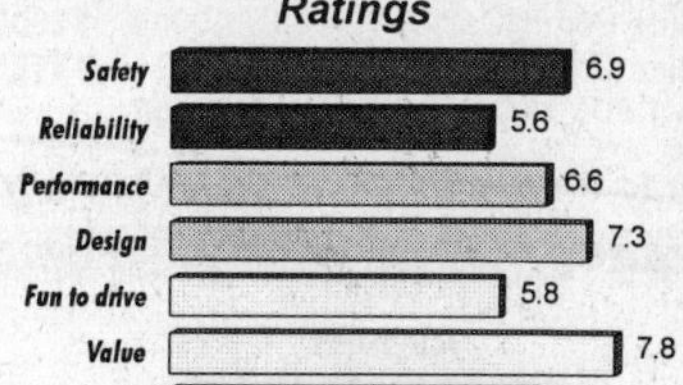

4WD/AT/PS/AC

Model/Body/Type	BaseList	Whlse	Retail
2 Dr Utility	16485	**9800**	**12050**

REFER TO 90 CHEV. TRUCK OPTIONS TABLE Pg 77

Model/Body/Type	BaseList	Whlse	Retail

C1500/C2500/C3500 PKUP V8 1990

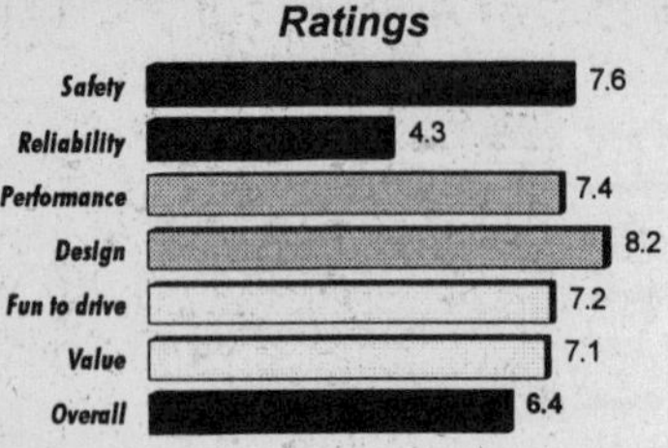

AT/PS/AC

Model/Body/Type	BaseList	Whlse	Retail
C1500 Pickup 1/2 Ton			
Fleetside WT 8' (V6)	10445	**6750**	**8775**
Sportside 6 1/2'	11625	**8100**	**10175**
Fleetside 6 1/2'	11300	**7950**	**10025**
Fleetside 8'	11580	**8050**	**10125**
Fleetside Ext Cab 6 1/2'	12210	**8900**	**11100**
Fleetside Ext Cab 8'	12490	**9000**	**11200**
Fleetside 454SS	18295	**10375**	**12750**
C2500 Pickup 3/4 Ton			
Fleetside 8'	12205	**8500**	**10600**
Fleetside Ext Cab 6 1/2'	13275	**9350**	**11575**
Fleetside Ext Cab 8'	13555	**9450**	**11675**
C3500 Pickup 1 Ton			
Fleetside 8'	13828	**9050**	**11800**
Fleetside Ext Cab 8'	14484	**9975**	**12850**
Fleetside Bonus Cab 8'	15383	**10000**	**12900**
Fleetside Crew Cab 8'	15913	**10175**	**13125**

DEDUCT FOR 90 C1500/C2500/C3500 PKUP:

V6 Eng -315

REFER TO 90 CHEV. TRUCK OPTIONS TABLE Pg 77

CAMARO 1990

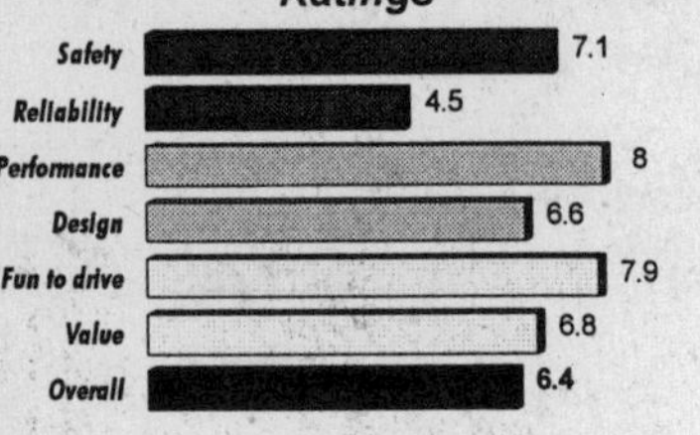

AT/PS/AC

Model/Body/Type	BaseList	Whlse	Retail
V6 Models			
2 Dr RS Cpe	10995	**5350**	**7075**
V8 Models			
2 Dr RS Cpe	11345	**5775**	**7475**
2 Dr RS Conv	16880	**9625**	**11675**
2 Dr IROC-Z Cpe	14555	**8175**	**10075**
2 Dr IROC-Z Conv	20195	**11975**	**14425**

ADD FOR 90 CAMARO:

5.7L V8 Eng +465	*Cass +60*
CD Player +115	*Cruise Ctrl +75*
Delco/Bose Mus Sys +100	*Leather Seats +115*
Pwr Locks +60	*Pwr Seat +75*
Pwr Wndw +75	*T-Top +465*

DEDUCT FOR 90 CAMARO:

No AC -430	*No Auto Trans -390*

CAPRICE V8 1990

Ratings

Safety	6.5
Reliability	6.7
Performance	6.1
Design	7.7
Fun to drive	5.7
Value	8
Overall	6.6

AT/PS/AC

Model/Body/Type	BaseList	Whlse	Retail
4 Dr Sdn	14525	**4225**	**5875**
4 Dr Classic Sdn	15125	**5475**	**7300**
4 Dr 3 Seat Classic Wgn	15725	**5825**	**7675**
4 Dr Classic Brougham Sdn	16325	**6275**	**8175**
4 Dr Classic Brougham LS Sdn	17525	**7025**	**9000**

ADD FOR 90 CAPRICE:

Cass +75	*Cruise Ctrl +100*
Custom Paint +35	*Custom Whls/Cvrs +115*
Estate Equip +130	*Leather Seats +130*
Luggage Rack +35	*Pwr Locks +60*
Pwr Seat +100	*Pwr Wndw +100*
Tilt Whl +60	*Vinyl Rf(Std Brghm) +60*

Model/Body/Type	BaseList	Whlse	Retail

CAVALIER 1990

Ratings

Rating	Score
Safety	6.7
Reliability	4.5
Performance	7.1
Design	7.7
Fun to drive	6.9
Value	7.1
Overall	6.1

FWD/AT/PS/AC

Model/Body/Type	BaseList	Whlse	Retail
4 Cyl Models			
4 Dr VL Sdn	7777	**3075**	**4350**
2 Dr VL Cpe	7577	**2975**	**4225**
4 Dr VL Wgn	8165	**3275**	**4600**
4 Dr Sdn	8820	**3500**	**4825**
2 Dr Cpe	8620	**3400**	**4725**
4 Dr RS Wgn	9195	**3750**	**5075**
V6 Models			
2 Dr Z24 Cpe	11505	**5875**	**7450**

ADD FOR 90 CAVALIER:

Cass +35
Cruise Ctrl +60
Custom Whls/Cvrs +75
Luggage Rack +35
Pwr Locks +35
Pwr Wndw +60
RS Sport Pkg +130
Sunroof +100
Tilt Whl +35
V6 Eng(Std Z24) +230

DEDUCT FOR 90 CAVALIER:

No AC -345
No Auto Trans -320
No Pwr Steering -100

CELEBRITY 1990

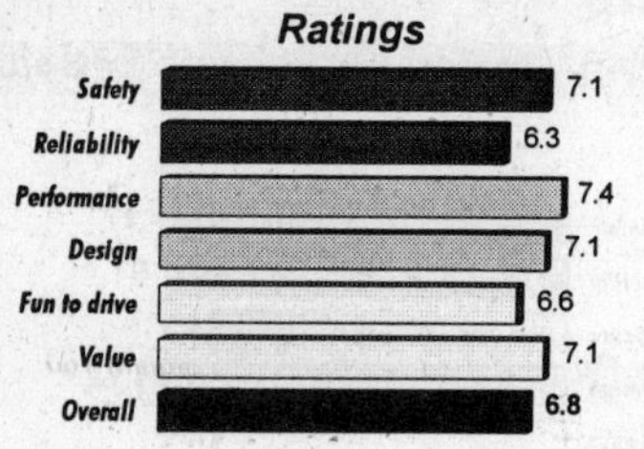

FWD/AT/PS/AC

Model/Body/Type	BaseList	Whlse	Retail
4 Cyl Models			
4 Dr 2 Seat Wgn	12395	**4000**	**5525**
V6 Models			
4 Dr 2 Seat Wgn	13055	**4400**	**5950**

ADD FOR 90 CELEBRITY:

Cass +60
Cruise Ctrl +75
Custom Whls/Cvrs +115
Eurosport Pkg +160
Luggage Rack +35
Pwr Locks +60
Pwr Seat +75
Pwr Wndw +75
Third Seat +100
Tilt Whl +60

DEDUCT FOR 90 CELEBRITY:

No AC -430

CORSICA 1990

Ratings

Rating	Score
Safety	7.1
Reliability	4.1
Performance	7.5
Design	7.3
Fun to drive	7.5
Value	7.3
Overall	6.2

FWD/AT/PS/AC

Model/Body/Type	BaseList	Whlse	Retail
4 Cyl Models			
4 Dr LT Nbk	9495	**3975**	**5325**
4 Dr LT Hbk	9875	**4175**	**5575**
V6 Models			
4 Dr LT Nbk	10180	**4325**	**5725**
4 Dr LT Hbk	10580	**4525**	**5950**
4 Dr LTZ Nbk	12795	**5700**	**7200**

ADD FOR 90 CORSICA:

Cass +35
Cruise Ctrl +60
Custom Whls/Cvrs +75
Pwr Locks +35
Pwr Wndw +60
Sunroof +100
Tilt Whl +35

DEDUCT FOR 90 CORSICA:

No AC -345
No Auto Trans -320

CHEVROLET 90

Model/Body/Type	BaseList	Whlse	Retail

CORVETTE V8 — 1990

Ratings

Rating	Score
Safety	8
Reliability	5.6
Performance	9.7
Design	7.9
Fun to drive	9
Value	7.1
Overall	7.5

AT-6SP

Model/Body/Type	BaseList	Whlse	Retail
2 Dr Hbk Cpe	31979	**15825**	**18900**
2 Dr Conv	37264	**19600**	**23025**
2 Dr ZR1 Cpe	58995	**25150**	**29025**

ADD FOR 90 CORVETTE:

CD Player(Std ZR1) +130
Delco/Bose Music Sys(Std ZR1) +130
Lthr Seats(Std ZR1) +160 Removable Glass Rf +390
Removable Hardtop +625

G10/G20/G30 VANS V8 — 1990

Ratings

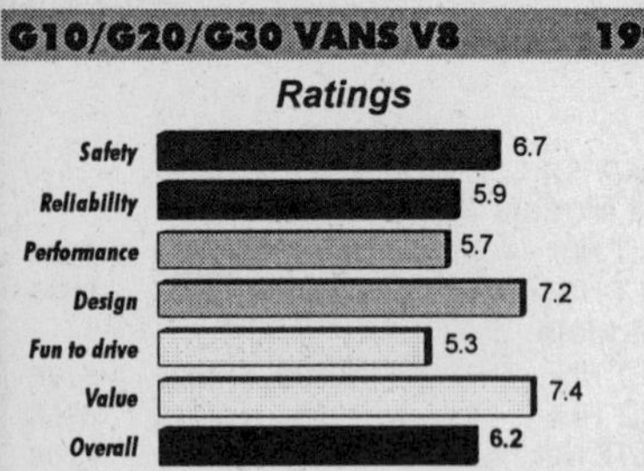

AT/PS/AC

Model/Body/Type	BaseList	Whlse	Retail
G10 Van 1/2 Ton			
Chevy Van	12650	**6575**	**8525**
Sportvan	14565	**7800**	**9900**
Beauville	16320	**8750**	**10925**
G20 Van 3/4 Ton			
Chevy Van	12820	**6675**	**8675**
Sportvan	15615	**8025**	**10100**
Beauville	16460	**8875**	**11050**
G30 Van 1 Ton			
Chevy Van	13367	**7025**	**9475**
Sportvan	17592	**8250**	**10850**
Beauville	18437	**9100**	**11850**
Ext Chevy Van	15439	**7475**	**9975**
Ext Sportvan	18446	**8725**	**11450**
Ext Beauville	19226	**9575**	**12350**

DEDUCT FOR 90 G10/G20/G30 VAN:

V6 Eng -315

REFER TO 90 CHEV. TRUCK OPTIONS TABLE Pg 77

LUMINA — 1990

Ratings

Rating	Score
Safety	6.2
Reliability	5.7
Performance	7.6
Design	7.4
Fun to drive	7.4
Value	7.5
Overall	6.5

FWD/AT/PS/AC

Model/Body/Type	BaseList	Whlse	Retail
4 Cyl Models			
4 Dr Sdn	12340	**3475**	**4875**
2 Dr Cpe	12140	**3475**	**4875**
V6 Models			
4 Dr Sdn	13000	**3875**	**5350**
2 Dr Cpe	12800	**3875**	**5350**
4 Dr Euro Sdn	14240	**4925**	**6600**
2 Dr Euro Cpe	14040	**4925**	**6600**

ADD FOR 90 LUMINA:

Cass +60 *Cruise Ctrl +75*
Custom Whls/Cvrs +115 *Pwr Locks +60*
Pwr Seat +75 *Pwr Wndw +75*
Tilt Whl +60

DEDUCT FOR 90 LUMINA:

No AC -430

LUMINA APV V6 — 1990

Ratings

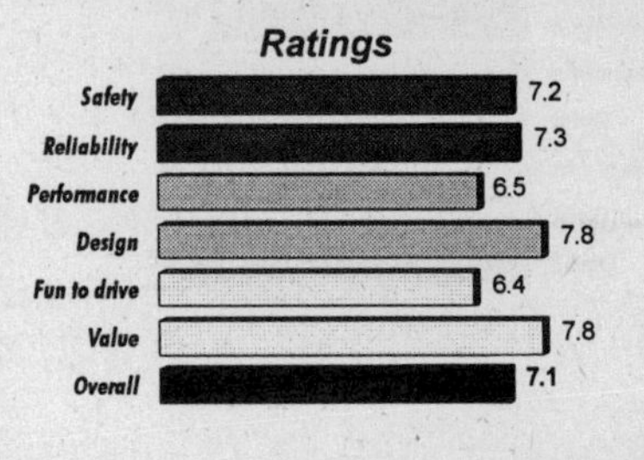

CHEVROLET

Model/Body/Type	BaseList	Whlse	Retail
FWD/AT/PS/AC			
Cargo Van	12895	**5200**	**7075**
Wagon	13995	**7025**	**9025**
CL Wagon	15745	**7500**	**9575**

REFER TO 90 CHEV. TRUCK OPTIONS TABLE Pg 77

S10 BLAZER V6 1/2 Ton — 1990

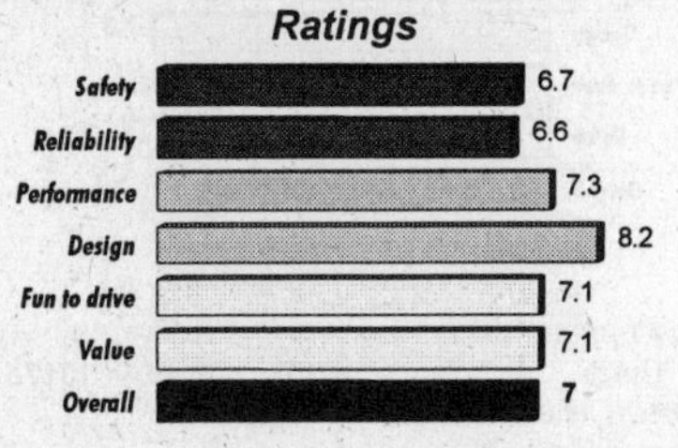

Model/Body/Type	BaseList	Whlse	Retail
AT/PS/AC			
2 Dr Utility	12930	**7150**	**9175**
2 Dr 4WD Utility	14595	**8625**	**10725**
4 Dr 4WD Utility	16905	**9225**	**11450**

ADD FOR 90 S10 BLAZER:
Sport Pkg +470

REFER TO 90 CHEV. TRUCK OPTIONS TABLE Pg 77

S10 PICKUPS V6 1/2 Ton — 1990

Ratings

Rating	Score
Safety	6.6
Reliability	5.2
Performance	7.6
Design	8.2
Fun to drive	7.4
Value	7.3
Overall	6.5

Model/Body/Type	BaseList	Whlse	Retail
AT/PS/AC			
Fleetside EL 6' (4 cyl,5 spd)	7975	**4050**	**5725**
Fleetside 6'	9215	**4850**	**6650**
Fleetside 7 1/3'	9380	**4925**	**6750**
Fleetside Ext Cab 6'	10165	**5750**	**7625**

ADD FOR 90 S10 PICKUP:
Durango Pkg +115 *Tahoe Pkg +315*

DEDUCT FOR 90 S10 PICKUP:
4 Cyl Eng -275

REFER TO 90 CHEV. TRUCK OPTIONS TABLE Pg 77

SUBURBAN V8 — 1990

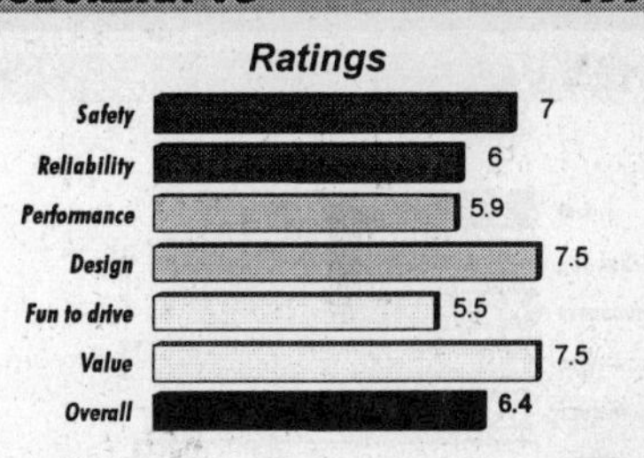

Model/Body/Type	BaseList	Whlse	Retail
AT/PS/AC			
R1500 Suburbn 1/2 Ton	15615	**11000**	**13500**
R2500 Suburbn 3/4 Ton	16238	**11475**	**14025**

ADD FOR 90 SUBURBAN:
Silverado Pkg +470

REFER TO 90 CHEV. TRUCK OPTIONS TABLE Pg 77

90 CHEVROLET TRUCK OPTIONS TABLE

ADD FOR ALL 90 CHEVROLET TRUCKS:
- *15 Pass Seating +250*
- *4-Whl Drive(Std Blazer V8) +1080*
- *AC-Rear +185*
- *CD Player +80*
- *Custom Whls(Std S-10 Blazer Sport) +80*
- *Dual Rear Whls +290*
- *Fiberglass Cap +125*
- *Leather Seats +125*
- *Privacy Glass(Std Suburban Silverado) +80*
- *Running Boards +80*
- *Towing Pkg +80*
- *V8 6.2L Diesel Engine +350*

DEDUCT FOR ALL 90 CHEVROLET TRUCKS:
- *No AC -250*
- *No Auto Trans -170*

CHEVROLET 89

Model/Body/Type	BaseList	Whlse	Retail

1989 CHEVROLET

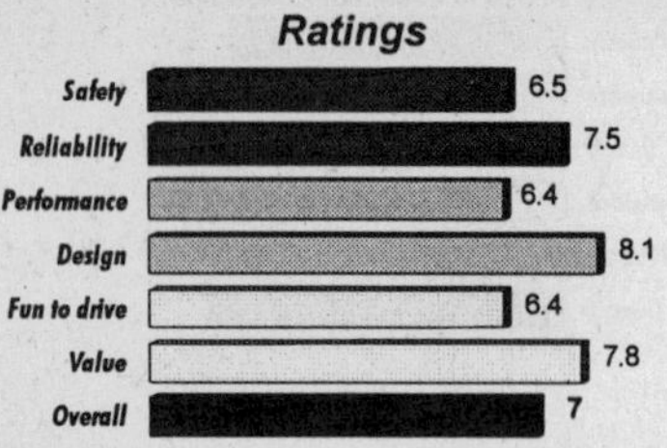

AT/PS/AC			
Cargo Van	10950	**4725**	**6525**
CS Van	11900	**5925**	**7825**
CL Van	12633	**6375**	**8300**
LT Van	14144	**6925**	**8925**

DEDUCT FOR 89 ASTRO VAN:

4 Cyl Eng -230

REFER TO 89 CHEV. TRUCK OPTIONS TABLE Pg 81

BERETTA 1989

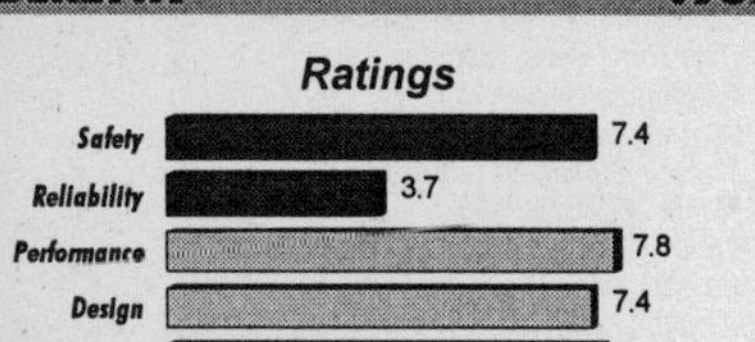

FWD/AT/PS/AC

4 Cyl Models			
2 Dr Cpe	10575	**3175**	**4475**
V6 Models			
2 Dr Cpe	11235	**3475**	**4800**
2 Dr GT Cpe	12685	**4350**	**5775**

ADD FOR 89 BERETTA:

Cass +20 *Cruise Ctrl +35*
Custom Whls/Cvrs +35 *Pwr Locks +20*
Pwr Wndw +35 *Sunroof +75*
Tilt Whl +20

DEDUCT FOR 89 BERETTA:

No AC -320 *No Auto Trans -275*

BLAZER V8 1/2 Ton 1989

Ratings

Safety 6.9
Reliability 5.6
Performance 6.6
Design 7.3
Fun to drive 5.8
Value 7.8
Overall 6.4

4WD/AT/PS/AC			
2 Dr Utility	15355	**8100**	**10175**

ADD FOR 89 BLAZER:

Silverado Pkg +390

REFER TO 89 CHEV. TRUCK OPTIONS TABLE Pg 81

C1500/C2500/C3500 PKUP V8 1989

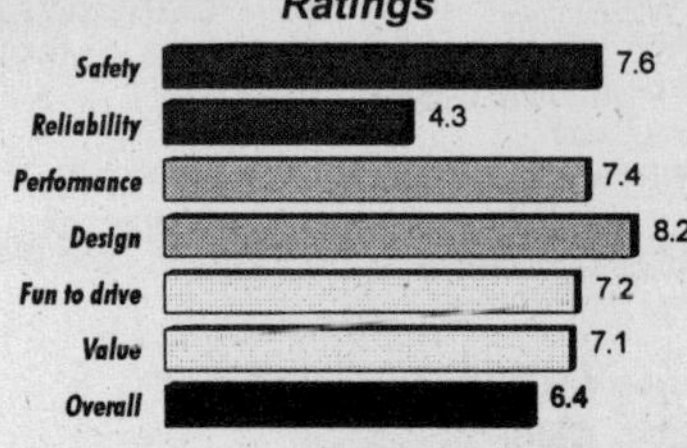

AT/PS/AC			
C1500 Pickup 1/2 Ton			
Sportside 6 1/2'	11108	**6850**	**8850**
Fleetside 6 1/2'	10890	**6725**	**8725**
Fleetside 8'	11090	**6850**	**8850**
Fleetside Ext Cab 6 1/2'	11817	**7575**	**9650**
Fleetside Ext Cab 8'	12022	**7675**	**9775**
C2500 Pickup 3/4 Ton			
Fleetside 8'	11698	**7225**	**9275**
Fleetside Ext Cab 8'	13053	**8075**	**10150**
Fleetside Bonus Cab 8'	14163	**8125**	**10200**
Fleetside Crew Cab 8'	14663	**8325**	**10400**
C3500 Pickup 1 Ton			
Fleetside 8'	12778	**7725**	**10275**
Fleetside Ext Cab 8'	13813	**8575**	**11200**
Fleetside Bonus Cab 8'	14362	**8625**	**11250**
Fleetside Crew Cab 8'	14871	**8825**	**11550**

ADD FOR 89 C1500/C2500/C3500 PKUP:
Scottsdale Pkg +115 *Silverado Pkg +350*
DEDUCT FOR 89 C1500/C2500/C3500 PKUP:
V6 Eng -275
REFER TO 89 CHEV. TRUCK OPTIONS TABLE Pg 81

CAMARO 1989

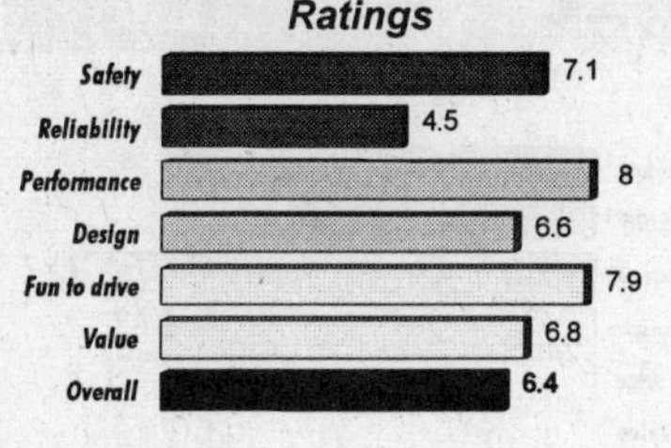

AT/PS/AC

Model/Body/Type	BaseList	Whlse	Retail
V6 Models			
2 Dr RS Cpe	11495	**4050**	**5575**
V8 Models			
2 Dr RS Cpe	11895	**4425**	**5975**
2 Dr RS Conv	16995	**8075**	**9975**
2 Dr IROC-Z Cpe	14145	**6600**	**8375**
2 Dr IROC-Z Conv	18945	**10200**	**12425**

ADD FOR 89 CAMARO:
5.7L V8 Eng +430 *Cass +35*
CD Player +75 *Cruise Ctrl +60*
Delco/Bose Mus Sys +75 *Leather Seats +75*
Pwr Locks +35 *Pwr Seat +60*
Pwr Wndw +60 *T-Top +405*
Tilt Whl +35
DEDUCT FOR 89 CAMARO:
No AC -390 *No Auto Trans -345*

CAPRICE V8 1989

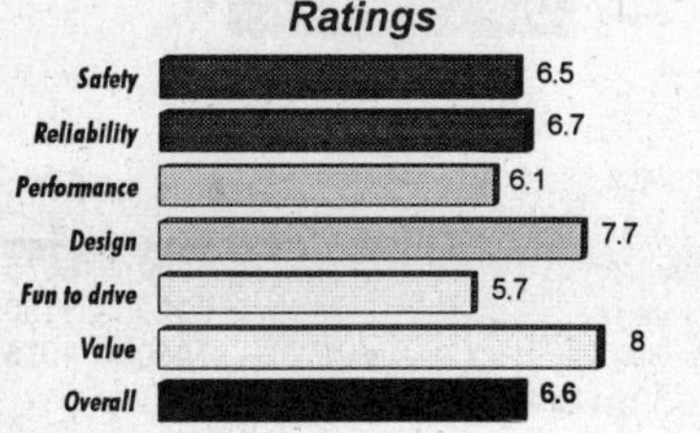

AT/PS/AC

Model/Body/Type	BaseList	Whlse	Retail
4 Dr Sdn	13865	**3200**	**4725**
4 Dr Classic Sdn	14445	**4400**	**6125**
4 Dr 3 Seat Classic Wgn	15025	**4700**	**6425**
4 Dr Classic Brougham Sdn	15615	**5050**	**6875**
4 Dr Classic Brougham LS Sdn	16835	**5750**	**7600**

ADD FOR 89 CAPRICE:
Cass +60 *Cruise Ctrl +75*
Custom Whls/Cvrs +75 *Estate Equip +100*
Leather Seats +115 *Luggage Rack +20*
Pwr Locks +35 *Pwr Seat +75*
Pwr Wndw +75 *Tilt Whl +35*
Vinyl Rf(Std Brghm) +35

CAVALIER 1989

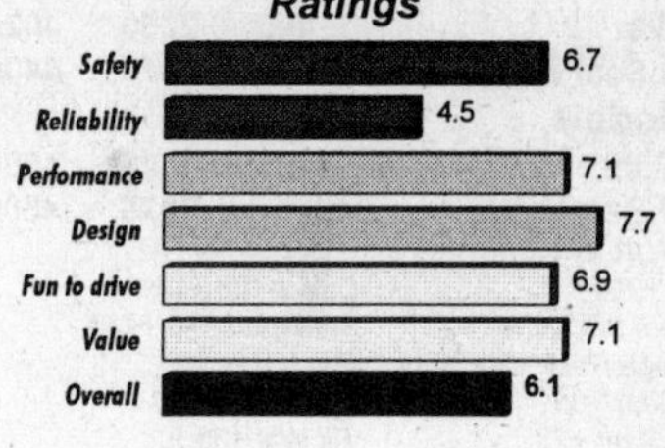

FWD/AT/PS/AC

Model/Body/Type	BaseList	Whlse	Retail
4 Cyl Models			
4 Dr Sdn	8595	**2300**	**3425**
2 Dr VL Cpe	7375	**1800**	**2850**
2 Dr Cpe	8395	**2225**	**3325**
4 Dr Wgn	8975	**2500**	**3650**
V6 Models			
2 Dr Z24 Cpe	11325	**4425**	**5850**
2 Dr Z24 Conv	16615	**6700**	**8450**

ADD FOR 89 CAVALIER:
Cass +20 *Cruise Ctrl +35*
Custom Whls/Cvrs +35 *Luggage Rack +20*
Pwr Locks(Std Conv) +20 *Pwr Wndw(Std Conv) +35*
RS Pkg +115 *Sunroof +75*
Tilt Whl +20 *V6 Eng(Std Z24) +215*
DEDUCT FOR 89 CAVALIER:
No AC -320 *No Auto Trans -275*
No Pwr Steering -75

Model/Body/Type	BaseList	Whlse	Retail

CELEBRITY 1989

Ratings

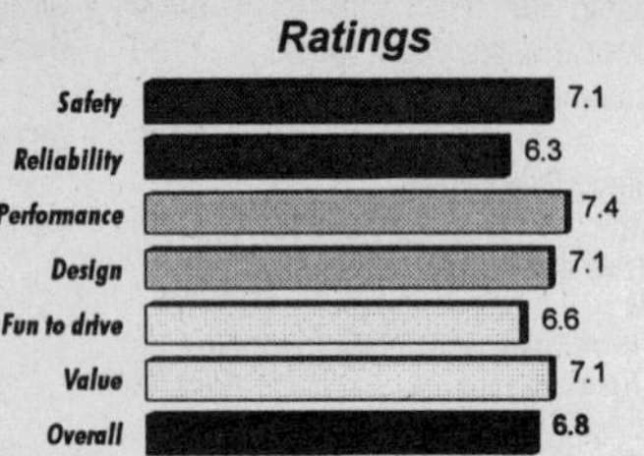

FWD/AT/PS/AC

Model/Body/Type	BaseList	Whlse	Retail
4 Cyl Models			
4 Dr Sdn	11495	**2750**	**4025**
4 Dr 2 Seat Wgn	11925	**3050**	**4400**
V6 Models			
4 Dr Sdn	12105	**3125**	**4500**
4 Dr 2 Seat Wgn	12535	**3375**	**4800**

ADD FOR 89 CELEBRITY:

Cass +35 *Cruise Ctrl +60*
Custom Whls/Cvrs +75 *Eurosport Pkg +130*
Luggage Rack +20 *Pwr Locks +35*
Pwr Seat +60 *Pwr Wndw +60*
Third Seat +75 *Tilt Whl +35*

DEDUCT FOR 89 CELEBRITY:

No AC -390

CORSICA 1989

Ratings

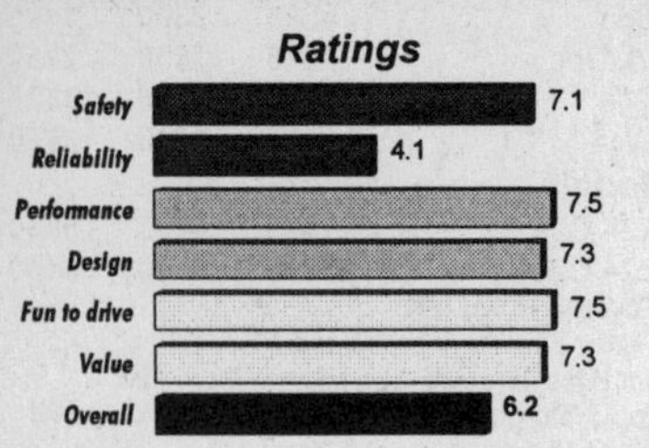

FWD/AT/PS/AC

Model/Body/Type	BaseList	Whlse	Retail
4 Cyl Models			
4 Dr Nbk	9985	**2700**	**3875**
4 Dr Hbk	10375	**2900**	**4150**
V6 Models			
4 Dr Nbk	10645	**3025**	**4275**
4 Dr Hbk	11035	**3200**	**4500**
4 Dr LTZ Nbk	12825	**4075**	**5475**

ADD FOR 89 CORSICA:

Cass +20 *Cruise Ctrl +35*
Custom Whls/Cvrs +35 *Pwr Locks +20*
Pwr Wndw +35 *Sunroof +75*
Tilt Whl +20

DEDUCT FOR 89 CORSICA:

No AC -320 *No Auto Trans -275*

CORVETTE V8 1989

Ratings

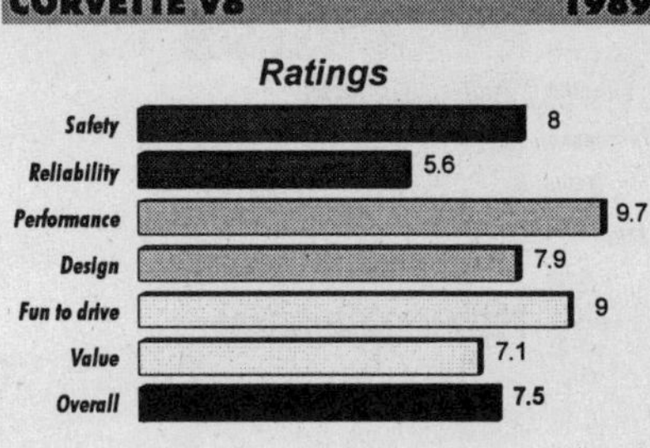

AT-6SP

Model/Body/Type	BaseList	Whlse	Retail
2 Dr Cpe	31545	**13700**	**16625**
2 Dr Conv	36785	**17075**	**20300**

ADD FOR 89 CORVETTE:

Delco/Bose Mus Sys +115 *Leather Seats +130*
Removable Glass Rf +330 *Removable Hardtop +565*

G10/G20/G30 VANS V8 1989

Ratings

Safety 6.7
Reliability 5.9
Performance 5.7
Design 7.2
Fun to drive 5.3
Value 7.4
Overall 6.2

AT/PS/AC

Model/Body/Type	BaseList	Whlse	Retail
G10 Van 1/2 Ton			
Chevy Van	11700	**5000**	**6875**
Sportvan	13193	**6225**	**8150**
Beauville	14776	**7050**	**9075**
G20 Van 3/4 Ton			
Chevy Van	12210	**5100**	**7000**
Sportvan	13676	**6400**	**8350**
Beauville	14995	**7150**	**9175**

G30 Van 1 Ton

Model/Body/Type	BaseList	Whlse	Retail
Chevy Van	13057	**5325**	**7525**
Sportvan	15494	**6550**	**8925**
Beauville	16813	**7275**	**9775**

DEDUCT FOR 89 G10/G20/G30 VAN:
V6 Eng -275
REFER TO 89 CHEV. TRUCK OPTIONS TABLE Pg 81

S10 BLAZER V6 1/2 Ton — 1989

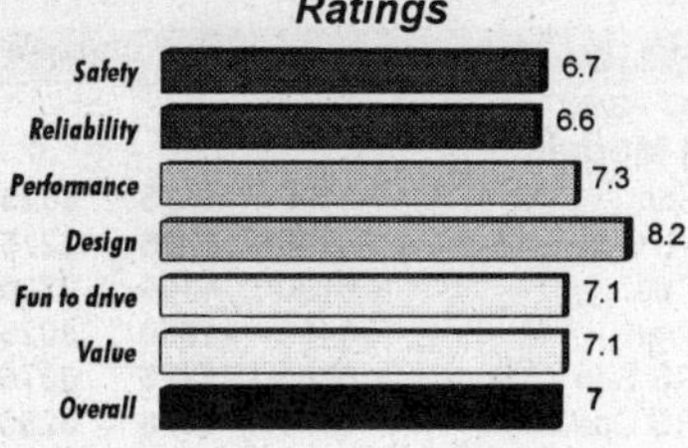

AT/PS/AC

Model/Body/Type	BaseList	Whlse	Retail
2 Dr Utility	11935	**5600**	**7475**
2 Dr 4WD Utility	13510	**7000**	**9000**

ADD FOR 89 S10 BLAZER:
Sport Pkg +390 *Tahoe Pkg +230*
REFER TO 89 CHEV. TRUCK OPTIONS TABLE Pg 81

S10 PICKUPS V6 1/2 Ton — 1989

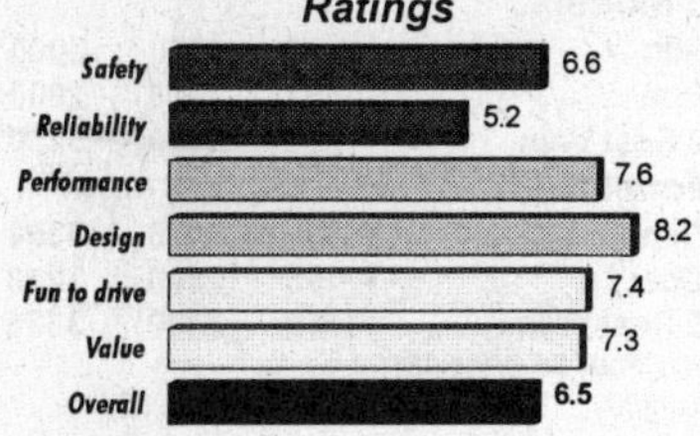

AT/PS/AC

Model/Body/Type	BaseList	Whlse	Retail
Fleetside EL 6' (4 cyl,5 spd)	7474	**3200**	**4725**
Fleetside 6'	9135	**3875**	**5550**
Fleetside 7 1/3'	9300	**3975**	**5675**
Fleetside Ext Cab 6'	9985	**4675**	**6425**

ADD FOR 89 S10 PICKUP:
Tahoe Pkg +230
DEDUCT FOR 89 S10 PICKUP:
4 Cyl Eng -230
REFER TO 89 CHEV. TRUCK OPTIONS TABLE Pg 81

SUBURBAN V8 — 1989

Ratings

Rating	Score
Safety	7
Reliability	6
Performance	5.9
Design	7.5
Fun to drive	5.5
Value	7.5
Overall	6.4

AT/PS/AC

Model/Body/Type	BaseList	Whlse	Retail
R1500 Suburbn 1/2 Ton	14585	**9025**	**11225**
R2500 Suburbn 3/4 Ton	15223	**9475**	**11700**

ADD FOR 89 SUBURBAN:
Silverado Pkg +390
REFER TO 89 CHEV. TRUCK OPTIONS TABLE Pg 81

89 CHEVROLET TRUCK OPTIONS TABLE

ADD FOR ALL 89 CHEVROLET TRUCKS:
15 Pass Seating +205
4-Whl Drive(Std Blazer V8) +975
AC-Rear +145
Dual Rear Whls +250
Fiberglass Cap +80
Leather Seats +80
V8 6.2L Diesel Engine +290
DEDUCT FOR ALL 89 CHEVROLET TRUCKS:
No AC -185
No Auto Trans -80

1988 CHEVROLET

ASTRO VAN V6 1/2 Ton — 1988

AT/PS/AC

Model/Body/Type	BaseList	Whlse	Retail
Cargo Van	9585	**3550**	**5125**
CS Van	10696	**4650**	**6400**
CL Van	11489	**5000**	**6875**
LT Van	12828	**5525**	**7400**

DEDUCT FOR 88 ASTRO VAN:
4 Cyl Eng -195
REFER TO 88 CHEV. TRUCK OPTIONS TABLE Pg 83

BERETTA — 1988

FWD/AT/PS/AC

Model/Body/Type	BaseList	Whlse	Retail
4 Cyl Models			
2 Dr Cpe	9555	**2425**	**3575**
V6 Models			
2 Dr Cpe	10215	**2725**	**3900**

ADD FOR 88 BERETTA:
GT Pkg +230
DEDUCT FOR 88 BERETTA:
No AC -250 *No Auto Trans -230*

CHEVROLET

CHEVROLET 88

BLAZER V8 1/2 Ton — 1988

4WD/AT/PS/AC

Model/Body/Type	BaseList	Whlse	Retail
2 Dr Utility	14509	**6825**	**8825**

ADD FOR 88 BLAZER:
Silverado Pkg +315
REFER TO 88 CHEV. TRUCK OPTIONS TABLE Pg 83

C1500/C2500/C3500 PKUP V8 — 1988

AT/PS/AC

Model/Body/Type	BaseList	Whlse	Retail
C1500 Pickup 1/2 Ton			
Sportside 6 1/2'	10472	**4975**	**6825**
Fleetside 6 1/2'	10264	**4925**	**6750**
Fleetside 8'	10454	**5025**	**6900**
Fleetside Ext Cab 8'	11661	**5850**	**7725**
C2500/R20 Pickup 3/4 Ton			
Fleetside 8'	11291	**5375**	**7250**
Fleetside Ext Cab 8'	12611	**6200**	**8125**
Fleetside Bonus Cab 8'	13632	**6250**	**8175**
Fleetside Crew Cab 8'	14068	**6450**	**8400**
C3500/R30 Pickup 1 Ton			
Fleetside 8'	11860	**5850**	**8150**
Fleetside Ext Cab 8'	13033	**6650**	**9050**
Fleetside Bonus Cab 8'	13828	**6675**	**9125**
Fleetside Crew Cab 8'	14268	**6900**	**9350**

ADD FOR 88 C1500/C2500/C3500 PKUP:
Silverado Pkg +275
DEDUCT FOR 88 C1500/C2500/C3500 PKUP:
V6 Eng -230
REFER TO 88 CHEV. TRUCK OPTIONS TABLE Pg 83

CAMARO — 1988

AT/PS/AC

Model/Body/Type	BaseList	Whlse	Retail
V6 Models			
2 Dr Cpe	10995	**3100**	**4475**
V8 Models			
2 Dr Cpe	11395	**3400**	**4825**
2 Dr Conv	16255	**6700**	**8525**
2 Dr IROC-Z Cpe	13490	**5350**	**7075**
2 Dr IROC-Z Conv	18015	**8700**	**10700**

ADD FOR 88 CAMARO:
5.7L V8 Eng +390 *T-Top +345*
DEDUCT FOR 88 CAMARO:
No AC -330 *No Auto Trans -290*

CAPRICE — 1988

AT/PS/AC

Model/Body/Type	BaseList	Whlse	Retail
V6 Models			
4 Dr Sdn	12030	**1400**	**2500**
4 Dr Classic Sdn	12575	**2575**	**3925**
4 Dr Classic Brougham Sdn	13645	**3150**	**4700**
4 Dr Classic Brougham LS Sdn	14820	**3725**	**5325**
V8 Models			
4 Dr Sdn	12470	**1850**	**3100**
4 Dr Classic Sdn	13015	**3075**	**4575**
4 Dr 3 Seat Classic Wgn	14340	**3250**	**4775**
4 Dr Classic Brougham Sdn	14085	**3625**	**5200**
4 Dr Classic Brougham LS Sdn	15260	**4225**	**5875**

DEDUCT FOR 88 CAPRICE:
No AC -375

CAVALIER — 1988

FWD/AT/PS/AC

Model/Body/Type	BaseList	Whlse	Retail
4 Cyl Models			
4 Dr Sdn	8195	**1775**	**2825**
2 Dr VL Cpe	6995	**1325**	**2275**
2 Dr Cpe	8120	**1700**	**2700**
4 Dr Wgn	8490	**1950**	**3025**
4 Dr RS Sdn	9385	**2275**	**3375**
2 Dr RS Cpe	9175	**2175**	**3250**
V6 Models			
2 Dr Z24 Cpe	10725	**3600**	**4925**
2 Dr Z24 Conv	15990	**5775**	**7325**

ADD FOR 88 CAVALIER:
V6 Eng(Std Z24) +200
DEDUCT FOR 88 CAVALIER:
No AC -250 *No Auto Trans -230*
No Pwr Steering -60

CELEBRITY — 1988

FWD/AT/PS/AC

Model/Body/Type	BaseList	Whlse	Retail
4 Cyl Models			
4 Dr Sdn	11025	**1850**	**3000**
2 Dr Cpe	10585	**1775**	**2900**
4 Dr 2 Seat Wgn	11350	**2100**	**3250**
V6 Models			
4 Dr Sdn	11635	**2175**	**3350**
2 Dr Cpe	11195	**2100**	**3250**
4 Dr 2 Seat Wgn	11960	**2400**	**3625**

DEDUCT FOR 88 CELEBRITY:
No AC -330 *No Auto Trans -290*

CORSICA — 1988

FWD/AT/PS/AC

Model/Body/Type	BaseList	Whlse	Retail
4 Cyl Models			
4 Dr Nbk	8995	**1975**	**3050**
V6 Models			
4 Dr Nbk	9655	**2250**	**3350**

DEDUCT FOR 88 CORSICA:
No AC -250 *No Auto Trans -230*

Model/Body/Type	BaseList	Whlse	Retail

CORVETTE V8 — 1988

AT-4SP

Model/Body/Type	BaseList	Whlse	Retail
2 Dr Cpe	29480	**11800**	**14625**
2 Dr Conv	34820	**15025**	**18050**

ADD FOR 88 CORVETTE:
Removable Glass Rf +320

G10/G20/G30 VANS V8 — 1988

AT/PS/AC

Model/Body/Type	BaseList	Whlse	Retail
G10 Van 1/2 Ton			
Chevy Van	10735	**3800**	**5425**
Sportvan	12417	**4550**	**6275**
Bonaventure	13576	**5050**	**6925**
Beauville	13984	**5200**	**7075**
G20 Van 3/4 Ton			
Chevy Van	11360	**3875**	**5550**
Sportvan	12918	**4675**	**6425**
Bonaventure	13825	**5125**	**7000**
Beauville	14231	**5275**	**7150**
G30 Van 1 Ton			
Chevy Van	12594	**4050**	**6050**
Sportvan	14663	**4775**	**6900**
Bonaventure	15571	**5250**	**7450**
Beauville	15976	**5400**	**7625**

DEDUCT FOR 88 G10/G20/G30 VAN:
V6 Eng -230
REFER TO 88 CHEV. TRUCK OPTIONS TABLE Pg 83

MONTE CARLO — 1988

AT/PS/AC

Model/Body/Type	BaseList	Whlse	Retail
V6 Models			
2 Dr LS Cpe	12330	**3275**	**4700**
V8 Models			
2 Dr LS Cpe	12770	**3675**	**5100**
2 Dr SS Sport Cpe	14320	**5650**	**7300**

DEDUCT FOR 88 MONTE CARLO:
No AC -330

NOVA 4 Cyl — 1988

FWD/AT/PS/AC

Model/Body/Type	BaseList	Whlse	Retail
5 Dr Hbk	9050	**2100**	**3175**
4 Dr Nbk	8795	**2000**	**3100**
4 Dr Twin Cam Nbk	11395	**2525**	**3675**

DEDUCT FOR 88 NOVA:
No AC -250 *No Auto Trans -200*
No Pwr Steering -60

S10 BLAZER V6 1/2 Ton — 1988

AT/PS/AC

Model/Body/Type	BaseList	Whlse	Retail
2 Dr Utility	10505	**4350**	**6100**
2 Dr 4WD Utility	12737	**5650**	**7500**

ADD FOR 88 S10 BLAZER:
Sport Pkg +275 *Tahoe Pkg +160*
DEDUCT FOR 88 S10 BLAZER:
4 Cyl Eng -195
REFER TO 88 CHEV. TRUCK OPTIONS TABLE Pg 83

S10 PICKUPS V6 1/2 Ton — 1988

AT/PS/AC

Model/Body/Type	BaseList	Whlse	Retail
Fleetside EL 6'(4 cyl,5 spd)	6595	**2475**	**3875**
Fleetside 6'	8238	**3000**	**4500**
Fleetside 7 1/3'	8412	**3100**	**4600**
Fleetside Ext Cab 6'	9257	**3700**	**5275**

ADD FOR 88 S10 PICKUP:
Sport Pkg +275 *Tahoe Pkg +160*
DEDUCT FOR 88 S10 PICKUP:
4 Cyl Eng -195
REFER TO 88 CHEV. TRUCK OPTIONS TABLE Pg 83

SPECTRUM 4 Cyl — 1988

FWD/AT/PS/AC

Model/Body/Type	BaseList	Whlse	Retail
2 Dr Express Hbk	6495	**675**	**1475**
4 Dr Nbk	8160	**1350**	**2300**
2 Dr Hbk	7720	**1275**	**2200**
4 Dr Turbo Nbk	10665	**1750**	**2775**

DEDUCT FOR 88 SPECTRUM:
No AC -215 *No Auto Trans -200*

SPRINT 3 Cyl — 1988

5SP/AC/FWD

Model/Body/Type	BaseList	Whlse	Retail
4 Dr Hbk	6585	**1100**	**2000**
2 Dr Hbk	6380	**1000**	**1900**
2 Dr Metro Hbk	5495	**875**	**1725**
2 Dr Turbo Hbk	8240	**1375**	**2325**

ADD FOR 88 SPRINT:
Auto Trans +200
DEDUCT FOR 88 SPRINT:
No AC -215

SUBURBAN V8 — 1988

AT/PS/AC

Model/Body/Type	BaseList	Whlse	Retail
R10 Suburbn 1/2 Ton	13945	**7075**	**9100**
R20 Suburbn 3/4 Ton	14559	**7450**	**9525**

ADD FOR 88 SUBURBAN:
Silverado Pkg +315
REFER TO 88 CHEV. TRUCK OPTIONS TABLE Pg 83

88 CHEVROLET TRUCK OPTIONS TABLE

ADD FOR ALL 88 CHEVROLET TRUCKS:
15 Pass Seating +170
4-Whl Drive(Std Blazer V8) +850
AC-Rear +105
Dual Rear Whls +185
V8 6.2L Diesel Engine +195
DEDUCT FOR ALL 88 CHEVROLET TRUCKS:
No AC -125

1987 CHEVROLET

ASTRO VAN V6 1/2 Ton — 1987

AT/PS/AC

Model/Body/Type	BaseList	Whlse	Retail
Cargo Van	8797	2800	4275
Van	9833	3800	5425
CS Van	10314	3900	5575
CL Van	11079	4100	5800
LT Van	12370	4650	6400

DEDUCT FOR 87 ASTRO VAN:
4 Cyl Eng -160
REFER TO 87 CHEV. TRUCK OPTIONS TABLE Pg 85

BERETTA 4 Cyl — 1987

FWD/AT/PS/AC

Model/Body/Type	BaseList	Whlse	Retail
2 Dr Cpe	11165	2100	3175

ADD FOR 87 BERETTA:
V6 Engine +215

BLAZER V8 1/2 Ton — 1987

4WD/AT/PS/AC

Model/Body/Type	BaseList	Whlse	Retail
2 Dr Utility	13066	5525	7400

ADD FOR 87 BLAZER:
Silverado Pkg +230
REFER TO 87 CHEV. TRUCK OPTIONS TABLE Pg 85

CAMARO V8 — 1987

AT/PS/AC

Model/Body/Type	BaseList	Whlse	Retail
2 Dr Cpe	10395	2350	3575
2 Dr LT Cpe	11917	2700	3975
2 Dr Z28 Cpe	12819	3700	5125
2 Dr IROC-Z Cpe	13488	4200	5725

ADD FOR 87 CAMARO:
5.7L V8 Eng +345
DEDUCT FOR 87 CAMARO:
V6 Engine -250

CAPRICE V8 — 1987

AT/PS/AC

Model/Body/Type	BaseList	Whlse	Retail
4 Dr Sdn	11435	1525	2650
4 Dr Wgn	11995	1625	2775
4 Dr Classic Sdn	12000	2575	3925
2 Dr Classic Sport Cpe	11832	2425	3750
4 Dr Classic Wgn	12586	2675	4050
4 Dr Classic Brougham Sdn	12989	3050	4550
4 Dr Classic Brougham LS Sdn	14245	3350	4900

DEDUCT FOR 87 CAPRICE:
V6 Engine -375

CAVALIER — 1987

FWD/AT/PS/AC

Model/Body/Type	BaseList	Whlse	Retail
4 Cyl Models			
4 Dr Sdn	7449	1350	2300
2 Dr Cpe	7255	1275	2200
4 Dr Wgn	7615	1475	2425
4 Dr CS Sdn	7953	1475	2425
2 Dr CS Hbk	7978	1475	2425
4 Dr CS Wgn	8140	1600	2575
4 Dr RS Sdn	8499	1675	2650
2 Dr RS Cpe	8318	1575	2550
2 Dr RS Hbk	8520	1675	2650
2 Dr RS Conv	13446	3475	4800
4 Dr RS Wgn	8677	1775	2800
V6 Models			
2 Dr Z24 Cpe	9913	2825	4075
2 Dr Z24 Hbk	10115	2925	4175

ADD FOR 87 CAVALIER:
V6 Eng(Std Z24) +175

CELEBRITY V6 — 1987

FWD/AT/PS/AC

Model/Body/Type	BaseList	Whlse	Retail
4 Dr Sdn	10875	1550	2600
2 Dr Cpe	10605	1450	2500
4 Dr Wgn	11035	1750	2875

DEDUCT FOR 87 CELEBRITY:
4 Cyl Engine -250

CHEVETTE 4 Cyl — 1987

AT/PS/AC

Model/Body/Type	BaseList	Whlse	Retail
4 Dr CS Hbk	5495	850	1700
2 Dr CS Hbk	4995	750	1575

CORSICA 4 Cyl — 1987

FWD/AT/PS/AC

Model/Body/Type	BaseList	Whlse	Retail
4 Dr Nbk	10605	1650	2625

ADD FOR 87 CORISCA:
V6 Engine +205

CORVETTE V8 — 1987

AT-4SP

Model/Body/Type	BaseList	Whlse	Retail
2 Dr Cpe	27999	9875	12450
2 Dr Conv	33172	12900	15775

EL CAMINO V8 1/2 Ton — 1987

AT/PS/AC

Model/Body/Type	BaseList	Whlse	Retail
Pkup	10453	4725	6525
SS Pkup	10784	5050	6925

DEDUCT FOR 87 EL CAMINO:
V6 Eng -195
REFER TO 87 CHEV. TRUCK OPTIONS TABLE Pg 85

G10/G20/G30 VANS V8 — 1987

AT/PS/AC

Model/Body/Type	BaseList	Whlse	Retail
G10 Van 1/2 Ton			
Chevy Van	9464	2975	4475
Sportvan	11162	3825	5475
Bonaventure	12279	4275	5975
Beauville	12631	4425	6150

G20 Van 3/4 Ton

Model/Body/Type	BaseList	Whlse	Retail
Chevy Van	10131	3025	4525
Sportvan	11609	3900	5575
Bonaventure	12483	4325	6050
Beauville	12833	4475	6200
G30 Van 1 Ton			
Chevy Van	12110	3125	4875
Sportvan	14004	4000	5975
Bonaventure	14879	4500	6550
Beauville	15228	4675	6725

DEDUCT FOR 87 G10/G20/G30 VAN:
V6 Eng -195
REFER TO 87 CHEV. TRUCK OPTIONS TABLE Pg 85

MONTE CARLO 1987

AT/PS/AC

Model/Body/Type	BaseList	Whlse	Retail
V6 Models			
2 Dr LS Cpe	11306	2300	3525
V8 Models			
2 Dr SS Cpe	13463	4250	5800

ADD FOR 87 MONTE CARLO:
V8 Engine +290

NOVA 4 Cyl 1987

FWD/AT/PS/AC

Model/Body/Type	BaseList	Whlse	Retail
5 Dr Hbk	8510	1650	2625
4 Dr Nbk	8258	1550	2525

R10/R20/R30 PICKUPS V8 1987

AT/PS/AC

Model/Body/Type	BaseList	Whlse	Retail
R10 Pickup 1/2 Ton			
Stepside 6 1/2'	8651	4375	6125
Fleetside 6 1/2'	8503	4425	6150
Fleetside 8'	8687	4525	6275
R20 Pickup 3/4 Ton			
Stepside 8'	10077	4750	6550
Fleetside 8'	9924	4800	6625
Fleetside Bonus Cab 8'	12475	5600	7475
Fleetside Crew Cab 8'	12842	5800	7675
R30 Pickup 1 Ton			
Stepside 8'	11712	5125	7300
Fleetside 8'	11565	5175	7350
Fleetside Bonus Cab 8'	12664	6000	8325
Fleetside Crew Cab 8'	13034	6200	8550

ADD FOR 87 R10/R20/R30 PICKUP:
Silverado Pkg +195
DEDUCT FOR 87 R10/R20/R30 PICKUP:
V6 Eng -195
REFER TO 87 CHEV. TRUCK OPTIONS TABLE Pg 85

S10 BLAZER V6 1/2 Ton 1987

AT/PS/AC

Model/Body/Type	BaseList	Whlse	Retail
2 Dr Utility	10124	3200	4725
2 Dr 4WD Utility	11588	4325	6050

ADD FOR 87 S10 BLAZER:
Sport Pkg +195
DEDUCT FOR 87 S10 BLAZER:
4 Cyl Eng -160
REFER TO 87 CHEV. TRUCK OPTIONS TABLE Pg 85

S10 PICKUPS V6 1/2 Ton 1987

AT/PS/AC

Model/Body/Type	BaseList	Whlse	Retail
Fleetside EL 6' (4 cyl,5 spd)	6595	2300	3675
Fleetside 6'	7435	2550	3975
Fleetside 7 1/3'	7702	2650	4075
Fleetside Ext Cab 6'	8167	3175	4700

ADD FOR 87 S10 PICKUP:
Sport Pkg +195
DEDUCT FOR 87 S10 PICKUP:
4 Cyl Eng -160
REFER TO 87 CHEV. TRUCK OPTIONS TABLE Pg 85

SPECTRUM 4 Cyl 1987

FWD/AT/PS/AC

Model/Body/Type	BaseList	Whlse	Retail
2 Dr Express Hbk	6495	525	1325
4 Dr Nbk	7709	1125	2025
2 Dr Hbk	7412	1025	1925
4 Dr Turbo Nbk	9735	1375	2325

SPRINT 3 Cyl 1987

5SP/AC/FWD

Model/Body/Type	BaseList	Whlse	Retail
4 Dr Hbk	6195	875	1700
2 Dr Hbk	5995	775	1600
2 Dr ER Hbk	6110	825	1650
2 Dr Turbo Hbk	7690	1125	2025

SUBURBAN V8 1987

AT/PS/AC

Model/Body/Type	BaseList	Whlse	Retail
R10 Suburbn 1/2 Ton	12477	7075	9100
R20 Suburbn 3/4 Ton	13077	7450	9525

ADD FOR 87 SUBURBAN:
Silverado Pkg +195
REFER TO 87 CHEV. TRUCK OPTIONS TABLE Pg 85

87 CHEVROLET TRUCK OPTIONS TABLE

ADD FOR ALL 87 CHEVROLET TRUCKS:
15 Pass Seating +125
4-Whl Drive(Std Blazer V8) +680
Dual Rear Whls +125
DEDUCT FOR ALL 87 CHEVROLET TRUCKS:
No AC -80

1986 CHEVROLET

Model/Body/Type	BaseList	Whlse	Retail
ASTRO VAN			**1986**
Cargo Van	8431	1950	3350
Van	9037	2900	4500
CS Van	9492	3000	4600
CL Van	10216	3150	4775
BLAZER 1/2 Ton			**1986**
4WD			
Utility	12034	4350	6125
C10/C20/C30 PICKUPS			**1986**
C10 Pickup 1/2 Ton			
Stepside 6 1/2'	7904	3250	4850
Fleetside 6 1/2'	7764	3250	4900
Fleetside 8'	7938	3325	4975
C20 Pickup 3/4 Ton			
Stepside 8'	9253	3525	5200
Fleetside 8'	9113	3575	5250
Fleetside Bonus Cab 8'	11103	4150	5925
Fleetside Crew Cab 8'	11451	4350	6125
C30 Pickup 1 Ton			
Stepside 8'	10381	3850	5575
Fleetside 8'	10242	3900	5650
Fleetside Bonus Cab 8'	11282	4475	6275
Fleetside Crew Cab 8'	11633	4650	6500

ADD FOR 86 C10/C20/C30 PICKUP:
4-Whl Drive +495 *Dual Rear Whls +80*

Model/Body/Type	BaseList	Whlse	Retail
CAMARO			**1986**
2 Dr Cpe	9685	2025	3225
2 Dr Berlinetta Cpe	12302	2525	3800
2 Dr Z28 Cpe	11902	3175	4550
2 Dr IROC-Z Cpe	12597	3550	4950
CAPRICE			**1986**
4 Dr Sdn	10633	1250	2500
4 Dr Classic Sdn	11185	2025	3450
2 Dr Classic Sport Cpe	11025	1900	3300
4 Dr Classic Brougham Sdn	11819	2400	3925
4 Dr Classic Wgn	11511	2150	3600
CAVALIER			**1986**
FWD			
4 Dr Sdn	6888	1075	2100
2 Dr Cpe	6706	975	2000
4 Dr Wgn	7047	1100	2150
4 Dr CS Sdn	7350	1125	2175
2 Dr CS Hbk	7373	1125	2175
4 Dr CS Wgn	7525	1175	2200
4 Dr RS Sdn	7811	1275	2300
2 Dr RS Cpe	7640	1200	2225
2 Dr RS Hbk	7830	1275	2300
2 Dr RS Conv	12530	2650	3925
4 Dr RS Wgn	7979	1300	2350
2 Dr Z24 Cpe	8878	2025	3200
2 Dr Z24 Hbk	9068	2100	3275
CELEBRITY			**1986**
FWD			
4 Dr Sdn	9366	1175	2200
2 Dr Cpe	9170	1075	2125
4 Dr Wgn	9516	1275	2325
CHEVETTE			**1986**
4 Dr CS Hbk	5959	500	1450
2 Dr CS Hbk	5645	425	1350
CORVETTE			**1986**
2 Dr Cpe	27027	9425	11575
2 Dr Conv	32480	12325	14725
EL CAMINO 1/2 Ton			**1986**
Pkup	9572	3675	5350
SS Pkup	9885	3925	5675
G10/G20/G30 VANS			**1986**
G10 Van 1/2 Ton			
Chevy Van	8626	2175	3650
Sportvan	10232	2875	4450
Bonaventure	11290	3125	4725
Beauville	11622	3200	4825
G20 Van 3/4 Ton			
Chevy Van	9257	2250	3725
Sportvan	10655	2925	4525
Bonaventure	11482	3175	4800
Beauville	11813	3250	4875
G30 Van 1 Ton			
Chevy Van	11128	2300	3825
Sportvan	13173	3025	4625

ADD FOR 86 G10/G20/G30 VAN:
15 Pass Pkg +80

Model/Body/Type	BaseList	Whlse	Retail
MONTE CARLO			**1986**
2 Dr Cpe	10241	1850	3050
2 Dr SS Cpe	12466	3600	5000
NOVA			**1986**
5 Dr Hbk	7669	1225	2250
4 Dr Nbk	7435	1125	2175
S10 BLAZER 1/2 Ton			**1986**
2 Dr Utility	9582	2450	4000
2 Dr 4WD Utility	10698	3250	4900

Model/Body/Type	BaseList	Whlse	Retail
S10 PICKUPS 1/2 Ton			**1986**
Fleetside 6'	6999	1800	3225
Fleetside 7 1/3'	7234	1875	3275
Fleetside Ext Cab 6'	7686	2275	3800
ADD FOR 86 S10 PICKUP:			
4-Whl Drive +495			
SPECTRUM			**1986**
FWD			
4 Dr Nbk	6925	850	1800
2 Dr Hbk	6658	775	1725
SPRINT			**1986**
FWD			
4 Dr Hbk	5580	600	1550
2 Dr Hbk	5380	500	1450
2 Dr ER Hbk	5765	525	1475
SUBURBAN			**1986**
C10 Suburbn 1/2 Ton	11476	4600	6425
C20 Suburbn 3/4 Ton	12297	4925	6825
ADD FOR 86 SUBURBAN:			
4-Whl Drive +495			

1985 CHEVROLET

Model/Body/Type	BaseList	Whlse	Retail
ASTRO VAN			**1985**
Cargo Van	7821	1425	2750
Van	8195	2275	3800
CS Van	8623	2350	3875
CL Van	9359	2450	4000
BLAZER			**1985**
4WD Utility	11223	3300	4950
C10/C20/C30 PICKUPS			**1985**
C10 Pickup 1/2 Ton			
Stepside 6 1/2'	7428	2550	4100
Fleetside 6 1/2'	7295	2600	4150
Fleetside 8'	7461	2675	4225
C20 Pickup 3/4 Ton			
Stepside 8'	8677	2825	4400
Fleetside 8'	8543	2875	4450
Fleetside Bonus Cab 8'	9902	3300	4950
Fleetside Crew Cab 8'	10238	3475	5150
C30 Pickup 1 Ton			
Stepside 8'	9167	3125	4725
Fleetside 8'	9033	3150	4775
Fleetside Bonus Cab 8'	10033	3625	5300
Fleetside Crew Cab 8'	10371	3800	5525
ADD FOR 85 C10/C20/C30 PICKUP:			
4-Whl Drive +250			
CAMARO			**1985**
2 Dr Cpe	8998	1675	2800
2 Dr Berlinetta Cpe	11360	2125	3300
2 Dr Z28 Cpe	11080	2650	3950
2 Dr IROC-Z Cpe	11739	3100	4450
CAPRICE			**1985**
4 Dr Classic Sdn	10278	1325	2600
2 Dr Classic Cpe	10128	1200	2450
4 Dr Classic Wgn	10714	1350	2675
CAVALIER			**1985**
FWD			
4 Dr Sdn	6477	600	1550
4 Dr Wgn	6633	650	1625
2 Dr Type-10 Cpe	6737	650	1625
2 Dr Type-10 Hbk	6919	750	1700
2 Dr Type-10 Conv	11693	2000	3175
4 Dr CS Sdn	6900	725	1700
4 Dr CS Wgn	7066	800	1750
CELEBRITY			**1985**
FWD			
4 Dr Sdn	8548	950	1975
2 Dr Cpe	8362	900	1875
4 Dr Wgn	8739	1075	2100
CHEVETTE			**1985**
4 Dr CS Hbk	5690	275	1225
2 Dr CS Hbk	5340	200	1125
CITATION II			**1985**
FWD			
4 Dr Hbk	7090	675	1650
2 Dr Hbk	6940	600	1550
CORVETTE			**1985**
2 Dr Cpe	24403	8575	10675
EL CAMINO			**1985**
Pkup	8933	2875	4475
SS Pkup	9198	3075	4700

Model/Body/Type	BaseList	Whlse	Retail
G10/G20/G30 VANS			**1985**
G10 Van 1/2 Ton			
Chevy Van	7987	1550	2900
Sportvan	9517	2150	3600
Bonaventure	10514	2300	3825
Beauville	10827	2400	3925
G20 Van 3/4 Ton			
Chevy Van	8581	1600	2975
Sportvan	9915	2200	3675
Bonaventure	10695	2375	3900
Beauville	11007	2450	4000
G30 Van 1 Ton			
Chevy Van	10342	1675	3050
Sportvan	12291	2250	3750
IMPALA			**1985**
4 Dr Sdn	9759	650	1800
MONTE CARLO			**1985**
2 Dr Cpe	9540	1450	2550
2 Dr SS Cpe	11657	2925	4250
NOVA			**1985**
FWD			
4 Dr Nbk	7195	925	1925
S10 BLAZER			**1985**
2 Dr Utility	8881	1975	3400
2 Dr 4WD Utility	9994	2600	4150
S10 PICKUPS 1/2 Ton			**1985**
Fleetside 6'	5990	1600	2950
Fleetside 7 1/3'	6702	1650	3025
Fleetside Ext Cab 6'	7167	1975	3400
ADD FOR 85 S10 PICKUP:			
4-Whl Drive +250			
SPECTRUM			**1985**
FWD			
4 Dr Hbk	6575	625	1600
2 Dr Hbk	6295	550	1500
SPRINT			**1985**
FWD			
2 Dr Hbk	4949	225	1150
SUBURBAN			**1985**
C10 Suburbn 1/2 Ton	10700	3475	5150
C20 Suburbn 3/4 Ton	10953	3825	5550
ADD FOR 85 SUBURBAN:			
4-Whl Drive +250			

CHRYSLER USA

1990 Chrysler LeBaron GTC Coupe

For a Chrysler dealer in your area, see our Dealer Directory (pg 217)

1994 CHRYSLER

CONCORDE V6 — 1994

Model/Body/Type	BaseList	Whlse	Retail
FWD/AT/PS/AC			
4 Dr Sdn	19457	**16475**	**19300**

ADD FOR 94 CONCORDE:

3.5L V6 Engine +365
Anti-Theft/Recovery Sys +365
Car Phone +230 *CD Player +275*
Custom Whls/Cvrs +230 *Infinity Ster Sys +230*
Leather Seats +320 *Pwr Locks +135*
Pwr Seat +180 *Pwr Sunroof +590*
Pwr Wndw +180

LE BARON SDN/CONV V6 — 1994

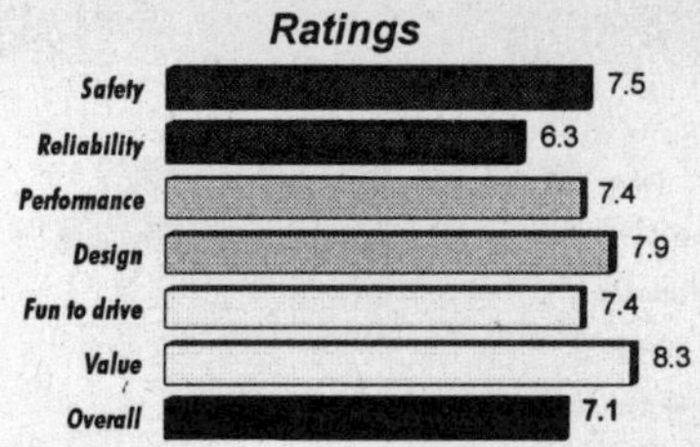

Model/Body/Type	BaseList	Whlse	Retail
FWD/AT/PS/AC			
4 Dr LE Sdn (4 Cyl)	15121	**10325**	**12550**
4 Dr LE Sdn	16551	**10925**	**13275**
4 Dr Landau Sdn	17933	**12025**	**14500**
2 Dr GTC Conv	17024	**14475**	**17025**

ADD FOR 94 LE BARON:

ABS +430
Anti-Theft/Recovery Sys +365
Cass(Std Landau,Conv) +115
CD Player +230
Cruise Ctrl(Std LE,Landau) +160
Custom Whls/Cvrs +205 *Lthr Seats +275*
Pwr Locks(Std LE,Landau) +115
Pwr Seat +160
Tilt Whl(Std LE,Landau) +115

NEW YORKER V6 — 1994

Model/Body/Type	BaseList	Whlse	Retail
FWD/AT/PS/AC			
4 Dr Sdn	25386	**17325**	**20375**

ADD FOR 94 NEW YORKER:

Anti-Theft/Recovery Sys +365
Car Phone +230
CD Player +340 *Custom Whls/Cvrs +275*
Infinity Ster Sys +295 *Leather Seats +365*
Power Sunroof +635

TOWN & COUNTRY V6 — 1994

Model/Body/Type	BaseList	Whlse	Retail
FWD/AT/PS/AC			
Wgn	27184	**21900**	**25325**

ADD FOR 94 TOWN & COUNTRY:

AC-Rear +375 *All Whl Drive +1275*
CD Player +205 *Running Boards +145*
Sunroof-Manual +145 *Towing Pkg +180*

See the Automobile Dealer Directory on page 379 for a Dealer near you!

1993 CHRYSLER

CONCORDE V6 1993

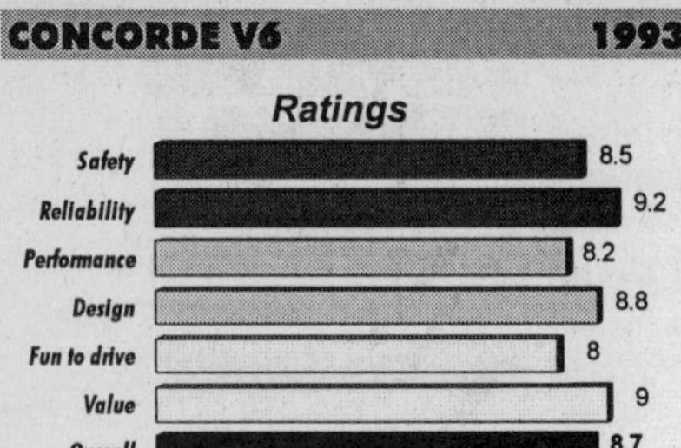

FWD/AT/PS/AC

Model/Body/Type	BaseList	Whlse	Retail
4 Dr Sdn	18341	**15300**	**18075**

ADD FOR 93 CONCORDE:

Car Phone +175 *Cass +115*
CD Player +230 *Cruise Ctrl +160*
Custom Whls/Cvrs +195 *Infinity Ster Sys +195*
Leather Seats +275 *Pwr Locks +115*
Pwr Seat +160 *Pwr Wndw +160*

IMPERIAL V6 1993

Ratings

Safety 7.7
Reliability 5.2
Performance 6.8
Design 8.1
Fun to drive 6.7
Value 8.3
Overall 6.6

FWD/AT/PS/AC

Model/Body/Type	BaseList	Whlse	Retail
4 Dr Sdn	29381	**15000**	**18025**

ADD FOR 93 IMPERIAL:

Car Phone +175 *CD Player +290*
Infinity Ster Sys +250 *Leather Seats +315*

LE BARON COUPE/CONV 1993

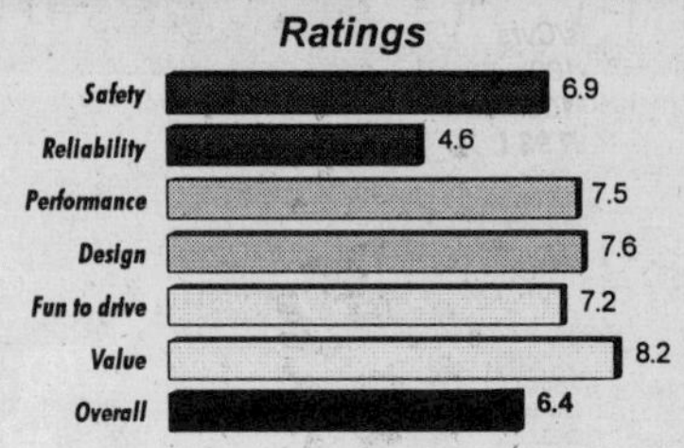

FWD/AT/PS/AC

Model/Body/Type	BaseList	Whlse	Retail
4 Cyl Models			
2 Dr Cpe	13999	**9350**	**11375**
2 Dr Conv	17399	**12075**	**14550**
V6 Models			
2 Dr Cpe	14693	**9875**	**12025**
2 Dr Conv	18093	**12625**	**15100**
2 Dr LX Cpe	16676	**10925**	**13275**
2 Dr LX Conv	21165	**13725**	**16250**

ADD FOR 93 LE BARON COUPE/CONV:

ABS +390 *CD Player +195*
Cruise Ctrl(Std LX) +135 *Custom Whls/Cvrs +175*
GTC Pkg +1445 *Lthr Seats(Std LXCnv) +230*
Pwr Locks(Std LX) +100 *Pwr Seat(Std LXCnv) +135*
Cass(Std LXCnv) +100 *Tilt Whl(Std LX) +100*

DEDUCT FOR 93 LE BARON COUPE/CONV:

No AC -545

LE BARON SEDAN V6 1993

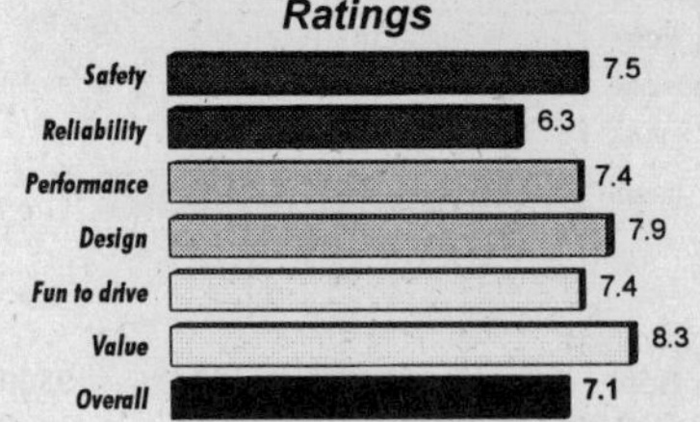

FWD/AT/PS/AC

Model/Body/Type	BaseList	Whlse	Retail
4 Dr LE Sdn (4 Cyl)	14497	**9400**	**11425**
4 Dr LE Sdn	15191	**9925**	**12075**
4 Dr Landau Sdn	17119	**10850**	**13200**

ADD FOR 93 LE BARON SEDAN:

ABS +390 | CD Player +195
Custom Whls/Cvrs +175 | Leather Seats +230
Pwr Locks +100 | Pwr Seat +135
Pwr Wndw +135 | Cass(Std Lan) +100

DEDUCT FOR 93 LE BARON SEDAN:

No AC -545

NEW YORKER 5TH AVENUE V6 1993

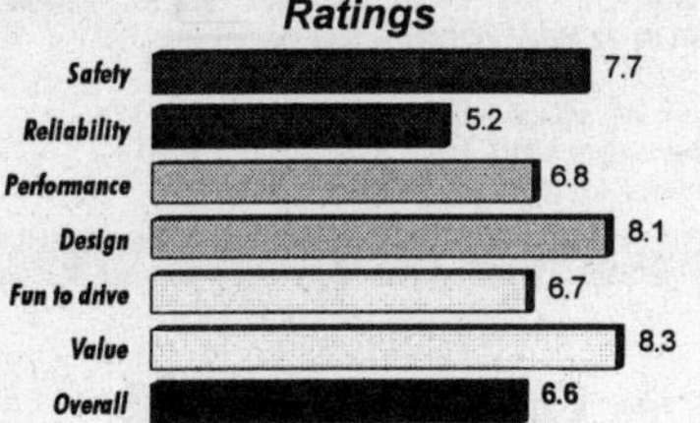

Model/Body/Type	BaseList	Whlse	Retail
FWD/AT/PS/AC			
4 Dr Sdn	21948	**13500**	**16150**

ADD FOR 93 NEW YORKER 5TH AVE:

ABS +390 | Car Phone +175
CD Player +230 | Custom Whls/Cvrs +195
Infinity Ster Sys +195 | Leather Seats +275

NEW YORKER SALON V6 1993

Model/Body/Type	BaseList	Whlse	Retail
FWD/AT/PS/AC			
4 Dr Sdn	18705	**11850**	**14425**

ADD FOR 93 NEW YORKER SALON:

ABS +390 | Car Phone +175
Custom Whls/Cvrs +195 | Infinity Ster Sys +195
Leather Seats +275 | Vinyl Roof +115

TOWN & COUNTRY V6 1993

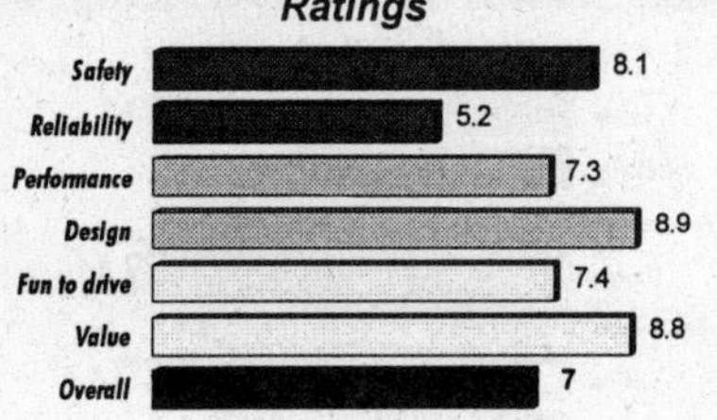

Model/Body/Type	BaseList	Whlse	Retail
FWD/AT/PS/AC			
Wgn	25538	**18725**	**21900**

ADD FOR 93 TOWN & COUNTRY:

AC-Rear +375 | All Whl Drive +1265
CD Player +205 | Running Boards +145
Sunroof-Manual +145 | Towing Pkg +180

1992 CHRYSLER

IMPERIAL V6 1992

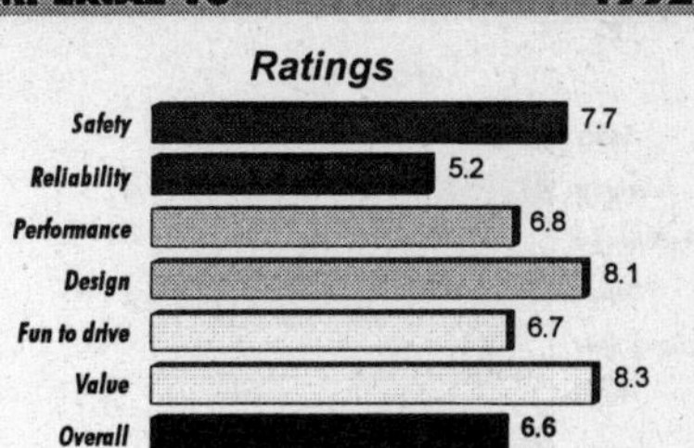

Model/Body/Type	BaseList	Whlse	Retail
FWD/AT/PS/AC			
4 Dr Sdn	28453	**15000**	**18025**

ADD FOR 92 IMPERIAL:

Car Phone +160 | Infinity Ster Sys +230
Leather Seats +275

LE BARON COUPE/CONV 1992

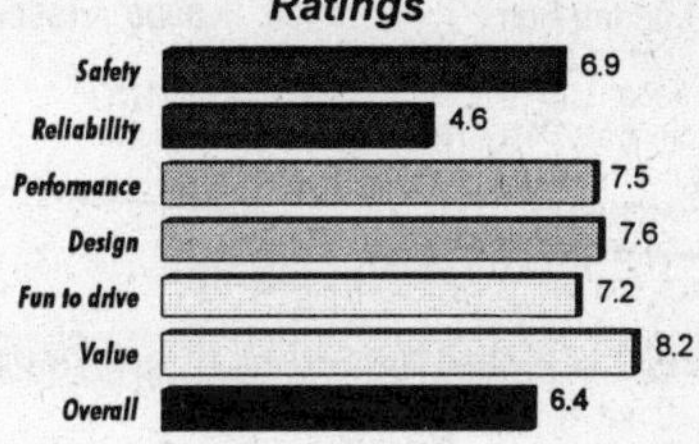

Model/Body/Type	BaseList	Whlse	Retail
FWD/AT/PS/AC			
4 Cyl Models			
2 Dr Cpe	13488	**7750**	**9675**
2 Dr Conv	16884	**10375**	**12600**
V6 Models			
2 Dr Cpe	14182	**8250**	**10150**
2 Dr Conv	17578	**10875**	**13225**
2 Dr LX Cpe	16094	**9225**	**11250**
2 Dr LX Conv	20280	**11850**	**14300**

CHRYSLER 92-91

Model/Body/Type	BaseList	Whlse	Retail

ADD FOR 92 LE BARON COUPE/CONV:

4 Cyl Turbo Eng +230 — *ABS +350*
Cass +75 — *CD Player +175*
Cruise Ctrl(Std LX) +115 — *Custom Whls/Cvrs +160*
GTC Pkg +1340 — *Lthr Seats(Std LXCnv) +195*
Pwr Locks(Std LX) +75 — *Pwr Seat +115*
Tilt Whl(Std LX) +75

DEDUCT FOR 92 LE BARON COUPE/CONV:

No AC -505 — *No Auto Trans -470*

LE BARON SEDAN 1992

Ratings

Safety 7.5
Reliability 6.3
Performance 7.4
Design 7.9
Fun to drive 7.4
Value 8.3
Overall 7.1

FWD/AT/PS/AC

Model/Body/Type	BaseList	Whlse	Retail
4 Cyl Models			
4 Dr Sdn	13998	**7450**	**9325**
4 Dr Landau Sdn	15710	**8400**	**10300**
V6 Models			
4 Dr Sdn	14692	**7950**	**9875**
4 Dr LX Sdn	15287	**8475**	**10375**
4 Dr Landau Sdn	16404	**8900**	**10900**

ADD FOR 92 LE BARON SEDAN:

ABS +350 — *Cass(Std Lan) +75*
Custom Whls/Cvrs +160 — *Leather Seats +195*
Pwr Locks +75 — *Pwr Seat +115*
Pwr Wndw +115

DEDUCT FOR 92 LE BARON SEDAN:

No AC -505

NEW YORKER 5TH AVENUE V6 1992

Ratings

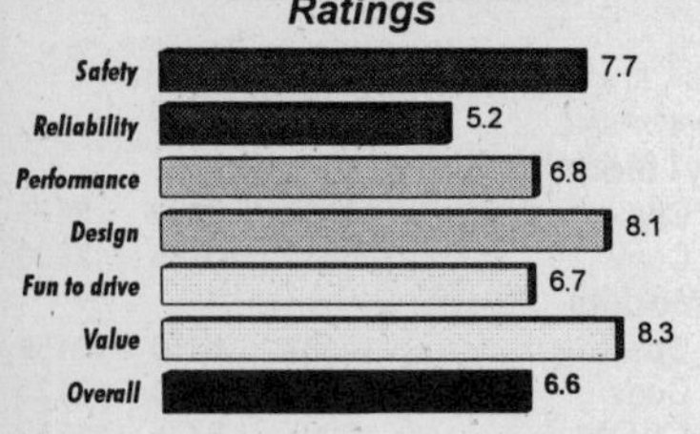

FWD/AT/PS/AC

Model/Body/Type	BaseList	Whlse	Retail
4 Dr Sdn	22074	**11875**	**14450**

ADD FOR 92 NEW YORKER 5TH AVE:

ABS +350 — *Car Phone +160*
Custom Whls/Cvrs +175 — *Infinity Ster Sys +175*
Leather Seats +230 — *Pwr Sunroof +430*

NEW YORKER SALON V6 1992

FWD/AT/PS/AC

Model/Body/Type	BaseList	Whlse	Retail
4 Dr Sdn	18849	**9825**	**12050**

ADD FOR 92 NEW YORKER SALON:

ABS +350 — *Car Phone +160*
Custom Whls/Cvrs +175 — *Infinity Ster Sys +175*
Leather Seats +230 — *Pwr Sunroof +430*
Vinyl Roof +100

TOWN & COUNTRY V6 1992

Ratings

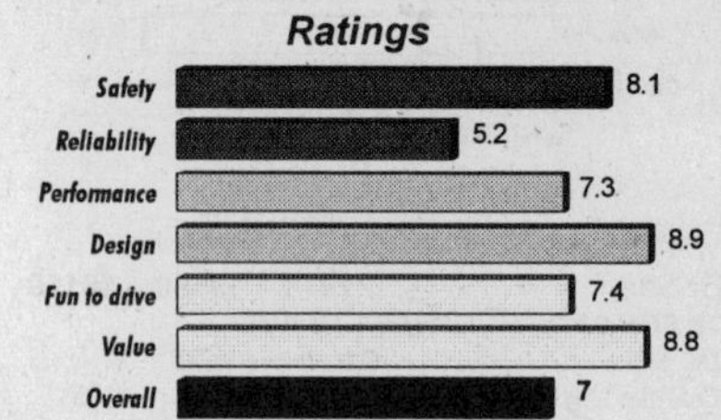

FWD/AT/PS/AC

Model/Body/Type	BaseList	Whlse	Retail
Wgn	24621	**15550**	**18425**

ADD FOR 92 TOWN & COUNTRY:

AC-Rear +315 — *All Whl Drive +1200*
Running Boards +125 — *Sunroof-Manual +105*

1991 CHRYSLER

IMPERIAL V6 1991

Ratings

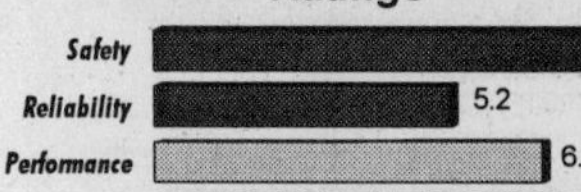

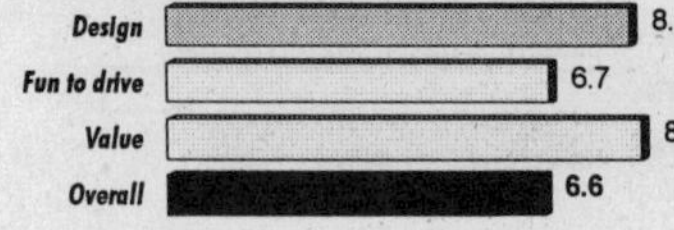

FWD/AT/PS/AC

Model/Body/Type	BaseList	Whlse	Retail
4 Dr Sdn	26705	**9850**	**12425**

CHRYSLER

ADD FOR 91 IMPERIAL:
Car Phone +135 · *Infinity Ster Sys +195* · *Mark Cross Pkg +315*

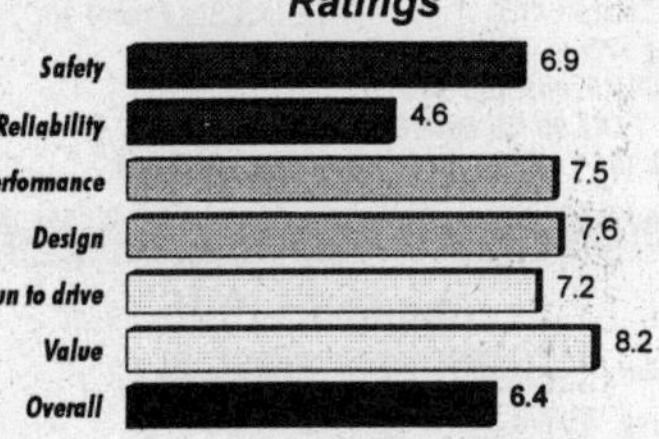

FWD/AT/PS/AC

Model/Body/Type	BaseList	Whlse	Retail
4 Cyl Models			
2 Dr Cpe	13160	**5825**	**7525**
2 Dr Conv	15705	**8375**	**10275**
V6 Models			
2 Dr Cpe	13854	**6275**	**8025**
2 Dr Conv	16399	**8825**	**10825**
2 Dr LX Cpe	15685	**7150**	**9000**
2 Dr LX Conv	18955	**9700**	**11800**

ADD FOR 91 LE BARON COUPE/CONV:
4 Cyl Turbo Eng +215 · *Cass +60* · *CD Player +160* · *Cruise Ctrl(Std LX) +100* · *Custom Whls/Cvrs +135* · *GTC Perf Pkg +1750* · *GTC Pkg +1310* · *Lthr Seats(Std LXCnv) +160* · *Pwr Locks(Std LX) +60* · *Pwr Sts(Std LXCnv) +100* · *Sunroof +160* · *Tilt Whl(Std LX) +60*

DEDUCT FOR 91 LE BARON COUPE/CONV:
No AC -470 · *No Auto Trans -430*

LE BARON SEDAN V6 1991

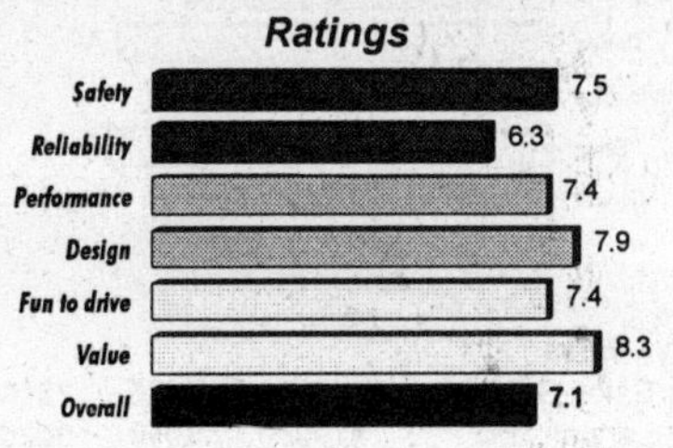

FWD/AT/PS/AC

Model/Body/Type	BaseList	Whlse	Retail
4 Dr Sdn	16699	**7350**	**9225**

ADD FOR 91 LE BARON SEDAN:
ABS +315 · *Custom Whls/Cvrs +135* · *Leather Seats +160* · *Pwr Locks +60* · *Pwr Seat +100* · *Pwr Wndw +100*

NEW YORKER 5TH AVENUE V6 1991

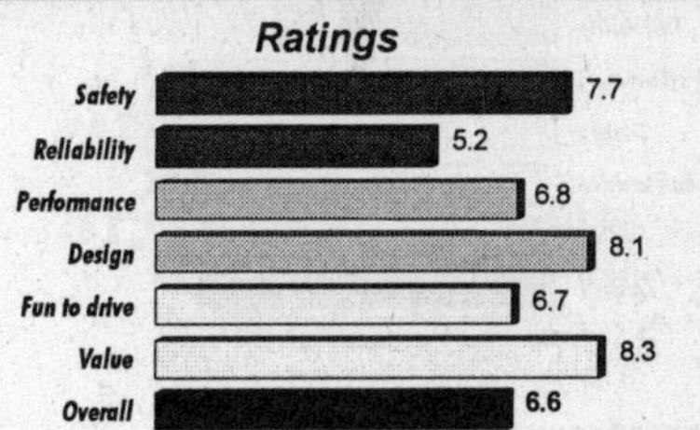

FWD/AT/PS/AC

Model/Body/Type	BaseList	Whlse	Retail
4 Dr Sdn	20875	**8975**	**11050**

ADD FOR 91 NEW YORKER 5TH AVE:
ABS +315 · *Car Phone +135* · *Custom Whls/Cvrs +160* · *Infinity Ster Sys +135* · *Mark Cross Pkg +800* · *Pwr Sunroof +390*

NEW YORKER SALON V6 1991

FWD/AT/PS/AC

Model/Body/Type	BaseList	Whlse	Retail
4 Dr Sdn	17899	**7575**	**9625**

ADD FOR 91 NEW YORKER SALON:
ABS +315 · *Car Phone +135* · *Custom Whls/Cvrs +160* · *Infinity Ster Sys +135* · *Leather Seats +195* · *Pwr Sunroof +390*

TOWN & COUNTRY V6 1991

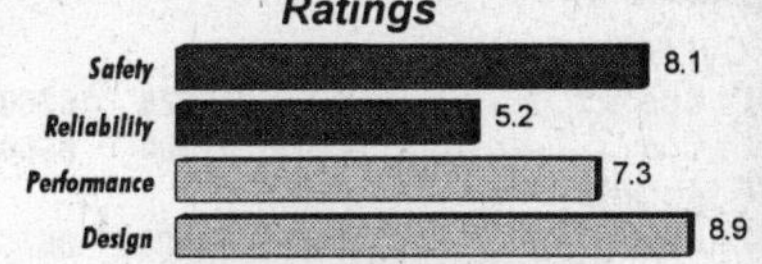
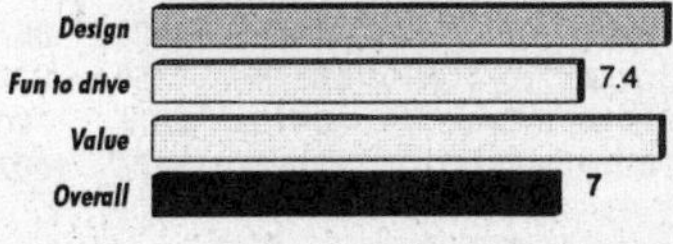

FWD/AT/PS/AC

Model/Body/Type	BaseList	Whlse	Retail
Wgn	25905	**13225**	**15950**

ADD FOR 91 TOWN & COUNTRY:
AC-Rear +250 · *Air Bag +230* · *Running Boards +145* · *Sunroof-Manual +80*

1990 CHRYSLER

IMPERIAL V6 1990

Ratings

Rating	Score
Safety	7.7
Reliability	5.2
Performance	6.8
Design	8.1
Fun to drive	6.7
Value	8.3
Overall	6.6

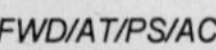

FWD/AT/PS/AC

Model/Body/Type	BaseList	Whlse	Retail
4 Dr Sdn	25495	**8450**	**10675**

ADD FOR 90 IMPERIAL:

Infinity Ster Sys +135 *Leather Seats +160*

LE BARON COUPE/CONV 1990

Ratings

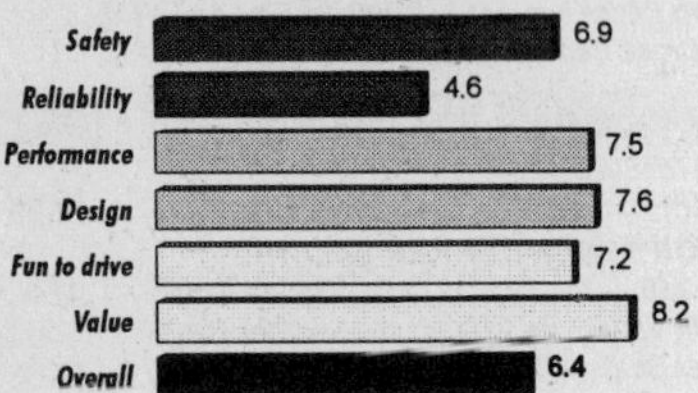

FWD/AT/PS/AC

Model/Body/Type	BaseList	Whlse	Retail
4 Cyl Models			
2 Dr Cpe	12495	**4675**	**6250**
2 Dr Conv	14995	**7000**	**8800**
V6 Models			
2 Dr Cpe	13175	**5025**	**6675**
2 Dr Conv	15675	**7350**	**9225**
2 Dr Premium Cpe	16415	**5875**	**7600**
2 Dr Premium Conv	19595	**8175**	**10075**

ADD FOR 90 LE BARON COUPE/CONV:

4 Cyl Turbo Eng +195 *Cass(Std PremCnv) +60*
CD Player +115
Cruise Ctrl(Std PremCnv) +75
Custom Paint +25 *Custom Whls/Cvrs +115*
GTC Pkg +1035 *GTC Turbo Pkg +1585*
Leather Seats +115 *Pwr Dr Lks(Std Prem) +60*
Pwr Seat +75 *Sunroof +115*
Tilt Whl(Std PremCnv) +60

DEDUCT FOR 90 LE BARON COUPE/CONV:

No AC -430 *No Auto Trans -390*

LE BARON SEDAN V6 1990

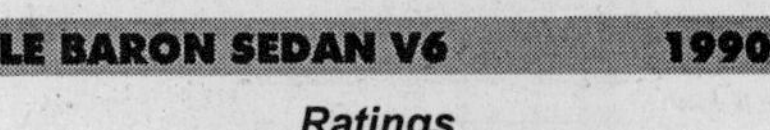

Ratings

Rating	Score
Safety	7.5
Reliability	6.3
Performance	7.4
Design	7.9
Fun to drive	7.4
Value	8.3
Overall	7.1

FWD/AT/PS/AC

Model/Body/Type	BaseList	Whlse	Retail
4 Dr Sdn	15995	**5975**	**7700**

ADD FOR 90 LE BARON SEDAN:

Custom Whls/Cvrs +115 *Leather Seats +115*
Pwr Locks +60 *Pwr Seat +75*
Pwr Wndw +75

NEW YORKER V6 1990

Ratings

FWD/AT/PS/AC

Model/Body/Type	BaseList	Whlse	Retail
4 Dr Salon Sdn	16342	**6125**	**7975**
4 Dr Landau Sdn	19080	**7050**	**9025**

ADD FOR 90 NEW YORKER:

ABS +275 *Custom Whls/Cvrs +115*
Infinity Ster Sys +115 *Mark Cross Pkg +680*
Pwr Sunroof +350

NEW YORKER 5TH AVENUE V6 1990

FWD/AT/PS/AC

Model/Body/Type	BaseList	Whlse	Retail
4 Dr Sdn	20860	**7200**	**9200**

ADD FOR 90 NEW YORKER 5TH AVENUE:
ABS +275 *Custom Whls/Cvrs +115*
Infinity Ster Sys +115 *Mark Cross Pkg +680*
Pwr Sunroof +350

TOWN & COUNTRY V6 1990

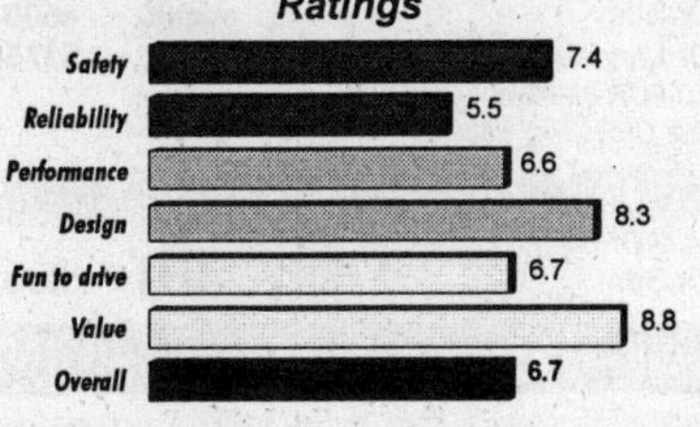

FWD/AT/PS/AC

Model/Body/Type	BaseList	Whlse	Retail
Wgn	25000	10650	13150

1989 CHRYSLER

CONQUEST 4 Cyl Turbo 1989

AT/PS/AC

Model/Body/Type	BaseList	Whlse	Retail
2 Dr TSi Hbk	18974	**4275**	**5825**

ADD FOR 89 CONQUEST:
Leather Seats +115 *Sunroof +115*
DEDUCT FOR 89 CONQUEST:
No AC -430 *No Auto Trans -230*

FIFTH AVENUE V8 1989

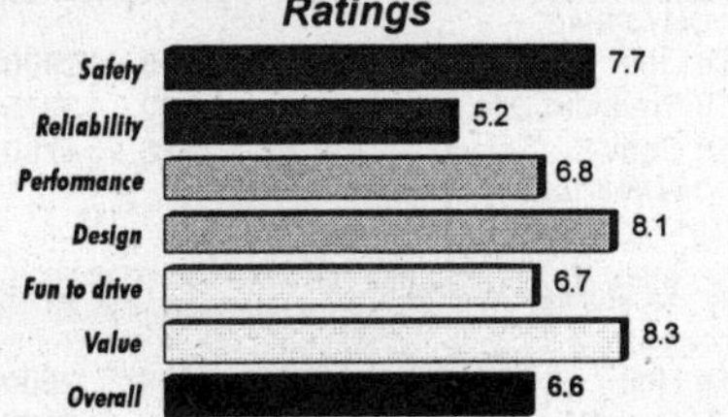

FWD/AT/PS/AC

Model/Body/Type	BaseList	Whlse	Retail
4 Dr Sdn	18345	**4075**	**5725**

ADD FOR 89 FIFTH AVENUE:
Custom Whls/Cvrs +75 *Leather Seats +115*
Pwr Sunroof +290

LE BARON 4 Cyl 1989

FWD/AT/PS/AC

Model/Body/Type	BaseList	Whlse	Retail
4 Dr Lbk	11495	**3475**	**4875**
4 Dr Premium Lbk	13495	**4025**	**5550**
4 Dr GTS Turbo Lbk	17095	**5150**	**6850**

ADD FOR 89 LE BARON:
4 Cyl Turbo Eng +175 *Cass(Std GTS) +35*
Cruise Ctrl(Std GTS) +60 *Custom Whls/Cvrs +75*
Leather Seats +75
Pwr Locks(Std Prem,GTS) +35
Pwr Seat +60 *Pwr Sunroof +250*
Pwr Wndw(Std GTS) +60
Tilt Whl(Std GTS) +35
DEDUCT FOR 89 LE BARON:
No AC -390 *No Auto Trans -350*

LE BARON COUPE/CONV 4 Cyl 1989

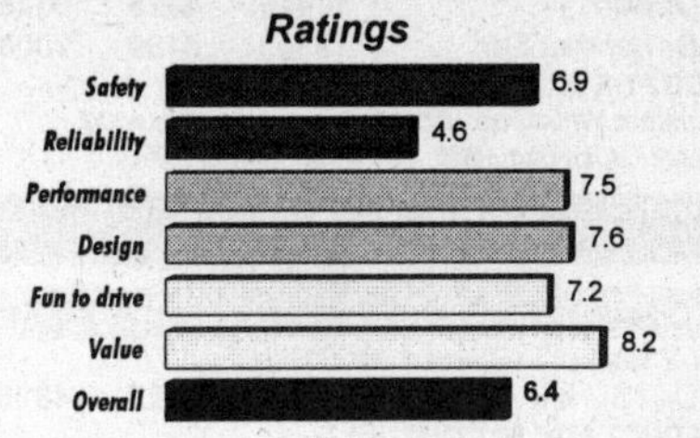

FWD/AT/PS/AC

Model/Body/Type	BaseList	Whlse	Retail
2 Dr Cpe	11495	**3300**	**4725**
2 Dr Conv	13995	**5200**	**6900**
2 Dr Premium Cpe	14695	**4025**	**5550**
2 Dr Premium Conv	18195	**5950**	**7675**

ADD FOR 89 LE BARON COUPE/CONV:
4 Cyl Turbo Eng +175 *Cass(Std PremCnv) +35*
CD Player +75
Cruise Ctrl(Std Prem Cnv) +60
Custom Whls/Cvrs +75 *GT Turbo Pkg +835*
GTC Turbo Pkg +1310 *Leather Seats +75*
Pwr Dr Lks(Std Prem) +35 *Pwr Seat(Std PremCnv) +60*
Pwr Wndw(Std Cnv) +60 *Sunroof +100*
Tilt Whl(Std PremCnv) +35
DEDUCT FOR 89 LE BARON COUPE/CONV:
No AC -390 *No Auto Trans -350*

CHRYSLER 89-87

Model/Body/Type	BaseList	Whlse	Retail

NEW YORKER V6 — 1989

Ratings

Rating	Score
Safety	7.7
Reliability	5.2
Performance	6.8
Design	8.1
Fun to drive	6.7
Value	8.3
Overall	6.6

FWD/AT/PS/AC

Model/Body/Type	BaseList	Whlse	Retail
4 Dr Sdn	17416	**4325**	**6025**
4 Dr Landau Sdn	19509	**5150**	**7000**

ADD FOR 89 NEW YORKER:
Custom Whls/Cvrs +75 *Infinity Ster Sys +100*
Mark Cross Pkg +585 *Pwr Sunroof +290*

1988 CHRYSLER

CONQUEST 4 Cyl Turbo — 1988

AT/PS/AC

Model/Body/Type	BaseList	Whlse	Retail
2 Dr TSi Hbk	18155	**3225**	**4625**

DEDUCT FOR 88 CONQUEST:
No AC -370 *No Auto Trans -195*

FIFTH AVENUE V8 — 1988

AT/PS/AC

Model/Body/Type	BaseList	Whlse	Retail
4 Dr Sdn	17243	**3050**	**4550**

LE BARON 4 Cyl — 1988

FWD/AT/PS/AC

Model/Body/Type	BaseList	Whlse	Retail
4 Dr Sdn	11286	**2200**	**3375**
4 Dr Town & Cntry Wgn	12889	**2900**	**4250**

ADD FOR 88 LE BARON:
4 Cyl Turbo Eng +160
DEDUCT FOR 88 LE BARON:
No AC -330

LE BARON COUPE/CONV 4 Cyl 1988

FWD/AT/PS/AC

Model/Body/Type	BaseList	Whlse	Retail
2 Dr Cpe	11473	**2200**	**3375**
2 Dr Conv	13959	**3800**	**5275**
2 Dr Premium Cpe	13830	**2750**	**4025**
2 Dr Premium Conv	18079	**4375**	**5925**

ADD FOR 88 LE BARON COUPE/CONV:
4 Cyl Turbo Eng +160
DEDUCT FOR 88 LE BARON COUPE/CONV:
No AC -330 *No Auto Trans -290*

LE BARON GTS 4 Cyl — 1988

FWD/AT/PS/AC

Model/Body/Type	BaseList	Whlse	Retail
4 Dr Hbk	12971	**2200**	**3375**

ADD FOR 88 LE BARON GTS:
4 Cyl Turbo Eng +160
DEDUCT FOR 88 LE BARON GTS:
No AC -330 *No Auto Trans -290*

NEW YORKER V6 — 1988

FWD/AT/PS/AC

Model/Body/Type	BaseList	Whlse	Retail
4 Dr Sdn	17416	**3000**	**4500**
4 Dr Landau Sdn	19509	**3775**	**5375**

ADD FOR 88 NEW YORKER:
Mark Cross Pkg +530

NEW YORKER TURBO 4 Cyl — 1988

FWD/AT/PS/AC

Model/Body/Type	BaseList	Whlse	Retail
4 Dr Sdn	17373	**2625**	**3975**

1987 CHRYSLER

CONQUEST 4 Cyl Turbo — 1987

AT/PS/AC

Model/Body/Type	BaseList	Whlse	Retail
2 Dr Hbk	14417	**2250**	**3425**

ADD FOR 87 CONQUEST:
TSi Intercooler +175

FIFTH AVENUE V8 — 1987

AT/PS/AC

Model/Body/Type	BaseList	Whlse	Retail
4 Dr Sdn	15666	**2200**	**3475**

LE BARON 4 Cyl — 1987

FWD/AT/PS/AC

Model/Body/Type	BaseList	Whlse	Retail
4 Dr Sdn	10707	**1575**	**2650**
4 Dr Town & Cntry Wgn	12019	**2200**	**3375**

ADD FOR 87 LE BARON:
4 Cyl Turbo Eng +135

LE BARON COUPE/CONV 4 Cyl 1987

FWD/AT/PS/AC

Model/Body/Type	BaseList	Whlse	Retail
2 Dr Cpe	11295	**1775**	**2900**
2 Dr Premium Cpe	12288	**2200**	**3375**
2 Dr Conv	13974	**3275**	**4700**

ADD FOR 87 LE BARON COUPE/CONV:
4 Cyl Turbo Eng +135

LE BARON GTS 4 Cyl — 1987

FWD/AT/PS/AC

Model/Body/Type	BaseList	Whlse	Retail
4 Dr Hbk	9774	**1450**	**2500**
4 Dr Prem Hbk	11389	**1775**	**2925**

ADD FOR 87 LE BARON GTS:
4 Cyl Turbo Eng +135

NEW YORKER 4 Cyl — 1987

FWD/AT/PS/AC

Model/Body/Type	BaseList	Whlse	Retail
4 Dr Sdn	14193	**2075**	**3300**

ADD FOR 87 NEW YORKER:
4 Cyl Turbo Eng +135

Model/Body/Type	BaseList	Whlse	Retail
1986 CHRYSLER			
FIFTH AVENUE 1986			
4 Dr Sdn	14717	2025	3225
LASER 1986			
FWD			
2 Dr Hbk	9398	1050	2075
2 Dr XE Hbk	11486	1375	2475
LE BARON 1986			
FWD			
4 Dr Sdn	9992	1150	2175
2 Dr Cpe	9842	1075	2100
2 Dr Conv	12593	2000	3175
2 Dr Mark Cross Conv	16619	2400	3650
LE BARON GTS 1986			
FWD			
4 Dr Hbk	9683	1075	2100
4 Dr Premium Hbk	11365	1325	2400
LE BARON TOWN & COUNTRY 1986			
FWD			
4 Dr Wgn	11235	1675	2800
2 Dr Mark Cross Conv	17606	3025	4350
NEW YORKER 1986			
FWD			
4 Dr Sdn	13465	1700	2850

Model/Body/Type	BaseList	Whlse	Retail
1985 CHRYSLER			
FIFTH AVENUE 1985			
4 Dr Sdn	13978	1675	2800
LASER 1985			
FWD			
2 Dr Hbk	8854	825	1775
2 Dr XE Hbk	10776	1075	2100
LE BARON 1985			
FWD			
4 Dr Sdn	9309	975	2000
2 Dr Cpe	9460	900	1900
2 Dr Conv	11889	1775	2950
2 Dr Mark Cross Conv	15994	2175	3350
LE BARON GTS 1985			
FWD			
4 Dr Hbk	9024	900	1875
4 Dr Premium Hbk	9970	1125	2175
LE BARON TOWN & COUNTRY 1985			
FWD			
4 Dr Wgn	10363	1450	2550
2 Dr Mark Cross Conv	16994	2675	3975
NEW YORKER 1985			
FWD			
4 Dr Sdn	12865	1525	2625

Model/Body/Type	BaseList	Whlse	Retail

DAIHATSU Japan

1992 Daihatsu Rocky

For a dealer in your area, see our Dealer Directory (pg 217)

1992 DAIHATSU

CHARADE			1992
FWD/PS/AC			
3 Cyl Models			
2 Dr SE Hbk	6797	3900	5250
4 Cyl Models			
4 Dr SE Sdn	8797	4400	5825
4 Dr SX Sdn (auto)	9997	5025	6550

ROCKY 4 Cyl			1992
4WD/PS/AC			
SE Utility Conv	11697	8025	9875
SE Utility Hardtop	12497	8175	10000
SX Utility Hardtop	13497	8725	10600

ADD FOR ALL 92 DAIHATSU:
4 Cyl Eng(Hbk) +275
Auto Trans(Std Charade SX) +390
Cass +60
Off Road Pkg +175

DEDUCT FOR ALL 92 DAIHATSU:
No AC -430
No Pwr Steering -135

1991 DAIHATSU

CHARADE			1991
FWD/PS/AC			
3 Cyl Models			
2 Dr SE Hbk	6397	3000	4250
4 Cyl Models			
4 Dr SE Sdn	8497	3350	4700
4 Dr SX Sdn(auto)	9697	3950	5300

ROCKY 4 Cyl			1991
4WD/PS/AC			
SE Utility Conv	11297	7000	8725
SE Utility Hardtop	12097	7125	8875
SX Utility Hardtop	12997	7475	9275

ADD FOR ALL 91 DAIHATSU:
4 Cyl Eng(Hbk) +230
Auto Trans(Std Charade SX) +350
Cass +35
Off Road Pkg +135

DEDUCT FOR ALL 91 DAIHATSU:
No AC -390
No Pwr Steering -115

1990 DAIHATSU

CHARADE			1990
FWD/PS/AC			
3 Cyl Models			
2 Dr SE Hbk	6497	2225	3325
2 Dr SX Hbk	6997	2475	3625
4 Cyl Models			
4 Dr SE Sdn	7997	2600	3750
4 Dr SX Sdn	8697	2875	4125

ROCKY 4 Cyl			1990
4WD/PS/AC			
SE Utility Conv	10897	5425	7000
SX Utility Conv	11597	5725	7275
SE Utility Hardtop	11697	5600	7150
SX Utility Hardtop	12497	5875	7450

ADD FOR ALL 90 DAIHATSU:
4 Cyl Eng(Hbk) +175
Auto Trans +315
Cass +35
Off Road Pkg +75

DEDUCT FOR ALL 90 DAIHATSU:
No AC -350
No Pwr Steering -100

1989 DAIHATSU

CHARADE 3 Cyl 1989

FWD/PS/AC

Model/Body/Type	BaseList	Whlse	Retail
2 Dr CES Hbk	6197	**1375**	**2325**
2 Dr CLS Hbk	6697	**1625**	**2600**
2 Dr CLX Hbk	7497	**1800**	**2850**

ADD FOR ALL 89 DAIHATSU:
4 Cyl Eng +160
Auto Trans +275
Cass +25

DEDUCT FOR ALL 89 DAIHATSU:
No AC -315
No Pwr Steering -75

1988 DAIHATSU

CHARADE 3 Cyl 1988

FWD/AC

Model/Body/Type	BaseList	Whlse	Retail
2 Dr CLS Hbk	6397	**1000**	**1900**
2 Dr CLX Hbk	7650	**1200**	**2125**
2 Dr CSX Hbk	9232	**1400**	**2350**

ADD FOR ALL 88 DAIHATSU:
Cass(Std CSX) +25

DEDUCT FOR ALL 88 DAIHATSU:
No AC -250

Model/Body/Type	BaseList	Whlse	Retail

DODGE

USA

1990 Dodge Caravan

For a Dodge dealer in your area, see our Dealer Directory (pg 217)

1994 DODGE

B-SERIES RAM VANS V8 — 1994

Ratings

Rating	Score
Safety	6.6
Reliability	5.6
Performance	6.1
Design	6.6
Fun to drive	5.5
Value	8.2
Overall	6.1

AT/PS/AC

Model/Body/Type	BaseList	Whlse	Retail
B150 Van 1/2 Ton			
Wagon	14491	**14425**	**17200**
Van	12951	**13025**	**15725**
B250 Van 3/4 Ton			
Wagon	18260	**14875**	**17700**
Maxiwagon	19546	**15575**	**18450**
Van	15911	**13325**	**16050**
Maxivan	17266	**14225**	**17000**
B350 Van 1 Ton			
Wagon	19548	**15225**	**18650**
Maxiwagon	20565	**15925**	**19400**
Van	17559	**13875**	**17175**
Maxivan	18524	**14550**	**17900**

ADD FOR 94 B150/B250/B350 VAN:
LE Pkg +955 *4 Wheel ABS +430*
DEDUCT FOR 93 B150/B250/B350 VAN:
V6 Eng -590
REFER TO 94 DODGE TRUCK OPTIONS TABLE Pg102

BR-SERIES RAM PICKUPS V8 — 1994

AT/PS/AC

Model/Body/Type	BaseList	Whlse	Retail
BR1500 Pickup 1/2 Ton			
Sweptline S 6 1/2' (V6)	11824	-	-
Sweptline S 8' (V6)	12096	-	-
Sweptline 6 1/2'	14389	**14775**	**17600**
Sweptline 8'	14661	**14875**	**17700**
BR2500 Pickup 3/4 Ton			
Sweptline 8'	15916	**15725**	**18600**
Heavy Duty 8'	17102	-	-
BR3500 Pickup 1 Ton			
Sweptline 8'	18417	-	-

ADD FOR 94 BR1500/BR2500/BR3500 PICKUP:
4 Wheel ABS +430
6 Cyl 5.9L Trb Dsl Eng +1820
Laramie SLT Pkg +775 *ST Pkg +230*
DEDUCT FOR 94 BR1500/BR2500/BR3500 PICKUP:
V6 Eng -590
REFER TO 94 DODGE TRUCK OPTIONS TABLE Pg102

CARAVAN V6 — 1994

FWD/AT/PS/AC

Model/Body/Type	BaseList	Whlse	Retail
Caravan C/V	14412	-	-
Extended Caravan C/V	16866	-	-
Caravan	14919	**14275**	**17025**
Caravan SE	18139	**15375**	**18225**
Caravan LE	21963	**16575**	**19600**
Grand Caravan	18178	**15600**	**18475**
Grand Caravan SE	19304	**16450**	**19375**
Grand Caravan LE	22883	**17600**	**20725**

ADD FOR 94 CARAVAN:
4 Wheel ABS +4320 *All Wheel Drive +1275*
ES Pkg +500
DEDUCT FOR 94 CARAVAN:
4 Cyl Eng -545
REFER TO 94 DODGE TRUCK OPTIONS TABLE Pg102

COLT 4 Cyl — 1994

FWD/AT/PS/AC

Model/Body/Type	BaseList	Whlse	Retail
2 Dr Cpe (5 spd)	9120	-	-
4 Dr Sdn	11428	-	-
2 Dr ES Cpe	10060	-	-
4 Dr ES Sdn	12181	-	-

Model/Body/Type	BaseList	Whlse	Retail

DAKOTA V6 1/2 Ton — 1994

AT/PS/AC

Model/Body/Type	BaseList	Whlse	Retail
Sweptline S 6 1/2'	9560	-	-
Sweptline S 8'	11085	-	-
Sweptline 6 1/2'	11432	**10450**	**12850**
Sweptline 8'	12282	**10575**	**12950**
Sweptline Sport 6 1/2'	10742	**10150**	**12525**
Club Cab 6 1/2'	11275	**12075**	**14750**
Club Cab Sport 6 1/2'	14042	**11800**	**14450**

ADD FOR 94 DAKOTA:

4 Wheel ABS +430 *SLT Pkg +410*
V8 Eng +590

DEDUCT FOR 94 DAKOTA:

4 Cyl Eng -545

REFER TO 94 DODGE TRUCK OPTIONS TABLE Pg102

INTREPID V6 — 1994

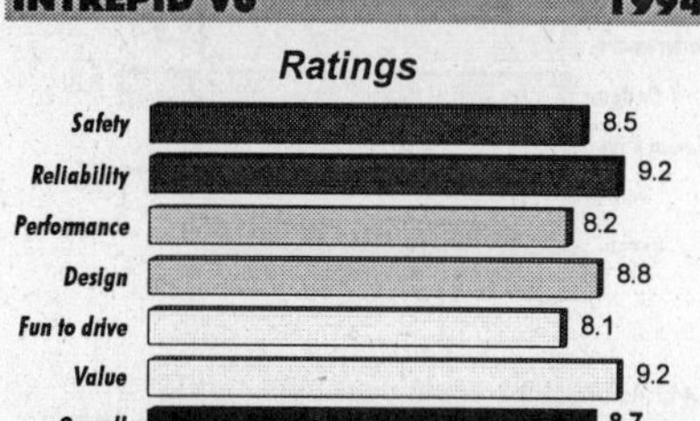

FWD/AT/PS/AC

Model/Body/Type	BaseList	Whlse	Retail
4 Dr Sdn	17251	**15075**	**17825**
4 Dr ES Sdn	19191	**17200**	**20225**

ADD FOR 94 INTREPID:

3.5L V6 Eng +365 *ABS +430*
Anti-Theft/Recovery Sys +365 *Car Phone +230*
Cass(Std ES) +135 *CD Player +275*
Cruise Ctrl(Std ES) +180 *Custom Whls/Cvrs +230*
Infinity Ster Sys +230 *Leather Seats +320*
Pwr Locks +135 *Pwr Seat +180*
Pwr Sunroof +590 *Pwr Wndw +180*

SHADOW 4 Cyl — 1994

Ratings

Rating	Score
Safety	6.7
Reliability	6.1
Performance	7.1
Design	7.5
Fun to drive	6.9
Value	7.6
Overall	6.7

FWD/AT/PS/AC

Model/Body/Type	BaseList	Whlse	Retail
4 Dr Hbk	9206	**8250**	**10100**
2 Dr Hbk	8806	**8150**	**9975**
4 Dr ES Hbk	10652	**9500**	**11450**
2 Dr ES Hbk	10252	**9400**	**11325**

ADD FOR 94 SHADOW:

ABS +430
Anti-Theft/Recovery Sys +365
Cass +90 *CD Player +205*
Cruise Ctrl +135 *Custom Whls/Cvrs +180*
Pwr Locks +90 *Pwr Seat +135*
Pwr Wndw +135 *Sunroof +275*
Tilt Whl +90 *V6 Eng +455*

DEDUCT FOR 94 SHADOW:

No AC -590 *No Auto Trans -500*

SPIRIT — 1994

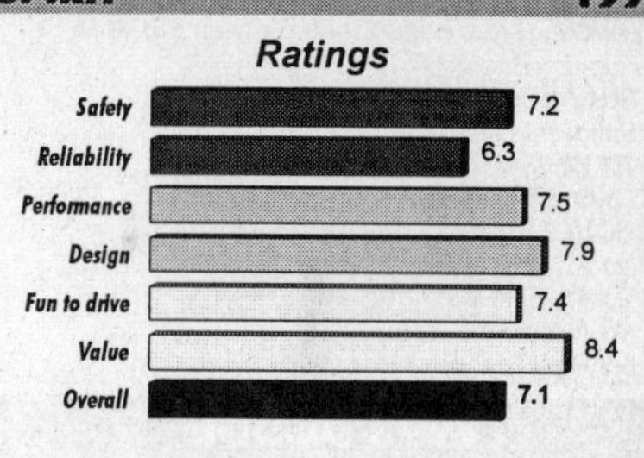

FWD/AT/PS/AC

Model/Body/Type	BaseList	Whlse	Retail
4 Cyl Models			
4 Dr Sdn	12470	**9250**	**11275**
V6 Models			
4 Dr Sdn	13195	**9825**	**12000**

ADD FOR 94 SPIRIT:

ABS +430
Anti-Theft/Recovery Sys +365
Cass +115 *Custom Whls/Cvrs +205*
Pwr Locks +115 *Pwr Seat +160*
Pwr Wndw +160

STEALTH V6 — 1994

FWD/AT/PS/AC

Model/Body/Type	BaseList	Whlse	Retail
2 Dr Lbk	20935	-	-
2 Dr R/T Lbk	23680	-	-
2 Dr R/T Turb 4WD Lbk (6 spd)	37512	-	-

See the Automobile Dealer Directory on page 379 for a Dealer near you!

DODGE

DODGE 94-93

Model/Body/Type	BaseList	Whlse	Retail

94 DODGE TRUCK OPTIONS TABLE

ADD FOR ALL 94 DODGE TRUCKS:

15 Pass Seating +375
4-Whl Drive +1265
AC-Rear +375
Bed Liner +125
Cass(Std B150/250LE,CrvnSE/LE/ES,Dak LE) +105
CD Player +205
Cruise Ctrl(Std Caravan LE/ES) +125
Custom Whls +145
Dual Rear Whls +415
Fiberglass Cap +250
Leather Seats +250
Luggage Rack(Std Caravan LE) +80
Privacy Glass(Std B150/250LE,Caravan ES) +145
Pwr Locks(Std B150/250LE,Caravan LE) +105
Pwr Seats(Std Caravan ES) +125
Pwr Wndw(Std B150/250LE,Caravan ES) +145
Running Boards +145
Slider Wndw(Std Dakota LE) +80
Sunroof-Manual +145
Tilt Whl(Std Caravan SE/LE/ES) +105
Towing Pkg +185

DEDUCT FOR ALL 94 DODGE TRUCKS

No AC -435
No AM/FM Radio -105
No Auto Trans -415
No Pwr Steering -185

1993 DODGE

B150/B250/B350 VANS V8 — 1993

Ratings

Safety	6.6
Reliability	5.6
Performance	6.1
Design	6.6
Fun to drive	5.5
Value	8.2
Overall	6.1

AT/PS/AC

Model/Body/Type	BaseList	Whlse	Retail
B150 Van 1/2 Ton			
Wagon	16160	**13100**	**15800**
Van	14564	**11775**	**14425**
B250 Van 3/4 Ton			
Wagon	17662	**13525**	**16250**
Maxiwagon	18948	**14175**	**16950**
Van	15112	**12025**	**14650**
Maxivan	16793	**12825**	**15525**
B350 Van 1 Ton			
Wagon	18950	**13875**	**17175**
Maxiwagon	19967	**14525**	**17850**
Van	17086	**12525**	**15750**
Maxivan	18051	**13175**	**16450**

ADD FOR 93 B150/B250/B350 VAN:

LE Pkg +745

DEDUCT FOR 93 B150/B250/B350 VAN:

V6 Eng -470

REFER TO 93 DODGE TRUCK OPTIONS TABLE Pg106

CARAVAN V6 — 1993

Ratings

Safety	8.1
Reliability	5.2
Performance	7.3
Design	8.9
Fun to drive	7.4
Value	8.8
Overall	7

FWD/AT/PS/AC

Model/Body/Type	BaseList	Whlse	Retail
Caravan C/V	13566	**10800**	**13300**
Extended Caravan C/V	16020	**11800**	**14475**
Caravan	14073	**12025**	**14675**
Caravan SE	16101	**13075**	**15775**
Caravan LE	20841	**14175**	**16950**
Grand Caravan	17555	**13275**	**16000**
Grand Caravan SE	17935	**14100**	**16875**
Grand Caravan LE	21784	**15150**	**18000**

ADD FOR 93 CARAVAN:

ABS +390 *ES Pkg +390*

DEDUCT FOR 93 CARAVAN:

4 Cyl Eng -430

REFER TO 93 DODGE TRUCK OPTIONS TABLE Pg106

COLT 4 Cyl — 1993

Ratings

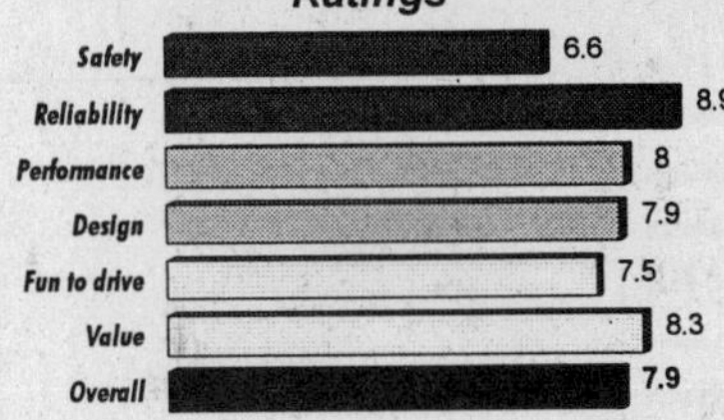

DODGE

Model/Body/Type	BaseList	Whlse	Retail
FWD/AT/PS/AC			
2 Dr Cpe	7806	**5725**	**7250**
4 Dr Sdn	9448	**7175**	**8950**
2 Dr GL Cpe	8705	**6650**	**8275**
4 Dr GL Sdn	10423	**7775**	**9625**

ADD FOR 93 COLT:
ABS +390 *Cass +75*
Cruise Ctrl +115 *Custom Whls/Cvrs +160*
Pwr Locks +75 *Pwr Wndw +115*
Tilt Whl +75

DEDUCT FOR 93 COLT:
No AC -430 *No Auto Trans -390*
No Pwr Steering -135

D-SERIES PICKUPS V8 1993

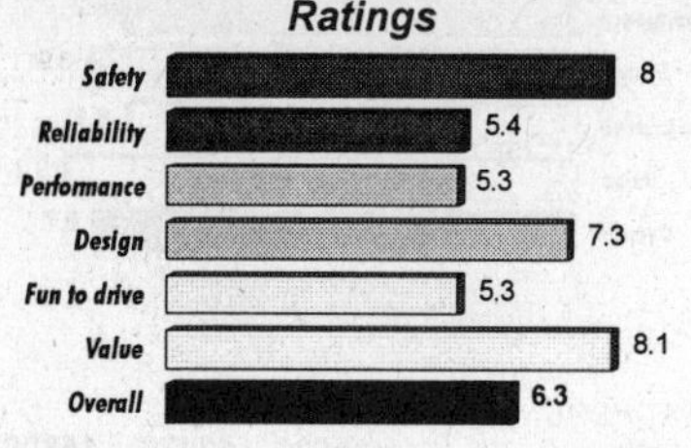

Model/Body/Type	BaseList	Whlse	Retail
AT/PS/AC			
D150 Pickup 1/2 Ton			
Sweptline 6 1/2'	13733	**10300**	**12675**
Sweptline 8'	13950	**10400**	**12775**
Club Cab 6 1/2'	15815	**11950**	**14575**
Club Cab 8'	16034	**12025**	**14675**
D250 Pickup 3/4 Ton			
Sweptline 8'	15010	**11150**	**13675**
Club Cab 8'	17175	**12775**	**15450**
D350 Pickup 1 Ton			
Sweptline 8'	15876	**11700**	**14825**
Club Cab 8' (Diesel)	22060	**14775**	**18175**

ADD FOR 93 D-SERIES PICKUPS:
5.8L Turbo Diesel Eng +1090

DEDUCT FOR 93 D-SERIES PICKUP:
V6 Eng -470

REFER TO 93 DODGE TRUCK OPTIONS TABLE Pg106

DAKOTA V6 1/2 Ton 1993

Ratings

Rating	Score
Safety	6.9
Reliability	6.4
Performance	6.7
Design	8.4
Fun to drive	6.6
Value	8.3
Overall	6.9

Model/Body/Type	BaseList	Whlse	Retail
AT/PS/AC			
Sweptline S 6 1/2' (4 cyl,5 spd)	9154	**7975**	**10050**
Sweptline 6 1/2'	11162	**9250**	**11475**
Sweptline 8'	11345	**9350**	**11575**
Sweptline Sport 6 1/2'	9943	**9025**	**11225**
Club Cab 6 1/2'	12414	**10575**	**12975**

ADD FOR 93 DAKOTA:
LE Pkg +625 *V8 Eng +470*

DEDUCT FOR 93 DAKOTA:
4 Cyl Eng -430

REFER TO 93 DODGE TRUCK OPTIONS TABLE Pg106

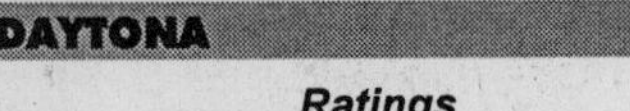

Ratings

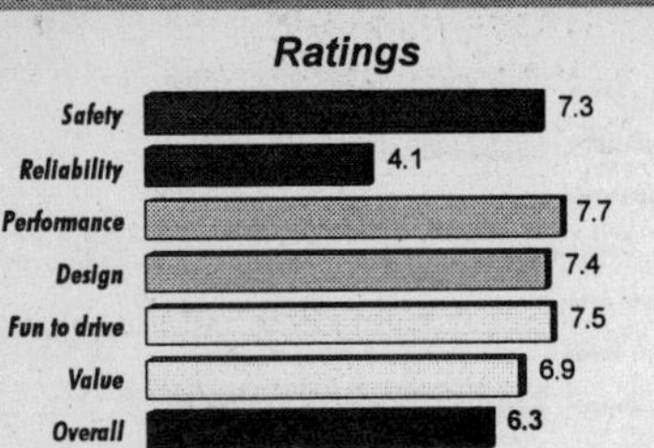

Model/Body/Type	BaseList	Whlse	Retail
FWD/AT/PS/AC			
4 Cyl Models			
2 Dr Hbk	10874	**8400**	**10300**
2 Dr ES Hbk	12018	**9300**	**11325**
V6 Models			
2 Dr Hbk	11568	**8950**	**10950**
2 Dr ES Hbk	12712	**9825**	**12000**
2 Dr IROC Hbk	13309	**10325**	**12550**

ADD FOR 93 DAYTONA:

ABS +390 | *Cass +100*
CD Player +195 | *Cruise Ctrl +135*
Custom Whls/Cvrs +175 | *Leather Seats +230*
Pwr Locks +100 | *Pwr Seat +135*
Pwr Wndw +135 | *R/T Trbo Pkg +170*
Sunroof +230 | *Tilt Whl +100*

DEDUCT FOR 93 DAYTONA:

No AC -545 | *No Auto Trans -430*

DYNASTY 1993

Ratings

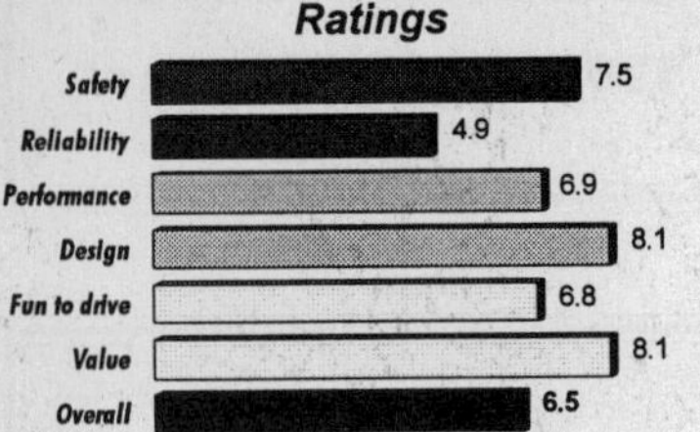

Model/Body/Type	BaseList	Whlse	Retail
FWD/AT/PS/AC			
4 Cyl Models			
4 Dr Sdn	14736	**8750**	**10825**
V6 Models			
4 Dr Sdn	15430	**9350**	**11475**
4 Dr LE Sdn	16267	**10125**	**12400**

ADD FOR 93 DYNASTY:

ABS +390 | *Car Phone +175*
Cass +115 | *Cruise Ctrl +160*
Custom Whls/Cvrs +195 | *Infinity Ster Sys +195*
Leather Seats +275 | *Pwr Locks +115*
Pwr Seat +160 | *Pwr Wndw +160*
Tilt Whl +115 | *Vinyl Roof +115*

DEDUCT FOR 93 DYNASTY:

No AC -585

INTREPID V6 1993

Ratings

Safety 8.5
Reliability 9.2
Performance 8.2
Design 8.8
Fun to drive 8.1
Value 9.2
Overall 8.7

Model/Body/Type	BaseList	Whlse	Retail
FWD/AT/PS/AC			
4 Dr Sdn	15930	**13175**	**15800**
4 Dr ES Sdn	17189	**14925**	**17675**

ADD FOR 93 INTREPID:

ABS +390 | *Car Phone +175*
Cass +115 | *CD Player +230*
Cruise Ctrl +160 | *Custom Whls/Cvrs +195*
Infinity Ster Sys +195 | *Leather Seats +275*
Pwr Locks +115 | *Pwr Seat +160*
Pwr Wndw +160

DEDUCT FOR 93 INTREPID:

No AC -585

RAM 50 4 Cyl 1/2 Ton 1993

Ratings

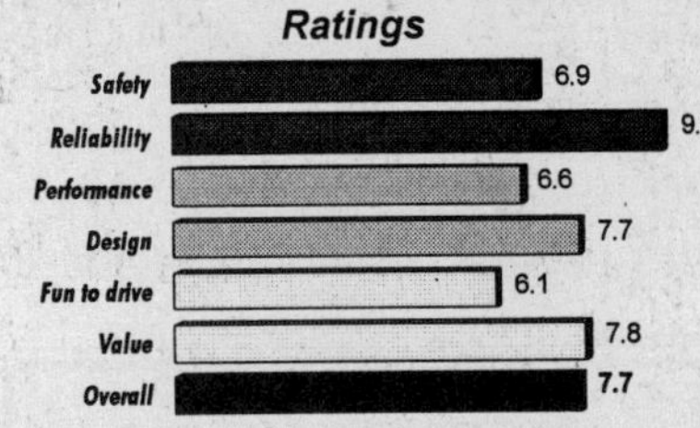

Model/Body/Type	BaseList	Whlse	Retail
AT/PS/AC			
LB Pkup	9432	**7525**	**9600**
Pkup	8865	**7650**	**9750**
SE Pkup	10035	**7975**	**10050**

REFER TO 93 DODGE TRUCK OPTIONS TABLE Pg106

RAMCHARGER V8 1/2 Ton 1993

AT/PS/AC

Model/Body/Type	BaseList	Whlse	Retail
2 Dr 150 S Utility	17636	**13050**	**15750**
2 Dr 150 S 4WD Utility	19985	**14675**	**17450**
2 Dr 150 Utility	19926	**14100**	**16875**
2 Dr 150 4WD Utility	21696	**15700**	**18575**

ADD FOR 93 RAMCHARGER:

Canyon Sport Pkg +700 *LE Pkg +585*

REFER TO 93 DODGE TRUCK OPTIONS TABLE Pg106

SHADOW 4 Cyl 1993

Ratings

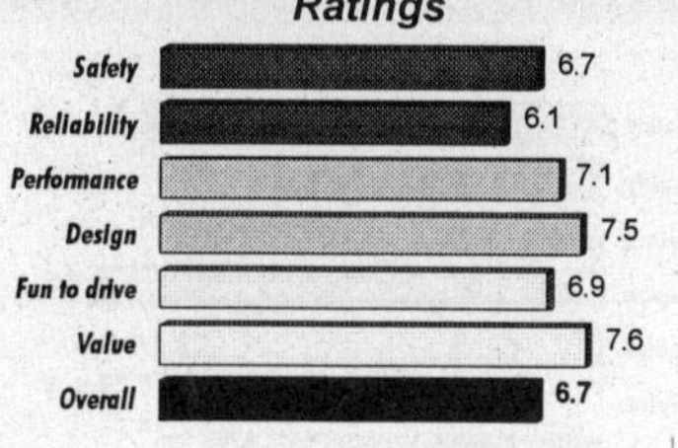

FWD/AT/PS/AC

Model/Body/Type	BaseList	Whlse	Retail
4 Dr Hbk	8797	**7000**	**8725**
2 Dr Hbk	8397	**6875**	**8600**
2 Dr Conv	14028	**10200**	**12300**
4 Dr ES Hbk	10204	**8125**	**9975**
2 Dr ES Hbk	9804	**8025**	**9875**
2 Dr ES Conv	14167	**11375**	**13700**

ADD FOR 93 SHADOW:

ABS +390 *Cass +75*
CD Player +175 *Cruise Ctrl +115*
Custom Whls/Cvrs +160 *Pwr Locks +75*
Pwr Seat +115 *Pwr Wndw(Std Cnv) +115*
Sunroof +195 *Tilt Whl +75*
V6 Eng +350

DEDUCT FOR 93 SHADOW:

No AC -470 *No Auto Trans -430*

SPIRIT 1993

Ratings

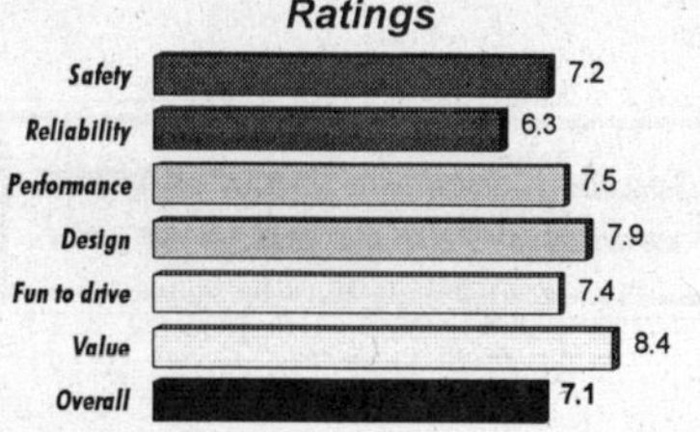

FWD/AT/PS/AC

Model/Body/Type	BaseList	Whlse	Retail
4 Cyl Models			
4 Dr Sdn	11941	**7900**	**9825**
4 Dr ES Sdn	14715	**9250**	**11275**
V6 Models			
4 Dr Sdn	12666	**8450**	**10350**
4 Dr ES Sdn	15440	**9800**	**11925**

ADD FOR 93 SPIRIT:

ABS +390 *Cass +100*
CD Player +195 *Cruise Ctrl(Std ES) +135*
Pwr Locks +100 *Pwr Seat +135*
Pwr Wndw +135 *Tilt Whl(Std ES) +100*

DEDUCT FOR 93 SPIRIT:

No AC -545 *No Auto Trans -505*

STEALTH V6 1993

Ratings

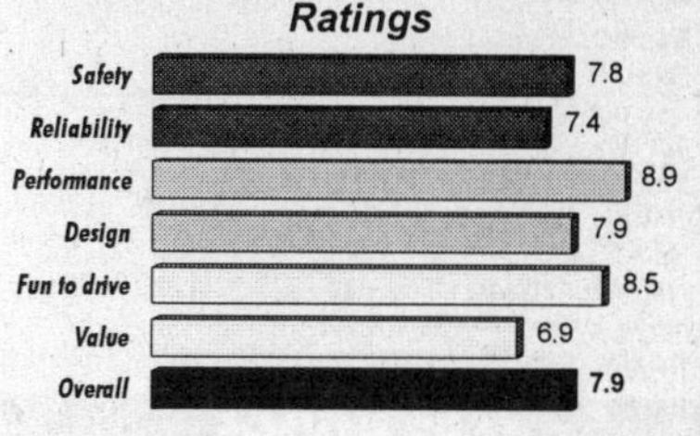

FWD/AT/PS/AC

Model/Body/Type	BaseList	Whlse	Retail
2 Dr Lbk	18506	**14675**	**17375**
2 Dr ES Lbk	20322	**15950**	**18750**
2 Dr R/T Lbk	27366	**19575**	**22750**
2 Dr R/T Turb AWD Lbk	33107	**22550**	**25925**

ADD FOR 93 STEALTH:

ABS(Std R/T) +390 *Car Phone +175*
Cass(Std R/T) +115 *CD Player +230*
CruiseCtrl(Std R/T) +160 *Custom Whls/Cvrs +195*
Leather Seats +275 *Pwr Dr Lks(Std R/T) +115*
Pwr Wndw(Std R/T) +160 *Sunroof +275*

DEDUCT FOR 93 STEALTH:

No AC -585 *No Auto Trans -545*

DODGE 93-92

93 DODGE TRUCK OPTIONS TABLE

ADD FOR ALL 93 DODGE TRUCKS:

15 Pass Seating +375
4-Whl Drive +1265
AC-Rear +375
Bed Liner +125
Cass(Std B150/250LE,CrvnSE/LE/ES,Dak LE) +105
CD Player +205
Cruise Ctrl(Std Caravan LE/ES) +125
Custom Whls(Std Ram50SE,RamchrgCynSpt) +145
Dual Rear Whls +415
Fiberglass Cap +250
Leather Seats +250
Luggage Rack(Std Caravan LE) +80
Privacy Glass(Std B150/250LE, Caravan ES,Ramcharger Cnyn Spt) +145
Pwr Locks(Std B150/250LE,Caravan LE) +105
Pwr Seats(Std Caravan ES) +125
Pwr Wndw(Std B150/250LE,Caravan ES) +145
Running Boards +145
Slider Wndw(Std Dakota LE) +80
Sunroof-Manual +145
Tilt Whl(Std Caravan SE/LE/ES) +105
Towing Pkg +185

DEDUCT FOR ALL 93 DODGE TRUCKS

No AC -435
No AM/FM Radio -105
No Auto Trans -415
No Pwr Steering -185

1992 DODGE

B150/B250/B350 VANS V8 — 1992

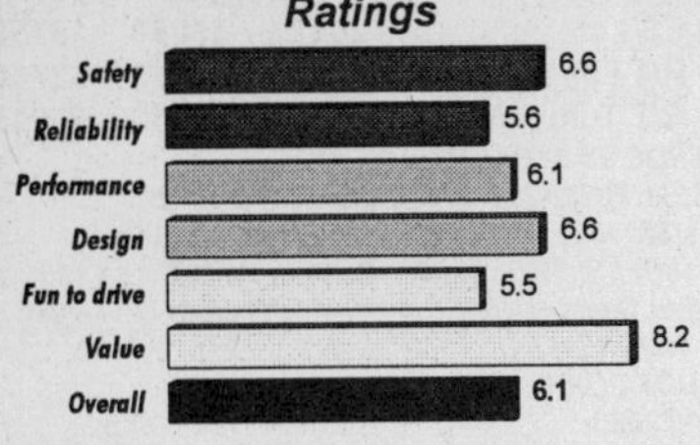

AT/PS/AC

Model/Body/Type	BaseList	Whlse	Retail
B150 Van 1/2 Ton			
Wagon	15167	**11475**	**14025**
Van	13779	**10150**	**12525**
B250 Van 3/4 Ton			
Wagon	16669	**11800**	**14475**
Maxiwagon	17955	**12375**	**15025**
Van	14077	**10350**	**12725**
Maxivan	16008	**11075**	**13600**
B350 Van 1 Ton			
Wagon	17957	**12100**	**15275**
Maxiwagon	19244	**12675**	**15900**
Van	15951	**10800**	**13850**
Maxivan	17266	**11375**	**14475**

ADD FOR 92 B150/B250/B350 VAN:

LE Pkg +535

DEDUCT FOR 92 B150/B250/B350 VAN:

V6 Eng -430

REFER TO 92 DODGE TRUCK OPTIONS TABLE Pg110

CARAVAN V6 — 1992

Ratings

Rating	Score
Safety	8.1
Reliability	5.2
Performance	7.3
Design	8.9
Fun to drive	7.4
Value	8.8
Overall	7

FWD/AT/PS/AC

Model/Body/Type	BaseList	Whlse	Retail
Caravan C/V	12820	**7800**	**9900**
Extended Caravan C/V	15209	**8775**	**10950**
Caravan	13706	**9000**	**11200**
Caravan SE	15679	**9975**	**12275**
Caravan LE	20102	**10875**	**13400**
Grand Caravan	17281	**10100**	**12425**
Grand Caravan SE	17511	**10900**	**13425**
Grand Caravan LE	20822	**11850**	**14500**

ADD FOR 92 CARAVAN:

ABS +350 *ES Pkg +315*

DEDUCT FOR 92 CARAVAN:

4 Cyl Eng -390

REFER TO 92 DODGE TRUCK OPTIONS TABLE Pg110

See the Automobile Dealer Directory on page 379 for a Dealer near you!

COLT 4 Cyl — 1992

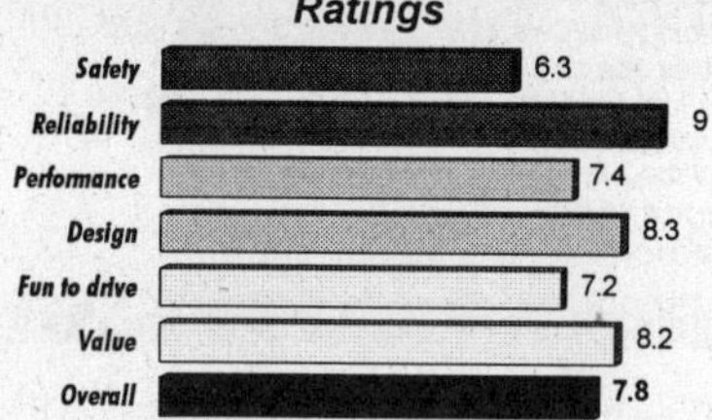

Model/Body/Type	BaseList	Whlse	Retail
FWD/AT/PS/AC			
3 Dr Hbk	7302	**3975**	**5325**
3 Dr GL Hbk	8122	**4650**	**6125**

ADD FOR 92 COLT:
Cass +60

DEDUCT FOR 92 COLT
No AC -390 *No Auto Trans -350*
No Pwr Steering -115

D-SERIES PICKUPS V8 — 1992

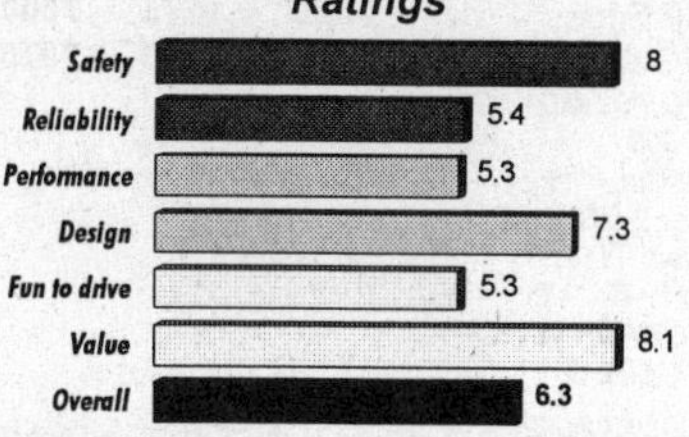

Model/Body/Type	BaseList	Whlse	Retail
AT/PS/AC			
D150 Pickup 1/2 Ton			
Sweptline 6 1/2'	13083	**9675**	**11950**
Sweptline 8'	13300	**9775**	**12025**
Club Cab 6 1/2'	15165	**11050**	**13575**
Club Cab 8'	15384	**11150**	**13675**
D250 Pickup 3/4 Ton			
Sweptline 8'	14241	**10300**	**12675**
Club Cab 8'	16925	**11750**	**14400**
D350 Pickup 1 Ton			
Sweptline 8'	15790	**10900**	**13950**
Club Cab 8' (Diesel)	21620	**13725**	**17000**

ADD FOR 92 D-SERIES PICKUP:
5.9L Turbo Diesel Eng +895

DEDUCT FOR 92 D-SERIES PICKUP:
V6 Eng -430

REFER TO 92 DODGE TRUCK OPTIONS TABLE Pg110

DAKOTA V6 1/2 Ton — 1992

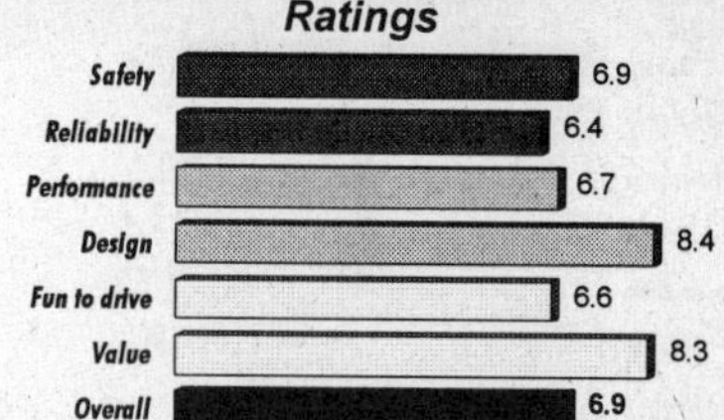

Model/Body/Type	BaseList	Whlse	Retail
AT/PS/AC			
Sweptline S 6 1/2' (4 cyl,5 spd)	8995	**7125**	**9150**
Sweptline 6 1/2'	10705	**8250**	**10325**
Sweptline 8'	10988	**8350**	**10425**
Club Cab 6 1/2'	11872	**9500**	**11725**

ADD FOR 92 DAKOTA:
LE Pkg +585 *V8 Eng +430*

DEDUCT FOR 92 DAKOTA:
4 Cyl Eng -390

REFER TO 92 DODGE TRUCK OPTIONS TABLE Pg110

DODGE 92

Model/Body/Type	BaseList	Whlse	Retail

DAYTONA 1992

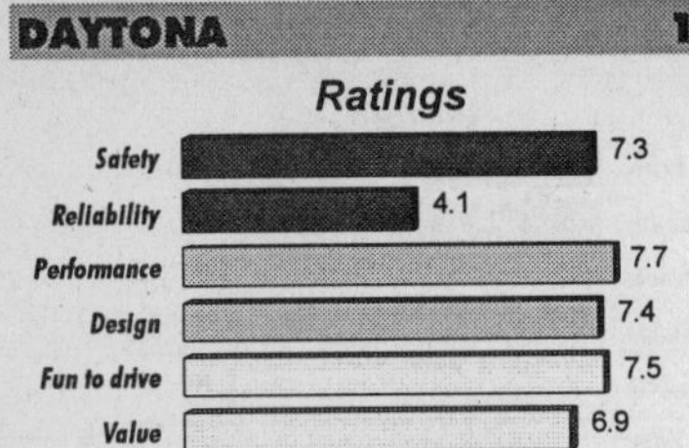

FWD/AT/PS/AC

Model/Body/Type	BaseList	Whlse	Retail
4 Cyl Models			
2 Dr Hbk	10997	**7125**	**8950**
2 Dr ES Hbk	11871	**7825**	**9750**
V6 Models			
2 Dr Hbk	11691	**7600**	**9500**
2 Dr ES Hbk	12565	**8325**	**10225**
2 Dr IROC Hbk	13333	**8850**	**10850**

ADD FOR 92 DAYTONA:

ABS +350
Cass +75
CD Player +175
Cruise Ctrl +115
Custom Whls/Cvrs +160
Leather Seats +195
Pwr Locks +75
Pwr Seat +115
Pwr Wndw +115
Sunroof +195
Tilt Whl +75

DEDUCT FOR 92 DAYTONA MODELS

No AC -505
No Auto Trans -390

DYNASTY 1992

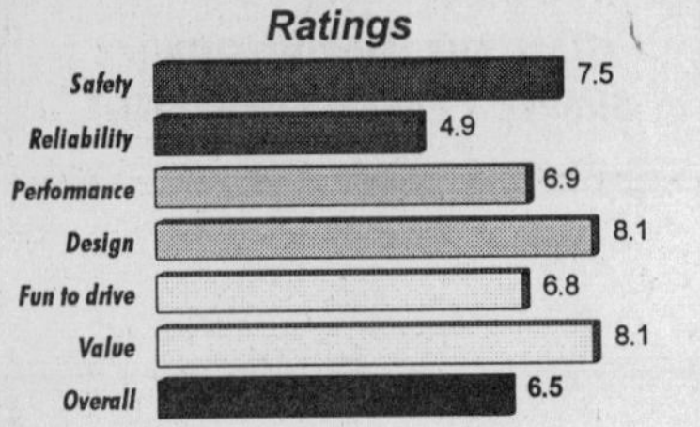

FWD/AT/PS/AC

Model/Body/Type	BaseList	Whlse	Retail
4 Cyl Models			
4 Dr Sdn	14477	**6025**	**7900**
V6 Models			
4 Dr Sdn	15171	**6575**	**8500**
4 Dr LE Sdn	15967	**7250**	**9275**

ADD FOR 92 DYNASTY:

ABS +350
Car Phone +160
Cass +100
Cruise Ctrl +135
Custom Whls/Cvrs +175
Infinity Ster Sys +175
Leather Seats +230
Pwr Locks +100
Pwr Seat +135
Pwr Sunroof +430
Pwr Wndw +135
Tilt Whl +100
Vinyl Roof +100

DEDUCT FOR 92 DYNASTY:

No AC -545

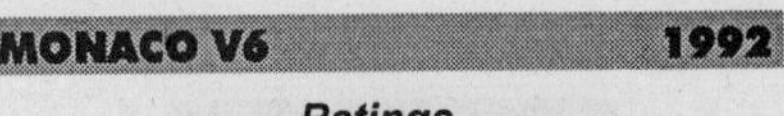

MONACO V6 1992

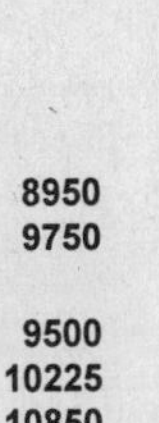

Ratings

Safety 7
Reliability 4.5
Performance 7.9
Design 7.8
Fun to drive 7.9
Value 7.1
Overall 6.4

FWD/AT/PS/AC

Model/Body/Type	BaseList	Whlse	Retail
4 Dr LE Sdn	14354	**5275**	**7000**
4 Dr ES Sdn	17203	**6150**	**7875**

ADD FOR 92 MONACO:

ABS +350
Cass(Std ES) +75
Cruise Ctrl +115
Custom Whls/Cvrs +160
Leather Seats +195
Pwr Locks +75
Pwr Seat +115
Pwr Wndw +115
Tilt Whl +75

DEDUCT FOR 92 MONACO:

No AC -505

RAM 50 4 Cyl 1/2 Ton 1992

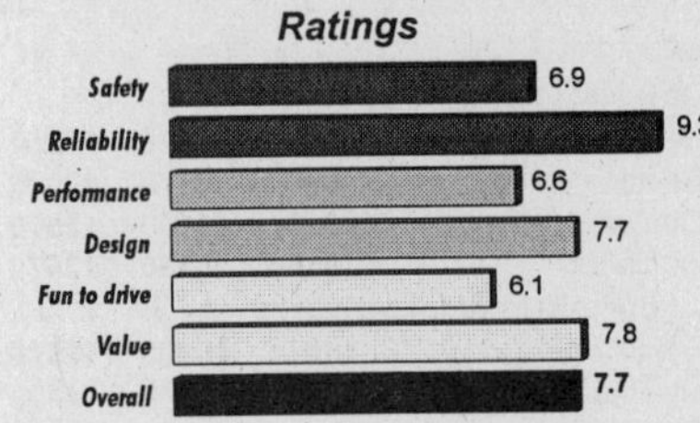

AT/PS/AC

Model/Body/Type	BaseList	Whlse	Retail
Pkup	8178	**5650**	**7500**
LB Pkup	8723	**5750**	**7625**
SE Pkup	9298	**6025**	**7925**

REFER TO 92 DODGE TRUCK OPTIONS TABLE Pg110

DODGE

RAMCHARGER V8 1/2 Ton 1992

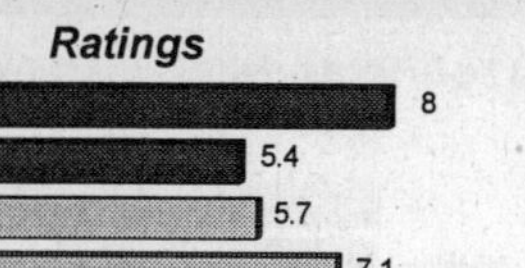
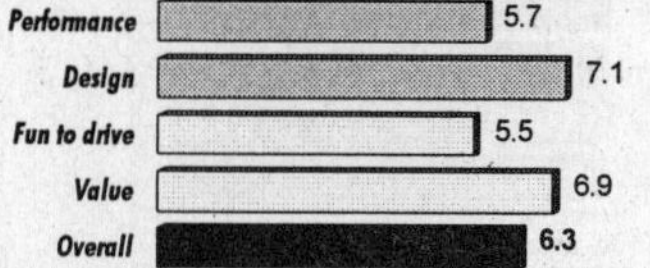

AT/PS/AC

Model/Body/Type	BaseList	Whlse	Retail
2 Dr 150 S Utility	16545	**10425**	**12800**
2 Dr 150 S 4WD Utility	17939	**12025**	**14650**
2 Dr 150 Utility	18764	**11425**	**13975**
2 Dr 150 4WD Utility	19595	**13000**	**15700**

ADD FOR 92 RAMCHARGER:

Canyon Sport Pkg +625 *LE Pkg +545*

REFER TO 92 DODGE TRUCK OPTIONS TABLE Pg110

SHADOW 4 Cyl 1992

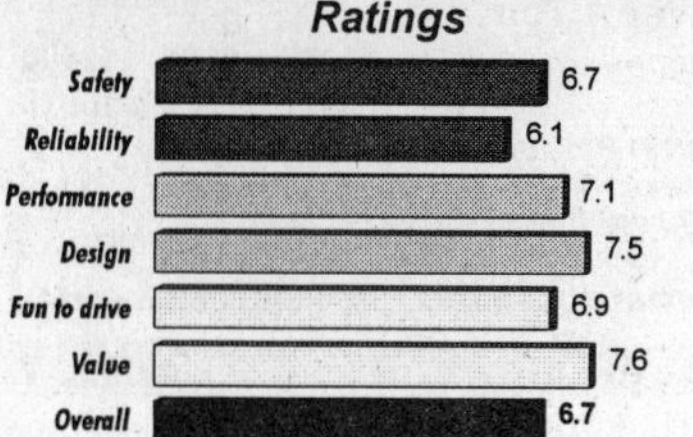

FWD/AT/PS/AC

Model/Body/Type	BaseList	Whlse	Retail
4 Dr America Hbk	8384	**4850**	**6350**
2 Dr America Hbk	7984	**4775**	**6250**
4 Dr Hbk	9646	**5575**	**7125**
2 Dr Hbk	9246	**5475**	**7000**
2 Dr Conv	13457	**8650**	**10500**
4 Dr ES Hbk	11234	**6600**	**8225**
2 Dr ES Hbk	10912	**6500**	**8125**
2 Dr ES Conv	14685	**9675**	**11675**

ADD FOR 92 SHADOW:

4 Cyl Turbo Eng +230 *Cass +60*
Cruise Ctrl +100 *Custom Whls/Cvrs +135*
Pwr Locks +60 *Pwr Seat +100*
Pwr Wndw(Std Cnv) +100 *Sunroof +160*
Tilt Whl +60 *V6 Eng +315*

DEDUCT FOR 92 SHADOW:

No AC -430 *No Auto Trans -390*

SPIRIT 1992

Ratings

Rating	Score
Safety	7.2
Reliability	6.3
Performance	7.5
Design	7.9
Fun to drive	7.4
Value	8.4
Overall	7.1

FWD/AT/PS/AC

Model/Body/Type	BaseList	Whlse	Retail
4 Cyl Models			
4 Dr Sdn	11470	**5650**	**7300**
4 Dr LE Sdn	13530	**6275**	**8025**
4 Dr ES Turbo Sdn	14441	**7100**	**8925**
4 Dr R/T Turbo Sdn	18674	**7850**	**9800**
V6 Models			
4 Dr Sdn	12195	**6125**	**7850**
4 Dr LE Sdn	14255	**6750**	**8600**
4 Dr ES Sdn	14441	**7275**	**9150**

ADD FOR 92 SPIRIT:

4 Cyl Turbo Eng +230 *ABS +350*
Cass(Std ES,R/T) +75 *Cruise Ctrl +115*
Custom Whls/Cvrs +160 *Pwr Locks +75*
Pwr Seat +115 *Pwr Wndw +115*
Tilt Whl +75

DEDUCT FOR 92 SPIRIT:

No AC -505 *No Auto Trans -470*

DODGE 92-91

STEALTH V6 — 1992

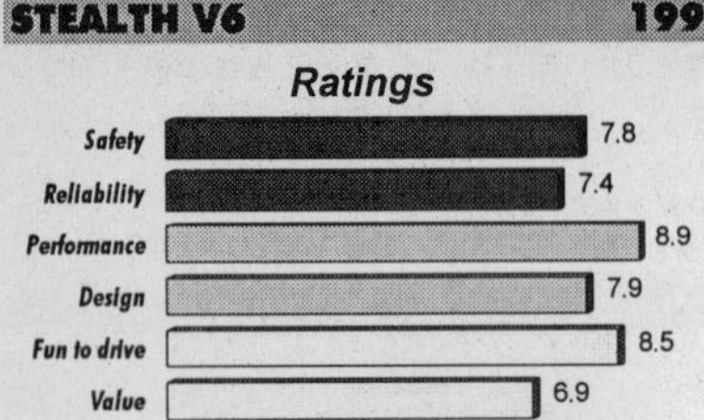

Model/Body/Type	BaseList	Whlse	Retail
FWD/AT/PS/AC			
2 Dr Lbk	17155	**11750**	**14325**
2 Dr ES Lbk	19028	**12825**	**15450**
2 Dr R/T Lbk	25500	**16000**	**18800**
2 Dr R/T Turb AWD Lbk	30885	**18925**	**22050**

ADD FOR 92 STEALTH:
ABS(Std R/T) +350
Cass(Std R/T) +100
CruiseCtrl(Std R/T) +135
Leather Seats +230
Pwr Wndw(Std R/T) +135
Car Phone +160
CD Player +195
Custom Whls/Cvrs +175
Pwr Dr Lks(Std R/T) +100
Sunroof +215

DEDUCT FOR 92 STEALTH:
No AC -545
No Auto Trans -470

92 DODGE TRUCK OPTIONS TABLE

ADD FOR ALL 92 DODGE TRUCKS:
15 Pass Seating +330
4-Whl Drive +1200
AC-Rear +315
Bed Liner +105
Cass(Std B150/250LE,CrvnSE/LE/ES,Dak LE) +80
Cruise Ctrl(Std Caravan LE/ES) +80
Custom Whls(Std CaravanES, Ram 50SE,Ramcharger Cnyn Spt) +125
Dual Rear Whls +375
Fiberglass Cap +205
Leather Seats +205
Privacy Glass(Std B150/250LE, Caravan ES,Ramcharger Cnyn Spt) +125
Pwr Locks(Std B150/250LE,Caravan LE) +80
Pwr Seats(Std Caravan ES) +105
Pwr Wndw(Std B150/250LE,Caravan LE/ES) +105
Running Boards +125
Sunroof-Manual +105
Towing Pkg +145

DEDUCT FOR ALL 92 DODGE TRUCKS
No AC -375
No Auto Trans -330
No Pwr Steering -145

1991 DODGE

B150/B250/B350 VANS V8 — 1991

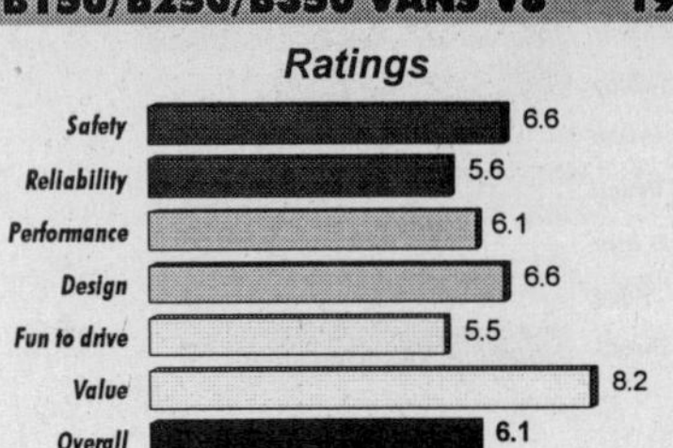

Model/Body/Type	BaseList	Whlse	Retail
AT/PS/AC			
B150 Van 1/2 Ton			
Wagon	14882	**9050**	**11250**
Van	12975	**7750**	**9825**
B250 Van 3/4 Ton			
Wagon	16345	**9325**	**11550**
Van	13216	**7900**	**9975**
B350 Van 1 Ton			
Wagon	17526	**9625**	**12400**
Van	15042	**8325**	**10925**

ADD FOR 91 B150/B250/B350 VAN:
LE Pkg +415

DEDUCT FOR 91 B150/B250/B350 VAN:
V6 Eng -390

REFER TO 91 DODGE TRUCK OPTIONS TABLE Pg114

CARAVAN V6 — 1991

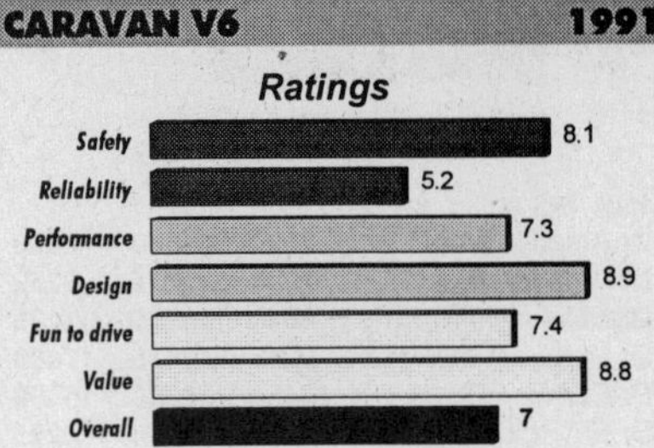

DODGE

Model/Body/Type	BaseList	Whlse	Retail
FWD/AT/PS/AC			
Caravan C/V	12266	**5725**	**7600**
Extended Caravan C/V	14006	**6625**	**8575**
Caravan	13195	**6925**	**8925**
Caravan SE	14325	**7800**	**9900**
Caravan LE	17625	**8650**	**10750**
Grand Caravan SE	16175	**8700**	**10875**
Grand Caravan LE	19435	**9550**	**11800**

ADD FOR 91 CARAVAN:

Air Bag +230 *ES Pkg +275*

DEDUCT FOR 91 CARAVAN:

4 Cyl Eng -350

REFER TO 91 DODGE TRUCK OPTIONS TABLE Pg114

COLT 4 Cyl 1991

Ratings

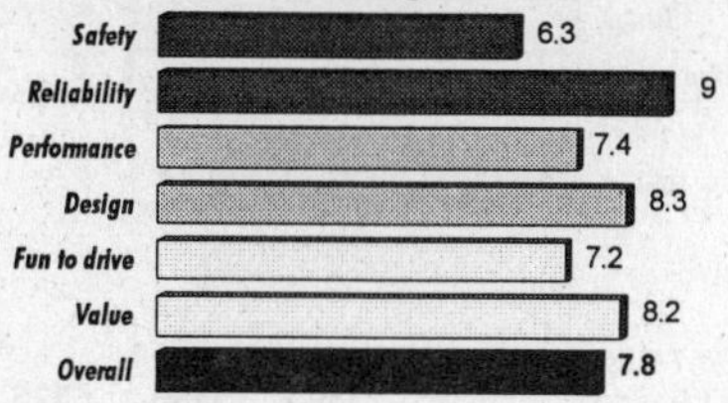

Rating	Score
Safety	6.3
Reliability	9
Performance	7.4
Design	8.3
Fun to drive	7.2
Value	8.2
Overall	7.8

Model/Body/Type	BaseList	Whlse	Retail
FWD/AT/PS/AC			
3 Dr Hbk	6949	**2675**	**3850**
3 Dr GL Hbk	7845	**3275**	**4600**
4 Dr Vista Wgn	11941	**5700**	**7200**
4 Dr 4WD Vista Wgn (5 Spd)	13167	**5975**	**7550**

ADD FOR 91 COLT:

Cass +35 *Cruise Ctrl +75*
Custom Whls/Cvrs +115 *Luggage Rack +35*
Pwr Locks +35 *Pwr Wndw +75*

DEDUCT FOR 91 COLT:

No AC -350 *No Auto Trans -315*
No Pwr Steering -100

D-SERIES PICKUPS V8 1991

Ratings

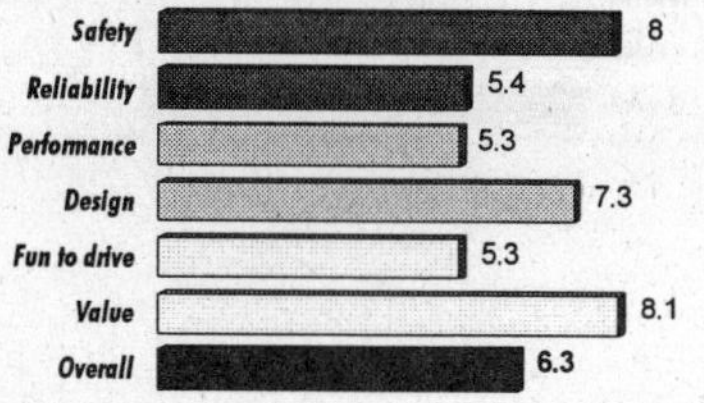

Rating	Score
Safety	8
Reliability	5.4
Performance	5.3
Design	7.3
Fun to drive	5.3
Value	8.1
Overall	6.3

Model/Body/Type	BaseList	Whlse	Retail
AT/PS/AC			
D150 Pickup 1/2 Ton			
Sweptline S 6 1/2'	10841	**7200**	**9250**
Sweptline S 8'	11050	**7300**	**9375**
Sweptline 6 1/2'	12063	**8000**	**10075**
Sweptline 8'	12271	**8100**	**10175**
Club Cab 6 1/2'	14104	**9150**	**11350**
Club Cab 8'	14313	**9250**	**11475**
D250 Pickup 3/4 Ton			
Sweptline 8'	13083	**8650**	**10750**
Club Cab 8'	15700	**9800**	**12050**
D350 Pickup 1 Ton			
Sweptline 8'	14601	**9200**	**11950**

ADD FOR 91 D-SERIES PICKUP:

5.9L Turbo Diesel Eng +745
LE Pkg +545 *SE Pkg +350*

DEDUCT FOR 91 D-SERIES PICKUP:

V6 Eng -390

REFER TO 91 DODGE TRUCK OPTIONS TABLE Pg114

DAKOTA V6 1/2 Ton 1991

Ratings

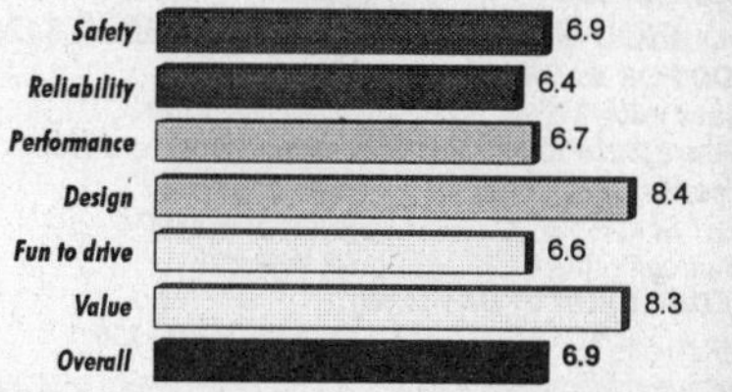

Rating	Score
Safety	6.9
Reliability	6.4
Performance	6.7
Design	8.4
Fun to drive	6.6
Value	8.3
Overall	6.9

Model/Body/Type	BaseList	Whlse	Retail
AT/PS/AC			
Sweptline S 6 1/2' (4 cyl,5 spd)	8396	**5950**	**7850**
Sweptline 6 1/2'	10172	**7000**	**8975**
Sweptline LB 8'	10323	**7075**	**9100**
Sweptline Sport 6 1/2'	12874	**7750**	**9825**
Club Cab 6 1/2'	11241	**8000**	**10075**
Club Cab Sport 6 1/2'	13993	**8800**	**11000**

ADD FOR 91 DAKOTA:

V8 Eng +390

DEDUCT FOR 91 DAKOTA:

4 Cyl Eng -350

REFER TO 91 DODGE TRUCK OPTIONS TABLE Pg114

DAYTONA 1991

Ratings

Rating	Score
Safety	7.3
Reliability	4.1
Performance	7.7
Design	7.4
Fun to drive	7.5
Value	6.9
Overall	6.3

FWD/AT/PS/AC

Model/Body/Type	BaseList	Whlse	Retail
4 Cyl Models			
2 Dr Hbk	10150	**5075**	**6750**
2 Dr ES Hbk	11395	**5725**	**7425**
V6 Models			
2 Dr Hbk	10844	**5550**	**7225**
2 Dr ES Hbk	12089	**6175**	**7900**
2 Dr IROC Hbk	12940	**6650**	**8425**

ADD FOR 91 DAYTONA:

Cass +60
CD Player +160
Cruise Ctrl +100
Custom Whls/Cvrs +135
Leather Seats +160
Pwr Locks +60
Pwr Seat +100
Pwr Wndw +100
Sunroof +160
Tilt Whl +60

DEDUCT FOR 91 DAYTONA:

No AC -470
No Auto Trans -350

DYNASTY 1991

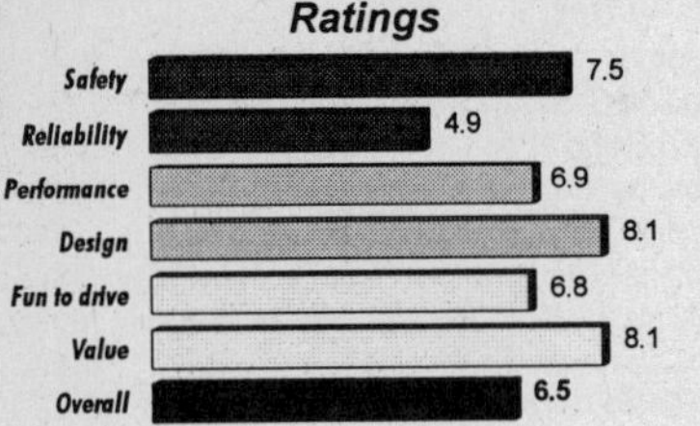

FWD/AT/PS/AC

Model/Body/Type	BaseList	Whlse	Retail
4 Cyl Models			
4 Dr Sdn	13625	**4625**	**6350**
V6 Models			
4 Dr Sdn	14319	**5075**	**6925**
4 Dr LE Sdn	15065	**5725**	**7575**

ADD FOR 91 DYNASTY:

ABS +315
Car Phone +135
Cass +75
Cruise Ctrl +115
Custom Whls/Cvrs +160
Infinity Ster Sys +135
Leather Seats +195
Pwr Locks +75
Pwr Seat +115
Pwr Sunroof +390
Pwr Wndw +115
Tilt Whl +75

DEDUCT FOR 91 DYNASTY:

No AC -505

MONACO V6 1991

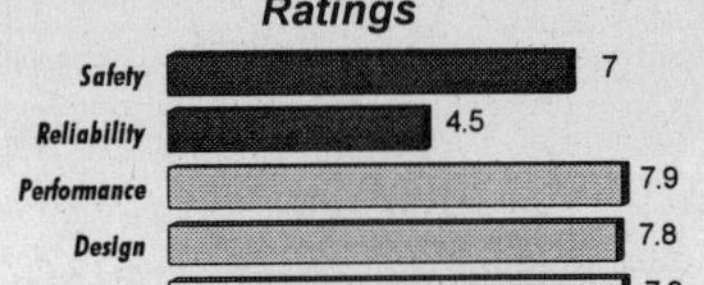

FWD/AT/PS/AC

Model/Body/Type	BaseList	Whlse	Retail
4 Dr LE Sdn	13895	**3850**	**5325**
4 Dr ES Sdn	16595	**4650**	**6225**

ADD FOR 91 MONACO:

ABS +315
Cass(Std ES) +60
CD Player +160
Cruise Ctrl +100
Custom Whls/Cvrs +135
Leather Seats +160
Pwr Locks +60
Pwr Seat +100
Pwr Wndw +100
Tilt Whl +60

DEDUCT FOR 91 MONACO:

No AC -470

RAM 50 4 Cyl 1/2 Ton 1991

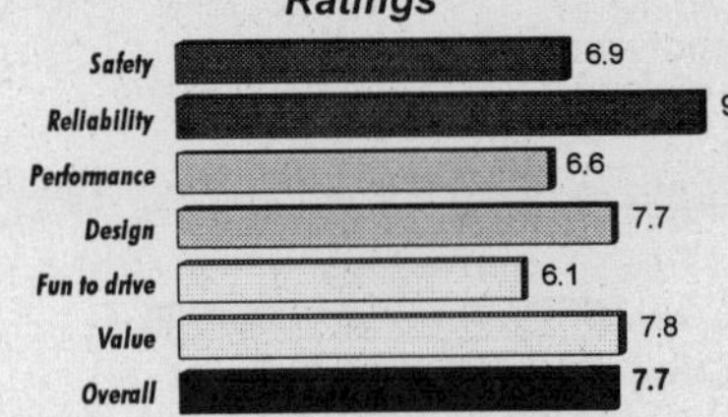

Model/Body/Type	BaseList	Whlse	Retail
AT/PS/AC			
Pkup	7787	**4700**	**6500**
LB Pkup	8320	**4825**	**6650**
SE Pkup	8498	**4975**	**6825**
Sports Cab Pkup	8826	**5500**	**7350**
LE Sports Cab Pkup	10727	**6250**	**8175**
SE Sports Cab 4WD Pkup (V6)	12885	**7575**	**9650**

ADD FOR 91 RAM 50:

6 Cyl Eng +350

REFER TO 91 DODGE TRUCK OPTIONS TABLE Pg114

RAMCHARGER V8 1/2 Ton 1991

Ratings

- Safety: 8
- Reliability: 5.4
- Performance: 5.7
- Design: 7.1
- Fun to drive: 5.5
- Value: 6.9
- Overall: 6.3

Model/Body/Type	BaseList	Whlse	Retail
AT/PS/AC			
2 Dr 150 S Utility	15003	**7875**	**9975**
2 Dr 150 S 4WD Utility	17196	**9425**	**11650**
2 Dr 150 Utility	16360	**8825**	**11000**
2 Dr 150 4WD Utility	18005	**10300**	**12675**

ADD FOR 91 RAMCHARGER:

LE Pkg +505

REFER TO 91 DODGE TRUCK OPTIONS TABLE Pg114

SHADOW 4 Cyl 1991

Ratings

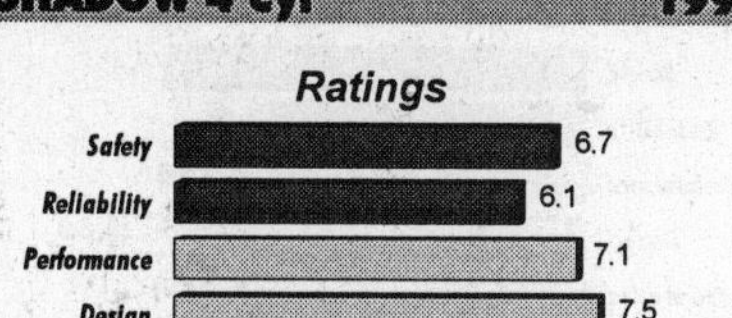

Model/Body/Type	BaseList	Whlse	Retail
FWD/AT/PS/AC			
4 Dr America Hbk	7799	**3850**	**5200**
2 Dr America Hbk	7599	**3750**	**5075**
4 Dr Hbk	9270	**4500**	**5925**
2 Dr Hbk	9070	**4400**	**5825**
2 Dr Conv	12995	**7375**	**9175**
4 Dr ES Hbk	10745	**5350**	**6900**
2 Dr ES Hbk	10545	**5250**	**6775**
2 Dr ES Conv	14068	**8275**	**10125**

ADD FOR 91 SHADOW:

4 Cyl Turbo Eng +215
Cass +35
Cruise Ctrl +75
Custom Whls/Cvrs +115
Pwr Locks +35
Pwr Seat +75
Pwr Wndw(Std Conv) +75
Sunroof +115
Tilt Whl +35

DEDUCT FOR 91 SHADOW:

No AC -390
No Auto Trans -350

SPIRIT 1991

Ratings

- Safety: 7.2
- Reliability: 6.3
- Performance: 7.5
- Design: 7.9
- Fun to drive: 7.4
- Value: 8.4
- Overall: 7.1

Model/Body/Type	BaseList	Whlse	Retail
FWD/AT/PS/AC			
4 Cyl Models			
4 Dr Sdn	10905	**4475**	**6050**
4 Dr LE Sdn	12905	**5025**	**6675**
4 Dr ES Turbo Sdn	13689	**5725**	**7425**
4 Dr R/T Turbo Sdn	17800	**6425**	**8175**
V6 Models			
4 Dr Sdn	11599	**4875**	**6550**
4 Dr LE Sdn	13599	**5500**	**7175**
4 Dr ES Sdn	14383	**5875**	**7625**

ADD FOR 91 SPIRIT:

4 Cyl Turbo Eng +215
ABS +315
Cass(Std ES,R/T) +60
Cruise Ctrl +100
Custom Whls/Cvrs +135
Pwr Locks +60
Pwr Seat +100
Pwr Wndw +100
Sunroof +160
Tilt Whl +60

DEDUCT FOR 91 SPIRIT:

No AC -470
No Auto Trans -430

STEALTH V6 1991

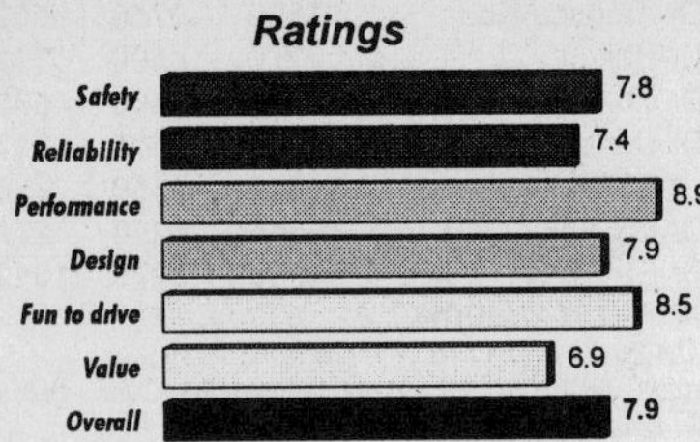

Model/Body/Type	BaseList	Whlse	Retail
FWD/AT/PS/AC			
2 Dr Lbk	16293	**10175**	**12475**
2 Dr ES Lbk	18056	**11100**	**13550**
2 Dr R/T Lbk	24155	**14025**	**16700**
2 Dr R/T Turb AWD Lbk	29267	**16675**	**19625**

ADD FOR 91 STEALTH:

ABS(Std R/T) +315
Car Phone +135
Cass(Std R/T) +75
CD Player +160
CruiseCtrl(Std R/T) +115
Custom Whls/Cvrs +160
Leather Seats +195
Pwr Dr Lks(Std R/T) +75
Pwr Wndw(Std R/T) +115

DEDUCT FOR 91 STEALTH:

No AC -505
No Auto Trans -430

91 DODGE TRUCK OPTIONS TABLE

ADD FOR ALL 91 DODGE TRUCKS:

15 Pass Seating +290
4-Whl Drive +1140
AC-Rear +250
Bed Liner +80
Custom Whls(Std Caravan ES) +105
Dual Rear Whls +330
Fiberglass Cap +170
Leather Seats +170
Privacy Glass(Std Ramcharger LE) +105
Pwr Seats +80
Pwr Wndw(Std Caravan LE/ES) +80
Running Boards +105
Sunroof-Manual +80
Towing Pkg +105

DEDUCT FOR ALL 91 DODGE TRUCKS:

No AC -315
No Auto Trans -250
No Pwr Steering -105

1990 DODGE

B150/B250/B350 VANS V8 1990

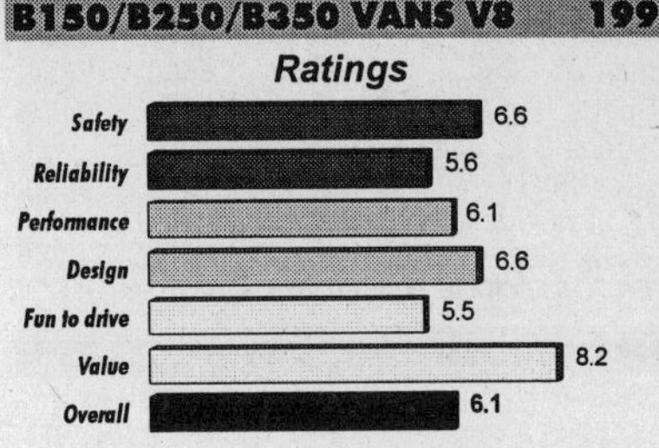

Model/Body/Type	BaseList	Whlse	Retail
AT/PS/AC			
B150 Van 1/2 Ton			
Wagon	14145	**7675**	**9775**
Van	12345	**6450**	**8400**
B250 Van 3/4 Ton			
Wagon	15545	**7900**	**9975**
Van	12575	**6575**	**8525**
B350 Van 1 Ton			
Wagon	16675	**8125**	**10700**
Van	14325	**6900**	**9350**

ADD FOR 90 B150/B250/B350 VAN:

LE Pkg +330

DEDUCT FOR 90 B150/B250/B350 VAN:

V6 Eng -315

REFER TO 90 DODGE TRUCK OPTIONS TABLE Pg117

CARAVAN V6 1990

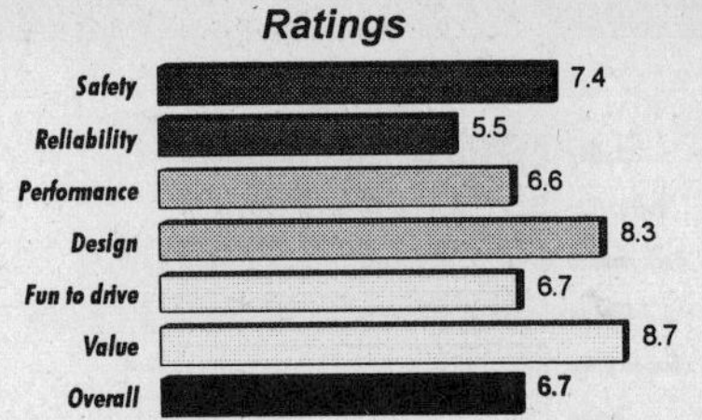

Model/Body/Type	BaseList	Whlse	Retail
FWD/AT/PS/AC			
Caravan C/V	11125	**4825**	**6650**
Extended Caravan C/V	13450	**5675**	**7525**
Caravan	11995	**5975**	**7875**
Caravan SE	12675	**6750**	**8775**
Caravan LE	16125	**7450**	**9525**

Model/Body/Type	BaseList	Whlse	Retail
Grand Caravan SE	15395	**7575**	**9650**
Grand Caravan LE	18325	**8275**	**10350**

ADD FOR 90 CARAVAN:
ES Pkg +230
DEDUCT FOR 90 CARAVAN:
4 Cyl Eng -275 *2.5L Turbo Eng -115*
REFER TO 90 DODGE TRUCK OPTIONS TABLE Pg117

COLT 4 Cyl 1990

Ratings

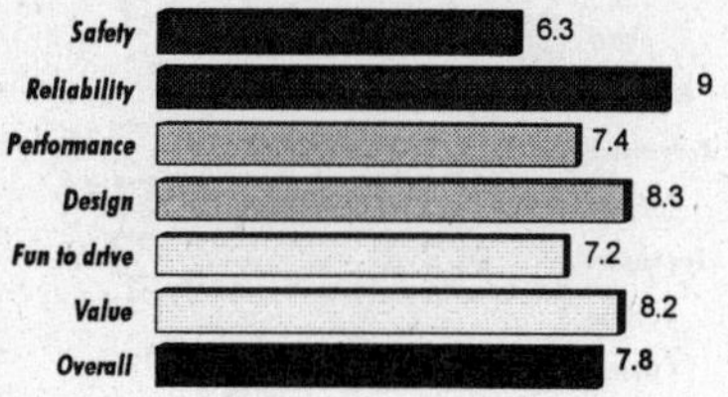

Rating	Score
Safety	6.3
Reliability	9
Performance	7.4
Design	8.3
Fun to drive	7.2
Value	8.2
Overall	7.8

FWD/AT/PS/AC

Model/Body/Type	BaseList	Whlse	Retail
3 Dr Hbk	6851	**1625**	**2600**
3 Dr GL Hbk	7909	**2500**	**3650**
3 Dr GT Hbk	9121	**3100**	**4375**
4 Dr DL Wgn	9316	**3450**	**4775**
5 Spd 4WD DL S/W	11145	**3750**	**5075**
4 Dr Vista Wgn	11941	**4675**	**6125**
4 Dr 4WD Vista Wgn (5 Spd)	13167	**4925**	**6450**

ADD FOR 90 COLT:
Cass +35 *Cruise Ctrl +60*
Custom Whls/Cvrs +75 *Luggage Rack +35*
Pwr Locks +35 *Pwr Wndw +60*
DEDUCT FOR 90 COLT:
No AC -315 *No Auto Trans -275*
No Pwr Steering -75

D-SERIES PICKUPS V8 1990

Ratings

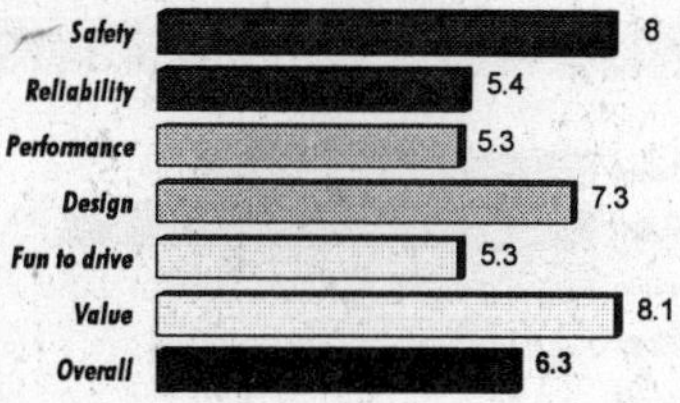

Rating	Score
Safety	8
Reliability	5.4
Performance	5.3
Design	7.3
Fun to drive	5.3
Value	8.1
Overall	6.3

AT/PS/AC

Model/Body/Type	BaseList	Whlse	Retail
D150 Pickup 1/2 Ton			
Sweptline S 6 1/2'	10450	**5800**	**7675**
Sweptline S 8'	10650	**5875**	**7800**
Sweptline 6 1/2'	11425	**6600**	**8550**
Sweptline 8'	11625	**6675**	**8675**
Club Cab 6 1/2'	13375	**7525**	**9600**
Club Cab 8'	13575	**7625**	**9725**
D250 Pickup 3/4 Ton			
Sweptline 8'	12400	**7150**	**9175**
Club Cab 8'	14900	**8075**	**10150**
D350 Pickup 1 Ton			
Sweptline 8'	13850	**7675**	**10200**

ADD FOR 90 D-SERIES PICKUP:
5.9L Turbo Dsl Eng +700 *Diesel Eng +315*
LE Pkg +430 *SE Pkg +315*
DEDUCT FOR 90 D-SERIES PICKUP:
V6 Eng -315
REFER TO 90 DODGE TRUCK OPTIONS TABLE Pg117

DAKOTA V6 1/2 Ton 1990

Ratings

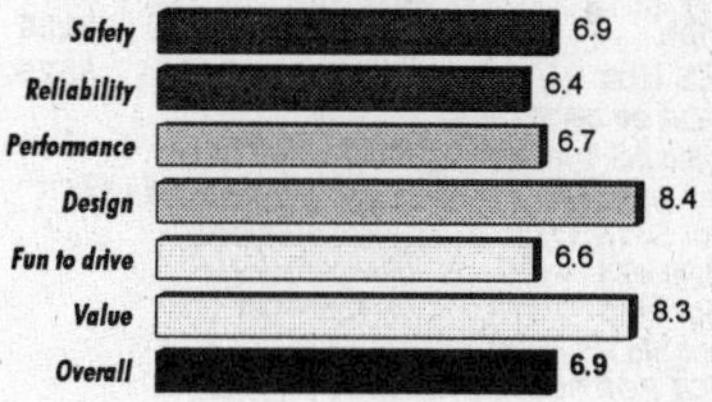

Rating	Score
Safety	6.9
Reliability	6.4
Performance	6.7
Design	8.4
Fun to drive	6.6
Value	8.3
Overall	6.9

AT/PS/AC

Model/Body/Type	BaseList	Whlse	Retail
Sweptline S 6 1/2' (4 cyl,5 spd)	7995	**4350**	**6100**
Sweptline 6 1/2'	9700	**5125**	**7000**
Sweptline 8'	9845	**5225**	**7100**
Sweptline Sport 6 1/2'	12225	**5850**	**7725**
Sweptline Conv 6 1/2'	13345	**5850**	**7725**
Sweptline Conv Spt 6 1/2'	15500	**6550**	**8500**
Club Cab 6 1/2'	10725	**6050**	**7950**
Club Cab Sport 6 1/2'	13300	**6725**	**8725**

ADD FOR 90 DAKOTA:
LE Pkg +470 *SE Pkg +315*
REFER TO 90 DODGE TRUCK OPTIONS TABLE Pg117

DODGE 90

DAYTONA 1990

Ratings

Safety 7.3
Reliability 4.1
Performance 7.7
Design 7.4
Fun to drive 7.5
Value 6.9
Overall 6.3

FWD/AT/PS/AC

Model/Body/Type	BaseList	Whlse	Retail
4 Cyl Models			
2 Dr Hbk	9745	**4225**	**5775**
2 Dr ES Hbk	10995	**4750**	**6375**
2 Dr ES Turbo Hbk	12895	**5425**	**7150**
2 Dr Shelby Hbk	14057	**6000**	**7725**
V6 Models			
2 Dr Hbk	10425	**4625**	**6200**
2 Dr ES Hbk	11675	**5125**	**6825**

ADD FOR 90 DAYTONA:
Cass(Std ES Turbo,Shelby) +60
Cruise Ctrl +75 *Custom Whls/Cvrs +115*
Leather Seats +115 *Pwr Locks +60*
Pwr Seat +75 *Pwr Wndw +75*
Sunroof +115 *T-Top +470*
Tilt Whl(Std ES Turbo,Shelby) +60
DEDUCT FOR 90 DAYTONA:
No AC -430 *No Auto Trans -315*

DYNASTY 1990

Ratings

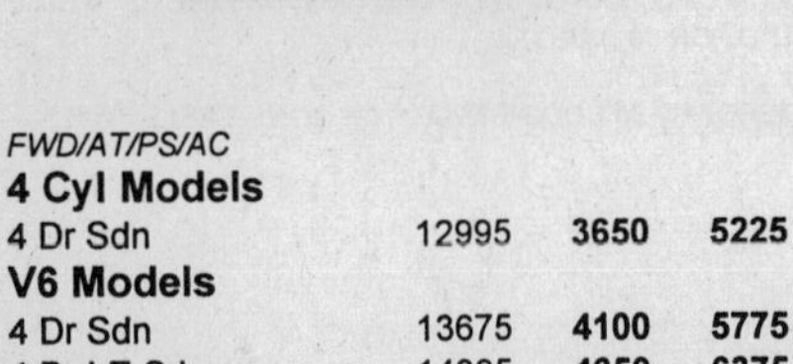

FWD/AT/PS/AC

Model/Body/Type	BaseList	Whlse	Retail
4 Cyl Models			
4 Dr Sdn	12995	**3650**	**5225**
V6 Models			
4 Dr Sdn	13675	**4100**	**5775**
4 Dr LE Sdn	14395	**4650**	**6375**

ADD FOR 90 DYNASTY:
ABS +275 *Cass +75*
Cruise Ctrl +100 *Custom Whls/Cvrs +115*
Infinity Ster Sys +115 *Pwr Locks +60*
Pwr Seat +100 *Pwr Sunroof +350*
Pwr Wndw +100 *Tilt Whl +60*
DEDUCT FOR 90 DYNASTY:
No AC -470

MONACO V6 1990

Ratings

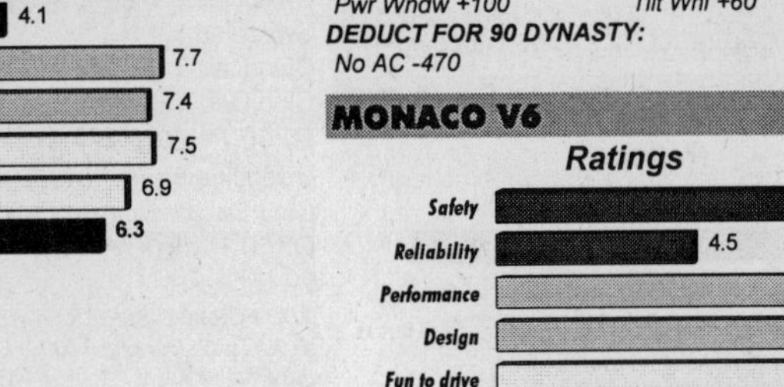

FWD/AT/PS/AC

Model/Body/Type	BaseList	Whlse	Retail
4 Dr LE Sdn	14995	**2975**	**4325**
4 Dr ES Sdn	17595	**3650**	**5075**

ADD FOR 90 MONACO:
Cass(Std ES) +60 *Cruise Ctrl +75*
Custom Whls/Cvrs +115 *Leather Seats +115*
Pwr Locks +60 *Pwr Seat +75*
Pwr Sunroof +315 *Pwr Wndw +75*
Tilt Whl +60
DEDUCT FOR 90 MONACO:
No AC -430

OMNI 4 Cyl 1990

FWD/AT/PS/AC

Model/Body/Type	BaseList	Whlse	Retail
4 Dr Hbk	6995	**2150**	**3225**

ADD FOR 90 OMNI:
Cass +35
DEDUCT FOR 90 OMNI:
No AC -315 *No Auto Trans -275*
No Pwr Steering -75

RAM 50 4 Cyl 1/2 Ton 1990

Ratings

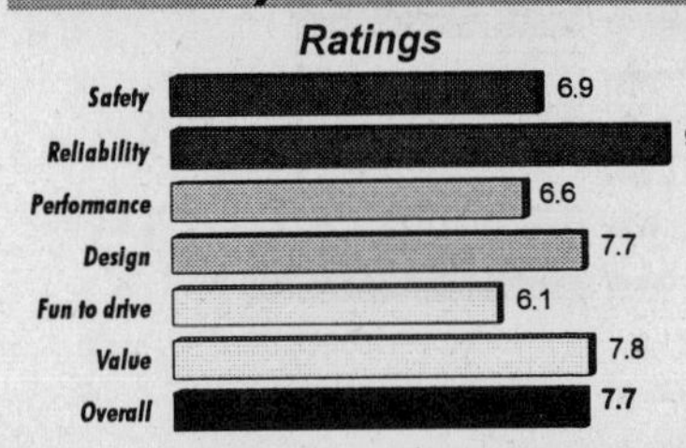

DODGE

AT/PS/AC

Model/Body/Type	BaseList	Whlse	Retail
Pkup	7787	**3925**	**5600**
LB Pkup	8320	**4050**	**5725**
SE Pkup	8530	**4125**	**5825**
Sports Cab Pkup	8826	**4625**	**6375**
LE Sports Cab Pkup	10890	**5125**	**7000**
SE Sports Cab 4WD Pkup (V6)	13058	**6600**	**8550**

ADD FOR 90 RAM 50:

6 Cyl Eng +275

REFER TO 90 DODGE TRUCK OPTIONS TABLE Pg117

RAMCHARGER V8 1/2 Ton — 1990

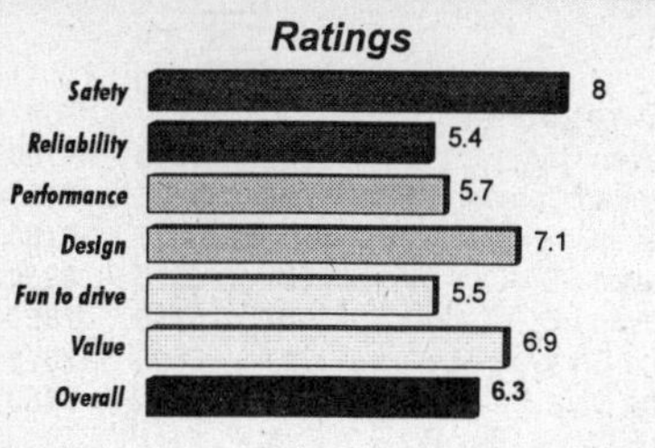

AT/PS/AC

Model/Body/Type	BaseList	Whlse	Retail
2 Dr 150 S Utility	14275	**5950**	**7850**
2 Dr 150 S 4WD Utility	15575	**7425**	**9500**
2 Dr 150 Utility	16375	**6850**	**8850**
2 Dr 150 4WD Utility	17150	**8325**	**10400**

ADD FOR 90 RAMCHARGER:

LE Pkg +470

REFER TO 90 DODGE TRUCK OPTIONS TABLE Pg117

SHADOW 4 Cyl — 1990

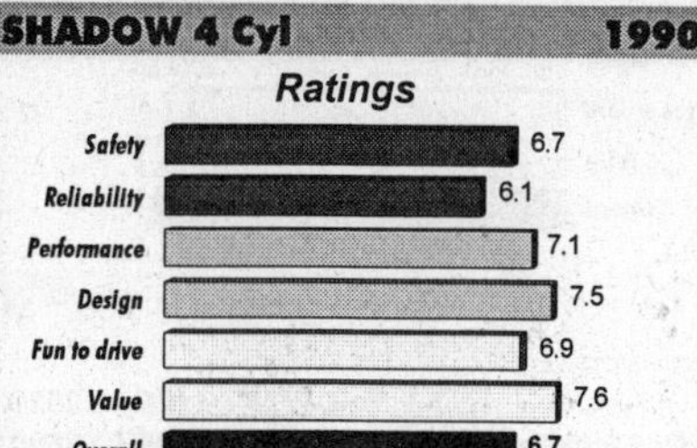

FWD/AT/PS/AC

Model/Body/Type	BaseList	Whlse	Retail
4 Dr Lbk	8985	**3250**	**4575**
2 Dr Lbk	8785	**3175**	**4475**

ADD FOR 90 SHADOW:

4 Cyl Turbo Eng +195 · *Cass +35*
Cruise Ctrl +60 · *Custom Whls/Cvrs +75*
ES Pkg +430 · *Pwr Locks +35*
Pwr Seat +60 · *Pwr Wndw +60*
Sunroof +100 · *Tilt Whl +35*

DEDUCT FOR 90 SHADOW:

No AC -350 · *No Auto Trans -315*

SPIRIT — 1990

Ratings

Safety 7.2
Reliability 6.3
Performance 7.5
Design 7.9
Fun to drive 7.4
Value 8.4
Overall 7.1

FWD/AT/PS/AC

Model/Body/Type	BaseList	Whlse	Retail
4 Cyl Models			
4 Dr Sdn	10495	**3250**	**4675**
4 Dr LE Sdn	11905	**3725**	**5200**
4 Dr ES Turbo Sdn	13205	**4400**	**5950**
V6 Models			
4 Dr Sdn	11175	**3650**	**5075**
4 Dr LE Sdn	12585	**4125**	**5675**
4 Dr ES Sdn	13205	**4550**	**6125**

ADD FOR 90 SPIRIT:

4 Cyl Turbo Eng +195 · *Cass(Std ES) +60*
Cruise Ctrl(Std LE,ES) +75 · *Custom Whls/Cvrs +115*
Pwr Locks +60 · *Pwr Seat +75*
Pwr Wndw +75 · *Sunroof +115*
Tilt Whl(Std LE,ES) +60

DEDUCT FOR 90 SPIRIT:

No AC -430 · *No Auto Trans -390*

90 DODGE TRUCK OPTIONS TABLE

ADD FOR ALL 90 DODGE TRUCKS:

15 Pass Seating +250
4-Whl Drive +1080
AC-Rear +185
Custom Whls(Std Caravan ES) +80
Dual Rear Whls +290
Fiberglass Cap +125
Privacy Glass +80
Running Boards +80
Sunroof-Pwr +205
Towing Pkg +80

DEDUCT FOR ALL 90 DODGE TRUCKS

No AC -250
No Auto Trans -170

Model/Body/Type	BaseList	Whlse	Retail

1989 DODGE

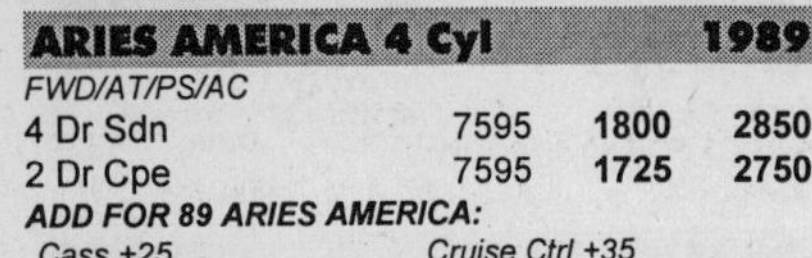

ARIES AMERICA 4 Cyl 1989

FWD/AT/PS/AC

Model/Body/Type	BaseList	Whlse	Retail
4 Dr Sdn	7595	**1800**	**2850**
2 Dr Cpe	7595	**1725**	**2750**

ADD FOR 89 ARIES AMERICA:

Cass +25 · *Cruise Ctrl +35* · *Pwr Locks +25* · *Tilt Whl +25*

DEDUCT FOR 89 ARIES AMERICA:

No AC -315 · *No Auto Trans -275* · *No Pwr Steering -75*

B150/B250/B350 VANS V8 1989

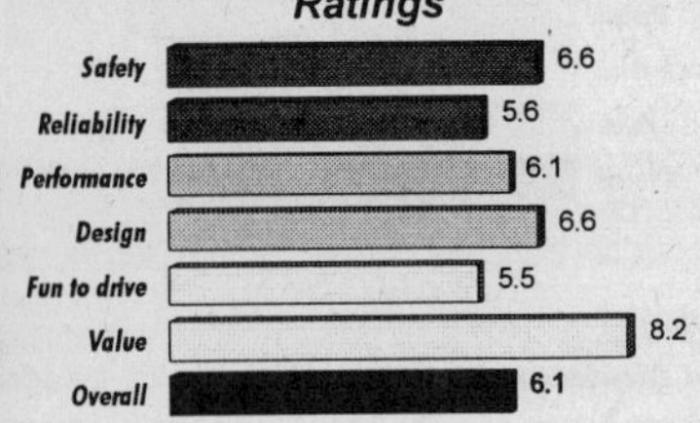

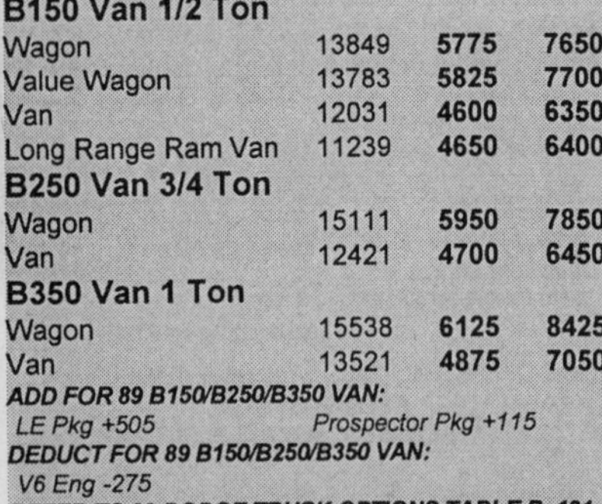

AT/PS/AC

Model/Body/Type	BaseList	Whlse	Retail
B150 Van 1/2 Ton			
Wagon	13849	**5775**	**7650**
Value Wagon	13783	**5825**	**7700**
Van	12031	**4600**	**6350**
Long Range Ram Van	11239	**4650**	**6400**
B250 Van 3/4 Ton			
Wagon	15111	**5950**	**7850**
Van	12421	**4700**	**6450**
B350 Van 1 Ton			
Wagon	15538	**6125**	**8425**
Van	13521	**4875**	**7050**

ADD FOR 89 B150/B250/B350 VAN:

LE Pkg +505 · *Prospector Pkg +115*

DEDUCT FOR 89 B150/B250/B350 VAN:

V6 Eng -275

REFER TO 89 DODGE TRUCK OPTIONS TABLE Pg121

CARAVAN V6 1989

Ratings

Safety 7.4
Reliability 5.5
Performance 6.6
Design 8.3
Fun to drive 6.7
Value 8.7
Overall 6.7

FWD/AT/PS/AC

Model/Body/Type	BaseList	Whlse	Retail
Caravan C/V	10592	**3525**	**5100**
Extended Caravan C/V	12708	**4225**	**5925**
Caravan	11312	**4425**	**6150**
Caravan SE	12039	**5075**	**6950**
Caravan LE	13987	**5750**	**7625**
Grand Caravan SE	13741	**5800**	**7675**
Grand Caravan LE	16362	**6450**	**8400**

ADD FOR 89 CARAVAN:

Royal Pkg +230

DEDUCT FOR 89 CARAVAN:

2.5L Turbo Eng -100 · *4 Cyl Eng -230*

REFER TO 89 DODGE TRUCK OPTIONS TABLE Pg121

COLT 4 Cyl 1989

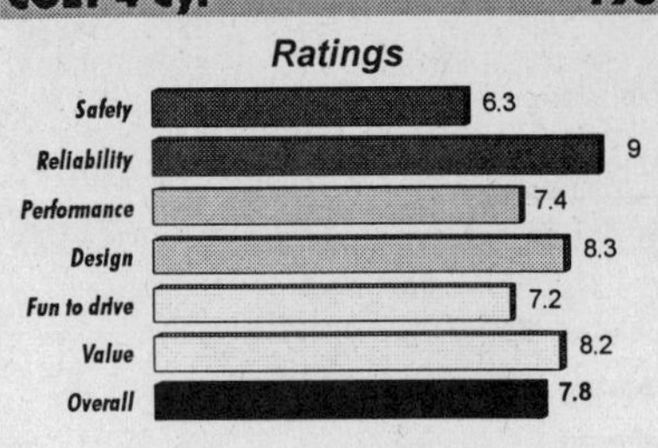

FWD/AT/PS/AC

Model/Body/Type	BaseList	Whlse	Retail
3 Dr Hbk	6477	**1125**	**2025**
3 Dr E Hbk	7279	**1625**	**2600**
3 Dr GT Hbk	8620	**2475**	**3625**
4 Dr DL Wgn	9316	**2700**	**3875**
5 Spd 4WD DL S/W	11145	**3000**	**4250**
4 Dr Vista Wgn	11518	**3800**	**5150**
4 Dr 4WD Vista Wgn(5 Spd)	12828	**4100**	**5500**

Model/Body/Type	BaseList	Whlse	Retail

ADD FOR 89 COLT:
Cass +25 · *Cruise Ctrl +35*
Custom Whls/Cvrs +35 · *GT Turbo Pkg +350*
Pwr Locks +25 · *Pwr Wndw +35*
DEDUCT FOR 89 COLT:
No AC -275 · *No Auto Trans -230*

D-SERIES PKUP V8 — 1989

Ratings

Rating	Score
Safety	8
Reliability	5.4
Performance	5.3
Design	7.3
Fun to drive	5.3
Value	8.1
Overall	6.3

AT/PS/AC

Model/Body/Type	BaseList	Whlse	Retail
D100 Pickup 1/2 Ton			
Sweptline 6 1/2'	9883	**5150**	**7025**
Sweptline 8'	10069	**5250**	**7150**
D150 Pickup 1/2 Ton			
Sweptline 6 1/2'	11203	**5475**	**7325**
Sweptline 8'	11403	**5575**	**7450**
D250 Pickup 3/4 Ton			
Sweptline 8'	12155	**5975**	**7875**
D350 Pickup 1 Ton			
Sweptline 8'	13239	**6500**	**8850**

ADD FOR 89 D-SERIES PICKUP:
5.9L Trbo Dsl Eng +625 · *LE Pkg +330*
Prospector Pkg +115
DEDUCT FOR 89 D-SERIES PICKUP:
V6 Eng -275
REFER TO 89 DODGE TRUCK OPTIONS TABLE Pg121

DAKOTA V6 1/2 Ton — 1989

Ratings

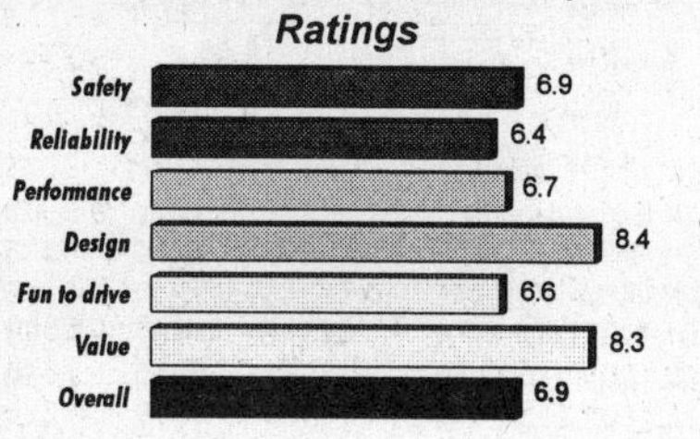

AT/PS/AC

Model/Body/Type	BaseList	Whlse	Retail
Sweptline S 6 1/2' (4 cyl,5 spd)	7469	**3525**	**5100**
Sweptline 6 1/2'	9580	**4225**	**5925**
Sweptline LB 8'	9746	**4325**	**6050**
Sweptline Sport 6 1/2'	11058	**4800**	**6625**
Sweptline Shelby (V8)	-	**5500**	**7350**
Sweptline Sport Conv	-	**5275**	**7150**

ADD FOR 89 DAKOTA:
LE Pkg +390 · *SE Pkg +230*
DEDUCT FOR 89 DAKOTA:
4 Cyl Eng -230
REFER TO 89 DODGE TRUCK OPTIONS TABLE Pg121

DAYTONA 4 Cyl — 1989

Ratings

Rating	Score
Safety	7.3
Reliability	4.1
Performance	7.7
Design	7.4
Fun to drive	7.5
Value	6.9
Overall	6.3

FWD/AT/PS/AC

Model/Body/Type	BaseList	Whlse	Retail
2 Dr Hbk	9295	**2775**	**4100**
2 Dr ES Hbk	10395	**3250**	**4650**
2 Dr ES Turbo Hbk	11995	**3850**	**5325**
2 Dr Shelby Hbk	13295	**4325**	**5875**

ADD FOR 89 DAYTONA:
4 Cyl Turbo Eng(Std ES Turbo,Shelby) +175
Cass(Std ES Turbo,Shelby) +35
CD Player +75 · *Cruise Ctrl +60*
Custom Whls/Cvrs +75 · *Leather Seats +75*
Pwr Locks +35 · *Pwr Seat +60*
Pwr Wndw +60 · *Sunroof +100*
T-Top +410
Tilt Whl(Std ES Turbo,Shelby) +35
DEDUCT FOR 89 DAYTONA:
No AC -390 · *No Auto Trans -275*

DIPLOMAT V8 — 1989

AT/PS/AC

Model/Body/Type	BaseList	Whlse	Retail
4 Dr Salon Sdn	11995	**1600**	**2750**
4 Dr SE Sdn	14795	**2275**	**3550**

ADD FOR 89 DIPLOMAT:
Cass +60 · *Cruise Ctrl(Std SE) +75*
Custom Whls/Cvrs +75 · *Pwr Locks +35*
Pwr Seat +75 · *Pwr Sunroof +290*
Pwr Wndw +75 · *Vinyl Roof(Std SE) +35*
DEDUCT FOR 89 DIPLOMAT:
No AC -430

DODGE 89

Model/Body/Type	BaseList	Whlse	Retail

DYNASTY 1989

Ratings

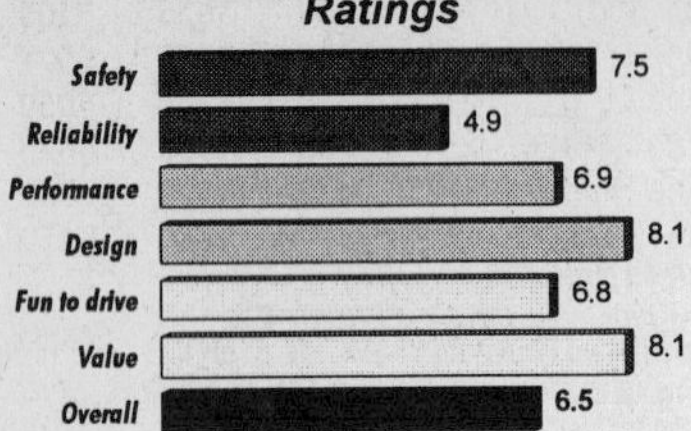

FWD/AT/PS/AC

Model/Body/Type	BaseList	Whlse	Retail
4 Cyl Models			
4 Dr Sdn	12295	**2350**	**3675**
V6 Models			
4 Dr Sdn	13069	**2775**	**4250**
4 Dr LE Sdn	13595	**3200**	**4725**

ADD FOR 89 DYNASTY:
Cass +60 — *Cruise Ctrl +75*
Custom Whls/Cvrs +75 — *Infinity Ster Sys +100*
Pwr Locks +35 — *Pwr Seat +75*
Pwr Sunroof +290 — *Pwr Wndw +75*
Tilt Whl +35

DEDUCT FOR 89 DYNASTY:
No AC -430

LANCER 4 Cyl 1989

FWD/AT/PS/AC

Model/Body/Type	BaseList	Whlse	Retail
4 Dr Sport Lbk	11195	**3225**	**4625**
4 Dr Sport ES Lbk	13695	**3750**	**5225**
4 Dr Sport Shelby Lbk	17395	**4825**	**6500**

ADD FOR 89 LANCER:
4 Cyl Turbo Eng(Std ES,Shelby) +175
Cass(Std Shelby) +35 — *Cr Ctrl(Std Shelby) +60*
Custom Whls/Cvrs +75 — *Lthr Seats(Std Shelby) +75*
Pwr Locks(Std ES,Shlby) +35
Pwr Seat(Std Shlby) +60 — *Pwr Sunroof +250*
PwrWndw(Std Shlby) +60 — *Tilt Whl(Std Shlby) +35*

DEDUCT FOR 89 LANCER:
No AC -390 — *No Auto Trans -350*

OMNI AMERICA 4 Cyl 1989

FWD/AT/PS/AC

Model/Body/Type	BaseList	Whlse	Retail
4 Dr Hbk	6595	**1550**	**2525**

ADD FOR 89 OMNI AMERICA:
Cass +25

DEDUCT FOR 89 OMNI AMERICA:
No AC -275 — *No Auto Trans -230*

RAIDER 6 Cyl 1989

4WD/AT/PS/AC

Model/Body/Type	BaseList	Whlse	Retail
2 Dr Utility	12550	**4825**	**6650**

DEDUCT FOR 89 RAIDER:
4 Cyl Eng -230

REFER TO 89 DODGE TRUCK OPTIONS TABLE Pg121

RAM 50 4 Cyl 1/2 Ton 1989

Ratings

Safety 6.9
Reliability 9.3
Performance 6.6
Design 7.7
Fun to drive 6.1
Value 7.8
Overall 7.7

AT/PS/AC

Model/Body/Type	BaseList	Whlse	Retail
Pkup 6'	7664	**3025**	**4525**
LB Pkup	8320	**3125**	**4650**
Sport Pkup	9496	**3450**	**5000**
Custom LB Pkup	8769	**3400**	**4950**
Extended Cab Pkup	8680	**3625**	**5200**
Sport Ext Cab Pkup	10407	**4100**	**5800**
Custom Ext Cab 4WD Pkup	11620	**5275**	**7150**

REFER TO 89 DODGE TRUCK OPTIONS TABLE Pg121

RAMCHARGER V8 1/2 Ton 1989

Ratings

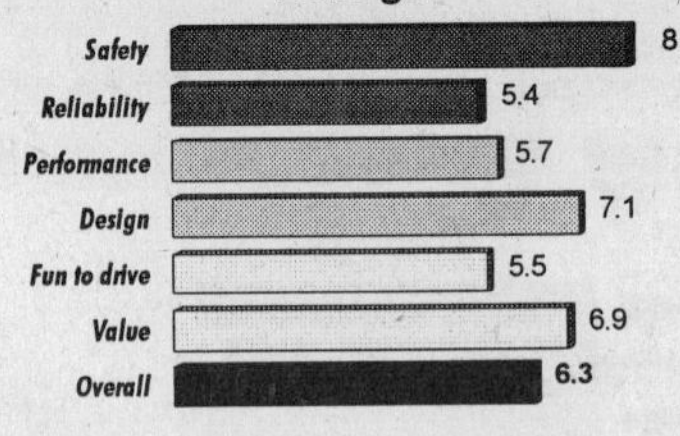

AT/PS/AC

Model/Body/Type	BaseList	Whlse	Retail
2 Dr 100 Utility	12302	**4600**	**6350**
2 Dr 100 4WD Utility	13361	**5975**	**7875**
2 Dr 150 Utility	14409	**5350**	**7225**
2 Dr 150 4WD Utility	15523	**6750**	**8775**

ADD FOR 89 RAMCHARGER:
LE Pkg +390 — *Prospector Pkg +160*

REFER TO 89 DODGE TRUCK OPTIONS TABLE Pg121

SHADOW 4 Cyl — 1989

Ratings

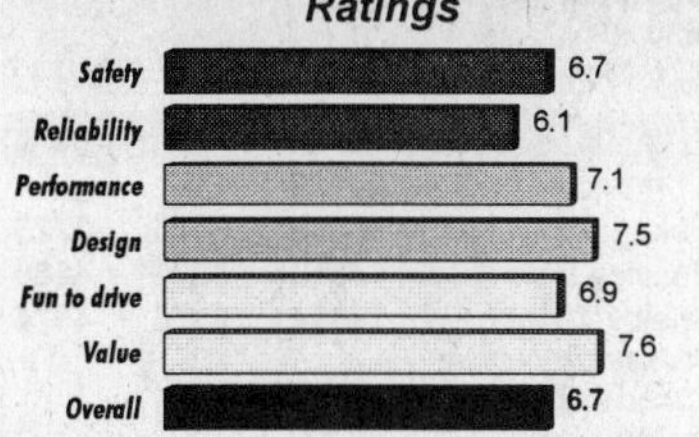

FWD/AT/PS/AC

Model/Body/Type	BaseList	Whlse	Retail
4 Dr Lbk	8595	**2600**	**3750**
2 Dr Lbk	8395	**2500**	**3650**

ADD FOR 89 SHADOW:

4 Cyl Turbo Eng +175 — *Cass +25*
Cruise Ctrl +35 — *Custom Whls/Cvrs +35*
ES Pkg +370 — *Pwr Locks +25*
Pwr Seat +35 — *Pwr Wndw +35*
Sunroof +75 — *Tilt Whl +25*

DEDUCT FOR 89 SHADOW:

No AC -315 — *No Auto Trans -275*

SPIRIT — 1989

Ratings

Safety 7.2
Reliability 6.3
Performance 7.5
Design 7.9
Fun to drive 7.4
Value 8.4
Overall 7.1

FWD/AT/PS/AC

Model/Body/Type	BaseList	Whlse	Retail
4 Cyl Models			
4 Dr Sdn	9995	**2400**	**3625**
4 Dr LE Sdn	11195	**2850**	**4175**
4 Dr ES Turbo Sdn	12495	**3400**	**4825**
V6 Models			
4 Dr ES Sdn	12495	**3475**	**4875**

ADD FOR 89 SPIRIT:

4 Cyl Turbo Eng +175 — *Cass(Std ES) +35*
Cruise Ctrl(Std LE,ES) +60 — *Custom Whls/Cvrs +75*
Pwr Locks +35 — *Pwr Seat +60*
Pwr Wndw +60 — *Sunroof +100*
Tilt Whl(Std LE,ES) +35

DEDUCT FOR 89 SPIRIT:

No AC -390 — *No Auto Trans -350*

89 DODGE TRUCK OPTIONS TABLE

ADD FOR ALL 89 DODGE TRUCKS:

15 Pass Seating +205
4-Whl Drive +975
AC-Rear +145
Dual Rear Whls +250
Fiberglass Cap +80
Sunroof-Pwr +145

DEDUCT FOR ALL 89 DODGE TRUCKS

No AC -185
No Auto Trans -80

1988 DODGE

600 4 Cyl — 1988

FWD/AT/PS/AC

Model/Body/Type	BaseList	Whlse	Retail
4 Dr Sdn	10659	**1725**	**2850**
4 Dr SE Sdn	11628	**2050**	**3200**

ADD FOR 88 600:

4 Cyl Turbo Eng +160

DEDUCT FOR 88 600:

No AC -330

ARIES AMERICA 4 Cyl — 1988

FWD/AT/PS/AC

Model/Body/Type	BaseList	Whlse	Retail
4 Dr Sdn	6995	**1325**	**2275**
2 Dr Cpe	6995	**1275**	**2175**
4 Dr Wgn	7695	**1700**	**2700**

DEDUCT FOR 88 ARIES AMERICA:

No AC -250 — *No Auto Trans -230*
No Pwr Steering -60

B150/B250/B350 VANS V8 — 1988

AT/PS/AC

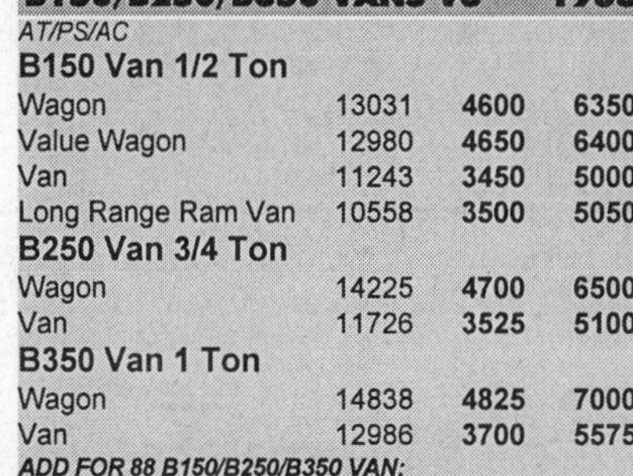

Model/Body/Type	BaseList	Whlse	Retail
B150 Van 1/2 Ton			
Wagon	13031	**4600**	**6350**
Value Wagon	12980	**4650**	**6400**
Van	11243	**3450**	**5000**
Long Range Ram Van	10558	**3500**	**5050**
B250 Van 3/4 Ton			
Wagon	14225	**4700**	**6500**
Van	11726	**3525**	**5100**
B350 Van 1 Ton			
Wagon	14838	**4825**	**7000**
Van	12986	**3700**	**5575**

ADD FOR 88 B150/B250/B350 VAN:

LE Pkg +390

DEDUCT FOR 88 B150/B250/B350 VAN:

V6 Eng -230

REFER TO 88 DODGE TRUCK OPTIONS TABLE Pg123

Model/Body/Type	BaseList	Whlse	Retail

CARAVAN V6 1988

FWD/AT/PS/AC

Model/Body/Type	BaseList	Whlse	Retail
Caravan	10887	3775	5400
Caravan SE	11587	4325	6050
Caravan LE	13462	4850	6650
Grand Caravan SE	13162	4850	6675
Grand Caravan LE	15509	5400	7275

DEDUCT FOR 88 CARAVAN:
4 Cyl Eng -195
REFER TO 88 DODGE TRUCK OPTIONS TABLE Pg123

COLT 4 Cyl 1988

FWD/AT/PS/AC

Model/Body/Type	BaseList	Whlse	Retail
3 Dr Hbk	5899	625	1425
4 Dr E Sdn	7624	1150	2050
3 Dr E Hbk	6318	900	1750
4 Dr DL Sdn	8048	1350	2300
3 Dr DL Hbk	7625	1275	2200
4 Dr DL Wgn	8663	1600	2575
4 Dr Premier Sdn	8943	1800	2850
4 Dr Vista Wgn	11122	2525	3675
4 Dr 4WD Vista Wgn(5 Spd)	12405	2850	4100

ADD FOR 88 COLT:
4 Cyl Turbo Eng +160
DEDUCT FOR 88 COLT:
No AC -215 *No Auto Trans -195*

D-SERIES PICKUP V8 1988

AT/PS/AC

Model/Body/Type	BaseList	Whlse	Retail
D100 Pickup 1/2 Ton			
Sweptline 6 1/2'	9304	3925	5600
Sweptline 8'	9483	4025	5725
D150 Pickup 1/2 Ton			
Sweptline 6 1/2'	10499	4200	5875
Sweptline 8'	10690	4300	6025
D250 Pickup 3/4 Ton			
Sweptline 8'	11528	4650	6400
D350 Pickup 1 Ton			
Sweptline 8'	12096	5050	7225

ADD FOR 88 D-SERIES PICKUP:
LE Pkg +275
DEDUCT FOR 88 D-SERIES PICKUP:
6 Cyl Eng -230
REFER TO 88 DODGE TRUCK OPTIONS TABLE Pg123

DAKOTA V6 1/2 Ton 1988

AT/PS/AC

Model/Body/Type	BaseList	Whlse	Retail
Sweptline S 6 1/2' (4 cyl,5 spd)	7011	2675	4100
Sweptline 6 1/2'	8653	3175	4700
Sweptline LB 8'	8931	3250	4800
Sweptline Sport 6 1/2'	9995	3650	5225

ADD FOR 88 DAKOTA:
LE Pkg +315
DEDUCT FOR 88 DAKOTA:
4 Cyl Eng -195
REFER TO 88 DODGE TRUCK OPTIONS TABLE Pg123

DAYTONA 4 Cyl 1988

FWD/AT/PS/AC

Model/Body/Type	BaseList	Whlse	Retail
2 Dr Hbk	9823	2075	3225
2 Dr Pacifica Hbk	14513	3200	4600
2 Dr Shelby Z Hbk	13394	3175	4575

ADD FOR 88 DAYTONA:
4 Cyl Turbo Eng(Std Pacifica,Shelby) +160
T-Top +350
DEDUCT FOR 88 DAYTONA:
No AC -330 *No Auto Trans -230*

DIPLOMAT V8 1988

AT/PS/AC

Model/Body/Type	BaseList	Whlse	Retail
4 Dr Sdn	12127	1550	2675
4 Dr Salon Sdn	11407	1250	2275
4 Dr SE Sdn	14221	1850	3100

DEDUCT FOR 88 DIPLOMAT:
No AC -370

DYNASTY 1988

FWD/AT/PS/AC

Model/Body/Type	BaseList	Whlse	Retail
4 Cyl Models			
4 Dr Sdn	11666	1900	3125
4 Dr Premium Sdn	12226	2175	3450
V6 Models			
4 Dr Sdn	12326	2275	3550
4 Dr Premium Sdn	12886	2550	3900

DEDUCT FOR 88 DYNASTY:
No AC -370

LANCER 4 Cyl 1988

FWD/AT/PS/AC

Model/Body/Type	BaseList	Whlse	Retail
4 Dr Lbk	10482	2175	3350
4 Dr ES Lbk	12715	2625	3875

ADD FOR 88 LANCER:
4 Cyl Turbo Eng +160 *Shelby Pkg +725*
DEDUCT FOR 88 LANCER:
No AC -330 *No Auto Trans -290*

MINI RAM VAN 6 Cyl 1988

FWD/AT/PS/AC

Model/Body/Type	BaseList	Whlse	Retail
Van	9717	2975	4475

DEDUCT FOR 88 MINI RAM VAN:
4 Cyl Eng -195
REFER TO 88 DODGE TRUCK OPTIONS TABLE Pg123

OMNI AMERICA 4 Cyl 1988

FWD/AT/PS/AC

Model/Body/Type	BaseList	Whlse	Retail
4 Dr Hbk	5999	1025	1925

DEDUCT FOR 88 OMNI AMERICA:
No AC -215 *No Auto Trans -195*

RAIDER 6 Cyl — 1988

Model/Body/Type	BaseList	Whlse	Retail
4WD/AT/PS/AC			
2 Dr Utility	11083	3875	5550

REFER TO 88 DODGE TRUCK OPTIONS TABLE Pg123

RAM 50 4 Cyl 1/2 Ton — 1988

Model/Body/Type	BaseList	Whlse	Retail
AT/PS/AC			
Pkup 6'	6845	2225	3575
LB Pkup	7456	2325	3700
Sport Pkup	8544	2575	4000
Custom LB Pkup	7966	2525	3950
Extended Cab Pkup	7670	2800	4275
Sport Ext Cab Pkup	9241	3150	4700
Custom Ext Cab 4WD Pkup	10584	4250	5950

REFER TO 88 DODGE TRUCK OPTIONS TABLE Pg123

RAMCHARGER V8 1/2 Ton — 1988

Model/Body/Type	BaseList	Whlse	Retail
AT/PS/AC			
2 Dr 100 Utility	11776	3575	5150
2 Dr 100 4WD Utility	12589	4850	6650
2 Dr 150 Utility	13640	4175	5875
2 Dr 150 4WD Utility	14490	5425	7300

ADD FOR 88 RAMCHARGER:
LE Pkg +315

REFER TO 88 DODGE TRUCK OPTIONS TABLE Pg123

SHADOW 4 Cyl — 1988

Model/Body/Type	BaseList	Whlse	Retail
FWD/AT/PS/AC			
4 Dr Lbk	8075	1650	2625
2 Dr Lbk	7875	1550	2525

ADD FOR 88 SHADOW:
4 Cyl Turbo Eng +160
DEDUCT FOR 88 SHADOW:
No Auto Trans -230 *No AC -250*

88 DODGE TRUCK OPTIONS TABLE

ADD FOR ALL 88 DODGE TRUCKS:
15 Pass Seating +170
4-Whl Drive +850
AC-Rear +105
Dual Rear Whls +185
Sunroof-Pwr +80
DEDUCT FOR ALL 88 DODGE TRUCKS
No AC -125

1987 DODGE

600 4 Cyl — 1987

Model/Body/Type	BaseList	Whlse	Retail
FWD/AT/PS/AC			
4 Dr Sdn	9891	1200	1475
4 Dr SE Sdn	10553	1475	2525

ADD FOR 87 600:
4 Cyl Turbo Eng +135

ARIES 4 Cyl — 1987

Model/Body/Type	BaseList	Whlse	Retail
FWD/AT/PS/AC			
4 Dr Sdn	7655	925	1800
2 Dr Cpe	7655	875	1700
4 Dr LE Sdn	8134	1100	2000
2 Dr LE Cpe	8134	1000	1900
4 Dr LE Wgn	8579	1400	2350

B150/B250/B350 VANS V8 — 1987

Model/Body/Type	BaseList	Whlse	Retail
AT/PS/AC			
B150 Van 1/2 Ton			
Wagon	11673	3500	5050
Value Wagon	11634	3550	5125
Van	9620	2425	3825
Long Range Ram Van	9694	2475	3875
B250 Van 3/4 Ton			
Wagon	12254	3575	5150
Van	10089	2475	3875
B350 Van 1 Ton			
Wagon	13820	3675	5550
Van	11698	2600	4300

ADD FOR 87 B150/B250/B350 VAN:
LE Pkg +315
DEDUCT FOR 87 B150/B250/B350 VAN:
6 Cyl Eng -195

REFER TO 87 DODGE TRUCK OPTIONS TABLE Pg124

CARAVAN 4 Cyl — 1987

Model/Body/Type	BaseList	Whlse	Retail
FWD/AT/PS/AC			
Caravan	10333	2950	4425
Caravan SE	10810	3350	4900
Caravan LE	11674	3800	5425
Grand Caravan SE (V6)	11751	4050	5725
Grand Caravan LE (V6)	12561	4500	6225

ADD FOR 87 CARAVAN:
V6 Eng +160

REFER TO 87 DODGE TRUCK OPTIONS TABLE Pg124

CHARGER 4 Cyl — 1987

Model/Body/Type	BaseList	Whlse	Retail
FWD/AT/PS/AC			
2 Dr Hbk	6999	1100	2000
2 Dr Shelby Hbk	9840	1550	2525

COLT 4 Cyl — 1987

Model/Body/Type	BaseList	Whlse	Retail
FWD/AT/PS/AC			
4 Dr E Sdn	7290	650	1450
3 Dr E Hbk	6056	550	1350
4 Dr DL Sdn	7677	1000	1900
3 Dr DL Hbk	7152	900	1775
4 Dr Premier Sdn	8638	1425	2375
4 Dr Vista Wgn	10158	2000	3100
4 Dr 4WD Vista Wgn(5 Spd)	11371	2400	3550

ADD FOR 87 COLT:
4 Cyl Turbo Eng +135

Model/Body/Type	BaseList	Whlse	Retail
D-SERIES PICKUPS V8			**1987**
AT/PS/AC			
D100 Pickup 1/2 Ton			
Sweptline 6 1/2'	7653	**2825**	**4300**
Sweptline 8'	7825	**2925**	**4400**
D150 Pickup 1/2 Ton			
Sweptline 6 1/2'	8550	**3075**	**4575**
Sweptline 8'	8735	**3150**	**4700**
D250 Pickup 3/4 Ton			
Sweptline 8'	10226	**3425**	**4975**
D350 Pickup 1 Ton			
Sweptline 8'	12053	**3825**	**5800**

ADD FOR 87 D-SERIES PICKUP:
LE Pkg +195
REFER TO 87 DODGE TRUCK OPTIONS TABLE Pg124

Model/Body/Type	BaseList	Whlse	Retail
DAKOTA V6 1/2 Ton			**1987**
AT/PS/AC			
Sweptline S 6 1/2' (4 cyl,5 spd)	6590	**2275**	**3625**
Sweptline 6 1/2'	7529	**2500**	**3900**
Sweptline 8'	7764	**2600**	**4025**

ADD FOR 87 DAKOTA:
LE Pkg +230
DEDUCT FOR 87 DAKOTA:
4 Cyl Eng -160
REFER TO 87 DODGE TRUCK OPTIONS TABLE Pg124

Model/Body/Type	BaseList	Whlse	Retail
DAYTONA 4 Cyl			**1987**
FWD/AT/PS/AC			
2 Dr Hbk	9799	**1550**	**2600**
2 Dr Pacifica Hbk	13912	**2350**	**3575**
2 Dr Shelby Z Hbk	12749	**2325**	**3550**

ADD FOR 87 DAYTONA:
4 Cyl Turbo Eng(Std Pacifica,Shelby) +135

Model/Body/Type	BaseList	Whlse	Retail
DIPLOMAT V8			**1987**
AT/PS/AC			
4 Dr Salon Sdn	10598	**925**	**1925**
4 Dr SE Sdn	11678	**1500**	**2625**
LANCER 4 Cyl			**1987**
FWD/AT/PS/AC			
4 Dr Hbk	9474	**1450**	**2500**
4 Dr ES Hbk	11678	**1775**	**2925**

ADD FOR 87 LANCER:
4 Cyl Turbo Eng +135

Model/Body/Type	BaseList	Whlse	Retail
MINI RAM VAN 4 Cyl			**1987**
FWD/AT/PS/AC			
Van	8965	**2225**	**3575**
Royal Van	9767	**2400**	**3800**

ADD FOR 87 MINI RAM VAN:
6 Cyl Eng +160
REFER TO 87 DODGE TRUCK OPTIONS TABLE Pg124

Model/Body/Type	BaseList	Whlse	Retail
OMNI 4 Cyl			**1987**
FWD/AT/PS/AC			
4 Dr America Hbk	5499	**775**	**1600**
RAIDER 4 Cyl			**1987**
4WD/AT/PS/AC			
2 Dr Utility	10165	**3150**	**4700**

REFER TO 87 DODGE TRUCK OPTIONS TABLE Pg124

Model/Body/Type	BaseList	Whlse	Retail
RAM 50 4 Cyl 1/2 Ton			**1987**
AT/PS/AC			
Pkup 6'	6302	**1650**	**2850**
LB Pkup	6999	**1750**	**3000**
Sport Pkup	7659	**1875**	**3150**
Custom LB Pkup	7059	**1850**	**3125**

REFER TO 87 DODGE TRUCK OPTIONS TABLE Pg124

Model/Body/Type	BaseList	Whlse	Retail
RAMCHARGER V8 1/2 Ton			**1987**
AT/PS/AC			
2 Dr Utility	12637	**3075**	**4575**
2 Dr 4WD Utility	13538	**4175**	**5875**

ADD FOR 87 RAMCHARGER:
LE Pkg +195
REFER TO 87 DODGE TRUCK OPTIONS TABLE Pg124

Model/Body/Type	BaseList	Whlse	Retail
SHADOW 4 Cyl			**1987**
FWD/AT/PS/AC			
4 Dr Lbk	7499	**1325**	**2250**
2 Dr Lbk	7699	**1250**	**2175**

ADD FOR 87 SHADOW:
4 Cyl Turbo Eng +135

87 DODGE TRUCK OPTIONS TABLE
ADD FOR ALL 87 DODGE TRUCKS:
15 Pass Seating +125
4-Whl Drive +680
Dual Rear Whls +125
DEDUCT FOR ALL 87 DODGE TRUCKS
No AC -80

1986 DODGE

Model/Body/Type	BaseList	Whlse	Retail
600			**1986**
FWD			
4 Dr Sdn	9156	**900**	**1875**
2 Dr Cpe	9390	**825**	**1775**
4 Dr SE Sdn	9813	**1125**	**2175**
2 Dr Conv	11523	**2025**	**3200**
2 Dr ES Turbo Conv	14780	**2425**	**3675**

DODGE

Model/Body/Type	BaseList	Whlse	Retail
ARIES			**1986**
FWD			
4 Dr Sdn	7179	**700**	**1675**
2 Dr Cpe	7062	**600**	**1575**
4 Dr SE Sdn	7634	**825**	**1775**
2 Dr SE Cpe	7514	**750**	**1700**
4 Dr SE Wgn	8002	**1000**	**2025**
4 Dr LE Sdn	8082	**950**	**1975**
2 Dr LE Cpe	7962	**900**	**1875**
4 Dr LE Wgn	8812	**1175**	**2200**
B150/B250/B350 VANS			**1986**
B150 Van 1/2 Ton			
Wagon	10987	**2725**	**4300**
Van	9040	**2075**	**3500**
B250 Van 3/4 Ton			
Wagon	11535	**2800**	**4375**
Van	9489	**2125**	**3575**
B350 Van 1 Ton			
Wagon	12650	**2875**	**4475**
Van	10716	**2200**	**3675**
ADD FOR 86 B150/250/350 VAN:			
15 Pass Seating +80			
CARAVAN			**1986**
FWD			
Caravan	9506	**2275**	**3800**
Caravan SE	9785	**2450**	**4000**
Caravan LE	10528	**2675**	**4250**
CHARGER			**1986**
FWD			
2 Dr Hbk	6741	**750**	**1700**
2 Dr 2.2 Hbk	7686	**925**	**1925**
2 Dr Shelby Hbk	9315	**1250**	**2275**
COLT			**1986**
FWD			
4 Dr E Sdn	6310	**425**	**1350**
3 Dr E Hbk	5431	**350**	**1275**
4 Dr DL Sdn	6629	**675**	**1650**
3 Dr DL Hbk	6318	**600**	**1550**
4 Dr Premier Sdn	7624	**950**	**1975**
4 Dr Vista Wgn	8814	**1500**	**2600**
4 Dr 4WD Vista Wgn (5 Spd)	9913	**1900**	**3100**
CONQUEST			**1986**
2 Dr Hbk	13417	**1625**	**2750**
D-SERIES PICKUPS			**1986**
AT/PS/AC			
D100 Pickup 1/2 Ton			
Sweptline 6 1/2'	7291	**2050**	**3475**
Sweptline 8'	7515	**2100**	**3550**
D150 Pickup 1/2 Ton			
Sweptline 6 1/2'	8010	**2150**	**3600**
Sweptline 8'	8184	**2200**	**3675**
D250 Pickup 3/4 Ton			
Sweptline 8'	9333	**2400**	**3950**
D350 Pickup 1 Ton			
Sweptline 8'	11311	**2725**	**4300**
ADD FOR 86 D-SERIES PICKUP:			
4-Whl Drive +495			
DAYTONA			**1986**
FWD			
2 Dr Hbk	9066	**1125**	**2175**
2 Dr Turbo Z Hbk	11368	**1750**	**2925**
DIPLOMAT			**1986**
4 Dr Salon Sdn	9947	**775**	**1725**
4 Dr SE Sdn	11022	**1100**	**2150**
LANCER			**1986**
FWD			
4 Dr Hbk	9354	**1150**	**2175**
4 Dr ES Hbk	10250	**1375**	**2450**
MINI RAM VAN			**1986**
FWD			
Van	8308	**1625**	**3000**
Royal Van	9125	**1775**	**3150**
OMNI			**1986**
FWD			
4 Dr Hbk	6209	**475**	**1425**
4 Dr SE Hbk	6558	**750**	**1700**
4 Dr GLH Hbk	7918	**950**	**1975**
RAM 50 1/2 Ton			**1986**
Pkup	5788	**1275**	**2550**
Sport Pkup	6712	**1450**	**2800**
RAMCHARGER 1/2 Ton			**1986**
2 Dr Utility	11534	**2600**	**4150**
2 Dr 4WD Utility	12763	**3400**	**5050**

1985 DODGE

Model/Body/Type	BaseList	Whlse	Retail
600			**1985**
FWD			
4 Dr SE Sdn	8953	**725**	**1700**
2 Dr Cpe	9060	**625**	**1600**
2 Dr Conv	10889	**1550**	**2650**
2 Dr ES Turbo Conv	13995	**1850**	**3050**

DODGE 85

ARIES 1985

Model/Body/Type	BaseList	Whlse	Retail
FWD			
4 Dr Sdn	7039	**675**	**1650**
2 Dr Cpe	6924	**600**	**1550**
4 Dr SE Sdn	7439	**775**	**1725**
2 Dr SE Cpe	7321	**675**	**1650**
4 Dr SE Wgn	7909	**925**	**1925**
4 Dr LE Sdn	7792	**850**	**1800**
2 Dr LE Cpe	7659	**775**	**1725**
4 Dr LE Wgn	8348	**1000**	**2025**

B150/B250/B350 VANS 1985

Model/Body/Type	BaseList	Whlse	Retail
B150 Van 1/2 Ton			
Wagon	10118	**1900**	**3300**
Van	8432	**1325**	**2600**
B250 Van 3/4 Ton			
Wagon	10641	**1950**	**3375**
Van	8824	**1350**	**2675**
B350 Van 1 Ton			
Wagon	11705	**2025**	**3450**
Van	9929	**1425**	**2750**

CARAVAN 1985

Model/Body/Type	BaseList	Whlse	Retail
FWD			
Caravan	9147	**1700**	**3100**
Caravan SE	9393	**1800**	**3225**
Caravan LE	10005	**1975**	**3400**

CHARGER 1985

Model/Body/Type	BaseList	Whlse	Retail
FWD			
2 Dr Hbk	6584	**525**	**1475**
2 Dr 2.2 Hbk	7515	**700**	**1675**
2 Dr Shelby Hbk	9553	**900**	**1900**

COLT 1985

Model/Body/Type	BaseList	Whlse	Retail
FWD			
4 Dr E Hbk	6029	**375**	**1300**
2 Dr E Hbk	5372	**275**	**1225**
4 Dr DL Sdn	6492	**475**	**1425**
2 Dr DL Hbk	6177	**400**	**1325**
4 Dr Premier Sdn	7409	**800**	**1750**
4 Dr Vista Wgn	8721	**1225**	**2250**
4 Dr 4WD Vista Wgn	9809	**1550**	**2675**

CONQUEST 1985

Model/Body/Type	BaseList	Whlse	Retail
2 Dr Hbk	12564	**1150**	**2175**

See the Automobile Dealer Directory on page 379 for a Dealer near you!

D-SERIES PICKUPS 1985

Model/Body/Type	BaseList	Whlse	Retail
D100 Pickup 1/2 Ton			
Sweptline 6 1/2'	6775	**1600**	**2950**
Sweptline 8'	6991	**1650**	**3025**
D150 Pickup 1/2 Ton			
Utiline 6 1/2'	7589	**1625**	**3000**
Sweptline 6 1/2'	7456	**1675**	**3050**
Utiline 8'	7755	**1700**	**3075**
Sweptline 8'	7622	**1725**	**3125**
D250 Pickup 3/4 Ton			
Utiline 8'	8522	**1850**	**3250**
Sweptline 8'	8389	**1900**	**3300**
D350 Pickup 1 Ton			
Sweptline 8'	9331	**2175**	**3650**
Swept Crew Cab 6 1/2'	10535	**2750**	**4325**
Sweptline Crew Cab 8'	10629	**2825**	**4400**

DAYTONA 1985

Model/Body/Type	BaseList	Whlse	Retail
FWD			
2 Dr Hbk	8505	**875**	**1825**
2 Dr Turbo Hbk	10286	**1100**	**2150**
2 Dr Turbo Z Hbk	11620	**1375**	**2475**

DIPLOMAT 1985

Model/Body/Type	BaseList	Whlse	Retail
4 Dr Salon Sdn	9399	**600**	**1550**
4 Dr SE Sdn	10418	**900**	**1875**

LANCER 1985

Model/Body/Type	BaseList	Whlse	Retail
FWD			
4 Dr Hbk	8713	**900**	**1900**
4 Dr ES Hbk	9690	**1100**	**2150**

MINI RAM VAN 1985

Model/Body/Type	BaseList	Whlse	Retail
FWD			
Van	7972	**1125**	**2350**
Royal Van	8760	**1250**	**2500**

OMNI 1985

Model/Body/Type	BaseList	Whlse	Retail
FWD			
4 Dr Hbk	5977	**300**	**1250**
4 Dr SE Hbk	6298	**500**	**1450**
4 Dr GLH Hbk	7620	**725**	**1700**

RAM 50 PICKUP 1985

Model/Body/Type	BaseList	Whlse	Retail
Custom Pkup	5684	**1000**	**2225**
Royal Pkup	6290	**1125**	**2350**
Sport Pkup	7018	**1175**	**2400**

RAMCHARGER 1985

Model/Body/Type	BaseList	Whlse	Retail
2 Dr Utility	10471	**1900**	**3300**
2 Dr 4WD Utility	11581	**2500**	**4050**

DODGE

EAGLE

USA

1992 Eagle Talon TSi AWD

For an Eagle dealer in your area, see our Dealer Directory (pg 217)

1994 EAGLE

SUMMIT 4 Cyl — 1994

Model/Body/Type	BaseList	Whlse	Retail
FWD/AT/PS/AC			
2 Dr DL Cpe(5 spd)	9120	**5285**	**6870**
2 Dr ES Cpe	10060	-	-
4 Dr ES Sdn	12181	-	-
4 Dr LX Sdn	11428	-	-
3 Dr DL Wgn	12979	-	-
3 Dr LX Wgn	14194	-	-
3 Dr 4WD Wgn	14884	-	-

ADD FOR 94 SUMMIT:

Tilt Whl(Std LX S/W,4WD) +75

TALON 4 Cyl — 1994

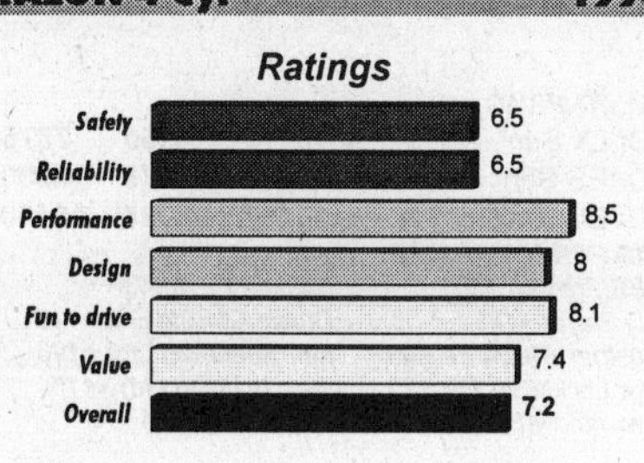

Model/Body/Type	BaseList	Whlse	Retail
FWD/AT/PS/AC			
2 Dr DL Lbk	11892	-	-
2 Dr ES Lbk	14362	-	-
2 Dr TSi Turbo Lbk	15885	-	-
2 Dr 4WD TSi Turbo Lbk	17978	-	-

VISION V6 — 1994

Ratings

Rating	Score
Safety	8.5
Reliability	9.2
Performance	8.2
Design	8.8
Fun to drive	8.1
Value	8.8
Overall	8.7

Model/Body/Type	BaseList	Whlse	Retail
FWD/AT/PS/AC			
4 Dr ESi Sdn	19308	**15425**	**18050**
4 Dr TSi Sdn	22773	**18700**	**21650**

ADD FOR 94 VISION:

ABS(Std TSi) +430
Anti-Theft/Recovery Sys +365
Car Phone +230 — *CD Player +275*
Custom Whls/Cvrs +230 — *Infinity Ster Sys +230*
Leather Seats +320 — *Pwr Seat(Std TSi) +180*

1993 EAGLE

SUMMIT 4 Cyl — 1993

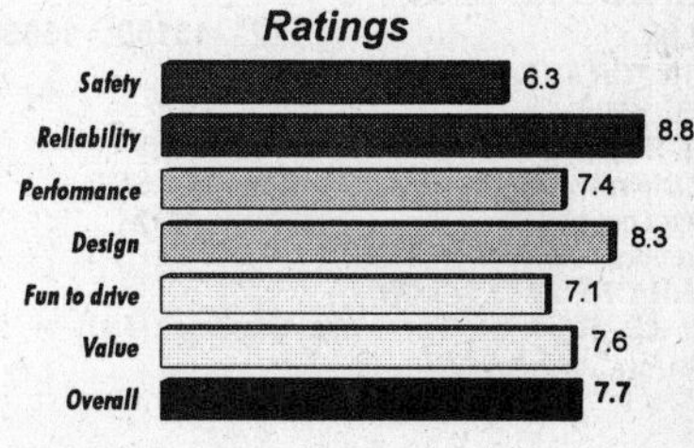

EAGLE

FWD/AT/PS/AC

Model/Body/Type	BaseList	Whlse	Retail
2 Dr DL Cpe	7806	**5700**	**7200**
4 Dr DL Sdn	9448	**7150**	**8925**
2 Dr ES Cpe	8705	**6625**	**8250**
4 Dr ES Sdn	10423	**7750**	**9600**
4 Dr DL Wgn	11455	**9350**	**11275**
4 Dr LX Wgn	12368	**9800**	**11800**
4 Dr AWD Wgn	13539	**10150**	**12225**

ADD FOR 93 SUMMIT:

ABS +390
Cass +75
Cruise Ctrl +115
Custom Whls/Cvrs +160
Luggage Rack +75
Pwr Locks +75
Pwr Wndw +115
Tilt Whl(Std LX,AWD) +75

DEDUCT FOR 93 SUMMIT:

No AC -430
No Auto Trans -390
No Pwr Steering -135

TALON 4 Cyl — 1993

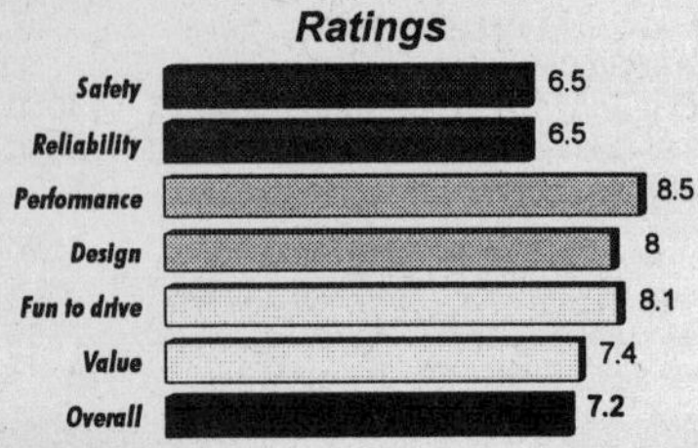

FWD/AT/PS/AC

Model/Body/Type	BaseList	Whlse	Retail
2 Dr DL Lbk	11752	**8900**	**10900**
2 Dr ES Lbk	14197	**10100**	**12275**
2 Dr TSi Turbo Lbk	15703	**11425**	**13800**
2 Dr AWD TSi Turbo Lbk	17772	**13150**	**15650**

ADD FOR 93 TALON:

ABS +390
Cass(DL) +100
CD Player +195
Cruise Ctrl +135
Custom Whls/Cvrs +175
Leather Seats +230
Pwr Locks +100
Pwr Wndw +135
Sunroof +230

DEDUCT FOR 93 TALON:

No AC -545
No Auto Trans -430
No Pwr Steering -175

See the Automobile Dealer Directory on page 379 for a Dealer near you!

VISION V6 — 1993

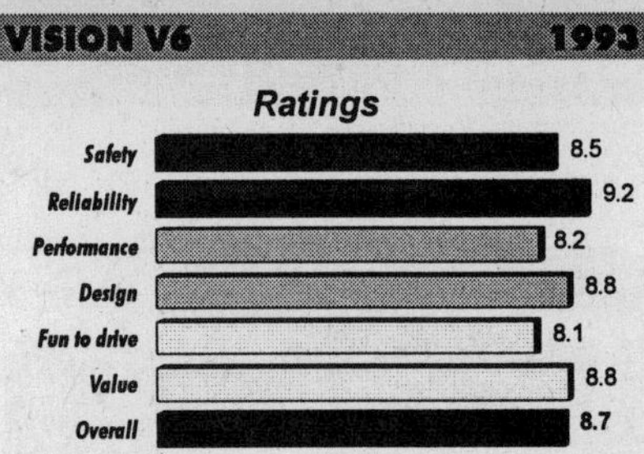

FWD/AT/PS/AC

Model/Body/Type	BaseList	Whlse	Retail
4 Dr ESi Sdn	17387	**12600**	**15075**
4 Dr TSi Sdn	21104	**15600**	**18250**

ADD FOR 93 VISION:

ABS(Std TSi) +390
Car Phone +175
Cass(Std TSi) +115
CD Player +230
CruiseCtrl(Std TSi) +160
Custom Whls/Cvrs +195
Leather Seats +275
Pwr Locks(Std TSi) +115
Pwr Seat +160
Pwr Wndw +160

1992 EAGLE

PREMIER V6 — 1992

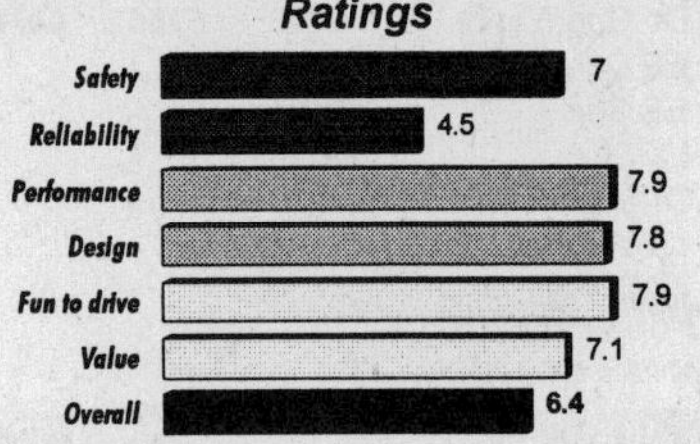

FWD/AT/PS/AC

Model/Body/Type	BaseList	Whlse	Retail
4 Dr LX Sdn	15716	**6150**	**7875**
4 Dr ES Sdn	18057	**7075**	**8900**
4 Dr ES Limited Sdn	20212	**8225**	**10150**

ADD FOR 92 PREMIER:

ABS(Std Ltd) +350
Cass(Std ES) +75
CD Player +175
Cruise Ctrl(Std ES) +115
Custom Whls/Cvrs +160
Lthr Seats(Std Ltd) +195
Pwr Locks(Std ES) +75
Pwr Seat(Std Ltd) +115
Pwr Wndw(Std Ltd) +115
Tilt Whl(Std ES) +75

Model/Body/Type	BaseList	Whlse	Retail

SUMMIT 4 Cyl — 1992

Ratings

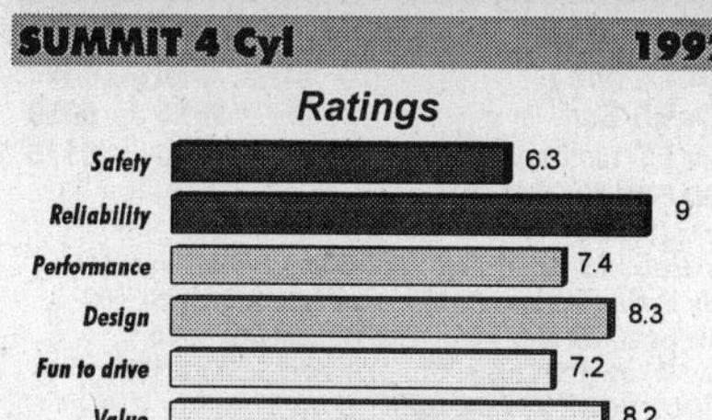

FWD/AT/PS/AC

Model/Body/Type	BaseList	Whlse	Retail
3 Dr Hbk	7602	**4025**	**5375**
3 Dr ES Hbk	8122	**4575**	**6000**
4 Dr Sdn	8981	**5025**	**6550**
4 Dr ES Sdn	9998	**5600**	**7150**
4 Dr DL Wgn	11397	**7200**	**8975**
4 Dr LX Wgn	12102	**7550**	**9375**
4 Dr AWD Wgn	13469	**7900**	**9775**

ADD FOR 92 SUMMIT:
ABS +350 | *Cass +60*
Cruise Ctrl +100 | *Custom Whls/Cvrs +135*
Luggage Rack +60 | *Pwr Locks +60*
Pwr Wndw +100

DEDUCT FOR 92 SUMMIT:
No AC -390 | *No Auto Trans -350*
No Pwr Steering -115

TALON 4 Cyl — 1992

Ratings

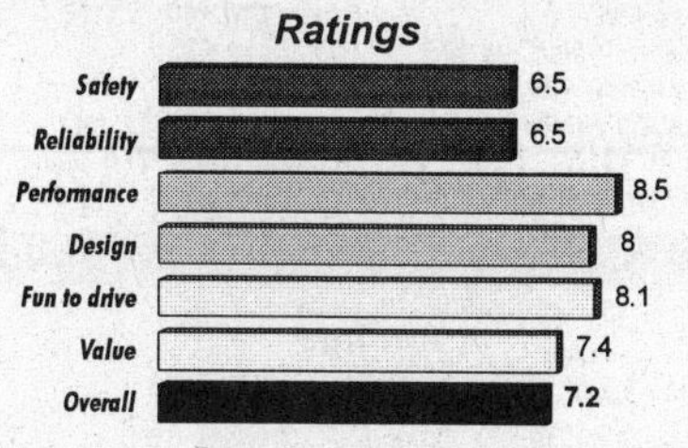

FWD/AT/PS/AC

Model/Body/Type	BaseList	Whlse	Retail
2 Dr Lbk	13631	**8650**	**10575**
2 Dr TSi Turbo Lbk	14963	**9925**	**12075**
2 Dr AWD TSi Turbo Lbk	16905	**11525**	**13900**

ADD FOR 92 TALON:
ABS +350 | *CD Player +175*
Cruise Ctrl +115 | *Leather Seats +195*
Pwr Locks +75 | *Pwr Wndw +115*
Sunroof +195

DEDUCT FOR 92 TALON:
No AC -505 | *No Auto Trans -390*

1991 EAGLE

PREMIER V6 — 1991

Ratings

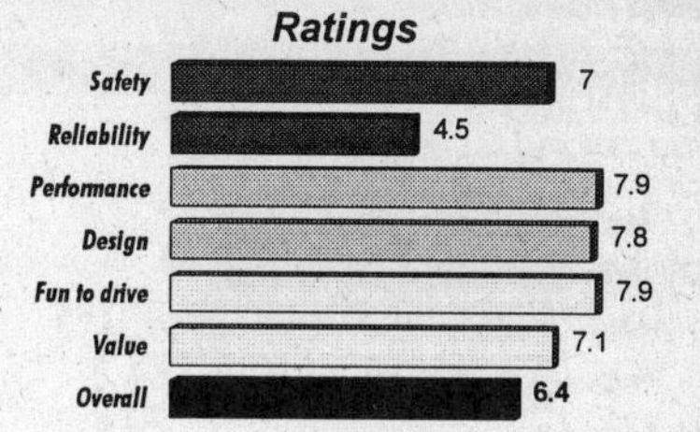

FWD/AT/PS/AC

Model/Body/Type	BaseList	Whlse	Retail
4 Dr LX Sdn	15250	**4000**	**5525**
4 Dr ES Sdn	17455	**4750**	**6375**
4 Dr ES Limited Sdn	19695	**5800**	**7500**

ADD FOR 91 PREMIER:
ABS(Std Ltd) +315 | *Cass(Std ES) +60*
CD Player +160 | *Cruise Ctrl(Std ES) +100*
Custom Whls/Cvrs +135 | *Lthr Seats(Std Ltd) +160*
Pwr Locks(Std ES) +60 | *Pwr Seat(Std Ltd) +100*
Pwr Wndw(Std Ltd) +100 | *Tilt Whl(Std ES) +60*

SUMMIT 4 Cyl — 1991

Ratings

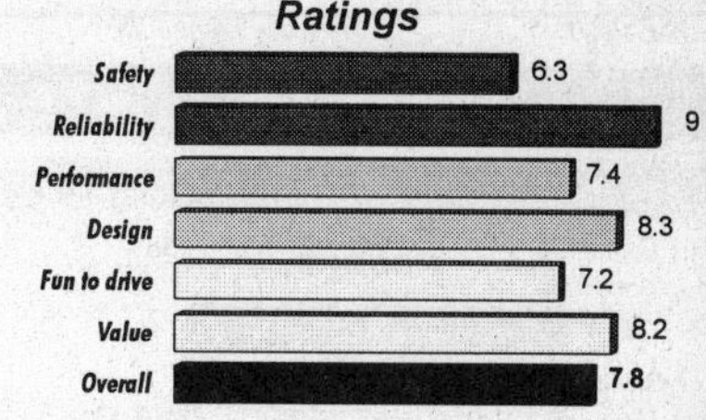

EAGLE 91-90

Model/Body/Type	BaseList	Whlse	Retail
FWD/AT/PS/AC			
3 Dr Hbk	6949	**3450**	**4775**
3 Dr ES Hbk	7845	**3900**	**5250**
4 Dr Sdn	8618	**4300**	**5725**
4 Dr ES Sdn	9623	**4725**	**6200**

ADD FOR 91 SUMMIT:

Cass +35 | *Cruise Ctrl +75*
Custom Whls/Cvrs +115 | *Pwr Locks +35*
Pwr Wndw +75

DEDUCT FOR 91 SUMMIT:

No AC -350 | *No Auto Trans -315*
No Pwr Steering -100

TALON 4 Cyl 1991

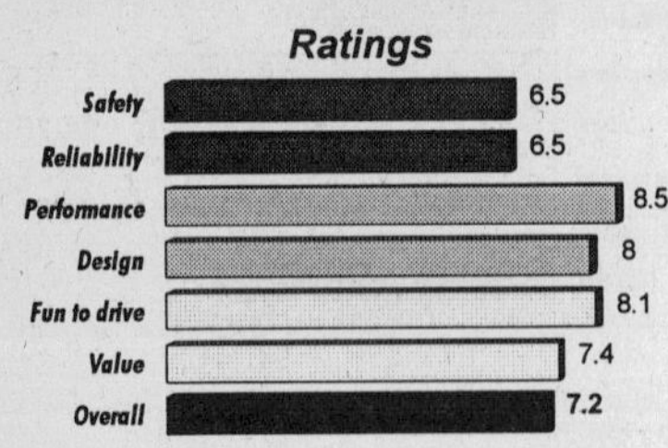

Model/Body/Type	BaseList	Whlse	Retail
FWD/AT/PS/AC			
2 Dr Lbk	12990	**6850**	**8675**
2 Dr TSi Turbo Lbk	14609	**8025**	**9950**
2 Dr AWD TSi Turbo Lbk	16513	**9525**	**11575**

ADD FOR 91 TALON:

ABS +315 | *CD Player +160*
Cruise Ctrl +100 | *Leather Seats +160*
Pwr Locks +60 | *Pwr Wndw +100*
Sunroof +160

DEDUCT FOR 91 TALON:

No AC -470 | *No Auto Trans -350*

1990 EAGLE

PREMIER V6 1990

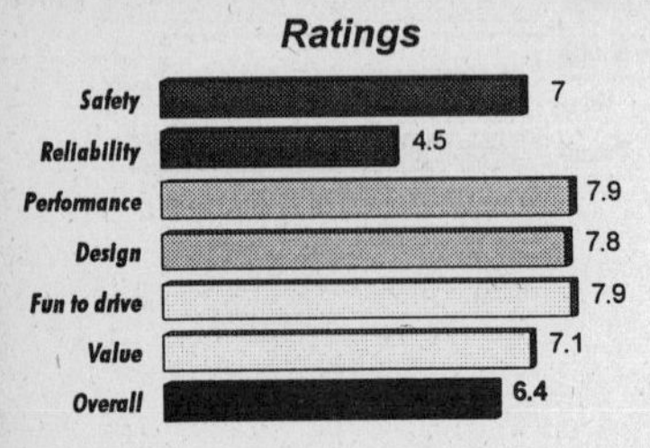

Model/Body/Type	BaseList	Whlse	Retail
FWD/AT/PS/AC			
4 Dr LX Sdn	15350	**2950**	**4300**
4 Dr ES Sdn	17845	**3625**	**5050**
4 Dr ES Limited Sdn	20284	**4600**	**6175**

ADD FOR 90 PREMIER:

Cass(Std ES) +60 | *CD Player +115*
CruiseCtrl(Std Ltd) +75 | *Custom Whls/Cvrs +115*
Lthr Seats(Std Ltd) +115 | *Pwr Locks(Std ES) +60*
Pwr Seat(Std Ltd) +75 | *Pwr Sunroof +315*
Pwr Wndw(Std Ltd) +75 | *Tilt Whl(Std Ltd) +60*

DEDUCT FOR 90 PREMIER:

No AC -430

SUMMIT 4 Cyl 1990

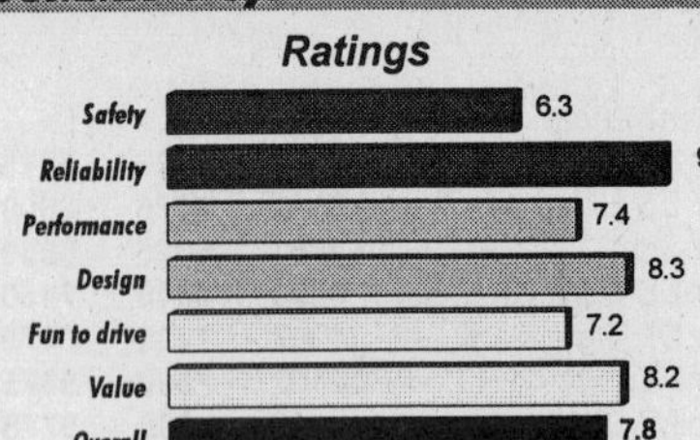

Model/Body/Type	BaseList	Whlse	Retail
FWD/AT/PS/AC			
4 Dr Sdn	8895	**2250**	**3350**
4 Dr DL Sdn	9456	**2525**	**3675**
4 Dr LX Sdn	10408	**3025**	**4275**
4 Dr ES Sdn	11257	**3350**	**4700**

ADD FOR 90 SUMMIT:

Cass +35 | *Cruise Ctrl +60*
Custom Whls/Cvrs +75 | *Pwr Locks +35*
Pwr Wndw +60

DEDUCT FOR 90 SUMMIT:

No AC -315 | *No Auto Trans -275*
No Pwr Steering -75

TALON 4 Cyl 1990

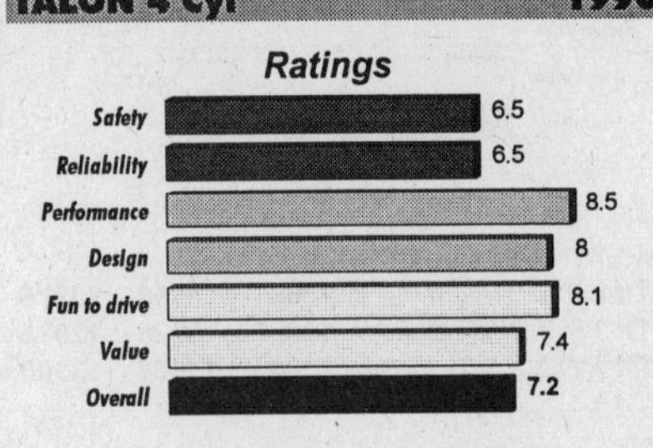

Model/Body/Type	BaseList	Whlse	Retail
FWD/AT/PS/AC			
2 Dr Lbk	12995	**5325**	**7025**
2 Dr TSi Turbo Lbk	14753	**6100**	**7800**
2 Dr AWD TSi Turbo Lbk	16437	**7375**	**9250**

ADD FOR 90 TALON:

CD Player +115 | *Cruise Ctrl +75*
Leather Seats +115 | *Pwr Locks +60*
Pwr Wndw +75 | *Sunroof +115*

DEDUCT FOR 90 TALON:

No AC -430 | *No Auto Trans -315*

1989 EAGLE

MEDALLION 4 Cyl 1989

Model/Body/Type	BaseList	Whlse	Retail
FWD/AT/PS/AC			
4 Dr DL Sdn	10405	**1275**	**2200**
4 Dr DL Wgn	11649	**1600**	**2575**
4 Dr LX Sdn	10938	**1425**	**2375**
4 Dr LX Wgn	12275	**1750**	**2775**

ADD FOR 89 MEDALLION:

Cass +25 | *Cruise Ctrl +35*
Custom Whls/Cvrs +35 | *Pwr Locks +25*
Pwr Sunroof +160 | *Pwr Wndw +35*
Third Seat +60

DEDUCT FOR 89 MEDALLION:

No AC -315 | *No Auto Trans -275*

PREMIER 1989

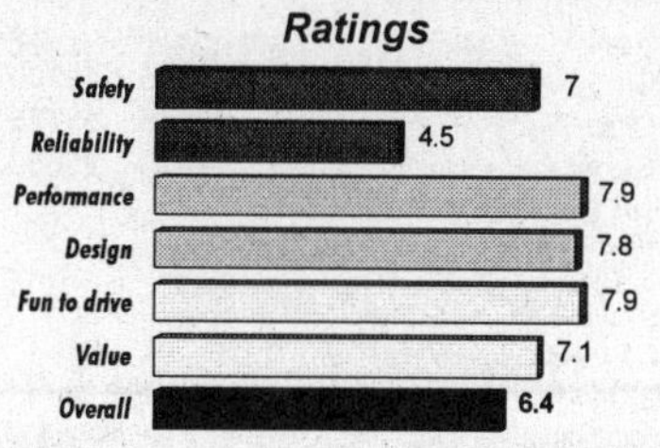

Model/Body/Type	BaseList	Whlse	Retail
FWD/AT/PS/AC			
4 Cyl Models			
4 Dr LX Sdn	13276	**1675**	**2750**
V6 Models			
4 Dr LX Sdn	13956	**2000**	**3150**
4 Dr ES Sdn	15259	**2475**	**3725**
4 Dr ES Limited Sdn	19181	**3375**	**4800**

ADD FOR 89 PREMIER:

Cass(Std Ltd) +35 | *CruiseCtrl(Std Ltd) +60*
Custom Whls/Cvrs +75 | *Lthr Seats(Std Ltd) +75*
Pwr Locks(Std Ltd) +35 | *Pwr Seat(Std Ltd) +60*
Pwr Wndw(Std Ltd) +60 | *Tilt Whl(Std Ltd) +35*

DEDUCT FOR 89 PREMIER:

No AC -390

SUMMIT 4 Cyl 1989

Ratings

Rating	Score
Safety	6.3
Reliability	9
Performance	7.4
Design	8.3
Fun to drive	7.2
Value	8.2
Overall	7.8

Model/Body/Type	BaseList	Whlse	Retail
FWD/AT/PS/AC			
4 Dr DL Sdn	9347	**1950**	**3025**
4 Dr LX Sdn	10364	**2450**	**3600**
4 Dr LX Sdn DOHC	11169	**2725**	**3900**

ADD FOR 89 SUMMIT:

Cass +25 | *Cruise Ctrl +35*
Custom Whls/Cvrs +455 | *Pwr Locks +25*
Pwr Wndw +35

DEDUCT FOR 89 SUMMIT:

No AC -275 | *No Auto Trans -230*

1988 EAGLE

EAGLE V6 1988

Model/Body/Type	BaseList	Whlse	Retail
AT/PS/AC			
4 Dr 4WD Wgn	12995	**1800**	**2950**

MEDALLION 4 Cyl 1988

Model/Body/Type	BaseList	Whlse	Retail
FWD/AT/PS/AC			
4 Dr DL Sdn	9965	**950**	**1825**
4 Dr DL Wgn	10693	**1250**	**2175**
4 Dr LX Sdn	10479	**1100**	**2000**

DEDUCT FOR 88 MEDALLION:

No AC -250 | *No Auto Trans -230*

PREMIER V6 1988

Model/Body/Type	BaseList	Whlse	Retail
FWD/AT/PS/AC			
4 Dr LX Sdn	13104	**1650**	**2725**
4 Dr ES Sdn	14079	**2025**	**3175**

DEDUCT FOR 88 PREMIER:

4 Cyl Eng -275 | *No AC -330*

FORD

FORD USA

1990 Ford Ranger

For a Ford dealer in your area, see our Dealer Directory (pg 217)

1994 FORD

AEROSTAR V6 ½ Ton 1994

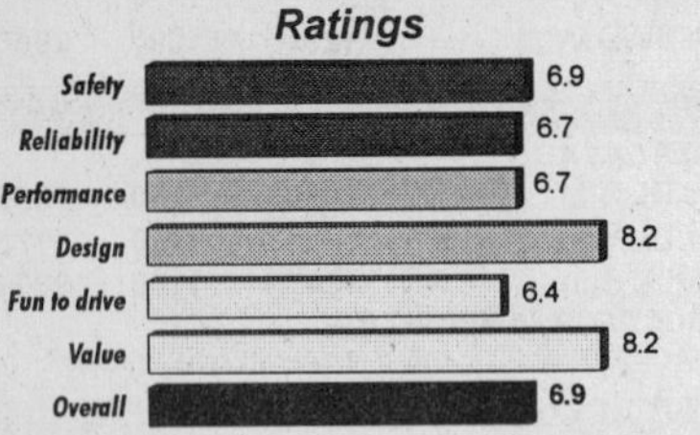

AT/PS/AC			
Cargo Van	15040	-	-
Wagon	14980	**14025**	**16800**
Window Van	15335	-	-
Extended Cargo Van	15590	-	-
Extended Wagon	16425	**15325**	**18175**
Extended Window Van	15885	-	-

ADD FOR 94 AEROSTAR:

All Whl Drive +1275 *Eddie Bauer Pkg +1590*
XLT Pkg +910

REFER TO 94 FORD TRUCK OPTIONS TABLE Pg 135

ASPIRE 4 Cyl 1994

AC/FWD			
2 Dr Hbk	8240	-	-
4 Dr Hbk	8855	-	-
2 Dr SE Hbk	8995	-	-

BRONCO V8 ½ Ton 1994

4WD/AT/PS/AC			
2 Dr Utility	21515	**18750**	**21925**

ADD FOR 94 BRONCO:

Eddie Bauer Pkg +1545 *XLT Pkg +910*

REFER TO 94 FORD TRUCK OPTIONS TABLE Pg 135

CLUB WAGON V8 ½-1 Ton 1994

Ratings

Rating	Score
Safety	8.3
Reliability	8.3
Performance	6
Design	8.7
Fun to drive	6.3
Value	7.7
Overall	7.7

AT/PS/AC			
E150 Club Wgn	18099	**16375**	**19300**
E350 Club Wgn	19344	**16775**	**19775**
E350 Super Club Wgn	21467	**17425**	**20550**

ADD FOR 94 CLUB WAGON:

Chateau Pkg +1410 *XLT Pkg +910*
V8 7.3L Dsl Eng +1000

DEDUCT FOR 94 CLUB WAGON:

6 Cyl Eng -590

REFER TO 94 FORD TRUCK OPTIONS TABLE Pg 135

CROWN VICTORIA V8 1994

AT/PS/AC			
4 Dr Sdn	19300	**14850**	**17600**
4 Dr LX Sdn	20715	**15750**	**18550**

ADD FOR 94 CROWN VICTORIA:

ABS +430
Anti-Theft/Recovery Sys +365
Car Phone +230 *Cass +135*
CD Player +275 *Cruise Ctrl +180*
Custom Whls/Cvrs +230 *JBL Stereo System +230*
Leather Seats +320 *Pwr Locks +135*
Pwr Seat(Std LX) +180

Model/Body/Type	BaseList	Whlse	Retail

ECONOLINE VAN V8 1994

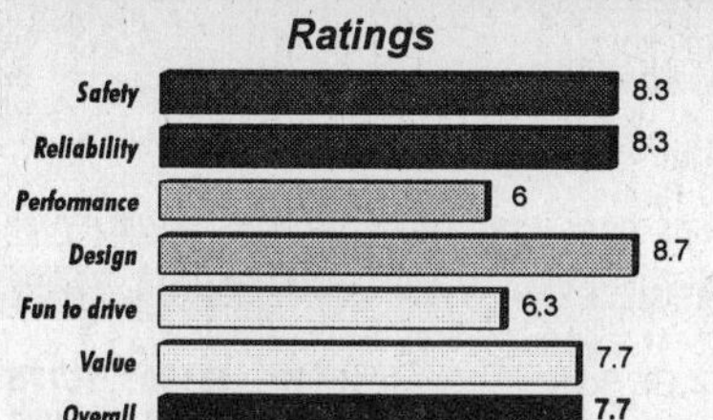

AT/PS/AC

Model/Body/Type	BaseList	Whlse	Retail
E150 Econoline Van ½ Ton			
Cargo Van	16115	**13725**	**16475**
E250 Econoline Van ¾ Ton			
Cargo Van	16473	**14025**	**16800**
Super Cargo Van	17450	**14700**	**17475**
E350 Econoline Van 1 Ton			
Cargo Van	17841	-	-
Super Cargo Van	18810	-	-

ADD FOR 94 ECONOLINE VAN:
4 Wheel ABS +430 *XL Pkg +480*
V8 7.3L Dsl Eng +1000
DEDUCT FOR 94 ECONOLINE VAN:
6 Cyl Eng -590
REFER TO 94 FORD TRUCK OPTIONS TABLE Pg 135

ESCORT 4 Cyl 1994

FWD/AT/PS/AC

Model/Body/Type	BaseList	Whlse	Retail
2 Dr Hbk	9035	**7900**	**9775**
2 Dr LX Hbk	9890	**8575**	**10425**
4 Dr LX Hbk	10325	**8875**	**10775**
4 Dr LX Sdn	10550	**9025**	**10925**
4 Dr LX Wgn	10880	**9625**	**11575**
2 Dr GT Hbk	12300	**10425**	**12550**

ADD FOR 94 ESCORT:
ABS +430
Anti-Theft/Recovery Sys +365
Cass(Std GT) +90 *CD Player +205*
Cruise Ctrl +135 *Custom Whls/Cvrs +180*
Luggage Rack(S/W) +115 *Pwr Locks +90*
Pwr Sunroof +410 *Pwr Wndw +135*
Tilt Whl +90
DEDUCT FOR 94 ESCORT:
No AC -545 *No Auto Trans -455*
No Pwr Steering -160

EXPLORER V6 ½ Ton 1994

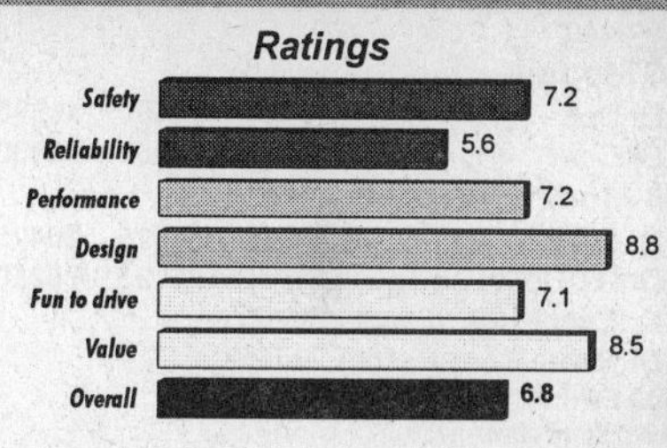

AT/PS/AC

Model/Body/Type	BaseList	Whlse	Retail
2 Dr Wgn	17240	**16900**	**19925**
4 Dr Wgn	18130	**18050**	**21225**
2 Dr 4WD Wgn	18990	**18550**	**21750**
4 Dr 4WD Wgn	19900	**19725**	**23000**

ADD FOR 94 EXPLORER:
Eddie Bauer Pkg +1545 *Limited Pkg +1865*
Sport Pkg +680 *XLT Pkg +910*
REFER TO 94 FORD TRUCK OPTIONS TABLE Pg 135

F-SERIES PICKUPS V8 1994

AT/PS/AC

Model/Body/Type	BaseList	Whlse	Retail
F150 Pickup ½ Ton			
Styleside S 6 ¾' (6 cyl)	12266	-	-
Styleside S 8' (6 cyl)	12772	-	-
Flareside 6 ¾'	14834	**13475**	**16200**
Styleside 6 ¾'	13956	**13075**	**15775**
Styleside Lightning 6 ¾'	-	-	-
Styleside 8'	14180	**13175**	**15875**
Styleside Supercab S 6 ¾'	14119	-	-
Styleside Supercab S 8'	14353	-	-
Flareside Supercab 6 ¾'	16268	**15325**	**18175**
Styleside Supercab 6 ¾'	15562	**14925**	**17750**
Styleside Supercab 8'	15805	**15025**	**17850**
F250 Pickup ¾ Ton			
Styleside 8'	14802	**14025**	**16800**
Heavy Duty 8'	15369	**14325**	**17075**
HD Supercab S 8'	16456	-	-
HD Supercab 8'	17900	**15875**	**18775**
F350 Pickup 1 Ton			
Styleside 8'	17639	**14650**	**18000**
Styleside Crew Cab 8'	19341	**16675**	**20250**
Styleside Supercab 8'	19732	**17575**	**21275**

ADD FOR 94 F-SERIES PICKUP:
V8 7.3L Dsl Eng +1000 *V8 7.3L Trb Dsl Eng +1000*
XLT Pkg +910
DEDUCT FOR 94 F-SERIES PICKUP:
6 Cyl Eng -590
REFER TO 94 FORD TRUCK OPTIONS TABLE Pg 135

FORD

Model/Body/Type	BaseList	Whlse	Retail

MUSTANG 1994

AT/PS/AC

Model/Body/Type	BaseList	Whlse	Retail
V6 Models			
2 Dr Cpe	13355	**14400**	**16975**
2 Dr Conv	20150	**18950**	**21900**
V8 Models			
2 Dr GT Cpe	17270	**17525**	**20425**
2 Dr GT Conv	21960	**22125**	**25250**
2 Dr Cobra Hbk (5 spd)	20765	-	-
2 Dr Cobra Conv (5 spd)	23535	-	-

ADD FOR 94 MUSTANG:
ABS(Std Cobra) +430
Anti-Theft/Recovery Sys +365
Cass +115 — *CD Player +230*
Cruise Ctrl +160 — *Custom Whls/Cvrs +205*
Leather Seats +275 — *Pwr Locks(Base Cpe) +115*
Pwr Wndw(Base Cpe) +160

DEDUCT FOR 94 MUSTANG:
No AC -680 — *No Auto Trans(V6) -500*

PROBE 1994

FWD/AT/PS/AC

Model/Body/Type	BaseList	Whlse	Retail
4 Cyl Models			
2 Dr Hbk	13685	**12425**	**14900**
V6 Models			
2 Dr GT Hbk	16015	**14750**	**17325**

ADD FOR 94 PROBE:
ABS +430
Anti-Theft/Recovery Sys +365
Cass +115 — *CD Player +230*
Cruise Ctrl +160 — *Custom Whls/Cvrs +205*
Leather Seats +275 — *Pwr Locks +115*
Pwr Seat +160 — *Pwr Sunroof +545*
Pwr Wndw +160 — *Tilt Whl +115*

DEDUCT FOR 94 PROBE:
No AC -680 — *No Auto Trans -500*

RANGER V6 ½ Ton 1994

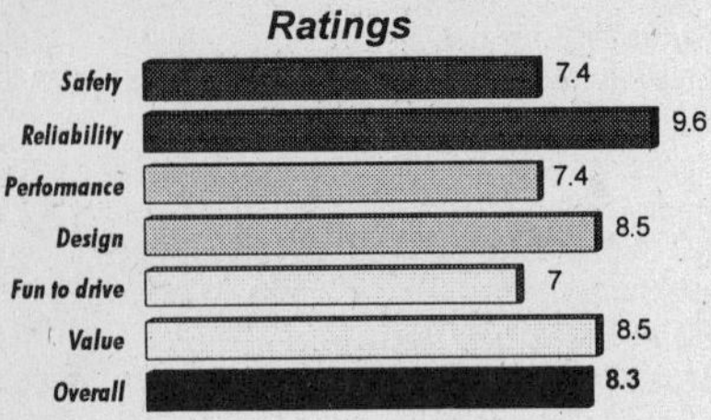

Ratings

Rating	Score
Safety	7.4
Reliability	9.6
Performance	7.4
Design	8.5
Fun to drive	7
Value	8.5
Overall	8.3

AT/PS/AC

Model/Body/Type	BaseList	Whlse	Retail
Styleside	9389	**9200**	**11425**
LB Styleside	9763	**9300**	**11525**
Flareside Splash	12845	**10425**	**12800**
Styleside Supercab	11832	**10775**	**13275**
Flareside Supercab Splash	14314	-	-

ADD FOR 94 RANGER:
STX Pkg +680 — *XLT Pkg +500*

DEDUCT FOR 94 RANGER:
4 Cyl Eng -545

REFER TO 94 FORD TRUCK OPTIONS TABLE Pg 135

TAURUS V6 1994

FWD/AT/PS/AC

Model/Body/Type	BaseList	Whlse	Retail
4 Dr GL Sdn	16140	**13150**	**15775**
4 Dr GL Wgn	17220	**14250**	**16950**
4 Dr LX Sdn	18785	**14800**	**17525**
4 Dr LX Wgn	20400	**15900**	**18700**
4 Dr SHO Sdn	24715	**18700**	**21825**

ADD FOR 94 TAURUS:
ABS(Std SHO) +430
Anti-Theft/Recovery Sys +365
Cass(Std SHO) +115 — *CD Player +230*
Cruise Ctrl(Std SHO) +160 — *Custom Whls/Cvrs +205*
JBL Stereo System +205 — *Leather Seats +275*
Pwr Locks(Std LX,SHO) +115
Pwr Seat(Std LX,SHO) +160
Pwr Sunroof +545
Pwr Wndw(Std LX,SHO) +160
Third Seat S/W +205

DEDUCT FOR 94 TAURUS:
No AC -680 — *No Auto Trans -590*

TEMPO 4 Cyl 1994

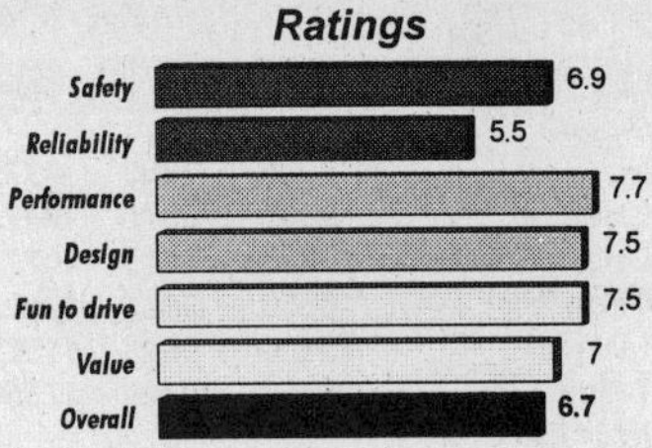

Ratings

Rating	Score
Safety	6.9
Reliability	5.5
Performance	7.7
Design	7.5
Fun to drive	7.5
Value	7
Overall	6.7

FWD/AT/PS/AC

Model/Body/Type	BaseList	Whlse	Retail
2 Dr GL Cpe	10735	**8825**	**10725**
4 Dr GL Sdn	10735	**8925**	**10825**
4 Dr LX Sdn	12560	**9950**	**12000**

ADD FOR 94 TEMPO:
Anti-Theft/Recovery Sys +365
Cass +75 — *Cruise Ctrl +135*
Custom Whls/Cvrs +180 — *Driver Side Airbag +340*
Pwr Locks(Std LX) +90 — *Pwr Seat +135*
Pwr Wndw +135 — *Tilt Whl(Std LX) +90*
V6 Eng +455

DEDUCT FOR 94 TEMPO:
No AC -590 — *No Auto Trans -500*

THUNDERBIRD 1994

AT/PS/AC

Model/Body/Type	BaseList	Whlse	Retail
V6 Models			
2 Dr LX Cpe	16830	**13050**	**15550**
2 Dr Super Cpe	22240	**17575**	**20450**
V8 Models			
2 Dr LX Cpe	17860	**13650**	**16175**

ADD FOR 94 THUNDERBIRD:

ABS(Std SC) +430
Anti-Theft/Recovery Sys +365
CD Player +230
Custom Whls/Cvrs +205
JBL Stereo System +205
Leather Seats +275
Pwr Sunroof +545

94 FORD TRUCK OPTIONS TABLE

ADD FOR ALL 94 FORD TRUCKS:

15 Pass Seating +375
4-Whl Drive +1265
AC-Rear(Std Aerostar Eddie Bauer) +375
Bed Liner +125
Cass(Std Aerostar Eddie B,Club Wgn Chat, Explorer XLT/Eddie B/Ltd) +105
CD Player +205
Cruise Ctrl(Std Aerostar XLT/Eddie B, Bronco XLT/Eddie B,Club Wgn Chat, Explorer XLT/Eddie B/Ltd) +125
Custom Whls(Std Aerostar XLT/Eddie B, Bronco Eddie B,Club Wgn Chat, Explorer Spt/XLT/EddieB/Ltd,RangerSpl) +145
Dual Rear Whls +415
Fiberglass Cap +250
Leather Seats(Std Explorer Ltd) +250
Luggage Rack(Std Aerostar Eddie B, Explorer Eddie B/Ltd) +80
Privacy Glass(Std Club Wgn Chat, Explorer Spt/XLT/Eddie B/Ltd) +145
Pwr Locks(Std Aerostar EddieB,Econo XL, ClubWgn XLT/Chat,Explr XLT/EddieB/Ltd) +105
Pwr Seats(Std Club Wgn Chat,Explorer Ltd) +125
Pwr Wndw(Std Aerostar Eddie B,Econo XL, ClubWgnXLT/Chat,Explr XLT/EddieB/Ltd) +145
Running Boards +145
Slider Wndw +80
Sunroof-Manual +145
Tilt Whl(Std Aerostar XLT/Eddie B, Bronco XLT/Eddie B/Club Wgn Chat, Explorer XLT/Eddie B/Ltd) +105
Towing Pkg(Std Club Wgn XLT/Chat) +185
V8 7.3 L Diesel Engine +745

DEDUCT FOR ALL 94 FORD TRUCKS

No AC -435
No AM/FM Radio -105
No Auto Trans -415
No Pwr Steering -185

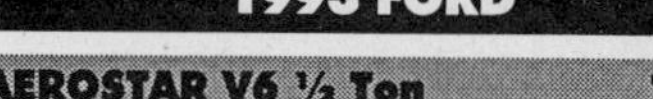

AEROSTAR V6 ½ Ton 1993

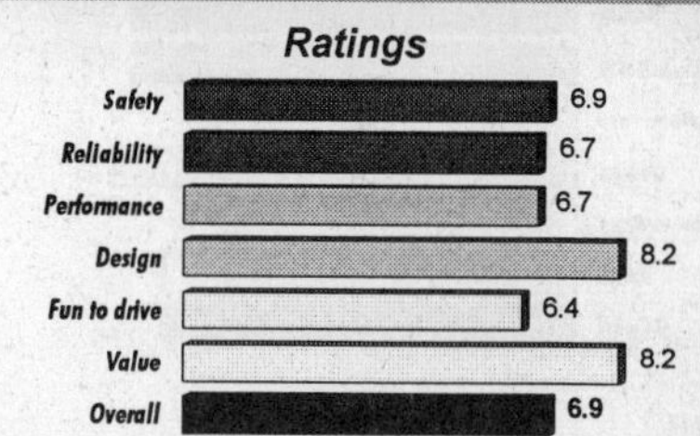

AT/PS/AC

Model/Body/Type	BaseList	Whlse	Retail
Cargo Van	14221	**10300**	**12675**
Wagon	14416	**11950**	**14575**
Window Van	14516	**10400**	**12775**
Extended Cargo Van	14968	**11600**	**14225**
Extended Wagon	16208	**13225**	**15950**
Extended Window Van	15264	**11700**	**14350**

ADD FOR 93 AEROSTAR:

Eddie Bauer Pkg +1290
XLT Pkg +700

REFER TO 93 FORD TRUCK OPTIONS TABLE Pg 139

BRONCO V8 ½ Ton 1993

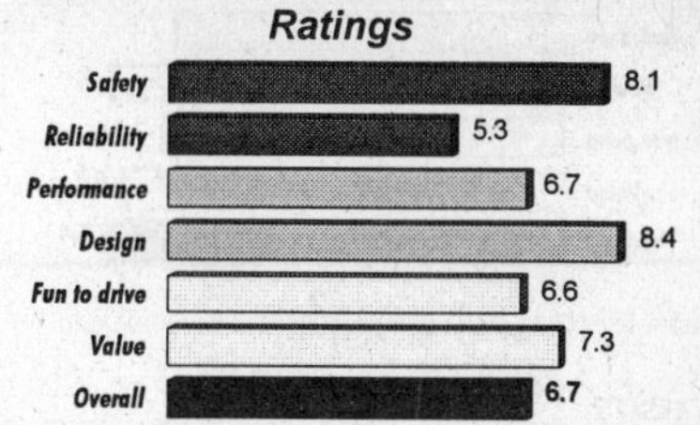

4WD/AT/PS/AC

Model/Body/Type	BaseList	Whlse	Retail
2 Dr Utility	20084	**16775**	**19775**

ADD FOR 93 BRONCO:

Eddie Bauer Pkg +1245
XLT Pkg +700

REFER TO 93 FORD TRUCK OPTIONS TABLE Pg 139

Model/Body/Type	BaseList	Whlse	Retail

CLUB WAGON V8 ½-1 Ton 1993

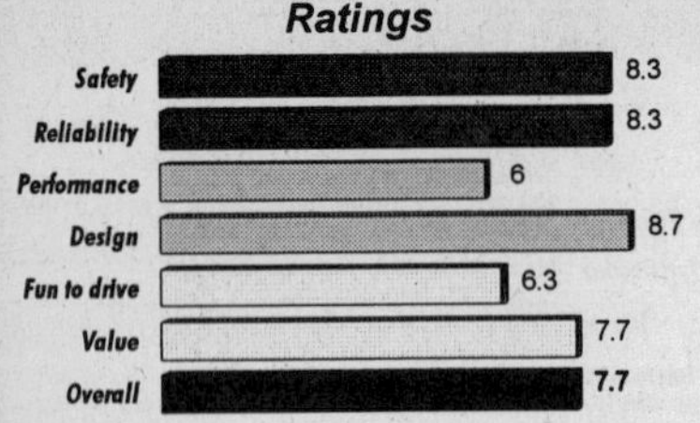

AT/PS/AC

Model/Body/Type	BaseList	Whlse	Retail
E150 Club Wgn	17459	**14075**	**16850**
E350 Club Wgn	18446	**14650**	**17425**
E350 Super Club Wgn	20497	**15275**	**18125**

ADD FOR 93 CLUB WAGON:
Chateau Pkg +1135 *XLT Pkg +700*
DEDUCT FOR 93 CLUB WAGON:
6 Cyl Eng -470
REFER TO 93 FORD TRUCK OPTIONS TABLE Pg 139

CROWN VICTORIA V8 1993

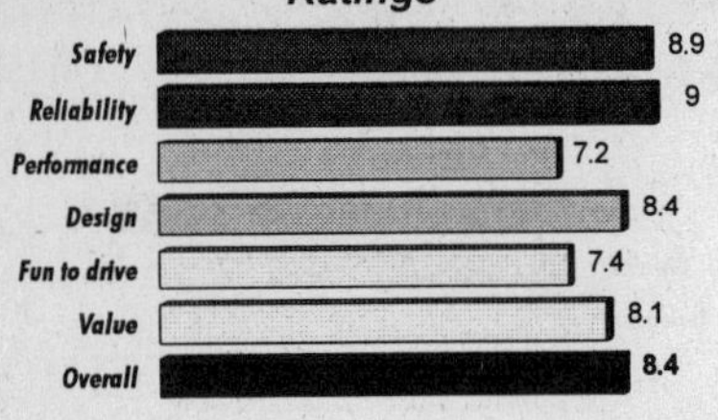

AT/PS/AC

Model/Body/Type	BaseList	Whlse	Retail
4 Dr Sdn	19972	**12350**	**14925**
4 Dr LX Sdn	21559	**13175**	**15800**

ADD FOR 93 CROWN VICTORIA:
ABS +390 *Car Phone +175*
Cass +115 *CD Player +230*
Cruise Ctrl +160 *Custom Whls/Cvrs +195*
JBL Stereo System +195 *Leather Seats +275*
Pass Side Airbag +315 *Pwr Locks +115*
Pwr Seat(Std LX) +160

ECONOLINE VAN V8 1993

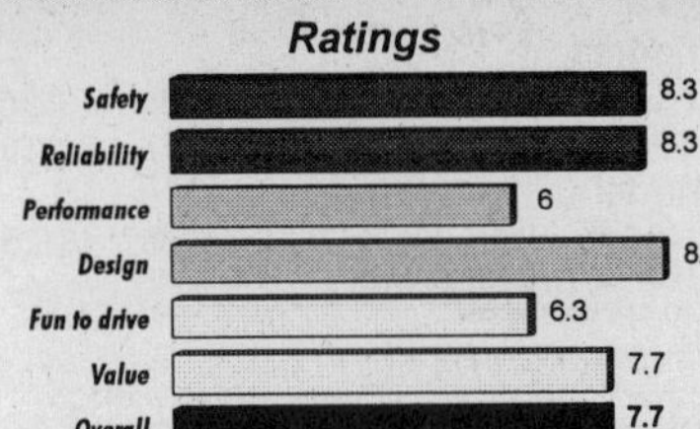

AT/PS/AC

Model/Body/Type	BaseList	Whlse	Retail
E150 Econoline Van ½ Ton			
Cargo Van	15436	**11925**	**14550**
E250 Econoline Van ¾ Ton			
Cargo Van	16093	**12150**	**14800**
Super Cargo Van	16743	**12800**	**15475**
E350 Econoline Van 1 Ton			
Cargo Van	17192	**12500**	**15725**
Super Cargo Van	18103	**13150**	**16425**

ADD FOR 93 ECONOLINE VAN:
XL Pkg +350
DEDUCT FOR 93 ECONOLINE VAN:
6 Cyl Eng -470
REFER TO 93 FORD TRUCK OPTIONS TABLE Pg 139

ESCORT 4 Cyl 1993

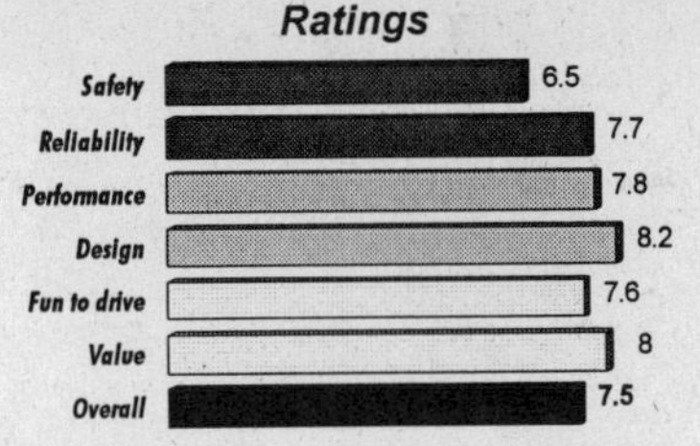

FWD/AT/PS/AC

Model/Body/Type	BaseList	Whlse	Retail
2 Dr Hbk	8355	**6225**	**7825**
2 Dr LX Hbk	9364	**6825**	**8550**
4 Dr LX Hbk	9797	**7125**	**8875**
4 Dr LX Sdn	10041	**7250**	**9050**
4 Dr LX Wgn	10367	**7800**	**9650**
4 Dr LX-E Sdn	11933	**8350**	**10175**
2 Dr GT Hbk	11871	**8550**	**10400**

ADD FOR 93 ESCORT:
Cass(Std GT,LX-E) +75 | *Cruise Ctrl +115*
Custom Whls/Cvrs +160 | *Luggage Rack +75*
Pwr Locks +75 | *Pwr Sunroof +315*
Pwr Wndw +115 | *Tilt Whl +75*

DEDUCT FOR 93 ESCORT:
No AC -430 | *No Auto Trans -390*
No Pwr Steering -135

EXPLORER V6 ½ Ton — 1993

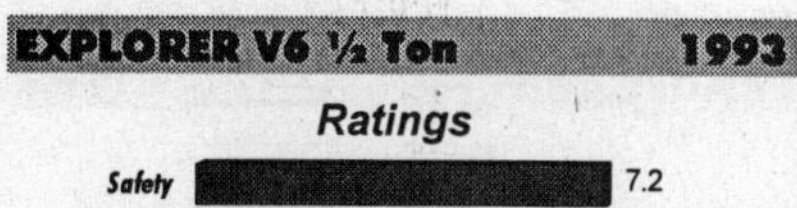

Ratings

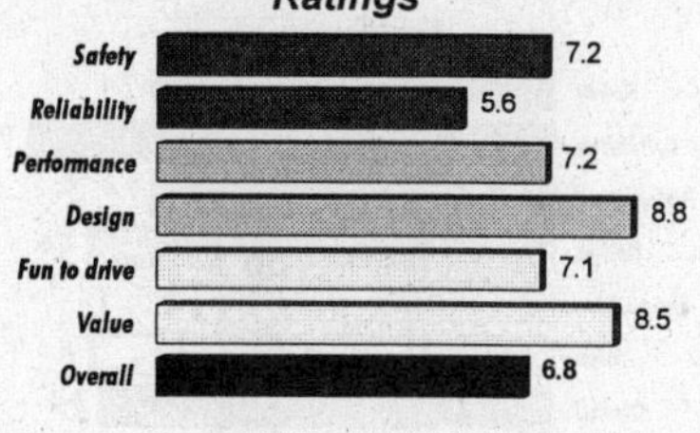

Model/Body/Type	BaseList	Whlse	Retail
AT/PS/AC			
2 Dr Wgn	16652	**14750**	**17550**
4 Dr Wgn	17416	**15825**	**18700**
2 Dr 4WD Wgn	18458	**16375**	**19300**
4 Dr 4WD Wgn	19246	**17425**	**20550**

ADD FOR 93 EXPLORER:
Eddie Bauer Pkg +1245 | *Limited Pkg +1480*
Sport Pkg +545 | *XLT Pkg +700*

REFER TO 93 FORD TRUCK OPTIONS TABLE Pg 139

F-SERIES PICKUPS V8 — 1993

Ratings

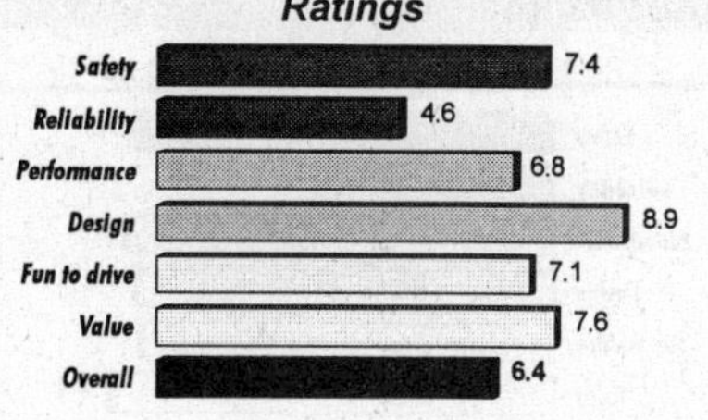

Model/Body/Type	BaseList	Whlse	Retail
AT/PS/AC			
F150 Pickup ½ Ton			
Styleside S 6 ¾' (6 cyl)	11033	**9475**	**11700**
Styleside S 8' (6 cyl)	11268	**9575**	**11800**
Flareside 6 ¾'	13916	**11200**	**13750**
Styleside 6 ¾'	13066	**10900**	**13425**
Styleside 8'	13310	**11000**	**13525**
Flare Supercab 6 ¾'	15215	**12825**	**15525**
Style Supercab 6 ¾'	14505	**12525**	**15200**
Styleside Supercab 8'	14739	**12625**	**15300**
F250 Pickup ¾ Ton			
Styleside 8'	14174	**11750**	**14400**
Heavy Duty 8'	14925	**12000**	**14625**
HD Supercab 8'	17381	**13375**	**16100**
F350 Pickup 1 Ton			
Styleside 8'	17046	**12275**	**15475**
Styleside Crew Cab 8'	18406	**13975**	**17250**
Styleside Supercab 8'	18973	**14875**	**18275**

ADD FOR 93 F-SERIES PICKUP:
Lightning Pkg +1745 | *XLT Pkg +700*

DEDUCT FOR 93 F-SERIES PICKUP:
6 Cyl Eng -470

REFER TO 93 FORD TRUCK OPTIONS TABLE Pg 139

FESTIVA 4 Cyl — 1993

Ratings

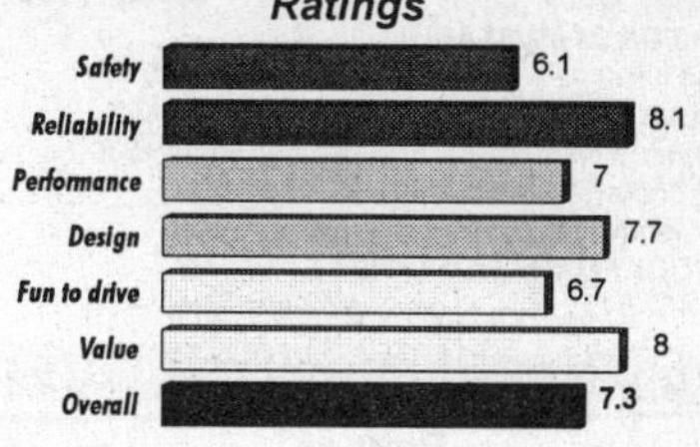

Model/Body/Type	BaseList	Whlse	Retail
AC/FWD			
2 Dr L Hbk	6941	**4850**	**6325**
2 Dr GL Hbk	7869	**5675**	**7175**

ADD FOR 93 FESTIVA:
Auto Trans +390 | *Cass +75*
Sunroof +195

DEDUCT FOR 93 FESTIVA:
No AC -430

FORD

MUSTANG 1993

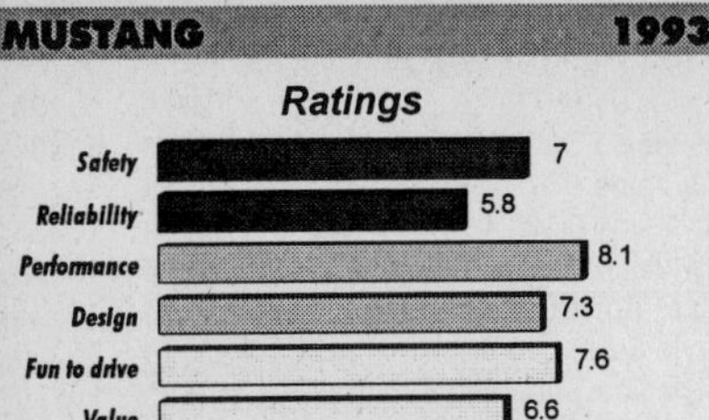

Model/Body/Type	BaseList	Whlse	Retail
AT/PS/AC			
4 Cyl Models			
2 Dr LX Cpe	10719	**7350**	**9225**
2 Dr LX Hbk	11224	**7500**	**9400**
2 Dr LX Conv	17548	**11375**	**13750**
V8 Models			
2 Dr LX Cpe	13926	**9200**	**11225**
2 Dr LX Hbk	14710	**9350**	**11375**
2 Dr LX Conv	20293	**13200**	**15700**
2 Dr GT Hbk	15747	**11575**	**13950**
2 Dr GT Conv	20848	**15450**	**18075**

ADD FOR 93 MUSTANG:

Cass +100 | *CD Player +195*
Cruise Ctrl +135 | *Custom Paint +75*
Custom Whls/Cvrs +175 | *Leather Seats +230*
Pwr Locks(Std Cnv) +100 | *Pwr Seat +135*
Pwr Wndw(Std Cnv) +135 | *Sunroof +230*

DEDUCT FOR 93 MUSTANG:

No AC -545 | *No Auto Trans -430*

PROBE 1993

Ratings

Safety 7.3
Reliability 8.4
Performance 8.5
Design 8
Fun to drive 8.4
Value 7.6
Overall 8.1

Model/Body/Type	BaseList	Whlse	Retail
FWD/AT/PS/AC			
4 Cyl Models			
2 Dr Hbk	12845	**10150**	**12350**
V6 Models			
2 Dr GT Hbk	15174	**12350**	**14800**

ADD FOR 93 PROBE:

ABS +390 | *Cass +100*
CD Player +195 | *Cruise Ctrl +135*
Custom Whls/Cvrs +175 | *Leather Seats +230*
Pwr Locks +100 | *Pwr Seat +135*
Pwr Sunroof +430 | *Pwr Wndw +135*
Tilt Whl +100

DEDUCT FOR 93 PROBE:

No AC -545 | *No Auto Trans -430*

RANGER V6 ½ Ton 1993

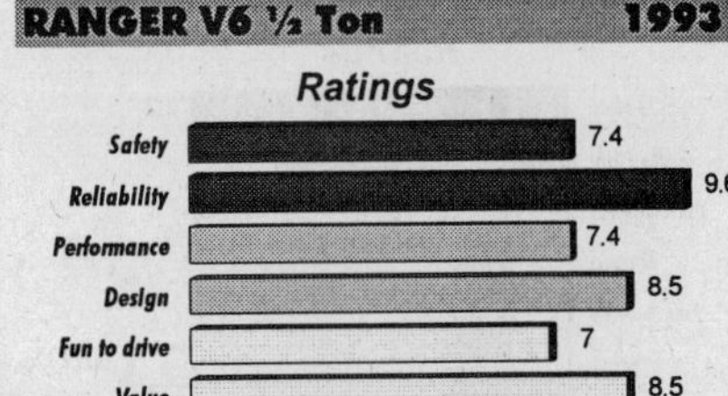

Model/Body/Type	BaseList	Whlse	Retail
AT/PS/AC			
Styleside	8781	**8175**	**10250**
LB Styleside	9026	**8275**	**10350**
Flareside Splash	12175	**9375**	**11600**
Styleside Supercab	11775	**9575**	**11800**

ADD FOR 93 RANGER:

STX Pkg +545 | *XLT Pkg +390*

DEDUCT FOR 93 RANGER:

4 Cyl Eng -430

REFER TO 93 FORD TRUCK OPTIONS TABLE Pg 139

TAURUS V6 1993

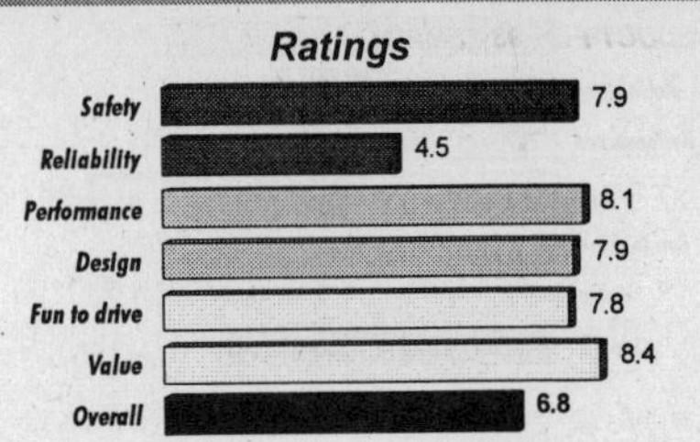

Model/Body/Type	BaseList	Whlse	Retail
FWD/AT/PS/AC			
4 Dr GL Sdn	15491	**10775**	**13200**
4 Dr GL Wgn	16656	**11775**	**14350**
4 Dr LX Sdn	18300	**12300**	**14875**
4 Dr LX Wgn	19989	**13300**	**15950**
4 Dr SHO Sdn	24829	**15800**	**18600**

Model/Body/Type	BaseList	Whlse	Retail

ADD FOR 93 TAURUS:
ABS(Std SHO) +390
Cass(Std SHO) +100
CD Player +195
CruiseCtrl(Std SHO) +135
Custom Whls/Cvrs +175
JBL Stereo System +175
Leather Seats +230
Pass Side Airbag +315
Pwr Locks(Std LX,SHO) +100
Pwr Seat(Std LX,SHO) +135
Pwr Sunroof +430
Pwr Wndw(Std LX,SHO) +135
Third Seat +160

DEDUCT FOR 93 TAURUS:
No AC -545
No Auto Trans -505

TEMPO 4 Cyl 1993

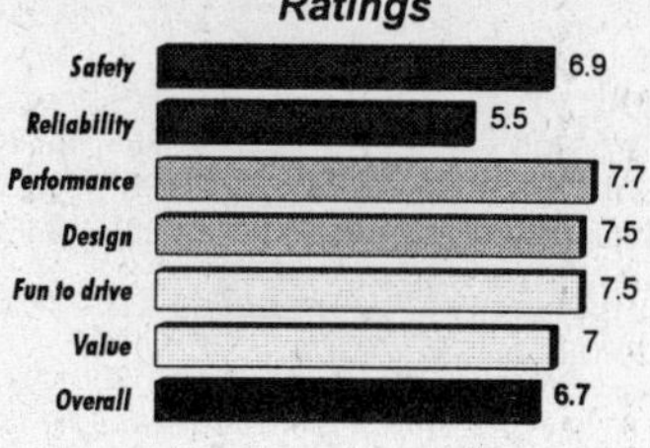

FWD/AT/PS/AC

Model/Body/Type	BaseList	Whlse	Retail
2 Dr GL Cpe	10267	**7300**	**9100**
4 Dr GL Sdn	10267	**7400**	**9200**
4 Dr LX Sdn	12135	**8275**	**10125**

ADD FOR 93 TEMPO:
Cass +75
Cruise Ctrl +115
Custom Whls/Cvrs +160
Driver Side Airbag +315
Pwr Locks(Std LX) +75
Pwr Seat +115
Pwr Wndw +115
Tilt Whl(Std LX) +75
V6 Eng +350

DEDUCT FOR 93 TEMPO:
No AC -470
No Auto Trans -430

THUNDERBIRD 1993

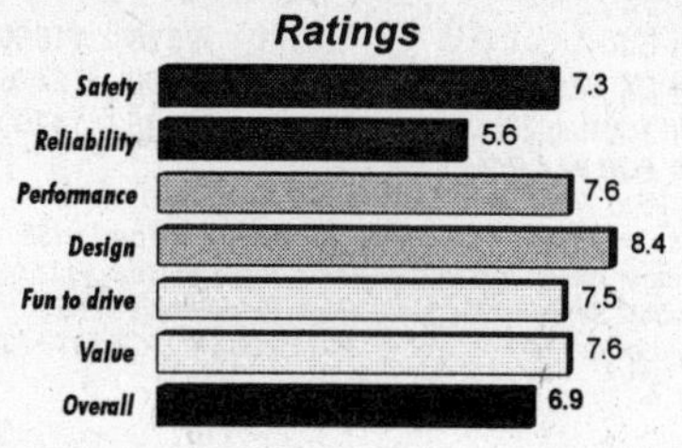

AT/PS/AC

Model/Body/Type	BaseList	Whlse	Retail
V6 Models			
2 Dr LX Cpe	15797	**10175**	**12400**
2 Dr Super Cpe	22030	**14500**	**17050**
V8 Models			
2 Dr LX Cpe	16883	**10725**	**13075**

ADD FOR 93 THUNDERBIRD:
ABS(Std SC) +390
CD Player +195
Custom Whls/Cvrs +175
JBL Stereo System +175
Leather Seats +230
Pwr Sunroof +430

93 FORD TRUCK OPTIONS TABLE

ADD FOR ALL 93 FORD TRUCKS:
15 Pass Seating +375
4-Whl Drive +1265
AC-Rear(Std Aerostar Eddie Bauer) +375
Bed Liner +125
Cass(Std Aerostar Eddie B,Club Wgn Chat, Explorer XLT/Eddie B/Ltd) +105
CD Player +205
Cruise Ctrl(Std Aerostar XLT/Eddie B, Bronco XLT/Eddie B,Club Wgn Chat, Explorer XLT/Eddie B/Ltd) +125
Custom Whls(Std Aerostar XLT/Eddie B, Bronco Eddie B,Club Wgn Chat, Explorer Spt/XLT/EddieB/Ltd,RangerSpl) +145
Dual Rear Whls +415
Fiberglass Cap +250
Leather Seats(Std Explorer Ltd) +250
Luggage Rack(Std Aerostar Eddie B, Explorer Eddie B/Ltd) +80
Privacy Glass(Std Club Wgn Chat, Explorer Spt/XLT/Eddie B/Ltd) +145
Pwr Locks(Std Aerostar EddieB,Econo XL, ClubWgn XLT/Chat,Explr XLT/EddieB/Ltd) +105
Pwr Seats(Std Club Wgn Chat,Explorer Ltd) +125
Pwr Wndw(Std Aerostar Eddie B, Econo XL,ClubWgnXLT/Chat, Explrorer XLT/EddieB/Ltd) +145
Running Boards +145
Slider Wndw +80
Sunroof-Manual +145
Tilt Whl(Std Aerostar XLT/Eddie B, Bronco XLT/Eddie B/Club Wgn Chat, Explorer XLT/Eddie B/Ltd) +105
Towing Pkg(Std Club Wgn XLT/Chat) +185
V8 7.3 L Diesel Engine +745

DEDUCT FOR ALL 93 FORD TRUCKS
No AC -435
No AM/FM Radio -105
No Auto Trans -415
No Pwr Steering -185

FORD

1992 FORD

AEROSTAR V6 ½ Ton 1992

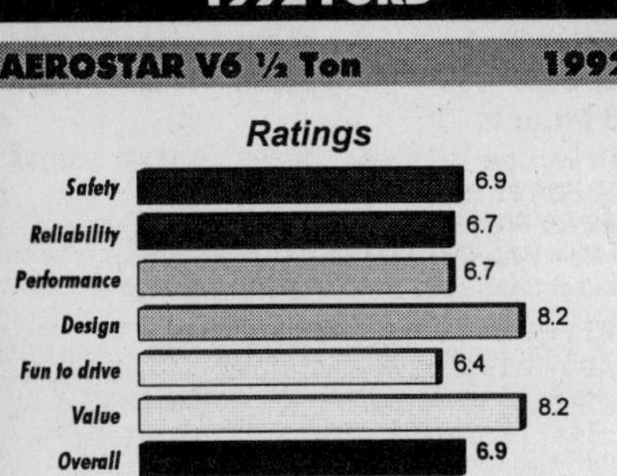

AT/PS/AC	BaseList	Whlse	Retail
Cargo Van	13772	**7800**	**9900**
Wagon	13739	**9350**	**11575**
Window Van	14099	**7900**	**9975**
Extended Cargo Van	14519	**9000**	**11200**
Extended Wagon	15531	**10475**	**12875**
Extended Window Van	14846	**9100**	**11300**

ADD FOR 92 AEROSTAR:

Eddie Bauer Pkg +1205 XLT Pkg +625

REFER TO 92 FORD TRUCK OPTIONS TABLE Pg 144

BRONCO V8 ½ Ton 1992

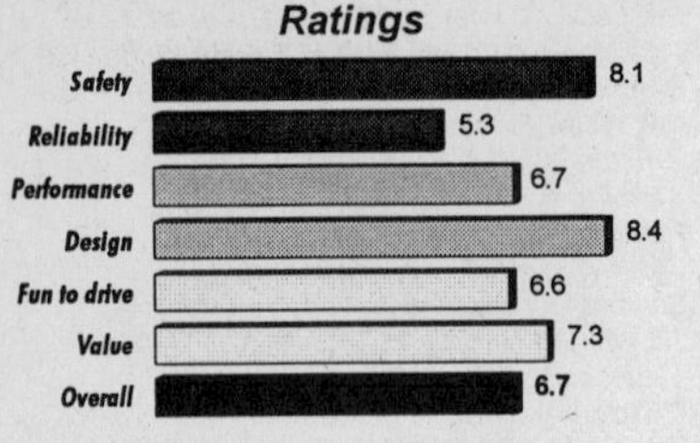

4WD/AT/PS/AC	BaseList	Whlse	Retail
2 Dr Utility	18852	**14550**	**17300**

ADD FOR 92 BRONCO:

Eddie Bauer Pkg +1175 Nite Pkg +780
XLT Pkg +625

DEDUCT FOR 92 BRONCO:

6 Cyl Eng -430

REFER TO 92 FORD TRUCK OPTIONS TABLE Pg 144

CLUB WAGON V8 ½-1 Ton 1992

Ratings

Safety 8.3
Reliability 8.3
Performance 6
Design 8.7
Fun to drive 6.3
Value 7.7
Overall 7.7

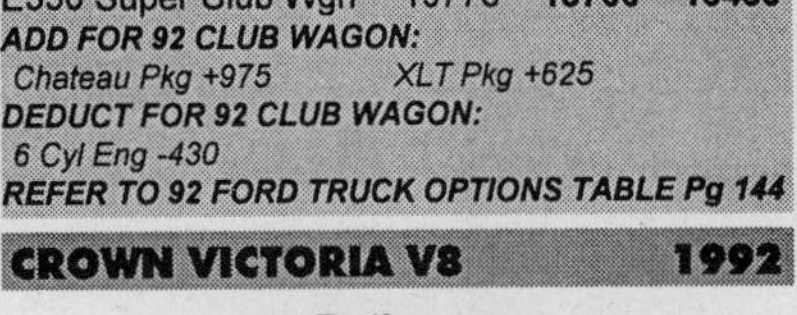

AT/PS/AC	BaseList	Whlse	Retail
E150 Club Wgn	16740	**12625**	**15300**
E350 Club Wgn	17728	**13125**	**15825**
E350 Super Club Wgn	19778	**13700**	**16450**

ADD FOR 92 CLUB WAGON:

Chateau Pkg +975 XLT Pkg +625

DEDUCT FOR 92 CLUB WAGON:

6 Cyl Eng -430

REFER TO 92 FORD TRUCK OPTIONS TABLE Pg 144

CROWN VICTORIA V8 1992

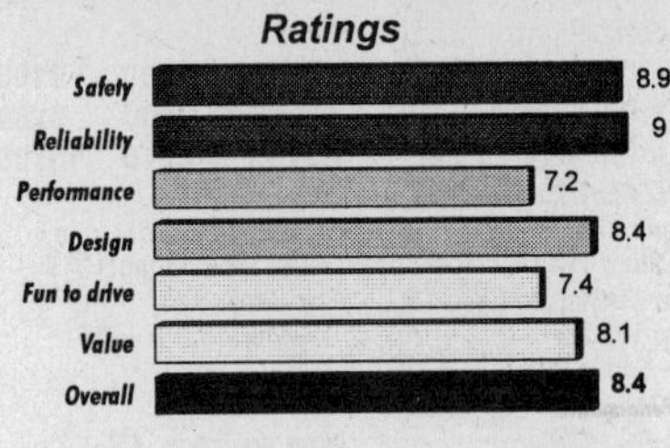

AT/PS/AC	BaseList	Whlse	Retail
4 Dr Sdn	19563	**9525**	**11650**
4 Dr LX Sdn	20887	**10150**	**12425**
4 Dr Touring Sdn	23832	**11625**	**14200**

ADD FOR 92 CROWN VICTORIA:

ABS(Std Tour) +350 Car Phone +160
Cass +100 CruiseCtrl(Std Tour) +135
Custom Whls/Cvrs +175 JBL Stereo System +175
Leather Seats +230 Pass Side Airbag +275
Pwr Locks +100 Pwr Seat(Std LX,Tour) +135

Model/Body/Type	BaseList	Whlse	Retail

ECONOLINE VAN V8 1992

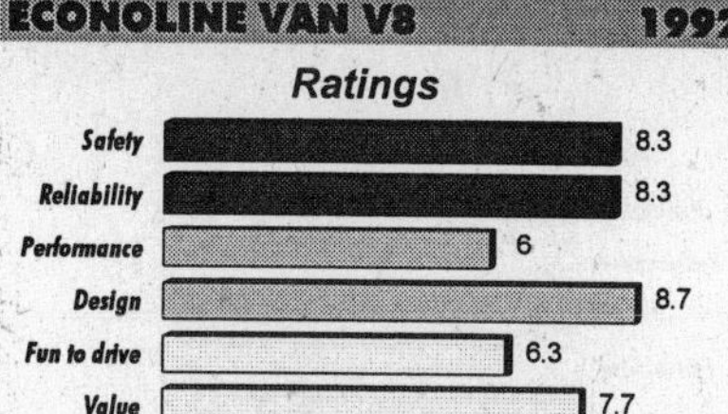

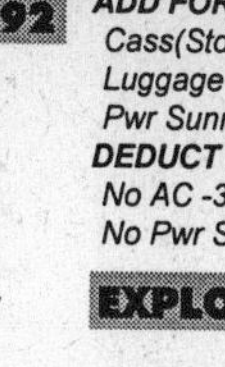

AT/PS/AC

Model/Body/Type	BaseList	Whlse	Retail
E150 Econoline Van ½ Ton			
Cargo Van	14960	**9950**	**12250**
E250 Econoline Van ¾ Ton			
Cargo Van	15374	**10125**	**12450**
Super Cargo Van	16024	**10675**	**13175**
E350 Econoline Van 1 Ton			
Cargo Van	16474	**10400**	**13375**
Super Cargo Van	17384	**11000**	**14025**

ADD FOR 92 ECONOLINE VAN:
XL Pkg +275

DEDUCT FOR 92 ECONOLINE VAN:
6 Cyl Eng -430

REFER TO 92 FORD TRUCK OPTIONS TABLE Pg 144

ESCORT 4 Cyl 1992

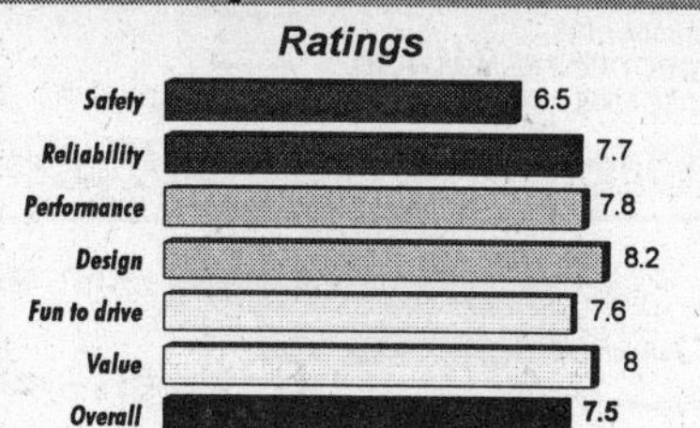

FWD/AT/PS/AC

Model/Body/Type	BaseList	Whlse	Retail
2 Dr Hbk	8355	**4500**	**5925**
2 Dr LX Hbk	9055	**5000**	**6525**
4 Dr LX Hbk	9483	**5300**	**6850**
4 Dr LX Sdn	9795	**5475**	**7000**
4 Dr LX Wgn	10067	**5975**	**7550**
4 Dr LX-E Sdn	11933	**6500**	**8125**
2 Dr GT Hbk	11871	**6625**	**8250**

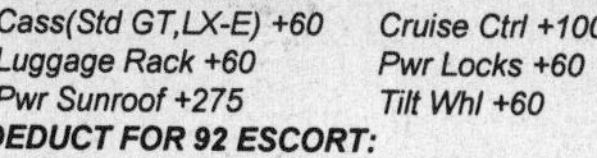

ADD FOR 92 ESCORT:
Cass(Std GT,LX-E) +60 *Cruise Ctrl +100*
Luggage Rack +60 *Pwr Locks +60*
Pwr Sunroof +275 *Tilt Whl +60*

DEDUCT FOR 92 ESCORT:
No AC -390 *No Auto Trans -350*
No Pwr Steering -115

EXPLORER V6 ½ Ton 1992

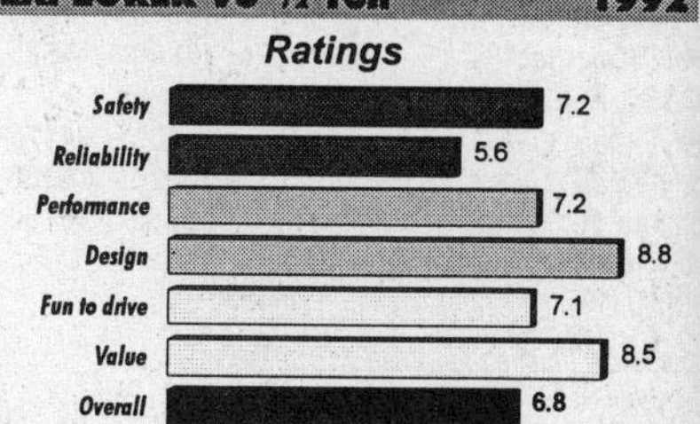

AT/PS/AC

Model/Body/Type	BaseList	Whlse	Retail
2 Dr Wgn	15854	**12525**	**15200**
4 Dr Wgn	16692	**13525**	**16250**
2 Dr 4WD Wgn	17644	**14125**	**16900**
4 Dr 4WD Wgn	18505	**15075**	**17925**

ADD FOR 92 EXPLORER:
Sport Pkg +470 *XLT Pkg +625*
Eddie Bauer Pkg +1175

REFER TO 92 FORD TRUCK OPTIONS TABLE Pg 144

F-SERIES PICKUPS V8 1992

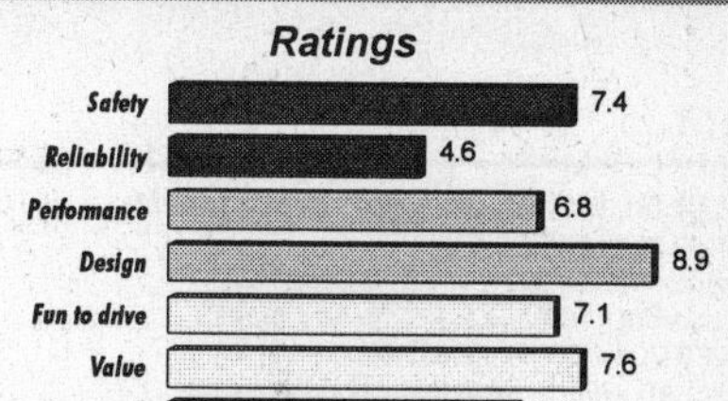

AT/PS/AC

Model/Body/Type	BaseList	Whlse	Retail
F150 Pickup ½ Ton			
Styleside S 6 ¾' (6 cyl)	10336	**8475**	**10575**
Styleside S 8' (6 cyl)	10572	**8575**	**10675**
Flareside 6 ¾'	14120	**10075**	**12400**
Styleside 6 ¾'	12807	**9850**	**12150**
Styleside 8'	13051	**9950**	**12250**
Styleside Supercab			
S 6 ¾'(6 cyl)	12739	**9900**	**12200**

FORD

FORD 92

Model/Body/Type	BaseList	Whlse	Retail
Styleside Supercab			
S 8'(6 cyl)	12965	9975	12300
Flare Supercab 6 ¾'	14173	11500	14050
Style Supercab 6 ¾'	14173	11250	13800
Styleside Supercab 8'	14407	11350	13900
F250 Pickup ¾ Ton			
Styleside 8'	13891	10500	12900
Heavy Duty 8'	14607	10750	13250
HD Supercab 8'	17002	11950	14575
F350 Pickup 1 Ton			
Styleside 8'	16728	11100	14175
Styleside Crew Cab 8'	18087	12625	15850
Styleside Supercab 8'	18594	13450	16750

ADD FOR 92 F-SERIES PICKUP:

Sport Pkg +470 *XL Pkg +275*
XLT Lariat Pkg +625 *XLT Nite Pkg +780*

DEDUCT FOR 92 F-SERIES PICKUP:

6 Cyl Eng -430

REFER TO 92 FORD TRUCK OPTIONS TABLE Pg 144

FESTIVA 4 Cyl 1992

Ratings

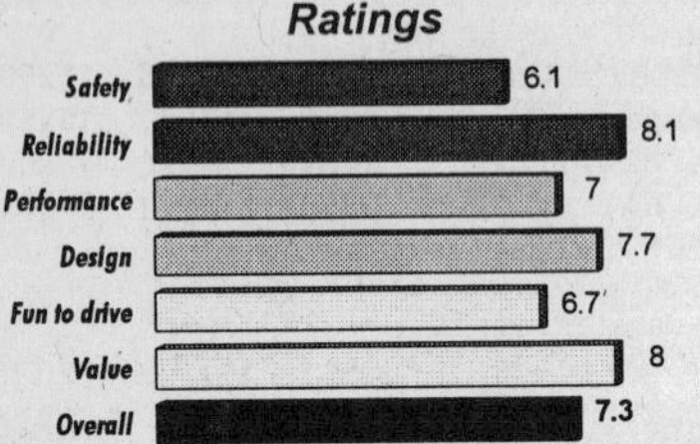

AC/FWD

Model/Body/Type	BaseList	Whlse	Retail
2 Dr L Hbk	6941	3525	4850
2 Dr GL Hbk	7980	4250	5675

ADD FOR 92 FESTIVA:

Auto Trans +350 *Cass +60*
Sunroof +160

DEDUCT FOR 92 FESTIVA:

No AC -390

MUSTANG 1992

Ratings

Safety 7
Reliability 5.8
Performance 8.1
Design 7.3
Fun to drive 7.6
Value 6.6
Overall 6.9

AT/PS/AC

Model/Body/Type	BaseList	Whlse	Retail
4 Cyl Models			
2 Dr LX Cpe	10215	6250	8000
2 Dr LX Hbk	10721	6400	8150
2 Dr LX Conv	16899	10000	12175
V8 Models			
2 Dr LX Cpe	13422	7925	9850
2 Dr LX Hbk	14207	8075	9975
2 Dr LX Conv	19644	11675	14125
2 Dr GT Hbk	15243	10025	12200
2 Dr GT Conv	20199	13650	16175

ADD FOR 92 MUSTANG:

Cass +75 *Cruise Ctrl +115*
Custom Paint +60 *Custom Whls/Cvrs +160*
Leather Seats +195 *Pwr Locks(Std Cnv) +75*
Pwr Seat +115 *Pwr Wndw(Std Cnv) +115*
Sunroof +195

DEDUCT FOR 92 MUSTANG:

No AC -505 *No Auto Trans -390*

PROBE 1992

Ratings

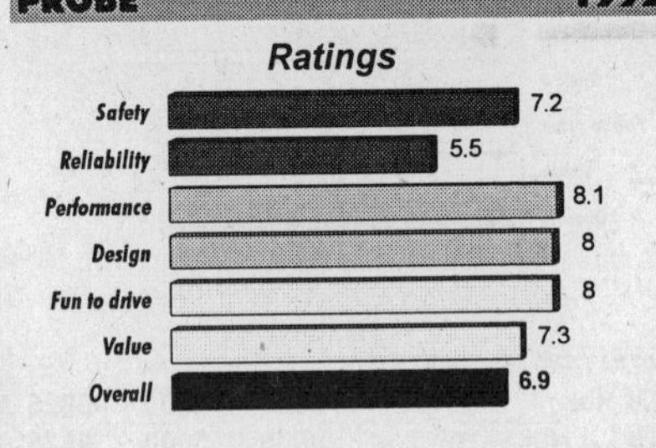

FWD/AT/PS/AC

Model/Body/Type	BaseList	Whlse	Retail
4 Cyl Models			
2 Dr Hbk	12257	7275	9150
2 Dr GT Turbo Hbk	13257	9425	11450

Model/Body/Type	BaseList	Whlse	Retail
V6 Models			
2 Dr LX Hbk	14857	**8325**	**10225**

ADD FOR 92 PROBE:

ABS +350 — *Cass +75*
CD Player +175 — *Cruise Ctrl +115*
Custom Whls/Cvrs +160 — *Leather Seats +195*
Pwr Locks +75 — *Pwr Seat +115*
Pwr Wndw +115 — *Sunroof +195*
Tilt Whl +75

DEDUCT FOR 92 PROBE:

No AC -505 — *No Auto Trans -390*

RANGER V6 ½ Ton 1992

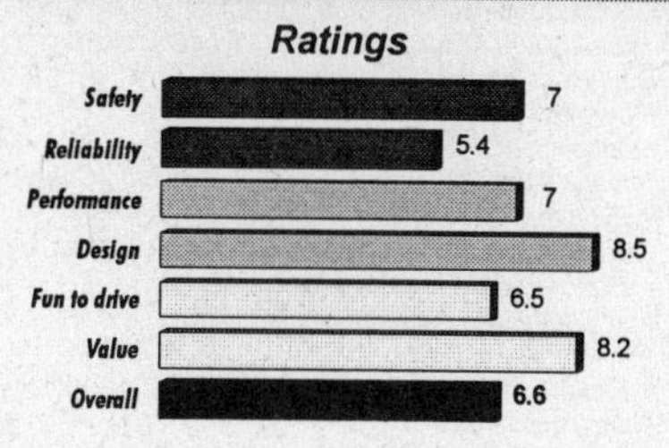

AT/PS/AC

Model/Body/Type	BaseList	Whlse	Retail
Styleside S (4 cyl,5 spd)	8930	**6150**	**8075**
Styleside	10147	**7275**	**9325**
LB Styleside	10176	**7375**	**9450**
Styleside Supercab	11568	**8525**	**10625**

ADD FOR 92 RANGER:

STX Pkg +470 — *XLT Pkg +350*

DEDUCT FOR 92 RANGER:

4 Cyl Eng -390

REFER TO 92 FORD TRUCK OPTIONS TABLE Pg 144

TAURUS V6 1992

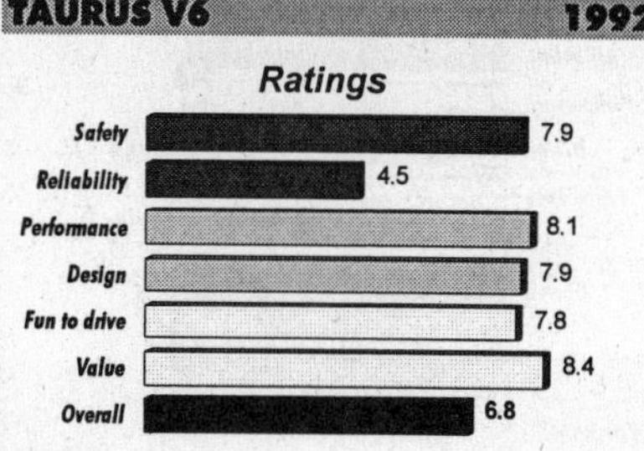

FWD/AT/PS/AC

Model/Body/Type	BaseList	Whlse	Retail
4 Dr L Sdn	14980	**6950**	**8900**
4 Dr L Wgn	16013	**7850**	**9900**
4 Dr GL Sdn	15280	**7725**	**9775**
4 Dr GL Wgn	16290	**8650**	**10700**
4 Dr LX Sdn	17775	**9175**	**11275**
4 Dr LX Wgn	19464	**10050**	**12325**
4 Dr SHO Sdn (5 spd)	23839	**12375**	**14950**

ADD FOR 92 TAURUS:

ABS(Std SHO) +350 — *Cass(Std SHO) +75*
CD Player +175 — *CruiseCtrl(Std SHO) +115*
Custom Whls/Cvrs +160 — *JBL Stereo System +160*
Leather Seats +195 — *Pass Side Airbag +275*
Pwr Locks(Std LX,SHO) +75
Pwr Seat(Std LX,SHO) +115
Pwr Sunroof +390
Pwr Wndw(Std LX,SHO) +115
Third Seat +135

DEDUCT FOR 92 TAURUS:

No AC -505

TEMPO 1992

Ratings

Rating	Score
Safety	6.9
Reliability	5.5
Performance	7.7
Design	7.5
Fun to drive	7.5
Value	7
Overall	6.7

FWD/AT/PS/AC

Model/Body/Type	BaseList	Whlse	Retail
4 Cyl Models			
2 Dr GL Cpe	9987	**5400**	**6950**
4 Dr GL Sdn	10137	**5525**	**7075**
4 Dr LX Sdn	11115	**6175**	**7750**
V6 Models			
2 Dr GLS Cpe	12652	**6425**	**8025**
4 Dr GLS Sdn	12800	**6525**	**8150**

ADD FOR 92 TEMPO:

Cass(Std GLS) +60 — *Cruise Ctrl +100*
Custom Whls/Cvrs +135 — *Driver Side Airbag +275*
Pwr Locks(Std LX) +60 — *Pwr Seat +100*
Pwr Wndw +100 — *Tilt Whl(Std LX) +60*
V6 Eng(Std GLS) +315

DEDUCT FOR 92 TEMPO:

No AC -430 — *No Auto Trans -390*

FORD

THUNDERBIRD 1992

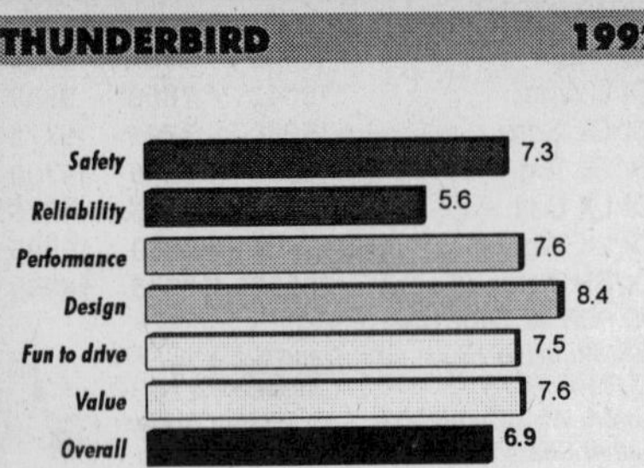

AT/PS/AC

Model/Body/Type	BaseList	Whlse	Retail
V6 Models			
2 Dr Cpe	16345	**8300**	**10200**
2 Dr LX Cpe	18783	**9350**	**11375**
2 Dr Super Cpe	22046	**12400**	**14850**
V8 Models			
2 Dr Cpe	17425	**8800**	**10800**
2 Dr Sport Cpe	18611	**9750**	**11875**
2 Dr LX Cpe	19863	**9825**	**12000**

ADD FOR 92 THUNDERBIRD:

ABS(Std SC) +350
CD Player +175
Custom Whls/Cvrs +160
Leather Seats +195
Pwr Seat(Std LX) +115
Tilt Whl(Std Spt,LX) +75
Cass(Std LX) +75
Cr Ctrl(Std Spt,LX) +115
JBL Stereo System +160
Pwr Locks(Std LX) +75
Pwr Sunroof +390

92 FORD TRUCK OPTIONS TABLE

ADD FOR ALL 92 FORD TRUCKS:

15 Pass Seating +330
4-Whl Drive +1200
AC-Rear(Std Aerostar Eddie Bauer) +315
Bed Liner +105
Cass(Std Aerostar EddieB,ClubWgn Chat, Explorer XLT/Eddie B) +80
CD Player +170
Cruise Ctrl(Std Aerostar XLT/Eddie B, Bronco XLT/Nite/Eddie B,ClubWgn Chat, Explorer XLT/Eddie B) +80
Custom Whls(Std Aerostar Eddie B, Bronco Nite/Eddie B,Club Wgn Chat, ExplrSpt/XLT/EdB/Ltd,F-Ser XLT Lar/Nite) +125
Dual Rear Whls +375
Fiberglass Cap +205
Leather Seats +205
Privacy Glass(Std Bronco Eddie B,Club Wgn Chat, Explorer XLT/Eddie B) +125
Pwr Locks(Std Econoline XL,ClubWgn XLT/Chat, Explorer XLT/Eddie B) +80
Pwr Seats(Std Club Wgn Chat) +105
Pwr Wndw(Std EconoXL,ClubWgn XLT/Chat, Explorer XLT/Eddie B) +105
Running Boards +125
Sunroof-Manual +105
Towing Pkg(Std Club Wgn XLT/Chat) +145
V8 7.3 L Diesel Engine +700

DEDUCT FOR ALL 92 FORD TRUCKS

No AC -375
No Auto Trans -330
No Pwr Steering -145

1991 FORD

AEROSTAR V6 ½ Ton 1991

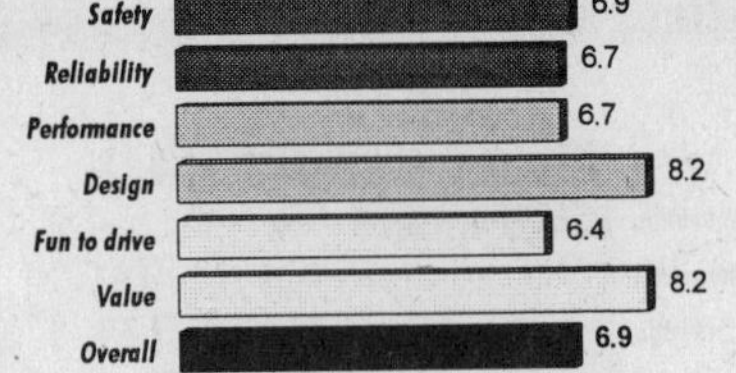

AT/PS/AC

Model/Body/Type	BaseList	Whlse	Retail
Cargo Van	12520	**6400**	**8350**
Wagon	13479	**7825**	**9925**
Window Van	12904	**6500**	**8450**
Extended Cargo Van	13267	**7375**	**9450**
Extended Wagon	14376	**8825**	**11000**
Extended Window Van	13651	**7475**	**9550**

Model/Body/Type	BaseList	Whlse	Retail

ADD FOR 91 AEROSTAR:
Eddie Bauer Pkg +1135 *XLT Pkg +545*
REFER TO 91 FORD TRUCK OPTIONS TABLE Pg 149

BRONCO V8 ½ Ton 1991

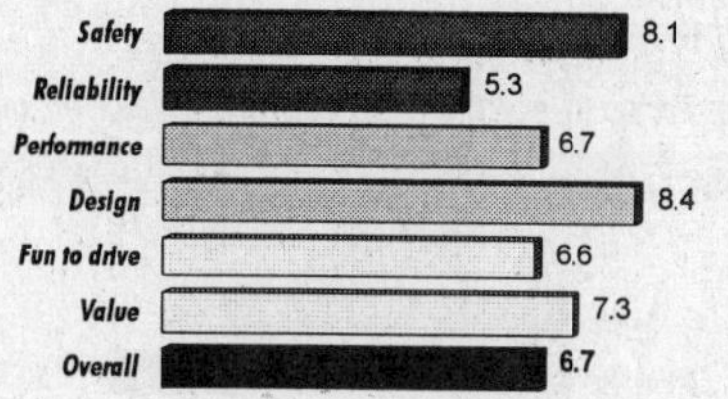

Model/Body/Type	BaseList	Whlse	Retail
4WD/AT/PS/AC			
2 Dr Utility	17620	**12300**	**14950**

ADD FOR 91 BRONCO:
Eddie Bauer Pkg +1090 *Silver Aniv Pkg +1455*
XLT Pkg +545
DEDUCT FOR 91 BRONCO:
6 Cyl Eng -390
REFER TO 91 FORD TRUCK OPTIONS TABLE Pg 149

CLUB WAGON V8 ½-1 Ton 1991

Model/Body/Type	BaseList	Whlse	Retail
AT/PS/AC			
E150 Club Wgn	17512	**9825**	**12100**
E250 Club Wgn	18037	**9975**	**12275**
E350 Super Club Wgn	19346	**10750**	**13250**

ADD FOR 91 CLUB WAGON:
XLT Pkg +545
DEDUCT FOR 91 CLUB WAGON:
6 Cyl Eng -390
REFER TO 91 FORD TRUCK OPTIONS TABLE Pg 149

ECONOLINE VAN V8 1991

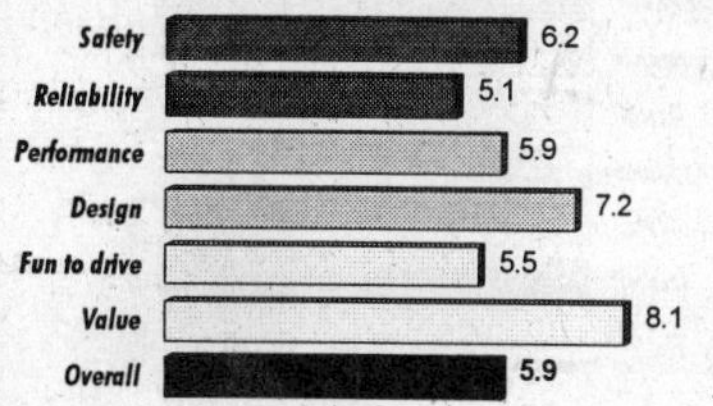

Model/Body/Type	BaseList	Whlse	Retail
AT/PS/AC			
E150 Econoline Van ½ Ton			
Cargo Van	13740	**8400**	**10500**
Super Cargo Van	14650	**8925**	**11125**
E250 Econoline Van ¾ Ton			
Cargo Van	14090	**8550**	**10650**
Super Cargo Van	14789	**9075**	**11275**
E350 Econoline Van 1 Ton			
Cargo Van	15085	**8850**	**11575**
Super Cargo Van	15960	**9375**	**12125**

ADD FOR 91 ECONOLINE VAN:
XL Pkg +230
DEDUCT FOR 91 ECONOLINE VAN:
6 Cyl Eng -390
REFER TO 91 FORD TRUCK OPTIONS TABLE Pg 149

ESCORT 4 Cyl 1991

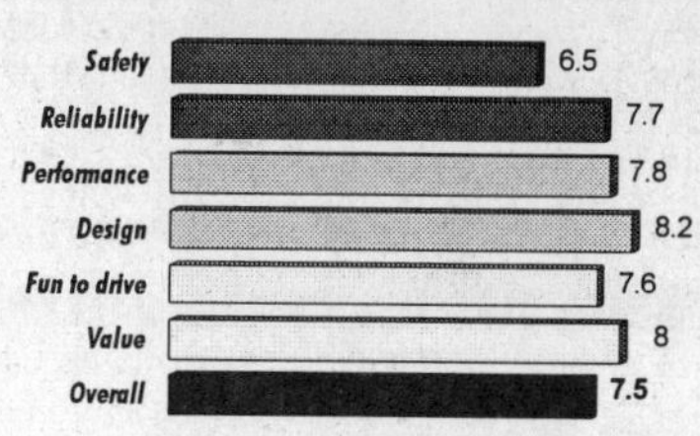

Model/Body/Type	BaseList	Whlse	Retail
FWD/AT/PS/AC			
2 Dr Pony Hbk	7976	**2950**	**4200**
2 Dr LX Hbk	8667	**3400**	**4725**
4 Dr LX Hbk	9075	**3700**	**5025**
4 Dr LX Wgn	9680	**4300**	**5725**
2 Dr GT Hbk	11484	**4900**	**6425**

ADD FOR 91 ESCORT:
Cass(Std GT) +35 *Cruise Ctrl +75*
Luggage Rack +35 *Pwr Locks +35*
Pwr Sunroof +230 *Tilt Whl +35*
DEDUCT FOR 91 ESCORT:
No AC -350 *No Auto Trans -315*
No Pwr Steering -100

FORD

EXPLORER V6 ½ Ton — 1991

Ratings

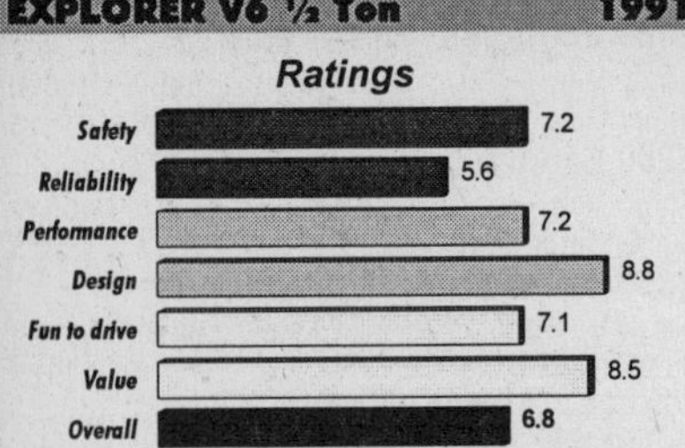

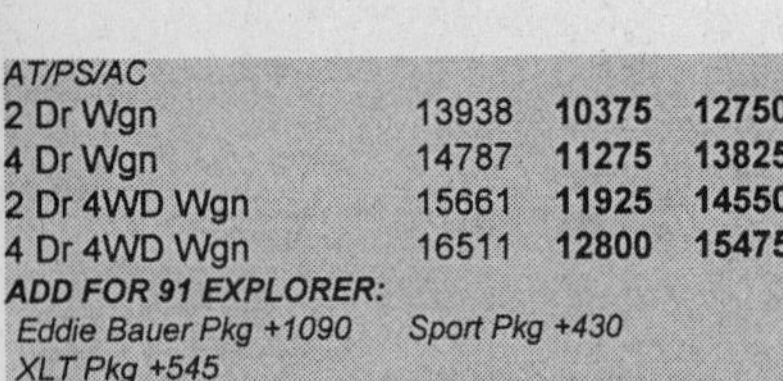

Model/Body/Type	BaseList	Whlse	Retail
AT/PS/AC			
2 Dr Wgn	13938	**10375**	**12750**
4 Dr Wgn	14787	**11275**	**13825**
2 Dr 4WD Wgn	15661	**11925**	**14550**
4 Dr 4WD Wgn	16511	**12800**	**15475**

ADD FOR 91 EXPLORER:
Eddie Bauer Pkg +1090 *Sport Pkg +430*
XLT Pkg +545

REFER TO 91 FORD TRUCK OPTIONS TABLE Pg 149

F-SERIES PICKUPS V8 — 1991

Ratings

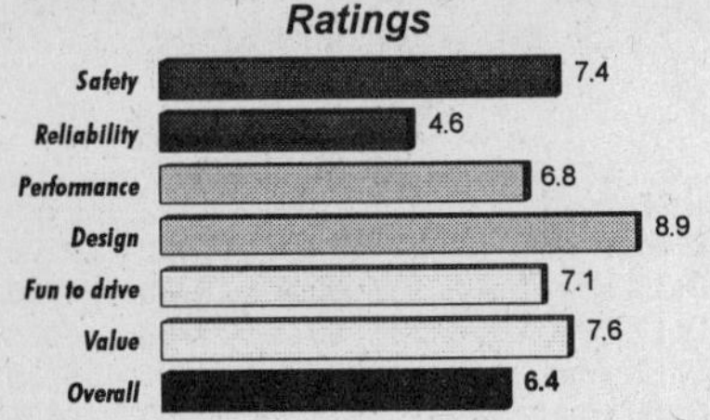

Model/Body/Type	BaseList	Whlse	Retail
AT/PS/AC			
F150 Pickup ½ Ton			
Styleside S 6 ¾' (6 cyl)	10971	**7525**	**9600**
Styleside S 8' (6 cyl)	11187	**7625**	**9725**
Styleside 6 ¾'	11967	**8825**	**11000**
Styleside 8'	12191	**8925**	**11125**
Style Supercab 6 ¾'	13317	**9950**	**12250**
Styleside Supercab 8'	13541	**10025**	**12350**
F250 Pickup ¾ Ton			
Styleside 8'	13392	**9475**	**11700**
Heavy Duty 8'	13967	**9700**	**11975**
HD Supercab 8'	15746	**10575**	**12950**
F350 Pickup 1 Ton			
Styleside 8'	15434	**9975**	**12875**
Styleside Crew Cab 8'	17263	**11350**	**14450**
Styleside Supercab 8'	17257	**11950**	**15100**

ADD FOR 91 F-SERIES PICKUP:
XL Pkg +230 *XLT Lariat Pkg +545*
XLT Nite Pkg +625

DEDUCT FOR 91 F-SERIES PICKUP:
6 Cyl Eng -315

REFER TO 91 FORD TRUCK OPTIONS TABLE Pg 149

FESTIVA 4 Cyl — 1991

Ratings

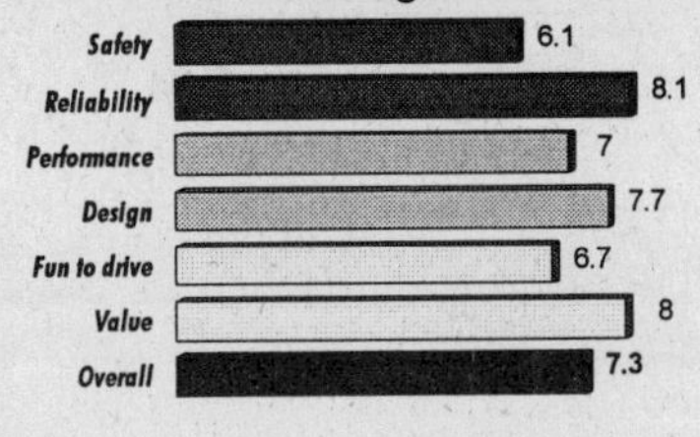

Model/Body/Type	BaseList	Whlse	Retail
AC/FWD			
2 Dr L Hbk	6620	**2275**	**3400**
2 Dr GL Hbk	7460	**2875**	**4125**

ADD FOR 91 FESTIVA:
Auto Trans +315 *Cass +35*
Pwr Steering +100 *Sunroof +115*

DEDUCT FOR 91 FESTIVA:
No AC -350

LTD CROWN VICTORIA V8 — 1991

Ratings

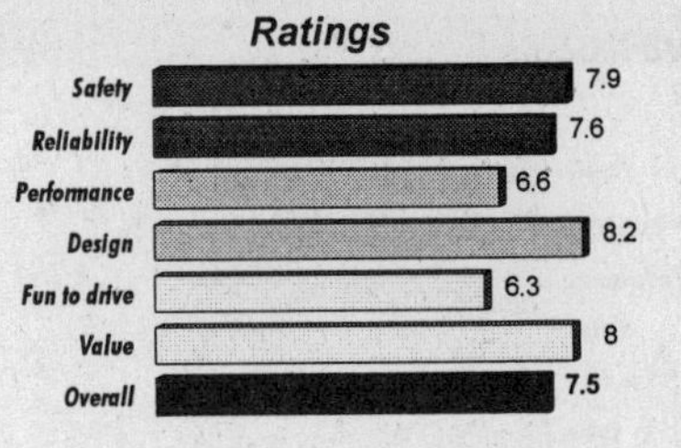

Model/Body/Type	BaseList	Whlse	Retail
AT/PS/AC			
4 Dr S Sdn	17045	**4825**	**6600**
4 Dr Sdn	18227	**6200**	**8075**
4 Dr LX Sdn	18863	**6850**	**8800**
DFRS Wgn	18298	**6125**	**8000**
2 Seat Wgn	18083	**5925**	**7775**
DFRS LX Wgn	18833	**6750**	**8725**
DFRS Cntry Squire Wgn	18550	**6625**	**8550**
2 Seat Cntry Squire Wgn	18335	**6425**	**8325**
DFRS LX Cntry Squire Wgn	19085	**7250**	**9275**

ADD FOR 91 LTD CROWN VICTORIA:

Brougham Roof +115 · *Car Phone +135*
Cass +75 · *Cruise Ctrl +115*
Custom Whls/Cvrs +160 · *Leather Seats +195*
Pwr Locks +75 · *Pwr Seat +115*

MUSTANG 1991

Ratings

Rating	Score
Safety	7
Reliability	5.8
Performance	8.1
Design	7.3
Fun to drive	7.6
Value	6.6
Overall	6.9

Model/Body/Type	BaseList	Whlse	Retail
AT/PS/AC			
4 Cyl Models			
2 Dr LX Cpe	10157	**5175**	**6875**
2 Dr LX Hbk	10663	**5325**	**7025**
2 Dr LX Conv	16222	**8650**	**10575**
V8 Models			
2 Dr LX Cpe	13270	**6725**	**8550**
2 Dr LX Hbk	14055	**6900**	**8725**
2 Dr LX Conv	19242	**10150**	**12325**
2 Dr GT Hbk	15034	**8525**	**10425**
2 Dr GT Conv	19864	**11775**	**14225**

ADD FOR 91 MUSTANG:

Cass +60 · *Cruise Ctrl +100*
Custom Paint +35 · *Custom Whls/Cvrs +135*
Leather Seats +160 · *Pwr Locks(Std Cnv) +60*
Pwr Wndw(Std Cnv) +100 · *Sunroof +160*

DEDUCT FOR 91 MUSTANG:

No AC -470 · *No Auto Trans -350*

PROBE 1991

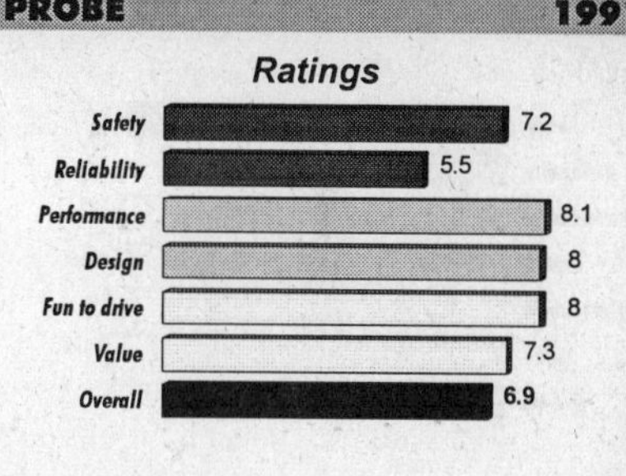

Model/Body/Type	BaseList	Whlse	Retail
FWD/AT/PS/AC			
4 Cyl Models			
2 Dr GL Hbk	11691	**5525**	**7200**
2 Dr GT Turbo Hbk	14964	**7525**	**9425**
V6 Models			
2 Dr LX Hbk	13229	**6500**	**8225**

ADD FOR 91 PROBE:

ABS +315 · *Cass +60*
CD Player +160 · *Cruise Ctrl +100*
Custom Whls/Cvrs +135 · *Leather Seats +160*
Pwr Locks +60 · *Pwr Seat +100*
Pwr Wndw +100 · *Sunroof +160*
Tilt Whl(Std LX,GT) +60

DEDUCT FOR 91 PROBE:

No AC -470 · *No Auto Trans -350*

RANGER V6 ½ Ton 1991

Ratings

Rating	Score
Safety	7
Reliability	5.4
Performance	7
Design	8.5
Fun to drive	6.5
Value	8.2
Overall	6.6

Model/Body/Type	BaseList	Whlse	Retail
AT/PS/AC			
Styleside S (4 cyl,5 spd)	8279	**4925**	**6750**
Styleside	9658	**5975**	**7875**
LB Styleside	9821	**6100**	**7975**
Styleside Supercab	11186	**7025**	**9025**

ADD FOR 91 RANGER:

STX Pkg +430 · *XLT Pkg +315*

DEDUCT FOR 91 RANGER:

4 Cyl Eng -350

REFER TO 91 FORD TRUCK OPTIONS TABLE Pg 149

FORD 91

TAURUS 1991

Ratings

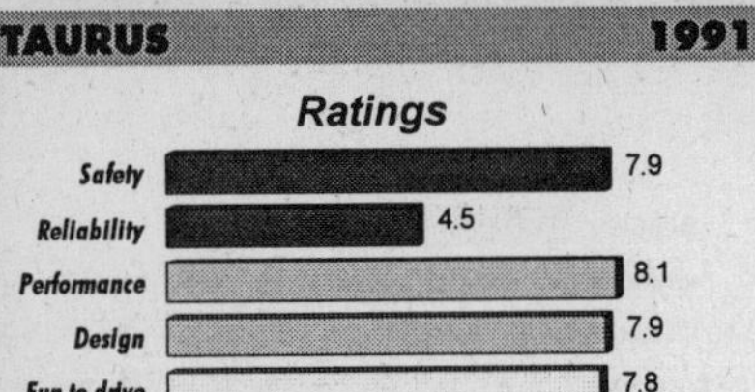

FWD/AT/PS/AC

Model/Body/Type	BaseList	Whlse	Retail
4 Cyl Models			
4 Dr L Sdn	13352	**4400**	**6125**
4 Dr GL Sdn	13582	**5050**	**6875**
V6 Models			
4 Dr L Sdn	13873	**4850**	**6650**
4 Dr L Wgn	14784	**5725**	**7575**
4 Dr GL Sdn	14103	**5575**	**7400**
4 Dr GL Wgn	14990	**6425**	**8325**
4 Dr LX Sdn	17373	**6925**	**8875**
4 Dr LX Wgn	18963	**7750**	**9800**
4 Dr SHO Sdn (5 spd)	22071	**9825**	**12050**

ADD FOR 91 TAURUS:

ABS(Std LX,SHO) +315
Cass(Std SHO) +60
CD Player +160
CruiseCtrl(Std SHO) +100
Custom Whls/Cvrs +135
JBL Stereo System +135
Leather Seats +160
Pwr Locks(Std LX,SHO) +60
Pwr Seat(Std LX,SHO) +100
Pwr Sunroof +350
Pwr Wndw(Std LX,SHO) +100
Third Seat +115

DEDUCT FOR 91 TAURUS:

No AC -470

TEMPO 4 Cyl 1991

Ratings

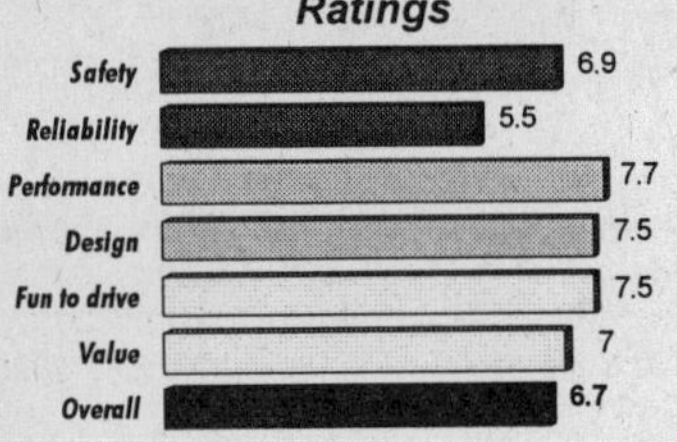

FWD/AT/PS/AC

Model/Body/Type	BaseList	Whlse	Retail
2 Dr L Cpe	8306	**3750**	**5075**
4 Dr L Sdn	8449	**3850**	**5200**
2 Dr GL Cpe	9541	**4325**	**5725**
4 Dr GL Sdn	9691	**4425**	**5850**
2 Dr GLS Cpe	10358	**4750**	**6225**
4 Dr GLS Sdn	10506	**4850**	**6325**
4 Dr LX Sdn	10663	**4950**	**6500**
4 Dr 4WD Sdn	11390	**5650**	**7150**

ADD FOR 91 TEMPO:

Cass(Std GLS) +35
Cruise Ctrl +75
Custom Whls/Cvrs +115
Driver Side Airbag +230
Pwr Locks(Std LX) +35
Pwr Seat +75
Pwr Wndw +75
Tilt Whl(Std LX) +35

DEDUCT FOR 91 TEMPO:

No AC -390
No Auto Trans -350

THUNDERBIRD 1991

Ratings

Rating	Score
Safety	7.3
Reliability	5.6
Performance	7.6
Design	8.4
Fun to drive	7.5
Value	7.6
Overall	6.9

AT/PS/AC

Model/Body/Type	BaseList	Whlse	Retail
V6 Models			
2 Dr Cpe	15318	**6825**	**8650**
2 Dr LX Cpe	17734	**7725**	**9650**
2 Dr Super Cpe	20999	**10525**	**12750**
V8 Models			
2 Dr Cpe	16398	**7250**	**9125**
2 Dr LX Cpe	18814	**8175**	**10075**

ADD FOR 91 THUNDERBIRD:

ABS(Std SC) +315
Cass(Std LX) +60
CD Player +160
Cruise Ctrl(Std LX) +100
Custom Whls/Cvrs +135
JBL Stereo System +135
Leather Seats +160
Pwr Locks(Std LX) +60
Pwr Seat(Std LX) +100
Pwr Sunroof +350
Tilt Whl(Std LX) +60

Model/Body/Type	BaseList	Whlse	Retail	Model/Body/Type	BaseList	Whlse	Retail

91 FORD TRUCK OPTIONS TABLE

ADD FOR ALL 91 FORD TRUCKS:

15 Pass Seating +290
4-Whl Drive +1140
AC-Rear(Std Aerostar Eddie Bauer) +250
Bed Liner +80
CD Player +125
Cstm Whls(Std Aerostar Eddie, Bronco SilvAn, Explorer Sport/Eddie B,F-Series Nite) +105
Dual Rear Whls +330
Fiberglass Cap +170
Leather Seats(Std Bronco Silver Ann) +170
Privacy Glass(Std Bronco XLT/Eddie B) +105
Pwr Wndw(Std Bronco XLT/Eddie/SilvAn, Explorer XLT/Eddie B) +80
Running Boards +105
Sunroof-Manual +80
Towing Pkg +105
V8 7.3 L Diesel Engine +665

DEDUCT FOR ALL 91 FORD TRUCKS

No AC -315
No Auto Trans -250
No Pwr Steering -105

1990 FORD

AEROSTAR V6 ½ Ton — 1990

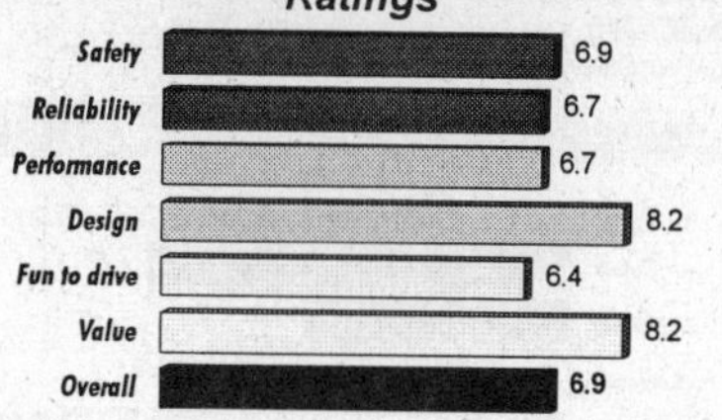

AT/PS/AC

Model/Body/Type	BaseList	Whlse	Retail
Cargo Van	11841	**5100**	**7000**
Wagon	12267	**6500**	**8425**
Window Van	12225	**5200**	**7075**
Extended Cargo Van	12588	**5950**	**7850**
Extended Wagon	13165	**7275**	**9325**
Extended Window Van	12972	**5400**	**7950**

ADD FOR 90 AEROSTAR:

Eddie Bauer Pkg +1050 XLT Pkg +430

REFER TO 90 FORD TRUCK OPTIONS TABLE Pg 153

BRONCO V8 ½ Ton — 1990

Ratings

Rating	Score
Safety	8.1
Reliability	5.3
Performance	6.7
Design	8.4
Fun to drive	6.6
Value	7.3
Overall	6.7

4WD/AT/PS/AC

Model/Body/Type	BaseList	Whlse	Retail
2 Dr Utility	16795	**9900**	**12200**

ADD FOR 90 BRONCO:

Eddie Bauer Pkg +1015 XLT Pkg +430

DEDUCT FOR 90 BRONCO:

6 Cyl Eng -315

REFER TO 90 FORD TRUCK OPTIONS TABLE Pg 153

BRONCO II V6 ½ Ton — 1990

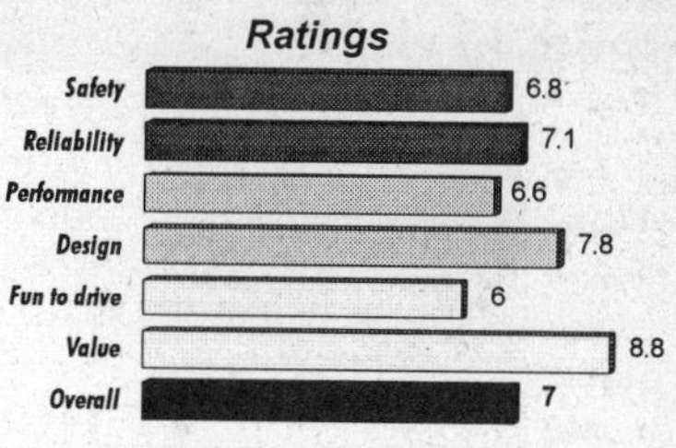

AT/PS/AC

Model/Body/Type	BaseList	Whlse	Retail
2 Dr Utility	13001	**6000**	**7900**
2 Dr 4WD Utility	14704	**7475**	**9550**

ADD FOR 90 BRONCO II:

Eddie Bauer Pkg +1015 XL Sport Pkg +350
XLT Pkg +430

REFER TO 90 FORD TRUCK OPTIONS TABLE Pg 153

FORD

FORD 90

CLUB WAGON V8 ½-1 Ton — 1990

Ratings

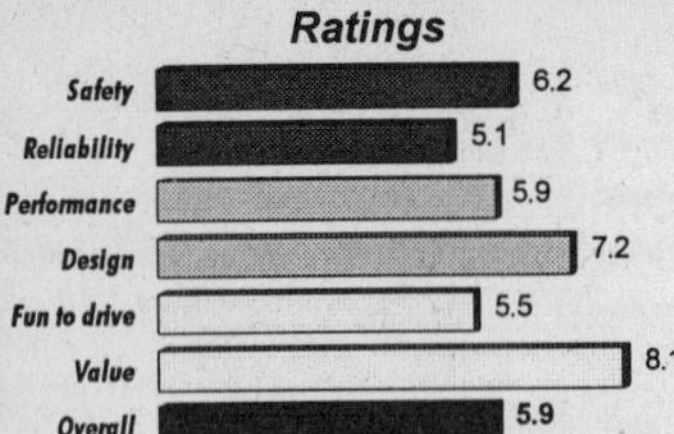

Model/Body/Type	BaseList	Whlse	Retail
AT/PS/AC			
E150 Club Wgn	16596	**8100**	**10175**
E250 Club Wgn	17120	**8225**	**10300**
E350 Super Club Wgn	18431	**8925**	**11125**

ADD FOR 90 CLUB WAGON:
XLT Pkg +430

DEDUCT FOR 90 CLUB WAGON:
6 Cyl Eng -315

REFER TO 90 FORD TRUCK OPTIONS TABLE Pg 153

ECONOLINE VAN V8 — 1990

Ratings

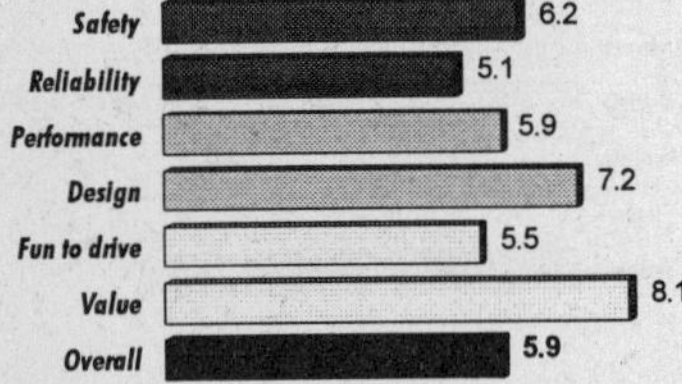

Model/Body/Type	BaseList	Whlse	Retail
AT/PS/AC			
E150 Econoline Van ½ Ton			
Cargo Van	12740	**6400**	**8350**
Super Cargo Van	13920	**7000**	**8975**
E250 Econoline Van ¾ Ton			
Cargo Van	13299	**6625**	**8575**
Super Cargo Van	14058	**7100**	**9125**
E350 Econoline Van 1 Ton			
Cargo Van	14111	**6850**	**9275**
Super Cargo Van	15229	**7300**	**9800**

ADD FOR 90 ECONOLINE VAN:
XL Pkg +195

DEDUCT FOR 90 ECONOLINE VAN:
6 Cyl Eng -315

REFER TO 90 FORD TRUCK OPTIONS TABLE Pg 153

ESCORT 4 Cyl — 1990

Ratings

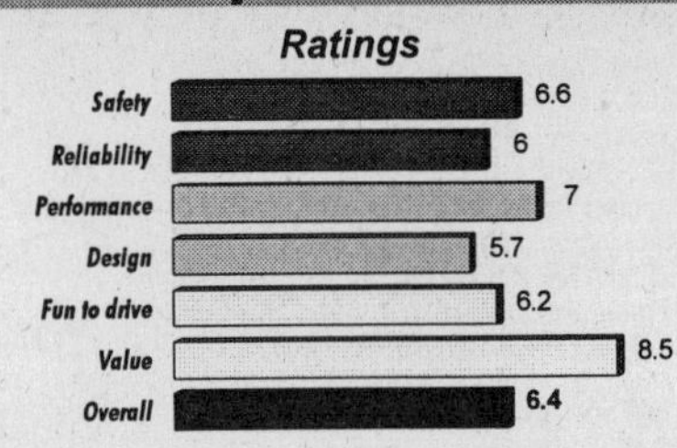

Model/Body/Type	BaseList	Whlse	Retail
FWD/AT/PS/AC			
2 Dr Pony Hbk	7402	**2225**	**3325**
2 Dr LX Hbk	7806	**2650**	**3825**
4 Dr LX Hbk	8136	**2750**	**3925**
4 Dr LX Wgn	8737	**2975**	**4225**
2 Dr GT Hbk	9844	**3575**	**4900**

ADD FOR 90 ESCORT:
Cass +35 — *Cruise Ctrl +60*
Custom Whls/Cvrs +75 — *Luggage Rack +35*
Tilt Whl +35

DEDUCT FOR 90 ESCORT:
No AC -315 — *No Auto Trans -275*
No Pwr Steering -75

F-SERIES PICKUPS V8 — 1990

Ratings

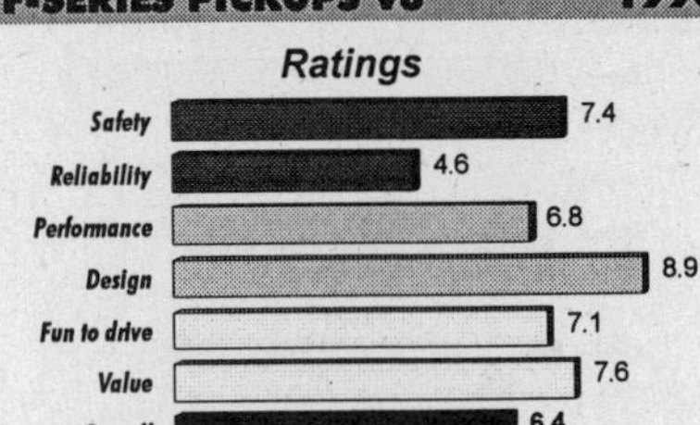

Model/Body/Type	BaseList	Whlse	Retail
AT/PS/AC			
F150 Pickup ½ Ton			
Styleside S 6 ¾' (6 cyl)	10249	**6275**	**8200**
Styleside S 8' (6 cyl)	10465	**6375**	**8300**
Styleside 6 ¾'	11211	**7450**	**9525**
Styleside 8'	11435	**7550**	**9625**
Style Supercab 6 ¾'	12561	**8400**	**10500**
Styleside Supercab 8'	12785	**8500**	**10600**
F250 Pickup ¾ Ton			
Styleside 8'	12156	**8000**	**10075**
Heavy Duty 8'	12605	**8200**	**10275**
HD Supercab 8'	14959	**8950**	**11150**

Model/Body/Type	BaseList	Whlse	Retail
F350 Pickup 1 Ton			
Styleside 8'	14647	**8550**	**11175**
Styleside Crew Cab 8'	16464	**9750**	**12575**
Styleside Supercab 8'	16470	**10175**	**13125**

ADD FOR 90 F-SERIES PICKUP:
XL Pkg +195 *XLT Lariat Pkg +430*
DEDUCT FOR 90 F-SERIES PICKUP:
6 Cyl Eng -315
REFER TO 90 FORD TRUCK OPTIONS TABLE Pg 153

FESTIVA 4 Cyl 1990

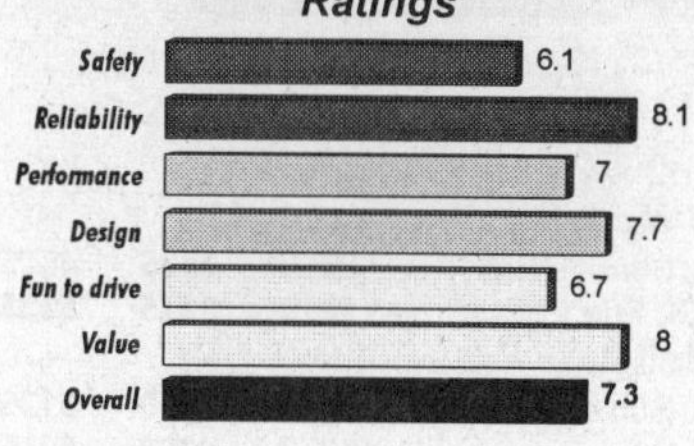

AC/FWD

Model/Body/Type	BaseList	Whlse	Retail
2 Dr L Hbk	6319	**1500**	**2450**
2 Dr L Plus Hbk	7111	**1725**	**2750**
2 Dr LX Hbk	7750	**2000**	**3100**

ADD FOR 90 FESTIVA:
Auto Trans +275 *Cass +35*
Custom Whls/Cvrs +75 *Pwr Steering +75*
Sunroof +100
DEDUCT FOR 90 FESTIVA:
No AC -315

LTD CROWN VICTORIA V8 1990

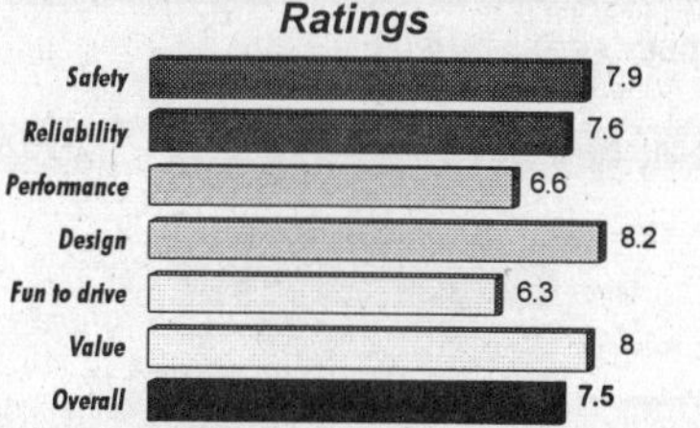

AT/PS/AC

Model/Body/Type	BaseList	Whlse	Retail
4 Dr S Sdn	16630	**3825**	**5425**
4 Dr Sdn	17257	**4975**	**6775**
4 Dr LX Sdn	17894	**5650**	**7475**
DFRS Wgn	17841	**4950**	**6750**
2 Seat Wgn	17668	**4800**	**6575**
DFRS LX Wgn	18418	**5600**	**7425**
DFRS Country Squire Wgn	18094	**5400**	**7250**
2 Seat Country Squire Wgn	17921	**5225**	**7075**
DFRS LX Country Squire Wgn	18671	**6050**	**7925**

ADD FOR 90 LTD CROWN VICTORIA:
Brougham Roof +75 *Cass +75*
Cruise Ctrl +100 *Custom Paint +35*
Custom Whls/Cvrs +115 *Leather Seats +135*
Pwr Locks +60 *Pwr Seat +100*

MUSTANG 1990

Ratings

Rating	Score
Safety	7
Reliability	5.8
Performance	8.1
Design	7.3
Fun to drive	7.6
Value	6.6
Overall	6.9

AT/PS/AC

Model/Body/Type	BaseList	Whlse	Retail
4 Cyl Models			
2 Dr LX Cpe	9456	**3675**	**5100**
2 Dr LX Hbk	9962	**3825**	**5300**
2 Dr LX Conv	15141	**6750**	**8600**
V8 Models			
2 Dr LX Cpe	12164	**5025**	**6675**
2 Dr LX Hbk	13007	**5175**	**6875**
2 Dr LX Conv	18183	**8150**	**10050**
2 Dr GT Hbk	13986	**6675**	**8500**
2 Dr GT Conv	18805	**9650**	**11700**

ADD FOR 90 MUSTANG:
Cass +60 *Cruise Ctrl +75*
Custom Paint +25 *Custom Whls/Cvrs +115*
Leather Seats +115 *Pwr Locks(Std Cnv) +60*
Pwr Wndw(Std Cnv) +75 *Sunroof +115*
DEDUCT FOR 90 MUSTANG:
No AC -430 *No Auto Trans -315*

FORD

FORD 90

PROBE 1990

Ratings

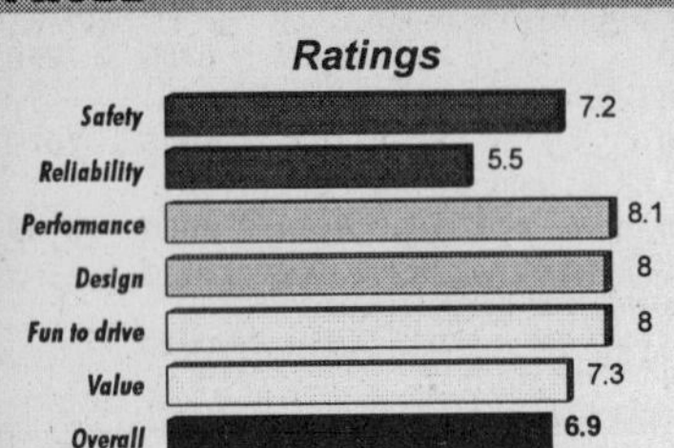

FWD/AT/PS/AC

Model/Body/Type	BaseList	Whlse	Retail
4 Cyl Models			
2 Dr GL Hbk	11470	**4450**	**6000**
2 Dr GT Turbo Hbk	14726	**6225**	**7975**
V6 Models			
2 Dr LX Hbk	13008	**5250**	**6950**

ADD FOR 90 PROBE:
ABS +275 | *Cass +60*
CD Player +115 | *Cruise Ctrl +75*
Custom Whls/Cvrs +115 | *Leather Seats +115*
Pwr Locks +60 | *Pwr Seat +75*
Pwr Wndw +75 | *Sunroof +115*
Tilt Whl(Std LX,GT) +60

DEDUCT FOR 90 PROBE:
No AC -430 | *No Auto Trans -315*

RANGER V6 ½ Ton 1990

Ratings

Rating	Score
Safety	7
Reliability	5.4
Performance	7
Design	8.5
Fun to drive	6.5
Value	8.2
Overall	6.6

AT/PS/AC

Model/Body/Type	BaseList	Whlse	Retail
Styleside S (4 cyl,5 spd)	7856	**4175**	**5875**
Styleside	9224	**4950**	**6775**
LB Styleside	9387	**5050**	**6925**
Styleside Supercab	10771	**5875**	**7775**

ADD FOR 90 RANGER:
STX Pkg +390 | *XLT Pkg +230*

DEDUCT FOR 90 RANGER:
4 Cyl Eng -275

REFER TO 90 FORD TRUCK OPTIONS TABLE Pg 153

TAURUS 1990

Ratings

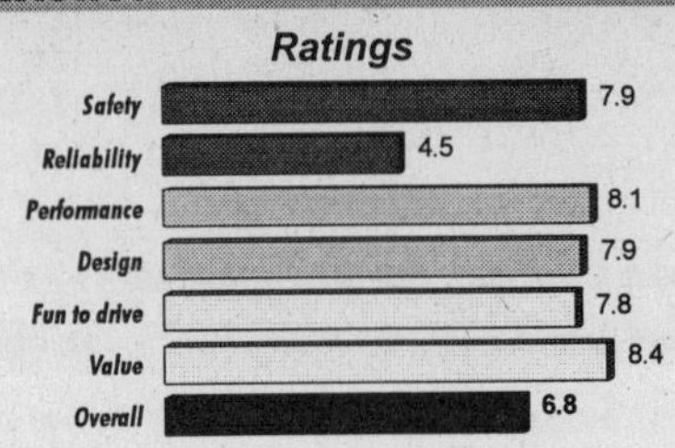

FWD/AT/PS/AC

Model/Body/Type	BaseList	Whlse	Retail
4 Cyl Models			
4 Dr L Sdn	12640	**3125**	**4675**
4 Dr GL Sdn	13113	**3725**	**5325**
V6 Models			
4 Dr L Sdn	13361	**3550**	**5125**
4 Dr L Wgn	14272	**4300**	**5975**
4 Dr GL Sdn	13834	**4175**	**5850**
4 Dr GL Wgn	14722	**4875**	**6675**
4 Dr LX Sdn	16180	**5275**	**7125**
4 Dr LX Wgn	17771	**6050**	**7925**
4 Dr SHO Sdn (5 spd)	21633	**7925**	**9975**

ADD FOR 90 TAURUS:
ABS(Std LX,SHO) +275 | *Cass(Std SHO) +60*
CD Player +115 | *CruiseCtrl(Std SHO) +75*
Custom Whls/Cvrs +115 | *JBL Stereo System +100*
Leather Seats +115
Pwr Locks(Std LX,SHO) +60
Pwr Seat(Std LX,SHO) +75
Pwr Sunroof +315
Pwr Wndw(Std LX,SHO) +75
Third Seat +100

DEDUCT FOR 90 TAURUS:
No AC -430

TEMPO 4 Cyl 1990

Ratings

Model/Body/Type	BaseList	Whlse	Retail
FWD/AT/PS/AC			
2 Dr GL Cpe	9483	**2950**	**4200**
4 Dr GL Sdn	8633	**3050**	**4300**
2 Dr GLS Cpe	10300	**3300**	**4650**
4 Dr GLS Sdn	10448	**3400**	**4725**
4 Dr LX Sdn	10605	**3525**	**4850**
4 Dr 4WD Sdn	11331	**4125**	**5525**

ADD FOR 90 TEMPO:
Cass(Std GLS) +35 — *Cruise Ctrl +60*
Custom Whls/Cvrs +75 — *GLS Sport Pkg +230*
Pwr Locks(Std LX) +35 — *Pwr Seat +60*
Pwr Wndw +60 — *Tilt Whl(Std LX) +35*

DEDUCT FOR 90 TEMPO:
No AC -350 — *No Auto Trans -315*

THUNDERBIRD V6 1990

Ratings

Rating	Score
Safety	7.3
Reliability	5.6
Performance	7.6
Design	8.4
Fun to drive	7.5
Value	7.6
Overall	6.9

Model/Body/Type	BaseList	Whlse	Retail
AT/PS/AC			
2 Dr Cpe	14980	**5475**	**7150**
2 Dr LX Cpe	17263	**6325**	**8075**
2 Dr Super Cpe	20390	**8725**	**10725**

ADD FOR 90 THUNDERBIRD:
ABS(Std SC) +275 — *Cass(Std LX) +60*
CD Player +115 — *Cruise Ctrl(Std LX) +75*
Custom Whls/Cvrs +115 — *JBL Stereo System +100*
Leather Seats +115 — *Pwr Locks(Std LX) +60*
Pwr Seat(Std LX) +75 — *Pwr Sunroof +315*
Tilt Whl(Std LX) +60

90 FORD TRUCK OPTIONS TABLE

ADD FOR ALL 90 FORD TRUCKS:
15 Pass Seating +250
4-Whl Drive +1080
AC-Rear(Std Aerostar Eddie Bauer) +185
Custom Whls(Std Aerostar Eddie B, Bronco Eddie B,BroncoII XL Spt/Eddie) +80
Dual Rear Whls +290
Fiberglass Cap +125
Privacy Glass(Std Aerostar XLT/Eddie B) +80
Running Boards +80
Towing Pkg +80
V8 7.3 L Diesel Engine +625

DEDUCT FOR ALL 90 FORD TRUCKS
No AC -250
No Auto Trans -170

1989 FORD

AEROSTAR V6 ½ Ton 1989

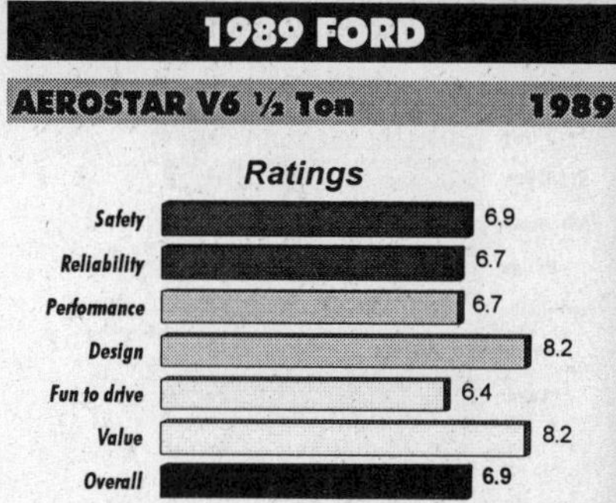

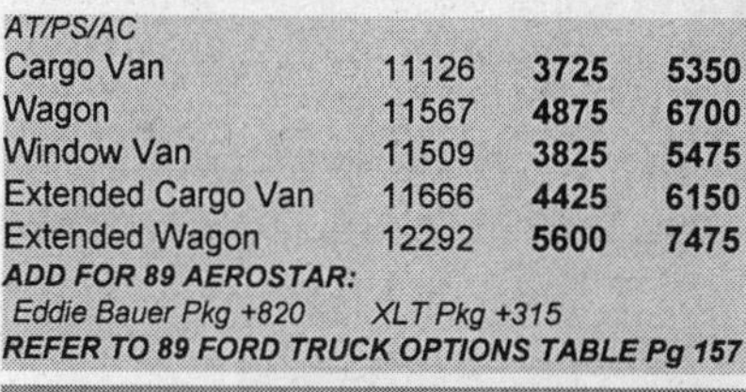

Model/Body/Type	BaseList	Whlse	Retail
AT/PS/AC			
Cargo Van	11126	**3725**	**5350**
Wagon	11567	**4875**	**6700**
Window Van	11509	**3825**	**5475**
Extended Cargo Van	11666	**4425**	**6150**
Extended Wagon	12292	**5600**	**7475**

ADD FOR 89 AEROSTAR:
Eddie Bauer Pkg +820 — *XLT Pkg +315*

REFER TO 89 FORD TRUCK OPTIONS TABLE Pg 157

BRONCO V8 ½ Ton 1989

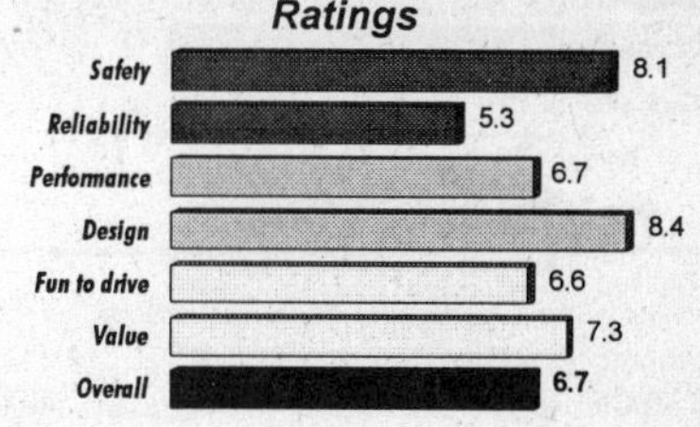

Model/Body/Type	BaseList	Whlse	Retail
4WD/AT/PS/AC			
2 Dr Utility	16526	**8275**	**10350**

ADD FOR 89 BRONCO:
Eddie Bauer Pkg +780 — *XLT Pkg +315*

DEDUCT FOR 89 BRONCO:
6 Cyl Eng -275

REFER TO 89 FORD TRUCK OPTIONS TABLE Pg 157

Model/Body/Type	BaseList	Whlse	Retail

BRONCO II V6 ½ Ton 1989

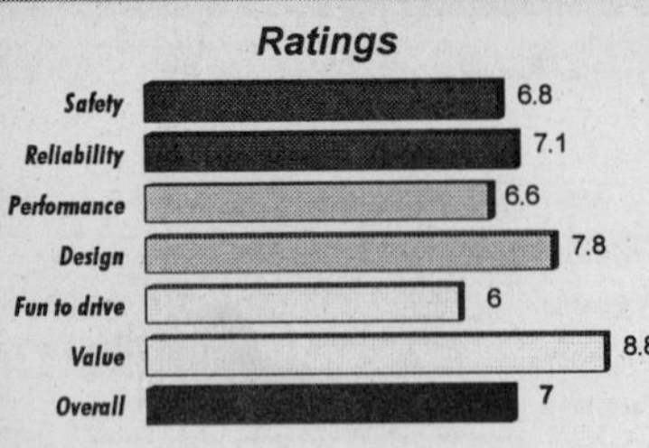

AT/PS/AC			
2 Dr Utility	12405	**4900**	**6725**
2 Dr 4WD Utility	13915	**6325**	**8250**

ADD FOR 89 BRONCO II:

Eddie Bauer Pkg +780 XL Sport Pkg +275

XLT Pkg +315

REFER TO 89 FORD TRUCK OPTIONS TABLE Pg 157

CLUB WAGON V8 ½-1 Ton 1989

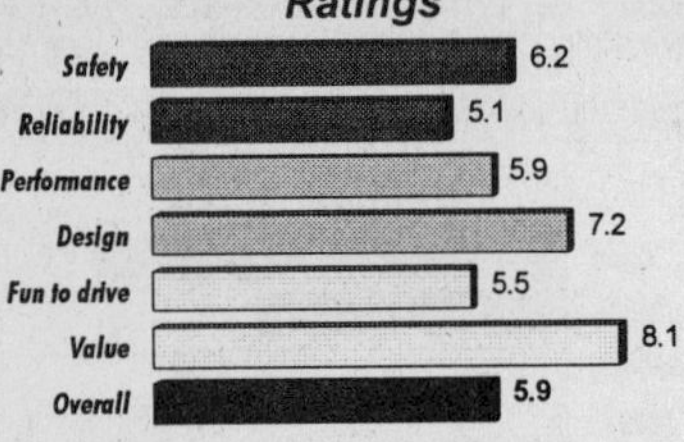

AT/PS/AC			
E150 Club Wgn	15797	**6575**	**8525**
E250 Club Wgn	16082	**6650**	**8650**
E350 Super Club Wgn	17522	**7225**	**9275**

ADD FOR 89 CLUB WAGON:

XLT Pkg +315

DEDUCT FOR 89 CLUB WAGON:

6 Cyl Eng -275

REFER TO 89 FORD TRUCK OPTIONS TABLE Pg 157

ECONOLINE VAN V8 1989

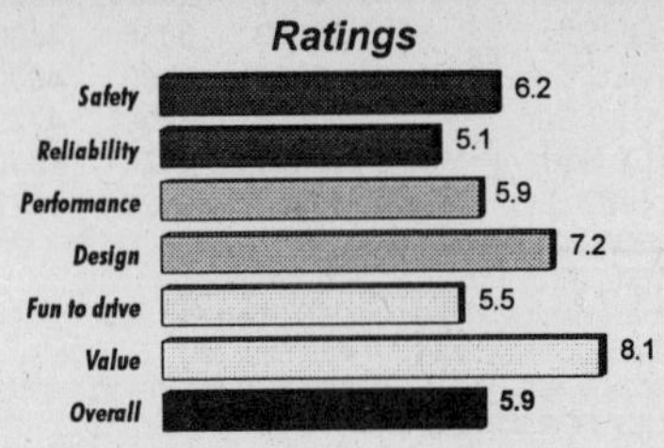

AT/PS/AC			
E150 Econoline Van ½ Ton			
Cargo Van	11902	**5025**	**6900**
Super Cargo Van	13678	**5550**	**7425**
E250 Econoline Van ¾ Ton			
Cargo Van	13301	**5200**	**7075**
Super Cargo Van	14017	**5675**	**7525**
E350 Econoline Van 1 Ton			
Cargo Van	14257	**5350**	**7550**
Super Cargo Van	15375	**5800**	**8100**

ADD FOR 89 ECONOLINE VAN:

XL Pkg +160

DEDUCT FOR 89 ECONOLINE VAN:

6 Cyl Eng -275

REFER TO 89 FORD TRUCK OPTIONS TABLE Pg 157

ESCORT 4 Cyl 1989

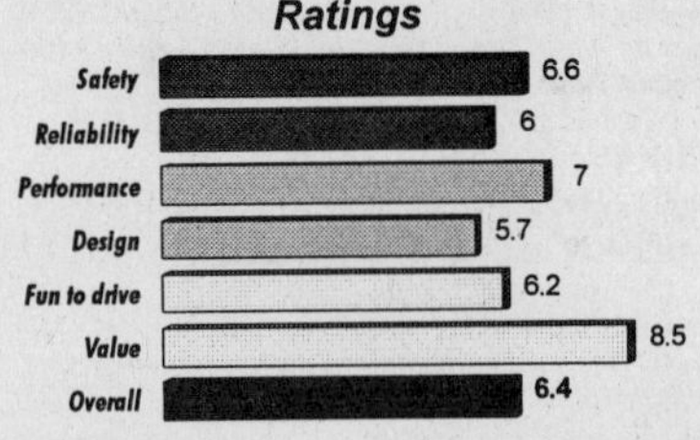

FWD/AT/PS/AC			
2 Dr Pony Hbk	6964	**1550**	**2525**
2 Dr LX Hbk	7349	**1900**	**2975**
4 Dr LX Hbk	7679	**2000**	**3100**
4 Dr LX Wgn	8280	**2175**	**3250**
2 Dr GT Hbk	9315	**2725**	**3900**

Model/Body/Type	BaseList	Whlse	Retail

ADD FOR 89 ESCORT:
Cass +25 *Cruise Ctrl +35*
Custom Whls/Cvrs +35 *Tilt Whl +25*
DEDUCT FOR 89 ESCORT:
No AC -275 *No Auto Trans -230*

F-SERIES PICKUPS V8 1989

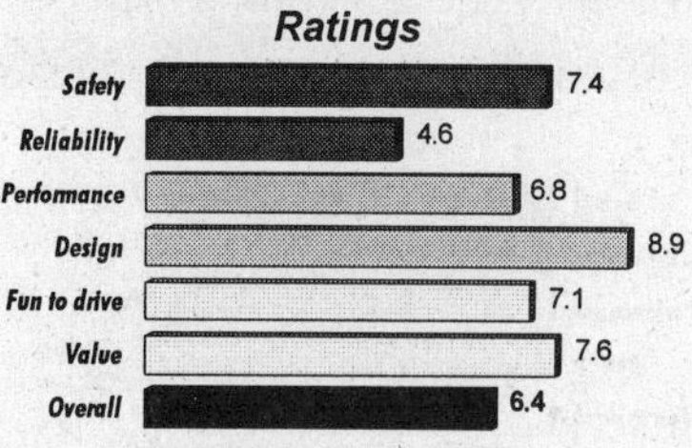

AT/PS/AC

Model/Body/Type	BaseList	Whlse	Retail
F150 Pickup ½ Ton			
Styleside S 6 ¾' (6 cyl)	10083	**4850**	**6675**
Styleside S 8' (6 cyl)	10272	**4950**	**6775**
Styleside 6 ¾'	11001	**5975**	**7875**
Styleside 8'	11193	**6100**	**7975**
Style Supercab 6 ¾'	12479	**6825**	**8825**
Styleside Supercab 8'	12668	**6925**	**8925**
F250 Pickup ¾ Ton			
Styleside 8'	11419	**6500**	**8425**
Heavy Duty 8'	11843	**6650**	**8650**
HD Supercab 8'	14250	**7300**	**9375**
F350 Pickup 1 Ton			
Styleside 8'	13985	**7000**	**9425**
Styleside Crew Cab 8'	15841	**8050**	**10625**
Styleside Supercab 8'	15780	**8450**	**11050**

ADD FOR 89 F-SERIES PICKUP:
XL Pkg +160 *XLT Lariat Pkg +315*
DEDUCT FOR 89 F-SERIES PICKUP:
6 Cyl Eng -275
REFER TO 89 FORD TRUCK OPTIONS TABLE Pg 157

FESTIVA 4 Cyl 1989

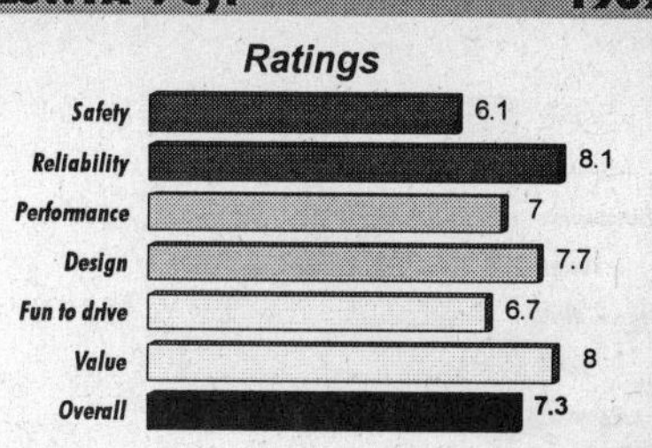

AC/FWD

Model/Body/Type	BaseList	Whlse	Retail
2 Dr L Hbk	5699	**1300**	**2225**
2 Dr L Plus Hbk	6372	**1475**	**2425**
2 Dr LX Hbk	7101	**1725**	**2750**

ADD FOR 89 FESTIVA:
Auto Trans +230 *Cass +25*
Custom Whls/Cvrs +35
DEDUCT FOR 89 FESTIVA:
No AC -275

LTD CROWN VICTORIA V8 1989

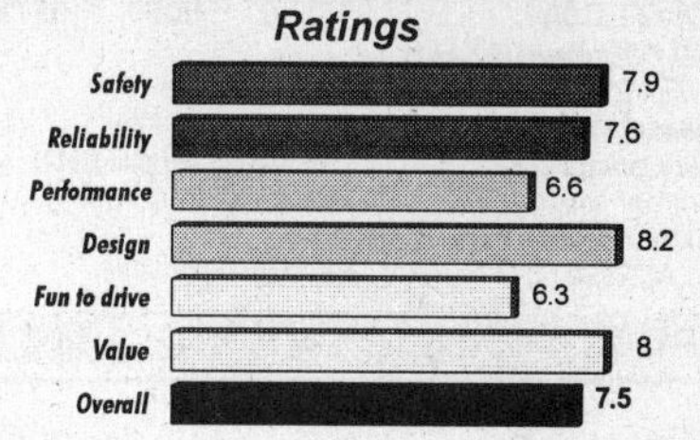

AT/PS/AC

Model/Body/Type	BaseList	Whlse	Retail
4 Dr S Sdn	15434	**2625**	**3975**
4 Dr Sdn	15851	**3650**	**5225**
4 Dr LX Sdn	16767	**4225**	**5875**
DFRS Wgn	16382	**3600**	**5175**
2 Seat Wgn	16209	**3475**	**5050**
DFRS LX Wgn	17238	**4175**	**5850**
DFRS Cntry Squire Wgn	16700	**4000**	**5675**
2 Seat Cntry Squire Wgn	16527	**3875**	**5525**
DFRS LX Cntry Squire Wgn	17556	**4575**	**6275**

ADD FOR 89 LTD CROWN VICTORIA:
Brougham Roof +60 *Cass +60*
Cruise Ctrl +75 *Custom Whls/Cvrs +75*
Leather Seats +115 *Pwr Locks +35*
Pwr Seat +75 *Pwr Wndw(Std LX) +75*
Tilt Whl +35

FORD 89

FORD

MUSTANG 1989

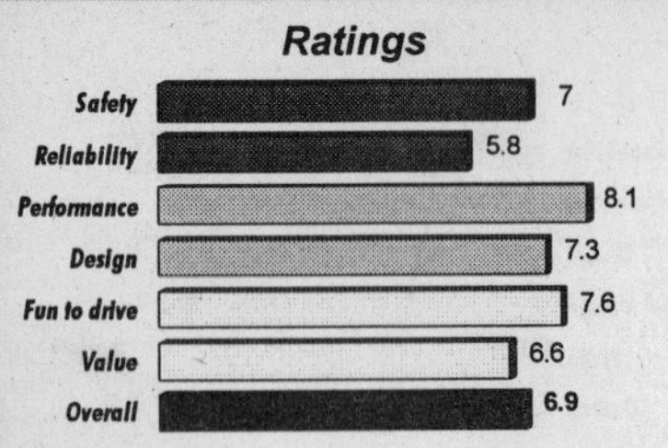

AT/PS/AC

Model/Body/Type	BaseList	Whlse	Retail
4 Cyl Models			
2 Dr LX Cpe	9050	**2600**	**3850**
2 Dr LX Hbk	9556	**2750**	**4025**
2 Dr LX Conv	14140	**5425**	**7150**
V8 Models			
2 Dr LX Cpe	11410	**3800**	**5275**
2 Dr LX Hbk	12265	**3950**	**5475**
2 Dr LX Conv	17001	**6675**	**8500**
2 Dr GT Hbk	13272	**5275**	**7000**
2 Dr GT Conv	17512	**8050**	**9975**

ADD FOR 89 MUSTANG:
Cass +35 — *Cruise Ctrl +60*
Custom Whls/Cvrs +75 — *Leather Seats +75*
Pwr Locks(Std Cnv) +35 — *Pwr Wndw(Std Cnv) +60*
Sunroof +100 — *Tilt Whl(Std GT) +35*

DEDUCT FOR 89 MUSTANG:
No AC -390 — *No Auto Trans -275*

PROBE 4 Cyl 1989

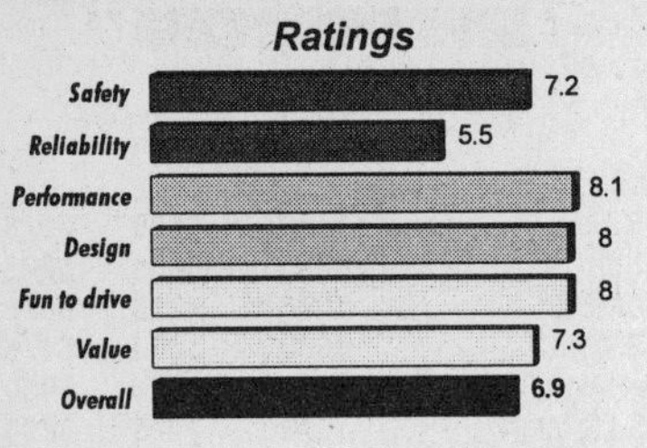

FWD/AT/PS/AC

Model/Body/Type	BaseList	Whlse	Retail
2 Dr GL Hbk	10459	**3375**	**4800**
2 Dr LX Hbk	11443	**3950**	**5475**
2 Dr GT Turbo Hbk	13593	**4700**	**6325**

ADD FOR 89 PROBE:
Cass +35 — *CD Player +75*
Cruise Ctrl +60 — *Custom Whls/Cvrs +75*
Pwr Locks +35 — *Pwr Seat +60*
Pwr Wndw +60 — *Sunroof +100*
Tilt Whl(Std LX,GT) +35

DEDUCT FOR 89 PROBE:
No AC -390 — *No Auto Trans -275*

RANGER V6 ½ Ton 1989

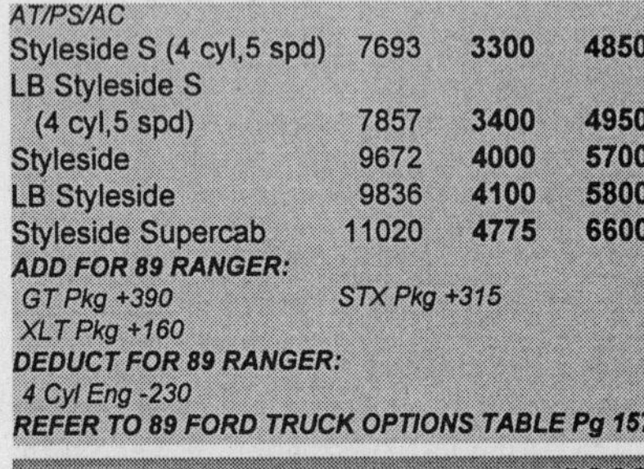

AT/PS/AC

Model/Body/Type	BaseList	Whlse	Retail
Styleside S (4 cyl,5 spd)	7693	**3300**	**4850**
LB Styleside S (4 cyl,5 spd)	7857	**3400**	**4950**
Styleside	9672	**4000**	**5700**
LB Styleside	9836	**4100**	**5800**
Styleside Supercab	11020	**4775**	**6600**

ADD FOR 89 RANGER:
GT Pkg +390 — *STX Pkg +315*
XLT Pkg +160

DEDUCT FOR 89 RANGER:
4 Cyl Eng -230

REFER TO 89 FORD TRUCK OPTIONS TABLE Pg 157

TAURUS 1989

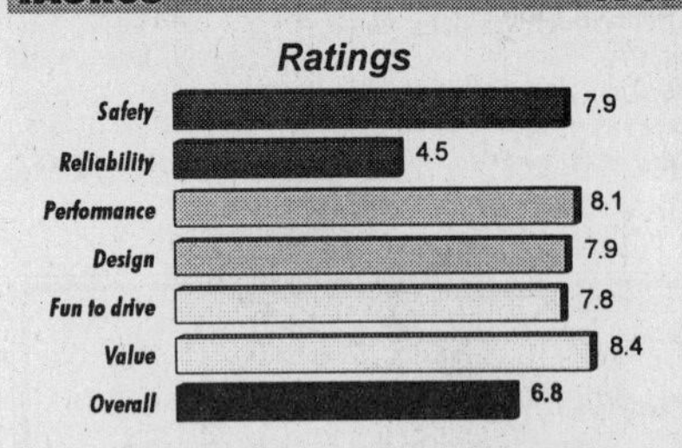

FWD/AT/PS/AC

Model/Body/Type	BaseList	Whlse	Retail
4 Cyl Models			
4 Dr L Sdn	11778	**2275**	**3600**
4 Dr GL Sdn	12202	**2825**	**4300**

Model/Body/Type	BaseList	Whlse	Retail
V6 Models			
4 Dr L Sdn	12450	**2700**	**4075**
4 Dr L Wgn	13143	**3275**	**4850**
4 Dr GL Sdn	12874	**3225**	**4750**
4 Dr GL Wgn	13544	**3825**	**5425**
4 Dr LX Sdn	15282	**4200**	**5875**
4 Dr LX Wgn	16524	**4800**	**6575**
4 Dr SHO Sdn (5 spd)	19739	**6275**	**8175**

ADD FOR 89 TAURUS:

Tilt Whl(Std LX,SHO) +35
Cass(Std SHO) +35
CruiseCtrl(Std SHO) +60
Custom Whls/Cvrs +75
JBL Stereo System +75
Leather Seats +75
Pwr Locks(Std LX,SHO) +35
Pwr Seat(Std LX,SHO) +60
Pwr Sunroof +250
Pwr Wndw(Std LX,SHO) +60
Third Seat +75

DEDUCT FOR 89 TAURUS:

No AC -390

TEMPO 4 Cyl — 1989

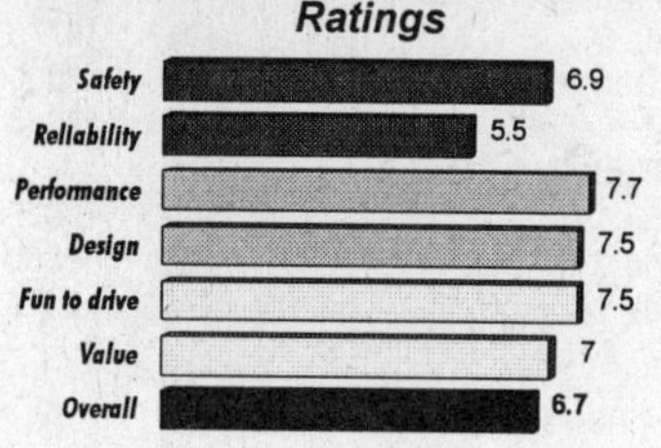

FWD/AT/PS/AC

Model/Body/Type	BaseList	Whlse	Retail
2 Dr GL Cpe	9057	**2175**	**3250**
4 Dr GL Sdn	9207	**2275**	**3375**
2 Dr GLS Cpe	9697	**2500**	**3650**
4 Dr GLS Sdn	9848	**2600**	**3750**
4 Dr LX Sdn	10156	**2725**	**3900**
4 Dr 4WD Sdn	10860	**3250**	**4550**

ADD FOR 89 TEMPO:

Cass(Std GLS) +25
Cruise Ctrl +35
Custom Whls/Cvrs +35
Pwr Locks(Std LX) +25
Pwr Seat +35
Pwr Wndw +35
Tilt Whl(Std LX) +25

DEDUCT FOR 89 TEMPO:

No AC -315
No Auto Trans -275

THUNDERBIRD V6 — 1989

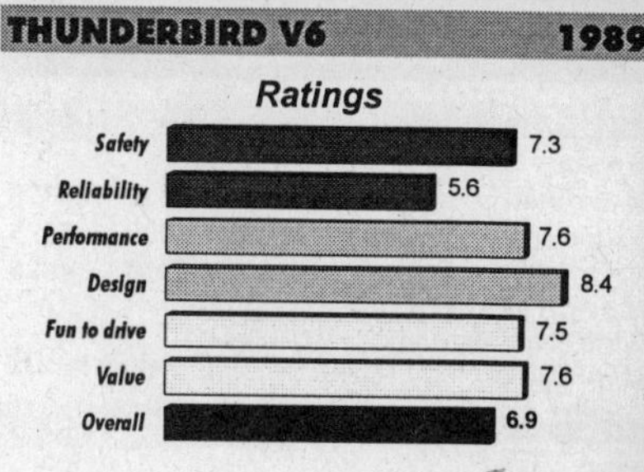

AT/PS/AC

Model/Body/Type	BaseList	Whlse	Retail
2 Dr Cpe	14612	**4400**	**5950**
2 Dr LX Cpe	16817	**5100**	**6775**
2 Dr Super Cpe	19823	**6850**	**8675**

ADD FOR 89 THUNDERBIRD:

Cass(Std LX) +35
CD Player +75
Cruise Ctrl(Std LX) +60
Custom Whls/Cvrs +75
JBL Stereo System +75
Leather Seats +75
Pwr Locks(Std LX) +35
Pwr Seat(Std LX) +60
Pwr Sunroof +250
Tilt Whl(Std LX) +35

89 FORD TRUCK OPTIONS TABLE

ADD FOR ALL 89 FORD TRUCKS:

15 Pass Seating +205
4-Whl Drive +975
AC-Rear(Std Aerostar Eddie Bauer) +145
Dual Rear Whls +250
Fiberglass Cap +80
V8 7.3 L Diesel Engine +505

DEDUCT FOR ALL 89 FORD TRUCKS

No AC -185
No Auto Trans -80

1988.5 FORD

ESCORT 4 Cyl — 1988.5

FWD/AT/PS/AC

Model/Body/Type	BaseList	Whlse	Retail
2 Dr Pony Hbk	6747	**1050**	**1950**
2 Dr LX Hbk	7127	**1250**	**2175**
4 Dr LX Hbk	7457	**1325**	**2250**
4 Dr LX Wgn	8058	**1475**	**2425**
2 Dr GT Hbk	9093	**2000**	**3100**
2 Dr EXP Luxury Hbk	8201	**1425**	**2375**

DEDUCT FOR 88.5 ESCORT:

No AC -215
No Auto Trans -195

Model/Body/Type	BaseList	Whlse	Retail

1988 FORD

AEROSTAR V6 ½ Ton — 1988

AT/PS/AC

Model/Body/Type	BaseList	Whlse	Retail
Cargo Van	10456	**2850**	**4325**
Wagon	11165	**3900**	**5575**
Window Van	10854	**2950**	**4425**

ADD FOR 88 AEROSTAR:
Eddie Bauer Pkg +585 *XLT Pkg +230*
REFER TO 88 FORD TRUCK OPTIONS TABLE Pg 159

BRONCO V8 ½ Ton — 1988

4WD/AT/PS/AC

Model/Body/Type	BaseList	Whlse	Retail
2 Dr Utility	15397	**7000**	**8975**

ADD FOR 88 BRONCO:
Eddie Bauer Pkg +545 *XLT Pkg +230*
DEDUCT FOR 88 BRONCO:
6 Cyl Eng -230
REFER TO 88 FORD TRUCK OPTIONS TABLE Pg 159

BRONCO II V6 ½ Ton — 1988

AT/PS/AC

Model/Body/Type	BaseList	Whlse	Retail
2 Dr Utility	11707	**3525**	**5100**
2 Dr 4WD Utility	13316	**4800**	**6625**

ADD FOR 88 BRONCO II:
Eddie Bauer Pkg +545 *XL Sport Pkg +230*
XLT Pkg +230
REFER TO 88 FORD TRUCK OPTIONS TABLE Pg 159

CLUB WAGON V8 ½-1 Ton — 1988

AT/PS/AC

Model/Body/Type	BaseList	Whlse	Retail
E150 Club Wgn	15177	**4975**	**6825**
E250 Club Wgn	15461	**5050**	**6925**
E350 Super Club Wgn	16731	**5600**	**7475**

ADD FOR 88 CLUB WAGON:
XLT Pkg +230
DEDUCT FOR 88 CLUB WAGON:
6 Cyl Eng -230
REFER TO 88 FORD TRUCK OPTIONS TABLE Pg 159

ECONOLINE VAN V8 — 1988

AT/PS/AC

Model/Body/Type	BaseList	Whlse	Retail
E150 Econoline Van ½ Ton			
Cargo Van	11456	**4450**	**6175**
Super Cargo Van	13192	**4850**	**6675**
E250 Econoline Van ¾ Ton			
Cargo Van	12006	**4575**	**6325**
Super Cargo Van	12639	**4925**	**6750**
E350 Econoline Van 1 Ton			
Cargo Van	12841	**4700**	**6750**
Super Cargo Van	13999	**5050**	**7225**

DEDUCT FOR 88 ECONOLINE VAN:
6 Cyl Eng -230
REFER TO 88 FORD TRUCK OPTIONS TABLE Pg 159

ESCORT 4 Cyl — 1988

FWD/AT/PS/AC

Model/Body/Type	BaseList	Whlse	Retail
2 Dr Pony Hbk	6632	**950**	**1825**
2 Dr GL Hbk	6949	**1150**	**2050**
4 Dr GL Hbk	7355	**1250**	**2175**
4 Dr GL Wgn	7938	**1375**	**2325**
2 Dr GT Hbk	9055	**1900**	**2975**
2 Dr EXP Luxury Hbk	8073	**1325**	**2275**

DEDUCT FOR 88 ESCORT:
No AC -215 *No Auto Trans -195*

F-SERIES PICKUPS V8 — 1988

AT/PS/AC

Model/Body/Type	BaseList	Whlse	Retail
F150 Pickup ½ Ton			
Styleside S 6 ¾' (6 cyl)	9732	**3550**	**5125**
Styleside S 8' (6 cyl)	9916	**3650**	**5225**
Styleside 6 ¾'	10650	**4550**	**6275**
Styleside 8'	10834	**4650**	**6400**
Style Supercab 6 ¾'	12106	**5300**	**7175**
Styleside Supercab 8'	12295	**5400**	**7275**
F250 Pickup ¾ Ton			
Styleside 8'	10849	**4950**	**6775**
Heavy Duty 8'	11288	**5125**	**7000**
HD Supercab 8'	13073	**5775**	**7650**
F350 Pickup 1 Ton			
Styleside 8'	13818	**5400**	**7625**
Styleside Crew Cab 8'	14855	**6500**	**8850**
Styleside Supercab 8'	15580	**6725**	**9175**

ADD FOR 88 F-SERIES PICKUP:
XLT Lariat Pkg +230
DEDUCT FOR 88 F-SERIES PICKUP:
6 Cyl Eng -230
REFER TO 88 FORD TRUCK OPTIONS TABLE Pg 159

FESTIVA 4 Cyl — 1988

AC/FWD

Model/Body/Type	BaseList	Whlse	Retail
2 Dr L Hbk	5765	**925**	**1800**
2 Dr L Plus Hbk	6072	**1100**	**2000**
2 Dr LX Hbk	6868	**1325**	**2250**

DEDUCT FOR 88 FESTIVA:
No AC -215

LTD CROWN VICTORIA V8 — 1988

AT/PS/AC

Model/Body/Type	BaseList	Whlse	Retail
4 Dr S Sdn	14653	**1975**	**3225**
4 Dr Sdn	15218	**2900**	**4400**
4 Dr LX Sdn	16134	**3350**	**4900**
DFRS Wgn	15353	**2775**	**4250**
DFRS LX Wgn	16210	**3250**	**4775**
DFRS Cntry Squire Wgn	15786	**3075**	**4575**
DFRS LX Cntry Squire Wgn	16643	**3525**	**5100**

Model/Body/Type	BaseList	Whlse	Retail

MUSTANG 1988

AT/PS/AC

Model/Body/Type	BaseList	Whlse	Retail
4 Cyl Models			
2 Dr LX Cpe	8726	**1850**	**3000**
2 Dr LX Hbk	9221	**2000**	**3150**
2 Dr LX Conv	13702	**4500**	**6100**
V8 Models			
2 Dr LX Cpe	10611	**2950**	**4300**
2 Dr LX Hbk	11106	**3100**	**4475**
2 Dr LX Conv	15587	**5650**	**7300**
2 Dr GT Hbk	12745	**4400**	**5950**
2 Dr GT Conv	16610	**7000**	**8800**

ADD FOR 88 MUSTANG:
T-Top +350
DEDUCT FOR 88 MUSTANG:
No AC -330 *No Auto Trans -230*

RANGER V6 ½ Ton 1988

AT/PS/AC

Model/Body/Type	BaseList	Whlse	Retail
Styleside S (4 cyl,5 spd)	6973	**2575**	**4000**
Styleside	8940	**3100**	**4600**
LB Styleside	9102	**3175**	**4700**
Styleside Supercab	10347	**3800**	**5425**

ADD FOR 88 RANGER:
GT Pkg +315 *STX Pkg +230*
DEDUCT FOR 88 RANGER:
4 Cyl Eng -195
REFER TO 88 FORD TRUCK OPTIONS TABLE Pg 159

TAURUS 1988

FWD/AT/PS/AC

Model/Body/Type	BaseList	Whlse	Retail
4 Cyl Models			
4 Dr MT5 Sdn (5 spd)	12835	**1675**	**2825**
V6 Models			
4 Dr L Sdn	12371	**1850**	**3100**
4 Dr L Wgn	12884	**2375**	**3700**
4 Dr GL Sdn	12872	**2300**	**3625**
4 Dr GL Wgn	13380	**2875**	**4350**
4 Dr LX Sdn	15295	**3150**	**4700**
4 Dr LX Wgn	15905	**3700**	**5300**

DEDUCT FOR 88 TAURUS:
4 Cyl Eng(Std MT5) -315 *No AC -330*

TEMPO 4 Cyl 1988

FWD/AT/PS/AC

Model/Body/Type	BaseList	Whlse	Retail
2 Dr GL Cpe	8658	**1650**	**2625**
4 Dr GL Sdn	8808	**1725**	**2750**
2 Dr GLS Cpe	9249	**1925**	**3000**
4 Dr GLS Sdn	9400	**2025**	**3125**
4 Dr LX Sdn	9737	**2100**	**3175**
4 Dr 4WD Sdn	10413	**2550**	**3700**

DEDUCT FOR 88 TEMPO:
No AC -250 *No Auto Trans -230*

THUNDERBIRD 1988

AT/PS/AC

Model/Body/Type	BaseList	Whlse	Retail
V6 Models			
2 Dr Cpe	13599	**2975**	**4325**
2 Dr LX Cpe	15885	**4050**	**5575**
V8 Models			
2 Dr Cpe	14320	**3325**	**4750**
2 Dr Sport Cpe	16030	**4075**	**5600**
2 Dr LX Cpe	16606	**4450**	**6000**
4 Cyl AT-5SP Models			
2 Dr Turbo Cpe	17250	**3575**	**5000**

88 FORD TRUCK OPTIONS TABLE

ADD FOR ALL 88 FORD TRUCKS:
15 Pass Seating +170
4-Whl Drive +850
AC-Rear +105
Dual Rear Whls +185
V8 7.3 L Diesel Engine +390
DEDUCT FOR ALL 88 FORD TRUCKS
No AC -125

1987 FORD

AEROSTAR V6 ½ Ton 1987

AT/PS/AC

Model/Body/Type	BaseList	Whlse	Retail
Cargo Van	9541	**2250**	**3600**
Wagon	10682	**3250**	**4775**
Window Van	10395	**2325**	**3700**

ADD FOR 87 AEROSTAR:
XLT Pkg +160
DEDUCT FOR 87 AEROSTAR:
4 Cyl Eng -160 *No AC -80*

BRONCO V8 ½ Ton 1987

4WD/AT/PS/AC

Model/Body/Type	BaseList	Whlse	Retail
2 Dr Utility	13924	**5650**	**7500**

ADD FOR 87 BRONCO:
Eddie Bauer Pkg +315 *XLT Pkg +160*
DEDUCT FOR 87 BRONCO:
No AC -80

BRONCO II V6 ½ Ton 1987

AT/PS/AC

Model/Body/Type	BaseList	Whlse	Retail
2 Dr Utility	11398	**2775**	**4250**
2 Dr 4WD Utility	12798	**3875**	**5550**

ADD FOR 87 BRONCO II:
Eddie Bauer Pkg +315 *XLT Pkg +160*
DEDUCT FOR 87 BRONCO II:
No AC -80

FORD 87

Model/Body/Type	BaseList	Whlse	Retail
CLUB WAGON V8 ½-1 Ton			**1987**
AT/PS/AC			
E150 Club Wgn	13171	**3925**	**5600**
E250 Club Wgn	14881	**3975**	**5675**
E350 Super Club Wgn	16103	**4450**	**6175**

ADD FOR 87 CLUB WAGON:
15-Pass Pkg +130 *V8 6.9L Diesel Eng +315*
XLT Pkg +160
DEDUCT FOR 87 CLUB WAGON:
6 Cyl Eng -195 *No AC -80*

Model/Body/Type	BaseList	Whlse	Retail
ECONOLINE VAN V8			**1987**
AT/PS/AC			
E150 Econoline Van ½ Ton			
Cargo Van	10449	**3075**	**4575**
Window Van	10740	**3150**	**4700**
Super Cargo Van	11599	**3425**	**4975**
Super Window Van	11890	**3425**	**5100**
E250 Econoline Van ¾ Ton			
Cargo Van	11589	**3125**	**4650**
Window Van	11880	**3225**	**4750**
Super Cargo Van	12301	**3475**	**5025**
E350 Econoline Van 1 Ton			
Cargo Van	12394	**3225**	**4975**
Window Van	12686	**3300**	**5100**
Super Cargo Van	13513	**3575**	**5425**
Super Window Van	13804	**3675**	**5550**

ADD FOR 87 ECONOLINE VAN:
15-Pass Pkg +125 *V8 6.9L Diesel Eng +315*
XLT Pkg +160
DEDUCT FOR 87 ECONOLINE VAN:
6 Cyl Eng -195 *No AC -80*

Model/Body/Type	BaseList	Whlse	Retail
ESCORT 4 Cyl			**1987**
FWD/AT/PS/AC			
2 Dr Pony Hbk	6436	**825**	**1650**
2 Dr GL Hbk	6801	**950**	**1825**
4 Dr GL Hbk	7022	**1050**	**1950**
4 Dr GL Wgn	7312	**1175**	**2100**
2 Dr GT Hbk	8724	**1700**	**2700**
2 Dr EXP Luxury Hbk	7622	**1075**	**1975**
2 Dr EXP Sport Hbk	8831	**1350**	**2300**

DEDUCT FOR 87 ESCORT:
4 Cyl Diesel Eng -565

Model/Body/Type	BaseList	Whlse	Retail
F-SERIES PICKUPS V8			**1987**
AT/PS/AC			
F150 Pickup ½ Ton			
Flareside 6 ½'	9772	**3800**	**5425**
Styleside 6 ¾'	9509	**3850**	**5525**
Styleside 8'	9693	**3950**	**5650**
Style Supercab 6 ¾'	11405	**4550**	**6275**
Styleside Supercab 8'	11613	**4650**	**6400**
F250 Pickup ¾ Ton			
Styleside 8'	10566	**4250**	**5950**
Heavy Duty 8'	10874	**4400**	**6125**
HD Supercab 8'	12686	**4900**	**6725**
F350 Pickup 1 Ton			
Styleside 8'	13109	**4650**	**6700**
Styleside Crew Cab 8'	14114	**5650**	**7850**

ADD FOR 87 F-SERIES PICKUP:
4-Whl Drive +80 *Dual Rear Whls +125*
V8 6.9L Diesel Eng +315 *XLT Lariat Pkg +160*
DEDUCT FOR 87 F-SERIES PICKUP:
6 Cyl Eng -195 *No AC -80*

Model/Body/Type	BaseList	Whlse	Retail
LTD CROWN VICTORIA V8			**1987**
AT/PS/AC			
4 Dr S Sdn	13860	**1225**	**2275**
4 Dr Sdn	14355	**1800**	**3025**
2 Dr Cpe	14727	**1700**	**2850**
4 Dr LX Sdn	15454	**2225**	**3500**
2 Dr LX Cpe	15421	**2100**	**3325**
4 Dr S Wgn	14228	**1025**	**2050**
4 Dr Wgn	14235	**1650**	**2800**
4 Dr LX Wgn	15623	**2050**	**3275**
4 Dr Cntry Squire Wgn	14507	**1850**	**3100**
4 Dr LX Cntry Squire Wgn	15896	**2275**	**3550**

Model/Body/Type	BaseList	Whlse	Retail
MUSTANG			**1987**
AT/PS/AC			
4 Cyl Models			
2 Dr LX Cpe	8043	**1475**	**2525**
3 Dr LX Hbk	8474	**1625**	**2700**
2 Dr LX Conv	12840	**3875**	**5350**
V8 Models			
3 Dr GT Hbk	11835	**3675**	**5100**
2 Dr GT Conv	15724	**6050**	**7775**

ADD FOR 87 MUSTANG:
V8 Engine(Std GT) +760

Model/Body/Type	BaseList	Whlse	Retail
RANGER V6 ½ Ton			**1987**
AT/PS/AC			
Styleside S (4 cyl,5 spd)	6593	**2000**	**3275**
Styleside	7684	**2225**	**3575**
LB Styleside	7845	**2300**	**3675**
Styleside Supercab	8846	**2850**	**4325**

ADD FOR 87 RANGER:
4-Whl Drive +680 *STX Pkg +115*
DEDUCT FOR 87 RANGER:
4 Cyl Eng -160 *No AC -80*

Model/Body/Type	BaseList	Whlse	Retail
TAURUS			**1987**
FWD/AT/PS/AC			
4 Cyl Models			
4 Dr MT5 Sdn (5 spd)	11966	**1325**	**2375**
4 Dr MT5 Wgn (5 spd)	12534	**1775**	**3000**

Model/Body/Type	BaseList	Whlse	Retail
V6 Models			
4 Dr L Sdn	11163	1450	2575
4 Dr L Wgn	11722	1925	3150
4 Dr GL Sdn	12170	1800	3025
4 Dr GL Wgn	12688	2275	3600
4 Dr LX Sdn	14613	2425	3750
4 Dr LX Wgn	15213	2950	4450

DEDUCT FOR 87 TAURUS:
4 Cyl Eng(Std MT5) -290

TEMPO 4 Cyl — 1987

FWD/AT/PS/AC

Model/Body/Type	BaseList	Whlse	Retail
2 Dr GL Cpe	8043	1150	2050
4 Dr GL Sdn	8198	1250	2175
2 Dr Sport GL Cpe	8888	1325	2250
4 Dr Sport GL Sdn	9043	1400	2350
2 Dr LX Cpe	9238	1400	2350
4 Dr LX Sdn	9444	1500	2450
2 Dr 4WD Cpe	9984	1800	2850
4 Dr 4WD Sdn	10138	1900	2975

THUNDERBIRD — 1987

AT/PS/AC

Model/Body/Type	BaseList	Whlse	Retail
V6 Models			
2 Dr Cpe	12972	2275	3475
2 Dr LX Cpe	15383	3250	4650
V8 Models			
2 Dr Sport Cpe	15079	3250	4675
4 Cyl AT-5SP Models			
2 Dr Turbo Cpe	16805	2775	4100

ADD FOR 87 THUNDERBIRD:
V8 Eng(Std Sport) +290

1986 FORD

AEROSTAR — 1986

Model/Body/Type	BaseList	Whlse	Retail
Cargo Van	8774	1500	2850
Wagon	9398	2400	3950
Window Van	9764	1600	2950

BRONCO — 1986

4WD

Model/Body/Type	BaseList	Whlse	Retail
2 Dr Utility	12782	4300	6100

BRONCO II — 1986

Model/Body/Type	BaseList	Whlse	Retail
2 Dr Utility	10279	2250	3725
2 Dr 4WD Utility	11501	3075	4675

CLUB WAGON — 1986

Model/Body/Type	BaseList	Whlse	Retail
E150 Club Wgn	12274	3225	4850
E250 Club Wgn	13838	3250	4900
E350 Super Club Wgn	14849	3625	5300

ADD FOR 86 E/150/E250/E350 CLUB WAGON:
15 Pass Pkg +80

ECONOLINE VAN — 1986

Model/Body/Type	BaseList	Whlse	Retail
E150 Econoline Van ½ Ton			
Cargo Van	9439	1850	3250
Window Van	9710	1925	3325
Super Cargo Van	10593	2100	3550
Super Window Van	10863	2175	3625
E250 Econoline Van ¾ Ton			
Cargo Van	10561	1925	3325
Window Van	10831	1975	3400
Super Cargo Van	11222	2175	3625
E350 Econoline Van 1 Ton			
Cargo Van	11264	2000	3425
Window Van	11534	2075	3500
Super Cargo Van	12322	2250	3725

ESCORT — 1986

FWD

Model/Body/Type	BaseList	Whlse	Retail
2 Dr Pony Hbk	6052	425	1350
2 Dr L Hbk	6327	550	1550
4 Dr L Hbk	6541	625	1600
4 Dr L Wgn	6822	725	1700
2 Dr LX Hbk	7234	825	1775
4 Dr LX Hbk	7448	900	1875
4 Dr LX Wgn	7729	950	1975
2 Dr GT Hbk	8112	1150	2175
2 Dr EXP Hbk	7186	725	1700
2 Dr EXP Sport Hbk	8235	950	1975

F-SERIES PICKUPS — 1986

Model/Body/Type	BaseList	Whlse	Retail
F150 Pickup ½ Ton			
Flareside 6 ½'	8625	2950	4550
Styleside 6 ¾'	8373	3000	4600
Styleside 8'	8548	3075	4675
Style Supercab 6 ¾'	10272	3500	5175
Styleside Supercab 8'	10446	3575	5250
F250 Pickup ¾ Ton			
Styleside 8'	9924	3250	4900
Heavy Duty 8'	10278	3375	5025
HD Supercab 8'	11994	3825	5550
F350 Pickup 1 Ton			
Styleside 8'	12228	3575	5250
Styleside Crew Cab 8'	13171	4350	6125

ADD FOR 86 F-SERIES PICKUP:
4-Whl Drive +495

LTD — 1986

Model/Body/Type	BaseList	Whlse	Retail
4 Dr Sdn	10032	1150	2175
4 Dr Brougham Sdn	10420	1425	2525
4 Dr Wgn	10132	1300	2350

FORD 86-85

Model/Body/Type	BaseList	Whlse	Retail
LTD CROWN VICTORIA			**1986**
4 Dr S Sdn	12188	1175	2200
4 Dr Sdn	12562	1700	2825
2 Dr Cpe	13022	1550	2675
4 Dr LX Sdn	13784	2000	3175
2 Dr LX Cpe	13752	1850	3050
4 Dr S Wgn	12468	950	1975
4 Dr Wgn	12405	1475	2575
4 Dr LX Wgn	13567	1775	2950
4 Dr Country Squire	12655	1700	2875
4 Dr LX Country Squire	13817	2025	3225
MUSTANG			**1986**
2 Dr LX Cpe	7189	1300	2350
3 Dr LX Sdn	7744	1400	2500
2 Dr LX Conv	12821	3375	4775
3 Dr GT Hbk	10691	2875	4200
2 Dr GT Conv	14523	4375	5875
RANGER ½ Ton			**1986**
Styleside	6834	1775	3150
LB Styleside	6991	1800	3225
Styleside Supercab	7822	2250	3725
ADD FOR 86 RANGER:			
4-Whl Drive +495			
TAURUS			**1986**
FWD			
4 Dr MT5 Sdn	10276	1225	2250
4 Dr MT5 Wgn	10741	1550	2675
4 Dr L Sdn	10256	1350	2425
4 Dr L Wgn	10763	1700	2875
4 Dr GL Sdn	11322	1600	2725
4 Dr GL Wgn	11790	1975	3150
4 Dr LX Sdn	13351	2025	3200
4 Dr LX Wgn	13860	2375	3625
TEMPO			**1986**
FWD			
2 Dr GL Cpe	7358	825	1775
4 Dr GL Sdn	7508	875	1850
2 Dr LX Cpe	8578	950	1975
4 Dr LX Sdn	8777	1050	2075
THUNDERBIRD			**1986**
2 Dr Cpe	11020	1700	2875
2 Dr elan Cpe	12554	2350	3600
2 Dr Turbo Cpe	14143	1925	3125

1985.5 FORD

Model/Body/Type	BaseList	Whlse	Retail
ESCORT			**1985.5**
FWD			
2 Dr Hbk	5856	375	1325
2 Dr L Hbk	6127	475	1425
4 Dr L Hbk	6341	575	1525
4 Dr L Wgn	6622	625	1600
2 Dr GL Hbk	6641	600	1575
4 Dr GL Hbk	6855	700	1675
4 Dr GL Wgn	7136	775	1725

1985 FORD

Model/Body/Type	BaseList	Whlse	Retail
BRONCO			**1985**
2 Dr 4WD Utility	11993	3275	4925
BRONCO II			**1985**
2 Dr 4WD Utility	10889	2375	3900
CLUB WAGON			**1985**
E150 5Pass Club Wgn	11502	2450	4000
E250 5Pass Club Wgn	12953	2525	4075
E350 5Pass Super Club Wgn	13931	2775	4350
ECONOLINE VAN			**1985**
E150 Econoline Van ½ Ton			
Cargo Van	8561	1400	2725
Window Van	8755	1450	2800
Display Van	8688	1450	2775
Super Cargo Van	9650	1575	2925
Super Window Van	9844	1625	3000
E250 Econoline Van ¾ Ton			
Cargo Van	9817	1450	2800
Window Van	10011	1525	2875
Display Van	9944	1500	2850
Super Cargo Van	10447	1625	3000
Super Window Van	10641	1700	3075
E350 Econoline Van 1 Ton			
Cargo Van	9949	1525	2875
Super Cargo Van	10948	1700	3075

See the Automobile Dealer Directory on page 379 for a Dealer near you!

ESCORT 1985

Model/Body/Type	BaseList	Whlse	Retail
FWD			
2 Dr Hbk	5620	**375**	**1300**
4 Dr Hbk	5827	**450**	**1375**
2 Dr L Hbk	5876	**475**	**1400**
4 Dr L Hbk	6091	**550**	**1500**
4 Dr L Wgn	6305	**600**	**1575**
2 Dr GL Hbk	6374	**600**	**1550**
4 Dr GL Hbk	6588	**675**	**1650**
4 Dr GL Wgn	6765	**750**	**1700**
4 Dr LX Hbk	7840	**775**	**1725**
4 Dr LX Wgn	7931	**825**	**1775**
2 Dr GT Hbk	7585	**850**	**1800**
2 Dr Turbo GT Hbk	8680	**875**	**1825**
3 Dr EXP Cpe	6697	**325**	**1275**
3 Dr EXP Luxury Cpe	7585	**500**	**1450**
3 Dr EXP Turbo Cpe	9997	**400**	**1325**

F-SERIES PICKUPS 1985

Model/Body/Type	BaseList	Whlse	Retail
F150 Pickup ½ Ton			
Flareside 6 ½'	7962	**2100**	**3550**
Styleside 6 ¾'	7799	**2150**	**3600**
Styleside 8'	7965	**2200**	**3675**
Style Supercab 6 ¾'	9134	**2600**	**4150**
Styleside Supercab 8'	9300	**2675**	**4225**
F250 Pickup ¾ Ton			
Styleside 8'	8951	**2375**	**3900**
Heavy Duty 8'	9276	**2450**	**4000**
HD Supercab 8'	10250	**2875**	**4450**
F350 Pickup 1 Ton			
Styleside 8'	10437	**2675**	**4250**
Styleside Crew Cab 8'	10993	**3300**	**4950**

ADD FOR 85 F-SERIES PICKUP:
4-Whl Drive +250

LTD 1985

Model/Body/Type	BaseList	Whlse	Retail
4 Dr Sdn	9292	**900**	**1875**
4 Dr Brougham Sdn	9680	**1125**	**2175**
4 Dr Wgn	9384	**1000**	**2025**
4 Dr LX Sdn	11421	**1400**	**2500**

LTD CROWN VICTORIA 1985

Model/Body/Type	BaseList	Whlse	Retail
4 Dr S Sdn	10609	**1075**	**2100**
4 Dr Sdn	11627	**1550**	**2650**
2 Dr Sdn	11627	**1400**	**2500**
4 Dr S Wgn	10956	**900**	**1875**
4 Dr Wgn	11559	**1325**	**2375**
4 Dr Country Squire	11809	**1550**	**2675**

MUSTANG 1985

Model/Body/Type	BaseList	Whlse	Retail
2 Dr LX Cpe	6885	**1150**	**2175**
3 Dr LX Hbk	7345	**1275**	**2325**
2 Dr LX Conv	11985	**2700**	**4000**
3 Dr GT Hbk	9885	**2275**	**3500**
2 Dr GT Conv	13585	**3700**	**5100**

RANGER ½ Ton 1985

Model/Body/Type	BaseList	Whlse	Retail
Styleside	6675	**1325**	**2625**
LB Styleside	6829	**1375**	**2700**

ADD FOR 85 RANGER:
4-Whl Drive +250

TEMPO 1985

Model/Body/Type	BaseList	Whlse	Retail
FWD			
2 Dr L Cpe	7052	**500**	**1450**
4 Dr L Sdn	7052	**600**	**1550**
2 Dr GL Cpe	7160	**650**	**1625**
4 Dr GL Sdn	7160	**750**	**1700**
2 Dr GLX Cpe	8253	**825**	**1775**
4 Dr GLX Sdn	8302	**900**	**1875**

THUNDERBIRD 1985

Model/Body/Type	BaseList	Whlse	Retail
2 Dr Cpe	10249	**1375**	**2450**
2 Dr elan Cpe	11916	**2000**	**3175**
2 Dr Fila Cpe	14974	**2125**	**3300**
2 Dr Turbo Cpe	13365	**1400**	**2500**

GEO — Japan

1992 Geo Prizm GSi

For a Geo dealer in your area, see our Dealer Directory (pg 217)

1994 GEO

METRO 3 Cyl — 1994

Ratings

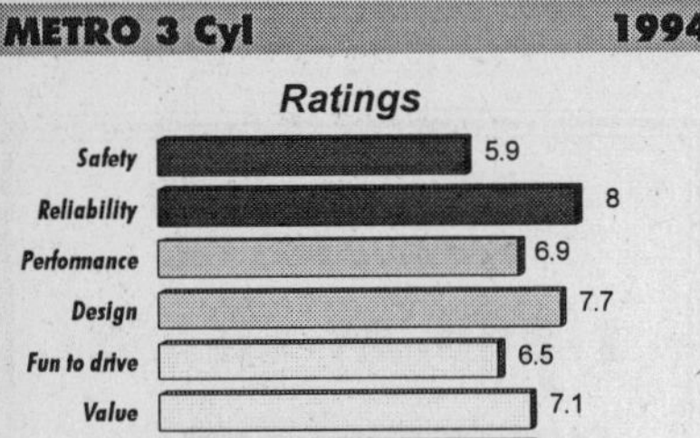

Model/Body/Type	BaseList	Whlse	Retail
FWD/5SP/PS/AC			
2 Dr XFi Hbk	7195	**6275**	**7900**
2 Dr Hbk	7195	**6650**	**8275**
4 Dr Hbk	7695	**6850**	**8575**

PRIZM 4 Cyl — 1994

Model/Body/Type	BaseList	Whlse	Retail
FWD/AT/PS/AC			
4 Dr Nbk	10730	**10575**	**12700**
4 Dr LSi Nbk	11500	**11175**	**13475**

TRACKER 4 Cyl — 1994

Model/Body/Type	BaseList	Whlse	Retail
4WD/5SP/PS/AC			
2 Dr Utility Conv (2WD)	10865	**9575**	**11525**
2 Dr Utility Hardtop	12295	**11150**	**13450**
2 Dr Utility Conv	12135	**11000**	**13300**

ADD FOR ALL 94 GEO:

ABS +430
Auto Trans (Metro,Tracker) +500
Anti-Theft/Recovery Sys +365
Cass +90
CD Player +205
Cruise Ctrl +135
Custom Whls +180
Leather Seats +230
Pwr Locks +90
Pwr Sunroof +410
Pwr Wndw +135
Tracker LSi Pkg +590

DEDUCT FOR ALL 93 GEO:

No AC -590
No Auto Trans -500
No Pwr Steering -180

1993 GEO

METRO 3 Cyl — 1993

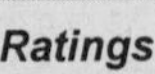

Model/Body/Type	BaseList	Whlse	Retail
FWD/5SP/PS/AC			
2 Dr XFi Hbk	6710	**4425**	**5850**
2 Dr Hbk	6710	**4800**	**6275**
2 Dr LSi Hbk	8199	**5375**	**6925**
4 Dr Hbk	7199	**4875**	**6375**
4 Dr LSi Hbk	8599	**5500**	**7025**
2 Dr LSi Conv	9999	**6825**	**8550**

See the Automobile Dealer Directory on page 379 for a Dealer near you!

PRIZM 4 Cyl — 1993

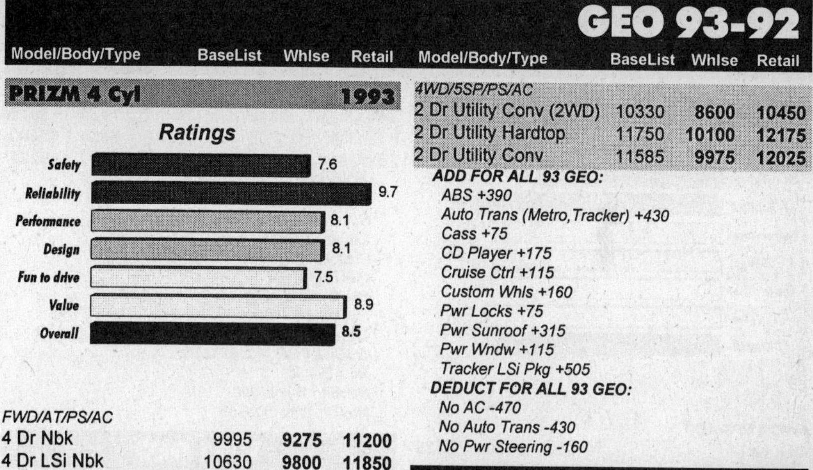

FWD/AT/PS/AC

Model/Body/Type	BaseList	Whlse	Retail
4 Dr Nbk	9995	**9275**	**11200**
4 Dr LSi Nbk	10630	**9800**	**11850**

STORM 4 Cyl — 1993

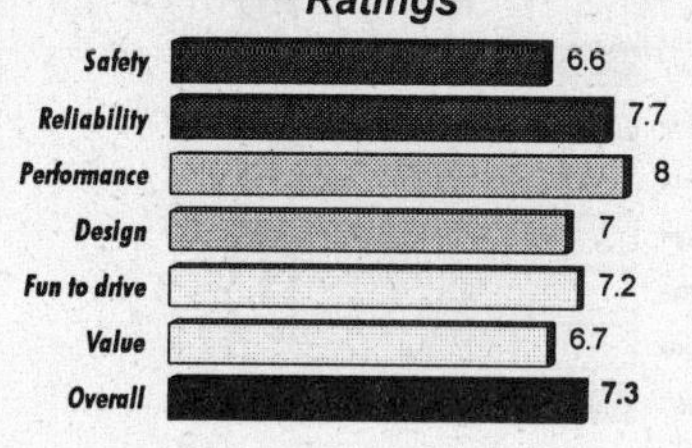

FWD/AT/PS/AC

Model/Body/Type	BaseList	Whlse	Retail
3 Dr 2+2 Cpe	11530	**7675**	**9600**
3 Dr 2+2 GSi Cpe	13495	**9175**	**11200**

TRACKER 4 Cyl — 1993

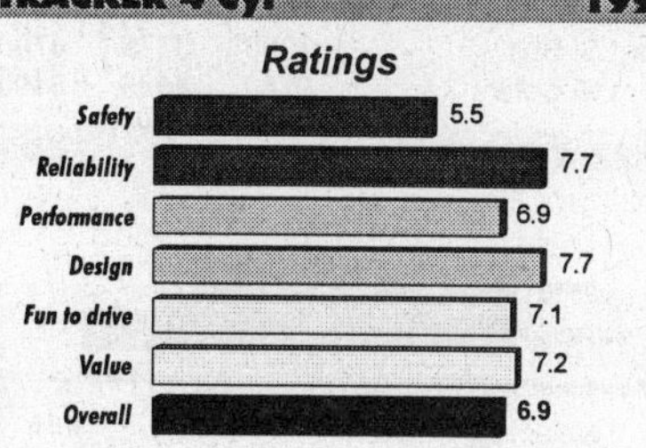

4WD/5SP/PS/AC

Model/Body/Type	BaseList	Whlse	Retail
2 Dr Utility Conv (2WD)	10330	**8600**	**10450**
2 Dr Utility Hardtop	11750	**10100**	**12175**
2 Dr Utility Conv	11585	**9975**	**12025**

ADD FOR ALL 93 GEO:

ABS +390
Auto Trans (Metro,Tracker) +430
Cass +75
CD Player +175
Cruise Ctrl +115
Custom Whls +160
Pwr Locks +75
Pwr Sunroof +315
Pwr Wndw +115
Tracker LSi Pkg +505

DEDUCT FOR ALL 93 GEO:

No AC -470
No Auto Trans -430
No Pwr Steering -160

1992 GEO

METRO 3 Cyl — 1992

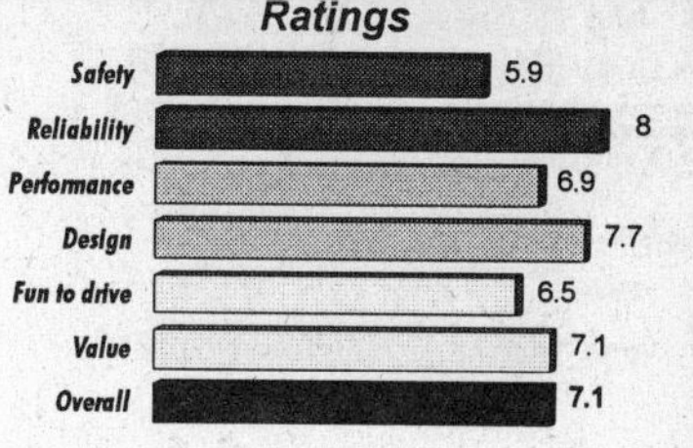

FWD/5SP/PS/AC

Model/Body/Type	BaseList	Whlse	Retail
2 Dr XFi Hbk	6999	**3425**	**4750**
2 Dr Hbk	6999	**3800**	**5150**
2 Dr LSi Hbk	8199	**4300**	**5725**
4 Dr Hbk	7399	**3900**	**5250**
4 Dr LSi Hbk	8599	**4400**	**5825**
2 Dr LSi Conv	9999	**5675**	**7175**

GEO 92-91

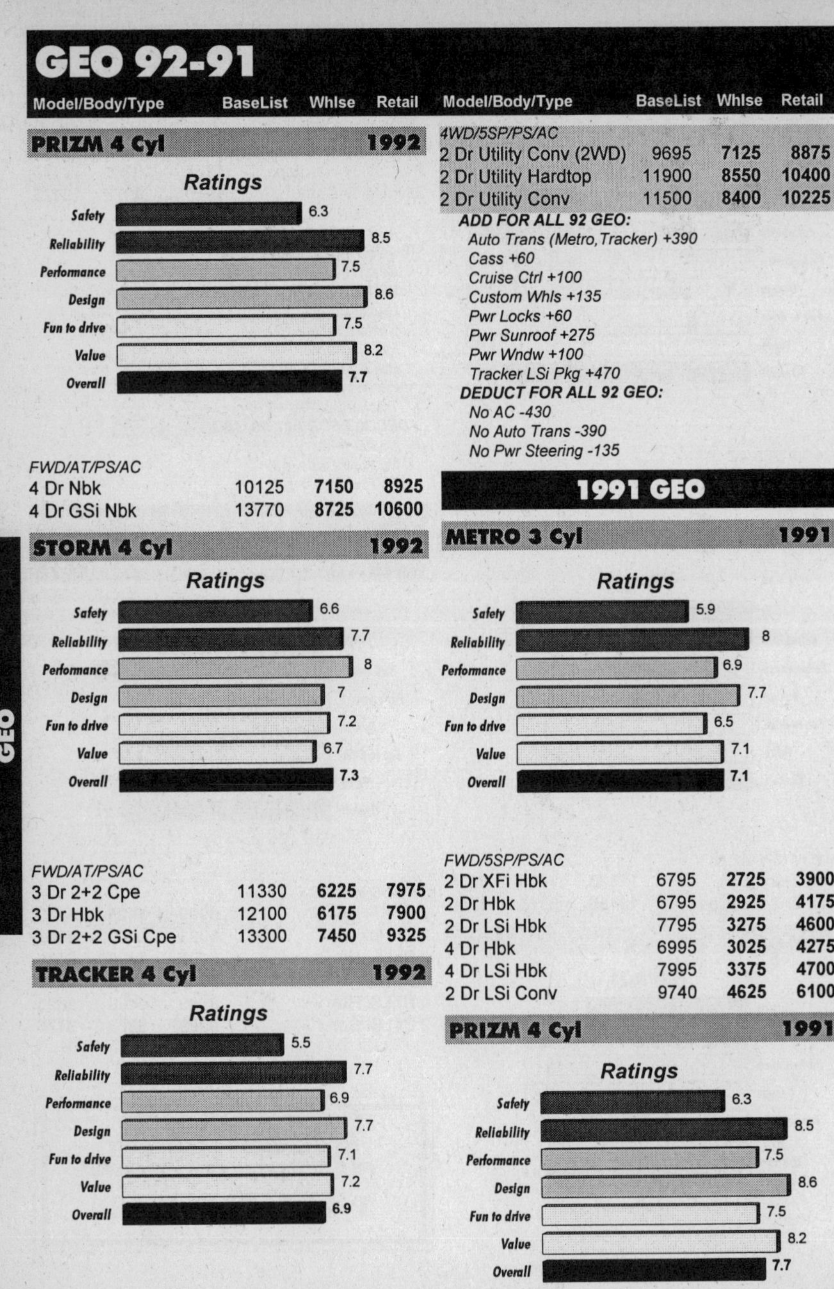

PRIZM 4 Cyl — 1992

FWD/AT/PS/AC

Model/Body/Type	BaseList	Whlse	Retail
4 Dr Nbk	10125	**7150**	**8925**
4 Dr GSi Nbk	13770	**8725**	**10600**

STORM 4 Cyl — 1992

Ratings: Safety 6.6; Reliability 7.7; Performance 8; Design 7; Fun to drive 7.2; Value 6.7; Overall 7.3

FWD/AT/PS/AC

Model/Body/Type	BaseList	Whlse	Retail
3 Dr 2+2 Cpe	11330	**6225**	**7975**
3 Dr Hbk	12100	**6175**	**7900**
3 Dr 2+2 GSi Cpe	13300	**7450**	**9325**

TRACKER 4 Cyl — 1992

Ratings: Safety 5.5; Reliability 7.7; Performance 6.9; Design 7.7; Fun to drive 7.1; Value 7.2; Overall 6.9

4WD/5SP/PS/AC

Model/Body/Type	BaseList	Whlse	Retail
2 Dr Utility Conv (2WD)	9695	**7125**	**8875**
2 Dr Utility Hardtop	11900	**8550**	**10400**
2 Dr Utility Conv	11500	**8400**	**10225**

ADD FOR ALL 92 GEO:

Auto Trans (Metro,Tracker) +390
Cass +60
Cruise Ctrl +100
Custom Whls +135
Pwr Locks +60
Pwr Sunroof +275
Pwr Wndw +100
Tracker LSi Pkg +470

DEDUCT FOR ALL 92 GEO:

No AC -430
No Auto Trans -390
No Pwr Steering -135

1991 GEO

METRO 3 Cyl — 1991

Ratings: Safety 5.9; Reliability 8; Performance 6.9; Design 7.7; Fun to drive 6.5; Value 7.1; Overall 7.1

FWD/5SP/PS/AC

Model/Body/Type	BaseList	Whlse	Retail
2 Dr XFi Hbk	6795	**2725**	**3900**
2 Dr Hbk	6795	**2925**	**4175**
2 Dr LSi Hbk	7795	**3275**	**4600**
4 Dr Hbk	6995	**3025**	**4275**
4 Dr LSi Hbk	7995	**3375**	**4700**
2 Dr LSi Conv	9740	**4625**	**6100**

PRIZM 4 Cyl — 1991

Ratings: Safety 6.3; Reliability 8.5; Performance 7.5; Design 8.6; Fun to drive 7.5; Value 8.2; Overall 7.7

GEO

Model/Body/Type	BaseList	Whlse	Retail
FWD/AT/PS/AC			
4 Dr Nbk	9680	**5675**	**7175**
4 Dr GSi Nbk	12195	**6650**	**8300**
5 Dr Hbk	10295	**5750**	**7300**
5 Dr GSi Hbk	12695	**6750**	**8500**

STORM 4 Cyl — 1991

Ratings

- Safety 6.6
- Reliability 7.7
- Performance 8
- Design 7
- Fun to drive 7.2
- Value 6.7
- Overall 7.3

Model/Body/Type	BaseList	Whlse	Retail
FWD/AT/PS/AC			
3 Dr 2+2 Cpe	10670	**5150**	**6850**
3 Dr Hbk	11450	**5100**	**6775**
3 Dr 2+2 GSi Cpe	12395	**6225**	**7975**

TRACKER 4 Cyl — 1991

Ratings

- Safety 5.5
- Reliability 7.7
- Performance 6.9
- Design 7.7
- Fun to drive 7.1
- Value 7.2
- Overall 6.9

Model/Body/Type	BaseList	Whlse	Retail
4WD/5SP/PS/AC			
2 Dr Utility Conv (2WD)	8999	**5975**	**7550**
2 Dr Utility Hardtop	11285	**7300**	**9100**
2 Dr Utility Conv	10885	**7150**	**8925**

ADD FOR ALL 91 GEO:

Auto Trans (Metro,Tracker) +350
Cass +35
Cruise Ctrl +75
Custom Whls +115
Pwr Locks +35
Pwr Sunroof +230
Pwr Wndw +75
Tracker LSi Pkg +430

DEDUCT FOR ALL 91 GEO:

No AC -390
No Auto Trans -350
No Pwr Steering -115

1990 GEO

METRO 3 Cyl — 1990

Ratings

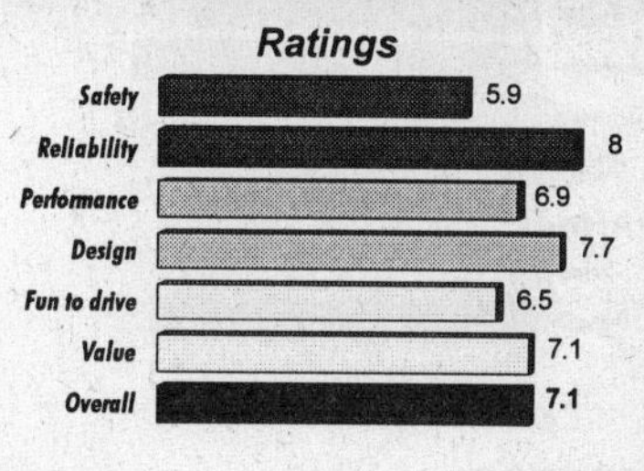

Model/Body/Type	BaseList	Whlse	Retail
FWD/5SP/PS/AC			
2 Dr XFi Hbk	5995	**1500**	**2450**
2 Dr Hbk	6695	**1700**	**2675**
2 Dr LSi Hbk	7495	**2050**	**3125**
4 Dr Hbk	6995	**1775**	**2800**
4 Dr LSi Hbk	7795	**2150**	**3225**
2 Dr LSi Conv	9740	**3100**	**4375**

PRIZM 4 Cyl — 1990

Ratings

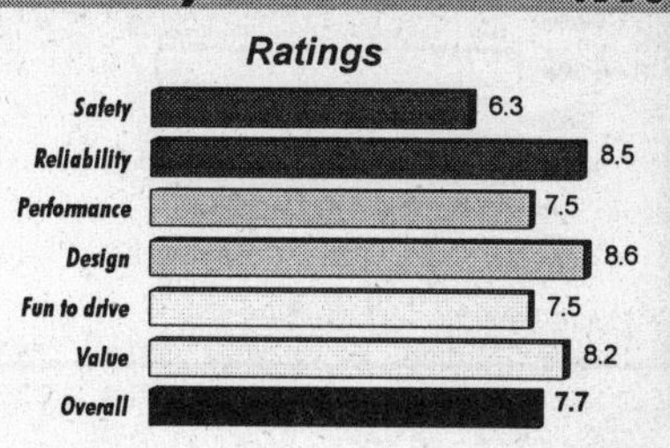

Model/Body/Type	BaseList	Whlse	Retail
FWD/AT/PS/AC			
4 Dr Nbk	9660	**4375**	**5800**
4 Dr GSi Nbk	11900	**5100**	**6625**
5 Dr Hbk	9960	**4475**	**5875**
5 Dr GSi Hbk	12285	**5200**	**6725**

GEO

GEO 90-89

Model/Body/Type	BaseList	Whlse	Retail

STORM 4 Cyl — 1990

Ratings

Rating	Score
Safety	6.6
Reliability	7.7
Performance	8
Design	7
Fun to drive	7.2
Value	6.7
Overall	7.3

Model/Body/Type	BaseList	Whlse	Retail
FWD/AT/PS/AC			
3 Dr 2+2 Cpe	10390	**4350**	**5875**
3 Dr 2+2 GSi Cpe	11650	**5150**	**6850**

TRACKER 4 Cyl — 1990

Ratings

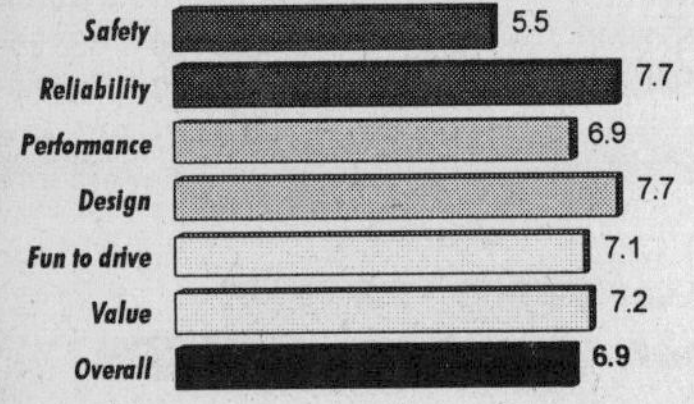

Model/Body/Type	BaseList	Whlse	Retail
4WD/5SP/PS/AC			
2 Dr Utility Hardtop	11035	**5950**	**7525**
2 Dr Utility Conv	10725	**5800**	**7350**

ADD FOR ALL 90 GEO:

Auto Trans (Metro,Tracker) +315
Cass +35
Cruise Ctrl +60
Custom Whls +75
Pwr Locks +35
Pwr Sunroof +195
Pwr Wndw +60
Tracker LSi Pkg +390

DEDUCT FOR ALL 90 GEO:

No AC -350
No Auto Trans -315
No Pwr Steering -100

1989 GEO

METRO 3 Cyl — 1989

Ratings

Rating	Score
Safety	5.9
Reliability	8
Performance	6.9
Design	7.7
Fun to drive	6.5
Value	7.1
Overall	7.1

Model/Body/Type	BaseList	Whlse	Retail
FWD/5SP/PS/AC			
2 Dr Hbk	5995	**1225**	**2150**
2 Dr LSi Hbk	6895	**1575**	**2550**
4 Dr LSi Hbk	7195	**1675**	**2650**

PRIZM 4 Cyl — 1989

Ratings

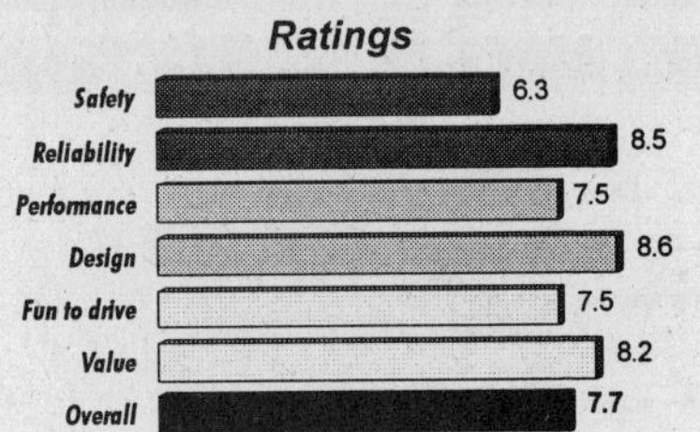

Model/Body/Type	BaseList	Whlse	Retail
FWD/AT/PS/AC			
4 Dr Nbk	-	**3325**	**4675**
5 Dr Hbk	-	**3425**	**4750**

SPECTRUM 4 Cyl — 1989

Model/Body/Type	BaseList	Whlse	Retail
FWD/AT/PS/AC			
2 Dr Hbk	7295	**2200**	**3300**
4 Dr Nbk	7795	**2350**	**3475**

See the Automobile Dealer Directory on page 379 for a Dealer near you!

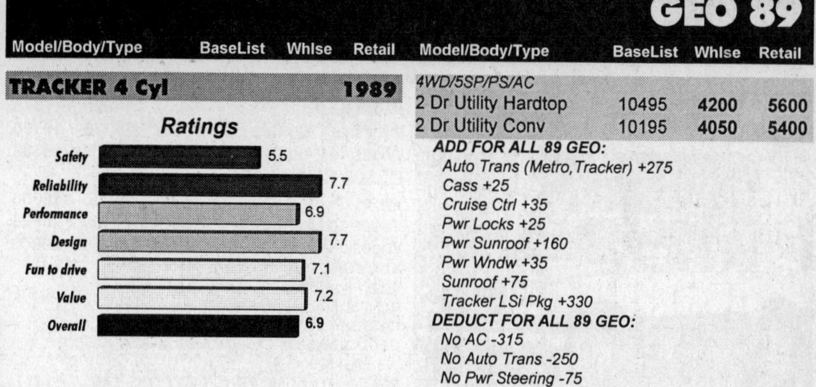

Model/Body/Type	BaseList	Whlse	Retail
TRACKER 4 Cyl 1989			
4WD/5SP/PS/AC			
2 Dr Utility Hardtop	10495	4200	5600
2 Dr Utility Conv	10195	4050	5400

ADD FOR ALL 89 GEO:

Auto Trans (Metro,Tracker) +275
Cass +25
Cruise Ctrl +35
Pwr Locks +25
Pwr Sunroof +160
Pwr Wndw +35
Sunroof +75
Tracker LSi Pkg +330

DEDUCT FOR ALL 89 GEO:

No AC -315
No Auto Trans -250
No Pwr Steering -75

Model/Body/Type	BaseList	Whlse	Retail

GMC

USA

1990 GMC C-2500 Club Coupe Pickup

For a GMC dealer in your area, see our Dealer Directory (pg 217)

1994 GMC

C1500/C2500/C3500 PKUP V8 1994

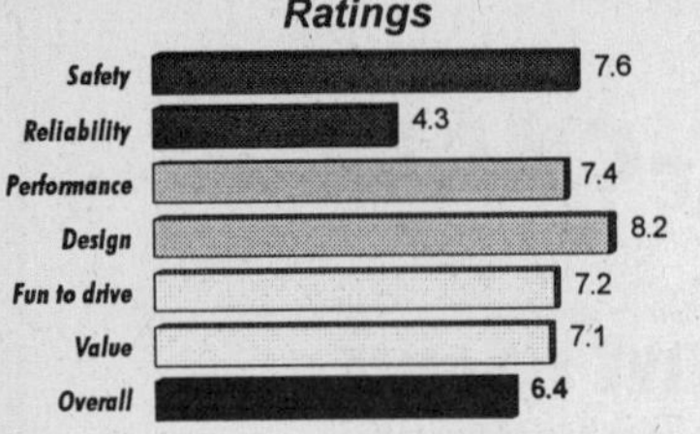

AT/PS/AC

Model/Body/Type	BaseList	Whlse	Retail
C1500 Pickup ½ Ton			
Wideside Special 6 ½'(V6)	12424	-	-
Wideside Special 8'(V6)	12424	-	-
Sportside 6 ½'	14930	**14075**	**16850**
Wideside 6 ½'	14267	**13675**	**16425**
Wideside 8'	14547	**13775**	**16525**
Wideside Club Cpe 6 ½'	16094	**15525**	**18400**
Wideside Club Cpe 8'	16937	**15625**	**18500**
Sportside Club Cpe 6 ½'	16506	**15925**	**18825**
C2500 Pickup ¾ Ton			
Wideside 8'	17022	**14600**	**17375**
Wideside Club Cpe 6 ½'	17882	**16375**	**19300**
Wideside Club Cpe 8'	18759	**16475**	**19400**
C3500 Pickup 1 Ton			
Wideside 8'	17019	**15225**	**18650**
Wideside Club Cpe 8'	20264	**17100**	**20725**
Wideside Crew Cab 8'	19358	**17250**	**20900**

ADD FOR 94 C1500/C2500/C3500 PKUP:
SLE Pkg +775 *Sport Pkg +820*
V8 6.5L Diesel Eng +730
V8 6.5L Turbo Diesel Eng +1045
DEDUCT FOR 94 C1500/C2500/C3500 PKUP:
V6 Eng -590
REFER TO 94 GMC TRUCK OPTIONS TABLE Pg 171

G1500/G2500/G3500 VAN V8 1994

AT/PS/AC

Model/Body/Type	BaseList	Whlse	Retail
G1500 Van ½ Ton			
Vandura	15779	**13450**	**16175**
G2500 Van ¾ Ton			
Vandura	15748	**13750**	**16500**
Rally Wgn	18859	**15300**	**18150**
G3500 Van 1 Ton			
Vandura	16012	-	-
Rally Wgn	20143	-	-
Extended Vandura	18132	-	-
Extended Rally Wgn	21299	-	-

ADD FOR 94 G1500/G2500/G3500 VAN:
STX Pkg +1230 *V8 6.5L Diesel Eng +730*
DEDUCT FOR 94 G1500/G2500/G3500 VAN:
V6 Eng -590
REFER TO 94 GMC TRUCK OPTIONS TABLE Pg 171

JIMMY V6 ½ Ton 1994

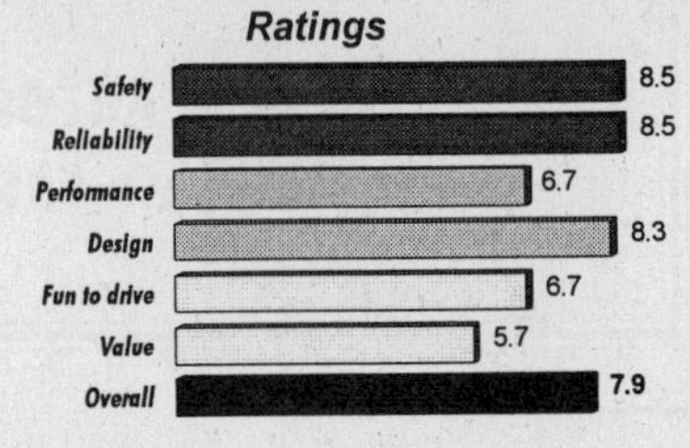

AT/PS/AC

Model/Body/Type	BaseList	Whlse	Retail
2 Dr Utility	15639	**15050**	**17875**
4 Dr Utility	16941	**16800**	**19800**
2 Dr 4WD Utility	17558	**16750**	**19750**
4 Dr 4WD Utility	19298	**18450**	**21650**
2 Dr AWD Typhoon	-	-	-

GMC

Model/Body/Type	BaseList	Whlse	Retail

ADD FOR 94 JIMMY:
SLE Pkg(Std 4 Dr) +775 *SLS Pkg +820*
SLT Pkg +1365
REFER TO 94 GMC TRUCK OPTIONS TABLE Pg 171

SAFARI V6 ½ Ton — 1994

AT/PS/AC

Model/Body/Type	BaseList	Whlse	Retail
Cargo Van	15414	-	-
Cargo Van XT	15887	-	-
SLX Van	16499	**14775**	**17575**
SLX Van XT	16801	**15825**	**18700**

ADD FOR 94 SAFARI:
All Whl Drv +1275 *SLE pkg +775*
SLT Pkg +1275
REFER TO 94 GMC TRUCK OPTIONS TABLE Pg 171

SONOMA PICKUPS V6 ½ Ton — 1994

AT/PS/AC

Model/Body/Type	BaseList	Whlse	Retail
Wideside 6'	9806	**9450**	**11675**
Wideside 7 1/3'	10106	**9550**	**11800**
Wideside Club Cpe 6'	12113	**11025**	**13550**

ADD FOR 94 SONOMA PICKUP:
SLE Pkg +680 *SLS Pkg +365*
DEDUCT FOR 94 SONOMA PICKUP:
4 Cyl Eng -545
REFER TO 94 GMC TRUCK OPTIONS TABLE Pg 171

SUBURBAN V8 — 1994

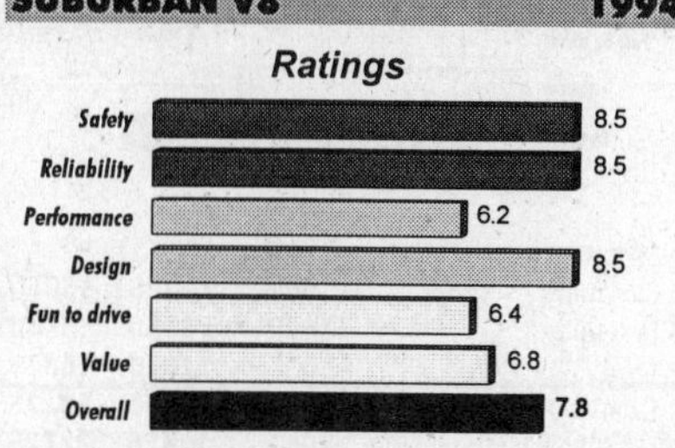

AT/PS/AC

Model/Body/Type	BaseList	Whlse	Retail
4 Dr Suburban C1500 ½ Ton	20236	**22100**	**25575**
4 Dr Suburban C2500 ¾ Ton	20522	**22850**	**26375**

ADD FOR 94 SUBURBAN:
SLE Pkg +910
V8 6.5L Turbo Diesel Eng +1045
REFER TO 94 GMC TRUCK OPTIONS TABLE Pg 171

YUKON V8 ½ Ton — 1994

Ratings

Rating	Score
Safety	8.5
Reliability	8.5
Performance	6.7
Design	8.3
Fun to drive	6.7
Value	5.7
Overall	7.9

4WD/AT/PS/AC

Model/Body/Type	BaseList	Whlse	Retail
2 Dr Utility	21195	**20625**	**23950**

ADD FOR 94 YUKON:
SLE Pkg +865 *Sport Pkg +1000*
V6 6.5L Turbo Diesel Eng +1045
REFER TO 94 GMC TRUCK OPTIONS TABLE Pg 171

94 GMC TRUCK OPTIONS TABLE

ADD FOR ALL 94 GMC TRUCKS:
15 Pass Seating +375
4-Whl Drive +1265
AC-Rear +375
Bed Liner +125
Cass +105
CD Player +205
Cruise Ctrl +125
Custom Whls(Std C1500/2500 Spt, Jimmy SLS/SLT/Typhoon, Yukon Spt) +145
Dual Rear Whls +415
Fiberglass Cap +250
Leather Seats +250
Luggage Rack +80
Privacy Glass +145
Pwr Locks(Std Jimmy SLT) +105
Pwr Seats +125
Pwr Wndw(Std Jimmy SLT) +145
Running Boards +145
Slider Wndw +80
Sunroof-Manual +145
Tilt Whl +105
Towing Pkg +185
V8 6.2L Diesel Engine +470
DEDUCT FOR ALL 94 GMC TRUCKS:
No AC -435
No AM/FM Radio -105
No Auto Trans -415

1993 GMC

C1500/C2500/C3500 PKUP V8 1993

Ratings

Rating	Score
Safety	7.6
Reliability	4.3
Performance	7.4
Design	8.2
Fun to drive	7.2
Value	7.1
Overall	6.4

AT/PS/AC

Model/Body/Type	BaseList	Whlse	Retail
C1500 Pickup ½ Ton			
Wideside Special 8'(V6)	11257	**10000**	**12325**
Sportside 6 ½'	14223	**11775**	**14425**
Wideside 6 ½'	13823	**11475**	**14025**
Wideside 8'	14123	**11575**	**14150**
Sport Club Cpe 6 ½'	15768	**13100**	**15800**
Wide Club Cpe 6 ½'	15368	**13200**	**15925**
Wideside Club Cpe 8'	15628	**13400**	**16125**
C2500 Pickup ¾ Ton			
Wideside 8'	14663	**12300**	**14950**
Wide Club Cpe 6 ½'	16478	**13850**	**16600**
Wideside Club Cpe 8'	16758	**13950**	**16700**
C3500 Pickup 1 Ton			
Wideside 8'	16335	**12850**	**16100**
Wideside Club Cpe 8'	17995	**14400**	**17700**
Wideside Crew Cab 8'	18315	**14550**	**17875**

ADD FOR 93 C1500/C2500/C3500 PKUP:
V8 6.5L Turbo Diesel Eng +700
SLE Pkg +545 *SLX Pkg +350*
Sport Pkg +545
DEDUCT FOR 93 C1500/C2500/C3500 PKUP:
V6 Eng -470
REFER TO 93 GMC TRUCK OPTIONS TABLE Pg 173

G1500/G2500/G3500 VAN V8 1993

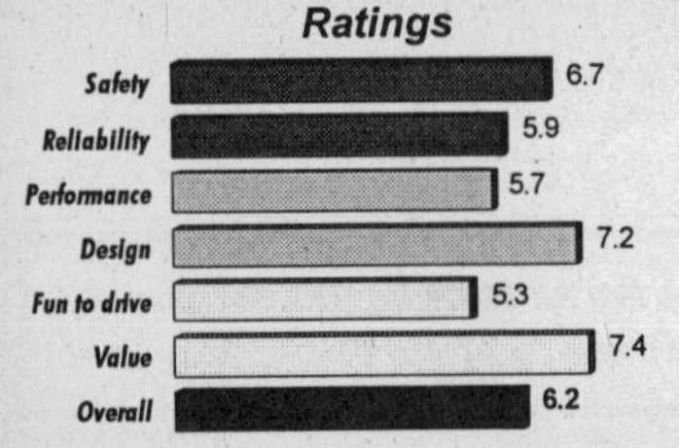

AT/PS/AC

Model/Body/Type	BaseList	Whlse	Retail
G1500 Van ½ Ton			
Vandura	14668	**11750**	**14400**
Rally Wgn	16569	**13075**	**15775**
G2500 Van ¾ Ton			
Vandura	14788	**12000**	**14625**
Rally Wgn	17459	**13500**	**16225**
G3500 Van 1 Ton			
Vandura	15942	**12500**	**15725**
Rally Wgn	19023	**13850**	**17150**
Extended Vandura	17532	**13150**	**16425**
Extended Rally Wgn	20628	**14500**	**17825**
Vandura Special	15954	**12450**	**15675**

DEDUCT FOR 93 G1500/G2500/G3500 VAN:
V6 Eng -470
REFER TO 93 GMC TRUCK OPTIONS TABLE Pg 173

JIMMY V6 ½ Ton 1993

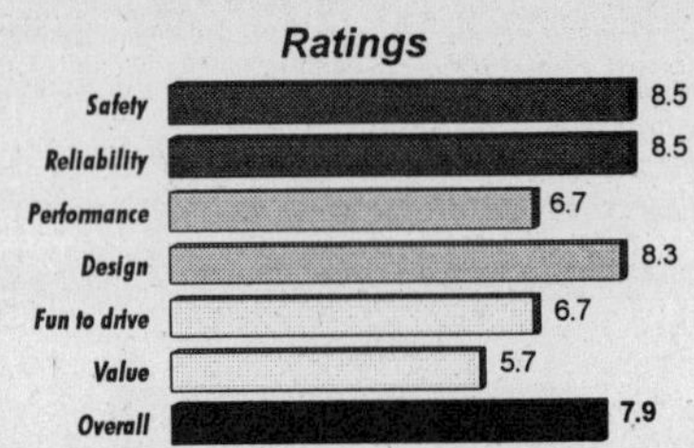

AT/PS/AC

Model/Body/Type	BaseList	Whlse	Retail
2 Dr Utility	15022	**12400**	**15050**
4 Dr Utility	15994	**13950**	**16700**
2 Dr 4WD Utility	16905	**14050**	**16825**
4 Dr 4WD Utility	18287	**15550**	**18425**
2 Dr AWD Typhoon	29320	**19475**	**22725**

ADD FOR 93 JIMMY:
SLE Pkg +545 *SLS Pkg(Std 4 Dr) +585*
SLT Pkg +1090
REFER TO 93 GMC TRUCK OPTIONS TABLE Pg 173

SAFARI V6 ½ Ton 1993

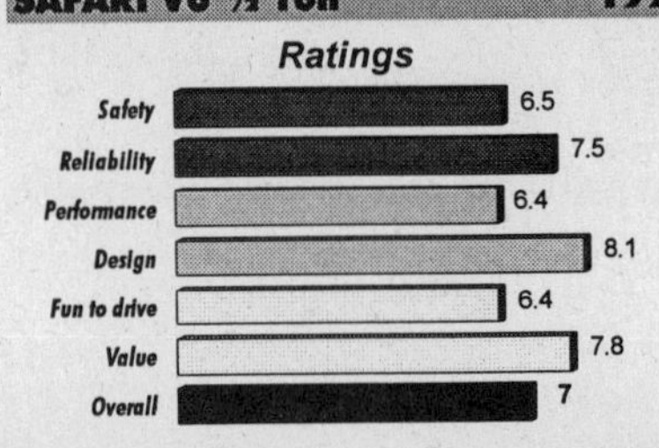

Model/Body/Type	BaseList	Whlse	Retail
AT/PS/AC			
Cargo Van	14763	**10525**	**12925**
Extended Cargo Van	15433	**11550**	**14125**
SLX Van	15824	**12150**	**14800**
Extended SLX Van	16514	**13175**	**15875**

ADD FOR 93 SAFARI:
Air Bag +275 *SLT Pkg +1015*
REFER TO 93 GMC TRUCK OPTIONS TABLE Pg 173

SONOMA PICKUPS V6 ½ Ton 1993

Ratings

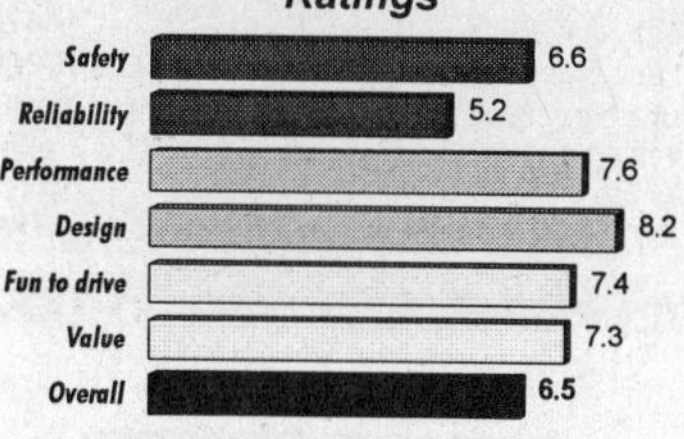

Model/Body/Type	BaseList	Whlse	Retail
AT/PS/AC			
Wideside Special 6'	8813	**7900**	**9975**
Wideside 6'	10329	**8125**	**10200**
Wideside 7 1/3'	10629	**8225**	**10300**
Wideside Club Cpe 6'	11829	**9525**	**11775**

ADD FOR 93 SONOMA PICKUP:
SLE Pkg +545 *SLS Pkg +275*
DEDUCT FOR 93 SONOMA PICKUP:
4 Cyl Eng -390
REFER TO 93 GMC TRUCK OPTIONS TABLE Pg 173

SUBURBAN V8 1993

Ratings

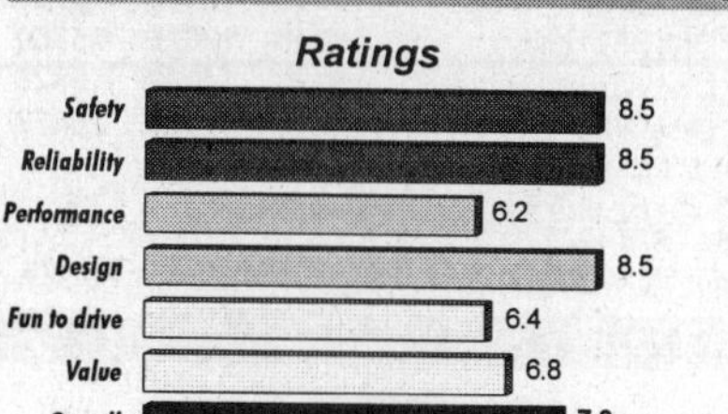

Model/Body/Type	BaseList	Whlse	Retail
AT/PS/AC			
4 Dr Suburban ½ Ton	19318	**18525**	**21725**
4 Dr Suburban ¾ Ton	20522	**19175**	**22400**

ADD FOR 93 SUBURBAN:
SLE Pkg +700
REFER TO 93 GMC TRUCK OPTIONS TABLE Pg 173

YUKON V8 ½ Ton 1993

Ratings

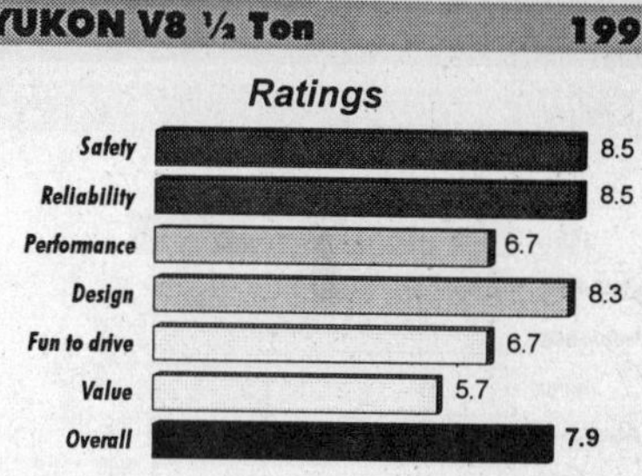

Model/Body/Type	BaseList	Whlse	Retail
4WD/AT/PS/AC			
2 Dr Utility	20243	**17025**	**20075**

ADD FOR 93 YUKON:
SLE Pkg +700 *Sport Pkg +780*
REFER TO 93 GMC TRUCK OPTIONS TABLE Pg 173

93 GMC TRUCK OPTIONS TABLE

ADD FOR ALL 93 GMC TRUCKS:
15 Pass Seating +375
4-Whl Drive(Std Typhoon) +1265
AC-Rear +375
Bed Liner +125
Cass(Std Typhoon,Sonoma GT) +105
CD Player +205
Cruise Ctrl(Std Typhoon,Sonoma GT) +125
Custom Whls(Std C1500/2500 Spt, Jimmy SLS/SLT/Typhoon,Yukon Spt) +145
Dual Rear Whls +415
Fiberglass Cap +250
Leather Seats(Std Typhoon) +250
Luggage Rack +80
Privacy Glass +145
Pwr Locks(Std Jimmy SLT/Typh,Sonoma GT) +105
Pwr Seats +125
Pwr Wndw(Std Jimmy SLT/Typh,Sonoma GT) +145
Running Boards +145
Slider Wndw +80
Sunroof-Manual +145
Tilt Whl(Std Typhoon,Sonoma GT) +105
Towing Pkg +185
V8 6.2L Diesel Engine +470
DEDUCT FOR ALL 93 GMC TRUCKS:
No AC -435
No AM/FM Radio -105
No Auto Trans -415

Model/Body/Type	BaseList	Whlse	Retail

1992 GMC

C1500/C2500/C3500 PKUP V8 1992

Ratings

Rating	Score
Safety	7.6
Reliability	4.3
Performance	7.4
Design	8.2
Fun to drive	7.2
Value	7.1
Overall	6.4

AT/PS/AC

Model/Body/Type	BaseList	Whlse	Retail
C1500 Pickup ½ Ton			
Wideside Special 8' (V6)	10602	**9200**	**11425**
Sportside 6 ½'	13733	**10775**	**13275**
Wideside 6 ½'	13333	**10525**	**12925**
Wideside 8'	13633	**10625**	**13125**
Sport Club Cpe 6 ½'	14683	**11975**	**14600**
Wide Club Cpe 6 ½'	14283	**12050**	**14725**
Wideside Club Cpe 8'	14573	**12200**	**14850**
C2500 Pickup ¾ Ton			
Wideside 8'	14273	**11225**	**13775**
Wide Club Cpe 6 ½'	15393	**12550**	**15225**
Wideside Club Cpe 8'	15673	**12650**	**15325**
C3500 Pickup 1 Ton			
Wideside 8'	15760	**11800**	**14975**
Wideside Club Cpe 8'	16830	**13150**	**16425**
Wideside Crew Cab 8'	17579	**13350**	**16625**

ADD FOR 92 C1500/C2500/C3500 PKUP:
SLE Pkg +505 *SLX Pkg +315*
Sport Pkg +545
V8 6.5L Turbo Diesel Eng +665
DEDUCT FOR 92 C1500/C2500/C3500 PKUP:
V6 Eng -430
REFER TO 92 GMC TRUCK OPTIONS TABLE Pg 175

G1500/G2500/G3500 VAN V8 1992

AT/PS/AC

Model/Body/Type	BaseList	Whlse	Retail
G1500 Van ½ Ton			
Vandura	14383	**10150**	**12525**
Rally Wgn	16199	**11475**	**14025**
G2500 Van ¾ Ton			
Vandura	14603	**10350**	**12725**
Rally Wgn	17339	**11800**	**14475**
G3500 Van 1 Ton			
Vandura	14577	**10800**	**13850**
Rally Wgn	19023	**12100**	**15275**
Extended Vandura	17347	**11375**	**14475**
Extended Rally Wgn	20553	**12675**	**15900**
Vandura Special	15027	**10475**	**13450**

DEDUCT FOR 92 G1500/G2500/G3500 VAN:
V6 Eng -430
REFER TO 92 GMC TRUCK OPTIONS TABLE Pg 175

JIMMY V6 ½ Ton 1992

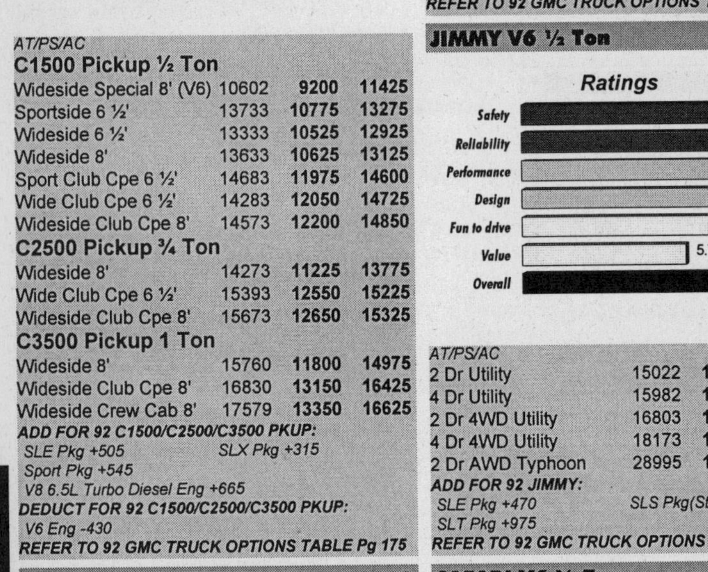

AT/PS/AC

Model/Body/Type	BaseList	Whlse	Retail
2 Dr Utility	15022	**11100**	**13625**
4 Dr Utility	15982	**12450**	**15125**
2 Dr 4WD Utility	16803	**12675**	**15350**
4 Dr 4WD Utility	18173	**14050**	**16825**
2 Dr AWD Typhoon	28995	**17350**	**20475**

ADD FOR 92 JIMMY:
SLE Pkg +470 *SLS Pkg(Std 4 Dr) +545*
SLT Pkg +975
REFER TO 92 GMC TRUCK OPTIONS TABLE Pg 175

SAFARI V6 ½ Ton 1992

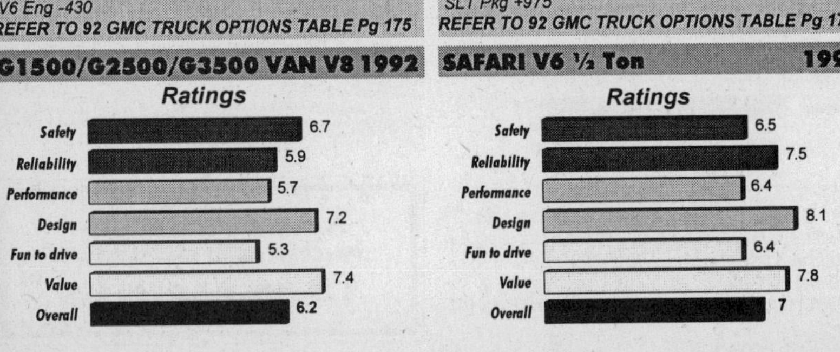

Model/Body/Type	BaseList	Whlse	Retail
AT/PS/AC			
Cargo Van	14063	**9000**	**11200**
Extended Cargo Van	14733	**9950**	**12250**
SLX Van	15404	**10475**	**12875**
Extended SLX Van	16094	**11450**	**14000**

ADD FOR 92 SAFARI:

SLT Pkg +975

REFER TO 92 GMC TRUCK OPTIONS TABLE Pg 175

SONOMA PICKUPS V6 ½ Ton 1992

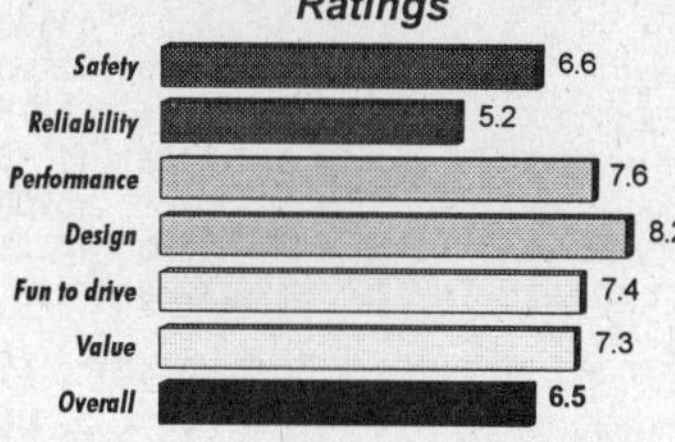

Model/Body/Type	BaseList	Whlse	Retail
AT/PS/AC			
Wideside Special 6'	8790	**6750**	**8775**
Wideside 6'	10057	**7000**	**8975**
Wideside 7 1/3'	10357	**7075**	**9100**
Wideside Club Cpe 6'	11557	**8200**	**10275**
Wideside GT 6'	16300	**9800**	**12050**
4WD Syclone	26995	**14800**	**17625**

ADD FOR 92 SONOMA PICKUP:

SLE Pkg +470 *SLS Pkg +185*

DEDUCT FOR 92 SONOMA PICKUP:

4 Cyl Eng -390

REFER TO 92 GMC TRUCK OPTIONS TABLE Pg 175

SUBURBAN V8 1992

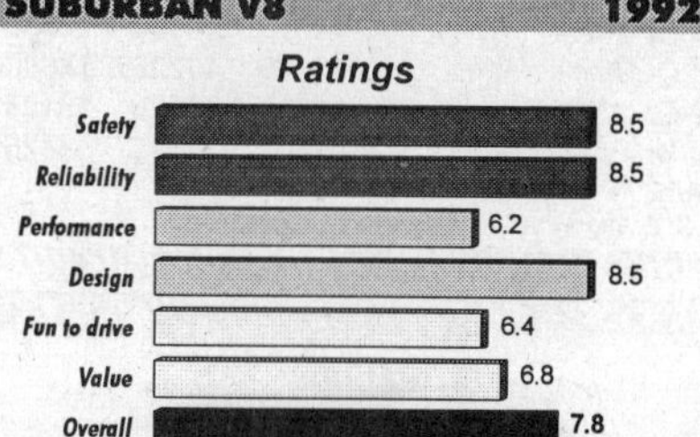

Model/Body/Type	BaseList	Whlse	Retail
AT/PS/AC			
4 Dr Suburban ½ Ton	18393	**15775**	**18650**
4 Dr Suburban ¾ Ton	19597	**16375**	**19300**

ADD FOR 92 SUBURBAN:

SLE Pkg +625

REFER TO 92 GMC TRUCK OPTIONS TABLE Pg 175

YUKON V8 ½ Ton 1992

Ratings

Rating	Score
Safety	8.5
Reliability	8.5
Performance	6.7
Design	8.3
Fun to drive	6.7
Value	5.7
Overall	7.9

Model/Body/Type	BaseList	Whlse	Retail
4WD/AT/PS/AC			
2 Dr Utility	19518	**14500**	**17250**

ADD FOR 92 YUKON:

SLE Pkg +625 *Sport Pkg +665*

REFER TO 92 GMC TRUCK OPTIONS TABLE Pg 175

92 GMC TRUCK OPTIONS TABLE

ADD FOR ALL 92 GMC TRUCKS:

15 Pass Seating +330
4-Whl Drive(Std Typhoon,Syclone) +1200
AC-Rear +315
Bed Liner +125
Cass(Std Typhoon,Sonoma GT/Syclone) +80
CD Player +170
Cruise Ctrl(Std Typh,Sonoma GT/Syclone) +125
Custom Whls(Std C1500/2500 Spt, Typhoon,Syclone,Yukon Spt) +125
Dual Rear Whls +375
Fiberglass Cap +205
Leather Seats(Std Typhoon) +205
Privacy Glass +125
Pwr Locks(Std JimmySLT/Typh,SonomaGT/Sy) +80
Pwr Seats +105
Pwr Wndw(Std JimmySLT/Typh,SonomGT/Sy) +105
Running Boards +125
Sunroof-Manual +105
Towing Pkg +145
V8 6.2L Diesel Engine +430

DEDUCT FOR ALL 92 GMC TRUCKS:

No AC -375
No Auto Trans -330
No Pwr Steering -145

GMC

1991 GMC

C1500/C2500/C3500 PKUP V8 1991

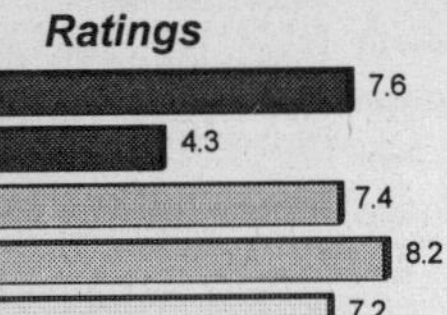

Model/Body/Type	BaseList	Whlse	Retail
AT/PS/AC			
C1500 Pickup ½ Ton			
Wideside Special 8' (V6)	10645	8000	10075
Sportside 6 ½'	12749	9500	11725
Wideside 6 ½'	12409	9300	11525
Wideside 8'	12709	9400	11625
Wide Club Cpe 6 ½'	13359	10375	12750
Wideside Club Cpe 8'	13649	10475	12875
C2500 Pickup ¾ Ton			
Wideside 8'	13349	9925	12225
Wide Club Cpe 6 ½'	14469	10925	13450
Wideside Club Cpe 8'	14749	11025	13550
C3500/R3500 Pickup 1 Ton			
Wideside 8'	16015	10425	13400
Wideside Club Cpe 8'	17085	11575	14650
Wideside Bonus Cab 8'	16409	11625	14775
Wideside Crew Cab 8'	16949	11800	14975

ADD FOR 91 C1500/C2500/C3500 PKUP:
SLE Pkg +470 *SLX Pkg +275*
Z71 Pkg +115
DEDUCT FOR 91 C1500/C2500/C3500 PKUP:
V6 Eng -390
REFER TO 91 GMC TRUCK OPTIONS TABLE Pg 177

G1500/G2500/G3500 VAN V8 1991

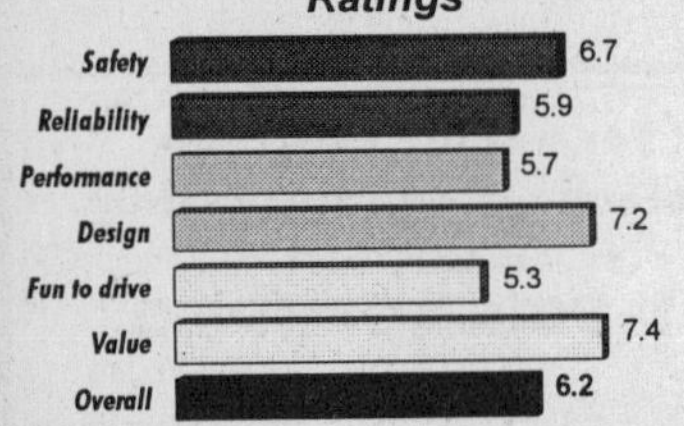

Model/Body/Type	BaseList	Whlse	Retail
AT/PS/AC			
G1500 Van ½ Ton			
Vandura	13694	7925	10000
Rally Wgn	15510	9225	11450
Rally STX Wgn	17370	10275	12650
G2500 Van ¾ Ton			
Vandura	13874	8075	10150
Rally Wgn	16610	9500	11725
Rally STX Wgn	17510	10425	12800
G3500 Van 1 Ton			
Vandura	13870	8500	11100
Rally Wgn	18336	9800	12625
Rally STX Wgn	19236	10725	13775
Extended Vandura	16660	9025	11775
Extended Rally Wgn	19866	10250	13200
Ext Rally STX Wgn	20696	11250	14325

DEDUCT FOR 91 G1500/G2500/G3500 VAN:
V6 Eng -390
REFER TO 91 GMC TRUCK OPTIONS TABLE Pg 177

S15 JIMMY V6 ½ Ton 1991

Ratings

Rating	Score
Safety	6.7
Reliability	6.6
Performance	7.3
Design	8.2
Fun to drive	7.1
Value	7.1
Overall	7

Model/Body/Type	BaseList	Whlse	Retail
AT/PS/AC			
2 Dr Utility	14060	9150	11350
4 Dr Utility	15300	10225	12600
2 Dr 4WD Utility	15811	10625	13125
4 Dr 4WD Utility	17451	11775	14425

ADD FOR 91 S15 JIMMY:
SLE Pkg +350 *SLS Pkg +505*
REFER TO 91 GMC TRUCK OPTIONS TABLE Pg 177

SAFARI V6 ½ Ton 1991

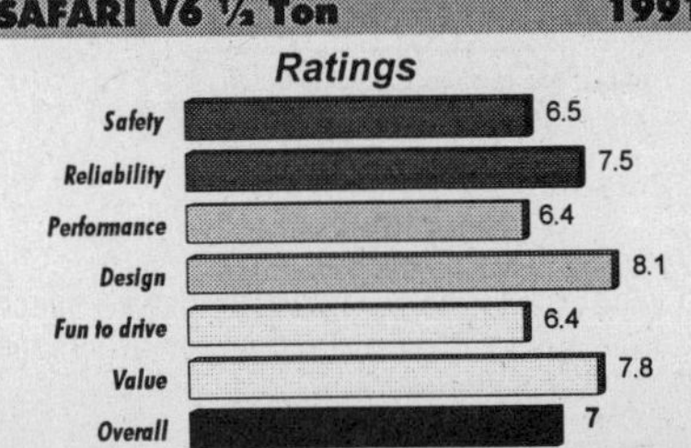

Model/Body/Type	BaseList	Whlse	Retail
AT/PS/AC			
Cargo Van	13544	**7750**	**9825**
Extended Cargo Van	14214	**8650**	**10750**
SLX Van	14815	**9200**	**11425**
SLE Van	15895	**9800**	**12050**
SLT Van	17445	**10325**	**12700**
Extended SLX Van	15505	**10050**	**12375**
Extended SLE Van	16585	**10625**	**13125**
Extended SLT Van	18135	**11225**	**13775**

REFER TO 91 GMC TRUCK OPTIONS TABLE Pg 177

SONOMA PICKUPS V6 ½ Ton — 1991

Ratings

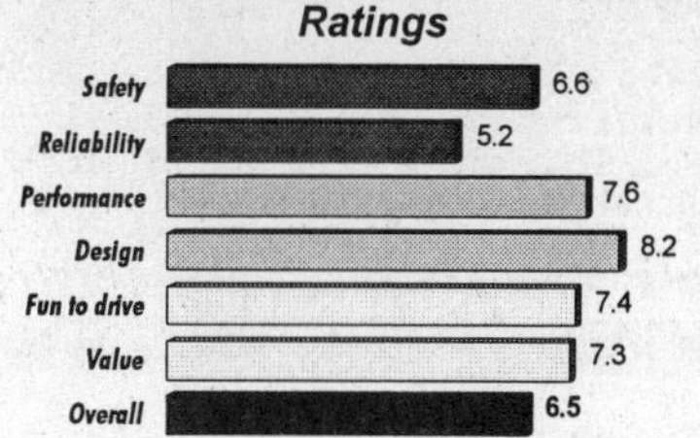

Model/Body/Type	BaseList	Whlse	Retail
AT/PS/AC			
Wideside Special 6' (4 cyl,5 spd)	8466	**4925**	**6750**
Wideside 6'	9915	**5975**	**7875**
Wideside 7 1/3'	10085	**6100**	**7975**
Wideside Club Cpe 6'	11185	**7025**	**9025**
4WD Syclone	25500	**13100**	**15800**

ADD FOR 91 SONOMA PICKUP:
SLE Pkg +350
DEDUCT FOR 91 SONOMA PICKUP:
4 Cyl Eng -350
REFER TO 91 GMC TRUCK OPTIONS TABLE Pg 177

SUBURBAN V8 — 1991

Ratings

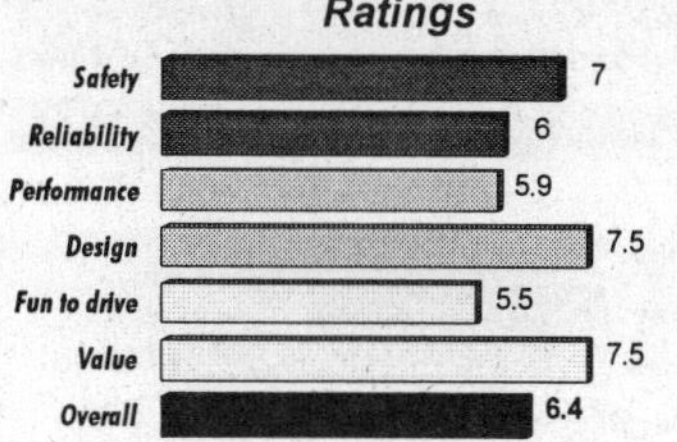

Model/Body/Type	BaseList	Whlse	Retail
AT/PS/AC			
4 Dr Suburban ½ Ton	16775	**13400**	**16125**
4 Dr Suburban ¾ Ton	18333	**13950**	**16700**

ADD FOR 91 SUBURBAN:
SLE Pkg +545
REFER TO 91 GMC TRUCK OPTIONS TABLE Pg 177

V1500 JIMMY V8 ½ Ton — 1991

Ratings

Rating	Score
Safety	6.9
Reliability	5.6
Performance	6.6
Design	7.3
Fun to drive	5.8
Value	7.8
Overall	6.4

Model/Body/Type	BaseList	Whlse	Retail
4WD/AT/PS/AC			
2 Dr Utility	17674	**11075**	**13600**

ADD FOR 91 V1500 JIMMY:
SLE Pkg +545
REFER TO 91 GMC TRUCK OPTIONS TABLE Pg 177

91 GMC TRUCK OPTIONS TABLE

ADD FOR ALL 91 GMC TRUCKS:
15 Pass Seating +290
4-Whl Drive(Std Syclone) +1140
AC-Rear +250
Bed Liner +80
Custom Whls(Std Syclone) +105
Dual Rear Whls +330
Fiberglass Cap +170
Leather Seats +170
Privacy Glass(Std Safari SLT) +105
Pwr Seats +80
Pwr Wndw(Std Syclone) +80
Running Boards +105
Sunroof-Manual +80
Towing Pkg +105
V8 6.2L Diesel Engine +390
DEDUCT FOR ALL 91 GMC TRUCKS:
No AC -315
No Auto Trans -250
No Pwr Steering -105

See the Automobile Dealer Directory on page 379 for a Dealer near you!

Model/Body/Type	BaseList	Whlse	Retail

1990 GMC

C1500/C2500/C3500 PKUP V8 1990

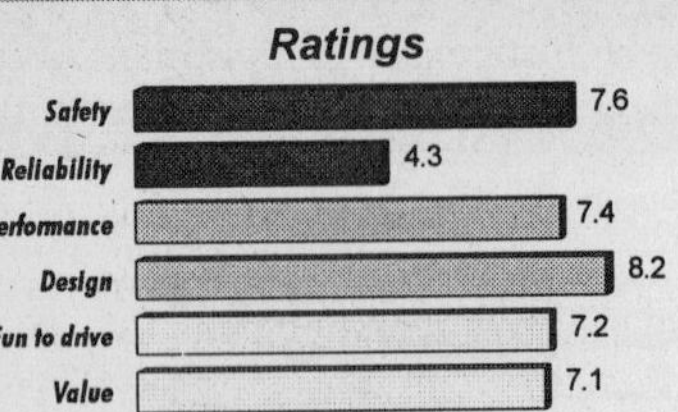

AT/PS/AC

Model/Body/Type	BaseList	Whlse	Retail
C1500 Pickup ½ Ton			
Wideside Special 8' (V6)	10445	**6825**	**8825**
Sportside 6 ½'	11897	**8150**	**10225**
Wideside 6 ½'	11572	**8000**	**10075**
Wideside 8'	11852	**8100**	**10175**
Wide Club Cpe 6 ½'	12482	**8950**	**11150**
Wideside Club Cpe 8'	12762	**9050**	**11250**
C2500 Pickup ¾ Ton			
Wideside 8'	12477	**8550**	**10650**
Wide Club Cpe 6 ½'	13547	**9400**	**11625**
Wideside Club Cpe 8'	13827	**9500**	**11725**
C3500/R3500 Pickup 1 Ton			
Wideside 8'	14038	**9100**	**11850**
Wideside Club Cpe 8'	15058	**10000**	**12900**
Wideside Bonus Cab 8'	15514	**10050**	**12950**
Wideside Crew Cab 8'	16044	**10225**	**13175**

ADD FOR 90 C1500/C2500/C3500 PKUP:
Sierra SLE Pkg +390 *Sierra SLX Pkg +195*
Z71 Pkg +100
DEDUCT FOR 90 C1500/C2500/C3500 PKUP:
V6 Eng -315
REFER TO 90 GMC TRUCK OPTIONS TABLE Pg 179

G1500/G2500/G3500 VAN V8 1990

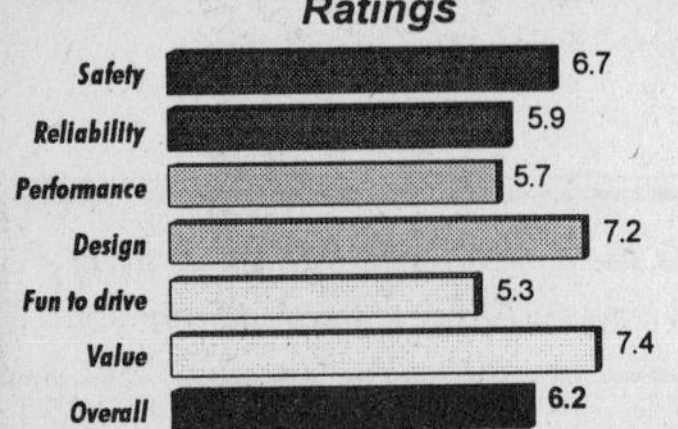

AT/PS/AC

Model/Body/Type	BaseList	Whlse	Retail
G1500 Van ½ Ton			
Vandura	12712	**6525**	**8475**
Rally Wgn	14713	**7750**	**9825**
Rally STX Wgn	16488	**8700**	**10875**
G2500 Van ¾ Ton			
Vandura	12882	**6650**	**8625**
Rally Wgn	15763	**7975**	**10050**
Rally STX Wgn	16628	**8825**	**11000**
G3500 Van 1 Ton			
Vandura	13367	**7000**	**9425**
Rally Wgn	17678	**8200**	**10775**
Rally STX Wgn	18543	**9050**	**11800**
Extended Vandura	15439	**7425**	**9925**
Extended Rally Wgn	18532	**8675**	**11375**
Ext Rally STX Wgn	19332	**9525**	**12275**

DEDUCT FOR 90 G1500/G2500/G3500 VAN:
V6 Eng -315
REFER TO 90 GMC TRUCK OPTIONS TABLE Pg 179

S15 JIMMY V6 ½ Ton 1990

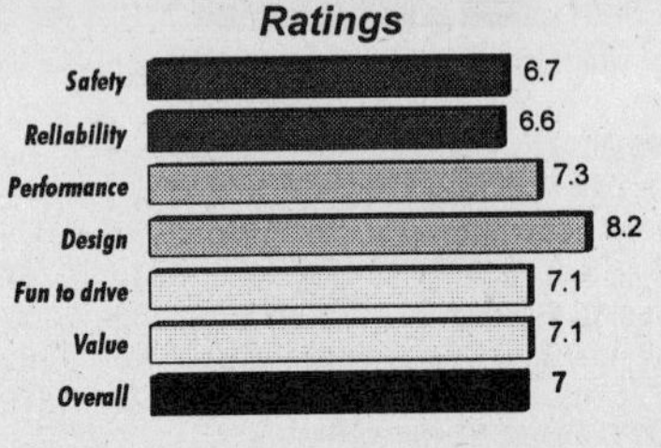

AT/PS/AC

Model/Body/Type	BaseList	Whlse	Retail
2 Dr Utility	13133	**7200**	**9250**
2 Dr 4WD Utility	14798	**8700**	**10875**
4 Dr 4WD Utility	17291	**9300**	**11525**

ADD FOR 90 S15 JIMMY:
Gypsy Pkg +470 *Sierra Classic Pkg +315*
REFER TO 90 GMC TRUCK OPTIONS TABLE Pg 179

S15 PICKUPS V6 ½ Ton 1990

Ratings

Safety 6.6
Reliability 5.2
Performance 7.6
Design 8.2
Fun to drive 7.4
Value 7.3
Overall 6.5

GMC

Model/Body/Type	BaseList	Whlse	Retail
AT/PS/AC			
Wideside Special 6' (4 cyl,5 spd)	8057	**4125**	**5825**
Wideside 6'	9425	**4900**	**6725**
Wideside 7 1/3'	9593	**5000**	**6875**
Wideside Club Cpe 6'	10378	**5825**	**7700**

ADD FOR 90 S15 PICKUP:
High Sierra Pkg +115 *Sierra Classic Pkg +315*
DEDUCT FOR 90 S15 PICKUP:
4 Cyl Eng -230
REFER TO 90 GMC TRUCK OPTIONS TABLE Pg 179

SAFARI V6 ½ Ton 1990

Ratings

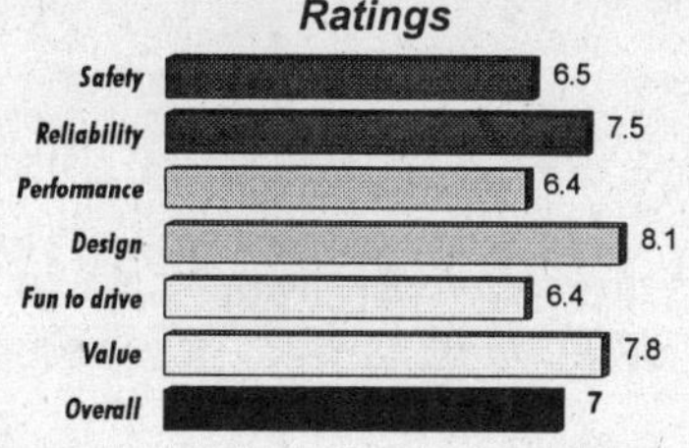

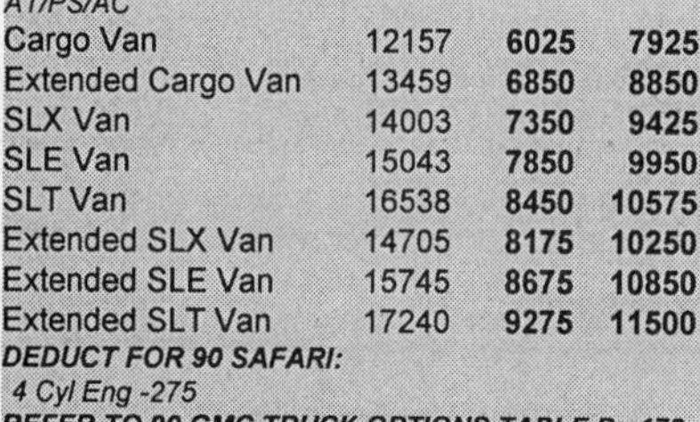

Model/Body/Type	BaseList	Whlse	Retail
AT/PS/AC			
Cargo Van	12157	**6025**	**7925**
Extended Cargo Van	13459	**6850**	**8850**
SLX Van	14003	**7350**	**9425**
SLE Van	15043	**7850**	**9950**
SLT Van	16538	**8450**	**10575**
Extended SLX Van	14705	**8175**	**10250**
Extended SLE Van	15745	**8675**	**10850**
Extended SLT Van	17240	**9275**	**11500**

DEDUCT FOR 90 SAFARI:
4 Cyl Eng -275
REFER TO 90 GMC TRUCK OPTIONS TABLE Pg 179

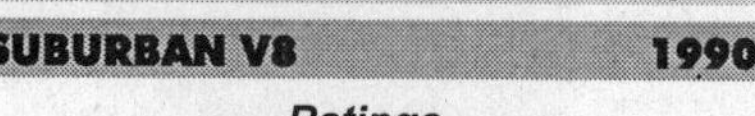

SUBURBAN V8 1990

Ratings

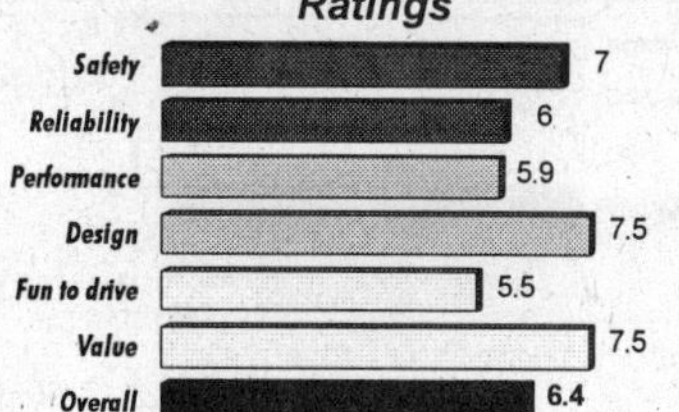

Model/Body/Type	BaseList	Whlse	Retail
AT/PS/AC			
4 Dr Suburban ½ Ton	15808	**11050**	**13575**
4 Dr Suburban ¾ Ton	16431	**11550**	**14125**

ADD FOR 90 SUBURBAN:
SLE Pkg +470
REFER TO 90 GMC TRUCK OPTIONS TABLE Pg 179

V1500 JIMMY V8 ½ Ton 1990

Ratings

Safety 6.9
Reliability 5.6
Performance 6.6
Design 7.3
Fun to drive 5.8
Value 7.8
Overall 6.4

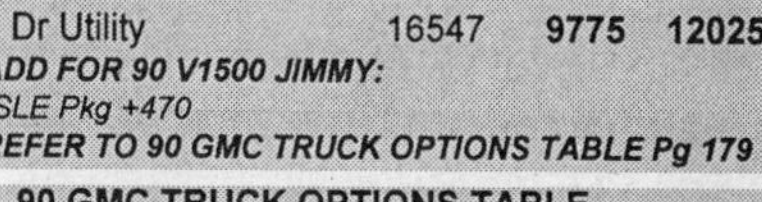

Model/Body/Type	BaseList	Whlse	Retail
4WD/AT/PS/AC			
2 Dr Utility	16547	**9775**	**12025**

ADD FOR 90 V1500 JIMMY:
SLE Pkg +470
REFER TO 90 GMC TRUCK OPTIONS TABLE Pg 179

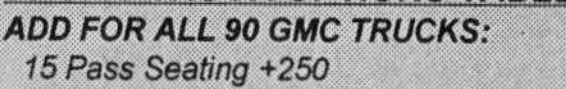

90 GMC TRUCK OPTIONS TABLE

ADD FOR ALL 90 GMC TRUCKS:

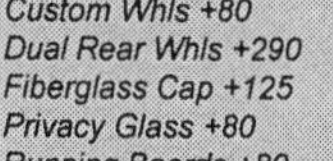

15 Pass Seating +250
4-Whl Drive +1080
AC-Rear +185
Custom Whls +80
Dual Rear Whls +290
Fiberglass Cap +125
Privacy Glass +80
Running Boards +80
Towing Pkg +80
V8 6.2L Diesel Engine +350

DEDUCT FOR ALL 90 GMC TRUCKS:
No AC -250
No Auto Trans -170

1989 GMC

C1500/C2500/C3500 PKUP V8 1989

Ratings

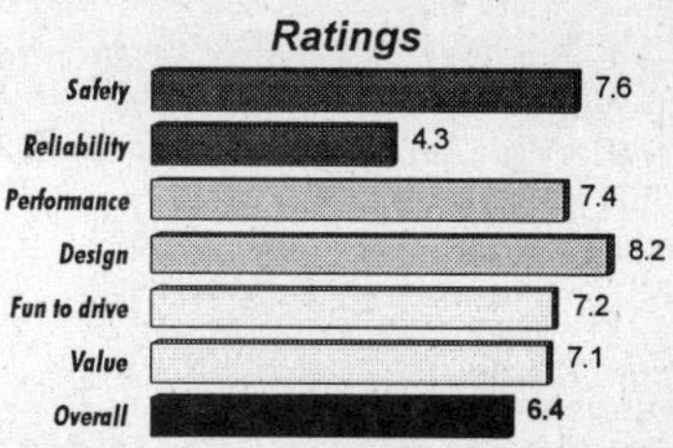

GMC 89

Model/Body/Type	BaseList	Whlse	Retail
AT/PS/AC			
C1500 Pickup ½ Ton			
Sportside 6 ½'	11168	**6850**	**8850**
Wideside 6 ½'	10950	**6725**	**8725**
Wideside 8'	11150	**6850**	**8850**
Wide Club Cpe 6 ½'	11877	**7575**	**9650**
Wideside Club Cpe 8'	12082	**7675**	**9775**
C2500 Pickup ¾ Ton			
Wideside 8'	11958	**7225**	**9275**
Wideside Club Cpe 8'	13473	**8075**	**10150**
Wide Bonus Cab 8'	14226	**8125**	**10200**
Wide Crew Cab 8'	14726	**8325**	**10400**
C3500/R3500 Pickup 1 Ton			
Wideside 8'	12778	**7725**	**10275**
Wideside Club Cpe 8'	13813	**8575**	**11200**
Wideside Bonus Cab 8'	14362	**8625**	**11250**
Wideside Crew Cab 8'	14871	**8825**	**11550**

ADD FOR 89 C1500/C2500/C3500 PKUP:
Sierra SLE Pkg +350 *Sierra SLX Pkg +115*
Z71 Pkg +80
DEDUCT FOR 89 C1500/C2500/C3500 PKUP:
V6 Eng -275
REFER TO 89 GMC TRUCK OPTIONS TABLE Pg 181

G1500/G2500/G3500 VAN V8 1989

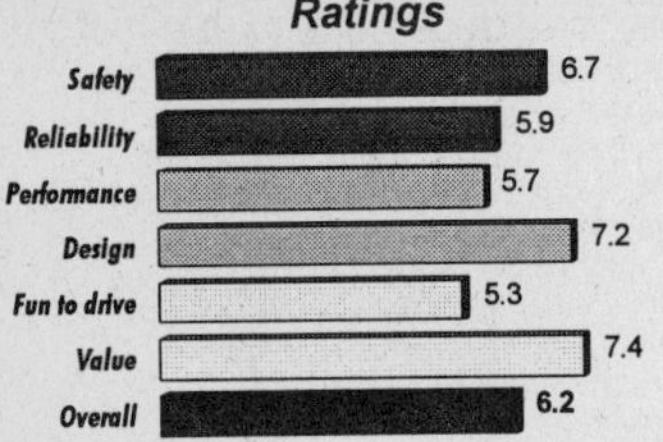

Model/Body/Type	BaseList	Whlse	Retail
AT/PS/AC			
G1500 Van ½ Ton			
Vandura	11760	**5050**	**6925**
Rally Wgn	13253	**6275**	**8200**
Rally STX Wgn	14836	**7100**	**9125**
G2500 Van ¾ Ton			
Vandura	12070	**5150**	**7025**
Rally Wgn	13736	**6450**	**8400**
Rally STX Wgn	15055	**7175**	**9225**
G3500 Van 1 Ton			
Vandura	13057	**5375**	**7575**
Rally Wgn	15494	**6600**	**8975**
Rally STX Wgn	16813	**7325**	**9800**

DEDUCT FOR 89 G1500/G2500/G3500 VAN:
V6 Eng -275
REFER TO 89 GMC TRUCK OPTIONS TABLE Pg 181

S15 JIMMY V6 ½ Ton 1989

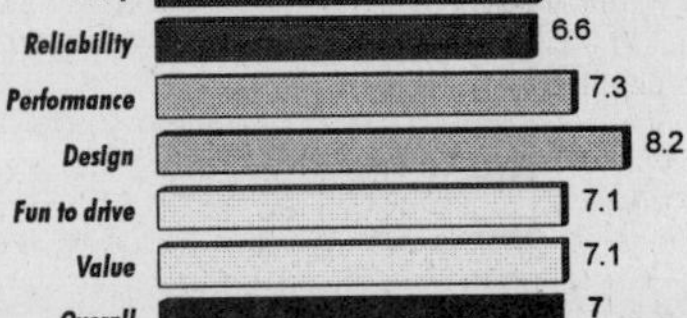

Model/Body/Type	BaseList	Whlse	Retail
AT/PS/AC			
2 Dr Utility	11993	**5725**	**7600**
2 Dr 4WD Utility	13568	**7125**	**9150**

ADD FOR 89 S15 JIMMY:
Gypsy Pkg +390 *Sierra Classic Pkg +230*
REFER TO 89 GMC TRUCK OPTIONS TABLE Pg 181

S15 PICKUPS V6 ½ Ton 1989

Model/Body/Type	BaseList	Whlse	Retail
AT/PS/AC			
Wideside Special 6' (4 cyl,5 spd)	7527	**3200**	**4725**
Wideside 6'	9191	**3875**	**5550**
Wideside 7 1/3'	9356	**3975**	**5675**
Wideside Club Cpe 6'	10041	**4675**	**6425**

ADD FOR 89 S15 PICKUP:
High Sierra Pkg +80 *Sierra Classic Pkg +230*
DEDUCT FOR 89 S15 PICKUP:
4 Cyl Eng -230
REFER TO 89 GMC TRUCK OPTIONS TABLE Pg 181

SAFARI V6 ½ Ton 1989

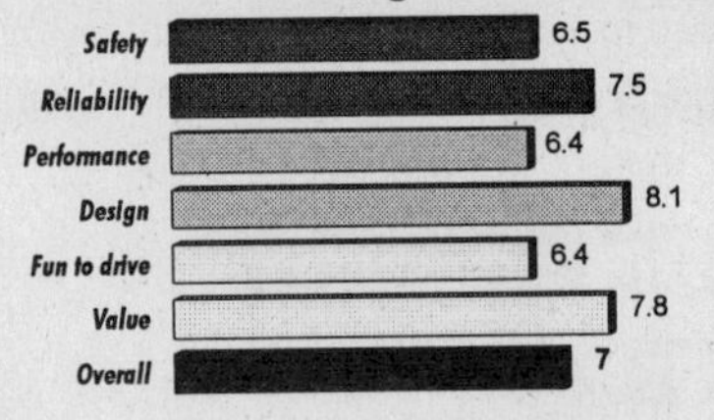

Model/Body/Type	BaseList	Whlse	Retail
AT/PS/AC			
Cargo Van	11007	**4825**	**6650**
SLX Van	11957	**6025**	**7925**
SLE Van	12690	**6500**	**8425**
SLT Van	14201	**7025**	**9025**

DEDUCT FOR 89 SAFARI:
4 Cyl Eng -230
REFER TO 89 GMC TRUCK OPTIONS TABLE Pg 181

Model/Body/Type	BaseList	Whlse	Retail

SUBURBAN V8 1989

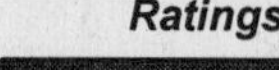

Ratings

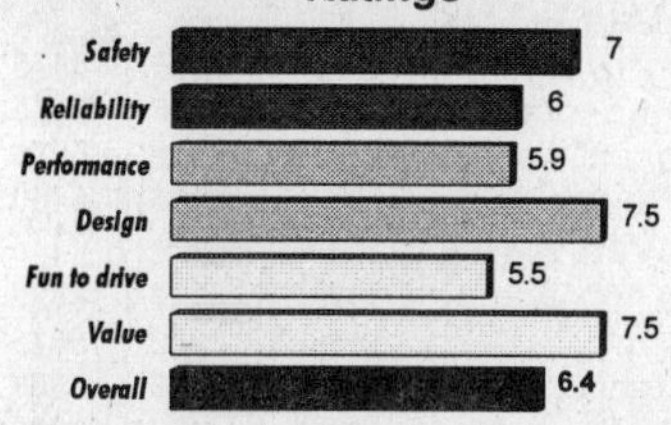

AT/PS/AC

Model/Body/Type	BaseList	Whlse	Retail
4 Dr Suburban ½ Ton	14585	**9100**	**11300**
4 Dr Suburban ¾ Ton	15223	**9550**	**11800**

ADD FOR 89 SUBURBAN:
SLE Pkg +390
REFER TO 89 GMC TRUCK OPTIONS TABLE Pg 181

V1500 JIMMY V8 ½ Ton 1989

Ratings

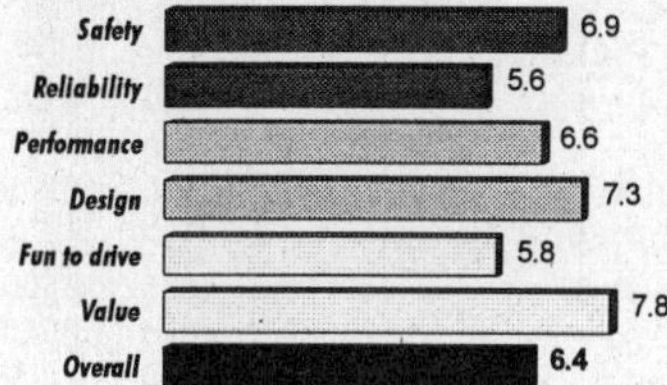

4WD/AT/PS/AC

Model/Body/Type	BaseList	Whlse	Retail
2 Dr Utility	15415	**8075**	**10150**

ADD FOR 89 V1500 JIMMY:
SLE Pkg +390
REFER TO 89 GMC TRUCK OPTIONS TABLE Pg 181

89 GMC TRUCK OPTIONS TABLE

ADD FOR ALL 89 GMC TRUCKS:
15 Pass Seating +205
4-Whl Drive +975
AC-Rear +145
Dual Rear Whls +250
Fiberglass Cap +80
V8 6.2L Diesel Engine +290
DEDUCT FOR ALL 89 GMC TRUCKS:
No AC -185
No Auto Trans -80

1988 GMC

C1500/C2500/C3500 PKUP V8 1988

AT/PS/AC

Model/Body/Type	BaseList	Whlse	Retail
C1500 Pickup ½ Ton			
Sportside 6 ½'	10523	**5075**	**6950**
Wideside 6 ½'	10315	**5025**	**6900**
Wideside 8'	10505	**5125**	**7000**
Wideside Club Cpe 8'	11712	**5950**	**7850**
C2500/R2500 Pickup ¾ Ton			
Wideside 8'	11342	**5500**	**7350**
Wideside Club Cpe 8'	12662	**6275**	**8225**
Wide Bonus Cab 8'	13683	**6350**	**8275**
Wide Crew Cab 8'	14119	**6550**	**8500**
C3500/R3500 Pickup 1 Ton			
Wideside 8'	11860	**5950**	**8275**
Wideside Club Cpe 8'	13033	**6725**	**9175**
Wideside Bonus Cab	13828	**6775**	**9225**
Wideside Crew Cab 8'	14268	**7000**	**9450**

ADD FOR 88 C1500/C2500/C3500 PKUP:
Sierra Pkg +275 *Sierra SLE Pkg +275*
DEDUCT FOR 88 C1500/C2500/C3500 PKUP:
V6 Eng -230
REFER TO 88 GMC TRUCK OPTIONS TABLE Pg 182

G1500/G2500/G3500 VAN V8 1988

AT/PS/AC

Model/Body/Type	BaseList	Whlse	Retail
G1500 Van ½ Ton			
Vandura	10786	**3800**	**5425**
Rally Wgn	12468	**4550**	**6275**
Rally Custom Wgn	13627	**5050**	**6925**
Rally STX Wgn	14035	**5200**	**7075**
G2500 Van ¾ Ton			
Vandura	11411	**3875**	**5550**
Rally Wgn	12969	**4675**	**6425**
Rally Custom Wgn	13876	**5125**	**7000**
Rally STX Wgn	14282	**5275**	**7150**
G3500 Van 1 Ton			
Vandura	13089	**4050**	**6050**
Rally Wgn	14663	**4775**	**6900**
Rally Custom Wgn	15571	**5250**	**7450**
Rally STX Wgn	15976	**5400**	**7625**

DEDUCT FOR 88 G1500/G2500/G3500 VAN:
V6 Eng -230
REFER TO 88 GMC TRUCK OPTIONS TABLE Pg 182

S15 JIMMY V6 ½ Ton 1988

AT/PS/AC

Model/Body/Type	BaseList	Whlse	Retail
2 Dr Utility	10675	**4425**	**6150**
2 Dr 4WD Utility	12784	**5725**	**7575**

ADD FOR 88 S15 JIMMY:
Gypsy Pkg +275 *Sierra Classic Pkg +160*
DEDUCT FOR 88 S15 JIMMY:
4 Cyl Eng -195
REFER TO 88 GMC TRUCK OPTIONS TABLE Pg 182

S15 PICKUPS V6 ½ Ton — 1988

AT/PS/AC

Model/Body/Type	BaseList	Whlse	Retail
Wideside Special 6' (4 cyl,5 spd)	6640	**2475**	**3875**
Wideside 6'	8285	**3000**	**4500**
Wideside 7 1/3'	8459	**3100**	**4600**
Wideside Club Cpe 6'	9304	**3700**	**5275**

ADD FOR 88 S15 PICKUP:
Gypsy Pkg +275 *High Sierra Pkg +160*
Sierra Classic Pkg +160
DEDUCT FOR 88 S15 PICKUP:
4 Cyl Eng -195
REFER TO 88 GMC TRUCK OPTIONS TABLE Pg 182

SAFARI V6 ½ Ton — 1988

AT/PS/AC

Model/Body/Type	BaseList	Whlse	Retail
Cargo Van	9634	**3550**	**5125**
SLX Van	10745	**4650**	**6400**
SLE Van	11538	**5000**	**6875**
SLT Van	12887	**5525**	**7400**

DEDUCT FOR 88 SAFARI:
4 Cyl Eng -195
REFER TO 88 GMC TRUCK OPTIONS TABLE Pg 182

SUBURBAN V8 — 1988

AT/PS/AC

Model/Body/Type	BaseList	Whlse	Retail
4 Dr Suburban ½ Ton	13997	**7200**	**9250**
4 Dr Suburban ¾ Ton	14611	**7600**	**9700**

ADD FOR 88 SUBURBAN:
Sierra Classic Pkg +315
REFER TO 88 GMC TRUCK OPTIONS TABLE Pg 182

V1500 JIMMY V8 ½ Ton — 1988

4WD/AT/PS/AC

Model/Body/Type	BaseList	Whlse	Retail
2 Dr Utility	14560	**6750**	**8775**

ADD FOR 88 V1500 JIMMY:
Sierra Classic Pkg +315
REFER TO 88 GMC TRUCK OPTIONS TABLE Pg 182

88 GMC TRUCK OPTIONS TABLE

ADD FOR ALL 88 GMC TRUCKS:
15 Pass Seating +170
4-Whl Drive +850
AC-Rear +105
Dual Rear Whls +185
V8 6.2L Diesel Engine +195
DEDUCT FOR ALL 88 GMC TRUCKS:
No AC -125

1987 GMC

CABALLERO V8 ½ Ton — 1987

AT/PS/AC

Model/Body/Type	BaseList	Whlse	Retail
Pkup	10504	**4725**	**6525**
Diablo Pkup	10835	**5050**	**6925**

DEDUCT FOR 87 CABALLERO:
V6 Eng -195 *No AC -80*

G1500/G2500/G3500 VAN V8 1987

AT/PS/AC

Model/Body/Type	BaseList	Whlse	Retail
G1500 Van ½ Ton			
Vandura	9515	**2975**	**4475**
Rally Wgn	11213	**3825**	**5475**
Rally Custom Wgn	12330	**4275**	**5975**
Rally STX Wgn	12682	**4425**	**6150**
G2500 Van ¾ Ton			
Vandura	10182	**3025**	**4525**
Rally Wgn	11660	**3900**	**5575**
Rally Custom Wgn	12534	**4325**	**6050**
Rally STX Wgn	12884	**4475**	**6200**
G3500 Van 1 Ton			
Vandura	12109	**3125**	**4875**
Rally Wgn	14004	**4000**	**5975**
Rally Custom Wgn	14879	**4425**	**6500**
Rally STX Wgn	15228	**4575**	**6625**

ADD FOR 87 G1500/G2500/G3500 VAN:
15 Pass Seating +125
DEDUCT FOR 87 G1500/G2500/G3500 VAN:
6 Cyl Eng -195 *No AC -80*

R1500/R2500/R3500 PKUP V8 1987

AT/PS/AC

Model/Body/Type	BaseList	Whlse	Retail
R1500 Pickup ½ Ton			
Fenderside 6 ½'	8702	**4400**	**6125**
Wideside 6 ½'	8554	**4450**	**6175**
Wideside 8'	8738	**4550**	**6275**
R2500 Pickup ¾ Ton			
Fenderside 8'	10128	**4775**	**6600**
Wideside 8'	9980	**4825**	**6650**
Wide Bonus Cab 8'	12522	**5650**	**7500**
Wide Crew Cab 8'	12889	**5825**	**7700**
R3500 Pickup 1 Ton			
Fenderside 8'	11712	**5150**	**7325**
Wideside 8'	11565	**5200**	**7400**
Wideside Bonus Cab 8'	12664	**6025**	**8350**
Wideside Crew Cab 8'	13034	**6225**	**8575**

ADD FOR 87 R1500/R2500/R3500 PKUP:
4-Whl Drive +680 *Dual Rear Whl +680*
Sierra Classic Pkg +195
DEDUCT FOR 87 R1500/R2500/R3500 PKUP:
No AC -80 *V6 Eng -195*

S15 JIMMY V6 ½ Ton — 1987

AT/PS/AC

Model/Body/Type	BaseList	Whlse	Retail
2 Dr Utility	10171	**3200**	**4725**
2 Dr 4WD Utility	11635	**4325**	**6050**

ADD FOR 87 S15 JIMMY:
Gypsy Pkg +195
DEDUCT FOR 87 S15 JIMMY:
4 Cyl Eng -160 *No AC -80*

Model/Body/Type	BaseList	Whlse	Retail
S15 PICKUPS V6 ½ Ton			**1987**
AT/PS/AC			
Wideside Special 6'			
(4 cyl,4 spd)	6640	2300	3675
Wideside 6'	7482	2550	3975
Wideside 7 1/3'	7749	2650	4075
Wideside Ext Cpe 6'	8214	3175	4700
ADD FOR 87 S15 PICKUP:			
4-Whl Drive +680	*Gypsy Pkg +195*		
DEDUCT FOR 87 S15 PICKUP:			
4 Cyl Eng -160	*No AC -80*		
SAFARI V6 ½ Ton			**1987**
AT/PS/AC			
Cargo Van	8846	2850	4325
SL Van	9882	3850	5525
SLX Van	10363	3950	5650
SLE Van	11128	4150	5850
SLT Van	12419	4700	6450
DEDUCT FOR 87 SAFARI:			
4 Cyl Eng -160	*No AC -80*		
SUBURBAN V8			**1987**
AT/PS/AC			
4 Dr Suburban ½ Ton	12529	5700	7550
4 Dr Suburban ¾ Ton	13129	6025	7925
ADD FOR 87 SUBURBAN:			
4-Whl Drive +680	*Sierra Classic Pkg +230*		
DEDUCT FOR 87 SUBURBAN:			
No AC -80			
V1500 JIMMY V8 ½ Ton			**1987**
4WD/AT/PS/AC			
2 Dr Utility	13117	5525	7400
ADD FOR 87 V1500 JIMMY:			
Sierra Classic Pkg +230			
DEDUCT FOR 87 V1500 JIMMY:			
No AC -80			

1986 GMC

Model/Body/Type	BaseList	Whlse	Retail
C1500/C2500/C3500 PKUP			**1986**
C1500 Pickup ½ Ton			
Fenderside 6 ½'	7955	3250	4875
Wideside 6 ½'	7815	3275	4925
Wideside 8'	7989	3350	5000
C2500 Pickup ¾ Ton			
Fenderside 8'	9304	3550	5225
Wideside 8'	9164	3600	5275
Wide Bonus Cab 8'	11154	4175	5950
Wide Crew Cab 8'	11502	4375	6150
C3500 Pickup 1 Ton			
Fenderside 8'	10381	3875	5600
Wideside 8'	10242	3925	5675
Wide Bonus Cab 8'	11282	4500	6275
Wide Crew Cab 8'	11633	4675	6500
ADD FOR 86 C1500/C2500/C3500 PKUP:			
4-Whl Drive +495			
CABALLERO ½ Ton			**1986**
AT/PS/AC			
Pkup	9623	3625	5300
Diablo Pkup	9936	3875	5600
G1500/G2500/G3500 VAN			**1986**
G1500 Van ½ Ton			
Vandura	8677	2225	3700
Rally Wgn	10283	2900	4500
Rally Custom Wgn	11341	3150	4775
Rally STX Wgn	11673	3250	4850
G2500 Van ¾ Ton			
Vandura	9308	2275	3775
Rally Wgn	10706	2975	4575
Rally Custom Wgn	11533	3225	4850
Rally STX Wgn	11864	3275	4925
G3500 Van 1 Ton			
Vandura	11129	2350	3875
Rally Wgn	13173	3075	4675
ADD FOR 86 G1500/G2500/G3500 VAN:			
15 Pass Seating +80			
K1500 JIMMY ½ Ton			**1986**
4WD			
2 Dr Utility	12085	4250	6025
S15 JIMMY ½ Ton			**1986**
2 Dr Utility	9312	2450	4000
2 Dr 4WD Utility	10745	3250	4900
S15 PICKUPS ½ Ton			**1986**
Wideside Special 6'(4 cyl)	5990	1620	2905
Wideside 6'	7046	1800	3225
Wideside 7 1/3'	7281	1875	3275
Wideside Ext Cpe 6'	7733	2275	3800
ADD FOR 86 S15 PICKUP:			
4-Whl Drive +495			
SAFARI ½ Ton			**1986**
Cargo Van	8945	1950	3350
SL Van	9086	2900	4500
SLX Van	9541	3000	4600
SLE Van	10265	3150	4775

Model/Body/Type	BaseList	Whlse	Retail
SUBURBAN			**1986**
4 Dr Suburban ½ Ton	11528	4700	6525
4 Dr Suburban ¾ Ton	12349	5000	6925
ADD FOR 86 SUBURBAN:			
4-Whl Drive +495			

1985 GMC

Model/Body/Type	BaseList	Whlse	Retail
C1500/C2500/C3500 PKUP			**1985**
C1500 Pickup ½ Ton			
Fenderside 6 ½'	7101	2500	4050
Wideside 6 ½'	6970	2550	4100
Wideside 8'	7127	2625	4175
C2500 Pickup ¾ Ton			
Fenderside 8'	8319	2775	4350
Wideside 8'	8188	2825	4400
Wide Bonus Cab 8'	9645	3250	4900
Wide Crew Cab 8'	9975	3450	5100
C3500 Pickup 1 Ton			
Fenderside 8'	8966	3075	4700
Wideside 8'	8834	3125	4725
Wide Bonus Cab 8'	9815	3575	5250
Wide Crew Cab 8'	10146	3750	5475
ADD FOR 85 C1500/C2500/C3500 PKUP:			
4-Whl Drive +250			
CABALLERO			**1985**
Pkup	8522	2825	4400
SS Diablo Pkup	8781	3025	4625
G1500/G2500/G3500 VAN			**1985**
G1500 Van ½ Ton			
Vandura	7541	1550	2900
Rally Wgn	9089	2150	3600
Rally Custom Wgn	10062	2300	3825
Rally STX Wgn	10327	2400	3925
G2500 Van ¾ Ton			
Vandura	8176	1600	2975
Rally Wgn	9477	2200	3675
Rally Custom Wgn	10238	2375	3900
Rally STX Wgn	10503	2450	4000
G3500 Van 1 Ton			
Vandura	9212	1675	3050
Rally Wgn	11964	2250	3750
K1500 JIMMY			**1985**
2 Dr 4WD Utility	10819	3200	4825
S15 JIMMY			**1985**
2 Dr Utility	8468	2100	3550
4WD Utility	9685	2725	4300
S15 PICKUPS ½ Ton			**1985**
Wideside 6'	6398	1600	2950
Wideside 7 1/3'	6551	1650	3025
Wideside Ext Cpe 6'	6924	1975	3400
ADD FOR 85 S15 PICKUP:			
4-Whl Drive +250			
SUBURBAN			**1985**
4 Dr Suburban ½ Ton	10368	3575	5250
4 Dr Suburban ¾ Ton	10599	3925	5675
ADD FOR 85 SUBURBAN:			
4-Whl Drive +250			

Model/Body/Type	BaseList	Whlse	Retail

HONDA

Japan

1992 HONDA Accord EX Sedan

For a Honda dealer in your area, see our Dealer Directory (pg 217)

1994 HONDA

ACCORD 4 Cyl — 1994

FWD/AT/PS/AC

Model/Body/Type	BaseList	Whlse	Retail
2 Dr DX Cpe	14130	**12575**	**15050**
2 Dr LX Cpe	17030	**14275**	**16850**
2 Dr EX Cpe	19550	**16425**	**19100**
4 Dr DX Sdn	14330	**12875**	**15375**
4 Dr LX Sdn	17230	**14550**	**17125**
4 Dr EX Sdn	19750	**16725**	**19500**
5 Dr LX Wgn	18180	-	-
5 Dr EX Wgn	20750	-	-

CIVIC 4 Cyl — 1994

FWD/AT/PS/AC

Model/Body/Type	BaseList	Whlse	Retail
3 Dr CX Hbk (5 spd)	9400	**9050**	**11050**
3 Dr DX Hbk	10800	**10375**	**12600**
3 Dr VX Hbk (5 spd)	11500	**10175**	**12400**
3 Dr Si Hbk (5 spd)	13170	**11375**	**13750**
2 Dr DX Cpe	11220	**11125**	**13500**
2 Dr EX Cpe	13600	**13100**	**15600**
4 Dr DX Sdn	11750	**11225**	**13600**
4 Dr LX Sdn	12950	**12050**	**14550**
4 Dr EX Sdn	15740	**13675**	**16200**

CIVIC DEL SOL 4 Cyl — 1994

FWD/AT/PS/AC

Model/Body/Type	BaseList	Whlse	Retail
2 Dr S Cpe	14100	**12400**	**14850**
2 Dr Si Cpe	16100	**13800**	**16350**
2 Dr VTEC Cpe (5 spd)	17500	-	-

PASSPORT 4 Cyl — 1994

AT/PS/AC

Model/Body/Type	BaseList	Whlse	Retail
4 Dr DX Utility (5 spd)	15600	-	-
4 Dr LX Utility	18870	-	-
4 Dr LX 4WD Utility	21350	-	-
4 Dr EX 4WD Utility	23900	-	-

PRELUDE 4 Cyl — 1994

FWD/AT/PS/AC

Model/Body/Type	BaseList	Whlse	Retail
2 Dr S Cpe	18100	**15400**	**18175**
2 Dr Si Cpe	21400	**17350**	**20425**
2 Dr 4WS Si Cpe	24160	-	-
2 Dr VTEC Cpe (5 spd)	24500	-	-

ADD FOR ALL 94 HONDA:

ABS(Civic EX 2D/Si/LX + Accord DX/LX) +430
Anti-Theft/Recovery Sys +365
Cass(VX +CX +DX +Del Sol S) +115
Custom Whls +205
Leather Seats(Std Prelude 4WS/VTEC) +275

DEDUCT FOR ALL 94 HONDA:

No AC -680
No Auto Trans -590

1993 HONDA

ACCORD 4 Cyl — 1993

Ratings

Rating	Score
Safety	7.5
Reliability	9.1
Performance	7.9
Design	8.8
Fun to drive	7.9
Value	8.1
Overall	8.3

FWD/AT/PS/AC

Model/Body/Type	BaseList	Whlse	Retail
2 Dr DX Cpe	13750	**11000**	**13350**
2 Dr LX Cpe	16350	**12475**	**14950**
2 Dr EX Cpe	18770	**14125**	**16675**
2 Dr SE Cpe	21520	**15425**	**18050**
4 Dr DX Sdn	13950	**11300**	**13675**
4 Dr LX Sdn	16550	**12775**	**15250**
4 Dr Anniversary Sdn	18300	**13825**	**16375**
4 Dr EX Sdn	18970	**14425**	**17000**
4 Dr SE Sdn	21720	**16025**	**18700**
5 Dr LX Wgn	17795	**13625**	**16150**
5 Dr EX Wgn	20425	**15225**	**17850**

HONDA 93-92

CIVIC 4 Cyl 1993

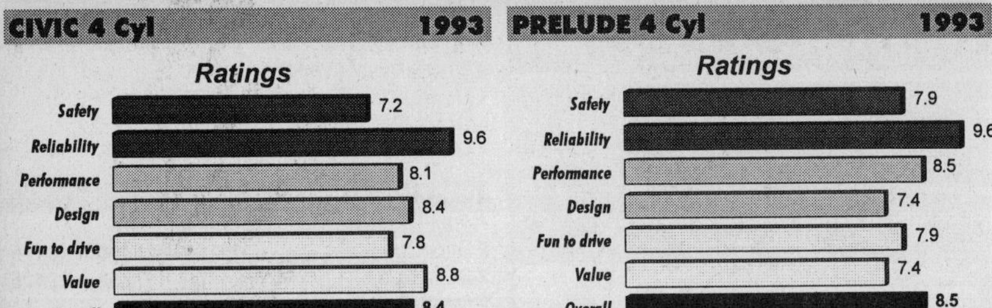

Model/Body/Type	BaseList	Whlse	Retail
FWD/AT/PS/AC			
3 Dr CX Hbk	8400	**7250**	**9125**
3 Dr DX Hbk	10100	**8650**	**10575**
3 Dr VX Hbk	10800	**8450**	**10350**
3 Dr Si Hbk	12200	**9500**	**11550**
2 Dr DX Cpe	10350	**9375**	**11425**
2 Dr EX Cpe	12400	**10900**	**13250**
4 Dr DX Sdn	11055	**9475**	**11525**
4 Dr LX Sdn	11885	**10125**	**12300**
4 Dr EX Sdn	15100	**11425**	**13800**

CIVIC DEL SOL 4 Cyl 1993

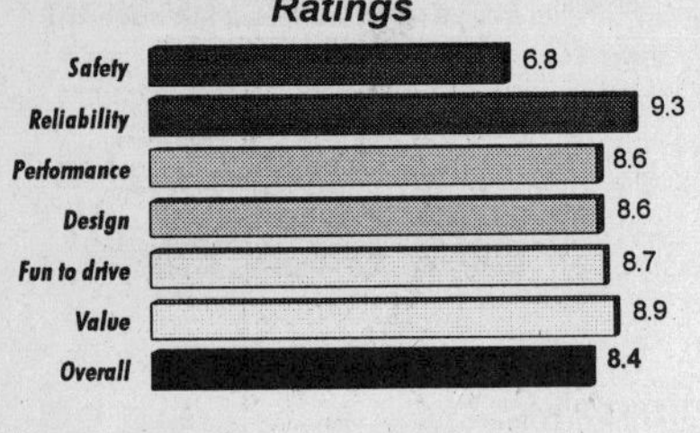

Model/Body/Type	BaseList	Whlse	Retail
FWD/AT/PS/AC			
2 Dr S Cpe	13200	**11250**	**13625**
2 Dr Si Cpe	15000	**12325**	**14775**

PRELUDE 4 Cyl 1993

Model/Body/Type	BaseList	Whlse	Retail
FWD/AT/PS/AC			
2 Dr S Cpe	17000	**14025**	**16700**
2 Dr Si Cpe	20000	**15575**	**18350**
2 Dr 4WS Si Cpe	22320	**16475**	**19300**
2 Dr VTEC Si Cpe (5 spd)	22690	**16775**	**19725**

ADD FOR ALL 93 HONDA:
Cass(Std Acc LX/EX/SE/Ann,Cvc EX,Prel) +100
Custom Whls +175

DEDUCT FOR ALL 93 HONDA:
No AC -545
No Auto Trans -505
No Pwr Steering -160

1992 HONDA

ACCORD 4 Cyl 1992

Ratings

Safety	7.5
Reliability	9.1
Performance	7.9
Design	8.8
Fun to drive	7.9
Value	8.1
Overall	8.3

Model/Body/Type	BaseList	Whlse	Retail
FWD/AT/PS/AC			
2 Dr DX Cpe	13025	**9400**	**11425**
2 Dr LX Cpe	15625	**10425**	**12650**
2 Dr EX Cpe	18045	**11875**	**14325**
4 Dr DX Sdn	13225	**9700**	**11800**
4 Dr LX Sdn	15825	**10725**	**13075**
4 Dr EX Sdn	18245	**12150**	**14625**
5 Dr LX Wgn	17450	**11575**	**13950**
5 Dr EX Wgn	19900	**13000**	**15500**

CIVIC 4 Cyl 1992

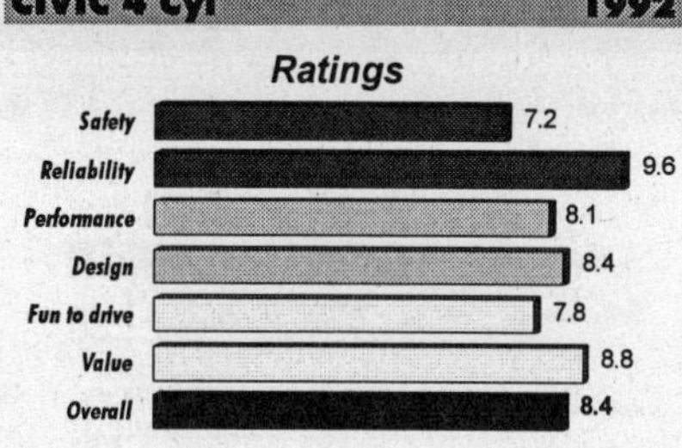

Model/Body/Type	BaseList	Whlse	Retail
FWD/AT/PS/AC			
3 Dr CX Hbk (5 spd)	7900	**5875**	**7600**
3 Dr DX Hbk	9650	**7200**	**9075**
3 Dr VX Hbk (5 spd)	10350	**7025**	**8850**
3 Dr Si Hbk (5 spd)	11700	**7625**	**9525**
4 Dr DX Sdn	10553	**7975**	**9900**
4 Dr LX Sdn	11385	**8600**	**10525**
4 Dr EX Sdn	13575	**9525**	**11575**

PRELUDE 4 Cyl 1992

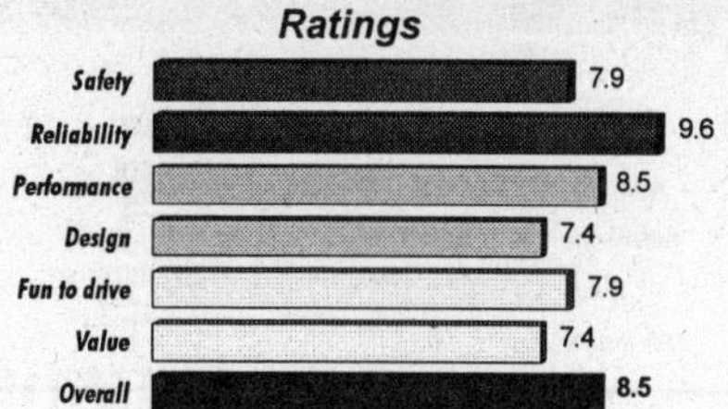

Model/Body/Type	BaseList	Whlse	Retail
FWD/AT/PS/AC			
2 Dr S Cpe	16250	**12350**	**14925**
2 Dr Si Cpe	19250	**13550**	**16200**
2 Dr 4WS Si Cpe	21570	**14350**	**17025**

ADD FOR ALL 92 HONDA:
Cass(Std Accord LX/EX,Prelude) +75
Custom Whls +160

DEDUCT FOR ALL 92 HONDA:
No AC -505
No Auto Trans -470
No Pwr Steering -135

1991 HONDA

ACCORD 4 Cyl 1991

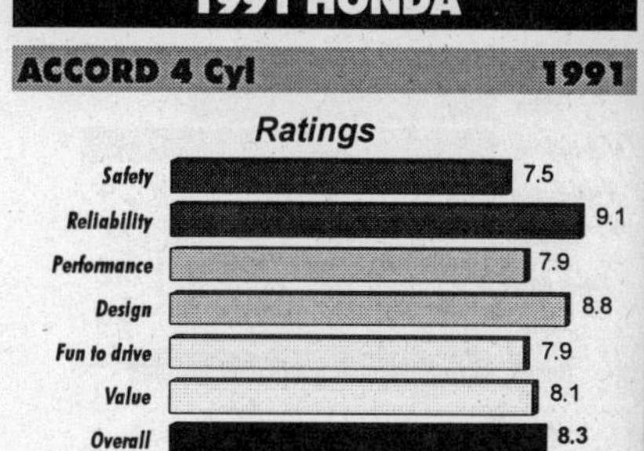

Model/Body/Type	BaseList	Whlse	Retail
FWD/AT/PS/AC			
2 Dr DX Cpe	12345	**7800**	**9725**
2 Dr LX Cpe	14895	**8800**	**10800**
2 Dr EX Cpe	16595	**9975**	**12125**
4 Dr DX Sdn	12545	**8100**	**10000**
4 Dr LX Sdn	15095	**9100**	**11125**
4 Dr EX Sdn	16795	**10225**	**12450**
4 Dr SE Sdn	19545	**11200**	**13575**
5 Dr LX Wgn	17300	**9900**	**12050**
5 Dr EX Wgn	19050	**11050**	**13400**

CIVIC 4 Cyl 1991

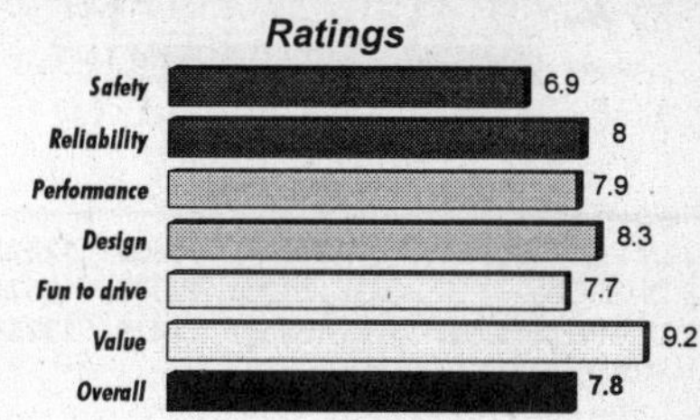

Model/Body/Type	BaseList	Whlse	Retail
FWD/AT/PS/AC			
3 Dr Hbk (5 spd)	6895	**4200**	**5725**
3 Dr DX Hbk	8745	**5725**	**7400**
3 Dr Si Hbk (5 spd)	10295	**6025**	**7750**
4 Dr DX Sdn	9490	**6425**	**8175**
4 Dr LX Sdn	10500	**7025**	**8850**
4 Dr EX Sdn	11195	**7350**	**9225**
4 Dr Wgn	10325	**6250**	**8000**
4 Dr 4WD Wgn	12410	**6900**	**8725**

Model/Body/Type	BaseList	Whlse	Retail

CIVIC CRX 4 Cyl 1991

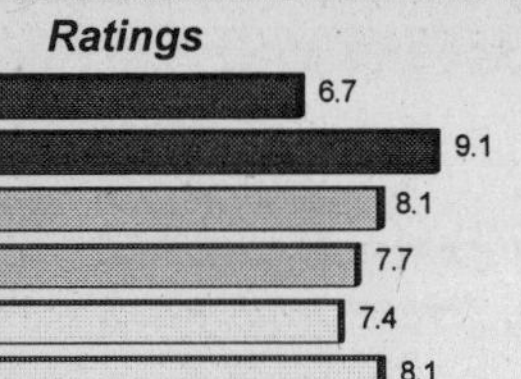

FWD/AT/PS/AC

Model/Body/Type	BaseList	Whlse	Retail
2 Dr HF Cpe (5 spd)	9145	**5675**	**7350**
2 Dr Cpe	9410	**6525**	**8300**
2 Dr Si Cpe (5 spd)	11130	**6950**	**8775**

PRELUDE 4 Cyl 1991

Ratings

Rating	Score
Safety	6.3
Reliability	9
Performance	7.8
Design	7.7
Fun to drive	7.5
Value	8.2
Overall	7.8

FWD/AT/PS/AC

Model/Body/Type	BaseList	Whlse	Retail
2 Dr 2.0 Si Cpe	14945	**10300**	**12625**
2 Dr Si Cpe	17165	**11075**	**13525**
2 Dr 4WS Si Cpe	18450	**11475**	**13950**

ADD FOR ALL 91 HONDA:

ABS (Prelude Si) +315
Cass(Std Accord LX/EX/SE,Prelude) +60
Custom Whls +135
Pwr Locks (Prelude) +60

DEDUCT FOR ALL 91 HONDA:

No AC -470
No Auto Trans -430
No Pwr Steering -115

See the Automobile Dealer Directory on page 379 for a Dealer near you!

1990 HONDA

ACCORD 4 Cyl 1990

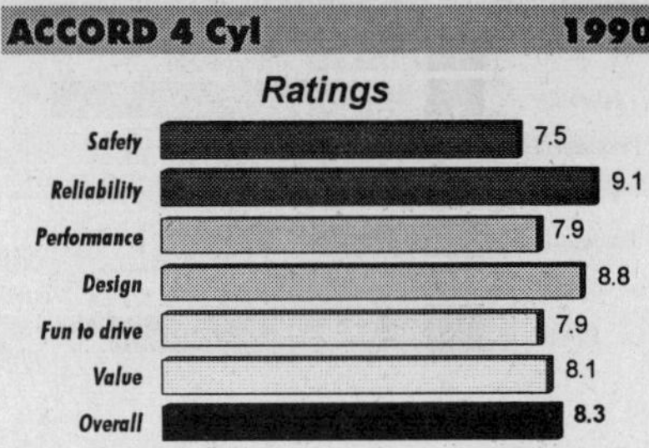

FWD/AT/PS/AC

Model/Body/Type	BaseList	Whlse	Retail
2 Dr DX Cpe	12145	**6500**	**8225**
2 Dr LX Cpe	14695	**7150**	**9025**
2 Dr EX Cpe	16395	**8150**	**10050**
4 Dr DX Sdn	12345	**6750**	**8600**
4 Dr LX Sdn	14895	**7450**	**9325**
4 Dr EX Sdn	16595	**8450**	**10350**

CIVIC 4 Cyl 1990

Ratings

Rating	Score
Safety	6.9
Reliability	8
Performance	7.9
Design	8.3
Fun to drive	7.7
Value	9.2
Overall	7.8

FWD/AT/PS/AC

Model/Body/Type	BaseList	Whlse	Retail
3 Dr Hbk (4 spd)	6635	**3250**	**4650**
3 Dr DX Hbk	8695	**4450**	**6000**
3 Dr Si Hbk (5 spd)	10245	**4700**	**6325**
4 Dr DX Sdn	9440	**5075**	**6750**
4 Dr LX Sdn	10450	**5675**	**7350**
4 Dr EX Sdn	11145	**5950**	**7675**
4 Dr Wgn	10325	**4900**	**6575**
4 Dr 4WD Wgn	12410	**5525**	**7200**

CIVIC CRX 4 Cyl — 1990

Ratings

Rating	Score
Safety	6.7
Reliability	9.1
Performance	8.1
Design	7.7
Fun to drive	7.4
Value	8.1
Overall	8

FWD/AT/PS/AC

Model/Body/Type	BaseList	Whlse	Retail
2 Dr HF Cpe (5 spd)	9145	**4425**	**5975**
2 Dr Cpe	9410	**5175**	**6875**
2 Dr Si Cpe (5 spd)	11130	**5475**	**7150**

PRELUDE 4 Cyl — 1990

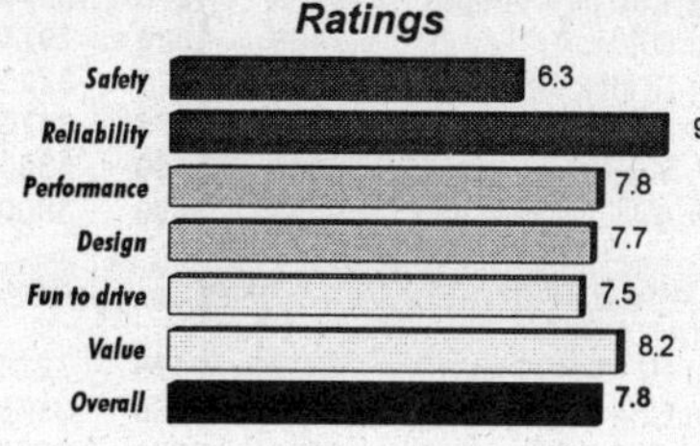

FWD/AT/PS/AC

Model/Body/Type	BaseList	Whlse	Retail
2 Dr 2.0 S Cpe	13945	**8175**	**10200**
2 Dr 2.0 Si Cpe	14945	**8675**	**10750**
2 Dr Si Cpe	16965	**9300**	**11425**
2 Dr 4WS Si Cpe	18450	**9650**	**11800**

ADD FOR ALL 90 HONDA:

ABS (Prelude Si) +275
Cass(Std Accord LX/EX,Prelude) +60
Custom Whls +115

DEDUCT FOR ALL 90 HONDA:

No AC -430
No Auto Trans -390
No Pwr Steering -100

1989 HONDA

ACCORD 4 Cyl — 1989

FWD/AT/PS/AC

Model/Body/Type	BaseList	Whlse	Retail
3 Dr DX Hbk	11230	**4875**	**6550**
3 Dr LXi Hbk	14530	**6050**	**7775**
2 Dr DX Cpe	11650	**5275**	**7000**
2 Dr LXi Cpe	14690	**6450**	**8200**
2 Dr SEi Cpe	16975	**7025**	**8850**
4 Dr DX Sdn	11770	**5650**	**7300**
4 Dr LX Sdn	14180	**5925**	**7650**
4 Dr LXi Sdn	15920	**6750**	**8600**
4 Dr SEi Sdn	17985	**7325**	**9200**

CIVIC 4 Cyl — 1989

Ratings

Rating	Score
Safety	6.9
Reliability	8
Performance	7.9
Design	8.3
Fun to drive	7.7
Value	9.2
Overall	7.8

FWD/AT/PS/AC

Model/Body/Type	BaseList	Whlse	Retail
3 Dr Hbk (4 spd)	6385	**2275**	**3500**
3 Dr DX Hbk	8445	**3350**	**4775**
3 Dr Si Hbk (5 spd)	9980	**3600**	**5025**
4 Dr DX Sdn	9190	**3975**	**5500**
4 Dr LX Sdn	10150	**4475**	**6050**
4 Dr Wgn	10125	**3800**	**5275**
4 Dr 4WD Wgn	12210	**4350**	**5875**

CIVIC CRX 4 Cyl — 1989

Ratings

Rating	Score
Safety	6.7
Reliability	9.1
Performance	8.1
Design	7.7
Fun to drive	7.4
Value	8.1
Overall	8

FWD/AT/PS/AC

Model/Body/Type	BaseList	Whlse	Retail
2 Dr HF Cpe (5 spd)	8895	**3375**	**4800**
2 Dr Cpe	9310	**4075**	**5600**
2 Dr Si Cpe (5 spd)	10930	**4350**	**5875**

HONDA 89-86

Model/Body/Type	BaseList	Whlse	Retail

PRELUDE 4 Cyl 1989

Ratings

Rating	Score
Safety	6.3
Reliability	9
Performance	7.8
Design	7.7
Fun to drive	7.5
Value	8.2
Overall	7.8

FWD/AT/PS/AC

Model/Body/Type	BaseList	Whlse	Retail
2 Dr S Cpe	13945	**6250**	**8125**
2 Dr Si Cpe	16965	**7100**	**9075**
2 Dr 4WS Si Cpe	18450	**7375**	**9400**

ADD FOR ALL 89 HONDA:
Cass(Std Accord LX/LXi/SEi,Prelude) +35
Custom Whls +75

DEDUCT FOR ALL 89 HONDA:
No AC -390
No Auto Trans -350
No Pwr Steering -75

1988 HONDA

ACCORD 4 Cyl 1988

FWD/AT/PS/AC

Model/Body/Type	BaseList	Whlse	Retail
3 Dr DX Hbk	10535	**3575**	**5000**
3 Dr LXi Hbk	13695	**4400**	**5950**
2 Dr DX Cpe	11335	**4025**	**5550**
2 Dr LXi Cpe	14295	**4825**	**6500**
4 Dr DX Sdn	11175	**4375**	**5925**
4 Dr LX Sdn	13460	**4575**	**6150**
4 Dr LXi Sdn	15200	**5150**	**6850**

CIVIC 4 Cyl 1988

FWD/AT/PS/AC

Model/Body/Type	BaseList	Whlse	Retail
3 Dr 1.3L Hbk (4 spd)	6095	**1550**	**2600**
3 Dr DX Hbk	7985	**2400**	**3625**
4 Dr DX Sdn	8795	**2975**	**4325**
4 Dr LX Sdn	9675	**3350**	**4775**
4 Dr Wgn	9948	**2800**	**4125**
4 Dr 4WD Wgn (6 spd)	11998	**2925**	**4275**

CIVIC CRX 4 Cyl 1988

FWD/AT/PS/AC

Model/Body/Type	BaseList	Whlse	Retail
2 Dr HF Cpe (5 spd)	8295	**2475**	**3725**
2 Dr Cpe	8635	**3075**	**4425**
2 Dr Si Cpe (5 spd)	10195	**3275**	**4700**

PRELUDE 4 Cyl 1988

FWD/AT/PS/AC

Model/Body/Type	BaseList	Whlse	Retail
2 Dr S Cpe	13495	**4925**	**6725**
2 Dr Si Cpe	16645	**5725**	**7525**
2 Dr 4WS Si Cpe	17945	**5950**	**7800**

DEDUCT FOR ALL 88 HONDA:
No AC -330
No Auto Trans -290

1987 HONDA

ACCORD 4 Cyl 1987

FWD/AT/PS/AC

Model/Body/Type	BaseList	Whlse	Retail
3 Dr DX Hbk	9795	**2775**	**4100**
3 Dr LXi Hbk	12785	**3425**	**4850**
4 Dr DX Sdn	10625	**3400**	**4825**
4 Dr LX Sdn	12799	**3600**	**5025**
4 Dr LXi Sdn	14429	**4100**	**5650**

CIVIC 4 Cyl 1987

FWD/AT/PS/AC

Model/Body/Type	BaseList	Whlse	Retail
3 Dr 1.3L Hbk (4 spd)	5799	**1275**	**2275**
3 Dr DX Hbk	7489	**1825**	**2975**
3 Dr Si Hbk (5 spd)	8899	**2075**	**3225**
4 Dr Sdn	8455	**2275**	**3475**
4 Dr Wgn	8330	**2150**	**3300**
4 Dr 4WD Wgn (6 spd)	9695	**2550**	**3800**

CIVIC CRX 4 Cyl 1987

FWD/AT/PS/AC

Model/Body/Type	BaseList	Whlse	Retail
2 Dr HF Cpe (5 spd)	7639	**2075**	**3225**
2 Dr Cpe	7975	**2350**	**3575**
2 Dr Si Cpe (5 spd)	9395	**2625**	**3875**

PRELUDE 4 Cyl 1987

FWD/AT/PS/AC

Model/Body/Type	BaseList	Whlse	Retail
2 Dr Cpe	11995	**4050**	**5725**
2 Dr Si Cpe	14945	**4550**	**6250**

DEDUCT FOR ALL 87 HONDA:
No AC -195
No Auto Trans -175

1986 HONDA

ACCORD 1986

FWD

Model/Body/Type	BaseList	Whlse	Retail
3 Dr DX Hbk	8429	**2250**	**3475**
3 Dr LXi Hbk	11149	**2800**	**4100**
4 Dr DX Sdn	9299	**2650**	**3950**
4 Dr LX Sdn	10995	**2850**	**4175**
4 Dr LXi Sdn	12675	**3200**	**4575**

Model/Body/Type	BaseList	Whlse	Retail
CIVIC			**1986**
FWD			
3 Dr 1.3L Hbk	5479	900	1875
3 Dr DX Hbk	6699	1300	2350
3 Dr Si Hbk (5 spd)	7999	1550	2650
4 Dr Sdn	7499	1675	2800
4 Dr Wgn	7395	1525	2625
4 Dr 4WD Wgn	8739	1925	3125
CIVIC CRX			**1986**
FWD			
2 Dr HF Cpe (5 spd)	6729	1525	2625
2 Dr Cpe	7049	1750	2925
2 Dr Si Cpe	8279	2025	3200
PRELUDE			**1986**
FWD			
2 Dr Cpe	10549	3125	4500
2 Dr Si Cpe	12995	3600	5000

1985 HONDA

Model/Body/Type	BaseList	Whlse	Retail
ACCORD			**1985**
3 Dr Hbk	7895	1375	2450
3 Dr LX Hbk	9095	1550	2650
4 Dr Sdn	8845	1700	2850
4 Dr LX Sdn	10295	1850	3050
4 Dr SE-i Sdn	12945	2225	3450
CIVIC			**1985**
3 Dr 1300 Hbk	5399	575	1525
2 Dr CRX HF Cpe	6479	1250	2275
2 Dr CRX Cpe	6855	1325	2400
2 Dr CRX Si Cpe	7999	1575	2700
3 Dr DX Hbk	6529	925	1950
3 Dr S Hbk	7129	1225	2250
4 Dr Sdn	7295	1250	2275
4 Dr Wgn	7195	1150	2175
4 Dr 4WD Wgn	8649	1500	2600
PRELUDE			**1985**
2 Dr Cpe	10345	2475	3750
2 Dr Si Cpe	12850	2925	4250

Model/Body/Type	BaseList	Whlse	Retail

HYUNDAI

Korea

1992 Hyundai Scoupe

For a Hyundai dealer in your area, see our Dealer Directory (pg 217)

1994 HYUNDAI

ELANTRA 4 Cyl — 1994

Model/Body/Type	BaseList	Whlse	Retail
FWD/AT/PS/AC			
4 Dr Sdn	9749	**8400**	**10225**
4 Dr GLS Sdn	10959	**9125**	**11025**

EXCEL 4 Cyl — 1994

Ratings

Rating	Score
Safety	6.2
Reliability	6.7
Performance	6.9
Design	8
Fun to drive	6.4
Value	7.1
Overall	6.7

Model/Body/Type	BaseList	Whlse	Retail
FWD/5SP/PS/AC			
3 Dr Hbk	7190	**6775**	**8525**
3 Dr GS Hbk	8099	**7300**	**9100**
4 Dr GL Sdn	8099	**7350**	**9150**

SCOUPE 4 Cyl — 1994

Model/Body/Type	BaseList	Whlse	Retail
FWD/AT/PS/AC			
2 Dr Cpe	9499	**8350**	**10175**
2 Dr LS Cpe	10599	**9100**	**11000**
2 Dr Turbo Cpe (5 spd)	11399	**9050**	**10950**

SONATA 4 Cyl — 1994

Ratings

Rating	Score
Safety	5.9
Reliability	4.6
Performance	7.3
Design	8.3
Fun to drive	7.6
Value	6.9
Overall	6.1

Model/Body/Type	BaseList	Whlse	Retail
FWD/AT/PS/AC			
4 Dr Sdn	12799	**10500**	**12725**
4 Dr GLS Sdn	14199	**11700**	**14150**

ADD FOR ALL 94 HYUNDAI:

ABS +430
Anti-Theft/Recovery Sys +365
Auto Trans (Excel) +500
Cass (Base Excel/Scoupe/Elantra) +90
CD Player +205
Cruise Ctrl (Std Sonata GLS) +135
Custom Whls +180
Leather Seats +275
Pwr Option Pkg(Std Sonata GLS) +430
Pwr Sunroof +410
Sunroof +275
V6 Eng +545

DEDUCT FOR ALL 94 HYUNDAI:

No AC -590
No Auto Trans -500
No Pwr Steering -180

HYUNDAI

ELANTRA 4 Cyl — 1993

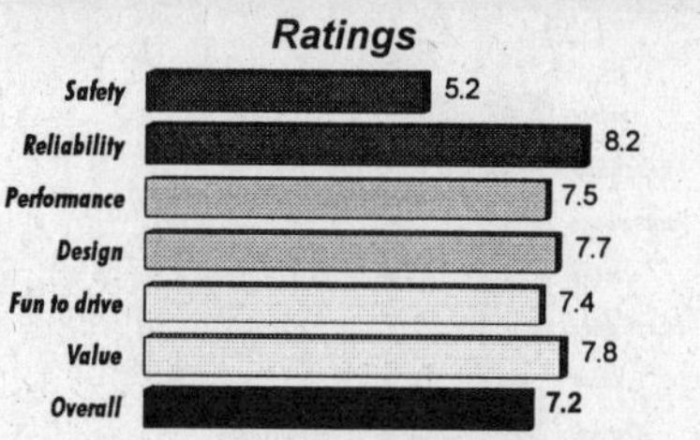

Model/Body/Type	BaseList	Whlse	Retail
FWD/AT/PS/AC			
4 Dr Sdn	8999	**7225**	**9025**
4 Dr GLS Sdn	10299	**7925**	**9800**

EXCEL 4 Cyl — 1993

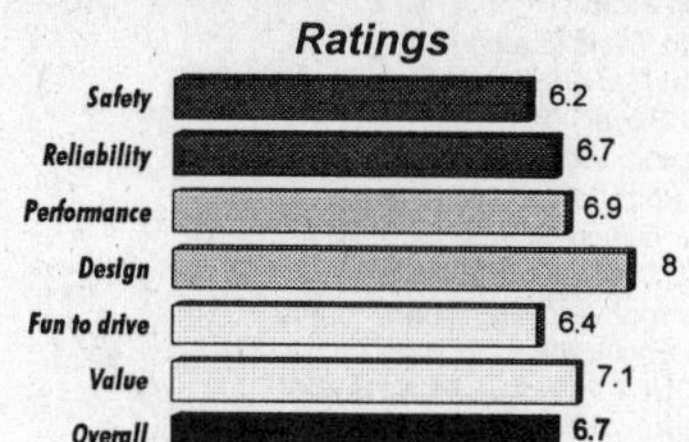

Model/Body/Type	BaseList	Whlse	Retail
FWD/5SP/PS/AC			
3 Dr Hbk (4 spd)	6799	**5550**	**7100**
4 Dr Sdn (4 spd)	7699	**5800**	**7350**
3 Dr GS Hbk	7699	**5875**	**7450**
4 Dr GL Sdn	8599	**6325**	**7925**

SCOUPE 4 Cyl — 1993

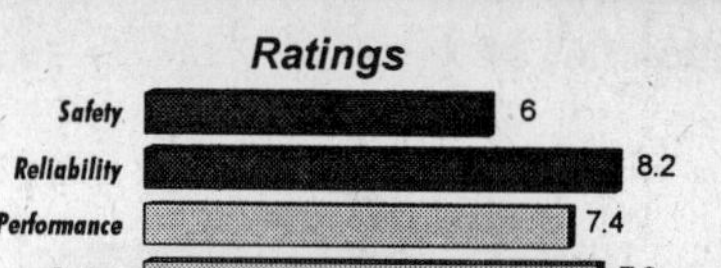

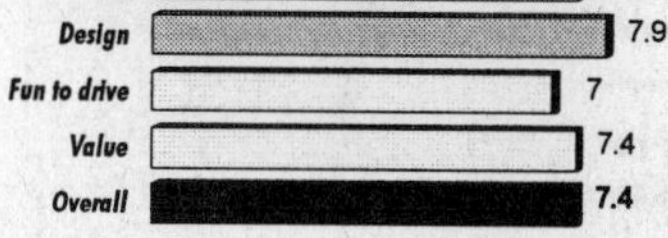

Model/Body/Type	BaseList	Whlse	Retail
FWD/AT/PS/AC			
2 Dr Cpe	9069	**7050**	**8800**
2 Dr LS Cpe	10199	**7725**	**9575**
2 Dr Turbo Cpe (5 spd)	10999	**7625**	**9450**

SONATA 4 Cyl — 1993

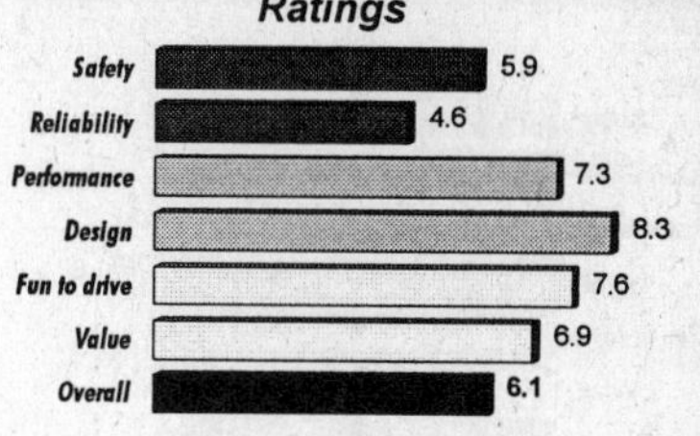

Model/Body/Type	BaseList	Whlse	Retail
FWD/AT/PS/AC			
4 Dr Sdn	12399	**8825**	**10825**
4 Dr GLS Sdn	13799	**9900**	**12050**

ADD FOR ALL 93 HYUNDAI:

ABS +390
Auto Trans (Excel) +430
Cass (Base Excel/Scoupe/Sonata) +75
CD Player +175
Cruise Ctrl (Elantra,Base Sonata) +135
Custom Whls +160
Leather Seats +230
Pwr Option Pkg(Std Sonata GLS) +315
Pwr Sunroof +315
Sunroof +195
V6 Eng +430

DEDUCT FOR ALL 93 HYUNDAI:

No AC -470
No Auto Trans -430
No Pwr Steering -160

HYUNDAI

1992 HYUNDAI

ELANTRA 4 Cyl 1992

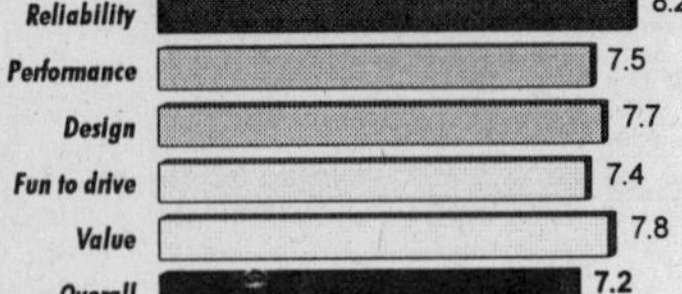

Model/Body/Type	BaseList	Whlse	Retail
FWD/AT/PS/AC			
4 Dr Sdn	8995	**5375**	**6925**
4 Dr GLS Sdn	9999	**5875**	**7475**

EXCEL 4 Cyl 1992

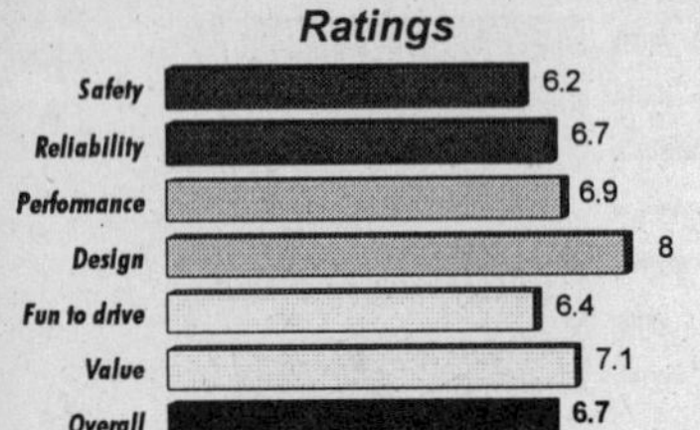

Model/Body/Type	BaseList	Whlse	Retail
FWD/5SP/PS/AC			
3 Dr Hbk (4 spd)	6595	**3975**	**5325**
4 Dr Sdn (4 spd)	7142	**4225**	**5650**
3 Dr GS Hbk	6821	**4300**	**5725**
4 Dr GL Sdn	7629	**4700**	**6150**

SCOUPE 4 Cyl 1992

Model/Body/Type	BaseList	Whlse	Retail
FWD/AT/PS/AC			
2 Dr Cpe	8799	**5875**	**7475**
2 Dr LS Cpe	9999	**6500**	**8125**

SONATA 4 Cyl 1992

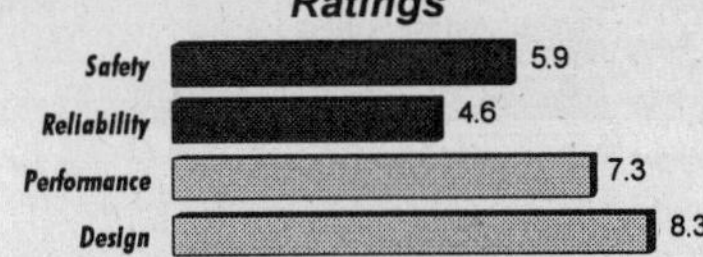

Model/Body/Type	BaseList	Whlse	Retail
FWD/AT/PS/AC			
4 Dr Sdn	11150	**7300**	**9175**
4 Dr GLS Sdn	13995	**8275**	**10175**

ADD FOR ALL 92 HYUNDAI:

ABS +350
Auto Trans (Excel) +390
Cass(Std GS,GL,LS,GLS,Sonata) +60
CD Player +160
Custom Whls +135
Leather Seats +195
Pwr Option Pkg(Std GLS) +250
Pwr Sunroof +275
Sunroof (Scoupe,Elantra) +160
V6 Eng +390

DEDUCT FOR ALL 92 HYUNDAI:

No AC -430
No Auto Trans -390
No Pwr Steering -135

1991 HYUNDAI

EXCEL 4 Cyl 1991

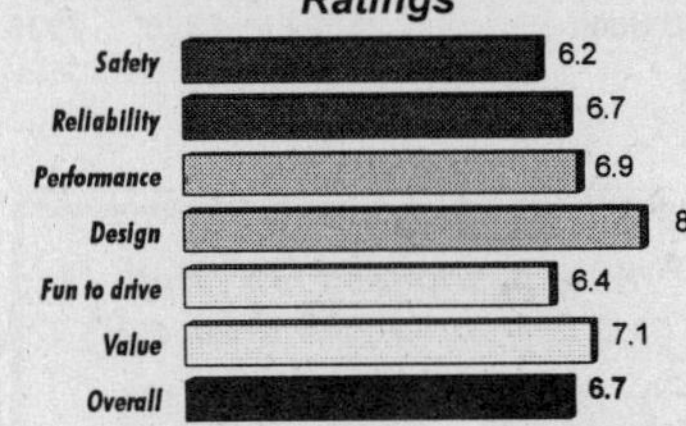

Model/Body/Type	BaseList	Whlse	Retail
FWD/5SP/PS/AC			
3 Dr Hbk (4 spd)	6275	**2675**	**3850**
4 Dr Sdn (4 spd)	7410	**2925**	**4175**
3 Dr GS Hbk	7145	**3000**	**4250**
4 Dr GL Sdn	8115	**3300**	**4650**
4 Dr GLS Sdn	8895	**3625**	**4950**

SCOUPE 4 Cyl — 1991

Ratings

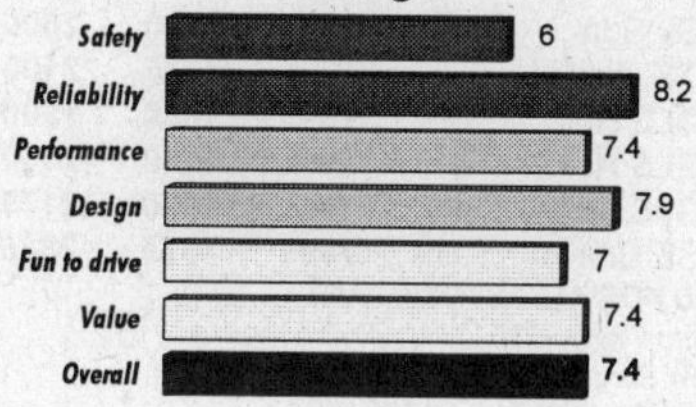

Rating	Score
Safety	6
Reliability	8.2
Performance	7.4
Design	7.9
Fun to drive	7
Value	7.4
Overall	7.4

Model/Body/Type	BaseList	Whlse	Retail
FWD/AT/PS/AC			
2 Dr Cpe	8395	**4250**	**5675**
2 Dr LS Cpe	9745	**4725**	**6200**

SONATA 4 Cyl — 1991

Ratings

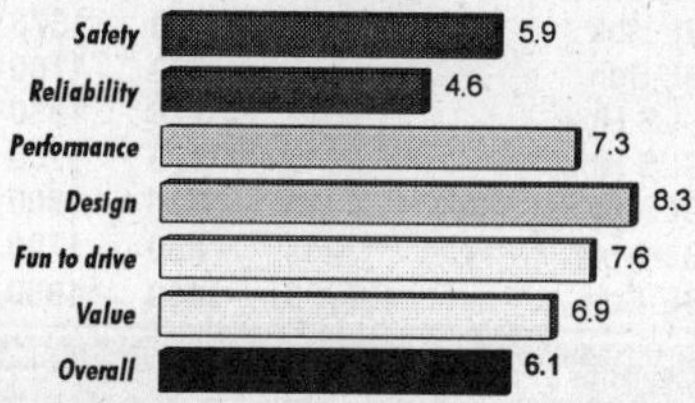

Rating	Score
Safety	5.9
Reliability	4.6
Performance	7.3
Design	8.3
Fun to drive	7.6
Value	6.9
Overall	6.1

Model/Body/Type	BaseList	Whlse	Retail
FWD/AT/PS/AC			
4 Dr Sdn	10700	**4975**	**6650**
4 Dr GLS Sdn	13250	**5800**	**7500**

ADD FOR ALL 91 HYUNDAI:

Auto Trans (Excel) +350
Cass(Std Sonata,Scoupe LS,Excel GLS) +35
CD Player +115
Custom Whls +115
Leather Seats +160
Pwr Option Pkg(Std Sonata GLS) +195
Pwr Sunroof +230
Sunroof (Scoupe) +115
V6 Eng +350

DEDUCT FOR ALL 91 HYUNDAI:

No AC -390
No Auto Trans -350
No Pwr Steering -115

1990 HYUNDAI

EXCEL 4 Cyl — 1990

Ratings

Rating	Score
Safety	6.2
Reliability	6.7
Performance	6.9
Design	8
Fun to drive	6.4
Value	7.1
Overall	6.7

Model/Body/Type	BaseList	Whlse	Retail
FWD/5SP/PS/AC			
3 Dr Hbk (4 spd)	5899	**1725**	**2750**
4 Dr Sdn (4 spd)	6999	**1950**	**3025**
3 Dr GS Hbk	6999	**2100**	**3175**
4 Dr GL Sdn	7879	**2300**	**3425**
5 Dr GL Hbk	7599	**2225**	**3325**
4 Dr GLS Sdn	8479	**2575**	**3725**

SONATA 4 Cyl — 1990

Ratings

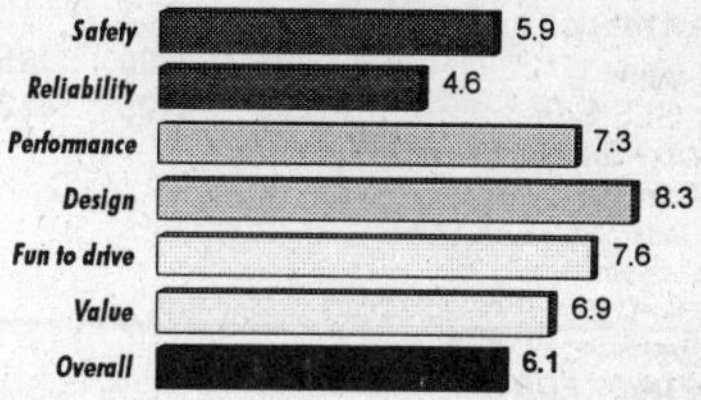

Rating	Score
Safety	5.9
Reliability	4.6
Performance	7.3
Design	8.3
Fun to drive	7.6
Value	6.9
Overall	6.1

Model/Body/Type	BaseList	Whlse	Retail
FWD/AT/PS/AC			
4 Dr Sdn	9999	**3850**	**5325**
4 Dr GLS Sdn	12349	**4550**	**6125**

ADD FOR ALL 90 HYUNDAI:

Auto Trans (Excel) +315
Cass(Std GLS) +35
CD Player +75
Custom Whls +75
Leather Seats +135
Pwr Option Pkg(Std Sonata GLS) +160
Pwr Sunroof +195
V6 Eng +315

DEDUCT FOR ALL 90 HYUNDAI:

No AC -350
No Auto Trans -315
No Pwr Steering -100

1989 HYUNDAI

EXCEL 4 Cyl — 1989

FWD/5SP/PS/AC

Model/Body/Type	BaseList	Whlse	Retail
3 Dr Hbk (4 spd)	5499	**900**	**1775**
4 Dr Sdn (4 spd)	6199	**1150**	**2050**
3 Dr GL Hbk	6699	**1250**	**2175**
5 Dr GL Hbk	6949	**1350**	**2300**
4 Dr GL Sdn	7149	**1450**	**2400**
3 Dr GS Hbk	7699	**1550**	**2525**
5 Dr GLS Hbk	7599	**1550**	**2525**
4 Dr GLS Sdn	7749	**1650**	**2625**

SONATA 4 Cyl — 1989

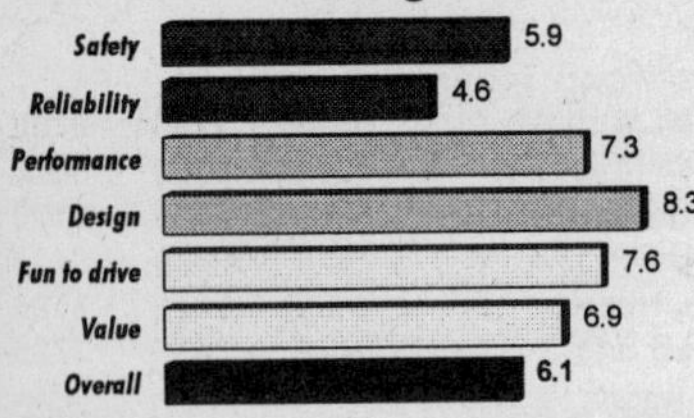

FWD/AT/PS/AC

Model/Body/Type	BaseList	Whlse	Retail
4 Dr Sdn	9695	**2600**	**3850**
4 Dr GLS Sdn	11695	**3125**	**4525**

ADD FOR ALL 89 HYUNDAI:
Auto Trans (Excel) +275
Cass(Std GS,GLS) +25
Custom Whls +35
Pwr Option Pkg(Std Sonata GLS) +100
Pwr Sunroof +160

DEDUCT FOR ALL 89 HYUNDAI:
No AC -315
No Auto Trans -275
No Pwr Steering -75

1988 HYUNDAI

EXCEL 4 Cyl — 1988

FWD/PS/AC

Model/Body/Type	BaseList	Whlse	Retail
3 Dr Hbk	5295	**650**	**1450**
5 Dr Hbk	5645	**800**	**1625**
4 Dr Sdn	5795	**875**	**1725**
3 Dr GL Hbk	6295	**875**	**1725**
5 Dr GL Hbk	6545	**1000**	**1900**
4 Dr GL Sdn	6695	**1100**	**2000**
3 Dr GS Hbk	7395	**1175**	**2100**
3 Dr GLS Hbk	7045	**1000**	**1900**
5 Dr GLS Hbk	7295	**1150**	**2050**
4 Dr GLS Sdn	7445	**1250**	**2175**
4 Dr SE Sdn	7999	**1375**	**2325**

ADD FOR ALL 88 HYUNDAI:
Auto Trans +230
Pwr Sunroof +100

DEDUCT FOR ALL 88 HYUNDAI:
No AC -250

1987 HYUNDAI

EXCEL 4 Cyl — 1987

FWD/PS/AC

Model/Body/Type	BaseList	Whlse	Retail
3 Dr L Hbk	4995	**475**	**1275**
5 Dr L Hbk	5295	**625**	**1425**
3 Dr GL Hbk	5995	**600**	**1400**
5 Dr GL Hbk	6295	**750**	**1575**
4 Dr GL Sdn	6445	**850**	**1700**
3 Dr GLS Hbk	6645	**725**	**1550**
5 Dr GLS Hbk	6945	**875**	**1700**
4 Dr GLS Sdn	7095	**925**	**1800**
3 Dr SE Hbk	7285	**850**	**1700**
4 Dr SE Sdn	7735	**1050**	**1950**

1986 HYUNDAI

EXCEL — 1986

FWD

Model/Body/Type	BaseList	Whlse	Retail
3 Dr Hbk	4995	**200**	**950**
5 Dr Hbk	4995	**200**	**1100**
3 Dr GL Hbk	5895	**200**	**1050**
5 Dr GL Hbk	5895	**275**	**1200**
4 Dr GL Sdn	6045	**350**	**1275**
3 Dr GLS Hbk	6395	**225**	**1150**
5 Dr GLS Hbk	6395	**350**	**1275**
4 Dr GLS Sdn	6545	**425**	**1350**

INFINITI

Japan

1992 Infiniti M30 Convertible

For an Infiniti dealer in your area, see our Dealer Directory (pg 217)

1994 INFINITI

G20 4 Cyl — 1994

Model/Body/Type	BaseList	Whlse	Retail
AT/PS/AC			
4 Dr Sdn	21975	-	-

J30 V6 — 1994

Model/Body/Type	BaseList	Whlse	Retail
AT/PS/AC			
4 Dr Sdn	36950	26400	30400

Q45 V8 — 1994

Model/Body/Type	BaseList	Whlse	Retail
AT/PS/AC			
4 Dr Q45 Sdn	47500	36050	39950
4 Dr Q45a Sdn	54100	37850	42375

ADD FOR ALL 94 INFINITI:
Anti-Theft/Recovery Sys +365
Car Phone +230
Touring Pkg +1365
Traction Ctrl(Std Q45a) +955

1993 INFINITI

G20 4 Cyl — 1993

Model/Body/Type	BaseList	Whlse	Retail
AT/PS/AC			
4 Dr Sdn	19500	13850	16800

J30 V6 — 1993

Ratings

Rating	Score
Safety	9.5
Reliability	9.7
Performance	8.2
Design	8.2
Fun to drive	7.9
Value	8.2
Overall	9

Model/Body/Type	BaseList	Whlse	Retail
AT/PS/AC			
4 Dr Sdn	33000	21950	25575

INFINITI 93-92

Model/Body/Type	BaseList	Whlse	Retail

Q45 V8 — 1993

Ratings

Rating	Score
Safety	8.8
Reliability	8.5
Performance	8.9
Design	8.3
Fun to drive	8.8
Value	7.2
Overall	8.6

AT/PS/AC

Model/Body/Type	BaseList	Whlse	Retail
4 Dr Q45 Sdn	45400	**29175**	**33275**
4 Dr Q45a Sdn	50400	**31150**	**35175**

ADD FOR ALL 93 INFINITI:

Car Phone +175
CD Player(Std J30) +290
Leather Seats(G20) +470
Pwr Sunroof (G20) +505
Touring Pkg +1035

DEDUCT FOR ALL 93 INFINITI:

No Auto Trans -585

1992 INFINITI

G20 4 Cyl — 1992

Ratings

Rating	Score
Safety	7.2
Reliability	9.6
Performance	8
Design	7.9
Fun to drive	7.9
Value	7.9
Overall	8.3

AT/PS/AC

Model/Body/Type	BaseList	Whlse	Retail
4 Dr Sdn	19200	**11150**	**13925**

M30 V6 — 1992

Ratings

Rating	Score
Safety	8.5
Reliability	9.5
Performance	7.6
Design	7.7
Fun to drive	7.4
Value	7.2
Overall	8.5

AT/PS/AC

Model/Body/Type	BaseList	Whlse	Retail
2 Dr Cpe	25000	**13975**	**16925**
2 Dr Conv	33000	**20350**	**23825**

Q45 V8 — 1992

Ratings

Rating	Score
Safety	8.8
Reliability	8.5
Performance	8.9
Design	8.3
Fun to drive	8.8
Value	7.2
Overall	8.6

AT/PS/AC

Model/Body/Type	BaseList	Whlse	Retail
4 Dr Q45 Sdn	42000	**23850**	**27600**
4 Dr Q45a Sdn	47000	**25600**	**29475**

ADD FOR ALL 92 INFINITI:

Car Phone +160
CD Player +250
Leather Seats(G20) +410
Pwr Sunroof(G20) +470
Touring Pkg +915

DEDUCT FOR ALL 92 INFINITI:

No Auto Trans -545

1991 INFINITI

G20 4 Cyl — 1991

Ratings

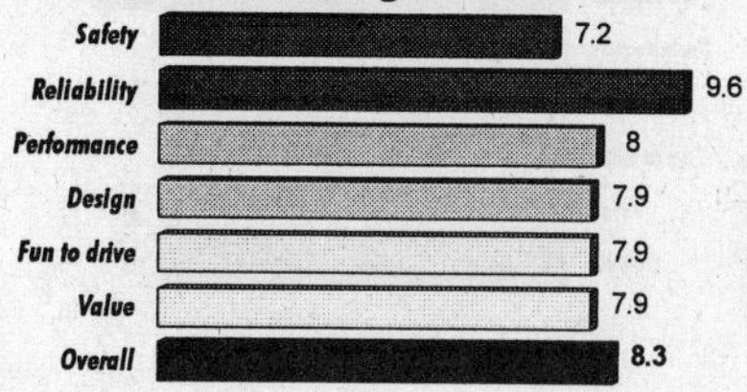

Category	Rating
Safety	7.2
Reliability	9.6
Performance	8
Design	7.9
Fun to drive	7.9
Value	7.9
Overall	8.3

Model/Body/Type	BaseList	Whlse	Retail
AT/PS/AC			
4 Dr Sdn	18300	**9775**	**12300**

M30 V6 — 1991

Ratings

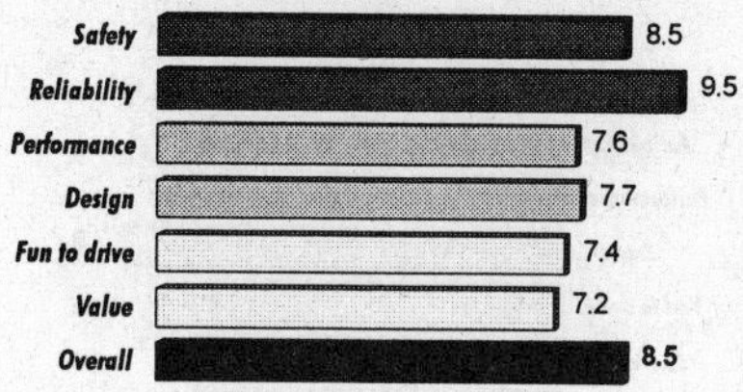

Category	Rating
Safety	8.5
Reliability	9.5
Performance	7.6
Design	7.7
Fun to drive	7.4
Value	7.2
Overall	8.5

Model/Body/Type	BaseList	Whlse	Retail
AT/PS/AC			
2 Dr Cpe	24000	**11525**	**14325**
2 Dr Conv	31000	**17075**	**20300**

Q45 V8 — 1991

Ratings

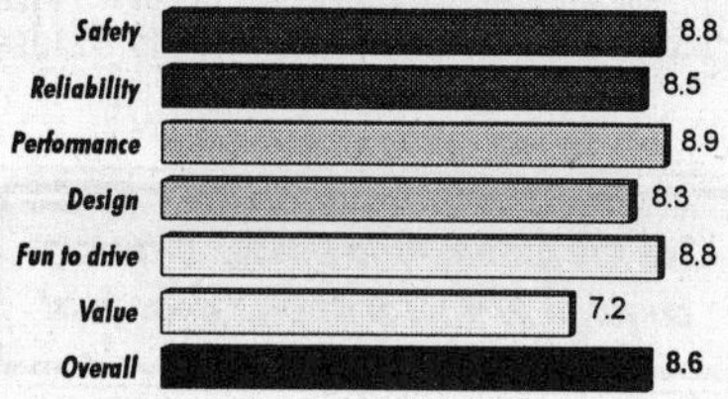

Category	Rating
Safety	8.8
Reliability	8.5
Performance	8.9
Design	8.3
Fun to drive	8.8
Value	7.2
Overall	8.6

Model/Body/Type	BaseList	Whlse	Retail
AT/PS/AC			
4 Dr Sdn	39000	**19525**	**22950**

ADD FOR ALL 91 INFINITI:
Car Phone +135
CD Player +195
Leather Seats(G20) +350
Pwr Sunroof(G20) +430
Touring Pkg +800

DEDUCT FOR ALL 91 INFINITI:
No Auto Trans -505

1990 INFINITI

M30 V6 — 1990

Ratings

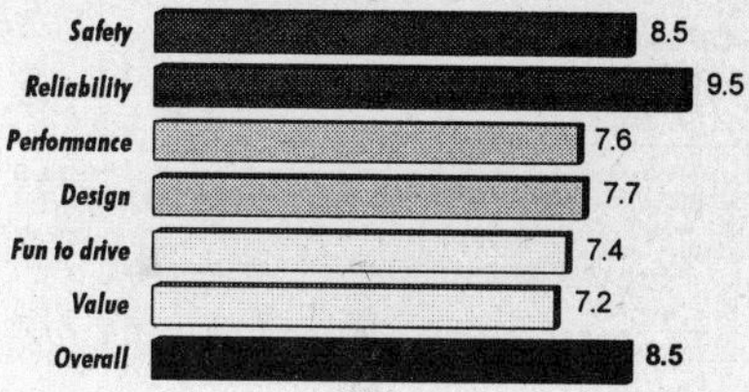

Category	Rating
Safety	8.5
Reliability	9.5
Performance	7.6
Design	7.7
Fun to drive	7.4
Value	7.2
Overall	8.5

Model/Body/Type	BaseList	Whlse	Retail
AT/PS/AC			
2 Dr Cpe	23500	**10150**	**12800**

Q45 V8 — 1990

Ratings

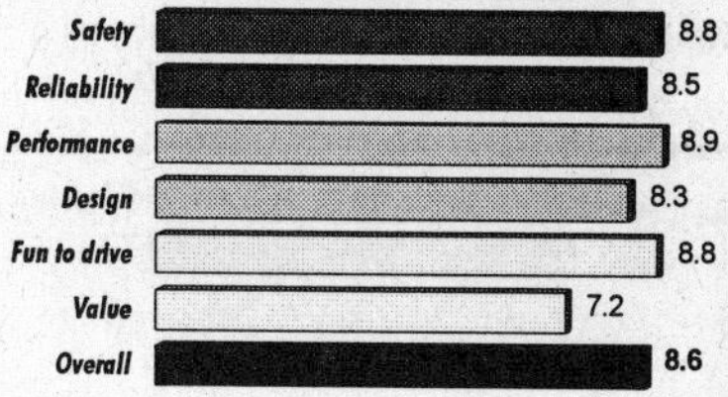

Category	Rating
Safety	8.8
Reliability	8.5
Performance	8.9
Design	8.3
Fun to drive	8.8
Value	7.2
Overall	8.6

Model/Body/Type	BaseList	Whlse	Retail
AT/PS/AC			
4 Dr Sdn	38000	**15600**	**18675**

ADD FOR ALL 90 INFINITI:
CD Player +135
Touring Pkg +700

Model/Body/Type	BaseList	Whlse	Retail

ISUZU

ISUZU

Japan

1990 Isuzu Trooper

For an Isuzu dealer in your area, see our Dealer Directory (pg 217)

1994 ISUZU

AMIGO 4 Cyl 1994

Ratings

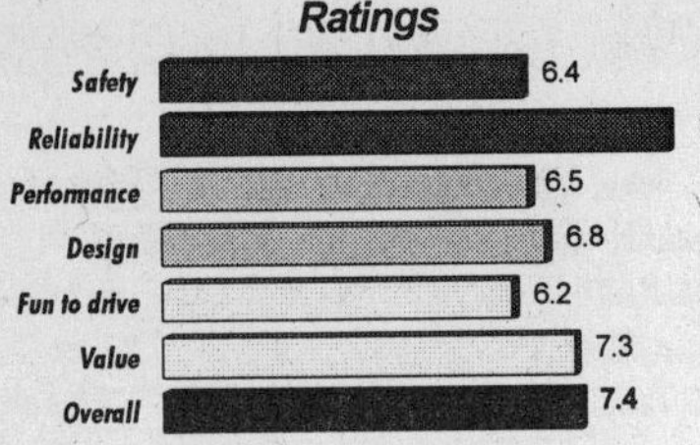

5SP/PS/AC	BaseList	Whlse	Retail
S Utility	14849	12150	14550
XS Utility	15499	-	-
S 4WD Utility	16799	13850	16325
XS 4WD Utility	17199	-	-

PICKUPS 4 Cyl 1994

Ratings

Rating	Score
Safety	6.5
Reliability	8.5
Performance	6.5
Design	7.3
Fun to drive	6.3
Value	7.8
Overall	7.3

5SP/PS/AC	BaseList	Whlse	Retail
S Pkup	9399	8000	9850
S LB Pkup	10809	8125	9975
S Spacecab Pkup	12709	9700	11700
S 4WD Pkup	13519	10725	13000

RODEO 1994

Ratings

Rating	Score
Safety	6.3
Reliability	6.5
Performance	6.7
Design	7.9
Fun to drive	6.3
Value	6.7
Overall	6.6

5SP/PS/AC	BaseList	Whlse	Retail
4 Cyl Models			
4 Dr S Utility	14968	13950	16500
V6 Models			
4 Dr LS Utility (AT)	22729	17850	20750
4 Dr 4WD S Utility	19249	16350	19025
4 Dr 4WD LS Utility	23799	19000	21925

See the Automobile Dealer Directory on page 379 for a Dealer near you!

Model/Body/Type	BaseList	Whlse	Retail

TROOPER V6 — 1994

Ratings

Safety 6.5
Reliability 8.3
Performance 7.4
Design 8.7
Fun to drive 7.1
Value 7.2
Overall 7.6

4WD/AT/PS/AC	BaseList	Whlse	Retail
4 Dr S Utility	21250	**18275**	**21200**
4 Dr LS Utility	26850	**22025**	**25150**
2 Dr RS Utility	24000	**20250**	**23275**

ADD FOR ALL 94 ISUZU:

ABS(Std Trooper LS) +430
Anti-Theft/Recovery Sys +365
Auto Trans (Pkup,Rodeo) +500
Cass(Std Trooper,Rodeo LS) +115
CD Player +230
Cruise Ctrl(Std Rodeo LS,Trooper LS/RS) +160
Custom Whls +205
Pwr Locks(Std Rodeo LS,Trooper LS/RS) +115
Pwr Sunroof +500
Pwr Wndw(Std Rodeo LS,Trooper LS/RS) +160
Sunroof +295
V6 Eng +680

DEDUCT FOR ALL 94 ISUZU:

No AC -635
No Auto Trans -590
No Pwr Steering -180

1993 ISUZU

AMIGO 4 Cyl — 1993

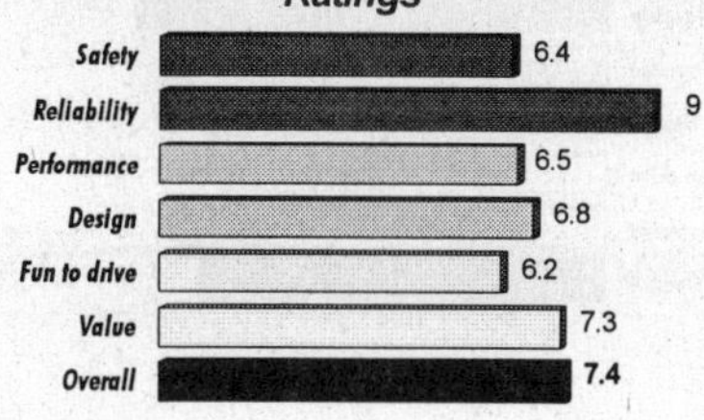

5SP/PS/AC	BaseList	Whlse	Retail
S Utility	11599	**10000**	**12050**
XS Utility	13139	**10775**	**13050**
S 4WD Utility	14649	**11575**	**13900**
XS 4WD Utility	15999	**12350**	**14750**

PICKUPS 4 Cyl — 1993

Ratings

Safety 6.5
Reliability 8.5
Performance 6.5
Design 7.3
Fun to drive 6.3
Value 7.8
Overall 7.3

5SP/PS/AC	BaseList	Whlse	Retail
S Pkup	8999	**6575**	**8200**
S LB Pkup	10099	**6675**	**8425**
S Spacecab Pkup	11549	**8000**	**9850**
S 4WD Pkup	12649	**9025**	**10925**

RODEO — 1993

Ratings

Safety 6.3
Reliability 6.5
Performance 6.7
Design 7.9
Fun to drive 6.3
Value 6.7
Overall 6.6

5SP/PS/AC	BaseList	Whlse	Retail
4 Cyl Models			
4 Dr S Utility	13699	**12350**	**14800**
V6 Models			
4 Dr LS Utility	18999	**14775**	**17350**
4 Dr 4WD S Utility	17899	**14575**	**17150**
4 Dr 4WD LS Utility	20999	**16450**	**19125**

ISUZU 93-92

Model/Body/Type	BaseList	Whlse	Retail

STYLUS 4 Cyl — 1993

Ratings

Safety	7
Reliability	7.7
Performance	8
Design	7
Fun to drive	7.2
Value	7.7
Overall	7.5

Model/Body/Type	BaseList	Whlse	Retail
FWD/AT/PS/AC			
4 Dr S Sdn	9599	**6875**	**8600**

TROOPER V6 — 1993

Ratings

Safety	6.5
Reliability	8.3
Performance	7.4
Design	8.7
Fun to drive	7.1
Value	7.2
Overall	7.6

Model/Body/Type	BaseList	Whlse	Retail
4WD/AT/PS/AC			
4 Dr S Utility	19750	**16525**	**19325**
4 Dr LS Utility	25000	**19650**	**22650**
2 Dr RS Utility	22350	**18175**	**21100**

ADD FOR ALL 93 ISUZU:

Auto Trans (Pkup,Amigo,Rodeo) +430
Bed Liner +125
Cass(Std Trooper,Rodeo LS) +75
CD Player +175
Cruise Ctrl(Std Rodeo LS,Trooper LS/RS) +115
Custom Whls(Std Amigo XS,4WD Rodeo XS, Trooper LS) +160
Fiberglass Cap +250
Luggage Rack +80
Privacy Glass(Std LS Spacecab,Trooper LS) +145
Pwr Locks(Std Rodeo LS,Trooper LS/RS) +75
Pwr Sunroof +315
Pwr Wndw(Std Rodeo LS,Trooper LS/RS) +115
Running Board +145
Slider Wndw +80
Sunroof-Manual +195
Tilt Whl(Std Amigo XS,Rodeo LS) +105
V6 Eng(Std Rodeo 4WD,Trooper) +430

DEDUCT FOR ALL 93 ISUZU:

No AC -470
No AM/FM Radio -105
No Auto Trans -430
No Pwr Steering -160

1992 ISUZU

AMIGO 4 Cyl — 1992

Ratings

Safety	6.4
Reliability	9
Performance	6.5
Design	6.8
Fun to drive	6.2
Value	7.3
Overall	7.4

Model/Body/Type	BaseList	Whlse	Retail
5SP/PS/AC			
S Utility	11099	**8550**	**10400**
XS Utility	12489	**9250**	**11175**
S 4WD Utility	13999	**10000**	**12050**
XS 4WD Utility	15349	**10675**	**12950**

IMPULSE 4 Cyl — 1992

Model/Body/Type	BaseList	Whlse	Retail
FWD/AT/PS/AC			
3 Dr XS Hbk	13099	**8100**	**10000**
3 Dr 2+2 XS Cpe	12499	**7900**	**9825**
2+2 AWD RS Turbo Cpe (5 spd)	15679	**9000**	**11000**

PICKUPS 4 Cyl — 1992

Ratings

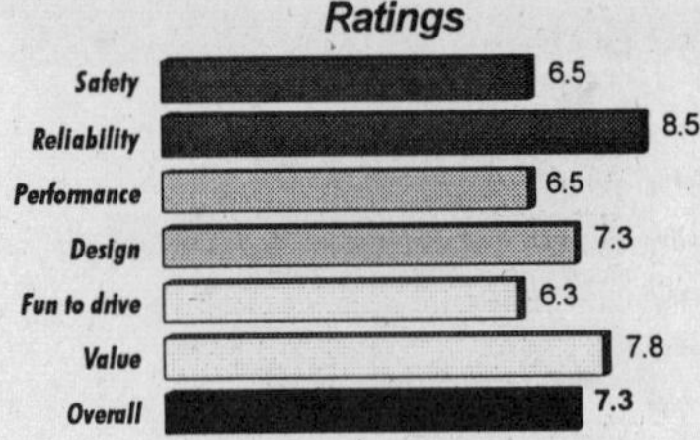

Model/Body/Type	BaseList	Whlse	Retail
5SP/PS/AC			
S Pkup	8349	**5000**	**6525**
S LB Pkup	9399	**5125**	**6650**
S 1 Ton LB Pkup	10639	**5400**	**6950**
S Spacecab Pkup	10439	**6275**	**7875**
LS Spacecab Pkup	13119	**7350**	**9150**
S 4WD Pkup	11879	**7350**	**9150**
LS 4WD Spacecab Pkup	15879	**9700**	**11700**

RODEO 1992

Ratings

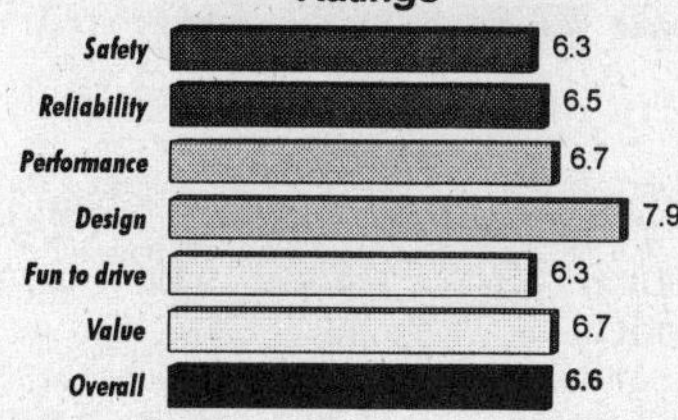

Model/Body/Type	BaseList	Whlse	Retail
5SP/PS/AC			
4 Cyl Models			
4 Dr S Utility	12919	**11300**	**13675**
V6 Models			
4 Dr XS Utility	14779	**12425**	**14900**
4 Dr LS Utility	16089	**13225**	**15725**
4 Dr 4WD S Utility	15549	**13375**	**15900**
4 Dr 4WD XS Utility	17529	**14025**	**16575**
4 Dr 4WD LS Utility	17849	**14775**	**17375**

STYLUS 4 Cyl 1992

Ratings

Safety 7
Reliability 7.7
Performance 8
Design 7
Fun to drive 7.2
Value 7.7
Overall 7.5

Model/Body/Type	BaseList	Whlse	Retail
FWD/AT/PS/AC			
4 Dr S Sdn	9249	**5875**	**7450**
4 Dr RS Sdn (5 spd)	10749	**6250**	**7850**

TROOPER V6 1992

Ratings

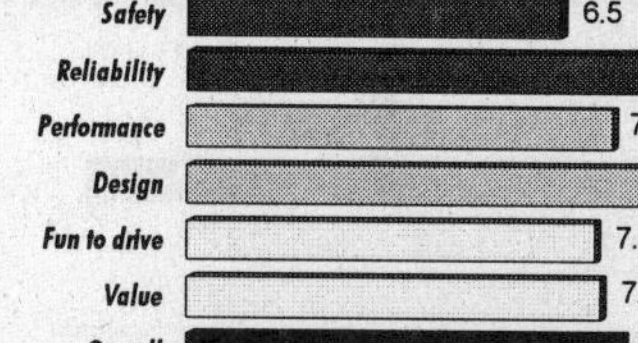

Model/Body/Type	BaseList	Whlse	Retail
4WD/AT/PS/AC			
4 Dr S Utility	18800	**14425**	**17000**
4 Dr LS Utility	24250	**17150**	**19950**

ADD FOR ALL 92 ISUZU:

Auto Trans (Pkup,Amigo,Rodeo) +390
Bed Liner +105
Cass(Std Impulse RS,LS,Trooper) +60
CD Player (Rodeo/Trooper LS) +160
Cruise Ctrl(Std Trooper LS) +100
Custom Whls(Std Amigo XS,4WD Rodeo XS, Impulse RS,Trooper LS) +135
Fiberglass Cap +205
Privacy Glass(Std LS Spacecab,Trooper LS) +125
Pwr Locks(Std Trooper LS) +60
Pwr Sunroof +275
Pwr Wndw(Std Trooper LS) +100
Running Board +125
Sunroof-Manual +160
V6 Eng(Std Rodeo 4WD,Trooper) +390

DEDUCT FOR ALL 92 ISUZU:

No AC -430
No Auto Trans -390
No Pwr Steering -135

1991 ISUZU

AMIGO 4 Cyl 1991

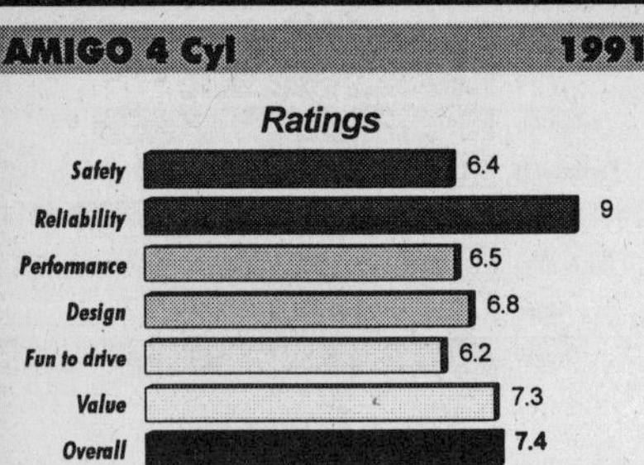

5SP/PS/AC

Model/Body/Type	BaseList	Whlse	Retail
S Utility	9799	6875	8600
XS Utility	11149	7450	9250
S 4WD Utility	12669	8250	10100
XS 4WD Utility	13949	8850	10750

IMPULSE 4 Cyl 1991

FWD/AT/PS/AC

Model/Body/Type	BaseList	Whlse	Retail
3 Dr 2+2 XS Cpe	12049	5825	7525
2+2 AWD RS Turbo Cpe (5 spd)	14849	6875	8700

PICKUPS 4 Cyl 1991

Ratings

Rating	Score
Safety	6.5
Reliability	8.5
Performance	6.5
Design	7.3
Fun to drive	6.3
Value	7.8
Overall	7.3

5SP/PS/AC

Model/Body/Type	BaseList	Whlse	Retail
S Pkup	7979	4300	5725
S LB Pkup	8809	4425	5850
S 1 Ton LB Pkup	9919	4650	6125
S Spacecab Pkup	9769	5400	6950
LS Spacecab Pkup	12249	6425	8025
S 4WD Pkup	11099	6500	8075
LS 4WD Pkup	13999	7450	9250
LS 4WD Spacecab Pkup	14859	8600	10450

RODEO 1991

Ratings

Rating	Score
Safety	6.3
Reliability	6.5
Performance	6.7
Design	7.9
Fun to drive	6.3
Value	6.7
Overall	6.6

5SP/PS/AC

Model/Body/Type	BaseList	Whlse	Retail
4 Cyl Models			
4 Dr S Utility	12499	9900	12050
V6 Models			
4 Dr XS Utility	13949	10900	13250
4 Dr LS Utility	15499	11700	14150
4 Dr 4WD S Utility	14399	11800	14250
4 Dr 4WD XS Utility	16019	12375	14825
4 Dr 4WD LS Utility	16799	13175	15675

STYLUS 4 Cyl 1991

Ratings

Rating	Score
Safety	7
Reliability	7.7
Performance	8
Design	7
Fun to drive	7.2
Value	7.7
Overall	7.5

FWD/AT/PS/AC

Model/Body/Type	BaseList	Whlse	Retail
4 Dr S Sdn	9199	4350	5775
4 Dr XS Sdn (5 spd)	11299	4750	6225

Model/Body/Type	BaseList	Whlse	Retail

TROOPER 1991

Ratings

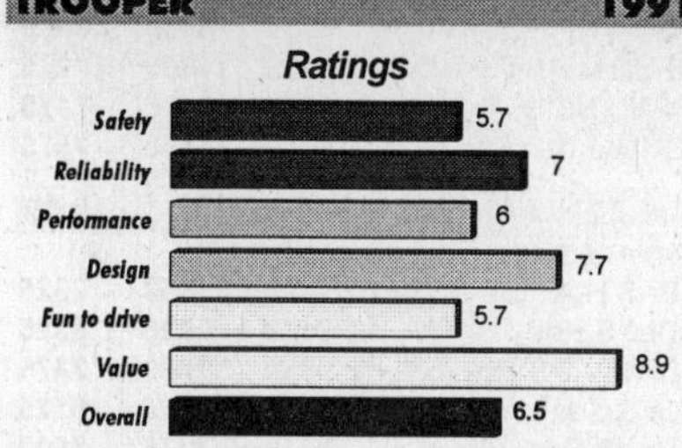

4WD/AT/PS/AC

Model/Body/Type	BaseList	Whlse	Retail
4 Cyl Models			
4 Dr S Utility	13699	**10425**	**12650**
V6 Models			
4 Dr XS Utility	15179	**11475**	**13850**
4 Dr SE Utility	15319	**11525**	**13900**
4 Dr LS Utility	17279	**12150**	**14625**

ADD FOR ALL 91 ISUZU:

ABS (Impulse RS) +315
Auto Trans (Pkup,Rodeo) +350
Bed Liner +80
Cass(Std Trooper,RS,Rodeo/Pkup LS) +35
Cruise Ctrl(Std Trooper LS) +75
Custom Whls(Std 4WD Amigo XS,Impulse RS, 4WD Rodeo XS,Trooper XS/LS) +115
Fiberglass Cap +170
Privacy Glass(Std 2WD LS Spacecb,Trper LS) +105
Pwr Locks(Std Trooper LS) +35
Pwr Sunroof +230
Pwr Wndw(Std Trooper LS) +75
Running Board +105
Sunroof-Manual +115
V6 Eng +350

DEDUCT FOR ALL 91 ISUZU:

No AC -390
No Auto Trans -350
No Pwr Steering -115

1990 ISUZU

AMIGO 4 Cyl 1990

Ratings

Rating	Score
Safety	6.4
Reliability	9
Performance	6.5
Design	6.8
Fun to drive	6.2
Value	7.3
Overall	7.4

5SP/PS/AC

Model/Body/Type	BaseList	Whlse	Retail
S Utility	8999	**5400**	**6950**
XS Utility	10269	**5875**	**7475**
S 4WD Utility	11769	**6700**	**8450**
XS 4WD Utility	12969	**7175**	**8950**

IMPULSE 4 Cyl 1990

FWD/AT/PS/AC

Model/Body/Type	BaseList	Whlse	Retail
3 Dr 2+2 XS Cpe	11999	**5250**	**6950**

PICKUPS 4 Cyl 1990

Ratings

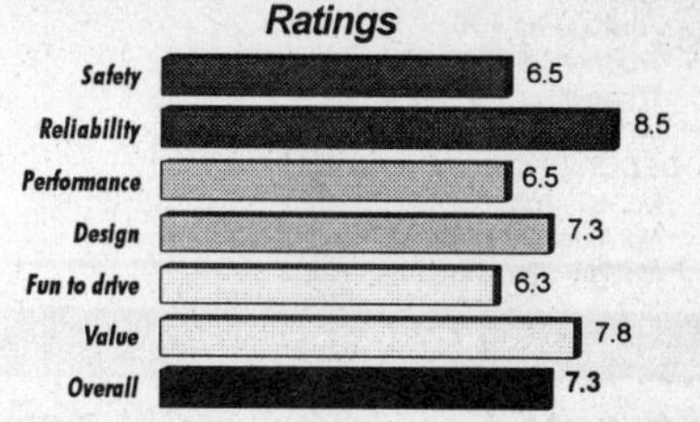

5SP/PS/AC

Model/Body/Type	BaseList	Whlse	Retail
S Pkup	7649	**3625**	**4950**
S LB Pkup	8509	**3750**	**5075**
S 1 Ton LB Pkup	9809	**3950**	**5300**
S Spacecab Pkup	9689	**4625**	**6100**
LS Pkup	10829	**4525**	**5950**
LS Spacecab Pkup	12059	**5500**	**7025**
S 4WD Pkup	10999	**5675**	**7175**
LS 4WD Pkup	13549	**6550**	**8175**
LS 4WD Spacecab Pkup	14679	**7525**	**9325**

ISUZU 90-89

Model/Body/Type	BaseList	Whlse	Retail

TROOPER 4 Cyl — 1990

Ratings

Safety 5.7
Reliability 7
Performance 6
Design 7.7
Fun to drive 5.7
Value 8.9
Overall 6.5

Model/Body/Type	BaseList	Whlse	Retail
4WD/AT/PS/AC			
4 Dr S Utility	13499	7725	9650
2 Dr RS Utility	15349	8000	9925

ADD FOR ALL 90 ISUZU:

Auto Trans (Pkup) +315
Cass(Std Pkup LS,Trooper,Impulse) +35
Cruise Ctrl(Std Trooper RS) +60
Custom Whls +75
Fiberglass Cap +125
Pkup XS Pkg +215
Privacy Glass +80
Pwr Locks +35
Pwr Wndw +60
Running Board +80
Sunroof +100
Towing Pkg +80
Trooper LS Pkg +585
Trooper XS Pkg +315
V6 Eng +315

DEDUCT FOR ALL 90 ISUZU:

No AC -350
No Auto Trans -315
No Pwr Steering -100

1989 ISUZU

AMIGO 4 Cyl — 1989

Ratings

Safety 6.4
Reliability 9
Performance 6.5
Design 6.8
Fun to drive 6.2
Value 7.3
Overall 7.4

Model/Body/Type	BaseList	Whlse	Retail
5SP/PS/AC			
S Utility	8999	4475	5875
XS Utility	10269	4800	6275
S 4WD Utility	11769	5675	7175
XS 4WD Utility	12969	6000	7575

I-MARK 4 Cyl — 1989

Model/Body/Type	BaseList	Whlse	Retail
FWD/AT/PS/AC			
3 Dr S Hbk	7779	1850	2925
3 Dr XS Hbk	9179	2225	3325
3 Dr 16V RS Hbk (5 spd)	9359	2350	3475
4 Dr S Sdn	8179	2025	3125
4 Dr XS Sdn	9379	2375	3500
4 Dr 16V RS Sdn (5 spd)	9559	2525	3675
4 Dr LS Turbo Sdn(5 spd)	11369	2575	3725

IMPULSE 4 Cyl — 1989

Model/Body/Type	BaseList	Whlse	Retail
AT/PS/AC			
2 Dr Sport Cpe	14329	4100	5650
2 Dr Turbo Sport Cpe	16329	4600	6175

PICKUPS 4 Cyl — 1989

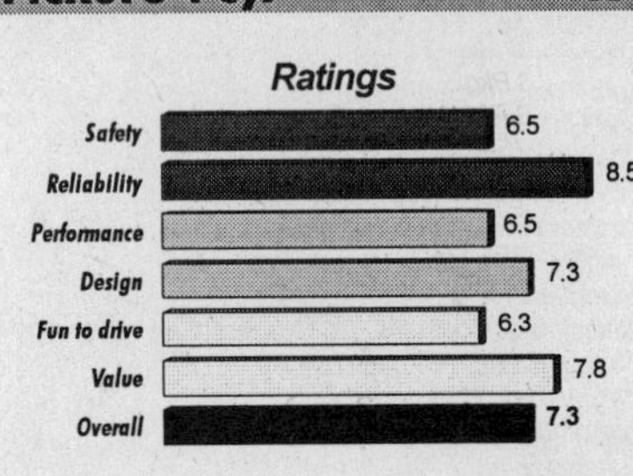

Model/Body/Type	BaseList	Whlse	Retail
5SP/PS/AC			
S Pkup	7649	2675	3850
S LB Pkup	8239	2800	4025
S 1 Ton LB Pkup	9479	2975	4225
LS Pkup	10429	3425	4750
LS Spacecab Pkup	11629	4375	5800
S 4WD Pkup	10579	4525	5950
LS 4WD Spacecab Pkup	14279	6250	7850

Model/Body/Type	BaseList	Whlse	Retail

TROOPER II 4 Cyl — 1989

Ratings

Safety 5.7
Reliability 7
Performance 6
Design 7.7
Fun to drive 5.7
Value 8.9
Overall 6.5

4WD/AT/PS/AC			
4 Dr S Utility	13149	6675	8500
2 Dr RS Utility	14899	6775	8625

ADD FOR ALL 89 ISUZU:
Auto Trans (Pkup) +275
Cass (S,XS) +25
Cruise Ctrl(Std Impulse,Trooper RS) +35
Fiberglass Cap +80
Pkup XS Pkg +160
Sunroof(Std I-Mark LS,Impulse) +75
Trooper LS Pkg +410
Trooper XS Pkg +250
V6 Eng +275
DEDUCT FOR ALL 89 ISUZU:
No AC -315
No Auto Trans -275
No Pwr Steering -75

1988 ISUZU

I-MARK 4 Cyl — 1988

FWD/AT/PS/AC			
3 Dr S Hbk	7439	1550	2525
3 Dr XS Hbk	8779	1825	2900
3 Dr Turbo Hbk (5 spd)	10409	1875	2950
3 Dr RS Turbo Hbk (5 spd)	9829	1850	2925
4 Dr S Sdn	7779	1700	2700
4 Dr XS Sdn	8959	2000	3100
4 Dr Turbo Sdn (5 spd)	10589	2050	3125
4 Dr LS Turbo Sdn (5 spd)	11189	2175	3250

IMPULSE 4 Cyl — 1988

AT/PS/AC			
2 Dr Sport Cpe	13629	2775	4100
2 Dr Turbo Sport Cpe	15529	3150	4550

PICKUPS 4 Cyl — 1988

5SP/PS/AC			
S Pkup	7199	1925	3000
S LB Pkup	7729	2050	3125
S 1 Ton LB Pkup	8999	2175	3250
LS Pkup	10249	2550	3700
LS Spacecab Pkup	11399	3400	4725
S 4WD Pkup	9949	3625	4950
LS 4WD Spacecab Pkup	13499	5150	6650

TROOPER II 4 Cyl — 1988

4WD/AT/PS/AC			
2 Dr S Utility (5 spd)	11909	5050	6725
4 Dr S Utility	12639	5775	7475
4 Dr Limited Utility	14499	6275	8025

ADD FOR ALL 88 ISUZU:
Auto Trans (Pkup) +230
Trooper LS Pkg +350
Trooper LX Pkg +545
Trooper XS Pkg +160
DEDUCT FOR ALL 88 ISUZU:
No AC -250
No Auto Trans -230

1987 ISUZU

I-MARK 4 Cyl — 1987

FWD/AT/PS/AC			
3 Dr S Hbk	7119	1000	1900
3 Dr Hbk	8239	1250	2175
3 Dr RS Turbo Hbk (5 spd)	9999	1300	2225
4 Dr S Sdn	7459	1175	2100
4 Dr Sdn	8419	1375	2325
4 Dr LS Turbo Sdn (5 spd)	10179	1450	2400

IMPULSE 4 Cyl — 1987

5SP/PS/AC			
2 Dr RS Turb Sport Cpe	14639	1925	3100

PICKUPS 4 Cyl — 1987

5SP/PS/AC			
Pkup	6519	1450	2400
LB Pkup	6769	1575	2550
LS Pkup	8469	1900	2975
MPG Diesel Pkup	7339	1000	1900
LB Diesel Pkup	7589	1125	2025
Spacecab Pkup	7719	2225	3325
Dlx Spacecab Pkup (auto)	8969	2650	3825
LS Spacecab Pkup	9969	2700	3875
4WD Pkup	8879	3050	4300
LS 4WD Pkup	10529	3500	4825
LS 4WD Spacecab Pkup	11629	4350	5775

TROOPER II 4 Cyl — 1987

4WD/5SP/PS/AC			
2 Dr Dlx Utility	10809	3425	4850
4 Dr Dlx Utility	11229	3675	5100

DEDUCT FOR ALL 87 ISUZU:
Diesel Eng -390

ISUZU 86-85

1986 ISUZU

Model/Body/Type	BaseList	Whlse	Retail
I-MARK			**1986**
FWD			
4 Dr Sdn	7249	825	1775
2 Dr Hbk	7149	650	1625
IMPULSE			**1986**
5SP/PS/AC			
2 Dr Sport Cpe	10949	1350	2425
2 Dr RS Turb Sport Cpe	13999	1550	2675
PICKUPS			**1986**
Pkup	5789	925	1950
LB Pkup	6279	1050	2075
MPG Diesel Pkup	6819	500	1450
Dlx Pkup	6749	1175	2200
Dlx LB Pkup	6929	1275	2300
Dlx Spacecab Pkup	7429	1825	3025
Dlx 4WD Pkup	8769	2700	4000
Dlx 4WD LB Pkup	8949	2825	4125
Dlx 4WD Spacecab Pkup	9199	3425	4825
TROOPER II			**1986**
4WD			
Dlx Utility	9449	2475	3750

DEDUCT FOR ALL 86 ISUZU:
Diesel Eng -275

1985 ISUZU

Model/Body/Type	BaseList	Whlse	Retail
I-MARK			**1985**
4 Dr Deluxe Sdn	6785	375	1325
4 Dr FWD Sdn	7249	475	1400
2 Dr FWD Hbk	7149	300	1250
IMPULSE			**1985**
2 Dr Sport Cpe	11048	1100	2150
2 Dr Turbo Sport Cpe	13499	1300	2350
PICKUPS			**1985**
Pkup	5775	500	1450
LB Pkup	5930	600	1550
Dlx Pkup	6519	675	1650
Dlx LB Pkup	6674	775	1725
Dlx 4WD Pkup	8189	1725	2900
Dlx 4WD LB Pkup	8344	1800	3000
TROOPER II			**1985**
4WD Utility	8683	1875	3075

JAGUAR

Britain

1988 Jaguar XJS Convertible

For a Jaguar dealer in your area, see our Dealer Directory (pg 217)

1994 JAGUAR

Model/Body/Type	BaseList	Whlse	Retail
XJ6 V6			**1994**
AT/PS/AC			
4 Dr XJ6 Sdn	51750	**37150**	**41650**
4 Dr XJ6 Vanden Plas Sdn	59400	**40500**	**45150**
4 Dr XJ12 Sedan (V12)	71750	**48975**	**53575**
XJS			**1994**
AT/PS/AC			
V6 Models			
2 Dr XJS6 Cpe	51950	-	-
2 Dr XJS6 Conv	59950	-	-
V12 Models			
2 Dr XJS12 Cpe	69950	-	-
2 Dr XJS12 Conv	79950	-	-

ADD FOR ALL 94 JAGUAR:
Anti-Theft/Recovery Sys +365
Car Phone +205
CD Player(Std XJ12) +340
Pwr Sunroof +635
DEDUCT FOR ALL 94 JAGUAR:
No Auto Trans -680

1993 JAGUAR

Model/Body/Type	BaseList	Whlse	Retail
XJ6 V6			**1993**
AT/PS/AC			
4 Dr Sdn	49750	**31300**	**35350**
4 Dr Vanden Plas Sdn	56750	**34000**	**37825**
XJS V12			**1993**
AT/PS/AC			
2 Dr Cpe	49750	**35500**	**39375**
2 Dr Conv	56750	**39125**	**43725**

ADD FOR ALL 93 JAGUAR:
Car Phone +175
CD Player +290
Pwr Sunroof +505
DEDUCT FOR ALL 93 JAGUAR:
No Auto Trans -635

1992 JAGUAR

Model/Body/Type	BaseList	Whlse	Retail
XJ6 V6			**1992**
AT/PS/AC			
4 Dr Sdn	44500	**24025**	**27775**
4 Dr Sovereign Sdn	49500	**26025**	**29925**
4 Dr Vanden Plas Sdn	54500	**28300**	**32325**
4 Dr Majestic Sdn	59500	**30075**	**34150**
XJS V12			**1992**
AT/PS/AC			
2 Dr Cpe	60500	**32400**	**36400**
2 Dr Conv	67500	**35950**	**39850**

ADD FOR ALL 92 JAGUAR:
Car Phone +160
CD Player +250

1991 JAGUAR

Model/Body/Type	BaseList	Whlse	Retail
XJ6 V6			**1991**
AT/PS/AC			
4 Dr Sdn	39900	**17975**	**21300**
4 Dr Sovereign Sdn	44900	**19825**	**23300**
4 Dr Vanden Plas Sdn	49900	**21850**	**25450**
XJS V12			**1991**
AT/PS/AC			
2 Dr Cpe	49900	**22125**	**25775**
2 Dr Conv	59900	**29925**	**34075**

ADD FOR ALL 91 JAGUAR:
Car Phone +135

1990 JAGUAR

Model/Body/Type	BaseList	Whlse	Retail
XJ6 V6			**1990**
AT/PS/AC			
4 Dr Sdn	39700	13975	16925
4 Dr Sovereign Sdn	43000	15625	18700
4 Dr Vanden Plas Sdn	48000	17275	20550
4 Dr Majestic Sdn	53000	18975	22325
XJS V12			**1990**
AT/PS/AC			
2 Dr Cpe	48000	16250	19375
2 Dr Conv	57000	23900	27650

1989 JAGUAR

Model/Body/Type	BaseList	Whlse	Retail
XJ6 V6			**1989**
AT/PS/AC			
4 Dr Sdn	43500	11225	14000
4 Dr Vanden Plas Sdn	47500	12450	15350
XJS V12			**1989**
AT/PS/AC			
2 Dr Cpe	47000	11325	14100
2 Dr Conv	56000	19150	22525

1988 JAGUAR

Model/Body/Type	BaseList	Whlse	Retail
XJ6 V6			**1988**
AT/PS/AC			
4 Dr Sdn	40500	8700	11000
4 Dr Vanden Plas Sdn	44500	9650	12025
XJS V12			**1988**
AT/PS/AC			
2 Dr Cpe	41500	9600	11975
2 Dr Cabriolet Cpe	47450	14100	17025
2 Dr Conv	49000	15000	18025

1987 JAGUAR

Model/Body/Type	BaseList	Whlse	Retail
XJ6 V6			**1987**
AT/PS/AC			
4 Dr Sdn	36300	7750	9975
4 Dr Vanden Plas Sdn	40100	8575	10825
XJS V12			**1987**
AT/PS/AC			
2 Dr Cpe	39700	8775	11100
2 Dr Cabriolet	44850	12975	15850

1986 JAGUAR

Model/Body/Type	BaseList	Whlse	Retail
XJ6			**1986**
4 Dr Sdn	32250	6725	8775
4 Dr Vanden Plas Sdn	35550	7475	9575
XJS			**1986**
2 Dr Cpe	36000	7850	9925

1985 JAGUAR

Model/Body/Type	BaseList	Whlse	Retail
XJ6			**1985**
4 Dr Sdn	32250	5725	7650
4 Dr Vanden Plas Sdn	35550	6375	8350
XJS			**1985**
2 Dr Cpe	36000	7000	9000

See the Automobile Dealer Directory on page 379 for a Dealer near you!

JEEP

USA

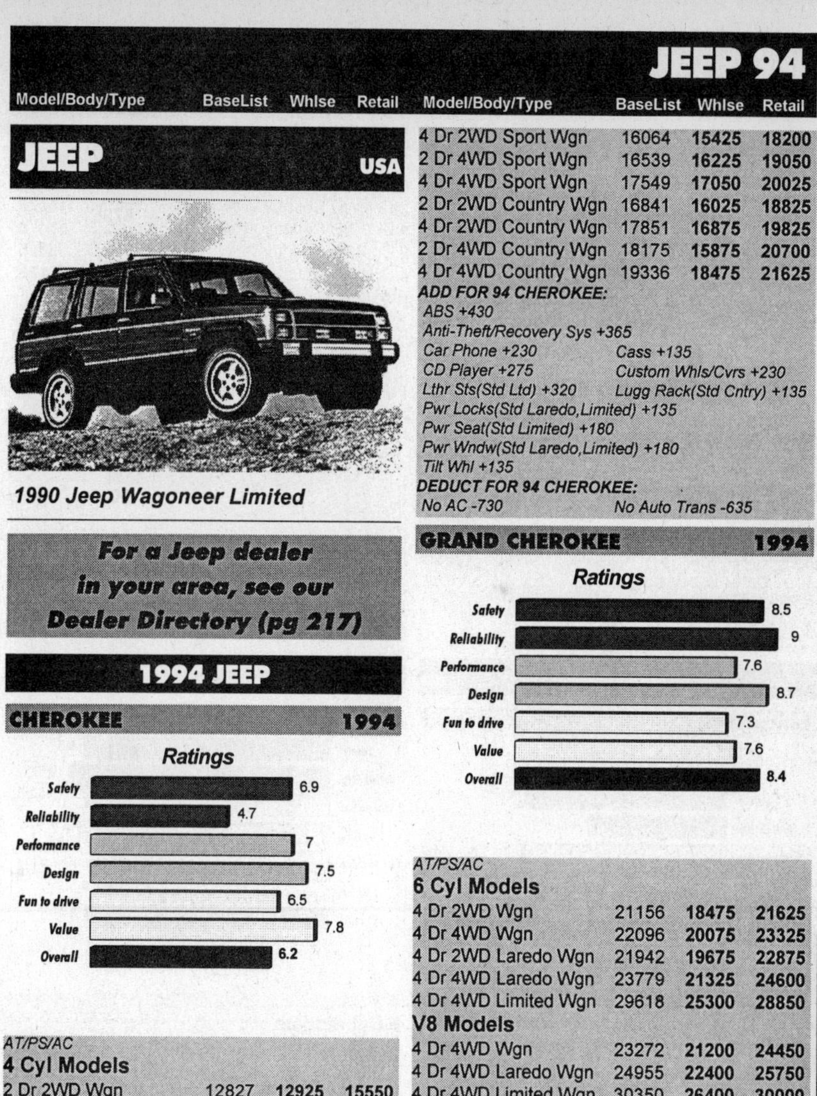

1990 Jeep Wagoneer Limited

For a Jeep dealer in your area, see our Dealer Directory (pg 217)

1994 JEEP

CHEROKEE 1994

Ratings

Rating	Score
Safety	6.9
Reliability	4.7
Performance	7
Design	7.5
Fun to drive	6.5
Value	7.8
Overall	6.2

AT/PS/AC

Model/Body/Type	BaseList	Whlse	Retail
4 Cyl Models			
2 Dr 2WD Wgn	12827	**12925**	**15550**
4 Dr 2WD Wgn	13907	**13775**	**16450**
2 Dr 4WD Wgn	14312	**14550**	**17250**
4 Dr 4WD Wgn	15322	**15375**	**18150**
6 Cyl Models			
2 Dr 2WD Wgn	13439	**13675**	**16350**
4 Dr 2WD Wgn	14519	**14525**	**17225**
2 Dr 4WD Wgn	14924	**15275**	**18050**
4 Dr 4WD Wgn	15934	**16125**	**18950**
2 Dr 2WD Sport Wgn	15054	**14600**	**17300**
4 Dr 2WD Sport Wgn	16064	**15425**	**18200**
2 Dr 4WD Sport Wgn	16539	**16225**	**19050**
4 Dr 4WD Sport Wgn	17549	**17050**	**20025**
2 Dr 2WD Country Wgn	16841	**16025**	**18825**
4 Dr 2WD Country Wgn	17851	**16875**	**19825**
2 Dr 4WD Country Wgn	18175	**15875**	**20700**
4 Dr 4WD Country Wgn	19336	**18475**	**21625**

ADD FOR 94 CHEROKEE:

ABS +430
Anti-Theft/Recovery Sys +365
Car Phone +230 *Cass +135*
CD Player +275 *Custom Whls/Cvrs +230*
Lthr Sts(Std Ltd) +320 *Lugg Rack(Std Cntry) +135*
Pwr Locks(Std Laredo,Limited) +135
Pwr Seat(Std Limited) +180
Pwr Wndw(Std Laredo,Limited) +180
Tilt Whl +135

DEDUCT FOR 94 CHEROKEE:

No AC -730 *No Auto Trans -635*

GRAND CHEROKEE 1994

Ratings

Rating	Score
Safety	8.5
Reliability	9
Performance	7.6
Design	8.7
Fun to drive	7.3
Value	7.6
Overall	8.4

AT/PS/AC

Model/Body/Type	BaseList	Whlse	Retail
6 Cyl Models			
4 Dr 2WD Wgn	21156	**18475**	**21625**
4 Dr 4WD Wgn	22096	**20075**	**23325**
4 Dr 2WD Laredo Wgn	21942	**19675**	**22875**
4 Dr 4WD Laredo Wgn	23779	**21325**	**24600**
4 Dr 4WD Limited Wgn	29618	**25300**	**28850**
V8 Models			
4 Dr 4WD Wgn	23272	**21200**	**24450**
4 Dr 4WD Laredo Wgn	24955	**22400**	**25750**
4 Dr 4WD Limited Wgn	30350	**26400**	**30000**

ADD FOR 94 GRAND CHEROKEE:

Anti-Theft/Recovery Sys +365
Car Phone +230 *CD Player +275*
Cruise Ctrl +180
Custom Whls/Cvrs +230 *Lthr Seats(Std Ltd) +320*
Pwr Locks(Std Laredo,Limited) +135
Pwr Seat(Std Limited) +180
Pwr Wndw(Std Laredo,Limited) +180

DEDUCT FOR 94 GRAND CHEROKEE:

No AC -730 *No Auto Trans -635*

Model/Body/Type	BaseList	Whlse	Retail

WRANGLER 6 Cyl — 1994

Ratings

Rating	Score
Safety	6.2
Reliability	5
Performance	6.3
Design	7.2
Fun to drive	7
Value	7.1
Overall	6

4WD/5SP/PS

Model/Body/Type	BaseList	Whlse	Retail
Jeep S (4 cyl)	11390	-	-
Jeep	14454	**13325**	**16050**
Jeep Sahara	16877	**14175**	**16950**
Jeep Renegade	18706	**14750**	**17550**

ADD FOR 94 WRANGLER:

4 Whl ABS +430 | *AC +730*
Auto Trans +500 | *Hard Top +590*
Sport Pkg +410

1993 JEEP

CHEROKEE — 1993

Ratings

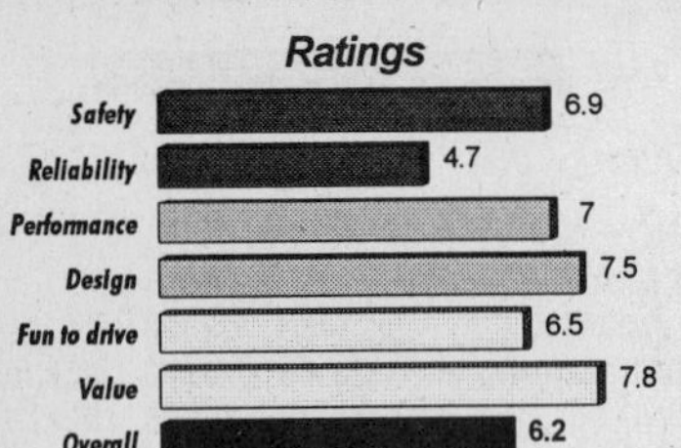

AT/PS/AC

Model/Body/Type	BaseList	Whlse	Retail
4 Cyl Models			
2 Dr 2WD Wgn	12137	**11225**	**13675**
4 Dr 2WD Wgn	13147	**11975**	**14550**
2 Dr 4WD Wgn	13622	**12750**	**15350**
4 Dr 4WD Wgn	14632	**13500**	**16150**
6 Cyl Models			
2 Dr 2WD Wgn	12749	**11925**	**14500**
4 Dr 2WD Wgn	13759	**12650**	**15250**
2 Dr 4WD Wgn	14234	**13450**	**16100**
4 Dr 4WD Wgn	15244	**14200**	**16900**
2 Dr 2WD Sport Wgn	14350	**12750**	**15350**
4 Dr 2WD Sport Wgn	15360	**13500**	**16150**
2 Dr 4WD Sport Wgn	15835	**14300**	**17000**
4 Dr 4WD Sport Wgn	16845	**15000**	**17750**
2 Dr 2WD Country Wgn	16038	**14050**	**16725**
4 Dr 2WD Country Wgn	17048	**14775**	**17475**
2 Dr 4WD Country Wgn	17523	**15550**	**18325**
4 Dr 4WD Country Wgn	18533	**16300**	**19125**

ADD FOR 93 CHEROKEE:

ABS +390
Car Phone +175
Cass(Std Laredo,Ltd) +115
CD Player +230
Cruise Ctrl(Std Laredo,Limited) +160
Custom Whls/Cvrs(Std Country,Laredo,Limited) +195
Leather Seats(Std Limited) +275
Luggage Rack(Std Country,Laredo,Limited) +100
Privacy Glass(Std Limited) +145
Pwr Locks(Std Limited) +115
Pwr Seat(Std Limited) +160
Pwr Wndw(Std Laredo,Limited) +160
Running Boards +145
Sunroof-Manual +145
Tilt Whl(Std Laredo,Limited) +115
Towing Pkg +185

DEDUCT FOR 93 CHEROKEE:

No AC -585 | *No Auto Trans -545*

GRAND CHEROKEE — 1993

Ratings

Rating	Score
Safety	8.5
Reliability	9
Performance	7.6
Design	8.7
Fun to drive	7.3
Value	7.6
Overall	8.4

AT/PS/AC

Model/Body/Type	BaseList	Whlse	Retail
6 Cyl Models			
4 Dr 2WD Wgn	18890	**16500**	**19325**
4 Dr 4WD Wgn	19700	**18000**	**21075**
4 Dr 2WD Laredo Wgn	20074	**17500**	**20550**
4 Dr 4WD Laredo Wgn	20884	**19050**	**22175**
4 Dr 4WD Limited Wgn	28440	**22600**	**25975**
V8 Models			
4 Dr 4WD Wgn	20844	**19050**	**22175**
4 Dr 4WD Laredo Wgn	22028	**20050**	**23300**
4 Dr 4WD Limited Wgn	29584	**23650**	**27075**

ADD FOR 93 GRAND CHEROKEE:

Car Phone +175
Cass(Std Laredo,Ltd) +115
CD Player +230
Cruise Ctrl(Std Laredo,Limited) +160
Custom Whls/Cvrs(Std Country,Laredo,Limited) +195
Leather Seats(Std Limited) +275
Luggage Rack(Std Country,Laredo,Limited) +100
Privacy Glass(Std Limited) +145
Pwr Locks(Std Limited) +115
Pwr Seat(Std Limited) +160
Pwr Wndw(Std Laredo,Limited) +160
Running Boards +145
Sunroof-Manual +145
Tilt Whl(Std Laredo,Limited) +115
Towing Pkg +185

DEDUCT FOR 93 GRAND CHEROKEE:

No AC -585 *No Auto Trans -545*

WRANGLER 6 Cyl 1993

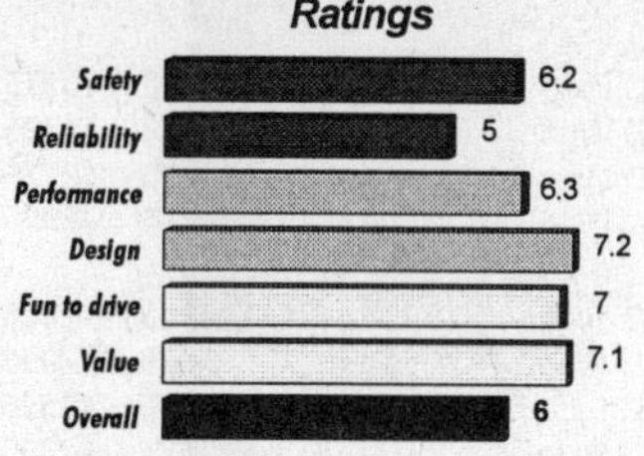

4WD/5SP/PS

Model/Body/Type	BaseList	Whlse	Retail
Jeep	13955	**11850**	**14500**
Jeep (4 cyl)	13343	**11300**	**13850**
Jeep S (4 cyl)	10925	**9525**	**11775**

ADD FOR 93 WRANGLER:

4 Whl ABS +390 *AC +585*
Auto Trans +390 *Cass +105*
Cust Whls(Std Ren) +145 *Hard Top +505*
Renegade Pkg +1015 *Sahara Pkg +585*
Sport Pkg +315 *Tilt Whl +105*

DEDUCT FOR 93 WRANGLER:

No AM/FM Radio -105 *No Pwr Steering -185*

1992 JEEP

CHEROKEE 1992

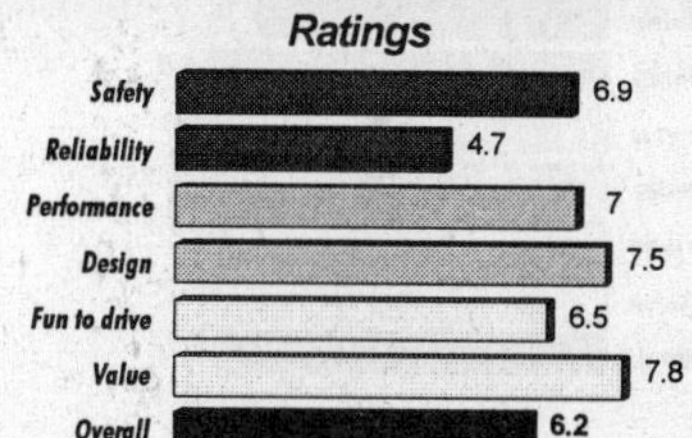

AT/PS/AC

Model/Body/Type	BaseList	Whlse	Retail
Cherokee 4 Cyl			
2 Dr 2WD Wgn	14346	**9925**	**12150**
4 Dr 2WD Wgn	15357	**10575**	**12875**
2 Dr 4WD Wgn	15832	**11325**	**13775**
4 Dr 4WD Wgn	16842	**12000**	**14550**
Cherokee 6 Cyl			
2 Dr 2WD Wgn	14458	**10500**	**12825**
4 Dr 2WD Wgn	15469	**11175**	**13625**
4 Dr 2WD Laredo Wgn	16550	**12600**	**15200**
2 Dr 4WD Wgn	15944	**11950**	**14525**
4 Dr 4WD Wgn	16954	**12600**	**15200**
2 Dr 4WD Laredo Wgn	18036	**13375**	**16025**
4 Dr 4WD Laredo Wgn	19046	**14050**	**16725**
4 Dr 4WD Limited Wgn	25334	**16400**	**19225**
4 Dr 4WD Briarwd Wgn	24799	**15900**	**18700**

ADD FOR 92 CHEROKEE:

ABS +350
Car Phone +160
Cass(Std Ltd,Briar) +100
CruiseCtrl(Std Limited,Briarwood) +135
Custom Whls/Cvrs(Std Sport,Laredo,Ltd,Briar) +175
Leather Seats(Std Limited,Briarwood) +230
Luggage Rack(Std Limited,Briarwood,Laredo) +75
Privacy Glass(Std Limited,Briarwood) +125
Pwr Locks(Std Limited,Briarwood) +100
Pwr Seat(Std Limited,Briarwood) +135
Pwr Wndw(Std Limited,Briarwood) +135
Run Boards +125 *Sport Pkg +290*
Sunroof +215 *Tilt Whl(Std Ltd,Briar) +100*
Towing Pkg +145

DEDUCT FOR 92 CHEROKEE:

No AC -545 *No Auto Trans -505*

COMANCHE 6 Cyl — 1992

Ratings

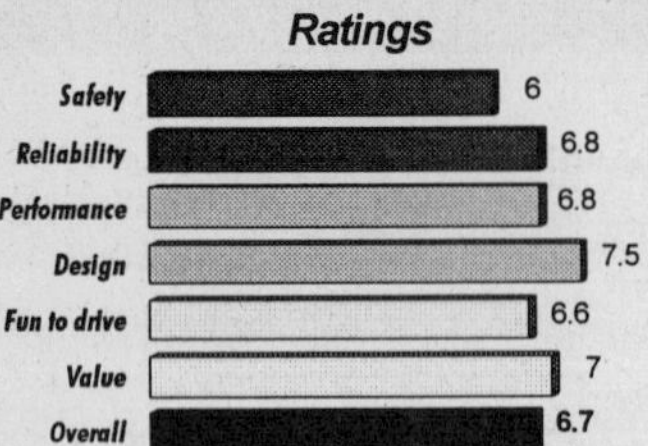

Model/Body/Type	BaseList	Whlse	Retail
AT/PS/AC			
Pkup	9329	**7075**	**9100**
LB Pkup	10026	**7150**	**9200**

ADD FOR 92 COMANCHE:
4-Whl Drive +1200 · *Bed Liner +105* · *Cass +80* · *Cruise Ctrl +80* · *Cust Whls(Std Sport) +125* · *Eliminator Pkg +545* · *Fiberglass Cap +205* · *Pioneer Pkg +350* · *Running Boards +125* · *Sport Pkg +195* · *Sunroof-Manual +105*

DEDUCT FOR 92 COMANCHE:
4 Cyl Eng -390 · *No AC -375* · *No Auto Trans -330* · *No Pwr Steering -145*

WRANGLER 6 Cyl — 1992

Ratings

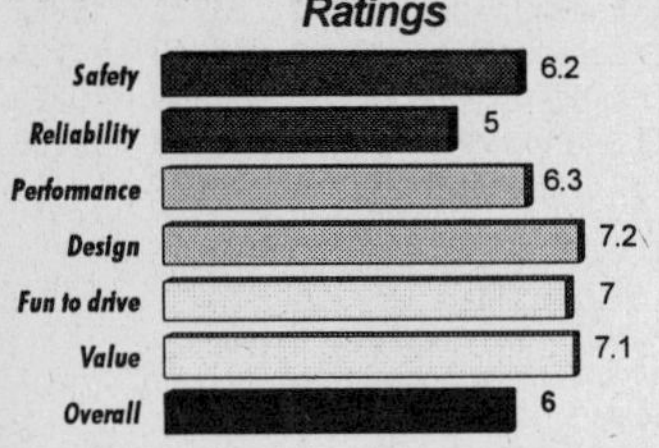

Model/Body/Type	BaseList	Whlse	Retail
4WD/5SP/PS			
Jeep	13451	**10575**	**12950**
Jeep (4 cyl)	12839	**10075**	**12400**
Jeep S (4 cyl)	10393	**8425**	**10525**

ADD FOR 92 WRANGLER:
AC +545 · *Auto Trans +350* · *Cass +80* · *Custom Whls(Std Ren) +125* · *Hard Top +470* · *Islander Pkg +315* · *Renegade Pkg +935* · *Sahara Pkg +545*

DEDUCT FOR 92 WRANGLER:
No Pwr Steering -145

CHEROKEE — 1991

Ratings

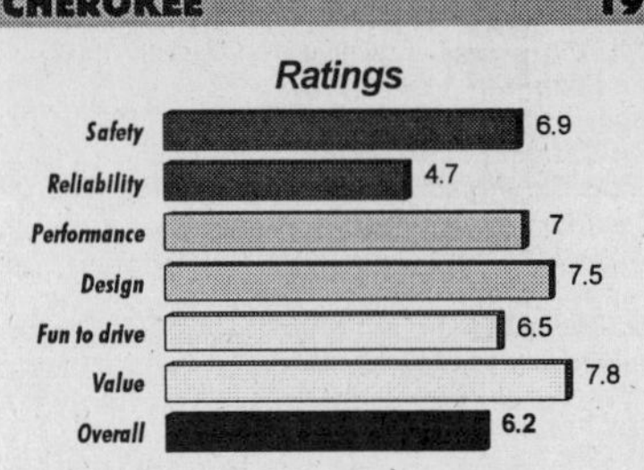

Model/Body/Type	BaseList	Whlse	Retail
AT/PS/AC			
Cherokee 4 Cyl			
2 Dr 2WD Wgn	13822	**8700**	**10775**
4 Dr 2WD Wgn	14699	**9300**	**11425**
2 Dr 4WD Wgn	15267	**10000**	**12275**
4 Dr 4WD Wgn	16144	**10575**	**12900**
Cherokee 6 Cyl			
2 Dr 2WD Wgn	14434	**9250**	**11350**
4 Dr 2WD Wgn	15311	**9825**	**12050**
4 Dr 2WD Laredo Wgn	15759	**11075**	**13525**
2 Dr 4WD Wgn	15879	**10525**	**12850**
4 Dr 4WD Wgn	16756	**11125**	**13575**
2 Dr 4WD Laredo Wgn	16996	**11800**	**14400**
4 Dr 4WD Laredo Wgn	17379	**12400**	**15000**
4 Dr 4WD Limited Wgn	25231	**14675**	**17375**
4 Dr 4WD Briarwd Wgn	24710	**14200**	**16900**

ADD FOR 91 CHEROKEE:
ABS +315 · *Car Phone +135* · *Cass(Std Ltd,Briar) +75* · *Cruise Ctrl(Std Ltd,Bri) +115* · *Custom Whls(Std Sport,Laredo,Ltd,Briar) +160* · *Lthr Seats(Std Ltd,Br) +170* · *Luggage Rack(Std Limited,Briarwood,Laredo) +60* · *Privacy Glass(Std Ltd,Br) +105* · *Pwr Sunroof +430* · *Pwr Locks(Std Limited,Briarwood) +75* · *Pwr Seats(Std Limited,Briarwood) +115* · *Pwr Wndw(Std Ltd) +115* · *Running Boards +105* · *Sport Pkg +250* · *Sunroof +175* · *Tilt Whl(Std Ltd,Briar) +75* · *Towing Pkg +105*

DEDUCT FOR 91 CHEROKEE:
No AC -505 · *No Auto Trans -470*

See the Automobile Dealer Directory on page 379 for a Dealer near you!

JEEP

COMANCHE 6 Cyl — 1991

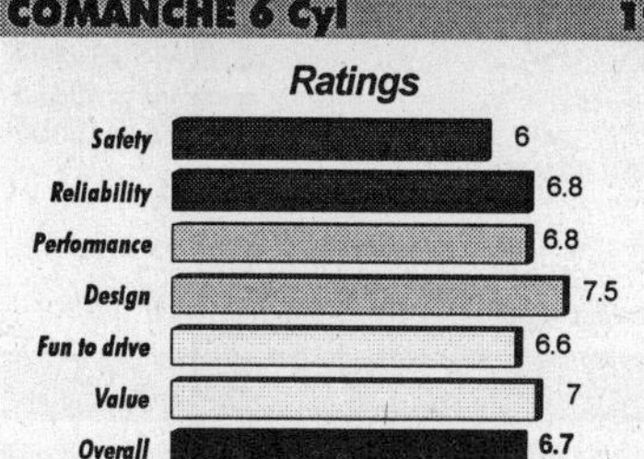

Model/Body/Type	BaseList	Whlse	Retail
AT/PS/AC			
Pkup	8537	**5600**	**7475**
LB Pkup	9454	**5725**	**7575**

ADD FOR 91 COMANCHE:
4-Whl Drive +1140 · *Bed Liner +80*
Cust Whls(Std Elim) +105 · *Eliminator Pkg +505*
Fiberglass Cap +170 · *Pioneer Pkg +275*
Running Boards +105 · *Sunroof-Manual +80*
Towing Pkg +105

DEDUCT FOR 91 COMANCHE:
4 Cyl Eng -350 · *No AC -315*
No Auto Trans -250 · *No Pwr Steering -105*

GRAND WAGONEER V8 — 1991

Model/Body/Type	BaseList	Whlse	Retail
4WD/AT/PS/AC			
4 Dr Wgn	29065	**12075**	**14675**

ADD FOR 91 GRAND WAGONEER:
Car Phone +135 · *Pwr Sunroof +390*
Running Boards +105 · *Sunroof +175*
Towing Pkg +105

WRANGLER 6 Cyl — 1991

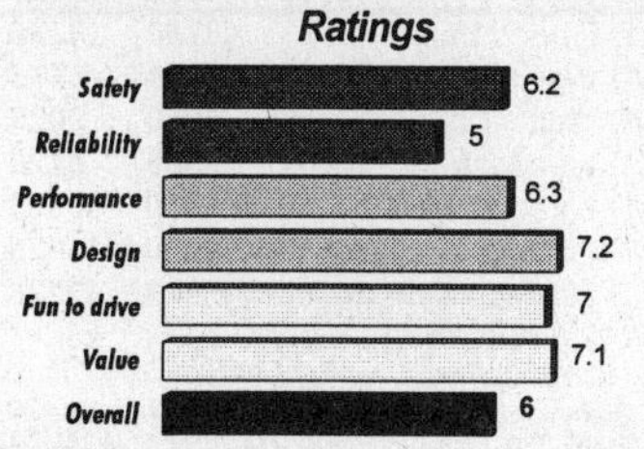

Model/Body/Type	BaseList	Whlse	Retail
4WD/5SP/PS			
Jeep	12800	**9525**	**11775**
Jeep (4 cyl)	12188	**9075**	**11275**
Jeep S (4 cyl)	9890	**7525**	**9600**

ADD FOR 91 WRANGLER:
AC +505 · *Auto Trans +315*
Cust Whls(Std Ren) +105 · *Hard Top +430*
Islander Pkg +275 · *Renegade Pkg +860*
Sahara Pkg +505

DEDUCT FOR 91 WRANGLER:
No Pwr Steering -105

1990 JEEP

CHEROKEE — 1990

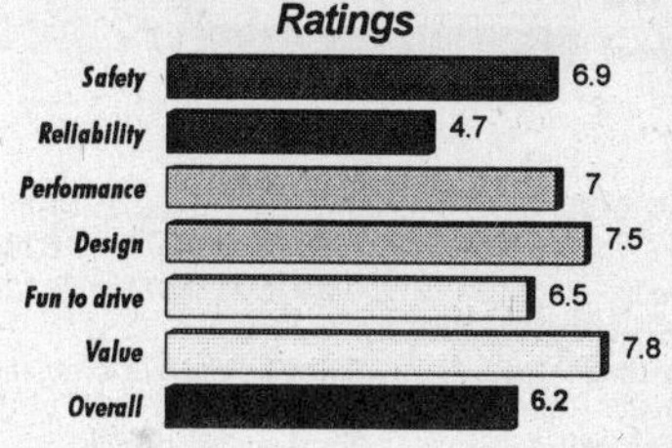

Model/Body/Type	BaseList	Whlse	Retail
AT/PS/AC			
Cherokee 4 Cyl			
2 Dr 2WD Wgn	13295	**6375**	**8275**
4 Dr 2WD Wgn	14145	**6875**	**8825**
2 Dr 4WD Wgn	14695	**7600**	**9650**
4 Dr 4WD Wgn	15545	**8100**	**10150**
Cherokee 6 Cyl			
2 Dr 2WD Wgn	13895	**6875**	**8825**
4 Dr 2WD Wgn	14745	**7350**	**9375**
4 Dr 2WD Laredo Wgn	17535	**8525**	**10575**
2 Dr 4WD Wgn	15295	**8100**	**10150**
4 Dr 4WD Wgn	16145	**8600**	**10650**
2 Dr 4WD Laredo Wgn	18085	**9275**	**11375**
4 Dr 4WD Laredo Wgn	18935	**9775**	**12000**
2 Dr 4WD Limited Wgn	24650	**11425**	**13850**
4 Dr 4WD Limited Wgn	25775	**11900**	**14475**

ADD FOR 90 CHEROKEE:
ABS +275 · *Cass(Std Ltd) +75*
Cruise Ctrl(Std Ltd) +100
Custom Whls/Cvrs(Std Laredo,Limited) +115
Lthr Seats(Std Ltd) +125 · *Lugg Rack(Std Ltd,Lar) +35*
Pioneer Pkg +250 · *Privacy Glass(Std Ltd) +80*
Pwr Locks(Std Ltd) +60 · *Pwr Seat(Std Ltd) +100*
Pwr Sunroof +350 · *Pwr Wndw(Std Ltd) +100*
Running Boards +80 · *Sport Pkg +195*
Sunroof +135 · *Tilt Whl(Std Ltd) +60*
Towing Pkg +80

DEDUCT FOR 90 CHEROKEE:
No AC -470 · *No Auto Trans -430*

JEEP 90-89

COMANCHE 6 Cyl — 1990

Ratings

Safety 6
Reliability 6.8
Performance 6.8
Design 7.5
Fun to drive 6.6
Value 7
Overall 6.7

Model/Body/Type	BaseList	Whlse	Retail
AT/PS/AC			
Pkup	8095	**4475**	**6200**
LB Pkup	8975	**4575**	**6325**

ADD FOR 90 COMANCHE:
4-Whl Drive +1080 · *Custom Whls(Std Elim) +80* · *Eliminator Pkg +430* · *Fiberglass Cap +125* · *Pioneer Pkg +195* · *Running Boards +80* · *Towing Pkg +80*

DEDUCT FOR 90 COMANCHE:
4 Cyl Eng -275 · *No AC -250* · *No Auto Trans -165*

WAGONEER — 1990

Model/Body/Type	BaseList	Whlse	Retail
4WD/AT/PS/AC			
Wagoneer 6 Cyl			
4 Dr Limited Wgn	24795	**11050**	**13475**
Grand Wagoneer V8			
4 Dr Wgn	27795	**8900**	**11000**

ADD FOR 90 WAGONEER:
ABS +275 · *Cass(Std GrWgnr) +75* · *Privacy Glass +80* · *Pwr Sunroof +350* · *Running Boards +80* · *Sunroof +135* · *Towing Pkg +80*

WRANGLER 6 Cyl — 1990

Ratings

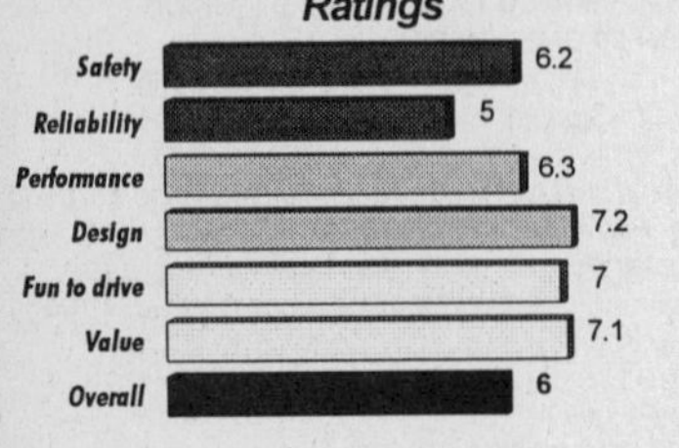

Model/Body/Type	BaseList	Whlse	Retail
4WD/5SP/PS			
Jeep	12029	**8100**	**10175**
Jeep (4 cyl)	11599	**7750**	**9825**
Jeep S (4 cyl)	9393	**6375**	**8300**

ADD FOR 90 WRANGLER:
AC +470 · *Auto Trans +275* · *Custom Whls(Std Islander,Laredo) +80* · *Hard Top +350* · *Islander Pkg +230* · *Laredo Pkg +700* · *Sahara Pkg +430*

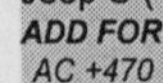

1989 JEEP

CHEROKEE — 1989

Ratings

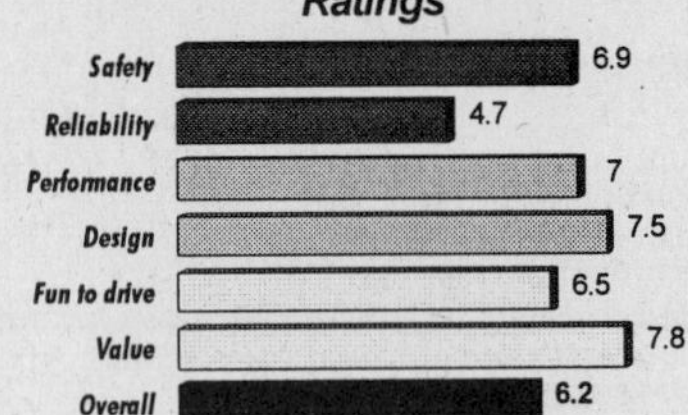

Model/Body/Type	BaseList	Whlse	Retail
AT/PS/AC			
Cherokee 4 Cyl			
2 Dr 2WD Wgn	12315	**4925**	**6725**
4 Dr 2WD Wgn	12950	**5425**	**7275**
2 Dr 4WD Wgn	13657	**6125**	**7975**
4 Dr 4WD Wgn	14293	**6600**	**8525**
Cherokee 6 Cyl			
2 Dr 2WD Wgn	12928	**5375**	**7225**
4 Dr 2WD Wgn	13563	**5875**	**7750**
4 Dr 2WD Laredo Wgn	16123	**6750**	**8725**
2 Dr 4WD Wgn	14270	**6550**	**8475**
4 Dr 4WD Wgn	14906	**7050**	**9025**
2 Dr 4WD Laredo Wgn	16652	**7400**	**9425**
4 Dr 4WD Laredo Wgn	17466	**7900**	**9950**
2 Dr 4WD Limited Wgn	23130	**9500**	**11625**
4 Dr 4WD Limited Wgn	24058	**9975**	**12225**

ADD FOR 89 CHEROKEE:
Cass(Std Ltd) +60 · *Cruise Ctrl(Std Ltd) +75* · *Custom Whls/Cvrs +75* · *Lugg Rack(Std Ltd,Lar) +20* · *Pioneer Pkg +230* · *Pwr Locks(Std Ltd) +35* · *Pwr Seat(Std Ltd) +75* · *Pwr Sunroof +290* · *Pwr Wndw(Std Ltd) +75* · *Sport Pkg +135* · *Sunroof +115* · *Tilt Whl(Std Ltd) +35*

DEDUCT FOR 89 CHEROKEE:
No AC -430 · *No Auto Trans -390*

Model/Body/Type	BaseList	Whlse	Retail

COMANCHE 6 Cyl 1989

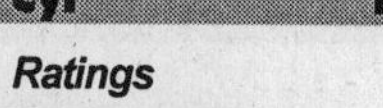

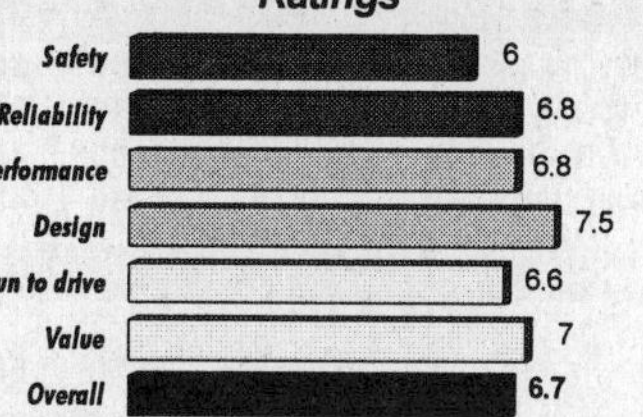

AT/PS/AC

Model/Body/Type	BaseList	Whlse	Retail
Pkup	8259	**3475**	**5025**
LB Pkup	9076	**3575**	**5150**

ADD FOR 89 COMANCHE:
Eliminator Pkg +390 *Pioneer Pkg +75*
DEDUCT FOR 89 COMANCHE:
4 Cyl Eng -230

WAGONEER 1989

4WD/AT/PS/AC

Model/Body/Type	BaseList	Whlse	Retail
Wagoneer 6 Cyl			
4 Dr Limited Wgn	23220	**9200**	**11300**
Grand Wagoneer V8			
4 Dr Wgn	26395	**7050**	**9025**

ADD FOR 89 WAGONEER:
Cass(Std GrWgnr) +60 *Custom Whls/Cvrs +75*
Pwr Sunroof +290 *Sunroof +115*
DEDUCT FOR 89 WAGONEER:
No AC -430 *No Auto Trans -390*

WRANGLER 6 Cyl 1989

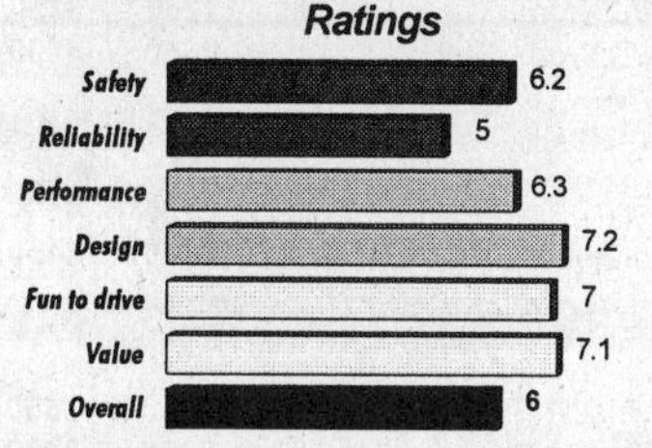

4WD/5SP/PS

Model/Body/Type	BaseList	Whlse	Retail
Jeep	11869	**7050**	**9075**
Jeep (4 cyl)	11452	**6725**	**8725**
Jeep S (4 cyl)	8995	**5525**	**7400**

ADD FOR 89 WRANGLER:
AC +390 *Auto Trans +230*
Hard Top +275 *Islander Pkg +160*
Laredo Pkg +545 *Sahara Pkg +350*

1988 JEEP

CHEROKEE 1988

AT/PS/AC

Model/Body/Type	BaseList	Whlse	Retail
Cherokee 4 Cyl			
2 Dr 2WD Wgn	11063	**3500**	**5075**
4 Dr 2WD Wgn	11675	**3950**	**5600**
2 Dr 4WD Wgn	12415	**4550**	**6250**
4 Dr 4WD Wgn	13027	**4950**	**6750**
Cherokee 6 Cyl			
2 Dr 2WD Wgn	11590	**3900**	**5550**
4 Dr 2WD Wgn	12202	**4350**	**6050**
2 Dr 4WD Wgn	12942	**4900**	**6700**
4 Dr 4WD Wgn	13554	**5350**	**7200**
2 Dr 4WD Limited Wgn	22260	**7500**	**9525**
4 Dr 4WD Limited Wgn	23153	**7950**	**9975**

ADD FOR 88 CHEROKEE:
Chief Pkg +315 *Laredo Pkg +530*
DEDUCT FOR 88 CHEROKEE:
No AC -370 *No Auto Trans -350*
No Pwr Steering -100

COMANCHE 6 Cyl 1988

AT/PS/AC

Model/Body/Type	BaseList	Whlse	Retail
Pkup	6995	**2625**	**4050**
LB Pkup	7787	**2725**	**4175**

ADD FOR 88 COMANCHE:
4-Whl Drive +850 *Chief Pkg +115*
Eliminator Pkg +290 *Laredo Pkg +195*
DEDUCT FOR 88 COMANCHE:
4 Cyl Eng -195 *No AC -125*

WAGONEER 1988

4WD/AT/PS/AC

Model/Body/Type	BaseList	Whlse	Retail
Wagoneer 6 Cyl			
4 Dr Limited Wgn	21926	**7150**	**9150**
Grand Wagoneer V8			
4 Dr Wgn	24623	**5200**	**7050**

DEDUCT FOR 88 WAGONEER:
No AC -370 *No Auto Trans -350*
No Pwr Steering -100

WRANGLER 6 Cyl 1988

4WD/5SP/PS

Model/Body/Type	BaseList	Whlse	Retail
Jeep	10981	**6100**	**7975**
Jeep (4 cyl)	10595	**5825**	**7700**
Jeep S (4 cyl)	8995	**4850**	**6675**

ADD FOR 88 WRANGLER:
AC +315 *Auto Trans +195*
Hard Top +195 *Laredo Pkg +390*
Sahara Pkg +275

JEEP 87-85

1987 JEEP

Model/Body/Type	BaseList	Whlse	Retail
CHEROKEE 6 Cyl			**1987**
AT/PS/AC			
2 Dr 2WD Wgn	10949	**2825**	**4300**
4 Dr 2WD Wgn	11493	**3250**	**4775**
2 Dr 4WD Wgn	12261	**3725**	**5325**
4 Dr 4WD Wgn	12806	**4175**	**5850**
4 Dr 4WD Limited Wgn	22104	**6450**	**8350**

ADD FOR 87 CHEROKEE:
Laredo Pkg +430
DEDUCT FOR 87 CHEROKEE:
4 Cyl Engine -275

Model/Body/Type	BaseList	Whlse	Retail
COMANCHE 6 Cyl			**1987**
AT/PS/AC			
Pkup	6495	**2075**	**3375**
LB Pkup	7860	**2175**	**3475**

ADD FOR 87 COMANCHE:
4-Whl Drive +680 *Laredo Pkg +115*
DEDUCT FOR 87 COMANCHE:
4 Cyl Eng -160

Model/Body/Type	BaseList	Whlse	Retail
JEEP PICKUPS V8			**1987**
4WD/AT/PS/AC			
J10 Pkup	11544	**4000**	**5700**
J20 Pkup	12941	**4350**	**6100**

ADD FOR 87 JEEP PICKUP:
Pioneer Pkg +75
DEDUCT FOR 87 JEEP PICKUP:
6 Cyl Eng -195

Model/Body/Type	BaseList	Whlse	Retail
WAGONEER			**1987**
4WD/AT/PS/AC			
Wagoneer 4 Cyl			
4 Dr Wgn	15126	**4655**	**6505**
4 Dr Limited Wgn	19995	**5400**	**7255**
Wagoneer 6 Cyl			
4 Dr Wgn	15634	**5075**	**6925**
4 Dr Limited Wgn	20503	**5850**	**7700**
Grand Wagoneer V8			
4 Dr Wgn	23560	**4100**	**5775**

Model/Body/Type	BaseList	Whlse	Retail
WRANGLER 6 Cyl			**1987**
4WD/5SP/PS			
Jeep	10274	**5025**	**6900**
Jeep (4 cyl)	9899	**4850**	**6650**
Jeep S (4 cyl)	8396	**4225**	**5925**

ADD FOR 87 WRANGLER:
AC +230 *Hard Top +135*
Laredo Pkg +230

1986 JEEP

Model/Body/Type	BaseList	Whlse	Retail
CHEROKEE			**1986**
2 Dr 2WD Wgn	9772	**2100**	**3550**
4 Dr 2WD Wgn	10387	**2400**	**3950**
2 Dr 4WD Wgn	11132	**2900**	**4500**
4 Dr 4WD Wgn	11757	**3250**	**4850**
CJ7			**1986**
4WD			
Jeep	7861	**3850**	**5575**
COMANCHE			**1986**
Pkup	7049	**1700**	**3100**

ADD FOR 86 COMANCHE:
4-Whl Drive +495

Model/Body/Type	BaseList	Whlse	Retail
JEEP PICKUPS			**1986**
4WD			
J10 Pkup	10870	**3050**	**4650**
J20 Pkup	12160	**3300**	**4950**
WAGONEER			**1986**
4WD			
Wagoneer			
4 Dr Wgn	14067	**3975**	**5725**
4 Dr Limited Wgn	19037	**4600**	**6425**
Grand Wagoneer			
4 Dr Wgn	21350	**3550**	**5225**

1985 JEEP

Model/Body/Type	BaseList	Whlse	Retail
CHEROKEE			**1985**
2 Dr 2WD Wgn	95447	**1600**	**2950**
4 Dr 2WD Wgn	10115	**1850**	**3250**
2 Dr 4WD Wgn	10754	**2250**	**3750**
4 Dr 4WD Wgn	11325	**2550**	**4100**
CJ			**1985**
4WD			
CJ7 Jeep	7282	**3075**	**4700**
Jeep Scrambler	7282	**2875**	**4450**
JEEP PICKUPS			**1985**
4WD			
J10 Townside Pkup	10311	**2100**	**3550**
J20 Townside Pkup	11275	**2325**	**3850**
WAGONEER			**1985**
4WD			
4 Dr Wagoneer	13604	**3200**	**4825**
4 Dr Limited Wagoneer	18302	**3750**	**5475**
4 Dr Grand Wagoneer	20462	**2950**	**4550**

Model/Body/Type	BaseList	Whlse	Retail	Model/Body/Type	BaseList	Whlse	Retail

LAND ROVER
Britain

1992 Land Rover Range Rover

For a Land Rover dealer in your area, see our Dealer Directory (pg 217)

1994 LAND ROVER

RANGE ROVER V8 1994

4WD/AT/PS/AC	BaseList	Whlse	Retail
4 Dr County Spt Utility	46900	-	-
4 Dr Cnty LWB Spt Util	50200	-	-

1993 LAND ROVER

RANGE ROVER V8 1993

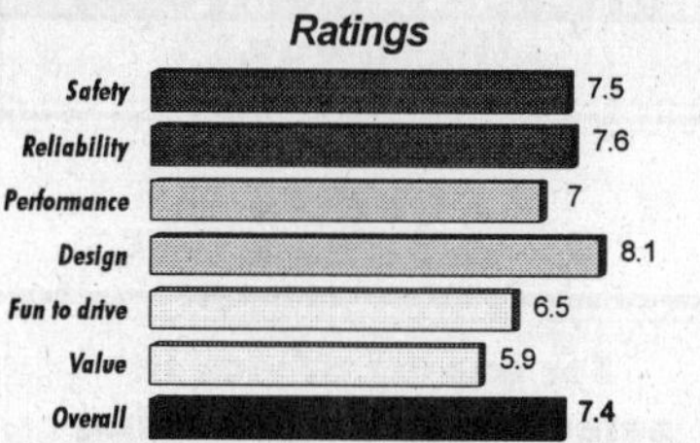

4WD/AT/PS/AC	BaseList	Whlse	Retail
4 Dr County Spt Utility	44500	32150	36375
4 Dr Cnty LWB Spt Util	49200	35250	39250

ADD FOR ALL 93 LAND ROVER
Car Phone +175

1992 LAND ROVER

RANGE ROVER V8 1992

Ratings

Rating	Score
Safety	7.5
Reliability	7.6
Performance	7
Design	8.1
Fun to drive	6.5
Value	5.9
Overall	7.4

4WD/AT/PS/AC	BaseList	Whlse	Retail
4 Dr Spt Utility	38900	27250	31300

ADD FOR ALL 92 LAND ROVER:
Car Phone +160
County Pkg +1400

1991 LAND ROVER

RANGE ROVER V8 1991

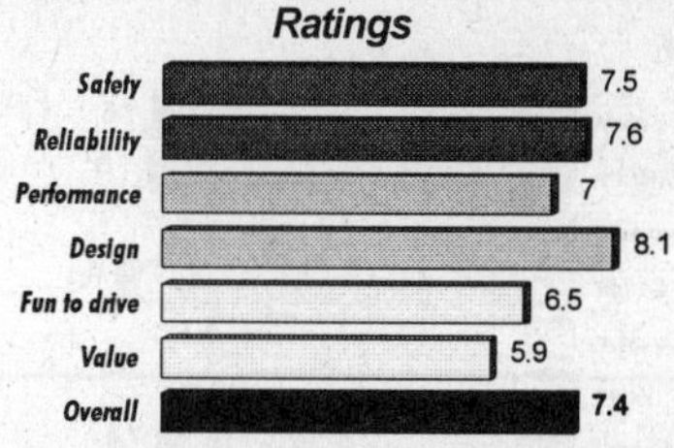

4WD/AT/PS/AC	BaseList	Whlse	Retail
4 Dr Spt Utility	42400	22200	25850

ADD FOR ALL 91 LAND ROVER:
Car Phone +135
CD Player +195
County SE Pkg +935
Pwr Sunroof +430

See the Automobile Dealer Directory on page 379 for a Dealer near you!

LAND ROVER

Model/Body/Type | BaseList | Whlse | Retail

1990 LAND ROVER

RANGE ROVER V8 — 1990

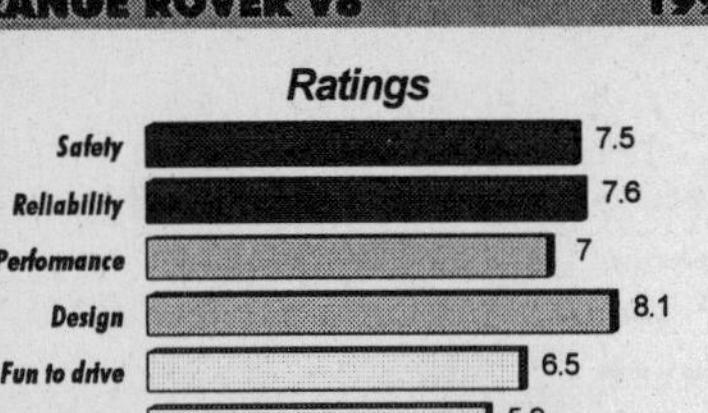

Model/Body/Type	BaseList	Whlse	Retail
4WD/AT/PS/AC			
4 Dr Spt Utility	38025	17800	21100

ADD FOR ALL 90 LAND ROVER:
CD Player +135
County Pkg +700
Pwr Sunroof +390

1989 LAND ROVER

RANGE ROVER V8 — 1989

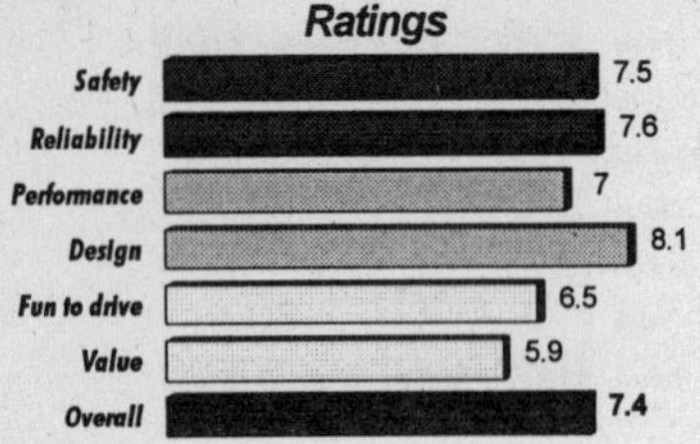

Model/Body/Type	BaseList	Whlse	Retail
4WD/AT/PS/AC			
4 Dr Spt Utility	36600	15000	18025

ADD FOR ALL 89 LAND ROVER:
County Pkg +1560

1988 LAND ROVER

RANGE ROVER V8 — 1988

Model/Body/Type	BaseList	Whlse	Retail
4WD/AT/PS/AC			
4 Dr Spt Utility	34400	11175	13950

1987 LAND ROVER

RANGE ROVER V8 — 1987

Model/Body/Type	BaseList	Whlse	Retail
4WD/AT/PS/AC			
4 Dr Spt Utility	30825	9375	11750

Model/Body/Type	BaseList	Whlse	Retail

LEXUS

Japan

1992 Lexus SC300

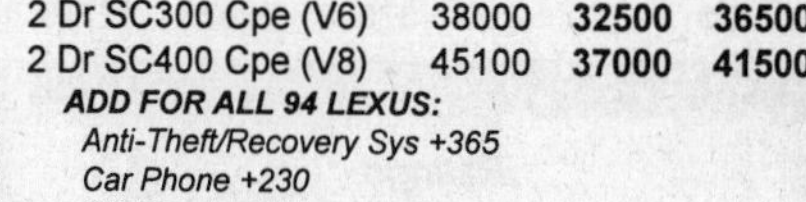

1994 LEXUS

ES300 V6 — 1994

AT/PS/AC

Model/Body/Type	BaseList	Whlse	Retail
4 Dr Sdn	30600	**24625**	**28450**

GS300 V8 — 1994

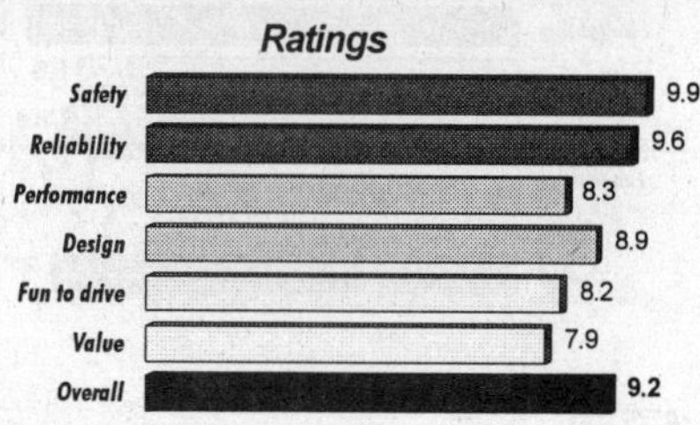

AT/PS/AC

Model/Body/Type	BaseList	Whlse	Retail
4 Dr Sdn	39900	**31150**	**35175**

LS400 V8 — 1994

AT/PS/AC

Model/Body/Type	BaseList	Whlse	Retail
4 Dr Sdn	49900	**38875**	**43450**

SC300/400 — 1994

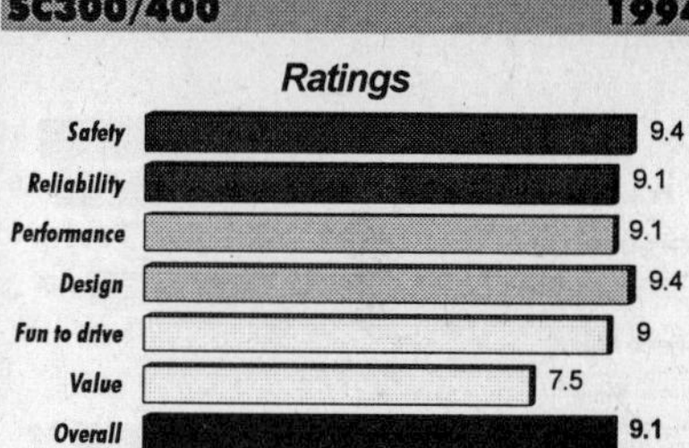

AT/PS/AC

Model/Body/Type	BaseList	Whlse	Retail
2 Dr SC300 Cpe (V6)	38000	**32500**	**36500**
2 Dr SC400 Cpe (V8)	45100	**37000**	**41500**

ADD FOR ALL 94 LEXUS:

Anti-Theft/Recovery Sys +365
Car Phone +230
CD Player +340
Leather Seats(Std SC400,LS400) +590
Nakamichi Stereo +410
Pwr Sunroof +635
Traction Ctrl +955

DEDUCT FOR ALL 94 LEXUS:

No Auto Trans -680

1993 LEXUS

ES300 V6 — 1993

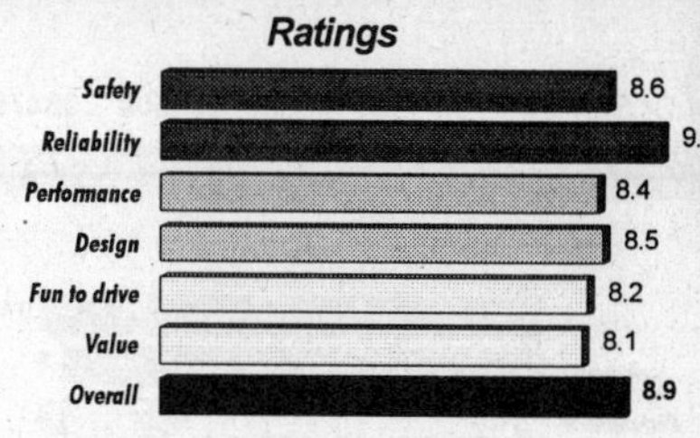

AT/PS/AC

Model/Body/Type	BaseList	Whlse	Retail
4 Dr Sdn	27500	**22250**	**25900**

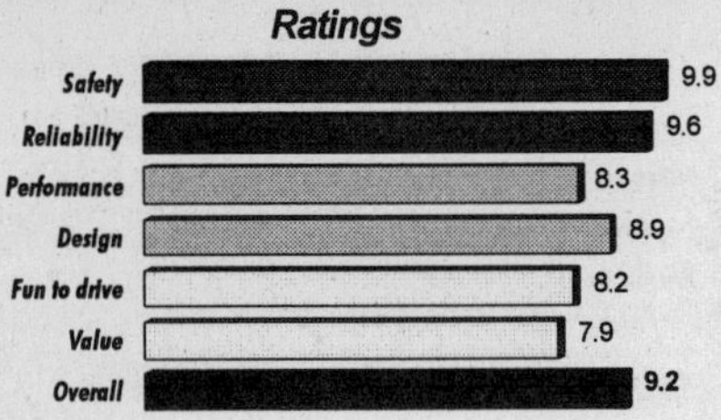

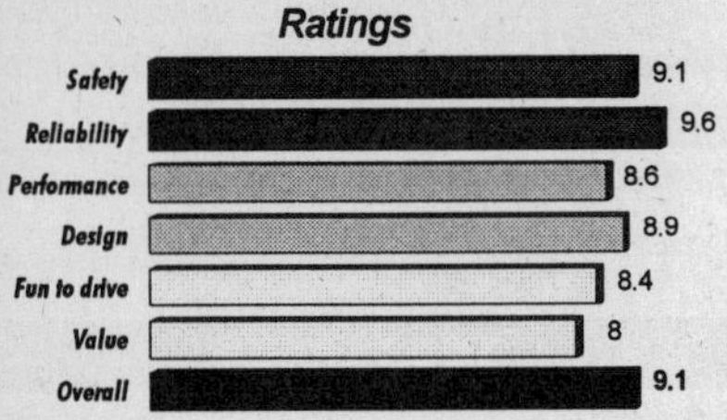

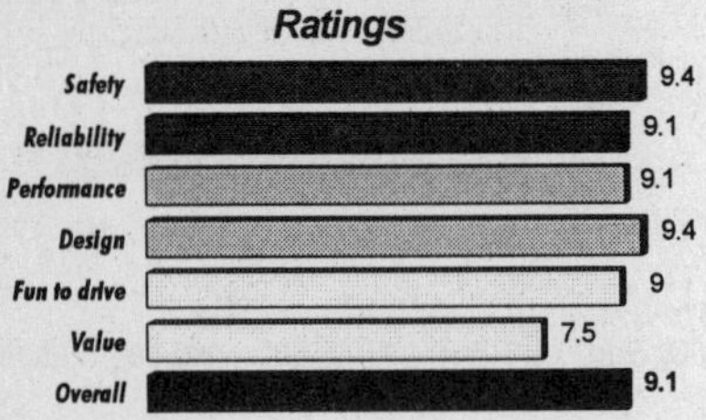

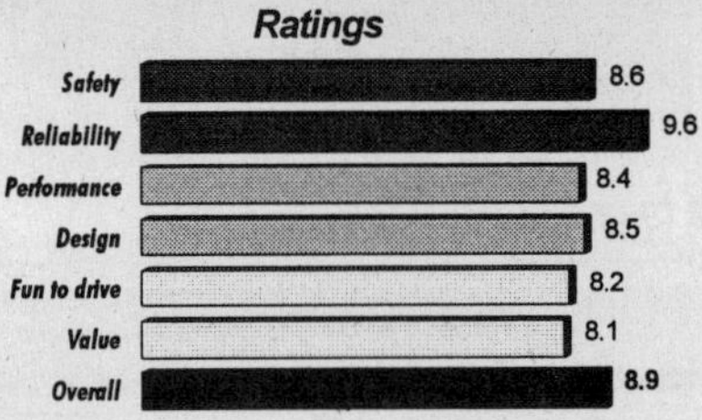

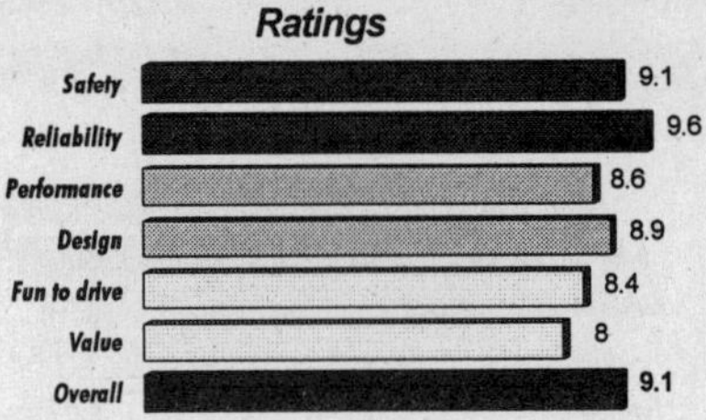

Model/Body/Type	BaseList	Whlse	Retail

GS300 V8 — 1993

Ratings

Rating	Score
Safety	9.9
Reliability	9.6
Performance	8.3
Design	8.9
Fun to drive	8.2
Value	7.9
Overall	9.2

AT/PS/AC	BaseList	Whlse	Retail
4 Dr Sdn	37500	**28675**	**32725**

LS400 V8 — 1993

Ratings

Rating	Score
Safety	9.1
Reliability	9.6
Performance	8.6
Design	8.9
Fun to drive	8.4
Value	8
Overall	9.1

AT/PS/AC	BaseList	Whlse	Retail
4 Dr Sdn	46600	**34500**	**38475**

SC300/400 — 1993

Ratings

Rating	Score
Safety	9.4
Reliability	9.1
Performance	9.1
Design	9.4
Fun to drive	9
Value	7.5
Overall	9.1

AT/PS/AC	BaseList	Whlse	Retail
2 Dr SC300 Cpe (V6)	34700	**29600**	**33750**
2 Dr SC400 Cpe (V8)	41400	**34200**	**38050**

ADD FOR ALL 93 LEXUS:

Car Phone +175
CD Player +290
Leather Seats(Std SC400,LS400) +470
Nakamichi Stereo +370
Pwr Sunroof +505

DEDUCT FOR ALL 93 LEXUS:

No Auto Trans -585

1992 LEXUS

ES300 V6 — 1992

Ratings

Rating	Score
Safety	8.6
Reliability	9.6
Performance	8.4
Design	8.5
Fun to drive	8.2
Value	8.1
Overall	8.9

AT/PS/AC	BaseList	Whlse	Retail
4 Dr Sdn	26150	**20175**	**23650**

LS400 V8 — 1992

Ratings

Rating	Score
Safety	9.1
Reliability	9.6
Performance	8.6
Design	8.9
Fun to drive	8.4
Value	8
Overall	9.1

AT/PS/AC	BaseList	Whlse	Retail
4 Dr Sdn	42200	**29175**	**33275**

See the Automobile Dealer Directory on page 379 for a Dealer near you!

Model/Body/Type	BaseList	Whlse	Retail

SC300/400 — 1992

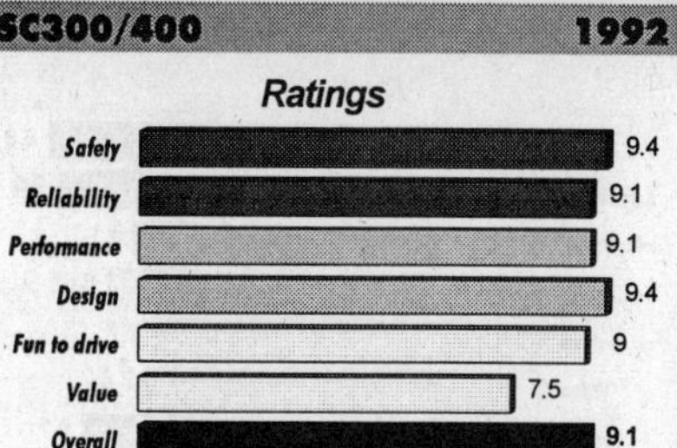

AT/PS/AC

Model/Body/Type	BaseList	Whlse	Retail
2 Dr SC300 Cpe (V6)	32000	**25100**	**29000**
2 Dr SC400 Cpe (V8)	37500	**29450**	**33575**

ADD FOR ALL 92 LEXUS:
Car Phone +160
CD Player +250
Leather Seats(Std SC400,LS400) +410
Nakamichi Stereo +315
Pwr Sunroof +470
DEDUCT FOR ALL 92 LEXUS:
No Auto Trans -545

1991 LEXUS

ES250 V6 — 1991

AT/PS/AC

Model/Body/Type	BaseList	Whlse	Retail
4 Dr Sdn	22050	**12250**	**15075**

LS400 V8 — 1991

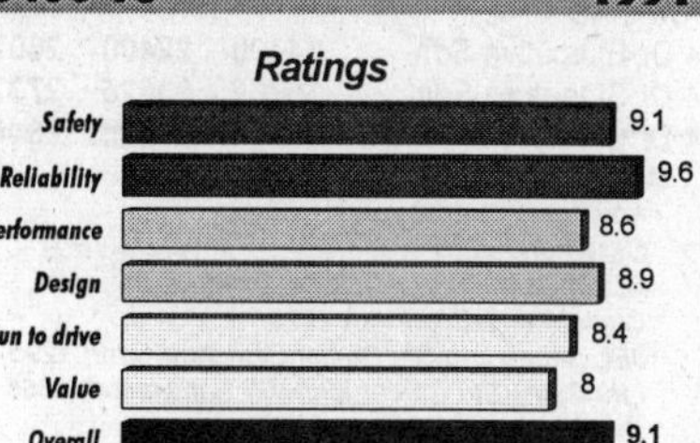

AT/PS/AC

Model/Body/Type	BaseList	Whlse	Retail
4 Dr Sdn	38000	**24950**	**28800**

ADD FOR ALL 91 LEXUS:
Car Phone +135
CD Player +195
Leather Seats +350
Nakamichi Stereo +275
Pwr Sunroof +430
DEDUCT FOR ALL 91 LEXUS:
No Auto Trans -505

1990 LEXUS

ES250 V6 — 1990

AT/PS/AC

Model/Body/Type	BaseList	Whlse	Retail
4 Dr Sdn	21800	**10425**	**13100**

LS400 V8 — 1990

AT/PS/AC

Model/Body/Type	BaseList	Whlse	Retail
4 Dr Sdn	35000	**21275**	**24750**

ADD FOR ALL 90 LEXUS:
CD Player +135
Leather Seats +290
Nakamichi Stereo +230
Pwr Sunroof +390
DEDUCT FOR ALL 90 LEXUS:
No Auto Trans -470

Model/Body/Type	BaseList	Whlse	Retail

LINCOLN USA

1992 Lincoln Mark VII

For a Lincoln dealer in your area, see our Dealer Directory (pg 217)

1994 LINCOLN

CONTINENTAL V6 1994

Ratings

FWD/AT/PS/AC

Model/Body/Type	BaseList	Whlse	Retail
4 Dr Executive Sdn	33850	**21625**	**25225**
4 Dr Signature Sdn	35750	**23250**	**26975**

See the Automobile Dealer Directory on page 379 for a Dealer near you!

MARK VIII V8 1994

Ratings

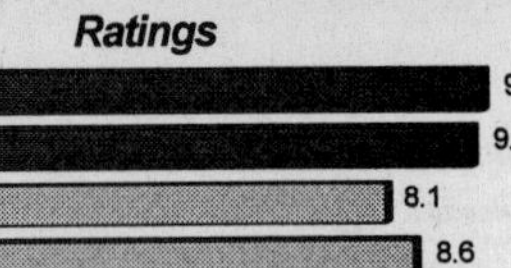

AT/PS/AC

Model/Body/Type	BaseList	Whlse	Retail
2 Dr Cpe	36890	**25650**	**29525**

TOWN CAR V8 1994

Ratings

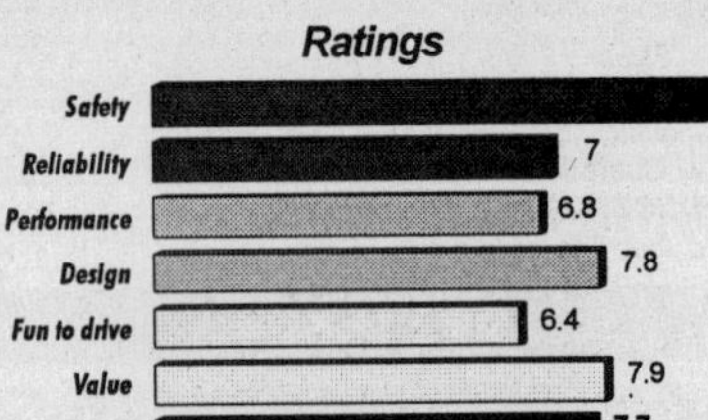

AT/PS/AC

Model/Body/Type	BaseList	Whlse	Retail
4 Dr Executive Sdn	34400	**22400**	**26075**
4 Dr Signature Sdn	35700	**23625**	**27375**
4 Dr Cartier Sdn	37800	**25525**	**29400**

ADD FOR ALL 94 LINCOLN:

Anti,Theft/Recovery Sys +365
Car Phone +230
CD Player +340
Custom Whls(MarkVIII) +275
JBL Stereo Sys(Std Cartier,Signature,Cont) +295
Lthr Seats(Std Cartier,MarkVIII,Continental) +365
Pwr Sunroof +635

1993 LINCOLN

CONTINENTAL V6 1993

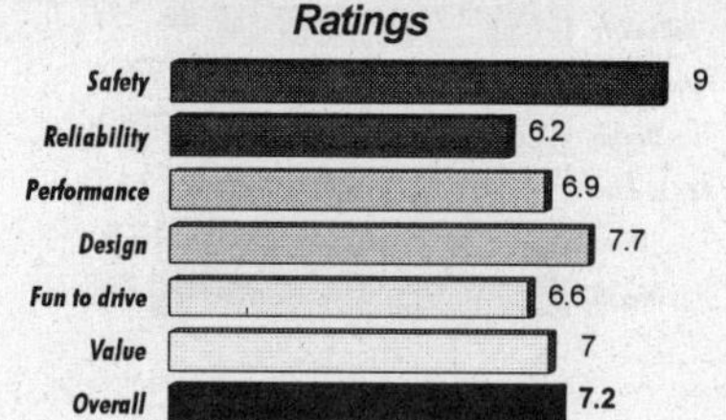

Model/Body/Type	BaseList	Whlse	Retail
FWD/AT/PS/AC			
4 Dr Executive Sdn	33328	**18275**	**21625**
4 Dr Signature Sdn	35319	**19800**	**23275**

MARK VIII V8 1993

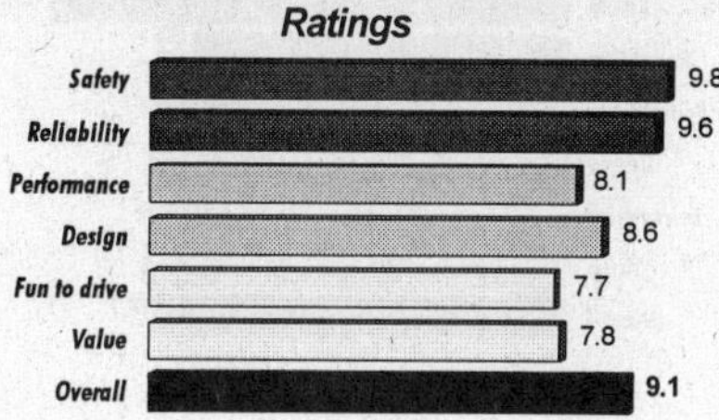

Model/Body/Type	BaseList	Whlse	Retail
AT/PS/AC			
2 Dr Cpe	36640	**23875**	**27625**

TOWN CAR V8 1993

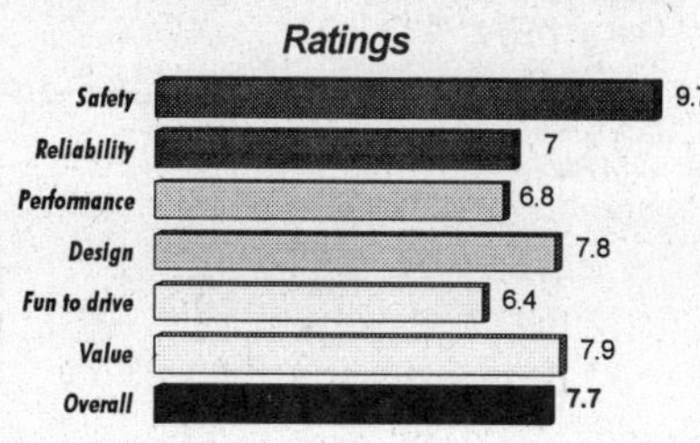

Model/Body/Type	BaseList	Whlse	Retail
AT/PS/AC			
4 Dr Executive Sdn	34190	**19725**	**23150**
4 Dr Signature Sdn	35494	**20875**	**24375**
4 Dr Cartier Sdn	37581	**22675**	**26350**

ADD FOR ALL 93 LINCOLN:

Car Phone +175
CD Player +290
JBL Stereo Sys(Std Cartier,Signature,Cont) +250
Leather Seats(Std Cartier,MarkVIII,Continental) +315
Pwr Sunroof +505
Vinyl Roof +175

1992 LINCOLN

CONTINENTAL V6 1992

Ratings

Rating	Score
Safety	9
Reliability	6.2
Performance	6.9
Design	7.7
Fun to drive	6.6
Value	7
Overall	7.2

Model/Body/Type	BaseList	Whlse	Retail
FWD/AT/PS/AC			
4 Dr Executive Sdn	32263	**14725**	**17700**
4 Dr Signature Sdn	34253	**16200**	**19300**

MARK VII V8 1992

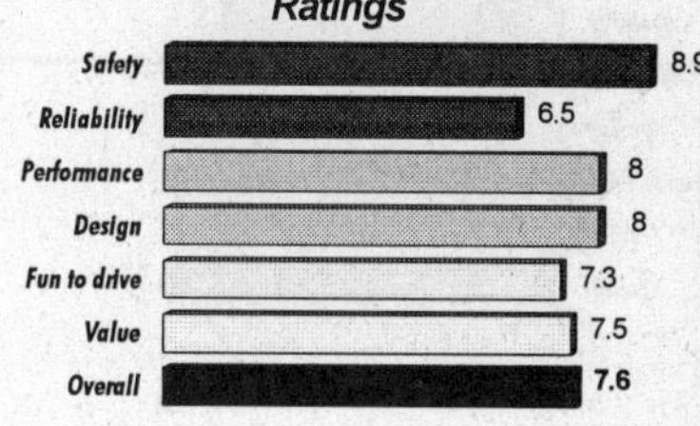

Model/Body/Type	BaseList	Whlse	Retail
AT/PS/AC			
2 Dr LSC Cpe	32032	**17050**	**20275**
2 Dr Bill Blass Cpe	32156	**17000**	**20200**

LINCOLN 92-91

TOWN CAR V8 — 1992

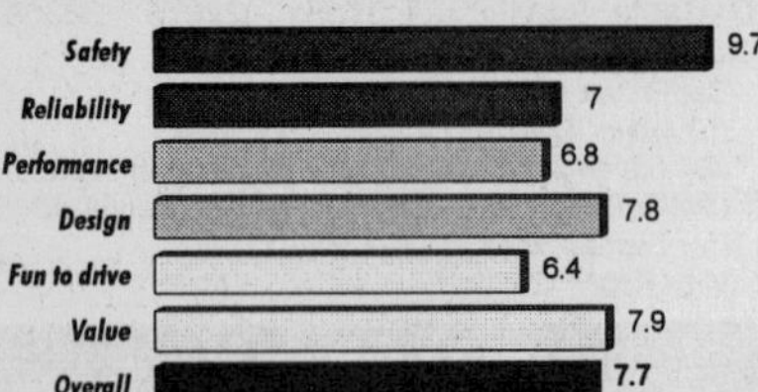

AT/PS/AC

Model/Body/Type	BaseList	Whlse	Retail
4 Dr Executive Sdn	31211	**15550**	**18625**
4 Dr Signature Sdn	34252	**17125**	**20375**
4 Dr Cartier Sdn	36340	**17900**	**21225**

ADD FOR ALL 92 LINCOLN:

Car Phone +160
CD Player +250
Custom Whls +215
JBL Stereo Sys(Std Cartier,Signature,Cont) +230
Leather Seats(Std Cartier,MarkVII,Continental) +275
Pwr Sunroof +470
Vinyl Roof +160

MARK VII V8 — 1991

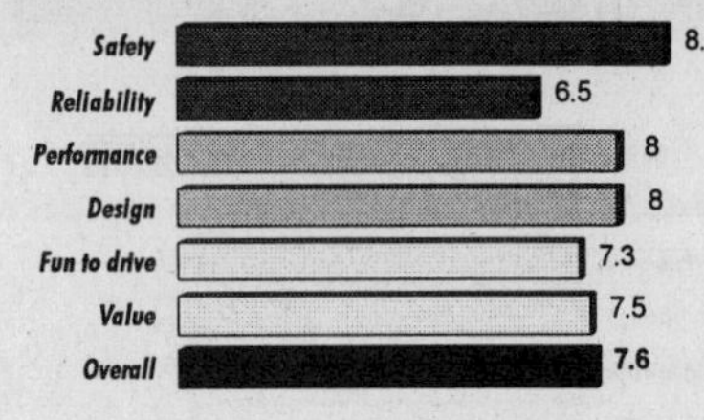

AT/PS/AC

Model/Body/Type	BaseList	Whlse	Retail
2 Dr LSC Cpe	30738	**13500**	**16425**
2 Dr Bill Blass Cpe	30862	**13450**	**16375**

TOWN CAR V8 — 1991

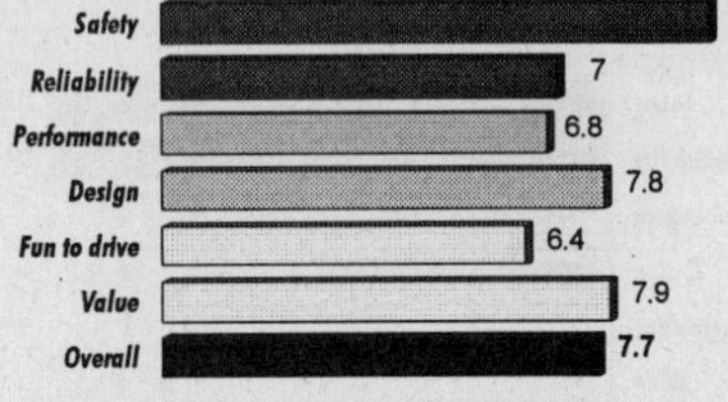

AT/PS/AC

Model/Body/Type	BaseList	Whlse	Retail
4 Dr Sdn	28581	**11850**	**14650**
4 Dr Signature Sdn	31540	**13275**	**16175**
4 Dr Cartier Sdn	33627	**14025**	**16975**

ADD FOR ALL 91 LINCOLN:

Car Phone +135
CD Player +195
Custom Whls +175
JBL Stereo Sys(Std Cartier) +195
Leather Seats(Std Cartier,MarkVII,Continental) +215
Pwr Sunroof +430
Vinyl Roof +135

1991 LINCOLN

CONTINENTAL V6 — 1991

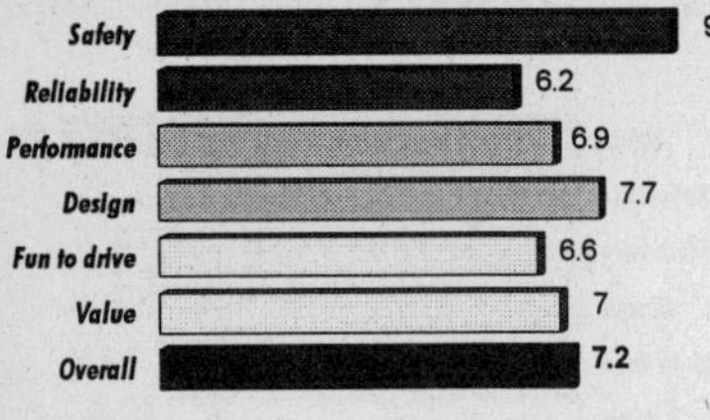

FWD/AT/PS/AC

Model/Body/Type	BaseList	Whlse	Retail
4 Dr Sdn	30395	**10525**	**13200**
4 Dr Signature Sdn	32304	**11875**	**14675**

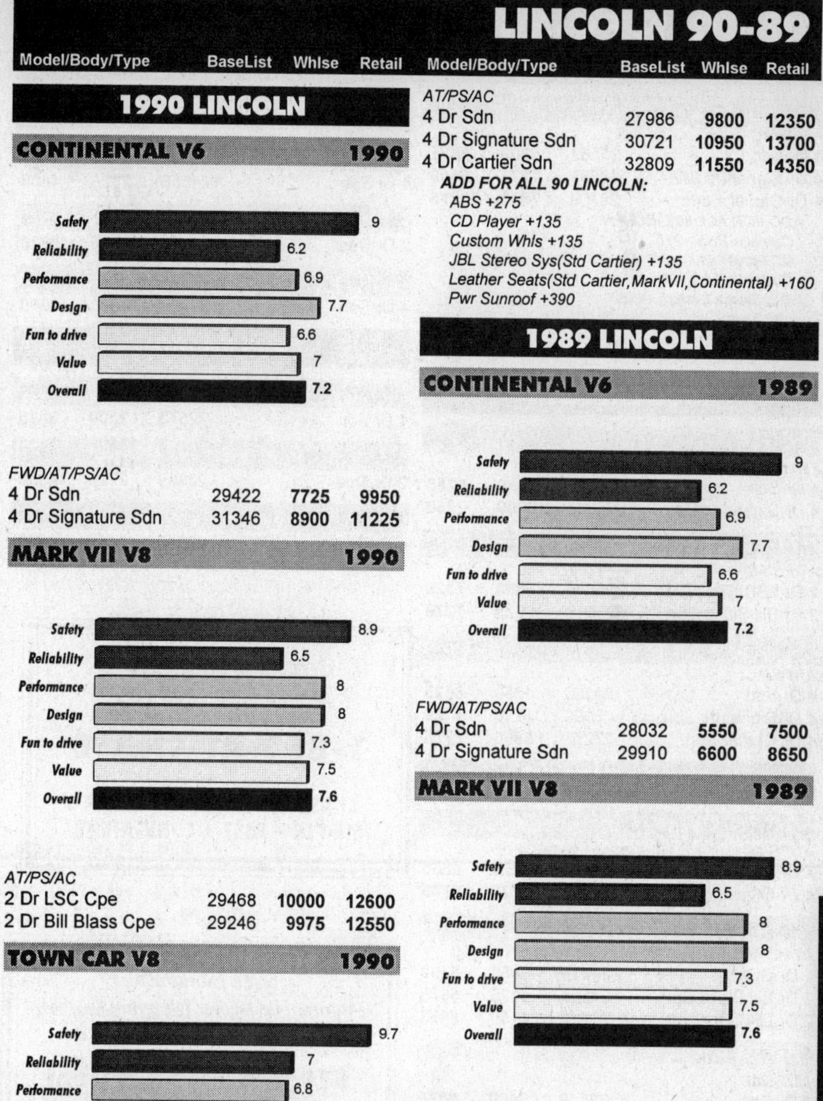

1990 LINCOLN

CONTINENTAL V6 1990

Rating	Score
Safety	9
Reliability	6.2
Performance	6.9
Design	7.7
Fun to drive	6.6
Value	7
Overall	7.2

FWD/AT/PS/AC

Model/Body/Type	BaseList	Whlse	Retail
4 Dr Sdn	29422	**7725**	**9950**
4 Dr Signature Sdn	31346	**8900**	**11225**

MARK VII V8 1990

Rating	Score
Safety	8.9
Reliability	6.5
Performance	8
Design	8
Fun to drive	7.3
Value	7.5
Overall	7.6

AT/PS/AC

Model/Body/Type	BaseList	Whlse	Retail
2 Dr LSC Cpe	29468	**10000**	**12600**
2 Dr Bill Blass Cpe	29246	**9975**	**12550**

TOWN CAR V8 1990

Rating	Score
Safety	9.7
Reliability	7
Performance	6.8
Design	7.8
Fun to drive	6.4
Value	7.9
Overall	7.7

AT/PS/AC

Model/Body/Type	BaseList	Whlse	Retail
4 Dr Sdn	27986	**9800**	**12350**
4 Dr Signature Sdn	30721	**10950**	**13700**
4 Dr Cartier Sdn	32809	**11550**	**14350**

ADD FOR ALL 90 LINCOLN:

ABS +275
CD Player +135
Custom Whls +135
JBL Stereo Sys(Std Cartier) +135
Leather Seats(Std Cartier,MarkVII,Continental) +160
Pwr Sunroof +390

1989 LINCOLN

CONTINENTAL V6 1989

Rating	Score
Safety	9
Reliability	6.2
Performance	6.9
Design	7.7
Fun to drive	6.6
Value	7
Overall	7.2

FWD/AT/PS/AC

Model/Body/Type	BaseList	Whlse	Retail
4 Dr Sdn	28032	**5550**	**7500**
4 Dr Signature Sdn	29910	**6600**	**8650**

MARK VII V8 1989

Rating	Score
Safety	8.9
Reliability	6.5
Performance	8
Design	8
Fun to drive	7.3
Value	7.5
Overall	7.6

AT/PS/AC

Model/Body/Type	BaseList	Whlse	Retail
2 Dr LSC Cpe	27569	**7250**	**9450**
2 Dr Bill Blass Cpe	27569	**7225**	**9425**

LINCOLN 89-85

Model/Body/Type	BaseList	Whlse	Retail
TOWN CAR V8			**1989**
AT/PS/AC			
4 Dr Sdn	25562	**6200**	**8225**
4 Dr Signature Sdn	28563	**7275**	**9500**
4 Dr Cartier Sdn	29709	**7875**	**10075**

ADD FOR ALL 89 LINCOLN:
Carriage Roof +215
CD Player +100
Custom Whls +100
JBL Stereo System +115
Lthr Seats(Std Cart,Mark,Cont) +135
Pwr Sunroof +330
Valino Coach Roof +75

1988 LINCOLN

Model/Body/Type	BaseList	Whlse	Retail
CONTINENTAL V6			**1988**
FWD/AT/PS/AC			
4 Dr Sdn	26078	**4450**	**6250**
4 Dr Signature Sdn	27944	**5300**	**7250**
MARK VII V8			**1988**
AT/PS/AC			
2 Dr LSC Cpe	25016	**5350**	**7325**
2 Dr Bill Blass Cpe	25016	**5325**	**7275**
TOWN CAR V8			**1988**
AT/PS/AC			
4 Dr Sdn	23126	**4250**	**6025**
4 Dr Signature Sdn	25990	**5150**	**7125**
4 Dr Cartier Sdn	27273	**5800**	**7775**

1987 LINCOLN

Model/Body/Type	BaseList	Whlse	Retail
CONTINENTAL V6			**1987**
AT/PS/AC			
4 Dr Sdn	26402	**3225**	**4825**
4 Dr Givenchy Sdn	28902	**4025**	**5775**
MARK VII V8			**1987**
AT/PS/AC			
2 Dr Cpe	24216	**3650**	**5300**
2 Dr Bill Blass Cpe	25863	**4125**	**5875**
2 Dr LSC Cpe	25863	**4150**	**5875**
TOWN CAR V8			**1987**
AT/PS/AC			
4 Dr Sdn	22549	**3400**	**5025**
4 Dr Signature Sdn	25541	**4275**	**6050**
4 Dr Cartier Sdn	26868	**4850**	**6725**

1986 LINCOLN

Model/Body/Type	BaseList	Whlse	Retail
CONTINENTAL			**1986**
4 Dr Sdn	24556	**2825**	**4400**
MARK VII			**1986**
2 Dr Cpe	22399	**3275**	**4925**
TOWN CAR			**1986**
4 Dr Sdn	20764	**3000**	**4600**

1985 LINCOLN

Model/Body/Type	BaseList	Whlse	Retail
CONTINENTAL			**1985**
4 Dr Sdn	22573	**2300**	**3825**
MARK VII			**1985**
2 Dr Cpe	22399	**2725**	**4300**
TOWN CAR			**1985**
4 Dr Sdn	19047	**2450**	**4000**

MAZDA

Japan

1990 Mazda MX-5 Miata

For a Mazda dealer in your area, see our Dealer Directory (pg 217)

1994 MAZDA

323 4 Cyl — 1994

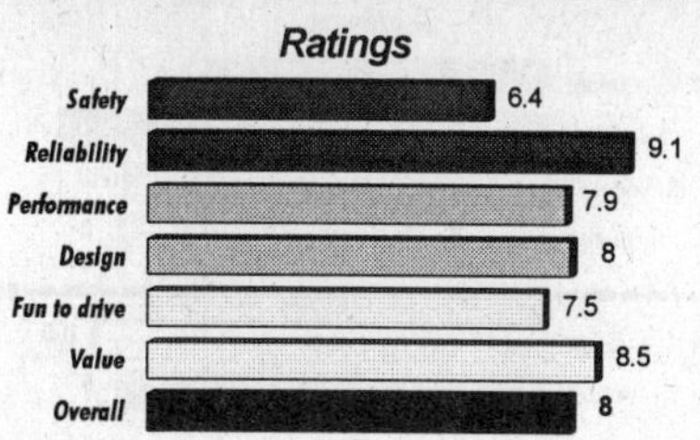

Model/Body/Type	BaseList	Whlse	Retail
FWD/AT/PS/AC			
3 Dr Hbk	7995	**8025**	**9875**

626 4 Cyl — 1994

Model/Body/Type	BaseList	Whlse	Retail
FWD/AT/PS/AC			
4 Dr DX Sdn	14255	**12900**	**15400**
4 Dr LX Sdn	16540	**14100**	**16650**
4 Dr ES Sdn (V6)	21545	**15450**	**18075**

929 V6 — 1994

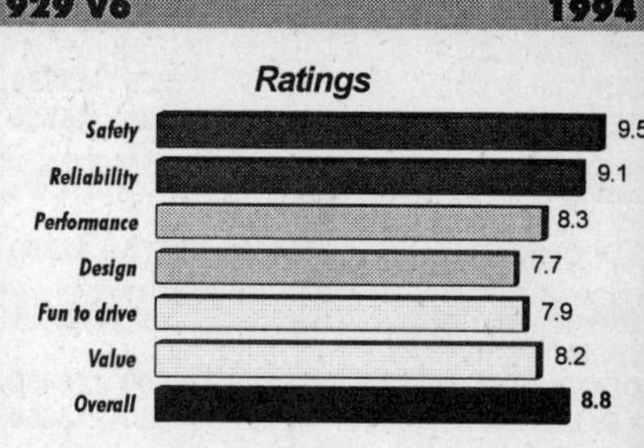

Model/Body/Type	BaseList	Whlse	Retail
AT/PS/AC			
4 Dr Sdn	30500	**22300**	**25650**

B-SERIES PICKUPS 4 Cyl — 1994

Ratings

Safety	7.4
Reliability	9.6
Performance	7.4
Design	8.5
Fun to drive	7
Value	8.5
Overall	8.3

Model/Body/Type	BaseList	Whlse	Retail
5SP/PS/AC			
4 Cyl Models			
Pkup	8780	**8050**	**9900**
SE Pkup	10550	**9050**	**10950**
Cab Plus Pkup	11995	**9750**	**11775**
V6 Models			
SE LB Pkup	11420	**9900**	**11950**
SE Cab Plus Pkup	13095	**11425**	**13750**
LE Cab Plus Pkup(AT)	15145	**12700**	**15100**
4WD Pkup	13250	**11525**	**13850**
SE 4WD Pkup	15145	**12500**	**14875**
4WD Cab Plus Pkup	15245	**13200**	**15625**
4WD SE Cab Plus Pkup	16595	**14200**	**16675**
4WD LE Cab Plus Pkup(AT)	18595	**15450**	**18000**

MPV 4 Cyl — 1994

Model/Body/Type	BaseList	Whlse	Retail
AT/PS/AC			
Wgn/Van	17795	**14550**	**17125**
Wgn	19195	**15275**	**17900**
4WD Wgn (V6)	22995	**17625**	**20500**

MAZDA

MAZDA 94-93

MX-3 V6 — 1994

Model/Body/Type	BaseList	Whlse	Retail
FWD/AT/PS/AC			
2 Dr Cpe (4 Cyl)	13595	**11275**	**13650**
2 Dr GS Cpe	16095	**11925**	**15750**

MX-5 MIATA 4 Cyl — 1994

Model/Body/Type	BaseList	Whlse	Retail
5SP/PS/AC			
2 Dr Conv	16450	**14775**	**17350**

MX-6 V6 — 1994

Model/Body/Type	BaseList	Whlse	Retail
FWD/AT/PS/AC			
2 Dr Cpe (4 Cyl)	17195	**13900**	**16450**
2 Dr LS Cpe	21195	**15950**	**18600**

NAVAJO V6 — 1994

Ratings

Rating	Score
Safety	7.2
Reliability	5.6
Performance	7.2
Design	8.8
Fun to drive	7.1
Value	8.5
Overall	6.8

Model/Body/Type	BaseList	Whlse	Retail
AT/PS/AC			
2WD DX Utility (5 spd)	17775	**15600**	**18250**
2WD LX Utility	18995	**17175**	**19975**
4WD DX Utility (5 spd)	19565	**17250**	**20125**
4WD LX Utility	20785	**18850**	**21800**

PROTEGE 4 Cyl — 1994

Ratings

Rating	Score
Safety	6.4
Reliability	9.1
Performance	7.9
Design	8
Fun to drive	7.5
Value	8.5
Overall	8

Model/Body/Type	BaseList	Whlse	Retail
FWD/AT/PS/AC			
4 Dr Sdn	8995	**8525**	**10375**
4 Dr DX Sdn	11295	**9975**	**12025**
4 Dr LX Sdn	12995	**11050**	**13350**

RX-7 — 1994

Model/Body/Type	BaseList	Whlse	Retail
5SP-AT/PS/AC			
2 Dr Turbo Cpe	34000	-	-

ADD FOR ALL 94 MAZDA:

ABS(Std ES,929,RX-7,Navajo) +430
Anti-Theft/Recovery Sys +365
Auto Trans(Miata,Pkup) +500
Car Phone(RX-7 +929) +230
Cass(Protege Base +DX +323 +BasePkup) +100
CD Player +230
Cruise Ctrl(Std LX,ES,LE,MX6,RX7,929) +160
Custom Whls +205
Detachable Hardtop +680
Dual AC +635
Leather Seats(Std ES) +320
Pwr Locks (MX-3,DX,SE,MPV) +115
Pwr Seats (Std ES,929) +160
Pwr Sunroof(Std ES,LS,929) +545
Pwr Wndw (MX-3,DX,SE,Miata,MPV) +160
Sunroof(Navajo) +320
V6 Eng +680

DEDUCT FOR ALL 94 MAZDA:

No AC -680
No Auto Trans -590
No Pwr Steering -180

1993 MAZDA

323 4 Cyl — 1993

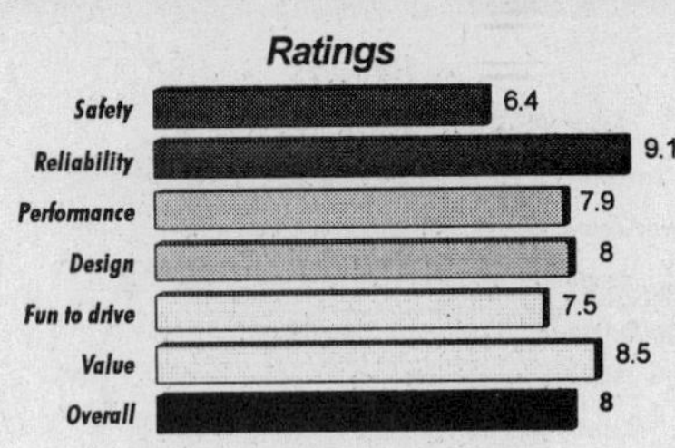

Model/Body/Type	BaseList	Whlse	Retail
FWD/AT/PS/AC			
3 Dr Hbk	7449	**6275**	**7875**
3 Dr SE Hbk	9129	**6950**	**8700**

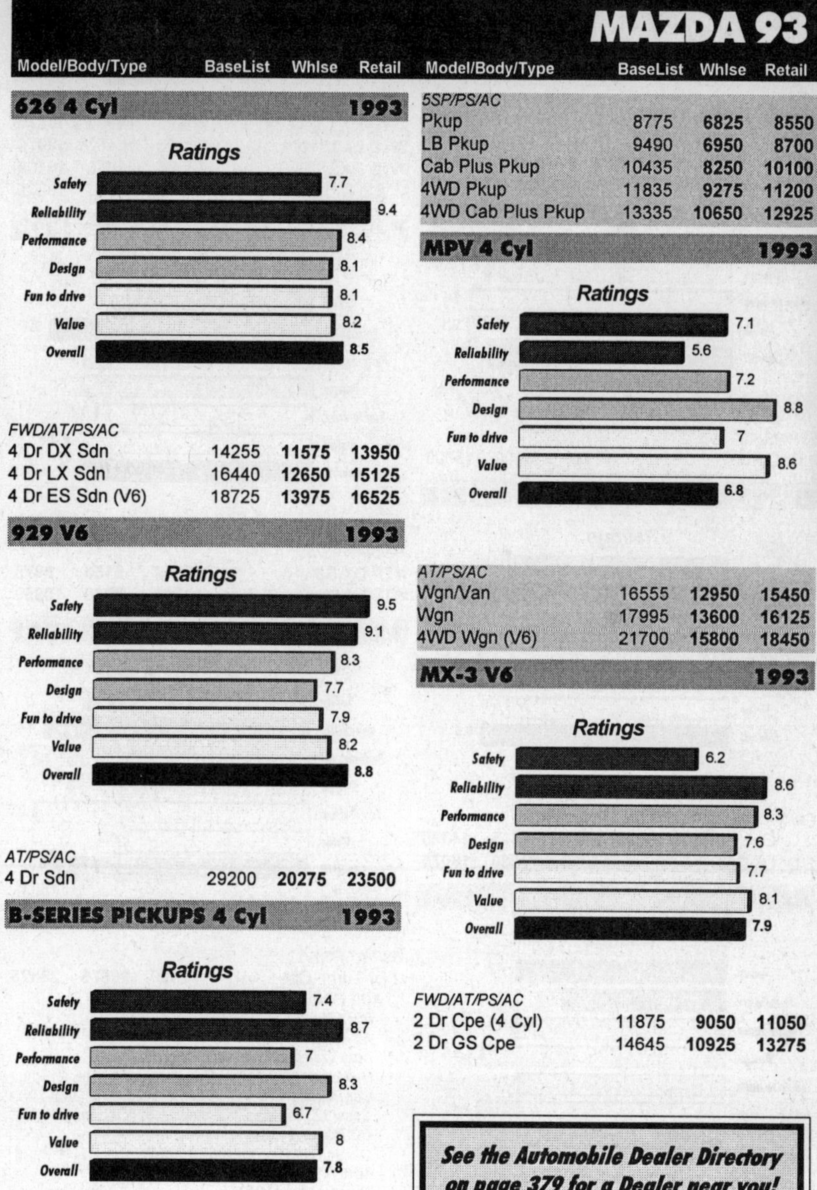

Model/Body/Type	BaseList	Whlse	Retail

626 4 Cyl — 1993

Ratings

Rating	Score
Safety	7.7
Reliability	9.4
Performance	8.4
Design	8.1
Fun to drive	8.1
Value	8.2
Overall	8.5

FWD/AT/PS/AC	BaseList	Whlse	Retail
4 Dr DX Sdn	14255	**11575**	**13950**
4 Dr LX Sdn	16440	**12650**	**15125**
4 Dr ES Sdn (V6)	18725	**13975**	**16525**

929 V6 — 1993

Ratings

Rating	Score
Safety	9.5
Reliability	9.1
Performance	8.3
Design	7.7
Fun to drive	7.9
Value	8.2
Overall	8.8

AT/PS/AC	BaseList	Whlse	Retail
4 Dr Sdn	29200	**20275**	**23500**

B-SERIES PICKUPS 4 Cyl — 1993

Ratings

Rating	Score
Safety	7.4
Reliability	8.7
Performance	7
Design	8.3
Fun to drive	6.7
Value	8
Overall	7.8

5SP/PS/AC	BaseList	Whlse	Retail
Pkup	8775	**6825**	**8550**
LB Pkup	9490	**6950**	**8700**
Cab Plus Pkup	10435	**8250**	**10100**
4WD Pkup	11835	**9275**	**11200**
4WD Cab Plus Pkup	13335	**10650**	**12925**

MPV 4 Cyl — 1993

Ratings

Rating	Score
Safety	7.1
Reliability	5.6
Performance	7.2
Design	8.8
Fun to drive	7
Value	8.6
Overall	6.8

AT/PS/AC	BaseList	Whlse	Retail
Wgn/Van	16555	**12950**	**15450**
Wgn	17995	**13600**	**16125**
4WD Wgn (V6)	21700	**15800**	**18450**

MX-3 V6 — 1993

Ratings

Rating	Score
Safety	6.2
Reliability	8.6
Performance	8.3
Design	7.6
Fun to drive	7.7
Value	8.1
Overall	7.9

FWD/AT/PS/AC	BaseList	Whlse	Retail
2 Dr Cpe (4 Cyl)	11875	**9050**	**11050**
2 Dr GS Cpe	14645	**10925**	**13275**

See the Automobile Dealer Directory on page 379 for a Dealer near you!

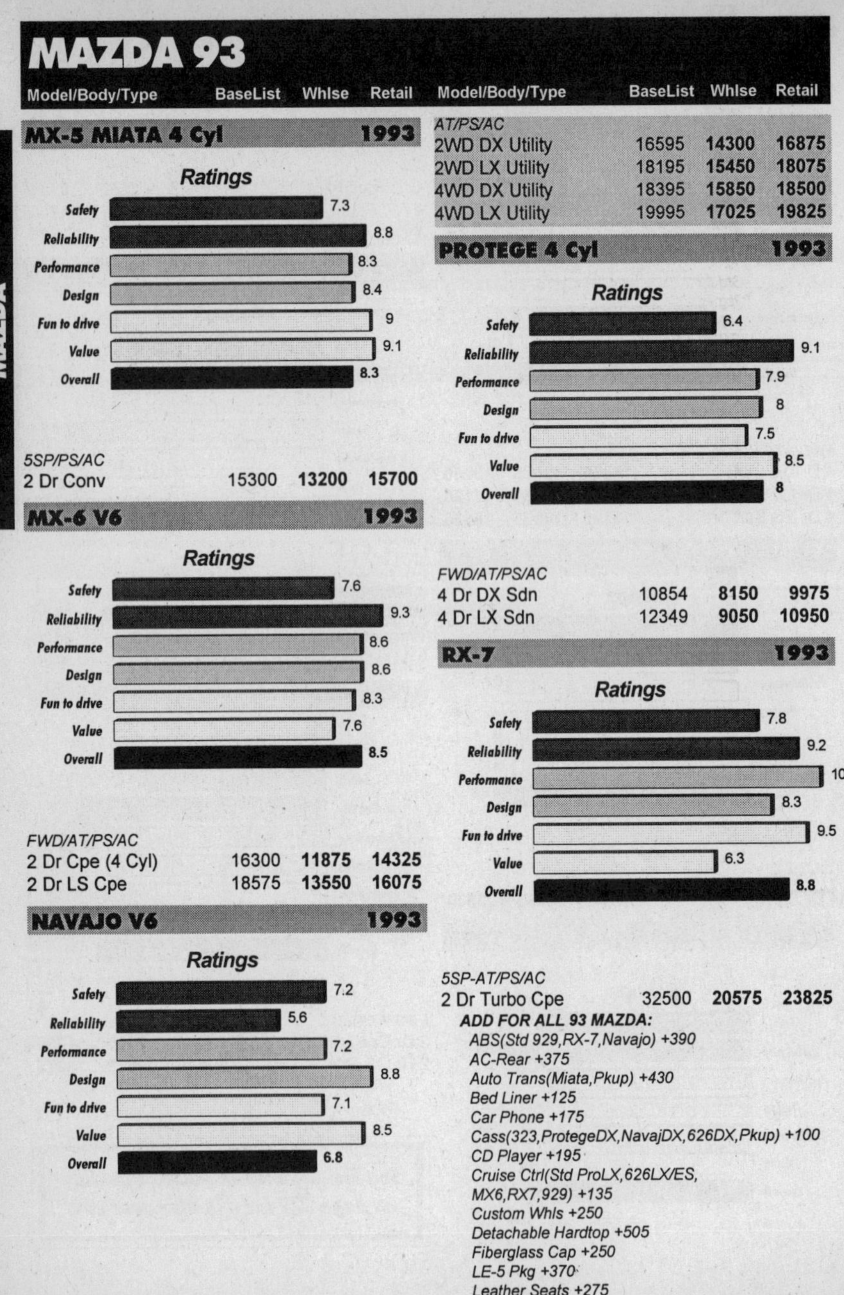

MAZDA 93

Model/Body/Type	BaseList	Whlse	Retail

MX-5 MIATA 4 Cyl — 1993

Ratings

Rating	Score
Safety	7.3
Reliability	8.8
Performance	8.3
Design	8.4
Fun to drive	9
Value	9.1
Overall	8.3

Model/Body/Type	BaseList	Whlse	Retail
5SP/PS/AC			
2 Dr Conv	15300	**13200**	**15700**

MX-6 V6 — 1993

Ratings

Rating	Score
Safety	7.6
Reliability	9.3
Performance	8.6
Design	8.6
Fun to drive	8.3
Value	7.6
Overall	8.5

Model/Body/Type	BaseList	Whlse	Retail
FWD/AT/PS/AC			
2 Dr Cpe (4 Cyl)	16300	**11875**	**14325**
2 Dr LS Cpe	18575	**13550**	**16075**

NAVAJO V6 — 1993

Ratings

Rating	Score
Safety	7.2
Reliability	5.6
Performance	7.2
Design	8.8
Fun to drive	7.1
Value	8.5
Overall	6.8

Model/Body/Type	BaseList	Whlse	Retail
AT/PS/AC			
2WD DX Utility	16595	**14300**	**16875**
2WD LX Utility	18195	**15450**	**18075**
4WD DX Utility	18395	**15850**	**18500**
4WD LX Utility	19995	**17025**	**19825**

PROTEGE 4 Cyl — 1993

Ratings

Rating	Score
Safety	6.4
Reliability	9.1
Performance	7.9
Design	8
Fun to drive	7.5
Value	8.5
Overall	8

Model/Body/Type	BaseList	Whlse	Retail
FWD/AT/PS/AC			
4 Dr DX Sdn	10854	**8150**	**9975**
4 Dr LX Sdn	12349	**9050**	**10950**

RX-7 — 1993

Ratings

Rating	Score
Safety	7.8
Reliability	9.2
Performance	10
Design	8.3
Fun to drive	9.5
Value	6.3
Overall	8.8

Model/Body/Type	BaseList	Whlse	Retail
5SP-AT/PS/AC			
2 Dr Turbo Cpe	32500	**20575**	**23825**

ADD FOR ALL 93 MAZDA:

ABS(Std 929,RX-7,Navajo) +390
AC-Rear +375
Auto Trans(Miata,Pkup) +430
Bed Liner +125
Car Phone +175
Cass(323,ProtegeDX,NavajDX,626DX,Pkup) +100
CD Player +195
Cruise Ctrl(Std ProLX,626LX/ES, MX6,RX7,929) +135
Custom Whls +250
Detachable Hardtop +505
Fiberglass Cap +250
LE-5 Pkg +370
Leather Seats +275

Model/Body/Type	BaseList	Whlse	Retail

Privacy Glass +145
Pwr Locks (MX-3,626 DX,MPV) +100
Pwr Seats (Navajo,626,MX-6) +135
Pwr Sunroof(Std 929) +430
Pwr Wndw (MX-3,Miata,626 DX,MPV) +135
Running Board +145
SE-5 Pkg +275
Slider Wndw +80
Sunroof +230
Tilt Whl(Std MPV) +105
Towing Pkg +185
V6 Eng +505

DEDUCT FOR ALL 93 MAZDA:

No AC -545
No AM/FM Radio -105
No Auto Trans -505
No Pwr Steering -160

1992 MAZDA

323 4 Cyl — 1992

Ratings

Category	Rating
Safety	6.4
Reliability	9.1
Performance	7.9
Design	8
Fun to drive	7.5
Value	8.5
Overall	8

FWD/AT/PS/AC	BaseList	Whlse	Retail
3 Dr Hbk	6999	**5225**	**6750**
3 Dr SE Hbk	8299	**5850**	**7400**

626 4 Cyl — 1992

Ratings

Category	Rating
Safety	7.2
Reliability	8.1
Performance	7.5
Design	8.3
Fun to drive	7.5
Value	7.8
Overall	7.7

FWD/AT/PS/AC	BaseList	Whlse	Retail
4 Dr DX Sdn	13025	**9000**	**11000**
4 Dr LX Sdn	14595	**9875**	**12025**

929 V6 — 1992

Ratings

Category	Rating
Safety	9.5
Reliability	9.1
Performance	8.3
Design	7.7
Fun to drive	7.9
Value	8.2
Overall	8.8

AT/PS/AC	BaseList	Whlse	Retail
4 Dr Sdn	27800	**17025**	**20000**

B-SERIES PICKUPS 4 Cyl — 1992

Ratings

Category	Rating
Safety	7.4
Reliability	8.7
Performance	7
Design	8.3
Fun to drive	6.7
Value	8
Overall	7.8

5SP/PS/AC	BaseList	Whlse	Retail
Pkup	8495	**5950**	**7525**
LB Pkup	9210	**6100**	**7650**
Cab Plus Pkup	9995	**7175**	**8950**
4WD Pkup	11495	**8275**	**10125**
4WD Cab Plus Pkup	12995	**9525**	**11475**

MPV 4 Cyl — 1992

Ratings

Category	Rating
Safety	7.1
Reliability	5.6
Performance	7.2
Design	8.8
Fun to drive	7
Value	8.6
Overall	6.8

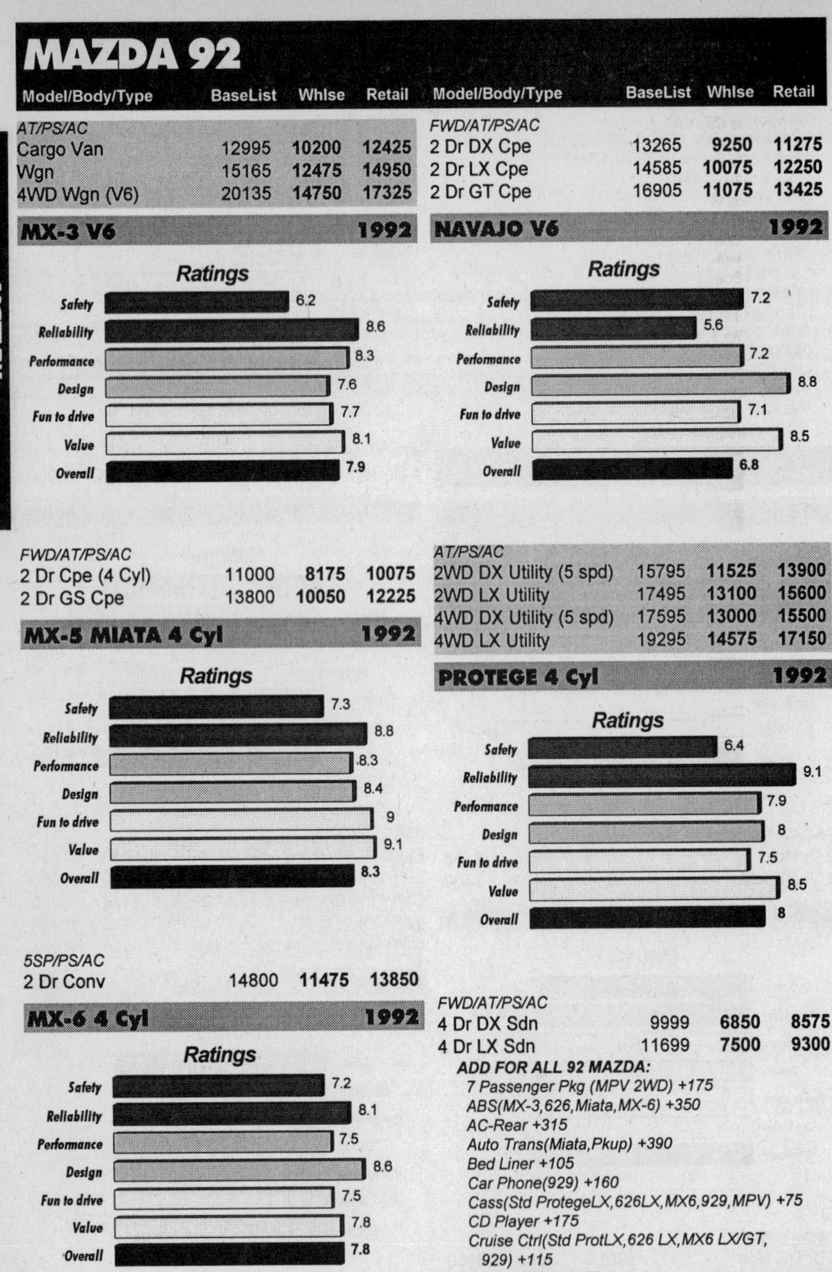

MAZDA

MAZDA 92

Model/Body/Type	BaseList	Whlse	Retail
AT/PS/AC			
Cargo Van	12995	**10200**	**12425**
Wgn	15165	**12475**	**14950**
4WD Wgn (V6)	20135	**14750**	**17325**

MX-3 V6 — 1992

Ratings

Rating	Score
Safety	6.2
Reliability	8.6
Performance	8.3
Design	7.6
Fun to drive	7.7
Value	8.1
Overall	7.9

Model/Body/Type	BaseList	Whlse	Retail
FWD/AT/PS/AC			
2 Dr Cpe (4 Cyl)	11000	**8175**	**10075**
2 Dr GS Cpe	13800	**10050**	**12225**

MX-5 MIATA 4 Cyl — 1992

Ratings

Rating	Score
Safety	7.3
Reliability	8.8
Performance	8.3
Design	8.4
Fun to drive	9
Value	9.1
Overall	8.3

Model/Body/Type	BaseList	Whlse	Retail
5SP/PS/AC			
2 Dr Conv	14800	**11475**	**13850**

MX-6 4 Cyl — 1992

Ratings

Rating	Score
Safety	7.2
Reliability	8.1
Performance	7.5
Design	8.6
Fun to drive	7.5
Value	7.8
Overall	7.8

Model/Body/Type	BaseList	Whlse	Retail
FWD/AT/PS/AC			
2 Dr DX Cpe	13265	**9250**	**11275**
2 Dr LX Cpe	14585	**10075**	**12250**
2 Dr GT Cpe	16905	**11075**	**13425**

NAVAJO V6 — 1992

Ratings

Rating	Score
Safety	7.2
Reliability	5.6
Performance	7.2
Design	8.8
Fun to drive	7.1
Value	8.5
Overall	6.8

Model/Body/Type	BaseList	Whlse	Retail
AT/PS/AC			
2WD DX Utility (5 spd)	15795	**11525**	**13900**
2WD LX Utility	17495	**13100**	**15600**
4WD DX Utility (5 spd)	17595	**13000**	**15500**
4WD LX Utility	19295	**14575**	**17150**

PROTEGE 4 Cyl — 1992

Ratings

Rating	Score
Safety	6.4
Reliability	9.1
Performance	7.9
Design	8
Fun to drive	7.5
Value	8.5
Overall	8

Model/Body/Type	BaseList	Whlse	Retail
FWD/AT/PS/AC			
4 Dr DX Sdn	9999	**6850**	**8575**
4 Dr LX Sdn	11699	**7500**	**9300**

ADD FOR ALL 92 MAZDA:

7 Passenger Pkg (MPV 2WD) +175
ABS(MX-3,626,Miata,MX-6) +350
AC-Rear +315
Auto Trans(Miata,Pkup) +390
Bed Liner +105
Car Phone(929) +160
Cass(Std ProtegeLX,626LX,MX6,929,MPV) +75
CD Player +175
Cruise Ctrl(Std ProtLX,626 LX,MX6 LX/GT, 929) +115
Custom Whls +160
Detachable Hardtop +470

Model/Body/Type	BaseList	Whlse	Retail
Fiberglass Cap +205			
LE-5 Pkg +330			
Leather Seats +230			
Privacy Glass +125			
Pwr Locks(MX-3,MPV) +75			
Pwr Seat(Navajo) +115			
Pwr Sunroof(Std 929) +390			
Pwr Wndw(MX-3,Miata,MPV) +115			
Running Board +125			
SE-5 Pkg +230			
Sunroof +195			
Towing Pkg +145			
V6 Eng +470			
DEDUCT FOR ALL 92 MAZDA:			
No AC -505			
No Auto Trans -470			
No Pwr Steering -135			

1991 MAZDA

323 4 Cyl — 1991

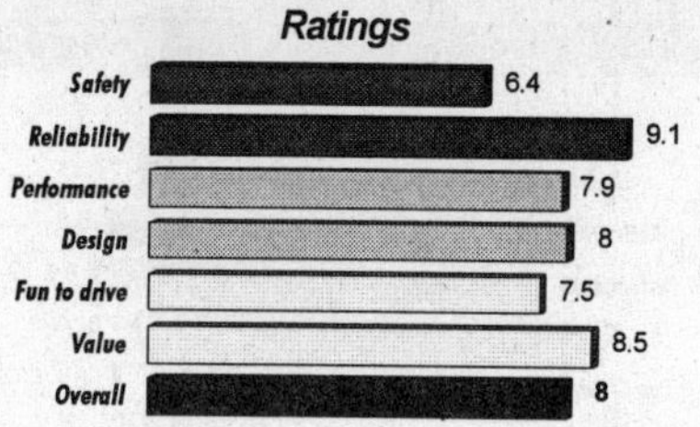

Ratings

Rating	Score
Safety	6.4
Reliability	9.1
Performance	7.9
Design	8
Fun to drive	7.5
Value	8.5
Overall	8

Model/Body/Type	BaseList	Whlse	Retail
FWD/AT/PS/AC			
3 Dr Hbk	6899	**4075**	**5475**
3 Dr SE Hbk	7849	**4600**	**6025**

626 4 Cyl — 1991

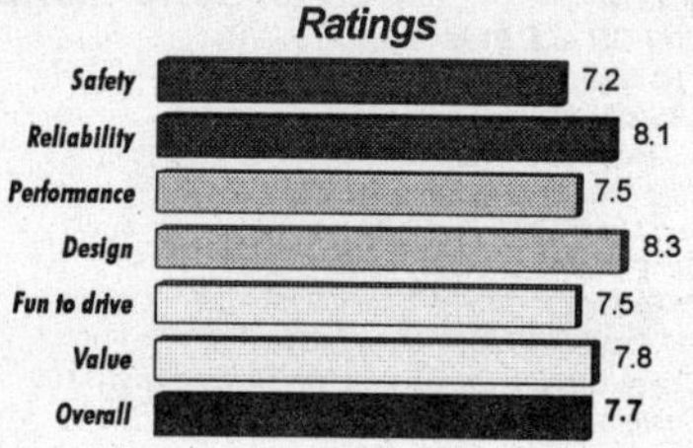

Ratings

Rating	Score
Safety	7.2
Reliability	8.1
Performance	7.5
Design	8.3
Fun to drive	7.5
Value	7.8
Overall	7.7

Model/Body/Type	BaseList	Whlse	Retail
FWD/AT/PS/AC			
4 Dr DX Sdn	12009	**7450**	**9125**
4 Dr LX Sdn	13929	**8100**	**10000**
5 Dr LX Hbk	14129	**8300**	**10200**
5 Dr GT Hbk	15729	**9075**	**11100**

929 V6 — 1991

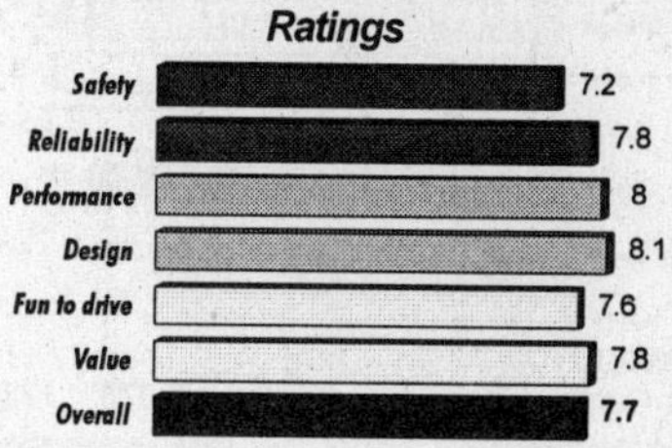

Ratings

Rating	Score
Safety	7.2
Reliability	7.8
Performance	8
Design	8.1
Fun to drive	7.6
Value	7.8
Overall	7.7

Model/Body/Type	BaseList	Whlse	Retail
AT/PS/AC			
4 Dr Sdn	23385	**11700**	**14275**
4 Dr S Sdn	24825	**12275**	**14850**

B-SERIES PICKUPS 4 Cyl — 1991

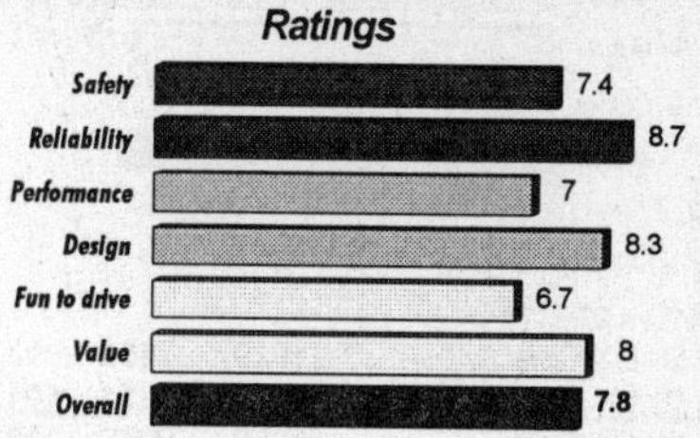

Ratings

Rating	Score
Safety	7.4
Reliability	8.7
Performance	7
Design	8.3
Fun to drive	6.7
Value	8
Overall	7.8

Model/Body/Type	BaseList	Whlse	Retail
5SP/PS/AC			
Pkup	7989	**5375**	**6925**
LB Pkup	8639	**5525**	**7075**
Cab Plus Pkup	9389	**6550**	**8175**
4WD Pkup	10989	**7575**	**9400**
4WD Cab Plus Pkup	12389	**8725**	**10600**

MPV 4 Cyl — 1991

Model/Body/Type	BaseList	Whlse	Retail
AT/PS/AC			
Cargo Van	12415	**8700**	**10700**
Wgn	13715	**10825**	**13175**
4WD Wgn (V6)	19435	**12900**	**15400**

MAZDA 91

Model/Body/Type	BaseList	Whlse	Retail

MX-5 MIATA 4 Cyl 1991

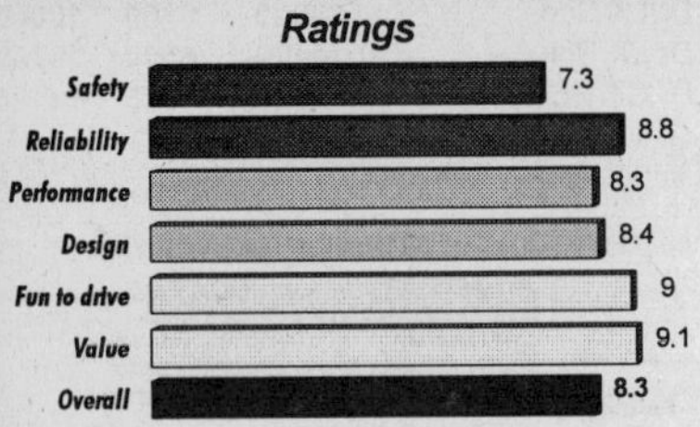

Ratings

Rating	Score
Safety	7.3
Reliability	8.8
Performance	8.3
Design	8.4
Fun to drive	9
Value	9.1
Overall	8.3

5SP/PS/AC			
2 Dr Conv	13800	**10075**	**12250**

MX-6 4 Cyl 1991

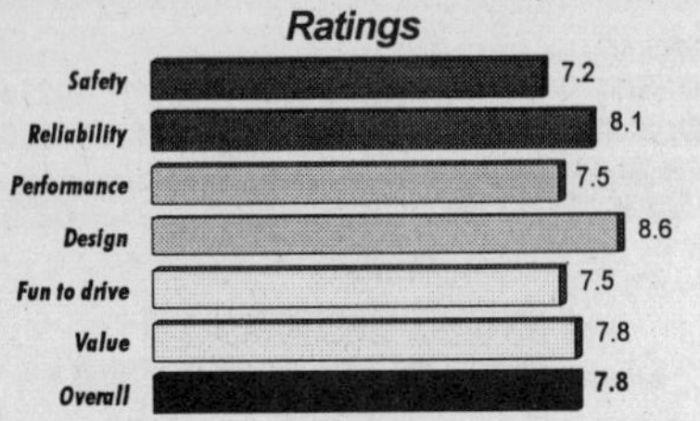

Ratings

Rating	Score
Safety	7.2
Reliability	8.1
Performance	7.5
Design	8.6
Fun to drive	7.5
Value	7.8
Overall	7.8

FWD/AT/PS/AC			
2 Dr DX Cpe	11829	**7450**	**9325**
2 Dr LX Cpe	13769	**8275**	**10175**
2 Dr GT Cpe	16059	**9075**	**11100**

NAVAJO V6 1991

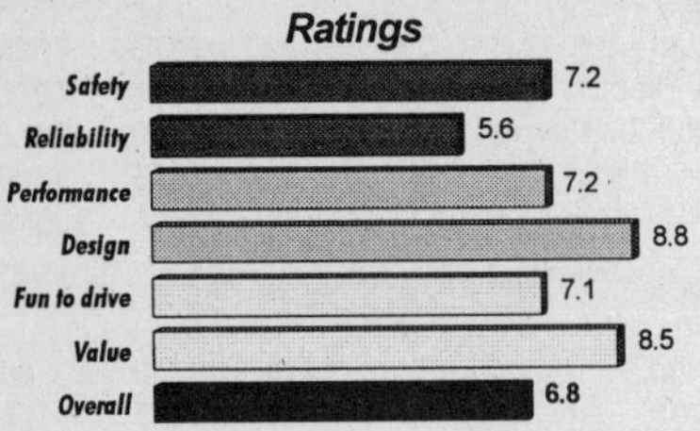

Ratings

Rating	Score
Safety	7.2
Reliability	5.6
Performance	7.2
Design	8.8
Fun to drive	7.1
Value	8.5
Overall	6.8

4WD/AT/PS/AC			
LX Utility	17560	**11975**	**14425**

Model/Body/Type	BaseList	Whlse	Retail

PROTEGE 4 Cyl 1991

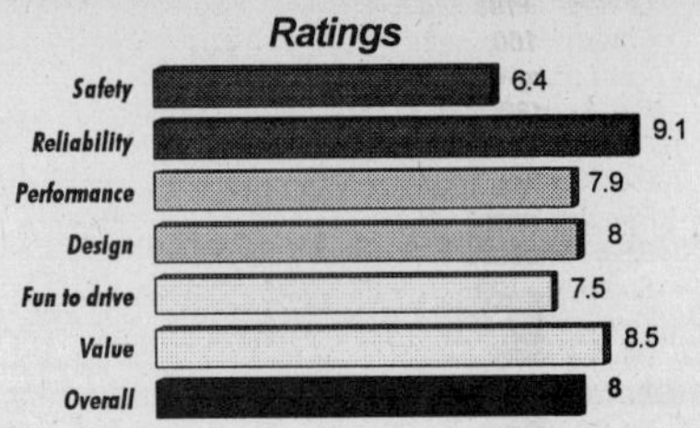

Ratings

Rating	Score
Safety	6.4
Reliability	9.1
Performance	7.9
Design	8
Fun to drive	7.5
Value	8.5
Overall	8

FWD/AT/PS/AC			
4 Dr DX Sdn	9359	**5550**	**7100**
4 Dr LX Sdn	10999	**6125**	**7675**
4 Dr 4WD Sdn	11239	**6200**	**7800**

RX-7 1991

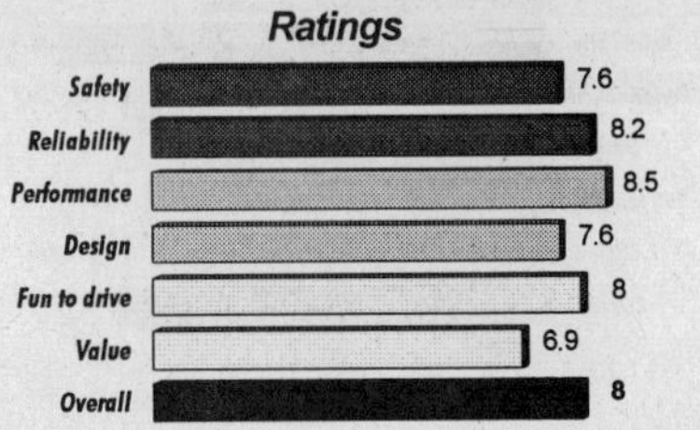

Ratings

Rating	Score
Safety	7.6
Reliability	8.2
Performance	8.5
Design	7.6
Fun to drive	8
Value	6.9
Overall	8

5SP-AT/PS/AC			
2 Dr Cpe	19335	**11050**	**13475**
2 Dr Turbo Cpe	26555	**14125**	**16825**
2 Dr Conv	27715	**15375**	**18150**

ADD FOR ALL 91 MAZDA:

7 Passenger Pkg(MPV 2WD) +135
ABS(626,Miata,MX-6) +315
AC-Rear +250
Auto Trans(Miata,Pkup) +350
Bed Liner +80
Car Phone(929,RX-7) +135
Cass(Std LX,GT,RX-7,MPV,929) +60
CD Player(Std RX-7 Conv) +160
Cruise Ctrl(Std LX,GT,929,RX-7 Trbo/Conv) +100
Custom Whls +135
Detachable Hardtop +430
Fiberglass Cap +170
LE-5 Pkg +290
Leather Seats(Std RX-7 Conv) +195
Privacy Glass +105
Pwr Locks(MPV) +60
Pwr Sunroof(Std RX-7 Turbo,929) +350

Model/Body/Type	BaseList	Whlse	Retail

Pwr Wndw(Miata,MPV) +100
Running Board +105
SE-5 Pkg +195
Sunroof +160
Towing Pkg +105
V6 Eng +430
DEDUCT FOR ALL 91 MAZDA:
No AC -470
No Auto Trans -430
No Pwr Steering -115

1990 MAZDA

323 4 Cyl — 1990

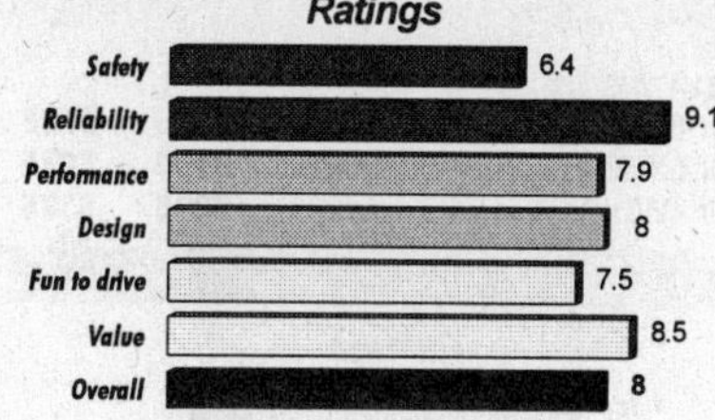

FWD/AT/PS/AC			
3 Dr Hbk	6599	**3225**	**4525**
3 Dr SE Hbk	8329	**3600**	**4925**

626 4 Cyl — 1990

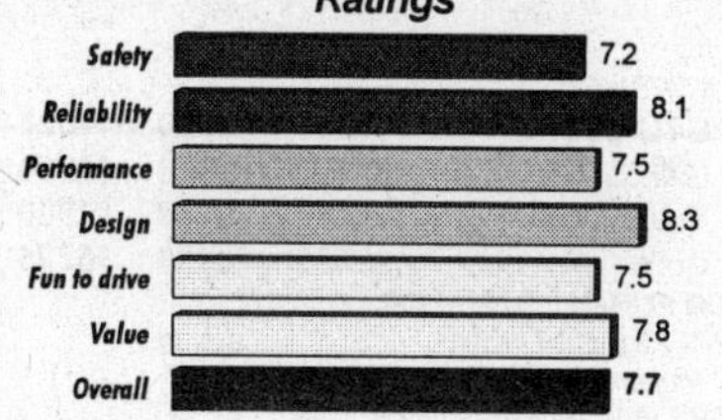

FWD/AT/PS/AC			
4 Dr DX Sdn	12459	**5975**	**7700**
4 Dr LX Sdn	13929	**6725**	**8550**
5 Dr LX Hbk	14129	**6950**	**8775**
5 Dr GT Hbk	15699	**7475**	**9375**

929 V6 — 1990

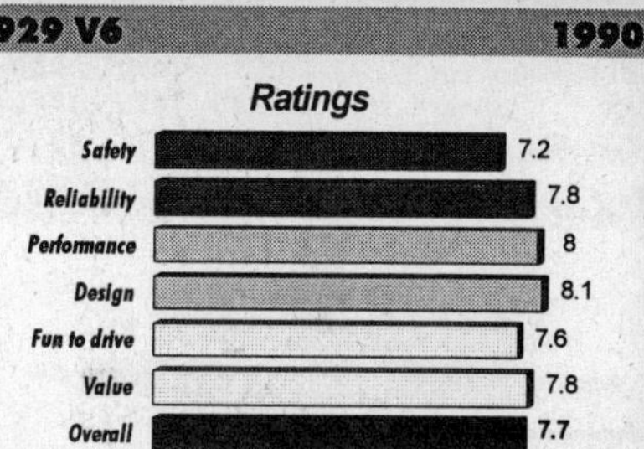

AT/PS/AC			
4 Dr Sdn	23300	**9650**	**11800**
4 Dr S Sdn	24800	**10150**	**12425**

B-SERIES PICKUPS 4 Cyl — 1990

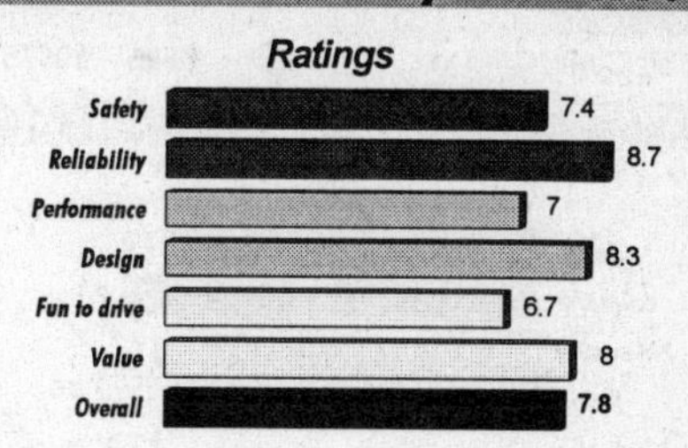

5SP/PS/AC			
Pkup	7949	**4425**	**5850**
LB Pkup	8599	**4550**	**5975**
Cab Plus Pkup	9349	**5375**	**6925**
4WD Pkup	10819	**6450**	**8050**
4WD Cab Plus Pkup	12579	**7425**	**9225**

MPV 4 Cyl — 1990

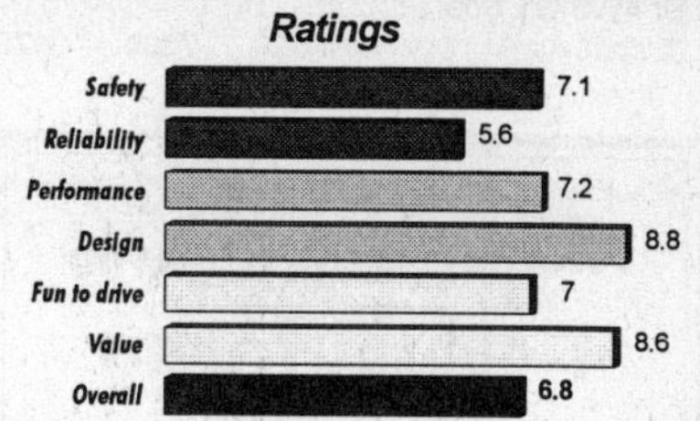

MAZDA 90

Model/Body/Type	BaseList	Whlse	Retail
AT/PS/AC			
Cargo Van	11699	**7400**	**9275**
Wgn	13699	**9400**	**11425**
4WD Wgn (V6)	18894	**11075**	**13425**

MX-5 MIATA 4 Cyl 1990

Ratings

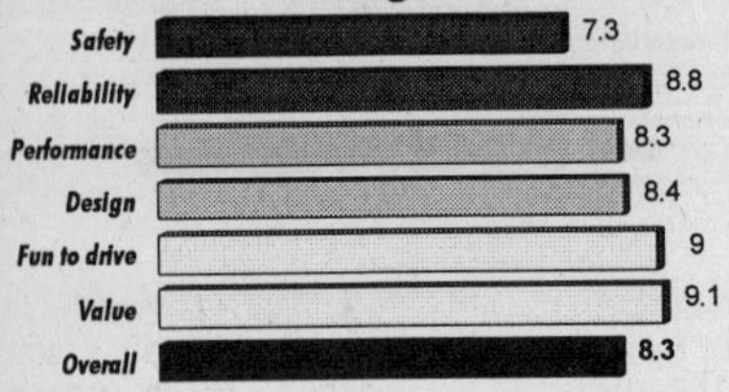

Rating	Score
Safety	7.3
Reliability	8.8
Performance	8.3
Design	8.4
Fun to drive	9
Value	9.1
Overall	8.3

Model/Body/Type	BaseList	Whlse	Retail
5SP/PS/AC			
2 Dr Conv	13800	**8625**	**10575**

MX-6 4 Cyl 1990

Ratings

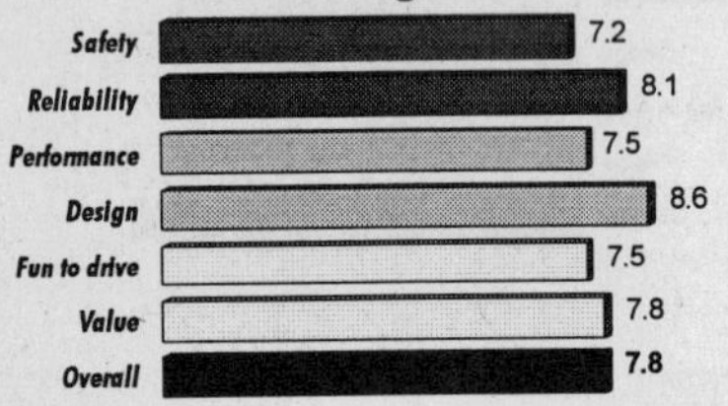

Rating	Score
Safety	7.2
Reliability	8.1
Performance	7.5
Design	8.6
Fun to drive	7.5
Value	7.8
Overall	7.8

Model/Body/Type	BaseList	Whlse	Retail
FWD/AT/PS/AC			
2 Dr DX Cpe	12279	**6150**	**7875**
2 Dr LX Cpe	13769	**6900**	**8725**
2 Dr GT Cpe	16029	**7450**	**9325**
2 Dr 4WS GT Cpe (5 spd)	17229	**7300**	**9175**

PROTEGE 4 Cyl 1990

Ratings

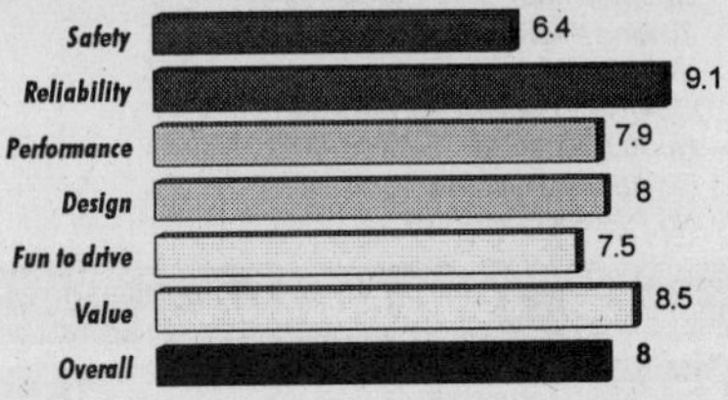

Rating	Score
Safety	6.4
Reliability	9.1
Performance	7.9
Design	8
Fun to drive	7.5
Value	8.5
Overall	8

Model/Body/Type	BaseList	Whlse	Retail
FWD/AT/PS/AC			
4 Dr SE Sdn	9339	**4325**	**5725**
4 Dr LX Sdn	10549	**4800**	**6275**
4 Dr 4WD Sdn	11239	**4875**	**6375**

RX-7 1990

Ratings

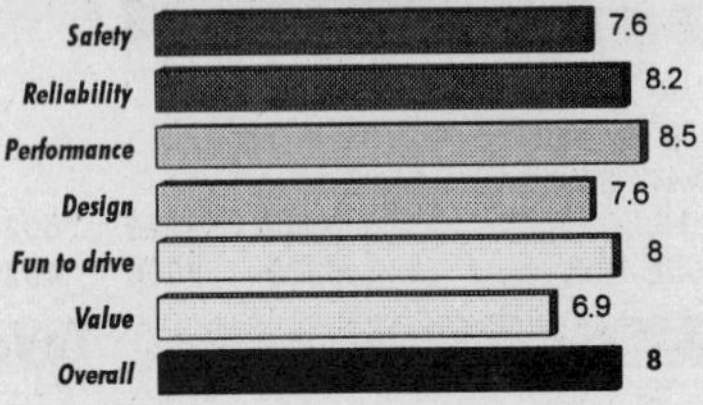

Rating	Score
Safety	7.6
Reliability	8.2
Performance	8.5
Design	7.6
Fun to drive	8
Value	6.9
Overall	8

Model/Body/Type	BaseList	Whlse	Retail
5SP-AT/PS/AC			
2 Dr GTU Cpe	17880	**8950**	**11025**
2 Dr GXL Cpe	22330	**9950**	**12200**
2 Dr Turbo Cpe	26530	**10575**	**12900**
2 Dr Conv	26530	**13100**	**15725**

ADD FOR ALL 90 MAZDA:

2+2 Pkg (RX-7) +135
7 Passenger Pkg (MPV 2WD) +115
ABS (626,MX-6,Base 929) +275
AC-Rear +185
Auto Trans (Pkup) +315
Cass(Std 626,MX-6,RX-7,929,MPV) +60
CD Player(Std RX-7 Conv) +115
Cruise Ctrl(Protege,626DX,MX6 DX,Miata,MPV) +75
Custom Whls +115
Detachable Hardtop +390
Fiberglass Cap +125
LE-5 Pkg +275
Leather Seats(Std RX-7 Conv) +135
Privacy Glass +80
Pwr Locks (Protege,MPV) +60
Pwr Sunroof(Std 4WS,GXL,Turbo,929) +315
Pwr Wndw (Protege,Miata,MPV) +75

Model/Body/Type	BaseList	Whlse	Retail
Running Board +80			
SE-5 Pkg +175			
Towing Pkg +80			
V6 Eng +390			
DEDUCT FOR ALL 90 MAZDA:			
No AC -430			
No Auto Trans -390			
No Pwr Steering -100			

1989 MAZDA

323 4 Cyl — 1989

Model/Body/Type	BaseList	Whlse	Retail
FWD/AT/PS/AC			
3 Dr Hbk	6299	**2725**	**3900**
3 Dr SE Hbk	7399	**3100**	**4375**
3 Dr 4WD GTX Hbk (5 spd)	12999	**5075**	**6600**
4 Dr SE Sdn	8299	**3475**	**4800**
4 Dr LX Sdn	9499	**3875**	**5225**

626 4 Cyl — 1989

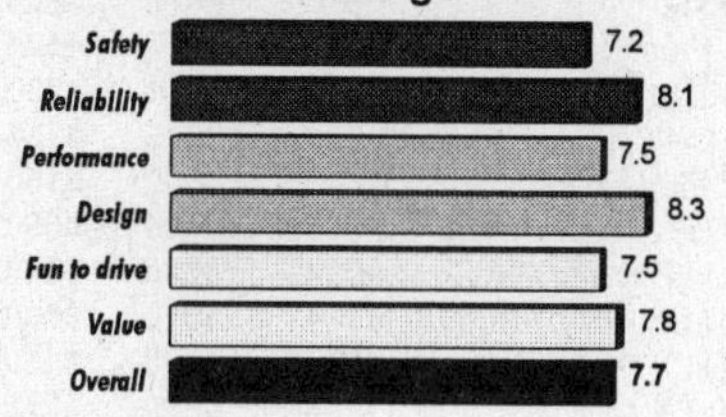

Model/Body/Type	BaseList	Whlse	Retail
FWD/AT/PS/AC			
4 Dr DX Sdn	11299	**4750**	**6375**
4 Dr LX Sdn	13199	**5400**	**7125**
5 Dr LX Touring Hbk	13399	**5650**	**7300**
5 Dr Touring Turbo Hbk	15049	**6100**	**7800**

929 V6 — 1989

Model/Body/Type	BaseList	Whlse	Retail
AT/PS/AC			
4 Dr Luxury Sdn	21920	**6650**	**8575**

B-SERIES PICKUPS 4 Cyl — 1989

Ratings

Rating	Score
Safety	7.4
Reliability	8.7
Performance	7
Design	8.3
Fun to drive	6.7
Value	8
Overall	7.8

Model/Body/Type	BaseList	Whlse	Retail
5SP/PS/AC			
Pkup	7799	**3100**	**4375**
LB Pkup	8299	**3200**	**4500**
Cab Plus LX Pkup	11099	**4750**	**6225**
4WD Pkup	10609	**4900**	**6425**
4WD Cab Plus LX Pkup	13779	**6650**	**8275**

MPV 4 Cyl — 1989

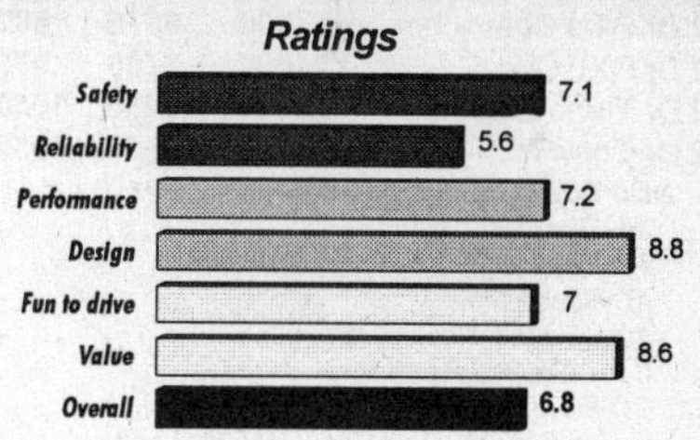

Model/Body/Type	BaseList	Whlse	Retail
AT/PS/AC			
Cargo Van	10989	**5700**	**7375**
Wgn	13759	**7450**	**9325**
4WD Wgn (V6)	18379	**9025**	**11025**

MX-6 4 Cyl — 1989

Ratings

Rating	Score
Safety	7.2
Reliability	8.1
Performance	7.5
Design	8.6
Fun to drive	7.5
Value	7.8
Overall	7.8

MAZDA 89-88

Model/Body/Type	BaseList	Whlse	Retail
FWD/AT/PS/AC			
2 Dr DX Cpe	11399	**4875**	**6550**
2 Dr LX Cpe	13299	**5550**	**7225**
2 Dr GT Cpe	15499	**6025**	**7750**
2 Dr 4WS GT Cpe (5 spd)	16699	**5875**	**7600**

RX-7 1989

Ratings

Rating	Score
Safety	7.6
Reliability	8.2
Performance	8.5
Design	7.6
Fun to drive	8
Value	6.9
Overall	8

Model/Body/Type	BaseList	Whlse	Retail
5SP-AT/PS/AC			
2 Dr GTU Cpe	17300	**6875**	**8825**
2 Dr GXL Cpe	21600	**7700**	**9750**
2 Dr Turbo Cpe	25950	**8450**	**10500**
2 Dr Conv	25600	**10900**	**13325**

ADD FOR ALL 89 MAZDA:

2+2 Pkg (RX-7) +115
7 Passenger Pkg (MPV 2WD) +100
AC-Rear +145
Auto Trans (Pkup) +275
Cass (DX,323,Pkup) +35
CD Player(Std RX-7 Conv) +75
Cruise Ctrl (323,DX,MPV,GTU,Pkup) +60
Custom Whls +75
Fiberglass Cap +80
Leather Seats(Std Conv) +115
Pwr Locks (323,DX,MPV,GTU,Pkup) +35
Pwr Sunroof(Std 4WS,RX-7 GXL/Turbo,929) +250
Pwr Wndw (323,DX,MPV,GTU,Pkup) +60
SE-5 Pkg +160
Sunroof +100
V6 Eng +350

DEDUCT FOR ALL 89 MAZDA:

No AC -390
No Auto Trans -350
No Pwr Steering -75

1988 MAZDA

323 4 Cyl 1988

Model/Body/Type	BaseList	Whlse	Retail
FWD/AT/PS/AC			
3 Dr Hbk	5999	**1825**	**2900**
3 Dr SE Hbk	6700	**2000**	**3100**
3 Dr 4WD GTX Hbk (5 spd)	12749	**4125**	**5525**
4 Dr Sdn	6949	**2200**	**3300**
4 Dr SE Sdn	7649	**2350**	**3475**
4 Dr LX Sdn	8999	**2700**	**3875**
4 Dr GT Sdn (5 spd)	11499	**3175**	**4475**
5 Dr Wgn	7849	**2300**	**3425**

626 4 Cyl 1988

Model/Body/Type	BaseList	Whlse	Retail
FWD/AT/PS/AC			
4 Dr DX Sdn	10499	**3500**	**4900**
4 Dr LX Sdn	12399	**3875**	**5350**
5 Dr LX Touring Hbk	12599	**4075**	**5600**
4 Dr Turbo Sdn	13999	**4350**	**5875**
5 Dr Touring Turbo Hbk	14199	**4550**	**6125**
4 Dr 4WS Turbo Sdn	17149	**4600**	**6175**

929 V6 1988

Model/Body/Type	BaseList	Whlse	Retail
AT/PS/AC			
4 Dr Luxury Sdn	18950	**5300**	**7150**

B-SERIES PICKUPS 4 Cyl 1988

Model/Body/Type	BaseList	Whlse	Retail
5SP/PS/AC			
Pkup	7099	**2350**	**3475**
LB Pkup	7599	**2475**	**3625**
Cab Plus Pkup	8599	**3225**	**4525**
LX Pkup	9049	**2950**	**4200**
LX LB Pkup	9549	**3075**	**4350**
Cab Plus LX Pkup	10099	**3800**	**5150**
4WD Pkup	9849	**4100**	**5500**
4WD LB Pkup	10349	**4225**	**5650**
4WD Cab Plus Pkup	11349	**4950**	**6500**
4WD LX Pkup	12049	**4700**	**6150**
4WD LX LB Pkup	12549	**4800**	**6275**
4WD Cab Plus LX Pkup	13099	**5575**	**7125**

MX-6 4 Cyl 1988

Model/Body/Type	BaseList	Whlse	Retail
FWD/AT/PS/AC			
2 Dr DX Cpe	10599	**3600**	**5025**
2 Dr LX Cpe	12499	**3975**	**5500**
2 Dr GT Cpe	14499	**4350**	**5875**

RX-7 1988

Model/Body/Type	BaseList	Whlse	Retail
5SP-AT/PS/AC			
2 Dr SE Cpe	15480	**4725**	**6500**
2 Dr GTU Cpe	17350	**4950**	**6750**
2 Dr GXL Cpe	19160	**5650**	**7475**
2 Dr Turbo Cpe	21800	**6125**	**8000**
2 Dr Conv	20500	**8500**	**10575**

ADD FOR ALL 88 MAZDA:

Auto Trans (Pkup) +230
SE-5 Pkg +135

DEDUCT FOR ALL 88 MAZDA:

No AC -330
No Auto Trans -290

1987 MAZDA

Model/Body/Type	BaseList	Whlse	Retail
323 4 Cyl			**1987**
FWD/AT/PS/AC			
3 Dr Hbk (4 spd)	5999	1450	2400
3 Dr SE Hbk	6699	1825	2900
3 Dr Dlx Hbk	7649	2050	3125
4 Dr Dlx Sdn	8199	2250	3350
4 Dr Luxury Sdn	8799	2425	3575
5 Dr Dlx Wgn	8799	2350	3475
626 4 Cyl			**1987**
FWD/AT/PS/AC			
4 Dr Dlx Sdn	9849	2400	3625
2 Dr Dlx Cpe	9899	2500	3750
4 Dr Luxury Sdn	11599	2750	4025
2 Dr Luxury Cpe	11799	2850	4175
5 Dr Luxury Touring Hbk	12299	2950	4300
4 Dr GT Sdn (5 spd)	13049	2800	4125
2 Dr GT Cpe (5 spd)	13349	2900	4250
5 Dr GT Touring Hbk (5 spd)	13949	3000	4350
B-SERIES PICKUPS 4 Cyl			**1987**
5SP/PS/AC			
Pkup	6395	2025	3125
LB Pkup	6595	2150	3225
Cab Plus Pkup	7795	2825	4075
LX Pkup	7895	2475	3625
LX LB Pkup	8095	2600	3750
Cab Plus LX Pkup	8995	3275	4600
4WD Pkup	9399	3625	4950
4WD LB Pkup	9799	3750	5075
4WD Cab Plus Pkup	10799	4475	5875
4WD LX Pkup	11499	4125	5525
4WD LX LB Pkup	11899	4250	5675
4WD Cab Plus LX Pkup	12449	4925	6450
RX-7			**1987**
5SP-AT/PS/AC			
2 Dr Cpe	14199	3275	4850
2 Dr GXL Cpe	18449	4100	5775
2 Dr Turbo Cpe	20195	4450	6150

ADD FOR ALL 87 MAZDA:
Sport Pkg (RX-7) +250
DEDUCT FOR ALL 87 MAZDA:
No AC -195
No Auto Trans -175

1986 MAZDA

Model/Body/Type	BaseList	Whlse	Retail
323			**1986**
FWD			
3 Dr Hbk	5495	900	1900
3 Dr Dlx Hbk	6495	1125	2175
3 Dr Luxury Hbk	7195	1275	2300
4 Dr Dlx Sdn	6995	1325	2375
4 Dr Luxury Sdn	7595	1450	2550
626			**1986**
FWD			
4 Dr Dlx Sdn	8695	1625	2750
2 Dr Dlx Cpe	8895	1700	2850
4 Dr Luxury Sdn	10295	1875	3075
2 Dr Luxury Cpe	10595	1975	3150
5 Dr Luxury Touring Hbk	11295	2075	3250
4 Dr GT Turbo Sdn	11945	1975	3150
2 Dr GT Turbo Cpe	12245	2050	3250
5 Dr GT Turbo Touring Hbk	12945	2175	3350
B2200 PICKUPS			**1986**
Pkup	5995	1500	2600
LB Pkup	6195	1600	2725
Cab Plus Pkup	6895	2200	3400
LX Pkup	6995	1900	3100
LX LB Pkup	7195	2025	3200
Cab Plus LX Pkup	7895	2625	3900
RX-7			**1986**
2 Dr Cpe	11995	2700	4000
2 Dr GXL Cpe	16695	3275	4675

1985 MAZDA

Model/Body/Type	BaseList	Whlse	Retail
626			**1985**
4 Dr Dlx Sdn	8495	1225	2275
2 Dr Dlx Cpe	8845	1300	2350
4 Dr Luxury Sdn	10245	1450	2550
2 Dr Luxury Cpe	10595	1550	2650
4 Dr Luxury Touring Sdn	11245	1625	2750
GLC			**1985**
3 Dr Hbk	5195	500	1450
3 Dr Dlx Hbk	6095	675	1650
3 Dr Luxury Hbk	6795	825	1775
4 Dr Dlx Sdn	6695	850	1800
4 Dr Luxury Sdn	7395	950	1975
RX-7			**1985**
2 Dr S Cpe	10945	1950	3125
2 Dr GS Cpe	11845	2025	3225
2 Dr GSL Cpe	13645	2275	3500
2 Dr GSL-SE Cpe	15645	2475	3750

MERCEDES Germany

1992 Mercedes-Benz 500SL

For a Mercedes-Benz dealer in your area, see our Dealer Directory (pg 217)

1994 MERCEDES-BENZ

Model/Body/Type	BaseList	Whlse	Retail
C-CLASS 6 CYL			**1994**
AT/PS/AC			
4 Dr C220 Sdn (4 Cyl)	29900	-	-
4 Dr C280 Sdn	34900	**29325**	**33425**
E-CLASS			**1994**
AT/PS/AC			
6 CYL Models			
4 Dr E320 Sdn	42500	**35100**	**39075**
4 Dr E320 Wgn	46200	-	-
2 Dr E320 Cpe	61600	-	-
2 Dr E320 Conv	77300	-	-
V8 Models			
4 Dr E420 Sdn	51000	-	-
4 Dr E500 Sdn	80800	-	-
S-CLASS			**1994**
AT/PS/AC			
6 CYL Models			
4 Dr S320 Sdn	70600	-	-
4 Dr S350D Turbo Sdn	70600	-	-
V8 Models			
4 Dr S420 Sdn	79500	**56550**	**60450**
4 Dr S500 Sdn	95300	-	-
2 Dr S500 Cpe	99800	-	-
SL-CLASS 6 CYL			**1994**
AT/PS/AC			
2 Dr SL320 Cpe/Roadster	85200	-	-
2 Dr SL500 Cpe/Roadster (V8)	99500	-	-

ADD FOR ALL 94 MERCEDES-BENZ:

Anti-Theft/Recovery Sys +365
Car Phone +230
CD Player +340
Lthr Seats(C280,E320 Wgn) +590
Traction Control(Std E500,S500,SL500) +955

1993 MERCEDES-BENZ

190 4 Cyl **1993**

Ratings

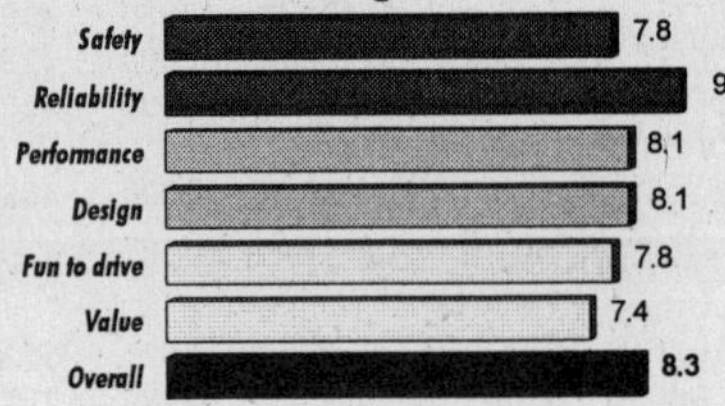

Model/Body/Type	BaseList	Whlse	Retail
AT/PS/AC			
190E 2.3 4 Dr Sdn	28950	**19575**	**23000**
190E 2.6 4 Dr Sdn (6 Cyl)	34000	**22350**	**26025**

300 6 Cyl 1993

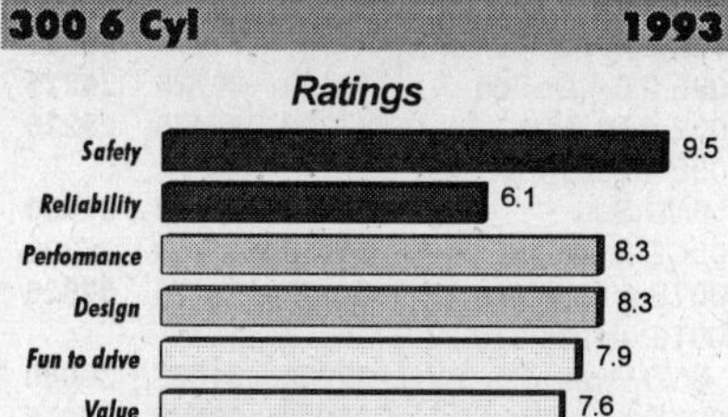

AT/PS/AC

Model/Body/Type	BaseList	Whlse	Retail
300D 2.5 4 Dr TurboSdn	43800	**29675**	**33825**
300E 2.8 4 Dr Sdn	43800	**28600**	**32650**
300E 4 Dr Sdn	49900	**32675**	**36700**
300E 4Matic 4 Dr 4WD Sdn	57700	**36325**	**40525**
300CE 2 Dr Cpe	61000	**39325**	**44050**
300CE 2 Dr Cabriolet	76500	**56750**	**61725**
300TE 4 Dr Wgn	54400	**36725**	**40925**
300TE 4Matic 4 Dr 4WD Wgn	61700	**40325**	**44950**
300SD 4 Dr Turbo Sdn	69900	**46675**	**51025**
300SE 4 Dr Sdn	69900	**47725**	**52125**
300SL 2 Dr Cpe/Rdstr	83300	**58250**	**64350**

400 V8 1993

AT/PS/AC

Model/Body/Type	BaseList	Whlse	Retail
400E 4 Dr Sdn	56400	**38175**	**42725**
400SEL 4 Dr Sdn	78700	**54075**	**57825**

500 V8 1993

AT/PS/AC

Model/Body/Type	BaseList	Whlse	Retail
500E 4 Dr Sdn	80000	**53550**	**58275**
500SEL 4 Dr Sdn	94400	**61450**	**67725**
500SEC 2 Dr Cpe	98900	**65950**	**72475**
500SL 2 Dr Cpe/Rdstr	98500	**69100**	**75800**

ADD FOR ALL 93 MERCEDES-BENZ:

Car Phone +175
CD Player +290
Leather Seats(190,300D/E2.8/TE) +470
Pwr Sunroof(190E 2.3) +505

DEDUCT FOR ALL 93 MERCEDES-BENZ:

No Auto Trans -585

1992 MERCEDES-BENZ

190 4 Cyl 1992

Ratings

Safety 7.8
Reliability 9
Performance 8.1
Design 8.1
Fun to drive 7.8
Value 7.4
Overall 8.3

AT/PS/AC

Model/Body/Type	BaseList	Whlse	Retail
190E 2.3 4 Dr Sdn	29850	**17700**	**21025**
190E 2.6 4 Dr Sdn (6 Cyl)	34900	**20250**	**23725**

300 6 Cyl 1992

Ratings

Safety 9.5
Reliability 6.1
Performance 8.3
Design 8.3
Fun to drive 7.9
Value 7.6
Overall 7.8

AT/PS/AC

Model/Body/Type	BaseList	Whlse	Retail
300D 2.5 4 Dr TurboSdn	42950	**26100**	**30000**
300E 2.6 4 Dr Sdn	42950	**25100**	**29000**
300E 4 Dr Sdn	49500	**29075**	**33150**
300E 4Matic 4 Dr 4WD Sdn	57100	**32750**	**36775**
300CE 2 Dr Cpe	60400	**35925**	**39825**
300TE 4 Dr Wgn	53900	**33350**	**37150**
300TE 4Matic 4 Dr 4WD Wgn	61100	**36700**	**40900**
300SD 4 Dr Turbo Sdn	69400	**42275**	**47025**
300SE 4 Dr Sdn	69400	**43125**	**47600**
300SL 2 Dr Cpe/Rdstr	83500	**56100**	**59975**

400 V8 1992

AT/PS/AC

Model/Body/Type	BaseList	Whlse	Retail
400E 4 Dr Sdn	54800	**34450**	**38425**
400SE 4 Dr Sdn	77900	**48900**	**53875**

MERCEDES-BENZ 92-90

Model/Body/Type	BaseList	Whlse	Retail
500 V8 — 1992			
AT/PS/AC			
500E 4 Dr Sdn	79200	**48975**	**53950**
500SEL 4 Dr Sdn	93500	**57200**	**62200**
500SL 2 Dr Cpe/Rdstr	97500	**63600**	**70000**

ADD FOR ALL 92 MERCEDES-BENZ:
Car Phone +160
CD Player +250
Leather Seats(190,300D/E2.6,TE) +410
Pwr Sunroof(190E 2.3) +470

DEDUCT FOR ALL 92 MERCEDES-BENZ:
No Auto Trans -545

1991 MERCEDES-BENZ

190 4 Cyl — 1991

Ratings

Rating	Score
Safety	7.8
Reliability	9
Performance	8.1
Design	8.1
Fun to drive	7.8
Value	7.4
Overall	8.3

Model/Body/Type	BaseList	Whlse	Retail
AT/PS/AC			
190E 2.3 4 Dr Sdn	28950	**14750**	**17725**
190E 2.6 4 Dr Sdn (6 Cyl)	33700	**17000**	**20200**

300 6 Cyl — 1991

Ratings

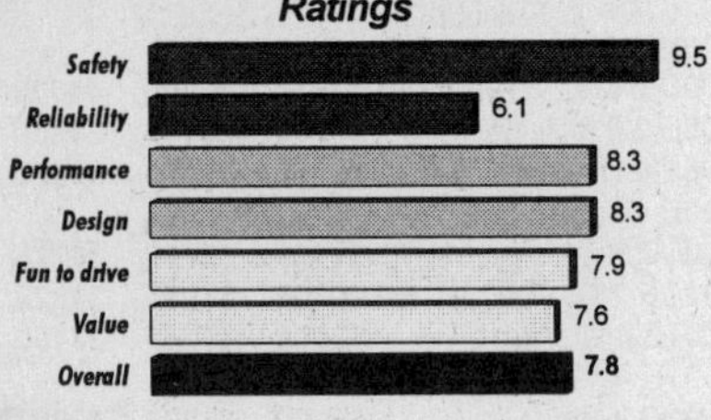

Model/Body/Type	BaseList	Whlse	Retail
AT/PS/AC			
300D 2.5 4 Dr TurboSdn	41000	**21475**	**25050**
300E 2.6 4 Dr Sdn	41000	**20725**	**24225**
300E 4 Dr Sdn	47200	**24425**	**28225**
300E 4Matic 4 Dr 4WD Sdn	54150	**27800**	**31850**
300CE 2 Dr Cpe	57350	**31250**	**35300**
300TE 4 Dr Wgn	51150	**28475**	**32525**
300TE 4Matic 4 Dr 4WD Wgn	57900	**31825**	**36000**
300SE 4 Dr Sdn	53900	**28525**	**32575**
300SEL 4 Dr Sdn	57800	**31100**	**35125**
300SL 2 Dr Cpe/Rdstr	78500	**49950**	**55475**
350SD 4 Dr Turbo Sdn	53900	**28325**	**32375**
350SDL 4 Dr Turbo Sdn	57800	**30900**	**34925**
420 V8 — 1991			
AT/PS/AC			
420SEL 4 Dr Sdn	63600	**33300**	**37100**
500 V8 — 1991			
AT/PS/AC			
500SL 2 Dr Cpe/Rdstr	89300	**57850**	**62875**
560SEL 4 Dr Sdn	75100	**37350**	**41850**
560SEC 2 Dr Cpe	82900	**41000**	**45675**

ADD FOR ALL 91 MERCEDES-BENZ:
Car Phone +135
Leather or Velour Seats(190,300D/E2.6,TE) +350
Pwr Sunroof(190E 2.3) +430

DEDUCT FOR ALL 91 MERCEDES-BENZ:
No Auto Trans -505

1990 MERCEDES-BENZ

190 6 CYL — 1990

Ratings

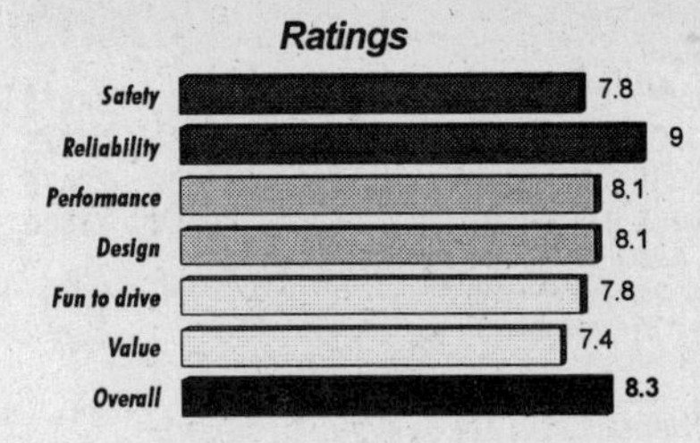

Model/Body/Type	BaseList	Whlse	Retail
AT/PS/AC			
190E 2.6 4 Dr Sdn	32500	**14825**	**17850**

Model/Body/Type	BaseList	Whlse	Retail

300 6 Cyl 1990

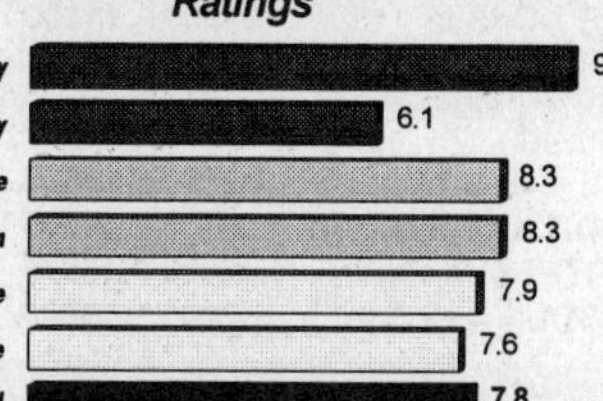

AT/PS/AC

Model/Body/Type	BaseList	Whlse	Retail
300E 2.6 4 Dr Sdn	39950	**17000**	**20200**
300D 2.5 4 Dr TurbSdn	39700	**17400**	**20675**
300E 4 Dr Sdn	45950	**20000**	**23475**
300E 4Matic 4WD Sdn	52550	**23200**	**26925**
300CE 2 Dr Cpe	55700	**26650**	**30650**
300TE 4 Dr Wgn	49650	**23600**	**27350**
300TE 4Matic 4WDWgn	56250	**26750**	**30775**
300SE 4 Dr Sdn	52950	**24075**	**27825**
300SEL 4 Dr Sdn	56800	**26225**	**30150**
300SL 2 Dr Cpe/Rdstr	73500	**45575**	**49875**
350SDL 4 Dr Turbo Sdn	56800	**26025**	**29925**

420 V8 1990

AT/PS/AC

Model/Body/Type	BaseList	Whlse	Retail
420SEL 4 Dr Sdn	62500	**28200**	**32225**

500 1990

AT/PS/AC

Model/Body/Type	BaseList	Whlse	Retail
500SL 2 Dr Cpe/Rdstr	83500	**53125**	**57825**
560SEL 4 Dr Sdn	73800	**32150**	**36375**
560SEC 2 Dr Cpe	81500	**35600**	**39475**

ADD FOR ALL 90 MERCEDES-BENZ:

Lthr or Velour Sts(190,300E 2.6,300D 2.5,TE) +290

DEDUCT FOR ALL 90 MERCEDES-BENZ:

No Auto Trans -470

1989 MERCEDES-BENZ

190 6 Cyl 1989

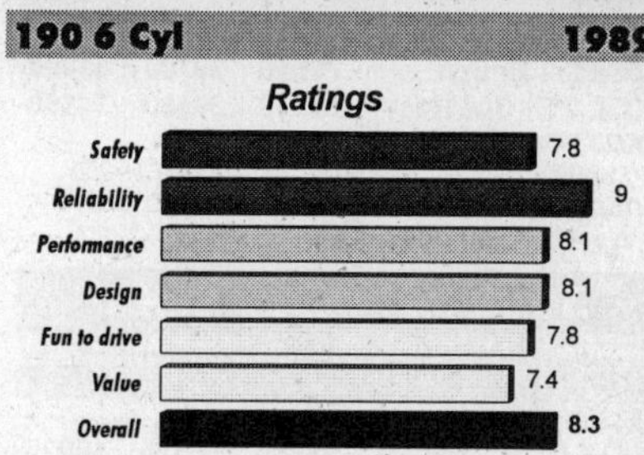

AT/PS/AC

Model/Body/Type	BaseList	Whlse	Retail
190D 4 Dr Sdn (5 Cyl)	30980	**10000**	**12600**
190E 2.6 4 Dr Sdn	31590	**12500**	**15350**

260 6 CYL 1989

AT/PS/AC

Model/Body/Type	BaseList	Whlse	Retail
260E 4 Dr Sdn	39200	**13325**	**16225**

300 6 Cyl 1989

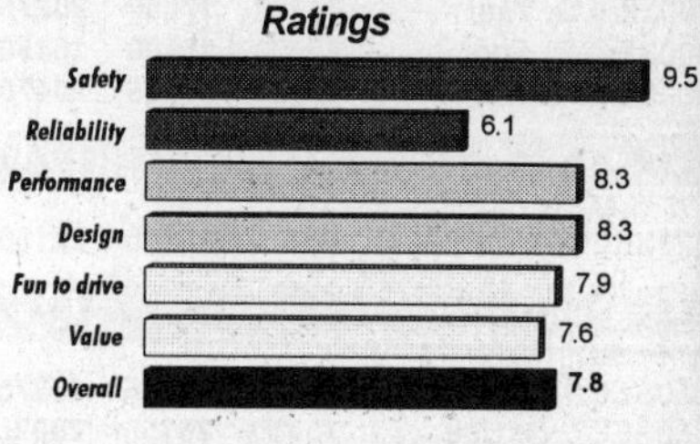

AT/PS/AC

Model/Body/Type	BaseList	Whlse	Retail
300E 4 Dr Sdn	44850	**16075**	**19175**
300CE 2 Dr Cpe	53880	**21625**	**25200**
300TE 4 Dr Wgn	48210	**19125**	**22500**
300SE 4 Dr Sdn	51400	**17800**	**21100**
300SEL 4 Dr Sdn	55100	**19900**	**23375**

420 V8 1989

AT/PS/AC

Model/Body/Type	BaseList	Whlse	Retail
420SEL 4 Dr Sdn	61210	**21625**	**25225**

MERCEDES-BENZ 89-85

MERCEDES-BENZ

Model/Body/Type	BaseList	Whlse	Retail
560 V8			**1989**
AT/PS/AC			
560SEL 4 Dr Sdn	72280	**25725**	**29600**
560SEC 2 Dr Cpe	79840	**29300**	**33400**
560SL 2 Dr Cpe/Rdstr	64230	**30550**	**34550**

ADD FOR ALL 89 MERCEDES-BENZ:
Leather or Velour Seats(190,260,300E/TE) +250
DEDUCT FOR ALL 89 MERCEDES-BENZ:
No Auto Trans -430

1988 MERCEDES-BENZ

Model/Body/Type	BaseList	Whlse	Retail
190			**1988**
AT/PS/AC			
190D 4 Dr Sdn (5 Cyl)	29960	**8575**	**10825**
190E 4 Dr Sdn (4 Cyl)	29190	**10025**	**12625**
190E 2.6 4 Dr Sdn (6 Cyl)	33500	**11050**	**13800**
260 6 CYL			**1988**
AT/PS/AC			
260E 4 Dr Sdn	37250	**12000**	**14775**
300 6 CYL			**1988**
AT/PS/AC			
300E 4 Dr Sdn	42680	**14175**	**17125**
300CE 2 Dr Cpe	52500	**19625**	**23050**
300TE 4 Dr Wgn	46980	**17050**	**20275**
300SE 4 Dr Sdn	49900	**15400**	**18450**
300SEL 4 Dr Sdn	52650	**17225**	**20475**
420 V8			**1988**
AT/PS/AC			
420SEL 4 Dr Sdn	58150	**18800**	**22150**
560 V8			**1988**
AT/PS/AC			
560SEL 4 Dr Sdn	68660	**21675**	**25275**
560SEC 2 Dr Cpe	75850	**25150**	**29025**
560SL 2 Dr Cpe/Rdstr	61130	**25200**	**29075**

ADD FOR ALL 88 MERCEDES-BENZ:
Leather or Velour Seats(190,260,300E/TE) +215
DEDUCT FOR ALL 88 MERCEDES-BENZ:
No Auto Trans -390

1987 MERCEDES-BENZ

Model/Body/Type	BaseList	Whlse	Retail
190 5 Cyl			**1987**
AT/PS/AC			
190D 4 Dr Sdn	27100	**7600**	**9825**
190D-T 4 Dr Sdn	29800	**8200**	**10400**
190E 4 Dr Sdn (4 Cyl)	27100	**8800**	**11125**
190E 2.6 4 Dr Sdn (6 Cyl)	31000	**9500**	**11875**
190E-16V 4 Dr Sdn (4 Cyl)	40300	**13600**	**16525**
260 6 Cyl			**1987**
AT/PS/AC			
260E 4 Dr Sdn	34500	**11200**	**13975**
300 6 Cyl			**1987**
AT/PS/AC			
300E 4 Dr Sdn	39500	**12875**	**15750**
300D-T 4 Dr Sdn	39500	**11900**	**14700**
300TD-T 4 Dr Wgn	42500	**13875**	**16825**
300SDL-T 4 Dr Sdn	47000	**15500**	**18550**
420 V8			**1987**
AT/PS/AC			
420SEL 4 Dr Sdn	52000	**16000**	**19100**
560 V8			**1987**
AT/PS/AC			
560SEL 4 Dr Sdn	61500	**19575**	**23000**
560SEC 2 Dr Cpe	68000	**23050**	**26750**
560SL 2 Dr Cpe/Rdstr	55300	**22150**	**25800**

DEDUCT FOR ALL 87 MERCEDES-BENZ:
No Auto Trans -230

1986 MERCEDES-BENZ

Model/Body/Type	BaseList	Whlse	Retail
MERCEDES-BENZ			**1986**
190D 4 Dr Sdn	24300	**7075**	**9125**
190E 4 Dr Sdn	24300	**7975**	**10050**
190E-16V 4 Dr Sdn	35400	**12375**	**14775**
300E 4 Dr Sdn	34700	**11925**	**14300**
300SDL 4 Dr Sdn	43800	**15100**	**17625**
420SEL 4 Dr Sdn	45100	**15400**	**17925**
560SEL 4 Dr Sdn	53300	**18400**	**21125**
560SEC 2 Dr Cpe	58700	**21900**	**24750**
560SL 2 Dr Cpe/Rdstr	48200	**21175**	**24050**

1985 MERCEDES-BENZ

Model/Body/Type	BaseList	Whlse	Retail
MERCEDES-BENZ			**1985**
190E 4 Dr Sdn	23430	**6500**	**8500**
190D 4 Dr Sdn	23510	**5650**	**7550**
300D-T 4 Dr Sdn	31940	**7750**	**9825**
300CD-T 2 Dr Cpe	35220	**9500**	**11650**
300TD-T 4 Dr Wgn	35310	**9150**	**11275**
300SD 4 Dr Sdn	39500	**10525**	**12800**
380SE 4 Dr Sdn	42730	**11950**	**14325**
380SL 2 Dr Cpe/Rdstr	43820	**18325**	**21050**
500SEL 4 Dr Sdn	51200	**13575**	**16025**
500SEC 2 Dr Cpe	56800	**17000**	**19600**

Model/Body/Type	BaseList	Whlse	Retail

MERCURY USA

1990 Mercury Cougar LS

For a Mercury dealer in your area, see our Dealer Directory (pg 217)

1994 MERCURY

CAPRI 4 Cyl — 1994

PS/AC/FWD

Model/Body/Type	BaseList	Whlse	Retail
2 Dr Conv	13265	-	-
2 Dr XR2 Turbo Conv	15015	-	-

COUGAR — 1994

AT/PS/AC

Model/Body/Type	BaseList	Whlse	Retail
V6 Models			
2 Dr XR-7 Cpe	14855	**13575**	**16225**
V8 Models			
2 Dr XR-7 Cpe	16045	**14175**	**16755**

ADD FOR 94 COUGAR:

ABS +430
Anti-Theft/Recovery Sys +365
CD Player +230 *Cruise Ctrl +160*
Custom Whls/Cvrs +205 *JBL Stereo System +205*
Leather Seats +275 *Pwr Locks +115*
Pwr Seat +160 *Pwr Sunroof +545*

GRAND MARQUIS V8 — 1994

AT/PS/AC

Model/Body/Type	BaseList	Whlse	Retail
4 Dr GS Sdn	22130	**15650**	**18425**
4 Dr LS Sdn	22690	**16400**	**19225**

ADD FOR 94 GRAND MARQUIS:

ABS +430
Anti-Theft/Recovery Sys +365
Car Phone +230 *Custom Whls/Cvrs +230*
Leather Seats +320

SABLE V6 — 1994

FWD/AT/PS/AC

Model/Body/Type	BaseList	Whlse	Retail
4 Dr GS Sdn	17460	**13400**	**16050**
4 Dr GS Wgn	18570	**14500**	**17200**
4 Dr LS Sdn	18540	**14500**	**17200**
4 Dr LS Wgn	19570	**15550**	**18325**

ADD FOR 94 SABLE:

ABS(Std LS) +430
Anti-Theft/Recovery Sys +365
Cass(Std LS) +115 *CD Player +230*
Cruise Ctrl +160 *Custom Whls/Cvrs +205*
Leather Seats +275 *Pwr Locks +115*
Pwr Seat(Std LS) +160 *Pwr Sunroof +545*
Pwr Wndw(Std LS) +160 *Third Seat S/W +205*

TOPAZ 4 Cyl — 1994

Ratings

Rating	Score
Safety	6.9
Reliability	5.5
Performance	7.7
Design	7.5
Fun to drive	7.5
Value	7
Overall	6.7

FWD/AT/PS/AC

Model/Body/Type	BaseList	Whlse	Retail
2 Dr GS Cpe	10900	**8925**	**10825**
4 Dr GS Sdn	10900	**9025**	**10925**

ADD FOR 94 TOPAZ:

Anti-Theft/Recovery Sys +365
Cass +90
Cruise Ctrl +135 *Custom Whls/Cvrs +180*
Driver Side Airbag +340 *Pwr Locks +90*
Pwr Seat +135 *Pwr Wndw +135*
Tilt Whl +90 *V6 Eng +455*

DEDUCT FOR 94 TOPAZ:

No AC -590 *No Auto Trans -500*

TRACER 4 Cyl — 1994

FWD/AT/PS/AC

Model/Body/Type	BaseList	Whlse	Retail
4 Dr Sdn	10155	**9050**	**10950**
4 Dr Wgn	10982	**9875**	**11925**
4 Dr LTS Sdn	12023	**10400**	**12525**

ADD FOR 94 TRACER:

ABS +430
Anti-Theft/Recovery Sys +365
Cass(Std LTS) +90 *CD Player +205*
Cruise Ctrl(Std LTS) +135 *Luggage Rack(S/W) +115*
Pwr Locks +90 *Pwr Sunroof +410*
Pwr Wndw +135 *Tilt Whl(Std LTS) +90*

DEDUCT FOR 94 TRACER:

No AC -545 *No Auto Trans -455*

MERCURY 94-93

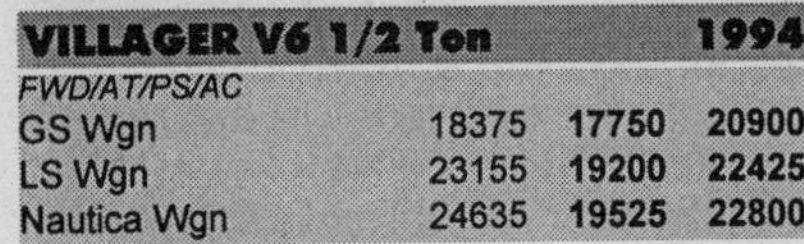

VILLAGER V6 1/2 Ton — 1994

Model/Body/Type	BaseList	Whlse	Retail
FWD/AT/PS/AC			
GS Wgn	18375	**17750**	**20900**
LS Wgn	23155	**19200**	**22425**
Nautica Wgn	24635	**19525**	**22800**

1993 MERCURY

CAPRI 4 Cyl — 1993

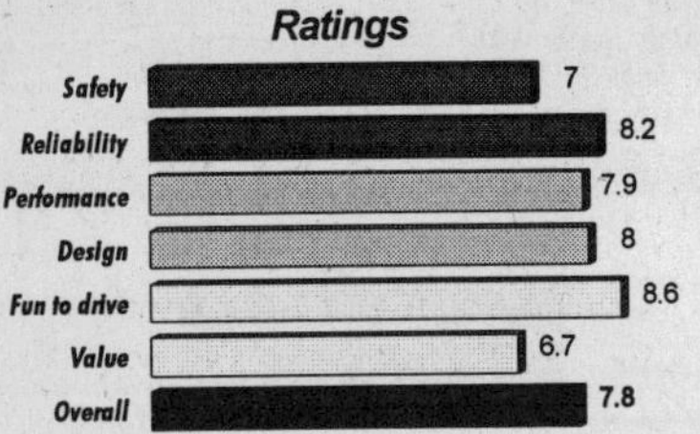

Model/Body/Type	BaseList	Whlse	Retail
PS/AC/FWD			
2 Dr Conv	14452	**9100**	**11125**
2 Dr XR2 Turbo Conv	17250	**10325**	**12550**

ADD FOR 93 CAPRI:

Auto Trans +430
Cass(Std XR2) +100
Cruise Ctrl(Std XR2) +135
Custom Whls/Cvrs +175
Leather Seats +230
Removable Hardtop +505

DEDUCT FOR 93 CAPRI:

No AC -545

COUGAR — 1993

Model/Body/Type	BaseList	Whlse	Retail
AT/PS/AC			
V6 Models			
2 Dr XR-7 Cpe	14855	**10950**	**13375**
V8 Models			
2 Dr XR-7 Cpe	16045	**11500**	**13875**

ADD FOR 93 COUGAR:

ABS +390
Cass +100
CD Player +195
Cruise Ctrl +135
Custom Whls/Cvrs +175
JBL Stereo System +175
Leather Seats +230
Pwr Locks +100
Pwr Seat +135
Pwr Sunroof +430
Tilt Whl +100

See the Automobile Dealer Directory on page 379 for a Dealer near you!

GRAND MARQUIS V8 — 1993

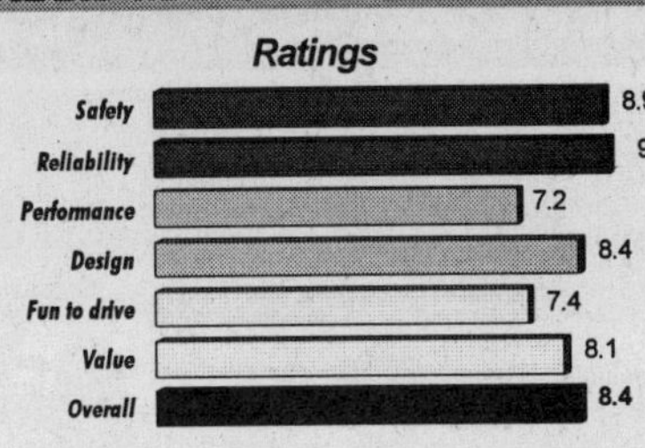

Model/Body/Type	BaseList	Whlse	Retail
AT/PS/AC			
4 Dr GS Sdn	22082	**13275**	**15925**
4 Dr LS Sdn	22609	**13975**	**16650**

ADD FOR 93 GRAND MARQUIS:

ABS +390
Car Phone +175
Custom Whls/Cvrs +195
Leather Seats +275
Vinyl Roof +160

SABLE V6 — 1993

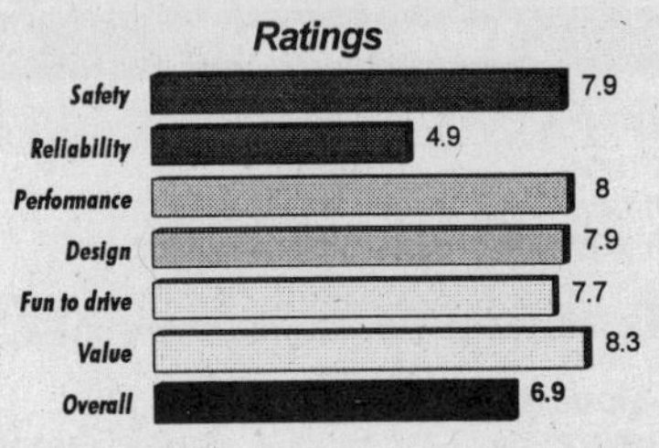

Model/Body/Type	BaseList	Whlse	Retail
FWD/AT/PS/AC			
4 Dr GS Sdn	17480	**11025**	**13450**
4 Dr GS Wgn	18459	**12025**	**14600**
4 Dr LS Sdn	18430	**12025**	**14600**
4 Dr LS Wgn	19457	**13000**	**15625**

ADD FOR 93 SABLE:

ABS +390
Cass +100
CD Player +195
Cruise Ctrl +135
Custom Whls/Cvrs +175
JBL Stereo System +175
Leather Seats +230
Pwr Locks +100
Pwr Seat +135
Pwr Sunroof +430
Pwr Wndw(Std LS) +135
Third Seat +160

Model/Body/Type	BaseList	Whlse	Retail

TOPAZ 4 Cyl — 1993

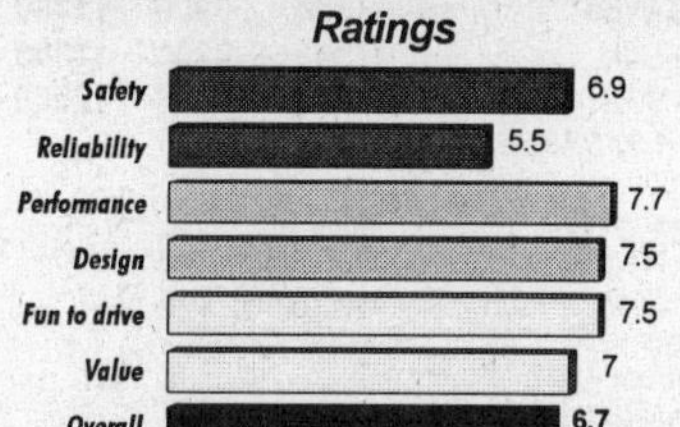

FWD/AT/PS/AC			
2 Dr GS Cpe	10809	**7450**	**9250**
4 Dr GS Sdn	10976	**7550**	**9375**

ADD FOR 93 TOPAZ:

Cass +75
Cruise Ctrl +115
Custom Whls/Cvrs +160
Driver Side Airbag +315
Pwr Locks +75
Pwr Seat +115
Pwr Wndw +115
Tilt Whl +75
V6 Eng +350

DEDUCT FOR 93 TOPAZ:

No AC -470
No Auto Trans -430

TRACER 4 Cyl — 1993

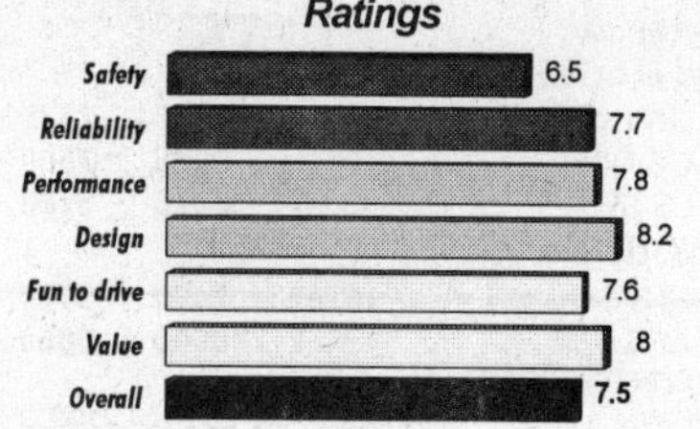

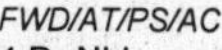

FWD/AT/PS/AC			
4 Dr Nbk	10155	**7325**	**9125**
4 Dr Wgn	10982	**8125**	**9975**
4 Dr LTS Nbk	12023	**8600**	**10450**

ADD FOR 93 TRACER:

Cass(Std LTS) +75
Cruise Ctrl(Std LTS) +115
Luggage Rack +75
Pwr Locks +75
Pwr Sunroof +315
Pwr Wndw +115
Tilt Whl(Std LTS) +75

DEDUCT FOR 93 TRACER:

No AC -430
No Auto Trans -390
No Pwr Steering -135

Model/Body/Type	BaseList	Whlse	Retail

VILLAGER V6 1/2 Ton — 1993

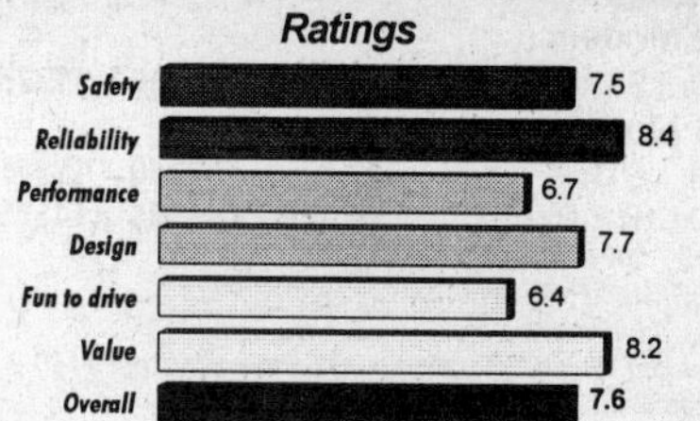

FWD/AT/PS/AC			
GS Wgn	16504	**16150**	**19050**
LS Wgn	21798	**17450**	**20575**

ADD FOR 93 VILLAGER:

AC-Rear +375
Cass(Std LS) +105
CD Player +205
Cruise Ctrl(Std LS) +125
Custom Whls +145
Leather Seats +250
Lugg Rack(Std LS) +80
Privacy Glass(Std LS) +145
Pwr Locks(Std LS) +105
Pwr Seats +125
Pwr Wndw(Std LS) +145
Running Boards +145
Sunroof-Manual +145
Sunroof-Pwr +390
Tilt Whl(Std LS) +105
Towing Pkg +185

DEDUCT FOR 93 VILLAGER:

No AC -440

1992 MERCURY

CAPRI 4 Cyl — 1992

Ratings

Safety	7
Reliability	8.2
Performance	7.9
Design	8
Fun to drive	8.6
Value	6.7
Overall	7.8

AC/FWD			
2 Dr Conv	14452	**7350**	**9225**
2 Dr XR2 Turbo Conv	17250	**8550**	**10450**

ADD FOR 92 CAPRI:

Auto Trans +390
Cass(Std XR2) +75
Cruise Ctrl(Std XR2) +115
Custom Whls/Cvrs +160
Leather Seats +195
Removable Hardtop +470

DEDUCT FOR 92 CAPRI:

No AC -505

COUGAR 1992

Model/Body/Type	BaseList	Whlse	Retail
AT/PS/AC			
V6 Models			
2 Dr LS Cpe	16460	**9250**	**11275**
V8 Models			
2 Dr LS Cpe	17450	**9750**	**11875**
2 Dr XR-7 Cpe	22054	**11925**	**14375**

ADD FOR 92 COUGAR:

ABS(Std XR-7) +350 | *Cass +75*
CD Player +175 | *Cruise Ctrl +115*
Custom Whls/Cvrs +160 | *JBL Stereo System +160*
Leather Seats +195 | *Pwr Locks +75*
Pwr Seat +115 | *Pwr Sunroof +390*
Tilt Whl +75

GRAND MARQUIS V8 1992

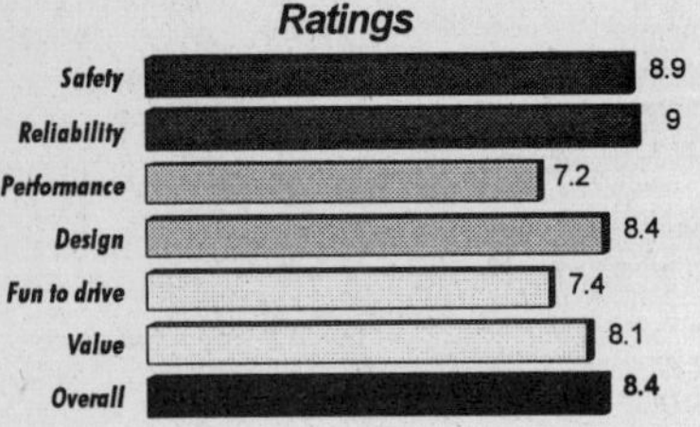

Model/Body/Type	BaseList	Whlse	Retail
AT/PS/AC			
4 Dr GS Sdn	20216	**10350**	**12675**
4 Dr LS Sdn	20644	**11025**	**13450**

ADD FOR 92 GRAND MARQUIS:

ABS +350 | *Car Phone +160*
Custom Whls/Cvrs +175 | *JBL Stereo System +175*
Leather Seats +230 | *Pass Side Airbag +275*
Vinyl Roof +135

SABLE V6 1992

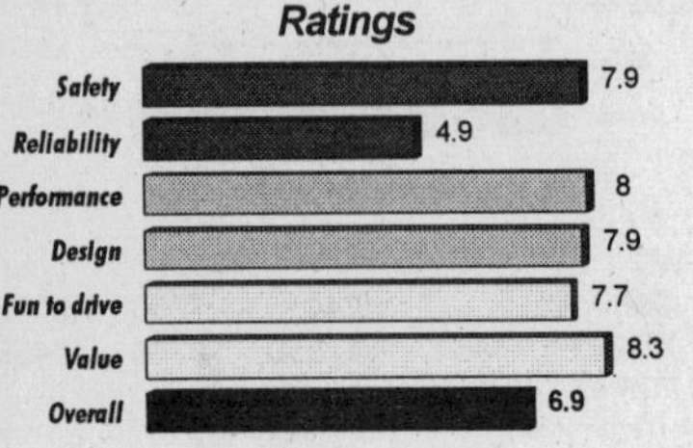

Model/Body/Type	BaseList	Whlse	Retail
FWD/AT/PS/AC			
4 Dr GS Sdn	16418	**8275**	**10300**
4 Dr GS Wgn	17396	**9200**	**11300**
4 Dr LS Sdn	17368	**9200**	**11300**
4 Dr LS Wgn	18395	**10075**	**12350**

ADD FOR 92 SABLE:

ABS +350 | *Cass +75*
CD Player +175 | *Cruise Ctrl +115*
Custom Whls/Cvrs +160 | *JBL Stereo System +160*
Leather Seats +195 | *Pass Side Airbag +275*
Pwr Locks +75 | *Pwr Seat +115*
Pwr Sunroof +390
Pwr Wndw(Std LS) +115
Third Seat +135

TOPAZ 1992

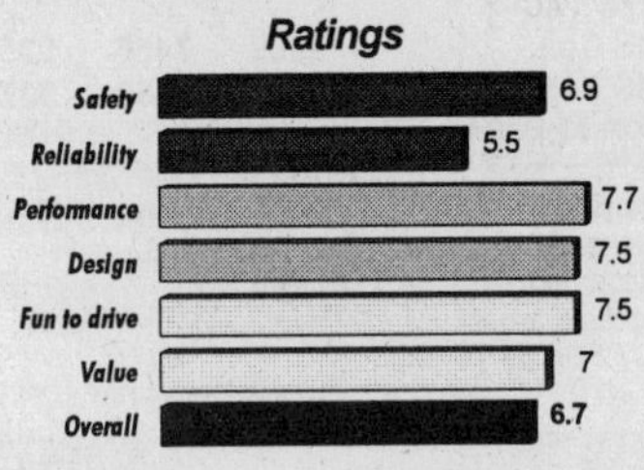

Model/Body/Type	BaseList	Whlse	Retail
FWD/AT/PS/AC			
4 Cyl Models			
2 Dr GS Cpe	10512	**5825**	**7375**
4 Dr GS Sdn	10678	**5925**	**7500**
4 Dr LS Sdn	12057	**6625**	**8250**
V6 Models			
4 Dr LTS Sdn	14244	**7400**	**9200**
2 Dr XR5 Cpe	13452	**6900**	**8650**

ADD FOR 92 TOPAZ:

Cass +60 | *Cr Ctrl(Std LS,LTS) +100*
Custom Whls/Cvrs +135 | *Driver Side Airbag +275*
Pwr Locks(Std LS,LTS) +60
Pwr Seat(Std LTS) +100
Pwr Wndw(Std LS,LTS) +100
Tilt Whl +60 | *V6 Eng(Std XR5,LTS) +315*

DEDUCT FOR 92 TOPAZ:

No AC -430 | *No Auto Trans -390*

TRACER 4 Cyl — 1992

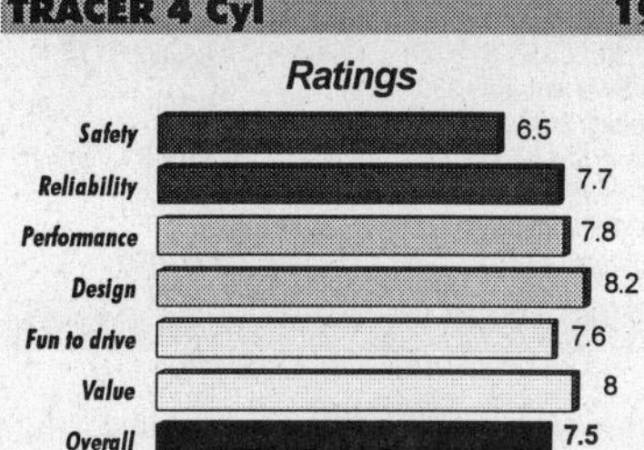

FWD/AT/PS/AC

Model/Body/Type	BaseList	Whlse	Retail
4 Dr Nbk	9773	**5525**	**7075**
4 Dr Wgn	10794	**6225**	**7825**
4 Dr LTS Nbk	12023	**6725**	**8475**

ADD FOR 92 TRACER:

Cass(Std LTS) +60 — *CruiseCtrl(Std LTS) +100*
Luggage Rack +60 — *Pwr Locks +60*
Pwr Sunroof +275 — *Pwr Wndw +100*
Tilt Whl(Std LTS) +60

DEDUCT FOR 92 TRACER:

No AC -390 — *No Auto Trans -350*
No Pwr Steering -115

1991 MERCURY

CAPRI 4 Cyl — 1991

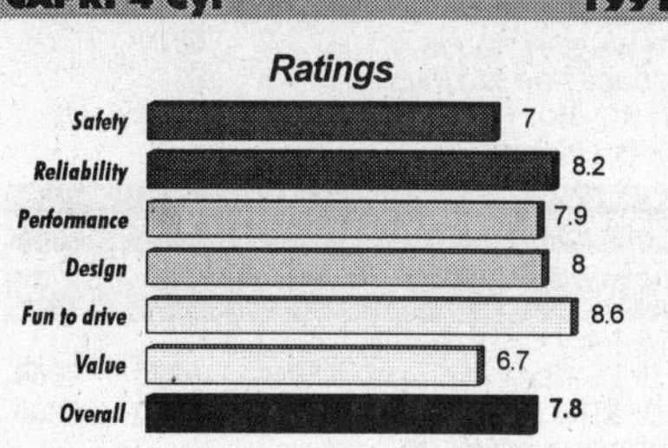

AC/FWD

Model/Body/Type	BaseList	Whlse	Retail
2 Dr Conv	12588	**6025**	**7750**
2 Dr XR2 Turbo Conv	15522	**7100**	**8925**

ADD FOR 91 CAPRI:

Auto Trans +350 — *Cass(Std XR2) +60*
Custom Whls/Cvrs +135 — *Pwr Locks(Std XR2) +60*
Removable Hardtop +430

DEDUCT FOR 91 CAPRI:

No AC -470

COUGAR — 1991

AT/PS/AC

Model/Body/Type	BaseList	Whlse	Retail
V6 Models			
2 Dr LS Cpe	16094	**7400**	**9275**
V8 Models			
2 Dr LS Cpe	17278	**7850**	**9800**
2 Dr XR-7 Cpe	21139	**9925**	**12075**

ADD FOR 91 COUGAR:

ABS(Std XR-7) +315 — *Cass +60*
CD Player +160 — *Cruise Ctrl +100*
Custom Whls/Cvrs +135 — *JBL Stereo System +135*
Leather Seats +160 — *Pwr Locks +60*
Pwr Seat +100 — *Pwr Sunroof +350*
Tilt Whl +60

GRAND MARQUIS V8 — 1991

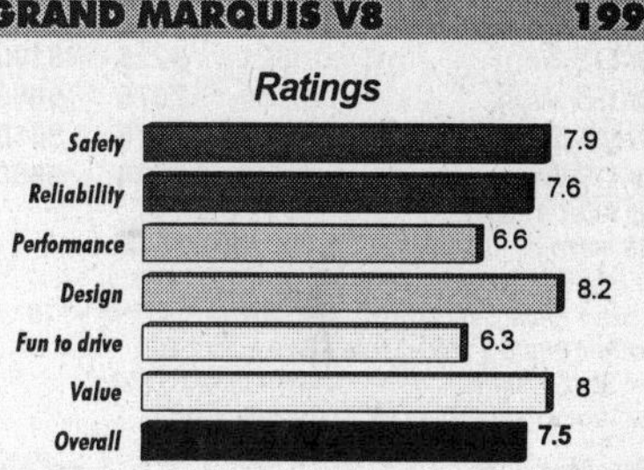

AT/PS/AC

Model/Body/Type	BaseList	Whlse	Retail
4 Dr GS Sdn	18199	**7150**	**9150**
4 Dr LS Sdn	18699	**7800**	**9850**
DFRS GS Colony Park	19133	**7800**	**9850**
2 Seat GS Colony Park	18918	**7600**	**9650**
DFRS LS Colony Park	19705	**8450**	**10500**
2 Seat LS Colony Park	19490	**8250**	**10275**

ADD FOR 91 GRAND MARQUIS:

Car Phone +135 — *Carriage Roof +230*
Custom Whls/Cvrs +160 — *Formal Coach Roof +115*
Leather Seats +195

Model/Body/Type	BaseList	Whlse	Retail

SABLE V6 — 1991

Ratings

Safety	7.9
Reliability	4.9
Performance	8
Design	7.9
Fun to drive	7.7
Value	8.3
Overall	6.9

FWD/AT/PS/AC

Model/Body/Type	BaseList	Whlse	Retail
4 Dr GS Sdn	15821	**6225**	**8100**
4 Dr GS Wgn	16766	**7075**	**9050**
4 Dr LS Sdn	16823	**7075**	**9050**
4 Dr LS Wgn	17794	**7900**	**9950**

ADD FOR 91 SABLE:

ABS +315 | *Cass +60*
CD Player +160 | *Cruise Ctrl +100*
Custom Whls/Cvrs +135 | *JBL Stereo System +135*
Leather Seats +160 | *Pwr Locks +60*
Pwr Seat +100 | *Pwr Sunroof +350*
Pwr Wndw(Std LS) +100 | *Third Seat +115*

TOPAZ 4 Cyl — 1991

Ratings

FWD/AT/PS/AC

Model/Body/Type	BaseList	Whlse	Retail
2 Dr GS Cpe	10448	**4475**	**5875**
4 Dr GS Sdn	10605	**4575**	**6000**
4 Dr LS Sdn	11984	**5175**	**6675**
4 Dr LTS Sdn	13008	**5725**	**7275**
2 Dr XR5 Cpe	11447	**5025**	**6550**

ADD FOR 91 TOPAZ:

4 Whl Drive +545 | *Cass +35*
Cr Ctrl(Std LS,LTS) +75 | *Custom Whls/Cvrs +115*
Driver Side Airbag +230
Pwr Locks(Std LS,LTS) +35
Pwr Seat(Std LTS) +75 | *Pwr Wndw(Std LS,LTS) +75*
Tilt Whl +35

DEDUCT FOR 91 TOPAZ:

No AC -390 | *No Auto Trans -350*

TRACER 4 Cyl — 1991

Ratings

Safety	6.5
Reliability	7.7
Performance	7.8
Design	8.2
Fun to drive	7.6
Value	8
Overall	7.5

FWD/AT/PS/AC

Model/Body/Type	BaseList	Whlse	Retail
4 Dr Nbk	8969	**4175**	**5575**
4 Dr Wgn	9990	**4750**	**6225**
4 Dr LTS Nbk	11219	**5300**	**6850**

ADD FOR 91 TRACER:

Cass(Std LTS) +35 | *CruiseCtrl(Std LTS) +75*
Luggage Rack +35 | *Pwr Locks +35*
Pwr Sunroof +230 | *Pwr Wndw +75*
Tilt Whl(Std LTS) +35

DEDUCT FOR 91 TRACER:

No AC -350 | *No Auto Trans -315*
No Pwr Steering -100

1990 MERCURY

COUGAR V6 — 1990

AT/PS/AC

Model/Body/Type	BaseList	Whlse	Retail
2 Dr LS Cpe	15816	**5925**	**7650**
2 Dr XR-7 Cpe	20213	**7850**	**9800**

ADD FOR 90 COUGAR:

ABS(Std XR-7) +275 | *Cass +60*
CD Player +115 | *Cruise Ctrl +75*
Custom Whls/Cvrs +115 | *JBL Stereo System +100*
Leather Seats +115 | *Pwr Locks +60*
Pwr Seat +75 | *Pwr Sunroof +315*
Tilt Whl +60

GRAND MARQUIS V8 — 1990

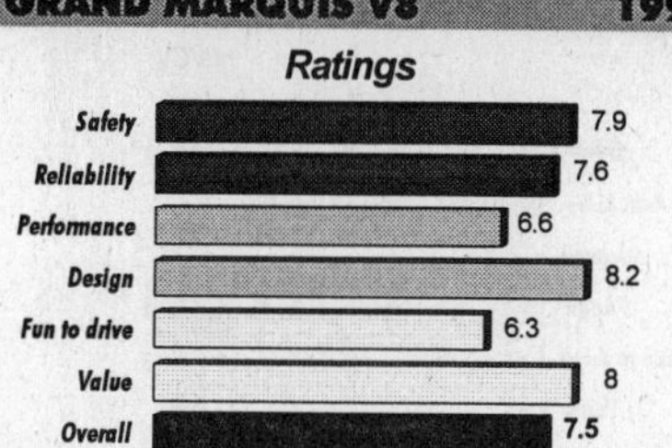

Model/Body/Type	BaseList	Whlse	Retail
AT/PS/AC			
4 Dr GS Sdn	17784	**5550**	**7375**
4 Dr LS Sdn	18284	**6175**	**8050**
DFRS GS Colony Park	18677	**6125**	**8000**
2 Seat GS Colony Park	18504	**5950**	**7800**
DFRS LS Colony Park	19249	**6725**	**8700**
2 Seat LS Colony Park	19076	**6575**	**8500**

ADD FOR 90 GRAND MARQUIS:

Custom Paint +35 — *Custom Whls/Cvrs +115*
Formal Coach Roof +75 — *Leather Seats +135*

SABLE V6 — 1990

Ratings

Rating	Score
Safety	7.9
Reliability	4.9
Performance	8
Design	7.9
Fun to drive	7.7
Value	8.3
Overall	6.9

Model/Body/Type	BaseList	Whlse	Retail
FWD/AT/PS/AC			
4 Dr GS Sdn	15065	**4675**	**6400**
4 Dr GS Wgn	16010	**5375**	**7225**
4 Dr LS Sdn	16067	**5425**	**7275**
4 Dr LS Wgn	17038	**6200**	**8075**

ADD FOR 90 SABLE:

ABS +275 — *Cass +60*
CD Player +115 — *Cruise Ctrl +75*
Custom Whls/Cvrs +115 — *JBL Stereo System +100*
Leather Seats +115 — *Pwr Locks +60*
Pwr Seat +75 — *Pwr Sunroof +315*
Pwr Wndw(Std LS) +75 — *Third Seat +100*

TOPAZ 4 Cyl — 1990

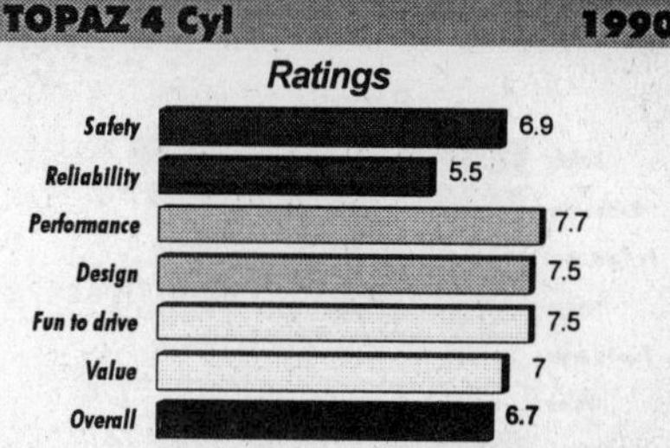

Model/Body/Type	BaseList	Whlse	Retail
FWD/AT/PS/AC			
2 Dr GS Cpe	10007	**3250**	**4550**
4 Dr GS Sdn	10164	**3325**	**4675**
4 Dr LS Sdn	11543	**3925**	**5275**
4 Dr LTS Sdn	12567	**4375**	**5800**
2 Dr XR5 Cpe	11006	**3775**	**5100**

ADD FOR 90 TOPAZ:

4 Whl Drive +505 — *Cass +35*
Cr Ctrl(Std LS,LTS) +60 — *Custom Whls/Cvrs +75*
Pwr Locks(Std LS,LTS) +35
Pwr Seat(Std LTS) +60 — *Pwr Wndw(Std LS,LTS) +60*
Tilt Whl +35

DEDUCT FOR 90 TOPAZ:

No AC -350 — *No Auto Trans -315*

1989 MERCURY

COUGAR V6 — 1989

Model/Body/Type	BaseList	Whlse	Retail
AT/PS/AC			
2 Dr LS Cpe	15448	**4775**	**6425**
2 Dr XR-7 Cpe	19650	**6525**	**8300**

ADD FOR 89 COUGAR:

Cass +35 — *CD Player +75*
Cruise Ctrl +60 — *Custom Whls/Cvrs +75*
JBL Stereo System +75 — *Leather Seats +75*
Pwr Locks +35 — *Pwr Seat +60*
Pwr Sunroof +250 — *Tilt Whl +35*

See Edmund's Automobile Dealer Directory (page 379)
and the back of this book to enter our
$10,000 Wheel N'Deal Giveaway.

GRAND MARQUIS V8 — 1989

Ratings

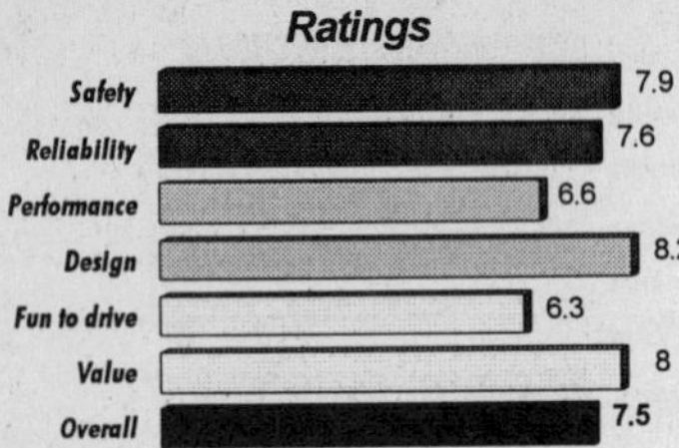

AT/PS/AC

Model/Body/Type	BaseList	Whlse	Retail
4 Dr GS Sdn	16701	**4525**	**6225**
4 Dr LS Sdn	17213	**5050**	**6875**
DFRS GS Colony Park	17511	**4950**	**6750**
2 Seat GS Colony Park	17338	**4850**	**6650**
DFRS LS Colony Park	18095	**5550**	**7375**
2 Seat LS Colony Park	17922	**5400**	**7250**

ADD FOR 89 GRAND MARQUIS:

Custom Whls/Cvrs +75 — *Formal Coach Roof +60*
Leather Seats +115

SABLE V6 — 1989

Ratings

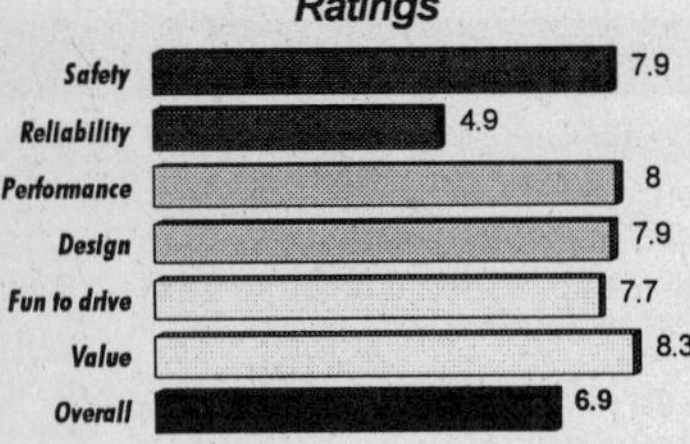

FWD/AT/PS/AC

Model/Body/Type	BaseList	Whlse	Retail
4 Dr GS Sdn	14101	**3400**	**4950**
4 Dr GS Wgn	14804	**4025**	**5700**
4 Dr LS Sdn	15094	**4100**	**5775**
4 Dr LS Wgn	15872	**4700**	**6500**

ADD FOR 89 SABLE:

Cass +35 — *Cruise Ctrl +60*
Custom Whls/Cvrs +75 — *JBL Stereo System +75*
Leather Seats +75 — *Pwr Locks +35*
Pwr Seat +60 — *Pwr Sunroof +250*
Pwr Wndw(Std LS) +60 — *Third Seat +75*
Tilt Whl +35

TOPAZ 4 Cyl — 1989

Ratings

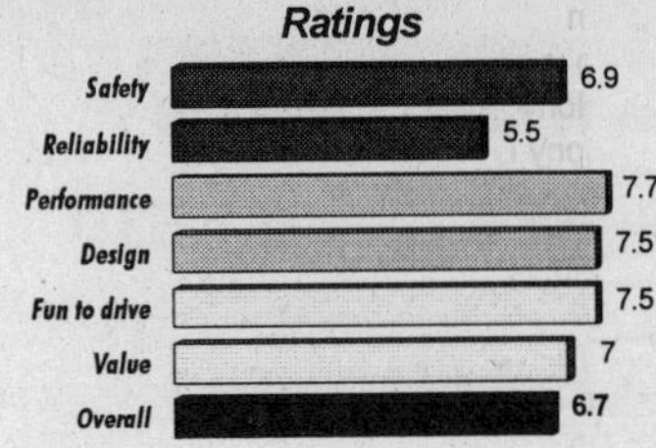

FWD/AT/PS/AC

Model/Body/Type	BaseList	Whlse	Retail
2 Dr GS Cpe	9577	**2225**	**3325**
4 Dr GS Sdn	9734	**2300**	**3425**
4 Dr LS Sdn	11030	**2850**	**4100**
4 Dr LTS Sdn	11980	**3200**	**4500**
2 Dr XR5 Cpe	10498	**2700**	**3875**

ADD FOR 89 TOPAZ:

4 Whl Drive +470 — *Cass +25*
Cruise Ctrl(Std LS,LTS) +35
Custom Whls/Cvrs +35 — *Pwr Locks(Std LS,LTS) +25*
Pwr Seat(Std LTS) +35 — *Pwr Wndw(Std LS,LTS) +35*
Tilt Whl +25

DEDUCT FOR 89 TOPAZ:

No AC -315 — *No Auto Trans -275*

TRACER 4 Cyl — 1989

FWD/AT/PS/AC

Model/Body/Type	BaseList	Whlse	Retail
4 Dr Hbk	9242	**1950**	**3025**
2 Dr Hbk	8556	**1800**	**2850**
4 Dr Wgn	9726	**2225**	**3325**

ADD FOR 89 TRACER:

Cass +25 — *Cruise Ctrl +35*
Custom Whls/Cvrs +35

DEDUCT FOR 89 TRACER:

No AC -275 — *No Auto Trans -230*

1988 MERCURY

COUGAR — 1988

AT/PS/AC

Model/Body/Type	BaseList	Whlse	Retail
V6 Models			
2 Dr LS	14134	**3350**	**4775**
V8 Models			
2 Dr LS	14855	**3750**	**5225**
2 Dr XR-7	16266	**4475**	**6050**

Model/Body/Type	BaseList	Whlse	Retail
GRAND MARQUIS V8			**1988**
AT/PS/AC			
4 Dr GS Sdn	16100	**3250**	**4775**
4 Dr LS Sdn	16612	**3725**	**5325**
4 Dr GS Colony Park	16514	**3250**	**4775**
4 Dr LS Colony Park	17099	**3725**	**5325**
SABLE V6			**1988**
FWD/AT/PS/AC			
4 Dr GS Sdn	14145	**2450**	**3775**
4 Dr GS Wgn	14665	**3025**	**4525**
4 Dr LS Sdn	15138	**3075**	**4575**
4 Dr LS Wgn	15683	**3600**	**5175**
TOPAZ 4 Cyl			**1988**
FWD/AT/PS/AC			
2 Dr GS Cpe	9166	**1700**	**2675**
4 Dr GS Sdn	9323	**1775**	**2800**
4 Dr LS Sdn	10591	**2225**	**3325**
4 Dr LTS Sdn	11541	**2550**	**3700**
2 Dr XR5 Cpe	10058	**2100**	**3175**

ADD FOR 88 TOPAZ:
4 Whl Drive +430
DEDUCT FOR 88 TOPAZ:
No AC -250 *No Auto Trans -230*

Model/Body/Type	BaseList	Whlse	Retail
TRACER 4 Cyl			**1988**
FWD/AT/PS/AC			
4 Dr Hbk	8364	**1450**	**2400**
2 Dr Hbk	7926	**1325**	**2250**
4 Dr Wgn	8727	**1675**	**2650**

DEDUCT FOR 88 TRACER:
No AC -215 *No Auto Trans -195*

1987 MERCURY

Model/Body/Type	BaseList	Whlse	Retail
COUGAR			**1987**
AT/PS/AC			
V6 Models			
2 Dr LS	13595	**2500**	**3750**
V8 Models			
2 Dr XR-7	15832	**3475**	**4875**

ADD FOR 87 COUGAR:
V8 Engine(Std XR-7) +290

Model/Body/Type	BaseList	Whlse	Retail
GRAND MARQUIS V8			**1987**
AT/PS/AC			
4 Dr GS Sdn	15198	**2175**	**3450**
4 Dr LS Sdn	15672	**2600**	**3950**
2 Dr LS Cpe	15523	**2450**	**3775**
4 Dr GS Colony Park	15462	**2300**	**3625**
4 Dr LS Colony Park	16010	**2750**	**4125**
LYNX 4 Cyl			**1987**
FWD/AT/PS/AC			
3 Dr L Hbk	6569	**775**	**1600**
3 Dr GS Hbk	6951	**950**	**1825**
5 Dr GS Hbk	7172	**1050**	**1950**
4 Dr GS Wgn	7462	**1175**	**2100**
3 Dr XR3 Hbk	8808	**1675**	**2650**

DEDUCT FOR 87 LYNX:
4 Cyl Diesel Eng -390

Model/Body/Type	BaseList	Whlse	Retail
SABLE V6			**1987**
FWD/AT/PS/AC			
4 Dr GS Sdn	12240	**2000**	**3250**
4 Dr GS Wgn	12793	**2475**	**3825**
4 Dr LS Sdn	14522	**2475**	**3825**
4 Dr LS Wgn	15054	**3000**	**4500**
TOPAZ 4 Cyl			**1987**
FWD/AT/PS/AC			
2 Dr GS Cpe	8562	**1150**	**2050**
4 Dr GS Sdn	8716	**1250**	**2175**
2 Dr GS Sport Cpe	9308	**1325**	**2250**
4 Dr GS Sport Sdn	9463	**1400**	**2350**
4 Dr LS Sdn	10213	**1500**	**2450**

ADD FOR 87 TOPAZ:
4 Whl Drive +390

1986 MERCURY

Model/Body/Type	BaseList	Whlse	Retail
CAPRI			**1986**
3 Dr GS Hbk	8331	**1075**	**2100**
3 Dr 5.0L Hbk	10950	**2750**	**4050**
COUGAR			**1986**
2 Dr GS	11421	**1775**	**2950**
2 Dr LS	12757	**2275**	**3500**
2 Dr Turbo	14377	**2025**	**3200**
GRAND MARQUIS			**1986**
4 Dr Sdn	13504	**1800**	**3225**
2 Dr Cpe	13480	**1700**	**3100**
4 Dr LS Sdn	13952	**2125**	**3575**
2 Dr LS Cpe	13929	**2000**	**3425**
4 Dr Colony Park	13724	**1850**	**3250**
LYNX			**1986**
FWD			
3 Dr Hbk	6182	**425**	**1350**
3 Dr L Hbk	6472	**550**	**1500**
5 Dr L Hbk	6686	**625**	**1600**
4 Dr L Wgn	6967	**725**	**1700**
3 Dr GS Hbk	7162	**825**	**1775**
5 Dr GS Hbk	7376	**900**	**1875**
4 Dr GS Wgn	7657	**950**	**1975**
3 Dr XR3 Hbk	8193	**1150**	**2175**

MERCURY 86-85

Model/Body/Type	BaseList	Whlse	Retail
MARQUIS			**1986**
4 Dr Sdn	10154	1025	2275
4 Dr Brougham Sdn	10542	1325	2625
4 Dr Wgn	10254	1200	2450
4 Dr Brougham Wgn	10613	1450	2800
SABLE			**1986**
FWD			
4 Dr GS Sdn	11311	1825	3025
4 Dr GS Wgn	11776	2225	3425
4 Dr LS Sdn	12574	2250	3475
4 Dr LS Wgn	13068	2650	3925
TOPAZ			**1986**
FWD			
2 Dr GS Cpe	8085	850	1800
4 Dr GS Sdn	8235	900	1900
2 Dr LS Cpe	9224	1000	2025
4 Dr LS Sdn	9494	1075	2125

1985.5 MERCURY

Model/Body/Type	BaseList	Whlse	Retail
LYNX			**1985.5**
FWD			
3 Dr Hbk	5753	375	1300
3 Dr L Hbk	6216	475	1400
5 Dr L Hbk	6430	550	1500
4 Dr L Wgn	6712	600	1575
3 Dr GS Hbk	6845	600	1550
5 Dr GS Hbk	7059	675	1650
4 Dr GS Wgn	7341	750	1700

1985 MERCURY

Model/Body/Type	BaseList	Whlse	Retail
CAPRI			**1985**
3 Dr GS Hbk	7944	950	1975
3 Dr 5.0L Hbk	10223	2100	3275
COUGAR			**1985**
2 Dr	10650	1450	2550
2 Dr LS	11850	1850	3050
2 Dr Turbo	13599	1500	2600
GRAND MARQUIS			**1985**
4 Dr Sdn	12305	1675	3050
2 Dr Cpe	12240	1550	2900
4 Dr LS Sdn	12854	1950	3350
2 Dr LS Cpe	12789	1800	3225
4 Dr Colony Park	12511	1700	3075
LYNX			**1985**
FWD			
3 Dr Hbk	5750	350	1275
3 Dr L Hbk	6170	450	1375
5 Dr L Hbk	6384	525	1475
4 Dr L Wgn	6508	600	1550
3 Dr GS Hbk	6707	575	1525
5 Dr GS Hbk	6921	650	1625
4 Dr GS Wgn	6973	725	1700
MARQUIS			**1985**
4 Dr Sdn	9414	850	2025
4 Dr Wgn	9506	925	2175
4 Dr Brougham Sdn	9741	1050	2275
4 Dr Brougham Wgn	9805	1200	2425
TOPAZ			**1985**
FWD			
2 Dr GS Cpe	7767	625	1600
4 Dr GS Sdn	7767	725	1700
2 Dr LS Cpe	8931	825	1775
4 Dr LS Sdn	8980	875	1850

Model/Body/Type	BaseList	Whlse	Retail

MERKUR

Germany

1988 Merkur Scorpio

For a dealer in your area, see our Dealer Directory (pg 217)

1989 MERKUR

XR4Ti 4 Cyl — 1989

AT/PS/AC

Model/Body/Type	BaseList	Whlse	Retail
3 Dr Turbo Hbk	19759	4550	6250

SCORPIO V6 — 1989

AT/PS/AC

Model/Body/Type	BaseList	Whlse	Retail
5 Dr Hbk	25052	5400	7250

ADD FOR ALL 89 MERKUR:
Leather Seats +115
Pwr Sunroof +290
Sunroof +115
DEDUCT FOR ALL 89 MERKUR:
No Auto Trans -390

1988 MERKUR

XR4Ti 4 Cyl — 1988

AT/PS/AC

Model/Body/Type	BaseList	Whlse	Retail
3 Dr Turbo Hbk	19065	3425	4975

SCORPIO V6 — 1988

AT/PS/AC

Model/Body/Type	BaseList	Whlse	Retail
5 Dr Hbk	23248	3775	5375

DEDUCT FOR ALL 88 MERKUR:
No Auto Trans -350

1987 MERKUR

XR4Ti 4 Cyl — 1987

AT/PS/AC

Model/Body/Type	BaseList	Whlse	Retail
3 Dr Turbo Hbk	17832	2350	3675

1986 MERKUR

XR4Ti — 1986

Model/Body/Type	BaseList	Whlse	Retail
3 Dr Turbo Hbk	16361	1700	3075

1985 MERKUR

XR4Ti — 1985

Model/Body/Type	BaseList	Whlse	Retail
3 Dr Turbo Hbk	16361	1325	2650

MITSUBISHI 94

MITSUBISHI Japan

1992 Mitsubishi Diamante LS

For a Mitsubishi dealer in your area, see our Dealer Directory (pg 217)

1994 MITSUBISHI

Model/Body/Type	BaseList	Whlse	Retail
3000GT V6			**1994**
5SP-FWD/AT/PS/AC			
2 Dr Cpe	27175	**20150**	**23375**
2 Dr SL Cpe	31650	**23725**	**27150**
4WD VR-4 Turbo Cpe	40900	**30625**	**34325**
DIAMANTE V6			**1994**
FWD/AT/PS/AC			
4 Dr ES Sdn	25525	**11405**	**20825**
4 Dr LS Sdn	32500	**21900**	**25225**
4 Dr ES Wgn	25850	**17175**	**20175**
ECLIPSE 4 Cyl			**1994**

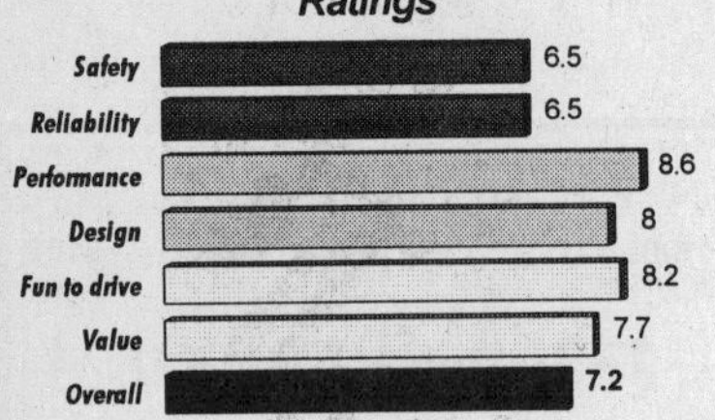

Model/Body/Type	BaseList	Whlse	Retail
FWD/AT/PS/AC			
2 Dr Cpe	11979	**10800**	**13150**
2 Dr GS Cpe	14089	**11700**	**14150**
2 Dr GS/16V Cpe	15819	**13275**	**15775**
2 Dr GS/16V Turbo Cpe	18529	**13975**	**16525**
2 Dr GSX/16V 4WD Turbo Cpe	21269	**16725**	**19500**
EXPO 4 Cyl			**1994**
FWD/AT/PS/AC			
3 Dr LRV Wgn	13019	**12650**	**15250**
3 Dr LRV Sport Wgn	16799	**14625**	**17325**
4 Dr Wgn	15689	**14450**	**17125**
4 Dr 4WD Wgn	17129	**15200**	**17950**
GALANT 4 Cyl			**1994**
FWD/AT/PS/AC			
4 Dr S Sdn	13600	**12025**	**14525**
4 Dr ES Sdn	16775	**13525**	**16050**
4 Dr LS Sdn	18215	**14125**	**16675**
4 Dr GS Sdn	20494	**15975**	**18625**
MIRAGE 4 Cyl			**1994**
FWD/AT/PS/AC			
2 Dr S Cpe (5 spd)	8989	**7600**	**9425**
2 Dr ES Cpe	10359	**9350**	**11275**
2 Dr LS Cpe	11879	**9925**	**11975**
4 Dr S Sdn	11369	**9975**	**12025**
4 Dr ES Sdn	11929	**10575**	**12700**
4 Dr LS Sdn	14529	**11175**	**13475**
MONTERO V6			**1994**
4WD/AT/PS/AC			
4 Dr LS Utility	23975	**20325**	**23350**
4 Dr SR Utility	31475	**24100**	**27350**
PICKUPS 4 Cyl			**1994**

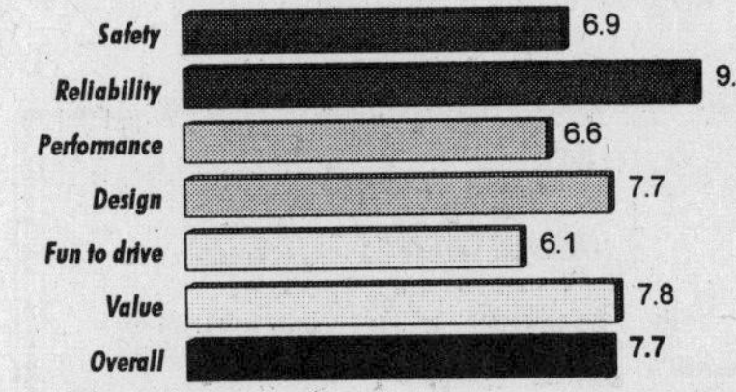

Model/Body/Type	BaseList	Whlse	Retail
5SP/PS/AC			
Mighty Max	9429	**8075**	**9925**
Mighty Max Macrocab	10899	**9775**	**11800**
4WD Mighty Max (V6)	14219	**11550**	**13875**

Model/Body/Type	BaseList	Whlse	Retail

ADD FOR ALL 94 MITSUBISHI:

ABS(Std MonSR,DiamLS, Eclipse,GSX,GT,SL/VR4) +430
Anti-Theft/Recovery Sys +365
Auto Trans(Pkup) +500
Car Phone(Diamante,GT) +230
Cass(Std MirageLS,EclipseGS/GSX) +115
CD Player(Std GalantGS,EclGS Turbo/GSX) +230
Cruise Ctrl(Std Mirage LS 4Dr, EclipseGS 16V Trb/GSX) +160
Custom Whls +205
Leather Seats(Std Diamante LS,GT VR-4) +275
Pwr Locks(Std Mirage LS 4Dr, EclipseGS Trb/GSX) +115
Pwr Sunroof +545
Pwr Wndw(Std Mirage LS 4Dr, EclipseGS Trb/GSX) +160
Sunroof +320

DEDUCT FOR ALL 94 MITSUBISHI:

No AC -680
No Auto Trans -590
No Pwr Steering -180

1993 MITSUBISHI

3000GT V6 1993

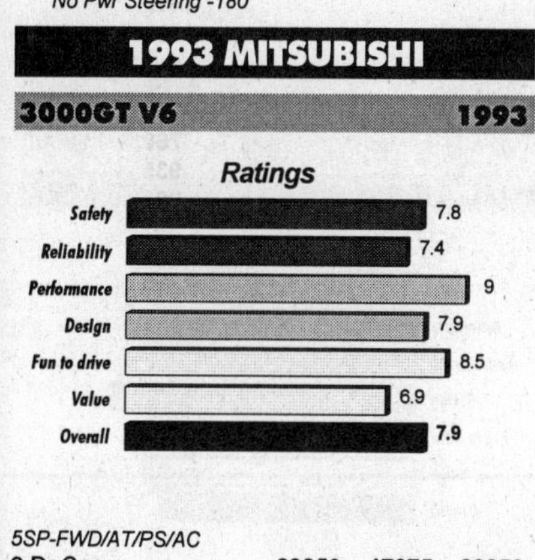

Model/Body/Type	BaseList	Whlse	Retail
5SP-FWD/AT/PS/AC			
2 Dr Cpe	23659	**17075**	**20050**
2 Dr SL Cpe	28709	**20325**	**23550**
AWD VR-4 Turbo Cpe	37250	**24400**	**27850**

DIAMANTE V6 1993

Ratings

Safety	7.7
Reliability	9.2
Performance	8.2
Design	7.5
Fun to drive	7.9
Value	6.9
Overall	8.3

Model/Body/Type	BaseList	Whlse	Retail
FWD/AT/PS/AC			
4 Dr ES Sdn	22399	**14950**	**17700**
4 Dr LS Sdn	29850	**18700**	**21825**
4 Dr ES Wgn	22399	**14400**	**17075**

ECLIPSE 4 Cyl 1993

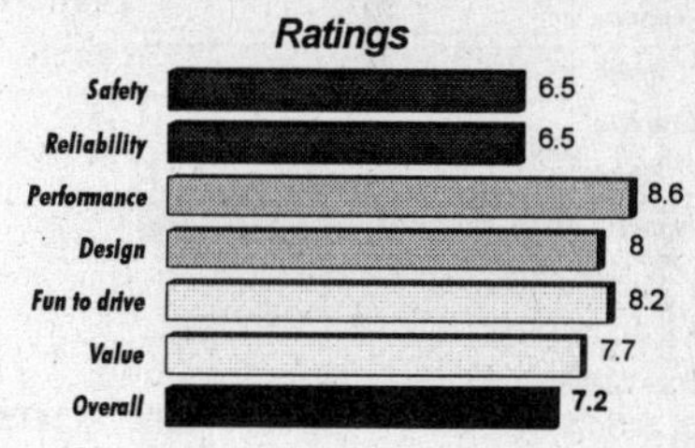

Model/Body/Type	BaseList	Whlse	Retail
FWD/AT/PS/AC			
2 Dr Cpe	11719	**9975**	**12150**
2 Dr GS Cpe	13429	**10650**	**12975**
2 Dr GS/16V Cpe	14359	**11550**	**13925**
2 Dr GS/16V Turbo Cpe	18049	**12525**	**15000**
2 Dr GSX/16V AWD Turbo Cpe	20769	**14975**	**17575**

EXPO 4 Cyl 1993

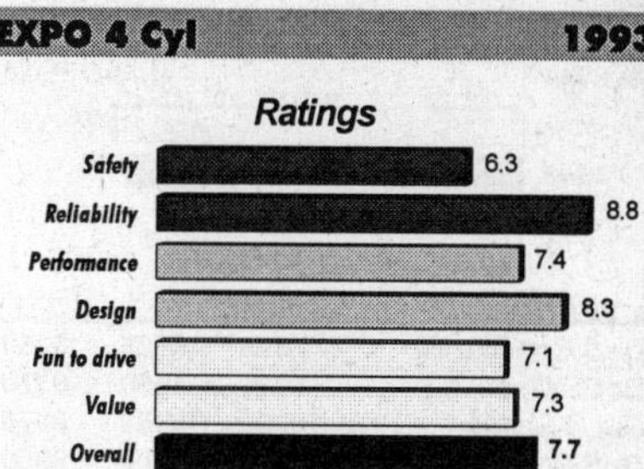

Model/Body/Type	BaseList	Whlse	Retail
FWD/AT/PS/AC			
3 Dr LRV Wgn	11429	**10825**	**13250**
3 Dr LRV AWD Wgn	13169	**11925**	**14500**
3 Dr LRV Sport Wgn	14269	**12300**	**14875**
4 Dr Wgn	13569	**12500**	**15100**
4 Dr AWD Wgn	14889	**13250**	**15900**
4 Dr SP Wgn	15669	**13650**	**16325**
4 Dr SP AWD Wgn	17019	**14400**	**17075**

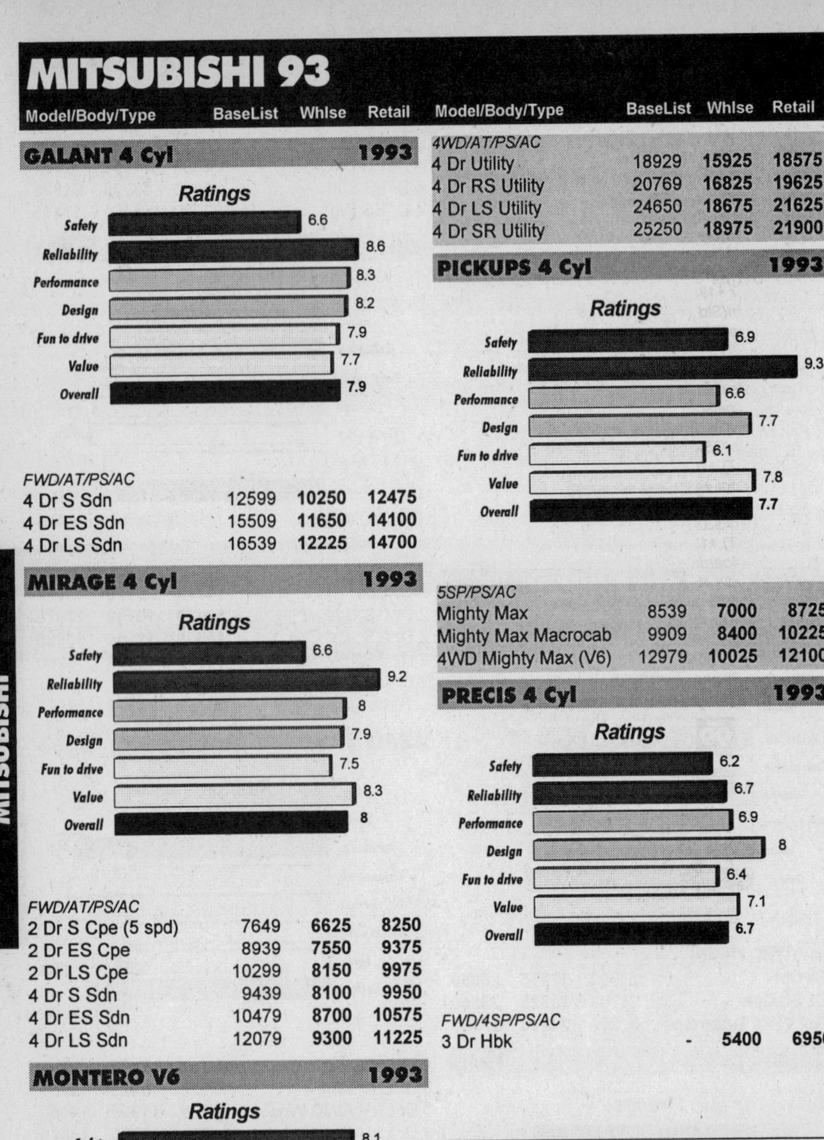

MITSUBISHI 93

GALANT 4 Cyl — 1993

Ratings

Rating	Score
Safety	6.6
Reliability	8.6
Performance	8.3
Design	8.2
Fun to drive	7.9
Value	7.7
Overall	7.9

Model/Body/Type	BaseList	Whlse	Retail
FWD/AT/PS/AC			
4 Dr S Sdn	12599	**10250**	**12475**
4 Dr ES Sdn	15509	**11650**	**14100**
4 Dr LS Sdn	16539	**12225**	**14700**

MIRAGE 4 Cyl — 1993

Ratings

Rating	Score
Safety	6.6
Reliability	9.2
Performance	8
Design	7.9
Fun to drive	7.5
Value	8.3
Overall	8

Model/Body/Type	BaseList	Whlse	Retail
FWD/AT/PS/AC			
2 Dr S Cpe (5 spd)	7649	**6625**	**8250**
2 Dr ES Cpe	8939	**7550**	**9375**
2 Dr LS Cpe	10299	**8150**	**9975**
4 Dr S Sdn	9439	**8100**	**9950**
4 Dr ES Sdn	10479	**8700**	**10575**
4 Dr LS Sdn	12079	**9300**	**11225**

MONTERO V6 — 1993

Ratings

Rating	Score
Safety	8.1
Reliability	9.2
Performance	6.6
Design	7.9
Fun to drive	6.3
Value	8.1
Overall	8.1

Model/Body/Type	BaseList	Whlse	Retail
4WD/AT/PS/AC			
4 Dr Utility	18929	**15925**	**18575**
4 Dr RS Utility	20769	**16825**	**19625**
4 Dr LS Utility	24650	**18675**	**21625**
4 Dr SR Utility	25250	**18975**	**21900**

PICKUPS 4 Cyl — 1993

Ratings

Rating	Score
Safety	6.9
Reliability	9.3
Performance	6.6
Design	7.7
Fun to drive	6.1
Value	7.8
Overall	7.7

Model/Body/Type	BaseList	Whlse	Retail
5SP/PS/AC			
Mighty Max	8539	**7000**	**8725**
Mighty Max Macrocab	9909	**8400**	**10225**
4WD Mighty Max (V6)	12979	**10025**	**12100**

PRECIS 4 Cyl — 1993

Ratings

Rating	Score
Safety	6.2
Reliability	6.7
Performance	6.9
Design	8
Fun to drive	6.4
Value	7.1
Overall	6.7

Model/Body/Type	BaseList	Whlse	Retail
FWD/4SP/PS/AC			
3 Dr Hbk	-	**5400**	**6950**

See the Automobile Dealer Directory on page 379 for a Dealer near you!

MITSUBISHI

Model/Body/Type	BaseList	Whlse	Retail

ADD FOR ALL 93 MITSUBISHI:

ABS(Std Diam LS,GSX, Montero LS/SR GT SL/VR4) +390
Auto Trans(Precis,Pkup) +430
Bed Liner +125
Car Phone(Diamante,GT) +175
Cass(Std Mont RS/LS/SR, ExpoSP/Spt,GT,Dia,EclGS/GSX,Mirag LS) +100
CD Player +195
Cruise Ctrl(Std Mirage LS Sdn,Glnt ES/LS, GS Turb/GSX,Mont LS/SR,Expo SP/Spt, Diam,GT) +135
Custom Whls +175
Fiberglass Cap +250
Leather Seats(Std Diamante LS,GT VR-4) +230
Pwr Locks(Std Mirage LS Sdn,Glnt ES/LS, GS Turb/GSX,Mont LS/SR,Expo SP/Spt, Diam,GT) +100
Pwr Sunroof +430
Pwr Wndw(Std Mirage LS Sdn,Glnt ES/LS, GS Turb/GSX,Mont LS/SR,Expo SP/Spt, Diam,GT) +135
Running Boards +145
Slider Wndw +80
Sunroof +230

DEDUCT FOR ALL 93 MITSUBISHI:

No AC -545
No AM/FM Radio -105
No Auto Trans -505
No Pwr Steering -160

1992 MITSUBISHI

3000GT V6 — 1992

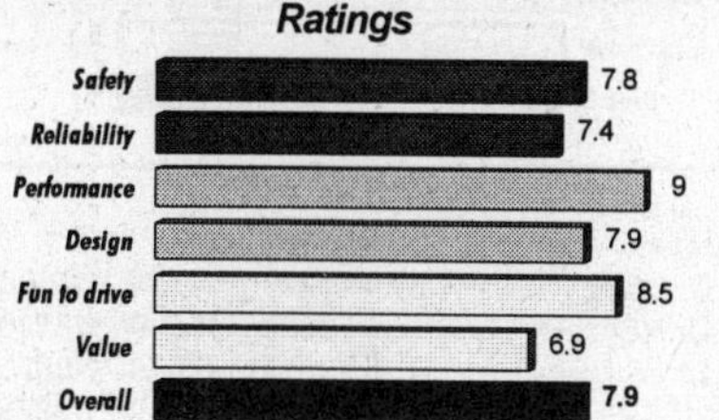

5SP-FWD/AT/PS/AC

Model/Body/Type	BaseList	Whlse	Retail
2 Dr Cpe	20049	**13950**	**16625**
2 Dr SL Cpe	26209	**17000**	**19950**
AWD VR-4 Turbo Cpe	32800	**20225**	**23450**

DIAMANTE V6 — 1992

Ratings

Rating	Score
Safety	7.7
Reliability	9.2
Performance	8.2
Design	7.5
Fun to drive	7.9
Value	6.9
Overall	8.3

FWD/AT/PS/AC

Model/Body/Type	BaseList	Whlse	Retail
4 Dr Sdn	19939	**13100**	**15725**
4 Dr LS Sdn	25135	**15850**	**18650**

ECLIPSE 4 Cyl — 1992

Ratings

Rating	Score
Safety	6.5
Reliability	6.5
Performance	8.6
Design	8
Fun to drive	8.2
Value	7.7
Overall	7.2

FWD/AT/PS/AC

Model/Body/Type	BaseList	Whlse	Retail
2 Dr Cpe	11259	**8200**	**10100**
2 Dr GS Cpe	12529	**8800**	**10800**
2 Dr GS/16V Cpe	13469	**9600**	**11650**
2 Dr GS/16V Turbo Cpe	17109	**10525**	**12750**
2 Dr GSX/16V AWD Turbo Cpe	18849	**11725**	**14175**

MITSUBISHI 92

EXPO 4 Cyl — 1992

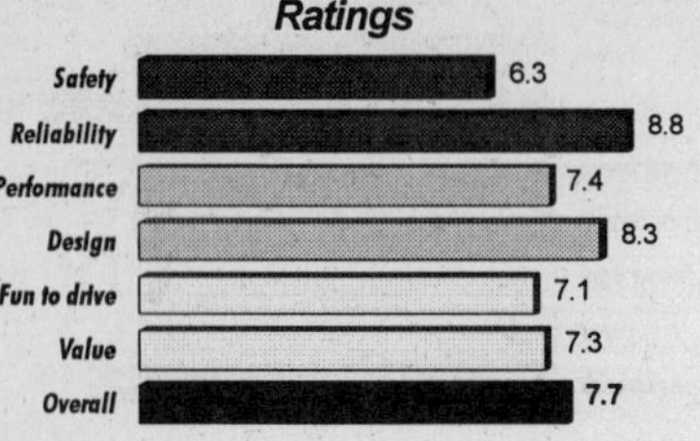

Model/Body/Type	BaseList	Whlse	Retail
FWD/AT/PS/AC			
3 Dr LRV Wgn	11169	**8950**	**11025**
3 Dr LRV Sport Wgn	11989	**9250**	**11350**
3 Dr LRV AWD Wgn	13889	**9925**	**12150**
4 Dr Wgn	13549	**10475**	**12800**
4 Dr SP Wgn	14509	**10900**	**13325**
4 Dr SP AWD Wgn	15839	**11600**	**14175**

GALANT 4 Cyl — 1992

Ratings
Safety 6.6
Reliability 8.6
Performance 8.3
Design 8.2
Fun to drive 7.9
Value 7.7
Overall 7.9

Model/Body/Type	BaseList	Whlse	Retail
FWD/AT/PS/AC			
4 Dr Sdn	11699	**8350**	**10250**
4 Dr LS Sdn	14809	**9100**	**11125**
4 Dr GS Sdn	15179	**9925**	**12075**
4 Dr GSR Sdn (5 spd)	16689	**10025**	**12200**
4 Dr GSX AWD Sdn	17729	**10575**	**12800**
VR-4 AWD Turbo Sdn (5 spd)	22500	**13150**	**15650**

MIRAGE 4 Cyl — 1992

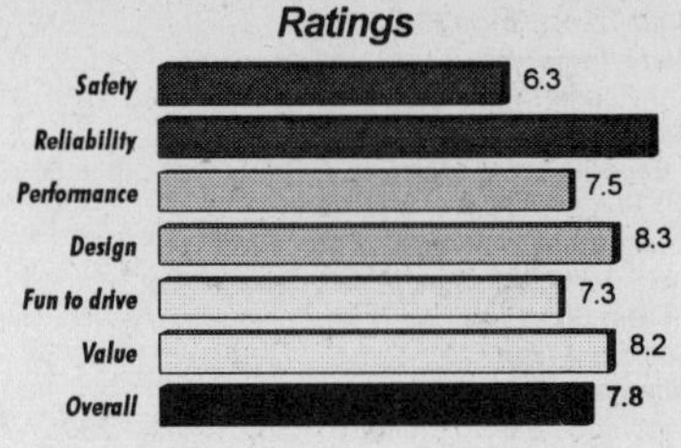

Model/Body/Type	BaseList	Whlse	Retail
FWD/AT/PS/AC			
3 Dr VL Hbk	7319	**5375**	**6925**
3 Dr Hbk	7919	**6175**	**7750**
4 Dr Sdn	8939	**6375**	**7975**
4 Dr LS Sdn	9489	**6650**	**8275**
4 Dr GS Sdn	10899	**7325**	**9125**

MONTERO V6 — 1992

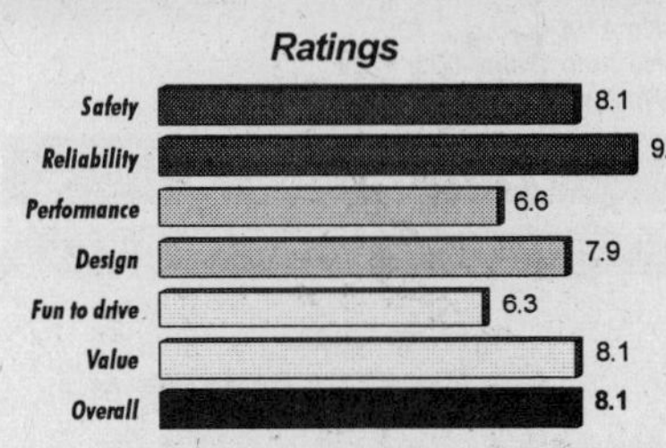

Model/Body/Type	BaseList	Whlse	Retail
4WD/AT/PS/AC			
4 Dr Utility	17929	**14725**	**17300**
4 Dr RS Utility	19599	**15500**	**18125**
4 Dr LS Utility	23019	**17075**	**19875**
4 Dr SR Utility	22429	**17175**	**19975**

MITSUBISHI

Model/Body/Type	BaseList	Whlse	Retail

PICKUPS 4 Cyl 1992

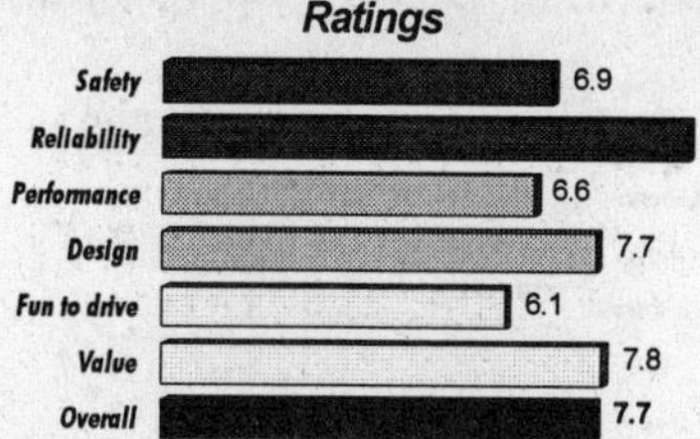

5SP/PS/AC			
Mighty Max	8079	**5725**	**7250**
Mighty Max Macrocab	9379	**6950**	**8700**
1 Ton LB Mighty Max	9429	**6050**	**7625**
4WD Mighty Max (V6)	12289	**8625**	**10475**

PRECIS 4 Cyl 1992

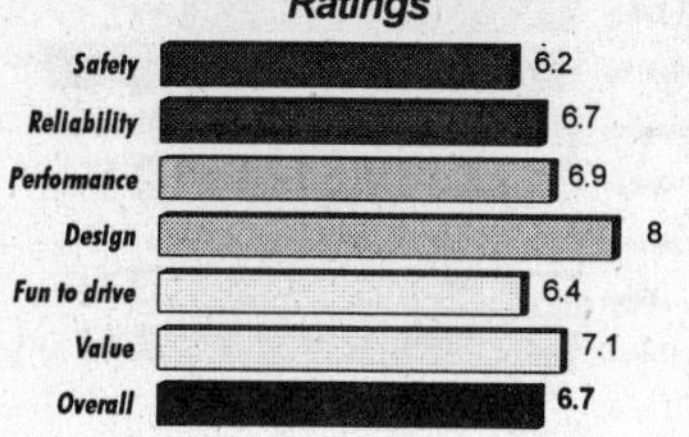

FWD/4SP/PS/AC			
3 Dr Hbk	6579	**4225**	**5650**

ADD FOR ALL 92 MITSUBISHI:

ABS(Std Diamnt LS,SL,VR-4,Mont LS) +350
Auto Trans(Precis,Pkup) +390
Bed Liner +105
Car Phone(Diamante,3000GT) +160
Cass(Prec,Mirage,Pkup,LRV,Base,Galant/ Eclipse/Mont/4D Exp) +75
CD Player +175
Cruise Ctrl(Std Diamante LS,Turbo,GSX, Galant LS/GS/GSR,SL,Mont LS/SR) +115
Custom Whls +160
Fiberglass Cap +205
Leather Seats(Std Galant VR-4) +195
Pwr Locks(Std Diamante,Turbo,GSX, Galant LS/GS/GSR,SL,Mont LS/SR) +75
Pwr Sunroof +390
Pwr Wndw(Std Diam,Turbo,GSX, Galant LS/GS/GSR,SL,Mont LS/SR) +135
Running Board +125
Sunroof +195

DEDUCT FOR ALL 92 MITSUBISHI:

No AC -505
No Auto Trans -470
No Pwr Steering -135

1991 MITSUBISHI

3000GT V6 1991

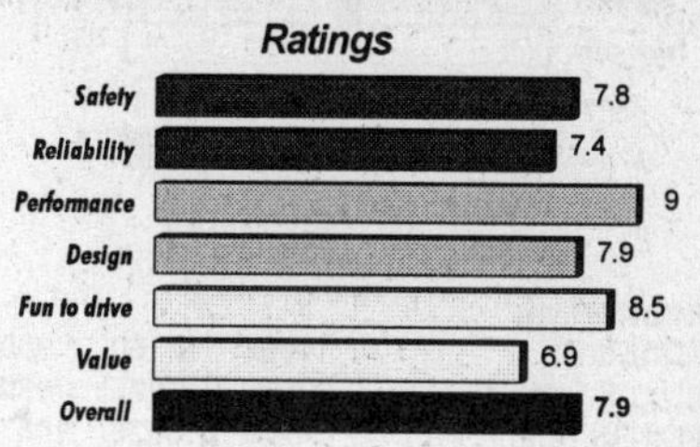

5SP-FWD/AT/PS/AC			
2 Dr Cpe	19059	**12450**	**15050**
2 Dr SL Cpe	24749	**15350**	**18125**
AWD VR-4 Turbo Cpe	30800	**18425**	**21550**

ECLIPSE 4 Cyl 1991

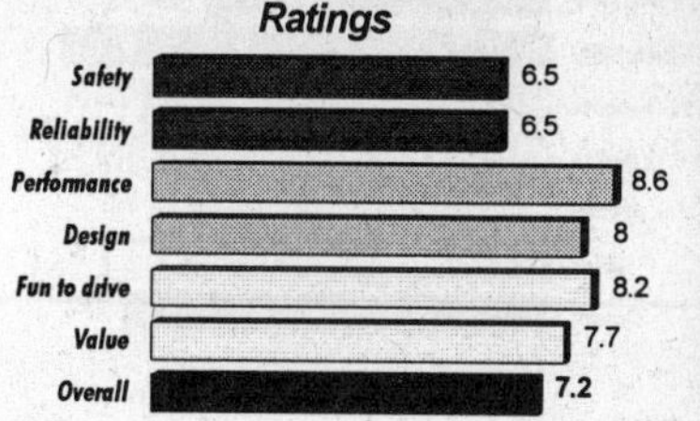

FWD/AT/PS/AC			
2 Dr Cpe	10859	**6650**	**8450**
2 Dr GS Cpe	11889	**7200**	**9075**
2 Dr GS/16V Cpe	12789	**7700**	**9625**
2 Dr GS/16V Turbo Cpe	15099	**8625**	**10575**
2 Dr GSX/16V AWD Turbo Cpe	16759	**9800**	**11925**

GALANT 4 Cyl — 1991

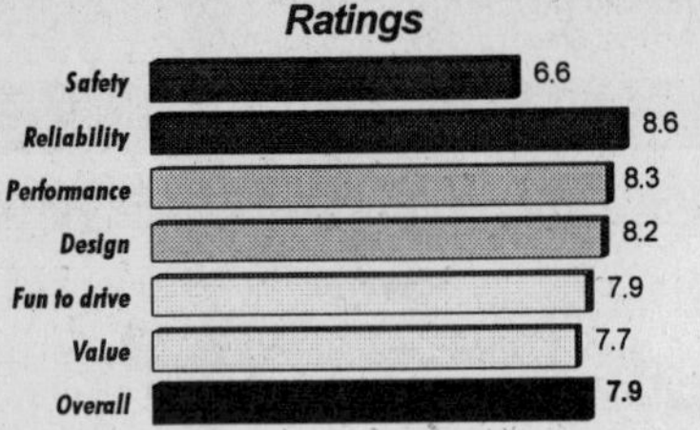

Model/Body/Type	BaseList	Whlse	Retail
FWD/AT/PS/AC			
4 Dr Sdn	10999	**7150**	**9000**
4 Dr LS Sdn	13979	**7875**	**9800**
4 Dr GS Sdn	14259	**8625**	**10575**
4 Dr GSR Sdn (5 spd)	16569	**8825**	**10825**
4 Dr GSX AWD Sdn	16959	**9225**	**11250**
VR-4 AWD Turbo Sdn (5 spd)	21000	**11800**	**14250**

MIRAGE 4 Cyl — 1991

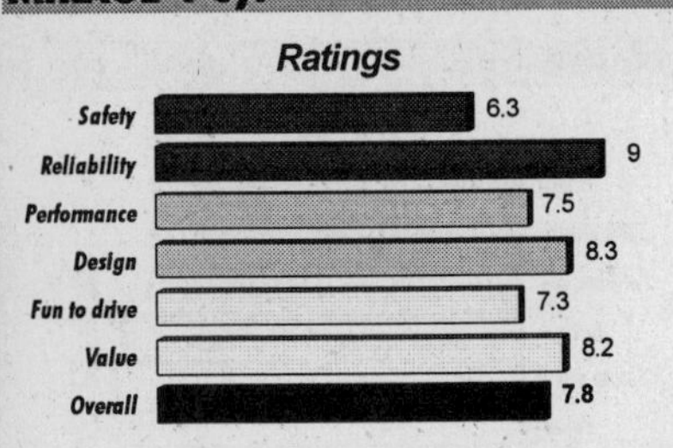

Model/Body/Type	BaseList	Whlse	Retail
FWD/AT/PS/AC			
3 Dr VL Hbk	7029	**3950**	**5300**
3 Dr Hbk	7609	**4600**	**6025**
4 Dr Sdn	8539	**4775**	**6250**
4 Dr LS Sdn	9109	**4950**	**6500**
4 Dr GS Sdn	10509	**5650**	**7150**

MONTERO V6 — 1991

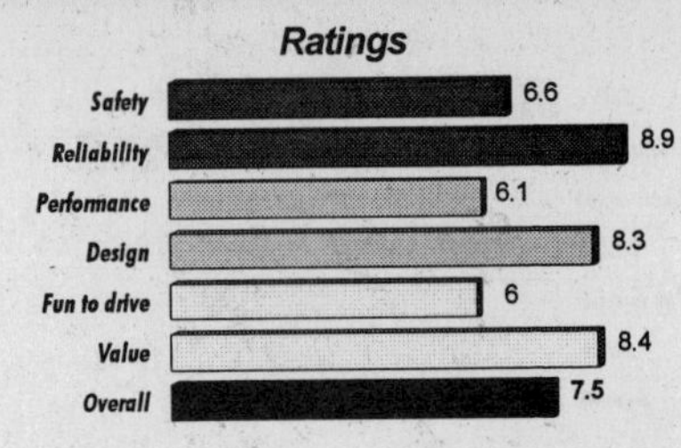

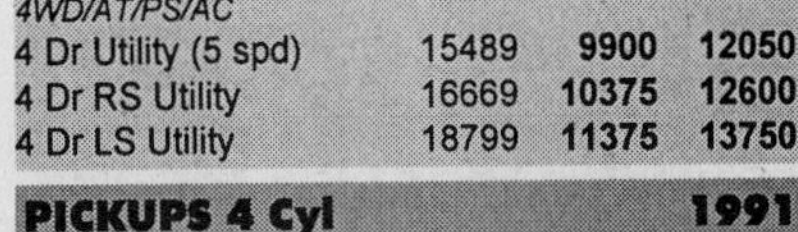

Model/Body/Type	BaseList	Whlse	Retail
4WD/AT/PS/AC			
4 Dr Utility (5 spd)	15489	**9900**	**12050**
4 Dr RS Utility	16669	**10375**	**12600**
4 Dr LS Utility	18799	**11375**	**13750**

PICKUPS 4 Cyl — 1991

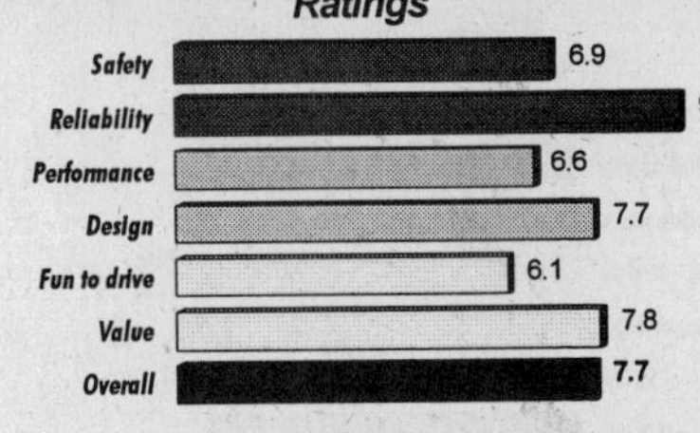

Model/Body/Type	BaseList	Whlse	Retail
5SP/PS/AC			
Mighty Max	7689	**4325**	**5725**
Mighty Max Macrocab	8919	**5425**	**7000**
1 Ton LB Mighty Max	8979	**4625**	**6100**
4WD Mighty Max (V6)	11699	**7050**	**8800**

PRECIS 4 Cyl — 1991

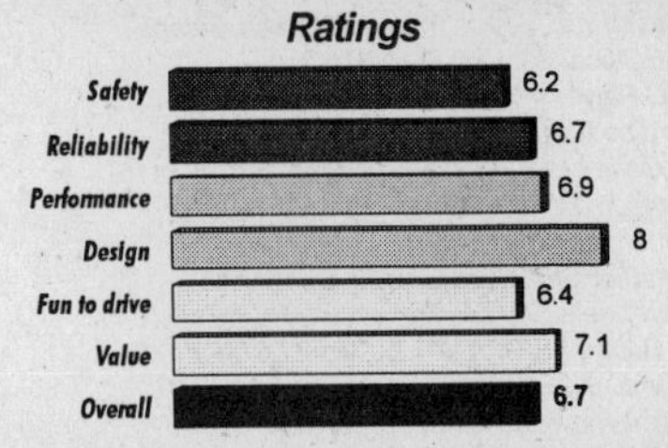

Model/Body/Type	BaseList	Whlse	Retail
FWD/PS/AC			
3 Dr Hbk (4 spd)	6469	**2875**	**4125**
3 Dr RS Hbk (5 spd)	6929	**3100**	**4375**

ADD FOR ALL 91 MITSUBISHI:

ABS(3000Base,GSX,GSTurbo,Galant GS) +315
Auto Trans(Precis,Pkup) +350
Bed Liner +80
Car Phone(3000GT) +135
Cass(Std Eclipse/Galant LS,GS,GSR,GSX, VR-4,GT,Mont LS) +60
CD Player +160
Cruise Ctrl(Std Turbo,SL, Galant LS/GS/GSX/GSR,Mont LS) +100
Custom Whls +135
Fiberglass Cap +170
Leather Seats(Std Galant VR-4) +160
Pwr Locks(Std VR-4,SL, Galant LS/GS/GSX/GSR,Mont LS) +60
Pwr Sunroof +350
Pwr Wndw(Std VR-4,SL, GalantLS/GS/GSX/GSR,Mont LS) +100
Running Board +105
Sunroof +160

DEDUCT FOR ALL 91 MITSUBISHI:

No AC -470
No Auto Trans -430
No Pwr Steering -115

1990 MITSUBISHI

ECLIPSE 4 Cyl — 1990

Ratings

Rating	Score
Safety	6.5
Reliability	6.5
Performance	8.6
Design	8
Fun to drive	8.2
Value	7.7
Overall	7.2

Model/Body/Type	BaseList	Whlse	Retail
FWD/AT/PS/AC			
2 Dr Cpe	10397	**6000**	**7725**
2 Dr GS Cpe	11409	**6500**	**8250**
2 Dr GS/16V Cpe	12239	**6850**	**8675**
2 Dr GS/16V Turbo Cpe (5 spd)	14169	**7175**	**9050**
AWD GSX/16V Turbo Cpe (5 spd)	16449	**8375**	**10275**

GALANT 4 Cyl — 1990

Ratings

Rating	Score
Safety	6.6
Reliability	8.6
Performance	8.3
Design	8.2
Fun to drive	7.9
Value	7.7
Overall	7.9

Model/Body/Type	BaseList	Whlse	Retail
FWD/AT/PS/AC			
4 Dr Sdn	10989	**5525**	**7200**
4 Dr LS Sdn	13969	**6125**	**7850**
4 Dr GS Sdn	15669	**7025**	**8850**
4 Dr GSX AWD Sdn (5 spd)	16369	**7325**	**9200**

MIRAGE 4 Cyl — 1990

Ratings

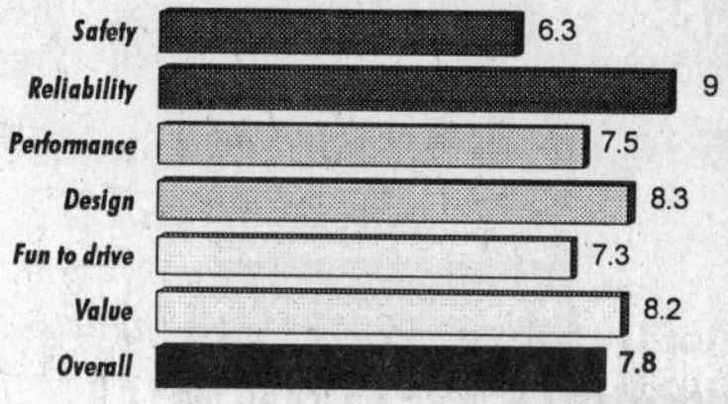

Rating	Score
Safety	6.3
Reliability	9
Performance	7.5
Design	8.3
Fun to drive	7.3
Value	8.2
Overall	7.8

Model/Body/Type	BaseList	Whlse	Retail
FWD/AT/PS/AC			
3 Dr VL Hbk (4 spd)	6929	**2175**	**3250**
3 Dr Hbk	7839	**3250**	**4550**
3 Dr RS Hbk (5 spd)	8759	**3025**	**4275**
4 Dr Sdn	8559	**3425**	**4750**
4 Dr RS Sdn	9509	**3675**	**5000**

See the Automobile Dealer Directory on page 379 for a Dealer near you!

MITSUBISHI 90-89

Model/Body/Type	BaseList	Whlse	Retail

MONTERO V6 1990

Ratings

- Safety 6.6
- Reliability 8.9
- Performance 6.1
- Design 8.3
- Fun to drive 6
- Value 8.4
- Overall 7.5

4WD/AT/PS/AC			
2 Dr SP Utility	13949	8175	10075
2 Dr Sport Utility	15409	8275	10175
4 Dr Utility	15519	8950	10950
4 Dr RS Utility	18139	9450	11500

PICKUPS 4 Cyl 1990

5SP/PS/AC			
Mighty Max	7689	3550	4875
Mighty Max Macrocab	8919	4550	5975
1 Ton LB Mighty Max	8979	3825	5175
4WD Mighty Max (V6)	11459	6100	7650

PRECIS 4 Cyl 1990

Ratings

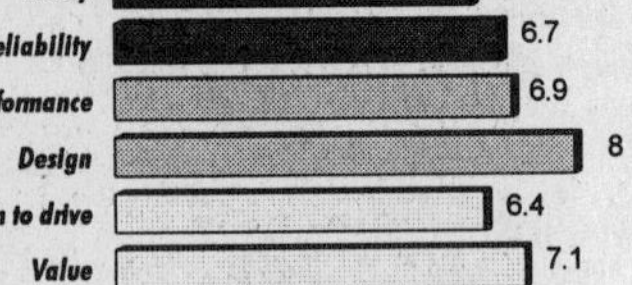

FWD/PS/AC			
3 Dr Hbk (4 spd)	5899	1975	3050
3 Dr RS Hbk (5 spd)	6999	2425	3575

SIGMA V6 1990

FWD/AT/PS/AC			
4 Dr Sdn	17879	6650	8575

VAN/WAGON 4 Cyl 1990

AT/PS/AC			
Cargo Van	11229	4875	6550
Wagon	14929	7200	9075

ADD FOR ALL 90 MITSUBISHI:

ABS(GS,GSX,Sigma) +275
Auto Trans(Precis,Pkup) +315
Cass(Std LS/GS/GSX,Sigma,Mont Spt/RS) +60
CD Player +115
Cruise Ctrl(Std LS/GS/GSX,Sigma,Mont RS) +75
Custom Whls +115
Dual AC(Wgn) +315
exe Pkg(Mirage) +230
Fiberglass Cap +125
Leather Seats +115
LS Pkg(Wgn,Mont) +505
Pwr Locks(Std LS/GS/GSX,Sig,MontRS, Van/Wg) +60
Pwr Sunroof +315
Pwr Wndw(Std LS/GS/GSX,Sigma,Mont RS) +75
Running Board +80
Sunroof +115

DEDUCT FOR ALL 90 MITSUBISHI:

No AC -430
No Auto Trans -390
No Pwr Steering -100

1989 MITSUBISHI

GALANT 4 Cyl 1989

Ratings

FWD/AT/PS/AC			
4 Dr Sdn	10971	4175	5725
4 Dr LS Sdn	13579	4650	6325
4 Dr GS Sdn (5 spd)	15269	5000	6650

MIRAGE 4 Cyl 1989

Ratings

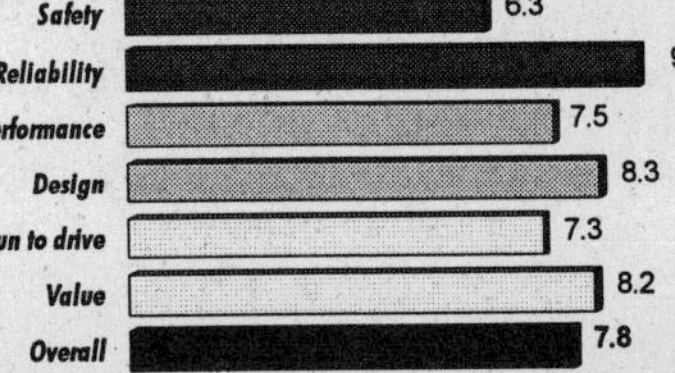

MITSUBISHI

Model/Body/Type	BaseList	Whlse	Retail
FWD/AT/PS/AC			
3 Dr Hbk	9159	**2400**	**3550**
3 Dr Turbo Hbk (5 spd)	11969	**2800**	**4025**
4 Dr Sdn	8859	**2600**	**3750**
4 Dr LS Sdn	10209	**2925**	**4175**

MONTERO 1989

Ratings

Safety	6.6
Reliability	8.9
Performance	6.1
Design	8.3
Fun to drive	6
Value	8.4
Overall	7.5

Model/Body/Type	BaseList	Whlse	Retail
4WD/AT/PS/AC			
4 Cyl Models			
2 Dr SP Utility (5 spd)	12299	**6375**	**8125**
V6 Models			
2 Dr Sport Utility	15399	**7050**	**8875**
4 Dr Utility	17099	**8025**	**9950**

PICKUPS 4 Cyl 1989

Ratings

Safety	6.9
Reliability	9.3
Performance	6.6
Design	7.7
Fun to drive	6.1
Value	7.8
Overall	7.7

Model/Body/Type	BaseList	Whlse	Retail
5SP/PS/AC			
Mighty Max	7599	**2850**	**4100**
1 Ton LB Mighty Max	8869	**3100**	**4375**
Mighty Max Sport	8489	**3250**	**4575**
LB Mighty Max Sport	9079	**3375**	**4700**
Mighty Max Macrocab	8809	**3750**	**5075**
SPX Macrocab	10179	**4450**	**5875**
4WD Mighty Max	10559	**4700**	**6150**
4WD LB Mighty Max Spt	11889	**5225**	**6750**
4WD SPX Pkup	12109	**5350**	**6900**
4WD SPX Macro Pkup	13019	**6325**	**7925**

PRECIS 4 Cyl 1989

Model/Body/Type	BaseList	Whlse	Retail
FWD/5SP/PS/AC			
3 Dr Hbk (4 spd)	5499	**1425**	**2375**
3 Dr RS Hbk	6699	**1700**	**2700**
3 Dr LS Hbk	7349	**2050**	**3125**
5 Dr LS Hbk	7599	**2175**	**3250**

SIGMA V6 1989

Model/Body/Type	BaseList	Whlse	Retail
FWD/AT/PS/AC			
4 Dr Sdn	17069	**5175**	**7025**

STARION 4 Cyl 1989

Model/Body/Type	BaseList	Whlse	Retail
5SP/PS/AC			
2 Dr ESI-R Sport Cpe	19859	**5525**	**7350**

VAN/WAGON 4 Cyl 1989

Model/Body/Type	BaseList	Whlse	Retail
AT/PS/AC			
Cargo Van	11229	**2550**	**3800**
Wagon	14929	**4500**	**6100**

ADD FOR ALL 89 MITSUBISHI:

Auto Trans(Precis,Pkup,Mont SP) +275
Cass(Std Precis LS,Galant LS/GS, Sigma,Starion,Mont Spt/4Dr) +35
Cruise Ctrl(Std Galant LS/GS,Sigma,Starion) +60
Custom Whls +75
Fiberglass Cap +80
Leather Seats(Starion,Sigma) +75
LS Pkg(Wgn,Mont 4Dr) +370
Pwr Sunroof +250
Pwr Wndw(Std Galant LS/GS,Sigma,Starion) +60
Sunroof +100
V6 Eng +350

DEDUCT FOR ALL 89 MITSUBISHI:

No AC -390
No Auto Trans -350
No Pwr Steering -75

1988 MITSUBISHI

CORDIA 4 Cyl 1988

Model/Body/Type	BaseList	Whlse	Retail
FWD/AT/PS/AC			
3 Dr L Hbk	10569	**1975**	**3225**
3 Dr Turbo Hbk (5 spd)	12089	**1850**	**3100**

GALANT 4 Cyl 1988

Model/Body/Type	BaseList	Whlse	Retail
FWD/AT/PS/AC			
4 Dr Sigma Sdn	16549	**3250**	**4650**

MIRAGE 4 Cyl 1988

Model/Body/Type	BaseList	Whlse	Retail
FWD/AT/PS/AC			
4 Dr L Sdn	8349	**1850**	**2925**
2 Dr Turbo Hbk (5 spd)	8829	**1525**	**2475**

MONTERO 4 Cyl 1988

Model/Body/Type	BaseList	Whlse	Retail
4WD/AT/PS/AC			
SP Utility	10969	**4450**	**6000**
Sport Utility	13109	**4950**	**6625**

MITSUBISHI 88-86

Model/Body/Type	BaseList	Whlse	Retail
PICKUPS 4 Cyl			**1988**
5SP/PS/AC			
Mighty Max	6799	2175	3250
1 Ton LB Mighty Max	7899	2350	3475
Mighty Max Sport	7729	2500	3650
LB Mighty Max Sport	8269	2625	3775
Mighty Max Macrocab	7759	3025	4275
SPX Macrocab Pkup	9199	3625	4950
4WD Mighty Max	9739	3875	5225
4WD LB Mighty Max Sport	10999	4375	5800
4WD SPX Pkup	11129	4525	5950
4WD SPX Macro Pkup	11879	5375	6925
PRECIS 4 Cyl			**1988**
FWD/5SP/PS/AC			
3 Dr Hbk (4 spd)	5295	1100	2000
3 Dr RS Hbk	6299	1325	2250
3 Dr LS Hbk	7049	1575	2550
5 Dr LS Hbk	7299	1700	2700
STARION 4 Cyl			**1988**
5SP/PS/AC			
2 Dr ESI Sport Cpe	16649	3400	4950
2 Dr ESI-R Sport Cpe	19259	3875	5525
VAN/WAGON 4 Cyl			**1988**
AT/PS/AC			
Cargo Van	10189	2025	3175
Wagon	13679	3575	5000

ADD FOR ALL 88 MITSUBISHI:
Auto Trans(Precis,Starion,Pkup) +230
DEDUCT FOR ALL 88 MITSUBISHI:
No AC -330
No Auto Trans -290

1987 MITSUBISHI

Model/Body/Type	BaseList	Whlse	Retail
CORDIA 4 Cyl			**1987**
FWD/AT/PS/AC			
3 Dr L Hbk	9759	1450	2575
3 Dr Turbo Hbk (5 spd)	11329	1425	2525
GALANT 4 Cyl			**1987**
FWD/AT/PS/AC			
4 Dr Luxury Sdn	13999	2150	3300
MIRAGE 4 Cyl			**1987**
FWD/AT/PS/AC			
2 Dr Hbk (4 spd)	6059	1150	2050
2 Dr L Hbk	7319	1500	2450
4 Dr Sdn	7859	1700	2675
2 Dr Turbo Hbk	8479	1475	2425
MONTERO 4 Cyl			**1987**
4WD/AT/PS/AC			
Utility	9739	3375	4800
Sport Utility	11899	3725	5200
PICKUPS 4 Cyl			**1987**
5SP/PS/AC			
Mighty Max	6289	1350	2300
1 Ton LB Mighty Max	7039	1550	2525
Mighty Max Sport	7129	1650	2625
LB Mighty Max Sport	7349	1750	2775
SPX Pkup	7519	1800	2850
4WD Mighty Max	8949	2850	4100
4WD LB Mighty Max	9169	2975	4225
4WD SPX Pkup	9999	3300	4650
PRECIS 4 Cyl			**1987**
FWD/5SP/PS/AC			
3 Dr Hbk (4 spd)	5195	700	1525
3 Dr LS Hbk	6499	1025	1925
5 Dr LS Hbk	6799	1175	2100
STARION 4 Cyl			**1987**
5SP/PS/AC			
2 Dr LE Sport Cpe	15469	2700	4075
2 Dr ESI-R Sport Cpe	17989	3100	4600
TREDIA 4 Cyl			**1987**
FWD/AT/PS/AC			
4 Dr L Sdn	9369	1375	2325
4 Dr Turbo Sdn (5 spd)	10429	1350	2300
VAN/WAGON 4 Cyl			**1987**
AT/PS/AC			
Cargo Van	9839	1550	2600
Wagon	12789	2750	4025

1986 MITSUBISHI

Model/Body/Type	BaseList	Whlse	Retail
CORDIA			**1986**
FWD			
3 Dr L Hbk	8689	875	1850
3 Dr Sport Turbo Hbk	10369	875	1825
GALANT			**1986**
FWD			
4 Dr Luxury Sdn	12699	1625	2750
MIRAGE			**1986**
FWD			
2 Dr Hbk	5459	600	1550
2 Dr L Hbk	6539	700	1675
2 Dr Sport Turbo Hbk	7879	675	1650

Model/Body/Type	BaseList	Whlse	Retail
MONTERO			**1986**
4WD			
Utility	9839	2650	3925
PICKUPS			**1986**
Mighty Max	5799	625	1600
Mighty Max Sport	6259	850	1800
SPX Pkup	7029	975	2000
4WD Mighty Max	8299	2150	3325
4WD SPX Pkup	9319	2500	3775
STARION			**1986**
2 Dr LE Sport Cpe	14829	2000	3175
2 Dr ESI-R Sport Cpe	17299	2200	3400
TREDIA			**1986**
FWD			
4 Dr Sdn	7199	700	1675
4 Dr L Sdn	8379	825	1775
4 Dr Turbo Sdn	9689	800	1750

1985 MITSUBISHI

Model/Body/Type	BaseList	Whlse	Retail
CORDIA			**1985**
3 Dr L Hbk	8449	560	1505
3 Dr Turbo Hbk	9959	550	1480
GALANT			**1985**
4 Dr Luxury Sdn	11989	1270	2300
MIRAGE			**1985**
2 Dr Hbk	5389	260	1200
2 Dr L Hbk	6189	300	1295
2 Dr LS Hbk	6669	400	1350
2 Dr Turbo Hbk	7689	300	1250
MONTERO			**1985**
4WD Utility	9639	2100	3285
PICKUPS			**1985**
Mighty Max	5749	285	1225
SP Pkup	6669	480	1400
SPX Pkup	7239	630	1580
4WD SPX Pkup	9229	1650	2800
STARION			**1985**
2 Dr LS Sport Cpe	12629	1380	2460
2 Dr LE Sport Cpe	14869	1580	2685
2 Dr ES Sport Cpe	14489	1720	2880
2 Dr ESI Sport Cpe	15279	1875	3020
TREDIA			**1985**
4 Dr Sdn	6989	375	1320
4 Dr L Sdn	8189	460	1400
4 Dr Turbo Sdn	9279	430	1375

NISSAN Japan

1992 Nissan Maxima SE

For a Nissan dealer in your area, see our Dealer Directory (pg 217)

1994 NISSAN

240SX 4 Cyl — 1994

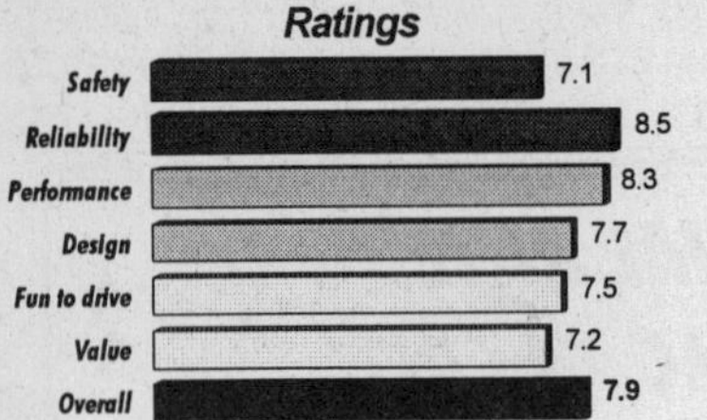

Model/Body/Type	BaseList	Whlse	Retail
AT/PS/AC			
2 Dr SE Conv	23969	-	-

300ZX V6 — 1994

Model/Body/Type	BaseList	Whlse	Retail
5SP-AT/PS/AC			
2 Dr Cpe	33699	-	-
2 Dr 2+2 Cpe	36489	-	-
2 Dr Turbo Cpe	40099	-	-
2 Dr Conv	40879	-	-

ALTIMA 4 Cyl — 1994

Model/Body/Type	BaseList	Whlse	Retail
FWD/AT/PS/AC			
4 Dr XE Sdn	13739	**12800**	**15275**
4 Dr GXE Sdn	14859	**13400**	**15925**
4 Dr SE Sdn	18179	**14775**	**17350**
4 Dr GLE Sdn	19179	**15750**	**18400**

MAXIMA V6 — 1994

Ratings

Rating	Score
Safety	7.2
Reliability	8.7
Performance	8.3
Design	7.8
Fun to drive	8.2
Value	7.6
Overall	8.1

Model/Body/Type	BaseList	Whlse	Retail
FWD/AT/PS/AC			
4 Dr SE Sdn	23299	**16975**	**19925**
4 Dr GXE Sdn	22199	**15125**	**17875**

PATHFINDER V6 — 1994

Model/Body/Type	BaseList	Whlse	Retail
4WD/AT/PS/AC			
4 Dr XE Utility (2WD)	19429	**17675**	**20750**
4 Dr XE Utility	21099	**19375**	**22525**
4 Dr SE Utility	25009	**21350**	**24625**
4 Dr LE Utility	28999	-	-

PICKUPS 1994

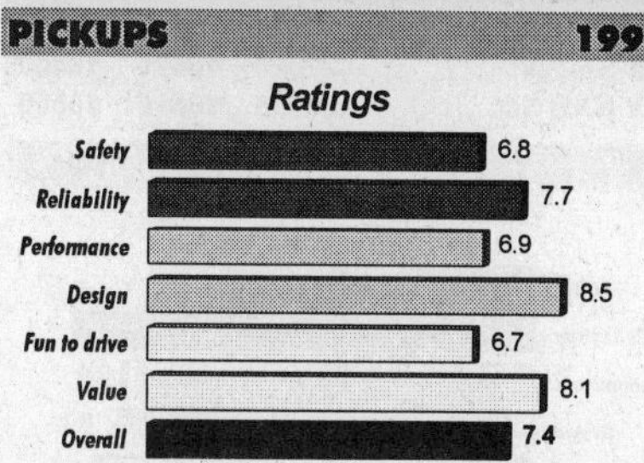

5SP/PS/AC

Model/Body/Type	BaseList	Whlse	Retail
4 Cyl Models			
Std Pkup	9359	**8600**	**10450**
XE Pkup	10129	**9300**	**11225**
XE King Cab Pkup	11679	**10925**	**13225**
4WD XE Pkup	13619	**12025**	**14400**
4WD XE King Cab Pkup	15089	**13700**	**16150**
V6 Models			
LB Pkup	11189	**9475**	**11425**
SE King Cab Pkup	14279	**12100**	**14500**
4WD XE King Cab Pkup	15879	**14450**	**16950**
4WD SE King Cab Pkup	16379	**14850**	**17375**

QUEST V6 1994

FWD/AT/PS/AC

Model/Body/Type	BaseList	Whlse	Retail
XE Van	18529	**16825**	**19625**
GXE Van	23039	**19650**	**22650**

SENTRA 4 Cyl 1994

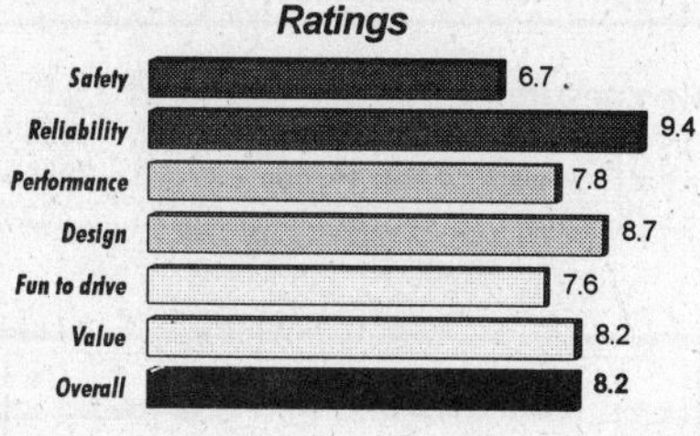

FWD/AT/PS/AC

Model/Body/Type	BaseList	Whlse	Retail
2 Dr E Cpe	10049	**9100**	**11000**
4 Dr E Sdn	10599	**9200**	**11125**
2 Dr XE Cpe	12099	**9825**	**11875**
4 Dr XE Sdn	12299	**9925**	**11975**
2 Dr SE Cpe	12599	**10000**	**12050**
2 Dr SE-R Cpe	13799	**10775**	**13050**
4 Dr GXE Sdn	14669	**11275**	**13600**

ADD FOR FOR ALL 94 NISSAN:

ABS(Std ZX,QuestGXE) +430
AC-Rear(Std Quest GXE) +590
Air Bag(Sentra E/XE/SE/SE-R,Quest) +340
Anthi-Theft/Recovery Sys +365
Auto Trans(Pkup) +500
Car Phone(ZX,Maxima) +230
Cass(Sentra E/SE/SE-R,Altima XE/GXE, Pkup Base/XE) +115
CD Player(Std AltimaGLE,PathLE) +230
Cruise Ctrl(SentraSE/SE-R,AltimaXE/GXE, QuestXE,PathXE,PkupXE) +160
Custom Whls +205
Leather Seats(Std ZX Conv,PathLE) +320
Pwr Locks(Quest XE,Path XE,Pkup SE) +115
Pwr Seats(Std 300ZX Conv) +160
Pwr Sunroof(Std Altima SE +GLE) +545
Pwr Wndw(Quest XE,Path XE,Pkup SE) +160
Sunroof(Std Path SE/LE) +320

DEDUCT FOR ALL 94 NISSAN:

No AC -680
No Auto Trans -590
No Pwr Steering -180

1993 NISSAN

240SX 4 Cyl 1993

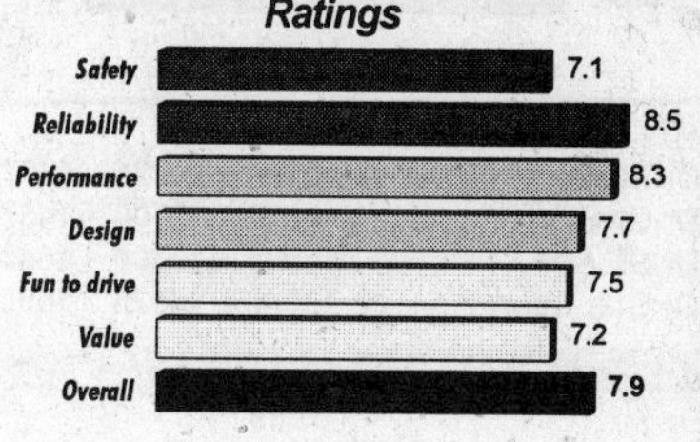

AT/PS/AC

Model/Body/Type	BaseList	Whlse	Retail
2 Dr Cpe	14755	**11575**	**13950**
3 Dr Fbk	15475	**11675**	**14125**
2 Dr SE Cpe	17220	**12850**	**15325**
3 Dr SE Fbk	17675	**12950**	**15450**
2 Dr SE Conv	22345	**15400**	**18025**

Model/Body/Type	BaseList	Whlse	Retail

300ZX V6 — 1993

Ratings

Rating	Score
Safety	7.9
Reliability	7.6
Performance	9
Design	8.4
Fun to drive	8.7
Value	7.4
Overall	8.1

Model/Body/Type	BaseList	Whlse	Retail
5SP-AT/PS/AC			
2 Dr Cpe	30095	**21775**	**25075**
2 Dr 2+2 Cpe	33525	**23050**	**26450**
2 Dr Turbo Cpe	37090	**26050**	**29625**
2 Dr Conv	35995	**25900**	**29475**

ALTIMA 4 Cyl — 1993

Ratings

Rating	Score
Safety	7.9
Reliability	9.6
Performance	8.4
Design	8.2
Fun to drive	8.4
Value	8.7
Overall	8.7

Model/Body/Type	BaseList	Whlse	Retail
FWD/AT/PS/AC			
4 Dr XE Sdn	12999	**11625**	**14075**
4 Dr GXE Sdn	14024	**12100**	**14575**
4 Dr SE Sdn	16524	**13300**	**15800**
4 Dr GLE Sdn	18349	**14325**	**16900**

MAXIMA V6 — 1993

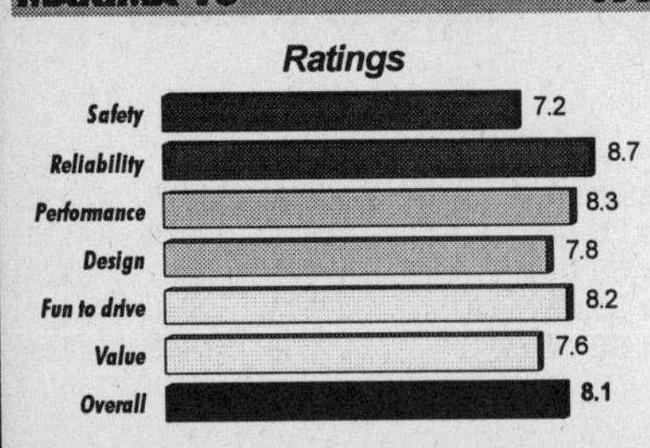

Model/Body/Type	BaseList	Whlse	Retail
FWD/AT/PS/AC			
4 Dr SE Sdn	22025	**15625**	**18400**
4 Dr GXE Sdn	20960	**13875**	**16550**

NX 4 Cyl — 1993

Ratings

Rating	Score
Safety	6.3
Reliability	9.4
Performance	8.4
Design	8.7
Fun to drive	8.9
Value	7.7
Overall	8.3

Model/Body/Type	BaseList	Whlse	Retail
FWD/AT/PS/AC			
2 Dr 1600 Cpe	11635	**8800**	**10800**
2 Dr 2000 Cpe	14720	**10425**	**12650**

PATHFINDER V6 — 1993

Ratings

Rating	Score
Safety	6.7
Reliability	9
Performance	7.1
Design	8.1
Fun to drive	6.5
Value	7.8
Overall	7.8

Model/Body/Type	BaseList	Whlse	Retail
4WD/AT/PS/AC			
4 Dr XE Utility (2WD)	18090	**16225**	**19050**
4 Dr XE Utility	19810	**17775**	**20850**
4 Dr SE Utility	23230	**19375**	**22525**

Model/Body/Type	BaseList	Whlse	Retail

PICKUPS 1993

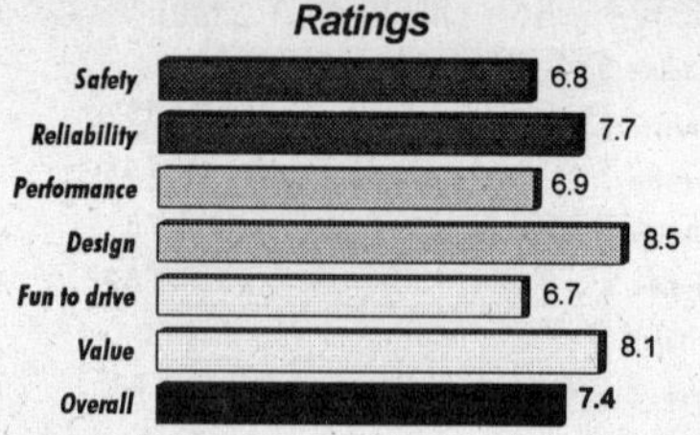

5SP/PS/AC

Model/Body/Type	BaseList	Whlse	Retail
4 Cyl Models			
Std Pkup	9195	**7325**	**9125**
King Cab Pkup	11495	**8775**	**10650**
4WD Std Pkup	12550	**9800**	**11800**
4WD King Cab Pkup	14665	**11175**	**13475**
V6 Models			
LB Pkup	10665	**8100**	**9950**
SE King Cab Pkup	14055	**10650**	**12925**
4WD SE King Cab Pkup	16200	**13100**	**15525**

QUEST V6 1993

Ratings

Safety	7.8
Reliability	8.4
Performance	6.7
Design	7.7
Fun to drive	6.4
Value	7.7
Overall	7.7

FWD/AT/PS/AC

Model/Body/Type	BaseList	Whlse	Retail
XE Van	17145	**15625**	**18275**
GXE Van	21450	**18150**	**21075**

SENTRA 4 Cyl 1993

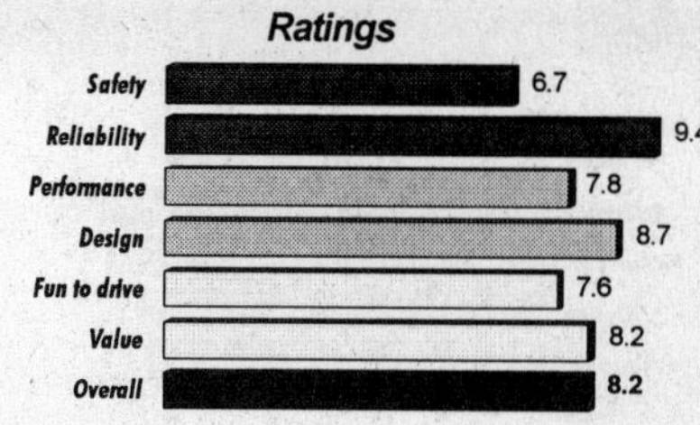

FWD/AT/PS/AC

Model/Body/Type	BaseList	Whlse	Retail
2 Dr E Cpe	8715	**7600**	**9425**
4 Dr E Sdn	10165	**7700**	**9550**
2 Dr XE Cpe	10500	**8300**	**10150**
4 Dr XE Sdn	11190	**8400**	**10225**
2 Dr SE Cpe	10900	**8450**	**10275**
2 Dr SE-R Cpe	12455	**9175**	**11100**
4 Dr GXE Sdn	14145	**9700**	**11700**

ADD FOR FOR ALL 93 NISSAN:

ABS(Std ZX) +390
AC-Rear(Std Quest GXE) +375
Auto Trans(Pkup) +430
Bed Liner +125
Car Phone(ZX,Maxima) +175
Cass(Sentra,NX1600,Altima XE/GXE,Pkup) +100
CD Player(Std Altima GLE) +195
Cruise Ctrl(NX,Sentra,Altima XE/GXE) +135
Custom Whls +175
Fiberglass Cap +250
Leather Seats(Std ZX Conv) +275
Luggage Rack(Std Quest GXE) +80
Privacy Glass +145
Pwr Locks(NX,Quest XE,Path XE,Pkp SE) +100
Pwr Seats +135
Pwr Sunroof(Std Altima GLE) +390
Pwr Wndw(NX,Quest XE,Path XE,Pkp SE) +135
Running Board +145
Slider Wndw +80
Sunroof +230
T-Top(NX1600,Base ZX) +545

DEDUCT FOR ALL 93 NISSAN:

No AC -545
No Auto Trans -505
No Pwr Steering -160

Model/Body/Type	BaseList	Whlse	Retail

1992 NISSAN

240SX 4 Cyl — 1992

Model/Body/Type	BaseList	Whlse	Retail
AT/PS/AC			
2 Dr Cpe	14515	**10225**	**12450**
3 Dr Fbk	14785	**10325**	**12550**
2 Dr SE Cpe	16690	**11425**	**13800**
3 Dr SE Fbk	16885	**11525**	**13900**
3 Dr LE Fbk	18725	**12500**	**14975**
2 Dr SE Conv	21995	**13650**	**16175**

300ZX V6 — 1992

Model/Body/Type	BaseList	Whlse	Retail
5SP-AT/PS/AC			
2 Dr Cpe	29120	**18925**	**22050**
2 Dr 2+2 Cpe	32440	**20075**	**23325**
2 Dr Turbo Cpe	35890	**22825**	**26200**

See the Automobile Dealer Directory on page 379 for a Dealer near you!

MAXIMA V6 — 1992

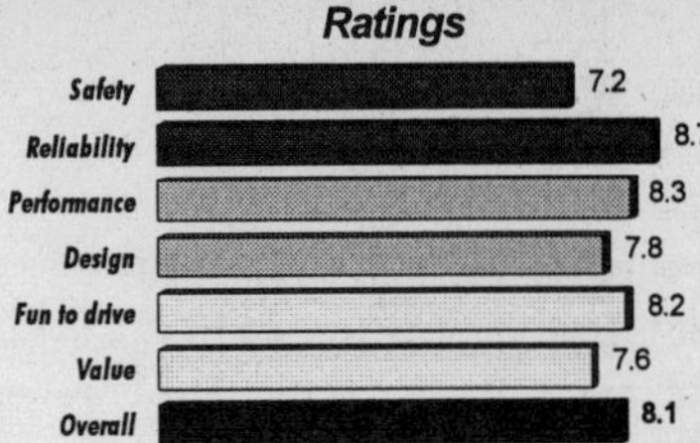

Model/Body/Type	BaseList	Whlse	Retail
FWD/AT/PS/AC			
4 Dr SE Sdn	20815	**13625**	**16275**
4 Dr GXE Sdn	19695	**12025**	**14625**

NX 4 Cyl — 1992

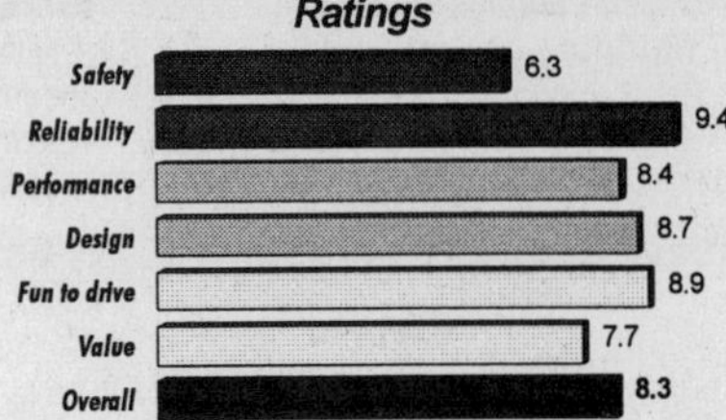

Model/Body/Type	BaseList	Whlse	Retail
FWD/AT/PS/AC			
2 Dr 1600 Cpe	11300	**7550**	**9450**
2 Dr 2000 Cpe	13480	**8950**	**10950**

PATHFINDER V6 — 1992

Model/Body/Type	BaseList	Whlse	Retail
4WD/AT/PS/AC			
4 Dr XE Utility (2WD)	17265	**15125**	**17875**
4 Dr XE Utility	18910	**16625**	**19575**
4 Dr SE Utility	21980	**17975**	**21050**

PICKUPS 1992

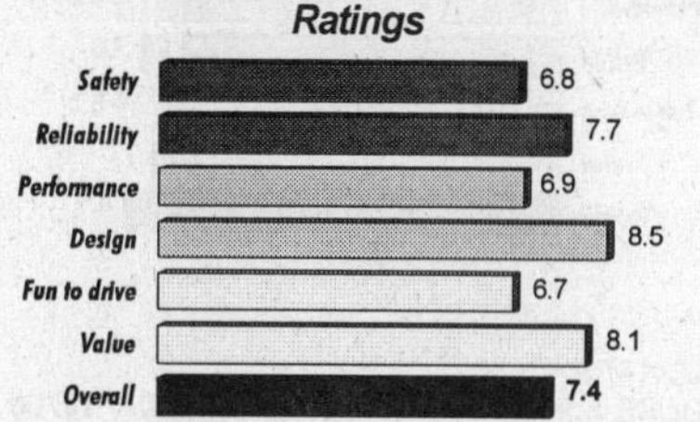

Model/Body/Type	BaseList	Whlse	Retail
5SP/PS/AC			
4 Cyl Models			
Std Pkup	8865	**6200**	**7800**
King Cab Pkup	10525	**7425**	**9225**
4WD Std Pkup	11880	**8525**	**10375**
4WD King Cab Pkup	13765	**9775**	**11800**
V6 Models			
LB Pkup	10280	**6925**	**8675**
SE King Cab Pkup	13505	**8975**	**10875**
4WD SE King Cab Pkup	15620	**11250**	**13575**

SENTRA 4 Cyl 1992

Ratings

- Safety 6.7
- Reliability 9.4
- Performance 7.8
- Design 8.7
- Fun to drive 7.6
- Value 8.2
- Overall 8.2

Model/Body/Type	BaseList	Whlse	Retail
FWD/AT/PS/AC			
2 Dr E Cpe	8495	**6100**	**7650**
4 Dr E Sdn	9550	**6175**	**7750**
2 Dr XE Cpe	9880	**6700**	**8450**
4 Dr XE Sdn	10565	**6825**	**8550**
2 Dr SE Cpe	10560	**6875**	**8600**
2 Dr SE-R Cpe (5 spd)	11850	**7450**	**9250**
4 Dr GXE Sdn	12950	**7950**	**9800**

STANZA 4 Cyl 1992

Ratings

- Safety 6.3
- Reliability 8.7
- Performance 7.9
- Design 8.1
- Fun to drive 8.2
- Value 8.4
- Overall 7.8

Model/Body/Type	BaseList	Whlse	Retail
FWD/AT/PS/AC			
4 Dr XE Sdn	12750	**8150**	**10050**
4 Dr SE Sdn	16690	**9550**	**11600**
4 Dr GXE Sdn	17070	**9300**	**11325**

ADD FOR ALL 92 NISSAN:

Auto Trans(Pkup) +390
Bed Liner +105
Car Phone(300ZX,Maxima) +160
Cass(Sentra,NX1600,Stanza XE,Pkup) +75
CD Player +175
Cruise Ctrl(XE,NX,Sentra SE/SE-R) +115
Custom Whls +160
Fiberglass Cap +205
Leather Seats(Std 240SX LE) +230
Privacy Glass +125
Pwr Locks(NX,Stanz XE,Path XE,Pkp SE) +75
Pwr Seats(Maxima) +115
Pwr Sunroof +390
Pwr Wndw(NX,Stanz XE,Path XE,Pkp SE) +115
Running Board +125
Sunroof +195
T-Top(NX,Base ZX) +485
ABS(Std 300ZX) +350

DEDUCT FOR ALL 92 NISSAN:

No AC -505
No Auto Trans -470
No Pwr Steering -135

1991 NISSAN

240SX 4 Cyl — 1991

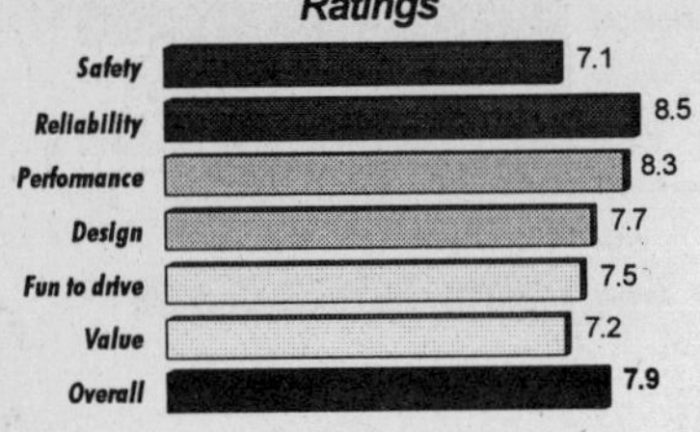

AT/PS/AC	BaseList	Whlse	Retail
2 Dr Cpe	13609	**8950**	**10950**
3 Dr Fbk	13859	**9050**	**11050**
2 Dr SE Cpe	15649	**10000**	**12175**
3 Dr SE Fbk	15834	**10100**	**12275**
3 Dr LE Fbk	17559	**11000**	**13325**

300ZX V6 — 1991

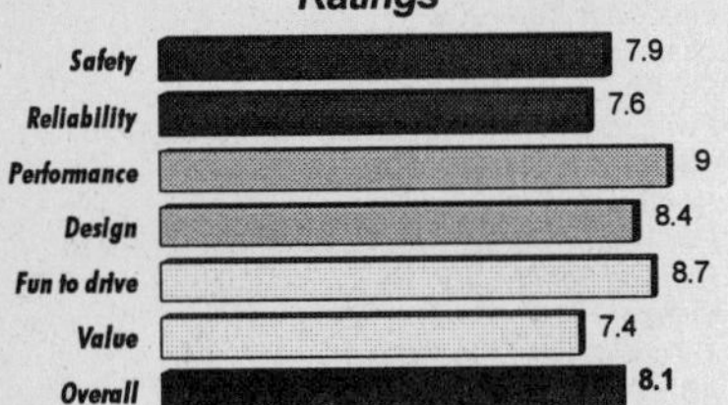

5SP-AT/PS/AC	BaseList	Whlse	Retail
2 Dr Cpe	27300	**16025**	**18825**
2 Dr 2+2 Cpe	30300	**17175**	**20175**
2 Dr Turbo Cpe	33500	**18875**	**22000**

MAXIMA V6 — 1991

FWD/AT/PS/AC	BaseList	Whlse	Retail
4 Dr SE Sdn	19449	**11250**	**13700**
4 Dr GXE Sdn	18399	**9850**	**12075**

NX 4 Cyl — 1991

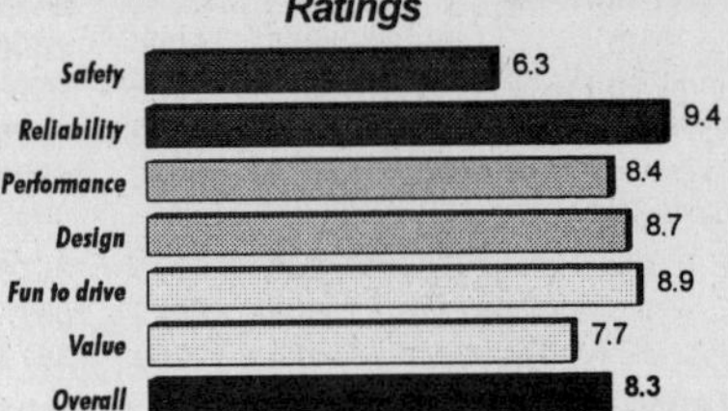

FWD/AT/PS/AC	BaseList	Whlse	Retail
2 Dr 1600 Cpe	11090	**6350**	**8100**
2 Dr 2000 Cpe	12970	**7625**	**9525**

PATHFINDER V6 — 1991

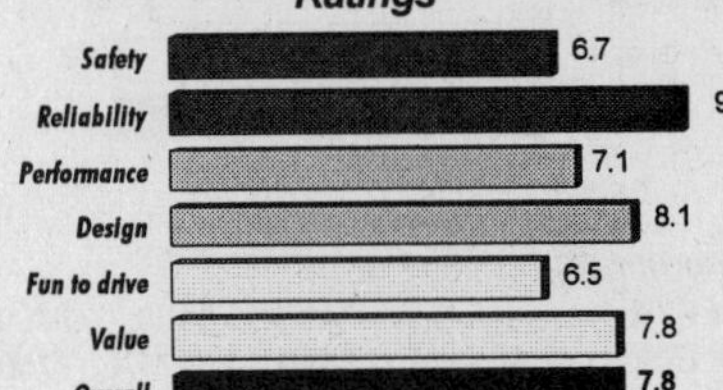

Model/Body/Type	BaseList	Whlse	Retail
4WD/AT/PS/AC			
4 Dr XE Utility (2WD)	16120	**13475**	**16125**
4 Dr XE Utility	17695	**14825**	**17550**
4 Dr SE Utility	20549	**15925**	**18725**

PICKUPS 1991

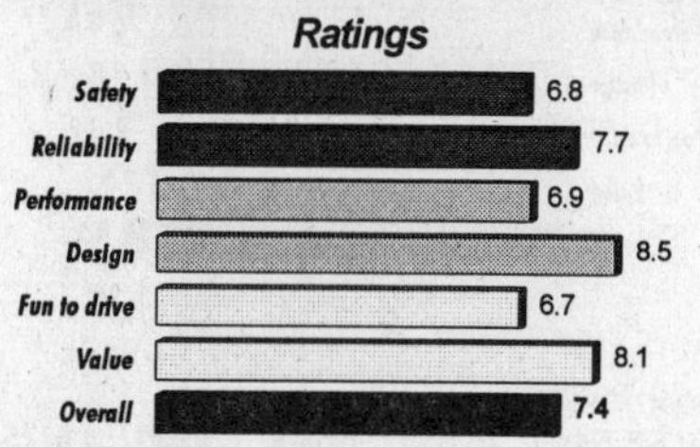

Model/Body/Type	BaseList	Whlse	Retail
5SP/PS/AC			
4 Cyl Models			
Std Pkup	8279	**5100**	**6625**
King Cab Pkup	9849	**6275**	**7875**
4WD Std Pkup	11124	**7300**	**9100**
4WD King Cab Pkup	12949	**8450**	**10275**
V6 Models			
LB Pkup	9624	**5800**	**7350**
SE King Cab Pkup	12699	**7750**	**9600**
4WD SE King Cab Pkup	14749	**9925**	**11975**

SENTRA 4 Cyl 1991

Ratings

Rating	Score
Safety	6.7
Reliability	9.4
Performance	7.8
Design	8.7
Fun to drive	7.6
Value	8.2
Overall	8.2

Model/Body/Type	BaseList	Whlse	Retail
FWD/AT/PS/AC			
2 Dr E Cpe	7999	**4975**	**6500**
4 Dr E Sdn	8900	**5075**	**6600**
2 Dr XE Cpe	9100	**5600**	**7150**
4 Dr XE Sdn	9760	**5725**	**7250**
2 Dr SE Cpe	9755	**5750**	**7300**
2 Dr SE-R Cpe (5 spd)	10970	**6100**	**7650**
4 Dr GXE Sdn	12050	**6775**	**8525**

STANZA 4 Cyl 1991

Ratings

Rating	Score
Safety	6.3
Reliability	8.7
Performance	7.9
Design	8.1
Fun to drive	8.2
Value	8.4
Overall	7.8

Model/Body/Type	BaseList	Whlse	Retail
FWD/AT/PS/AC			
4 Dr XE Sdn	11900	**6675**	**8500**
4 Dr GXE Sdn	15225	**7775**	**9700**

ADD FOR ALL 91 NISSAN:

ABS(Std 300ZX) +315
Auto Trans(Pkup) +350
Bed Liner +80
Car Phone(ZX,Maxima) +135
Cass(Sent,NX1600,Stanza XE,Pkup) +60
CD Player +160
Cruise Ctrl(Sentra XE,Stanza XE) +100
Custom Whls +135
Fiberglass Cap +170
Leather Seats(Std 240SX LE) +195
Privacy Glass +105
Pwr Locks(Stanza XE,Path XE,Pkup SE) +60
Pwr Seats +100
Pwr Sunroof(Std Maxima SE) +350
Pwr Wndw(Stanza XE,Path XE,Pkup SE) +100
Running Board +105
Sunroof +160
T-Top(NX2000,Base 300ZX) +450

DEDUCT FOR ALL 91 NISSAN:

No AC -470
No Auto Trans -430
No Pwr Steering -115

Model/Body/Type	BaseList	Whlse	Retail

1990 NISSAN

240SX 4 Cyl — 1990

Ratings

Rating	Score
Safety	7.1
Reliability	8.5
Performance	8.3
Design	7.7
Fun to drive	7.5
Value	7.2
Overall	7.9

Model/Body/Type	BaseList	Whlse	Retail
AT/PS/AC			
2 Dr XE Cpe	13249	**6750**	**8600**
3 Dr SE Fbk	13499	**6875**	**8700**

300ZX V6 — 1990

Ratings

Rating	Score
Safety	7.9
Reliability	7.6
Performance	9
Design	8.4
Fun to drive	8.7
Value	7.4
Overall	8.1

Model/Body/Type	BaseList	Whlse	Retail
5SP-AT/PS/AC			
2 Dr GS Cpe	27300	**12900**	**15525**
2 Dr 2+2 GS Cpe	28500	**13200**	**15825**
2 Dr Turbo Cpe	33000	**15525**	**18300**

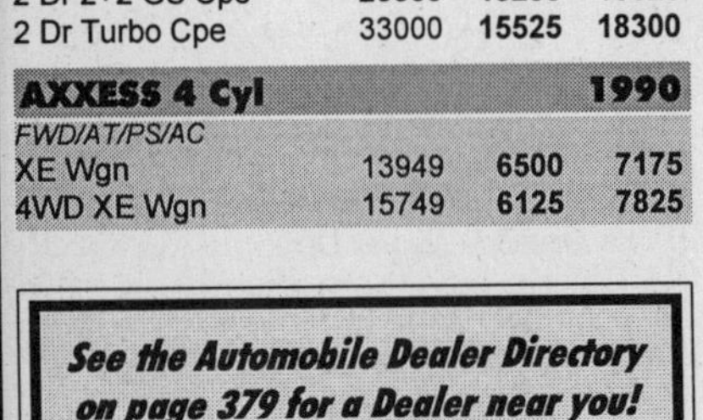

AXXESS 4 Cyl — 1990

Model/Body/Type	BaseList	Whlse	Retail
FWD/AT/PS/AC			
XE Wgn	13949	**6500**	**7175**
4WD XE Wgn	15749	**6125**	**7825**

See the Automobile Dealer Directory on page 379 for a Dealer near you!

MAXIMA V6 — 1990

Ratings

Rating	Score
Safety	7.2
Reliability	8.7
Performance	8.3
Design	7.8
Fun to drive	8.2
Value	7.6
Overall	8.1

Model/Body/Type	BaseList	Whlse	Retail
FWD/AT/PS/AC			
4 Dr SE Sdn	18749	**9350**	**11475**
4 Dr GXE Sdn	17699	**8050**	**10100**

PATHFINDER V6 — 1990

Ratings

Rating	Score
Safety	6.7
Reliability	9
Performance	7.1
Design	8.1
Fun to drive	6.5
Value	7.8
Overall	7.8

Model/Body/Type	BaseList	Whlse	Retail
4WD/AT/PS/AC			
4 Dr XE Utility (2WD)	15720	**11350**	**13800**
4 Dr XE Utility	17295	**12625**	**15225**
2 Dr SE Utility	21814	**13125**	**15750**
4 Dr SE Utility	20149	**13625**	**16275**

PICKUPS — 1990

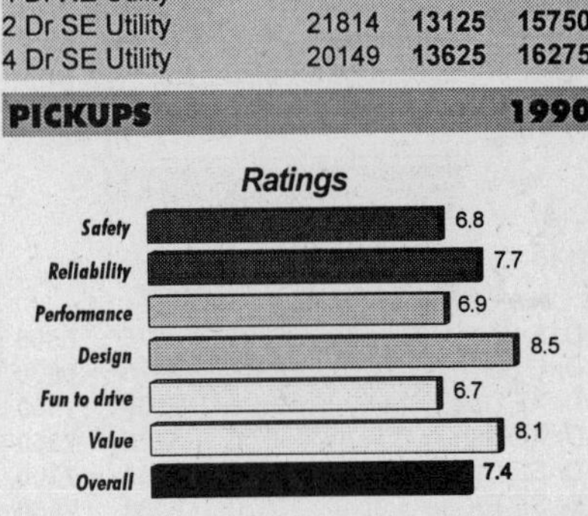

Ratings

Rating	Score
Safety	6.8
Reliability	7.7
Performance	6.9
Design	8.5
Fun to drive	6.7
Value	8.1
Overall	7.4

NISSAN

Model/Body/Type	BaseList	Whlse	Retail
5SP/PS/AC			
4 Cyl Models			
Std Pkup	8149	4300	5725
King Cab Pkup	9749	5250	6775
4WD Std Pkup	10574	6325	7925
4WD King Cab Pkup	12599	7300	9100
V6 Models			
LB Pkup	9524	4875	6375
SE King Cab Pkup	12599	6700	8450
4WD Pkup	12574	6825	8550
4WD SE King Cab Pkup	14749	8750	10625

PULSAR NX 4 Cyl 1990

Model/Body/Type	BaseList	Whlse	Retail
FWD/AT/PS/AC			
2 Dr XE Cpe	12249	5700	7375

SENTRA 4 Cyl 1990

Ratings

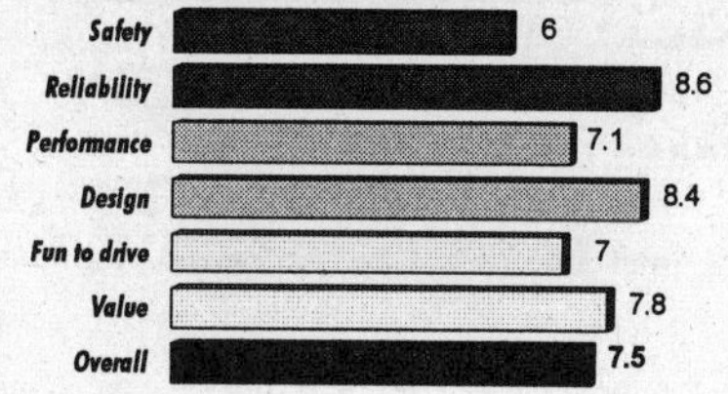

Rating	Score
Safety	6
Reliability	8.6
Performance	7.1
Design	8.4
Fun to drive	7
Value	7.8
Overall	7.5

Model/Body/Type	BaseList	Whlse	Retail
FWD/AT/PS/AC			
2 Dr Std(4 spd) Cpe	7299	2350	3475
2 Dr XE Cpe	8549	3600	4925
4 Dr XE Sdn	9149	3700	5025
5 Dr XE Wgn	9899	3975	5325
2 Dr XE Cpe	10999	4375	5800
2 Dr SE Cpe	12299	4800	6275

STANZA 4 Cyl 1990

Ratings

Rating	Score
Safety	6.3
Reliability	8.7
Performance	7.9
Design	8.1
Fun to drive	8.2
Value	8.4
Overall	7.8

Model/Body/Type	BaseList	Whlse	Retail
FWD/AT/PS/AC			
4 Dr XE Sdn	11450	5525	7200
4 Dr GXE Sdn	14775	6500	8225

VAN 4 Cyl 1990

Model/Body/Type	BaseList	Whlse	Retail
AT/PS/AC			
XE Van	14799	4375	5925
GXE Van	17449	4900	6575

ADD FOR ALL 90 NISSAN:

ABS(Std 300ZX) +275
Auto Trans(Pkup) +315
Cass(Std GXE,Maxima,ZX,Path,Pkp SE,Axx) +60
Cruise Ctrl(Stanza XE,SX,Axxess) +75
Custom Whls +115
Dual Sunroof(Van) +430
Fiberglass Cap +125
Leather Seats +135
Privacy Glass +80
Pwr Locks(Stanza XE,SX,Path XE,Pkp SE) +60
Pwr Seats +75
Pwr Sunroof(Std Maxima SE,Axxess SE) +315
Pwr Wndw(Stanza XE,SX,Path XE,Pkp SE) +75
Running Board +80
SE Pkg(Axxess) +625
Sunroof(Std Sentra SE,Path SE) +115

DEDUCT FOR ALL 90 NISSAN:

No AC -430
No Auto Trans -390
No Pwr Steering -100

1989 NISSAN

240SX 4 Cyl 1989

Ratings

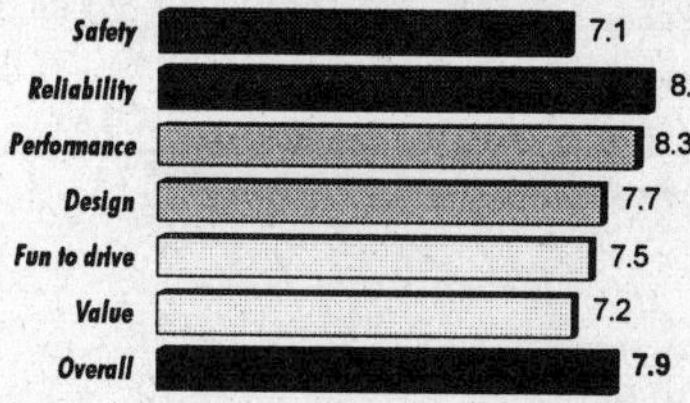

Rating	Score
Safety	7.1
Reliability	8.5
Performance	8.3
Design	7.7
Fun to drive	7.5
Value	7.2
Overall	7.9

Model/Body/Type	BaseList	Whlse	Retail
AT/PS/AC			
2 Dr XE Cpe	12999	5525	7200
3 Dr SE Fbk	13199	5650	7300

300ZX V6 1989

Model/Body/Type	BaseList	Whlse	Retail
5SP-AT/PS/AC			
2 Dr GS Cpe	22299	8475	10525
2 Dr 2+2 GS Cpe	23449	8625	10675
2 Dr Turbo Cpe	24699	9275	11375

NISSAN 89

MAXIMA V6 — 1989

Model/Body/Type	BaseList	Whlse	Retail
FWD/AT/PS/AC			
4 Dr SE Sdn	17999	**7675**	**9725**
4 Dr GXE Sdn	16999	**6675**	**8650**

PATHFINDER V6 — 1989

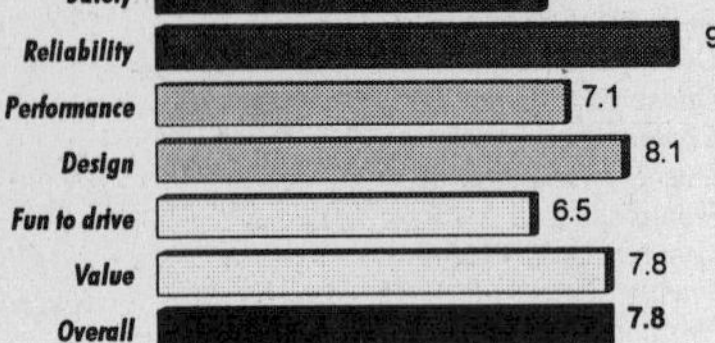

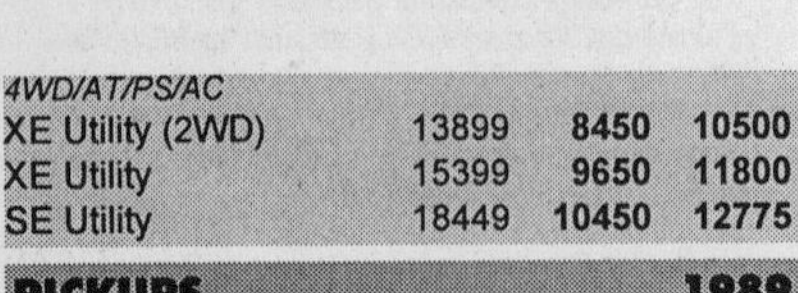

Model/Body/Type	BaseList	Whlse	Retail
4WD/AT/PS/AC			
XE Utility (2WD)	13899	**8450**	**10500**
XE Utility	15399	**9650**	**11800**
SE Utility	18449	**10450**	**12775**

PICKUPS — 1989

Ratings

Rating	Score
Safety	6.8
Reliability	7.7
Performance	6.9
Design	8.5
Fun to drive	6.7
Value	8.1
Overall	7.4

Model/Body/Type	BaseList	Whlse	Retail
5SP/PS/AC			
4 Cyl Models			
Std Pkup	7549	**3400**	**4725**
Special Pkup	8549	**3850**	**5200**
King Cab Pkup	8549	**4350**	**5775**
Special King Cab Pkup	9549	**4775**	**6250**
4WD Pkup	9999	**5250**	**6775**
4WD Special Pkup	10999	**5725**	**7275**
4WD King Cab Pkup	10999	**6225**	**7825**
4WD Special King Cab Pkup	11999	**6650**	**8300**

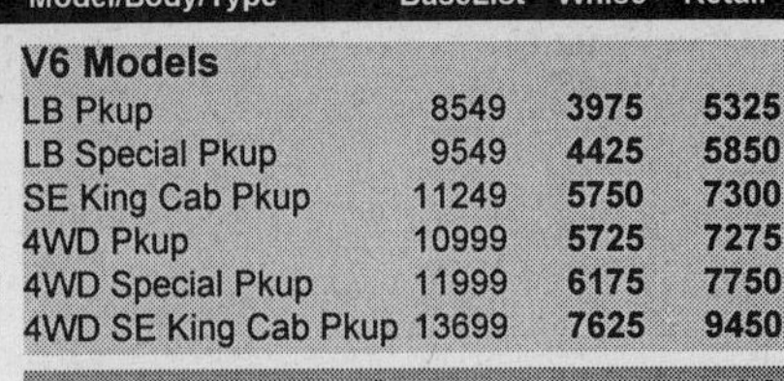

Model/Body/Type	BaseList	Whlse	Retail
V6 Models			
LB Pkup	8549	**3975**	**5325**
LB Special Pkup	9549	**4425**	**5850**
SE King Cab Pkup	11249	**5750**	**7300**
4WD Pkup	10999	**5725**	**7275**
4WD Special Pkup	11999	**6175**	**7750**
4WD SE King Cab Pkup	13699	**7625**	**9450**

PULSAR NX 4 Cyl — 1989

Model/Body/Type	BaseList	Whlse	Retail
FWD/AT/PS/AC			
2 Dr XE Cpe	11749	**4275**	**5825**
2 Dr SE/16V Cpe	12999	**4725**	**6350**

SENTRA 4 Cyl — 1989

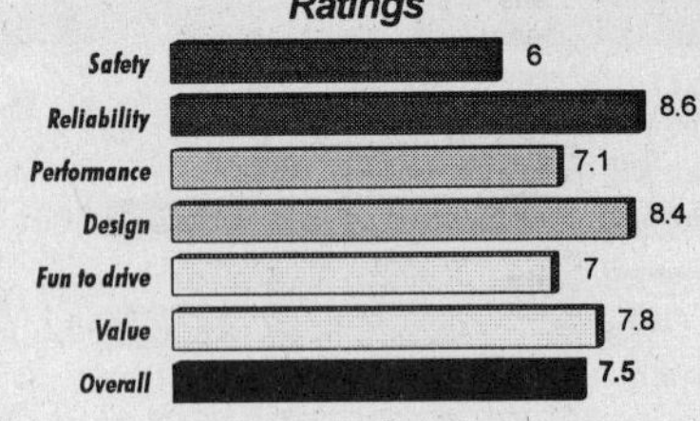

Model/Body/Type	BaseList	Whlse	Retail
FWD/AT/PS/AC			
2 Dr Cpe (4 spd)	6849	**1575**	**2550**
2 Dr E Cpe	7999	**2675**	**3850**
4 Dr E Sdn	8549	**2775**	**4000**
5 Dr E Wgn	9224	**3025**	**4275**
2 Dr XE Cpe	9649	**3075**	**4350**
4 Dr XE Sdn	10299	**3150**	**4450**
5 Dr XE Wgn	10724	**3375**	**4700**
5 Dr XE 4WD Wgn	11524	**3925**	**5275**
2 Dr XE Cpe	10674	**3375**	**4700**
2 Dr SE Cpe	11924	**3750**	**5075**

STANZA 4 Cyl — 1989

Model/Body/Type	BaseList	Whlse	Retail
FWD/AT/PS/AC			
4 Dr E Nbk	11849	**4400**	**5950**
4 Dr GXE Nbk	13799	**4900**	**6575**

NISSAN

Model/Body/Type	BaseList	Whlse	Retail

ADD FOR ALL 89 NISSAN:

Auto Trans(Pkup) +275
Cass(Std GXE,Maxima,ZX,Path, Pkup Spec 4WD/SE,2WD) +35
CD Player +75
Cruise Ctrl(Std Stanza GXE,Maxima,ZX, PathSE,Pkup SE) +60
Custom Whls +75
Fiberglass Cap +125
Leather Seats +115
Pwr Locks(Std Stanza GXE,Max,ZX,Path SE) +60
Pwr Seats +60
Pwr Sunroof(Std Maxima SE) +250
Pwr Wndw(Std Stanz GXE,Max,ZX,Path SE) +60
Sunroof(Std Sentra SE) +100

DEDUCT FOR ALL 89 NISSAN:

No AC -390
No Auto Trans -350
No Pwr Steering -75

1988 NISSAN

200SX — 1988

AT/PS/AC

Model/Body/Type	BaseList	Whlse	Retail
4 Cyl Models			
2 Dr XE Nbk	11899	3475	4875
2 Dr XE Hbk	12149	3575	5000
V6 Models			
2 Dr SE Hbk	14949	4150	5700

300ZX V6 — 1988

5SP-AT/PS/AC

Model/Body/Type	BaseList	Whlse	Retail
2 Dr GS Cpe	20649	6375	8275
2 Dr 2+2 GS Cpe	21799	6500	8375
2 Dr Turbo Cpe	23149	7000	8950

MAXIMA V6 — 1988

FWD/AT/PS/AC

Model/Body/Type	BaseList	Whlse	Retail
4 Dr SE Sdn	17199	5225	7075
4 Dr GXE Sdn	16949	4750	6525
4 Dr GXE Wgn	18199	4700	6500

PATHFINDER V6 — 1988

4WD/AT/PS/AC

Model/Body/Type	BaseList	Whlse	Retail
XE Utility	14999	7825	9875
SE Utility	17049	8450	10500

PICKUPS — 1988

5SP/PS/AC

Model/Body/Type	BaseList	Whlse	Retail
4 Cyl Models			
Std Pkup (4 spd)	7199	2725	3900
E Pkup	7499	3100	4375
E LB Pkup	8199	3200	4500
E King Cab	8499	3950	5300
XE King Cab	9949	4375	5800
4WD E Pkup	9999	4825	6275
4WD E LB Pkup	10699	4925	6450
4WD E King Cab	10999	5725	7275
4WD XE King Cab	12499	6150	7725
V6 Models			
SE King Cab	11099	4850	6325
4WD E Pkup	10999	5200	6725
4WD SE Pkup	12649	5750	7300
4WD SE King Cab	13599	6650	8275

PULSAR NX 4 Cyl — 1988

FWD/AT/PS/AC

Model/Body/Type	BaseList	Whlse	Retail
2 Dr XE Cpe	11649	3250	4675
2 Dr SE/16V Cpe	12999	3700	5125

SENTRA 4 Cyl — 1988

FWD/AT/PS/AC

Model/Body/Type	BaseList	Whlse	Retail
2 Dr Cpe (4 spd)	6499	1275	2175
2 Dr E Cpe	7299	2100	3175
4 Dr E Sdn	8499	2175	3250
3 Dr E Hbk	7199	2000	3100
5 Dr E Wgn	8949	2375	3500
2 Dr XE Cpe	8999	2400	3550
4 Dr XE Sdn	9599	2500	3650
5 Dr XE Wgn	9899	2725	3900
5 Dr XE 4WD S/W (5 spd)	10699	2850	4100
4 Dr GXE Sdn	10199	2700	3875
2 Dr XE Cpe	9849	2775	4000
2 Dr SE Cpe	11099	3100	4375

STANZA 4 Cyl — 1988

FWD/AT/PS/AC

Model/Body/Type	BaseList	Whlse	Retail
4 Dr E Nbk	11109	3400	4825
4 Dr GXE Nbk	12999	3825	5300
XE Wgn	12049	3575	5000
4WD XE Wgn	13704	4075	5600

VAN 4 Cyl — 1988

AT/PS/AC

Model/Body/Type	BaseList	Whlse	Retail
XE Van	14349	2775	4100

ADD FOR ALL 88 NISSAN:

Auto Trans(Pkup) +230
Cass(Std Stanz GXE,Max,ZX,Path SE) +25
Cruise Ctrl(Std Stanz GXE,Max,ZX,Path SE) +35
Custom Whls +35
GXE Pkg(Van) +275
Leather Seats +75
Pwr Locks(Std Stanz GXE,Max,ZX,Path SE) +25
Pwr Seats(Std Maxima) +35
Pwr Sunroof(Std Maxima SE & Wgn) +160
Pwr Wndw(Std Stanza GXE,SX SE, Max,ZX,Path SE) +35
SportBak Pkg(Pulsar) +100
Sunroof(Std Sentra SE) +60

DEDUCT FOR ALL 88 NISSAN:

No AC -330
No Auto Trans -290

NISSAN 87-86.5

1987 NISSAN

Model/Body/Type	BaseList	Whlse	Retail
200SX			**1987**
AT/PS/AC			
4 Cyl Models			
2 Dr XE Nbk	10849	**2675**	**3950**
2 Dr XE Hbk	11199	**2775**	**4100**
V6 Models			
2 Dr SE Hbk	14499	**3275**	**4700**
300ZX V6			**1987**
5SP-AT/PS/AC			
2 Dr GS Cpe	18499	**4775**	**6550**
2 Dr 2+2 GS Cpe	20649	**4850**	**6650**
2 Dr Turbo Cpe	21399	**5200**	**7050**
MAXIMA V6			**1987**
FWD/AT/PS/AC			
4 Dr SE Sdn	15199	**3800**	**5400**
4 Dr GXE Sdn	15199	**4850**	**6650**
4 Dr GXE Wgn	16149	**3475**	**5050**
PATHFINDER			**1987**
4WD/AT/PS/AC			
4 Cyl Models			
E Utility (5 spd)	12299	**5925**	**7775**
V6 Models			
XE Utility	13999	**6875**	**8825**
SE Utility	15399	**7225**	**9225**
PICKUPS			**1987**
5SP/PS/AC			
4 Cyl Models			
Std Pkup	6699	**2250**	**3350**
E Pkup	7299	**2525**	**3675**
E LB Pkup	7749	**2650**	**3825**
XE LB Pkup	8799	**3025**	**4275**
E King Cab	8599	**3325**	**4675**
XE King Cab	9649	**3700**	**5025**
4WD E Pkup	9749	**4175**	**5575**
4WD XE LB Pkup	11299	**4675**	**6125**
4WD XE King Cab	12049	**5350**	**6900**
V6 Models			
SE Pkup	10049	**3350**	**4700**
SE King Cab	11149	**4200**	**5600**
4WD SE Pkup	12499	**5000**	**6525**
4WD SE King Cab	13649	**5875**	**7450**
PULSAR NX 4 Cyl			**1987**
FWD/AT/PS/AC			
2 Dr XE Cpe	10599	**2275**	**3500**
2 Dr SE/16V Cpe (5 spd)	11799	**2325**	**3550**
SENTRA 4 Cyl			**1987**
FWD/AT/PS/AC			
2 Dr Cpe (5 spd)	5999	**1025**	**1925**
2 Dr E Cpe	6999	**1700**	**2675**
4 Dr E Sdn	7399	**1775**	**2800**
3 Dr E Hbk	7199	**1600**	**2575**
5 Dr E Wgn	8449	**1950**	**3025**
2 Dr XE Cpe	7849	**1850**	**2925**
4 Dr XE Sdn	8199	**1950**	**3025**
3 Dr XE Hbk	7999	**1775**	**2800**
5 Dr XE Wgn	8499	**2150**	**3225**
5 Dr XE 4WD S/W (5 spd)	10149	**2550**	**3700**
4 Dr GXE Sdn	9099	**2175**	**3250**
5 Dr GXE Wgn	9399	**2325**	**3450**
2 Dr XE Cpe	8699	**2175**	**3250**
2 Dr SE Cpe	9699	**2500**	**3650**
STANZA 4 Cyl			**1987**
FWD/AT/PS/AC			
4 Dr E Nbk	9999	**2550**	**3800**
4 Dr GXE Nbk	11299	**2900**	**4250**
5 Dr XE Hbk	10999	**2650**	**3900**
XE Wgn	11349	**2675**	**3950**
4WD XE Wgn (5 spd)	12749	**3125**	**4500**
VAN 4 Cyl			**1987**
AT/PS/AC			
XE Van	11999	**1875**	**3050**

ADD FOR ALL 87 NISSAN:
GXE Pkg(Van) +195

1986.5 NISSAN

Model/Body/Type	BaseList	Whlse	Retail
PICKUPS			**1986.5**
5SP/PS/AC			
4 Cyl Models			
Std Pkup	6299	**1700**	**2875**
E Pkup	6949	**1925**	**3125**
E LB Pkup	7249	**2025**	**3225**
XE LB Pkup	7899	**2325**	**3575**
E King Cab	8049	**2650**	**3925**
XE King Cab	8699	**2975**	**4300**
4WD E Pkup	9249	**3525**	**4900**
4WD XE LB Pkup	10549	**3975**	**5400**
4WD XE King Cab	11299	**4625**	**6150**
V6 Models			
SE Pkup	9099	**2650**	**3950**
SE King Cab	10199	**3375**	**4775**
4WD SE Pkup	11399	**4300**	**5800**
4WD SE King Cab	12799	**5025**	**6650**

NISSAN

1986 NISSAN

Model/Body/Type	BaseList	Whlse	Retail
200SX			**1986**
2 Dr E Nbk	9199	1900	3100
2 Dr XE Nbk	10499	2025	3225
2 Dr E Hbk	9499	2000	3175
2 Dr XE Hbk	11099	2125	3300
2 Dr Turbo Hbk	12599	2175	3375
300ZX			**1986**
2 Dr Cpe	17599	3875	5300
2 Dr Turbo Cpe	20099	4275	5750
MAXIMA			**1986**
FWD			
4 Dr SE Sdn	13699	3125	4475
4 Dr GL Sdn	13699	3075	4425
4 Dr GL Wgn	14599	3075	4400
PICKUPS			**1986**
Std Pkup	5999	1700	2825
Dlx Pkup	7295	1875	3075
Std LB Pkup	6299	1775	2950
ST LB Pkup	8445	2250	3475
Std King Cab	7395	2375	3625
Dlx King Cab	7895	2600	3875
4WD Std Pkup	8395	3250	4650
4WD Dlx Pkup	9095	3475	4850
4WD Dlx LB Pkup	9245	3575	4975
4WD Dlx King Cab	9695	4250	5725
PULSAR NX			**1986**
FWD			
2 Dr Cpe	8349	1275	2325
SENTRA			**1986**
FWD			
2 Dr Cpe	5499	625	1600
2 Dr Dlx Cpe	6699	925	1950
4 Dr Dlx Sdn	6899	1025	2050
4 Dr Dlx Wgn	7399	1150	2175
2 Dr MPG Diesel Cpe	7149	475	1400
2 Dr XE Cpe	7349	1075	2125
4 Dr XE Sdn	7549	1175	2200
4 Dr XE Wgn	8049	1275	2325
2 Dr XE Hbk	7849	1175	2200
2 Dr SE Hbk	8749	1400	2500
STANZA			**1986**
FWD			
4 Dr GL Nbk	9649	1575	2700
XE Wgn	9949	1600	2725
4WD XE Wgn	11149	2025	3200

DEDUCT FOR ALL 86 NISSAN:

Diesel Eng(Std MPG) -390

1985 NISSAN

Model/Body/Type	BaseList	Whlse	Retail
200SX			**1985**
2 Dr Deluxe Nbk	8999	1500	2600
2 Dr XE Nbk	10249	1600	2710
2 Dr Deluxe Hbk	9199	1600	2710
2 Dr XE Hbk	10749	1650	2810
2 Dr Turbo Hbk	12349	1650	2810
300ZX			**1985**
2 Dr Cpe	17199	3000	4375
2 Dr Turbo Cpe	19699	3325	4710
MAXIMA			**1985**
4 Dr SE Sdn	13499	2570	3850
4 Dr GL Sdn	13499	2520	3800
4 Dr GL Wgn	14399	2520	3780
PICKUPS			**1985**
Std Pkup	5999	1350	2380
Dlx Pkup	7295	1500	2580
Std LB Pkup	6299	1400	2480
ST LB Pkup	8445	1755	2910
Std King Cab	7395	1810	2980
Dlx King Cab	7895	1990	3150
4WD Std Pkup	8395	2400	3675
4WD Dlx Pkup	9095	2600	3875
4WD Dlx LB Pkup	9245	2670	3975
4WD Dlx King Cab	9695	3100	4475
PULSAR			**1985**
2 Dr NX Cpe	8249	1030	2070
SENTRA			**1985**
2 Dr Cpe	5499	490	1460
2 Dr Dlx Cpe	6649	715	1660
4 Dr Dlx Sdn	6849	785	1730
4 Dr Dlx Wgn	7349	875	1900
2 Dr MPG Diesel Cpe	7099	280	1225
2 Dr XE Cpe	7299	800	1800
4 Dr XE Sdn	7499	875	1900
4 Dr XE Wgn	7999	1010	2045
2 Dr XE Hbk	7799	875	1900
2 Dr SE Hbk	8699	1100	2120
STANZA			**1985**
4 Dr XE Hbk	8949	1255	2275
4 Dr GL Nbk	9549	1325	2365

OLDSMOBILE USA

1992 Oldsmobile Cutlass Supreme

For a Oldsmobile dealer in your area, see our Dealer Directory (pg 217)

1994 OLDSMOBILE

ACHIEVA 1994

FWD/AT/PS/AC

Model/Body/Type	BaseList	Whlse	Retail
Quad 4 Models			
4 Dr S Sdn	14175	**10850**	**13200**
2 Dr S Cpe	14075	**10850**	**13200**
4 Dr SL Sdn	17475	**12300**	**14775**
2 Dr SC Cpe	17475	**12300**	**14775**
V6 Models			
4 Dr S Sdn	14585	**11050**	**13400**
2 Dr S Cpe	14585	**11050**	**13400**
4 Dr SL Sdn	17335	**12500**	**14975**
2 Dr SC Cpe	17335	**12500**	**14975**

ADD FOR 94 ACHIEVA:

Anti-Theft/Recovery Sys +365
Cass(S) +115 *CD Player +230*
Cruise Ctrl(S) +160 *Custom Whls/Cvrs +205*
Leather Seats +275 *Pwr Seat +160*
Pwr Sunroof +545 *Pwr Wndw +160*

DEDUCT FOR 94 ACHIEVA:

No AC -680 *No Auto Trans -590*

See the Automobile Dealer Directory on page 379 for a Dealer near you!

BRAVADA V6 1/2 Ton 1994

Ratings

Rating	Score
Safety	7
Reliability	6.6
Performance	6.3
Design	8.2
Fun to drive	6
Value	6.5
Overall	6.8

4WD/AT/PS/AC

Model/Body/Type	BaseList	Whlse	Retail
4 Dr Utility	26320	**21025**	**24375**

CUTLASS CIERA V6 1994

FWD/AT/PS/AC

Model/Body/Type	BaseList	Whlse	Retail
4 Dr S Sdn (4 Cyl)	15675	**11575**	**13950**
4 Dr S Sdn	16485	**12150**	**14625**
2 Seat Cruiser S Wgn	17175	**12700**	**15175**

ADD FOR 94 CUTLASS CIERA:

Anti-Theft/Recovery Sys +365
Cass +115 *Cruise Ctrl +160*
Custom Whls/Cvrs +205 *Leather Seats +275*
Luggage Rack(S/W) +115 *Pwr Seat +160*
Pwr Wndw +160 *Third Seat S/W +205*
Woodgrain +180

CUTLASS SUPREME V6 1994

FWD/AT/PS/AC

Model/Body/Type	BaseList	Whlse	Retail
4 Dr S Sdn	17475	**13550**	**16075**
2 Dr S Cpe	17375	**13550**	**16075**
2 Dr Conv	25275	**19950**	**23000**

ADD FOR 94 CUTLASS SUPREME:

Anti-Theft/Recovery Sys +365
Cass(Std Conv) +115 *CD Player +230*
Cruise Ctrl(Std Conv) +160 *Custom Whls/Cvrs +205*
Lthr Sts(Std Conv) +275 *Pwr Seat(Std Conv) +160*
Pwr Sunroof +545 *Pwr Wndw(Std Conv) +160*

EIGHTY-EIGHT ROYALE V6 1994

FWD/AT/PS/AC

Model/Body/Type	BaseList	Whlse	Retail
4 Dr Sdn	20875	**15875**	**18675**
4 Dr LS Sdn	22875	**17300**	**20350**

ADD FOR 94 EIGHTY-EIGHT ROYALE:

Anti-Theft/Recovery Sys +365 *Car Phone +230*
Cass(Std LS) +135 *CD Player +275*
Cruise Ctrl(Std LS) +180 *Custom Whls/Cvrs +230*
Leather Seats +320 *LSS Pkg +455*
Pwr Seat +180

NINETY-EIGHT V6 1994

FWD/AT/PS/AC

Model/Body/Type	BaseList	Whlse	Retail
4 Dr Regency Sdn	25875	**20325**	**23800**
4 Dr Regency Elite Sdn	27975	**21625**	**25225**

ADD FOR 94 NINETY-EIGHT:

Anti-Theft/Recovery Sys +365
Car Phone +230 *CD Player +340*
Custom Whls/Cvrs +275 *Leather Seats +365*
Pwr Sunroof +635 *Supercharged V6 Eng +545*

SILHOUETTE V6 1994

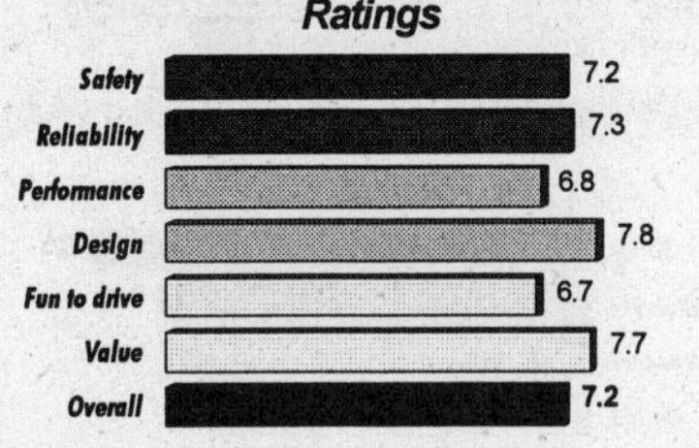

FWD/AT/PS/AC

Model/Body/Type	BaseList	Whlse	Retail
Wagon	20465	**16900**	**19925**

ADD FOR 94 SILHOUETTE:

3.8L V6 Eng +455 *Pwr Sliding Dr +320*

1993 OLDSMOBILE

ACHIEVA 1993

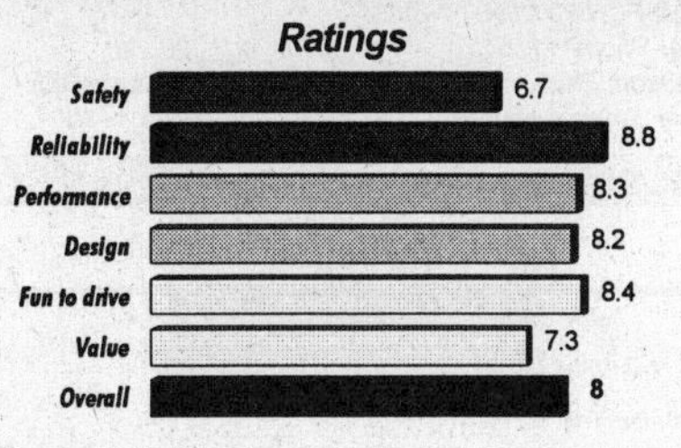

FWD/AT/PS/AC

Model/Body/Type	BaseList	Whlse	Retail
Quad 4 Models			
4 Dr S Sdn	13149	**8925**	**10925**
2 Dr S Cpe	13049	**8925**	**10925**
4 Dr SL Sdn	14949	**9875**	**12025**
2 Dr SL Cpe	14849	**9875**	**12025**
V6 Models			
2 Dr S Cpe	13509	**9125**	**11150**
4 Dr SL Sdn	14999	**10050**	**12225**
2 Dr SL Cpe	14899	**10050**	**12225**

ADD FOR 93 ACHIEVA:

Cass(Std SL) +100 *CD Player +195*
Cruise Ctrl +135 *Custom Whls/Cvrs +175*
Pwr Seat +135 *Pwr Wndw +135*
SC Pkg +760 *SCX Pkg +605*
Tilt Whl +100

DEDUCT FOR 93 ACHIEVA:

No AC -545 *No Auto Trans -505*

BRAVADA V6 1/2 Ton 1993

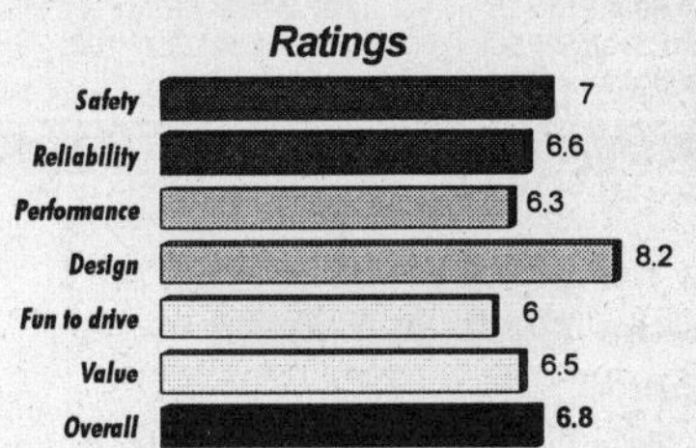

4WD/AT/PS/AC

Model/Body/Type	BaseList	Whlse	Retail
4 Dr Utility	25349	**17575**	**20700**

ADD FOR 93 BRAVADA:

CD Player +205 *Leather Seats +250*
Running Boards +145 *Sunroof-Manual +145*
Towing Pkg +190

CUTLASS CIERA 1993

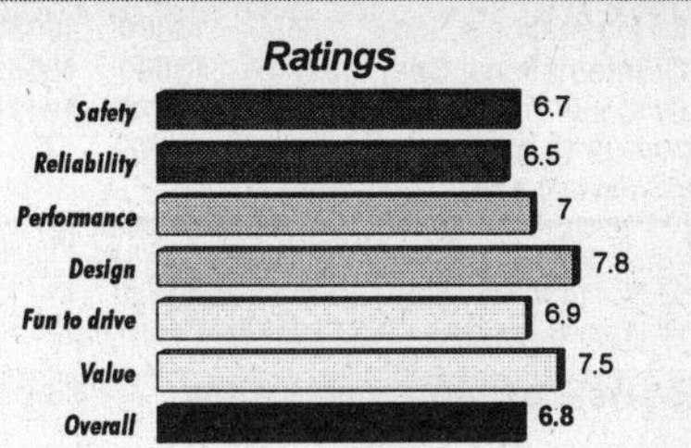

FWD/AT/PS/AC

Model/Body/Type	BaseList	Whlse	Retail
4 Cyl Models			
4 Dr S Sdn	14199	**9250**	**11275**
2 Seat Cruiser S Wgn	14899	**9750**	**11875**

OLDSMOBILE 93

Model/Body/Type	BaseList	Whlse	Retail
V6 Models			
4 Dr S Sdn	14859	**9800**	**11925**
2 Seat Cruiser S Wgn	15559	**10225**	**12450**
4 Dr SL Sdn	17899	**10575**	**12800**
3 Seat Cruiser SL Wgn	18399	**11275**	**13650**

ADD FOR 93 CUTLASS CIERA:

Cass(Std SL) +100 | *Cruise Ctrl +135*
Custom Whls/Cvrs +175 | *Driver Airbag(Std SL) +315*
Leather Seats +230 | *Luggage Rack +75*
Pwr Seat +135 | *Pwr Wndw +135*
Third Seat(Std SL) +160 | *Tilt Whl(Std SL) +100*
Woodgrain +160

CUTLASS SUPREME V6 1993

Ratings

Rating	Score
Safety	7.3
Reliability	6.4
Performance	7.4
Design	7.8
Fun to drive	6.8
Value	7.6
Overall	7

Model/Body/Type	BaseList	Whlse	Retail
FWD/AT/PS/AC			
4 Dr S Sdn	15795	**10350**	**12575**
2 Dr S Cpe	15695	**10350**	**12575**
4 Dr International Sdn	22899	**13800**	**16350**
2 Dr International Cpe	22799	**13800**	**16350**
2 Dr Conv	22699	**16475**	**19175**

ADD FOR 93 CUTLASS SUPREME:

ABS(Std Intl) +390 | *Cass +100*
CD Player +195 | *CruiseCtrl(Std Intl) +135*
Custom Whls/Cvrs +175 | *Leather Seats +230*
Pwr Seat(Std Intl) +135 | *Pwr Sunroof +430*
Pwr Wndw(Std Conv) +135 | *Tilt Whl(Std Intl) +100*

EIGHTY-EIGHT ROYALE V6 1993

Ratings

Rating	Score
Safety	8.7
Reliability	8.6
Performance	7.7
Design	8.1
Fun to drive	7.8
Value	8.7
Overall	8.4

Model/Body/Type	BaseList	Whlse	Retail
FWD/AT/PS/AC			
4 Dr Sdn	19549	**12875**	**15500**
4 Dr LS Sdn	21949	**14225**	**16925**

ADD FOR 93 EIGHTY-EIGHT ROYALE:

Car Phone +175 | *Cass(Std LS) +115*
CD Player +230 | *Cruise Ctrl(Std LS) +160*
Custom Whls/Cvrs +195 | *Leather Seats +275*
LSS Pkg +315 | *Pwr Locks(Std LS) +115*
Pwr Seat +160

NINETY-EIGHT V6 1993

Ratings

Model/Body/Type	BaseList	Whlse	Retail
FWD/AT/PS/AC			
4 Dr Regency Sdn	24999	**16375**	**19475**
4 Dr Regency Elite Sdn	26999	**17475**	**20775**
4 Dr Touring Sdn	29699	**19600**	**23025**

ADD FOR 93 NINETY-EIGHT:

Car Phone +175 | *CD Player +290*
Custom Paint +115 | *Lthr Seats(Std Tour) +315*
Pwr Sunroof +505 | *Supercharged V6 +435*

SILHOUETTE V6 1993

Ratings

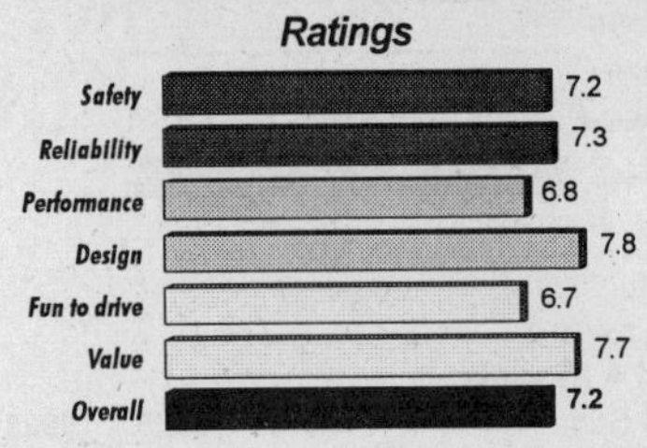

Model/Body/Type	BaseList	Whlse	Retail
FWD/AT/PS/AC			
Wagon	19499	**13450**	**16175**

ADD FOR 93 SILHOUETTE:

AC-Rear +375 | *Cass +105*
CD Player +205 | *Cruise Ctrl +125*
Leather Seats +250 | *Luggage Rack +80*
Pwr Locks +105 | *Pwr Seats +125*
Pwr Wndw +145 | *Running Boards +145*
Sunroof-Manual +145 | *Towing Pkg +190*

1992 OLDSMOBILE

ACHIEVA 1992

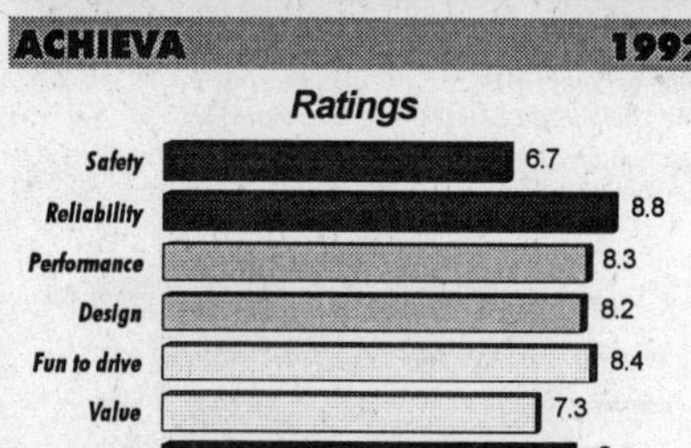

FWD/AT/PS/AC

Model/Body/Type	BaseList	Whlse	Retail
Quad 4 Models			
4 Dr S Sdn	12815	**7350**	**9225**
2 Dr S Cpe	12715	**7350**	**9225**
4 Dr SL Sdn	14595	**8200**	**10100**
2 Dr SL Cpe	14495	**8200**	**10100**
V6 Models			
2 Dr S Cpe	15075	**7550**	**9450**
4 Dr SL Sdn	14645	**8400**	**10300**
2 Dr SL Cpe	14545	**8400**	**10300**

ADD FOR 92 ACHIEVA:

Cass(Std SL) +75 | *CD Player +175*
Cruise Ctrl +115 | *Custom Whls/Cvrs +160*
Pwr Seat +115 | *Pwr Wndw +115*
SC Pkg +700 | *SCX Pkg +545*
Sport Perf Pkg +530 | *Tilt Whl +75*

DEDUCT FOR 92 ACHIEVA:

No AC -505 | *No Auto Trans -470*

BRAVADA V6 1/2 Ton 1992

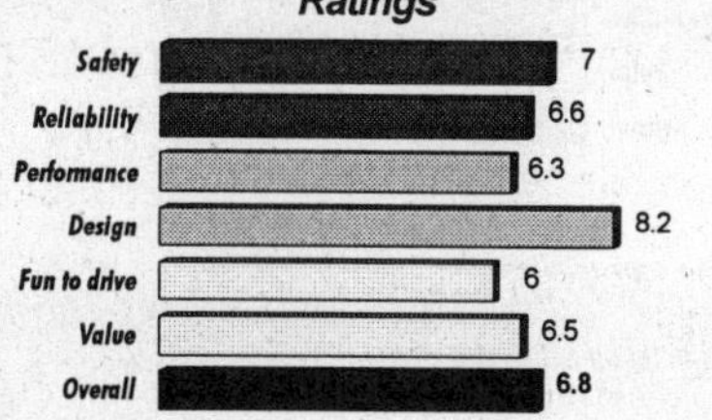

4WD/AT/PS/AC

Model/Body/Type	BaseList	Whlse	Retail
4 Dr Utility	24595	**15000**	**17825**

ADD FOR 92 BRAVADA:

CD Player +170 | *Leather Seats +205*
Running Boards +125 | *Sunroof-Manual +105*
Towing Pkg +150

CUSTOM CRUISER V8 1992

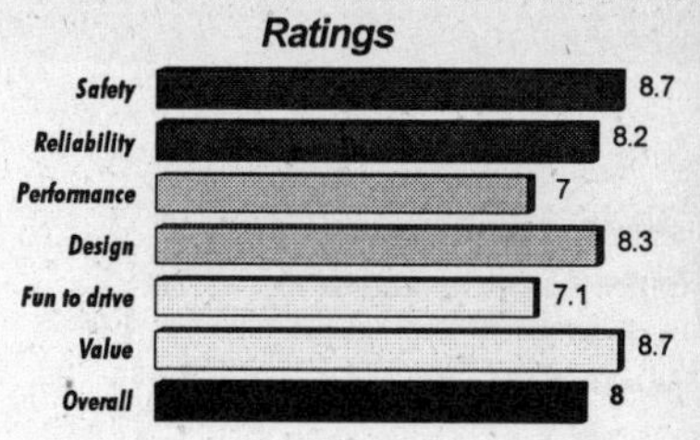

AT/PS/AC

Model/Body/Type	BaseList	Whlse	Retail
3 Seat Wgn	20995	**13200**	**15825**

ADD FOR 92 CUSTOM CRUISER:

Car Phone +160 | *CD Player +195*
Custom Whls/Cvrs +175 | *Leather Seats +230*

CUTLASS CIERA 1992

Ratings

Safety 6.7
Reliability 6.5
Performance 7
Design 7.8
Fun to drive 6.9
Value 7.5
Overall 6.8

FWD/AT/PS/AC

Model/Body/Type	BaseList	Whlse	Retail
4 Cyl Models			
4 Dr S Sdn	12755	**6775**	**8625**
2 Seat Cruiser S Wgn	13860	**7225**	**9100**
V6 Models			
4 Dr S Sdn	13465	**7275**	**9150**
2 Seat Cruiser S Wgn	14570	**7725**	**9650**
4 Dr SL Sdn	16895	**8000**	**9925**
3 Seat Cruiser SL Wgn	17395	**8625**	**10575**

OLDSMOBILE 92

Model/Body/Type | BaseList | Whlse | Retail

ADD FOR 92 CUTLASS CIERA:

- *Cass(Std SL) +75*
- *Cruise Ctrl +115*
- *Custom Whls/Cvrs +160*
- *Leather Seats +195*
- *Luggage Rack +60*
- *Pwr Seat +115*
- *Pwr Wndw +115*
- *Third Seat(Std SL) +135*
- *Tilt Whl +75*
- *Woodgrain +135*

DEDUCT FOR 92 CUTLASS CIERA:

- *No AC -505*

CUTLASS SUPREME V6 — 1992

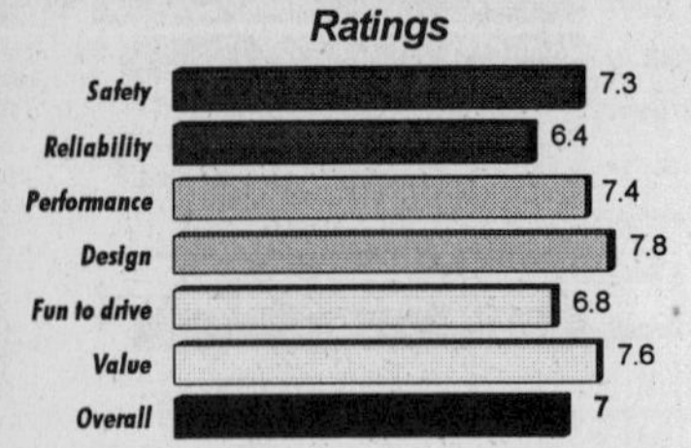

FWD/AT/PS/AC

Model/Body/Type	BaseList	Whlse	Retail
4 Dr S Sdn	15795	**8225**	**10150**
2 Dr S Cpe	15695	**8225**	**10150**
4 Dr International Sdn	21895	**10650**	**12975**
2 Dr International Cpe	21795	**10650**	**12975**
2 Dr Conv	21995	**14075**	**16625**

ADD FOR 92 CUTLASS SUPREME:

- *ABS(Std Intl) +350*
- *Cass +75*
- *CD Player +175*
- *Cruise Ctrl(Std Intl) +115*
- *Custom Whls/Cvrs +160*
- *Leather Seats +195*
- *Pwr Locks(Std Intl) +75*
- *Pwr Seat +115*
- *Pwr Sunroof +390*
- *Pwr Wndw(Std Conv) +115*
- *Tilt Whl(Std Intl) +75*

EIGHTY-EIGHT ROYALE V6 — 1992

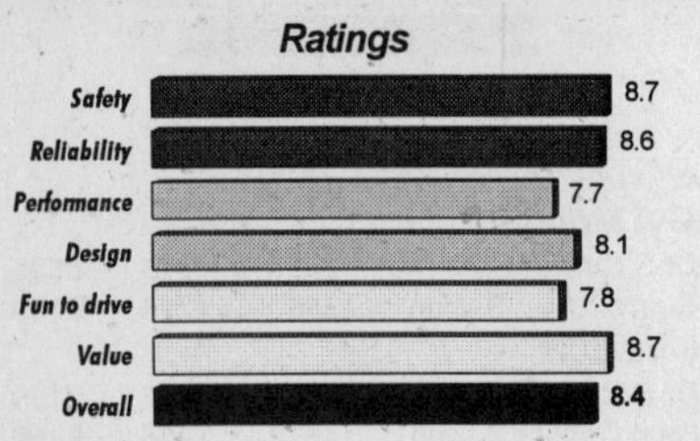

FWD/AT/PS/AC

Model/Body/Type	BaseList	Whlse	Retail
4 Dr Sdn	18495	**10300**	**12625**
4 Dr LS Sdn	21395	**11525**	**14000**

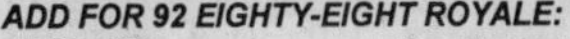

ADD FOR 92 EIGHTY-EIGHT ROYALE:

- *ABS +350*
- *Car Phone +160*
- *Cass(Std LS) +100*
- *CD Player +195*
- *Cruise Ctrl(Std LS) +135*
- *Custom Whls/Cvrs +175*
- *Leather Seats +230*
- *LSS Pkg +250*
- *Pwr Locks(Std LS) +100*
- *Pwr Seat +135*

NINETY-EIGHT V6 — 1992

FWD/AT/PS/AC

Model/Body/Type	BaseList	Whlse	Retail
4 Dr Regency Sdn	24595	**12100**	**14925**
4 Dr Regency Elite Sdn	26195	**13150**	**16050**
4 Dr Touring Sdn	28995	**15050**	**18075**

ADD FOR 92 NINETY-EIGHT:

- *Car Phone +160*
- *CD Player +250*
- *Custom Paint +100*
- *Lthr Seats(Std Tour) +275*
- *Pwr Sunroof +470*
- *Supercharged V6 +350*

SILHOUETTE V6 — 1992

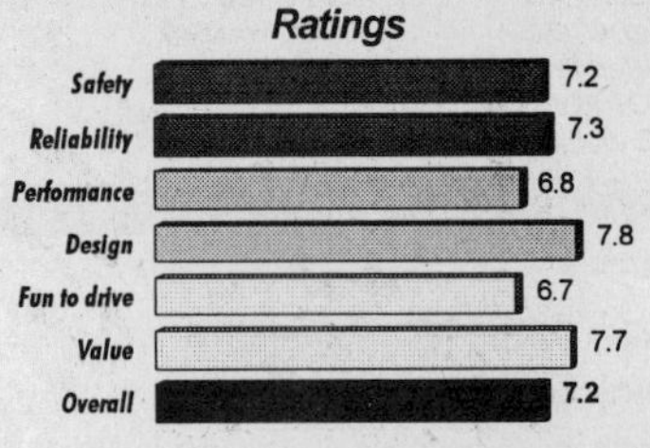

FWD/AT/PS/AC

Model/Body/Type	BaseList	Whlse	Retail
Wagon	19095	**11525**	**14075**

ADD FOR 92 SILHOUETTE:

- *AC-Rear +315*
- *Cass +80*
- *CD Player +170*
- *Cruise Ctrl +80*
- *Leather Seats +205*
- *Pwr Locks +80*
- *Pwr Seats +105*
- *Pwr Wndw +105*
- *Running Boards +125*
- *Sunroof-Manual +105*
- *Towing Pkg +150*

Model/Body/Type	BaseList	Whlse	Retail

TORONADO V6 1992

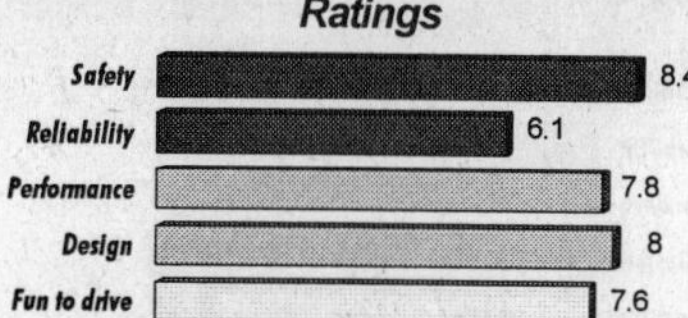

FWD/AT/PS/AC

Model/Body/Type	BaseList	Whlse	Retail
2 Dr Cpe	24695	**13475**	**16400**
2 Dr Trofeo Cpe	27295	**15525**	**18600**

ADD FOR 92 TORONADO:

Car Phone +160 *CD Player +250*
Custom Paint +100 *Lthr Seats(Std Trof) +275*
Pwr Sunroof +470

1991 OLDSMOBILE

BRAVADA V6 1/2 Ton 1991

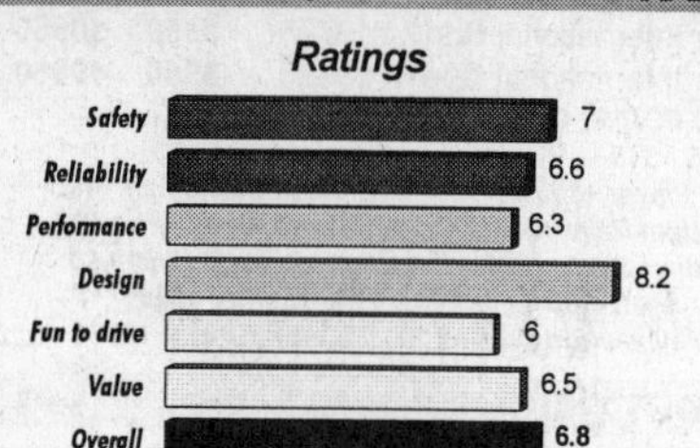

4WD/AT/PS/AC

Model/Body/Type	BaseList	Whlse	Retail
4 Dr Utility	23795	**13350**	**16075**

ADD FOR 91 BRAVADA:

Leather Seats +170 *Running Boards +105*
Sunroof-Manual +80 *Towing Pkg +105*

CUSTOM CRUISER V8 1991

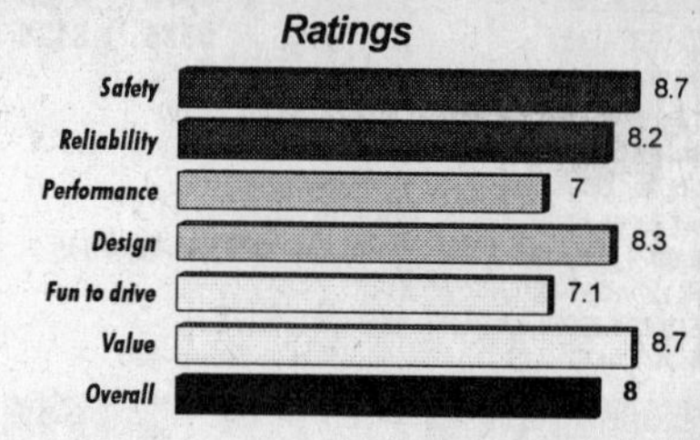

AT/PS/AC

Model/Body/Type	BaseList	Whlse	Retail
3 Seat Wgn	20495	**10725**	**13150**

ADD FOR 91 CUSTOM CRUISER:

Car Phone +135 *CD Player +160*
Custom Whls/Cvrs +160 *Leather Seats +195*

CUTLASS CALAIS 1991

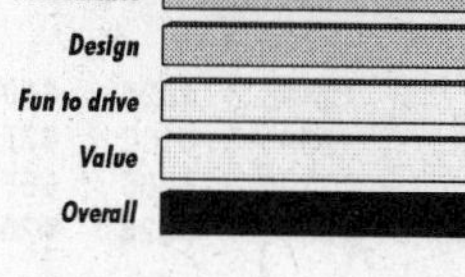

FWD/AT/PS/AC

Model/Body/Type	BaseList	Whlse	Retail
4 Cyl Models			
4 Dr Sdn	10295	**5000**	**6650**
2 Dr Cpe	10295	**5000**	**6650**
4 Dr S Sdn	11595	**5500**	**7175**
2 Dr S Cpe	11495	**5500**	**7175**
Quad 4 Models			
4 Dr SL Sdn	15195	**6325**	**8075**
2 Dr SL Cpe	15095	**6325**	**8075**
4 Dr International Sdn	16395	**7400**	**9275**
2 Dr International Cpe	16295	**7400**	**9275**

OLDSMOBILE

OLDSMOBILE

Model/Body/Type	BaseList	Whlse	Retail
V6 Models			
4 Dr SL Sdn	15245	**6375**	**8125**
2 Dr SL Cpe	15145	**6375**	**8125**

ADD FOR 91 CUTLASS CALAIS:

Cass(Std SL,Intl) +60 | *CD Player +160*
Cruise Ctrl +100 | *Custom Whls/Cvrs +135*
Leather Seats +160 | *Pwr Locks +60*
Pwr Seat +100 | *Pwr Wndw +100*
Quad 4 Eng +275 | *Quad 442 Perf Pkg +545*
Tilt Whl(Std Intl) +60

DEDUCT FOR 91 CUTLASS CALAIS:

No AC -470 | *No Auto Trans -430*

CUTLASS CIERA 1991

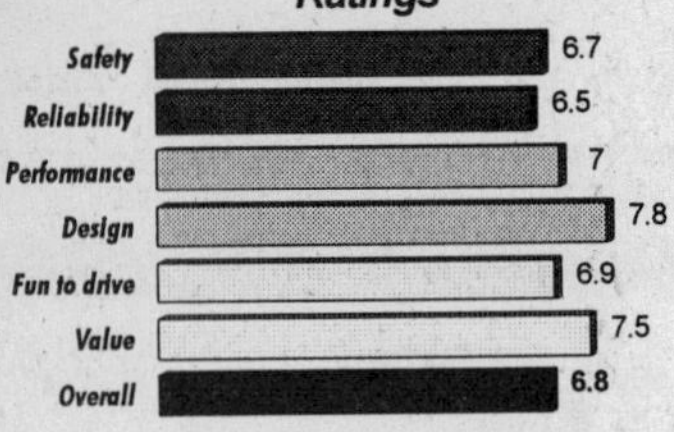

FWD/AT/PS/AC

Model/Body/Type	BaseList	Whlse	Retail
4 Cyl Models			
4 Dr Sdn	12495	**4825**	**6500**
4 Dr S Sdn	12995	**5100**	**6775**
2 Dr S Cpe	13395	**5000**	**6650**
2 Seat Cruiser S Wgn	13895	**5525**	**7200**
V6 Models			
4 Dr Sdn	13205	**5250**	**6950**
4 Dr S Sdn	13705	**5575**	**7250**
2 Dr S Cpe	14105	**5475**	**7150**
2 Seat Cruiser S Wgn	14605	**5975**	**7700**
4 Dr SL Sdn	15895	**6150**	**7875**
3 Seat Cruiser SL Wgn	16595	**6675**	**8500**

ADD FOR 91 CUTLASS CIERA:

Cass(Std SL) +60 | *Cruise Ctrl +100*
Custom Whls/Cvrs +135 | *Leather Seats +160*
Luggage Rack +35 | *Pwr Locks +60*
Pwr Seat +100 | *Pwr Wndw +100*
Third Seat(Std SL) +115 | *Tilt Whl +60*
Woodgrain +115

DEDUCT FOR 91 CUTLASS CIERA:

No AC -470

CUTLASS SUPREME 1991

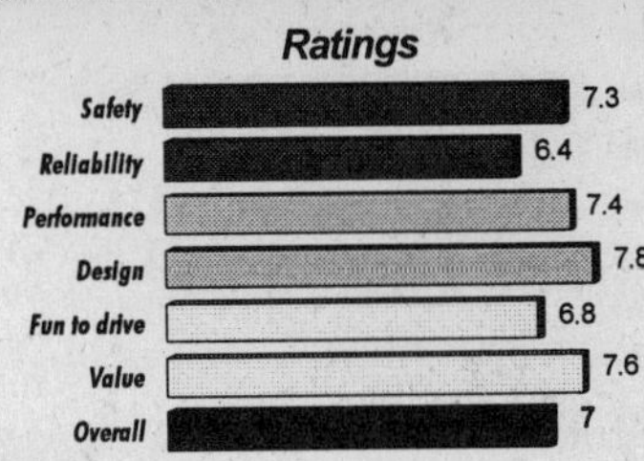

FWD/AT/PS/AC

Model/Body/Type	BaseList	Whlse	Retail
Quad 4 Models			
4 Dr Sdn	15095	**6650**	**8450**
2 Dr Cpe	14995	**6650**	**8450**
V6 Models			
4 Dr Sdn	15270	**6875**	**8700**
2 Dr Cpe	15170	**6875**	**8700**
2 Dr Conv	20995	**12350**	**14800**
4 Dr SL Sdn	16995	**7600**	**9500**
2 Dr SL Cpe	16895	**7600**	**9500**
4 Dr International Sdn	19795	**8950**	**10950**
2 Dr International Cpe	19695	**8950**	**10950**

ADD FOR 91 CUTLASS SUPREME:

ABS +315 | *Cass +60*
CD Player +160 | *Cruise Ctrl(Std Intl) +100*
Custom Paint +35 | *Custom Whls/Cvrs +135*
Leather Seats +160 | *Pwr Locks(Std Intl) +60*
Pwr Seat +100 | *Pwr Sunroof +350*
Pwr Wndw(Std Cnv) +100 | *Tilt Whl(Std Intl) +60*

EIGHTY-EIGHT ROYALE V6 1991

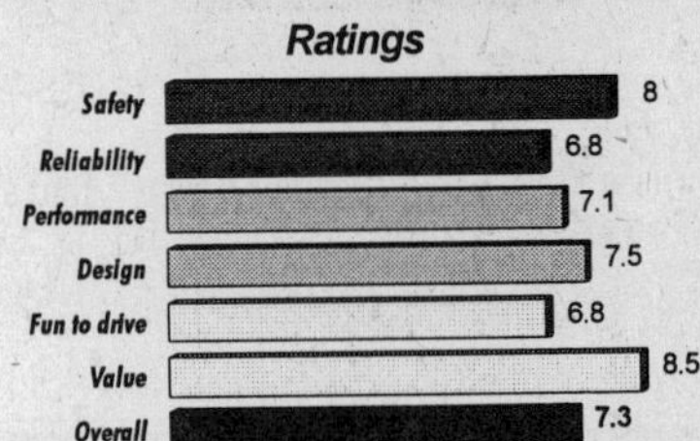

FWD/AT/PS/AC

Model/Body/Type	BaseList	Whlse	Retail
4 Dr Sdn	17195	**7325**	**9350**
2 Dr Cpe	17095	**7175**	**9175**
4 Dr Brougham Sdn	18795	**8250**	**10275**
2 Dr Brougham Cpe	18695	**8100**	**10150**

ADD FOR 91 EIGHTY-EIGHT ROYALE:

ABS +315 | *Car Phone +135*
Cass(Std Brghm) +75 | *CD Player +160*
Cruise Ctrl +115 | *Custom Whls/Cvrs +160*
Driver Side Airbag +230 | *Leather Seats +195*
Pwr Locks +75 | *Pwr Seat +115*
Pwr Wndw +115 | *Vinyl Roof +75*

NINETY-EIGHT V6 1991

Ratings

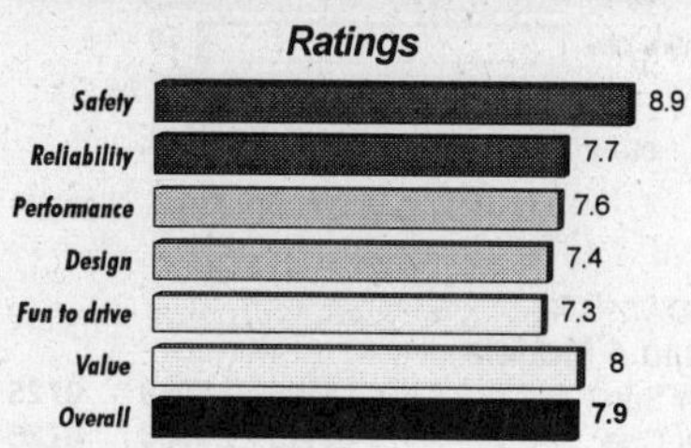

FWD/AT/PS/AC

Model/Body/Type	BaseList	Whlse	Retail
4 Dr Regency Elite Sdn	23695	**10175**	**12825**
4 Dr Touring Sdn	28595	**12000**	**14775**

ADD FOR 91 NINETY-EIGHT:

Car Phone +135 | *CD Player +195*
Custom Paint +75 | *Lthr Seats(Std Tour) +215*
Pwr Sunroof +430

SILHOUETTE V6 1991

Ratings

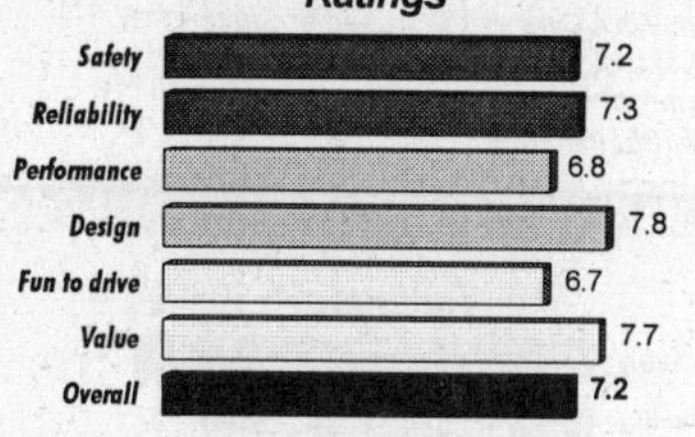

FWD/AT/PS/AC

Model/Body/Type	BaseList	Whlse	Retail
Wagon	18195	**9775**	**12025**

ADD FOR 91 SILHOUETTE:

CD Player +125 | *Leather Seats +170*
Pwr Seats +80 | *Pwr Wndw +80*
Running Boards +105 | *Sunroof-Manual +85*

TORONADO V6 1991

Ratings

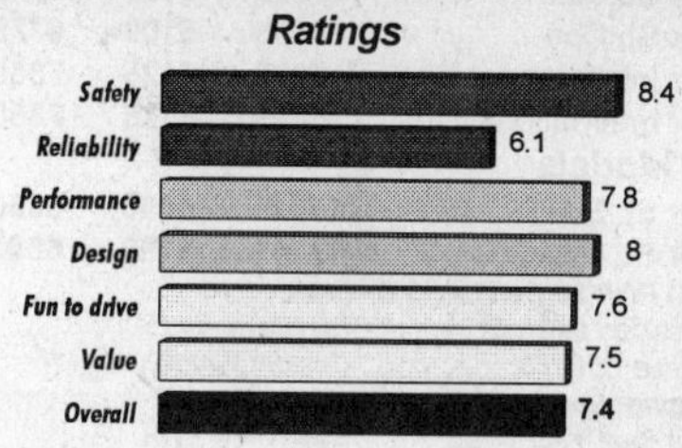

FWD/AT/PS/AC

Model/Body/Type	BaseList	Whlse	Retail
2 Dr Cpe	23795	**10325**	**12975**
2 Dr Trofeo Cpe	26495	**12050**	**14875**

ADD FOR 91 TORONADO:

Car Phone +135 | *CD Player +195*
Custom Paint +75 | *Lthr Seats(Std Trofeo) +215*
Pwr Sunroof +430

1990 OLDSMOBILE

CUSTOM CRUISER V8 1990

AT/PS/AC

Model/Body/Type	BaseList	Whlse	Retail
3 Seat Wgn	17595	**5425**	**7275**

ADD FOR 90 CUSTOM CRUISER:

Custom Whls/Cvrs +115 | *Luggage Rack +35*
Woodgrain +135

CUTLASS CALAIS 1990

Ratings

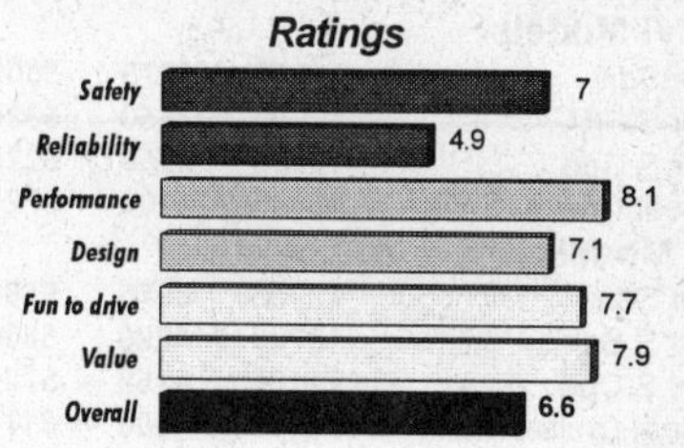

FWD/AT/PS/AC

4 Cyl Models

Model/Body/Type	BaseList	Whlse	Retail
4 Dr Sdn	9995	**3950**	**5475**
2 Dr Cpe	9995	**3950**	**5475**
4 Dr S Sdn	10995	**4375**	**5925**
2 Dr S Cpe	10895	**4375**	**5925**

OLDSMOBILE 90

Model/Body/Type	BaseList	Whlse	Retail
Quad 4 Models			
4 Dr SL Sdn	13295	**5100**	**6775**
2 Dr SL Cpe	13195	**5100**	**6775**
4 Dr International Sdn	14995	**6125**	**7850**
2 Dr International Cpe	14895	**6125**	**7850**
V6 Models			
4 Dr SL Sdn	13345	**5150**	**6850**
2 Dr SL Cpe	13245	**5150**	**6850**

ADD FOR 90 CUTLASS CALAIS:

Cass(Std Intl) +60 | *CD Player +115*
Cruise Ctrl +75 | *Custom Whls/Cvrs +115*
Leather Seats +115 | *Pwr Locks +60*
Pwr Seat +75 | *Pwr Wndw +75*
Quad 4 Eng +230 | *Quad 442 Perf Pkg +485*
Sunroof +115 | *Tilt Whl(Std Intl) +60*

DEDUCT FOR 90 CUTLASS CALAIS:

No AC -430 | *No Auto Trans -390*

CUTLASS CIERA 1990

Ratings

Safety	6.7
Reliability	6.5
Performance	7
Design	7.8
Fun to drive	6.9
Value	7.5
Overall	6.8

FWD/AT/PS/AC

Model/Body/Type	BaseList	Whlse	Retail
4 Cyl Models			
4 Dr Sdn	11995	**3575**	**5000**
4 Dr S Sdn	12995	**3850**	**5325**
2 Dr S Cpe	12395	**3750**	**5225**
2 Seat Cruiser S Wgn	13395	**4200**	**5725**
V6 Models			
4 Dr Sdn	12705	**3975**	**5500**
4 Dr S Sdn	13705	**4250**	**5800**
2 Dr S Cpe	13105	**4150**	**5700**
2 Seat Cruiser S Wgn	14105	**4600**	**6175**
4 Dr SL Sdn	14695	**4750**	**6375**
3 Seat Cruiser SL Wgn	15295	**5200**	**6900**
4 Dr International Sdn	16795	**6025**	**7750**
2 Dr International Cpe	15995	**5925**	**7650**

ADD FOR 90 CUTLASS CIERA:

Cass(Std SL,Intl) +60 | *Cruise Ctrl +75*
Custom Whls/Cvrs +115 | *Leather Seats +115*
Luggage Rack +35 | *Pwr Locks +60*
Pwr Seat +75 | *Pwr Sunroof +315*
Pwr Wndw +75 | *Third Seat(Std SL) +100*
Tilt Whl(Std Intl) +60 | *Woodgrain +100*

DEDUCT FOR 90 CUTLASS CIERA:

No AC -430

CUTLASS SUPREME 1990

Ratings

Safety	7.3
Reliability	6.4
Performance	7.4
Design	7.8
Fun to drive	6.8
Value	7.6
Overall	7

FWD/AT/PS/AC

Model/Body/Type	BaseList	Whlse	Retail
Quad 4 Models			
4 Dr Sdn	14595	**5050**	**6725**
2 Dr Cpe	14495	**5050**	**6725**
4 Dr International Sdn	17995	**6925**	**8750**
2 Dr International Cpe	17995	**6925**	**8750**
V6 Models			
4 Dr Sdn	15095	**5250**	**6950**
2 Dr Cpe	14995	**5250**	**6950**
4 Dr SL Sdn	16195	**5950**	**7675**
2 Dr SL Cpe	16095	**5950**	**7675**
4 Dr International Sdn	18495	**7125**	**8950**
2 Dr International Cpe	18495	**7125**	**8950**

ADD FOR 90 CUTLASS SUPREME:

ABS +275 | *Cass +60*
CD Player +115 | *Cruise Ctrl +75*
Custom Whls/Cvrs +115 | *Leather Seats +115*
Pwr Locks(Std Intl) +60 | *Pwr Seat +75*
Pwr Sunroof +315 | *Pwr Wndw +75*
Tilt Whl(Std Intl) +60

EIGHTY-EIGHT ROYALE V6 1990

Ratings

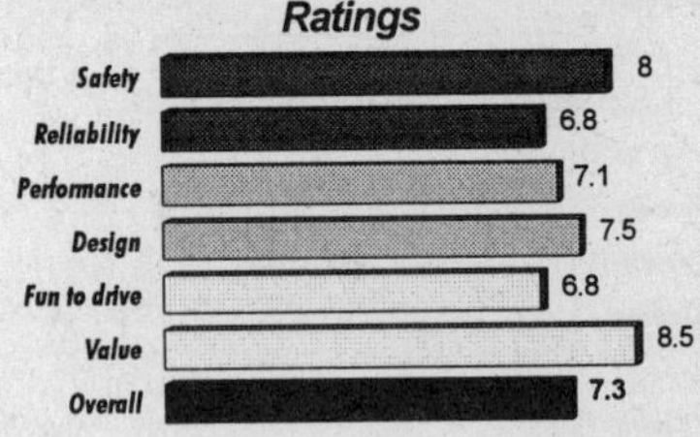

FWD/AT/PS/AC

Model/Body/Type	BaseList	Whlse	Retail
4 Dr Sdn	15995	**5950**	**7800**
2 Dr Cpe	15895	**5800**	**7650**
4 Dr Brougham Sdn	17395	**6775**	**8750**
2 Dr Brougham Cpe	17295	**6650**	**8575**

ADD FOR 90 EIGHTY-EIGHT ROYALE:

ABS +275	Cass(Std Brghm) +75
CD Player +115	Cruise Ctrl +100
Custom Whls/Cvrs +115	Leather Seats +135
Pwr Locks +60	Pwr Seat +100
Pwr Wndw +100	Tilt Whl +60
Vinyl Roof +60	

NINETY-EIGHT V6 — 1990

FWD/AT/PS/AC

Model/Body/Type	BaseList	Whlse	Retail
4 Dr Regency Sdn	19995	**6775**	**8950**
4 Dr Reg Brghm Sdn	21595	**7650**	**9875**
4 Dr Touring Sdn	26795	**9350**	**11700**

ADD FOR 90 NINETY-EIGHT:

ABS(Std Tour) +275	CD Player +135
Delco/Bose Mus Sys +135	Lthr Seats(Std Tour) +160
Pwr Sunroof +390	Vinyl Roof +100

SILHOUETTE V6 — 1990

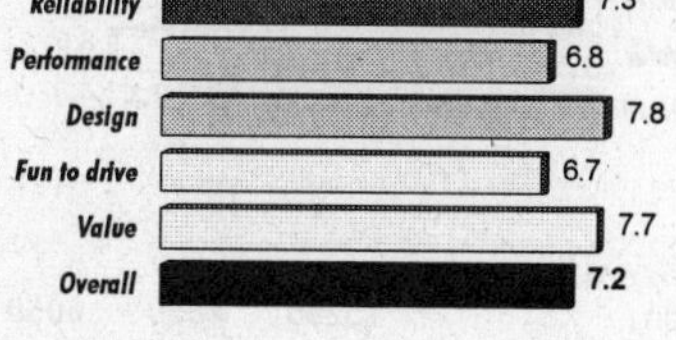

FWD/AT/PS/AC

Model/Body/Type	BaseList	Whlse	Retail
Wagon	17195	**8500**	**10600**

ADD FOR 90 SILHOUETTE:

CD Player +80	Leather Seats +125
Running Boards +85	

TORONADO V6 — 1990

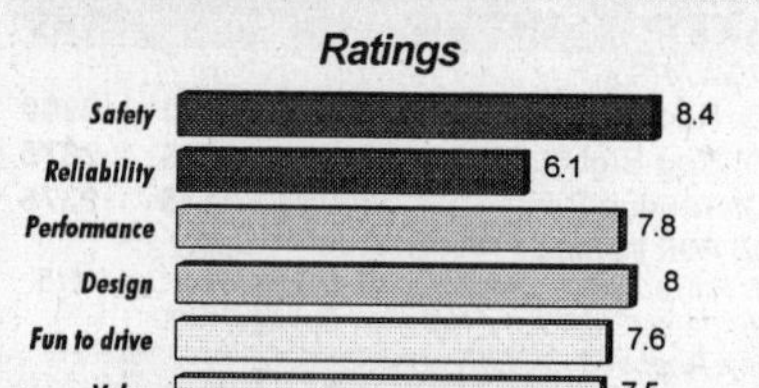

FWD/AT/PS/AC

Model/Body/Type	BaseList	Whlse	Retail
2 Dr Cpe	21995	**7825**	**10025**
2 Dr Trofeo Cpe	24995	**9300**	**11650**

ADD FOR 90 TORONADO:

ABS(Std Trofeo) +275	CD Player +135
Delco/Bose Mus Sys +135	Lthr Seats(Std Trof) +160
Pwr Sunroof +390	Vinyl Roof +100

1989 OLDSMOBILE

CUSTOM CRUISER V8 — 1989

AT/PS/AC

Model/Body/Type	BaseList	Whlse	Retail
3 Seat Wgn	16795	**4300**	**5975**

ADD FOR 89 CUSTOM CRUISER:

Custom Whls/Cvrs +75	Luggage Rack +25
Woodgrain +100	

CUTLASS CALAIS — 1989

Ratings

Safety	7
Reliability	4.9
Performance	8.1
Design	7.1
Fun to drive	7.7
Value	7.9
Overall	6.6

FWD/AT/PS/AC

Model/Body/Type	BaseList	Whlse	Retail
4 Cyl Models			
4 Dr Sdn	9995	**3025**	**4375**
2 Dr Cpe	9995	**3025**	**4375**
4 Dr S Sdn	10995	**3400**	**4825**
2 Dr S Cpe	10895	**3400**	**4825**
4 Dr SL Sdn	11995	**3775**	**5250**
2 Dr SL Cpe	11895	**3775**	**5250**
Quad 4 Models			
4 Dr International Sdn	14495	**4775**	**6425**
2 Dr International Cpe	14395	**4775**	**6425**
V6 Models			
4 Dr S Sdn	11705	**3725**	**5200**
2 Dr S Cpe	11605	**3725**	**5200**
4 Dr SL Sdn	12705	**4100**	**5650**
2 Dr SL Cpe	12605	**4100**	**5650**

ADD FOR 89 CUTLASS CALAIS:

Cass(Std Intl) +35	Cruise Ctrl +60
Custom Whls/Cvrs +75	Leather Seats +75
Pwr Locks +35	Pwr Seat +60
Pwr Wndw +60	Quad 4 Eng(Std Intl) +215
Quad 4 Appr Pkg +330	Sunroof +100
Tilt Whl(Std Intl) +35	

DEDUCT FOR 89 CUTLASS CALAIS:

No AC -390	No Auto Trans -350

OLDSMOBILE

OLDSMOBILE 89

CUTLASS CIERA 1989

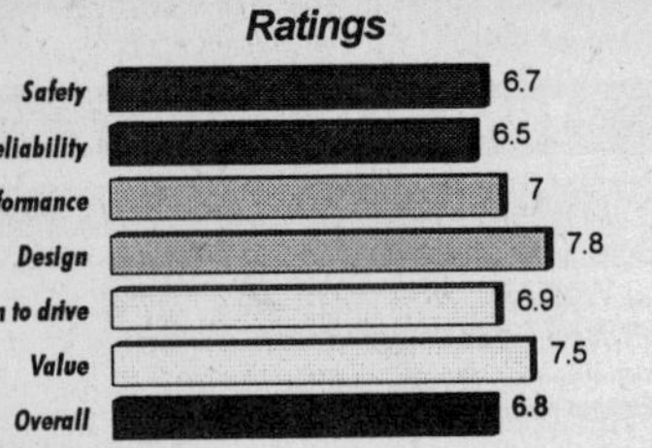

FWD/AT/PS/AC

Model/Body/Type	BaseList	Whlse	Retail
4 Cyl Models			
4 Dr Sdn	12195	**3125**	**4500**
2 Dr Cpe	11695	**3025**	**4375**
2 Seat Cruiser Wgn	12995	**3375**	**4800**
4 Dr SL Sdn	13495	**3550**	**4975**
2 Dr SL Cpe	12695	**3450**	**4850**
3 Seat Cruiser SL Wgn	13995	**3975**	**5500**
V6 Models			
4 Dr Sdn	12805	**3450**	**4850**
2 Dr Cpe	12305	**3350**	**4775**
2 Seat Cruiser Wgn	13605	**3750**	**5225**
4 Dr SL Sdn	14105	**3925**	**5400**
2 Dr SL Cpe	13305	**3825**	**5300**
3 Seat Cruiser SL Wgn	14605	**4325**	**5875**
4 Dr International Sdn	16795	**5000**	**6650**
2 Dr International Cpe	15995	**4900**	**6575**

ADD FOR 89 CUTLASS CIERA:

Cass(Std SL,Intl) +35 · *Cruise Ctrl +60* · *Custom Whls/Cvrs +75* · *Leather Seats +75* · *Luggage Rack +25* · *Pwr Locks +35* · *Pwr Seat +60* · *Pwr Sunroof +250* · *Pwr Wndw +60* · *Third Seat(Std SL) +75* · *Tilt Whl(Std Intl) +35* · *Woodgrain +75*

DEDUCT FOR 89 CUTLASS CIERA:

No AC -390

CUTLASS SUPREME V6 1989

Ratings

Safety 7.3
Reliability 6.4
Performance 7.4
Design 7.8
Fun to drive 6.8
Value 7.6
Overall 7

FWD/AT/PS/AC

Model/Body/Type	BaseList	Whlse	Retail
2 Dr Cpe	14295	**4225**	**5775**
2 Dr SL Cpe	15195	**4800**	**6450**
2 Dr International Cpe	16995	**5750**	**7450**

ADD FOR 89 CUTLASS SUPREME:

Cass(Std SL,Intl) +35 · *CD Player +75* · *Cruise Ctrl +60* · *Custom Whls/Cvrs +75* · *Leather Seats +75* · *Pwr Locks(Std Intl) +35* · *Pwr Seat +60* · *Pwr Sunroof +250* · *Pwr Wndw +60* · *Tilt Whl(Std Intl) +35*

DEDUCT FOR 89 CUTLASS SUPREME:

No Auto Trans -350

EIGHTY-EIGHT ROYALE V6 1989

Ratings

Safety 8
Reliability 6.8
Performance 7.1
Design 7.5
Fun to drive 6.8
Value 8.5
Overall 7.3

FWD/AT/PS/AC

Model/Body/Type	BaseList	Whlse	Retail
4 Dr Sdn	15295	**4350**	**6050**
2 Dr Cpe	15195	**4200**	**5875**
4 Dr Brougham Sdn	16395	**5075**	**6925**
2 Dr Brougham Cpe	16295	**4925**	**6725**

ADD FOR 89 EIGHTY-EIGHT ROYALE:

Cass +60 · *CD Player +100* · *Cruise Ctrl +75* · *Custom Whls/Cvrs +75* · *Leather Seats +115* · *Pwr Locks +35* · *Pwr Seat +75* · *Pwr Wndw +75* · *Tilt Whl +35* · *Vinyl Roof +35*

NINETY-EIGHT V6 1989

FWD/AT/PS/AC

Model/Body/Type	BaseList	Whlse	Retail
4 Dr Regency Sdn	19295	**4950**	**6900**
4 Dr Reg Brghm Sdn	20495	**5725**	**7675**
4 Dr Touring Sdn	25995	**7175**	**9375**

ADD FOR 89 NINETY-EIGHT:

CD Player +100 · *Delco/Bose Mus Sys +115* · *Lthr Seats(Std Tour) +135* · *Pwr Sunroof +330* · *Vinyl Roof +75*

TORONADO V6 — 1989

Ratings

Rating	Score
Safety	8.4
Reliability	6.1
Performance	7.8
Design	8
Fun to drive	7.6
Value	7.5
Overall	7.4

FWD/AT/PS/AC

Model/Body/Type	BaseList	Whlse	Retail
2 Dr Cpe	21995	**6350**	**8375**
2 Dr Trofeo Cpe	24995	**7325**	**9550**

ADD FOR 89 TORONADO:

CD Player +100 · *Delco/Bose Mus Sys +115*
Lthr Seats(Std Trof) +135 · *Pwr Sunroof +330*
Vinyl Roof +75

1988 OLDSMOBILE

CUSTOM CRUISER V8 — 1988

AT/PS/AC

Model/Body/Type	BaseList	Whlse	Retail
3 Seat Wgn	15655	**2825**	**4300**

CUTLASS CALAIS — 1988

FWD/AT/PS/AC

Model/Body/Type	BaseList	Whlse	Retail
4 Cyl Models			
4 Dr Sdn	10320	**2350**	**3575**
2 Dr Cpe	10320	**2350**	**3575**
4 Dr SL Sdn	11195	**2700**	**3975**
2 Dr SL Cpe	11195	**2700**	**3975**
Quad 4 Models			
4 Dr International Sdn	13695	**3350**	**4775**
2 Dr International Cpe	13695	**3350**	**4775**
V6 Models			
4 Dr Sdn	10980	**2650**	**3900**
2 Dr Cpe	10980	**2650**	**3900**
4 Dr SL Sdn	11855	**3000**	**4350**
2 Dr SL Cpe	11855	**3000**	**4350**

ADD FOR 88 CUTLASS CALAIS:

Quad 4 Eng(Std International) +195

DEDUCT FOR 88 CUTLASS CALAIS:

No AC -330 · *No Auto Trans -290*

CUTLASS CIERA — 1988

FWD/AT/PS/AC

Model/Body/Type	BaseList	Whlse	Retail
4 Cyl Models			
4 Dr Sdn	11656	**2275**	**3475**
2 Dr Cpe	10995	**2175**	**3350**
2 Seat Cruiser Wgn	12320	**2500**	**3750**
4 Dr Brougham Sdn	12625	**2675**	**3950**
2 Dr Brougham SL Cpe	11845	**2575**	**3825**
2 Seat Brougham Cruiser SL Wgn	12995	**2925**	**4275**
V6 Models			
4 Dr Sdn	12266	**2600**	**3850**
2 Dr Cpe	11605	**2500**	**3750**
2 Seat Cruiser Wgn	12930	**2850**	**4175**
4 Dr Brougham Sdn	13235	**3025**	**4375**
2 Dr Brougham SL Cpe	12455	**2925**	**4275**
2 Seat Brougham Cruiser SL Wgn	13605	**3250**	**4650**
4 Dr International Sdn	15825	**3900**	**5375**
2 Dr International Cpe	14995	**3800**	**5275**

DEDUCT FOR 88 CUTLASS CIERA:

No AC -330

CUTLASS SUPREME V6 — 1988

FWD/AT/PS/AC

Model/Body/Type	BaseList	Whlse	Retail
2 Dr Cpe	12846	**3275**	**4700**
2 Dr SL Cpe	13495	**3775**	**5250**
2 Dr International Cpe	15644	**4425**	**5975**

DEDUCT FOR 88 CUTLASS SUPREME:

No AC -330 · *No Auto Trans -290*

CUTLASS SUPREME CLASSIC V8 — 1988

AT/PS/AC

Model/Body/Type	BaseList	Whlse	Retail
2 Dr Cpe	13163	**3750**	**5225**
2 Dr Brougham Cpe	13995	**4275**	**5825**

DEDUCT FOR 88 CUTLASS SUPREME:

No AC -330

DELTA 88 ROYALE V6 — 1988

FWD/AT/PS/AC

Model/Body/Type	BaseList	Whlse	Retail
4 Dr Sdn	14498	**3025**	**4525**
2 Dr Cpe	14498	**2875**	**4350**
4 Dr Brougham Sdn	15451	**3650**	**5225**
2 Dr Brougham Cpe	15451	**3500**	**5075**

FIRENZA 4 Cyl — 1988

FWD/AT/PS/AC

Model/Body/Type	BaseList	Whlse	Retail
4 Dr Sdn	9295	**2275**	**3375**
2 Dr Cpe	9295	**2175**	**3250**
4 Dr Cruiser Wgn	9995	**2425**	**3575**

DEDUCT FOR 88 FIRENZA:

No AC -250 · *No Auto Trans -230*
No Pwr Steering -60

OLDSMOBILE 88-86

Model/Body/Type	BaseList	Whlse	Retail
NINETY-EIGHT V6			**1988**
FWD/AT/PS/AC			
4 Dr Regency Sdn	17995	**3375**	**5000**
4 Dr Reg Brghm Sdn	19371	**4000**	**5725**
4 Dr Touring Sdn	24470	**5200**	**7150**
TORONADO V6			**1988**
FWD/AT/PS/AC			
2 Dr Cpe	20598	**4025**	**5775**
2 Dr Trofeo Cpe	22695	**4700**	**6600**

1987 OLDSMOBILE

Model/Body/Type	BaseList	Whlse	Retail
CALAIS 4 Cyl			**1987**
FWD/AT/PS/AC			
4 Dr Sdn	9741	**1800**	**2950**
2 Dr Cpe	9741	**1800**	**2950**
4 Dr Supreme Sdn	10397	**2100**	**3250**
2 Dr Supreme Cpe	10397	**2100**	**3250**
ADD FOR 87 CALAIS:			
V6 Engine +215			
CUSTOM CRUISER V8			**1987**
AT/PS/AC			
4 Dr Wgn	14420	**2000**	**3250**
CUTLASS V6			**1987**
AT/PS/AC			
4 Dr Supreme Sdn	11539	**2250**	**3425**
2 Dr Supreme Cpe	11539	**2425**	**3650**
4 Dr Suprm Brghm Sdn	12378	**2525**	**3775**
2 Dr Suprm Brghm Cpe	12378	**2725**	**4000**
2 Dr Salon Cpe	12697	**3125**	**4525**
2 Dr Supreme 442 Cpe	14706	**4450**	**6000**
ADD FOR 87 CUTLASS:			
V8 Engine(Std 442) +290			
CUTLASS CIERA V6			**1987**
FWD/AT/PS/AC			
4 Dr Sdn	11550	**1775**	**2925**
2 Dr S Cpe	11550	**1700**	**2800**
4 Dr Cruiser Wgn	12043	**2000**	**3150**
4 Dr Brougham Sdn	12357	**2150**	**3300**
2 Dr Brougham SL Cpe	12357	**2050**	**3200**
4 Dr Brghm Cruiser Wgn	12705	**2325**	**3550**
ADD FOR 87 CUTLASS CIERA:			
GT Pkg +350			
DEDUCT FOR 87 CUTLASS CIERA:			
4 Cyl Engine -250			
DELTA 88 ROYALE V6			**1987**
FWD/AT/PS/AC			
4 Dr Sdn	13639	**2450**	**3775**
2 Dr Cpe	13639	**2300**	**3625**
4 Dr Brougham Sdn	14536	**3025**	**4525**
2 Dr Brougham Cpe	14536	**2875**	**4350**
FIRENZA			**1987**
FWD/AT/PS/AC			
4 Cyl Models			
4 Dr Sdn	8499	**1700**	**2700**
2 Dr Cpe	8541	**1625**	**2600**
2 Dr S Hbk	8976	**1700**	**2700**
4 Dr LX Sdn	9407	**1925**	**3000**
2 Dr LC Cpe	9639	**1825**	**2900**
4 Dr Cruiser Wgn	9146	**1800**	**2850**
V6 Models			
2 Dr GT Hbk	11034	**2375**	**3500**
NINETY-EIGHT V6			**1987**
FWD/AT/PS/AC			
4 Dr Regency Sdn	17371	**2525**	**3975**
4 Dr Reg Brghm Sdn	18388	**3050**	**4625**
2 Dr Reg Brghm Cpe	18388	**2900**	**4450**
ADD FOR 87 NINETY-EIGHT:			
Touring Sdn Pkg +1245			
TORONADO V6			**1987**
FWD/AT/PS/AC			
2 Dr Brougham Cpe	19938	**3200**	**4800**
ADD FOR 87 TORONADO:			
Trofeo Pkg +470			

1986 OLDSMOBILE

Model/Body/Type	BaseList	Whlse	Retail
CALAIS			**1986**
FWD			
4 Dr Sdn	9478	**1300**	**2350**
2 Dr Cpe	9283	**1300**	**2350**
4 Dr Supreme Sdn	9863	**1525**	**2625**
2 Dr Supreme Cpe	9668	**1525**	**2625**
CUSTOM CRUISER			**1986**
4 Dr Wgn	13416	**1450**	**2800**
CUTLASS CIERA			**1986**
FWD			
4 Dr LS Sdn	10789	**1375**	**2450**
2 Dr LS Cpe	10588	**1300**	**2350**
2 Dr S LS Cpe	11309	**1450**	**2550**
4 Dr Cruiser LS Wgn	11169	**1525**	**2625**
4 Dr Brougham Sdn	11303	**1675**	**2800**
2 Dr Brougham Cpe	11080	**1575**	**2700**
2 Dr Brougham SL Cpe	11764	**1725**	**2900**
CUTLASS SALON			**1986**
2 Dr Cpe	11728	**2350**	**3600**
2 Dr 442 Cpe	14343	**3725**	**5125**

Model/Body/Type	BaseList	Whlse	Retail
CUTLASS SUPREME			**1986**
4 Dr Sdn	10872	1750	2925
2 Dr Cpe	10698	1925	3125
4 Dr Brougham Sdn	11551	2050	3250
2 Dr Brougham Cpe	11408	2225	3425
DELTA 88 ROYALE			**1986**
FWD			
4 Dr Sdn	12760	1750	3125
2 Dr Cpe	12760	1625	3000
4 Dr Brougham Sdn	13461	2125	3575
2 Dr Brougham Cpe	13461	2000	3425
FIRENZA			**1986**
FWD			
4 Dr Sdn	8035	1225	2250
2 Dr Cpe	7782	1125	2175
2 Dr S Hbk	7941	1225	2250
4 Dr LX Sdn	8626	1375	2475
2 Dr LC Cpe	8611	1325	2375
4 Dr Cruiser Wgn	8259	1275	2300
2 Dr GT Hbk	9774	1750	2925
NINETY-EIGHT			**1986**
FWD			
4 Dr Regency Sdn	15989	1975	3400
2 Dr Regency Cpe	16062	1850	3250
4 Dr Reg Brghm Sdn	16979	2275	3800
2 Dr Reg Brghm Cpe	17052	2175	3650
TORONADO			**1986**
FWD			
2 Dr Brougham Cpe	19418	2650	4200

1985 OLDSMOBILE

Model/Body/Type	BaseList	Whlse	Retail
CALAIS			**1985**
FWD			
2 Dr Cpe	8499	1200	2225
2 Dr Supreme Cpe	8844	1350	2400
CUSTOM CRUISER			**1985**
4 Dr Wgn	11627	1375	2700
CUTLASS CIERA			**1985**
FWD			
4 Dr LS Sdn	9757	1200	2240
2 Dr LS Cpe	9567	1100	2165
4 Dr Cruiser LS Wgn	10118	1320	2365
4 Dr Brougham Sdn	10258	1400	2475
2 Dr Brougham Cpe	10047	1355	2400
CUTLASS SALON			**1985**
2 Dr Cpe	10770	1780	3000
2 Dr 442 Cpe	12435	3100	4450
CUTLASS SUPREME			**1985**
4 Dr Sdn	9961	1275	2350
2 Dr Cpe	9797	1430	2475
4 Dr Brougham Sdn	10602	1500	2610
2 Dr Brougham Cpe	10468	1675	2800
DELTA 88 ROYALE			**1985**
4 Dr Sdn	10986	1385	2700
2 Dr Cpe	10878	1290	2545
4 Dr Brougham Sdn	11452	1680	3050
2 Dr Brougham Cpe	11358	1550	2900
4 Dr LS Brougham Sdn	14331	2000	3425
FIRENZA			**1985**
FWD			
4 Dr Sdn	7528	900	1875
2 Dr Cpe	7439	825	1795
4 Dr LX Sdn	8091	1050	2095
2 Dr SX Cpe	8238	950	1995
4 Dr Cruiser Wgn	7753	935	1975
4 Dr LX Cruiser Wgn	8316	1100	2175
NINETY-EIGHT			**1985**
FWD			
4 Dr Regency Sdn	14665	1625	2995
2 Dr Regency Cpe	14735	1475	2845
4 Dr Reg Brghm Sdn	15864	1890	3315
2 Dr Reg Brghm Cpe	15932	1795	3175
TORONADO			**1985**
FWD			
2 Dr Cpe	16798	2050	3450

Model/Body/Type	BaseList	Whlse	Retail

PEUGEOT

France

1990 Peugeot 405S Sportwagon

For a dealer in your area, see our Dealer Directory (pg 217)

1991 PEUGEOT

405 4 Cyl — 1991

FWD/AT/PS/AC

Model/Body/Type	BaseList	Whlse	Retail
4 Dr DL Sdn	15950	4625	6350
4 Dr S Sdn	18350	5600	7425
4 Dr Mi16 Sdn (5 spd)	21700	6675	8650
4 Dr DL Sportswagon	16640	5075	6925
4 Dr S Sportswagon	19145	6125	7975

505 4 Cyl — 1991

AT/PS/AC

Model/Body/Type	BaseList	Whlse	Retail
DL Wgn	19240	6050	7925
SW8 2.2 Wgn	21050	7300	9325
SW8 Turbo Wgn	26100	9775	12000

ADD FOR ALL 91 PEUGEOT:
Car Phone +135
Pwr Sunroof(405 S) +390
DEDUCT FOR ALL 91 PEUGEOT:
No Auto Trans -470

1990 PEUGEOT

405 4 Cyl — 1990

FWD/AT/PS/AC

Model/Body/Type	BaseList	Whlse	Retail
4 Dr DL Sdn	14850	3600	5175
4 Dr DL Sportswagon	15990	4000	5675
4 Dr S Sportswagon	18495	4775	6550

DEDUCT FOR ALL 90 PEUGEOT:
No Auto Trans -430

1989 PEUGEOT

405 4 Cyl — 1989

FWD/AT/PS/AC

Model/Body/Type	BaseList	Whlse	Retail
4 Dr DL Sdn	14500	2375	3700
4 Dr S Sdn	17700	3125	4675
4 Dr Mi16 Sdn (5 spd)	20700	4125	5800

505 — 1989

AT/PS/AC

Model/Body/Type	BaseList	Whlse	Retail
4 Cyl Models			
4 Dr S Sdn	19295	3575	5150
4 Dr Turbo Sdn	26335	6150	8025
DL Wgn	17590	2825	4300
SW8 Wgn	19995	3900	5550
Turbo Wgn	25540	6450	8350
SW8 Turbo Wgn	25695	6625	8550
V6 Models			
4 Dr S Sdn	21435	4025	5700
4 Dr STX Sdn	25895	5875	7750

ADD FOR ALL 89 PEUGEOT:
Leather Seats(405 S,505 Turbo Sdn) +115
DEDUCT FOR ALL 89 PEUGEOT:
No Auto Trans -390

1988 PEUGEOT

505 — 1988

AT/PS/AC

Model/Body/Type	BaseList	Whlse	Retail
4 Cyl Models			
4 Dr DL Sdn	15495	2250	3525
4 Dr GLS Sdn	17775	2725	4100
4 Dr Turbo S Sdn	24615	4425	6125
4 Dr STI Sdn	20295	3100	4600
DL Wgn	16485	2500	3850
GLS Wgn	17995	3000	4500
SW8 Wgn	18545	3300	4850
Turbo S Wgn	23645	4700	6425
V6 Models			
4 Dr GLX Sdn	19850	3125	4675
4 Dr STX Sdn	23995	4325	6025

ADD FOR ALL 88 PEUGEOT:
Leather Seats +75
DEDUCT FOR ALL 88 PEUGEOT:
No Auto Trans -350

See the Automobile Dealer Directory on page 379 for a Dealer near you!

Model/Body/Type	BaseList	Whlse	Retail

1987 PEUGEOT

505			1987
AT/PS/AC			
4 Cyl Models			
4 Dr GL Sdn	13900	**1575**	2700
4 Dr GLS Sdn	15950	**1975**	3225
4 Dr Turbo Sdn	18650	**2575**	3925
4 Dr Turbo S Sdn	22600	**3375**	4925
4 Dr STI Sdn	18400	**2300**	3625
4 Dr Liberte Sdn	15600	**1825**	3075
Liberte Wgn	16600	**2075**	3300
Turbo Wgn	19980	**2825**	4300
Turbo S Wgn	22250	**3625**	5200
V6 Models			
4 Dr STI Sdn	20700	**2650**	4025
4 Dr STX Sdn	23250	**3275**	4850

DEDUCT FOR ALL 87 PEUGEOT:
No AC -230
No Auto Trans -195

1986 PEUGEOT

505			1986
4 Dr GL Sdn	12615	900	1900
4 Dr S Sdn	15965	**1275**	2300
4 Dr S Turbo Diesel Sdn	17950	900	1900
4 Dr STI Sdn	17065	**1475**	2575
4 Dr GL Turbo Sdn	16465	**1275**	2300
4 Dr Turbo Sdn	18740	**1700**	2850
GL Wgn	13185	**1075**	2100
S Wgn	17130	**1400**	2500
S Turbo Diesel Wgn	19600	**1075**	2100
Turbo Wgn	20435	**1850**	3050

1985 PEUGEOT

505			1985
4 Dr GL Sdn	11900	570	1500
4 Dr GL Turb Diesel Sdn	13220	200	1120
4 Dr S Sdn	15580	890	1840
4 Dr S Turbo Diesel Sdn	16900	520	1450
4 Dr STI Sdn	16630	1040	2040
4 Dr STI Turb Diesel Sdn	17950	700	1645
4 Dr Turbo Sdn	18150	1200	2220
GL Wgn	12440	700	1650
GL Turbo Diesel Wgn	13860	325	1250
S Wgn	17075	995	2000
S Turbo Diesel Wgn	17965	650	1600

PLYMOUTH USA

1992 Plymouth Acclaim

For a Plymouth dealer in your area, see our Dealer Directory (pg 217)

1994 PLYMOUTH

ACCLAIM V6 1994

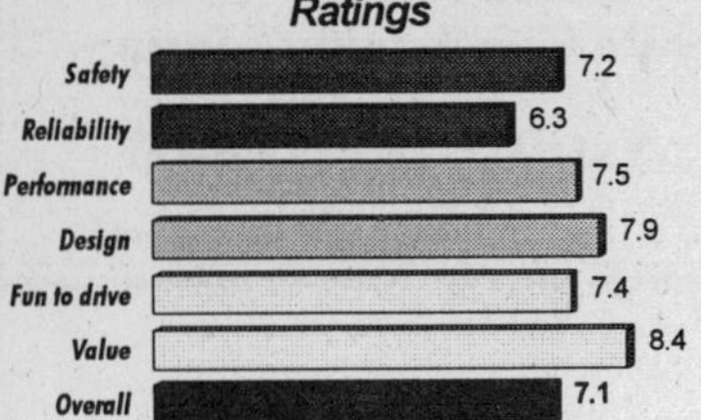

FWD/AT/PS/AC

Model/Body/Type	BaseList	Whlse	Retail
4 Dr Sdn (4 Cyl)	12470	9250	11275
4 Dr Sdn	13195	9825	12000

ADD FOR 94 ACCLAIM:

ABS +430
Anti-Theft/Recovery Sys +365
Cass +115 — *Custom Whls/Cvrs +205*
Pwr Locks +115 — *Pwr Seat +160*
Pwr Wndw +160

COLT 4 Cyl 1994

FWD/AT/PS/AC

Model/Body/Type	BaseList	Whlse	Retail
2 Dr Cpe(5 spd)	9120	5400	6980
4 Dr Sdn	11428	-	-
2 Dr GL Cpe	10060	-	-
4 Dr GL Sdn	12181	-	-
3 Dr Vista Wgn	12979	-	-
3 Dr Vista SE Wgn	14194	-	-
3 Dr Vista 4WD Wgn	14884	-	-

ADD FOR 94 COLT:

ABS
Anti-Theft/Recovery Sys
Cass — *Cruise Ctrl*
Custom Whls/Cvrs — *Luggage Rack(S/W)*
Pwr Locks(Std Vista SE) — *Pwr Wndw*
Tilt Whl(Std Vista)

DEDUCT FOR 94 COLT:

No AC — *No Auto Trans*
No Pwr Steering

LASER 4 Cyl 1994

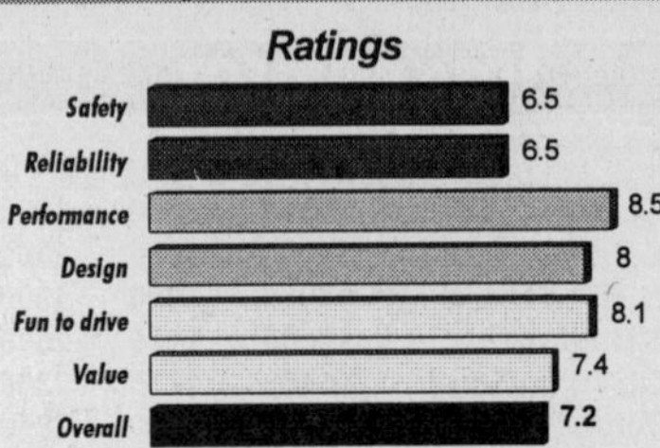

FWD/AT/PS/AC

Model/Body/Type	BaseList	Whlse	Retail
3 Dr Hbk	11542	-	-
3 Dr RS Hbk	13910	-	-
3 Dr RS Turbo Hbk	15444	-	-
3 Dr RS Turb 4WD Hbk	17572	-	-

ADD FOR 94 LASER:

ABS
Anti-Theft/Recovery Sys
Cass(Std RS) — *CD Player*
Cruise Ctrl — *Custom Whls/Cvrs*
Pwr Locks — *Pwr Wndw*
Sunroof

DEDUCT FOR 94 LASER:

PLYMOUTH

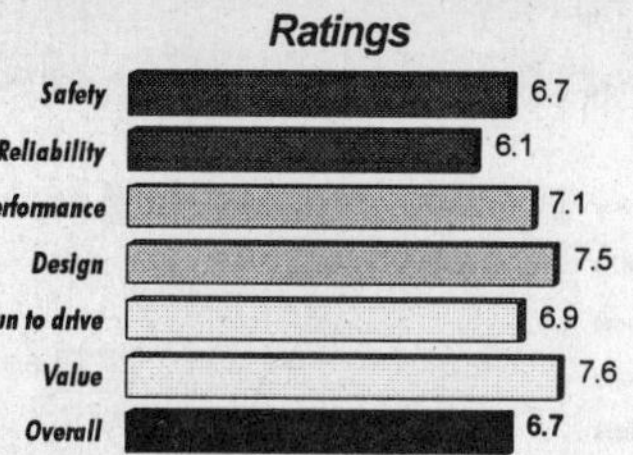

FWD/AT/PS/AC

Model/Body/Type	BaseList	Whlse	Retail
4 Cyl Models			
4 Dr Hbk	9206	8250	10100
2 Dr Hbk	8806	8150	9975
V6 Models			
4 Dr Duster Hbk	11346	9975	12025
2 Dr Duster Hbk	10946	9875	11925

ADD FOR 94 SUNDANCE:

ABS +430
Anti-Theft/Recovery Sys +365
Cass +90 | *CD Player +205*
Cruise Ctrl +135 | *Custom Whls/Cvrs +180*
Pwr Locks +90 | *Pwr Seat +135*
Pwr Wndw +135 | *Sunroof +275*
Tilt Whl +90

DEDUCT FOR 94 SUNDANCE:

4 Cyl Eng(Duster) -500 | *No AC -590*
No Auto Trans -500

VOYAGER V6 1994

FWD/AT/PS/AC

Model/Body/Type	BaseList	Whlse	Retail
Voyager	14819	14300	17050
Voyager SE	18039	15400	18250
Voyager LE	21863	16600	19625
Grand Voyager	18078	15625	18500
Grand Voyager SE	19204	16475	19400
Grand Voyager LE	22783	17575	20700

ADD FOR 94 VOYAGER:

All-Whl Drive +1275 | *ABS +430*
LX Pkg +500

DEDUCT FOR 94 VOYAGER:

4 Cyl Eng -545

1993 PLYMOUTH

ACCLAIM V6 1993

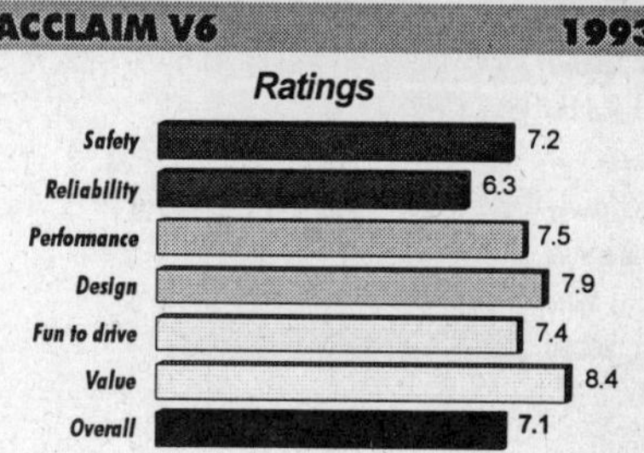

FWD/AT/PS/AC

Model/Body/Type	BaseList	Whlse	Retail
4 Dr Sdn (4 Cyl)	11470	7925	9850
4 Dr Sdn	12195	8475	10375

ADD FOR 93 ACCLAIM:

ABS +390 | *Cass +100*
CD Player +195 | *Cruise Ctrl +135*
Pwr Locks +100 | *Pwr Seat +135*
Pwr Wndw +135 | *Tilt Whl +100*

DEDUCT FOR 93 ACCLAIM:

No AC -545 | *No Auto Trans -505*

COLT 4 Cyl 1993

FWD/AT/PS/AC

Model/Body/Type	BaseList	Whlse	Retail
2 Dr Cpe	7806	5725	7250
4 Dr Sdn	9448	7175	8950
2 Dr GL Cpe	8705	6650	8275
4 Dr GL Sdn	10423	7775	9625
4 Dr Vista Wgn	11455	9375	11300
4 Dr Vista SE Wgn	12368	9800	11850
4 Dr Vista AWD Wgn	13539	10150	12250

ADD FOR 93 COLT:

ABS +390 | *Cass +75*
Cruise Ctrl +115 | *Custom Whls/Cvrs +160*
Luggage Rack +75 | *Pwr Locks +75*
Pwr Wndw +115 | *Tilt Whl +75*

DEDUCT FOR 93 COLT:

No AC -430 | *No Auto Trans -390*
No Pwr Steering -135

See the Automobile Dealer Directory on page 379 for a Dealer near you!

Model/Body/Type	BaseList	Whlse	Retail

LASER 4 Cyl — 1993

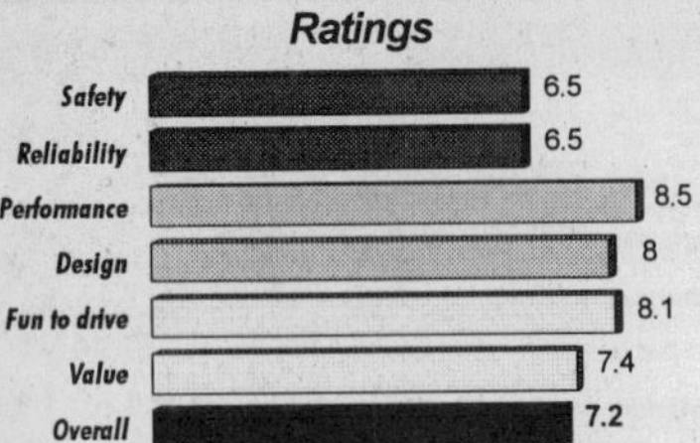

FWD/AT/PS/AC

Model/Body/Type	BaseList	Whlse	Retail
3 Dr Hbk	11405	8950	10950
3 Dr RS Hbk	13749	10150	12325
3 Dr RS Turbo Hbk	15267	11475	13850
3 Dr RS Turb AWD Hbk	17371	13200	15700

ADD FOR 93 LASER:
ABS +390 | *Cass(Std RS) +100*
CD Player +195 | *Cruise Ctrl +135*
Custom Whls/Cvrs +175 | *Pwr Locks +100*
Pwr Wndw +135 | *Sunroof +230*

DEDUCT FOR 93 LASER:
No AC -545 | *No Auto Trans -430*
No Pwr Steering -175

SUNDANCE — 1993

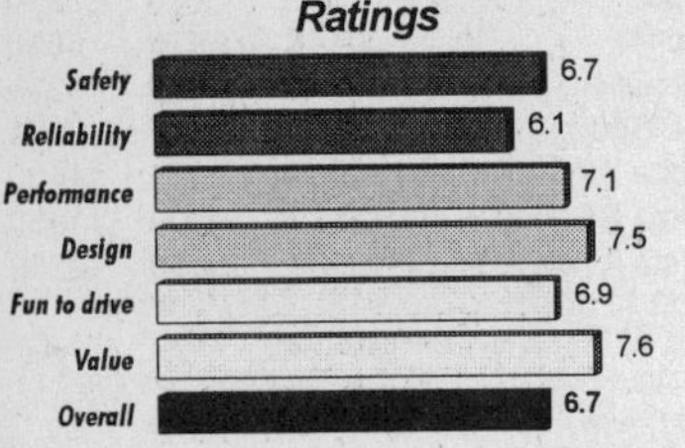

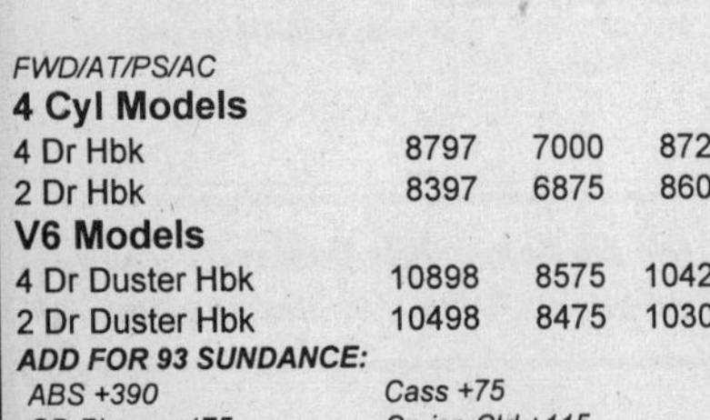

FWD/AT/PS/AC

Model/Body/Type	BaseList	Whlse	Retail
4 Cyl Models			
4 Dr Hbk	8797	7000	8725
2 Dr Hbk	8397	6875	8600
V6 Models			
4 Dr Duster Hbk	10898	8575	10425
2 Dr Duster Hbk	10498	8475	10300

ADD FOR 93 SUNDANCE:
ABS +390 | *Cass +75*
CD Player +175 | *Cruise Ctrl +115*
Custom Whls/Cvrs +160 | *Pwr Locks +75*
Pwr Seat +115 | *Pwr Wndw +115*
Sunroof +195 | *Tilt Whl +75*

DEDUCT FOR 93 SUNDANCE:
4 Cyl Eng -350 | *No AC -470*
No Auto Trans -430

VOYAGER V6 — 1993

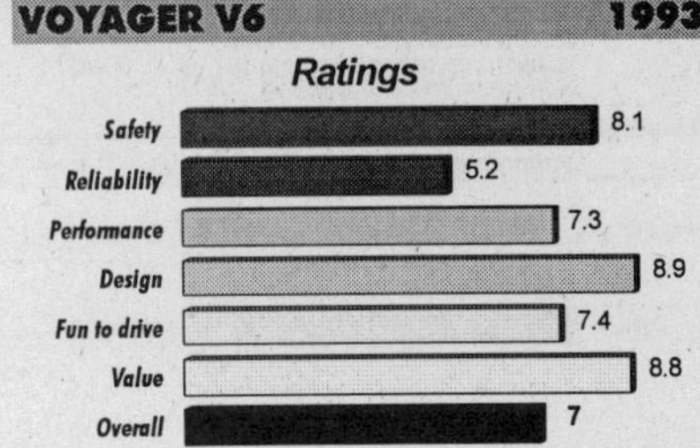

FWD/AT/PS/AC

Model/Body/Type	BaseList	Whlse	Retail
Voyager	14073	12150	14800
Voyager SE	16101	13200	15925
Voyager LE	20703	14300	17050
Grand Voyager	17555	13400	16125
Grand Voyager SE	17935	14225	17000
Grand Voyager LE	21735	15275	18125

ADD FOR 93 VOYAGER:
4-Whl Drive +1265 | *ABS +390*
AC-Rear +375 | *Cass(Std LX) +105*
CD Player +205 | *Cruise Ctrl(Std LE) +125*
Custm Whls(Std LX) +145 | *Leather Seats +250*
Luggage Rack +80 | *LX Pkg +390*
Privacy Glass(Std LX) +145
Pwr Locks(Std LE) +105
Pwr Seats(Std LX) +125 | *Pwr Wndw(Std LE,LX) +145*
Running Boards +145 | *Sunroof-Manual +145*
Tilt Whl(Std LE) +105 | *Towing Pkg +185*

DEDUCT FOR 93 VOYAGER:
4 Cyl Eng -430 | *No AC -435*
No Auto Trans -415

1992 PLYMOUTH

ACCLAIM V6 — 1992

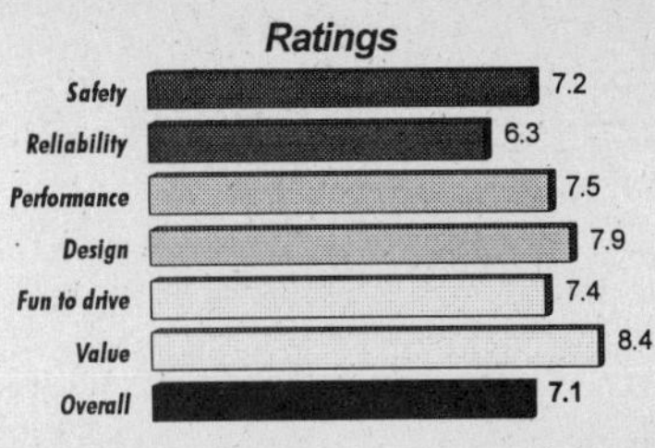

Model/Body/Type	BaseList	Whlse	Retail
FWD/AT/PS/AC			
4 Dr Sdn (4 Cyl)	11470	5675	7350
4 Dr Sdn	12195	6150	7875

ADD FOR 92 ACCLAIM:

ABS +350	*Cass +75*
Cruise Ctrl +115	*Custom Whls/Cvrs +160*
Pwr Locks +75	*Pwr Seat +115*
Pwr Wndw +115	*Tilt Whl +75*

DEDUCT FOR 92 ACCLAIM:

No AC -505	*No Auto Trans -470*

COLT 4 Cyl — 1992

Model/Body/Type	BaseList	Whlse	Retail
FWD/AT/PS/AC			
3 Dr Hbk	7302	3975	5325
3 Dr GL Hbk	8122	4650	6125
4 Dr Vista Wgn	11397	7275	9075
4 Dr Vista SE Wgn	12102	7625	9450
4 Dr Vista AWD Wgn	13469	7975	9825

ADD FOR 92 COLT:

ABS +350	*Cass +60*
Cruise Ctrl +100	*Luggage Rack +60*
Pwr Locks +60	*Pwr Wndw +100*

DEDUCT FOR 92 COLT:

No AC -390	*No Auto Trans -350*
No Pwr Steering -115	

LASER 4 Cyl — 1992

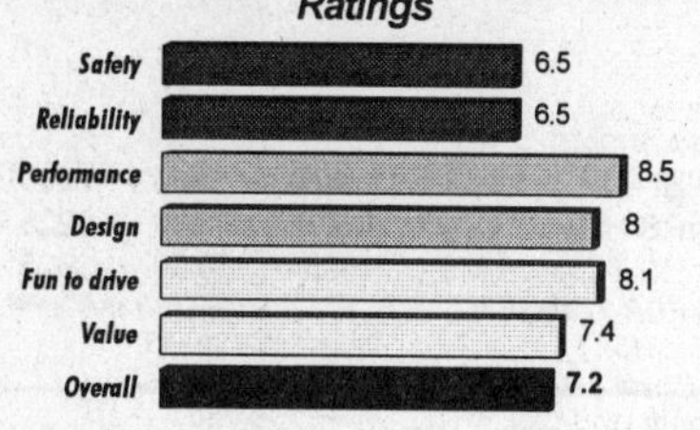

Model/Body/Type	BaseList	Whlse	Retail
FWD/AT/PS/AC			
3 Dr Hbk	11184	7050	8875
3 Dr RS Hbk	13332	7750	9675
3 Dr RS Turbo Hbk	14811	9050	11050
3 Dr RS Turb AWD Hbk	16853	10175	12400

ADD FOR 92 LASER:

ABS +350	*Cass(Std RS) +75*
CD Player +175	*Cruise Ctrl +115*
Custom Whls/Cvrs +160	*Pwr Locks +75*
Pwr Wndw +115	*Sunroof +195*

DEDUCT FOR 92 LASER:

No AC -505	*No Auto Trans -390*
No Pwr Steering -160	

SUNDANCE — 1992

Ratings

Rating	Score
Safety	6.7
Reliability	6.1
Performance	7.1
Design	7.5
Fun to drive	6.9
Value	7.6
Overall	6.7

Model/Body/Type	BaseList	Whlse	Retail
FWD/AT/PS/AC			
4 Cyl Models			
4 Dr America Hbk	8384	4850	6350
2 Dr America Hbk	7984	4775	6250
4 Dr Hbk	9646	5575	7125
2 Dr Hbk	9246	5475	7000
V6 Models			
4 Dr Duster Hbk	10249	6425	8025
2 Dr Duster Hbk	9849	6325	7925

ADD FOR 92 SUNDANCE:

Cass +60	*CD Player +160*
Cruise Ctrl +100	*Custom Whls/Cvrs +135*
Pwr Locks +60	*Pwr Seat +100*
Pwr Wndw +100	*Sunroof +160*
Tilt Whl +60	

DEDUCT FOR 92 SUNDANCE:

No AC -430	*No Auto Trans -390*

VOYAGER V6 — 1992

Ratings

Rating	Score
Safety	8.1
Reliability	5.2
Performance	7.3
Design	8.9
Fun to drive	7.4
Value	8.8
Overall	7

Model/Body/Type	BaseList	Whlse	Retail
FWD/AT/PS/AC			
Voyager	13706	9050	11250
Voyager SE	15679	10000	12325
Voyager LE	19964	10925	13450
Grand Voyager	17281	10150	12500
Grand Voyager SE	17511	10950	13475
Grand Voyager LE	20773	11950	14575

PLYMOUTH 92-91

Model/Body/Type	BaseList	Whlse	Retail

ADD FOR 92 VOYAGER:

4-Whl Drive +1200 | *ABS +350*
AC-Rear +315 | *Cass(Std LX) +80*
CD Player +170 | *Cruise Ctrl(Std LE) +80*
Custm Whls(Std LX) +145 | *Leather Seats +205*
LX Pkg +315 | *Privacy Glass(Std LX) +125*
Pwr Locks(Std LE) +80 | *Pwr Seats(Std LX) +105*
Pwr Wndw(Std LE,LX) +105
Running Boards +125
Sunroof-Manual +105 | *Towing Pkg +145*

DEDUCT FOR 92 VOYAGER:

4 Cyl Eng -390 | *No AC -375*
No Auto Trans -330

1991 PLYMOUTH

ACCLAIM 1991

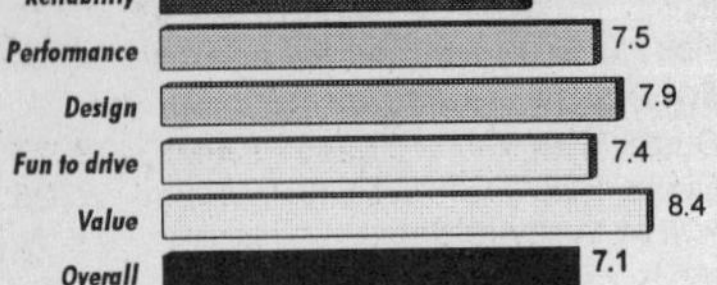

FWD/AT/PS/AC

Model/Body/Type	BaseList	Whlse	Retail
4 Cyl Models			
4 Dr Sdn	10805	4500	6100
4 Dr LE Sdn	12860	5050	6725
V6 Models			
4 Dr Sdn	11499	4900	6575
4 Dr LE Sdn	13554	5525	7200
4 Dr LX Sdn	14360	6125	7850

ADD FOR 91 ACCLAIM:

ABS +315 | *Cass +60*
CruiseCtrl(Std LE,LX) +100 | *Custom Whls/Cvrs +135*
Pwr Locks +60 | *Pwr Seat +100*
Pwr Wndw +100 | *Sunroof +160*
Tilt Whl(Std LE,LX) +60

DEDUCT FOR 91 ACCLAIM:

No AC -470 | *No Auto Trans -430*

COLT 4 Cyl 1991

FWD/AT/PS/AC

Model/Body/Type	BaseList	Whlse	Retail
3 Dr Hbk	6949	2675	3850
3 Dr GL Hbk	7845	3275	4600
4 Dr Vista Wgn	11941	5700	7200
4 Dr Vista 4WD Wgn (5 spd)	13167	5975	7550

ADD FOR 91 COLT:

Cass +35 | *Cruise Ctrl +75*
Custom Whls/Cvrs +115 | *Luggage Rack +35*
Pwr Locks +35 | *Pwr Wndw +75*

DEDUCT FOR 91 COLT:

No AC -350 | *No Auto Trans -315*
No Pwr Steering -100

LASER 4 Cyl 1991

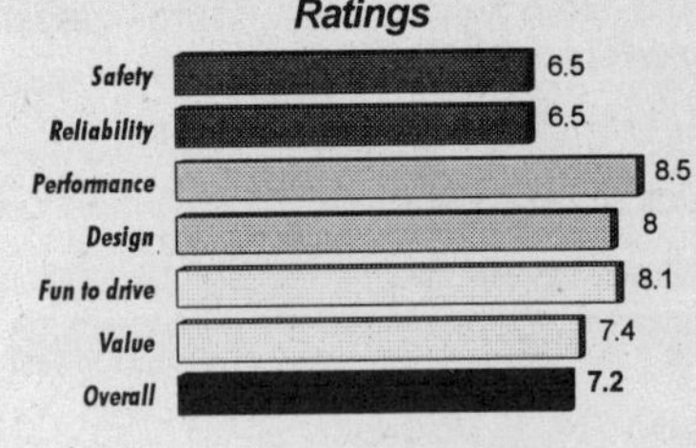

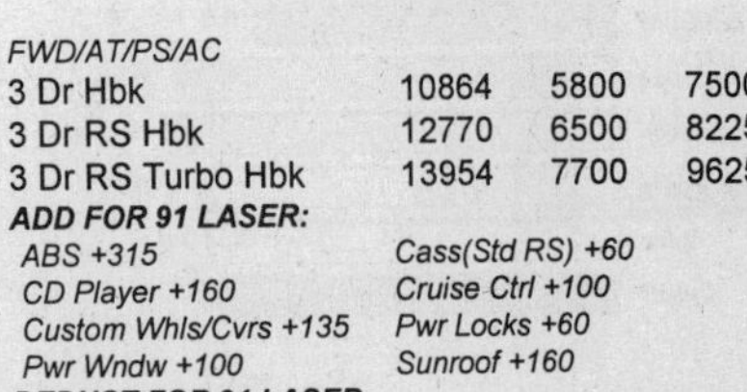

FWD/AT/PS/AC

Model/Body/Type	BaseList	Whlse	Retail
3 Dr Hbk	10864	5800	7500
3 Dr RS Hbk	12770	6500	8225
3 Dr RS Turbo Hbk	13954	7700	9625

ADD FOR 91 LASER:

ABS +315 | *Cass(Std RS) +60*
CD Player +160 | *Cruise Ctrl +100*
Custom Whls/Cvrs +135 | *Pwr Locks +60*
Pwr Wndw +100 | *Sunroof +160*

DEDUCT FOR 91 LASER:

No AC -470 | *No Auto Trans -350*
No Pwr Steering -135

SUNDANCE 4 Cyl 1991

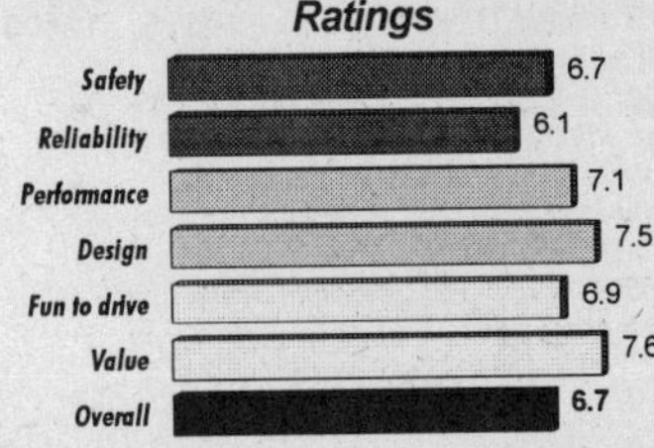

PLYMOUTH

Model/Body/Type	BaseList	Whlse	Retail
FWD/AT/PS/AC			
4 Dr America Hbk	7799	3850	5200
2 Dr America Hbk	7599	3750	5075
4 Dr Hbk	9270	4500	5925
2 Dr Hbk	9070	4400	5825
4 Dr RS Hbk	10495	5350	6900
2 Dr RS Hbk	10270	5250	6775

ADD FOR 91 SUNDANCE:

4 Cyl Turbo Eng +215 | *Cass(Std RS) +35*
Cruise Ctrl +75 | *Custom Whls/Cvrs +115*
Pwr Locks +35 | *Pwr Seat +75*
Pwr Wndw +75 | *Sunroof +115*
Tilt Whl +35

DEDUCT FOR 91 SUNDANCE:

No AC -390 | *No Auto Trans -350*

VOYAGER V6 — 1991

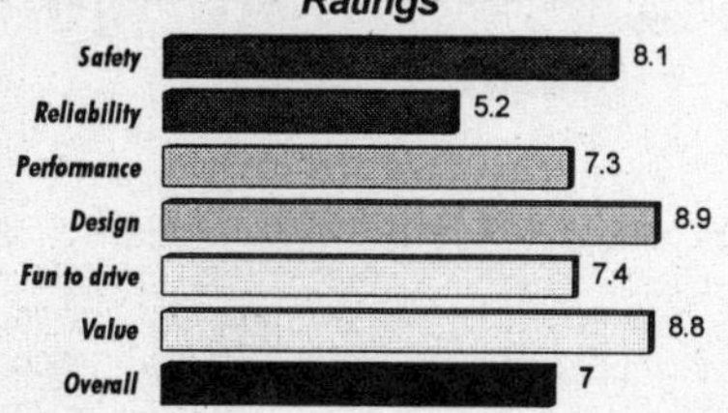

Model/Body/Type	BaseList	Whlse	Retail
FWD/AT/PS/AC			
Voyager	13195	7050	9075
Voyager SE	14325	7925	10000
Voyager LE	17625	8775	10950
Grand Voyager SE	16175	8825	11000
Grand Voyager LE	19435	9675	11950

ADD FOR 91 VOYAGER:

4-Whl Drive +1140 | *AC-Rear +250*
Air Bag +230 | *CD Player +125*
Custm Whls(Std LX) +105 | *Leather Seats +170*
LX Pkg +275 | *Privacy Glass(Std LX) +105*
Pwr Seats(Std LX) +80 | *Pwr Wndw(Std LE,LX) +80*
Running Boards +105 | *Sunroof-Manual +80*
Towing Pkg +105

DEDUCT FOR 91 VOYAGER:

4 Cyl Eng -350 | *No AC -315*
No Auto Trans -250

1990 PLYMOUTH

ACCLAIM — 1990

Ratings

Rating	Score
Safety	7.2
Reliability	6.3
Performance	7.5
Design	7.9
Fun to drive	7.4
Value	8.4
Overall	7.1

Model/Body/Type	BaseList	Whlse	Retail
FWD/AT/PS/AC			
4 Cyl Models			
4 Dr Sdn	10395	3250	4675
4 Dr LE Sdn	11875	3725	5200
V6 Models			
4 Dr Sdn	11075	3650	5075
4 Dr LE Sdn	12555	4125	5675
4 Dr LX Sdn	13865	4725	6350

ADD FOR 90 ACCLAIM:

4 Cyl Turbo Eng +195 | *Cass(Std LX) +60*
CruiseCtrl(Std LE,LX) +75 | *Custom Whls/Cvrs +115*
Pwr Locks +60 | *Pwr Seat +75*
Pwr Wndw +75 | *Sunroof +115*
Tilt Whl(Std LE,LX) +60

DEDUCT FOR 90 ACCLAIM:

No AC -430 | *No Auto Trans -390*

COLT 4 Cyl — 1990

Model/Body/Type	BaseList	Whlse	Retail
FWD/AT/PS/AC			
3 Dr Hbk	6851	1625	2600
3 Dr GL Hbk	7909	2500	3650
3 Dr GT Hbk	9121	3100	4375
4 Dr DL Wgn	9316	3450	4775
4WD DL (5 spd)	11145	3750	5075
4 Dr Vista Wgn	11941	4675	6125
4WD Vista (5 spd)	13167	4925	6450

ADD FOR 90 COLT:

Cass +35 | *Cruise Ctrl +60*
Custom Whls/Cvrs +75 | *GT Pkg +485*
Luggage Rack +35 | *Pwr Locks +35*
Pwr Wndw +60

DEDUCT FOR 90 COLT:

No AC -315 | *No Auto Trans -275*
No Pwr Steering -75

PLYMOUTH 90-89

HORIZON 4 Cyl — 1990

Model/Body/Type	BaseList	Whlse	Retail
FWD/AT/PS/AC			
4 Dr Hbk	6995	2150	3225

ADD FOR 90 HORIZON:
Cass +35

DEDUCT FOR 90 HORIZON:
No AC -315 | *No Auto Trans -275*
No Pwr Steering -75

LASER 4 Cyl — 1990

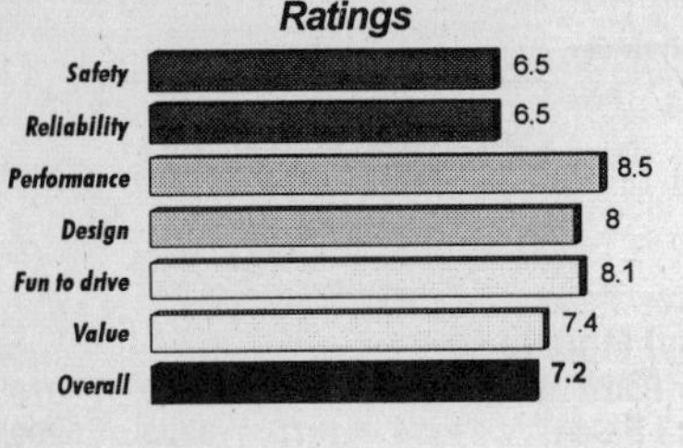

Model/Body/Type	BaseList	Whlse	Retail
FWD/AT/PS/AC			
3 Dr Hbk	10397	4400	5950
3 Dr RS Hbk	11417	4950	6625
3 Dr RS Turbo Hbk	13394	5775	7475

ADD FOR 90 LASER:
16 Valve Eng +230 | *Cass(Std RS) +60*
CD Player +115 | *Cruise Ctrl +75*
Custom Whls/Cvrs +115 | *Pwr Locks +60*
Pwr Wndw +75 | *Sunroof +115*

DEDUCT FOR 90 LASER:
No AC -430 | *No Auto Trans -315*
No Pwr Steering -115

SUNDANCE 4 Cyl — 1990

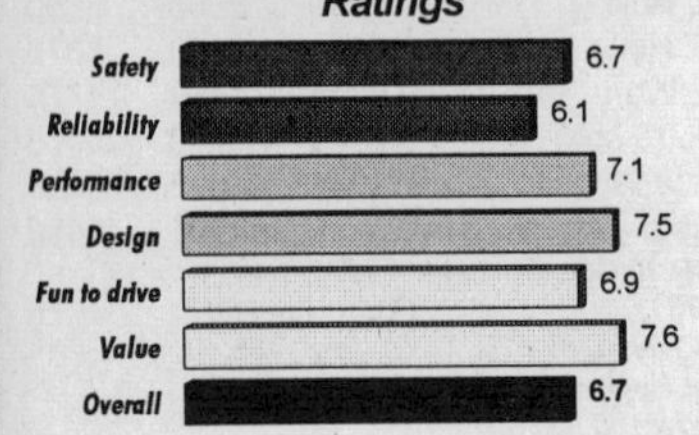

Model/Body/Type	BaseList	Whlse	Retail
FWD/AT/PS/AC			
4 Dr Lbk	9045	3200	4500
2 Dr Lbk	8845	3125	4400

ADD FOR 90 SUNDANCE:
4 Cyl Turbo Eng +195 | *Cass +35*
Cruise Ctrl +60 | *Custom Whls/Cvrs +75*
Pwr Locks +35 | *Pwr Seat +60*
Pwr Wndw +60 | *RS Pkg +230*
Sunroof +100 | *Tilt Whl +35*

DEDUCT FOR 90 SUNDANCE:
No AC -350 | *No Auto Trans -315*

VOYAGER V6 — 1990

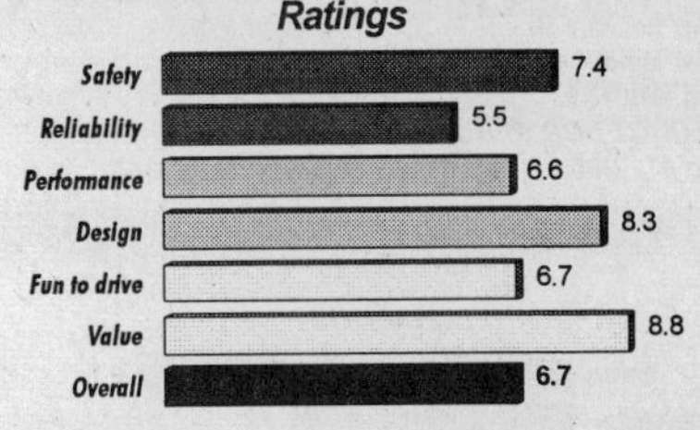

Model/Body/Type	BaseList	Whlse	Retail
FWD/AT/PS/AC			
Voyager	11995	5950	7850
Voyager SE	12675	6725	8725
Voyager LE	16125	7425	9500
Grand Voyager SE	15395	7550	9625
Grand Voyager LE	18325	8250	10325

ADD FOR 90 VOYAGER:
AC-Rear +185 | *Custom Whls +80*
Leather Seats +125 | *LX Pkg +230*
Privacy Glass +80 | *Running Boards +80*
Sunroof-Pwr +205 | *Towing Pkg +80*

DEDUCT FOR 90 VOYAGER:
2.5L 4Cyl Trbo Eng -115 | *4 Cyl Eng -275*

1989 PLYMOUTH

ACCLAIM 4 Cyl — 1989

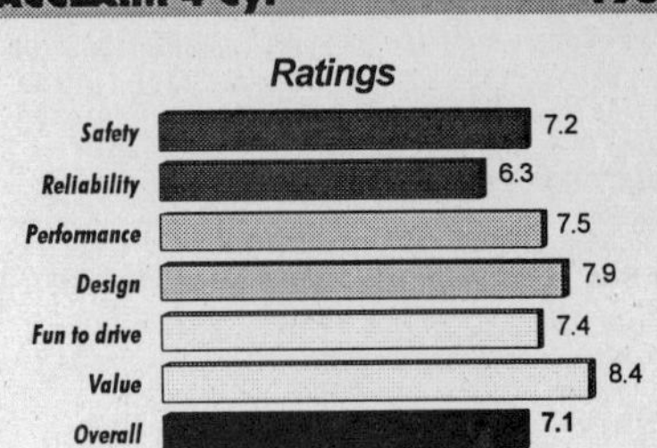

Model/Body/Type	BaseList	Whlse	Retail
FWD/AT/PS/AC			
4 Dr Sdn	9920	2400	3625
4 Dr LE Sdn	11295	2850	4175
4 Dr LX Sdn (V6)	13195	3725	5200

ADD FOR 89 ACCLAIM:

4 Cyl Turbo Eng +175 | *Cass(Std LX) +35*
CruiseCtrl(Std LE,LX) +60 | *Pwr Locks +35*
Pwr Seat +60 | *Pwr Wndw +60*
Sunroof +100
Tilt Whl(Std LE,LX) +35

DEDUCT FOR 89 ACCLAIM:

No AC -390 | *No Auto Trans -350*

COLT 4 Cyl 1989

Model/Body/Type	BaseList	Whlse	Retail
FWD/AT/PS/AC			
3 Dr Hbk	6477	1125	2025
3 Dr E Hbk	7279	1625	2600
3 Dr GT Hbk	8620	2475	3625
4 Dr DL Wgn	9316	2700	3875
4WD DL (5 spd)	11145	3000	4250
4 Dr Vista Wgn	11518	3800	5150
4WD Vista (5 spd)	12828	4100	5500

ADD FOR 89 COLT:

Cass +25 | *Cruise Ctrl +35*
Custom Whls/Cvrs +35 | *GT Pkg +350*
Pwr Locks +25 | *Pwr Wndw +35*

DEDUCT FOR 89 COLT:

No AC -275 | *No Auto Trans -230*

GRAN FURY SALON V8 1989

Model/Body/Type	BaseList	Whlse	Retail
AT/PS/AC			
4 Dr Sdn	11995	1600	2750

ADD FOR 89 GRAN FURY:

Cass +60 | *Cruise Ctrl +75*
Custom Whls/Cvrs +75 | *Pwr Locks +35*
Pwr Wndw +75 | *Vinyl Roof +35*

DEDUCT FOR 89 GRAN FURY:

No AC -430

HORIZON AMERICA 4 Cyl 1989

Model/Body/Type	BaseList	Whlse	Retail
FWD/AT/PS/AC			
4 Dr Hbk	6595	1550	2525

ADD FOR 89 HORIZON AMERICA:

Cass +25

DEDUCT FOR 89 HORIZON AMERICA:

No AC -275 | *No Auto Trans -230*

RELIANT AMERICA 4 Cyl 1989

Model/Body/Type	BaseList	Whlse	Retail
FWD/AT/PS/AC			
4 Dr Sdn	7595	1800	2850
2 Dr Cpe	7595	1725	2750

ADD FOR 89 RELIANT AMERICA:

Cass +25 | *Cruise Ctrl +35*
Pwr Locks +25 | *Tilt Whl +25*

DEDUCT FOR 89 RELIANT AMERICA:

No AC -315 | *No Auto Trans -275*
No Pwr Steering -75

SUNDANCE 4 Cyl 1989

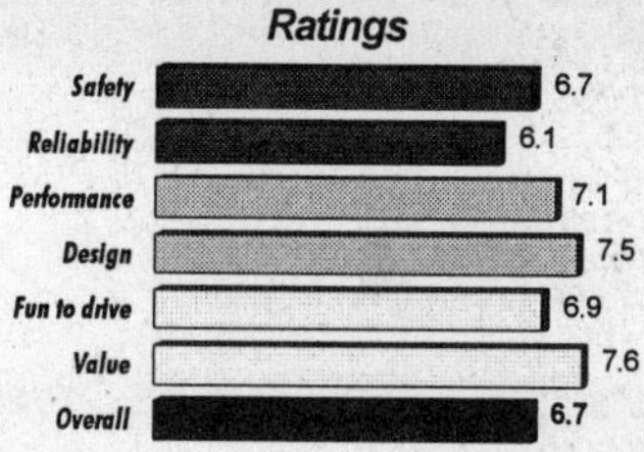

Ratings

Rating	Score
Safety	6.7
Reliability	6.1
Performance	7.1
Design	7.5
Fun to drive	6.9
Value	7.6
Overall	6.7

Model/Body/Type	BaseList	Whlse	Retail
FWD/AT/PS/AC			
4 Dr Lbk	8595	2625	3775
2 Dr Lbk	8395	2525	3675

ADD FOR 89 SUNDANCE:

4 Cyl Turbo Eng +175 | *Cass +25*
Cruise Ctrl +35 | *Custom Whls/Cvrs +35*
Pwr Locks +25 | *Pwr Seat +35*
Pwr Wndw +35 | *RS Pkg +195*
Sunroof +75 | *Tilt Whl +25*

DEDUCT FOR 89 SUNDANCE:

No AC -315 | *No Auto Trans -275*

VOYAGER V6 1989

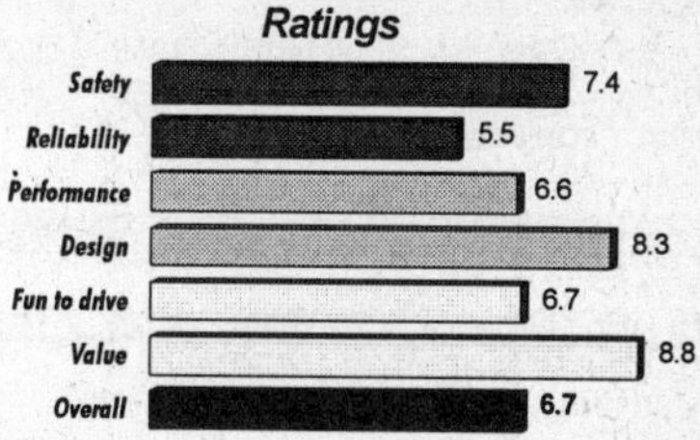

Ratings

Rating	Score
Safety	7.4
Reliability	5.5
Performance	6.6
Design	8.3
Fun to drive	6.7
Value	8.8
Overall	6.7

Model/Body/Type	BaseList	Whlse	Retail
FWD/AT/PS/AC			
Voyager	11312	4425	6150
Voyager SE	12039	5075	6950
Voyager LE	13987	5750	7625
Grand Voyager SE	13741	5800	7675
Grand Voyager LE	16362	6450	8400

ADD FOR 89 VOYAGER:

AC-Rear +145 | *Leather Seats +80*
Sunroof-Pwr +205

DEDUCT FOR 89 VOYAGER:

2.5L 4Cyl Trbo Eng -100 | *4 Cyl Eng -230*

1988 PLYMOUTH

Model/Body/Type	BaseList	Whlse	Retail
CARAVELLE 4 Cyl 1988			
FWD/AT/PS/AC			
4 Dr Sdn	10659	1850	3000
4 Dr SE Sdn	11628	2175	3350

ADD FOR 88 CARAVELLE:
4 Cyl Turbo Eng +160
DEDUCT FOR 88 CARAVELLE:
No AC -330

Model/Body/Type	BaseList	Whlse	Retail
COLT 4 Cyl 1988			
FWD/AT/PS/AC			
3 Dr Hbk	5899	625	1425
4 Dr E Sdn	7624	1150	2050
3 Dr E Hbk	6318	900	1750
4 Dr DL Sdn	8048	1350	2300
3 Dr DL Hbk	7625	1275	2200
4 Dr DL Wgn	8663	1600	2575
4 Dr Premier Sdn	8943	1800	2850
4 Dr Vista Wgn	11122	2525	3675
4WD Vista (5 spd)	12405	2850	4100

ADD FOR 88 COLT:
4 Cyl Turbo Eng +160
DEDUCT FOR 88 COLT:
No AC -215 *No Auto Trans -195*

Model/Body/Type	BaseList	Whlse	Retail
GRAN FURY V8 1988			
AT/PS/AC			
4 Dr Salon Sdn	11407	1250	2275
4 Dr Sdn	12127	1550	2675

DEDUCT FOR 88 GRAN FURY:
No AC -370

Model/Body/Type	BaseList	Whlse	Retail
HORIZON AMERICA 4 Cyl 1988			
FWD/AT/PS/AC			
4 Dr Hbk	5999	1025	1925

DEDUCT FOR 88 HORIZON AMERICA:
No AC -215 *No Auto Trans -195*

Model/Body/Type	BaseList	Whlse	Retail
RELIANT AMERICA 4 Cyl 1988			
FWD/AT/PS/AC			
4 Dr Sdn	6995	1325	2275
2 Dr Cpe	6995	1275	2175
4 Dr Wgn	7695	1700	2700

DEDUCT FOR 88 RELIANT:
No AC -250 *No Auto Trans -230*
No Pwr Steering -60

Model/Body/Type	BaseList	Whlse	Retail
SUNDANCE 4 Cyl 1988			
FWD/AT/PS/AC			
4 Dr Lbk	8175	1650	2625
2 Dr Lbk	7975	1550	2525

ADD FOR 88 SUNDANCE:
4 Cyl Turbo Eng +160
DEDUCT FOR 88 SUNDANCE:
No AC -250 *No Auto Trans -230*

Model/Body/Type	BaseList	Whlse	Retail
VOYAGER V6 1988			
FWD/AT/PS/AC			
Voyager	10887	3825	5475
Voyager SE	11587	4375	6125
Voyager LE	13462	4875	6700
Grand Voyager SE	13162	4900	6725
Grand Voyager LE	15509	5475	7325

ADD FOR 88 VOYAGER:
AC-Rear +105 *Sunroof-Pwr +80*
DEDUCT FOR 88 VOYAGER:
4 Cyl Eng -195

1987 PLYMOUTH

Model/Body/Type	BaseList	Whlse	Retail
CARAVELLE 4 Cyl 1987			
FWD/AT/PS/AC			
4 Dr Sdn	9762	1200	2175
4 Dr SE Sdn	10335	1475	2525

ADD FOR 87 CARAVELLE:
4 Cyl Turbo Eng +135

Model/Body/Type	BaseList	Whlse	Retail
COLT 4 Cyl 1987			
FWD/AT/PS/AC			
4 Dr E Sdn	7290	650	1450
3 Dr E Hbk	6056	550	1350
4 Dr DL Sdn	7677	1000	1900
3 Dr DL Hbk	7152	900	1775
4 Dr Premier Sdn	8638	1425	2375
4 Dr Vista Wgn	10158	2000	3100
4WD Vista (5 spd)	11371	2400	3550

ADD FOR 87 COLT:
4 Cyl Turbo Eng +135

Model/Body/Type	BaseList	Whlse	Retail
GRAN FURY V8 1987			
AT/PS/AC			
4 Dr Salon Sdn	10598	925	1925
HORIZON 4 Cyl 1987			
FWD/AT/PS/AC			
4 Dr America Hbk	5799	775	1600
RELIANT 4 Cyl 1987			
FWD/AT/PS/AC			
4 Dr Sdn	7655	925	1800
2 Dr Cpe	7655	875	1700
4 Dr LE Sdn	8134	1100	2000
2 Dr LE Cpe	8134	1000	1900
4 Dr LE Wgn	8579	1400	2350
SUNDANCE 4 Cyl 1987			
FWD/AT/PS/AC			
4 Dr Lbk	7799	1325	2250
2 Dr Lbk	7599	1250	2175

ADD FOR 87 SUNDANCE:
4 Cyl Turbo Eng +135

Model/Body/Type	BaseList	Whlse	Retail
TURISMO 4 Cyl			**1987**
FWD/AT/PS/AC			
2 Dr Hbk	7199	1100	2000
VOYAGER 4 Cyl			**1987**
FWD/AT/PS/AC			
Voyager	10333	2925	4400
Voyager SE	10810	3325	4875
Voyager LE	11674	3775	5400
Grand Voyager SE (V6)	11751	4025	5725
Grand Voyager LE (V6)	12561	4475	6200
ADD FOR 87 VOYAGER:			
V6 Eng +160			

1986 PLYMOUTH

Model/Body/Type	BaseList	Whlse	Retail
CARAVELLE			**1986**
FWD			
4 Dr Sdn	9026	875	1825
4 Dr SE Sdn	9595	1075	2125
COLT			**1986**
FWD			
4 Dr E Sdn	6310	375	1325
3 Dr E Hbk	5431	300	1250
4 Dr DL Sdn	6629	675	1650
3 Dr DL Hbk	6318	600	1550
4 Dr Premier Sdn	7624	950	1975
4 Dr Vista Wgn	8814	1500	2600
4WD Vista (5 spd)	9913	1900	3100
CONQUEST			**1986**
2 Dr Hbk	13417	1625	2750
GRAN FURY			**1986**
4 Dr Salon Sdn	9947	600	1750
HORIZON			**1986**
FWD			
4 Dr Hbk	6209	475	1425
4 Dr SE Hbk	6558	750	1700
RELIANT			**1986**
FWD			
4 Dr Sdn	7179	700	1675
2 Dr Cpe	7062	600	1575
4 Dr SE Sdn	7634	825	1775
2 Dr SE Cpe	7514	750	1700
4 Dr SE Wgn	8002	1000	2025
4 Dr LE Sdn	8082	950	1975
2 Dr LE Cpe	7962	900	1875
4 Dr LE Wgn	8812	1175	2200
TURISMO			**1986**
FWD			
2 Dr Hbk	6741	750	1700
2 Dr 2.2 Hbk	7686	925	1925
VOYAGER			**1986**
FWD			
Voyager	9506	2275	3800
Voyager SE	9785	2450	4000
Voyager LE	10528	2675	4250

1985 PLYMOUTH

Model/Body/Type	BaseList	Whlse	Retail
CARAVELLE			**1985**
4 Dr SE Sdn	8879	650	1625
COLT			**1985**
4 Dr E Hbk	6029	375	1300
2 Dr E Hbk	5372	275	1225
4 Dr DL Sdn	6492	475	1425
2 Dr DL Hbk	6177	400	1325
4 Dr Premier Sdn	7409	800	1750
4 Dr Vista Wgn	8721	1225	2250
4 Dr 4WD Vista Wgn	9809	1550	2675
CONQUEST			**1985**
2 Dr Hbk	12564	1075	2125
GRAN FURY			**1985**
4 Dr Salon Sdn	9399	375	1500
HORIZON			**1985**
4 Dr Hbk	5977	325	1275
4 Dr SE Hbk	6298	525	1475
RELIANT			**1985**
4 Dr Sdn	7039	625	1600
2 Dr Cpe	6924	550	1500
4 Dr SE Sdn	7439	725	1700
2 Dr SE Cpe	7321	625	1600
4 Dr SE Wgn	7909	900	1875
4 Dr LE Sdn	7792	825	1775
2 Dr LE Cpe	7659	725	1700
4 Dr LE Wgn	8348	950	1975
TURISMO			**1985**
2 Dr Hbk	6584	550	1500
2 Dr 2.2 Hbk	7515	725	1700
VOYAGER			**1985**
Voyager	9147	1700	3100
Voyager SE	9393	1800	3225
Voyager LE	10005	1975	3400

Model/Body/Type	BaseList	Whlse	Retail

PONTIAC

PONTIAC USA

1992 Pontiac Bonneville SSEi

For a Pontiac dealer in your area, see our Dealer Directory (pg 217)

1994 PONTIAC

BONNEVILLE V6 1994

FWD/AT/PS/AC

Model/Body/Type	BaseList	Whlse	Retail
4 Dr SE Sdn	20424	**15450**	**18225**
4 Dr SSE Sdn	25884	**20325**	**23550**

ADD FOR 94 BONNEVILLE:

Anti-Theft/Recovery Sys +365
Car Phone +230 | *Cass(Std SSE) +135*
CD Player +275 | *Cruise Ctrl(Std SSE) +180*
Custom Whls/Cvrs +230 | *Head-Up Display +135*
Lthr Seats +320 | *Pwr Seat(Std SSE) +180*
Pwr Sunroof +590
SSEi Supercharged Pkg +865

FIREBIRD 1994

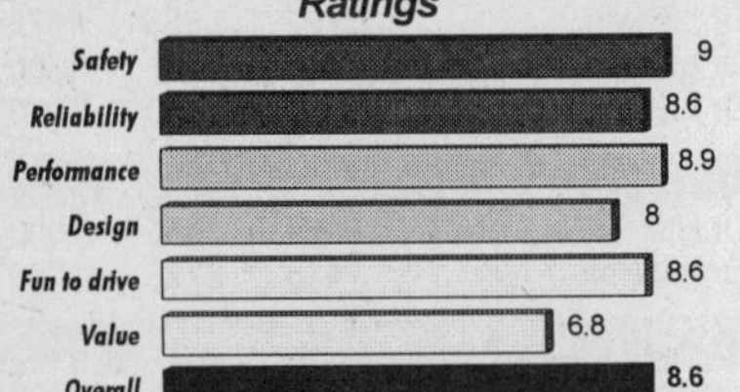

AT/PS/AC

Model/Body/Type	BaseList	Whlse	Retail
V6 Models			
2 Dr Cpe	13995	-	-
2 Dr Conv	21179	-	-
V8 Models			
2 Dr Formula Cpe	17995	-	-
2 Dr Formula Conv	24279	-	-
2 Dr Trans Am Cpe	19895	-	-
2 Dr Trans Am GT Cpe	21395	-	-
2 Dr Trans Am GT Conv	26479	-	-

ADD FOR 94 FIREBIRD:

Anti-Theft/Recovery Sys | *CD Player*
Cruise Ctrl(Std T/A,Conv) | *Leather Seats*
Pwr Locks(Std T/A,Conv) | *Pwr Seat*
Pwr Wndw(Std T/A,Conv) | *T-Top*

DEDUCT FOR 93 FIREBIRD:

No AC | *No Auto Trans(V6)*

GRAND AM 1994

FWD/AT/PS/AC

Model/Body/Type	BaseList	Whlse	Retail
Quad 4 Models			
4 Dr SE Sdn	12614	**11425**	**13775**
2 Dr SE Cpe	12514	**11425**	**13775**
4 Dr GT Sdn	15114	**13275**	**15775**
2 Dr GT Cpe	15114	**13275**	**15775**
V6 Models			
4 Dr SE Sdn	13024	**11600**	**14050**
2 Dr SE Cpe	13024	**11600**	**14050**

ADD FOR 94 GRAND AM:

Anti-Theft/Recovery Sys +365
Cass +115 | *CD Player +230*
Cruise Ctrl +160 | *Custom Whls/Cvrs +205*
Leather Seats +275 | *Pwr Seat +160*
Pwr Wndw +160 | *Tilt Whl(Std GT) +115*

DEDUCT FOR 94 GRAND AM:

No AC -680 | *No Auto Trans -590*

GRAND PRIX V6 1994

FWD/AT/PS/AC

Model/Body/Type	BaseList	Whlse	Retail
4 Dr SE Sdn	16174	**13500**	**16025**
2 Dr SE Cpe	13950	**12125**	**16025**

ADD FOR 94 GRAND PRIX:

ABS +430
Anti-Theft/Recovery Sys +365
Cass(Std Cpe) +115 | *CD Player +230*
Cruise Ctrl(Std Cpe) +160 | *Custom Whls/Cvrs +205*
Head-Up Display +135 | *Leather Seats +275*
Pwr Seat +160 | *Pwr Sunroof +545*

See the Automobile Dealer Directory on page 379 for a Dealer near you!

Model/Body/Type	BaseList	Whlse	Retail

SUNBIRD 4 Cyl — 1994

Ratings

Rating	Score
Safety	6.7
Reliability	4.1
Performance	7.1
Design	7.2
Fun to drive	7
Value	7.4
Overall	6

FWD/AT/PS/AC

Model/Body/Type	BaseList	Whlse	Retail
4 Dr LE Sdn	9764	**8550**	**10400**
2 Dr LE Cpe	9764	**8450**	**10275**
2 Dr LE Conv	15524	**12375**	**14775**
2 Dr SE Cpe (V6)	12424	-	-

ADD FOR 94 SUNBIRD:

Anti-Theft/Recovery Sys +365
Cass +90 — *CD Player +205*
Cruise Ctrl +135 — *Custom Whls/Cvrs +180*
Pwr Wndw(Std Conv) +135
Sunroof +275 — *Tilt Whl +90*
V6 Eng(Std SE) +455

DEDUCT FOR 94 SUNBIRD:

No AC -590 — *No Auto Trans -500*

TRANS SPORT V6 — 1994

FWD/AT/PS/AC

Model/Body/Type	BaseList	Whlse	Retail
SE Wagon	17369	**15150**	**18000**

ADD FOR 94 TRANS SPORT:

3.8L V6 Eng +455 — *Pwr Sliding Dr +320*

1993 PONTIAC

BONNEVILLE V6 — 1993

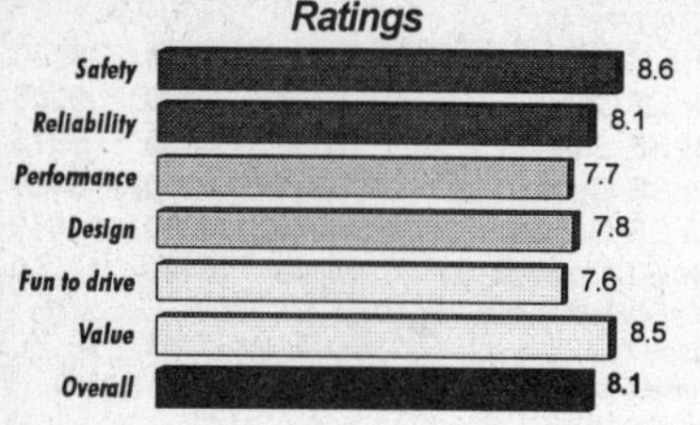

FWD/AT/PS/AC

Model/Body/Type	BaseList	Whlse	Retail
4 Dr SE Sdn	19444	**12850**	**15475**
4 Dr SSE Sdn	24844	**17275**	**20325**
4 Dr SSEi Sdn	29444	**19450**	**22600**

ADD FOR 93 BONNEVILLE:

Car Phone +175 — *Cass(Std SSE,SSEi) +115*
CD Player +230
Cruise Ctrl(Std SSE,SSEi) +160
Custom Whls/Cvrs +195 — *Lthr Seats(Std SSEi) +275*
Pass Side Airbag(Std SSEi) +315
Pwr Seat(Std SSE,SSEi) +160
Pwr Sunroof +470
Supercharged V6(Std SSEi) +435

FIREBIRD V8 — 1993

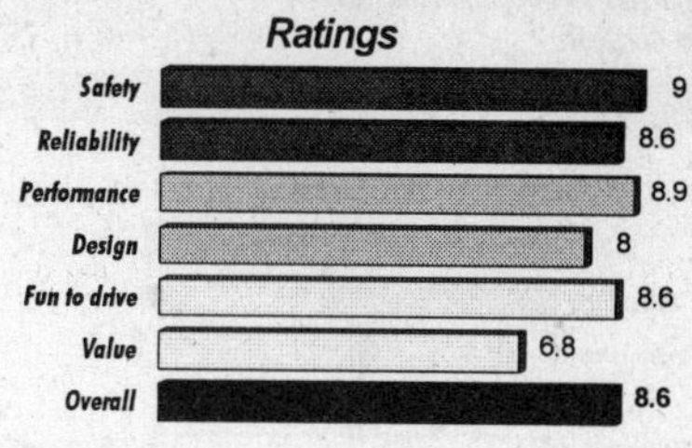

AT/PS/AC

Model/Body/Type	BaseList	Whlse	Retail
2 Dr Cpe (V6)	13995	**13200**	**15700**
2 Dr Formula Cpe	17995	**16600**	**19400**
2 Dr Trans Am Cpe	21395	**17750**	**20650**

ADD FOR 93 FIREBIRD:

CD Player +195 — *Cruise Ctrl(Std T/A) +135*
Leather Seats +230 — *Pwr Locks(Std T/A) +100*
Pwr Seat +135 — *Pwr Wndw(Std T/A) +135*
T-Top +625

DEDUCT FOR 93 FIREBIRD:

No AC -545 — *No Auto Trans(V6) -505*

GRAND AM — 1993

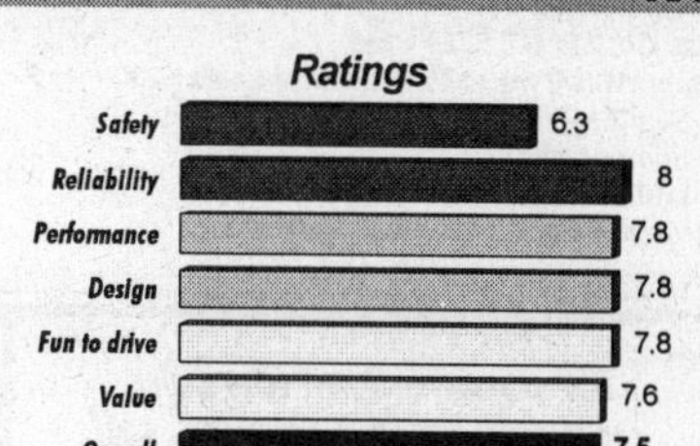

PONTIAC

PONTIAC

Model/Body/Type	BaseList	Whlse	Retail

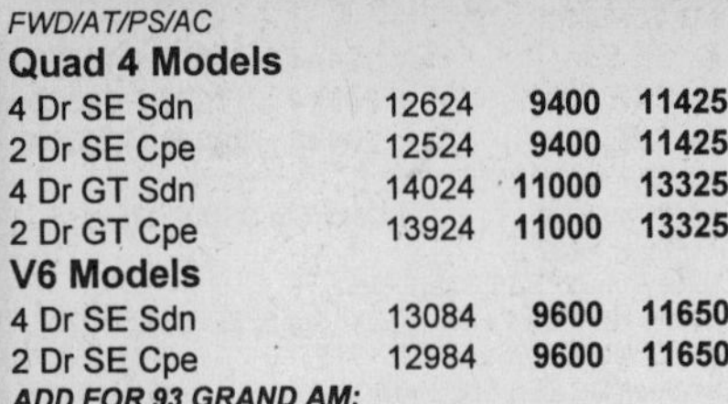

FWD/AT/PS/AC

Quad 4 Models			
4 Dr SE Sdn	12624	**9400**	**11425**
2 Dr SE Cpe	12524	**9400**	**11425**
4 Dr GT Sdn	14024	**11000**	**13325**
2 Dr GT Cpe	13924	**11000**	**13325**
V6 Models			
4 Dr SE Sdn	13084	**9600**	**11650**
2 Dr SE Cpe	12984	**9600**	**11650**

ADD FOR 93 GRAND AM:

Cass +100 *CD Player +195*
Cruise Ctrl +135 *Custom Whls/Cvrs +175*
Pwr Seat +135 *Pwr Wndw +135*
Tilt Whl +100

DEDUCT FOR 93 GRAND AM:

No AC -545 *No Auto Trans -505*

GRAND PRIX V6 — 1993

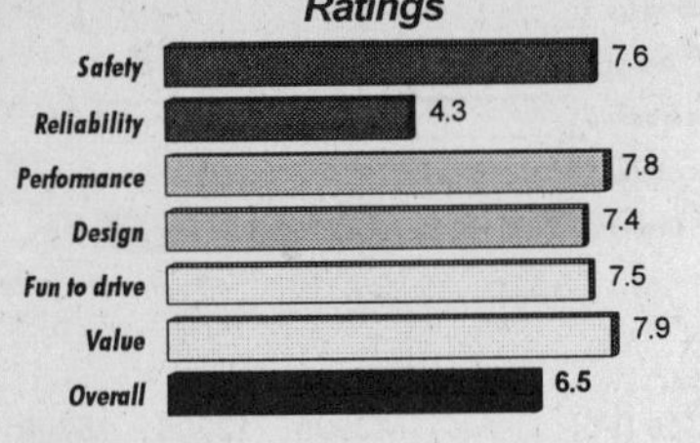

FWD/AT/PS/AC

Model/Body/Type	BaseList	Whlse	Retail
4 Dr LE Sdn	14890	**10150**	**12325**
4 Dr SE Sdn	16190	**11000**	**13325**
2 Dr SE Cpe	15390	**11000**	**13325**
4 Dr STE Sdn	21635	**13975**	**16525**
2 Dr GT Cpe	20340	**13475**	**16000**

ADD FOR 93 GRAND PRIX:

ABS(Std GT,STE) +390 *Cass(Std GT,STE) +100*
CD Player +195
Cruise Ctrl(Std GT,STE) +135
Custom Whls/Cvrs +175 *Leather Seats +230*
Pwr Seat(StdGT,STE) +135
Pwr Sunroof +430
Pwr Wndw(Std GT,STE) +135
Tilt Whl(Std GT,STE) +100

LE MANS 4 Cyl — 1993

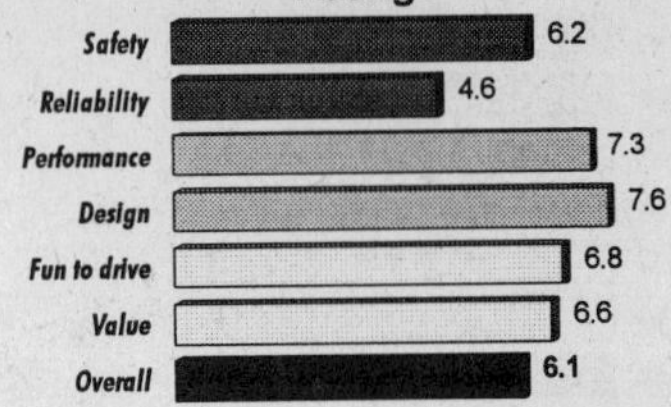

FWD/AT/PS/AC

Model/Body/Type	BaseList	Whlse	Retail
3 Dr Aerocoupe (4 spd)	8154	**4550**	**5975**
3 Dr SE Aerocoupe	9054	**5725**	**7275**
4 Dr SE Sdn	9854	**5975**	**7550**

ADD FOR 93 LE MANS:

Cass +75 *Sunroof +195*

DEDUCT FOR 93 LE MANS:

No AC -430 *No Auto Trans -390*
No Pwr Steering -135

SUNBIRD 4 Cyl — 1993

Ratings

Rating	Score
Safety	6.7
Reliability	4.1
Performance	7.1
Design	7.2
Fun to drive	7
Value	7.4
Overall	6

FWD/AT/PS/AC

Model/Body/Type	BaseList	Whlse	Retail
4 Dr LE Sdn	9382	**7500**	**9300**
2 Dr LE Cpe	9382	**7400**	**9200**
4 Dr SE Sdn	10380	**8150**	**9975**
2 Dr SE Cpe	10380	**8050**	**9900**
2 Dr SE Conv	15405	**11700**	**14050**
2 Dr GT Cpe (V6)	12820	**10150**	**12250**

ADD FOR 93 SUNBIRD:

Cass +75 *CD Player +175*
Cruise Ctrl +115 *Custom Whls/Cvrs +160*
Pwr Wndw(Std Conv) +115 *Sunroof +195*
Tilt Whl +75 *V6 Eng(Std GT) +350*

DEDUCT FOR 93 SUNBIRD:

No AC -470 *No Auto Trans -430*

PONTIAC

TRANS SPORT V6 — 1993

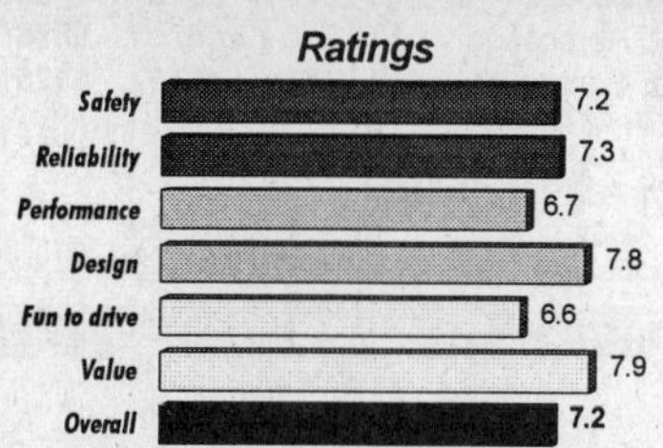

FWD/AT/PS/AC

Model/Body/Type	BaseList	Whlse	Retail
SE Wagon	16689	**12550**	**15225**

ADD FOR 93 TRANS SPORT:

AC-Rear +375, *Cass +105*, *CD Player +205*, *Cruise Ctrl +125*, *Custom Whls +145*, *Leather Seats +250*, *Luggage Rack +80*, *Privacy Glass +145*, *Pwr Locks +105*, *Pwr Seats +125*, *Pwr Wndw +145*, *Running Boards +145*, *Sunroof-Manual +145*, *Tilt Whl +105*, *Towing Pkg +185*

DEDUCT FOR 93 TRANS SPORT:

No AC -435

1992 PONTIAC

BONNEVILLE V6 — 1992

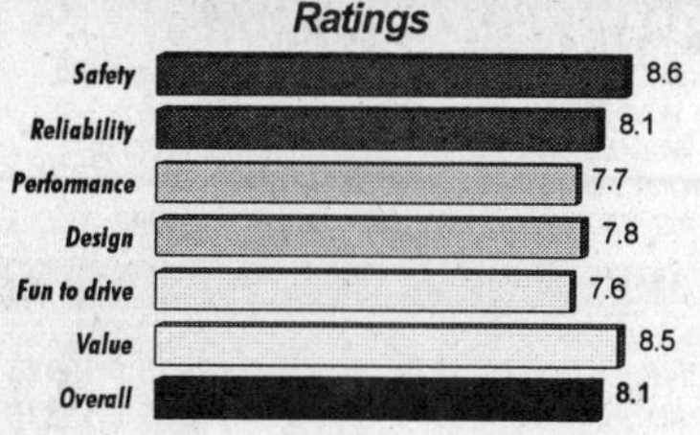

FWD/AT/PS/AC

Model/Body/Type	BaseList	Whlse	Retail
4 Dr SE Sdn	18599	**10600**	**13000**
4 Dr SSE Sdn	23999	**14725**	**17425**
4 Dr SSEi Sdn	28045	**16675**	**19625**

ADD FOR 92 BONNEVILLE:

ABS(Std SSE,SSEi) +350, *Car Phone +160*, *Cass(Std SSE,SSEi) +100*, *CD Player +195*, *CruiseCtrl(Std SSEi) +135*, *Custom Whls/Cvrs +175*, *Leather Seats +230*, *Pass Airbag(Std SSEi) +275*, *Pwr Sunroof +430*, *Pwr Seat(Std SSE,SSEi) +135*, *Supercharged V6(Std SSEi) +350*

FIREBIRD — 1992

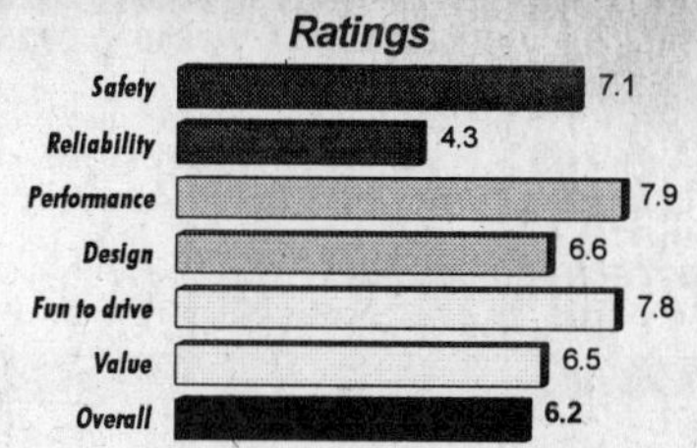

AT/PS/AC

Model/Body/Type	BaseList	Whlse	Retail
V6 Models			
2 Dr Cpe	12505	**9075**	**11100**
2 Dr Conv	19375	**13275**	**15775**
V8 Models			
2 Dr Cpe	12874	**9575**	**11625**
2 Dr Conv	19744	**13775**	**16300**
2 Dr Formula Cpe	16205	**10400**	**12625**
2 Dr Trans Am Cpe	18105	**12350**	**14800**
2 Dr Trans Am Conv	23875	**16600**	**19400**
2 Dr GTA Cpe	25880	**14475**	**17025**

ADD FOR 92 FIREBIRD:

5.7L V8Eng(Std GTA) +605, *CD Player +175*, *Cruise Ctrl(Std GTA) +115*, *Leather Seats +195*, *Pwr Locks(Std GTA) +75*, *Pwr Wndw(Std GTA) +115*, *T-Top +565*

DEDUCT FOR 92 FIREBIRD:

No AC -505, *No Auto Trans -470*

GRAND AM — 1992

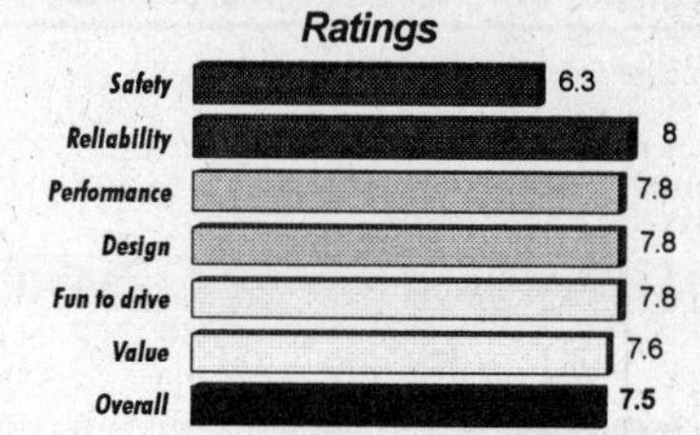

FWD/AT/PS/AC

Model/Body/Type	BaseList	Whlse	Retail
Quad 4 Models			
4 Dr SE Sdn	11999	**7600**	**9500**
2 Dr SE Cpe	11899	**7600**	**9500**
4 Dr GT Sdn	13799	**9050**	**11050**
2 Dr GT Cpe	13699	**9050**	**11050**

PONTIAC 92

PONTIAC

Model/Body/Type	BaseList	Whlse	Retail
V6 Models			
4 Dr SE Sdn	12459	**7800**	**9725**
2 Dr SE Cpe	12359	**7800**	**9725**

ADD FOR 92 GRAND AM:

Cass +75 | *CD Player +175*
Cruise Ctrl +115 | *Custom Whls/Cvrs +160*
Pwr Seat +115 | *Pwr Wndw +115*
Tilt Whl +75

DEDUCT FOR 92 GRAND AM:

No AC -505 | *No Auto Trans -470*

GRAND PRIX V6 — 1992

Ratings

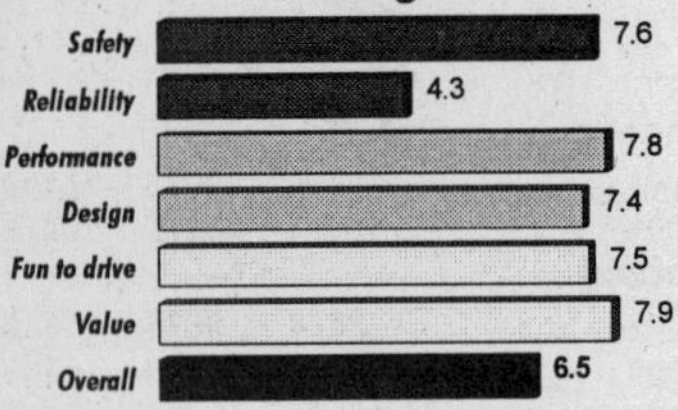

Rating	Score
Safety	7.6
Reliability	4.3
Performance	7.8
Design	7.4
Fun to drive	7.5
Value	7.9
Overall	6.5

Model/Body/Type	BaseList	Whlse	Retail
FWD/AT/PS/AC			
4 Dr LE Sdn	14890	**7800**	**9725**
4 Dr SE Sdn	16190	**8500**	**10400**
2 Dr SE Cpe	15390	**8500**	**10400**
4 Dr STE Sdn	21635	**11025**	**13375**
2 Dr GT Cpe	20340	**10525**	**12750**

ADD FOR 92 GRAND PRIX:

ABS(Std GT,STE) +350 | *Cass(Std GT,STE) +75*
CD Player +175
Cruise Ctrl(Std GT,STE) +115
Custom Paint +60 | *Custom Whls/Cvrs +160*
Leather Seats +195
Pwr Locks(Std GT,STE) +75
Pwr Seat(Std GT,STE) +115
Pwr Sunroof +390
Pwr Wndw(Std GT,STE) +115
Tilt Whl(Std GT,STE) +75

LE MANS 4 Cyl — 1992

Ratings

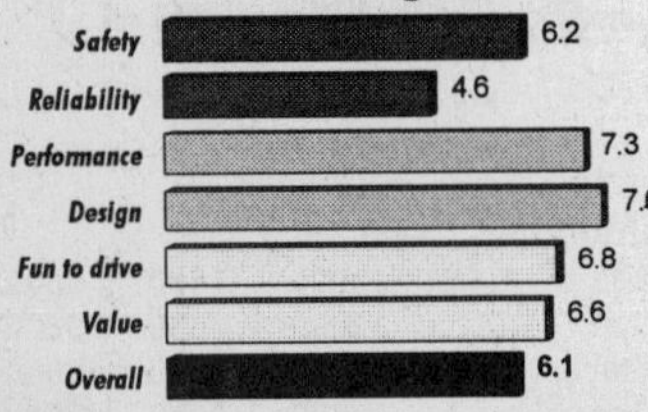

Rating	Score
Safety	6.2
Reliability	4.6
Performance	7.3
Design	7.6
Fun to drive	6.8
Value	6.6
Overall	6.1

Model/Body/Type	BaseList	Whlse	Retail
FWD/AT/PS/AC			
3 Dr Aerocoupe (4 spd)	8050	**3375**	**4700**
3 Dr SE Aerocoupe	8750	**4475**	**5875**
4 Dr SE Sdn	9465	**4675**	**6125**

ADD FOR 92 LE MANS:

Cass +60 | *Sunroof +160*

DEDUCT FOR 92 LE MANS:

No AC -390 | *No Auto Trans -350*
No Pwr Steering -115

SUNBIRD 4 Cyl — 1992

Ratings

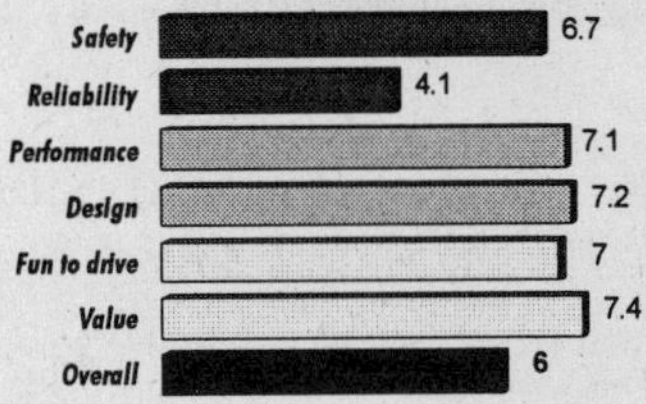

Rating	Score
Safety	6.7
Reliability	4.1
Performance	7.1
Design	7.2
Fun to drive	7
Value	7.4
Overall	6

Model/Body/Type	BaseList	Whlse	Retail
FWD/AT/PS/AC			
4 Dr LE Sdn	9720	**6450**	**8050**
2 Dr LE Cpe	9620	**6350**	**7950**
4 Dr SE Sdn	10480	**7050**	**8800**
2 Dr SE Cpe	10380	**6950**	**8700**
2 Dr SE Conv	15345	**10400**	**12525**
2 Dr GT Cpe (V6)	12820	**8975**	**10875**

ADD FOR 92 SUNBIRD:

Cass +60 | *CD Player +160*
Cruise Ctrl +100 | *Custom Whls/Cvrs +135*
Pwr Wndw(Std Conv) +100 | *Sunroof +160*
Tilt Whl +60 | *V6 Eng(Std GT) +315*

DEDUCT FOR 92 SUNBIRD:

No AC -430 | *No Auto Trans -390*

TRANS SPORT V6 — 1992

Model/Body/Type	BaseList	Whlse	Retail
FWD/AT/PS/AC			
SE Wagon	16225	**10525**	**12925**
GT Wagon	20935	**11325**	**13875**

ADD FOR 92 TRANS SPORT:

AC-Rear +315 | *Cass +80*
CD Player +170 | *Cruise Ctrl(Std GT) +80*
Custom Whls(Std GT) +125
Privacy Glass(Std GT) +125
Pwr Locks +80 | *Pwr Seats +105*
Pwr Wndw +105 | *Running Boards +125*
Sunroof-Manual +105 | *Towing Pkg +145*

DEDUCT FOR 92 TRANS SPORT:

No AC -375

Model/Body/Type	BaseList	Whlse	Retail

1991 PONTIAC

6000 V6 1991

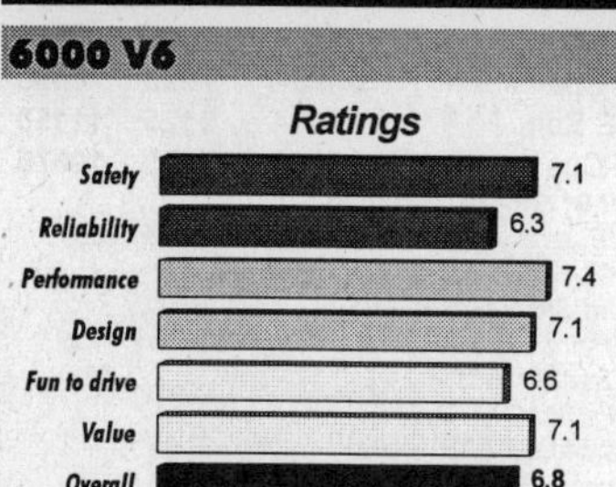

FWD/AT/PS/AC

Model/Body/Type	BaseList	Whlse	Retail
4 Dr LE Sdn (4 Cyl)	12999	**5050**	**6725**
4 Dr LE Sdn	13659	**5525**	**7200**
4 Dr LE Wgn	16699	**5925**	**7650**
4 Dr SE Sdn	18399	**6500**	**8225**

ADD FOR 91 6000:
Cass(Std SE) +60 CD Player +160
Cruise Ctrl(Std SE) +100 Custom Paint +35
Custom Whls/Cvrs +135 Pwr Locks(Std SE) +60
Pwr Seat +100 PwrWndw(Std SE) +100
Tilt Whl(Std SE) +60 Woodgrain +115

DEDUCT FOR 91 6000:
No AC -470

BONNEVILLE V6 1991

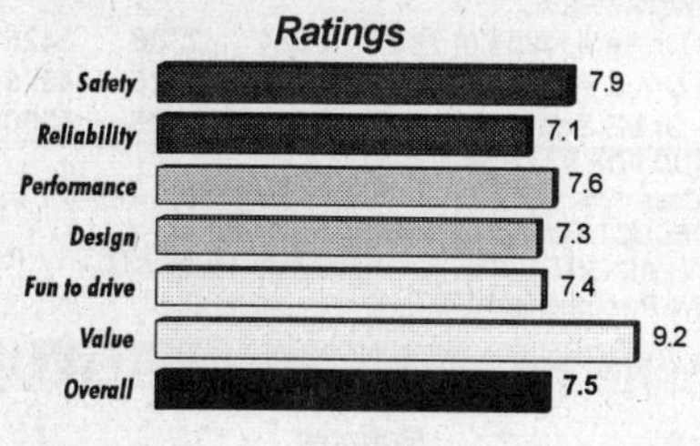

FWD/AT/PS/AC

Model/Body/Type	BaseList	Whlse	Retail
4 Dr LE Sdn	16834	**7225**	**9225**
4 Dr SE Sdn	20464	**8575**	**10625**
4 Dr SSE Sdn	25264	**11800**	**14375**

ADD FOR 91 BONNEVILLE:
ABS(Std SSE) +315 Car Phone +135
Cass(Std SE,SSE) +75 CD Player +160
Cruise Ctrl(Std SE,SSE) +115
Custom Paint +60 Custom Whls/Cvrs +160
Leather Seats +195
Pwr Locks(Std SE,SSE) +75
Pwr Seat(Std SE,SSE) +115
Pwr Sunroof +390
Pwr Wndw(Std SE,SSE) +115
Tilt Whl(Std SE,SSE) +75

FIREBIRD 1991

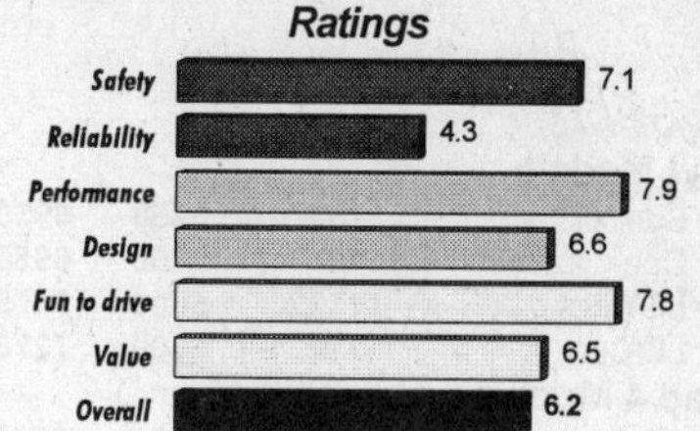

AT/PS/AC

Model/Body/Type	BaseList	Whlse	Retail
V6 Models			
2 Dr Cpe	12690	**7350**	**9225**
2 Dr Conv	19159	**11375**	**13750**
V8 Models			
2 Dr Cpe	13040	**7800**	**9725**
2 Dr Conv	19509	**11800**	**14275**
2 Dr Formula Cpe	15530	**8575**	**10475**
2 Dr Trans Am Cpe	17530	**10300**	**12525**
2 Dr Trans Am Conv	22980	**14375**	**16950**
2 Dr GTA Cpe	24530	**12575**	**15050**

ADD FOR 91 FIREBIRD:
5.7L V8 Eng(Std GTA) +545
CD Player +160 CruiseCtrl(Std GTA) +100
Leather Seats +160 Pwr Locks(Std GTA) +60
Pwr Wndw(Std GTA) +100 T-Top +530

DEDUCT FOR 91 FIREBIRD:
No AC -470 No Auto Trans -430

PONTIAC

Model/Body/Type	BaseList	Whlse	Retail

GRAND AM 1991

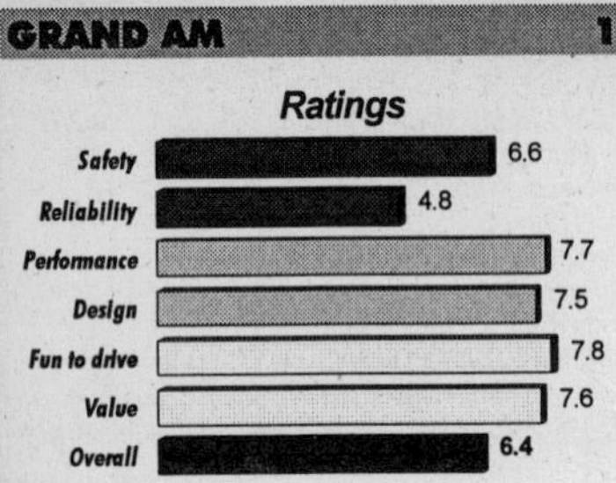

FWD/AT/PS/AC

Model/Body/Type	BaseList	Whlse	Retail
4 Cyl Models			
4 Dr Sdn	10374	**5250**	**6950**
2 Dr Cpe	10174	**5250**	**6950**
4 Dr LE Sdn	11324	**5600**	**7275**
2 Dr LE Cpe	11124	**5600**	**7275**
Quad 4 Models			
4 Dr SE Sdn	16544	**6925**	**8750**
2 Dr SE Cpe	16344	**6925**	**8750**

ADD FOR 91 GRAND AM:

Cass(Std SE) +60 | *CD Player +160*
Cruise Ctrl(Std SE) +100 | *Custom Paint +60*
Custom Whls/Cvrs +135 | *Pwr Locks(Std SE) +60*
Pwr Seat +100 | *Pwr Wndw(Std SE) +100*
Quad 4 Eng(Std SE) +275 | *Sunroof +160*
Tilt Whl(Std SE) +60

DEDUCT FOR 91 GRAND AM:

No AC -470 | *No Auto Trans -430*

GRAND PRIX 1991

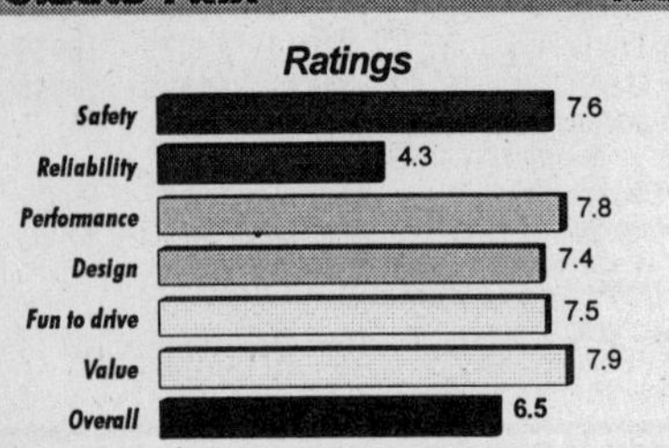

FWD/AT/PS/AC

Model/Body/Type	BaseList	Whlse	Retail
Quad 4 Models			
4 Dr LE Sdn	14294	**6275**	**8025**
4 Dr SE Sdn	15284	**6825**	**8650**
2 Dr SE Cpe	14894	**6825**	**8650**
V6 Models			
4 Dr LE Sdn	14294	**6500**	**8225**
4 Dr SE Sdn	15284	**7025**	**8850**
2 Dr SE Cpe	14894	**7025**	**8850**
4 Dr STE Sdn	19994	**9125**	**11150**
2 Dr GT Cpe	19154	**8675**	**10675**

ADD FOR 91 GRAND PRIX:

ABS +315 | *Cass(Std GT,STE) +60*
CD Player +160
Cruise Ctrl(Std GT,STE) +100
Custom Paint +35 | *Custom Whls/Cvrs +135*
Leather Seats +160
Pwr Locks(Std GT,STE) +60
Pwr Seat(Std GT,STE) +100
Pwr Sunroof +350
Pwr Wndw(Std GT,STE) +100
Tilt Whl(Std GT,STE) +60

LE MANS 4 Cyl 1991

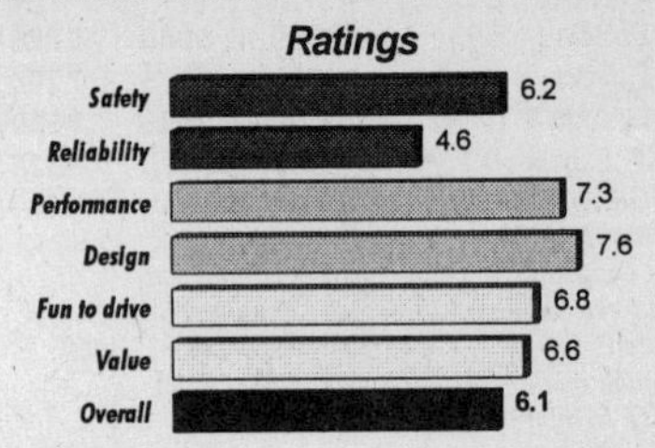

FWD/AT/PS/AC

Model/Body/Type	BaseList	Whlse	Retail
3 Dr Aerocoupe (4 spd)	7574	**2300**	**3425**
3 Dr LE Aerocoupe	8304	**3325**	**4675**
4 Dr LE Sdn	8754	**3525**	**4850**

ADD FOR 91 LE MANS:

Cass +35 | *Sunroof +115*

DEDUCT FOR 91 LE MANS:

No AC -350 | *No Auto Trans -315*
No Pwr Steering -100

SUNBIRD 1991

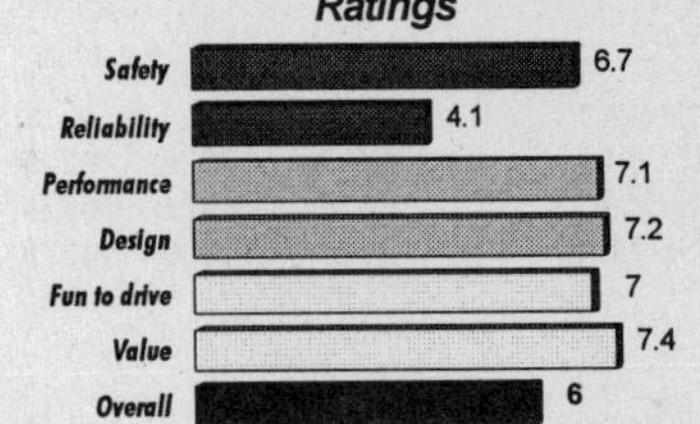

Model/Body/Type	BaseList	Whlse	Retail
FWD/AT/PS/AC			
4 Cyl Models			
4 Dr Sdn	8784	**4350**	**5775**
2 Dr Cpe	8684	**4250**	**5675**
4 Dr LE Sdn	9544	**4850**	**6350**
2 Dr LE Cpe	9444	**4775**	**6250**
2 Dr LE Conv	14414	**7725**	**9575**
2 Dr SE Cpe	10694	**5400**	**6950**
V6 Models			
2 Dr GT Cpe	12444	**7025**	**8775**

ADD FOR 91 SUNBIRD:

Cass(Std GT) +35 — *CD Player +115*
Cruise Ctrl +75 — *Custom Whls/Cvrs +115*
Pwr Locks(Std Cnv) +35 — *Pwr Wndw(Std Cnv) +75*
Sunroof +115 — *Tilt Whl +35*
V6 Eng(Std GT) +275

DEDUCT FOR 91 SUNBIRD:

No AC -390 — *No Auto Trans -350*

TRANS SPORT V6 — 1991

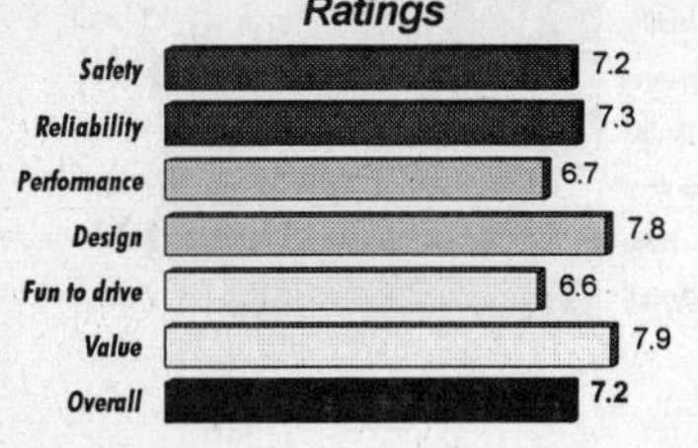

Model/Body/Type	BaseList	Whlse	Retail
FWD/AT/PS/AC			
Wagon	15619	**9675**	**11950**
SE Wagon	18889	**10200**	**12575**

ADD FOR 91 TRANS SPORT:

CD Player +125 — *Custom Whls(Std SE) +105*
Privacy Glass(Std SE) +105
Pwr Seats +80 — *Pwr Wndw +80*
Running Boards +105 — *Sunroof-Manual +80*

DEDUCT FOR 91 TRANS SPORT:

No AC -315

1990 PONTIAC

6000 V6 — 1990

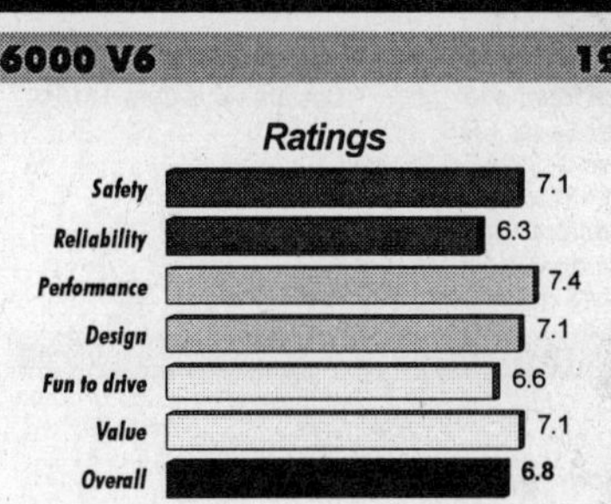

Model/Body/Type	BaseList	Whlse	Retail
FWD/AT/PS/AC			
4 Dr LE Sdn (4 Cyl)	12149	**3600**	**5025**
4 Dr LE Sdn	12809	**4000**	**5525**
4 Dr LE Wgn	15309	**4350**	**5875**
4 Dr SE Sdn	16909	**4850**	**6525**
4 Dr SE Wgn	18509	**5200**	**6900**

ADD FOR 90 6000:

All Whl Drive +1035 — *Cass(Std SE) +60*
CD Player +115 — *Cruise Ctrl(Std SE) +75*
Custom Paint +25 — *Custom Whls/Cvrs +115*
Pwr Locks(Std SE) +60 — *Pwr Seat +75*
Pwr Wndw(Std SE) +75 — *Tilt Whl(Std SE) +60*
Woodgrain +100

DEDUCT FOR 90 6000:

No AC -430

BONNEVILLE V6 — 1990

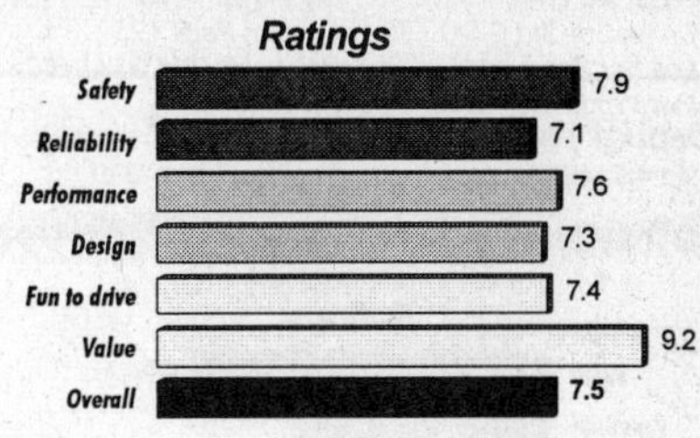

Model/Body/Type	BaseList	Whlse	Retail
FWD/AT/PS/AC			
4 Dr LE Sdn	15774	**5675**	**7500**
4 Dr SE Sdn	19144	**6850**	**8800**
4 Dr SSE Sdn	23994	**9700**	**11925**

Model/Body/Type	BaseList	Whlse	Retail

ADD FOR 90 BONNEVILLE:
ABS(Std SSE) +275 *Cass(Std SE,SSE) +75*
CD Player +115
Cruise Ctrl(Std SE,SSE) +100
Custom Paint +35 *Custom Whls/Cvrs +115*
Leather Seats +135
Pwr Locks(Std SE,SSE) +60
Pwr Seat(Std SE,SSE) +100
Pwr Sunroof +350
Pwr Wndw(Std SE,SSE) +100
Tilt Whl(Std SE,SSE) +60

FIREBIRD V8 1990

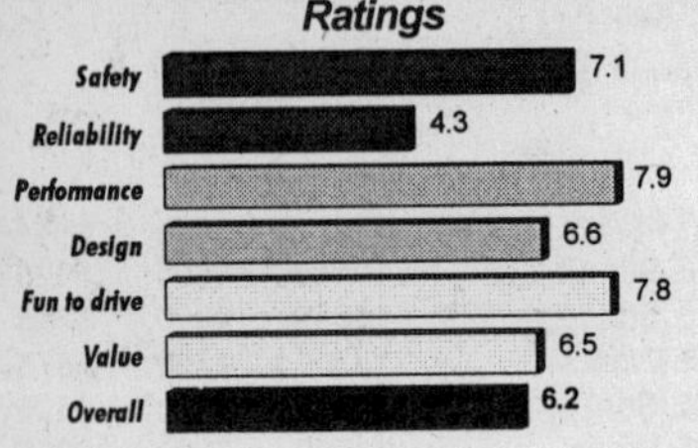

AT/PS/AC

Model/Body/Type	BaseList	Whlse	Retail
2 Dr Cpe (V6)	11320	**6150**	**7875**
2 Dr Cpe	11670	**6550**	**8325**
2 Dr Formula Cpe	14610	**7200**	**9075**
2 Dr Trans Am Cpe	16510	**8950**	**10950**
2 Dr GTA Cpe	23320	**11100**	**13450**

ADD FOR 90 FIREBIRD:
5.7L V8 Eng(Std GTA) +470
Cass(Std GTA) +60 *CD Player +115*
CruiseCtrl(Std GTA) +75 *Custom Paint +25*
Leather Seats +115 *Pwr Locks(Std GTA) +60*
Pwr Wndw(Std GTA) +75 *T-Top +470*
DEDUCT FOR 90 FIREBIRD:
No AC -430 *No Auto Trans -390*

GRAND AM 1990

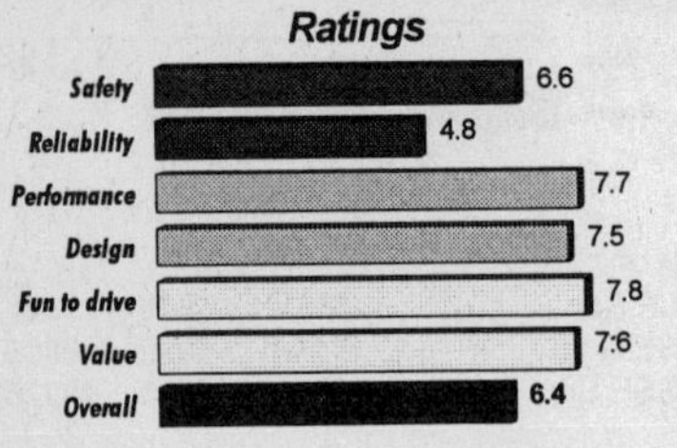

FWD/AT/PS/AC

Model/Body/Type	BaseList	Whlse	Retail
4 Cyl Models			
4 Dr LE Sdn	10744	**4650**	**6225**
2 Dr LE Cpe	10544	**4650**	**6225**
Quad 4 Models			
4 Dr SE Sdn	15194	**5825**	**7525**
2 Dr SE Cpe	14894	**5825**	**7525**

ADD FOR 90 GRAND AM:
Cass(Std SE) +60 *CD Player +115*
Cruise Ctrl(Std SE) +75 *Custom Paint +25*
Custom Whls/Cvrs +115 *Pwr Locks(Std SE) +60*
Pwr Seat +75 *Pwr Wndw(Std SE) +75*
Quad 4 Eng(Std SE) +230 *Sunroof +115*
Tilt Whl(Std SE) +60
DEDUCT FOR 90 GRAND AM:
No AC -430 *No Auto Trans -390*

GRAND PRIX 1990

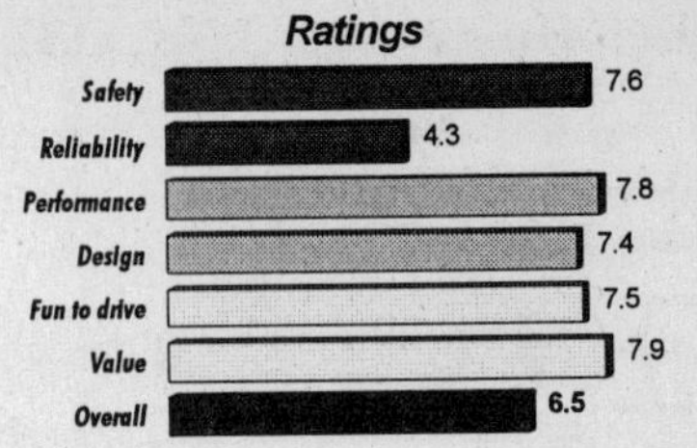

FWD/AT/PS/AC

Model/Body/Type	BaseList	Whlse	Retail
Quad 4 Models			
4 Dr LE Sdn	14564	**5150**	**6850**
2 Dr LE Cpe	14564	**5150**	**6850**
V6 Models			
4 Dr LE Sdn	14564	**5350**	**7075**
2 Dr LE Cpe	14564	**5350**	**7075**
4 Dr STE Sdn	18539	**7500**	**9400**
2 Dr SE Cpe	17684	**6850**	**8675**

ADD FOR 90 GRAND PRIX:
ABS +270 *Cass(Std SE,STE) +60*
CD Player +115
Cruise Ctrl(Std SE,STE) +75
Custom Paint +25 *Custom Whls/Cvrs +115*
Leather Seats +115
Pwr Locks(Std SE,STE) +60
Pwr Seat(Std SE,STE) +75
Pwr Sunroof +315
Pwr Wndw(Std SE,STE) +75
Tilt Whl(Std SE,STE) +60
Turbo Eng Pkg +800
DEDUCT FOR 90 GRAND PRIX:
No Auto Trans -390

Model/Body/Type | BaseList | Whlse | Retail

LE MANS 4 Cyl — 1990

Ratings

Rating	Score
Safety	6.2
Reliability	4.6
Performance	7.3
Design	7.6
Fun to drive	6.8
Value	6.6
Overall	6.1

FWD/AT/PS/AC	BaseList	Whlse	Retail
3 Dr Aerocoupe (4 spd)	7254	**1525**	**2475**
3 Dr LE Aerocoupe	8554	**2400**	**3550**
3 Dr GSE Aerocoupe	10764	**3075**	**4350**
4 Dr LE Sdn	8904	**2600**	**3750**

ADD FOR 90 LE MANS:
Cass +35 *Sunroof +100*

DEDUCT FOR 90 LE MANS:
No AC -315 *No Auto Trans -275*
No Pwr Steering -75

SUNBIRD 4 Cyl — 1990

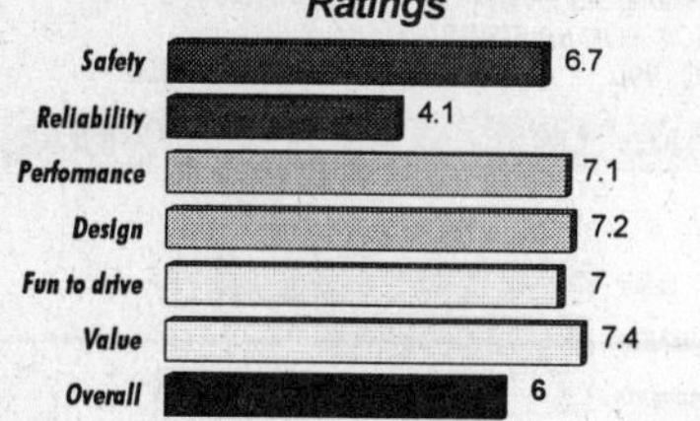

FWD/AT/PS/AC	BaseList	Whlse	Retail
4 Dr VL Sdn	7958	**3250**	**4575**
2 Dr VL Cpe	7858	**3175**	**4475**
4 Dr LE Sdn	8899	**3725**	**5050**
2 Dr LE Cpe	8799	**3625**	**4950**
2 Dr LE Conv	13924	**6425**	**8025**
2 Dr SE Cpe	9204	**3950**	**5300**
2 Dr GT Turbo Cpe	11724	**5675**	**7175**

ADD FOR 90 SUNBIRD:
4 Cyl Turbo Engine(Std GT) +215
Cass(Std GT) +35 *CD Player +75*
Cruise Ctrl +60 *Custom Whls/Cvrs +75*
Pwr Locks(Std Cnv) +35 *Pwr Wndw(Std Cnv) +60*
Sunroof +100 *Tilt Whl +35*

DEDUCT FOR 90 SUNBIRD:
No AC -350 *No Auto Trans -315*
No Pwr Steering -100

TRANS SPORT V6 — 1990

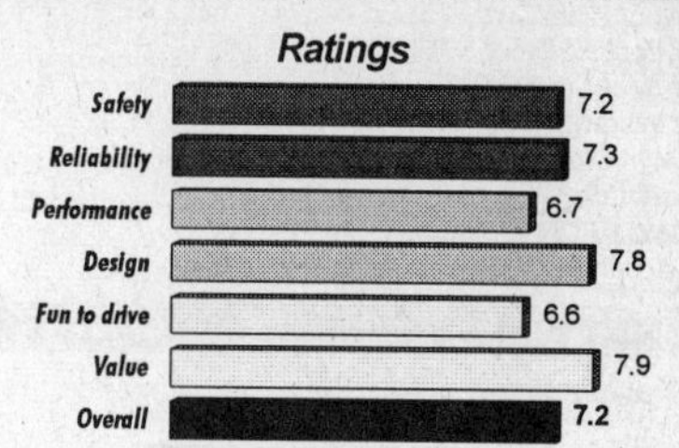

FWD/AT/PS/AC	BaseList	Whlse	Retail
Wagon	15495	**8150**	**10225**
SE Wagon	18625	**8550**	**10650**

ADD FOR 90 TRANS SPORT:
CD Player +80 *Custom Whls(Std SE) +80*
Privacy Glass(Std SE) +80
Running Boards +80

DEDUCT FOR 90 TRANS SPORT:
No AC -250

1989 PONTIAC

6000 V6 — 1989

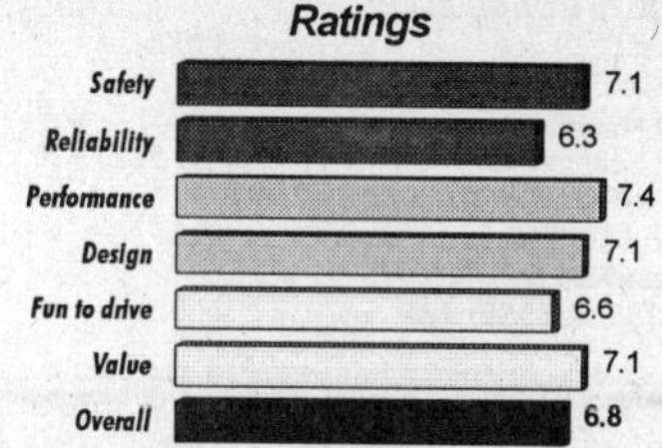

Model/Body/Type	BaseList	Whlse	Retail
FWD/AT/PS/AC			
4 Dr LE Sdn (4 Cyl)	11969	**2875**	**4225**
4 Dr LE Sdn	12579	**3225**	**4625**
4 Dr LE Wgn	13769	**3500**	**4900**
4 Dr SE Sdn	15399	**3900**	**5375**
4 Dr SE Wgn	16699	**3900**	**5375**
4 Dr STE AWD Sdn	22599	**4200**	**5725**

ADD FOR 89 6000:

Cass(Std SE,STE) +35 *CD Player +75*
Cruise Ctrl(Std SE,STE) +60
Custom Whls/Cvrs +75
Pwr Locks(Std SE,STE) +35
Pwr Seat(Std SE,STE) +60
Pwr Wndw(Std SE,STE) +60
Tilt Whl(Std SE,STE) +35
Woodgrain +75

DEDUCT FOR 89 6000:

No AC -390

BONNEVILLE V6 1989

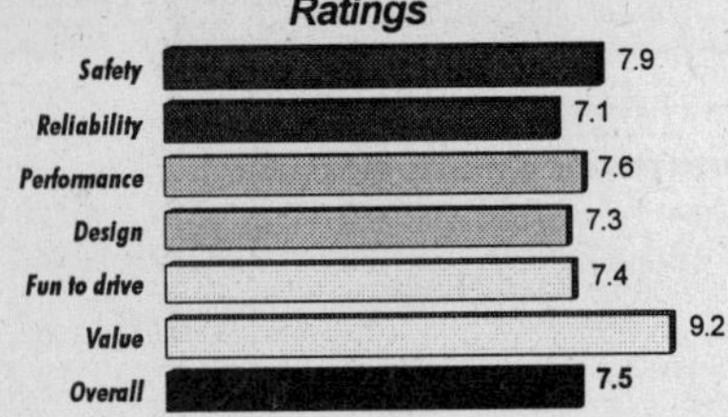

Model/Body/Type	BaseList	Whlse	Retail
FWD/AT/PS/AC			
4 Dr LE Sdn	14829	**4450**	**6150**
4 Dr SE Sdn	17199	**5400**	**7250**
4 Dr SSE Sdn	22899	**7650**	**9700**

ADD FOR 89 BONNEVILLE:

Cass(Std SSE) +60 *CD Player +100*
Cruise Ctrl(Std SE,SSE) +75
Custom Whls/Cvrs +75
Leather Seats +115 *Pwr Locks(Std SSE) +35*
Pwr Seat(Std SE,SSE) +75
Pwr Sunroof +290
Pwr Wndw(Std SE,SSE) +75
Tilt Whl(Std SE,SSE) +35

See the Automobile Dealer Directory on page 379 for a Dealer near you!

FIREBIRD 1989

Ratings

Safety 7.1
Reliability 4.3
Performance 7.9
Design 6.6
Fun to drive 7.8
Value 6.5
Overall 6.2

Model/Body/Type	BaseList	Whlse	Retail
AT/PS/AC			
V6 Models			
2 Dr Cpe	11999	**4650**	**6225**
V8 Models			
2 Dr Cpe	12399	**4975**	**6650**
2 Dr Formula Cpe	13949	**5575**	**7250**
2 Dr Trans Am Cpe	15999	**7175**	**9050**
2 Dr GTA Cpe	20339	**9125**	**11150**

ADD FOR 89 FIREBIRD:

5.7L V8Eng(Std GTA) +430 *Cass(Std GTA) +35*
CD Player +75 *Cruise Ctrl(Std GTA) +60*
Leather Seats +75 *Pwr Locks(Std GTA) +35*
Pwr Wndw(Std GTA) +60 *T-Top +410*

DEDUCT FOR 89 FIREBIRD:

No AC -390 *No Auto Trans -350*

GRAND AM 4 Cyl 1989

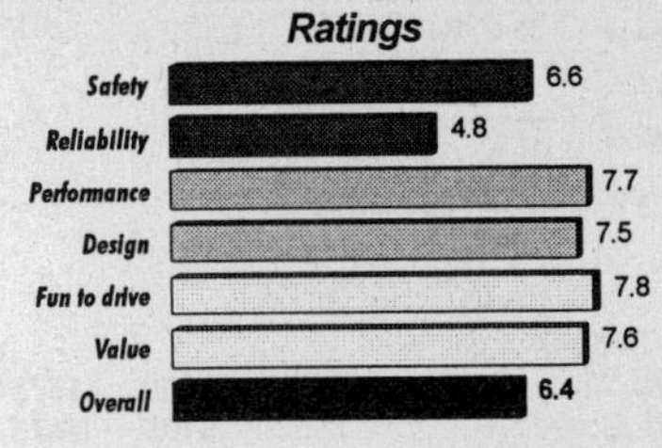

Model/Body/Type	BaseList	Whlse	Retail
FWD/AT/PS/AC			
4 Dr LE Sdn	10669	**3525**	**4950**
2 Dr LE Cpe	10469	**3525**	**4950**
4 Dr SE Turbo Sdn	13799	**4525**	**6125**
2 Dr SE Turbo Cpe	13599	**4525**	**6125**

Model/Body/Type	BaseList	Whlse	Retail

ADD FOR 89 GRAND AM:

Cass(Std SE) +35
Cruise Ctrl(Std SE) +60
Pwr Locks(Std SE) +35
Pwr Wndw +60
Sunroof +100
CD Player +75
Custom Whls/Cvrs +75
Pwr Seat +60
Quad 4 Eng +215
Tilt Whl(Std SE) +35

DEDUCT FOR 89 GRAND AM:

No AC -390
No Auto Trans -350

GRAND PRIX V6 — 1989

Ratings

Rating	Score
Safety	7.6
Reliability	4.3
Performance	7.8
Design	7.4
Fun to drive	7.5
Value	7.9
Overall	6.5

FWD/AT/PS/AC

Model/Body/Type	BaseList	Whlse	Retail
2 Dr Cpe	13899	**4225**	**5775**
2 Dr LE Cpe	14849	**4750**	**6375**
2 Dr SE Cpe	15999	**5650**	**7300**

ADD FOR 89 GRAND PRIX:

Cass +35
Custom Whls/Cvrs +75
Pwr Locks +35
Pwr Sunroof +250
Pwr Wndw(Std LE,SE) +60
Tilt Whl(Std SE) +35
Cruise Ctrl(Std SE) +60
Leather Seats +75
Pwr Seat +60

DEDUCT FOR 89 GRAND PRIX:

No Auto Trans -350

LE MANS 4 Cyl — 1989

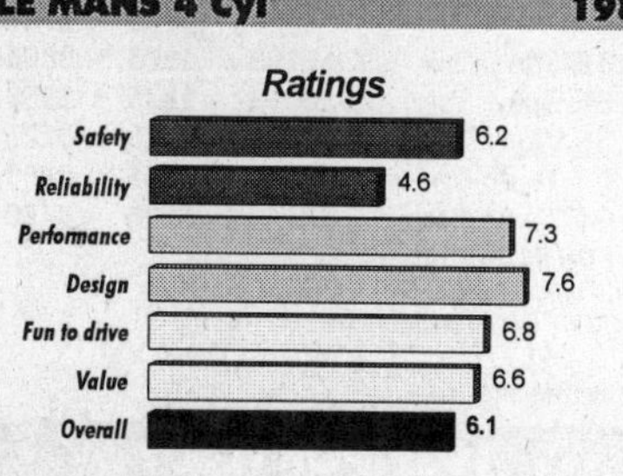

FWD/AT/PS/AC

Model/Body/Type	BaseList	Whlse	Retail
3 Dr Aerocoupe (4 spd)	6399	**650**	**1450**
3 Dr LE Aerocoupe	7699	**1400**	**2350**
3 Dr GSE Aerocoupe	9149	**1850**	**2925**
4 Dr LE Sdn	7999	**1600**	**2575**
4 Dr SE Sdn	9429	**2000**	**3100**

ADD FOR 89 LE MANS:

Cass +25
Sunroof +75
Cruise Ctrl +35

DEDUCT FOR 89 LE MANS:

No AC -275
No Auto Trans -230

SAFARI V8 — 1989

AT/PS/AC

Model/Body/Type	BaseList	Whlse	Retail
4 Dr Wgn	15659	**4150**	**5825**

ADD FOR 89 SAFARI:

Cass +60
Custom Whls/Cvrs +75
Pwr Locks +35
Pwr Wndw +75
Woodgrain +100
Cruise Ctrl +75
Luggage Rack +25
Pwr Seat +75
Tilt Whl +35

SUNBIRD 4 Cyl — 1989

Ratings

Rating	Score
Safety	6.7
Reliability	4.1
Performance	7.1
Design	7.2
Fun to drive	7
Value	7.4
Overall	6

FWD/AT/PS/AC

Model/Body/Type	BaseList	Whlse	Retail
4 Dr LE Sdn	8949	**2825**	**4075**
2 Dr LE Cpe	8849	**2725**	**3900**
2 Dr SE Cpe	9099	**2925**	**4175**
2 Dr GT Turbo Cpe	11399	**4400**	**5825**
2 Dr GT Turbo Conv	16899	**6675**	**8425**

ADD FOR 89 SUNBIRD:

4 Cyl Turbo Engine(Std GT) +195
Cass +25
Cruise Ctrl +35
Pwr Locks(Std Cnv) +25
Sunroof +75
CD Player +60
Custom Whls/Cvrs +35
Pwr Wndw(Std Cnv) +35
Tilt Whl +25

DEDUCT FOR 89 SUNBIRD:

No AC -315
No Pwr Steering -75
No Auto Trans -275

1988 PONTIAC

6000 — 1988

FWD/AT/PS/AC

Model/Body/Type	BaseList	Whlse	Retail
4 Cyl Models			
4 Dr Sdn	11199	**1775**	**2925**
4 Dr Safari Wgn	11639	**2025**	**3175**
4 Dr LE Sdn	11839	**2150**	**3300**
4 Dr LE Safari Wgn	12299	**2350**	**3575**
V6 Models			
4 Dr Sdn	11809	**2125**	**3275**
4 Dr Safari Wgn	12249	**2325**	**3550**
4 Dr LE Sdn	12449	**2450**	**3700**
4 Dr LE Safari Wgn	12909	**2700**	**3975**
4 Dr SE Sdn	12739	**2725**	**4000**
4 Dr SE Safari Wgn	13639	**2975**	**4325**
4 Dr STE Sdn	18699	**4525**	**6125**

DEDUCT FOR 88 6000:
No AC -330 *No Auto Trans -290*

BONNEVILLE V6 — 1988

FWD/AT/PS/AC

Model/Body/Type	BaseList	Whlse	Retail
4 Dr LE Sdn	14099	**3000**	**4500**
4 Dr SE Sdn	16299	**3700**	**5300**
4 Dr SSE Sdn	21879	**5925**	**7775**

FIERO — 1988

AT/AC

Model/Body/Type	BaseList	Whlse	Retail
4 Cyl Models			
2 Dr Cpe	8999	**2125**	**3275**
V6 Models			
2 Dr Formula Cpe	10999	**3200**	**4600**
2 Dr GT Cpe	13999	**4375**	**5925**

DEDUCT FOR 88 FIERO:
No AC -330 *No Auto Trans -230*

FIREBIRD — 1988

AT/PS/AC

Model/Body/Type	BaseList	Whlse	Retail
V6 Models			
2 Dr Cpe	10999	**3250**	**4675**
V8 Models			
2 Dr Cpe	11399	**3600**	**5025**
2 Dr Formula Cpe	11999	**4000**	**5525**
2 Dr Trans Am Cpe	13999	**5575**	**7250**
2 Dr GTA Cpe	19299	**7150**	**9025**

ADD FOR 88 FIREBIRD:
5.7L V8 Eng(Std GTA) +390
T-Top +350
DEDUCT FOR 88 FIREBIRD:
No AC -330 *No Auto Trans -290*

GRAND AM 4 Cyl — 1988

FWD/AT/PS/AC

Model/Body/Type	BaseList	Whlse	Retail
4 Dr Sdn	10069	**2200**	**3375**
2 Dr Cpe	9869	**2200**	**3375**
4 Dr LE Sdn	10769	**2525**	**3775**
2 Dr LE Cpe	10569	**2525**	**3775**
4 Dr SE Turbo Sdn	13099	**3150**	**4550**
2 Dr SE Turbo Cpe	12869	**3150**	**4550**

ADD FOR 88 GRAND AM:
4 Cyl Turbo Eng(Std SE) +230
Quad 4 Eng +195
DEDUCT FOR 88 GRAND AM:
No AC -330 *No Auto Trans -290*

GRAND PRIX V6 — 1988

FWD/AT/PS/AC

Model/Body/Type	BaseList	Whlse	Retail
2 Dr Cpe	12539	**3125**	**4525**
2 Dr LE Cpe	13239	**3550**	**4975**
2 Dr SE Cpe	15249	**4300**	**5850**

DEDUCT FOR 88 GRAND PRIX:
No AC -330 *No Auto Trans -290*

LE MANS 4 Cyl — 1988

FWD/AT/PS/AC

Model/Body/Type	BaseList	Whlse	Retail
3 Dr Aerocoupe (4 spd)	5995	**425**	**1250**
3 Dr Aerocoupe	7325	**1075**	**1975**
4 Dr Sdn	7925	**1275**	**2175**
4 Dr SE Sdn	8399	**1525**	**2475**

DEDUCT FOR 88 LE MANS:
No AC -215 *No Auto Trans -195*

SAFARI V8 — 1988

AT/PS/AC

Model/Body/Type	BaseList	Whlse	Retail
4 Dr Wgn	14519	**2850**	**4325**

SUNBIRD 4 Cyl — 1988

FWD/AT/PS/AC

Model/Body/Type	BaseList	Whlse	Retail
4 Dr Sdn	8499	**1725**	**2750**
4 Dr SE Sdn	8799	**1975**	**3050**
2 Dr SE Cpe	8599	**1875**	**2950**
4 Dr SE Wgn	9399	**2150**	**3225**
2 Dr GT Turbo Cpe	10899	**3125**	**4400**
2 Dr GT Turbo Conv	16199	**5225**	**6750**

ADD FOR 88 SUNBIRD:
4 Cyl Turbo Eng(Std GT) +175
DEDUCT FOR 88 SUNBIRD:
No AC -250 *No Auto Trans -230*
No Pwr Steering -60

1987 PONTIAC

1000 4 Cyl — 1987

AT/PS/AC

Model/Body/Type	BaseList	Whlse	Retail
5 Dr Hbk	6099	**850**	**1700**
3 Dr Hbk	5959	**750**	**1575**

6000 V6 — 1987

FWD/AT/PS/AC

Model/Body/Type	BaseList	Whlse	Retail
4 Dr Sdn	11109	**1500**	**2550**
2 Dr Cpe	11109	**1400**	**2450**
4 Dr Safari Wgn	11509	**1700**	**2800**
4 Dr LE Sdn	11709	**1775**	**2925**
4 Dr LE Safari Wgn	12109	**2000**	**3150**
4 Dr SE Sdn	12389	**2075**	**3225**
4 Dr SE Safari Wgn	13049	**2275**	**3475**
4 Dr STE Sdn	18099	**3400**	**4825**

DEDUCT FOR 87 6000:
4 Cyl Engine -250

BONNEVILLE V6 — 1987

FWD/AT/PS/AC

Model/Body/Type	BaseList	Whlse	Retail
4 Dr Sdn	13399	**2425**	**3750**
4 Dr LE Sdn	14866	**3075**	**4575**

ADD FOR 87 BONNEVILLE:
SE Pkg +275

FIERO — 1987

AT/AC

4 Cyl Models

Model/Body/Type	BaseList	Whlse	Retail
2 Dr Cpe	8299	**1300**	**2300**
2 Dr Sport Cpe	9989	**1575**	**2650**
2 Dr SE Cpe	11239	**2125**	**3275**

V6 Models

Model/Body/Type	BaseList	Whlse	Retail
2 Dr GT Cpe	13489	**3450**	**4850**

ADD FOR 87 FIERO:
V6 Eng(Std GT) +275

FIREBIRD V8 — 1987

AT/PS/AC

Model/Body/Type	BaseList	Whlse	Retail
2 Dr Cpe	10759	**2450**	**3700**
2 Dr Formula Cpe	11829	**2800**	**4125**
2 Dr Trans Am Cpe	13259	**3800**	**5275**
2 Dr GTA Cpe	14104	**5300**	**7000**

ADD FOR 87 FIREBIRD:
5.7L V8 Eng(Std GTA) +350
DEDUCT FOR 87 FIREBIRD:
V6 Engine -250

GRAND AM 4 Cyl — 1987

FWD/AT/PS/AC

Model/Body/Type	BaseList	Whlse	Retail
4 Dr Sdn	9499	**1800**	**2950**
2 Dr Cpe	9299	**1800**	**2950**
4 Dr LE Sdn	10199	**2100**	**3250**
2 Dr LE Cpe	9999	**2100**	**3250**
4 Dr SE Sdn	12239	**2675**	**3950**
2 Dr SE Cpe	11999	**2675**	**3950**

ADD FOR 87 GRAND AM:
V6 Engine +215

GRAND PRIX V6 — 1987

FWD/AT/PS/AC

Model/Body/Type	BaseList	Whlse	Retail
2 Dr Cpe	11069	**2275**	**3475**
2 Dr LE Cpe	11799	**2500**	**3750**
2 Dr Brougham Cpe	12519	**2875**	**4225**

ADD FOR 87 GRAND PRIX:
V8 Engine +290

SAFARI V8 — 1987

AT/PS/AC

Model/Body/Type	BaseList	Whlse	Retail
4 Dr Wgn	13959	**2000**	**3250**

SUNBIRD 4 Cyl — 1987

FWD/AT/PS/AC

Model/Body/Type	BaseList	Whlse	Retail
4 Dr Sdn	7999	**1325**	**2275**
4 Dr Safari Wgn	8529	**1450**	**2400**
2 Dr SE Cpe	7979	**1475**	**2425**
3 Dr SE Hbk	8499	**1575**	**2550**
2 Dr SE Conv	13799	**3375**	**4700**
4 Dr GT Turbo Sdn	10349	**2425**	**3575**
2 Dr GT Turbo Cpe	10299	**2325**	**3450**
3 Dr GT Turbo Hbk	10699	**2425**	**3575**
2 Dr GT Turbo Conv	15569	**4250**	**5675**

ADD FOR 87 SUNBIRD:
4 Cyl Turbo Eng(Std GT) +100

1986 PONTIAC

1000 — 1986

Model/Body/Type	BaseList	Whlse	Retail
5 Dr Hbk	5969	**450**	**1378**
3 Dr Hbk	5749	**375**	**1300**

6000 — 1986

FWD

Model/Body/Type	BaseList	Whlse	Retail
4 Dr Sdn	10164	**1175**	**2200**
2 Dr Cpe	9984	**1075**	**2125**
4 Dr Safari Wgn	10530	**1300**	**2350**
4 Dr LE Sdn	10630	**1325**	**2400**
2 Dr LE Cpe	10484	**1275**	**2300**
4 Dr LE Safari Wgn	11014	**1475**	**2575**
4 Dr SE Sdn	11179	**1550**	**2675**
4 Dr SE Safari Wgn	11825	**1700**	**2850**
4 Dr STE Sdn	15949	**2250**	**3475**

BONNEVILLE V6 — 1986

Model/Body/Type	BaseList	Whlse	Retail
4 Dr Sdn	10249	**1275**	**2550**
4 Dr LE Sdn	10529	**1450**	**2775**
4 Dr Brougham Sdn	11079	**1700**	**3075**

FIERO — 1986

Model/Body/Type	BaseList	Whlse	Retail
2 Dr Cpe	8949	**1100**	**2150**
2 Dr Sport Cpe	9449	**1400**	**2500**
2 Dr SE Cpe	10595	**1775**	**2975**
2 Dr GT Cpe	12875	**2450**	**3725**

Model/Body/Type	BaseList	Whlse	Retail
FIREBIRD			**1986**
2 Dr Cpe	10029	2125	3300
2 Dr SE Cpe	12395	2625	3900
2 Dr Trans Am Cpe	12395	3250	4650
GRAND AM			**1986**
FWD			
4 Dr Sdn	8749	1400	2500
2 Dr Cpe	8549	1400	2500
4 Dr LE Sdn	9279	1625	2750
2 Dr LE Cpe	9079	1625	2750
4 Dr SE Sdn	11749	2175	3350
2 Dr SE Cpe	11499	2175	3350
GRAND PRIX			**1986**
2 Dr Cpe	10259	1675	3050
2 Dr LE Cpe	10795	1850	3250
2 Dr Brougham Cpe	11579	2125	3575
PARISIENNE			**1986**
4 Dr Sdn	11559	1650	3025
4 Dr Brougham Sdn	12339	2025	3450
4 Dr Wgn	11779	1775	3150
SUNBIRD			**1986**
FWD			
4 Dr Sdn	7495	1000	2025
4 Dr Wgn	7879	1075	2125
2 Dr SE Cpe	7469	1100	2150
3 Dr SE Hbk	7829	1200	2225
2 Dr SE Conv	12779	2550	3825
4 Dr GT Turbo Sdn	9499	1700	2825
2 Dr GT Turbo Cpe	9459	1600	2725
3 Dr GT Turbo Hbk	9819	1700	2825
2 Dr GT Turbo Conv	14399	3100	4450

1985 PONTIAC

Model/Body/Type	BaseList	Whlse	Retail
1000			**1985**
5 Dr Hbk	5445	275	1225
3 Dr Hbk	5695	200	1125
6000			**1985**
FWD			
4 Dr Sdn	9514	1025	2050
2 Dr Cpe	9334	925	1950
4 Dr Wgn	9870	1150	2175
4 Dr LE Sdn	9974	1200	2225
2 Dr LE Cpe	9820	1100	2150
4 Dr LE Wgn	10304	1300	2350
4 Dr STE Sdn	14829	1850	3050
BONNEVILLE			**1985**
4 Dr Sdn	9549	1025	2275
4 Dr LE Sdn	9789	1200	2450
4 Dr Brougham Sdn	10279	1350	2675
FIERO			**1985**
2 Dr Cpe	8495	925	1925
2 Dr Sport Cpe	8995	1225	2275
2 Dr SE Cpe	9995	1525	2625
2 Dr GT Cpe	11795	2175	3375
FIREBIRD			**1985**
2 Dr Cpe	9357	1675	2800
2 Dr SE Cpe	12015	2125	3300
2 Dr Trans Am Cpe	11079	2650	3950
GRAND AM			**1985**
FWD			
2 Dr Cpe	7995	1225	2275
2 Dr LE Cpe	8485	1375	2450
GRAND PRIX			**1985**
2 Dr Cpe	9569	1125	2350
2 Dr LE Cpe	10049	1275	2550
2 Dr Brougham Cpe	10749	1500	2850
PARISIENNE			**1985**
4 Dr Sdn	10635	1325	2650
4 Dr Brougham Sdn	11365	1675	3050
4 Dr Wgn	10945	1450	2775
SUNBIRD			**1985**
FWD			
4 Dr Sdn	6995	850	1800
2 Dr Cpe	6875	775	1725
3 Dr Hbk	7215	850	1800
4 Dr Wgn	7335	900	1875
4 Dr LE Sdn	7725	1000	2025
2 Dr LE Cpe	7555	925	1925
2 Dr LE Conv	12035	2125	3300
4 Dr LE Wgn	8055	1075	2100
4 Dr SE Sdn	9455	1300	2350
2 Dr SE Cpe	9285	1225	2275
3 Dr SE Hbk	9765	1300	2350

Model/Body/Type	BaseList	Whlse	Retail

PORSCHE
Germany

1990 Porsche 928

For an Porsche dealer in your area, see our Dealer Directory (pg 217)

1994 PORSCHE

Model/Body/Type	BaseList	Whlse	Retail
968 4 Cyl			**1994**
AC			
2 Dr Cpe	39950	-	-
2 Dr Cabriolet	51900	-	-
911 6 Cyl			**1994**
AC			
2 Dr Carrera 2 Cpe	64990	-	-
2 Dr Carrera 2 Targa	66600	-	-
2 Dr Carrera 2 Cabriolet	74190	-	-
2 Dr Carrera 4 Cpe	78450	-	-
928 GTS V8			**1994**
AC			
2 Dr Cpe	82260	-	-

ADD FOR ALL 94 PORSCHE:
Anti-Theft/Recovery Sys
Car Phone
CD Player
Leather Seats(Std 928)
Tiptronic Trans

1993 PORSCHE

Model/Body/Type	BaseList	Whlse	Retail
968 4 Cyl			**1993**
AC			
2 Dr Cpe	39950	**28775**	**32850**
2 Dr Cabriolet	51900	**34650**	**38600**
911 6 Cyl			**1993**
AC			
2 Dr Carrera 2 Cpe	64990	**45050**	**49325**
2 Dr Carrera 2 Targa	66600	**46000**	**50325**
2 Dr Carrera 2 Cabriolet	74190	**50800**	**56375**
2 Dr Carrera 4 Cpe	77050	**50200**	**55750**
2 Dr Carrera 4 Targa	78660	**51150**	**56750**
2 Dr Carrera 4 Cabriolet	86250	**56900**	**60825**
2 Dr RS America Cpe	53900	-	-
2 Dr America Rdstr	89350	-	-
928 GTS V8			**1993**
AC			
2 Dr Cpe	82260	**55450**	**59275**

ADD FOR ALL 93 PORSCHE:
Car Phone +175
CD Player +290
Leather Seats +470
Tiptronic Trans +860

1992 PORSCHE

Model/Body/Type	BaseList	Whlse	Retail
968 4 Cyl			**1992**
AC			
2 Dr Cpe	39850	**26450**	**30450**
2 Dr Cabriolet	51000	**32050**	**36225**
911 6 Cyl			**1992**
AC			
2 Dr Carrera 2 Cpe	63900	**43000**	**47775**
2 Dr Carrera 2 Targa	65500	**43700**	**48200**
2 Dr Carrera 2 Cabriolet	72900	**48325**	**53275**
2 Dr Carrera 4 Cpe	75780	**47625**	**52525**
2 Dr Carrera 4 Targa	77380	**48475**	**53425**
2 Dr Carrera 4 Cabriolet	84780	**53250**	**57975**

ADD FOR ALL 92 PORSCHE:
Car Phone +160
CD Player +250
Leather Seats +410
Tiptronic Trans +780

Model/Body/Type	BaseList	Whlse	Retail

1991 PORSCHE

911 6 Cyl — 1991

AC

Model/Body/Type	BaseList	Whlse	Retail
2 Dr Carrera 2 Cpe	60700	37350	41850
2 Dr Carrera 2 Targa	62200	38125	42675
2 Dr Carrera 2 Cabriolet	69300	42900	47675
2 Dr Carrera 4 Cpe	72000	42300	47050
2 Dr Carrera 4 Targa	73500	43075	47875
2 Dr Carrera 4 Cabriolet	80600	47800	52225

928 S4 V8 — 1991

AC

Model/Body/Type	BaseList	Whlse	Retail
2 Dr Cpe	77500	38300	42850

944 S2 4 Cyl — 1991

AC

Model/Body/Type	BaseList	Whlse	Retail
2 Dr Cpe	43350	19850	23325
2 Dr Cabriolet	50350	23650	27400

ADD FOR ALL 91 PORSCHE:

Car Phone +135
CD Player +195
Leather Seats(Std 928) +350
Tiptronic Trans +745

1990 PORSCHE

911 6 Cyl — 1990

AC

Model/Body/Type	BaseList	Whlse	Retail
2 Dr Carrera 2 Cpe	58500	32150	36375
2 Dr Carrera 2 Targa	59900	32650	36875
2 Dr Carrera 2 Cabriolet	66800	37050	41550
2 Dr Carrera 4 Cpe	69500	36600	40800
2 Dr Carrera 4 Targa	70900	37050	41550
2 Dr Carrera 4 Cabriolet	77800	41700	46400

928 S4 V8 — 1990

AC

Model/Body/Type	BaseList	Whlse	Retail
2 Dr Cpe	74545	32150	36375

944 S2 4 Cyl — 1990

AC

Model/Body/Type	BaseList	Whlse	Retail
2 Dr Cpe	41900	16700	19850
2 Dr Cabriolet	48600	20175	23650

ADD FOR ALL 90 PORSCHE:

CD Player +135
Leather Seats(Std 928) +290

1989 PORSCHE

911 6 Cyl — 1989

AC

Model/Body/Type	BaseList	Whlse	Retail
2 Dr Carrera Cpe	51205	25875	29775
2 Dr Carrera Targa	52435	26525	30525
2 Dr Carrera Cabriolet	59200	30525	34525

928 S4 V8 — 1989

AC

Model/Body/Type	BaseList	Whlse	Retail
2 Dr Cpe	74545	25250	29125

944 4 Cyl — 1989

AC

Model/Body/Type	BaseList	Whlse	Retail
2 Dr Cpe	36360	11475	14250
2 Dr Turbo Cpe	47600	15300	18350
2 Dr S2 Cpe	45285	13150	16050

ADD FOR ALL 89 PORSCHE:

CD Player +100
Leather Seats(Std 928) +250

1988 PORSCHE

911 6 Cyl — 1988

AC

Model/Body/Type	BaseList	Whlse	Retail
2 Dr Carrera Cpe	42730	21950	25575
2 Dr Carrera Targa	44930	22550	26225
2 Dr Carrera Cabriolet	49325	26300	30225

924 S 4 Cyl — 1988

AC

Model/Body/Type	BaseList	Whlse	Retail
2 Dr Cpe	24935	4775	6650

928 S4 V8 — 1988

AC

Model/Body/Type	BaseList	Whlse	Retail
2 Dr Cpe	65400	20025	23500

944 4 Cyl — 1988

AC

Model/Body/Type	BaseList	Whlse	Retail
2 Dr Cpe	29100	8750	11050
2 Dr S Cpe	34580	10025	12625
2 Dr Turbo Cpe	37335	11800	14625

See the Automobile Dealer Directory on page 379 for a Dealer near you!

Model/Body/Type	BaseList	Whlse	Retail

1987 PORSCHE

911 6 Cyl			1987
AC			
2 Dr Carrera Cpe	38500	19725	23150
2 Dr Carrera Targa	40500	20275	23750
2 Dr Carrera Cabriolet	44500	23800	27550

924 S 4 Cyl			1987
AC			
2 Dr Cpe	19900	3675	5325

928 S4 V8			1987
AC			
2 Dr Cpe	58900	17100	20325

944 4 Cyl			1987
AC			
2 Dr Cpe	25500	6850	9000
2 Dr S Cpe	28250	7475	9700
2 Dr Turbo Cpe	33250	9625	12000

1986 PORSCHE

911			1986
2 Dr Carrera Cpe	31950	18675	21425
2 Dr Carrera Targa	33450	19175	21925
2 Dr Carrera Cabriolet	36450	22200	25100

928 S			1986
2 Dr Cpe	50000	13425	15850

944			1986
2 Dr Cpe	22950	6000	7950
2 Dr Turbo Cpe	29500	8275	10350

1985 PORSCHE

911			1985
2 Dr Carrera Cpe	31950	17500	20175
2 Dr Carrera Targa	33450	17925	20625
2 Dr Carrera Cabriolet	36450	20900	23750

928 S			1985
2 Dr Cpe	50000	12100	14500

944			1985
2 Dr Cpe	21440	5050	7000

SAAB Sweden

1991 Saab 900 Turbo Convertible

For a Saab dealer in your area, see our Dealer Directory (pg 217)

1994 SAAB

900 4 Cyl 1994

FWD/AT/PS/AC

Model/Body/Type	BaseList	Whlse	Retail
3 Dr S Hbk	22290	-	-
5 Dr S Sdn	20990	-	-
3 Dr SE Turbo Sdn	27280	-	-
5 Dr SE Sdn	25460	-	-
2 Dr S Conv	33275	-	-
2 Dr Turbo Conv	38415	-	-

9000 4 Cyl 1994

FWD/AT/PS/AC

Model/Body/Type	BaseList	Whlse	Retail
5 Dr CS Sdn	28725	-	-
5 Dr CS Turbo Sdn	31780	-	-
4 Dr CDE Turbo Sdn	36685	-	-
5 Dr CSE Sdn	33045	-	-
5 Dr CSE Turbo Sdn	36100	-	-
5 Dr Aero Turbo Sdn	38690	-	-

ADD FOR ALL 94 SAAB:

Anti-Theft/Recovery Sys
Car Phone
Leather Seats(900S,9000CS)
Pwr Seats(900S)
Pwr Sunroof(900S)
V6 Engine(900S)

DEDUCT FOR ALL 94 SAAB:

No Auto Trans

1993 SAAB

900 4 Cyl 1993

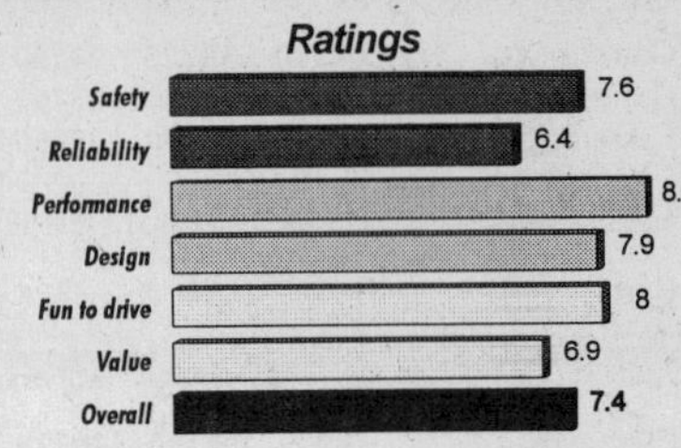

FWD/AT/PS/AC

Model/Body/Type	BaseList	Whlse	Retail
3 Dr S Hbk	20345	**15800**	**18600**
4 Dr S Sdn	20960	**15900**	**18700**
2 Dr S Conv	32160	**19900**	**23375**
3 Dr Turbo Hbk	30555	**21675**	**24950**
2 Dr Turbo Conv	37060	**22800**	**26500**

9000 4 Cyl 1993

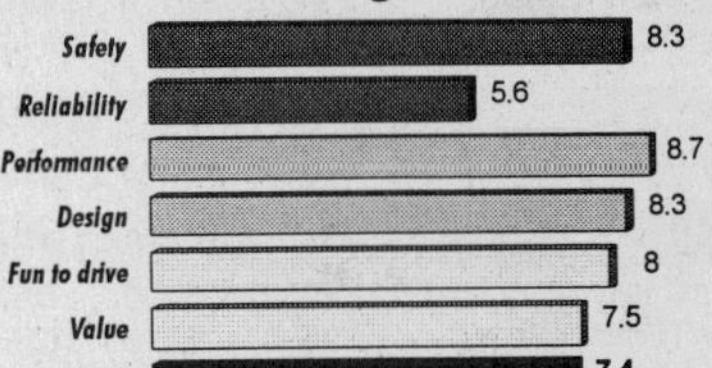

FWD/AT/PS/AC

Model/Body/Type	BaseList	Whlse	Retail
4 Dr CD Sdn	24825	**18200**	**21525**
4 Dr CD Turbo Sdn	28820	**20625**	**24125**
5 Dr CS Sdn	25725	**18400**	**21750**
5 Dr CS Turbo Sdn	29720	**20825**	**24325**
4 Dr CDE Sdn	30830	**19850**	**23325**
4 Dr CDE Turbo Sdn	34825	**22300**	**25950**
5 Dr CSE Sdn	31060	**20050**	**23525**
5 Dr CSE Turbo Sdn	35055	**22500**	**26175**

ADD FOR ALL 93 SAAB:

Car Phone +175
Leather Seats(900S,9000CD/CS) +315
Pwr Seats(9000CD/CS) +175
Pwr Sunroof(900S,9000CD/CS) +505

DEDUCT FOR ALL 93 SAAB:

No Auto Trans -545

SAAB

Model/Body/Type	BaseList	Whlse	Retail

1992 SAAB

900 4 Cyl 1992

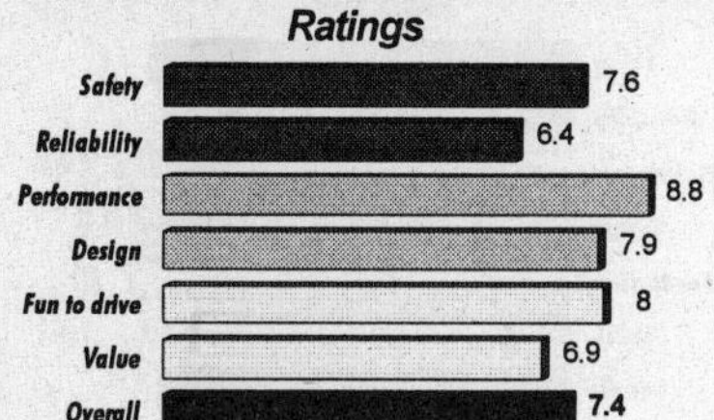

FWD/AT/PS/AC			
3 Dr Hbk	19395	**11475**	**13950**
4 Dr Sdn	19995	**11575**	**14050**
3 Dr S Hbk	23395	**13550**	**16200**
4 Dr S Sdn	23995	**13650**	**16325**
2 Dr S Conv	30595	**17950**	**21275**
3 Dr Turbo Hbk	28645	**16650**	**19600**
2 Dr Turbo Conv	35345	**20625**	**24125**

9000 4 Cyl 1992

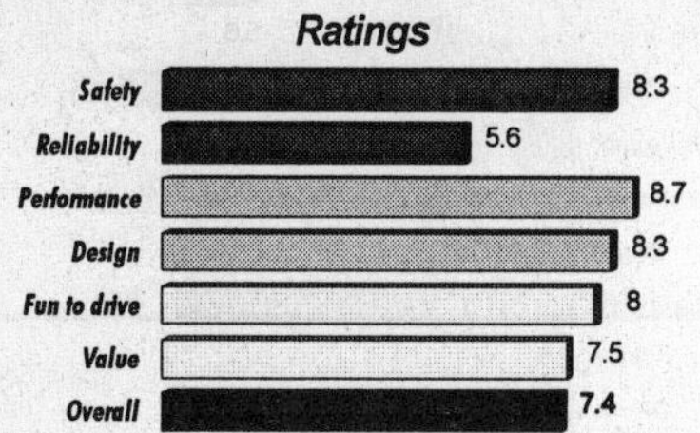

FWD/AT/PS/AC			
5 Dr Sdn	24845	**14425**	**17350**
5 Dr S Sdn	28095	**15975**	**19075**
4 Dr CD Sdn	30195	**16300**	**19425**
5 Dr Turbo Sdn	36045	**19875**	**23350**
4 Dr CD Turbo Sdn	36695	**20375**	**23850**

ADD FOR ALL 92 SAAB:
Car Phone +160
DEDUCT FOR ALL 92 SAAB:
No Auto Trans -505

1991 SAAB

900 4 Cyl 1991

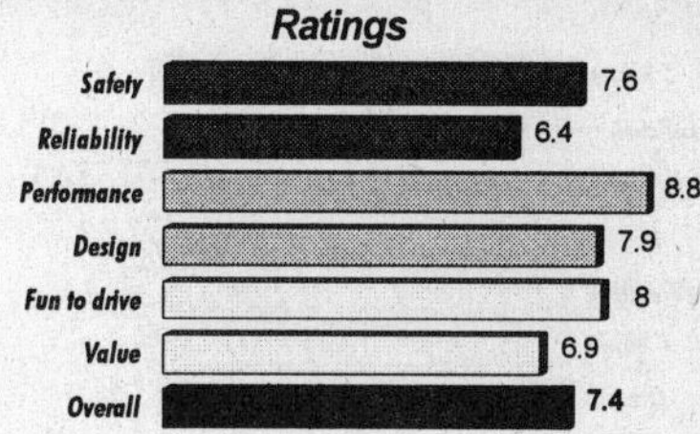

FWD/AT/PS/AC			
3 Dr Hbk	18295	**9275**	**11375**
4 Dr Sdn	18815	**9375**	**11500**
3 Dr S Hbk	22445	**11175**	**13625**
4 Dr S Sdn	22995	**11275**	**13725**
2 Dr S Conv	28295	**15525**	**18600**
3 Dr Turbo Hbk	26295	**13400**	**16050**
2 Dr Turbo Conv	33295	**17925**	**21250**

9000 4 Cyl 1991

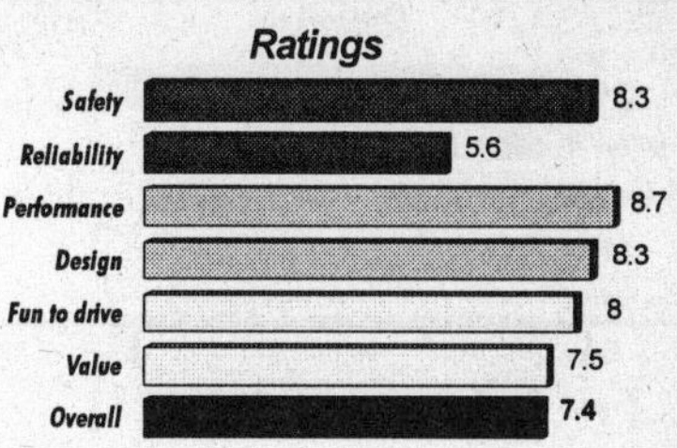

FWD/AT/PS/AC			
5 Dr Sdn	22895	**10725**	**13450**
5 Dr S Sdn	26995	**11925**	**14725**
4 Dr CD Sdn	28995	**12300**	**15125**
5 Dr Turbo Sdn	32995	**15350**	**18400**
4 Dr CD Turbo Sdn	33995	**15675**	**18750**

ADD FOR ALL 91 SAAB:
Car Phone +135
SPG Pkg +780
DEDUCT FOR ALL 91 SAAB:
No Auto Trans -470

SAAB 90-89

1990 SAAB

900 4 Cyl — 1990

Ratings

Safety	7.6
Reliability	6.4
Performance	8.8
Design	7.9
Fun to drive	8
Value	6.9
Overall	7.4

FWD/AT/PS/AC

Model/Body/Type	BaseList	Whlse	Retail
3 Dr Hbk	16995	**7500**	**9525**
4 Dr Sdn	17515	**7600**	**9650**
3 Dr S Hbk	20995	**9200**	**11300**
4 Dr S Sdn	21545	**9300**	**11425**
3 Dr Turbo Hbk	25495	**11125**	**13575**
4 Dr Turbo Sdn	26045	**11225**	**13675**
2 Dr Turbo Conv	32995	**14775**	**17750**

9000 4 Cyl — 1990

Ratings

Safety	8.3
Reliability	5.6
Performance	8.7
Design	8.3
Fun to drive	8
Value	7.5
Overall	7.4

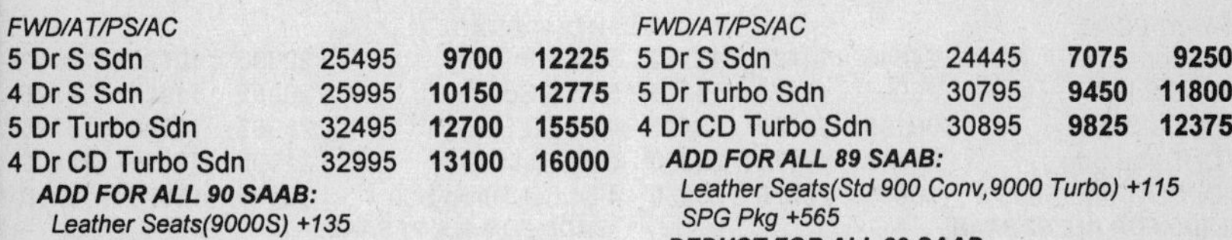

FWD/AT/PS/AC

Model/Body/Type	BaseList	Whlse	Retail
5 Dr S Sdn	25495	**9700**	**12225**
4 Dr S Sdn	25995	**10150**	**12775**
5 Dr Turbo Sdn	32495	**12700**	**15550**
4 Dr CD Turbo Sdn	32995	**13100**	**16000**

ADD FOR ALL 90 SAAB:
Leather Seats(9000S) +135
SPG Pkg +700

DEDUCT FOR ALL 90 SAAB:
No Auto Trans -430

1989 SAAB

900 4 Cyl — 1989

Ratings

Safety	7.6
Reliability	6.4
Performance	8.8
Design	7.9
Fun to drive	8
Value	6.9
Overall	7.4

FWD/AT/PS/AC

Model/Body/Type	BaseList	Whlse	Retail
3 Dr Hbk	16995	**5650**	**7475**
4 Dr Sdn	17515	**5725**	**7575**
3 Dr S Hbk	19695	**6900**	**8850**
4 Dr S Sdn	20245	**7000**	**8975**
3 Dr Turbo Hbk	23795	**8550**	**10600**
4 Dr Turbo Sdn	24345	**8650**	**10700**
2 Dr Turbo Conv	32095	**12850**	**15725**

9000 4 Cyl — 1989

Ratings

Safety	8.3
Reliability	5.6
Performance	8.7
Design	8.3
Fun to drive	8
Value	7.5
Overall	7.4

FWD/AT/PS/AC

Model/Body/Type	BaseList	Whlse	Retail
5 Dr S Sdn	24445	**7075**	**9250**
5 Dr Turbo Sdn	30795	**9450**	**11800**
4 Dr CD Turbo Sdn	30895	**9825**	**12375**

ADD FOR ALL 89 SAAB:
Leather Seats(Std 900 Conv,9000 Turbo) +115
SPG Pkg +565

DEDUCT FOR ALL 89 SAAB:
No Auto Trans -390

1988 SAAB

Model/Body/Type	BaseList	Whlse	Retail
900 4 Cyl			**1988**
FWD/AT/PS/AC			
3 Dr Hbk	14983	4000	5675
4 Dr Sdn	15471	4100	5775
3 Dr S Hbk	18718	4850	6650
4 Dr S Sdn	19206	4950	6750
3 Dr Turbo Hbk	21995	6125	8000
2 Dr Turbo Conv	29740	10350	13000
9000 4 Cyl			**1988**
FWD/AT/PS/AC			
5 Dr S Sdn	23337	4950	6900
5 Dr Turbo Sdn	28141	6175	8175

ADD FOR ALL 88 SAAB:
SPG Pkg +450
DEDUCT FOR ALL 88 SAAB:
No Auto Trans -350

1987 SAAB

Model/Body/Type	BaseList	Whlse	Retail
900 4 Cyl			**1987**
FWD/AT/PS/AC			
3 Dr Hbk	14115	2700	7050
4 Dr Sdn	14515	2800	4275
3 Dr S Hbk	17585	3250	4800
4 Dr S Sdn	17985	3350	4900
3 Dr Turbo Hbk	20405	4150	5825
2 Dr Turbo Conv	26580	8875	11200
9000 4 Cyl			**1987**
FWD/AT/PS/AC			
5 Dr S Sdn	21805	3750	5425
5 Dr Turbo Sdn	25515	4550	6350

ADD FOR ALL 87 SAAB:
SPG Pkg +350

1986 SAAB

Model/Body/Type	BaseList	Whlse	Retail
900			**1986**
FWD			
3 Dr Hbk	12285	1875	3075
4 Dr Sdn	12685	1975	3150
2 Dr S Sdn	15595	2225	3450
3 Dr S Hbk	15895	2300	3550
4 Dr S Sdn	16295	2400	3650
3 Dr Turbo Hbk	18695	3025	4350
9000			**1986**
FWD			
5 Dr Turbo Sdn	21945	3375	4775

1985 SAAB

Model/Body/Type	BaseList	Whlse	Retail
900			**1985**
3 Dr Hbk	11850	1525	2625
4 Dr Sdn	12170	1600	2725
3 Dr S Hbk	15040	1900	3100
4 Dr S Sdn	15510	2000	3175
3 Dr Turbo Hbk	18150	2475	3750
4 Dr Turbo Sdn	18620	2575	3850

SATURN USA

1991 Saturn SL1 Sedan

For an Saturn dealer in your area, see our Dealer Directory (pg 217)

1994 SATURN

SATURN 4 Cyl 1994

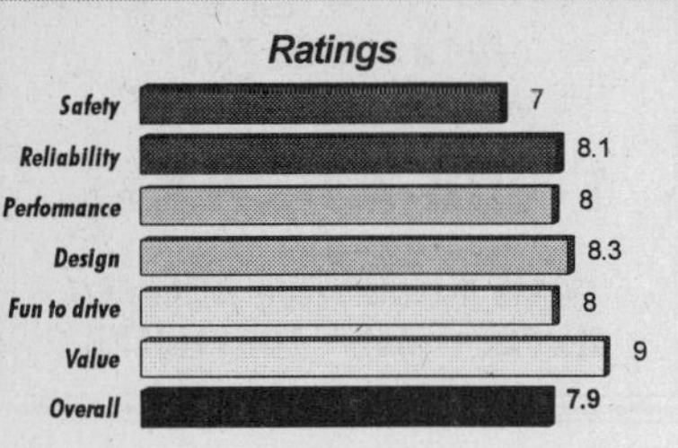

Model/Body/Type	BaseList	Whlse	Retail
FWD/AT/PS/AC			
4 Dr SL Sdn(5 spd)	9995	**7055**	**8830**
4 Dr SL1 Sdn	10795	-	-
4 Dr SL2 Sdn	11795	**10675**	**12950**
2 Dr SC1 Cpe	11695	-	-
2 Dr SC2 Cpe	12895	-	-
4 Dr SW1 Wgn	11695	-	-
4 Dr SW2 Wgn	12595	-	-

ADD FOR 94 SATURN:

ABS +430
Anti-Theft/Recovery Sys +365
Cass +90 *CD Player +205*
Cruise Ctrl +135 *Custom Whls/Cvrs +180*
Leather Seats +230 *Pwr Locks +90*
Pwr Sunroof +410 *Pwr Wndw +135*

DEDUCT FOR 93 SATURN:

No AC -590 *No Auto Trans -500*

1993 SATURN

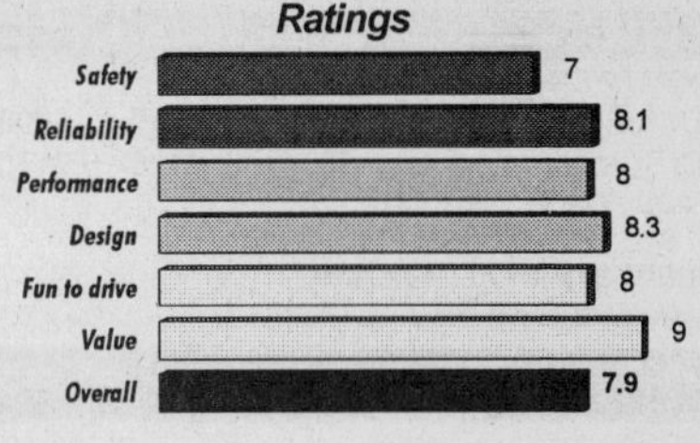

SATURN 4 Cyl 1993

Model/Body/Type	BaseList	Whlse	Retail
FWD/AT/PS/AC			
4 Dr SL Sdn	9195	**7300**	**9100**
4 Dr SL1 Sdn	9995	**8325**	**10150**
4 Dr SL2 Sdn	11495	**10025**	**12100**
2 Dr SC1 Cpe	10995	**9725**	**11750**
2 Dr SC2 Cpe	12795	**11200**	**13525**
4 Dr SW1 Wgn	10895	**9800**	**11850**
4 Dr SW2 Wgn	12195	**10600**	**12875**

ADD FOR 93 SATURN:

ABS +390 *Cass +75*
CD Player +175 *Cruise Ctrl +115*
Custom Whls/Cvrs +160 *Leather Seats +195*
Pwr Locks +75 *Pwr Sunroof +315*
Pwr Wndw +115

DEDUCT FOR 93 SATURN:

No AC -470 *No Auto Trans -430*

See the Automobile Dealer Directory on page 379 for a Dealer near you!

1992 SATURN

SATURN 4 Cyl 1992

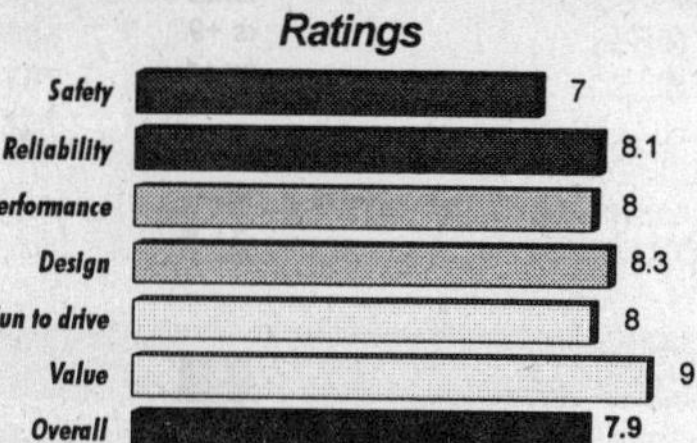

Model/Body/Type	BaseList	Whlse	Retail
FWD/AT/PS/AC			
4 Dr SL Sdn	8195	**5850**	**7400**
4 Dr SL1 Sdn	8995	**6850**	**8575**
4 Dr SL2 Touring Sdn	10395	**8525**	**10375**
2 Dr SC Cpe	11875	**9675**	**11675**

ADD FOR 92 SATURN:

ABS +350 *Cass +60*
CD Player +160 *Cruise Ctrl +100*
Custom Whls/Cvrs +135 *Driver Side Airbag +275*
Leather Seats +160 *Pwr Locks +60*
Pwr Sunroof +275 *Pwr Wndw +100*

DEDUCT FOR 92 SATURN:

No AC -430 *No Auto Trans -390*

1991 SATURN

SATURN 4 Cyl 1991

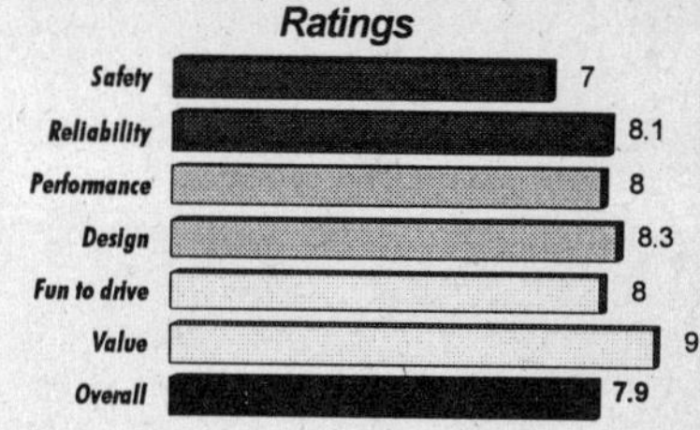

Model/Body/Type	BaseList	Whlse	Retail
FWD/AT/PS/AC			
4 Dr SL Sdn	7995	**4775**	**6250**
4 Dr SL1 Sdn	8595	**5725**	**7275**
4 Dr SL2 Touring Sdn	10295	**7350**	**9150**
2 Dr SC Cpe	11775	**8425**	**10250**

ADD FOR 91 SATURN:

ABS +315 *Cass +35*
CD Player +115 *Cruise Ctrl +75*
Pwr Locks +35 *Pwr Sunroof +230*
Pwr Wndw +75

DEDUCT FOR 91 SATURN:

No AC -390 *No Auto Trans -350*

STERLING — Britain

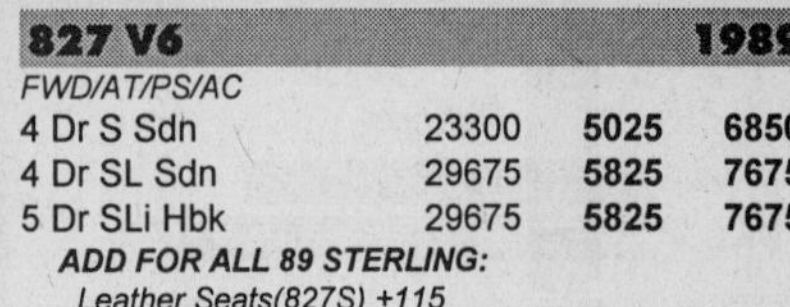

1990 Sterling 827 Si Sedan

For a dealer in your area, see our Dealer Directory (pg 217)

1991 STERLING

Model/Body/Type	BaseList	Whlse	Retail
827 V6			**1991**
FWD/AT/PS/AC			
4 Dr Si Sdn	26500	**8325**	**10350**
4 Dr SL Sdn	28500	**9200**	**11300**
5 Dr SLi Hbk	28500	**9200**	**11300**

ADD FOR ALL 91 STERLING:
Car Phone +135
CD Player +160
DEDUCT FOR ALL 91 STERLING:
No Auto Trans -470

1990 STERLING

Model/Body/Type	BaseList	Whlse	Retail
827 V6			**1990**
FWD/AT/PS/AC			
4 Dr S Sdn	23350	**6725**	**8700**
4 Dr Si Sdn	26500	**7250**	**9275**
4 Dr SL Sdn	28500	**7875**	**9925**
5 Dr SLi Hbk	28500	**7875**	**9925**

ADD FOR ALL 90 STERLING:
ABS(827S) +275
CD Player +115
Leather Seats(827S) +135
DEDUCT FOR ALL 90 STERLING:
No Auto Trans -430

1989 STERLING

Model/Body/Type	BaseList	Whlse	Retail
827 V6			**1989**
FWD/AT/PS/AC			
4 Dr S Sdn	23300	**5025**	**6850**
4 Dr SL Sdn	29675	**5825**	**7675**
5 Dr SLi Hbk	29675	**5825**	**7675**

ADD FOR ALL 89 STERLING:
Leather Seats(827S) +115
DEDUCT FOR ALL 89 STERLING:
No Auto Trans -390

1988 STERLING

Model/Body/Type	BaseList	Whlse	Retail
825 V6			**1988**
FWD/AT/PS/AC			
4 Dr S Sdn	20804	**3500**	**5150**
4 Dr SL Sdn	25995	**4050**	**5725**

DEDUCT FOR ALL 88 STERLING:
No Auto Trans -350

1987 STERLING

Model/Body/Type	BaseList	Whlse	Retail
825 V6			**1987**
FWD/AT/PS/AC			
4 Dr S Sdn	19000	**2750**	**4125**
4 Dr SL Sdn	23900	**3100**	**4600**

Model/Body/Type	BaseList	Whlse	Retail

SUBARU

Japan

1992 Subaru SVX

For a Subaru dealer in your area, see our Dealer Directory (pg 217)

1994 SUBARU

IMPREZA 4 Cyl — 1994

FWD/AT/PS/AC

Model/Body/Type	BaseList	Whlse	Retail
4 Dr Sdn (5 spd)	11200	-	-
4 Dr L Sdn	12000	-	-
4 Dr L 4WD Wgn	13500	-	-
4 Dr LS 4WD Wgn	18550	-	-
L Sportwagon	12400	-	-
L 4WD Sportwagon	13900	-	-
LS 4WD Sportwagon	18950	-	-

JUSTY 3 Cyl — 1994

FWD/5SP/PS/AC

Model/Body/Type	BaseList	Whlse	Retail
3 Dr Hbk	7749	6650	8300
5 Dr GL 4WD Hbk	9603	-	-

See the Automobile Dealer Directory on page 379 for a Dealer near you!

LEGACY 4 Cyl — 1994

Ratings

Rating	Score
Safety	7.2
Reliability	7.5
Performance	8.2
Design	8.4
Fun to drive	8.2
Value	7.8
Overall	7.7

FWD/AT/PS/AC

Model/Body/Type	BaseList	Whlse	Retail
4 Dr L Sdn	13999	**11800**	**14575**
4 Dr L 4WD Sdn	18050	**13150**	**15650**
4 Dr LS Sdn	19700	**14350**	**16925**
4 Dr LS 4WD Sdn	21300	**15350**	**17975**
4 Dr Sport Turbo 4WD Sdn	21400	-	-
5 Dr L Wgn	14999	**13000**	**15500**
5 Dr L 4WD Wgn	16499	**14050**	**16600**
5 Dr LS Wgn	20400	**15200**	**17825**
5 Dr LS 4WD Wgn	22000	**16250**	**18925**
5 Dr Turbo 4WD Wgn	23200	-	-

LOYALE 4 Cyl — 1994

FWD/AT/PS/AC

Model/Body/Type	BaseList	Whlse	Retail
5 Dr 4WD Wgn	13553	-	-

SVX V6 — 1994

4WD/AT/PS/AC

Model/Body/Type	BaseList	Whlse	Retail
2 Dr L Cpe	23900	-	-
2 Dr LS Cpe	28550	-	-
2 Dr LSi 4WD Cpe	33850	-	-

ADD FOR ALL 94 SUBARU:

ABS(Legacy L,Impresa L) +430
Anti-Theft/Recovery Sys +365
Cass(Legacy L) +115
CD Player(Legacy L) +230
Cruise Ctrl(Legacy L) +160
Custom Whls +205
Leather Seats(Legacy LS) +275
Passenger Air Bag(Impr L)
Pwr Locks(Leg L,Impr L) +115
Pwr Wndw(Leg L,Impr L) +160

DEDUCT FOR ALL 94 SUBARU:

No AC -680
No Auto Trans -590

1993 SUBARU

IMPREZA 4 Cyl — 1993

Ratings

Rating	Score
Safety	7.2
Reliability	9.2
Performance	7.9
Design	8.3
Fun to drive	7.5
Value	7
Overall	8.2

Model/Body/Type	BaseList	Whlse	Retail
FWD/AT/PS/AC			
4 Dr Sdn (5 spd)	10999	**7025**	**8775**
4 Dr L Sdn	11499	**8625**	**10475**
4 Dr LS Sdn	15699	**9700**	**11700**
4 Dr L AWD Wgn	14499	**9625**	**11575**
4 Dr LS AWD Wgn	17199	**10625**	**12900**
L Sportwagon	13399	**9425**	**11350**
LS Sportwagon	16099	**10425**	**12550**
L AWD Sportwagon	14899	**10350**	**12475**
LS AWD Sportwagon	17599	**11425**	**13750**

JUSTY 3 Cyl — 1993

Model/Body/Type	BaseList	Whlse	Retail
FWD/5SP/PS/AC			
3 Dr Hbk	7209	**4400**	**5825**
3 Dr GL Hbk (auto)	8984	**5725**	**7250**
3 Dr GL 4WD Hbk (auto)	9784	**6350**	**7950**
5 Dr GL 4WD Hbk	9349	**5950**	**7525**

LEGACY 4 Cyl — 1993

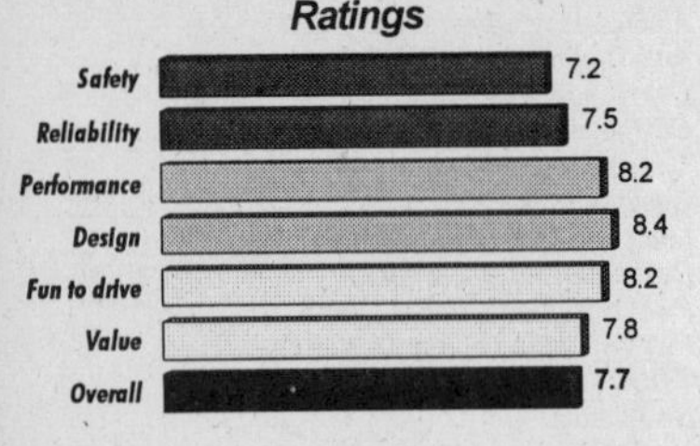

Model/Body/Type	BaseList	Whlse	Retail
FWD/AT/PS/AC			
4 Dr L Sdn	16250	**10075**	**12250**
4 Dr L 4WD Sdn	17850	**11050**	**13400**
4 Dr LS Sdn	19150	**12175**	**14650**
4 Dr LS 4WD Sdn	20750	**13175**	**15675**
4 Dr Sport Turbo 4WD Sdn	20850	**13975**	**16525**
5 Dr L Wgn	16950	**10850**	**13200**
5 Dr L 4WD Wgn	18550	**11850**	**14300**
5 Dr LS Wgn	19850	**12975**	**15475**
5 Dr LS 4WD Wgn	21450	**13975**	**16525**
5 Dr Turbo 4WD Wgn	22650	**14750**	**17325**

LOYALE 4 Cyl — 1993

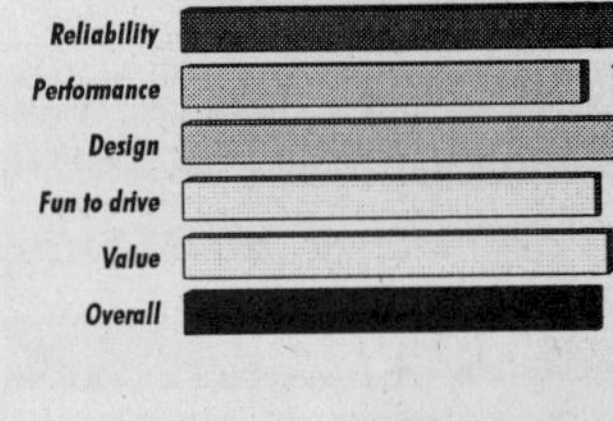

Model/Body/Type	BaseList	Whlse	Retail
FWD/AT/PS/AC			
4 Dr Sdn	10349	**7600**	**9425**
4 Dr 4WD Sdn	11699	**8600**	**10450**
5 Dr Wgn	11199	**8400**	**10225**
5 Dr 4WD Wgn	12699	**9400**	**11325**

SVX V6 — 1993

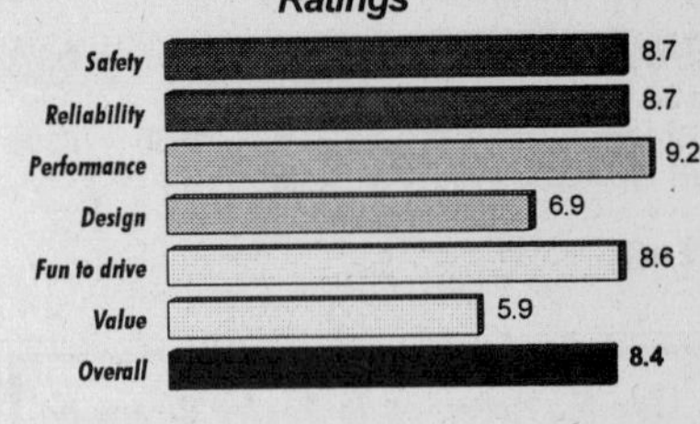

Model/Body/Type	BaseList	Whlse	Retail
4WD/AT/PS/AC			
2 Dr LS-L Touring Cpe	-	**21075**	**24350**

Model/Body/Type	BaseList	Whlse	Retail

ADD FOR ALL 93 SUBARU:
ABS(Legacy L 4WD Wgn) +390
Auto Trans(Justy) +430
Cass(Std Legacy,Impreza LS) +100
CD Player +195
Cruise Ctrl(Std Legacy,Impreza LS) +135
Custom Whls +175
Leather Seats(Legacy LS) +230
Pwr Locks(Std Leg,Impr L Wgn/LS,Loy) +100
Pwr Wndw(Std Leg,Impr L Wgn/LS,Loy) +135
DEDUCT FOR ALL 93 SUBARU:
No AC -545
No Auto Trans -505
No Pwr Steering -545

1992 SUBARU

JUSTY 3 Cyl — 1992

FWD/5SP/PS/AC

Model/Body/Type	BaseList	Whlse	Retail
3 Dr DL Hbk	6645	**3400**	**4725**
3 Dr GL Hbk	8049	**4175**	**5575**
3 Dr GL 4WD Hbk	8849	**4750**	**6225**
5 Dr GL 4WD Hbk	8949	**4875**	**6375**

LEGACY 4 Cyl — 1992

Ratings

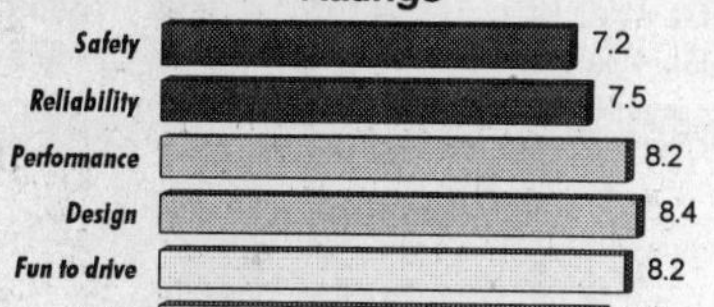

FWD/AT/PS/AC

Model/Body/Type	BaseList	Whlse	Retail
4 Dr L Sdn	13499	**8525**	**10425**
4 Dr L 4WD Sdn	16099	**9425**	**11450**
4 Dr LS Sdn	18499	**10500**	**12725**
4 Dr LS 4WD Sdn	19999	**11425**	**13775**
4 Dr Sport Turbo 4WD Sdn	19799	**12075**	**14550**
5 Dr L Wgn	13999	**9225**	**11250**
5 Dr L 4WD Wgn	15599	**10075**	**12250**
5 Dr LS Wgn	18999	**11200**	**13575**
5 Dr LS 4WD Wgn	20499	**12075**	**14550**
5 Dr LE Turbo 4WD Wgn	21645	**12775**	**15250**

LOYALE 4 Cyl — 1992

Ratings

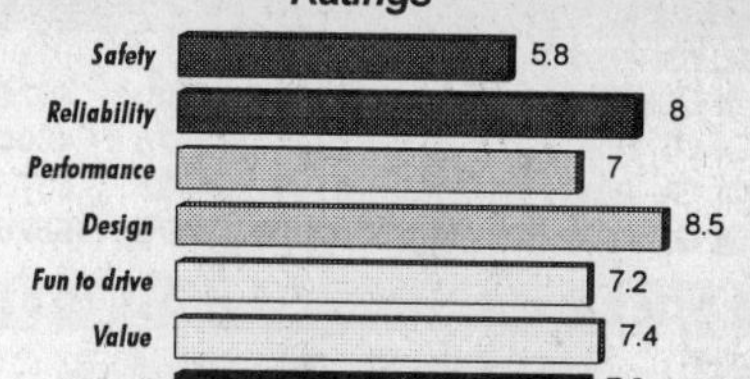

FWD/AT/PS/AC

Model/Body/Type	BaseList	Whlse	Retail
4 Dr Sdn	9799	**6325**	**7925**
4 Dr 4WD Sdn	11149	**7200**	**8975**
5 Dr Wgn	10649	**7025**	**8775**
5 Dr 4WD Wgn	12149	**7900**	**9775**

SVX V6 — 1992

Ratings

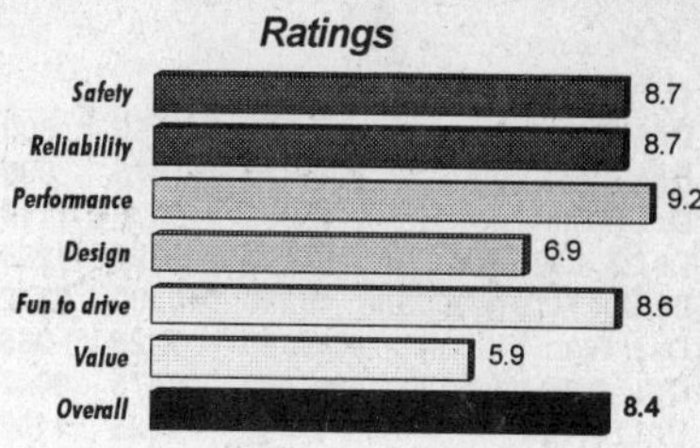

4WD/AT/PS/AC

Model/Body/Type	BaseList	Whlse	Retail
2 Dr LS Cpe	25000	**15325**	**18100**
2 Dr LS-L Touring Cpe	28000	**16675**	**19625**

ADD FOR ALL 92 SUBARU:
ABS(Std Leg LS,Spt,LE,SVX) +350
Air Bag(Std SVX) +275
Auto Trans(Justy) +390
Car Phone(SVX) +160
Cass(Std Leg LS,Spt,LE,SVX) +75
CD Player +175
Cruise Ctrl(Std Leg LS,Spt,LE,SVX) +115
Custom Whls +160
Leather Seats(Leg LS) +195
Pwr Locks(Legacy L) +75
Pwr Wndw(Legacy L) +115
DEDUCT FOR ALL 92 SUBARU:
No AC -505
No Auto Trans -470
No Pwr Steering -135

SUBARU 91-90

1991 SUBARU

JUSTY 3 Cyl — 1991

Model/Body/Type	BaseList	Whlse	Retail
FWD/5SP/PS/AC			
3 Dr DL Hbk	5995	**2800**	**4025**
3 Dr GL Hbk	7399	**3475**	**4800**
3 Dr GL 4WD Hbk	8199	**4025**	**5375**
5 Dr GL 4WD Hbk	8299	**4175**	**5575**

LEGACY 4 Cyl — 1991

Ratings

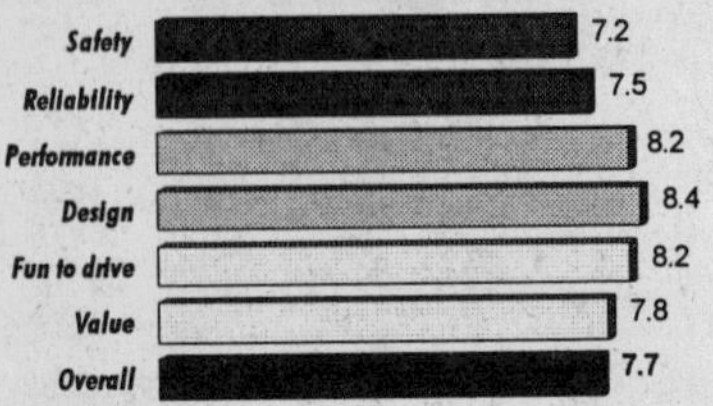

Model/Body/Type	BaseList	Whlse	Retail
FWD/AT/PS/AC			
4 Dr L Sdn	12599	**7150**	**9000**
4 Dr L 4WD Sdn	15849	**7975**	**9900**
4 Dr LS Sdn	16999	**9075**	**11100**
4 Dr LS 4WD Sdn	18499	**9900**	**12050**
4 Dr Spt Turb 4WD Sdn	18899	**10200**	**12425**
5 Dr L Wgn	13199	**7725**	**9650**
5 Dr L 4WD Wgn	14499	**8575**	**10475**
5 Dr LS Wgn	17599	**9725**	**11850**
5 Dr LS 4WD Wgn	18999	**10500**	**12725**

LOYALE 4 Cyl — 1991

Ratings

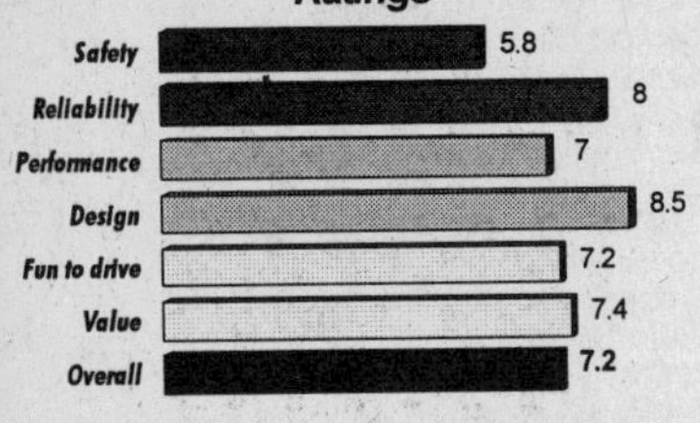

Model/Body/Type	BaseList	Whlse	Retail
FWD/AT/PS/AC			
4 Dr Sdn	9499	**5575**	**7125**
4 Dr 4WD Sdn	10599	**6425**	**8025**
5 Dr Wgn	10299	**6175**	**7750**
5 Dr 4WD Wgn	11299	**7025**	**8775**

XT V6 — 1991

Model/Body/Type	BaseList	Whlse	Retail
FWD/AT/PS/AC			
2 Dr GL Cpe (4 Cyl)	13438	**7025**	**8775**
2 Dr XT6 Cpe	17478	**8075**	**9925**
2 Dr XT6 4WD Cpe	18318	**8925**	**10825**

ADD FOR ALL 91 SUBARU:

ABS(Std Leg LS,Spt) +315
Auto Trans(Justy) +350
Cass(Std Leg LS,Spt,XT6) +60
CD Player +160
Cruise Ctrl(Std Leg LS,Spt,XT6) +100
Custom Whls +135
Leather Seats +160
Pwr Locks(Legacy L) +60
Pwr Wndw(Legacy L) +100

DEDUCT FOR ALL 91 SUBARU:

No AC -470
No Auto Trans -430
No Pwr Steering -115

1990 SUBARU

JUSTY 3 Cyl — 1990

Model/Body/Type	BaseList	Whlse	Retail
FWD/5SP/PS/AC			
3 Dr DL Hbk	5866	**2200**	**3300**
3 Dr GL Hbk	7251	**2725**	**3900**
3 Dr GL 4WD Hbk	7951	**3200**	**4500**
5 Dr GL 4WD Hbk	8156	**3325**	**4675**

LEGACY 4 Cyl — 1990

Ratings

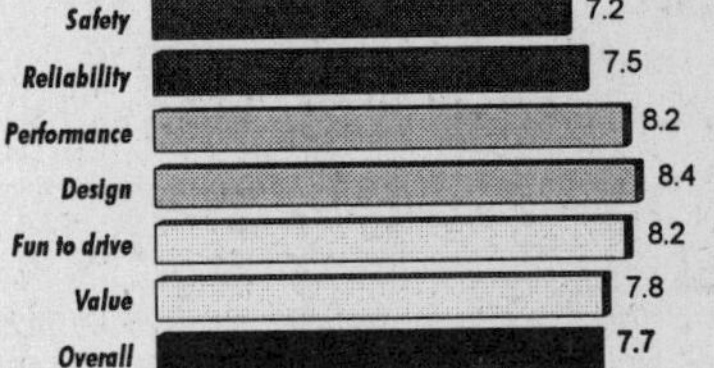

Model/Body/Type	BaseList	Whlse	Retail
FWD/AT/PS/AC			
4 Dr Sdn	11299	**5050**	**6725**
4 Dr L Sdn	12499	**5775**	**7475**
4 Dr L 4WD Sdn	13699	**6500**	**8225**
5 Dr Wgn	11849	**5500**	**7175**
5 Dr L Wgn	13049	**6200**	**7950**
5 Dr L 4WD Wgn	14249	**6900**	**8725**

Model/Body/Type	BaseList	Whlse	Retail

LOYALE 4 Cyl — 1990

Ratings

Rating	Score
Safety	5.8
Reliability	8
Performance	7
Design	8.5
Fun to drive	7.2
Value	7.4
Overall	7.2

FWD/AT/PS/AC

Model/Body/Type	BaseList	Whlse	Retail
3 Dr Cpe	9599	**3775**	**5100**
3 Dr RS 4WD Cpe	11024	**4475**	**5875**
3 Dr RS Turb 4WD Cpe	13699	**4700**	**6175**
4 Dr Sdn	9299	**3875**	**5225**
4 Dr 4WD Sdn	10374	**4575**	**6000**
5 Dr Wgn	9999	**4300**	**5725**
5 Dr 4WD Wgn	10999	**4950**	**6500**

ADD FOR ALL 90 SUBARU:

ABS +275
Auto Trans(Justy) +315
Cass +60
Cruise Ctrl +75
Custom Whls +115
LS Pkg(Legacy L) +470
Touring Wgn +100
Turbo Eng +195

DEDUCT FOR ALL 90 SUBARU:

No AC -430
No Auto Trans -390
No Pwr Steering -100

1989 SUBARU

DL 4 Cyl — 1989

FWD/AT/PS/AC

Model/Body/Type	BaseList	Whlse	Retail
3 Dr Cpe	10031	**2675**	**3850**
4 Dr Sdn	9731	**2775**	**4000**
4 Dr Wgn	10181	**3025**	**4275**
4 Dr 4WD Wgn (5 spd)	10881	**3125**	**4400**

GL 4 Cyl — 1989

FWD/AT/PS/AC

Model/Body/Type	BaseList	Whlse	Retail
3 Dr Hbk	8596	**2000**	**3100**
3 Dr 4WD Hbk (5 spd)	9269	**2100**	**3175**
3 Dr Cpe	11821	**3100**	**4375**
3 Dr 4WD Cpe	12521	**3600**	**4925**
3 Dr RX 4WD Turb Cpe	16361	**4200**	**5600**
4 Dr Sdn	11521	**3175**	**4475**
4 Dr 4WD Sdn	12221	**3700**	**5025**
4 Dr Wgn	11971	**3400**	**4725**
4 Dr 4WD Wgn	12671	**3950**	**5300**

JUSTY 3 Cyl — 1989

FWD/5SP/PS/AC

Model/Body/Type	BaseList	Whlse	Retail
3 Dr DL Hbk	5866	**1325**	**2250**
3 Dr GL Hbk	7251	**1725**	**2750**
3 Dr GL 4WD Hbk	7951	**2150**	**3225**
3 Dr RS 4WD Hbk	8351	**2300**	**3425**

XT V6 — 1989

FWD/AT/PS/AC

Model/Body/Type	BaseList	Whlse	Retail
3 Dr GL Cpe	13071	**4050**	**5400**
3 Dr GL 4WD Cpe	13771	**4600**	**6025**
3 Dr XT6 Cpe	17111	**5000**	**6525**
3 Dr XT6 4WD Cpe	17951	**5575**	**7125**

ADD FOR ALL 89 SUBARU:

Auto Trans(Justy) +275
Cass(Std XT6) +35
Cruise Ctrl(Std XT6) +60
Custom Whls +75
GL-10 Pkg +410
Touring Wgn +75
Turbo Eng(Std RX) +175

DEDUCT FOR ALL 89 SUBARU:

No AC -390
No Auto Trans -350
No Pwr Steering -75

1988 SUBARU

DL 4 Cyl — 1988

FWD/AT/PS/AC

Model/Body/Type	BaseList	Whlse	Retail
3 Dr Cpe	9295	**2325**	**3450**
4 Dr Sdn	8995	**2425**	**3575**
4 Dr Wgn	9595	**2650**	**3825**
4 Dr 4WD Wgn (5 spd)	9995	**2775**	**4000**

SUBARU 88-86

Model/Body/Type	BaseList	Whlse	Retail
GL 4 Cyl			**1988**
FWD/AT/PS/AC			
3 Dr Hbk	7995	**1775**	**2825**
3 Dr 4WD Hbk (5 spd)	8795	**1900**	**2975**
3 Dr Cpe	10695	**2625**	**3775**
3 Dr 4WD Cpe	11395	**3125**	**4400**
3 Dr RX 4WD Turbo Cpe (5 spd)	14995	**3275**	**4600**
4 Dr Sdn	10395	**2725**	**3900**
4 Dr 4WD Sdn	11095	**3200**	**4500**
4 Dr RX 4WD Turbo Sdn (5 spd)	14995	**3375**	**4700**
4 Dr Wgn	10995	**2950**	**4200**
4 Dr 4WD Wgn	11695	**3400**	**4725**
JUSTY 3 Cyl			**1988**
FWD/5SP/PS/AC			
3 Dr DL Hbk	5695	**825**	**1650**
3 Dr GL Hbk	6595	**1125**	**2025**
3 Dr GL 4WD Hbk	7195	**1475**	**2425**
3 Dr RS 4WD Hbk	7666	**1625**	**2600**
XT V6			**1988**
FWD/AT/PS/AC			
3 Dr DL Cpe (5 spd)	10195	**1775**	**2825**
3 Dr GL Cpe	12195	**2775**	**4000**
3 Dr GL 4WD Cpe (5 spd)	12895	**2900**	**4150**
3 Dr XT6 Cpe	16995	**3425**	**4750**
3 Dr XT6 4WD Cpe	17745	**3925**	**5275**

ADD FOR ALL 88 SUBARU:
GL-10 Pkg +215
Turbo Eng(Std RX) +160
DEDUCT FOR ALL 88 SUBARU:
No AC -330
No Auto Trans -290

1987 SUBARU

Model/Body/Type	BaseList	Whlse	Retail
BRAT 4 Cyl			**1987**
4WD/4SP/PS/AC			
Brat GL	8338	**1275**	**2175**
DL 4 Cyl			**1987**
FWD/AT/PS/AC			
3 Dr Cpe (5 spd)	9108	**1425**	**2375**
4 Dr Sdn	8808	**1700**	**2700**
4 Dr Wgn	9208	**1875**	**2950**
4 Dr 4WD Wgn (5 spd)	9598	**2275**	**3400**
GL 4 Cyl			**1987**
FWD/AT/PS/AC			
3 Dr Hbk	7588	**1150**	**2050**
3 Dr 4WD Hbk (5 spd)	8293	**1550**	**2525**
3 Dr Cpe	10138	**1800**	**2850**
3 Dr 4WD Cpe	10608	**2225**	**3325**
4 Dr Sdn	9838	**1900**	**2975**
4 Dr 4WD Sdn	10308	**2300**	**3425**
4 Dr Wgn	10238	**2100**	**3175**
4 Dr 4WD Wgn	10708	**2500**	**3650**
4 Dr RX 4WD Turbo Sdn (5 spd)	13833	**2325**	**3450**
JUSTY 3 Cyl			**1987**
FWD/5SP/PS/AC			
3 Dr DL Hbk	5725	**625**	**1425**
3 Dr GL Hbk	6525	**775**	**1600**
STANDARD 4 Cyl			**1987**
FWD/5SP/PS/AC			
3 Dr Hbk	5398	**250**	**1050**
XT V6			**1987**
FWD/AT/PS/AC			
2 Dr DL Cpe (5 spd)	9593	**1100**	**2000**
2 Dr GL Cpe	11518	**1800**	**2850**
2 Dr GL 4WD Cpe	12628	**2225**	**3325**

ADD FOR ALL 87 SUBARU:
GL-10 Pkg +160
Turbo Eng(Std RX) +135

1986 SUBARU

Model/Body/Type	BaseList	Whlse	Retail
BRAT			**1986**
4WD			
Brat GL	7783	**800**	**1750**
DL			**1986**
FWD			
3 Dr Sdn	7960	**1000**	**2025**
4 Dr Sdn	7391	**1075**	**2100**
4 Dr Wgn	7692	**1225**	**2250**
4 Dr 4WD Wgn	8242	**1600**	**2725**
GL			**1986**
FWD			
3 Dr Hbk	6883	**550**	**1500**
3 Dr 4WD Hbk	7508	**925**	**1950**
3 Dr Sdn	8585	**1125**	**2175**
3 Dr 4WD Sdn	9680	**1525**	**2625**
4 Dr Sdn	7991	**1200**	**2225**
4 Dr 4WD Sdn	9114	**1575**	**2700**
4 Dr RX 4WD Turb Sdn	11627	**1675**	**2800**
4 Dr Wgn	8292	**1325**	**2375**
4 Dr 4WD Wgn	8842	**1700**	**2875**

Model/Body/Type	BaseList	Whlse	Retail
STANDARD			**1986**
FWD			
3 Dr Hbk	4989	200	900
XT			**1986**
FWD			
2 Dr DL Cpe	8371	825	1775
2 Dr GL Cpe	10097	1200	2225
2 Dr GL-10 4WD Turbo Cpe	13771	1775	2950

1985 SUBARU

Model/Body/Type	BaseList	Whlse	Retail
BRAT			**1985**
4WD Brat GL	7783	400	1325
DL			**1985**
4 Dr Sdn	7096	625	1600
4 Dr Wgn	7334	800	1750
4 Dr 4WD Wgn	7884	1125	2175
GL			**1985**
3 Dr Hbk	6924	425	1350
3 Dr 4WD Hbk	7474	825	1775
4 Dr Sdn	7646	775	1725
4 Dr 4WD Sdn	9104	1100	2150
4 Dr RX 4WD Turb Sdn	10743	1200	2225
4 Dr 4WD Turbo Sdn	11130	1375	2450
4 Dr Wgn	7884	900	1875
4 Dr 4WD Wgn	8434	1250	2275
STANDARD			**1985**
3 Dr Hbk	4989	175	850
XT			**1985**
2 Dr DL Cpe	7889	500	1450
2 Dr GL Cpe	9899	875	1825
2 Dr GL-10 4WD Turbo Cpe	13589	1325	2375

Model/Body/Type	BaseList	Whlse	Retail

SUZUKI

Japan

1992 Suzuki Samurai

For a Suzuki dealer in your area, see our Dealer Directory (pg 217)

1994 SUZUKI

SAMURAI 4 Cyl — 1994

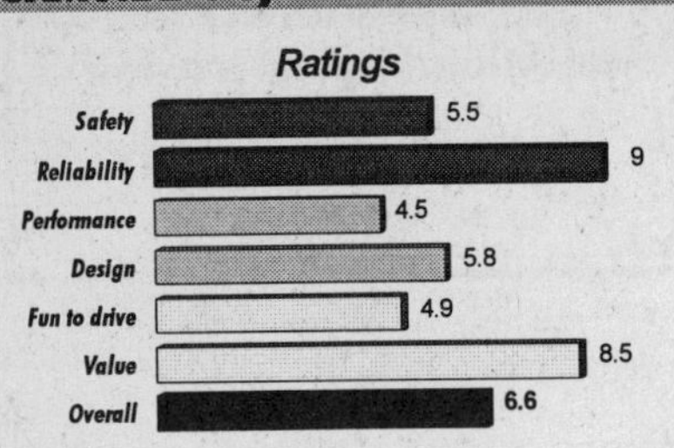

PS/AC	BaseList	Whlse	Retail
JL 4WD Conv	9469	**8450**	**10275**

See the Automobile Dealer Directory on page 379 for a Dealer near you!

SIDEKICK 4 Cyl — 1994

Ratings

Rating	Score
Safety	5.5
Reliability	7.7
Performance	6.9
Design	7.7
Fun to drive	7.1
Value	7.2
Overall	6.9

4WD/PS/AC	BaseList	Whlse	Retail
2 Dr JS 2WD Conv	11449	**9425**	**11350**
2 Dr JX Conv	12849	**10850**	**13150**
4 Dr JS 2WD Hardtop	12849	**9575**	**11525**
4 Dr JX Hardtop	14079	**11000**	**13300**
4 Dr JLX Hardtop	15429	**11800**	**14175**

SWIFT 4 Cyl — 1994

Ratings

Rating	Score
Safety	5.9
Reliability	8
Performance	7.2
Design	7.7
Fun to drive	6.8
Value	7.4
Overall	7.2

FWD/PS/AC	BaseList	Whlse	Retail
3 Dr GA Hbk	7549	**6550**	**8175**
3 Dr GT Hbk	10659	**8425**	**10250**
4 Dr GA Sdn	8529	**6725**	**8475**
4 Dr GS Sdn	10029	**7525**	**9325**

ADD FOR ALL 94 SUZUKI:

Auto Trans +500
Anti-Theft/Recovery Sys +365
Cass(Std 4D Sidekick,Swift GT/GS) +90
CD Player +205

DEDUCT FOR ALL 94 SUZUKI:

No AC -590

Model/Body/Type	BaseList	Whlse	Retail

1993 SUZUKI

SAMURAI 4 Cyl 1993

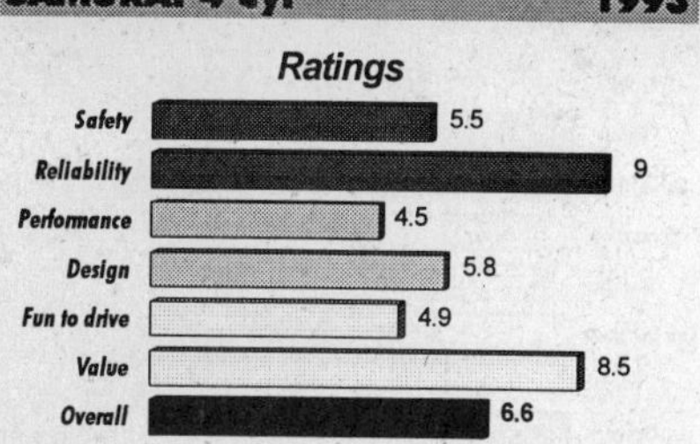

PS/AC			
JA 2WD Conv	6699	4850	6350
JL 4WD Conv	8599	6625	8250

SIDEKICK 4 Cyl 1993

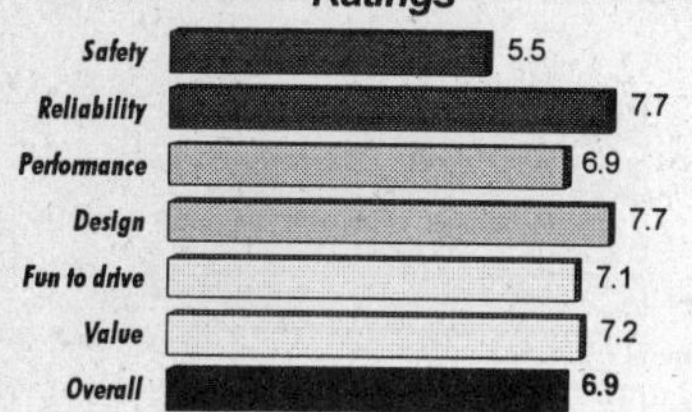

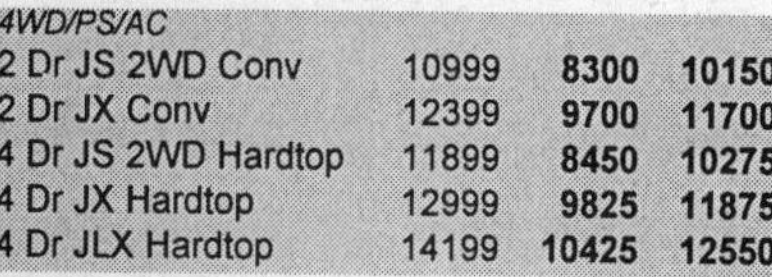

4WD/PS/AC			
2 Dr JS 2WD Conv	10999	8300	10150
2 Dr JX Conv	12399	9700	11700
4 Dr JS 2WD Hardtop	11899	8450	10275
4 Dr JX Hardtop	12999	9825	11875
4 Dr JLX Hardtop	14199	10425	12550

SWIFT 4 Cyl 1993

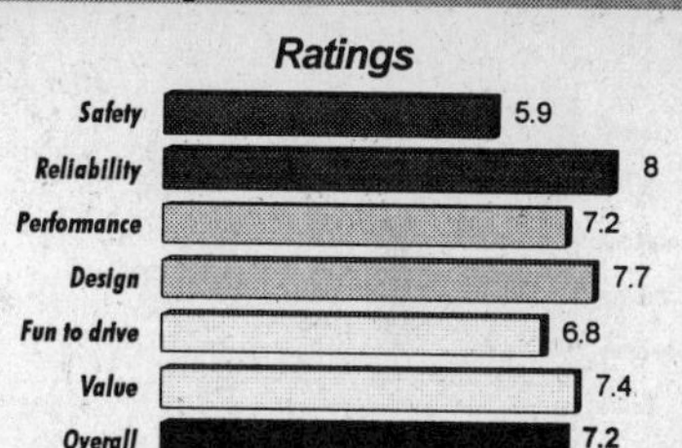

FWD/PS/AC			
3 Dr GA Hbk	7299	5225	6750
3 Dr GT Hbk	9999	6950	8700
4 Dr GA Sdn	7999	5375	6925
4 Dr GS Sdn	9399	6125	7675

ADD FOR ALL 93 SUZUKI:

Auto Trans +430
Cass(Std 4D Sidekick,Swift GT/GS) +75
CD Player +175
Custom Whls +145
Sunroof +145

DEDUCT FOR ALL 93 SUZUKI:

No AC -470
No Pwr Steering -160

1992 SUZUKI

SAMURAI 4 Cyl 1992

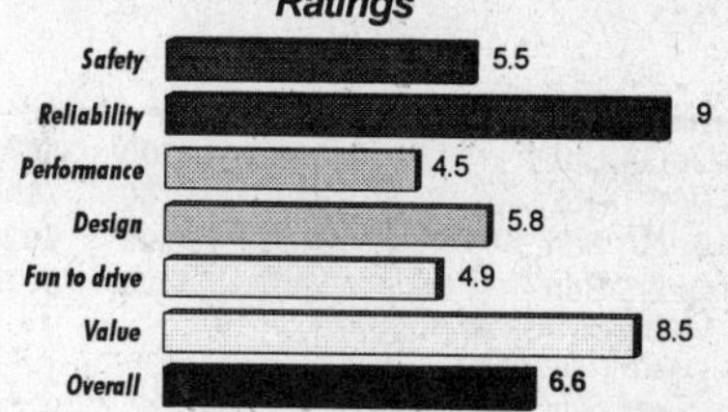

PS/AC			
JA 2WD Conv	6299	3950	5300
JL 4WD Conv	8199	5575	7125

SUZUKI

SUZUKI

SIDEKICK 4 Cyl — 1992

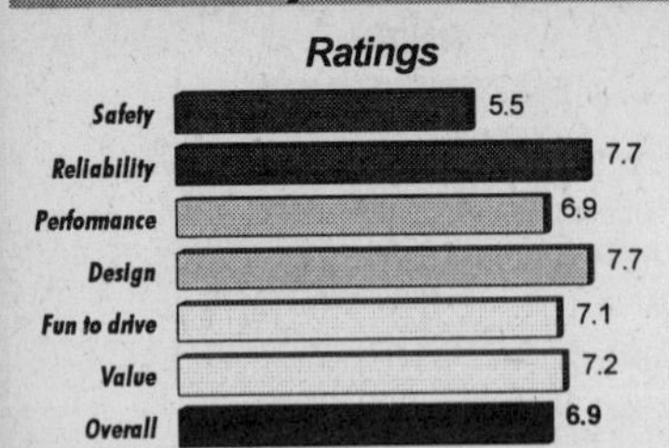

Model/Body/Type	BaseList	Whlse	Retail
4WD/PS/AC			
2 Dr JS 2WD Conv	10699	**6950**	**8700**
2 Dr JX Conv	11999	**8225**	**10075**
4 Dr JX Hardtop	12499	**8375**	**10200**
4 Dr JLX Hardtop	13699	**8975**	**10875**

SWIFT 4 Cyl — 1992

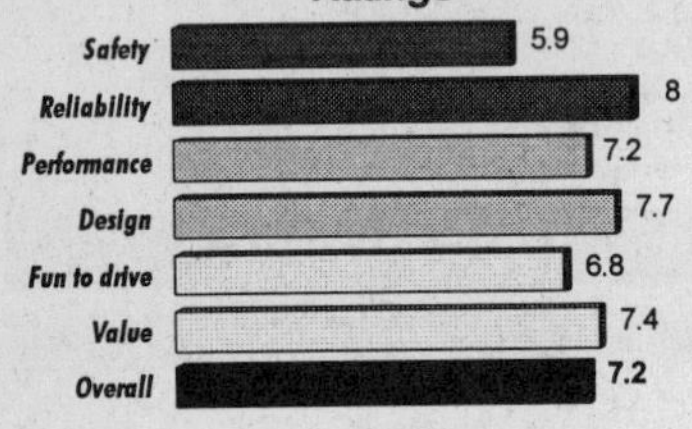

Model/Body/Type	BaseList	Whlse	Retail
FWD/PS/AC			
3 Dr GA Hbk	6899	**4350**	**5775**
3 Dr GT Hbk	9599	**5750**	**7300**
4 Dr GA Sdn	7699	**4500**	**5925**
4 Dr GS Sdn	9099	**5100**	**6625**

ADD FOR ALL 92 SUZUKI:

Auto Trans +390
Cass(Std 4D Sidekick,Swift GT/GS) +60
Custom Whls +125
Sunroof +105

DEDUCT FOR ALL 92 SUZUKI:

No AC -430
No Pwr Steering -135

1991 SUZUKI

SAMURAI 4 Cyl — 1991

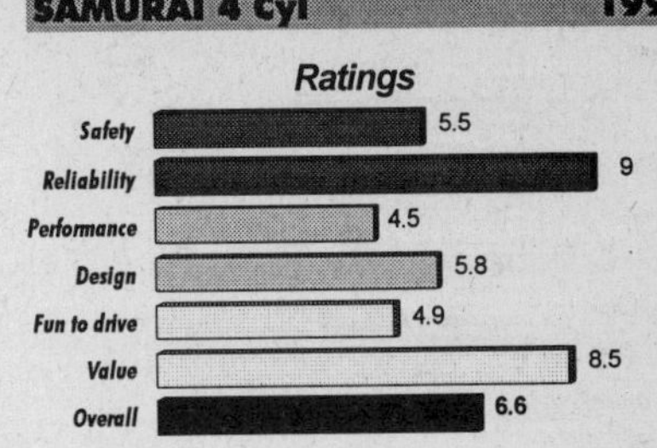

Model/Body/Type	BaseList	Whlse	Retail
AC			
JA 2WD Conv	5999	**3200**	**4500**
JS 2WD Conv	6999	**3575**	**4900**
JL 4WD Conv	8299	**4750**	**6225**

SIDEKICK 4 Cyl — 1991

Ratings

Rating	Score
Safety	5.5
Reliability	7.7
Performance	6.9
Design	7.7
Fun to drive	7.1
Value	7.2
Overall	6.9

Model/Body/Type	BaseList	Whlse	Retail
4WD/AC			
2 Dr JS 2WD Conv	10299	**5825**	**7375**
2 Dr JL Conv	10999	**6625**	**8250**
2 Dr JX Conv	11799	**7025**	**8775**
4 Dr JX Hardtop	11999	**7150**	**8925**
4 Dr JLX Hardtop	12999	**7550**	**9375**

SWIFT 4 Cyl — 1991

Ratings

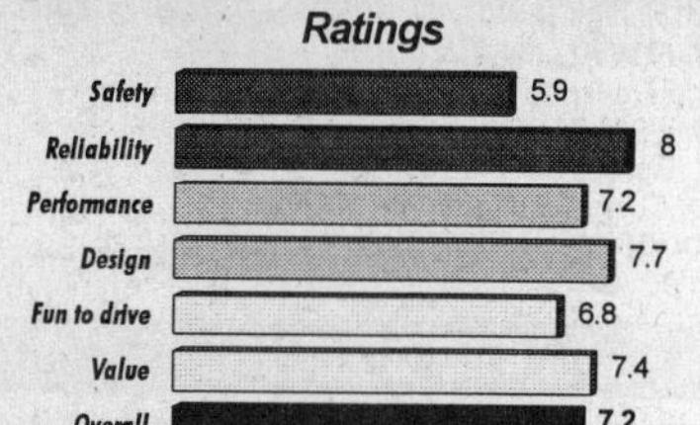

Model/Body/Type	BaseList	Whlse	Retail
FWD/AC			
3 Dr GA Hbk	6399	**3400**	**4725**
3 Dr GT Hbk	9399	**4600**	**6025**
4 Dr GA Sdn	7499	**3550**	**4875**
4 Dr GS Sdn	8599	**4175**	**5575**

ADD FOR ALL 91 SUZUKI:

Auto Trans +350
Cass(Std Sidekick JX/JLX,Swift GT/GS) +35
Custom Whls +125
Sunroof +105

DEDUCT FOR ALL 91 SUZUKI:

No AC -390

1990 SUZUKI

SAMURAI 4 Cyl — 1990

Ratings

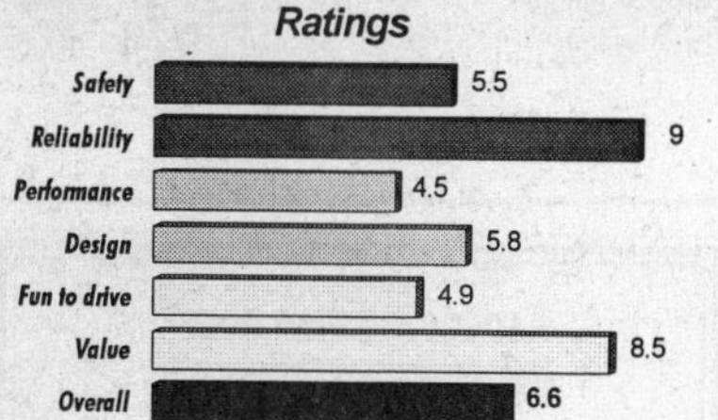

Model/Body/Type	BaseList	Whlse	Retail
4WD/AC			
Conv Utility	7999	**3600**	**4925**

SIDEKICK 4 Cyl — 1990

Ratings

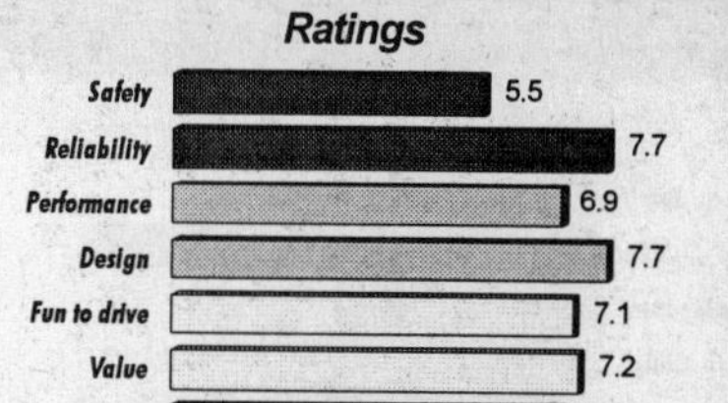

Model/Body/Type	BaseList	Whlse	Retail
4WD/AC			
JS 2WD Conv	9999	**5000**	**6525**
JX Conv	10799	**5850**	**7400**
JX Hardtop	11099	**6000**	**7575**

SWIFT 4 Cyl — 1990

Ratings

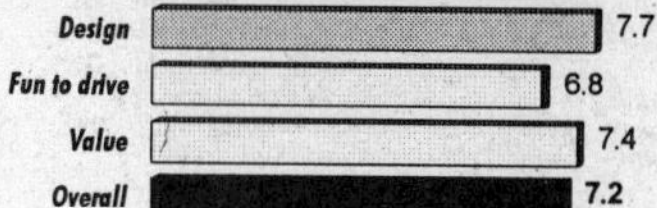

Model/Body/Type	BaseList	Whlse	Retail
FWD/AC			
3 Dr GA Hbk	6399	**2350**	**3475**
3 Dr GT Hbk	9399	**3400**	**4725**
4 Dr GA Sdn	7399	**2500**	**3650**
4 Dr GS Sdn	8599	**3000**	**4250**

ADD FOR ALL 90 SUZUKI:

Auto Trans +315
Cass(Std Swift GS/GT,Sidekick JX) +35
Custom Whls +80
GL Pkg(Swift GA) +75
JLX Custom Pkg(Sidekick) +275

DEDUCT FOR ALL 90 SUZUKI:

No AC -350

SUZUKI 89-86

1989 SUZUKI

SAMURAI 4 Cyl 1989

Ratings

Rating	Score
Safety	5.5
Reliability	9
Performance	4.5
Design	5.8
Fun to drive	4.9
Value	8.5
Overall	6.6

Model/Body/Type	BaseList	Whlse	Retail
4WD/AC			
Conv Utility	8595	2825	4075
Hardtop Utility	8495	2675	3850

SIDEKICK 4 Cyl 1989

Ratings

Rating	Score
Safety	5.5
Reliability	7.7
Performance	6.9
Design	7.7
Fun to drive	7.1
Value	7.2
Overall	6.9

Model/Body/Type	BaseList	Whlse	Retail
4WD/AC			
JA Conv Utility	8995	3450	4775
JX Conv Utility (auto)	12495	4825	6275
JX DLX Hardtop Utility	10995	4200	5600

SWIFT 4 Cyl 1989

Ratings

Rating	Score
Safety	5.9
Reliability	8
Performance	7.2
Design	7.7
Fun to drive	6.8
Value	7.4
Overall	7.2

Model/Body/Type	BaseList	Whlse	Retail
FWD/AC			
3 Dr GTi Hbk	8995	2075	3150
5 Dr GLX Hbk (auto)	7495	1800	2850

ADD FOR ALL 89 SUZUKI:
Auto Trans(Std GLX,JX Hardtop) +275
Cass(Std GTi,Sidekick JX) +25
JX Pkg(Samurai) +215
JLX Custom Pkg(Sidekick) +230
DEDUCT FOR ALL 89 SUZUKI:
No AC -315

1988 SUZUKI

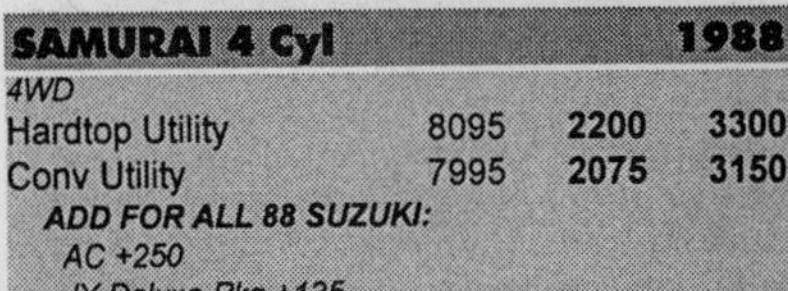

SAMURAI 4 Cyl 1988

Model/Body/Type	BaseList	Whlse	Retail
4WD			
Hardtop Utility	8095	2200	3300
Conv Utility	7995	2075	3150

ADD FOR ALL 88 SUZUKI:
AC +250
JX Deluxe Pkg +135

1987 SUZUKI

SAMURAI 4 Cyl 1987

Model/Body/Type	BaseList	Whlse	Retail
4WD			
Hardtop Utility	7100	1825	2900
Conv Utility	6895	1700	2700

1986 SUZUKI

SAMURAI 1986

Model/Body/Type	BaseList	Whlse	Retail
4WD			
Hardtop Utility	6700	1350	2425
Conv Utility	6550	1225	2275

Model/Body/Type	BaseList	Whlse	Retail

TOYOTA

Japan

1992 Toyota MR2 Coupe

For a Toyota dealer in your area, see our Dealer Directory (pg 217)

1994 TOYOTA

4RUNNER V6 — 1994

4WD/AT/PS/AC

Model/Body/Type	BaseList	Whlse	Retail
4 Dr SR5 Wgn (5 spd,4 Cyl)	19998	**19200**	**22150**
4 Dr 2WD SR5 Wgn	21028	**18900**	**21850**
4 Dr SR5 Wgn	21938	**20575**	**23625**

CAMRY — 1994

FWD/AT/PS/AC

Model/Body/Type	BaseList	Whlse	Retail
4 Cyl Models			
2 Dr DX Cpe	16148	**14100**	**16650**
2 Dr LE Cpe	18938	**15100**	**17725**
4 Dr DX Sdn	16438	**14200**	**16750**
4 Dr LE Sdn	19228	**15200**	**17825**
4 Dr XLE Sdn	21258	**18250**	**21175**
5 Dr DX Wgn	18648	**14775**	**17350**
5 Dr LE Wgn	20618	**15800**	**18450**
V6 Models			
2 Dr SE Cpe	22238	**17250**	**20125**
4 Dr SE Sdn	22528	**17350**	**20225**

CELICA 4 Cyl — 1994

FWD/AT/PS/AC

Model/Body/Type	BaseList	Whlse	Retail
2 Dr ST Cpe	16168	**13575**	**16100**
3 Dr ST Lbk	16508	**13825**	**16375**
2 Dr GT Cpe	18428	**15475**	**18100**
3 Dr GT Lbk	18898	**15725**	**18375**

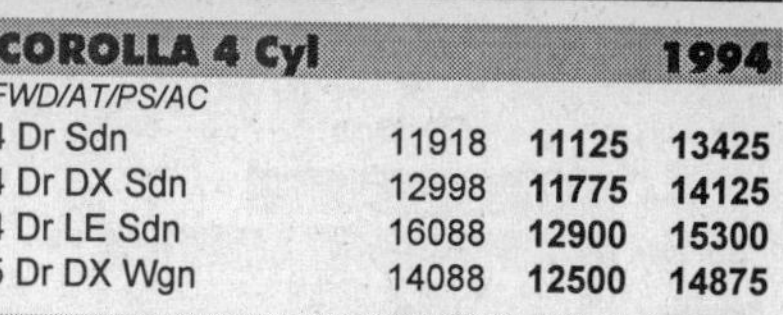

COROLLA 4 Cyl — 1994

FWD/AT/PS/AC

Model/Body/Type	BaseList	Whlse	Retail
4 Dr Sdn	11918	**11125**	**13425**
4 Dr DX Sdn	12998	**11775**	**14125**
4 Dr LE Sdn	16088	**12900**	**15300**
5 Dr DX Wgn	14088	**12500**	**14875**

LAND CRUISER V6 — 1994

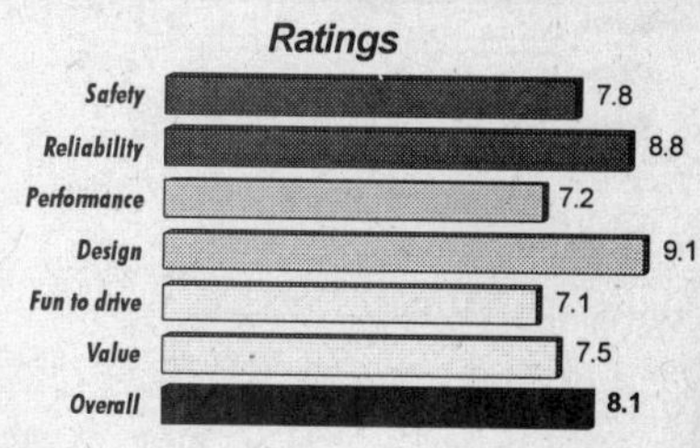

4WD/AT/PS/AC

Model/Body/Type	BaseList	Whlse	Retail
4 Dr Wgn	34268	**34200**	**37625**

MR2 4 Cyl — 1994

AT/PS/AC

Model/Body/Type	BaseList	Whlse	Retail
2 Dr Cpe	22538	-	-
2 Dr Turbo Cpe (5 spd)	27588	-	-

PASEO 4 Cyl — 1994

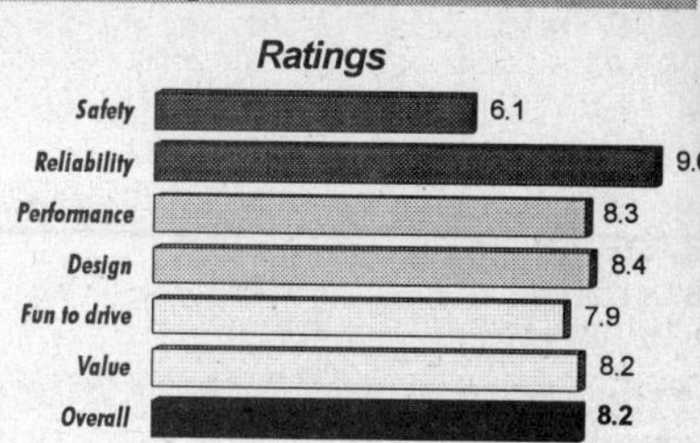

FWD/AT/PS/AC

Model/Body/Type	BaseList	Whlse	Retail
2 Dr Cpe	12468	**10825**	**13125**

See the Automobile Dealer Directory on page 379 for a Dealer near you!

TOYOTA

Model/Body/Type	BaseList	Whlse	Retail

PICKUPS 1994

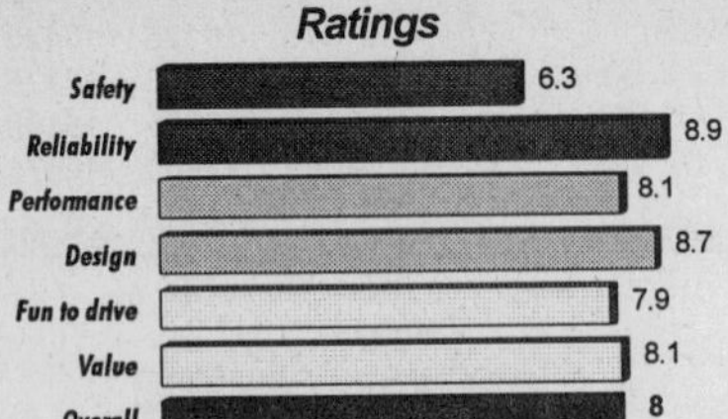

Model/Body/Type	BaseList	Whlse	Retail
5SP/PS/AC			
4 Cyl Models			
Pkup	9818	**8675**	**10575**
DX Pkup	10908	**9275**	**11200**
DX X-Cab Pkup	12458	**10900**	**13200**
DX 4WD Pkup	14448	**12000**	**14475**
DX X-Cab 4WD Pkup	15988	**13675**	**16200**
V6 Models			
SR5 X-Cab Pkup	15558	**12875**	**15275**
SR5 X-Cab 4WD Pkup	19148	**15625**	**18275**

PREVIA 4 Cyl 1994

Model/Body/Type	BaseList	Whlse	Retail
AT/PS/AC			
DX Wgn	22148	**18775**	**21725**
LE Wgn	25798	**21150**	**24225**
LE S/C Wgn	28158	-	-
DX All-Trac Wgn	25388	**20500**	**23450**
LE All-Trac Wgn	28848	**22875**	**25975**
LE S/C All-Trac Wgn	31298	-	-

SUPRA V6 1994

Model/Body/Type	BaseList	Whlse	Retail
5/6SP/PS/AC			
3 Dr Lbk	35800	-	-
3 Dr Turbo Lbk	42800	-	-

T100 PICKUPS V6 1994

Model/Body/Type	BaseList	Whlse	Retail
AT/PS/AC			
Pkup	12998	-	-
DX Pkup	14698	**12150**	**14625**
SR5 Pkup	16768	-	-
1-Ton Pkup	15438	-	-
DX 4WD Pkup	18168	**14450**	**17000**
SR5 4WD Pkup	20178	-	-

TERCEL 4 Cyl 1994

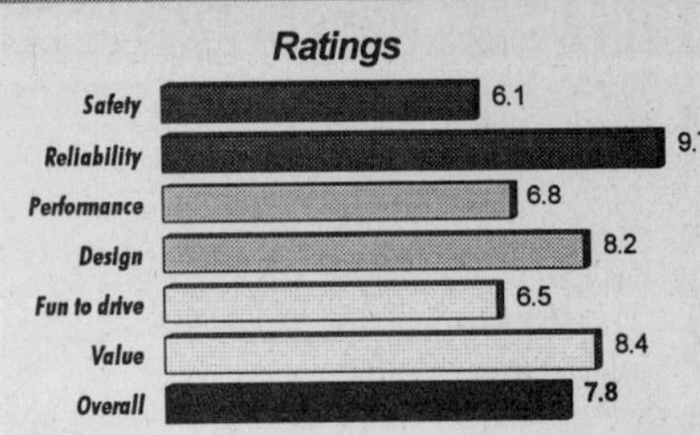

Model/Body/Type	BaseList	Whlse	Retail
FWD/AT/PS/AC			
2 Dr Cpe (4 spd)	8698	**7850**	**9725**
2 Dr DX Cpe	10148	**10000**	**12050**
4 Dr DX Sdn	10248	**10100**	**12175**

ADD FOR ALL 94 TOYOTA:

ABS(Std Supra) +430
Anti-Theft/Recovery Sys +365
Auto Trans(Pkup) +500
Car Phone(Land Cruiser,Supra) +230
Cass(Std Celica GT,MR2) +115
CD Player +230
Cruise Ctrl(Std Corolla LE) +160
Custom Whls +205
Dual Sunroof(Previa LE 2WD) +820
Leather Seats +320
Pwr Locks(Std CorollaLE,CelicaGT) +115
Pwr Seat(Std Supra,CamryXLE) +160
Pwr Sunroof(Std Camry XLE) +545
Pwr Wndw(Std CorollaLE,CelicaGT) +160
Removable Roof(Std MR2 Turbo)
Sunroof +320
V6 Eng +680

DEDUCT FOR ALL 94 TOYOTA:

No AC -680
No Auto Trans -590
No Pwr Steering -180

1993 TOYOTA

4RUNNER V6 1993

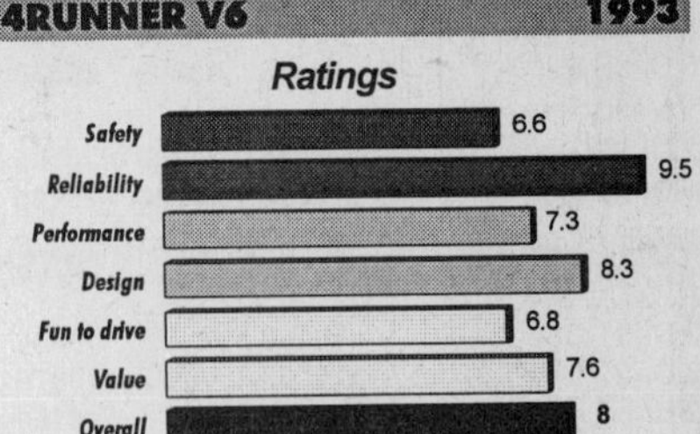

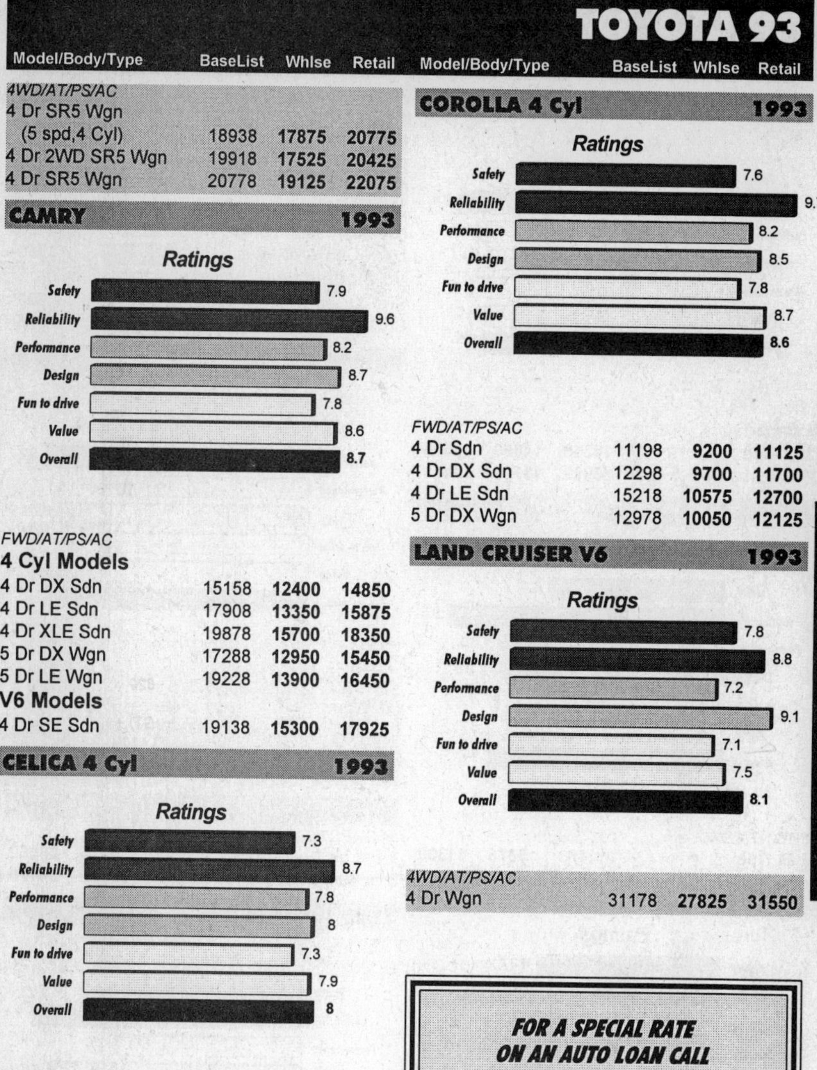

Model/Body/Type	BaseList	Whlse	Retail
4WD/AT/PS/AC			
4 Dr SR5 Wgn (5 spd,4 Cyl)	18938	17875	20775
4 Dr 2WD SR5 Wgn	19918	17525	20425
4 Dr SR5 Wgn	20778	19125	22075

CAMRY 1993

Ratings

Rating	Score
Safety	7.9
Reliability	9.6
Performance	8.2
Design	8.7
Fun to drive	7.8
Value	8.6
Overall	8.7

Model/Body/Type	BaseList	Whlse	Retail
FWD/AT/PS/AC			
4 Cyl Models			
4 Dr DX Sdn	15158	12400	14850
4 Dr LE Sdn	17908	13350	15875
4 Dr XLE Sdn	19878	15700	18350
5 Dr DX Wgn	17288	12950	15450
5 Dr LE Wgn	19228	13900	16450
V6 Models			
4 Dr SE Sdn	19138	15300	17925

CELICA 4 Cyl 1993

Ratings

Rating	Score
Safety	7.3
Reliability	8.7
Performance	7.8
Design	8
Fun to drive	7.3
Value	7.9
Overall	8

Model/Body/Type	BaseList	Whlse	Retail
FWD/AT/PS/AC			
2 Dr ST Cpe	14198	11175	13550
2 Dr GT Cpe	16708	12500	14975
3 Dr GT Lbk	16848	12600	15075
3 Dr GT-S Lbk	18428	13850	16400
All-Trac Turbo Lbk	28298	17450	20325
2 Dr GT Conv	21768	16700	19475

COROLLA 4 Cyl 1993

Ratings

Rating	Score
Safety	7.6
Reliability	9.7
Performance	8.2
Design	8.5
Fun to drive	7.8
Value	8.7
Overall	8.6

Model/Body/Type	BaseList	Whlse	Retail
FWD/AT/PS/AC			
4 Dr Sdn	11198	9200	11125
4 Dr DX Sdn	12298	9700	11700
4 Dr LE Sdn	15218	10575	12700
5 Dr DX Wgn	12978	10050	12125

LAND CRUISER V6 1993

Ratings

Rating	Score
Safety	7.8
Reliability	8.8
Performance	7.2
Design	9.1
Fun to drive	7.1
Value	7.5
Overall	8.1

Model/Body/Type	BaseList	Whlse	Retail
4WD/AT/PS/AC			
4 Dr Wgn	31178	27825	31550

TOYOTA

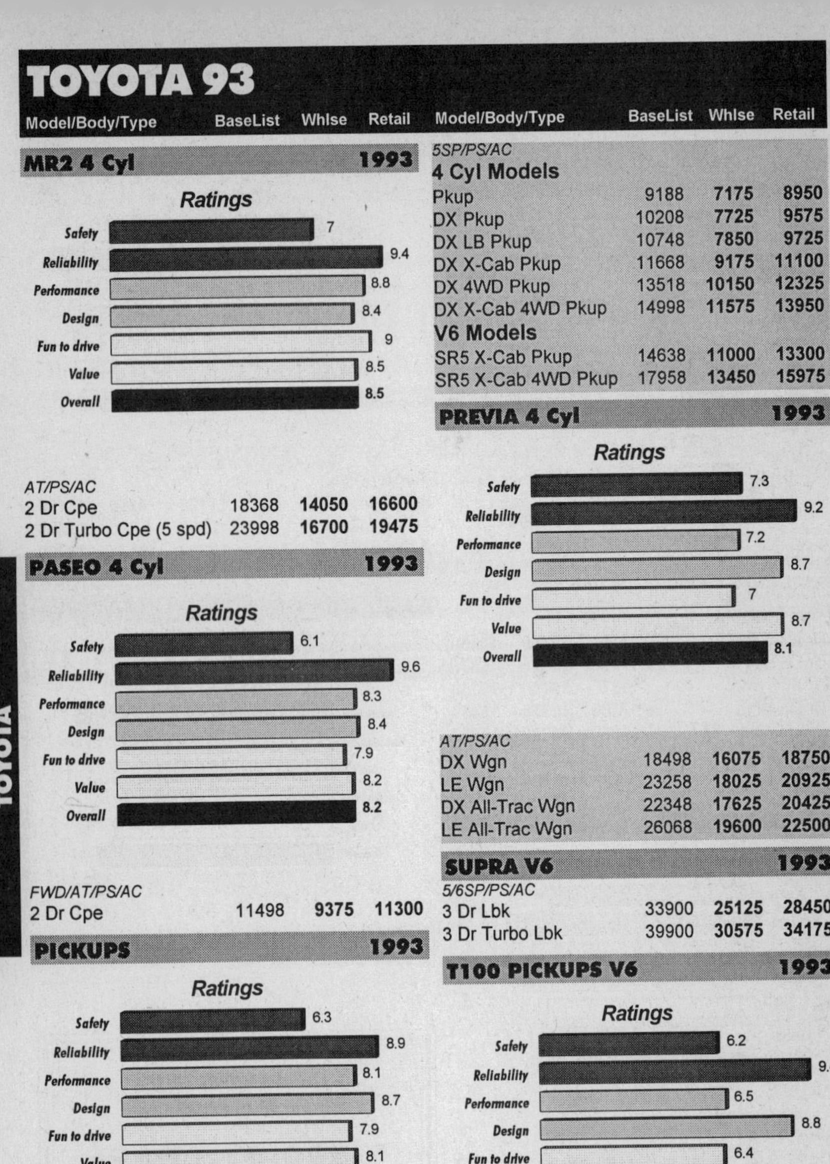

TOYOTA 93

MR2 4 Cyl — 1993

Ratings

Rating	Score
Safety	7
Reliability	9.4
Performance	8.8
Design	8.4
Fun to drive	9
Value	8.5
Overall	8.5

Model/Body/Type	BaseList	Whlse	Retail
AT/PS/AC			
2 Dr Cpe	18368	**14050**	**16600**
2 Dr Turbo Cpe (5 spd)	23998	**16700**	**19475**

PASEO 4 Cyl — 1993

Ratings

Rating	Score
Safety	6.1
Reliability	9.6
Performance	8.3
Design	8.4
Fun to drive	7.9
Value	8.2
Overall	8.2

Model/Body/Type	BaseList	Whlse	Retail
FWD/AT/PS/AC			
2 Dr Cpe	11498	**9375**	**11300**

PICKUPS — 1993

Ratings

Rating	Score
Safety	6.3
Reliability	8.9
Performance	8.1
Design	8.7
Fun to drive	7.9
Value	8.1
Overall	8

Model/Body/Type	BaseList	Whlse	Retail
5SP/PS/AC			
4 Cyl Models			
Pkup	9188	**7175**	**8950**
DX Pkup	10208	**7725**	**9575**
DX LB Pkup	10748	**7850**	**9725**
DX X-Cab Pkup	11668	**9175**	**11100**
DX 4WD Pkup	13518	**10150**	**12325**
DX X-Cab 4WD Pkup	14998	**11575**	**13950**
V6 Models			
SR5 X-Cab Pkup	14638	**11000**	**13300**
SR5 X-Cab 4WD Pkup	17958	**13450**	**15975**

PREVIA 4 Cyl — 1993

Ratings

Rating	Score
Safety	7.3
Reliability	9.2
Performance	7.2
Design	8.7
Fun to drive	7
Value	8.7
Overall	8.1

Model/Body/Type	BaseList	Whlse	Retail
AT/PS/AC			
DX Wgn	18498	**16075**	**18750**
LE Wgn	23258	**18025**	**20925**
DX All-Trac Wgn	22348	**17625**	**20425**
LE All-Trac Wgn	26068	**19600**	**22500**

SUPRA V6 — 1993

Model/Body/Type	BaseList	Whlse	Retail
5/6SP/PS/AC			
3 Dr Lbk	33900	**25125**	**28450**
3 Dr Turbo Lbk	39900	**30575**	**34175**

T100 PICKUPS V6 — 1993

Ratings

Rating	Score
Safety	6.2
Reliability	9.4
Performance	6.5
Design	8.8
Fun to drive	6.4
Value	7.6
Overall	7.7

Model/Body/Type	BaseList	Whlse	Retail
AT/PS/AC			
Pkup	13998	**10125**	**12300**
SR5 Pkup	15718	**11425**	**13775**
1-Ton Pkup	14718	**10575**	**12775**
4WD Pkup	17368	**12275**	**14750**
SR5 4WD Pkup	19028	**13575**	**16100**

TERCEL 4 Cyl — 1993

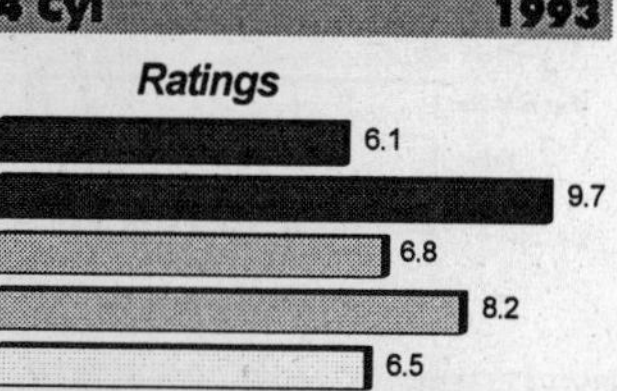

Model/Body/Type	BaseList	Whlse	Retail
FWD/AT/PS/AC			
2 Dr Cpe (4 spd)	7848	**6325**	**7925**
2 Dr DX Cpe	9678	**8400**	**10225**
4 Dr DX Sdn	9778	**8500**	**10325**
4 Dr LE Sdn	11308	**9100**	**11000**

ADD FOR ALL 93 TOYOTA:

ABS(Std Celica Turbo) +390
Auto Trans(Pkup) +430
Bed Liner +125
Car Phone(Land Cruiser) +175
Cass(Std Prev LE,Cam LE/XLE,Turbo,GTS,MR2, Cam SE,Land Cruiser) +100
CD Player(Std Celica Turbo) +195
Cruise Ctrl(Std Prev LE,Cam LE/XLE,Supra, Corolla LE,Land Cruiser) +135
Custom Whls +175
Dual Sunroof(Previa LE 2WD) +665
Fiberglass Cap +250
Leather Seats(Std Celica Turbo) +275
Privacy Glass +145
Pwr Locks(Std PrvLE,CamLE/XLE,Turb,CorLE, Land Cruiser) +100
Pwr Seat(Std Celica Turbo) +135
Pwr Sunroof(Std Celica Turbo,Cam XLE) +430
Pwr Wndw(Std PrvLE,CamLE/XLE,Turb,CorLE, Land Cruiser) +135
Removable Roof(Std MR2 Turbo) +545
Running Board +145
Slider Wndw +80
Sunroof +230
Towing Pkg +185
V6 Eng +505

DEDUCT FOR ALL 93 TOYOTA:

No AC -545
No Auto Trans -505
No Pwr Steering -160

4RUNNER V6 — 1992

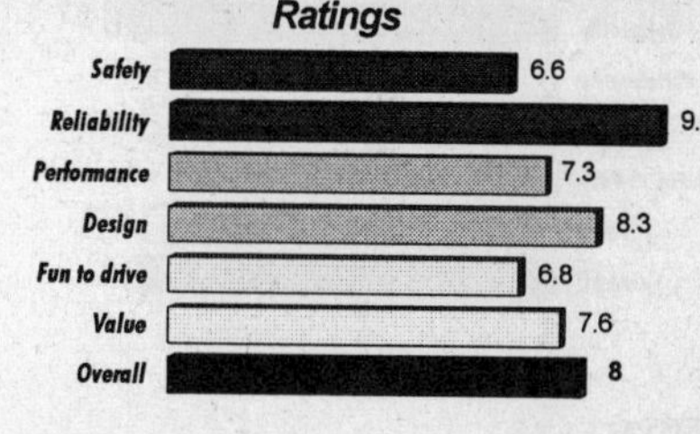

Model/Body/Type	BaseList	Whlse	Retail
4WD/AT/PS/AC			
4 Dr SR5 Wgn (4 Cyl)	18018	**17200**	**20000**
2 Dr SR5 Wgn (5 spd)	20428	**16675**	**19450**
4 Dr SR5 2WD Wgn	19198	**16325**	**19000**

CAMRY 4 Cyl — 1992

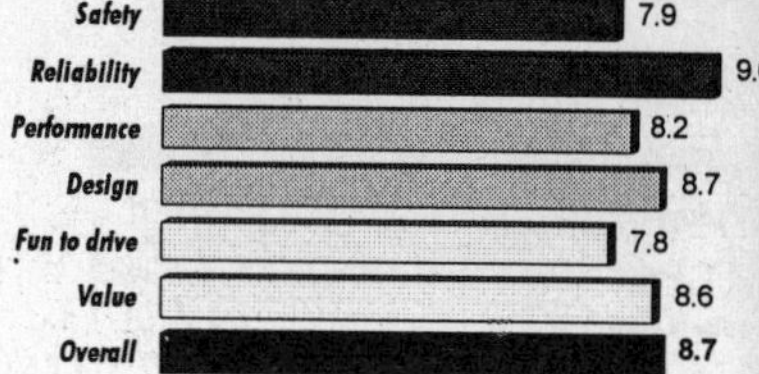

Model/Body/Type	BaseList	Whlse	Retail
FWD/AT/PS/AC			
4 Dr DX Sdn	14368	**10800**	**13150**
4 Dr LE Sdn	16998	**11675**	**14125**
4 Dr XLE Sdn	18848	**13750**	**16275**
5 Dr DX Wgn	16898	**11300**	**13675**
5 Dr LE Wgn	18798	**12150**	**14625**
4 Dr SE Sdn (V6)	18528	**13450**	**15975**

CELICA 4 Cyl 1992

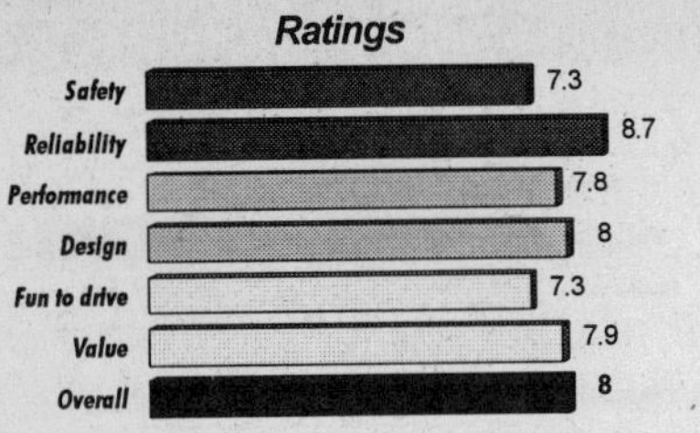

Ratings

Rating	Score
Safety	7.3
Reliability	8.7
Performance	7.8
Design	8
Fun to drive	7.3
Value	7.9
Overall	8

FWD/AT/PS/AC	BaseList	Whlse	Retail
2 Dr ST Cpe	13378	**10125**	**12300**
2 Dr GT Cpe	15708	**11250**	**13625**
3 Dr GT Lbk	15838	**11350**	**13725**
3 Dr GT-S Lbk	17328	**12475**	**14950**
3 Dr All-Trac Turbo Lbk (5 spd)	22048	**14025**	**16575**
2 Dr GT Conv	20468	**15100**	**17725**

COROLLA 4 Cyl 1992

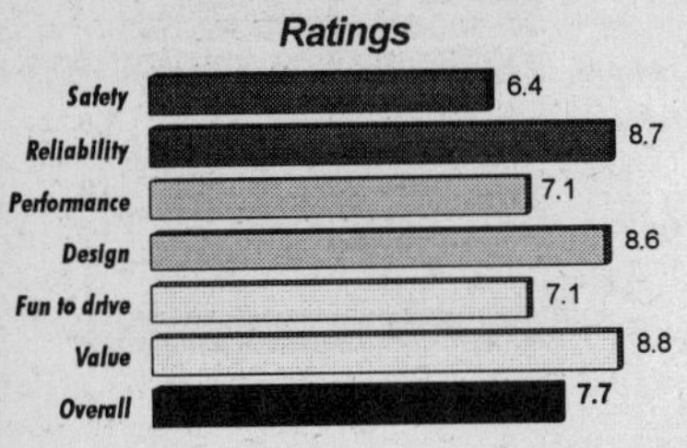

Ratings

Rating	Score
Safety	6.4
Reliability	8.7
Performance	7.1
Design	8.6
Fun to drive	7.1
Value	8.8
Overall	7.7

FWD/AT/PS/AC	BaseList	Whlse	Retail
4 Dr Sdn	9418	**6850**	**8575**
4 Dr DX Sdn	10408	**7275**	**9075**
4 Dr LE Sdn	12598	**7925**	**9800**
5 Dr DX Wgn	11078	**7625**	**9450**
5 Dr DX All-Trac Wgn	12688	**8325**	**10150**

CRESSIDA V6 1992

AT/PS/AC	BaseList	Whlse	Retail
4 Dr Sdn	23488	**15325**	**18100**

LAND CRUISER V6 1992

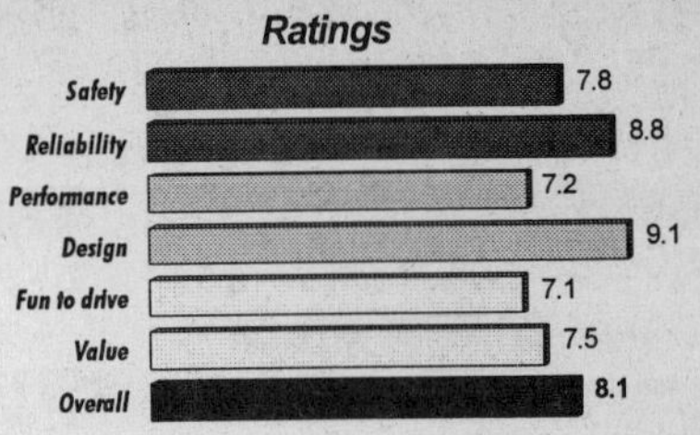

Ratings

Rating	Score
Safety	7.8
Reliability	8.8
Performance	7.2
Design	9.1
Fun to drive	7.1
Value	7.5
Overall	8.1

4WD/AT/PS/AC	BaseList	Whlse	Retail
4 Dr Wgn	25628	**24600**	**28100**

MR2 4 Cyl 1992

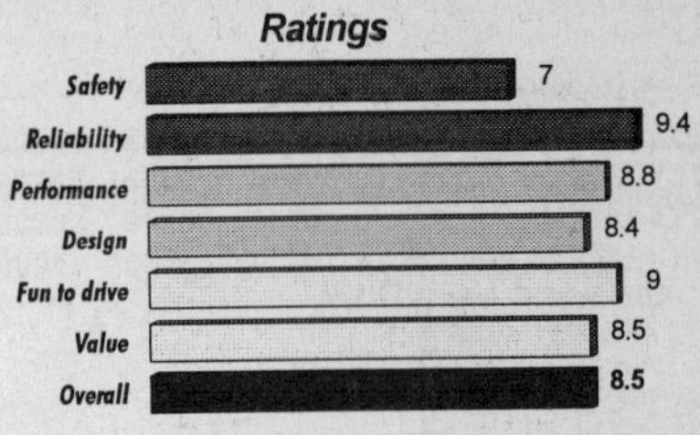

Ratings

Rating	Score
Safety	7
Reliability	9.4
Performance	8.8
Design	8.4
Fun to drive	9
Value	8.5
Overall	8.5

AT/PS/AC	BaseList	Whlse	Retail
2 Dr Cpe	16048	**12200**	**14675**
2 Dr Turbo Cpe (5 spd)	19378	**13250**	**15750**

PASEO 4 Cyl 1992

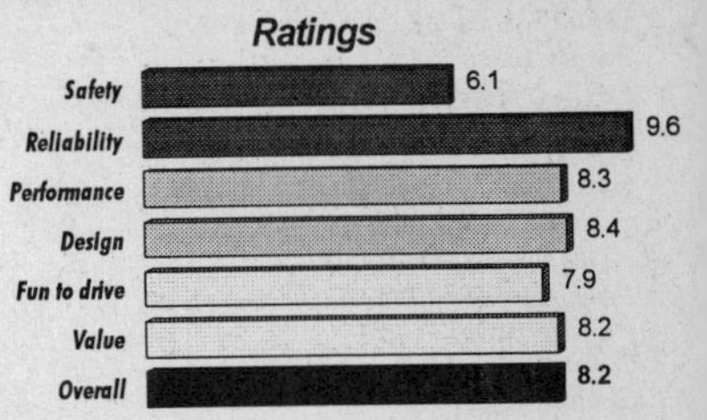

Ratings

Rating	Score
Safety	6.1
Reliability	9.6
Performance	8.3
Design	8.4
Fun to drive	7.9
Value	8.2
Overall	8.2

FWD/AT/PS/AC	BaseList	Whlse	Retail
2 Dr Cpe	10338	**7750**	**9600**

Model/Body/Type	BaseList	Whlse	Retail

PICKUPS 1992

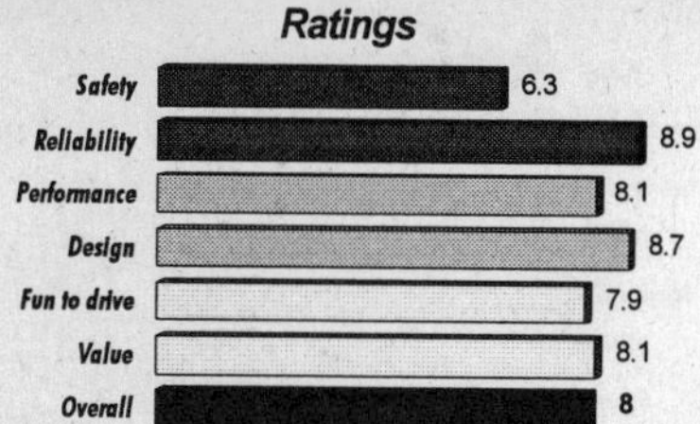

5SP/PS/AC

Model/Body/Type	BaseList	Whlse	Retail
4 Cyl Models			
Pkup	8998	**6250**	**7850**
DX Pkup	9868	**6725**	**8475**
DX LB Pkup	10398	**6875**	**8600**
DX X-Cab Pkup	11108	**7975**	**9825**
DX 4WD Pkup	12818	**9075**	**11100**
DX 4WD LB Pkup	13428	**9200**	**11225**
DX X-Cab 4WD Pkup	14068	**10250**	**12475**
V6 Models			
SR5 X-Cab Pkup	14058	**9475**	**11425**
1-Ton LB Pkup	12088	**7225**	**9100**
SR5 X-Cab 4WD Pkup	16988	**11750**	**14200**

PREVIA 4 Cyl 1992

Ratings

Rating	Score
Safety	7.3
Reliability	9.2
Performance	7.2
Design	8.7
Fun to drive	7
Value	8.7
Overall	8.1

AT/PS/AC

Model/Body/Type	BaseList	Whlse	Retail
DX Wgn	16518	**14425**	**17000**
LE Wgn	21448	**16150**	**18825**
DX All-Trac Wgn	19128	**15850**	**18425**
LE All-Trac Wgn	24058	**17575**	**20350**

SUPRA V6 1992

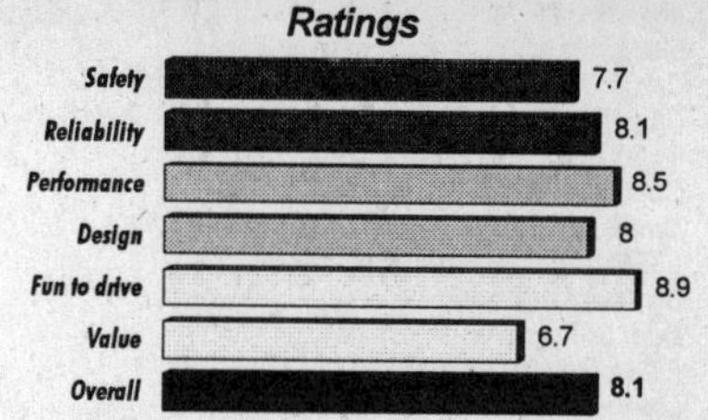

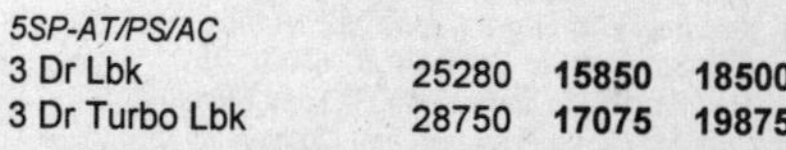

5SP-AT/PS/AC

Model/Body/Type	BaseList	Whlse	Retail
3 Dr Lbk	25280	**15850**	**18500**
3 Dr Turbo Lbk	28750	**17075**	**19875**

TERCEL 4 Cyl 1992

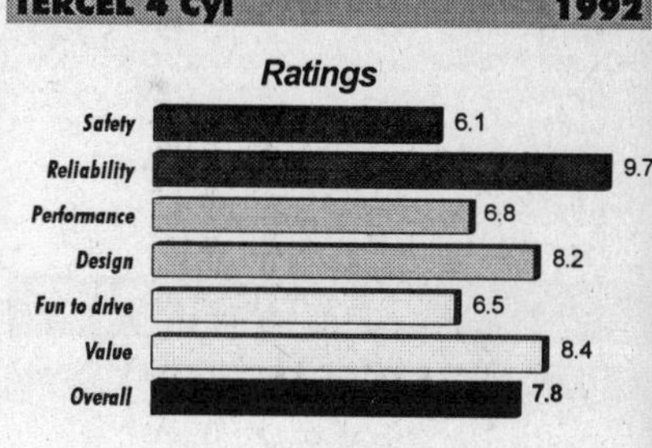

FWD/AT/PS/AC

Model/Body/Type	BaseList	Whlse	Retail
2 Dr Cpe (4 spd)	6998	**4475**	**5875**
2 Dr DX Cpe	8428	**6400**	**8000**
4 Dr DX Sdn	8528	**6500**	**8125**
4 Dr LE Sdn	9908	**7025**	**8775**

TOYOTA

Model/Body/Type	BaseList	Whlse	Retail

ADD FOR ALL 92 TOYOTA:

ABS(Std Supra Turbo) +350
Auto Trans(Pkup) +390
Bed Liner +105
Car Phone(Supra,Cress,Land Cruiser) +160
Cass(Std Cam LE/XLE,Cress,Supra,GTS,Turbo, Cam SE,Land Cruiser) +75
CD Player +175
Cruise Ctrl(Std Camry LE/XLE,Cress,Supra, Celica Trbo,Previa LE) +115
Custom Whls +160
Dual Sunroof(Previa LE 2WD) +585
Fiberglass Cap +205
Leather Seats +230
Privacy Glass +125
Pwr Locks(Std Cam LE/XLE,Cress,Supra, Celica Turbo,Prev LE,Land Cruiser) +75
Pwr Seat(Std Supra,Camry XLE) +115
Pwr Sunroof(Std Camry XLE) +390
Pwr Wndw(Std Cam LE/XLE,Cress,Supra, Celica Turbo,Prev LE,Land Cruiser) +115
Removable Roof +485
Running Board +125
Sunroof +195
Towing Pkg +145
V6 Eng +470

DEDUCT FOR ALL 92 TOYOTA:

No AC -505
No Auto Trans -470
No Pwr Steering -135

1991 TOYOTA

4RUNNER 4 Cyl — 1991

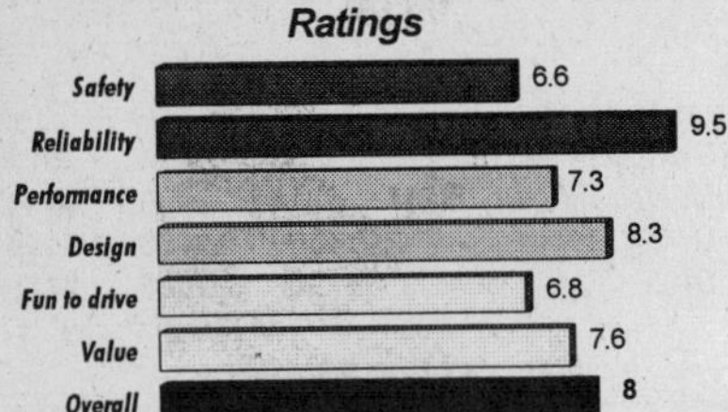

4WD/AT/PS/AC

Model/Body/Type	BaseList	Whlse	Retail
2 Dr SR5 Wgn	16718	**14450**	**17000**
4 Dr SR5 2WD Wgn	15898	**13550**	**16075**
4 Dr SR5 Wgn	16708	**14900**	**17500**

CAMRY — 1991

Ratings

Rating	Score
Safety	7.2
Reliability	7.5
Performance	8
Design	9.1
Fun to drive	8.2
Value	9.1
Overall	7.8

FWD/AT/PS/AC

Model/Body/Type	BaseList	Whlse	Retail
4 Cyl Models			
4 Dr Sdn	11948	**7500**	**9400**
4 Dr DX Sdn	12688	**8200**	**10100**
4 Dr LE Sdn	15028	**9000**	**11000**
4 Dr DX All-Trac Sdn	15358	**8850**	**10850**
4 Dr LE All-Trac Sdn	17018	**9650**	**11700**
5 Dr DX Wgn	14158	**8650**	**10575**
V6 Models			
5 Dr LE Wgn	18208	**9975**	**12125**

CELICA 4 Cyl — 1991

Ratings

Rating	Score
Safety	7.3
Reliability	8.7
Performance	7.8
Design	8
Fun to drive	7.3
Value	7.9
Overall	8

FWD/AT/PS/AC

Model/Body/Type	BaseList	Whlse	Retail
2 Dr ST Cpe	12698	**7975**	**9900**
2 Dr GT Cpe	14368	**8975**	**11000**
3 Dr GT Lbk	14618	**9075**	**11100**
3 Dr GT-S Lbk	16668	**10125**	**12300**
3 Dr All-Trac Turbo Lbk (5 spd)	21408	**11350**	**13725**
2 Dr GT Conv	19228	**12325**	**14775**

Model/Body/Type	BaseList	Whlse	Retail

COROLLA 4 Cyl — 1991

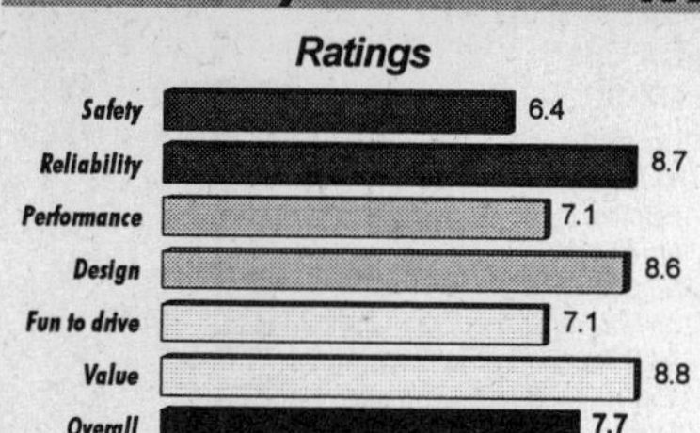

FWD/AT/PS/AC			
4 Dr Sdn	8998	**5725**	**7275**
4 Dr DX Sdn	9998	**6125**	**7700**
4 Dr LE Sdn	11478	**6700**	**8450**
5 Dr DX Wgn	10668	**6450**	**8050**
5 Dr DX All-Trac Wgn	12368	**7100**	**8850**
2 Dr SR5 Cpe	11418	**7000**	**8725**
2 Dr GT-S Cpe (5 spd)	13588	**7350**	**9150**

CRESSIDA V6 — 1991

AT/PS/AC			
4 Dr Sdn	22198	**12775**	**15375**

LAND CRUISER V6 — 1991

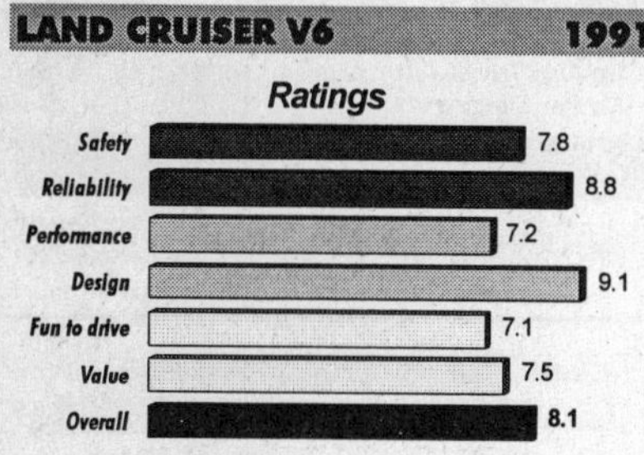

4WD/AT/PS/AC			
4 Dr Wgn	21998	**20075**	**23325**

MR2 4 Cyl — 1991

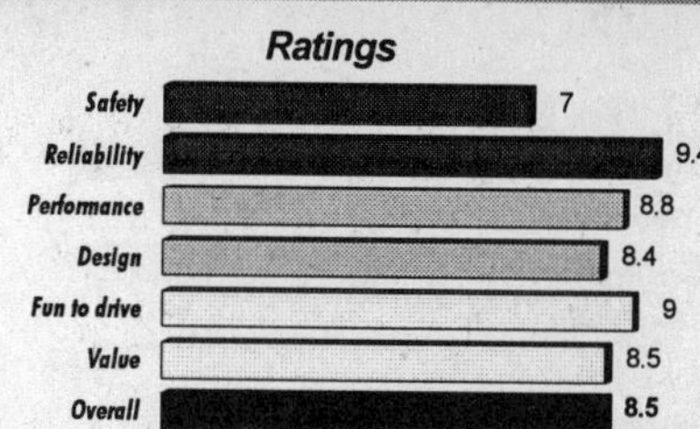

AT/PS/AC			
2 Dr Cpe	14898	**9750**	**11875**
2 Dr Turbo Cpe (5 spd)	18228	**10650**	**12975**

PICKUPS — 1991

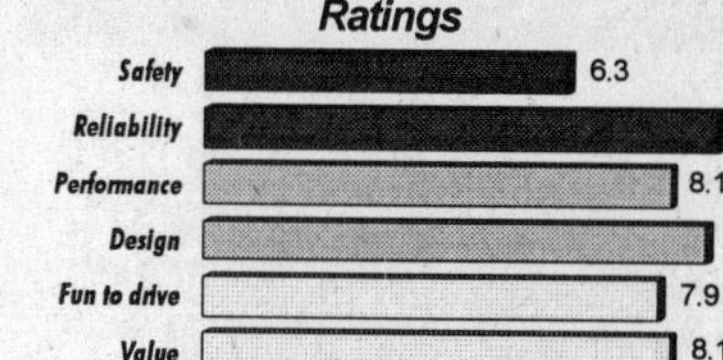

5SP/PS/AC			
4 Cyl Models			
Pkup	8198	**5250**	**6775**
DX Pkup	9018	**5725**	**7275**
DX LB Pkup	9548	**5850**	**7400**
DX X-Cab Pkup	10258	**6875**	**8600**
DX 4WD Pkup	11638	**7900**	**9825**
DX 4WD LB Pkup	12248	**8025**	**9950**
DX X-Cab 4WD Pkup	12888	**9050**	**11050**
V6 Models			
SR5 X-Cab Pkup	13258	**8050**	**9900**
1-Ton LB Pkup	11318	**6175**	**7900**
SR5 X-Cab 4WD Pkup	15928	**10175**	**12400**

TOYOTA 91-90

Model/Body/Type	BaseList	Whlse	Retail

PREVIA 4 Cyl — 1991

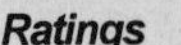

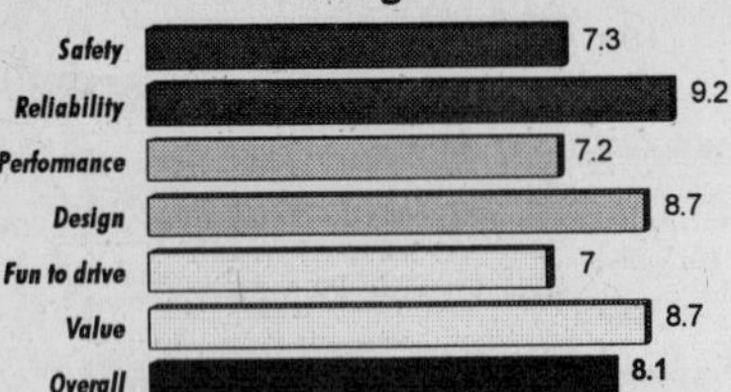

AT/PS/AC			
DX Wgn	13998	**11850**	**14300**
LE Wgn	18698	**13225**	**15725**
DX All-Trac Wgn	16608	**13200**	**15625**
LE All-Trac Wgn	21308	**14575**	**17075**

SUPRA V6 — 1991

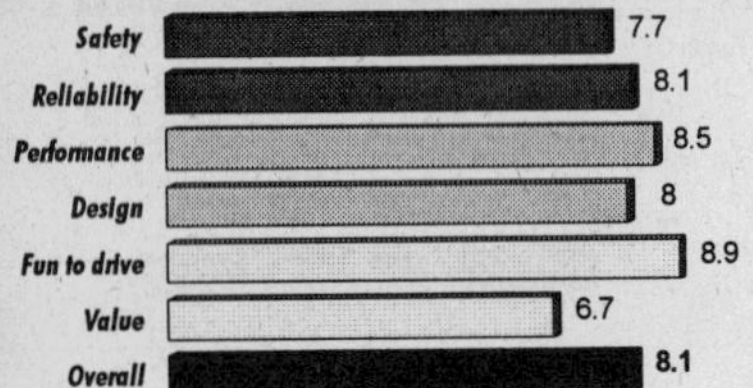

5SP-AT/PS/AC			
3 Dr Lbk	23820	**13200**	**15700**
3 Dr Turbo Lbk	27290	**14250**	**16825**

TERCEL 4 Cyl — 1991

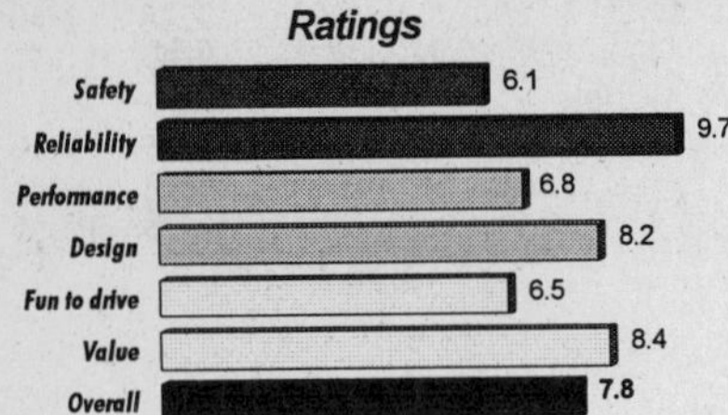

FWD/AT/PS/AC			
2 Dr Cpe (4 spd)	6488	**3350**	**4700**
2 Dr DX Cpe	7798	**5200**	**6725**
4 Dr DX Sdn	7898	**5300**	**6850**
4 Dr LE Sdn	9478	**5775**	**7325**

ADD FOR ALL 91 TOYOTA:

ABS(Std Supra Turbo) +315
Auto Trans(Pkup) +350
Bed Liner +80
Car Phone(Supra,Cress,Land Cruiser) +135
Cass(Std Cam LE V6,Supra,Cress,Turbo, Celica GTS,Land Cruiser) +60
CD Player +160
Cruise Ctrl(Std Cam LE V6,Supra,Cress, Celica Turbo,Previa LE) +100
Custom Whls +135
Fiberglass Cap +170
Leather Seats +195
Privacy Glass +105
Pwr Locks(Std CamLEV6,Supra,Cress, Cel Trbo,PrvLE) +60
Pwr Seat(Std Supra) +100
Pwr Sunroof +350
Pwr Wndw(Std CamLE V6,Supra,Cres, Celica Trbo) +100
Removable Roof +450
Running Board +105
Sunroof +160
Towing Pkg +105
V6 Eng +430

DEDUCT FOR ALL 91 TOYOTA:

No AC -470
No Auto Trans -430
No Pwr Steering -115

1990 TOYOTA

4RUNNER 4 Cyl — 1990

4WD/AT/PS/AC			
2 Dr SR5 Wgn	16718	**12450**	**14925**
4 Dr SR5 2WD Wgn	15498	**11675**	**14125**
4 Dr SR5 Wgn	16218	**12950**	**15450**

CAMRY 1990

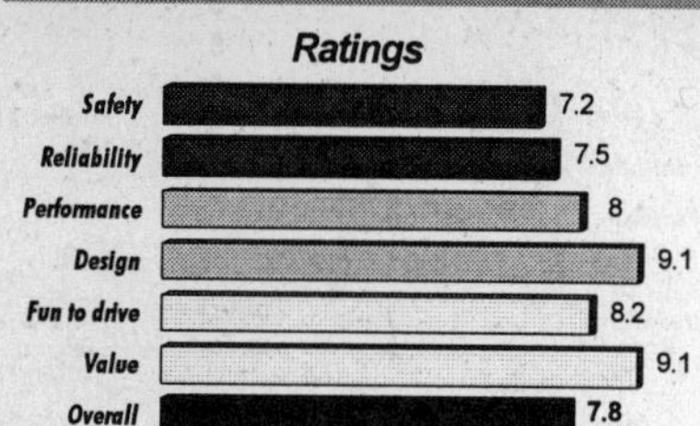

FWD/AT/PS/AC

Model/Body/Type	BaseList	Whlse	Retail
4 Cyl Models			
4 Dr Sdn	11588	**5950**	**7675**
4 Dr Dlx Sdn	12388	**6550**	**8325**
4 Dr LE Sdn	14658	**7250**	**9125**
4 Dr Dlx All-Trac Sdn	14168	**7150**	**9000**
4 Dr LE All-Trac Sdn	16648	**7850**	**9800**
5 Dr Dlx Wgn	13768	**7000**	**8800**
V6 Models			
5 Dr LE Wgn	17218	**8175**	**10075**

CELICA 4 Cyl 1990

Ratings

Rating	Score
Safety	7.3
Reliability	8.7
Performance	7.8
Design	8
Fun to drive	7.3
Value	7.9
Overall	8

FWD/AT/PS/AC

Model/Body/Type	BaseList	Whlse	Retail
2 Dr ST Cpe	12268	**6450**	**8200**
2 Dr GT Cpe	13938	**7225**	**9100**
3 Dr GT Lbk	14188	**7325**	**9200**
3 Dr GT-S Lbk	16268	**8375**	**10275**
3 Dr All-Trac Turbo Lbk (5 spd)	21008	**9625**	**11675**

COROLLA 4 Cyl 1990

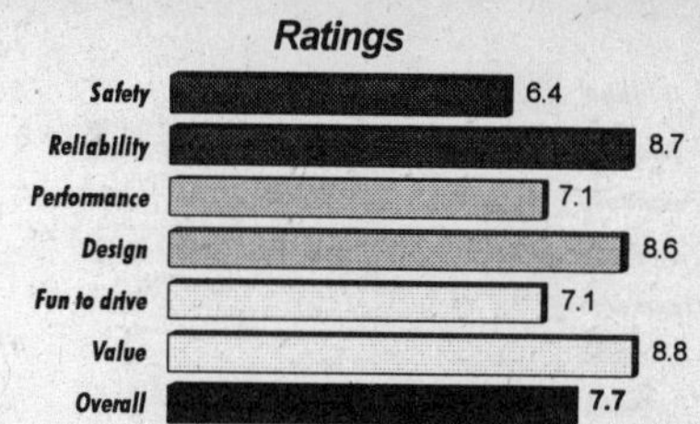

FWD/AT/PS/AC

Model/Body/Type	BaseList	Whlse	Retail
4 Dr Sdn	8748	**4350**	**5775**
4 Dr Dlx Sdn	9488	**4700**	**6150**
4 Dr LE Sdn	10928	**5200**	**6725**
5 Dr Dlx Wgn	10128	**4950**	**6500**
4 Dr Dlx All-Trac Sdn	10758	**5250**	**6775**
5 Dr Dlx All-Trac Wgn	11838	**5575**	**7125**
5 Dr SR5 All-Trac S/W (5 spd)	13238	**5825**	**7375**
2 Dr SR5 Cpe	11068	**5475**	**7000**
2 Dr GT-S Cpe (5 spd)	13238	**5775**	**7325**

CRESSIDA V6 1990

AT/PS/AC

Model/Body/Type	BaseList	Whlse	Retail
4 Dr Luxury Sdn	21498	**10250**	**12550**

LAND CRUISER V6 1990

Ratings

Rating	Score
Safety	7.8
Reliability	8.8
Performance	7.2
Design	9.1
Fun to drive	7.1
Value	7.5
Overall	8.1

4WD/AT/PS/AC

Model/Body/Type	BaseList	Whlse	Retail
4 Dr Wgn	20898	**13975**	**16650**

Model/Body/Type	BaseList	Whlse	Retail

PICKUPS 4 Cyl — 1990

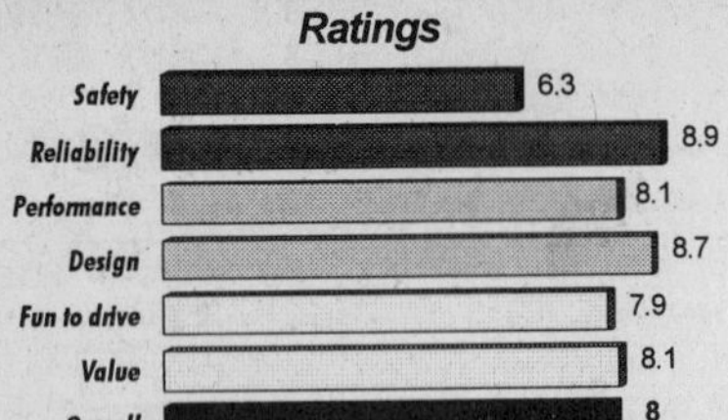

5SP/PS/AC	BaseList	Whlse	Retail
Pkup	7998	**4250**	**5675**
Dlx Pkup	8588	**4675**	**6125**
Dlx LB Pkup	9118	**4775**	**6250**
SR5 LB Pkup	9988	**5325**	**6875**
Dlx X-Cab Pkup	9758	**5675**	**7175**
SR5 X-Cab Pkup	10988	**6225**	**7825**
Dlx 4WD Pkup	11318	**6675**	**8500**
Dlx 4WD LB Pkup	11928	**6825**	**8650**
SR5 4WD Pkup	12218	**7250**	**9125**
Dlx X-Cab 4WD Pkup	12568	**7675**	**9600**
SR5 X-Cab 4WD Pkup	13528	**8250**	**10150**
Dlx 1-Ton LB Pkup (V6)	11038	**5400**	**7125**

SUPRA V6 — 1990

Ratings

Rating	Score
Safety	7.7
Reliability	8.1
Performance	8.5
Design	8
Fun to drive	8.9
Value	6.7
Overall	8.1

5SP-AT/PS/AC	BaseList	Whlse	Retail
3 Dr Lbk	22860	**10875**	**13225**
3 Dr Turbo Lbk	25200	**11800**	**14275**

See the Automobile Dealer Directory on page 379 for a Dealer near you!

TERCEL 4 Cyl — 1990

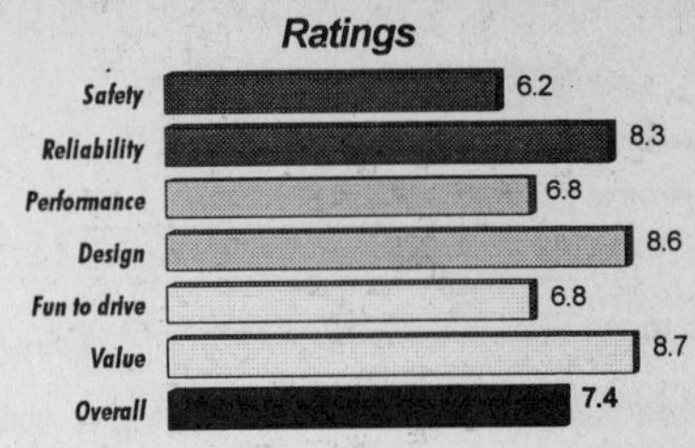

FWD/AT/PS/AC	BaseList	Whlse	Retail
3 Dr EZ Lbk (4 spd)	6488	**2250**	**3350**
3 Dr Lbk	7558	**3300**	**4650**
2 Dr Cpe	7618	**3400**	**4725**
2 Dr Dlx Cpe	9028	**4000**	**5350**

ADD FOR ALL 90 TOYOTA:

ABS +275
Auto Trans(Pkup) +315
Cass(Std Celica GTS/Turbo,Supra,Cressida) +60
CD Player +115
Cruise Ctrl(Std Celica Trbo,Supra,Cress) +75
Custom Whls +115
Fiberglass Cap +125
Leather Seats +135
Privacy Glass +80
Pwr Locks(Std Celica Trbo,Supra,Cress) +60
Pwr Seat +75
Pwr Sunroof +315
Pwr Wndw(Std Celica Trbo,Supra,Cress) +75
Removable Roof +390
Running Board +80
Sunroof +115
Towing Pkg +80
V6 Eng +390

DEDUCT FOR ALL 90 TOYOTA:

No AC -430
No Auto Trans -390
No Pwr Steering -100

1989 TOYOTA

4RUNNER 4 Cyl — 1989

4WD/AT/PS/AC	BaseList	Whlse	Retail
Dlx Utility	13988	**8950**	**10950**
Dlx Wgn	14668	**9350**	**11375**
SR5 Wgn	16318	**10075**	**12250**

CAMRY 4 Cyl — 1989

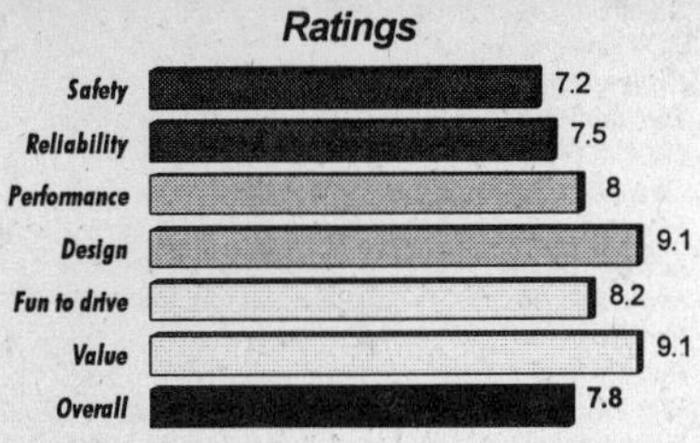

Ratings

Rating	Score
Safety	7.2
Reliability	7.5
Performance	8
Design	9.1
Fun to drive	8.2
Value	9.1
Overall	7.8

Model/Body/Type	BaseList	Whlse	Retail
FWD/AT/PS/AC			
4 Dr Sdn	11488	**4725**	**6350**
4 Dr Dlx Sdn	12328	**5225**	**6925**
4 Dr LE Sdn	14658	**5825**	**7525**
4 Dr Dlx All-Trac Sdn	14108	**5800**	**7500**
4 Dr LE All-Trac Sdn	16648	**6375**	**8125**
5 Dr Dlx Wgn	13018	**5675**	**7350**
5 Dr LE Wgn	15438	**6225**	**7975**

CELICA 4 Cyl — 1989

Model/Body/Type	BaseList	Whlse	Retail
FWD/AT/PS/AC			
2 Dr ST Cpe	11808	**4850**	**6500**
2 Dr GT Cpe	13408	**5575**	**7250**
3 Dr GT Lbk	13658	**5700**	**7375**
2 Dr GT-S Cpe	15388	**6500**	**8225**
3 Dr GT-S Lbk (5 spd)	15738	**6125**	**7850**
3 Dr All-Trac Turbo Lbk (5 spd)	20878	**7800**	**9725**
2 Dr GT Conv	18318	**8625**	**10575**

COROLLA 4 Cyl — 1989

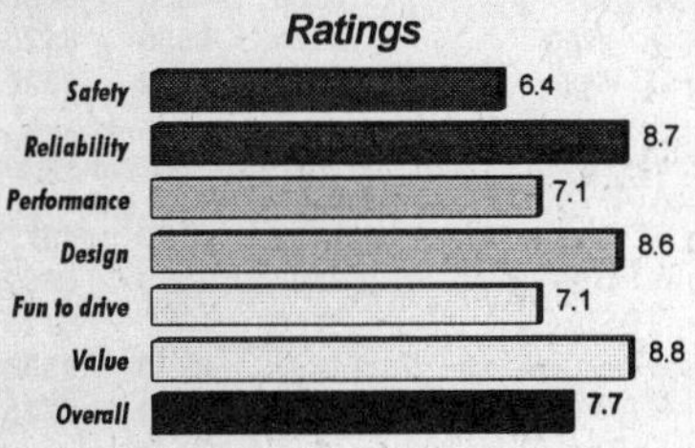

Ratings

Rating	Score
Safety	6.4
Reliability	8.7
Performance	7.1
Design	8.6
Fun to drive	7.1
Value	8.8
Overall	7.7

Model/Body/Type	BaseList	Whlse	Retail
FWD/AT/PS/AC			
4 Dr Dlx Sdn	9198	**4075**	**5475**
4 Dr LE Sdn	10418	**4600**	**6025**
5 Dr Dlx Wgn	9788	**4350**	**5775**
4 Dr Dlx All-Trac Sdn	10608	**4625**	**6100**
5 Dr Dlx All-Trac Wgn	11498	**4850**	**6350**
5 Dr SR5 All-Trac S/W (5 spd)	13088	**5100**	**6625**
2 Dr SR5 Cpe	10628	**4700**	**6150**
2 Dr GT-S Cpe (5 spd)	12728	**4925**	**6450**

CRESSIDA V6 — 1989

Model/Body/Type	BaseList	Whlse	Retail
AT/PS/AC			
4 Dr Luxury Sdn	21498	**8425**	**10475**

LAND CRUISER V6 — 1989

Model/Body/Type	BaseList	Whlse	Retail
4WD/AT/PS/AC			
4 Dr Wgn	20898	**11075**	**13525**

MR2 4 Cyl — 1989

Model/Body/Type	BaseList	Whlse	Retail
AT/PS/AC			
2 Dr Cpe	13798	**5825**	**7525**
2 Dr Supercharged Cpe	17628	**6775**	**8625**

PICKUPS 4 Cyl — 1989

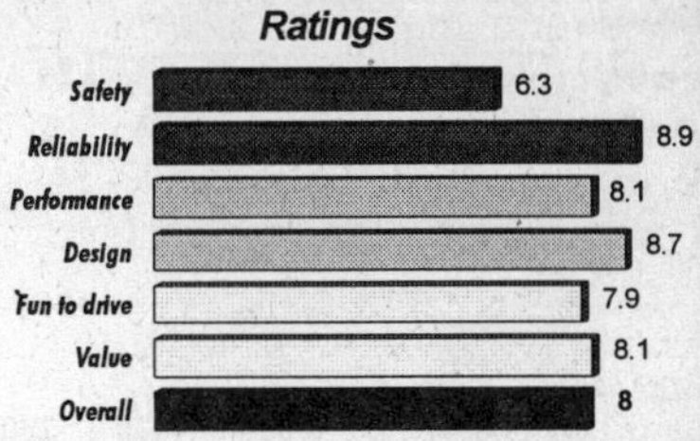

Ratings

Rating	Score
Safety	6.3
Reliability	8.9
Performance	8.1
Design	8.7
Fun to drive	7.9
Value	8.1
Overall	8

Model/Body/Type	BaseList	Whlse	Retail
5SP/PS/AC			
Pkup	7998	3300	4650
Dlx Pkup	8458	3675	5000
Dlx LB Pkup	8988	3800	5150
SR5 LB Pkup	9888	4350	5775
Dlx X-Cab Pkup	9628	4625	6100
SR5 X-Cab Pkup	10888	5125	6650
Dlx 4WD Pkup	11138	5550	7225
Dlx 4WD LB Pkup	11748	5700	7375
SR5 4WD Pkup	12068	6125	7825
Dlx X-Cab 4WD Pkup	12388	6500	8250
SR5 X-Cab 4WD Pkup	13378	7050	8875
Dlx 1-Ton LB Pkup (V6)	10908	4375	5925

TOYOTA 89-88

SUPRA V6 — 1989

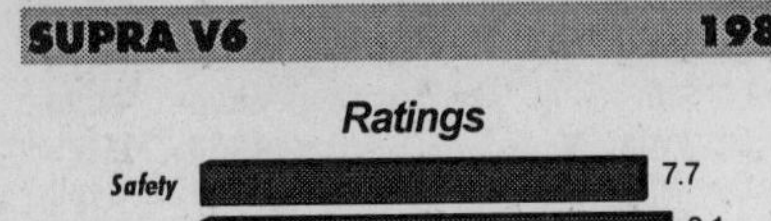
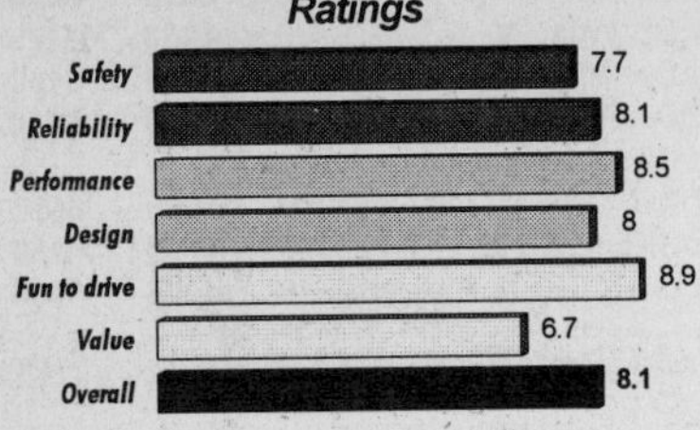

Model/Body/Type	BaseList	Whlse	Retail
5SP-AT/PS/AC			
3 Dr Lbk	22360	**8550**	**10450**
3 Dr Turbo Lbk	24700	**9300**	**11325**

TERCEL 4 Cyl — 1989

Ratings

Rating	Score
Safety	6.2
Reliability	8.3
Performance	6.8
Design	8.6
Fun to drive	6.8
Value	8.7
Overall	7.4

Model/Body/Type	BaseList	Whlse	Retail
FWD/AT/PS/AC			
3 Dr EZ Lbk (4 spd)	6328	**1825**	**2900**
3 Dr Lbk	7178	**2675**	**3850**
3 Dr Dlx Lbk	8298	**3175**	**4475**
5 Dr Dlx Lbk	8538	**3250**	**4575**
2 Dr Cpe	7338	**2775**	**4000**
2 Dr Dlx Cpe	8398	**3250**	**4575**

VAN 4 Cyl — 1989

Model/Body/Type	BaseList	Whlse	Retail
AT/PS/AC			
Window Van	11058	**4275**	**5700**
Panel Van	10758	**3925**	**5275**
Deluxe Van	13608	**5775**	**7325**
LE Van	15538	**6500**	**8075**
4WD Panel Van	14018	**4875**	**6550**
4WD Deluxe Van	16068	**6750**	**8600**
4WD LE Van	18448	**7450**	**9325**

ADD FOR ALL 89 TOYOTA:

Auto Trans(Pkup) +275
Cass(Std Celica Trbo,Supr,Cress) +35
CD Player +75
Cruise Ctrl(Std Supra,Cressida) +60
Custom Whls +75
Dual AC +275
Dual Sunroof +350
Fiberglass Cap +80
Leather Seats +115
Pwr Locks(Std Celica Trbo,Supra,Cres,Van LE) +35
Pwr Seat +60
Pwr Sunroof +250
Pwr Wndw(Std Celica Turbo,Supra,Cressida) +60
Removable Roof(Std Supercharged MR2) +330
Sunroof +100
V6 Eng +350

DEDUCT FOR ALL 89 TOYOTA:

No AC -390
No Auto Trans -350
No Pwr Steering -75

1988 TOYOTA

4RUNNER 4 Cyl — 1988

Model/Body/Type	BaseList	Whlse	Retail
4WD/AT/PS/AC			
Dlx Utility	13138	**7575**	**9475**
SR5 Utility	14718	**8275**	**10175**
Dlx Wgn (5 spd)	13698	**7600**	**9500**
SR5 Wgn (V6)	16118	**9075**	**11100**

CAMRY 4 Cyl — 1988

Model/Body/Type	BaseList	Whlse	Retail
FWD/AT/PS/AC			
4 Dr Sdn	10898	**3850**	**5325**
4 Dr Dlx Sdn	11698	**4250**	**5800**
4 Dr LE Sdn	14058	**4700**	**6275**
4 Dr Dlx All-Trac Sdn (5 spd)	13428	**4375**	**5925**
4 Dr LE All-Trac Sdn (5 spd)	15068	**4800**	**6450**
5 Dr Dlx Wgn	12388	**4550**	**6125**
5 Dr LE Wgn	14828	**4950**	**6625**

CELICA 4 Cyl — 1988

Model/Body/Type	BaseList	Whlse	Retail
FWD/AT/PS/AC			
2 Dr ST Cpe	11198	**3550**	**4975**
2 Dr GT Cpe	12888	**4100**	**5650**
3 Dr GT Lbk	13138	**4200**	**5725**
2 Dr GT-S Cpe	14898	**4875**	**6550**
3 Dr GT-S Lbk (5 spd)	15248	**4650**	**6225**
3 Dr All-Trac Turbo Lbk (5 spd)	20298	**6100**	**7800**
2 Dr GT Conv	17848	**6675**	**8500**

Model/Body/Type	BaseList	Whlse	Retail
COROLLA 4 Cyl			**1988**
FWD/AT/PS/AC			
4 Dr Dlx Sdn	8898	3125	4425
4 Dr LE Sdn	10148	3525	4850
5 Dr Dlx Wgn	9248	3350	4700
5 Dr Dlx All-Trac Wgn	10948	3850	5200
5 Dr SR5 All-Trac S/W (5 spd)	12418	4000	5350
2 Dr SR5 Cpe	9898	3600	4925
2 Dr GT-S Cpe (5 spd)	12028	3925	5275
3 Dr FX Lbk	7948	1875	2950
3 Dr FX16 Lbk	9978	2500	3650
3 Dr FX16 GT-S Lbk	10968	3025	4275
CRESSIDA V6			**1988**
AT/PS/AC			
4 Dr Luxury Sdn	20250	6325	8225
LAND CRUISER V6			**1988**
4WD/AT/PS/AC			
4 Dr Wgn	19998	8975	11050
MR2 4 Cyl			**1988**
AT/PS/AC			
2 Dr Cpe	12808	4575	6150
2 Dr Supercharged Cpe	16418	5500	7175
PICKUPS 4 Cyl			**1988**
5SP/PS/AC			
Pkup	7538	2650	3825
LB Pkup	8208	2775	4000
Dlx LB Pkup	8418	3125	4400
X-Cab LB Pkup	8668	3625	4950
Dlx X-Cab LB Pkup	8958	3975	5325
SR5 X-Cab Pkup	10358	4325	5725
SR5 X-Cab Turbo Pkup	11518	4550	5975
1-Ton LB Pkup	9078	2925	4275
Std 4WD Pkup	10348	4400	5950
Dlx 4WD LB Pkup	11168	4850	6500
Dlx X-Cab 4WD Pkup	11398	5650	7300
SR5 4WD Pkup	12198	5175	6875
SR5 X-Cab 4WD Pkup	12688	6125	7825
SUPRA V6			**1988**
5SP-AT/PS/AC			
3 Dr Lbk	21290	6275	8025
3 Dr Turbo Lbk	23760	6925	8750
TERCEL 4 Cyl			**1988**
FWD/AT/PS/AC			
3 Dr EZ Lbk (4 spd)	5948	1225	2150
3 Dr Lbk	6698	1900	2975
3 Dr Dlx Lbk	7798	2275	3375
5 Dr Dlx Lbk	8038	2350	3475
2 Dr Cpe	6898	2000	3100
2 Dr Dlx Cpe	7948	2350	3475
Dlx 4WD Wgn	10488	3000	4250
SR5 4WD Wgn (6 spd)	11508	3050	4300
VAN 4 Cyl			**1988**
AT/PS/AC			
Window Van	10198	3350	4700
Panel Van	9898	3150	4450
Deluxe Van	12588	4425	5850
LE Van	14658	4975	6500
4WD Panel Van	12318	4025	5550
4WD LE Van	16728	5875	7625

ADD FOR ALL 88 TOYOTA:
Auto Trans(Pkup) +230
Cass(Std Celica Trbo,Supr,Cress) +25
Cruise Ctrl(Std Supra,Cressida) +35
Custom Whls +35
Dual AC +230
Dual Sunroof +230
Leather Seats +75
Pwr Locks(Std Celica Trbo,Supra,Cres,Van LE) +25
Pwr Seat +35
Pwr Sunroof +160
Pwr Wndw(Std Celica Trbo,Supra,Cress) +35
Removable Roof(Std Supercharged MR2) +215
Sunroof +60
V6 Eng +315

DEDUCT FOR ALL 88 TOYOTA:
No AC -330
No Auto Trans -290

1987 TOYOTA

Model/Body/Type	BaseList	Whlse	Retail
4RUNNER 4 Cyl			**1987**
4WD/AT/PS/AC			
Dlx Utility (5 spd)	12998	5925	7650
SR5 Utility	14548	6825	8650
SR5 Wgn (5 spd)	15248	7025	8850
SR5 Turbo Wgn	18568	7375	9250
CAMRY 4 Cyl			**1987**
FWD/AT/PS/AC			
4 Dr Sdn	10648	3125	4500
4 Dr Deluxe Sdn	10798	3400	4825
4 Dr LE Sdn	13398	3900	5375
5 Dr Deluxe Wgn	11488	3650	5075
5 Dr LE Wgn	14168	4150	5700
CELICA 4 Cyl			**1987**
FWD/AT/PS/AC			
2 Dr ST Cpe	10598	2950	4300
2 Dr GT Cpe	12038	3400	4825
3 Dr GT Lbk	12288	3500	4900
2 Dr GT-S Cpe	13978	4100	5650
3 Dr GT-S Lbk (5 spd)	14328	4200	5725
2 Dr GT Conv	16798	5700	7375

TOYOTA 87-86

Model/Body/Type	BaseList	Whlse	Retail
COROLLA 4 Cyl — 1987			
FWD/AT/PS/AC			
4 Dr Dlx Sdn	8178	**2325**	**3450**
5 Dr Dlx Lbk	9038	**2425**	**3575**
4 Dr LE Sdn	9278	**2625**	**3775**
2 Dr SR5 RWD Cpe	9548	**2775**	**4000**
2 Dr GT-S RWD Cpe (5 spd)	10368	**3025**	**4275**
3 Dr FX Lbk	7878	**1425**	**2375**
3 Dr FX16 Lbk	9678	**2000**	**3100**
3 Dr FX16 GT-S Lbk	10668	**2425**	**3575**
CRESSIDA 4 Cyl — 1987			
AT/PS/AC			
4 Dr Luxury Sdn	19350	**4800**	**6575**
5 Dr Luxury Wgn	19410	**4750**	**6525**
LAND CRUISER 4 Cyl — 1987			
4WD/4SP/PS/AC			
4 Dr Wgn	17198	**7375**	**9400**
MR2 4 Cyl — 1987			
AT/PS/AC			
2 Dr Cpe	12548	**3150**	**4550**
PICKUPS 4 Cyl — 1987			
5SP/PS/AC			
Pkup	6598	**2275**	**3400**
LB Pkup	7518	**2400**	**3550**
Dlx LB Pkup	7868	**2725**	**3900**
X-Cab LB Pkup	8068	**3225**	**4525**
Dlx X-Cab LB Pkup	8578	**3525**	**4850**
SR5 X-Cab Pkup	10188	**3800**	**5150**
SR5 X-Cab Turbo Pkup	12488	**3975**	**5325**
1-Ton LB Pkup	8478	**2525**	**3775**
Std 4WD Pkup	9548	**3925**	**5400**
4WD Turbo Pkup	11238	**4075**	**5600**
Dlx 4WD LB Pkup	10598	**4375**	**5925**
Dlx X-Cab 4WD Pkup	10828	**5050**	**6725**
SR5 4WD Pkup	11888	**4650**	**6225**
SR5 X-Cab 4WD Pkup	12368	**5475**	**7150**
SR5 X-Cab 4WD Turbo Pkup	14418	**5650**	**7300**
SUPRA 4 Cyl — 1987			
5SP-AT/PS/AC			
3 Dr Lbk	19990	**5025**	**6675**
3 Dr Turbo Lbk	22260	**5675**	**7350**
TERCEL 4 Cyl — 1987			
FWD/AT/PS/AC			
3 Dr EZ Lbk (4 spd)	5848	**1050**	**1950**
3 Dr Lbk (4 spd)	5898	**1100**	**2000**
3 Dr Dlx Lbk	7358	**1650**	**2625**
5 Dr Dlx Lbk	7988	**1725**	**2750**
2 Dr Cpe	6548	**1350**	**2300**
2 Dr Dlx Cpe	8088	**1700**	**2675**
5 Dr Dlx Wgn	8398	**1850**	**2925**
4 Dr Dlx 4WD Wgn	9588	**2275**	**3375**
4 Dr SR5 4WD Wgn (6 spd)	10638	**2375**	**3500**
VAN 4 Cyl — 1987			
AT/PS/AC			
Window Van	9548	**2050**	**3125**
Panel Van	9248	**1850**	**2925**
Deluxe Van	11688	**2900**	**4150**
LE Van	14228	**3300**	**4650**
4WD Panel Van	11568	**2600**	**3850**
4WD LE Van	15598	**4100**	**5650**

1986 TOYOTA

Model/Body/Type	BaseList	Whlse	Retail
4RUNNER — 1986			
4WD			
Std Utility	11118	**4950**	**6550**
Dlx Utility	12378	**5400**	**7025**
SR5 Utility	13058	**5775**	**7375**
CAMRY — 1986			
FWD			
4 Dr Deluxe Sdn	9378	**2425**	**3675**
5 Dr LE Lbk	11488	**2825**	**4150**
4 Dr LE Sdn	10538	**2800**	**4100**
CELICA — 1986			
FWD			
2 Dr ST Cpe	9098	**2200**	**3400**
2 Dr GT Cpe	10148	**2525**	**3800**
3 Dr GT Lbk	10398	**2625**	**3900**
2 Dr GT-S Cpe	11998	**3100**	**4450**
3 Dr GT-S Lbk	12348	**3175**	**4550**
COROLLA — 1986			
FWD			
4 Dr Dlx Sdn	7148	**1675**	**2800**
5 Dr Dlx Lbk	7408	**1725**	**2900**
4 Dr LE Sdn	7698	**1875**	**3075**
4 Dr LE Ltd Sdn	9818	**2075**	**3250**
2 Dr SR5 RWD Cpe	8158	**2000**	**3175**
2 Dr GT-S RWD Cpe	9248	**2350**	**3600**
3 Dr SR5 RWD Lbk	8338	**1975**	**3150**
3 Dr GT-S RWD Lbk	9428	**2325**	**3575**
CRESSIDA — 1986			
4 Dr Luxury Sdn	16130	**3800**	**5225**
5 Dr Luxury Wgn	16190	**3800**	**5200**
LAND CRUISER — 1986			
4WD			
4 Dr Wgn	15998	**6425**	**8100**

Model/Body/Type	BaseList	Whlse	Retail
MR2			**1986**
2 Dr Cpe	11298	2425	3700
PICKUPS			**1986**
Pkup	5998	1775	2950
LB Pkup	6498	1875	3075
Dlx LB Pkup	6748	2150	3325
X-Cab Pkup	7458	2750	4050
1-Ton LB Pkup	7768	2025	3225
SR5 LB Pkup	8318	2450	3725
SR5 X-Cab Pkup	8498	3100	4450
Std 4WD Pkup	8398	3350	4750
Dlx 4WD LB Pkup	9258	3750	5150
Dlx X-Cab 4WD Pkup	9498	4400	5875
SR5 4WD Pkup	10328	4000	5425
SR5 4WD LB Pkup	10678	4100	5575
SR5 X-Cab 4WD Pkup	10858	4750	6275
SUPRA			**1986**
3 Dr Lbk	16558	4175	5675
3 Dr Lbk (1986.5)	17990	4450	5950
TERCEL			**1986**
FWD			
3 Dr Lbk	5448	850	1800
3 Dr Dlx Lbk	6438	1100	2150
5 Dr Dlx Lbk	6588	1200	2225
5 Dr Dlx Wgn	7038	1275	2300
4 Dr Dlx 4WD Wgn	8328	1675	2800
4 Dr SR5 4WD Wgn	8898	1925	3125
VAN			**1986**
Cargo Van	8498	1275	2300
Deluxe Van	9998	2000	3175
LE Van	12208	2350	3600

1985 TOYOTA

Model/Body/Type	BaseList	Whlse	Retail
4RUNNER			**1985**
4WD			
Std Utility	10668	4125	5600
Dlx Utility	12068	4475	5975
SR5 Utility	12568	4800	6375
CAMRY			**1985**
4 Dr Deluxe Sdn	8948	1925	3125
5 Dr Deluxe Lbk	9988	1975	3150
4 Dr LE Sdn	10898	2225	3450
5 Dr LE Lbk	11248	2275	3500
CELICA			**1985**
2 Dr ST Cpe	8449	1625	2750
2 Dr GT Cpe	9639	1950	3125
3 Dr GT Lbk	9989	2025	3225
2 Dr GT-S Cpe	11199	2350	3600
3 Dr GT-S Lbk	11549	2425	3700
2 Dr GT-S Conv	17669	5175	6750
3 Dr L Supra	15998	3075	4400
3 Dr Supra	16558	3425	4825
COROLLA			**1985**
4 Dr Dlx Sdn	6938	1325	2400
5 Dr Dlx Lbk	7198	1400	2500
4 Dr LE Sdn	7738	1525	2625
5 Dr LE Lbk	8358	1600	2725
4 Dr LE Ltd Sdn	9258	1650	2775
2 Dr SR5 Cpe	8058	1550	2675
2 Dr GT-S Cpe	9298	1800	3000
3 Dr SR5 Lbk	8238	1550	2650
3 Dr GT-S Lbk	9538	1775	2975
CRESSIDA			**1985**
4 Dr Luxury Sdn	15690	3075	4425
5 Dr Luxury Wgn	15750	3075	4400
LAND CRUISER			**1985**
4 Dr 4WD Wgn	14568	5350	7000
MR2			**1985**
2 Dr Cpe	10999	2100	3275
PICKUPS			**1985**
Std Pkup	5998	1475	2575
LB Pkup	6498	1550	2675
Dlx LB Pkup	6898	1775	2950
Dlx X-Cab Pkup	7288	2200	3400
SR5 Pkup	8098	1900	3100
SR5 LB Pkup	8268	2000	3175
SR5 X-Cab Pkup	8448	2400	3650
1-Ton LB Pkup	7338	1675	2800
Std 4WD Pkup	8398	2600	3875
Dlx 4WD LB Pkup	9058	2925	4250
Dlx X-Cab 4WD Pkup	9298	3325	4725
SR5 4WD Pkup	10258	3075	4400
SR5 4WD LB Pkup	10428	3125	4500
SR5 X-Cab 4WD Pkup	10648	3550	4950
TERCEL			**1985**
3 Dr Std Lbk	5348	650	1625
3 Dr Dlx Lbk	6338	875	1825
5 Dr Dlx Lbk	6488	925	1925
5 Dr Dlx Wgn	6918	975	2000
5 Dr Dlx 4WD Wgn	8208	1325	2400
5 Dr SR5 4WD Wgn	8778	1650	2775
VAN			**1985**
Cargo Van	9198	900	1900
Deluxe Van	9748	1450	2550
LE Van	11348	1775	2975

Model/Body/Type	BaseList	Whlse	Retail

VOLKSWAGEN Germany

1992 Volkswagen Passat CL

For a Volkswagen dealer in your area, see our Dealer Directory (pg 217)

1994 VOLKSWAGEN

CORRADO V6 — 1994

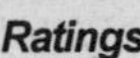

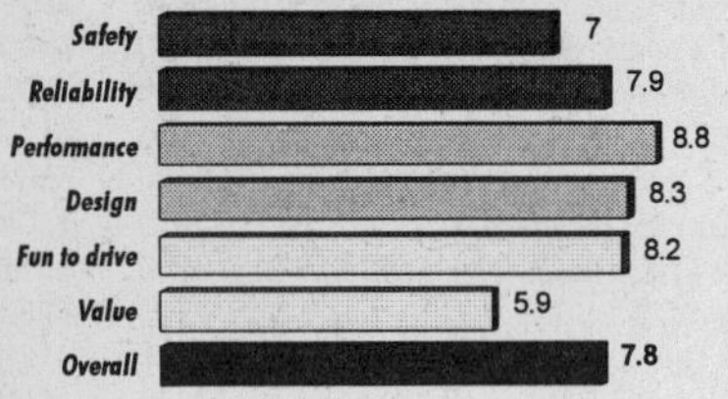

Model/Body/Type	BaseList	Whlse	Retail
FWD/5SP-AT/PS/AC			
2 Dr SLC Cpe	25150	-	-

GOLF III 4 Cyl — 1994

Model/Body/Type	BaseList	Whlse	Retail
FWD/AT/PS/AC			
2 Dr GL Hbk	12325	**10575**	**12700**
4 Dr GL Hbk	11900	**10675**	**12950**

JETTA III — 1994

Model/Body/Type	BaseList	Whlse	Retail
FWD/AT/PS/AC			
4 Cyl Models			
4 Dr GL Sdn	13125	**11600**	**14050**
4 Dr GLS Sdn	15700	**13075**	**15575**
V6 Models			
4 Dr GLX Sdn	19975	-	-

PASSAT V6 — 1994

Model/Body/Type	BaseList	Whlse	Retail
FWD/AT/PS/AC			
4 Dr GLX Sdn	23075	-	-
4 Dr GLX Wgn	23500	-	-

ADD FOR ALL 94 VOLKSWAGEN:

ABS(GL,GLS) +430
Anti-Theft/Recovery Sys +365
Cass(GL) +115
CD Player +230
Cruise Ctrl(GL) +160
Custom Whls +205
Leather Seats(Std Corrado) +275
Pwr Sunroof(Std Passat) +545

DEDUCT FOR ALL 94 VOLKSWAGEN:

No AC -680
No Auto Trans -590

1993 VOLKSWAGEN

CABRIOLET 4 Cyl — 1993

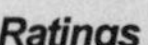

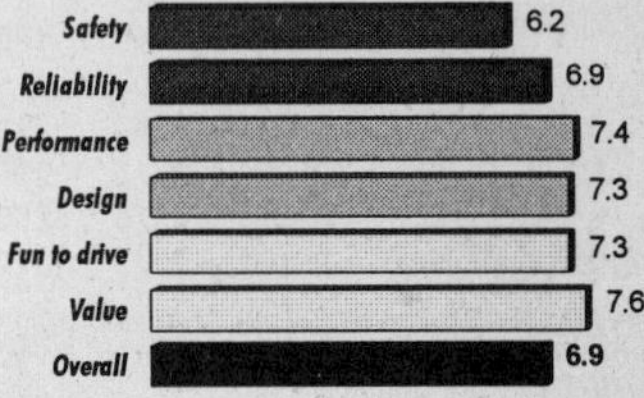

Model/Body/Type	BaseList	Whlse	Retail
FWD/AT/PS/AC			
2 Dr Conv	18380	**13100**	**15525**

CORRADO V6 — 1993

Ratings

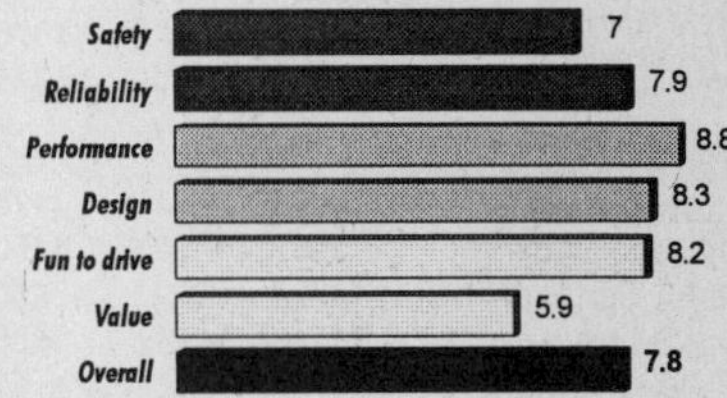

Model/Body/Type	BaseList	Whlse	Retail
FWD/5SP-AT/PS/AC			
2 Dr SLC Cpe	22870	**15525**	**18150**

EUROVAN 5 Cyl — 1993

FWD/AT/PS/AC

Model/Body/Type	BaseList	Whlse	Retail
CL Van	16640	**11975**	**14425**
GL Van	20420	**13950**	**16500**
MV Van	21850	**15075**	**17675**

FOX 4 Cyl — 1993

FWD/5SP/PS/AC

Model/Body/Type	BaseList	Whlse	Retail
2 Dr Wolfsburg Cpe	8690	**5675**	**7175**
4 Dr GL Wolfsburg Sdn	9520	**6450**	**8050**

PASSAT — 1993

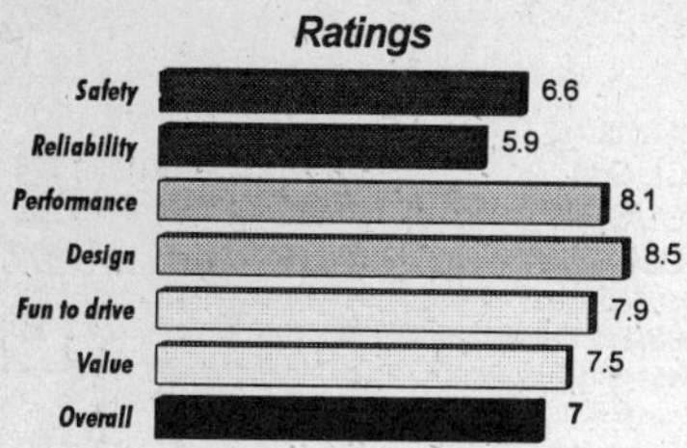

FWD/AT/PS/AC

Model/Body/Type	BaseList	Whlse	Retail
4 Cyl Models			
4 Dr GL Sdn	17610	**12475**	**14950**
V6 Models			
4 Dr GLX Sdn	21130	**14300**	**16875**
4 Dr GLX Wgn	21560	**14575**	**17150**

ADD FOR ALL 93 VOLKSWAGEN:

ABS(Std Passat GLX,Corrado) +390
Cass(Fox,EuroVan CL) +100
CD Player +195
Cruise Ctrl(EuroVan) +135
Custom Whls +175
Dual AC(Std Eurovan GL,MV) +470
Leather Seats +230
Pwr Locks(EuroVan) +100
Pwr Sunroof(Std Passat GLX) +430
Pwr Wndw(EuroVan) +135
Weekender Pkg +1245

DEDUCT FOR ALL 93 VOLKSWAGEN:

No AC -545
No Auto Trans -505
No Pwr Steering -160

1992 VOLKSWAGEN

CABRIOLET 4 Cyl — 1992

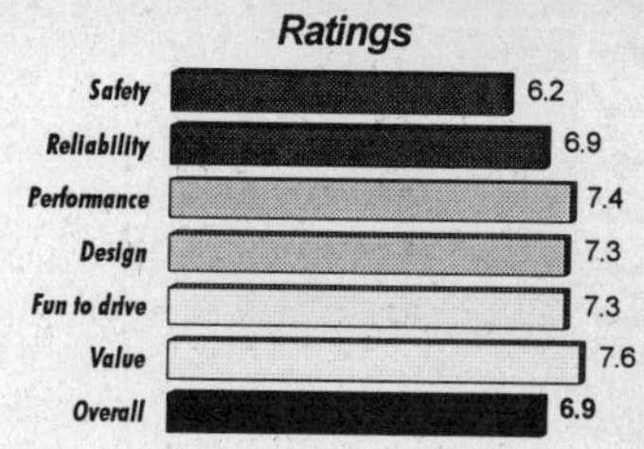

FWD/AT/PS/AC

Model/Body/Type	BaseList	Whlse	Retail
2 Dr Conv	17320	**12025**	**14400**

CORRADO — 1992

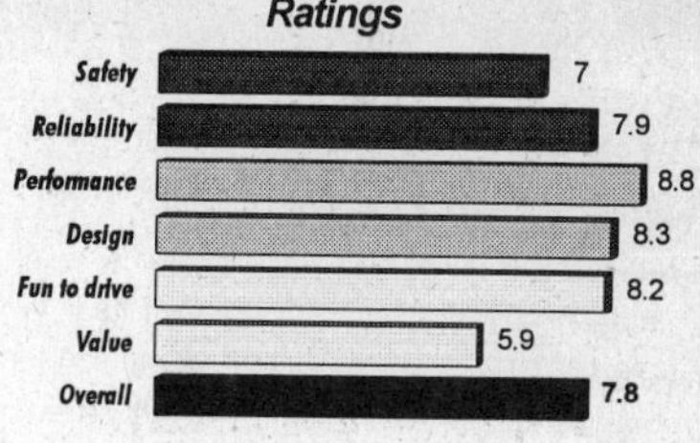

FWD/5SP-AT/PS/AC

Model/Body/Type	BaseList	Whlse	Retail
4 Cyl Models			
2 Dr G60 Cpe	19860	**11125**	**13500**
V6 Models			
2 Dr SLC Cpe	22170	**12700**	**15175**

FOX 4 Cyl — 1992

FWD/PS/AC

Model/Body/Type	BaseList	Whlse	Retail
2 Dr Cpe (4 spd)	7670	**4300**	**5725**
4 Dr GL Sdn (5 spd)	8890	**5050**	**6575**

GOLF 4 Cyl 1992

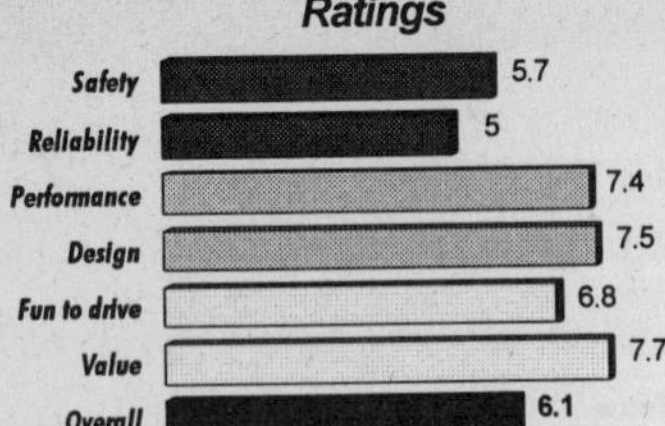

Model/Body/Type	BaseList	Whlse	Retail
FWD/AT/PS/AC			
2 Dr GL Hbk	9640	**7500**	**9300**
4 Dr GL Hbk	9950	**7600**	**9425**
2 Dr GTI Hbk	11110	**8425**	**10250**
2 Dr GTI/16V Hbk (5 spd)	13910	**9525**	**11475**

JETTA 4 Cyl 1992

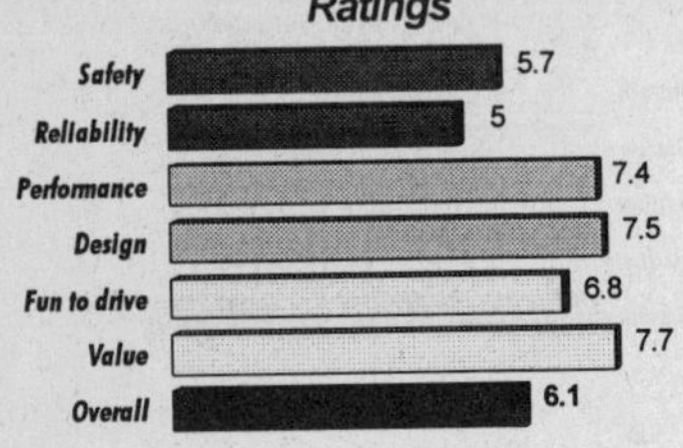

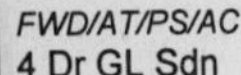

Model/Body/Type	BaseList	Whlse	Retail
FWD/AT/PS/AC			
4 Dr GL Sdn	11370	**7800**	**9725**
4 Dr GL Diesel Sdn (5 spd)	11670	**6700**	**8525**
4 Dr GL Carat Sdn	12390	**8350**	**10250**
4 Dr GLI/16V Sdn (5 spd)	15480	**9700**	**11800**

PASSAT 4 Cyl 1992

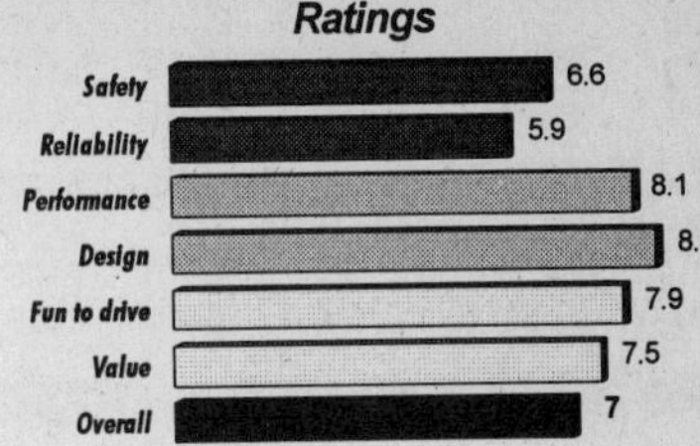

Model/Body/Type	BaseList	Whlse	Retail
FWD/AT/PS/AC			
4 Dr CL Sdn	14950	**9300**	**11325**
4 Dr GL Sdn	17550	**10800**	**13150**
4 Dr GL Wgn	17970	**11050**	**13400**

ADD FOR ALL 92 VOLKSWAGEN:

ABS(Std Corrado SLC) +350
Cass(Std Corrado,GLI 16V,Cabrio,PassGL) +75
Cruise Ctrl(Jetta GL/GLI) +115
Custom Whls +160
Leather Seats(Passat GL) +195
Pwr Sunroof +390
Pwr Wndw(Jetta GLI) +115
Sunroof +195

DEDUCT FOR ALL 92 VOLKSWAGEN:

No AC -505
No Auto Trans -470
No Pwr Steering -135

1991 VOLKSWAGEN

CABRIOLET 4 Cyl 1991

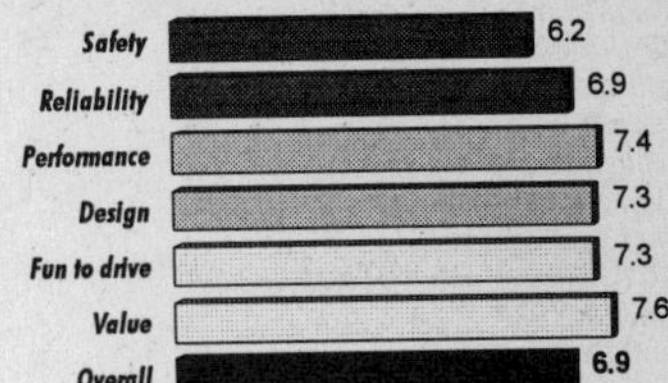

Model/Body/Type	BaseList	Whlse	Retail
FWD/AT/PS/AC			
2 Dr Conv	16175	**10450**	**12575**

CORRADO 4 Cyl — 1991

Ratings

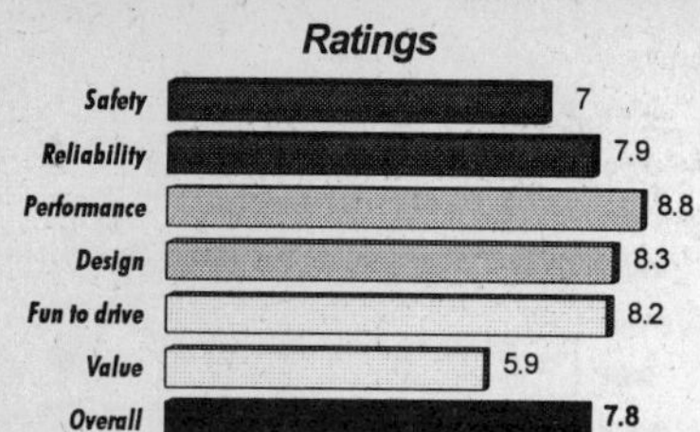

Model/Body/Type	BaseList	Whlse	Retail
FWD/5SP-AT/PS/AC			
2 Dr Cpe	18675	**9475**	**11525**

FOX 4 Cyl — 1991

Model/Body/Type	BaseList	Whlse	Retail
FWD/PS/AC			
2 Dr Cpe (4 spd)	7225	**3575**	**4900**
4 Dr GL Sdn (5 spd)	8395	**4350**	**5775**

GOLF 4 Cyl — 1991

Ratings

Rating	Score
Safety	5.7
Reliability	5
Performance	7.4
Design	7.5
Fun to drive	6.8
Value	7.7
Overall	6.1

Model/Body/Type	BaseList	Whlse	Retail
FWD/AT/PS/AC			
2 Dr GL Hbk	9055	**6025**	**7600**
4 Dr GL Hbk	9355	**6125**	**7700**
2 Dr GTI Hbk	10440	**6725**	**8475**
2 Dr GTI/16V Hbk (5 spd)	13070	**8000**	**9850**

JETTA 4 Cyl — 1991

Ratings

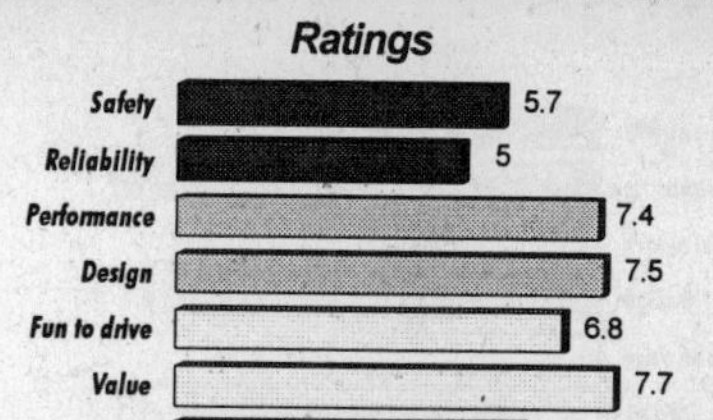

Model/Body/Type	BaseList	Whlse	Retail
FWD/AT/PS/AC			
2 Dr GL Cpe	10385	**6175**	**7900**
4 Dr GL Sdn	10685	**6375**	**8125**
4 Dr GL Diesel Sdn (5 spd)	10685	**5300**	**7000**
4 Dr Carat Sdn	11640	**6875**	**8700**
4 Dr GLI/16V Sdn (5 spd)	14550	**8200**	**10100**

PASSAT 4 Cyl — 1991

Ratings

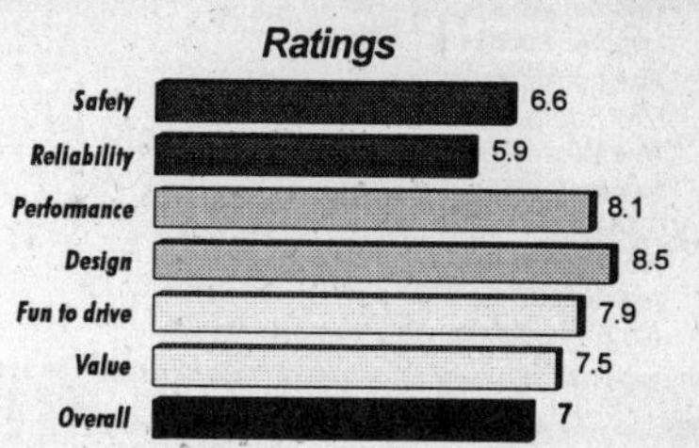

Model/Body/Type	BaseList	Whlse	Retail
FWD/AT/PS/AC			
4 Dr GL Sdn	15240	**9000**	**11000**
4 Dr GL Wgn	15650	**9250**	**11275**

VOLKSWAGEN 91-90

VANAGON 4 Cyl — 1991

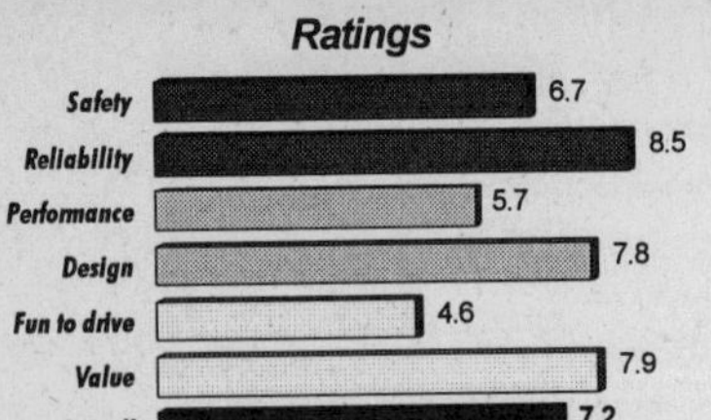

Model/Body/Type	BaseList	Whlse	Retail
AT/PS/AC			
Wgn	14575	**8875**	**10875**
GL Wgn	17070	**10900**	**13250**
Carat Wgn	18735	**12150**	**14625**
GL Camper	21730	**14250**	**16825**

ADD FOR ALL 91 VOLKSWAGEN:

4WD/Synchro +1070
ABS +315
Cass(Std Corrado,GLI 16V,Cabrio) +60
Cruise Ctrl(Base Van/GL,JettaGL/GLI,Pass) +100
Custom Whls +135
Leather Seats +160
Pwr Locks(Base Van/GL,Passat) +60
Pwr Sunroof +350
Pwr Wndw(Base Van/GL,GLI,Passat) +100
Sunroof +160

DEDUCT FOR ALL 91 VOLKSWAGEN:

No AC -470
No Auto Trans -430
No Pwr Steering -115

1990 VOLKSWAGEN

CABRIOLET 4 Cyl — 1990

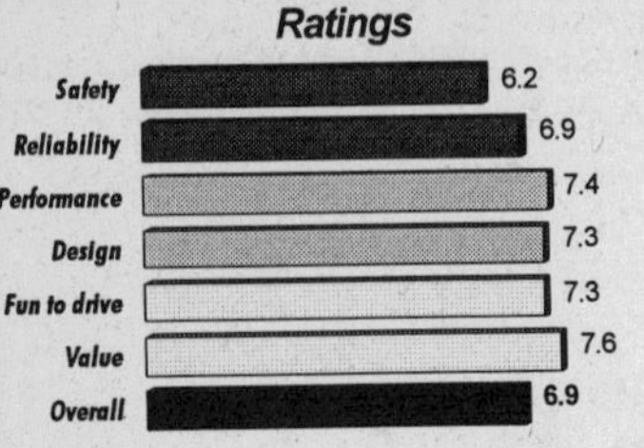

Model/Body/Type	BaseList	Whlse	Retail
FWD/AT/PS/AC			
2 Dr Conv	15485	**8875**	**10775**

CORRADO 4 Cyl — 1990

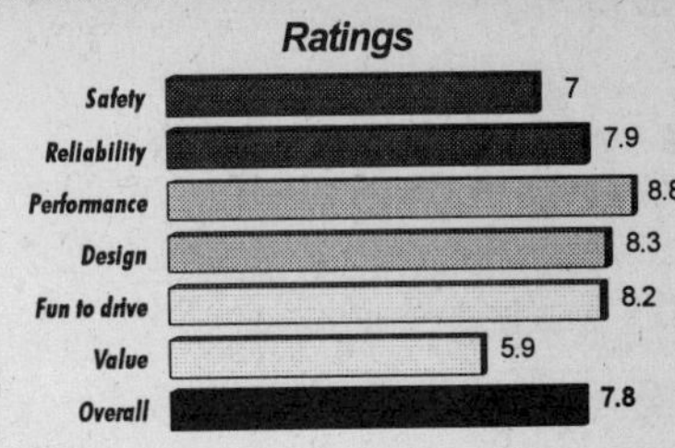

Model/Body/Type	BaseList	Whlse	Retail
FWD/5SP/PS/AC			
2 Dr Cpe	17900	**7700**	**9625**

FOX 4 Cyl — 1990

Model/Body/Type	BaseList	Whlse	Retail
FWD/4SP/PS/AC			
2 Dr Cpe	7225	**2700**	**3875**
4 Dr GL Sdn	8310	**3400**	**4725**
2 Dr GL Wgn	8550	**3425**	**4750**
2 Dr GL Sport Sdn (5 spd)	8595	**3550**	**4875**

GOLF 4 Cyl — 1990

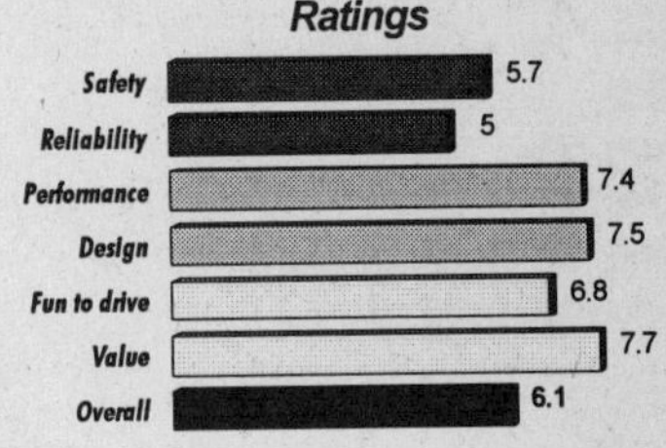

Model/Body/Type	BaseList	Whlse	Retail
FWD/AT/PS/AC			
2 Dr GL Hbk	8695	**4625**	**6100**
4 Dr GL Hbk	8995	**4700**	**6175**
2 Dr GTI Hbk (5 spd)	9995	**4850**	**6325**

See the Automobile Dealer Directory on page 379 for a Dealer near you!

Model/Body/Type	BaseList	Whlse	Retail

JETTA 4 Cyl — 1990

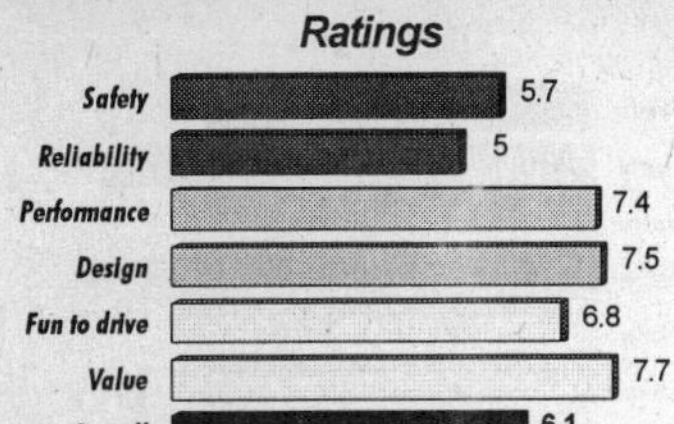

FWD/AT/PS/AC	BaseList	Whlse	Retail
2 Dr GL Cpe	9995	**4700**	**6325**
4 Dr GL Sdn	10295	**4875**	**6550**
4 Dr GL Diesel Sdn (5 spd)	10495	**3925**	**5400**
4 Dr Carat Sdn	10990	**5275**	**7000**
4 Dr GLI/16V Sdn (5 spd)	13750	**6650**	**8425**

PASSAT 4 Cyl — 1990

Ratings

Rating	Score
Safety	6.6
Reliability	5.9
Performance	8.1
Design	8.5
Fun to drive	7.9
Value	7.5
Overall	7

FWD/AT/PS/AC	BaseList	Whlse	Retail
4 Dr GL Sdn	14770	**7175**	**9050**
4 Dr GL Wgn	15885	**7350**	**9225**

VANAGON 4 Cyl — 1990

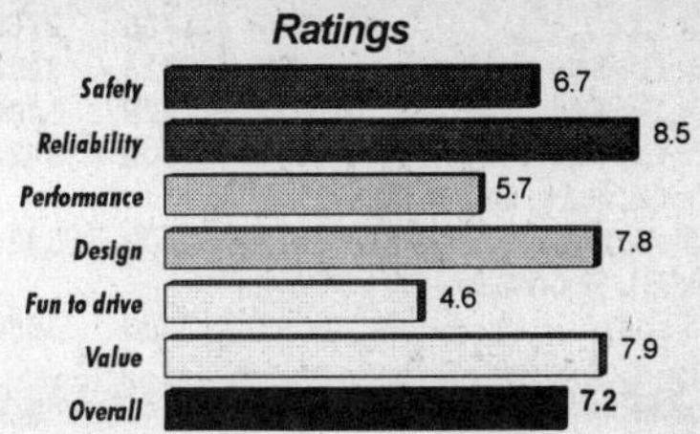

AT/PS/AC	BaseList	Whlse	Retail
Wgn	14080	**6900**	**8725**
GL Wgn	16490	**8875**	**10875**
Carat Wgn	18670	**9925**	**12075**
GL Camper	20990	**12000**	**14475**

ADD FOR ALL 90 VOLKSWAGEN:

4WD/Synchro +860
ABS +275
Cass(Std Corrado,Cabrio) +60
Cruise Ctrl(Std Corrado,Van Carat) +75
Custom Whls +115
Leather Seats +115
Pwr Locks(Vanagon) +60
Pwr Sunroof +315
Pwr Wndw(Std Corrado,Cabrio,Van Carat) +75
Sunroof +115

DEDUCT FOR ALL 90 VOLKSWAGEN:

No AC -430
No Auto Trans -390
No Pwr Steering -100

1989 VOLKSWAGEN

CABRIOLET 4 Cyl — 1989

Ratings

Rating	Score
Safety	6.2
Reliability	6.9
Performance	7.4
Design	7.3
Fun to drive	7.3
Value	7.6
Overall	6.9

FWD/AT/PS/AC	BaseList	Whlse	Retail
2 Dr Conv	15195	**7600**	**9425**

VOLKSWAGEN 89-88

FOX 4 Cyl — 1989

Model/Body/Type	BaseList	Whlse	Retail
FWD/4SP/PS/AC			
2 Dr Cpe	6890	**1700**	**2700**
2 Dr GL Sdn	7720	**2125**	**3200**
4 Dr GL Sdn	7920	**2275**	**3400**
2 Dr GL Wgn	8150	**2300**	**3425**
2 Dr GL Sport Cpe (5 spd)	8195	**2300**	**3425**
4 Dr GL Sport Sdn (5 spd)	8395	**2500**	**3650**

GOLF 4 Cyl — 1989

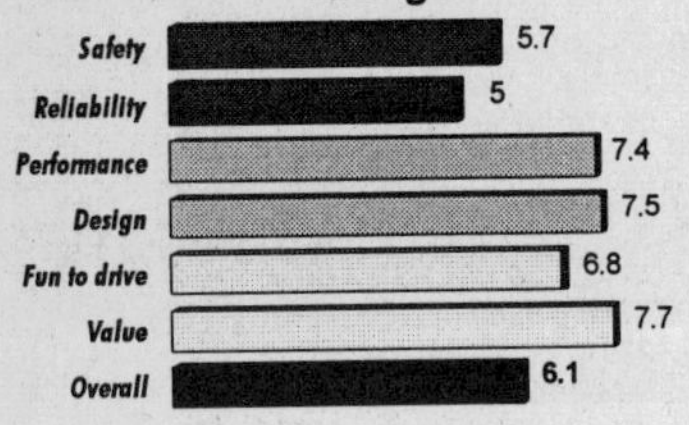

Model/Body/Type	BaseList	Whlse	Retail
FWD/AT/PS/AC			
2 Dr Hbk	8465	**3400**	**4725**
2 Dr GL Hbk	9170	**3800**	**5150**
4 Dr GL Hbk	9380	**3900**	**5250**
2 Dr GTI/16V Hbk (5 spd)	13650	**5300**	**6850**

JETTA 4 Cyl — 1989

Ratings

Rating	Score
Safety	5.7
Reliability	5
Performance	7.4
Design	7.5
Fun to drive	6.8
Value	7.7
Overall	6.1

Model/Body/Type	BaseList	Whlse	Retail
FWD/AT/PS/AC			
2 Dr Cpe	9690	**3975**	**5500**
4 Dr Sdn	9910	**4175**	**5725**
4 Dr GL Sdn	11120	**4525**	**6125**
4 Dr Carat Sdn	15140	**5000**	**6650**
4 Dr GLI/16V Sdn (5 spd)	14770	**5725**	**7400**

VANAGON 4 Cyl — 1989

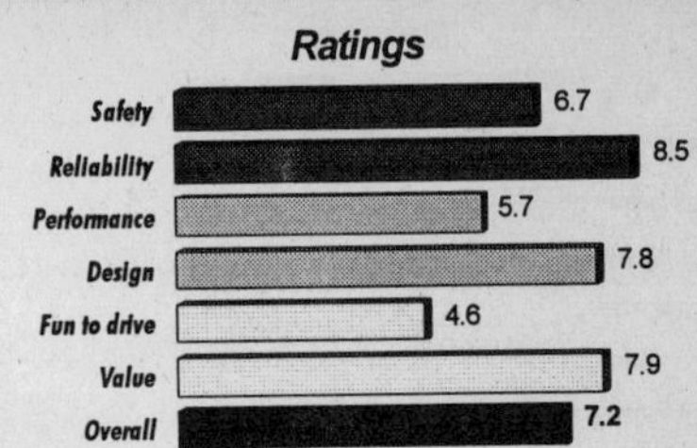

Model/Body/Type	BaseList	Whlse	Retail
AT/PS/AC			
GL Wgn	17035	**7600**	**9500**
GL Camper	22235	**10525**	**12750**
Carat Wgn	19355	**8650**	**10575**

ADD FOR ALL 89 VOLKSWAGEN:

4WD/Synchro +780
Cass(Std Cabrio,Jetta Carat) +35
Cruise Ctrl(Std Jetta Carat) +60
Custom Whls +75
Leather Seats +75
Pwr Locks(Std Carat) +35
Pwr Wndw(Std Jetta Carat) +60
Sunroof +100
Weekender Pkg(Std Vanagon Carat) +35

DEDUCT FOR ALL 89 VOLKSWAGEN:

No AC -390
No Auto Trans -350
No Pwr Steering -75

1988 VOLKSWAGEN

CABRIOLET 4 Cyl — 1988

Model/Body/Type	BaseList	Whlse	Retail
FWD/AT/PS/AC			
2 Dr Conv	14450	**6450**	**8050**

FOX 4 Cyl — 1988

Model/Body/Type	BaseList	Whlse	Retail
FWD/4SP/PS/AC			
2 Dr Cpe	5990	**1275**	**2175**
4 Dr GL Sdn	6890	**1675**	**2650**
2 Dr GL Wgn	6990	**1700**	**2675**

GOLF 4 Cyl — 1988

Model/Body/Type	BaseList	Whlse	Retail
FWD/AT/PS/AC			
2 Dr Hbk	7990	**2450**	**3600**
2 Dr GL Hbk	8490	**2725**	**3900**
4 Dr GL Hbk	8700	**2825**	**4075**
2 Dr GT Hbk	9975	**3225**	**4525**
4 Dr GT Hbk	10185	**3300**	**4650**
2 Dr GTI/16V Hbk(5spd)	12725	**3975**	**5325**

Model/Body/Type	BaseList	Whlse	Retail
JETTA 4 Cyl			**1988**
FWD/AT/PS/AC			
2 Dr Cpe	8990	3200	4600
4 Dr Sdn	9210	3375	4800
4 Dr GL Sdn	10340	3550	4975
4 Dr Carat Sdn	14200	3925	5400
4 Dr GLI/16V Sdn(5spd)	13725	4625	6200
QUANTUM 5 Cyl			**1988**
FWD/AT/PS/AC			
4 Dr GL Sdn	17525	3625	5050
4 Dr GL Wgn	17925	3650	5075
SCIROCCO 4 Cyl			**1988**
FWD/5SP/PS/AC			
2 Dr 16V Hbk	14090	4175	5725
VANAGON 4 Cyl			**1988**
AT/PS/AC			
GL Wgn	16240	5300	7000
GL Camper	21180	8100	10000

ADD FOR ALL 88 VOLKSWAGEN:
4WD/Synchro +605
DEDUCT FOR ALL 88 VOLKSWAGEN:
No AC -330
No Auto Trans -290

1987 VOLKSWAGEN

Model/Body/Type	BaseList	Whlse	Retail
CABRIOLET 4 Cyl			**1987**
FWD/AT/PS/AC			
2 Dr Conv	13250	4925	6450
FOX 4 Cyl			**1987**
FWD/4SP/PS/AC			
2 Dr Cpe	5690	900	1750
4 Dr GL Sdn	6490	1275	2200
2 Dr GL Wgn	6590	1300	2225
GOLF 4 Cyl			**1987**
FWD/AT/PS/AC			
2 Dr GL Hbk	8190	1975	3050
4 Dr GL Hbk	8400	2075	3150
2 Dr GT Hbk	9675	2325	3450
4 Dr GT Hbk	9885	2425	3575
2 Dr GTI Hbk(5 spd)	10325	2650	3825
2 Dr GTI/16V Hbk(5 spd)	12240	3075	4350
JETTA 4 Cyl			**1987**
FWD/AT/PS/AC			
2 Dr Cpe	9290	2250	3425
4 Dr Sdn	9510	2425	3650
4 Dr GL Sdn	9990	2575	3825
4 Dr GLI Sdn	11690	3100	4475
4 Dr GLI/16V Sdn (5 spd)	13725	3275	4700
QUANTUM 5 Cyl			**1987**
FWD/AT/PS/AC			
4 Dr GL Sdn	14985	2275	3475
4 Dr Wgn	13450	1900	3075
SCIROCCO 4 Cyl			**1987**
FWD/5SP-AT/PS/AC			
2 Dr Hbk	10680	2825	4150
2 Dr 16V Hbk	12980	3350	4775
VANAGON 4 Cyl			**1987**
AT/PS/AC			
Wgn	11560	2975	4325
GL Wgn	14730	4125	5675
Camper	16660	5175	6875
GL Camper	19225	6675	8500

ADD FOR ALL 87 VOLKSWAGEN:
4WD/Synchro +505
DEDUCT FOR ALL 87 VOLKSWAGEN:
Diesel Eng -390

1986 VOLKSWAGEN

Model/Body/Type	BaseList	Whlse	Retail
CABRIOLET			**1986**
FWD			
2 Dr Conv	11895	3700	5100
GOLF			**1986**
FWD			
2 Dr Hbk	7190	1275	2300
4 Dr Hbk	7400	1325	2400
2 Dr GTI Hbk	9190	1850	3050
JETTA			**1986**
FWD			
2 Dr Cpe	8150	1725	2900
4 Dr Sdn	8370	1900	3100
4 Dr GL Sdn	8670	2025	3200
4 Dr GLI Sdn	10190	2350	3600
QUANTUM			**1986**
FWD			
4 Dr GL Sdn	13595	1550	2675
5 Dr Wgn	11870	1250	2275
SCIROCCO			**1986**
FWD			
2 Dr Hbk	9980	1700	2875
2 Dr 16V Hbk	-	2175	3375

Model/Body/Type	BaseList	Whlse	Retail
VANAGON			**1986**
Wgn	10120	2350	3600
L Wgn	12290	2975	4300
GL Wgn	13140	3250	4650
Camper	14700	4175	5675
GL Camper	17190	5225	6825

DEDUCT FOR:
Diesel Eng -390

1985 VOLKSWAGEN

Model/Body/Type	BaseList	Whlse	Retail
CABRIOLET			**1985**
2 Dr Conv	11595	3050	4375
GOLF			**1985**
2 Dr Hbk	6990	925	1950
4 Dr Hbk	7200	1025	2050
2 Dr GTI Hbk	8990	1500	2600
JETTA			**1985**
2 Dr Cpe	7975	1375	2475
4 Dr Sdn	8195	1475	2575
4 Dr GL Sdn	8495	1550	2675
4 Dr GLI Sdn	9995	1875	3075
QUANTUM			**1985**
4 Dr GL Sdn	13295	1175	2200
5 Dr Wgn	11570	925	1925
SCIROCCO			**1985**
2 Dr Hbk	9980	1300	2350
VANAGON			**1985**
L Wgn	12290	2225	3425
GL Wgn	13140	2475	3750
Camper	17190	3450	4850

Model/Body/Type	BaseList	Whlse	Retail

VOLVO

Sweden

1987 Volvo 740 Sedan

For a Volvo dealer in your area, see our Dealer Directory (pg 217)

1994 VOLVO

850 5 Cyl — 1994

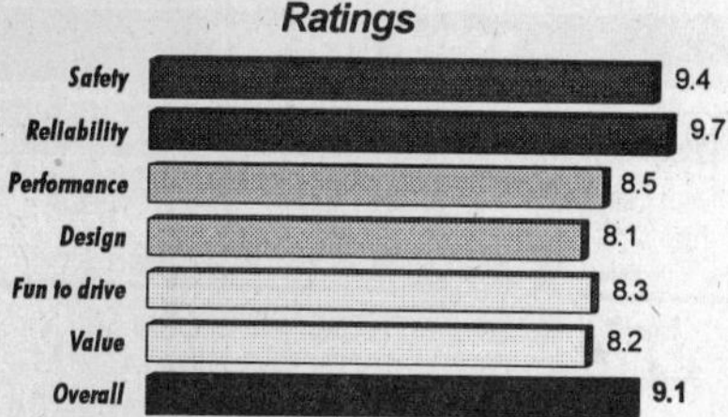

FWD/AT/PS/AC

Model/Body/Type	BaseList	Whlse	Retail
4 Dr Sdn	24300	**22250**	**25900**
4 Dr Wgn	27695	**23450**	**27175**
4 Dr Turbo Sdn	29985	-	-
4 Dr Turbo Wgn	30985	-	-

940 4 Cyl — 1994

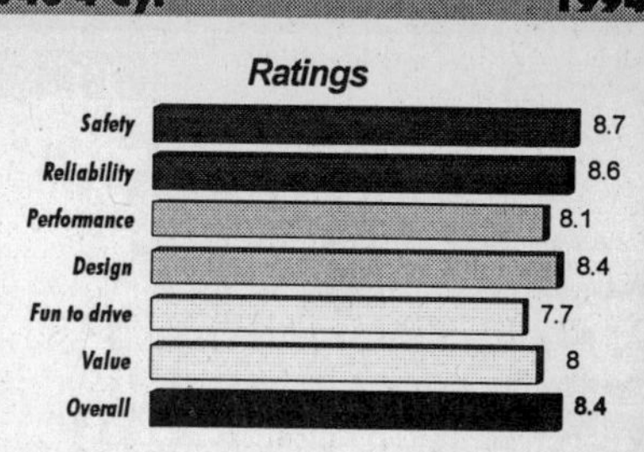

AT/PS/AC

Model/Body/Type	BaseList	Whlse	Retail
4 Dr Sdn	22900	**18000**	**21325**
4 Dr Wgn	24000	**19200**	**22575**
4 Dr Turbo Sdn	26295	**21075**	**24575**
4 Dr Turbo Wgn	27295	**22250**	**25900**

960 V6 — 1994

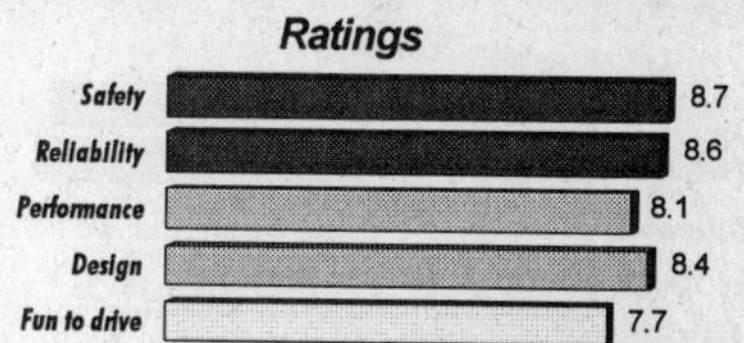

AT/PS/AC

Model/Body/Type	BaseList	Whlse	Retail
4 Dr Sdn	28950	**23450**	**27175**
4 Dr Wgn	34450	**25700**	**29575**

ADD FOR ALL 94 VOLVO:

Anti-Theft/Recovery Sys +365
Car Phone +230
Leather Seats(Std 850 Turbo,960 Wgn) +365
Pwr Sunroof(Std 850 Turbo,960 Wgn) +635

DEDUCT FOR ALL 94 VOLVO:

No Auto Trans -680

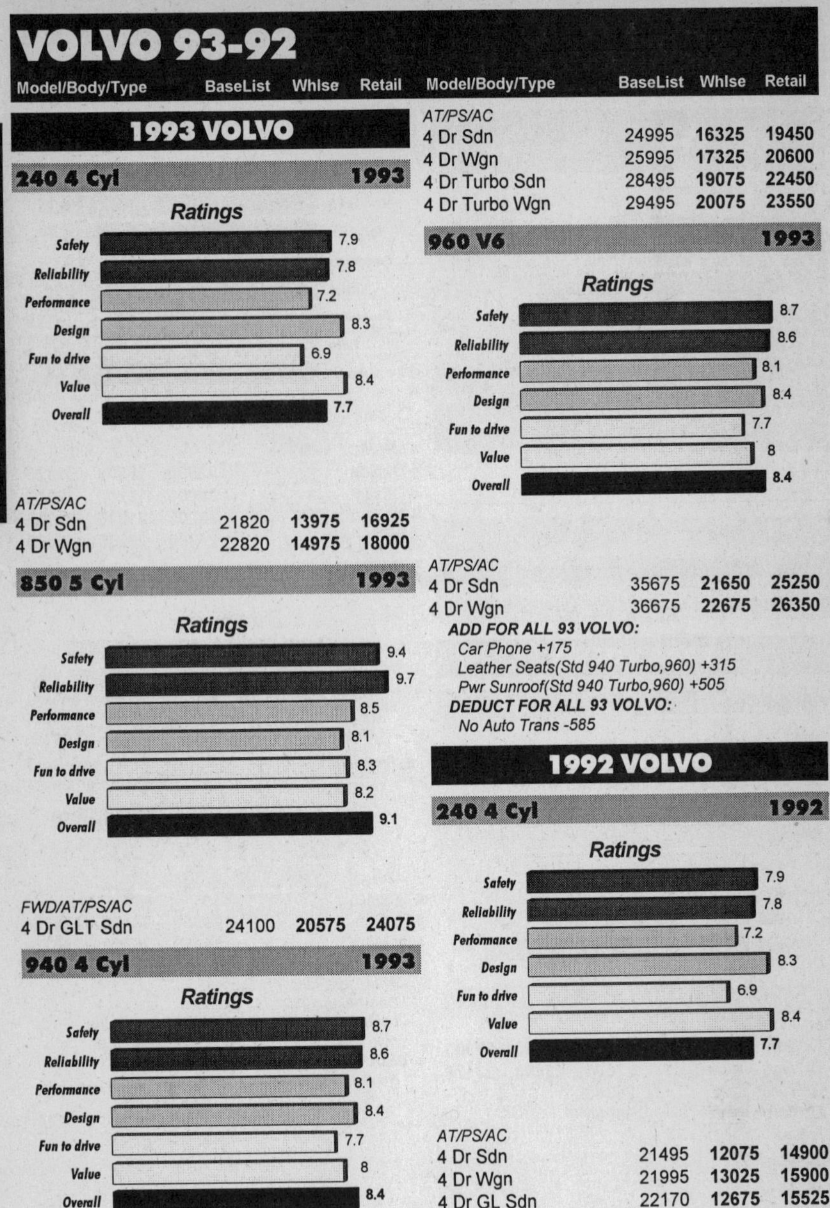

VOLVO 93-92

Model/Body/Type	BaseList	Whlse	Retail

1993 VOLVO

240 4 Cyl — 1993

Ratings

Rating	Score
Safety	7.9
Reliability	7.8
Performance	7.2
Design	8.3
Fun to drive	6.9
Value	8.4
Overall	7.7

AT/PS/AC

Model/Body/Type	BaseList	Whlse	Retail
4 Dr Sdn	21820	**13975**	**16925**
4 Dr Wgn	22820	**14975**	**18000**

850 5 Cyl — 1993

Ratings

Rating	Score
Safety	9.4
Reliability	9.7
Performance	8.5
Design	8.1
Fun to drive	8.3
Value	8.2
Overall	9.1

FWD/AT/PS/AC

Model/Body/Type	BaseList	Whlse	Retail
4 Dr GLT Sdn	24100	**20575**	**24075**

940 4 Cyl — 1993

Ratings

Rating	Score
Safety	8.7
Reliability	8.6
Performance	8.1
Design	8.4
Fun to drive	7.7
Value	8
Overall	8.4

AT/PS/AC

Model/Body/Type	BaseList	Whlse	Retail
4 Dr Sdn	24995	**16325**	**19450**
4 Dr Wgn	25995	**17325**	**20600**
4 Dr Turbo Sdn	28495	**19075**	**22450**
4 Dr Turbo Wgn	29495	**20075**	**23550**

960 V6 — 1993

Ratings

Rating	Score
Safety	8.7
Reliability	8.6
Performance	8.1
Design	8.4
Fun to drive	7.7
Value	8
Overall	8.4

AT/PS/AC

Model/Body/Type	BaseList	Whlse	Retail
4 Dr Sdn	35675	**21650**	**25250**
4 Dr Wgn	36675	**22675**	**26350**

ADD FOR ALL 93 VOLVO:

Car Phone +175
Leather Seats(Std 940 Turbo,960) +315
Pwr Sunroof(Std 940 Turbo,960) +505

DEDUCT FOR ALL 93 VOLVO:

No Auto Trans -585

1992 VOLVO

240 4 Cyl — 1992

Ratings

Rating	Score
Safety	7.9
Reliability	7.8
Performance	7.2
Design	8.3
Fun to drive	6.9
Value	8.4
Overall	7.7

AT/PS/AC

Model/Body/Type	BaseList	Whlse	Retail
4 Dr Sdn	21495	**12075**	**14900**
4 Dr Wgn	21995	**13025**	**15900**
4 Dr GL Sdn	22170	**12675**	**15525**

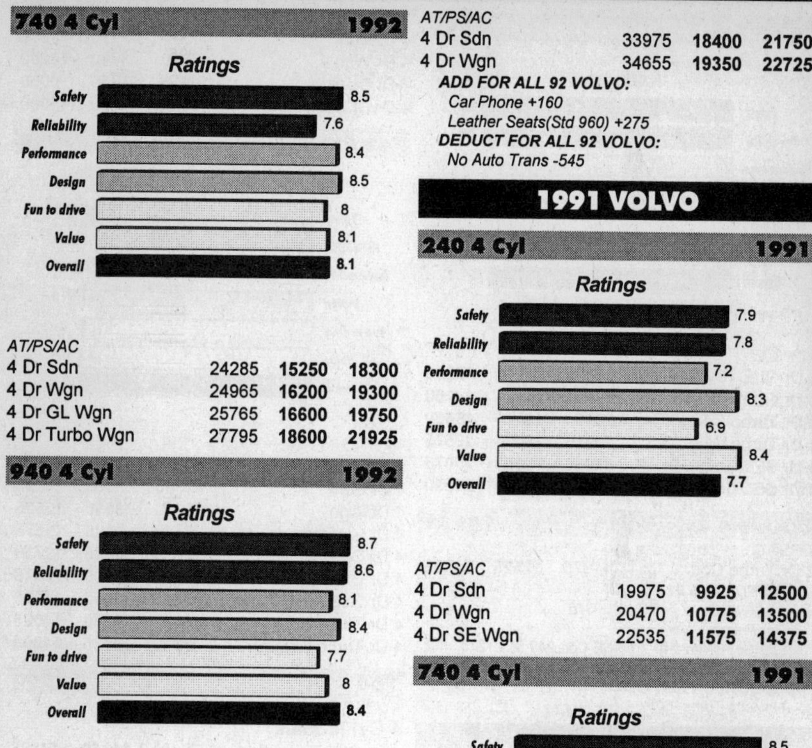

Model/Body/Type	BaseList	Whlse	Retail

740 4 Cyl — 1992

Ratings

Rating	Score
Safety	8.5
Reliability	7.6
Performance	8.4
Design	8.5
Fun to drive	8
Value	8.1
Overall	8.1

AT/PS/AC	BaseList	Whlse	Retail
4 Dr Sdn	24285	**15250**	**18300**
4 Dr Wgn	24965	**16200**	**19300**
4 Dr GL Wgn	25765	**16600**	**19750**
4 Dr Turbo Wgn	27795	**18600**	**21925**

940 4 Cyl — 1992

Ratings

Rating	Score
Safety	8.7
Reliability	8.6
Performance	8.1
Design	8.4
Fun to drive	7.7
Value	8
Overall	8.4

AT/PS/AC	BaseList	Whlse	Retail
4 Dr GL Sdn	24995	**15150**	**18175**
4 Dr Turbo Sdn	30795	**17300**	**20575**
4 Dr Turbo Wgn	31475	**18250**	**21625**

960 V6 — 1992

Ratings

Rating	Score
Safety	8.7
Reliability	8.6
Performance	8.1
Design	8.4
Fun to drive	7.7
Value	8
Overall	8.4

AT/PS/AC	BaseList	Whlse	Retail
4 Dr Sdn	33975	**18400**	**21750**
4 Dr Wgn	34655	**19350**	**22725**

ADD FOR ALL 92 VOLVO:
Car Phone +160
Leather Seats(Std 960) +275

DEDUCT FOR ALL 92 VOLVO:
No Auto Trans -545

1991 VOLVO

240 4 Cyl — 1991

Ratings

Rating	Score
Safety	7.9
Reliability	7.8
Performance	7.2
Design	8.3
Fun to drive	6.9
Value	8.4
Overall	7.7

AT/PS/AC	BaseList	Whlse	Retail
4 Dr Sdn	19975	**9925**	**12500**
4 Dr Wgn	20470	**10775**	**13500**
4 Dr SE Wgn	22535	**11575**	**14375**

740 4 Cyl — 1991

Ratings

Rating	Score
Safety	8.5
Reliability	7.6
Performance	8.4
Design	8.5
Fun to drive	8
Value	8.1
Overall	8.1

AT/PS/AC	BaseList	Whlse	Retail
4 Dr Sdn	22755	**11425**	**14200**
4 Dr Wgn	23435	**12300**	**15125**
4 Dr Turbo Sdn	25485	**13500**	**16425**
4 Dr Turbo Wgn	26165	**14400**	**17325**
4 Dr SE Turbo Sdn	27955	**14300**	**17250**
4 Dr SE Turbo Wgn	28635	**15150**	**18175**

VOLVO 91-90

940 4 Cyl — 1991

Ratings

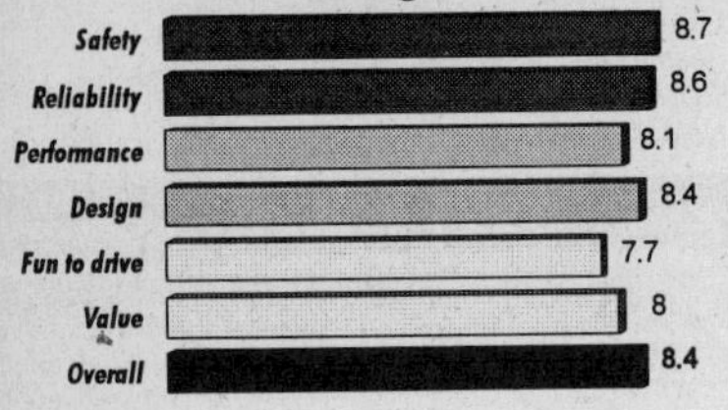

Rating	Score
Safety	8.7
Reliability	8.6
Performance	8.1
Design	8.4
Fun to drive	7.7
Value	8
Overall	8.4

Model/Body/Type	BaseList	Whlse	Retail
AT/PS/AC			
4 Dr GLE 16V Sdn	27885	**14275**	**17225**
4 Dr GLE 16V Wgn	28565	**15125**	**18150**
4 Dr Turbo Sdn	29295	**15575**	**18650**
4 Dr Turbo Wgn	29975	**16475**	**19575**
4 Dr SE Turbo Sdn	32950	**16900**	**20075**
4 Dr SE Turbo Wgn	33630	**17750**	**21050**

COUPE 4 Cyl — 1991

Model/Body/Type	BaseList	Whlse	Retail
T/PS/AC			
2 Dr Turbo Cpe	41975	**17525**	**20825**

ADD FOR ALL 91 VOLVO:
ABS(240 Base,740 Base) +315
Car Phone +135
Lthr Seats(Std 940 Trbo SE,Cpe,240 SE) +215
Pwr Sunroof(Std 740 Trbo,940,Cpe) +430
DEDUCT FOR ALL 91 VOLVO:
No Auto Trans -505

1990 VOLVO

240 4 Cyl — 1990

Ratings

Rating	Score
Safety	7.9
Reliability	7.8
Performance	7.2
Design	8.3
Fun to drive	6.9
Value	8.4
Overall	7.7

Model/Body/Type	BaseList	Whlse	Retail
AT/PS/AC			
4 Dr Sdn	17370	**7150**	**9350**
4 Dr Wgn	17860	**8000**	**10200**
4 Dr DL Sdn	19095	**7850**	**10050**
4 Dr DL Wgn	19585	**8700**	**11000**

740 4 Cyl — 1990

Ratings

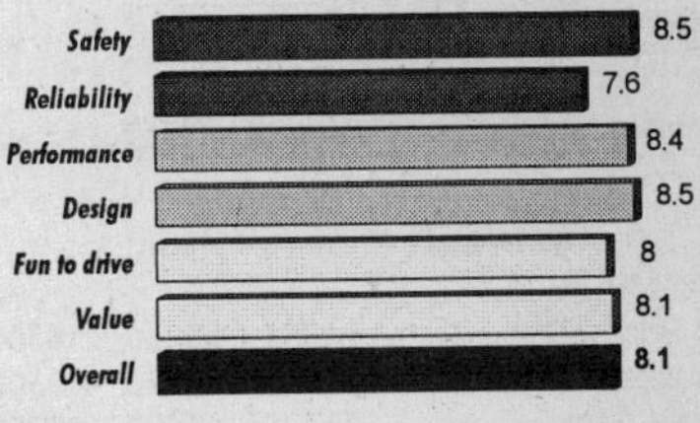

Rating	Score
Safety	8.5
Reliability	7.6
Performance	8.4
Design	8.5
Fun to drive	8
Value	8.1
Overall	8.1

Model/Body/Type	BaseList	Whlse	Retail
AT/PS/AC			
4 Dr Sdn	21330	**8800**	**11125**
4 Dr Wgn	22010	**9650**	**12025**
4 Dr GL Sdn	22345	**9325**	**11675**
4 Dr GL Wgn	23025	**10125**	**12750**
4 Dr GLE/16V Sdn	25995	**10500**	**13175**
4 Dr GLE/16V Wgn	26675	**11350**	**14125**
4 Dr Turbo Sdn	26330	**11250**	**14025**
4 Dr Turbo Wgn	27010	**12075**	**14900**

760 — 1990

Model/Body/Type	BaseList	Whlse	Retail
AT/PS/AC			
4 Cyl Models			
4 Dr GLE Turbo Sdn	33965	**11350**	**14125**
4 Dr GLE Turbo Wgn	33965	**12200**	**15025**
V6 Models			
4 Dr GLE Sdn	33185	**13050**	**15925**

780 — 1990

Model/Body/Type	BaseList	Whlse	Retail
AT/PS/AC			
4 Cyl Models			
2 Dr Turbo Cpe	39950	**14500**	**17450**
V6 Models			
2 Dr Cpe	38735	**13725**	**16650**

ADD FOR ALL 90 VOLVO:
ABS(740 Base,GL) +275
Leather Seats(Std 760,780) +160
Pwr Sunroof(Sdn 240 DL,740 GL) +390
Pwr Wndw(240 Base) +115
DEDUCT FOR ALL 90 VOLVO:
No AC -505
No Auto Trans -470

1989 VOLVO

240 4 Cyl — 1989

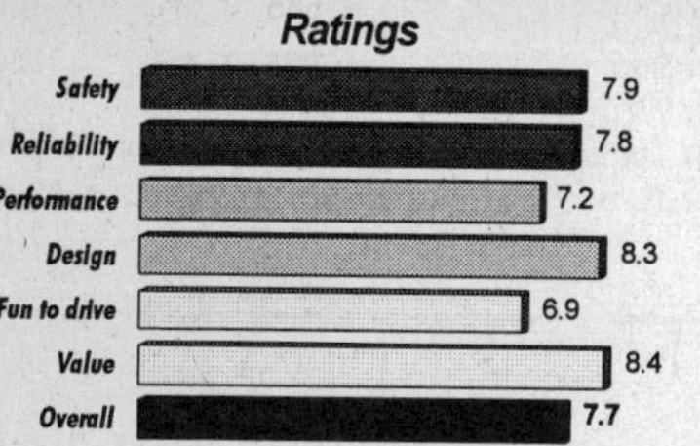

AT/PS/AC

Model/Body/Type	BaseList	Whlse	Retail
4 Dr DL Sdn	17250	**6325**	**8350**
4 Dr DL Wgn	17740	**7125**	**9300**
4 Dr GL Sdn	20035	**7400**	**9625**
4 Dr GL Wgn	20775	**8350**	**10575**

740 4 Cyl — 1989

Ratings

Rating	Score
Safety	8.5
Reliability	7.6
Performance	8.4
Design	8.5
Fun to drive	8
Value	8.1
Overall	8.1

AT/PS/AC

Model/Body/Type	BaseList	Whlse	Retail
4 Dr GL Sdn	19985	**7875**	**10075**
4 Dr GL Wgn	20665	**8675**	**11000**
4 Dr GLE/16V Sdn	24475	**8925**	**11250**
4 Dr GLE/16V Wgn	26050	**9850**	**12425**
4 Dr Turbo Sdn	24925	**9575**	**11950**
4 Dr Turbo Wgn	25605	**10300**	**12950**

760 — 1989

AT/PS/AC

Model/Body/Type	BaseList	Whlse	Retail
4 Cyl Models			
4 Dr GLE Turbo Sdn	32940	**10325**	**12975**
4 Dr GLE Turbo Wgn	32940	**11125**	**13875**
V6 Models			
4 Dr GLE Sdn	32155	**9775**	**12300**

780 — 1989

AT/PS/AC

Model/Body/Type	BaseList	Whlse	Retail
4 Cyl Models			
2 Dr Turbo Cpe	38975	**12500**	**15350**
V6 Models			
2 Dr Cpe	37790	**12000**	**14775**

ADD FOR ALL 89 VOLVO:

Lthr Seats(Std 780,760,240 GLWgn,GLE Wgn) +135

Pwr Wndw(DL) +100

DEDUCT FOR ALL 89 VOLVO:

No Auto Trans -430

1988 VOLVO

240 4 Cyl — 1988

AT/PS/AC

Model/Body/Type	BaseList	Whlse	Retail
4 Dr DL Sdn	16585	**4925**	**6875**
4 Dr DL Wgn	17075	**5675**	**7625**
4 Dr GL Sdn	19280	**5750**	**7725**
4 Dr GL Wgn	20020	**6450**	**8500**

740 4 Cyl — 1988

AT/PS/AC

Model/Body/Type	BaseList	Whlse	Retail
4 Dr GLE Sdn	21450	**6625**	**8675**
4 Dr GLE Wgn	23025	**7300**	**9525**
4 Dr GLE Turbo Sdn	24525	**7375**	**9600**
4 Dr GLE Turbo Wgn	25205	**8075**	**10275**

760 V6 — 1988

AT/PS/AC

Model/Body/Type	BaseList	Whlse	Retail
4 Dr GLE Sdn	31200	**7900**	**10100**
4 Dr GLE Turbo Sdn	31985	**8575**	**10825**
4 Dr GLE Turbo Wgn	31985	**9275**	**11625**

780 V6 — 1988

AT/PS/AC

Model/Body/Type	BaseList	Whlse	Retail
2 Dr GLE Cpe	37790	**10100**	**12700**

DEDUCT FOR ALL 88 VOLVO:

No Auto Trans -390

1987 VOLVO

240 4 Cyl — 1987

AT/PS/AC

Model/Body/Type	BaseList	Whlse	Retail
4 Dr DL Sdn	15175	**4050**	**5800**
4 Dr DL Wgn	15665	**4700**	**6525**
4 Dr GL Sdn	17845	**4775**	**6650**
4 Dr GL Wgn	18495	**5400**	**7375**

VOLVO 87-85

Model/Body/Type	BaseList	Whlse	Retail
740 4 Cyl			**1987**
AT/PS/AC			
4 Dr GLE Sdn	19605	5025	7000
4 Dr GLE Wgn	21015	5725	7675
4 Dr GLE Turbo Sdn	21585	5575	7525
4 Dr GLE Turbo Wgn	22185	6225	8250
760 4 Cyl			**1987**
AT/PS/AC			
4 Dr GLE Turbo Sdn	27280	5725	7675
4 Dr GLE Turbo Wgn	26705	6350	8375
780 V6			**1987**
AT/PS/AC			
2 Dr GLE Cpe	34785	7825	10025

1986 VOLVO

Model/Body/Type	BaseList	Whlse	Retail
240			**1986**
4 Dr DL Sdn	14370	3550	4925
4 Dr DL Wgn	14860	4050	5525
4 Dr GL Sdn	16425	4075	5550
4 Dr GL Wgn	17010	4600	6125
740			**1986**
4 Dr GLE Sdn	18240	4050	5525
4 Dr GLE Wgn	19465	4575	6125
4 Dr GLE TD Sdn	20095	3375	4775
4 Dr GLE TD Wgn	21320	3900	5325
4 Dr Turbo Sdn	20220	4475	5975
4 Dr Turbo Wgn	20710	4950	6550
760			**1986**
4 Dr GLE Sdn	22960	4250	5725
4 Dr GLE Turbo Sdn	23975	4650	6175
4 Dr GLE Turbo Wgn	24920	5150	6725

1985 VOLVO

Model/Body/Type	BaseList	Whlse	Retail
740			**1985**
4 Dr GLE Sdn	16845	3250	4625
4 Dr GLE Wgn	19360	3625	5025
4 Dr GLE TD Sdn	19015	2750	4050
4 Dr GLE TD Wgn	20760	3125	4500
4 Dr Turbo Sdn	20130	3550	4950
4 Dr Turbo Wgn	21340	3975	5400
760			**1985**
4 Dr GLE Sdn	21485	3300	4700
4 Dr GLE Turbo Sdn	22625	3650	5050
4 Dr Turbo Wgn	23440	4050	5525
4 Dr GLE TD Sdn	22470	2825	4150
4 Dr TD Wgn	23660	3225	4600
DL			**1985**
4 Dr Sdn	12940	2875	4200
4 Dr Wgn	13415	3250	4650
GL			**1985**
4 Dr Sdn	15985	3175	4550
4 Dr Wgn	16515	3550	4950
4 Dr Turbo Sdn	18420	3500	4875
4 Dr Turbo Wgn	18950	3900	5325

See the Automobile Dealer Directory
on page 379 for a Dealer near you!

Automobile Dealer Directory

BMW

CONNECTICUT

BMW SAAB OF DARIEN
140 Ledge Road
Darien
Contact: Charles or Ron 203/656-1804

NEW YORK

PACE BMW
25 E. Main
New Rochelle
Contact: Jerry or Dave 914/636-2000

BUICK

CALIFORNIA

MAGNUSSEN PONTIAC-BUICK-GMC
550 El Camino Real
Menlo Park
Contact: Steve Bridges 415/326-4100

MICHIGAN

SUPERIOR BUICK
15101 Michigan Avenue
Dearborn
Contact: Joe 313/846-0040

OREGON

WALLACE BUICK
3515 NE Sandy Blvd
Portland
Contact: Don Forni 503/234-0221

CADILLAC

FLORIDA

ED MORSE CADILLAC
101 E. Fletcher Avenue
Tampa
Contact: Phil Raskin 813/968-8222

MASSACHUSETTS

FROST CADILLAC
399 Washington Street
Newton
Contact: Mark Gablehart 617/630-3000

CHEVROLET / GEO

ARIZONA

COURTESY CHEVROLET
1233 E. Camelback Road
Phoenix
Contact: Commercial Fleet Dept 602/279-3232

CALIFORNIA

CONNELL CHEVROLET
2828 Harbour Blvd
Costa Mesa
Contact: Eddie Cuadra or Gail Dalton 714/546-1200

AMERICAN CHEVROLET & GEO
1234 McHenry Avenue
Modesto
Contact: Commercial Sales 209/575-1606

MASSACHUSETTS

MCLAUGHLIN CHEVROLET INC.
741 Temple St. RT 27
Whitman
Contact: Ed Valante 617/447-4401

LANNAN CHEVROLET OLDSMOBILE GEO, INC.
40 Winn,
Woburn
Contact: Steve Alesse 617/935-2000

MINNESOTA

FRIENDLY CHEVROLET/GEO INC.
7501 N.E. Hwy 65
Fridley
Contact: John Langworthy
or Howie Lee 612/786-6100

NEWJERSEY

FISHER CHEVROLET/OLDSMOBILE
210 S. Washington Ave.
Bergenfield
Contact: Pat Sabino 201/384-5800

PINE BELT CHEVROLET/GEO
1088 State HWY 88
Lakewood
Contact: Gil Casorla **908/363-2900**

NEW YORK

AMITY CHEVROLET INC.
20 Merick Road
Amityville
Contact: Chris Sadusky 516/264-0909

SOUNDVIEW CHEVROLET/GEO INC.
291 Main Street
New Rochelle
Contact: Mitch Kronengold 914/632-6400

NORTH CAROLINA

POWERS-SWAIN CHEVROLET/GEO
4709 Bragg Boulevard
Fayetteville
Contact: Gary Brown 800/467-5135

PENNSYLVANIA

CASTRIOTA CHEVROLET/GEO INC.
1701 West Liberty Avenue
Pittsburgh
Contact: Rocco 412/343-2100 x351

DAVID PENSKE CHEVROLET/GEO
On Mall Boulevard across
from King of Prussia Mall
Contact: Mark Degnan 610/337-3100 x20

TEXAS

NORMAN FREDE CHEVROLET
16801 Feather Craft
Houston
Contact: Bob Ondrias **713/486-2200**

CHRYSLER/PLYMOUTH

CALIFORNIA

CHASE CHRYSLER/ PLYMOUTH/SUZUKI
2979 Auto Center Circle
Stockton
Contact: Ted Yee .... 209/956-7600 or 209/956-7617

For a Dealer in your area dial 1-800-996-Auto

Automobile Dealer Directory

CONNECTICUT

CALLARI CHRYSLER/PLYMOUTH JEEP/EAGLE
840 E. Main Street
Stamford
Contact: Anthony Viola 203/326-7800

MASSACHUSETTS

DEDHAM–WEST ROXBURY CHRYSLER/PLYMOUTH INC.
17 Eastern Avenue at Dedham Square
Dedham
Contact: Marshall Satter 617/326-4040

OHIO

BOB CALDWELL CHRYSLER/PLYMOUTH
1888 Morse
Columbus
Contact: Doug Berger 614/888-2331

PENNSYLVANIA

MAINLINE CHRYSLER/PLYMOUTH
663 Lancaster Avenue
Bryn Mahr
Contact: Jim Maloney or David Rapp 610/525-6670

SOUTH HILLS CHRYSLER/PLYMOUTH
3344 Washington Road
McMurray
Contact: Larry Winter 412/941-4300

DODGE

MASSACHUSETTS

MOTOR MART DODGE
800 Washington Street
S. Attleboro
Contact: Martin Lamarro 508/761-5400

WESTMINSTER DODGE INC.
720 Morrissey Blvd.
Boston
Contact: Bob Bickford 800/274-9922

NEW JERSEY

MOTOR WORLD DODGE HYUNDAI
315 Rt 4 West
Paramus
Contact: Phil Bell 201/488-9000

SUBURBAN DODGE
85 Central Avenue
Metuchen
Contact: Frank Salbo 908/548-3500

PENNSYLVANIA

DEVON HILL DODGE
20 West Lancaster Avenue
Devon
Contact: Chuck O'Keefe 610/687-9350

LANCASTER DODGE
1475 Manheim Pike
Lancaster
Contact: Jerry Cutler or Russ Osborne 717/393-0625

NORWIN DODGE
13230 Rt 30
N. Hungtington
Contact: Jack Butler or Scott Gutshall 412/864-0140

WASHINGTON

TACOMA DODGE
4101 S. Tacoma Way
Tacoma
Contact: Bob Ward/John R. 206/475-7300

WISCONSIN

DODGE CITY
4640 South 27th
Milwaukee
Contact: Frank Brugger 414/281-9100

FORD

ARIZONA

BELL FORD
2401 West Bell Road
Phoenix
Contact: Larry Barnes 602/866-1776

CALIFORNIA

AIRPORT MARINA FORD
5880 Centinela Avenue
Los Angeles
Contact: Bob Garcia 310/649-3673

EL CAJON FORD
1595 E. Main Street
El Cajon
Contact: Phil Smithey 619/579-8888

HANSEL FORD
3075 Corby Avenue
Santa Rosa
Contact: Joe, Ed or Paul 707/525-3688
or 800/956-5556

S & C FORD & CITY LEASING
2001 Market Street
San Francisco
Contact: Ron Fields 415/861-6000

SUN VALLEY AUTO PLAZA
2285 Diamond Blvd.
Concord
Contact: Geoff Dettlinger or Dan Stillman . 510/686-3325

HAWAII

CUTTER FORD/ISUZU INC.
98-015 Kamehameha Highway
Aiea
Contact: Tom Nakama or Dennis Ouchi 808/487-3811

ILLINOIS

JOE COTTON FORD
175 West North Avenue
Carol Stream
Contact: Kimberly Schweppe 708/682-9200

ARLINGTON HEIGHTS FORD
801 West Dundee Road
Arlington Heights
Contact: Randy Malkiewicz
or Richard Jacobsen 708/870-1300

MASSACHUSETTS

MAIN STREET AUTO SALES
1022 main Street
Waltham
Contact: Justin Barrett or Julius Simon 617/894-8000

For a Dealer in your area dial 1-800-996-Auto

MINNESOTA

FREEWAY FORD
9700 Lyndale Avenue
Minneapolis
Contact: Kevin Johanson 612/888-9481

MISSOURI

CAVALIER FORD INC.
7501 Manchester Avenue
St. Louis
Contact: Jim Danner 314/645-2780

NEW JERSEY

KEATS FORD
2865 Brunswick Park
Lawrenceville
Contact: Joseph Keats or Gary Glauser 609/883-3400

LARSON FORD, INC.
1150 State HWY 88
Lakewood
Contact: Bob Taurosa or Bob Eden 908/363-8100

MULLANE FORD
241 N. Washington Avenue
Bergenfield
Contact: Pat Moran 201/385-6500

NEW YORK

ASPEN FORD INC.
855 65-th Street
Brooklyn
Contact: Pat DiDomenico or Rich Willis 718/921-9100

OHIO

PEFFLEY FORD
4600 N. Main Street
Dayton
Contact: Jake Cabay 513/278-7921

OREGON

HARVEST FORD LINCOLN/MERCURY
2833 Washburn Way
Klamath Falls
Contact: Gary Creese 503/884-3121

PENNSYLVANIA

McKEAN FORD
5151 Liberty Avenue
Pittsburgh
Contact: Fred Orendi 412/622-8800

NORRISTOWN FORD
Ridge Pike & Trooper
Norristown
Contact: Joe Lutz or Andy Stratz 215/539-5400

TEXAS

LEE JARMON FORD
1635 I-35 East
Carrollton
Contact: John Prouty 214/242-0682

LONE STAR FORD INC.
8477 North Freeway
Houston
Contact: Charlie Bradt or Teddy Dikas 713/931-3300

HONDA

CALIFORNIA

GOUDY HONDA
1400 W. Main Street
Alhambra
Contact: Terry McCarton or Mike Tognetti .. 818/576-1114
213/283-7336, 800/423-1114

JIM DOTEN'S HONDA
2600 Shattuck Avenue
Berkley
Contact: Stewart Petersen, Fleet Dept 510/843-3704

SAN FRANCISCO HONDA/KIA
10 South Van Ness Ave.
San Francisco
Contact: Brent Miletich or Philip Mah 415/441-2000
Beeper 415/202-6361

CONNECTICUT

SCHALLER
HONDA OLDS MITSU SUB
1 Veterans Drive
New Britain
Contact: Gary Turchetta 203/223-2230

MASSACHUSETTS

DARTMOUTH HONDA/VOLVO
26 State Rd.
North Dartmouth
Contact: Jim Dicostanzo or Hank Costa 508/996-6800

HONDA VILLAGE
371 Washington Street
Newton
Contact: Mort Shapiro 617/965-8200

NEW JERSEY

HONDA OF ESSEX
1170 Bloomfield Ave.
West Caldwell
Contact: Sales Manager 201/808-9100

VIP HONDA
555 Somerset Street/Corner of Rt 22 East
North Plainfield
Contact: Ron Lombardi 908/371-3752

NEW YORK

BAY RIDGE HONDA
8801 4-th Avenue
Brooklyn
Contact: Phil Donati or Mark Knipstein 718/836-4600

PACE HONDA
25 E. Main
New Rochelle
Contact: Jerry or Dave 914/636-2000

OHIO

MOTORCARS–HONDA
2953 Mayfield
Cleveland Heights
Contact: Rick Gartman 216/932-2400

TEXAS

JIM ALLEE HONDA
11300 East Northwest Hwy
Dallas
Contact: Andy Kahn 214/348-7500

WISCONSIN

DAVID HOBBS HONDA
6100 North Green Bay Avenue
Milwaukee
Contact: Randy Wilson or Tim Hansen 414/352-6100

JEEP/EAGLE

MICHIGAN

MIKE MILLER JEEP/EAGLE
6540 South Cedar
Lansing
Contact: Mike Hornberger 517/394-2770

NEW JERSEY

SALERNO DUANE JEEP/EAGLE
267 Broad Street
Summit
Contact: Steve Memolo 908/277-6700

OREGON

WALLACE JEEP/EAGLE
3515 NE Sandy Blvd
Portland
Contact: Don Forni 503/234-0221

TEXAS

JIM ALLEE OLDSMOBILE JEEP/EAGLE
12277 Shiloh Rd.
Dallas
Contact: Steve Hess 214/321-5030

LEXUS

FLORIDA

LEXUS OF KENDALL
10943 South Dixie Highway
Miami
Contact: Terry Bean 305/669-0522 x450

NEW JERSEY

PRESTIGE LEXUS
955 State Hwy 17
Ramsey
Contact: Bill Berradino 201/825-5200

LINCOLN/MERCURY

CALIFORNIA

TORRANCE LINCOLN/MERCURY VOLKS/HYUNDAI
20460 Hawthorne Blvd.
Torrance
Contact: Carol Wagner 310/370-6311

MASSACHUSETTS

CLARK & WHITE LINCOLN/MERCURY
777 Washington Street
Newton
Contact: Tom Gibbs 617/254-7400

MICHIGAN

MIKE MILLER LINCOLN/MERCURY
6540 South Cedar
Lansing
Contact: Mike Hornberger **517/394-2770**

NEW JERSEY

WESTWOOD LINCOLN/MERCURY
55 Kinderkamack Road
Emerson
Contact: Charlie Featherstone 201/265-7700

NEW YORK

L & B LINCOLN/MERCURY
520 Montauk Highway
West Babylon
Contact: George Talley 516/669-2600

OREGON

HARVEST FORD LINCOLN/MERCURY
2833 Washburn Way
Klamath Falls
Contact: Gary Creese 503/884-3121

PENNSYLVANIA

NORTHEAST LINCOLN/MERCURY
7001 Roosevelt Blvd
Philadelphia
Contact: Lori Swenson 215/331-6600

SOUTH HILLS LINCOLN/MERCURY
2760 Washington Road
Pittsburgh
Contact: Dave Arbogast 412/941-1600

MITSUBISHI

FLORIDA
PAUL WEST MITSUBISHI
3111 N. Main Street
Gainesville
Contact: Mark Fish 904/371-3752

MASSACHUSETTS
BERNARDI MITSUBISHI
671 Worcester Rd.
Natick
Contact: Stephen Bianchi 508/655-8588

NEW JERSEY
SALERNO DUANE MITSUBISHI
267 Broad Street
Summit
Contact: Dave Walsh 908/277-6780

NISSAN

CALIFORNIA
CONCORD NISSAN INC.
1290 Concord Avenue
Concord
Contact: Jack Tarafevic, Shawn Mosley 510/676-4400

FLORIDA
PRECISION NISSAN
4600 N. Dale Mabry Hwy
Tampa
Contact: Gary Armstrong 813/870-3333

GEORGIA
TRONCALLI NISSAN
1625 Church Street
Decatur
Contact: Jeff Slocum **404/292-3853**

MASSACHUSETTS
FROST NISSAN
1180 Washington Street
West Newton
Contact: Dan Favre 617/630-3050

NEW JERSEY
CHERRY HILL NISSAN
State Hwy 39 & Cooper Landing
Cherry Hill
Contact: Marvin, Frank,
or Freeman **609/667-8300**

MOTOR WORLD NISSAN MAZDA VOLKS
340 Sylvan Avenue Rt 9W
Englewood Cliffs
Contact: Jeff Montemuro 201/568-4400
.... 201/567-9000

NEW YORK
GEIS NISSAN
Rt 6 & Westbrook Drive
Peekskill
Contact: Tom Conaty
or Steve Pinto 914/528-4347x859/878

PENNSYLVANIA
CONCORDVILLE NISSAN
RT 202 South
Concordville
Contact: Gregory Brown 215/459-8900

WISCONSIN
ROSEN NISSAN INC.
5505 South 27th
Milwaukee
Contact: Scott Levy 414/282-9300

OLDSMOBILE

TEXAS
**JIM ALLEE
OLDSMOBILE JEEP/EAGLE**
12277 Shiloh Rd.
Dallas
Contact: Steve Hess 214/321-5030

PONTIAC

CALIFORNIA
**MAGNUSSEN
PONTIAC-BUICK-GMC**
550 El Camino Real
Menlo Park
Contact: Steve Bridges 415/326-4100

ILLINOIS
**JOE COTTON
PONTIAC/GMC TRUCK, INC.**
271 East North Avenue
Glendale Heights
Contact: Kimberly Schweppe 708/682-9200

NEW YORK
GEIS PONTIAC BUICK OLDS CAD
Rt 6 & Westbrook Drive
Peekskill
Contact: Ed Rice or Jim Lockwood 914/528-4347x811/866

OHIO
MOTORCARS–PONTIAC
2953 Mayfield
Cleveland Heights
Contact: Chris Osborne 216/932-2400

OREGON
BRESLIN PONTIAC GMC
3515 N E Sandy Boulevard
Portland
Contact: Don Forni 503/234-0221

NEW JERSEY
SALERNO DUANE PONTIAC
267 Broad Street
Summit
Contact: Steve Memolo 908/277-6700

TOYOTA

ARIZONA
CAMELBACK TOYOTA
1500 East Camelback Road
Phoenix
Contact: Vic Schafer 602/274-9576

For a Dealer in your area dial 1-800-996-Auto

Automobile Dealer Directory

CALIFORNIA
TOYOTA OF NORTH HOLLYWOOD
4100 Lankershim
North Hollywood
Contact: Cam Sadighi 818/508-2900

CONNECTICUT
GIRARD TOYOTA/BMW
543 Colman Street
New London
Contact: Larry Main 203/447-3141

FLORIDA
KENDALL TOYOTA
10943 South Dixie Highway
Miami
Contact: Frank Marsala 305/665-6581 x323

PRECISION TOYOTA INC.
10909 N. Florida Avenue
Tampa
Contact: Brad Savelli or Matt Coffey 813/933-6402

MASSACHUSETTS
WOBURN FOREIGN MOTORS
394 Washington Street
Woburn
Contact: Stephan Harasim 617/933-1100

MINNESOTA
RUDY LUTHER'S TOYOTA
8801 Wayzata Blvd
Minneapolis
Contact: Larry Fenton or Curt Folstad 612/544-1313

NEW JERSEY
BOB CIASULLI MONMOUTH TOYOTA
700 State Hwy 36
Eatontown
Contact: Allison Guttman 908/544-1000

NEW YORK
GEIS TOYOTA
Rt 6 & Westbrook Drive
Peekskill
Contact: Joe Trabucco
or Pat Canavan 914/528-4347x880/894

OHIO
KINGS TOYOTA/SUZUKI
9500 Kings Automall Road
Cincinnati
Contact: Greg Plowman 513/683-5440

TEXAS
STERLING McCALL TOYOTA
9400 Southwest Freeway
Houston
Contact: Tanya Tolander 713/270-3974

VOLVO

VOLVO

MASSACHUSETTS
DARTMOUTH HONDA/VOLVO
26 State Rd.
North Dartmouth
Contact: Jim Dicostanzo or Hank Costa 508/996-6800